# INFORMATION TECHNOLOGY

## PRINCIPLES, PRACTICES, OPPORTUNITIES

### THIRD EDITION

JAMES A. SENN

**PEARSON**

Hall

Upper Saddle River, New Jersey 07458

Library of Congress Cataloging-in-Publication Data
Senn, James A.
    Information technology : principles, practices, opportunities /
James A. Senn.–3rd ed.
        p. cm.
    Includes bibliographical references and indexes.
    ISBN 0-13-143626-0
    1. Business–Data processing.   2. Information storage and
retrieval systems–Business.   3. Information technology.   I. Title:
Business.   II. Title.
HF5548.2.S4366     2004
650'.0285–dc22                                           2003021914

**Publisher and Vice President:** Natalie E. Anderson
**AVP/Executive Editor:** David Alexander
**Project Manager:** Kyle Hannon
**Editorial Assistant:** Robyn Goldenberg
**Senior Marketing Manager:** Sharon M. Koch
**Marketing Assistant:** Danielle Torio
**Permissions Supervisor:** Suzanne Grappi
**Manufacturing Buyer:** Arnold Vila
**Design Manager:** Maria Lange
**Art Director:** Patricia Smythe
**Interior Design:** Kathryn Foot
**Cover Design:** Bruce Kenselaar
**Cover Illustration/Photo:** Chris Cheadle/Getty Images, Inc.–Stone Allstock and Ryan McVay/Getty Images–Image Bank
**Manager, Print Production:** Christy Mahon
**Composition/Full-Service Project Management:** Caryl Wenzel and Sue Katkus, PreMediaONE, A Black Dot Group Company
**Photo Research Coordinator:** Kathy Zander, PreMediaONE, A Black Dot Group Company
**Photo Research:** Rae Grant, Judy Mason, and Billie L. Porter
**Printer/Binder:** RR Donnelley-Willard

Credits and acknowledgments borrowed from other sources and reproduced, with permission, in this textbook appear on page C-1.

Microsoft® and Windows® are registered trademarks of the Microsoft Corporation in the U.S.A. and other countries. Screen shots and icons reprinted with permission from the Microsoft Corporation. This book is not sponsored or endorsed by or affiliated with the Microsoft Corporation.

Pearson Education LTD.
Pearson Education Singapore, Pte. Ltd
Pearson Education, Canada, Ltd
Pearson Education–Japan
Printed in the United States of America

Pearson Education Australia PTY, Limited
Pearson Education North Asia Ltd
Pearson Educación de Mexico, S.A. de C.V.
Pearson Education Malaysia, Pte. Ltd

10 9 8 7 6 5 4 3 2 1
ISBN 013-143626-0

# To Christian

(Who sees opportunity in every challenge)

An inquisitive builder, with a special personality, who is always ready to lend a hand—invaluable assets for the opportunities that are yet to come.

You'll always be PaPa's buddy!

*J*im Senn has thirty years experience in the development and implementation of corporate and information technology strategy in service, manufacturing industries, and high tech industries. He is a dynamic speaker and highly regarded global consultant. His client list includes many well-known "blue chip" firms from Europe, Asia, and the Americas. He is also a highly regarded facilitator at corporate and technology planning sessions. He has been appointed to the Board of Directors of numerous public and private organizations, including both established and start-up enterprises.

Senn is a member of the faculty of the J. Mack Robinson College of Business at Georgia State University where he teaches in the Executive MBA program and the college's program in Computer Information Systems. Under his leadership as Chairman of the Department of Computer Information Systems, the department gained widespread international recognition for its programs and activities. It received an overall national ranking by *ComputerWorld* as the number two program (second to the Massachusetts Institute of Technology) in the United States and was identified as having the top curriculum in the nation.

Senn is regarded as a master teacher and has received numerous distinguished faculty teaching excellence awards at leading institutions. He is a founder of the Association for Information Systems, the International Conference on Information Systems, and the MIS Quarterly, where he served as its founding Associate Editor for practice. In the Southeast, he is also the founder of 1st Tuesday, a worldwide venture capital and entrepreneur society, the Society for Information Systems, Atlanta chapter, and Information Managers of Atlanta.

Senn is the author of several leading text and research books on information technology that have been translated into multiple languages for use in many countries. He has written numerous articles and papers appearing in leading professional and academic publications. A constant global traveler, Senn addresses audiences around the world on leadership strategies and corporate success.

# BRIEF CONTENTS

# CONTENTS

# PART 5    Developing Information Technology Applications

# PART 6   Information Technology Issues

The information technology revolution we've just lived through is nothing compared to the one that lies ahead. Indeed, information technology (IT) will likely be a defining feature of this, the first decade of the 21st Century.

As you think about what lies ahead, it is useful to take stock of where we are today:

- Spending for information technology is at an all-time high, even after adjustments for downturns that were triggered by the bust of so-called "dot-com" e-commerce companies.
- Computers, communication networks, and handheld, mobile computers and telephones are not only in widespread use, but in some regions have reached a saturation point, making it unlikely that the number of adopters will continue growing.
- Information technology is no longer a novelty, but a resource that nearly everyone in the United States and the world's other industrialized countries expect to always be available and accessible.
- The generations of students on college and university campuses and in K-12 grades today have never experienced a time when information technology was not available to them. Indeed, they have grown up participating in the marvelous advances of the last century, and they expect them to continue well into the future.

Yet, it is human nature to wonder about the future, including the future associated with information technology. Each of us undoubtedly has questions, such as the following:

- Will the accelerating pace of technological change that we've become accustomed to continue at the same pace?
- Who are the principal competitors for technology development leadership?
- In what areas will IT's greatest impact be felt in the decade ahead?
- Will the Internet continue to evolve, reshaping the lives of people and enterprises even more dramatically than it already has?
- Will everyone become skilled in the use of information technology, or will some folks fall farther and farther behind?
- How will digital content and communication networks change the way we live, work, learn, and play?
- Will the desktop personal computer remain dominant or will other kinds of technology take its place in the decade ahead?

A myriad of scenarios is emerging. However, one thing is certain: those who have a firm grasp on the capabilities and characteristics of the underlying information technology are most likely to influence, or at least capitalize on, their application to the world around them—personal or professional.

Those individuals and enterprises having the know-how to combine their resources in computers and communication systems—the principal elements of information technology—are most likely to be successful in their endeavors. Moreover, their application of the principals of IT, as well as awareness of leading practices, provides the greatest opportunity for their success.

Yet the changes are likely to be ongoing. Education for a lifetime is thus replaced by a lifetime of education—including those involving the principles and practices associated with information technology.

# The Third Edition

The book's title, *Information Technology: Principles, Practices, Opportunities* reflects the basic realities and promise of information technology, both globally and locally. It suggests the book's distinguishing characteristics:

- Focus on information technology
- Emphasis on problem solving
- Incorporation of the Internet and World Wide Web
- Exploration of both personal applications and enterprise systems
- Examination of real-world experiences
- Application to professional practice

This third edition includes extensive discussions of the practical uses of information technology (IT) in a variety of application settings, a distinguishing characteristic of the very successful first and second editions. You'll recognize the many examples of IT practice throughout the book, all chosen to show how successful people and the world's best-known firms are capitalizing on IT to create new opportunities for themselves and to serve their stakeholders effectively. Because IT is widely used, as you know, I've also included many examples that illustrate the impact of IT in creating opportunities in science, journalism, medicine, e-commerce, business, personal life . . . the list is almost endless.

# New Chapters Expand Principles and Practices

This edition features comprehensive new chapters on the Internet, including its most widely used resource, the World Wide Web, on digital commerce, and on Web-enabled applications. There are also new chapters on personal and PC database systems and enterprise databases and warehouses.

This book is organized into six parts. The first part, "Introduction to Information Technology," introduces the principles of information technology in the first chapter and describes the reasons for its extensive use in all types of applications. You'll find the two chapters "Essentials of Computing" and "Essentials of the Internet and World Wide Web" in this module. The Internet is introduced early so it can be used in all the chapters that follow. I incorporate applications of the Net, the Web, and e-commerce into many of the IT practices described throughout the rest of the book.

"Hardware Technology," the second part, describes in detail the components of computers, including hardware and programs. A vast array of business uses of these IT components is described through illustration. If you're already familiar with the technical aspects of IT, this part will be useful to review the most recent developments in IT.

Part 3, "Database Technology," contains two chapters. One deals with personal databases, describing how individuals can build and apply database systems as productivity tools. The second chapter in this segment addresses enterprise database systems. It carefully examines current practices and the ongoing evolution in object-oriented databases, including the integration of relational and object concepts into current database software.

"Network Technology," Part 4, explores the way businesses interconnect many users within departments and across work groups and throughout an enterprise. End-users also share IT resources that are distributed across miles, countries, or continents. Developing shared applications places special requirements on the know-how of IT professionals, as Part 4 also discusses. The chapter "Electronic Commerce and Electronic Business" describes the innovations in products and services for consumers and businesses. It examines in detail the impact of applying communications technology to interconnect supply chains.

Part 5, "Developing Information Technology Applications," includes three comprehensive chapters. "Launching Information Technology Applications" explores the origin of IT applications, discussed in the context of the systems development process. The second chapter in this section, "Creating Enterprise Applications," examines the tools and techniques of systems developers, including the growing reliance on objects and components. It also discusses the unified modeling language (UML) and, using a common application example, compares it to traditional development tools. The third chapter, "Creating Web-Enabled Applications," is both current and forward looking. It explores the widespread interest in using Internet browsers and features of the World Wide Web to enhance the value of legacy applications. In this chapter we also discuss the extensible markup language (XML) and its use in creating, publishing, and interconnecting with Web services.

Part 6, "Information Technology Issues," explores important challenges surrounding the use of information technology, including the issues of IT security, digital piracy, ethics, personal privacy, and IT reliability. This final part examines these issues in the context of both enterprises using IT and society depending on the assurance of appropriate information technology safeguards.

# Features Highlight Practice

The themes of principles, practices, and opportunities are integrated into the hundreds of company illustrations spanning the chapters of this book. I further highlight the themes in each chapter with special insert features. *Information Technology in Practice* windows discuss innovative and effective applications of IT that are making people and enterprises more successful. In these features you'll find a candid (and sometimes gritty) discussion of IT practices related to the chapter's focus. One feature describes how a physician in the rural south has grown to rely on PC databases as an integral instrument in treating her patients. Then there's the examination of the dangers of identity theft, one of the fastest growing crimes in the United States. We look at the role IT plays in this and how the U.S. Federal Trade Commission suggests you protect yourself against identify theft.

## Opening and Closing Chapter Cases

Each chapter opens with a case and ends with a different case. All deal with a story of real enterprises and real people. For example, you'll see how Wal-Mart, the world's largest retailer, relies on communications networks and data warehouses to manage its supply chain of vendors, a critical factor in the company's enormous success. You'll also go inside the innovative digital asset management project at CNN, a huge IT innovation that is reshaping the very essence of how this global news network captures, stores, and broadcasts the details of breaking events and other news around the clock. Then there's the fascinating story of Yahoo! and an inside glimpse of the company's origin and its IT strategy for staying out front of the niche it occupies in the Internet world. Or, take the case of the NASDAQ stock market, and how its foresight in IT planning enabled it to stay operational throughout the infamous 9/11 terrorist attacks on New York's World Trade Center Towers, located in the heart of Wall Street. You will see what everyone developing or using IT applications can learn from NASDAQ's experience.

New technology uses are featured in the cases as well. Digital MP3 music and high density DVDs are creating difficult digital piracy issues. We'll see how the Recording Industry Association and the Motion Picture Association of America are fighting piracy of digital content and how their actions will personally affect you. The use of wireless (WiFi) networks at Boeing Company is changing the way jumbo aircraft are manufactured. The scientific breakthroughs in nanotechnology are investigated through innovative research and development in IBM's world class labs. You'll see the new storage technology that will be introduced into the market in a few years as a direct result of this research. Another case focuses on the importance of building in safeguards for new technology as it examines a global attack on the Internet. The case describes how the attack was carried out and the knowledge that experts and users alike gleaned from this event.

## Cool Mobility Running Case

*Cool Mobility* is a running case/exercise designed to accompany the third edition.

Each of the 14 chapters of the book contains an exercise that requires students, acting as a consulting intern on assignment to the *Cool Mobility* company, to visit the company's Web site (www.CoolMobility.biz). Some of the chapter exercises are designed to enable students to become familiar with the Web site by retrieving information from the site. Others focus on the Web site's features, asking the student to evaluate them as a means of applying the concepts, tools, and practices described in the chapter. Still others request that additional features be designed in order to augment the capabilities of the Web site.

## Critical Connection Cases

Critical thinking is an important part of solving problems and capitalizing on opportunities. A special Critical Connection case feature emphasizes problem solving. Each chapter introduces a challenge facing an individual or company and draws on the principles and practices discussed in the chapter. At the end of the chapter, these experiences are revisited and conclusions are drawn. Each Critical Connection case concludes with a series of discussion questions. Like the other examples throughout the book, Critical Connection cases focus on a wide variety of applications such as Hotmail, the free e-mail service; the Disney Fast Pass systems in use at Walt Disney World and Disneyland; and the flight recorder system used on every commercial aircraft around the world.

## Reality Checks

I often find it useful to step back from what I'm doing or what I'm reading to consider the ramifications of what's happening. For this reason I've included a series of Reality Checks in every chapter. Each Reality Check is a personal assessment of a particular principle, practice, or opportunity, and is drawn from a vast array of IT experiences in the worlds of business, government, and research.

## Photo Essays

The "mind's eye" augments written descriptions by allowing us to visualize experience. To further share the experiences of people and companies, I've created a series of photo essays that tell stories through photographs, images, and display screens. Each photo essay tells a step-by-step story in pictures.

## Group Projects and Applications

Because people often learn best when learning from each other and gathering information firsthand, you'll find a set of group projects included in every chapter. The project descriptions focus on a current topic relevant to the subject of the chapter. Each describes a topic for investigation, divides up the responsibility among group members, suggests a means for assembling information, and presents an approach to present results to the class. The projects require team members to get into the field, visiting companies or interviewing businesspersons.

## Net_Work Projects Explore the Internet

Elements of the Internet are woven throughout this book. However, of special significance are the Net_Work projects included in each chapter. These projects, which can be completed by individuals or teams, are designed to showcase the many capabilities and features of the

Internet and the World Wide Web. Net_Work projects will visit corporate and government sites, utilize the search engines to locate information, teach how to download software and documents, explore the multimedia possibilities provided by plug-ins—even venture into cybercruiting to see the career opportunities that are posted at various Web sites. Net_Work projects begin in the first chapter where your campus Internet resources are identified.

## Additional Learning Aids

Each chapter includes a variety of other learning aids designed to assist readers in testing their understanding and ability to apply the principles and practices described in the chapter. Included in each chapter are:

- A detailed outline that previews the chapter's contents
- Learning objectives that focus readers on understanding key concepts and frameworks
- A running marginal glossary of key terms introduced in the chapter
- A chapter summary keyed to learning objectives
- Key terms useful for review
- Review questions that test understanding of the chapter
- Discussion questions that raise thought-provoking, often controversial, issues

# Supplements

## Instructor's Resource CD-ROM (0-13-143871-9)

Most of the support materials described in the following section are conveniently available for adopters on the Instructor's Resource CD-ROM. The CD includes the Instructor's Resource Manual, Test Item File, TestGen, and PowerPoint slides.

## Instructor's Manual (on Instructor's Resource CD-ROM)

The Instructor's Manual features not only suggested answers to Critical Connections, Review Questions, Discussion Questions, Group Projects & Applications, Net_Work, *Cool Mobility*, and chapter Case Studies, but also teaching objectives and teaching suggestions. This supplement can be downloaded from the secure faculty section of the Senn Web site and is also available on the Instructor's Resource CD-ROM.

## Test Item File (on Instructor's Resource CD-ROM)

The Test Item File is a comprehensive collection of true–false, multiple-choice, fill-in-the-blank, and essay questions. The questions are rated by difficulty level and the answers are referenced by page number. An electronic version of the Test Item File, known as TestGen, is available on the Instructor's Resource CD-ROM.

## PowerPoint Slides (on Web and Instructor's Resource CD-ROM)

Electronic color slides are available in Microsoft PowerPoint. The slides illuminate and build on key concepts in the text. Both student and faculty can download the PowerPoint slides from the Web site, and they are also provided on the Instructor's Resource CD-ROM.

## Companion Web Site (www.prenhall.com/senn)

There is a dedicated Web site for the text that provides a dynamic complement to the text. The site includes an Interactive Study Guide for students as well as video cases. Additional faculty supplements can be downloaded from the password protected section of the site.

## Videos

**Prentice Hall MIS Video, Volume 1 (0-13-027199-3)**   The first video in the Prentice Hall MIS Video Library includes custom clips created exclusively for Prentice Hall featuring real companies, such as Andersen Consulting, Lands' End, Lotus Development Corporation, Oracle Corporation, and Pillsbury Company.

**Prentice Hall MIS Video, Volume 2 (0-13-101500-1)**   Video clips are provided to adopters to enhance class discussion and projects. These clips highlight real-world corporations and organizations and illustrate key concepts found in the text.

## Materials for Your Online Course

Prentice Hall supports our adopters using online courses by providing files ready for upload into both WebCT and BlackBoard course management systems for our testing, quizzing, and other supplements. Please contact your local PH representative or mis_service@prenhall.com for further information on your particular course.

For instructors seeking Application Software support to use with this text, Prentice Hall is pleased to offer the PH Train IT CD-ROM and the Web-delivered PH Train & Assess IT for Office XP and Office 2003. These exciting tutorial and assessment products are fully certified up to the expert level of the Microsoft Office User Specialist (MOUS) Certification Program. These items are not available as stand-alone items but can be packaged with the Senn text at an additional charge. Please go to www.prenhall.com/phit for an on-line demonstration of these products or contact your local Prentice Hall representative for more details.

## Packaging Options

Prentice Hall provides a wealth of activities, lab manuals and computer-based training for Microsoft Office that can be packaged with this text at a discount. Check with your local PH representative or mis_service@prenhall.com for further information.

With *MIS Cases: Decision Making with Application Software* by M. Lisa Miller students will prepare to make management level decisions with the most complete and interactive Management Information Systems Casebook on the market! This casebook contains 20 cases rated on a 1-5 level of difficulty. The reader will be required to use spreadsheets, databases and web page development tools to find solutions to the problems in the cases. Tutorials on these tools are included at www.prenhall.com/miller to ensure success. Many cases will ask the reader to prepare written and oral presentations of their solutions, just as if the reader was making these decisions at an actual firm. The Casebook can be packaged with the Miller text at an additional charge.

What a difference a year or two makes! MIS graduates, for the first time in many years, are having to battle for employment. Using real data and recent research, Fran Quittel, noted career columnist for Computerworld, identifies the best entry-level jobs and career paths in *The Prentice Hall IT Career Guide*. She also provides strategies on how to network, intern and interview. Filled with current and pragmatic advice, this guide can benefit the brand new IT job seeker! This guide is available free of charge when packaged with this text.

For more details on these items or for additional packaging options, please contact your local Prentice Hall representative.

# Acknowledgments

The real stories and applications woven throughout this book are the result of the support of many enterprises and many exceptional business leaders.

**Business Leaders**   The opportunity to interact first-hand with CEOs, presidents, and operational managers, whether as friends, acquaintances, or clients is an invaluable resource for an author. After all, this is what makes a book *real*.

Many such business leaders from around the world–Asia, Europe, and the Americas–have played a role or influenced the vignettes that are included in this book. Their sharing of experiences and willingness to discuss successes and important challenges provided invaluable information to stimulate the learning of others. A large number are identified in this book through their company names. Their support and candor is both invaluable and highly appreciated.

**Research Support**    This book benefited tremendously from the support of skilled researchers who helped gather and verify facts, organize information, and review narrative discussions for accuracy and completeness. I'm indebted to the assistance of Maribel Herrera, Melissa Morris, Frank Lee, Cathy Luce, Melinda Alexander, Diane Austin, Rae Grant, Judy Mason, Billie L. Porter, Linda Muterspaugh, Teri Stratford, Suzanne Scully, John Blatt, and Kristen Knutson.

Maribel Herrera, Joan Waxman, Dirk Kemp, and David Alexander each played a pivotal role in bringing *Cool Mobility* into being, giving it a life of its own.

**Learning Support System**    Many participated in the development of this book's supplements. Instructors and students alike will benefit from the practical and forward looking information they have assembled.

The roots of this book can be traced to a most important focus group that stimulated and validated the vision and concept for this book. To this day, their comments and insights play a role in crafting the focus and personality of the book. Members of this group included:

| | |
|---|---|
| Frank Davis<br>*Bloomsburg University* | Adolph Katz<br>*AK Associated & Fairfield University* |
| Donald L. Dawley<br>*Miami University* | Robert T. Keim<br>*Arizona State University* |
| Richard Fenzl<br>*Syracuse University* | John Pagliarulo<br>*Rockland Community College* |
| Barry Floyd<br>*California Polytechnic State University* | John Sanford<br>*Philadelphia College of Textiles and Science* |

A set of thoughtful, caring, and skilled reviewers ensured that the objectives of this book served as the guide throughout even as they scrutinized the drafts for accuracy, completeness, and usability. A special thank you goes to:

Theresa Adams, *DeKalb College*
Theo Addo, *San Diego State University*
Kemal Altinkemer, *Purdue University*
Garry R. Armstrong, *Shippensburg University*
Anitesh Barua, *University of Texas at Austin*
Luverne Bierle, *Iowa Central Community College*
Catherine J. Brotherton, *Riverside Community College*
Bruce Brown, *Salt Lake Community College*
Donald L. Dawley, *Miami University*
Warren Dickson, *University of Central Oklahoma*
Lois T. Elliot, *George's Community College*
Mary Helen Fagan, *Salisbury State University*
Edward Fisher, *Central Michigan University*
Gary Fisher, *Angelo State University*
Stephen Haag, *University of Minnesota-Duluth*

Keith Herrel, *University of Tennessee-Martin*
Wade M. Jackson, *Memphis State University*
O. K. Johnson, *University of Utah*
Ernest A. Kallman, *Bentley College*
Adolph Katz, *AK Associates & Fairfield University*
Robert T. Keim, *Arizona State University*
Mohammed B. Khan, *California State University-Long Beach*
Constance A. Knapp, *Pace University*
Craig Knight, *University of Alabama-Huntsville*
Kenneth A. Kozar, *University of Colorado-Boulder*
Stanley Kroder, *University of Dallas*
Gerald F. Mackey, *Georgia Institute of Technology*
Tony L. McRae, *Colin County Community College*
Louis Mills, *Sonoma State University*
Pat Ormond, *University of Utah*
Beverly Oswalt, *Stephen F. Austin State University*
King Perry, *Delaware County Community College*
Tom Philpott, *University of Texas at Austin*
Armand Picou, *The University of Central Arkansas*
Brad Prince, *Aubum University*
John F. Sanford, *Philadelphi College of Textiles and Science*
John R. Schillak, *University of Wisconsin-Eau Claire*
Martin Skolnik, *Florida Atlantic University*
Vincent J. Skudma, *Baruch College*
Blair A. Smith, *University of Phoenix, Colorado Campus*
Ronald W. Stimson, *Eastfield College*
Susan Silvera, *Los Angeles Trade-Technical College*
Ajay S. Vinze, *Texas A&M University*
Fred Wells, *DeKalb College*
Doug White, *University of Northern Colorado*

David Alexander proved once again that with infinite patience, anything is possible. Of course, everyone knows that behind the scene, Kyle Hannon was the real glue holding things together. Add to that the infectious enthusiasm and keen market sense of Sharon Koch and the result is a "Gang of Three" that is "over the top." Yet this team stands on the shoulders of others who provided the foundation for the initial edition. The original team of Valerie Ashton, P. J. Boardman, Sandy Steiner, Joe Heider, Steve Rigolosi, and Will Ethridge laid the foundation of the book.

Mary Fernandez remains both a friend and my eyes and ears in the field. Her role in stimulating and positioning the components in this book will have long lasting effects.

On the editorial side and production side: Pat Smythe, Jayne Conte, Arnold Vila, Suzanne Grappi, Rae Grant, Judy Mason, Billie L. Porter, and PreMediaONE–Caryl Wenzel, Sue Katkus, Cathy Townsend, Christine Parker, and Kathy Zander.

## Special Acknowledgments

Everyone needs their own "Chief of Staff"–someone willing to make a long-term commitment while having large quantities of patience to deal with the daily challenges. For me, that was my wife Elaine, who shared in the adventures and experiences that accumulate during the creation of any book. Her willingness to run the interference essential for foiling unnecessary interruptions–grandkids excluded, of course–during manuscript development ensured that milestones and target dates were met. When coupled with her organization skills–she emphasized chief; I stressed staff–and her ever present warmth and affection, Elaine was indeed the special partner to this and all other projects.

# 1 Information Technology: Principles, Practices, and Opportunities

## LEARNING OBJECTIVES

When you have completed this chapter, you should be able to

1 Describe the six characteristics of the Information Age and discuss the role of information technology as the principal tool of the Information Age.

2 Explain the three primary components of information technology.

3 Identify the six information-handling functions and the four benefits of information technology.

4 Summarize the principles of business reengineering, while emphasizing the potential benefits to people and business.

5 Discuss the types of opportunities that information technology offers to people.

6 Describe the responsibilities of people who use information technology.

## Digital Sign Wizardry Helps
## You Keep in Touch

**Steelcase**

"*W*ait for me. I have great news!"

The team is waiting outside your office for the important meeting, and you are not there!

Unfortunately, the meeting you are just leaving—which produced *fantastic results* you cannot wait to share—ran a bit long. How can you get a message to your team, to let them know you are on the way? A telephone call to an administrative assistant near the group's meeting area works. Because you have the Wizard™ Web Sign on the wall outside your office door, the assistant can instantly post your digital message, "Wait for me. I have great news!" so that it is displayed for everyone to see.

Steelcase, one of the world's largest office furniture makers, developed this electronic version of the familiar name plate that is a standard fixture on office doors. The Steelcase digital sign is much more useful—on it you can post your daily schedule, summarize your project status, or tell the team you will be there in a few moments.

Another version, made for use outside conference and meeting rooms, displays daily meeting schedules and shows times when the room is vacant. The 6$\frac{1}{2}$-inch backlit screen also displays the name of the meeting leader and the topic being discussed.

With Steelcase's Wizard Web Signs, company staff can

- Display messages and meeting times on any Wizard sign via the the company intranet or LAN network
- Check the availability of a meeting room
- Reserve the appropriate room for the desired time
- Extend a room reservation via the sign's touch screen when a meeting is running long
- Quickly release a room for colleagues in need of space
- Instantly claim an available room for an impromptu meeting via the touch screen, thereby recording its use in the company system

Since the Wizard system can connect with e-mail and calendar systems used by companies, the information is accessible to anyone in the company. The Wizard even keeps track of room usage. Reports and charts can be produced that indicate how often rooms are in use, which projects use them most frequently, and how often the use is impromptu rather than scheduled. What was once just a room sign is now a digital assistant.

When you get down to it, information technology is changing the way we work, the way we live, and the way we play. We are in the midst of a revolution—a digital revolution. Yet what we have witnessed in the last few decades is nothing compared to what we will experience in the future. While innovations and technology helped shape the twentieth century, they will *define* the twenty-first century.

*M*any of the digital innovations of the last century are now commonplace: personal computers, cellular mobile phones, the Internet and World Wide Web, and video conferencing, to name a few. All of these innovations depend on information technology (IT) for their development and use.

Businesses are capitalizing on the explosion in information technology to move information faster and to coordinate many activities simultaneously. The goal is to respond to customers' needs with greater efficiency and accuracy than ever before. Here are examples of the breakthroughs companies have made with IT technology:

- Aetna U.S. Healthcare is one of the world's leading health provider companies. Headquartered in Hartford, Connecticut, Aetna emphasizes health maintenance to prevent the need for treatment of illnesses and diseases for its 15,000 members. A central information technology tool is a vital prevention resource. Through its U.S. Quality Algorithms affiliate, Aetna maintains a huge data warehouse containing information about its members, healthcare providers, and medical plan sponsors. The database holds medical, disability, and pharmacy information for every member. The data warehouse is routinely processed to help physicians understand the treatment and procedures that have been performed for a patient. Moreover, members are sent notices automatically, reminding them to go for examinations that are part of the services covered by their medical plan. Hence patients with diabetes do not have to depend on their memories to have routine eye examinations or special blood analyses. The data warehouse provides the necessary information to trigger the release of timely reminders and the basis for following up to see that patients receive appropriate treatment. Aetna relies on its information technology resources to help its policyholders maintain good health, a much better alternative than treating illnesses and diseases *after* they arise.

- Big Science Company, of Atlanta, which was later acquired by e-Gain, created a system that makes it possible to give visitors to the company's World Wide Web site instantaneous, correct answers to questions they pose. Its virtual agents (computer programs called Klones) can chat with humans and infer their needs and interests using plain English and interactive conversational dialogue. If a Klone cannot solve a problem, it can escalate to a live customer-support representative via e-mail or online communications links. Well-known consumer product and technology companies have incorporated this capability into their customer-support systems. Of course, Klones will never replace humans, but they can be a real boon to shoppers or potential customers trying to get answers in a hurry. Want to try for your self? Go to www.egain.com and talk to Eve, the electronic Klone who will answer your questions.

- Shopping for eyeglasses is frustrating. When trying on frames, it is difficult to see what various styles look like *on you*, because you are not wearing your glasses! Also, many stores do not carry a large selection of frames. Eyeglasses.com, an online store, uses the Internet to reach customers regardless of their geographic location. Customers can scan a photo of themselves at home and send it via e-mail to eyeglasses.com (www.eyeglasses.com). Company staff will use the photo to show how different frames look. Several possibilities can be viewed side by side by displaying the company's Web page on your display screen. Best of all, frames from eyeglasses.com cost the same or less than those you buy in a retail store.

There is no limit to the imaginative ways information technology can help in day-to-day activities, whether personal or business related. It all begins with the creation of innovative ideas. But make no mistake, the same information technology that offers these tremendous advantages can be misused, either through carelessness or through outright underhandedness. Even though companies are able to move information electronically at lightning speed, some still respond to customer information requests at a snail-like pace. Then there are electronic interlopers who eavesdrop on private conversations and snoop into sensitive records. Consider these events:

- Over a Thanksgiving weekend, an intruder entered a communications network at the General Electric Company, boring through the system's security protection. GE officials were particularly concerned because the break-in involved a system containing proprietary company information. This breach of security sent a chill through the corporate community about the dangers of online access and made executives wonder whether their own systems were adequately protected.
- In a recent, large-scale survey conducted by the Federal Bureau of Investigation (FBI) and the Computer Security Institute, 85 percent of the participants indicated they had suffered security breaches. The average reported loss was $2 million.
- Losses from fraudulent and misleading business transactions conducted over the Internet is expected to reach $15 billion annually by 2005 according to a recent report in *CIO Magazine.*
- More than 750,000 individual identities are stolen in a typical year. Identity theft, whereby the personal identification, financial, and credit-card records of an individual are taken over and used by someone else, is a growing concern globally. In the past, this occurred when someone stole traditional mail and correspondence and then used the identity information it contained. Now, this type of theft also often involves unauthorized access to personal information stored in computer databases.

Suffice it to say that creating innovations also includes the responsibility to provide safeguards against their unintended, hurtful uses.

This book explores the role of IT in today's world. As you will see, the applications of IT are virtually limitless. IT can turn ordinary products into smart products, such as the digital interactive office sign. At the very least, IT transforms the way we work and play.

Today whether you start, buy, sell, invent, build, manage, or finance companies, products, or services, you will find that a working knowledge of information technology principles and practices is essential—there are virtually no exceptions. Using IT capabilities effectively and creatively can be a key to your success, whether you are focusing on a professional, healthcare, entrepreneurial, manufacturing, or service career. If you plan to work in the field of information technology itself, including the Internet, where specialists create new types of IT and develop new uses for existing IT, you will require not only a good understanding of the technology but also insight into the most effective ways in which people can benefit from its use.

The pages that follow describe many ways in which people and companies are developing and using IT today and planning for its application tomorrow. Although a number of these examples come from different areas of society, most are taken from the business world. In today's quality- and productivity-conscious, globally competitive environment, it is businesspeople who drive the development of IT. Innovations in IT are providing business opportunities that could not have been imagined only a few years ago.

As you progress through this book, you will read a series of special features describing how companies (large and small) and people are capitalizing on information technology. Features titled *Information Technology in Practice* relate examples of successful IT use.

Two other features will help you further understand information technology. *Critical Connections* are brief case studies that are presented in two parts. The first part, which appears during the chapter, introduces a situation in which IT is used or can be used in a meaningful way. At the end of the chapter, Part II of each *Critical Connections* feature explains how the company connected information technology to good practice, thereby improving the performance of its people or products. Questions are raised to further heighten your critical thinking about the application.

Also throughout the chapter, you will find *Reality Check* features. These include candid comments from the author based on my personal experience working with high-tech companies, Internet companies, and traditional businesses in the United States and elsewhere. The *Reality Check* features are not only interesting to read, but they are a useful way of seeing still another dimension of the rapidly evolving world of information technology in business.

Our journey into the world of IT begins with a description of the Information Age and a discussion of what it means for us.

# Welcome to the Information Age

We live in a society where information is an essential resource and knowledge is valuable. Only in the last 30 to 40 years have information and knowledge been recognized as assets that a society needs to develop and manage. With that realization, the Information Age began. To help you appreciate the social transformation wrought by the Information Age, here is a look at how it evolved.

## The Evolution of the Information Age

**Agricultural Age**
The period up to the 1800s, when the majority of workers were farmers whose lives revolved around agriculture.

Until the 1800s, long before the day of the digital sign wizard, the great majority of the world's people led lives that revolved around agriculture. During the **Agricultural Age**, entire families worked in partnership with the land to provide enough food for themselves (Table 1.1). This is still the case in many developing countries today.

As new tools and techniques gradually improved and extended the land that farmers could exploit for growing crops or grazing their herds, it became possible to produce more food with fewer hours of labor. Now most farm families could produce more food than they needed for themselves, enabling them to barter or sell farm products in return for other goods and services. This led to the expansion of the nonagricultural sector and the evolution of society into the next stage.

**Industrial Age**
The period from the 1800s to 1957, when work processes were simplified through mechanization and automation.

With the coming of the **Industrial Age**—first to England in the early 1800s, slightly later to other countries—workers were assisted by machines, which greatly extended their capabilities. A partnership developed between people and machines. As the nineteenth century progressed, machines became the primary tool for the majority of workers. With the simplification of more processes through mechanization and automation, the number of people working in manufacturing and industry increased. By the middle of the twentieth century, the great majority of workers in advanced societies had shifted from farming to industry.

**Information Age**
The period that began in 1957, in which the majority of workers are involved in the creation, distribution, and application of information.

The **Information Age** began in the United States in 1957, the first year that white-collar workers outnumbered blue-collar workers. Although agriculture and manufacturing are still important, most of today's workers are involved in the creation, distribution,

| Table 1.1   The Evolution of the Information Age | | | |
| --- | --- | --- | --- |
|  | **AGRICULTURAL AGE** | **INDUSTRIAL AGE** | **INFORMATION AGE** |
| Time Period | Pre-1800s | 1800s to 1957 | 1957 to present |
| Majority of Workers | Farmers | Factory workers | Knowledge workers |
| Partnership | People and land | People and machines | People and people |
| Principal Tool | Hand tools | Machines | Information technology |

and application of information. These **knowledge workers** now outnumber those employed in agriculture and manufacturing throughout the developed world. In the Information Age, the partnership is one of people with other people, and the principal tool is information technology.

Knowledge workers are found across many different professions. Stockbrokers, bankers, accountants, financial planners, and risk managers come to mind immediately. Other types of knowledge workers are telecommunications specialists, physicians, attorneys, systems analysts, computer programmers, journalists, and medical researchers.

Knowledge workers often depend on front-line service workers for data. The counter attendants at your local McDonald's are not knowledge workers themselves, but they do capture data for others to analyze. When they enter the details of your order into a cash register/computer terminal, they are providing useful data to help knowledge workers manage inventory, order supplies, and schedule workers. Knowledge workers, in fact, use information generated throughout the organization—on the front line, in the back office, and in the executive suite.

## The Characteristics of the Information Age

Six characteristics distinguish the Information Age from previous ages:

1. An information-based society has arisen.
2. Businesses depend on information technology to get their work done.
3. Work processes are being transformed to increase productivity.
4. Information technology provides the means to rethink—that is, recreate or *reengineer*—conventional business processes.
5. Success in business is largely determined by the effectiveness with which information technology is used.
6. Information technology is embedded in many products and services.

Underlying all of these characteristics is the central importance of data and information processing in the day-to-day activities of most people in the industrialized world.[1] Following is a closer look at the characteristics that define the Information Age.

**An Information Society**   The first characteristic describes how the Information Age came about. Basically, it began with the rise of an information society that depends on information technology. In an **information society,** more people work at handling information than in the agriculture and manufacturing sectors combined. This is as true in the United States (Figure 1.1), as it is in Great Britain, Australia, and Japan—just a few of the countries that are information societies.

Person-to-person communications and IT links between individuals and businesses are important features of an information society. Effective use of IT enables a group of people working together to accomplish more than those same individuals could do working alone.

**Capitalizing on Information Technology**   As you will see throughout this book, the second characteristic of the Information Age is that an information society depends on knowing when and how to use computers. Equally important are the capabilities to communicate information and to interconnect people through information technology.

**Transformation of Work**   Thirdly, in addition to its startling new tools, the Information Age is characterized by the transformation of earlier tools and work processes. These changes have led to increased productivity and effectiveness in the workplace. Consider, for example, the transformation of agricultural work processes during the Industrial Age

**knowledge workers**
Workers involved in the creation, distribution, and application of information.

**information society**
A society in which more people work at handling information than at agriculture and manufacturing combined.

---

[1]*Data* are facts—details that describe people, places, objects, and events. In and of themselves, they have little value. When a set of facts about an item or issue of interest are gathered and synthesized into a useful form, they become *information*.

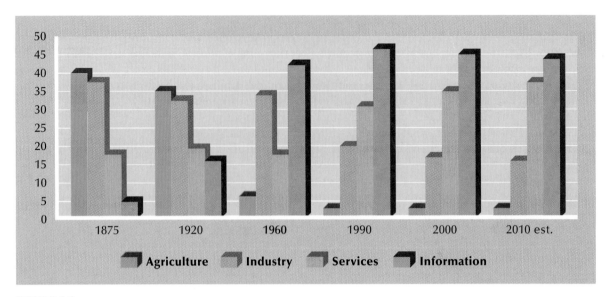

**FIGURE 1.1**

***U.S. Workforce by Sector***

In the U.S. information society, more people work at handling information than at agriculture and manufacturing combined.

*Source:* United States Department of Labor.

through mechanization. First, tractors that pulled plows, cultivators, and harvesters replaced horses and oxen. Then many agricultural-era tools were further mechanized to become self-propelled; not even a tractor was needed to pull them. The result of this mechanization was a vast improvement in productivity. More work could be accomplished in the same number of labor hours. In the Agricultural Age, it might have taken a family of four with one ox two weeks to plow a field; with mechanization, the work could be accomplished by one person in a day or two.

Today, information technology is generating new knowledge about what, when, and where to plant and how to care for the crops as they grow. Through information technology, the productivity of both farmers and the land is further increasing.

This farm example illustrates how work is transformed. New tools and work processes are combined with earlier tools and activities in ways that raise their productivity and effectiveness. **Work processes** are the activities that workers perform, the way they perform them, and the tools they use. **Productivity** is a measure of the amount of work that can be accomplished with a certain level of effort—that is, the specific level of output that is produced with a specific amount of input. **Effectiveness** is the extent to which desirable results are achieved.

**work processes**
The combination of activities that workers perform, the way they perform those activities, and the tools they use.

**productivity**
The relationship between the results of an activity (output) and the resources used to create those results (inputs).

**effectiveness**
The extent to which desirable results are achieved.

 **REALITY CHECK**
Too often, people seek magic solutions to the problems and challenges that confront them. Some look for a perfect pill that will enable them to eat all the fattening foods they want without gaining weight. Others spend beyond their means and hope that a lottery win will lift them out of debt.

But solutions to real-world problems are never that simple. Similarly, some businesspeople believe that installing and knowing how to use a computer is enough to guarantee success in the Information Age. However, success also requires an understanding of information technology's principles and practices, the opportunities it can offer, and its limitations. The true advantages of IT are realized when you use the information it provides in a way that creates opportunities and produces results. The knowledge that allows you to do the right thing at the right time can create tremendous advantages for you. ■

**Rethinking Business Practices**   The fourth characteristic of information technology is the capability it provides to rethink conventional business practices. When businesses introduced IT into their firms, they typically sought to use computer processing to automate routine tasks that workers had previously performed manually. The ways of conducting business did not really change; they just speeded up. More business transactions were conducted in a shorter period of time. If the activities of a business were a mess as a result of disorganization or faulty procedures, automation accomplished nothing more than *speeding up the mess*.

Properly used, information technology does more than simply speed up routine activities. It allows companies to rethink conventional ways of doing business. It provides the opportunity to reengineer what is being done in a company or in an entire industry. **Reengineering** is a concept that entered management vocabulary in 1990 with the publication of a *Harvard Business Review* article by professor and consultant Michael Hammer. Although the term is used less frequently today (a direct result of its inappropriate use by managers as a justification for taking many actions, whether they were truly reengineering or not), the principle behind it is *still* important. Reengineering involves:

- Rethinking business *practices*
- Focusing on business *processes*
- Introducing *radical improvements* to benefit both a business and its customers

**Business processes** are collections of *activities*, often spanning several departments, that take one or more kinds of input and create a result that is of value to a company's *customers* (Figure 1.2). The acceptance and processing of a customer's order for manufactured goods is a typical business process. In processing the order, the company's sales, inventory, manufacturing, shipping, and accounting departments all play a role. The activities they carry out make up the order fulfillment business process.

The first step in reengineering is to take a fresh look at a business process to see if it is fulfilling its objective and to determine whether it can be carried out in less time, using fewer steps, fewer resources, or fewer people. Reengineering does not seek incremental improvements of, say, 10 to 15 percent. Rather it seeks 100 to 200 percent improvements in the overall activity—a huge leap in performance.

The *Information Technology in Practice* feature, "Electronic Postage Arrives on the Internet," illustrates how the most ordinary, routine practices can be handled more efficiently by the combination of innovative thinking and creative use of information technology.

During the Industrial Age, greater productivity was attained by separating a work process into component tasks, with different workers specializing in each of the tasks. This is called **division of labor.** Today, greater productivity is achieved by connecting different workers so that they can share the same information to produce a joint result. In the Information Age, work is accomplished through

- **Teamwork**   People working together to accomplish a team outcome rather than an individual job.
- **Interconnection**   Individuals communicating, regardless of distance, to exchange ideas, experiences, and insights.

**reengineering**
The reshaping of business processes to remove barriers that prohibit an organization from providing better products and services and to help the organization capitalize on its strengths.

**business processes**
Collections of activities, often spanning several departments, that take one or more kinds of input and create a result that is of value to a company's customers.

**division of labor**
Separation of a work process into component tasks, with different workers specializing in each of the tasks.

---

 **REALITY CHECK**   Carelessly applied, reengineering is a euphemism for cost reduction through layoffs or an excuse to make employees work harder with less support. In these situations, changes are called *reengineering*, but the goal is really to reduce costs, lower the head count, or speed up work. *Reengineering* is also used as a buzzword to describe minimal improvements or minor adjustments to existing steps.

In other words, simply *calling* a change reengineering does not make it so. ■

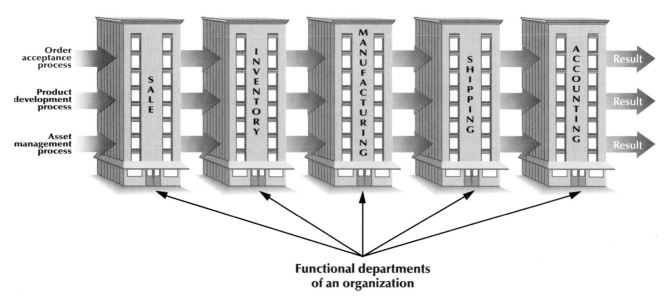

**FIGURE 1.2**

***Process Focus in Companies***

Business processes cut across the functional units of an enterprise.

- **Shared Information**   Communication networks making information available to several people simultaneously, instantaneously, or whenever they need it.

Continual concerns in the Information Age, therefore, are as follows: Is the needed information available? Can it be made available to appropriate staff members directly?

**Information Technology Influences Success**   The fifth characteristic of the Information Age is closely linked to the third: Information technology is to the Information Age what mechanization was to the Industrial Age.

It was hard to succeed in the Agricultural Age if you did not understand the capabilities and limitations of the horses, land, and farm implements you used. Likewise, in the Industrial Age, you had to know how to use and care for your machines. In the Information Age, the most successful people are those who know how to make the most of information technology. That involves more than just knowing how to key data into a computer or how to print reports. Success requires knowing what IT can do to improve your personal performance (quality, speed, and efficiency, for example) and how it can enhance your business's products and services in ways that add to their value for customers.

**Embedded Information Technology**   The sixth characteristic of the Information Age is that information technology is often a component in products and services. That is what *embedded* information technology means: IT is integrated with the other components of products and services. Products and services with embedded technology are sometimes called *knowledge-based* because knowledge about their function and performance are embedded within them.

The interactive Wizard Web Sign, for instance, is more than just an ordinary sign outside an office. The information technology embedded within it transforms the sign, giving it new features and capabilities that would be impossible for a traditional sign. The integration of information technology into the navigation and guidance system of a giant passenger aircraft or an electronic camera does the same thing—adds features and advanced capabilities to a traditional system.

An important point: Information technology is valuable only if the recipient finds the capabilities it provides desirable. Value may consist of convenience, quality, reliability, or novelty—any characteristic the consumer feels is useful. IT embedded within an aircraft navigation system is universally considered valuable. So is the information technology in

# INFORMATION TECHNOLOGY IN PRACTICE

## Electronic Postage Arrives on the Internet

Running out of stamps when you have something to mail is just plain frustrating. Trips to the post office to buy stamps often entail long lines, especially, it seems, when you are short on time. Now there is an alternative way to buy postage.

Stamps.com Internet postage takes the hassle out of buying stamps and preparing your mail. With Internet postage, you can buy and print your own postage right from your desktop computer. All that is required is the Stamps.com software, a standard laser or inkjet printer and an Internet connection. The Stamps.com software can be downloaded from the company's site on the World Wide Web (www. stamps.com).

With Stamps.com Internet postage, buying postage is easy. All you do is log into the Stamps.com software, buy postage via a credit card, and then the postage is credited to your account. When you need a stamp, you use the software to print postage directly on an envelope or postage labels. The eletronic stamp contains the amount of the postage as well as a 2-D bar code.

The post office benefits too. The greater the number of individuals buying and using electronic postage, the shorter the lines at the post office stamp window.

Electronic postage can be used for first-class, priority, and express mail, as well as parcel post, media mail and any mail going overseas. All are available with a keystroke—and without a trip to the post office.

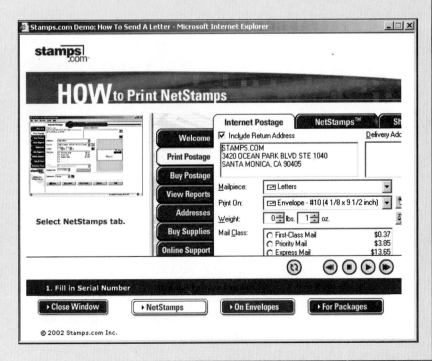

point-and-shoot electronic cameras. Regarding the Wizard Web Sign . . . we will have to wait for the value verdict from consumers.

The pervasiveness of knowledge-based products, services, and activities in today's society has so thoroughly changed the way we act that we often take this technology for granted. Consider the introduction of information technology into the personal travel industry (Figure 1.3). Today, many travelers shop for and book their tickets and reservations over the Internet, either with the airline directly or with an online travel service. Before online and computerized reservation systems were available, passengers and travel agents had to call an airline directly to make a reservation, providing the traveler's name, address, and telephone number verbally. Tickets were written by hand. Advance seat assignment was impossible. Either you got on the plane and took the first seat available, or you were assigned a seat at the gate just prior to boarding.

IT has not only enabled travelers and travel agents to make travel arrangements more efficiently, but it has also changed the nature of the services they use. In addition to making reservations and accepting payments, each can now obtain the advance assignment of seats, request special accommodations, and keep track of the number of miles the traveler has flown during the course of a year—all through an information system. Furthermore, a traveler's preferences in automobiles, hotels, and special services are entered into the computer network. Even though travel itself can still be a hassle

**FIGURE 1.3**

***Embedded IT in Personal Travel***

The travel industry has used IT to increase the number and quality of the services it offers.

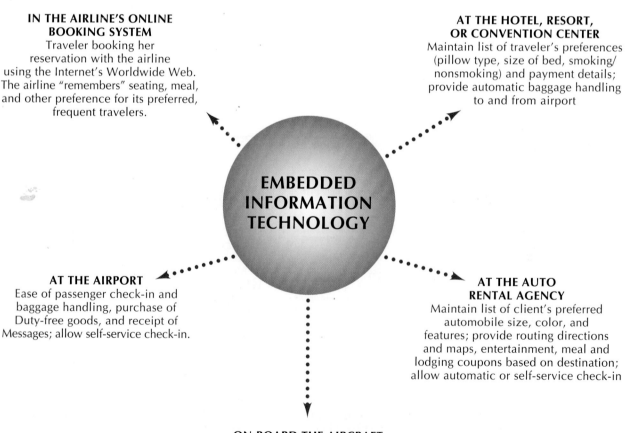

**IN THE AIRLINE'S ONLINE BOOKING SYSTEM**
Traveler booking her reservation with the airline using the Internet's Worldwide Web. The airline "remembers" seating, meal, and other preference for its preferred, frequent travelers.

**AT THE HOTEL, RESORT, OR CONVENTION CENTER**
Maintain list of traveler's preferences (pillow type, size of bed, smoking/nonsmoking) and payment details; provide automatic baggage handling to and from airport

**EMBEDDED INFORMATION TECHNOLOGY**

**AT THE AIRPORT**
Ease of passenger check-in and baggage handling, purchase of Duty-free goods, and receipt of Messages; allow self-service check-in.

**AT THE AUTO RENTAL AGENCY**
Maintain list of client's preferred automobile size, color, and features; provide routing directions and maps, entertainment, meal and lodging coupons based on destination; allow automatic or self-service check-in

**ON-BOARD THE AIRCRAFT**
Use telephone and fax, notebook computers, and send or receive electronic mail.

(e.g., getting to and from the airport, going through security checks, waiting through weather-related delays), making personal travel arrangements is much easier today than it was in the past.

Advances in travel and travel arrangement continue as the travel industry capitalizes on ever-more powerful capabilities in information technology. However, the same travel agents who today benefit from online computer reservations systems *yet who have not improved the services they offer compared to a few years ago* are finding themselves increasingly vulnerable. From an IT perspective, passengers and airlines are able to deal directly through electronic commerce on the Internet. If a travel agency does not offer additional value to the traveler, it will surely lose customers.

Embedded IT systems are also making the airlines more effective even as they make it possible for them to deal directly with their passengers. Passengers can now check flight schedules, prices, and seat assignments over the Internet. Airlines also issue electronic tickets, that is, they issue the *information* about the ticket, avoiding the necessity of printing and mailing or holding a paper ticket. All of this is more cost-efficient for the airline. It involves fewer staff, which in turn reduces the cost of booking and processing tickets before, during, and after the flight.

## What Is Information Technology?

By now, you probably have a good idea of what the term *information technology* means, but a careful definition should be helpful. **Information technology** refers to a wide variety of items and abilities used in the creation, storage, and dispersal of data and information as well as in the creation of knowledge. **Data** are raw facts, figures, and details. **Information** refers to an organized, meaningful, and useful interpretation of data, while **knowledge** is the awareness and understanding of a set of information and how that information can be put to the best use.

A simple example will clarify these distinctions. At a retail store, a specific customer order identifies the customer, the item(s) the customer purchased and in what quantity, and the price. These details are the raw data. At the end of the business period, the details of all customer orders are assembled, summarized, and compared with expected orders. This information tells managers whether the store's performance is better or worse than anticipated. This information may be combined with another set of information to create the knowledge that some customers are shopping at another store because of the competitor's new low price program. This knowledge may cause the store's managers to change their pricing strategy. There are many examples throughout this book of the role good information can play in improving a business's performance.

**information technology**
A term used to refer to a wide variety of items and abilities used in the creation, storage, and dispersal of data and information. Its three main components are computers, communications networks, and know-how.

**data**
Raw facts, figures, and details.

**information**
An organized, meaningful, and useful interpretation of data.

**knowledge**
An awareness and understanding of a set of information and how that information can be put to the best use.

Many of the world's airlines are rethinking their entire reservation and ticketing process. Even the capabilities provided by information technology just a few years ago are being rethought as new advances, such as the Internet, are widely accessible. Companies that fail to capitalize on these new advances frequently find themselves at a tremendous disadvantage. They may even be left out, or *disintermediated*, from the entire buyer chain of events. Such is the case with traditional travel agents, who risk being disintermediated as airlines and consumers realize they can *do away with the middleperson.*

Businesses of all types need to be like the airlines. *Standing still,* regardless of how well a company functions today, will put its success in jeopardy tomorrow. Rethinking business processes; capitalizing on Internet capabilities; dealing directly with customers to provide all available information whenever possible; and continuing to innovate as information technology evolves; are among the most important principles of business today. ■

## U.S. Postal Service Uses IT to Manage International Mail

Moving letters and packages internationally has been an important part of the U.S. Postal Service (USPS) for more than 70 years. In order to haul those parcels to and from international destinations, USPS works with a variety of different carriers; it does not maintain its own fleet of planes.

Postal workers visit each arriving or departing plane to verify the proper shipment of its many parcels loaded on each plane. Any unusual event is noted and recorded. For many years, postal employees noted *mail handling irregularities*—late arrivals, or missing or misrouted parcels—by recording the incident on a special form, along with an explanation (failure to load a parcel, poor weather, aircraft mechanical problem, etc.). Forms were then submitted to a processing center where the details were keyed into a database.

When analyzed, the USPS could identify and deal with recurring problems or with carriers that encountered more than the normal rate of difficulties.

Handheld computers are used today instead of paper forms. Since postal workers can enter parcel and carrier information directly into the handheld system, they are not only much more efficient, but there is never a question of illegible forms. Moreover, the parcel information can be electronically transferred directly into the USPS database without any intermediary steps.

Data and information are processed by information technology components. As Figure 1.4 shows, information technology is comprised of three primary components: computers, communications networks, and know-how. Combining these components in certain ways creates opportunities to be productive, effective, and successful.

## Computers

**computer**
An electronic system that can be instructed to accept, process, store, and present data and information.

The **computer,** any electronic system that can be instructed to accept, process, store, and present data and information, is ubiquitous in the daily lives of many people around the globe. In fact, it is difficult to think of *any* field that does not involve or is not affected by computers.

Computers do not always look the way you think they should. An automated teller machine (ATM), for instance, may not fit your image of a computer. But this cash dispenser is a computer, as is the automatic check-in terminal commonly found at today's large airports. At home, your microwave and your self-focusing camera also are (or use) small computers.

Computers come in four sizes: microcomputers, midrange computers, mainframes, and supercomputers.

**personal computer (PC)/ microcomputer**
A relatively compact type of computer, the most common of all, easily outsells all other types of computers annually for use in business and at home.

**Microcomputers**   The **personal computer,** or **PC,** is a **microcomputer.** This relatively compact type of computer, the most common of all, easily outsells all other types of computers annually. Millions of PCs are sold every year for use in business and at home. PCs are most frequently seen in one of the five following types:

FIGURE 1.4
*The Forces of Information Technology*
The three components of information technology are inseparable. Computers and communications are of little use without know-how.

1. **Desktop Computers** The original form of PC, **desktop computers** are designed so that their keyboard and display unit, and sometimes the processing unit, sit compactly on the surface of a desk or table (although frequently the processing unit of today's desktop computer sits on the floor). All components are connected to the processing unit by cables. Brand names include IBM, Dell, Compaq, Gateway, Hewlett-Packard, and Toshiba—all sold around the world. If you do not know desktop micromputers by name, you probably know them by what they do: word processing, e-mail, electronic spreadsheets, desktop publishing, account balancing, management of personal and business finances, creating visuals for presentations, and so on.

2. **Notebook Computers** About the size of a textbook, **notebook computers** are designed for portability. People can easily carry these 3- to 9-pound PCs wherever they go. Unlike desktop PCs, which may have detachable components, notebooks include all of their components (except a printer) in a single unit. Most desktop computer manufacturers also offer notebook computers.

3. **Tablet PCs** Lightweight PCs, **tablet PCs** weigh about three pounds and are the size of an ordinary tablet of writing paper. These PCs come in different shapes and sizes: wireless tablets that are controlled with a special pen and can be attached to a keyboard; notebook computers with a pen overlay; and convertibles in which the screen swivels and folds down on top of the keyboard, or can be detached to become a standalone tablet. Tablet PCs are used in many different situations. For example, law enforcement authorities use them to write electronic tickets for traffic violations, and insurance agents prepare damage claims on the spot by sketching details of the scene on the screen.

4. **Personal Digital Assistants** Small enough to be carried anywhere, and weighing less than a pound (454 grams), **personal digital assistants (PDAs)** are fast and powerful. Most PDAs have a pen-based capability. PDAs allow you to maintain multi-year appointment calendars, make to-do lists, keep extensive name and address directories, and jot down notes during meetings. If you want to send a fax to someone, many PDA models will retrieve the person's telephone number, dial it, and send the fax over the telephone to which it is connected. A growing number of PDAs also have wireless communications capabilities that enable them to send and receive both faxes and e-mail without being connected to a wire telephone line. The PDAs made by Palm, Handspring, and Sony dominate among PDA brands.

**desktop computer**
Designed so that their keyboard and display unit, and sometimes the processing unit, sit compactly on the surface of a desk or table (although frequently the processing unit of today's desktop computer sits on the floor).

**notebook computer/laptop computer**
Smaller versions of microcomputers that are designed for portability. All of their components, except a printer, are included in a single unit.

**tablet PC**
Weighing about three pounds and the size of an ordinary tablet of writing paper, these PCs come in different shapes and sizes (wireless tablets, notebook computers, and convertibles) or can be detached to become a standalone tablet.

**personal digital assistant (PDA)**
A portable computer generally used as a personal aid.

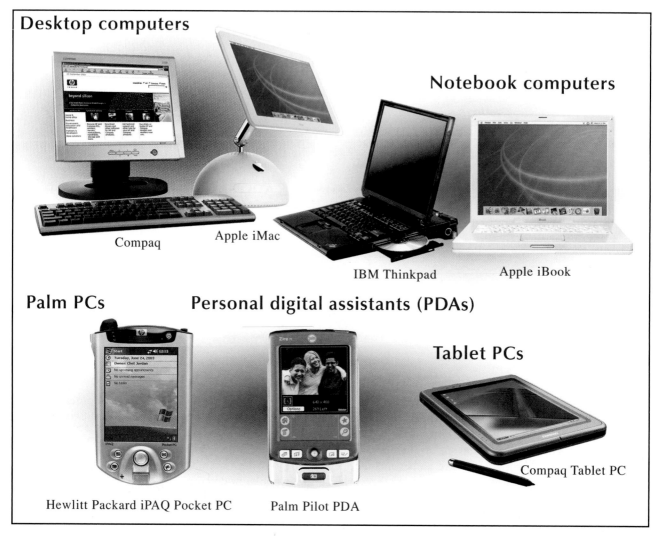

**FIGURE 1.5**

***Five Types of Microcomputer***

At one time, most microcomputers were found on desks or tabletops, but in the last decade, there has been an explosion of handheld and portable-sometimes even wearable-micros.

**palm PC**

A version of the microcomputer about the size of a pocket calculator, palmtops are used today for a small number of functions, such as maintaining personal calendars, name-and-address files, and electronic worksheets. But PC designers are building more power into these devices, so they will be used increasingly in such diverse settings as engineering and medicine where they serve to carry out calculations or to send and receive data.

**handheld computer**

A collective term for PDAs and Palm PCs, a name that is descriptive of the size and the fact that people can hold them in one hand as they enter and retrieve information with the other.

5. **Palm PCs**   **Palm PCs** are a version of the microcomputer that has grown rapidly in popularity. About the size of a pocket calculator, palmtops are used today for a small number of functions, such as maintaining personal calendars, name-and-address files, and electronic worksheets. But PC designers are building more power into these devices, so they will be used increasingly in such diverse settings as engineering and medicine where they serve to carry out calculations or to send and receive data and information. HP's iPAQ is among the most widely used Palm PCs. The number of Palm PCs in use is much smaller than the number of PDAs in use.

PDAs and Palm PCs are often collectively referred to as **handheld computers,** a name that is descriptive of the size and the fact that people can hold them in one hand as they enter and retrieve information with the other.

**Midrange and Mainframe Computers**   The computers most associated with medium- and large-size businesses are **midrange computers** (at one time called **minicomputers**) and **mainframes.** These types of computers interconnect people and large sets of information. The interconnection may be on an enterprise level—that is, across the many organizations or departments of an entire organization—or at the department level.

Mainframe computers (Figure 1.6) are generally larger, more expensive, and faster than midrange computers and permit the interconnection of a greater number of people. Mainframes also typically store larger volumes of data and information.

Midrange computers (Figure 1.7) are usually dedicated to performing specific functions when used in large corporations. For example, midrange computers are used to control complex manufacturing processes or to operate a hotel's reservation system. When used in smaller companies, midrange systems may be used for all business processing activities, including record keeping and financial systems.

One of the great advantages of mainframe systems is that they can be used for several purposes simultaneously. As midrange computers have become faster and more powerful, however, organizations have learned to use these specific-function computers to perform activities that once had to be run on a mainframe.

**Supercomputers** The most powerful of all computers, supercomputers were designed to solve problems consisting of long and difficult calculations (Figure 1.8). Since they can perform many millions of calculations per second, scientists find them highly useful for predicting weather patterns, preparing models of chemical and biological systems, mapping the surface of planets, and studying the neural network of the brain. Businesses use supercomputers to create and test new processes, machines, and products. Today, for example, when aircraft manufacturers design a new plane, they use a supercomputer to simulate the wind and weather conditions that planes encounter, and then *fly* the new plane under various simulated conditions before they attempt to build it. All of this happens in the supercomputer. Many automakers also design new vehicles on a supercomputer and then test them by simulating different driving conditions (including accidents) to evaluate the structure and safety of their designs before they invest resources in manufacturing the actual vehicle.

**Hardware, Software, and Business Systems** Computers and the equipment associated with them—monitors, printers, keyboards, and peripheral devices—are the **hardware.** This hardware can do nothing on its own. Rather, each component must be equipped with a **program** consisting of instructions that tell it how to carry out a particular task or set of tasks. **Software** refers to the instructions that manage the hardware. The computer will not function correctly unless it is properly programmed—that is, unless the software for all of its components is correct.

A **system** is a set of components—people, computers, other businesses, governmental agencies—that interact to accomplish a purpose. Systems are all around us: education

**midrange computer/ minicomputer**
A computer used to interconnect people and large sets of information. More powerful than a microcomputer, the minicomputer is usually dedicated to performing specific functions.

**mainframe**
Larger, faster, and more expensive than a midrange computer, this computer is used for several purposes simultaneously.

**hardware**
The computer and its associated equipment.

**program**
A set of instructions that directs a computer to perform certain tasks and produce certain results.

**software**
The general term for a set of instructions that controls a computer or a communications network.

**system**
A set of components that interact to accomplish a purpose.

**FIGURE 1.6**

***IBM Eserver Zseries 900***

**FIGURE 1.7**

***IBM AS/400***

**FIGURE 1.8**

*Blue Mountain Supercomputers at Los Alamos Labs*

**information system**

A business information system designed to produce the information needed for successful management of a structured problem, process, department, or business.

systems, transportation systems, and inventory systems, for example. In fact, everyone in the world lives according to an economic system, although not the same one.

Any business is also a system (Figure 1.9). Its components—marketing, manufacturing, sales, research, shipping, accounting, and human resources—all work together to create a product or service that benefits customers and therefore the employees and shareholders of the organization. Each of these components of a business is itself a system.

Contemporary businesses depend heavily on **information systems,** the systems by which data and information flow from one person or department to another. Information systems encompass everything from interoffice mail and telephone links to computer and communications systems that generate reports. They serve all of the systems of a business by linking the different components together so that they work effectively toward the same goal.

The *Information Technology in Practice* feature, "The Home Depot Way Depends on Information Technology," reveals that the world's largest do-it-yourself home improvement store simply could not exist without the broad array of IT applications it has created. Both company executives and store managers use their systems extensively throughout every business day.

**REALITY CHECK** Mainframes used to be defined by their size. While they can still fill an entire room, cost millions of dollars, and support thousands of users, there are now mainframes that can run on a laptop and support just a few individual users. Instead of size and cost, it is better today to think of a mainframe as combining two key distinguishing features: the ability to rapidly transfer a large volume of data from an array of giant capacity storage devices attached to the system, and the capability to gracefully adjust its services (i.e., temporarily terminate some services without effecting other services) in order to always keep the system running.

The names *mainframe* and *midrange computers* may be fading from the language of business and information technology. Recently, IBM, traditionally the leader in enterprise computing, announced a new family of computers, known as ⓔ-servers™, that will replace mainframes and midrange systems. Companies, large or small, can choose from a variety of ⓔ-servers™. While the models differ in performance, they all have similar design characteristics.

So now, if someone says ⓔ-server™, they may actually be referring to a computer with mainframe-like capabilities (and vice versa). ▪

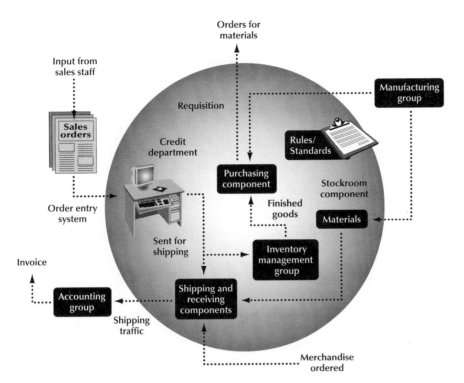

**FIGURE 1.9**

*A Typical Business System*
A system is a set of components that interact to accomplish a purpose. The business system shown here includes not only people and departments but also procedures for conducting the business efficiently.

## Communications Networks

The invention of the telephone by Alexander Graham Bell in 1876 did a great deal to foster communication. Today, you can call someone anywhere in the world *from* anywhere in the world, and when you speak into the telephone, your voice will reach its destination in less than one second, whether you are calling Great Britain, China, South Africa, or any other country across the globe. Moreover, your telephone may be the wireline version that was the norm for so many decades, or the now widely used wireless and highly mobile cellular telephone.

An integral part of information technology is **communication**—the sending and receiving of data and information over a communications network. A **communications network** consists of a set of stations at different locations that are interconnected through a medium that enables people to send and receive data and information. Telephone wires and cables are still common communications media, although as indicated above, wireless means are growing rapidly. **Data communication** is the transmission of data and information through a communications medium.

Communications networks are revolutionizing business products and services as well as our personal lives. Airlines use communications networks to communicate with one another and share information on passenger reservations, meal requirements, and baggage handling. Public networks, like America Online (AOL), Earthlink, Minitel, the Internet, and the World Wide Web—all of which offer a wide variety of commerce and other types of services—allow individuals to correspond with others electronically through their PCs. You will see many other uses of data communication in the IT practices covered in this book.

## Know-How

Information technology is only as good as the user's *know-how*. In other words, you have to *know how* to explore and take advantage of the opportunities this technology creates. Information technology **know-how** consists of

- Familiarity with the tools of IT, including the Internet
- Possession of the skills needed to use these tools
- An understanding of when to use IT to solve a problem or create an opportunity

**communication**
The sending and receiving of data and information over a communications network.

**communications network**
A set of locations, or nodes, consisting of hardware, programs, and information linked together as a system that transmits and receives data and information.

**data communication**
The transmission of data and information through a communications medium.

**know-how**
The capability to do something well.

# INFORMATION TECHNOLOGY IN PRACTICE

## The Home Depot Way Depends on Information Technology

The Home Depot, founded in 1978 in Atlanta, Georgia, is the world's largest home-improvement retailer, with over 1,500 stores in the United States, Canada, Puerto Rico, and Chile. It has been voted "America's Most Admired Specialty Retailer" by *Fortune* magazine for many consecutive years. Home Depot stores cater to do-it-yourselfers, as well as to home improvement, construction and building-maintenance professionals. Each store stocks approximately 40,000 to 50,000 different kinds of building and home-improvement tools and materials as well as lawn and garden products.

*The Home Depot Way* is the slogan for this company that excels in customer service. If you are unsure about proper use of tools or materials, or how to install a product, the associate will be certain you have the right information before you leave. Visit a Home Depot store on Saturday mornings and you will find clinics designed to help homeowners develop their do-it-yourself skills such as building, plumbing, electrical work, and floor covering. There are even clinics for kids where

they learn to hammer, saw, and assemble usable items (bird houses are a favorite). Each store also offers free design and decorating consultations, truck and tool rental, delivery, free potting, and many other services to accommodate customers' home improvement needs.

Low prices are another reason behind the company's excellent reputation, and a key element in *The Home Depot Way.* It does not run promotional sales that give customers a brief time to buy items at artificially low prices, only to return to higher prices after the sale. Instead, it features *every day low prices.* Products are always at the lowest possible price—lower than traditional home improvement stores.

The Home Depot's effective use of information technology (acknowledged through its many technology awards and by magazine publisher Forbes and others as a "best user of information technology") makes this possible. The company processes more than 1 billion customer transactions annually—enough so that if customers were lined up one behind the other they would circle the earth more than 14 times.

A large data center at the Atlanta corporate headquarters, consisting of interconnected mainframe computers holds the company's large database of financial, merchandising, distribution, and human resources data and information. A communications network of more than 2 million miles links every store to headquarters.

Each store has its own mid-range computer for merchandising

and inventory management. When a customer takes a product to the check out counter, the Home Depot associate scans the package, retrieving the product's price from the store computer. As each item is priced, the quantity on hand for the item is reduced in the store's inventory database. If the customer chooses to pay for the purchase by credit or debit card, the associate scans the card, instantly triggering the system to verify the validity of the card using the company's vast telecommunications network.

Each store manager is responsible for ensuring that merchandise is on hand when customers want it. To assist them, a wireless terminal mounted on a rolling cart, is used in the store to enter orders for items. As each requisition is entered, it is transmitted using infrared signals to the store computer. At the end of the day, the sales and order details accumulated in the store computer are transmitted to company headquarters where they are assembled and processed.

The Home Depot is a dramatic retailing success. Yet, the company as we know it could not exist without information technology.

Here is a simple analogy to demonstrate what this means:

You probably know someone who is a whiz at technical details—maybe concerning cars, sports, electronics, or medicine—but cannot put those details into a language and perspective that other people can understand or appreciate. The whiz is too focused on the technical specifics to see the big picture—the human, day-to-day use of the information.

Say you go to an athletic event with a couple of *technicians*. They know who holds all of the records; how fast the players run; how often they score; whether they perform better on rainy, sunny, or windy days; and the odds that they will attempt a risky play. They are so caught up in these details that they lose sight of the game being played. There is a time and a place for statistics, but most fans prefer the company of those who know the fundamentals but do not overwhelm them with details—friends who appreciate the game.

Like sports fans who concentrate so hard on memorizing stats that they lose sight of the actual game, people who focus too much on the technical details of IT often fail to grasp the big picture. The big picture encompasses what information technology can do today and what it might be able to do tomorrow. It involves knowing when an approach will work *and* when it will not.

Think of IT as you would an automobile. If you are a mechanic, you have to know how to diagnose an engine problem and how to take the engine apart to replace or repair parts. If you are not a mechanic, you do not need to know how to disassemble an engine and put it back together again. All you are interested in is what the automobile will do for you. This could be providing transportation for yourself or for your business, or presenting an opportunity to open a store that sells car-care products. Most users of IT are like the people who are not mechanics. They do not need to know the internal workings of IT. All they are interested in is reaping its benefits. For this, they simply need the know-how to use IT.

# The Principles of Information Technology

It is always rewarding to have the right answer to a question. In fact, anticipating questions and identifying answers can be an effective way to solve problems. It is also a method many people use in studying for examinations: They attempt to identify the questions that they will be asked and then master the answers to those questions. But what happens when the question has not been anticipated correctly or when it changes? The known *answer* may no longer apply; in fact, being prepared with this *wrong* answer may be downright counterproductive to solving the problem or answering the new question correctly.

The most effective way to learn a subject is to master the basic facts of that subject and to understand the principles underlying those facts. A *principle* is a fundamental rule, guideline, or motivating idea that, when applied to a situation, produces a desirable result. Focusing on principles rather than on a particular situation or set of facts prepares you to deal with a variety of problems and opportunities.

The first principle of information technology describes the purpose of IT: *Information technology's great usefulness is as an aid in solving problems, unlocking creativity, and making people more effective than they would be if they did not apply IT to their activities.*

Equally important to the effective application of information technology is the principle of high-tech/high-touch : *The more "high-tech" the information technology you are considering, the more important it is to consider the "high-touch" aspects of the matter—that is, "the people side."* A related principle stresses this: *Always fit information to people rather than asking people to adjust to information technology.*

## The Functions of Information Technology

What exactly can IT do? As Figure 1.10 shows, IT performs six information-handling functions: (1) capture, (2) processing, (3) generation, (4) storage, (5) retrieval, and (6) transmission. The way these functions are applied determines the impact IT will have.

**Capture**   It is often useful to compile detailed records of activities. This process, called data **capture,** is performed when you expect the data will be useful later. Here are some examples:

**capture**
The process of compiling detailed records of activities.

# CRITICAL CONNECTIONS 2

## Verizon Offers Directory Assistance by Computer

Verizon Communications, formed by the merger of Bell Atlantic and GTE, is one of the world's leading providers of communications services. Its companies are the largest providers of wireline and wireless communications in the United States.

Because Verizon Communications' wireless telephone service, serving some 30 million customers, spans across the United States, you can place a call from a seemingly unlimited number of locations. If you dial 411 to obtain a telephone number, the directory assistant who answers your information request may be a computer. This automated system—which is rapidly being developed at other telephone companies as well—was installed to reduce the cost to both directory assistance callers and Verizon. Relying on computer speech technology to answer the *millions* of daily information calls, the system asks the caller for the name and city and state of residence of the person or company whose number is being requested, and then hands the call over to an operator who looks up the number.

Verizon's call processing system detects and filters out the inevitable *ahs* and *ums* accompanying caller requests. It also knows to wait if the caller pauses or hesitates. But if the pause is too long, it will hand the caller over to an operator, who can provide needed assistance.

This system eliminates several seconds from every information request—a substantial time savings considering the large number of directory assistance calls the company receives each day.

- Whenever a book is checked out of the library, the name (or identification number) of the borrower and the title (or call number) of the book are captured.
- The theater box office records the assignment of every seat to an attendee as it is sold.
- A monitor records the pulse, heart rate, and white blood cell count of a hospital patient.
- When Maria Carey, the best selling vocalist, performs live, her singing is sometimes captured and transferred to a cassette tape, compact disk (CD), or computer storage for listening at a later time.
- The voice and data recorders in aircraft cockpits capture the pilots' conversations and record flight data about the aircraft's location and performance.
- When you order a book from an Internet bookstore, your name and address, billing information, and shipping information are captured along with the title of the book you are ordering.

**processing**
The process of converting, analyzing, computing, and synthesizing all forms of data or information.

**Processing**   The activity most often associated with computers, **processing,** is usually the purpose for which people and organizations purchase computers. The processing

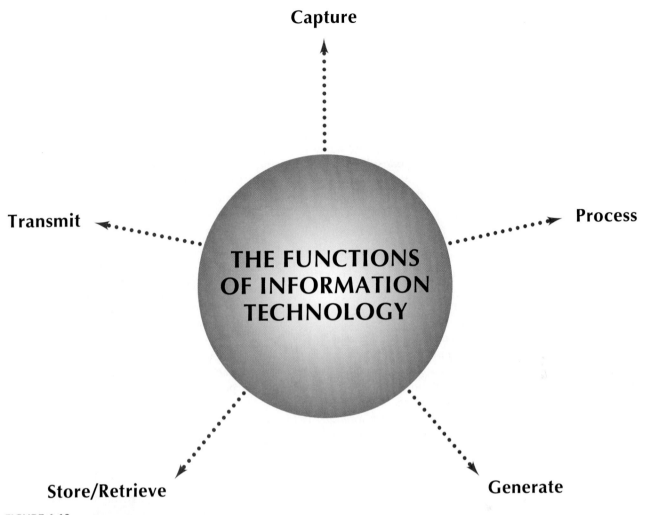

**FIGURE 1.10**

***The Six Functions of Information Technology***

The six functions of IT—capturing, processing, generating, storing and retrieving, and transmitting—may take place sequentially. In many cases, however, two or more functions take place simultaneously.

function entails converting, analyzing, computing, and synthesizing all forms of data or information.

One of the earliest business applications, **data processing**, focuses on taking data (raw numbers, symbols, and letters) and transforming them into information. An example of data processing is calculating the balance in a checkbook by taking the starting balance for the month, adding all deposits and subtracting all checks written (that is, the data) and determining the current balance.

**Information processing** is the transformation of any type of information into a different type of information. Text (reports, correspondence), sound (voice, music, tones), and images (visual information such as charts, graphs, drawings, and animated drawings) can all be processed. **Multimedia systems,** which are one type of information processing, have recently caught a lot of people's interest. These systems process multiple types of information simultaneously–for example, an animated presentation displayed on a computer screen will use information retrieved from within the computer, perhaps accompanied by music, voice, or other types of sound.

**data processing**
The process of handling data and transforming them into information.

**information processing**
A general term for the computer activity that entails processing any type of information and transforming it into a different type of information.

**multimedia system**
A computer system that can process multiple types of information simultaneously.

Other types of processing include the following:

- **Word Processing**   The creation of text-based documents, including reports, newsletters, and correspondence. Word-processing systems allow people to enter data, text, and images into a computer and transform them into a useful and attractive format.
- **Image Processing**   Converting visual information (graphics, drawings, and photos) into a format that can be managed within a computer system or transmitted between people and other computers. A process called *scanning* converts a print or film image into a form that a computer can use. (Scanners are discussed in Chapter 5).
- **Voice Processing**   The transformation and transmission of spoken information. Currently, voice information is most frequently entered into a computer system through a telephone or a microphone connected to the computer. Other systems are emerging that enable people to speak directly into a computer system to instruct it to take specific actions.

**generation**

The process of organizing information into a useful form, whether as numbers, text, sound, or visual image.

**Generation**   Information technology is frequently used to generate information through processing. **Generation** of information refers to the organization of data and information into a useful form, whether as numbers, text, sound, or visual image. Sometimes the information is regenerated in its original form. At other times, a new form is generated–for example recorded musical notes are *played* as sounds with rhythm and pauses (that is, as music).

Visualization generates information by converting data into a visual form. As a result, the meaning hidden in the detailed numbers can be revealed by viewing shapes, patterns, and relationships. Often visualization is performed to produce three-dimensional images, having height, width, and depth.

The *Information Technology in Practice* feature, "Chevron Texaco Makes a 3-D Picture Worth Millions," shows how scientific, business, and information technology principles are combined to aid in oil and gas exploration.

**storage**

The computer process of retaining information for future use.

**Storage and Retrieval**   **Storage** enables computers to keep data and information for later use. Stored data and information are placed on a storage medium (for example, a magnetic disk or CD-ROM optical disk–discussed in Chapter 5) that the computer can read when it needs to. The computer converts the data or information into a form that takes less space than the original source. For example, voice information is not stored in voice format, but rather in a specially coded electronic form that takes less space and that the computer can manage. The voice becomes, in a word, *digital.*

**retrieval**

The process by which a computer locates and copies stored data or information for further processing or for transmission to another user.

**Retrieval** entails locating and copying stored data or information for further processing or for transmission to another use. The computer user must keep track of the medium where the data or information is stored and make it available to the computer for processing.

**transmission**

The computer process of distributing information over a communications network.

**Transmission**   Sending data and information from one location to another is called **transmission.** As noted earlier, telephone systems transmit our conversation from a point of origin to a destination. Computer systems do precisely the same thing, often using telephone lines. Computer networks can also send data and information through other media, including satellites and light beams transmitted along plastic or glass optical fibers.

Modern communications networks, including the Internet, enable us to send information down the hall or around the world in an instant. PCs, mainframes, and supercomputers can be connected electronically to transmit data and information to and from one another.

There are two common forms of information transmission:

- **Electronic Mail, or E-Mail**   The acceptance, storage, and transmission of text and image messages between users of a computer system. Typically, the e-mail messages are entered through a computer keyboard and viewed on the receiving party's computer monitor (eliminating the need for sending paper messages). Frequently, additional information–images and photographs, additional text, or sound files may be

# INFORMATION TECHNOLOGY IN PRACTICE

## Chevron Texaco Makes a 3-D Picture Worth Millions

Every year, the world population grows by some 75 million people. Add this up over a period of years, and the reality is that by the middle of this century, the world's population will have grown from today's 6 billion to a whopping 9 billion people. Sadly, the greatest increase in population will be in the least developed areas of the world—places where access to telephones and even clean water is sometimes impossible.

Improving the day-to-day quality of life in both undeveloped and industrialized areas of the world depends on having energy that will permit cooking, heating, and other features often taken for granted. Projected shortages of known energy forms, notably oil and gas, mean that companies and researchers around the world are searching for new sources of energy. Yet, even though the search for new forms of energy continues, the need for exploration to find greater quantities of the forms of energy we use today becomes even more important.

Chevron Texaco Inc., of Houston, Texas, developed the world's largest

facility dedicated to oil exploration and production. It uses visualization technology to turn details about hidden oil and gas into pictures that show analysts underground energy sources. Visualization provides important information that aides Chevron Texaco in determining whether or not to drill deep into the earth for oil.

Geo-scientists—experts who explore for oil—at Chevron Texaco study earth formations, capturing data that describes the type and structure of rock found in areas of exploration. Thousands of bits of seismic data are captured in exploration databases to describe miles and miles of terrain. The scientists know that certain formations are more likely to lead to discovery of oil than others.

Geo-scientists for many years have analyzed the data with statistical, mathematical, and engineering processes. This resulted in detailed reports that require careful study and interpretation.

Chevron Texaco developed a powerful innovation to aid in identifying underground energy resources. At the company's 3-D Visualization Center in Houston, information technology enables the scientists to reduce the data to many meaningful pictures, each a very thin slice of subterranean rock structures. From the images, the scientists can estimate the likelihood of encountering hydrocarbons, that is, the presence of oil.

This 3-D visualization enables scientists to literally *see* inside and

outside million-year-old geological formations in three dimensions. The computer-generated visual renditions of geological data take advantage of the natural pattern-recognition powers of the human eye. The Visualization Center's state-of-the-art high-powered computers project subterranean pictures onto 9-foot tall, high resolution screens for easy viewing. The system is so powerful and speedy that it is interactive: Scientists explore the digital terrain from their desktop simply by giving the system instructions that it processes immediately, changing the image on the screen. Imagine the power to first see 3-D images of terrain thousands of miles away from the center, or miles below the surface, and then through IT's power, move them, or travel in and through them. When the cost of drilling oil wells in the wrong spot can exceed $50 million or needlessly disrupt the surrounding environment, a 3-D picture can easily be worth much more than the $3 million Chevron Texaco invested in development of the visualization center.

included with e-mail messages as *attachments*. In these instances, when the message is transmitted, the attachments are included in the transmission. E-mail messages can be sent between individuals or broadcast to a large number of people simultaneously.

- **Voice Messaging, or Voice Mail**    A form of voice processing in which callers leave spoken messages entered through their telephone receiver. The voice information is transmitted, stored, and retrieved *(played)* by the recipients.

Ships unloading at Singapore harbor.

**Singapore's TradeNetPlus: The Six IT Functions at Work**    The English-speaking Southeast Asian island city-nation of Singapore is widely applauded for the highly effective way in which it has integrated computing and communications capabilities into the handling of foreign trade. The Port of Singapore ranks among the busiest in the world, with no end in site to the growth possibilities, providing it can help ships move in and out more quickly and efficiently.

Several years ago, officials from the Singapore Trade and Development Board decided that it was taking too long to process customs documents for incoming and outgoing shipments. Turning to information technology as the tool, the board developed the world's first electronic trading document exchange system and launched it into operation on January 1, 1989. TradeNet, as it was named, is a 24-hour revolutionary electronic system that cuts exchange of information and granting of customs approvals from several days to less than three minutes. Accessible from the Internet, TradeNet allows traders to submit electronic trade declarations, describing the contents and value of shipments, to the various governmental authorities for approval and, if applicable, assessment of taxes. Moreover, since the electronic documentation can be submitted before a ship or plane nears the port, advance clearance and approval can further reduce the time in port, benefiting the shipper, recipient, and the port.

The board also created StatLink, a highly interactive trade database that is accessible from the Internet. StatLink subscribers can search the database by any of several thousand codes to examine the trading activities that have occurred. For instance, subscribers can specify any trade type (e.g., imports, exports, and re-exports), or a particular product category, all within a time frame they specify.

In 2001, the board expanded the systems features substantially, in what is called TradeNetPlus. The new system allows shippers to apply for letters of credit, insurance, and other shipping requirements online. The board wants to electronically integrate all trading activities and government departments, to further speed the movement of information, goods, and ships. The new system is saving shippers some $3 billion annually.

This TradeNetPlus example illustrates the six functions of information technology:

1. **Capture**    Incoming messages and documents are accepted electronically over the TradeLink network.
2. **Processing**    Trade declarations are evaluated to determine the acceptability of the shipment contents as well as to assess any taxes.
3. **Generation**    Notices of approval or disapproval as well as statements of taxes due are produced automatically, and typically within one to three minutes after the port authorities receive the trade declarations.
4. **Storage**    Details of all trade declarations are stored.
5. **Retrieval**    Details of trade declarations may be retrieved for a specific shipping transaction within the port, or in aggregate form through the StatLink subscriber service.
6. **Transmission**    All trading declarations can be transmitted to the port electronically and responses returned by the TradeLink network. In addition, StatLink subscribers can review the trading history database by means of the Internet.

## The Benefits of Information Technology

Computers linked through communications systems offer four major personal and business benefits to users: (1) speed, (2) consistency, (3) precision, (4) and reliability (see Figure 1.11).

# CRITICAL CONNECTIONS 3

## Free NetStations: A Good Idea That Didn't Quite Fly

**Get2Net**

Frequent business travelers depend on e-mail to stay in touch with their own offices as well as with important customers. Also, at times, they may need to search the Internet for valuable information. Yet, for those who connect with the Internet through laptop computers, finding an available phone line and computer jack in an airport (or an electrical outlet) can be a real challenge.

Get2Net Corp. of Denver, Colorado offered what it thought was the answer for informed business travelers. In major airports across the United States, it installed its NetStations. These NetStation terminals provided unlimited Internet access. Travelers did not need special software or interconnection to use NetStations. Best of all, they were able to use them anytime without charge.

---

**Speed**   Split-second thinking is an ability people admire in others and would like to have themselves. What exactly is split-second thinking? Clearly, the term implies *speed*– if a ball bounces in front of the car you are driving, you step on the brake pedal instantly to avoid hitting the child you suspect is chasing after the ball. You have only a fraction of a second to decide on and take the proper action. That is split-second thinking. Most tasks, however, take even the quickest thinkers longer than a split second. For instance, no one can write a sentence or add a list of 15 deposits and withdrawals in a split second.

Computers, on the other hand, do *everything* in fractions of seconds. They are much faster than people could ever hope to be at a myriad of tasks. They can perform complex calculations, recall stored information, transmit information from one location to another, and move objects around a computer screen almost instantly.

**FIGURE 1.11**

***The Benefits of Information Technology***

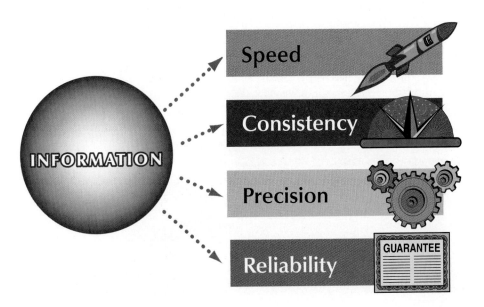

**Consistency**  People often have difficulty repeating their actions exactly. Indeed, doing something once is not nearly as difficult as doing it the same way, and with the same result, repeatedly.

Computers excel at repeating actions *consistently*. Whether running a spell checker built into a word processor or playing multimedia animations for training purposes, a computer will carry out the activity the same way every time.

**Precision**  In addition to being fast and consistent, computers are extremely *precise*. They can detect minute differences that people cannot see. In manufacturing an automobile, for example, the precise placement of a part, as directed by a computer, may make the difference between long use and early wear. Computers excel in managing the smallest differences, that is, in being precise.

**Reliability**  With speed, consistency, and precision comes reliability. When you know that the same procedure will be followed, rapidly, consistently, and precisely, you can expect *reliability of results*—that is, you can depend on getting the same result again and again. You can also count on computers and communications networks to be available and properly functioning when you need them—which is another kind of reliability, *reliability of use*.

In general, computers are very reliable. Many personal computers have never needed a service call. Communications networks are also very reliable and generally available whenever needed. You are seldom unable to use your telephone because the public telephone network is out of service. Usually, phone service is disrupted only when a bad storm has downed a line in your area or when power lines have been damaged by workers.

## Caterpillar's Virtual Reality Design

Caterpillar Inc., of Peoria, Illinois, is the world's leading manufacturer of the giant earthmoving equipment used in road building, digging, and construction. The firm designs and builds equipment in today's Information Age very differently from the way it did in the Industrial Age. Today, Caterpillar test-drives its machines *before* it builds them—an advantage made possible by virtual reality.

Virtual reality is the illusion of reality created by a computer. In Caterpillar's case, a supercomputer controls the projection of 3-D images on the four walls within a simulator—a 10-by-10-foot sound cave—and a high-quality sound system carries the noises created by the actions and motions of a mockup of a newly designed piece of equipment.

This is the system Caterpillar uses as a proving ground for all its new equipment designs. A mockup of the new machine (see Figure 1.12) is created on a screen displaying full-size images of the earthmover's frame, body, engine, shovel or blade, and hydraulic

**FIGURE 1.12**

***Virtual Reality Testing at Caterpillar***

Virtual reality testing has enabled Caterpillar to build equipment that is easier to use, with just the right features to do the intended job.

lines. Images of gauges and dials are shown on the dashboard, just as they will appear when the machine is built. The virtual roads, trees, buildings, people, and vehicles surrounding the earthmover are visible through the machine's window. From the operator's seat, the driver can turn the steering wheel and manipulate the levers to guide the machine ahead, backwards, or sideways as it moves the earth. As the driver turns the steering wheel, the machine also turns. Changes in direction and speed are visible through the window, as buildings, trees, and people appear nearer or more distant. The sounds of the powerful engine and the people around the vehicle, as well as sounds of moving rock, dirt, and sand, are clearly audible. The driver can stand up in the operator's compartment and move over to look out the windows. Unlike the more popular virtual reality systems you may be familiar with, no helmet, visor, or special gloves are needed to create the illusion, though lightweight glasses worn by the driver do enhance the images and ensure the proper perception of depth and dimension.

Virtual reality testing has enabled Caterpillar to build equipment that is easier to use, with just the right features to do the intended job. The ability to test designs this way before the equipment is built has helped Caterpillar maintain its position as the largest builder of earthmoving equipment in the world, even in the face of some tough foreign competition.

Caterpillar's virtual reality story demonstrates the four benefits of information technology:

1. **Speed**  Each action by the driver of the virtual earthmoving machine is sensed immediately and in a split second converted into motion that is displayed on the driver's screen. Since human senses can detect even an instant's delay, anything less than instant response would result in a contrived look and feel.
2. **Precision**  Each time a lever, button, shift, or wheel is moved, the direction, length, and speed of the movement is detected and the exact result computed and communicated to the visual display.
3. **Consistency**  Identical motions and instructions from the driver trigger the same actions by the system every time.
4. **Reliability**  Caterpillar can count on the availability of the virtual reality development system and on its ability to produce proper and accurate results.

## The Opportunities for Information Technology

IT provides many opportunities to help people and to solve problems.

**Helping People**  *How can I be more effective? More productive? More creative?* Asking these kinds of questions regularly will challenge you to perform at your best and fulfill your potential. Other questions focus your attention outward: *How can I help other people? How*

---

You have probably heard some lurid stories about computer failures—you may even have told a few yourself. Remember, though, it is important to distinguish between the inability to get the results you want from the computer and the failure of the computer (or the network) itself.

Early in the computer era, the failure rate of computers was high because the components used in the systems burned out after only a few hours of use. Today, however, we have extremely reliable computers and communications networks that operate for years without a hitch. Some systems—called *fail-safe* or *nonstop systems*—even include duplicate components; if one component malfunctions, the other will take over to keep the computer running.

Nonetheless, computers are not perfect. Computers and networks on some university campuses fail more often than others do. Generally, the cause of failure is excessive use. Because they are called upon to process a heavier load than anticipated when they were designed and implemented, the systems become overloaded and break down. ◼

# CRITICAL CONNECTIONS 4

## Pricewaterhouse Coopers Cuts Costs with Nomadic Hot-Desking Consultants

**Pricewaterhouse Coopers**

In Atlanta, Pricewaterhouse Coopers' consultants book small offices when they are in the company building. When they leave for the day, they take all their belongings with them because the office will be assigned to someone else the next working day. The practice of assigning a different temporary office to certain employees every day is known as *hot-desking.*

Pricewaterhouse Coopers' consultants, like many people in consulting, sales, and customer-service jobs, spend at least 70 percent of their time in the field. Since computer and communications systems allow them to stay in touch with headquarters and with their customers, the company's managing partners decided that setting aside an office for every consultant was an unnecessary cost of doing business.

Permanent offices may soon be an anachronism in companies whose employees spend most of their time in the field.

can I work toward providing affordable health care to all and jobs to all those who want them? How can I help to safeguard the environment; protect the air, water, and land from pollution; and save endangered species from extinction? How can my business improve the society in which I live? These questions are complex, challenging, and tremendously important. This book will shed light on IT's potential role in improving society. It will also describe many opportunities to use IT to assist people both in their personal lives and in their careers.

**problem**
A perceived difference between an existing condition and a desired condition.

**problem solving**
The process of recognizing a problem, identifying alternatives for solving it, and successfully implementing the chosen solution.

**Solving Problems** A **problem** is the perceived difference between an existing condition and a desired condition—for example, the study time you wish you had to prepare for an exam and the time you actually have to prepare. Problems can be as dramatic as accidents that cause serious harm or as mundane as traffic hassles. Dramatic or mundane, all problems can be challenging.

**Problem solving** is recognizing a problem, identifying alternatives for solving it, and successfully implementing the chosen solution. Information technology presents many opportunities to help people identify and solve problems. Using a word-processing program to prepare term papers and a spreadsheet program to analyze financial cases may help you solve a study-time problem, for example, because these programs enable you to accomplish more in a given amount of time.

## Information Technology Is All Around Us, Improving Our Lives

Information technology is everywhere. Here are some ways in which IT touches on and improves or lives every day—though we are usually not aware of it (Figure 1.13).

**Television** ABC, CBS, NBC, and Fox in the United States; CNN around the world; BBC in Britain and elsewhere; and TF TV in France all rely heavily on graphics and animation to illustrate weather patterns, present sports results, and report the

**a)** Stock trading is no longer done only on the trading room floor. New York's NASDAQ Exchange system allows stockbrokers to do all their trading electronically, through PCs and computer workstations.

**b)** Airlines around the world, including American, British Airways, and Lufthansa, use computer-controlled training systems to duplicate the interior of a cockpit and to simulate conditions identical to those that occur during real flights.

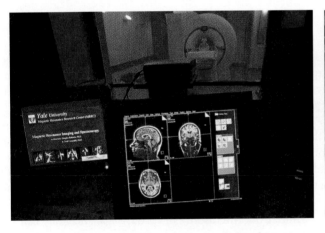

**c)** CAT scan technology, which allows physicians to look under a patient's skin without performing surgery, has become an important weapon in early cancer detection.

**d)** Robots used in manufacturing facilities throughout the world perform monotonous tasks tirelessly and precisely.

**FIGURE 1.13**

*The Uses of Information Technology in Business*

news. These graphics are produced on powerful microprocessors. Whether they are showing the movement of storm clouds across a region or the results of a public-opinion poll, graphics grab our attention in a way words might not.

**Education**  As companies seek to reduce the burden of travel for both customers and their own employees, a growing number are creating online learning systems to deliver product and service training. Cisco Systems, located in northern California's high-tech Silicon Valley region, is one of the most important suppliers of equipment that makes the Internet even possible. It delivers nearly all education about new products to customers and employees regardless of where they may be located throughout the world. Online education of this nature eliminates the need to travel to learn about the company's products and services.

**Training**  Some companies are using information technology in their employee training programs. For example, insurance adjusters in training at State Farm Insurance can view damage scenes (automobile accidents or natural disasters) on a computer display screen. The screen allows them to scrutinize photographs and images of the damage from any direction to estimate the extent of the repairs needed. Interacting with the

**REALITY CHECK**

Problems are usually perceived as causing trouble, harm, even destruction. But there is a brighter side to problems: They often create opportunities. Out of a difficult situation arises the chance to formulate innovative ways of dealing with the difficulty—to do something new, different, and better. In the business world, successful executives see problems as opportunities to create a distinct advantage in a product or service.

At one time, all automobile fenders rusted eventually and doors dented easily and stayed that way unless the car's owner undertook expensive repairs. These problems were seen as opportunities by the innovators of fiberglass fenders (which do not rust) and high-impact plastic for auto bodies (the kind in which a dent immediately pops back out).

Or take the problem of automobile tire wear. Many people are too busy to notice when the tread on their tires is worn down—a problem. Opportunity—tire manufacturers are developing technology that involves inserting into a new tire a microprocessor that senses wear and signals the driver it is time to replace the tire. Thus, the problem of unnoticed worn tires turned out to be an opportunity to develop a new product: smart tires.

Because we are surrounded by a seemingly endless stream of problems, we are also in the midst of an unending series of opportunities. ■

---

computer, the trainees ask questions and retrieve information about the damage. They get answers only to the questions they ask, however. At the end of the training session, the trainees receive suggestions about other questions they should have asked and other views of the damage they should have checked to produce a more accurate analysis.

Air France, British Airways, Lufthansa, JAL, SAS, American, Delta, United, and other airlines around the world conduct pilot training through flight simulators (Figure 1.13b). These computer-controlled training systems duplicate the cockpit of a plane and simulate conditions pilots encounter during real flights. They allow pilots to practice corrective actions under simulated emergency conditions they hope they will never have to face in the air.

**Entertainment**  Video games from Microsoft, Nintendo, Sega, and Sony can captivate young and old for hours as they display graphic villains and challenging hurdles on electronic display screens. Beneath the sleek covers of these digital interactive game machines you can find the same types of electronics components that are used in the information technology applications of huge companies.

**Shipping**  Couriers and package carriers around the world rely on information technology. FedEx, UPS, Airborne Express, DHL, and TNT use computer systems to keep track of every package they pick up and deliver. Their worldwide communications networks allow them to determine instantly the origin, current location, and destination of a package.

**Paperwork**  Despite early predictions, the age of the paperless office is not yet upon us. Most businesses still send, receive, and store huge quantities. Some, however, are taking steps to lighten their paper load. For example, whenever any correspondence about policies, claims, or premiums arrives at Texas-based USAA Insurance's mailroom, the sheets of paper are entered directly into the company's computer system using a scanner. An electronic image of the correspondence can then be seen in the desktop display screen of any customer-service agent (CSA) connected to the company's data communications network. When a customer telephones with an inquiry, the CSA can display the previous correspondence on the workstation simply by punching a few buttons. Several CSAs can display an image of the same correspondence simultaneously. The result is quicker service for the customer and less paper for the company.

**Money and Investments**  Stock markets around the world are in transition. On some trading floors, paper is disappearing. In fact, the trading floor itself is disappearing in some places. At New York's NASDAQ Exchange, stockbrokers to do all their trading electronically (Figure 1.13a). Brokers interconnected through a data communications network submit and receive bids using their PCs and computer workstations. Electronic trading will displace floor trading at investment markets around the world in the near future.

**Agriculture**   Several chemical and fertilizer companies now offer a planning service that combines their expertise in agriculture with effective use of information technology. Company advisors employ sophisticated computer programs to help farmers analyze alternative uses for their land. These programs evaluate different planting and fertilizing strategies while estimating crop sensitivity to rain and other environmental conditions. Each strategy can be analyzed to determine which will yield the most desirable results in terms of productivity and profits.

**Taxation and Accounting**   People do not like to pay taxes, and they do not like to fill out forms either. Nothing can be done about the first dislike, but the Internal Revenue Service (IRS) has installed a system that allows people to file their federal tax returns electronically using the PC in their home or office. Use of the electronic filing service has grown substantially every year since its inception in 1989. The IRS expects that soon 80 percent of all filings will be submitted electronically.

A growing number of accounting firms, as both a new service to their customers and as a way of getting ahead of their competitors, have developed the capability to file IRS tax returns electronically. H&R Block was the first to combine the IRS electronic filing process with its own Rapid Refund program. The happy results: Block's customers can receive a refund the same day they file their return.

**Health and Medicine**   It will come as no surprise that hospitals and clinics use computers to keep records and generate invoices. They also use computers to diagnose and treat patients' problems. For example, the CAT scanner is an imaging device that enables physicians to look beneath the patient's skin (Figure 1.13c). As the scanner passes over the patient, it displays an image of bone and tissue structures on a computer screen. The CAT scanner has become invaluable in identifying cancer and other conditions that benefit from early treatment.

**Manufacturing**   Robots have moved from the realm of science fiction to the factory floor over the last few decades. Automobiles made around the world, whether by Daimler-Chrysler, Peugeot, Ford, GM, Honda, or Toyota, are touched by robots at some point in the manufacturing process (Figure 1.13d). Robots do the monotonous jobs that people do not want, such as spraying paint and welding seams.

**Journalism**   Today you can read many of the world's great newspapers on the Internet. News has never been this accessible. Behind the scenes, reporters and journalists rely heavily on word processors to prepare news articles and write their columns. Typewriters are just not used anymore. Graphic designers who create the layout and procure the illustrations to accompany the text also use computers. At the offices of *USA Today*, the national U.S. newspaper sold throughout North America, Europe, and the Middle East, charts and graphs are produced on a PC that uses a special illustrator software program. Computer stores make this package (Adobe Illustrator) available to anyone for only a few hundred dollars.

**Energy**   Most gas pumps today accept credit cards. To use one of these pumps, you just place your credit card in the automated pump's reader and begin fueling your vehicle. The pump's built-in computer notes the cost of the fuel pumped, transmits the details of the transaction over communications lines to your bank or credit-card agency, and prints a receipt for you. You never have to wait for an attendant or go into the station. Automated gas pumps do not reduce the amount of fuel your vehicle consumes, but they do reduce the time and energy you burn in fueling up.

Large office buildings consume huge quantities of energy in both summer and winter. Thanks to information technology, this energy usage is better managed than ever before. Using a system of thermostats and sensors interconnected through a communications network, a computer constantly monitors temperatures around the clock, controlling heating and cooling devices to maintain the prespecified comfort level. At the end of the workday and on weekends, the system automatically adjusts the temperature, thus conserving additional energy. Some systems can also determine when a room is no longer occupied and shut off the lights.

**Sports** Auto racing draws enthusiasts around the world. In all of the auto circuits, including Formula 1, Indianapolis, IMSA, and NASCAR, computers are an integral part of race cars and a central element in racing strategy. Today's race cars are fitted with onboard computers and communications capabilities. Data regarding rate of fuel use, engine functions, braking patterns, and speed are monitored, displayed in the driver cockpit, and transmitted from the race car to the crew in the pits. These data provide information that can influence racing strategy and determine whether a team wins or loses.

## The Responsibilities of Using Information Technology

Implicit in using IT are three fundamental assumptions:

1. **To Be Informed** Users have to know how computers and networks can be applied in different situations, and the capabilities and limitations of IT in those situations.
2. **To Make Proper Use of IT** Users need to take responsibility for employing IT in desirable and ethical ways that help people and do not infringe on their privacy, rights, or well-being.
3. **To Safeguard** Users must take responsibility for protecting data and information that are in a computer or transmitted over a network against intentional or accidental damage or loss. They also need to guard against the failure of all processes that rely on information technology.

An important principle follows from these responsibilities: *People using information technology have the obligation to consider both the upside and the downside of introducing IT into any situation.*

# The Career Side of Information Technology

Information technology can help you in whatever career you pursue. Knowing how IT is used in organizations, acquiring demonstrable IT skills, and being able to list your IT accomplishments on your résumé will give you a solid advantage when you are competing for a job. In business as well as in the arts, the sciences, education medicine, law, and government, information technology—computers, communications networks, and know-how—is an essential tool.

You don't have to wait until you take the next step in your career to thinking about the role of IT in organizations. You can start right now.

# CRITICAL CONNECTIONS

## 1 Part II: U.S. Postal Service Uses IT to Manage International Mail

**UNITED STATES POSTAL SERVICE** The handheld computer has given USPS workers an efficient, mobile system for managing the movement of international parcels. International parcels are placed in large containers before they are loaded onto aircraft. Each container is uniquely identified with a bar-coded serial number, the flight number the container is assigned to for the next shipment, and its final destination. By passing the handheld computer over the bar code, USPS airport ramp workers automatically capture the container and shipment information.

Each week, airline and U.S. Postal Service workers meet to discuss any parcel hauling performance irregularities that have occurred. Data collected in the system provides the basis for finding ways to analyze trends in types of incidents, improving existing performance, and identifying routings that need to be changed. Because of the reliability and efficiency of the handheld computer in monitoring parcel movements, neither rain, nor sleet, nor snow can deter the USPS from carrying out its mission.

## Questions for Discussion

1. In what ways does the use of handheld computers improve overall productivity for the U.S. Postal Service?
2. How is the introduction of handheld computers and the ability to capture shipment data by scanning bar codes likely to improve the traceability of U.S. mail shipments?

## 2 Part II: Verizon Offers Directory Assistance by Computer

 While Verizon believes that using computer speech technology to assist in 411 information calls improves the company's productivity and reduces costs, it recognizes that some people will be uncomfortable with the computer's questions. Hence, it has built in an *old-fashioned alternative.* If at any time people want to speak to a human operator, all they have to do is press zero.

Although it does not currently plan to replace its telephone operators with computers, Verizon does not rule out that possibility in the future. The company's goal is to use information technology for what it does best and reserve employees for the kind of work better done by people.

### Questions for Discussion

1. As a telephone customer, what advantages and disadvantages do you see in Verizon's system?
2. How would you determine whether computer speech technology offers sufficient benefits to warrant its additional use?
3. Should Verizon entirely replace its directory assistance operators with information technology if such a move would make the company more competitive by reducing costs and if the company believes its customers will feel comfortable with such change?

## 3 Part II: Free NetStations: A Good Idea That Didn't Quite Fly

 Get2Net's NetStation terminals provided free and unlimited Internet access for travelers. In addition to airport locations, Get2Net had begun installing the terminals in restaurants and other travel venues.

Advertisers' interest in NetStations had begun to grow. Many companies were interested in having an electronic banner describing their products or services appear in front of the thousands of travelers who used the terminals each day. Moreover, Get2Net had developed a way of tailoring the advertising depending on the content categories the Internet users viewed—from news and weather to travel services and local information. Delivery of the advertisements was customizable by other sponsor-chosen criteria, including location, time of day, user profile and more. Get2Net's comprehensive reporting services let sponsors know exactly how effective their advertising message and placement on the terminal was. Their guidance helped the sponsor better target future ad messages and sharpen the focus of their creative advertising. Still, Get2Net recently ceased operating. It was unable to generate sufficient revenue from advertisers to remain in business. Its equipment and other assets have been acquired by another company that converted its terminals to provide *fee-based* access to the Internet.

### Questions for Discussion

1. As a traveler, do you think the Get2Net concept of providing free Internet access to travelers was a good idea? Why or why not?
2. As an advertiser, what features of the Get2Net plan for offering services to travelers do you find attractive? What features do you find unattractive?
3. Do you think travelers would be willing to pay a moderate fee for having access to the Internet by way of kiosks in airports, restaurants, and hotels? What is the reasoning behind your answer?

## 4 Part II: Pricewaterhouse Coopers Cuts Costs with Nomadic Hot-Desking Consultants

Pricewaterhouse Coopers' consultants and other hot-desking businesspeople need not lose touch with events at the office or within the company. Call forwarding permits the intended recipients to talk with callers regardless of their locations. When consultants are unable to take calls, voice-mail systems record the callers' messages. Consultants can later retrieve their messages from any telephone.

Wireless cellular telephones allow businesspeople to make or receive calls whether inside automobiles, on trains, or walking the streets. Notebook computers small enough to fit into a briefcase come equipped with fax machines so that messages can be sent or received anywhere.

Given IT's capabilities, people need never be out of touch. In many types of businesses today, the large office with its vast assemblage of employees may already be obsolete.

### Questions for Discussion

1. What does hot-desking imply for the costs of running companies and delivering services to customers?
2. The biggest impediment to the hot-desking revolution is management resistance. The majority of managers gauge their value and prestige at least partly by the size of the permanent office they are assigned. How can companies overcome this resistance?
3. Do you think hot-desking is a fad or a long-term trend made possible by information technology that will render ordinary offices obsolete? State the reasons underlying your answer.

# Summary of Learning Objectives

**1** **Describe the six characteristics of the Information Age and discuss the role of information technology (IT) as the principal tool of the Information Age.** The six characteristics of the Information Age are as follows: (1) the evolution of an information society in which more people work at handling information than at agriculture and manufacturing combined; (2) the dependence of businesses on information technology; (3) the transformation of work processes to increase their productivity and effectiveness; (4) the capability IT provides to rethink (reengineer) conventional business practices; (5) the importance of IT for business success; and (6) the embodiment of IT in many products and services.

**2** **Explain the three primary components of information technology.** The three components of information technology are as follows: (1) computers—electronic systems that can be instructed to accept, process, store, and present data and information; (2) communications networks—the interconnection of different locations through a medium that enables people to send and receive information; and (3) know-how—the familiarity with the tools of IT, the skills needed to use these tools, and the understanding of when to use them.

**3** **Identify the six information-handling functions and the four benefits of information technology.** The six information-handling functions of IT are as follows: (1) capture, or the compilation of detailed records of activities; (2) processing, or the conversion, analysis, computation, and synthesis of all forms of data or information; (3) generation, or the organization of information into a useful form, whether as text, sound, or visual image; (4) storage, or the maintenance of data and information for future use; (5) retrieval, or the locating and copying of stored data or information; and (6) transmission, or the sending of information from one location to another.

The four benefits of IT are speed, consistency, precision, and reliability.

**4** **Summarize the principles of business reengineering, emphasizing the potential benefits to people and businesses.** Reengineering emphasizes rethinking of business activities and introducing radical changes that benefit both a company's customers and its employees. Reengineering seeks to capitalize on the capabilities of information technology in a sensible and beneficial way to improve performance while using fewer steps, fewer resources, and fewer people.

**5** **Discuss the types of opportunities that information technology offers to people. IT can aid people in their personal lives as well as in their careers.** It also helps them to see the opportunities created by problems and to formulate solutions that capitalize on those opportunities.

**6** **Describe the responsibilities of people who use information technology.** IT users have three fundamental responsibilities: (1) *to be informed*—to know the capabilities and limitations of IT; (2) *to make proper use of IT*—to employ it in a desirable and ethical manner; and (3) *to safeguard*—to protect data and information against damage or loss.

# Key Terms

## Review Questions

1. What are the distinguishing characteristics of the Information Society?

2. Having the right knowledge is important to be successful in any job. Yet, some workers are called knowledge workers and others are not. What then is a knowledge worker and why are not all workers considered knowledge workers?

3. The terms *Information Age* and *Information Society* are frequently associated with applications of information technology. How do the meanings of the two terms differ with respect to information technology?

4. Distinguish between the Agricultural Age, Industrial Age, and Information Age. What developments brought about the onset of the Industrial Age and the Information Age?

5. Explain this statement: *The Information Age does not replace the activities of earlier ages. It transforms them.*

6. What are the six characteristics of the Information Age?

7. Define information technology. How are information technology and computers related?

8. What are work processes and how are they influenced by information technology?

9. How do work processes differ from business processes?

10. Reengineering is an idea and term that was first introduced in 1990, more than a decade ago. Is reengineering an obsolete idea in business today? Why or why not?

11. Distinguish among data, information, and knowledge.

12. Identify the four types of computers.

13. How are the different types of personal computers alike, and how do they differ?

14. How are hardware and software different? How are they related?

15. What role do communications networks play in an information society?

16. *Know-how* is neither a computer nor a data communications network. Why, then, is it a component of information technology?

17. Describe the principle of high-tech/high-touch.

18. What six functions does information technology perform? Briefly describe each one.

19. Describe four benefits of information technology.

20. What is meant by the term problem? By problem solving?

21. What three responsibilities does information technology create for its users?

## Discussion Questions

1. The executives and managers at Home Depot openly acknowledge that the company could not exist without its highly effective use of information technology. Considering the benefits provided by information technology in general, discuss the ways in which Home Depot uses these benefits to maintain its day-to-day activities throughout its many stores.

   The company is continuing to grow, adding many additional stores each year. Discuss the challenges Home Depot faces with respect to its IT capabilities as the company continues to add more stores.

2. Many retail and grocery stores have adopted the practice of displaying the price of an item on the store shelf, but not marking it on the item itself. Instead, the price is kept in the store computer. When the customer pays for the item, the sales assistant scans into the computer the item's unique identification number from the attached tag. The price is quickly retrieved, displayed for viewing, and added to the total.

   Analyze the pricing and payment process from the store's viewpoint. Considering the role and benefits of information technology, why have so many store managers chosen to incur the expense to buy the IT components enabling them to adopt this practice? That is, what benefits does the store gain?

   Consider the above practice from the customer's viewpoint. Does the customer benefit from the store's practice? Why or why not?

3. How might the illustration of a business process in Figure 1.9 be changed by applying the principles of business process reengineering described in this chapter? Apply these principles to two different situations: (1) a system that depends on paper documents from the sales staff and (2) one that depends on the electronic submission of sales orders.

4. The Internal Revenue Service (IRS) is encouraging filing of annual income tax returns by computer. Is this practice something that you now follow or will follow in the future? Why or why not?

   What factors related to information technology will determine whether the IRS achieves its goal of having more than 80 percent of all income tax filings made electronically?

5. *Computers don't make difficult things easier; they make impossible things possible.* Do you agree or disagree with this adage? Explain your answer.

6. Marks & Spencer, a leading British retailer, has top-of-the-line personal computers at the cash point where customers pay for purchases. Data from the transactions at each store—some 15,000 per *minute*—are captured at the point of sale and transmitted to a central database in London. At the end of the day, the company's computers analyze the sales and transmit restocking information to their suppliers who deliver the replacement goods before business the next day.

   The company's management recently suggested that the sales data be processed throughout the day in order to pick up customer buying trends right away. They thought that with rapid processing of the sales data and transmission to the suppliers, that goods for restocking, say of morning sales, could be brought in the afternoon, thus ensuring the stores are always properly stocked.

   Considering the benefits offered by information technology, what factors would determine whether the idea put forth by Marks & Spencer management is a good one?

7. How do you think the Information Age will change your personal and work life? What characteristics of the Information Age will have the greatest influence on your career?

# Group Projects and Applications

## Project 1

Make arrangements to meet with one of the staff members in the registration office of your institution. Discuss the role of information technology in registering and paying for classes. After your discussion,

- Identify the role information technology plays in enabling students to register for courses (including the way it prohibits students from registering from a course under various conditions).
- Identify the data and information that students and staff members must enter into the system to register or to support the registration process.
- Describe the components of information technology that comprise the system.

## Project 2

Visit your institution's library and search out the magazines and journals on information technology that are regularly received by the library. Then do the following:

- Make a list of the titles of the journals received in paper form.
- Make a list of the titles of the journals that are available online, in digital form.
- What are the procedures for locating and viewing the online journals? Can articles in each of the digital journals be printed on paper?

## Project 3

Information technology is ever more important in the management of different forms of public transportation—airlines, trains, subway systems, and bus systems. Select one of the public transportation companies near you and examine how it uses information technology to:

- Operate the system
- Manage the issuance or collection of tickets
- Disseminate information to customers and patrons

Write up your analysis of the company's use of IT, indicating where you think efficiency, productivity and convenience have benefited from good use of information technology, and where they have not.

Finally, check to see whether there is an Internet site from which you can obtain information about the transportation system or an individual transportation company. Include that information in your written analysis.

## Project 4

With a partner from your class, make arrangements to visit one of the following businesses:

- Retail store in the mall or downtown area
- Copy center
- Neighborhood restaurant

Arrange to interview the proprietor or staff and observe how customers or clients are served. Then do the following:

- Identify the roles played by information technology in the way business is conducted.
- Find out how IT has changed a particular business activity or process.
- Brainstorm ways that IT might be used to improve, or reengineer, other business processes or activities.
- Present a report of your findings and recommendations to the class.

## Project 5

Consult the help wanted ads in your weekend newspaper and summarize the characteristics of jobs open in your local job market. Then do the following:

- Estimate the percentage of ads that focus on (1) information technology occupations, (2) other occupations that require some IT skills, and (3) jobs that require no IT training. Bring in a sample of each of these three types of ads and estimate the entry-level salary range for each type.

- Based on your estimates, what is your overall view of the importance of information technology in making career choices?
- Include a section in your report identifying the limitations you will face if your peers have a higher level of IT know-how than you have.

## Project 6

As a class project, develop a file of real-world examples of IT in business. Your examples might focus on the following topics:

- Improving customer service
- Improving delivery time
- Improving quality
- Reaching new customers
- Increasing sales to existing customers
- Developing relationships with suppliers

Cast your net wide as you search for examples. Look in the business pages of your local newspaper; in business magazines such as *Fortune, Forbes,* and *Business Week;* and in online or Internet-based publications. You might also want to summarize examples that you have heard about through friends, relatives, or coworkers.

Each member of the class should bring in two examples for the file. Attach to each example a brief summary, along with complete information regarding its source.

# Net_Work

## Are You Networked?

Your institution probably provides a way for you to use the Internet through its computer center, through one of its academic departments, or through a local Internet service provider (i.e., a company whose business is providing an Internet connection for a fee). Chapter 3 discusses the Internet in detail.

To prepare for that discussion, you should establish an Internet account through your institution now, if you do not already have one.

When you have established an Internet account (required both to ensure that no one else can use the Internet under your name and to keep track of the time you are on the network), your institution or service provider will give you the information you need to use the system. Record the following information in a safe place so that you will have a reference for your network's characteristics:

- Your user name/account number
- Your password
- The name the institution has assigned to its computer

- Terminal emulation required so your computer will interact with the network properly (e.g., VT100; the computer center or service provider must give you this information)
- If using telephone dial-up access, choose one from each of these five parameters:
  - Transmission speed: 300/1200/2400/4800/9600/ 14400/28800
  - Parity: None/Even/Odd/Mark/Space
  - Data bits: 7/8
  - Stop bits: 1/2
  - Port: Com1/Com2/Com3/Com4
- Telephone number(s) to gain access to the Internet (if you are using dial-up access)
- Telephone number(s) to call if you need help (a service often known as a help desk)
- Name of communication software you must first start on your PC before you can use the Internet
- Name of the Internet browser program you will run on your computer (e.g., Netscape or Internet Exchange)
- The address (called a uniform resource locator–URL) of your institution or service provider's home page. It will appear similar to this: www.college.edu (URLs are discussed in Chapter 3).

# Cool Mobility

## On Assignment

Sometimes things just seem to go your way! As luck would have it, someone has recognized your tremendous talent and potential: You land a highly sought-after consulting residency. During your *virtual* residency, you will be engaged at the corporate offices of *Cool Mobility,* a young but already successful company operating in one of the most dynamic segments of the high-tech industry—wireless telecommunications. As you will see, *Cool Mobility,* is not your ordinary telecom company. The company's officers and staff specialize in what they call *cool to go. Cool*

*Mobility's*, story, as told by leading journalists and business writers, is one that has generated widespread interest *and envy* across the industry. You will soon see what all the hype is about; that is, you will become virtually part of the story.

For the duration of this term, you will be *on assignment* in a consulting residency. The residency will require some degree of integration of your ever-expanding knowledge and skills in the application of information technology. The founders and staff of *Cool Mobility,* together with an IT faculty member will interact with you throughout your term.

By the end of the residency, you should be able to

- Diagnose and solve problems and offer appropriate solutions related to *Cool Mobility*'s use of IT.
- Apply appropriate technologies, tools, and frameworks from all aspects of IT use to develop and defend recommendations related to successful customer and product support as well as employee and staff support.
- Work as a team member in setting goals, making decisions, allocating work, resolving conflicts, and meeting deadlines.
- Communicate ideas effectively through written documents and oral presentations.

## In Consultation

The energetic folks at *Cool Mobility* are anxiously awaiting your arrival, so let's get started. To begin your virtual residency, and to launch your consulting engagement, go to the front door of the company by pointing your Internet browser to www.CoolMobility.biz.

To help acquaint you with the company and prepare for your consultation responsibilities, explore its public Internet site and the employee intranet, assembling information to answer the following questions:

a. When was *Cool Mobility* founded?
b. Is the company *private* or *public*?
c. Explain the features of *Cool Mobility*'s innovative mobile phone products and services.
d. How many mobile service plans are offered and on what features do they differ?
e. What type of potential employee is *Cool Mobility* interested in? Are there any employment opportunities at the company?
f. How does an employee obtain a vacation request?
g. How does an employee submit a timesheet to the Human Resources Department?
h. By what characteristics can information about an employee be obtained through the intranet?

# Case Study

## Otis Raises Elevator Design to New Level of Service

**Otis**

Otis Elevator Company, a wholly owned subsidiary of United Technologies Corp., headquartered in Hartford, Connecticut, is the world's largest manufacturer installer and servicer of elevators, escalators, moving walkways and other horizontal transportation systems. Each year the company sells some 60,000 elevators for use in office buildings, hotels, apartments, condominiums, and parking garages.

### History of Elevators

From ancient times through the Middle Ages and into the thirteenth century, human or animal power was the driving force behind hoisting devices. By 1850, steam and hydraulic elevators had been introduced, but it was in 1852 that the landmark event in elevator history occurred: the invention of the world's first safety elevator by Elisha Graves Otis.

The first passenger elevator was installed by Otis in New York in 1857. After Otis's death in 1861, his sons, Charles and Norton, built on his heritage, creating Otis Brothers & Company in 1867. By 1873, over 2,000 Otis elevators were in use in office buildings, hotels and department stores across America, and five years later the first Otis hydraulic passenger elevator was installed.

In 1898, overseas business had added to the company's growth. To capitalize on the international possibilities, Otis Brothers merged with 14 other elevator entities to form the Otis Elevator Company.

In 1903, Otis introduced the design that would become the *backbone*

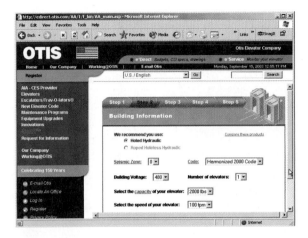

of the elevator industry: the gearless traction electric elevator, engineered and proven to outlast the building itself. This ushered in the age of high-rise skyscrapers, ultimately including New York's Empire State Building and the former World Trade Center, Chicago's John Hancock Center, and Toronto's CN Tower.

Throughout all these years, Otis introduced innovations one after the other. Currently, it is a world leader in developing computer technology. The company has revolutionized elevator controls, generating dramatic improvements in elevator response time and ride quality.

## Using Information Technology to Build Sales

Because each building is different, it is necessary for the building's architects and designers to prepare unique specifications for the elevators it will use. Otis managers know that the best chance of gaining the elevator business for new construction projects and rebuilding of historic structures is by making the job of the architects a little easier. To do so, Otis created a set of computer-based tools, called *Architect's Assistant,* which allows architects to work online with the Otis Internet site to create elevator designs and building plans and to determine the optimal elevator system for a building.

*Architect's Assistant* prompts the architect to enter structural information into the Internet application, including the building style, average population for each floor, the number of floors above and below the main entrance, and the characteristics of each floor (e.g., ceiling height). Another part of *Architect's Assistant* aides architects in preparing the necessary elevator specifications, including its desired dimensions, the capacity of each elevator car, and the location of the machine room that will house the equipment that will make movement of the elevator possible.

Capturing these details is important for more than the sake of appearance. Different elevator designs are required depending on the structure of the building. In geared or gearless traction systems (used in mid-rise and high-rise structures, respectively, where speed of moving passengers between floors is important), the elevator car is supported in a hoistway by several steel hoist ropes and a counterweight. In a hydraulic system (used primarily in low-rise installations, where moderate car speed is acceptable), a car is connected to the top of a long piston that moves up and down in a cylinder. The car moves up when oil is pumped into the cylinder from a reservoir, raising the piston. The car is lowered when the oil returns to the reservoir.

Otis's interactive Internet site also offers engineering drawings of elevators that architects can interactively manipulate over the company Internet site. For instance, with the Express Draw and OtisPLAN system components features, they can evaluate different dimensions or determine the impact of having machine rooms of different sizes and in alternative locations. They can view the graphically illustrated alternatives right on their computer screens or print them for later review. When they select their design, the details are already captured in electronic form and ready for processing.

## Processing Design Information

Otis processes the facts submitted by the architect to create the elevator engineering specifications, calculate the manufacturing costs, and formulate the final price quotation. While *Architect's Assistant's* capabilities make it easier for the architect to provide the information, Otis benefits too. Complex calculations to determine speed of motion, car weight, and braking requirements under different situations can be carried out quickly and reliably using the data already in the system. The task of examining the information, preparing the quotation, and responding to the architect now takes approximately 10 hours. Before the system was developed, Otis, like its competitors, required nearly 100 hours of time before it could respond.

Best of all, Otis stores all of the information entered into the system. Product design and marketing staff members periodically review the details to identify customer and product opportunities. Because Otis does business around the world, *Architect's Assistant* must be able to accommodate many different types of customers. The Internet-based system is available in more than 50 countries and 26 languages.

### Questions for Discussion

1. If you were an architect, would the Otis system be appealing to you? Why or why not?
2. In what ways are each of the six functions of information technology evident in the Otis *Architect's Assistant* system and how do they benefit the architects who use the system?
3. Identify and explain how each of the four roles of information technology is demonstrated in this system.
4. What factors should Otis managers examine in gauging the extent to which the benefits of the system compare with the cost of its development?

# Essentials of Computing

## LEARNING OBJECTIVES

When you have completed this chapter, you should be able to

1 Identify the five components of a computer system.

2 Explain the four categories of hardware and their functions.

3 Discuss the relationship between hardware and software.

4 Differentiate between an operating system and an application program.

5 Identify 10 types of software packages.

6 Explain the four components of information.

7 Distinguish between the users of information technology and IT professionals.

8 Describe the four types of procedures used in computer systems.

9 Explain the difference between single- and multiuser systems.

10 List the 13 information-processing activities associated with the five information-handling functions of IT.

# Continental's Information Technology Gets Cargo Right

One of the largest air carriers in the United States, Continental Airlines makes roughly 2,300 daily departures to some 200 domestic and international locations. The airline operates hubs in New York, Houston, Cleveland, and Guam. An industry leader, Continental Airlines has repeatedly been named by *Fortune* magazine as one of the 100 best places to work in the United States. Furthermore, industry publications consistently rate Continental high in customer satisfaction for both long- and short-haul flights.

Continental Airlines, like any air carrier, is successful only when it consistently meets customer needs and does so at an acceptable level of profitability. Continental is known for its high-quality passenger service. Yet the airline's ability to ship cargo for businesses also is essential to its operations.

Compared to passenger traffic, cargo can vary dramatically in both dimension and weight. For each flight, the airline must estimate the amount of space available for customer cargo, determine shipping costs, and provide the customer with a price quote. This is tricky business for any airline. To better meet this challenge, Continental implemented CargoProf, a Cargo Revenue Management system that has effectively managed the situation while adding millions of dollars to the airline's bottom line.

This is how the software works: Booking agents for cargo, like passenger travel agents, are linked electronically to Continental Airlines. When they seek to book space on a flight, the agents enter the details into Continental's cargo-reservation system. A five-step process is then activated at Continental to decide whether the requested shipment can be confirmed. The details of the requested shipment date, weight, and volume are transmitted from the cargo-reservation system to CargoProf. CargoProf in turn determines if there is enough weight and volume left on the requested flight based on a capacity forecast that takes expected passenger loads, baggage space, weather factors, and expected fuel requirements that are sent to CargoProf every evening. Once CargoProf determines there is enough space and weight for the shipment, it then evaluates the shipment based on its economic merits against a demand forecast that is generated nightly before accepting or rejecting the booking agent's request. If rejected, the agent will then have to decide whether to try a different flight, ship on another day, or pay a higher price for the shipment.

The transfer of information between the different computer-based systems is seamless and automatic. Without CargoProf, Continental would have to assign staff to evaluate each request; to pull information from the separate cargo, passenger, and flight control systems; and ultimately to make a decision. Compared to the CargoProf system, the old process is costly and time-consuming; and the results are less reliable. It's easy to see how CargoProf has become an invaluable aid to Continental Airlines and its agents.

The computers and programs used by Continental Airlines are important tools that contribute to the company's success. Because these tools are easy to handle, users can focus on the best way to price and schedule cargo rather than on mastering the intricacies of a difficult piece of technology.

*A*s the story of Continental's CargoProf suggests, information technology enables us to accomplish what we need to get done more quickly and more effectively. Cargo agents do not have to know all of the technical details of computers to do their jobs. All they need is a general understanding of how computers work and what they can do for them.

To see how a computer can make you more productive, you need to become familiar with its primary components. This chapter's guided tour of a computer system will give you a working knowledge of the basics. This should help you avoid some of the problems that often trip up computer users. An informed computer user is an effective user.

Computer systems are made up of five components: hardware, programs, information, people, and procedures (see Figure 2.1). This chapter will discuss each component—and the know-how you will need to use it effectively—in turn, starting with hardware.

# Hardware: Computing, Storing, and Communicating

The terms *computer* and *computer system* are often used loosely. We need to be more specific for this tour. As discussed in Chapter 1, a *computer* is any electronic system that can be instructed to accept, process, store, and present data and information. A *computer system* refers to a computer and all the hardware interconnected with it.

**hardware/computer hardware/devices**
The computer and its associated equipment.

**Hardware,** or **computer hardware,** is the general term for the machines (sometimes called **devices**) that carry out the activities of computing, storing, and communicating data (Figure 2.2). As Figure 2.3 shows, computer hardware falls into four categories of components:

- Input devices
- Processors
- Output devices
- Secondary storage devices

These components are part of most computer systems, regardless of their cost or size. However, some computer systems are designed to store all data and information internally and thus do not include secondary storage devices.

## Input Devices

**input**
The data or information entered into a computer or the process of entering data or information into the computer for processing, storage and retrieval, or transmission.

**Input** has two meanings: (1) as a noun, it refers to the data or information entered into a computer; (2) as a verb, it means the process of entering data or information into the computer for processing, storage and retrieval, or transmission.

FIGURE 2.1

*The Five Components of a Computer System*

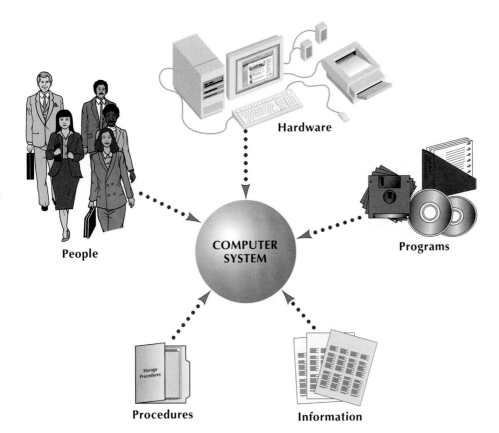

Seven different devices are commonly used to enter data or information into a computer:

1. **Keyboards**  Keyboards containing the letters of the alphabet, numbers, and frequently used symbols (such as $, &, and #) are the most common input devices. In some parts of the world, keyboards consist almost exclusively of symbols rather than alphabet letters. In Japan, for example, a popular keyboard contains the 5,000 symbols representing characters of the Kanji alphabet. The Kanji keyboard thus is much larger and contains many more symbols than the keyboards used in North and South America and Europe.

    Most keyboards also have a numeric keypad. Arranged in a layout similar to that used on handheld calculators, numeric keypads are useful for entering data quickly.

2. **Point-of-sale terminals**  A variation on the once common business cash register, these terminals typically do not contain alphabet letters. Rather, they consist of a numeric data pad and special-purpose function keys, such as those used for a sale, a refund, or a void. The numeric keypad can be used to enter the following: details of a purchase, such as the product or stock number; the cost of the product (if that information is not automatically retrieved from the computer when purchase details are entered); the amount of money tendered for a cash purchase; and the account number for a credit or debit card purchase.

3. **Mouse**  On the underside of the mouse is a ball that rotates as the mouse is moved, causing the corresponding movement of a pointer (a large arrow) on the display screen. A click of a button on the top side of the mouse lets the user invoke a command or initiate an action. A computer system can be controlled by pointing the mouse at commands on the screen rather than by entering them through the keyboard.

4. **Image scanners**  Image scanners can enter (that is, input) both words and images (including drawings, charts, and graphs) directly into a computer. A light illuminates the information one section at a time, and the information under the light is recognized and read into the computer. Image scanners range in size from those that fit into the palm of your hand to those the size of a newspaper page. Once in the computer's memory, images can be modified or combined with other information.

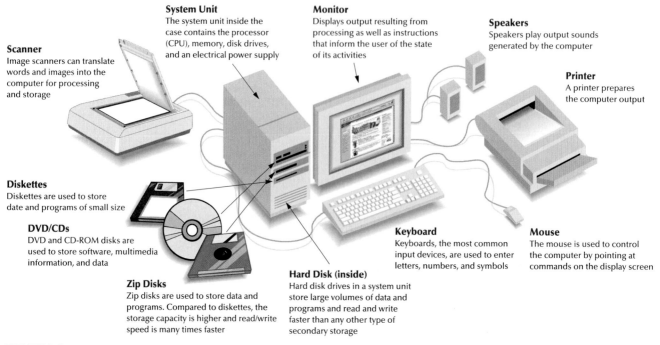

**System Unit**
The system unit inside the case contains the processor (CPU), memory, disk drives, and an electrical power supply

**Monitor**
Displays output resulting from processing as well as instructions that inform the user of the state of its activities

**Speakers**
Speakers play output sounds generated by the computer

**Scanner**
Image scanners can translate words and images into the computer for processing and storage

**Printer**
A printer prepares the computer output

**Diskettes**
Diskettes are used to store date and programs of small size

**DVD/CDs**
DVD and CD-ROM disks are used to store software, multimedia information, and data

**Zip Disks**
Zip disks are used to store data and programs. Compared to diskettes, the storage capacity is higher and read/write speed is many times faster

**Hard Disk (inside)**
Hard disk drives in a system unit store large volumes of data and programs and read and write faster than any other type of secondary storage

**Keyboard**
Keyboards, the most common input devices, are used to enter letters, numbers, and symbols

**Mouse**
The mouse is used to control the computer by pointing at commands on the display screen

**FIGURE 2.2**

***The Four Categories of Hardware and Commonly Used Media***

**bar code**
A computer-readable code consisting of bars or lines of varying widths or lengths.

**wand**
An input device used to read a bar code and input this information directly into a computer.

**multimedia**
A system that contains standard PC features but also has the capability to handle audio, video, animation, and graphics.

5. **Bar code scanners and wands**   Manual input of data or information takes time and is subject to error. Many retail stores have found that the scanning of bar code information on a package is a faster and more accurate process than entering the same information through a keyboard (Figure 2.4). A **bar code** is a computer-readable code consisting of bars or lines of varying widths or lengths. As the **wand,** a hand-held scanner, is waved across the bar code on the package, it recognizes the special letters and symbols embedded in the bar code and inputs this information directly into a PC, midrange computer, or point-of-sale terminal. There the code is translated into product and price information. Some stores, such as supermarkets, use a fixed scanner at the checkout counter instead of a wand. In this case, the package containing the bar code is passed over a scanner that is mounted under a piece of glass.

6. **Microphones**   Often used in multimedia systems, microphones capture voices or other sounds for use in computer processing (Figure 2.5). The microphone is attached to a computer by a cable that transmits the sounds.

7. **Prerecorded sources**   CD and DVD players, tape recorders, cassette decks, record players, and stereo amplifiers can be connected to a computer that captures sounds as they are played (Figure 2.6). This method of input allows high-quality music and voice reproductions to be merged with text and image information to produce **multimedia** presentations for education, training, and marketing. Multimedia incorporates basic PC features with audio, video, animation, and graphics.

**FIGURE 2.3**

***The Four Categories of Hardware***

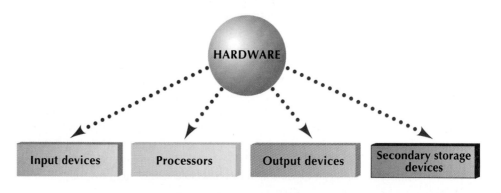

HARDWARE

Input devices | Processors | Output devices | Secondary storage devices

**a)** Bar code scanning is a fast and efficient way of inputting data. Here, a scientist uses bar codes to identify research samples.

**b)** Bar code scanning at checkout allows clerks to move customers much more quickly than cash registers do. It also permits managers to change the price of a product in an instant and to keep track of inventory.

**FIGURE 2.4**
*Bar Code Scanners*

Input devices can be either internal or external. For instance, some PCs and older terminals include the display screen and keyboard in a single case. In contrast, mice, scanners, wands, and microphones are usually separate devices attached to the computer by a cable. This setup is changing, however, with the development of wireless input devices (e.g., the wireless keyboard and mouse).

## The Processor

The center of action in a computer is the **processor,** also called the **central processing unit (CPU).** In microcomputers, the processor is a **microprocessor**–a central processor contained on a single computer chip.

A chip is a collection of electronic components in a very small, self-contained package. Chips perform the computer's processing actions, including arithmetic calculations and the generation of lines, images, and sounds. Some chips are general purpose and perform all types of actions. Others have a special purpose. Sound chips, for example, do exactly what their name suggests: They generate signals to be output as tones.

## System Board

The processor/CPU can take several forms. Microcomputers contain a specific microprocessor chip as their CPU. This chip is put into a protective package, and then mounted onto a board contained within the computer. This board is called a **system board** or **mother board** (Figure 2.7). The system board also contains other chips and circuitry that carry out processing activities.

**processor/central processing unit (CPU)**
A set of electronic circuits that perform the computer's processing actions.

**microprocessor**
The smallest type of processor, with all of the processing capabilities of the control unit and ALU located on a single chip.

**system board/mother board**
The system unit in a microcomputer, located on a board mounted on the bottom of a computer base.

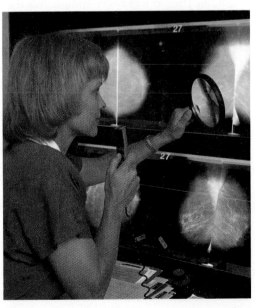

**FIGURE 2.5**
*A Microphone in a Medical Diagnosis System*
The computer captures the words spoken by the doctor into the microphone, then processes them to help him or her determine the best treatment for a patient.

Larger computer systems may have separate cabinets or freestanding units that contain the chips and circuits that make up the CPU. At one time, all mainframes and supercomputers had separate units housing the central processor. Today, thanks to the continued miniaturization of chips and circuits, separate units are not always necessary. Even in the most powerful central processors, chips and circuits can be integrated onto a few boards.

## Memory

**primary storage/main memory**

Storage within the computer itself. Primary memory holds data only temporarily, as the computer executes instructions.

Both system boards and separate processing units include space for memory, which is sometimes called **primary storage** or **main memory.** This is used by the central processing unit to carry out all computing activities. No processing takes place in memory. Instead, memory stores data, information, and instructions. When data enter the computer as input, they go into main memory until they are processed. After processing, the results—information—are retained in memory.

## CRITICAL CONNECTIONS 1

### McKesson Uses *Wearable* Computers to Tighten the Retailer-Distributor Link

**MCKESSON**
*Empowering Health*

If you had a splitting headache, you would not be pleased to find the drugstore shelf bare of aspirin. This, in a nutshell, summarizes the importance of distribution—the wholesale link between manufacturer and retailer. Few companies do distribution better than McKesson Corp., a San Francisco-based distributor of drugs and healthcare products.

In the pre-IT era, McKesson's customers ordered goods by telephone. Banks of telephone order takers completed order forms, while warehouse workers walked around handpicking the requested items off the shelves. The system was slow, expensive, and error-prone.

McKesson responded in the early 1970s by forging computer network links with manufacturers and retailers. Today, a retailer can walk through the store carrying a computer the size of a cellular phone. One swipe of a handheld laser scanner over a barcoded shelf label and—presto—an order is beamed to a McKesson warehouse. At the warehouse, a central computer radios the order to a revolutionary *wearable* computer strapped to a worker's forearm. This wearable computer combines a portable computer with a two-way radio (for receiving and sending order information), a handheld laser scanner (for choosing items from warehouse shelves), and a 3-inch screen that displays, among other things, the shortest route through the warehouse. When the worker has filled the order, the wearable computer sends a message back to the central computer, which creates an electronic bill for the retailer.

FIGURE 2.7
*A System Board*
The system board is often referred to
as the *motherboard*. In PCs, the CPU
is a single microprocessor chip that is
installed on the system board.

At any given time, a section of memory can hold either data and information or processing instructions. The allocation of memory at the time a program is running will determine whether a particular location will hold an instruction, a unit of data, or information. The CPU and primary memory will be discussed more fully in Chapter 4.

## Output Devices

People use computers to generate **output**–the results of entering and processing data and information. Output falls into two categories: (1) information that is presented to the user of the computer; and (2) information in the form of computer commands that are input to another device.

**output**
The results of inputting and processing data and information returned by the computer, either directly to the person using the system or to secondary storage.

Common forms of output are reports, schedules, budgets, newsletters, and correspondence. These results can be printed out, displayed on a computer screen, and sometimes played through the speaker built in or attached to a computer.

Output from computer processing that is entered as input to another device can perform various functions, including the following:

- **Control a printer**   Computer output can tell a printer when and what to print, including the location of text or images on a sheet of paper, film, or transparency. The dimensions of the image and the shades and colors used in the printout (assuming you have a color printer) can also be determined.
- **Direct a display**   Computers can display words, graphics, and shapes (either simultaneously or one at a time) on the computer display screen. Sometimes this screen is called a video display terminal (VDT) or monitor. These displays can be animated, so that words and shapes move across the screen. With animation, ideas can be demonstrated rather than described.
- **Control another device**   Output from computers can direct the actions of other computers and machinery. Devices such as computer-controlled manufacturing lathes, automobile ignition systems, and CAT scanners (which physicians use to look beneath the skin of a patient to view tissue and bone structures) accept computer output as their input–that is, instructions that guide the actions they perform.
- **Generate sounds**   Computer output can direct the computer itself to play music, simulate the sound of a jet powering up its engine, or replicate a human voice announcing train stops or telephone numbers. Driven by the need to cut costs while increasing responsiveness to callers, many businesses are augmenting their telephone switchboards with computer-generated voices that answer information inquiries or instruct callers on how to reach a certain party.

- **Initiate transmission of information**   Because computers are often connected to data communications networks, output is frequently sent over a communications link to another destination or to multiple destinations simultaneously.

Input and output devices will be discussed in more detail in a future chapter.

The *Information Technology in Practice* feature ("At American Airlines the Illusion of Flight Is Critical") describes how information technology is used to create an illusion of flight that seems amazingly real. In fact, it is so *real* that the airline substitutes time in a computer-controlled simulator for actual in-air training flights.

## Secondary Storage Devices

Computers that run multimedia and other complex programs require much storage capacity. For this reason, computer systems have several secondary storage options. **Secondary storage** provides enormous capacity to store data, information, or programs outside of the central processor.

The most widely used types of secondary storage are as follows:

**secondary storage**
A storage medium that is external to the computer, but that can be read by the computer; a way of storing data and information outside the computer itself.

**magnetic disk**
A general term referring to two types of storage disk: the flexible/floppy disk and the hard disk.

**zip disk**
Used to store data and programs. Compared to diskettes, the storage capacity is higher and read/write speed is many times faster.

**read only**
A type of disk that information can be read from but not written onto.

**CD-ROM disk**
Short for "compact disk—read only memory," an optical storage medium that permits storage of large amounts of information. CD-ROM disks can only be written to and cannot be erased.

**drive**
The device containing a secondary storage medium's read/write unit.

- **Diskettes**   Flexible, flat, oxide-coated disks on which data and information are stored magnetically (hence, they are sometimes called **magnetic disks**). Diskettes are 3½ inches. They can be removed from the computer when the user has finished using the data or information they contain. The data remain on the diskette.
- **Zip disks**   Similar to diskettes, but housed in a hard plastic case. Depending on the capacity of the zip disks, they store from 70 to 175 times more than diskettes. Also, data can be stored and retrieved from zip disks more quickly than from diskettes.
- **Hard disks**   Inflexible magnetic disks. Ranging from 2½ to 14 inches across (with standard sizes of 2½ and 3½ inches), hard disks can store more data than either diskettes or zip disks and provide for much more rapid storage and retrieval of data and information. Hard disks are usually mounted inside the computer and, unlike diskettes, are not easily removed.
- **Optical disks**   A storage medium similar in design to the compact discs (CDs) played on stereo systems. Many optical disks are **read only**, meaning that they can only be played—that is, data, information, and instructions can be read from these disks but not written onto them. This is why optical disks are sometimes known as **CD-ROM disks** (compact disks with read-only memory). Other types of optical disks allow the writing of information under certain circumstances. (More on the characteristics of optical disks is coming in Chapter 5.)
- **Magnetic tape**   Used to store large quantities of data and information, often as a second copy of data or information that exists elsewhere. Unlike diskettes, hard disks, and optical disks, which are circular, magnetic tape is linear and comes in reels or cartridges.

Information is written to or read from each type of secondary storage medium by a read/write unit contained in a **drive.** The drive rotates the medium during the read/write process. Disk and tape drives read information magnetically, in much the same way that stereo systems read information from cassette tapes. Optical drives use a laser beam to read information—just like an audio CD player.

## Peripheral Equipment

**peripheral equipment**
A general term used for any device that is attached to a computer system.

If you listen to computer professionals or systems engineers discussing the components of a computer system, you may hear them refer to *peripherals*. **Peripheral equipment** is a general term for any device that is attached, either physically or in wireless fashion, to a computer system—that is, to a PC, midrange, mainframe, or supercomputer. Peripherals include input devices, output devices, and secondary storage units. Any device that is ready to communicate with the computer is said to be *online*. One that is not ready to communicate is *off-line*.

# INFORMATION TECHNOLOGY IN PRACTICE

## At American Airlines the Illusion of Flight Is Critical

**AA** Properly used, illusion and deception are powerful tools. The computer-controlled flight simulators routinely used for pilot training are so successful that the Federal Aviation Administration (FAA) has approved their use since 1982 as the primary means for conducting aircraft training.

At the American Airlines Flight Academy near Dallas-Fort Worth International Airport, full-scale simulators are used to replicate the sensory experience of flying the Boeing 777, the world's most advanced wide-body airliner. American Airlines uses these simulators to train new pilots and to provide continuous training for current pilots.

Simulators recreate the cockpit flight deck of the American Airlines version of the Boeing 777 and the complete flying environment one experiences when in the pilot's seat. The cockpit contains every element of the aircraft design, including controls for the rudders, stick, flaps, speed brakes, and trim, with a virtual display giving the pilot a full view out the windows.

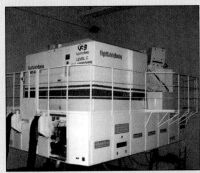

Everything the pilots see, hear, and feel must be indistinguishable from what they see, hear, and feel in the actual flying experience. For this reason, all commercial passenger airliner simulators are generally constructed using an actual cockpit built by Boeing or Airbus. Levers, buttons, and switches are identical. Computers powering the simulator operate behind the scene, controlling every view, motion, and sound, and responding to each and every action taken by the pilot.

The scenic display is not real, because the pilots cannot actually see out of the cockpit. The information is conveyed with graphics creating the scenery on a lifesize, 130-degree display. The visual system is the most demanding aspect of the simulator, for the human eye can instantly pick up even the most minor scenic discrepancies. The commercial airline simulators must project a display with near infinite focus, creating a scenario that appears to the pilot's eye to be many miles deep and wide. A global reference database, keyed to map coordinates, makes it possible to create computer-driven displays of the same scenery and landmarks

pilots would see during flight anywhere in the world. If the intent is to practice nighttime takeoffs and landings at Washington D.C.'s Reagan National Airport, pilots see an image identical to the airport's Runway 01, complete with lights, runway markers, and reflections.

The cockpit of the 777 simulator is perched some 10 feet above the ground on six hydraulic motion jacks that serve as moveable legs. The legs move up and down individually and collectively, acting out every movement of the virtual aircraft, no matter how large or small.

Whenever an instrument or lever is changed, the scenery is instantly adjusted to ensure the precise image on the visual display. Simultaneously, the pilots feel the result of their action. The simulator tips the cockpit down for braking or reduced engine thrust by shortening one or more of the jacks. For acceleration of speed or climbing to a higher altitude, the nose of the cabin is tipped up, creating the identical feel you would have when in a cockpit seat. Simulated crosswinds on takeoffs and landings create the same lurch that the pilot must correct to stay on course. Other computer-controlled hydraulic and electric machines apply pressure to flying controls, creating the feel of moving rudder pedals and the G force of tilting wings during flight.

Convincing sounds are just as important to the simulation of actual flight. Some 30 high-quality speakers, positioned invisibly around the cockpit, transmit the whining of jet engines as well as the fans of the onboard air conditioners. Seasoned

*continued*

pilots instinctively know the sounds of an aircraft's tires moving over a runway, the raising or lowering of landing gears, the hiss of air movement that becomes part of the background noise of a flight, and the chirp of tires hitting the runway upon landing. Even the lighting is controlled to reflect the brightness or gloominess of day, the reds and grays of dusk, and the blackness of nighttime.

American's 777 simulators are able to test pilots with unique scenarios, such as bad weather or unusual landing conditions. This is enormously helpful in training new pilots under different flying conditions as well as allowing seasoned pilots to practice skills they may not use in everyday flying scenarios.

How real is the environment in American's $15 million simulators? Pilots must go through the same checklist in preparing to fly the simulator as when seated in the 777, ready for takeoff. American Airlines maintains a separate maintenance log for every simulator where mechanics record each test, adjustment, and part replacement over the life of the simulator. All simulators are tested four times annually by the airline and at least once a year by the FAA. After all, when using simulators to train pilots who will fly thousands of people across the country and around the world, it is vital that the illusion is authentic.

---

**software**
The general term for a set of instructions that controls a computer or a communications network.

**program**
A set of instructions that directs a computer to perform certain tasks and produce certain results.

**communications program**
A program that manages the interaction between a computer system and a communications network and the transmission of data, programs, and information over the network.

**operating system**
A combination of programs that coordinates the actions of a computer, including its peripheral devices and memory.

**disk operating system (DOS)**
A combination of programs that coordinates the actions of a computer, including its peripheral devices and memory.

**Windows**
A single-user operating system that allows several programs to be operated simultaneously.

**graphical user interface (GUI)**
A link to an operating system that allows users to use icons rather than command words to start processing.

# Programs: In Charge of the Hardware

Today's general-purpose computer systems can perform many different tasks, moving between tasks in an instant. Because of the versatility of computers, businesspeople can create drawings and illustrations, write correspondence, prepare detailed financial analyses, maintain accounts payable, and control inventory—all on the same system.

The secret to the versatility of computers is programs. By itself, hardware is nothing but a collection of apparatus. Computer hardware is useless without software or programs. Though the terms *programs* and *software* are often used interchangeably, their meanings vary slightly. **Software** is the general term for a set of instructions that control a computer or a communications network, while a **program** is a specific sequence of instructions that tell a computer how to perform a particular action or solve a problem. For example, a **communications program** instructs the hardware how to send or receive information.

At the center of a computer's activities is the **operating system,** a combination of programs that coordinate the actions of the computer, including its peripheral devices and memory. Historically, one of the most common operating systems is DOS, a single-user personal computer operating system. **DOS** is an acronym for **disk operating system,** which means that the operating system's components reside on a disk and are brought into computer memory as needed. Today, most desktop microcomputers rely on **Windows.** This single-user PC **graphical user interface (GUI)** allows multitasking,

---

 **REALITY CHECK**

Video games—including those found in shopping-mall arcades as well as the Microsoft Xbox or Sony PlayStation in your home—are computers. They don't look like the PCs you find on desks and tables, but they have all of the characteristics of computers discussed so far. They use input, do processing, and generate output. (Some can be connected to computer networks so they can transmit information from one location to another. This allows "gamers" to play against each other over the Internet.)

A video game's input activities are the instructions that control the movement of the characters and vehicles as you use a joystick, button, steering wheel, or foot pedal. Processing takes place before your eyes as the computer translates your actions into the characters' activities. The output is what you see on the display screen and hear from the speakers. Processing also determines whether you have made good moves, assigning (or subtracting) points accordingly. If the computer chip inside senses that you have not made good moves, it will zap, trip, crash, or destroy you. When you have made too many mistakes, or when you have used up your allotted time, the chip will end the game. ■

which means that several programs can be operated concurrently, each in its own window or section of the computer screen. (An **interface** is the means by which a person interacts with a computer.) Using the GUI (pronounced "gooey") to interact with the operating system, the individual directs the computer through the window created by the software. A mouse is used to point to and click on an icon that will activate a program. Without the GUI interface, it would be necessary for the user to enter a command word to start processing. Most people prefer using GUI interfaces to entering operating system commands. Figure 2.8 explains Windows in more detail.

Other popular operating systems are Windows Server 2003, Windows 2000, and NT for PCs; UNIX and Linux for PCs, midrange systems, and mainframes; and MVS and VM, multiuser operating systems for the IBM mainframe computers used in business. Whether used on a PC, midrange, or supercomputer, all operating systems perform the same function: They enable people to interact with the computer and to control the movement, storage, and retrieval of data and information.

Another type of software is the *application program* (*application,* or *app* for short). An application program is actually several programs working together. The CargoProf program used by Continental Airlines is an application program. Likewise, the programs a bank uses to process charges, payments, and adjustments to an individual's credit card account are apps. So is the e-mail app that makes it possible to send and receive messages electronically.

## Software Packages

Many of the applications used on computers today are purchased as **software packages,** which are applications that focus on a particular subject. All software packages are accompanied by **documentation,** which is an instruction manual for the software. The most frequently used software packages allow users to do spreadsheet analysis, word processing, and desktop publishing; to create illustrations and graphics; to manage databases; to communicate with other computers; and to manage information systems.

Spreadsheet and word processing packages are the most common types of software purchased today. However, with the increased use of computers, other types of packages are growing in popularity (e.g., packages that teach foreign languages).

## Spreadsheet Programs

Employees at all levels of an organization—whether the organization is large or small, profit or nonprofit—spend a great deal of time reviewing business activities, recognizing problems, and identifying alternative ways to correct those problems. As discussed in Chapter 1, when they are addressed effectively, problems can become opportunities.

**interface**
The means by which a person interacts with a computer.

**software package**
An application that focuses on a particular subject, such as word processing, and is sold to businesses and the general public.

**documentation**
An instruction manual that accompanies software. Also, a technical, detailed written description of the specific facts of a program.

**FIGURE 2.8**
***Windows Interface***

 **REALITY CHECK**

You may hear IT users and professionals refer to *killer apps*. This term refers to a breakthrough in the form of an entirely new category of application. Killer apps are so revolutionary that they often change the way people work. They are so widely used that they are frequently the basis for any entirely new area of business or industry.

Spreadsheet software was considered a killer app when it was invented. So was desktop publishing. The Internet and the World Wide Web are more recent examples of killer apps.

What will be the next killer app? It's difficult to predict. However, you can be sure that creative entrepreneurs and ingenious information technology specialists are hard at work trying to identify the next breakthrough.

---

**spreadsheet**

A table of columns and rows used by people responsible for tracking revenues, expenses, profits, and losses.

Spreadsheet packages are designed to assist in problem solving. A **spreadsheet** consists of rows and columns of data or information. The intersection of each row and column (called a *cell*) can hold data or text, as Figure 2.9 illustrates. New information can be keyed in over old information, so the data in the spreadsheet can be easily updated and recalculated. It is also easy to instruct the software to add the contents of columns, determine percentages, and calculate trends.

Spreadsheet packages make the people using them more effective because they automate time-consuming and error-prone tasks like the adding and subtracting of columns of numbers. Users are then able to spend more time analyzing conditions and opportunities.

## Word Processing Programs

**Word processing (WP) program**

A program that allows the user to enter, change (edit), move, store, and print text information.

Correspondence (including letters, memoranda, and reports) is an important part of both business and personal life. **Word processing (WP) programs** allow you to enter, change (edit), move, store, and print text information (Figure 2.10). Many programs will also check your spelling, evaluate your grammar, and verify your punctuation.

Because word processing programs allow text to be stored and retrieved, they are frequently used to prepare tailor-made versions of correspondence and project proposals. The user can make the necessary changes to a stored document and print a new copy for distribution. Relieved of the task of re-keying an entire document manually, the user gains time to perform other, more important activities.

**FIGURE 2.9**

***Worksheet Created with Spreadsheet Software***

Spreadsheet software allows a user to change data and perform recalculations easily. For example, if rent were to increase to $12,000 per quarter, the spreadsheet software would automatically adjust both total expenses and gross profit to reflect that change.

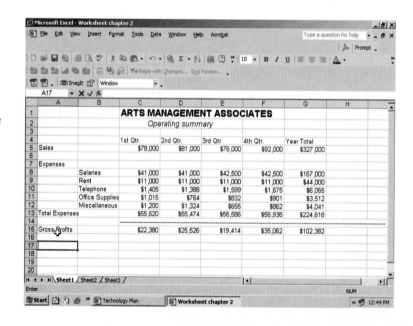

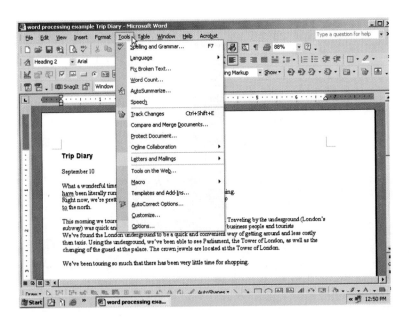

**FIGURE 2.10**

***Sample Word Processing Options***

In addition to allowing the user to lay out words in an aesthetically pleasing format, word processing software also checks spelling, grammar, and punctuation. Many newer programs offer graphics capabilities as well.

Software manufacturers are adding new features to word processing programs all the time. For example, many now provide the capability to insert graphics into the body of the text. In effect, word-processing software and desktop publishing software are converging.

## Desktop Publishing Programs

**Desktop publishing (DTP) programs** combine text and image-handling features with the capability to design documents. These programs give users more flexibility in positioning of text and images (whether drawings or photographs) on a page than word processing programs do. They also allow people to choose from a wide range of type styles and sizes to enhance the appearance of a document.

Desktop publishing was made possible by the introduction of powerful PCs and high-quality software and printers. Many organizations rely on a desktop publishing program to prepare newsletters, brochures, project proposals, advertisements, menus, and theater programs (Figure 2.11).

**desktop publishing (DTP) program**
A program that combines text and image-handling features with document-design capabilities.

---

**REALITY CHECK**

During the early days of information technology, the coming of the *paperless office* was proclaimed. Ideas would be entered through a keyboard and viewed on a computer screen, making it unnecessary to print the information. Some people even speculated that the general means of distribution of information throughout society would be magnetic disks, with newspapers, advertisements, magazines, and books being read on computer screens.

True, people are recording their thoughts on computers. But they are not generating any less paper. In fact, computers have led to a dramatic increase in paper use. It turns out we are unwilling to give up the printed word. In fact, when preparing a report or document, we tend to print it repeatedly to view changes and adjustments. (Of course, continual printing brings with it the social responsibility to recycle the excess paper generated—not to mention our old printer cartridges!)

In an effort to reduce this stubborn reliance on paper, more and more organizations are using electronic communications networks to send messages and documents that recipients print out only at their discretion. Perhaps one day, most business communication will be carried out in this manner. However, we have a long way to go before print is obsolete. ■

**FIGURE 2.11**

### Desktop Publishing Capabilities

Desktop publishing programs provide a great deal of flexibility in positioning text and images on a page. After the document designer has placed all the items in the desired locations (left), the document can be printed out and used as a master for making copies. Alternatively, the DTP system can be used to create a computer file that is sent on disk to a printer for printing (right). This process is more common with full-color publications.

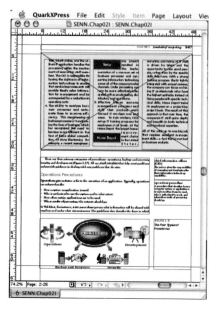
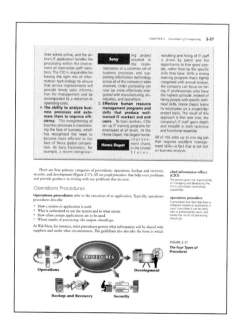

**business graphics**
Charts, graphs, and maps that are created using special graphics packages that translate data into visual representations.

## Graphic Presentation Programs

Presenting data in a form that describes trends, tracks performance levels, and compares categories frequently requires using charts, graphs, and maps. These **business graphics** can be created with special graphics packages that run on PCs, midrange systems, and mainframes (Figure 2.12). Often included in spreadsheet packages, graphics programs translate tables of data into visual representations. A one-page chart or graph, for example, may summarize many pages of detailed numeric data.

Graphics software programs prepare graphics more quickly and accurately than traditional manual methods. They not only help the user be more precise in drawing a chart or a map but also offer color, shading, and even the illusion of three dimensions to enhance the presentation.

Among the most widespread graphics programs are those designed to create electronic slides for speaker presentations. These programs, which run on desktop computers, combine text, drawings, and photos with business graphics. They also provide reduced copies of the slides that can be printed and distributed as audience handouts.

## Photo Editing Programs

Photo editing programs are used to work with digital versions of photographs, such as those captured by an image scanner. These programs will touch up, remove, or add features to a photograph. They can also be used to add special touches, such as feathering the edges of the photograph or distorting the shape of the image to create an unusual appearance (Figure 2.13).

Photo editing software is often used to prepare photos that will be inserted into graphic presentation slides or into pages created with desktop publishing programs.

## Illustration Programs

**illustration program**
A program in which the computer screen becomes a drawing board on which artists translate their ideas into visual form.

To draw images, create special effects, and translate ideas (rather than data) into visual form, people use **illustration programs.** These programs are the electronic equivalent of the artist's box of brushes, pens, and other devices. They turn the computer screen into a drawing board on which artists can bring their ideas to life (Figure 2.14). A finished illustration can be stored, retrieved, changed, and sent to a printer or similar device.

Illustration packages enable an artist to create any type of illustration with greater speed and precision than are possible by hand. Yet artistic creativity still originates with the user. The PC is but a tool that increases productivity; it is not a substitute for creativity and know-how. Illustration programs are discussed in detail in a future chapter.

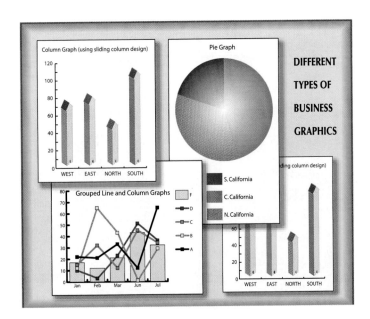

**FIGURE 2.12**
***Sample Graphics Program***
Graphics programs translate mountains of data into an easy-to-read, aesthetically pleasing format.

The *Information Technology in Practice* feature ("Rainforest Cafe Is a Wild Place to Shop and Eat! But Watch Out for Rapid Growth!") describes how information technology capabilities that successfully launched the Rainforest Cafe eventually had to be replaced when the chain grew in size.

## Database Management Programs

Businesses have a constant need to store and retrieve data and information. **Database management programs** let users store information as interrelated records that can be retrieved quickly. A record is a set of data pertaining to an item of interest. Information about a student, for example, is stored in a student record. Each record is composed of various fields, a collection of characters representing a single type of data. Thus, every student's record contains an address, a telephone number, and a date-of-birth field. A collection of related records (say, the freshman class or all biology majors, depending on how the database is organized) is called a *file*. The collection of all records about all students constitutes the **database.**

A database enables information about an item to be retrieved according to certain specified characteristics of the item. For example, a human resources manager could

**database management program**
A program that makes it possible for users to manage the data in ways that increase accessibility and productivity.

**database**
A collection of data and information describing items of interest to an organization.

**FIGURE 2.13**
***Photo Editing Program***

**FIGURE 2.14**

***Illustration Program Capabilities***

Illustration programs are like an electronic toolbox containing brushes, pens, boxes, circles, and color palettes.

ask a database system to select the records in an interviewee database and print a list of all interviewees who live in Houston and are experts on international commerce in the European Union (Figure 2.15). A utility company could use a database to keep a record of all the houses, apartment buildings, and businesses to which it provides electricity.

Like all other software, database management programs handle the storage, retrieval, changing, and formatting of the information for the individual user. Many packages are available for use on every size of computer. More on database management systems can be found in Chapters 6 and 7.

## Communications Programs

Data communication is an integral component of information technology and many computing applications. Communications programs manage the interaction between a computer system and a communications network and the transmission of data, information, and programs over the network. Some are designed specifically to link computers to the Internet. All provide the versatility needed to link different computers. Communications programs also establish the rules of data transmission and automatically manage electronic conversations to ensure users follow established rules. In addition, they control modems, the devices that allow computer-to-computer dialogue. Chapter 8 examines data communication from several different viewpoints.

**FIGURE 2.15**

***Records of Text and Data in a Job Database***

Each employee has his or her own individual record, which includes three fields: the employee's name, date of hire, and job title. Together, these records constitute a job database.

| NAME | DATE HIRED | JOB TITLE |
|------|-----------|-----------|
| Sally Thomas | 10/2/88 | Customer service representative |
| Morgan Fairfield | 5/4/91 | Advertising director |
| Bert Renoso | 3/2/76 | Customer service manager |
| James Jones Earl | 2/5/78 | Quality control supervisor |
| Ramon Vasquez | 6/3/85 | Customer service representative |
| Betty Lin | 1/4/65 | Operations manager |

Record of information ⎯ Fields ⎯ Database

# INFORMATION TECHNOLOGY IN PRACTICE

## Rainforest Cafe® Is a Wild Place to Shop and Eat®! But Watch Out for Rapid Growth!

Follow the trail into a rainforest and you'll find lush vegetation and spectacular wildlife. Step into the Rainforest Cafe and you will begin an adventure through the most realistic indoor rainforest ever created! Discover amazingly lush surroundings, cascading waterfalls, beautiful aquariums, and animals so lifelike in size and movement that some people are sure to believe they are real. At any moment, thunder and lightning and the tropical showers may convince even *you* that the forest is alive.

The Rainforest Cafe opened its first restaurant in Minneapolis in 1994. The sounds and smells of a tropical wonderland, an exotic menu, and the ever-present animals were an instant hit. Revenue grew more than 250 percent in a two-year period. Within the next few years the company successfully opened additional restaurants, and there was tremendous demand for even more of the unique restaurants.

Rapid growth is exciting, and a sure sign of success, so long as it can be effectively managed. And

good management means having business systems that can support the growth while keeping day-to-day operations under control.

But the rapid growth that the Rainforest Cafe experienced was quickly becoming a problem, and that problem was most visible in its information technology systems. Like many start-up companies, the management of the Rainforest Cafe began with an accounting system running on a PC. But the cafe's skyrocketing success meant not only that the company was outgrowing its PC-based systems, but that it also needed to add systems to manage an increasing number of restaurants spread over a growing geographic area. The need for improvement in the company's IT systems was evident, but the company did not have a permanent IT staff that could take on the development of these new systems.

Working with a computer services firm, Rainforest Cafe management created a new system that could scale up and evolve as the company added more restaurants. It featured powerful server computers that ran software packages capable of handling all

accounting, inventory, and financial management processes.

Because the company wanted to ensure that all restaurant managers were responsible and accountable for their own success, managers at each restaurant location have the capability to use the system to manage their own financial information. The system permits them to monitor their requisitions, the cost of food purchases, and staff labor costs. Headquarters managers can aggregate the same information by restaurant, by region, and company-wide. In each case, daily food and labor costs (the highest and most variable operating costs for restaurants) are available instantly. The online system also uses Internet capabilities to enable managers to access and share information with one another.

Rainforest Cafe's decision to restructure its IT capability has paid big dividends. The speedy system has been instrumental in reducing operating costs by hundreds of thousands of dollars annually, thereby paying for the system many times over. In addition, it has enabled further expansion of the company. Today, Rainforest Cafe can be found from coast-to-coast in the United States, and in international locations including Canada, France, Hong Kong, Japan, Mexico, Singapore, and the United Kingdom. The Rainforest Cafe proves how quickly you can grow a rainforest when you begin with little more than a PC and a keen imagination.

## Browsers

**Browsers** are software applications that work with communications programs to connect computers to the Internet. Browsers, such as Microsoft's Internet Explorer and Netscape's Communicator, interact with the Internet to retrieve and display text, image, and animated information in pages on an individual computer display. The browser also enables an individual to move between pages and display different pages of information.

## Information Systems Programs

Programs created to manage business activities made up the bulk of the software industry prior to the PC boom in the late 1970s and early 1980s. Even today, transaction processing applications account for huge expenditures of business funds in both large and small organizations. **Transaction processing** uses a combination of information technology and manual procedures to process data and information and to manage transactions. For years, businesses have used this system to process transaction data for payroll management, production management, personnel records management, inventory control, and accounting procedures. In today's world, however, companies often refer to other business management applications, called **information systems** or **management information systems (MIS).** In contrast to the processing of individual transactions, these applications help mangers oversee and make decisions about company or department operations.

Information systems therefore differ in an important way from spreadsheet packages and the other types of software discussed so far. Information systems focus on business processes (such as the processing of customer orders, the accounting process, the inventory management process, and increasing organizational productivity), while the other types of software focus on solving problems, aiding personal decision making, and increasing personal productivity. Information systems are covered in depth in Chapter 13.

## Programming Languages

Computer programs are not written in everyday language or as lines of text. Rather, they are created using a **computer programming language**–a series of commands and codes that the computer can translate into the electronic pulses that underlie all computing activities. When programmers write instructions in a programming language, they are telling the computer how and when to carry out arithmetic operations, read data from secondary storage, store data, and display or print information.

Some tasks are performed so frequently during processing that it would be extremely inefficient to code these activities into the program again and again. For this reason, programmers use special **utility programs** (sometimes called **utilities**) to perform such functions as sorting records and copying programs from one medium to another. Utilities can either be bundled into an operating system or purchased as software.

Many programming languages have been developed to suit the needs of people tackling different types of problems, with some more popular in business than others. One of the most commonly used business programming languages today is Java. Other common programming languages include C, C++, C#, and Visual Basic. At one time, COBOL (Common Business-Oriented Language) was the most commonly used business programming language. However, the other languages have largely replaced COBOL in business.

All the computer software packages discussed in the preceding section are written in a computer programming language. They eliminate the need for the user to know a programming language or know how to write a program.

## Custom Software

Not all software is prewritten and sold in package form. In fact, much of the software used in businesses is **custom software**, software designed for a particular firm by systems analysts and programmers (discussed later in this chapter). Applications software is the most common type of software developed by custom programmers (who write the application in a programming language). Custom applications may be developed by *in-house programmers*, who are employed by the company for which the application is developed, or by *contract programmers*, who are outside experts hired by the company to develop a certain program. The design and development of custom software is discussed in Chapters 10 and 11.

## Software Trends

Two trends are changing the sources of computer software:

- **Greater use of prewritten software packages**   You can buy software to fit virtually any need, either from a computer or office products retail store (such as CompUSA, MicroCenter, Staples, or Office Depot) that specializes in selling software or both software and hardware, or from a firm that develops and distributes software (such as Adobe, Microsoft, or IBM). When selecting software, you need to first determine your requirements and then evaluate the features and price of a particular software package.
- **Greater use of prewritten components**   One of the most fundamental trends in computer software today is the move away from writing software from scratch toward using prewritten components (frequently called *objects* in IT parlance). Under this approach, developers acquire and assemble components to create an application. (Note: The objects and components are created by specialists who write the software in a fashion that makes it reusable.)

Advances in the power and capabilities of computer hardware, coupled with the sky-rocketing demand for information technology at home, on campus, and at work, have led to advances in software development practices. Traditional software development practice is to use programming languages to create programs consisting of lengthy sections of computer instructions. Every time someone wants a new application written, the programmer has to write a separate programming procedure.

As you can imagine, many procedures are used repeatedly between applications. These procedures may be as subtle as date and time logging and customer account number validation routines in corporate accounting systems, or as visible as sound generation and graphics display modules in multimedia applications. There is no reason to keep writing these routine procedures over and over, regardless of which programming language is being used.

**Object-oriented programming** has evolved to simplify this situation. You might liken these new ways of developing software to the way consumer products have been manufactured for many years. A DVD or VCR, for instance, consists of the main circuit board, the disk or tape transport mechanism, and the chassis. Each of these components, in turn, consists of smaller components: The circuit board, for instance, is made up of chips and diodes.

**object-oriented programming**
Software development combining data and procedures into a single object.

**Objects** are independent software blocks that can be used in many different applications without changing the program code. The software equivalents of the DVD/VCR's circuit boards and chips in an accounting application are the invoice object and its component parts: the date module, the item analysis module, and the invoice tax and total module. Each object contains data and processing procedures (for example, how to determine and validate the date of the invoice). Using objects in application development reduces the time and effort put into creating an application. Each object can be reused, avoiding the need to write it from scratch.

**object**
A component that contains data about itself and how it is to be processed.

A growing number of applications, both custom and commercial, are being written using object-oriented programming. This will probably become the dominant programming method used by information technology professionals in the future. Both individuals and companies using software developed through object-oriented programming should benefit by getting better software more quickly. We will see how objects work in Chapters 7 and 11.

# Information: The Reason for Using Information Technology

**information**
An organized, meaningful, and useful interpretation of data.

**Information** is an organized, meaningful, and useful interpretation of data. Using information, you can determine conditions, assess whether a problem has occurred, evaluate alternative solutions, and select actions. But information is not composed solely of data. It may also include text, sound, and images. As Figure 2.16 shows, information technology helps us make the most effective use of information in any or all of these forms.

## Data

**data**
Raw facts, figures, and details.

The raw facts of a situation are **data.** Data can be numbers, letters, or symbols, or any combination of the three. Some examples of data are the average points scored by a team's leading player, the number of subscribers to a magazine, the attendance at a rock concert, the midday price for a corporate stock, and the number of English majors in the College of Arts and Sciences. Each piece of data describes a fact, a condition, an event, or the results of that event.

## Text

Text is written (narrative) information. It may be typed, printed, or handwritten. When you scan a newspaper, flip through a magazine, read a letter, or look at the fine print on a rental agreement, you are using text information.

Sports scores and statistics on athletic achievements tell only part of the story of a game. That's why newspapers and magazines always include a narrative highlighting key plays. Without this additional information, you could not possibly get the full story of the game.

## Sound

**spoken information**
Information that is conveyed by sound.

The same sports statistics that you can read in a newspaper may be broadcast to you by an announcer at the game. This is **spoken information**–information conveyed by sound. Have you ever called directory assistance to obtain a phone number and heard

**FIGURE 2.16**

***The Four Components of Information***

Data do not become information until they are organized logically and usefully. Information may also include text, sound, and images.

# CRITICAL CONNECTIONS 2

## Nevada Bob's—Where to Go If You Golf! NEVADA BOB'S GOLF

The game of golf, as we know it today, began in the 15th century on the eastern coast of Scotland. Back then, players would hit a pebble around a natural course using clubs made by wood craftsmen and bow makers from branches of beech or thornwood trees. Sand dunes lay in wait for anyone knocking the pebble off course.

During the next century, the Old Course at St. Andrews, Scotland, came into prominence. It is often credited with being the home of modern golf. To many people around the world, the name St. Andrews is synonymous with golf. However, for many others, the name they associate with golf is . . . Nevada Bob's.

Nevada Bob's is the world's largest chain of retail golf shops, providing the modern golfer with everything from clubs, bags, and balls to outerwear and practice gear. The more than 50 stores developed independently over a period of several years, beginning in 1962.

Bob's management believes that it is so successful because it takes care of the customer—providing customers with what they need when they need it. But that success created a significant challenge for the company. Because the number of Nevada Bob's stores grew over time, there was not a standard computer inventory control system for each store. This made it difficult for the company to keep track of what was on hand in a store, when an item sold, and when resupply was essential.

---

the number spoken in a humanlike—but definitely not human—voice? This, too, is spoken information—information conveyed by sound from a computer.

Virtually any sound can be captured in a computer system, transmitted over a network, or output through a computer-controlled device. It is now quite common for sound input to originate from people speaking into microphones connected to a computer. For example, when a telephone directory system asks you to say the name of the city and then the name of the party for whom you are seeking a telephone number, your voice response is sound input to the system.

### Images

An image is information in visual form. Images may be used to summarize data, as in charts and graphs. They may also take the form of lines, drawings, or photographs. Many *multimedia* presentations, which incorporate all four of the components of information, use animation to move words and images across the screen.

Most of the world's major league sports have a *Hall of Fame* where outstanding athletes and officials are honored. At the football Hall of Fame, you can find computer-controlled multimedia displays of great plays made in the game down through the decades. Sound and image information stored on optical disk is retrieved to re-create these memorable events for the viewer—right down to the athletes' grunts and groans and the cheers from the crowd. Best of all, the computer-managed displays can be maintained forever, providing a vivid historical record of the sport.

Many people think of computers as processing only data or text. That is an old-fashioned and limited view. As you will see throughout this book, sounds and images are as important as—and used almost as frequently as—data and text in computer systems.

## People: Users and Creators of IT Applications

People are the most important element in any computer system, for without them, there would be no need for computers. The people associated with information technology are its users and information technology professionals.

## Users

**user (end user)**
The people who use IT in their jobs or personal lives.

The people who employ information technology in their jobs or personal lives are called **users,** or sometimes **end users** because they are the ultimate users of a computer system.
There are four types of users:

- **Hands-on users**   These are the people who use computers or communications systems directly, interacting with them to enter data, do processing, store and retrieve information, transmit details, or produce output.
- **Indirect end users**   These individuals do not directly operate a computer but benefit from IT as the recipients of reports, electronic messages, communications, or multimedia presentations.
- **User managers**   People who have supervisory responsibility for activities that involve or are affected by information technology are known as user managers. Manufacturing managers, editors, and hospital administrators, for instance, may be in charge of departments or work groups that use IT. These managers may not use IT themselves, but they ensure that their staff members have reliable computer and communication capabilities. It is increasingly rare, however, to find a user manager who is not a hands-on user.
- **Senior managers**   These managers incorporate the capabilities of information technology into an organization's products, services, and overall competitive strategies. They also evaluate the organization's dependence on IT and identify the problems that could arise if appropriate operating procedures (discussed later in this chapter) are not established or followed.

The *Information Technology in Practice* feature ("The Role of CIOs in Creating Business Success") describes the importance of having an IT professional as part a company's senior management team.

## Wal-Mart: IT's a Success Story

The retail industry provides a good example of how information technology can span all levels of management and strongly influence a company's operations. Wal-Mart, the U.S. discount retailer, has become the world's largest retailer, with annual sales well in excess of $100 billion, through its use of IT. At the store level, cashiers (hands-on end users) enter sales data into point-of-sale terminals by waving a bar-code scanner across a package's bar-coded price and stock numbers. The price of the item is then retrieved from the store computer and appears on the point-of-sale terminal display. At the same time, the sale of the item is recorded.

Store and department managers who receive reports of store and department sales and inventory levels are indirect end users. They may not operate a computer directly, but they rely on the information captured and generated through the company's information system to make decisions. User managers help to ensure that Wal-Mart maintains remarkably low inventories (only about 10 percent of the company's square footage is devoted to inventory, compared to an industry average of 25 percent). The firm's senior managers, including the chief executive officer and corporate vice presidents, use IT to monitor store-by-store sales daily, a key step in ensuring that sales goals are achieved.

Together, senior and user managers have extended the reach of Wal-Mart's IT beyond the company. The majority of Wal-Mart's 5,000 vendors now receive point-of-sale information through an electronic link. They use this information to determine what goods are selling and to keep Wal-Mart sufficiently—but not overly—stocked to meet its sales needs. Yet the entire process begins with the activities of the hands-on end user who enters the details about each item sold at a Wal-Mart store.

## Information Technology Professionals

**information technology professional**
A person who is responsible for acquiring, developing, maintaining, or operating the hardware associated with computers and communications networks.

**Information technology professionals** are responsible for acquiring, developing, maintaining, or operating the hardware and software associated with computers and communications networks. The following IT professionals have the highest profile:

- **Programmers**  use programming languages to create computer and communications network software.
- **Systems analysts**  work with users to determine the requirements an application must meet. As part of their job, they may specify the purchase of a software package that gets the job done or order the development of custom software.
- **Systems designers**  formulate application specifications and design the features of custom software. In some organizations, the roles of programmer, systems analyst, and systems designer may be filled by one person called a **programmer/analyst.**
- **Web designers**  focus primarily on developing applications for the Internet and the World Wide Web. Often the apps they develop are referred to as *web-enabled* applications.
- **Project managers**  coordinate the development of a project and manage the team of programmer/analysts.
- **Network specialists**  design, operate, and manage computer communications networks, including networks that interconnect with the Internet.
- **Trainers**  work with end users, helping them to become comfortable with and skilled at using hardware or software.
- **Computer operators**  oversee the operations of computers in **data centers** (sometimes called **computer centers**), facilities where large and midrange computer systems are located. These systems are shared by many users who are interconnected with the system through communications links. Computer operators also perform support activities, such as starting applications, loading magnetic tape, and any other job that will ensure the smooth operation of computer facilities.

These IT professionals usually work for businesses that use computers or communications technology but do not design and manufacture the hardware they use. IT professionals in the business of manufacturing computers or computer-related components (such as communication cables and electrical power supplies) generally fall into two categories: **computer engineers,** who design, develop, and oversee the manufacturing of computer equipment; and **systems engineers,** who install and maintain hardware.

**programmer/analyst**
A person who has joint responsibility for determining system requirements and developing and implementing the systems.

**data center/computer center**
A facility at which large and midrange computer systems are located. These systems are shared by many users who are interconnected with the system through communications links.

**computer engineer**
An IT professional who designs, develops, and oversees the manufacturing of computer equipment.

**systems engineer**
An IT professional who installs and maintains hardware.

## Procedures: Processes to Use and Maintain IT

Good procedures are essential whether an application runs on a PC or a supercomputer or whether it is used by one person or by many people. A **procedure** is a step-by-step set of instructions—a process—for accomplishing specific results. Procedures, people, and applications together make up the know-how of IT.

There are four primary categories of procedures: operations, backup and recovery, security, and development (Figure 2.17). All are *people procedures* that help avert problems and provide guidance in dealing with any problems that do arise.

**procedure**
A step-by-step process or a set of instructions for accomplishing specific results.

**FIGURE 2.17**

*The Four Types of Procedures*

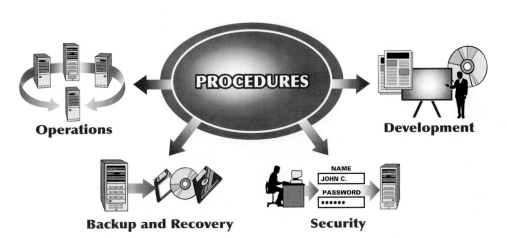

Operations — Development — Backup and Recovery — Security

# INFORMATION TECHNOLOGY IN PRACTICE

## The Role of CIOs in Creating Business Success

Because information technology is the lifeblood of business today, thousands of companies around the world have created the position of **chief information officer (CIO).** A CIO is essential to ensure that management's attention is focused on the effective use of information technology to enable the business to deliver its products and services. Often the CIO reports directly to the chief executive officer of the company. That way, each executive knows both the plans for the business and the role of information technology in meeting the company's goals.

CIO's backgrounds tend to vary. Some have extensive technical training and experience while others have MBAs but little or no technical experience. All share a keen awareness of what IT can do for their business.

What else does it take to be an effective CIO? DuWayne Peterson, one of the first-ever CIOs (having served at Merrill Lynch & Company and at Security Bank), and the

banking industry's first million-dollar salary CIO, identified five requirements for the successful CIO. They are as necessary today as when Peterson shared them in the 1980s:

1. **The knowledge that business strategy is the rudder that steers IT planning.** Sometimes a company's IT strategy calls for an entirely new vision of its business. The CIO of Simon & Schuster, for example, is charged with leading the giant publisher into the new world of electronic publishing. At other companies, the strategic goals are less radical but equally challenging. The CIO at Levi Strauss & Company is charged with using IT to help the company delegate authority and responsibility to its employees in the 100 countries where it does business. This has meant setting up computer networks that help store managers and suppliers maintain proper inventory levels without intervention from headquarters.

2. **A strong vision of what IT can do to achieve strategic objectives.** In the past, banks resigned themselves to the idea that customers come and go. As a result, most banks used IT for processing transactions in separate checking, savings, loan, and credit card accounts. Today, however, banks realize that retaining customers will make their business more profitable; and competition for loyal customers is heating up. Bank One

Corp. initiated a strategy **BankOne** that has become a banking trend: winning customer loyalty by pursuing *relationship banking*. At the heart of Bank One's campaign is a computer system that integrates 17 systems to create a comprehensive customer profile, which can then be used to market personalized services. With the help of this strategic application, Bank One's marketing department can identify customers who might need suggestions on anything from financing a college education to preparing for retirement.

3. **The technical ability to develop an IT structure that will provide low-cost, responsive services for all, as well as specialized services for individual business units.** At British Airways, executives seek to have the **British Airways** majority of their tickets booked over the Internet—a method of issuing tickets that until recently was technologically unavailable. To reach this goal, the company is investing tens of millions of pounds in IT infrastructure, marketing, and related expenses. Internet ticketing not only benefits the customer by providing quick service, anywhere, anytime, it also benefits the airline by reducing the number of staff needed to handle the booking of reservations. Customers book their tickets online, and the airline's

IT application handles the processing within the involvement of reservation staff members. The CIO is responsible for having the right mix of information technology to ensure that service improvements will provide timely sales information for management and be accompanied by a reduction in operating costs.

4. **The ability to analyze business processes and automate them to improve efficiency.** This *reengineering* of business processes is transforming the face of business, which has recognized the need to become more efficient in the face of fierce global competition. At Sony Electronics, for example, a recent reengineering project resulted in the

**Sony**

implementation of a common set of business processes and supporting information technology across all of the company's sales channels. Order processing can now be more effectively integrated with manufacturing, distribution, and operations.

5. **Effective human resource management programs and skills that produce well-trained IT workers and end users.** To train workers, CIOs set up IT training programs for employees at all levels. At the Home Depot, the largest home-improvement chain in the United States, recruiting and hiring of IT staff is driven by talent and the op-

**Home Depot**

portunity to hire good people, rather than by the specific skills they have. With a strong training program that's tightly integrated with annual reviews, the company can focus on hiring IT professionals who have the highest aptitude. Instead of hiring people with specific technical skills, Home Depot trains its employees on a project-by-project basis. The result of this approach is that over time, the company's IT staff gains depth and breadth in both technical and functional expertise.

All of this adds up to one big job that requires excellent management skills—a fact that is not lost on business analysts.

## Operations Procedures

**Operations procedures** refer to the execution of an application. Typically, operations procedures describe

- How a system or application is used.
- Who is authorized to use the system and to what extent.
- How often certain applications are to be used.
- Where results of processing–the output–should go.

At Wal-Mart, for instance, strict procedures govern what information will be shared with suppliers and under what circumstances. The guidelines also describe the form in which information is to be shared, indicating when raw data should be distributed and when only summary forms should be released.

If you use a PC, you probably follow a set of procedures for starting it up and shutting it down. Operators of mainframes in computer centers or midrange computers in offices must do the same thing. These procedures ensure that information will not be lost and that electrical components will not be damaged.

Depending on the application, operations procedures can be very simple ("Always make a backup copy of the day's work before shutting down the system") or quite involved ("At the end of every month, make a backup copy of all databases, a copy of all transactions, and reset all account totals to begin the next month").

## Backup and Recovery Procedures

You don't want to risk losing several days' work because a power line goes down or a diskette gets misplaced. **Backup procedures** describe when and how to make extra copies, called *backup copies*. **Backup copies** protect against loss of data, information, or software. Should any of these be lost or accidentally changed, they can then be restored from the backup copy. **Recovery procedures** describe what actions to take when data and information or software must be recovered.

**chief information officer (CIO)**
The person given the responsibility of managing and developing the firm's information technology capabilities.

**operations procedure**
A procedure that describes how a computer system or application is used, how often it can be used, who is authorized to use it, and where the results of processing should go.

**backup procedure**
A procedure that describes how and when to make extra copies of information or software to protect against losses.

**backup copies**
Extra copies of information or software made to protect against losses.

**recovery procedure**
An action taken when information or software must be restored.

## Security Procedures

**security procedure**
A procedure designed to safeguard data centers, communications networks, computers, and other IT components from accidental intrusion or intentional damage.

**security software**
Software that is designed to protect systems and data.

**Security procedures** are designed to safeguard data centers, communications networks, computers, and other IT components from accidental intrusion or intentional damage. Backup copies protect against loss; security procedures prevent actions that could lead to that loss. Common security procedures entail limiting access to certain databases and creating secret passwords that users must input into the computer to perform certain functions. **Security software** allows IT managers to restrict access to files and databases, to disk drives, and even to input/output devices.

Of particular importance is protection against viruses—hidden programs, residing on disk or in memory, which can alter (without any users realizing it) the way a computer operates or modify the data and programs stored on the computer. The virus copies itself onto other programs or to diskettes inserted into the system, thereby spreading itself from one computer to another—just as a biological virus spreads from one person to the next. If undetected, a virus can do a great deal of damage to stored information.

**antivirus software**
Software designed to scan incoming e-mail messages, documents, and other information to detect and remove viruses that may be attached.

**Antivirus software** scans incoming e-mail messages, documents, and other information to detect viruses that may be attached. They alert the user to the presence of a virus and offer alternatives for removing the virus. Viruses are discussed in more detail in Chapter 14.

## Development Procedures

**development procedure**
A procedure that explains how IT professionals should describe user needs and develop applications to meet those needs.

**Development procedures** tell IT professionals how to describe user needs and develop applications to meet those needs. These procedures may also prescribe when and how software should be acquired and put into use. The IT professional involved in a development procedure should begin by examining the business situation, and then evaluate alternative methods for improving that situation or capitalizing on an opportunity. In some firms, these findings are recorded according to specific *documentation procedures*.

It's the development procedures that will determine how successful an application will be.

Tho *Information Technology in Practice* feature ("Rethinking Société Générale's Global Business Systems") describes why a well-known bank chose to develop an IT application that dramatically altered the way it conducts business.

# An Introduction to Systems

Let's explore some of the differences between IT in personal systems and in multiuser systems. (Recall that a *system* is a set of components that interact to accomplish a purpose.)

**REALITY CHECK**

A fundamental principle of personal life has been humorously phrased in the form of Murphy's Law: If something can go wrong, it will. There are corollaries to this principle, including these:

- Nothing is as easy as it looks.
- Everything takes longer than you think.
- If you determine that there are exactly four ways in which something can go wrong, a fifth way will suddenly put in an appearance.
- Nature always takes the side of the hidden flaw.
- Applied to information technology, Murphy's Law dictates that you should always assume that sooner or later, data, information, and software will accidentally be erased, damaged, or lost. Therefore, make backup copies of *everything*. ■

## Personal/Single-User Systems

A **single-user system** is typically used by one person. It stands alone and is not interconnected with other companies or shared by other people. Often journalists and writers, financial analysts, and magazine illustrators using word processing, spreadsheets, and graphics illustration software respectively have powerful personal systems at hand. The most important benefit of personal systems is their ability to be customized to enhance the productivity and effectiveness of the person using them. In each case, effectiveness takes the form of being able to represent information in a usable and digestible format, while productivity derives from the system's ability to develop articles and reports, insights, or illustrations much more rapidly than they could by hand.

**single-user system**
An IT system used by only one person. A system that stands alone and is not interconnected with other companies or shared by other people.

## Multiuser Systems

People whose work requires them to exchange information find they can do so most quickly and effectively on computers that are interconnected. **Multiuser system** is the general term for a system in which more than one user shares one or more systems of hardware, programs, information, people, and procedures. The multiuser system has three purposes: (1) to increase the productivity and effectiveness of the people using the applications, (2) to increase the productivity and effectiveness of the organizations in which the applications are used, and (3) to improve the services provided to those who rely on the users of multiuser applications.

**multiuser system**
A communications system in which more than one user share hardware, programs, information, people, and procedures.

All of the following are reasons to use multiuser systems:

- **To share a computer**  *Example:* American Airlines, United Airlines, Delta Air Lines, Northwest, and Continental Airlines link thousands of travelers to their reservation computer over the Internet. They do the same for travel agents by allowing them to share a centralized mainframe system to check flight schedules for their customers. All use the centralized computer to book reservations. Other international air carriers have developed similar systems.

- **To share hardware**  *Example:* Artists working on separate projects at the *New York Times* share a printer on which they can produce their illustrations. Each artist's computer is connected to the printer through a communications cable.

- **To share software**  *Example:* Rather than requiring students to purchase individual copies of a multimedia biology education program, the University of Minnesota acquired a license from the manufacturer to allow many students to use the software. Students can share the software on a special network set up in the laboratory. The network interconnects separate PCs to a more powerful central PC on which the software is stored and made accessible to the separate student PCs.

- **To share information**  *Example:* Medical personnel at the Stanford Medical Center and at Massachusetts General Hospital can review all the diagnostic, test, and treatment information about a critically ill patient, including X rays, because it is all stored in a single database maintained at the hospital chosen by the patient.

- **To share communications**  *Example:* Product designers in a company can stay in touch with one another, regardless of their geographic locations, by means of an electronic mail system. Nokia, 3M, IBM, and many other companies interconnect their employees around the globe through their worldwide messaging networks. At Coca-Cola Company, employees use the same network to send and receive messages through their desktop, laptop, or notebook computers.

You can see how important multiuser systems are in manufacturing plants. Automobile makers in Japan, South Korea, throughout Europe, and in the United States rely on multiuser systems to interconnect production and assembly equipment, including robots. Networking allows activities to be synchronized so that all actions take place at the right time.

Multiuser systems are neither more nor less valuable than single-user systems. They just offer a different set of benefits. (Single-user systems are discussed in detail in Chapter 6 and multiuser systems in Chapters 7 and 8.)

# INFORMATION TECHNOLOGY IN PRACTICE

## Rethinking Société Générale's Global Business Systems

Société Générale, headquartered in Paris, is the sixth largest bank in the Euro zone, with €13 billion in assets under management. It consists of three lines of business: retail (consumer) banking, asset management and private banking, and corporate and investment banking. The bank's 81,000 employees—including 35,000 in France—are spread between 500 offices in 75 countries spanning North America, Asia, and Europe. It is the bank's strategy to continue growing both globally and in France.

Among the challenges in managing a company with global offices is devising a human resource system for support of the staff. As the Société Générale grew, it developed regionally unique and unconnected manual and computer-based human resource systems. Currencies varied between countries causing difficulties in managing salaries and other staff costs. More complications were caused by the fact that legal requirements for human resource systems (e.g., compensation, work force administration, career development, and payroll systems) in France were unique compared to those in other countries. Add to these hurdles France's 35-hour work week—significantly fewer hours than other countries—and it was easy to see how managing the bank globally was challenging.

Determining that the individual systems would ultimately hinder the bank's growth and overall performance, management decided to create a single, common human resource system in the Asian countries that would integrate into it a global payroll system. It also determined that centralizing the global human resource data and managing it with a single system was essential.

However, management also realized that an all-at-once worldwide restructuring was not likely to be successful. It decided to follow an evolutionary process. Capitalizing on the worldwide reach of the Internet, Société Générale first implemented computer software that enabled it to identify salary costs by region, track worldwide career paths for promotion and personal development, and maintain work histories for every employee of the investment bank.

Next it restructured the database so that the human resource system and a now global payroll process shared the same data. It also created a single computer interface so that users could access either system in the same way. At the end of this stage, all payrolls were denominated in a single currency, Euros.

In the final phase, global features for recruitment of new personnel, administration of benefits (e.g., health care and retirement), tracking career development and management succession planning, recording time off, and conducting employee reviews were added. The global system helps Société Générale manage individual work calendars and adhere to legal obligations. One component of the software was designed specifically to meet the unique French employment regulations under which the bank must operate in France.

Through its carefully planning adoption of information technology, Société Générale is now able to comply with local and regional laws while managing the investment bank globally.

# Information Technology in Practice at Starwood Hotels: An Example

Now that you have had a tour of the computer and have been introduced to its capabilities, let's see how it all fits together. Here is an example of PCs, mainframes, and communications networks working together to accomplish the day-to-day activities of a worldwide hotel system. Note how single-user and multiuser systems work together.

## Starwood Hotels

Starwood Hotels (Figure 2.18) headquartered in White Plains, New York, owns or operates more than 400 hotels around the world under such well-known names as Westin see Fig 2.19, Sheraton, Luxury Group, St. Regis, and W Hotels. Each hotel has a unique personality. Some are in downtown areas and cater to conventioneers and business travelers, while others are in resort areas and specialize in ensuring that vacationing guests can unwind and relax. Whatever a Starwood Hotel's characteristics, an important factor in its ability to meet its customers' needs is Starwood's property management system. This system is integral to providing services to guests and running day-to-day hotel operations.

## Starwood Worldwide Reservation System

Most guests make an advance reservation through Starwood's worldwide computer and communication system that is operated from the company's headquarters. Potential guests place a toll-free call to Starwood to check on the rates and availability of guest rooms at their chosen hotel. Reservation agents must have information at their fingertips telling them not only whether rooms are available but also the type of room (single bed, double bed, or suite), its location (oceanfront or mountain view, for example), and the daily rate. Rates vary according to the type of room, the season or dates of rental, and whether the guest is part of a convention or other large group booking rooms at the hotel. Starwood's reservation system also keeps track of information of this nature for each hotel.

Potential customers can contact Starwood's toll-free number (800-325-3535) for making reservations from anywhere in the world. When a reservation is made by phone, a reservation agent takes the call. All agents ask what location the caller is interested in. If the caller knows the city, but not a specific Starwood hotel within the city, the agent can call up a listing of all hotels in that city and information about their location. After the customer chooses a hotel and it is verified that a room is available on the desired dates, details of the reservation are entered into the database. The agent notes the name of the guest and all pertinent information, including address, dates and length of stay at the chosen hotel, and any special requirements. The reservation system issues a confirmation number that uniquely identifies the guest and the specific reservation (Figure 2.19). (Business travelers may have several reservations for different hotels on various dates entered for them in the system, and this unique number is the system's way of keeping them separate.)

Starwood's customer reservation system communicates with a computer system at each Starwood hotel. It retrieves information about the availability of rooms in order to respond to an inquiry from an individual guest. Likewise, details of reservations made through the reservation system are automatically passed to the local hotel through the communications link. (If a guest makes a reservation at the local hotel, or *walks in* to obtain a room on a specific day, this inventory information is also transmitted to Starwood's central reservation system.)

## Property Management System

Besides being connected to the Starwood headquarters system, each hotel in the Starwood chain operates its own independent systems. A property management system that runs on a local network of computers at the front desk of one of Starwood's hotels enables the staff to check in guests, registering them for the room, rate, and length of stay described in their reservation (Figure 2.20). All guest information originally entered

**FIGURE 2.18**
*A Modern Luxury Hotel Operated by Starwood Hotels*

**FIGURE 2.19**
*A Westin Hotel Representative Checking in an Arriving Guest*

through the reservation system is available to local hotel staff members. Front desk personnel can also enter additional details or make changes using the personal computer or workstation attached to the local hotel system.

During a guest's stay, the property management system keeps track of charges incurred by the guest in the hotel's restaurants and other facilities. At the guest's departure, a final bill is prepared and printed at the front desk (Figure 2.21). This bill reflects whether the guest is paying in cash or by credit card. Or the bill may be charged to a group account, which is paid later. All these details, entered into the property management system by the front desk attendant, are noted on the final printed statement.

Property management involves more than just running the hotel's front desk. The property management system supports other areas of the hotel, using the database of information maintained in the system. For example, the hotel telephone operator interacts with the database to answer callers' inquiries about the room number of a guest. Entering the name of the guest on a personal computer, the operator retrieves the room number from the system's database. (If the caller is not certain how the name is spelled, the operator enters a name by spelling it as it sounds, and the system displays all guests' names that sound similar, regardless of how they are spelled.) The operator also uses the property management system to key in messages callers leave for guests. The system keeps track of messages in the databases, noting when they are picked up by the guest.

The property management system also helps the hotel's housekeeping department, which is responsible for cleaning and servicing guest rooms (Figure 2.22). At the beginning of each day, a printer linked by a communication line to the property management system computer prepares a list of rooms to be serviced by each maid. Throughout the day, maids update the room database by entering the number and status information for each room as they clean it. They do this through the keyboard of a Touch-Tone telephone. The status information informs the front desk staff when rooms have been serviced and are ready for new guests.

## Back Office System

A hotel's property management system is visible to guests because they come into contact with it during check-in, throughout their stay, and at checkout time. Behind the scenes is another system, the back office system, which manages the hotel's overall operations.

At the end of each day, information from the property management system is transferred electronically to the back office system. Using desktop workstations linked to the

**FIGURE 2.20**

***Using the Property Management System at One of Starwood's Westin Hotels***

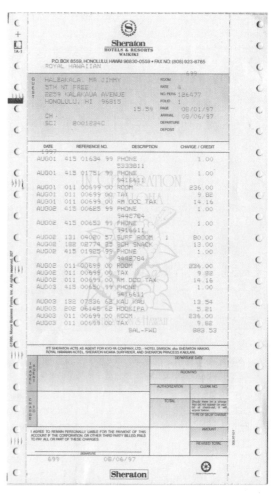

**FIGURE 2.21**

***Starwood's Property Management System Updates Billing***

back office system, the accounting staff reviews the previous day's work. Auditors check transactions for accuracy, and other staff members prepare the final bills to be mailed to groups that charged expenses.

Not all hotel transactions originate at the front desk. Some originate in banquets and special events (receptions, weddings, and business meetings). Back office staff members use desktop computers to enter these transactions into the database.

Still other transactions result from the purchase of supplies and services needed to keep the hotel running. Bills and invoices for these transactions are also submitted to the accounting staff, which enter details about them into the computer and prepare them for payment. Later, printed checks to suppliers are prepared on the back office system.

Juliette Reeves, the administrative coordinator for the executive offices of one of Starwood's hotels, is an effective information manager who works well with people. She believes in communicating face-to-face with managers, hotel staff members, and her own staff, but she also finds computers an invaluable tool for doing her job and for helping others to do theirs.

Reeves uses her PC to do five tasks: word processing, maintaining spreadsheets, maintaining departmental databases, doing departmental budgeting, and communicating electronically.

**Word Processing**  Reeves prepares many memos, letters, proposals, and reports, some of which are sent to people within the hotel, and others of which are sent to the business community, to potential guests, or to former guests. She prepares most of her written documents using word-processing software. Some of these documents are printed and mailed, while others are sent electronically over a network that connects management and staff of the hotel.

**FIGURE 2.22**

*The Property Management System Helps the Housekeeping Department Maintain the Hotel Facilities*

Reeves' office is currently extending its word-processing capabilities to include desktop publishing, which will enable the staff to prepare and print brochures and literature describing their specific hotel and the services it offers. These brochures will include photographs and graphic illustrations printed in color from a printer attached to her system.

**Spreadsheets**   Reeves routinely prepares and reviews guest occupancy projections, budgets, and proposals to enhance or repair specific facilities in the hotel. To keep this information accurate, she continually reviews and updates a spreadsheet containing the relevant categories of information.

Particularly important to Reeves and hotel managers are the *what if* analyses they perform using the spreadsheets. What if hotel occupancy increases by 10 percent next year? What if International Services Corp. requests a special price for the month-long use of a set of meeting rooms? By entering possible changes into the spreadsheets, Reeves is able to determine the likely effects of these changes.

**Departmental Databases**   Although the hotel's property management database contains a great deal of information on guest activities, facilities, operations activities, and maintenance, Reeves' department needs other information, which she maintains in separate databases on her PC. For instance, a special database contains personal information on managers and staff members (addresses and telephone numbers, e-mail addresses, employment histories). This database can also be used to retrieve the travel schedule of managers who are visiting corporate headquarters, attending planning meetings, or traveling on behalf of the hotel. It can also be used to prepare a directory of all the hotel's employees.

This special database resides only on Reeves' PC. It is maintained using a personal computer database management software package.

**Departmental Budgeting**   Although the property management system maintains a great deal of information on sales and guest activities, Reeves uses a software package running on her PC to maintain the hotel corporation's financial budget. This application includes information on actual and planned revenues, receipt of money, and expenses.

Periodically, Reeves prepares detailed listings itemizing the department's expenditures. Whenever she needs to determine the balance of a specific account, she can display or print a summary listing. She can even retrieve the details of a particular transaction for review.

**Electronic Communication**   A communications network links all of the PCs in the executive offices together. Thus, Reeves, like every other manager and staff member in the executive offices, as well as individual hotel departmental managers (such as the front desk, housekeeping, banquet, and sales managers), can send and retrieve messages or information about hotel activities and plans.

Because the back office system is connected to the property management system, Reeves can access any information contained in the property management system. She can display or print information, transferring it from the property management system to her PC. Transferring information makes it unnecessary to re-key data or information into the computer.

**The Executive Offices Staff**   Tanaka, Judy, Miguel, Tatiana, Roshawn, Carol, and Ruth are on the administrative staff at the local hotel's executive offices. All of them have a PC on their desk. Most use computers equipped with Windows, and a variety of PC-application packages for word processing, desktop publishing, spreadsheets, and graphics. However, Tatiana and Ruth use Apple iMac computers. Everyone's computer is outfitted with the same software, using versions either created for their respective computer.

All members of the administrative staff have customized their PCs to meet their needs. All PCs have a color monitor, keyboard, mouse, diskette drive, and internal hard disk. Many also have a CD-ROM drive. The PCs used by Roshawn and Carol have been set up to go right into the word-processing program when they are turned on. The others are set up so that the staff member must specify which application to use after turning the computer on.

In addition to a PC, Carol, along with several of the managers, has a notebook computer. The notebook, which is equipped with many of the same types of application software the PC has, can connect with a telephone line to send and receive information, including faxes. Its small size and portability mean it can easily be carried about so that Carol can enter information or connect with the hotel computers whenever the need arises.

All the personal computers used by the Executive Offices staff can be operated as stand-alone systems. Each is also connected to the hotel's computer network (Figure 2.20).

## Information Technology in Starwood's Reservation System

Starwood operates a large complex of mainframe and midrange computers. These multi-user computers at the corporation's computer center serve several purposes. One midrange computer, for example, is dedicated to the management of regional activities. Other, general-purpose midrange computers are shared by many people on the headquarters staff.

In addition to being the nexus of the worldwide reservation system, the computers in the computer center contain software that is shared by managers, planners, and other staff members. Shared mainframe software is usually expensive and requires capabilities that are beyond PCs or midrange computers. The administration also maintains centralized databases on Starwood's franchisees, facilities (buildings and equipment), employees, operating agreements, and finances. This information is accessible to some headquarters department administrators and staff members, who need it to operate their departments.

The Starwood corporate applications and databases reside on large systems, rather than PCs, because of the large volume of records that must be maintained. Large-scale applications require high-speed computing capabilities and large memory storage capacities. Mainframe computers can provide this capability while also providing access to large groups of people who wish to use the applications and databases.

## Information Processing

Chapter 1 introduced you to the five information-handling functions of IT: (1) capture, (2) processing, (3) generation, (4) storage and retrieval, and (5) transmission. At Starwood Hotels, 13 information-processing activities are associated with these information-handling functions.

### Capture

**Input**   Inputting is entering data into the system for processing. For example, a reservation agent can enter guest information through a PC, and a housekeeper can enter room and cleaning details through use of a Touch-Tone telephone. In both instances, the employees create transactions that are treated as *input* to the reservation and property management systems, respectively.

**Upload/Download**   Many hotel personnel receive information from another location that is part of the hotel or reservation network. For example, the administrative coordinator in the executive offices can download guest history information from the property management system. Likewise, reservation systems operators at headquarters upload information on conventions and room allocations at a local hotel. Sending information from a PC to a central mainframe is called **uploading.** Transferring information from a central system to a desktop computer is called **downloading.**

**uploading**
The process by which information is sent from a PC to a mainframe.

**downloading**
The transfer of information from a central system to a desktop computer.

### Processing

**Compute**   Computing is calculating results through addition, subtraction, and other arithmetic functions. For example, the front desk system computes the total bill to be paid by each guest on checkout. This tabulation adds up all charges incurred during the stay, deducting any adjustments, credits, or advance payments.

**Update**   Adding, deleting, or changing details (such as guest name, balance due, or method of payment) in records in the database is known as updating. Records can be updated in one of two ways. In **batch processing,** all transactions are grouped and processed at one time. For instance, all the day's guest records are processed at one time to produce a report of revenue for the day. In **real-time processing,** each transaction is processed as it occurs. For example, if a guest calls the reservation center and adds several days to a planned stay at a hotel, the change is added directly into the database through a terminal in real time.

**batch processing**
The grouping and processing of all transactions at one time.

**real-time processing**
The processing of each transaction as it occurs.

**Classify**   To classify is to categorize or group information according to a particular characteristic. For instance, the sales office groups customers by their company to determine the names of Starwood's biggest customers worldwide.

**Sort**   When information is arranged into a useful sequence (perhaps alphabetical or numerical order), it is said to be sorted. For example, the executive office of a local hotel prints an alphabetical listing of all employees, their departments and titles, and their telephone numbers.

**Summarize**   In this processing activity, a large volume of data is reduced into a concise, easy-to-use format that contains sufficient detail to meet the user's need. Average annual occupancy rates, for instance, are summarized by the number of rooms occupied, day by day, over the course of one year.

### Generate

**Output**   This activity consists of preparing a report to be printed or displayed for an intended recipient. For example, each day the front desk manager prepares a printed report that lists all charges and taxes associated with each guest.

**Issue**   This activity involves producing and printing a document. For example, the accounting department issues checks to pay suppliers, and the reservation system issues reservation confirmations that are mailed to guests who have booked a room in advance.

### Storage and Retrieval

**Inquire**   This activity involves satisfying a request for information through computation or retrieval of stored information. For example, the front desk manager may ask the system to produce a list of all guests scheduled to arrive on a specific day.

**Store**   Storing is retaining information for future use by recording the details on disk or diskette (for long-term storage) or in memory (for short-term storage). Guest history databases are generally recorded on magnetic disk for long-term retention.

**Retrieve**   Retrieving is locating and obtaining information specified in an inquiry. For example, a reservation agent may retrieve the record of a specific guest to verify or change occupation dates.

## Transmit

**Transmit**  Distributing information over a communications network is known as transmitting. For example, Starwood headquarters regularly transmits reservation details to local hotels over its communications network. At local hotels, e-mail networks are often used to send messages to staff members, either individually or collectively.

## A Final Word

While hardware and software are essential components of computing, the real reason for using them is to produce the information that people need. The information processing and information handling functions of IT are the means by which these components deliver useful results to their users.

# CRITICAL CONNECTIONS

## 1 Part II: McKesson's *Wearable* Computers Streamline the Retailer-Distributor Link

**MCKESSON**
*Empowering Healthcare*

McKesson Corp. estimates that its wearable computers have increased the productivity of its warehouse workers, reduced inventory levels, and cut order errors by 70 percent—all important considerations in an industry that operates on narrow profit margins. Moreover, McKesson's investment in IT enables it to offer retail customers such value-added services as improved inventory control, better recordkeeping, and even more accurate profit-and-loss statements.

### Questions for Discussion

1. Imagine that you are the CIO at McKesson in the 1970s. How would you try to convince the CEO to approve a multimillion-dollar investment in a networked computer system?
2. Using what you have learned about personal versus multiuser systems, how would you classify McKesson's wearable computers?
3. Major retailers such as Wal-Mart and JC Penney are among the more than 100,000 organizations worldwide that have adopted electronic data interchange (EDI), a standard way of representing and transferring order-related data electronically. These retailers benefit because the system eliminates the paperwork involved in communicating with any manufacturer using EDI. The manufacturers benefit because the giant retailers provide them with updated sales and inventory information that is useful in planning production. What does EDI mean for distributors like McKesson? For competition in the retail industry?

## 2 Part II: Nevada Bob's—A Golfer's Paradise

**NEVADA BOB'S GOLF**
*Your game. Your store.*

Seeking to enhance customer support in the more than 50 golf stores of Nevada Bob's, management adopted a retail management system that is identical in each store. The system consists of point-of-sale terminals in each store, all running the same software package, purchased from a leading IT vendor. The store systems are linked to corporate headquarters making it easy to exchange information. At the touch of a button, stores can receive new information or software updates. Because company managers can easily retrieve sales information from a store, they are able to quickly know when sales patterns are shifting or when a store is having a bad week.

Since the systems are identical, company IT personnel can quickly answer inquiries from new sales staff who use the system. They can also troubleshoot any problems much more quickly than before because they know the features of the system.

Nevada Bob's has benefited from improved inventory control and analysis at every store. In addition, customer information is maintained in a shared database, making it possible to send notices of discounts or new product announcements by mail to these customers. The game of golf is centuries old. But Nevada Bob's is using the latest information technology to provide excellent service to today's golfers.

### Questions for Discussion

1. When companies grow over time, why is it so common to find that the mix of information technology hardware and software varies between locations?
2. What is the drawback of having a mix of computer hardware and software that differs between locations?
3. What benefits do retail companies like Nevada Bob's gain if each store location uses identical information technology?
4. Are there any drawbacks to having an entire chain of stores using identical computer hardware and software?

# Summary of Learning Objectives

**1 Identify the five components of a computer system.** The five components of a computer system are (1) hardware, the machines (devices) that carry out the activities of computing, storing, and communicating data; (2) programs, the specific sequences of instructions that tell computers how to perform specific actions; (3) information, organized, meaningful, and useful sets of data; (4) people, the end users of IT or IT professionals; and (5) procedures, the step-by-step processes or sets of instructions for accomplishing specific results.

**2 Explain the four categories of hardware and their functions.** The four categories of hardware are (1) input devices, used to enter information or data into a computer; (2) processors, sets of electronic circuits used to perform the computer's processing actions, including arithmetic calculations; (3) output devices, used to present information to the user or to input information into another device; and (4) secondary storage devices, used to augment the computer's primary memory.

**3 Discuss the relationship between hardware and software.** By itself, a computer is merely a collection of computer apparatus. To be useful, hardware needs software or programs. Software is the general term for a set of instructions that controls a computer or communications network. A program is a specific sequence of instructions that tells a computer how to perform a particular action or solve a problem.

**4 Differentiate between an operating system and an application program.** An operating system is a combination of programs that coordinates the actions of a computer, including its peripheral devices and memory. It enables people to control the movement, storage, and retrieval of data and information. An application program consists of several programs working together.

**5 Identify eight types of software packages.** Eight types of software packages are (1) spreadsheet programs, (2) word-processing programs, (3) desktop publishing programs, (4) graphics programs, (5) illustration programs, (6) database management programs, (7) communications programs, and (8) information systems programs.

**6 Explain the four components of information.** The four components of information are (1) data, the raw facts of a situation; (2) text, or written (narrative) information; (3) sound, or spoken information; and (4) images, or visual information.

**7 Distinguish between the users of information technology and IT professionals.** Users are people who use information technology in their jobs or personal lives. There are four types of users: hands-on users, indirect end users, user managers, and senior managers.

IT professionals are responsible for acquiring, developing, maintaining, or operating the hardware and software associated with computers and communications networks. Some high-profile IT professionals are programmers, systems analysts, systems designers, project managers, network specialists, trainers, and computer operators.

**8 Describe the four types of procedures used in computer systems.** The four types of procedures used in computer systems are (1) operations procedures, which describe how a computer system or application is used, who is authorized to use it, how often it can be used, and where the results of processing should go; (2) backup and recovery procedures, which describe when and how to make extra copies of information and the steps to take when information or software must be recovered; (3) security procedures, which are designed to safeguard data centers, communications networks, computers, and other IT components from accidental intrusion or intentional damage; and (4) development procedures, which explain how IT professionals should describe user needs and develop applications to meet those needs.

**9 Explain the difference between single- and multiuser systems.** A single-user system is one that stands alone and is not connected with other computers or shared by other people. Multiuser system is the general term used to describe a system in which more than one user shares hardware, programs, information, people, and procedures.

**10 List the 13 information-processing activities associated with the five information-handling functions of IT.** The information-processing activities performed by IT are (1) input, (2) upload/download, (3) compute, (4) update, (5) classify, (6) sort, (7) summarize, (8) output, (9) issue, (10) inquire, (11) store, (12) retrieve, and (13) transmit.

# Key Terms

antivirus software   68
backup copies   67
backup procedure   67
bar code   46
batch processing   76
browser   60
business graphics   56
CD-ROM disk   50
chief information officer (CIO)   67
communications program   52
computer engineer   65
computer programming language   60
custom software   60
data   62
data center/computer center   65
database   57
database management program   57
desktop publishing (DTP) program   55
development procedure   68
disk operating system (DOS)   52
documentation   53
downloading   76
drive   50
graphical user interface (GUI)   52

hardware/computer
   hardware/devices   44
illustration program   56
information   62
information system or management
   information system (MIS)   60
information technology professional   64
input   44
interface   53
magnetic disk   50
microprocessor   47
multimedia   46
multiuser system   69
object   61
object-oriented programming   61
operating system   52
operations procedure   67
output   49
peripheral equipment   50
primary storage/main memory   48
procedure   65
processor/central processing
   unit (CPU)   47

program   52
programmer/analyst   65
read only   50
real-time processing   76
recovery procedure   67
secondary storage   50
security procedure   68
security software   68
single-user system   69
software   52
software package   53
spoken information   62
spreadsheet   54
system board/mother board   47
systems engineer   65
transaction processing   60
uploading   76
user (end user)   64
utility program (utilities)   60
wand   46
Windows   52
word processing (WP) program   54
zip disk   50

# Review Questions

1. To what does the term *hardware* refer in a computer system? List and describe the four categories of hardware.

2. What are the most common types of input devices? Why are there different types?

3. Do all computers, regardless of size, have a processing unit? Why or why not?

4. What is the purpose of the central processing unit? By what other names is this hardware component known?

5. What is the purpose of memory? Why is the memory in the central processor sometimes called primary storage?

6. Discuss the different actions can be triggered by computer output.

7. What is secondary storage? What is its relation to primary storage?

8. How do you distinguish between the characteristics of five types of secondary storage?

9. Why are some devices called peripheral equipment? What does *peripheral* mean?

10. What are the two types of software? What is the purpose of each?

11. List and briefly describe the 10 most popular types of software packages.

12. What is a computer programming language?

13. How do custom software and packaged software differ?

14. What are the two most important trends in the acquisition and development of computer software today?

15. How does the object-oriented approach to software change development practices?

16. What benefits are gained by the use of prewritten software components?

17. What are *killer apps* and why are they classified accordingly?

18. How do transaction processing and information system applications differ in purpose?

19. What is information? What are the four components of information?

20. What is meant by the term *user*? List and explain the four types of users.

21. Why have many companies created the job of chief information officer? How do CIOs differ from other IT professionals?

22. Identify the eight categories of information technology professionals. What function does each perform?

23. What are the four categories of procedures for managing and using information technology? Why is each needed?

24. How do single-user and multiuser systems differ? Is one type better than the other? Explain.

25. Describe each of the following information-processing activities: input, upload/download, compute, update, classify, sort, summarize, output, issue, inquire, store, retrieve, and transmit.

## Discussion Questions

1. The government motor vehicle departments in most states and regions rely heavily on computer-based systems for processing drivers' license applications and renewals and for the issuing of automobile, truck, bus, and motorcycle license plates. For what other reasons do they use computers?

2. Until the 1980s, administrative staff members in university and college academic departments relied heavily on typewriters for preparing the faculty's course materials, examinations, and academic manuscripts. Today, PCs typically are connected to communications networks and have replaced typewriters. Now faculty members use computers to *word process* (i.e., type, edit, and print) their own course materials and other documents. Word processing software is termed *productivity software*. Considering these changes, do you think that faculty members are generally more productive today compared to the era in which the department staff prepared the work on manual typewriters?

3. Make a list of the IT-based systems and applications you encounter in a typical day and discuss how IT affects your activities. Do you agree that people are the most important component of these computer systems? Explain.

4. Look over the list you made for Question 1 and list the different types of input devices you encountered. Why do you think there are so many different types of input devices besides the keyboard?

5. Why do you think that accounting departments were the first to install mainframe computers back in the early days of computing?

6. At Employers Health Insurance in Green Bay, Wisconsin, IT professionals spend 6- to 12-month "sabbaticals" in user departments interacting with users. The company's next move will be to assign IT managers to each of its business units, where they will present courses on how computer applications are developed. What benefit do these programs offer to Employers Health Insurance?

7. St. Agnes Medical Center of Fresno, California, has created a network that supports both critical patient-care applications and office productivity applications. Users can log onto the network from any PC in the medical center. Why do you think so many organizations like St. Agnes are developing computer networks of microcomputers?

## Group Projects and Applications

### Project 1

With a team of your colleagues, visit a set of three to five different supermarkets or discount department stores. Observe the checkout process in which customers have the total value of their purchases calculated so that payment can be made.

Then discuss the following questions:

- Note the following and compare the similarities and differences between stores: What information technology components are in use at the checkout counters?
- Are there specific IT capabilities that benefit or hinder the productivity of the individual handling the checkout process?
- What could go wrong to prevent or hinder an effective checkout process?
- What is your overall assessment of the way the checkout process works: very good, good, satisfactory, or unsatisfactory? What factors account for your assessment?

- If the number of transactions handled per hour increased by four times (i.e., 400 more customers to checkout ), could the store's system handle the increase? What does this tell you about the importance of *scalability* (i.e., the ability of a system to process greater numbers of transactions) when designing computer-based systems?

### Project 2

Visit the department offices in your college or university. Interview the administrative assistants about the process they use each term to assemble book requirements for the planned schedule of courses. Note whether the staff members in the different departments follow the same or different processes.

Be sure to address the following questions:

- What reports are used to assist the staff in asking faculty what books they wish to have students buy? Are the reports generated by computer or prepared manually?

- What software programs, if any, do the staff members use to accumulate the book requirements?
- Does the staff use spreadsheet or word processing programs as productivity aids in assembling the book request?
- How is the list of book requirements (i.e., the departmental book order) communicated to the college or university bookstore where the books are ultimately ordered by students who register for the courses?
- Does the Internet play a role in any part of the staff's book requirements process?
- What is your overall assessment of the role of IT use across departments for assembling and communicating book requirements to the bookstore?

## Project 3

With a partner or small group, visit a local business that uses information technology. Each member of your group should interview a person who uses information technology or manages one of the company's information technology applications.

### Questions to Ask IT Users:

- Which software programs or IT applications do you use on a daily basis?
- What are your job responsibilities? Do the IT applications you use help you become more efficient at your job?
- How did you learn to use IT in your job?

### Questions to Ask IT Professionals:

- What are your responsibilities in managing the company's IT application(s)?
- What procedures do you follow on a daily basis?
- What types of support do you offer to the company's IT users?

Each group should summarize its interviews and present the results to the class.

## Project 4

### Group Research Project

People in charge of IT systems must implement a series of security procedures to safeguard the system. Following is a list of words commonly used by network security specialists:

- Firewall
- Password
- Trojan Horse
- Digital signature encryption
- Hacker
- Trapdoor
- Antivirus program

With a partner or group, research each of these terms. What does each term mean? How is it related to network security?

Net_Work

## Your Digital Library

Visit your college or university library online by connecting over the Internet. (If your library does not maintain a digital library, locate another college or university library on the Internet that does.) Then check the online information section to identify and review the categories of library resources that are available in digital form over the Internet.

To help organize your research on digital libraries, begin by focusing on the following questions:

a. What types of information sources are accessible, in digital form, from your library?

b. What, if any, restrictions are there on use of the digital library resources (e.g., locations from which the library can be used, ability to print documents, and ability to store documents)?

c. Does the library limit access to its resources? If so, who is allowed to use the resources and how is use by others prohibited?

d. What benefits does having access to a digital library provide to students and faculty?

Also note any features or capabilities that you feel are particularly useful to library users. If any features you expected to be included are in fact not present, note them as well.

## Internet Access Providers

Providing access to the Internet has become a business. While use of the Internet itself is free—the costs being paid by organizations that maintain the Net's computers and communications links—getting access to it usually requires the payment of a fee to an access provider.

Many companies have been established to provide this service. To gain a better understanding of their costs and services and how they compete with one another, conduct a survey of Internet providers in your area by completing the following table (extending its size to accommodate the number of companies you survey). Be sure to consider telephone companies and cable companies servicing your area.

Based on your survey, which companies do you feel best meet your Internet needs? Why?

| CHARACTERISTIC | COMPANY #1 | COMPANY #2 | COMPANY #3 | COMPANY #4 | COMPANY #5 |
|---|---|---|---|---|---|
| Name of company | | | | | |
| Minimum monthly charge for service | | | | | |
| Hours of time included in monthly service charge | | | | | |
| Hours service is available (Monday – Friday; weekends) | | | | | |
| Additional charges (if any) for high-speed transmission service | | | | | |
| Additional charges (if any) for usage during peak times of the day | | | | | |
| Number of subscribers company has | | | | | |
| Is service accessible through a local (toll-free) call? | | | | | |
| Other services company provides | | | | | |
| Other factors that distinguish the company | | | | | |

## Cool Mobility

### On Assignment

Throughout your residency, the management and staff of *Cool Mobility* will engage you in various aspects of the company's business practice. They would like your insights on how information technology can support the company's day-to-day activities.

Today you meet with Tina Fuentes, CEO of *Cool Mobility,* to discuss the import role you will play for the company. Ms. Fuentes stresses the need for you to act as an independent observer. She indicates that you will be asked to apply your knowledge to evaluate the features and functions of the company Web site, www.CoolMobility.biz.

### In Consultation

During your meeting, Fuentes consults you about the company's Internet and intranet Web sites and gives the following assignments:

a. Examine the CoolMobility.biz Internet and intranet Web sites. Identify the information handling functions performed within each part of the site. Use a six-function framework to categorize 13 information-processing activities. Present your results in a table that includes one column for the public Internet site and another for the company's intranet activities.

b. Ms. Fuentes also asks, "Are we using all the components of information in what we present over our system?" As you evaluate CoolMobility.biz, recall the four components of information and how IT helps an enterprise make the most effective use of information in any or all of these forms. Using the four components as a guide, write a brief summary of the different types of information presented, highlighting any types not included in the system.

## Case Study

### CNN Digital Assets

Launched in 1980 as an innovation in news reporting, the Cable News Network (CNN), headquartered in Atlanta, Georgia, is a world leader in broadcast news and information delivery. Its familiar brand names include CNN, CNN Headline News, CNN International, CNN Airport Channel, CNN.com—in all, more than 20 distinct product lines. One factor is common to all: They focus on disseminating news and information to a global and national audience. CNN is available worldwide to more than 1 billion people in more than 200 countries. In the United States, it reaches more than 85 million homes. Over the Internet, a growing audience can view CNN.com on their desktop and on mobile devices, including personal digital assistants, palm computers, as well as wireless phones and laptop computers. Its 16 cable and satellite networks and 23 Web sites are critical resources for reaching its massive audience as well as for capturing news as it occurs.

CNN relies heavily on its 4,000-person global newsgathering team. As reporters and photographers capture the news, usually on videotape, it is transmitted electronically by satellite to CNN's world headquarters. There it is added to the networks' huge archive. The more than 150,000 hours of archive material is growing at a rate of approximately 20 percent annually.

Locating and retrieving footage in the archive, as well as preserving the quality of the archive itself, have long been of paramount importance to the company. Imagine having to locate a specific section of video footage from an archive in a matter of minutes so that it can be included in the live report of a breaking news story from the other side of the globe. It is impossible to manually search through the archive; you could not feasibly load all of the videotapes and scan them for a news clip. Remembering where a particular segment of news is stored is beyond anyone's capability.

The archive is a valuable asset. Finding ways to preserve the library is also a concern, because video footage tends to disintegrate due to age and repeated use.

Today CNN relies on information technology to achieve three important goals: (1) have the ability to distribute the archive's content in new ways, (2) preserve the network's archive, and (3) improve the efficiency of its news operation. Its digital asset system, created with the help of IBM and Sony Electronics, is the first of its type in the world. The digital asset system features an online library that makes it possible to locate video, share it across all business lines, and track its usage. Here is how it works.

Incoming video is captured, indexed, cataloged, and stored in digital form in its TV news library. CNN likens the digital news library to a virtual filing cabinet. The video is captured and stored in both high- and low-resolution format. The content is stored on an array of large-capacity magnetic disks attached to a computer server. All high-resolution video is stored on a Sony robotic tape library, compressed to reduce space requirements as well as to take less transmission time when a clip is retrieved.

Instead of the time-consuming and complex process of manually locating video, so characteristic of the past, CNN production assistants can now search the catalog from desktop computers connected to CNN's internal communications network. Using keywords (e.g., date or location of an event, or individuals' names) they can identify and retrieve video clips for review on their computer displays.

Eventually, CNN hopes to be able to search using facial characteristics, making it possible to find video even when the name of a person appearing in a segment of the news is not known at the time of cataloging.

Video clips are first retrieved in low-resolution format. The low-resolution format makes it possible to move the video over the network faster for review. Once the selection is made, the high-resolution version is retrieved for editing and use. CNN uses satellites and its own closed, internal network to distribute the content at a very high transmission speed to the location where it will be used.

CNN rewrote the rules for reporting the news when it began operations in 1980. Now it's rewriting the rules again through its digital content management system.

### Questions for Discussion

1. Besides avoiding wear and tear on the videotape itself, what benefits does CNN gain by having the archive stored in digital form?
2. Do you agree with the CNN strategy of storing the video clips twice (i.e., in both low- and high-resolution formats?
3. How can CNN determine whether the benefits of the digital asset library exceed its costs?
4. What are the challenges in searching the video library for facial images?

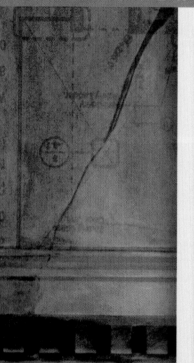

# 3

# Essentials of the Internet and World Wide Web

CNET Brings High-Tech Information to You

Origin of the Internet

Capabilities of the Internet

The Internet Community

Internet Addresses

Browsing the World Wide Web

A Final Word

Case Study: Do You Yahoo!?

## LEARNING OBJECTIVES

When you have completed this chapter, you should be able to

1  Explain how individual computers and server computers interact on the Internet.

2  Describe the three types of capabilities of the Internet.

3  Identify the 13 principal communication and retrieval capabilities of the Internet.

4  Summarize how the Internet knows the location of a particular user.

5  Describe how pages are used on the Web.

6  Explain the purpose of hyperlinks and their role on the Web.

7  Describe the characteristics of browser software and relate them to the types of information that can be included in a home page.

# CNET Brings High-Tech Information to You

To catch the latest buzz in the technology industry, many in the high-tech field turn to CNET Networks, found on the Internet. As a global source of information and commerce services, CNET Networks is a top Internet company with established Web sites in 20 countries, displaying content in 18 languages.

In fewer than 10 years, CNET Networks, headquartered in San Francisco, rose to prominence. Along with *The Wall Street Journal* and *BusinessWeek*, CNET is one of the most heralded sources of technology news and information. Each month, more than 60 million visitors gain access to CNET's editorial content via the Internet and to its digital print and broadcast information channels. In fact, CNET tops *Technology Marketing* magazine's "Media Influencer" list as the most influential information source on the Web.

If you visit CNET (www.cnet.com) you will likely find such items as breaking news on DVD pirates in Hollywood, a piercing review of Microsoft's latest software innovation, or frank commentary about leadership scuffles and resulting executive moves at a leading high-tech firm. Discussion groups allow you to join the battle of words (and opinions) about the competition among the major computer firms for leadership in a variety of computing components. You can read comments of high-tech insiders and experts, and if you care to, add your own view or raise a probing question.

For example, one report in CNET's series "Inside the Labs: A View of Leading Technology" took a candid and in-depth look at the future of the PC. Here is an interesting excerpt:

> With the deluge of personal digital assistants (PDAs), cell phones, and MP3 players, it's no longer just our PCs that need to be connected. As consumers, we are becoming increasingly dependent on an army of digital devices. We're also quickly becoming frustrated with how these devices are islands, typically incapable of communicating with each other and often sharing data with a PC in a very limited and proprietary fashion. Microsoft's vision is to have all our digital devices—PCs, TVs, phones, stereos, cameras, printers, digital photo frames, and so on—capable of communicating with each other, be they wired or wireless. I'm not sure if my digital photo frame needs to talk to my stereo, but it sure would be nice if my phone, PDA, and PC could all seamlessly communicate with each other.

In the "Vision Series," CNET examines how the leaders of the industry plan to guide their companies over the rough terrain of the ever-changing technology landscape. Television programs examine industry-related issues such as attempts of one company to acquire another, and the uneasy relationship of a top executive with government regulatory officials. Exclusive interviews highlight how industry leaders see the future; CNET editors add their commentary and rate the leader's chances for success.

CNET's family of brand names includes CNET.com, ZDNet.com, and TechRepublic.com. The online network also includes the award-winning news site, News.com and the leading online software download service, Download.com. In addition, Gamespot, the Internet's most highly trafficked gaming site, gives users instant access to game reviews, previews, downloads, hints, and more. The Computer Shopper and CNet Radio provide print and broadcast information respectively.

CNET generates revenue from advertisers, who position their product messages on CNET Web sites where they are viewed by millions of people. Who visits CNET Web sites? A recent study found that CNET sites reach 66 percent of all information technology professionals, and 74 percent of all CEOs, CFOs, and CIOs who use the Internet to make technology purchase decisions.

Clearly, the Internet is an essential tool and resource for businesses and individuals. It enables people to quickly and effectively gather, process, and deliver information. CNET Networks continues to build on its reputation as a media powerhouse as it helps consumers stay abreast of the latest trends in business and technology.

**Internet/the Net**
A communication network that is itself a connection of many other networks.

Several years ago, the Internet interested few people. Today, it's hard to read a newspaper, watch a television program, or get into a business discussion without hearing about the Internet or its popular graphical component, the World Wide Web. Whether you are an experienced, Internet-savvy individual or merely a novice, this chapter should uncover a few secrets or at least open a few doors on the World Wide Web. Don't miss out on one of the most revolutionary tools of our time! The **Internet**–commonly called the **Net**–is a communication network that itself is a connection of many other networks. Hence the name: *inter*connection of *net*works.

The Internet is used by hundreds of millions of people, and more people gain access to it every day. It is radically changing people's daily lives. In fact, enthusiasts believe the Internet is the most profound invention since the printing press or at least since the computer itself. It has given birth to many IT applications. For example, electronic mail or e-mail–written messages sent electronically over communication links–was born on the Internet. The Internet is quickly becoming the world's information superhighway, connecting people and businesses all over the world, and enabling them to share ideas and information.

## Origin of the Internet

The value of a network lies as much in *whom* it connects as in *how* it connects. The Internet, a network of networks, originated in the 1960s. The U.S. Department of Defense established the network to provide researchers and government officials with access to IT resources including radio telescopes, weather analysis programs, supercomputers, and specialized databases. From this origin–as a vehicle for the exclusive use of government and educational institutions–the Internet has expanded prodigiously. Today, the majority of U.S. Internet addresses belong to people who acquired them through a private employer or a commercial access provider.

Tens of thousands of new users join the Internet each day. Host computers are added daily, and the number of networks connected on the Internet has doubled every year. The rate of growth will continue to accelerate well into the future as people connect on campus, at the office, and at home.

The U.S. government, through the National Science Foundation, paid a decreasing share of the operating cost of the Internet through 1995, when all government funding was phased out. The bulk of the cost to operate the Internet is paid by the users. For example, universities and other institutions pay for operating their host computers and interconnecting them to the network. There is, however, no charge for sending a message from one computer to another.

The *Information Technology in Practice* feature, "Vinton Cerf, Father of the Internet," introduces a man who has done more than anyone else to democratize the Net.

## Computers on the Internet

The software you use to access the Internet runs on your individual workstation, or **client computer.** The client computer communicates with a **server computer** to access data and information. **Client-server computing** (Figure 3.1) is a characteristic of the Internet: Through the Internet, client computers interact with server computers, transmitting and receiving data and information. Data and information transmitted by the server computer are processed by the software running on the client computer (Figure 3.2).

**client computer**
The computer that accesses the information stored on a server computer.

**server computer**
The computer that contains data and information that can be accessed by a client computer.

**client-server computing**
A type of computing in which all data and information retrieval requests and responses pass over a network. Much of the processing is performed on the server and the results of the processing are transmitted to the client.

**surf (surfing)**
Moving among a number of networks that are linked together, or internetworked.

# INFORMATION TECHNOLOGY IN PRACTICE

## Vinton Cerf: Father of the Internet

Vinton Cerf is known as *father of the Internet* for his pioneering work in developing information technology to support the network and for his unending efforts to help the Internet grow. Cerf started with the principle that anyone should be able to talk to anyone else. Then he developed the TCP/IP protocol on which the Internet is built. This protocol greatly facilitated the Internet's growth by making networks open and thus permitting interconnection among them. Today, the ability to **surf** on the Internet—to ride freely from network to network the way a surfer rides from wave to wave—gives Internet users an endless wave of connectivity.

Cerf, who is part of the executive management team at MCI, headquartered in Washington, D.C., remains active in the field of information technology. In 1996, when the Internet was just becoming globally accessible, he shared his thoughts on the wonder of it:

I guess the surprises come because the spread of the system has been so rapid in unexpected quarters. And so when I get e-mail from people who are in obscure places around the world saying, "Hi, I'm on the Net," I'm always surprised. When I get e-mail from somebody in China and somebody in Africa, I'm always stunned. . . . Those are the kinds of surprises that are happening now, and of course the new applications that have come along, like Internet Multimedia and World chat, are surprises just because I almost invariably underestimate the amount of human creativity there is out there, especially with millions of people trying things.

The Internet makes it far easier for the individual voice to be heard than with any other communication medium. The most interesting question is: How will we take advantage of the opportunities provided by the Net?

*Source:* "Poet-Philosopher of the Net," *Educom Review,* Vol. 31 (May–June 1996), p. 38.

**FIGURE 3.1**
*Structure of the Internet*

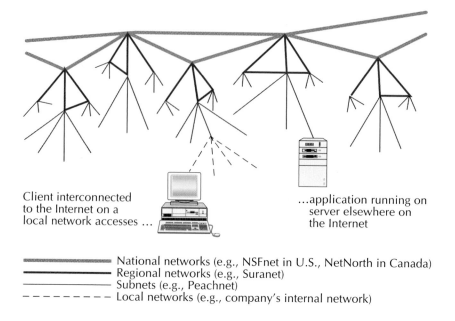

Client interconnected to the Internet on a local network accesses ...

...application running on server elsewhere on the Internet

━━━━━ National networks (e.g., NSFnet in U.S., NetNorth in Canada)
──── Regional networks (e.g., Suranet)
──── Subnets (e.g., Peachnet)
– – – – Local networks (e.g., company's internal network)

## Internet Addresses

Everyone on the Internet has an address from which to send and receive messages. Similarly, every location on the Internet has a unique address. If you know the address, you can find the person or place. If you don't, there are ways to search for it. We will explore Internet addresses in greater detail later. But first, it is important to understand the capabilities that the Internet offers.

# Capabilities of the Internet

There are three main functions of the Internet:

1. **Communicate**   You can contact and exchange information with friends and organizations anywhere in the world. The Internet's special features allow you to participate in conversations, sharing ideas, opinions, and news with other users.
2. **Retrieve**   You can access a broad range of data and information from other computers, or simply *sites,* on the network. You can also retrieve copies of information—including narratives, photographs, sound, music, and video—and bring them right into your own computer. The Internet's retrieval capability includes software. That is, computer software can be located and delivered immediately from commercial software manufacturers or from individuals who create and share software. Not long ago, overnight delivery of software was considered immediate. Now *immediately* means *instantly:* You can download copies of software, documents, and messages as soon as you ask (or pay) for them.

**FIGURE 3.2**
*Client/Server Computing*

**Client Computer**
(Individual User)

**Server Computer**
(on the Internet)

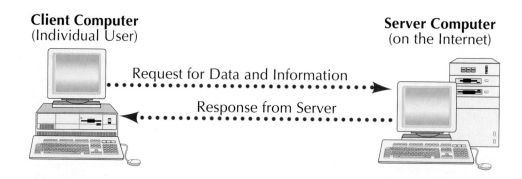

Request for Data and Information

Response from Server

3. **Shop, Buy, and Sell**   You can buy and sell goods and services on the Internet. This Internet capability has generated tremendous interest over the past few years, as well as tremendous disappointment for those who had unrealistic expectations for its use. However, there is little doubt that the Internet will substantially influence shopping and the buying and selling of goods and services for years to come.

## Communications Capabilities

The principal communications features of the Internet are e-mail, mailing lists, newsgroups, chat sessions, instant messages, Internet telephony, and Telnet (Table 3.1).

**E-Mail**   **E-mail**—short for **electronic mail**—is the most widely used function of the Internet. Anyone with e-mail access can transmit a message to anyone else with e-mail access on the Internet simply by including the intended recipient's e-mail address in the message. Anyone who sends you a message over the Internet must supply your address. The network processes your address to determine where you are located on the Internet and then routes the message to your computer. (More on electronic mail in Chapter 8).

**e-mail/electronic mail**
A service that transports text messages from a sender to one or more receivers via computer.

| Table 3.1   **Communication Capabilities on the Internet** | | |
|---|---|---|
| **INTERNET CAPABILITY** | **TOOL** | **DESCRIPTION** |
| Communication | Electronic mail (e-mail) | Sends and receives messages between locations on the Internet. |
| | Mailing lists | Each mailing list has subscribers who receive messages as part of an ongoing discussion of the list's topic. |
| | Newsgroups | Worldwide discussion areas where notices can be posted for anyone to view. |
| | Chat sessions | Interactive discussions in which parties on the network exchange ideas and observations electronically. |
| | Instant messages | A combination of real-time chat and e-mail by which short text messages are rapidly exchanged over the Internet, with messages appearing on recipient's display screen immediately upon arrival. |
| | Internet telephony | Real-time voice conversations transmitted between computers on the Internet. |
| | Telnet | A network capability that permits remote sign-on to any computer on the Internet from the computer an individual is using at that time. |
| Retrieval | FTP (File transfer protocol) | Used for transferring files containing documents or software between computers on the Internet. |
| | Web directory | A listing of Web sites and their URLs, categorized by topic. |
| | Search engines | Software programs that look through the Web to locate sites matching a keyword entered by the user. |
| | Portal | A gateway or hub on the Internet from which other sites can be visited. |
| | Webcasting | The prearranged delivery, or push, of information of interest to a user's desktop automatically. |
| | Streaming | An on-demand retrieval and playing of audio, video, or other media that can occur while the downloading is occurring. |
| Shopping, Buying, and Selling | Often called e-commerce | Conducting commercial activities on the Internet. |

Your computer need not be turned on for someone to send mail to you; the network will store any messages directed to you. Thus, the network acts as your *electronic mailbox*. When your computer is on and interacting with the network, you can ask it to display the messages currently in your mailbox. An e-mail message can be directed to an individual or to a group of recipients, large or small, so that each member of the group receives the same message at virtually the same time.

An e-mail message may be a sentence or two intended to communicate an idea or trigger an action. Or it may include a multipage document with photos, tables, or other graphics.

**Mailing Lists**    Mailing lists interconnect people who choose to participate in an ongoing discussion on a particular topic. Anyone—an individual, company, or organization—can establish a mailing list as long as it has the necessary information technology resources for doing so. A fee may be charged to those who want to receive the mailing list's messages. These messages might include comments and opinions; announcements; discussions of new products, tools, or services; reviews of books, articles, movies, music, or theater; or just about any other information of interest to a group of people.

Usually people join a mailing list by subscribing electronically. Information submitted by any group member is automatically sent to you and stored by the host computer to which you are attached. You are then electronically notified that you have received information.

**moderated**
A mailing list in which the messages are first screened by an individual to determine their suitability given the purpose of the list.

Some mailing lists are **moderated,** meaning that the messages are first screened by an individual to determine their suitability given the purpose of the list. For instance the moderator of a scientific research mailing list would probably not permit a message from a member soliciting contributions to an election campaign to be distributed to other members on the mailing list.

There are thousands of mailing lists on the Internet. You can join as many as you want—and have time to read!

# CRITICAL CONNECTIONS   1

## Hotmail Is Hot—And Free!

Hotmail

E-mail is a staple of today's Internet. Virtually all companies, large and small, rely on e-mail for communication. Likewise, individuals use e-mail to keep in touch with family, friends, and acquaintances. Some people pay for this wonderful service, while others get it for free!

Microsoft Corp.'s Hotmail service is one of the best-known e-mail sites on the Web. Some 100-million individuals scattered around the world use it. Yes, Hotmail is free. You can sign up at www.hotmail.com and begin using it within a few minutes.

Hotmail users can send or check for messages from any computer attached to the Internet, whether at home, at work, on campus, or in a public library. Hotmail also provides address books so you can keep track of the names and addresses of those with whom you wish to exchange messages. It also provides software *filters* that can screen out messages you do not wish to receive. Hotmail also provides storage space, which allows you to organize messages and attachments (such as photos and reports) into folders for archival purposes.

Free e-mail services like Hotmail have played an important role in making the Internet accessible to more people.

You may hear subscribers to mailing lists call it a *list serve*. This name comes from LISTSERV®, a widely used application that allows you to create, manage, and control electronic mailing lists on a corporate network or on the Internet. Since its inception in 1986 for IBM mainframes on the BITNET academic network, LISTSERV has become the predominant system in use today. LISTSERV is now available for many computer operating systems, including Microsoft Windows.

The LISTSERV program and documentation can be downloaded without charge from www.lsoft.com, the Web site of its developer, L-Soft. The developer also maintains a catalog of all *public* mailing lists around the world that can be found on the Internet. The catalog, known as the *Catalyst*, also can be found at the L-Soft Web site. ∎

**Newsgroups**   **Newsgroups** are discussion areas where any user can post a message (i.e., provide information, ask questions, or express opinions) to the group and read the responses from others. The collection of newsgroups available from the Internet is called **Usenet**, short for **User's Network.** There is a newsgroup for almost every topic imaginable. For example, there are Usenet discussion groups on recreation, computer technology, diabetes, and classic TV shows. (If no discussion group exists for the topic you are interested in, then start your own!)

Each newsgroup has a name that explains the purpose of the newsgroup, and each part of the name divides a larger topic into smaller topics. For example, *rec.music.collecting.cd* is in the general area of recreation. Within the broad category of recreation is a subcategory on music. Then to further narrow the topic, this newsgroup focuses on collecting music, specifically on compact discs.

Most newsgroups are unmoderated, meaning that anyone can participate and post anything they wish. Pressure from other members may keep individuals from repeatedly posting messages that are not consistent with the purpose of the newsgroup. (In a moderated newsgroup, the moderator would perform that function.)

Usenet host servers follow a format for messages and for transmission of news. You can read newsgroups using only your World Wide Web browser. However, some users feel that to get the most from newsgroups, you need a special program called a *NewsReader*, which is designed to handle news efficiently. NewsReader programs allow the user to easily navigate between newsgroups and articles by pointing and clicking on articles of interest. They also allow viewing of multiple articles simultaneously and on some systems even allow multiple connections to news servers simultaneously.

Although newsgroups on the Internet can be read from anywhere in the world, some newsgroups are only of local interest. For example, the alt.sports.baseball.atlanta.braves newsgroup will be of greatest interest to readers in the United States, both in the Atlanta area and elsewhere, who are interested in the Atlanta Braves major league baseball club. Figure 3.3 lists a representative set of newsgroups available on the Internet.

**Chat Sessions**   A live, interactive discussion—meaning all parties to the discussion are actually on the network, interacting through their computers—is known as a **chat session**, or **Internet relay chat (IRC).** For example, members of a consulting project team who cannot be at a single location at the same time might use the Internet's chat capability to exchange ideas through their PCs linked to the Internet.

Because chat sessions are conducted in real-time, each participant will see the others' comments simultaneously and be able to respond immediately. All you have to do is key your comments into the computer (Figure 3.4). The comments will appear simultaneously on the other members' computer display screens.

Chat sessions occur in a chat room, a section of a Web site devoted to real-time discussions. Chat rooms may be public or private, which means you need the proper password to gain access. Chat rooms are run by Internet service providers (e.g., AOL), by

**newsgroups**
Discussion areas where any user can post a message (i.e., provide information, ask questions, or express opinions) to the group and read the responses from others.

**Usenet/User's Network**
A system of worldwide discussion groups, not an actual physical network.

**chat session/Internet relay chat (IRC)**
A live interactive discussion where all parties are actually on the network, interacting through their computers.

**FIGURE 3.3**

*Alt Newsgroups Available on the Internet*

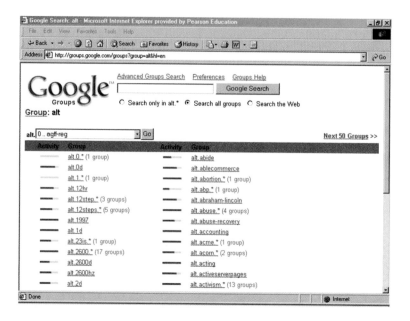

**portal**

A gateway or hub site, such as Yahoo!, that provides chat rooms.

**instant messages**

A short text message, exchanged over the internet, and appearing on recipient's display screen immediately after arrival.

**portals** (gateway or hub sites, such as Yahoo!), or by organizations or individuals interested in facilitating a discussion on a particular topic.

**Instant Messages** The use of **instant messages** on the Internet, a sort of combination of real-time chat and e-mail, has grown rapidly since it was introduced in the late 1990s. The best way to envision instant messaging is to think of a typed conversation, in which snippets of text are rapidly exchanged over the Internet. Each snippet appears on the recipient's screen as soon as it is sent. Unlike e-mail messages, which are automatically stored in servers and electronic mailboxes, instant messages disappear when a messaging session is closed.

Free instant messaging services are available from Internet service providers (ISPs), including AOL, which allows anyone to sign up for its instant messenger service. Corporations are investing in systems from leading information technology companies to provide a capability for instant conversation between employees and business partners.

The use of instant messages in companies has not been managed nearly as effectively as mainstream business applications. Hence, there is concern over the security of information transmitted in this manner. Even as companies rely more heavily on instant messages, managers are seeking ways to safeguard their contents.

**FIGURE 3.4**

*A Chat Session*

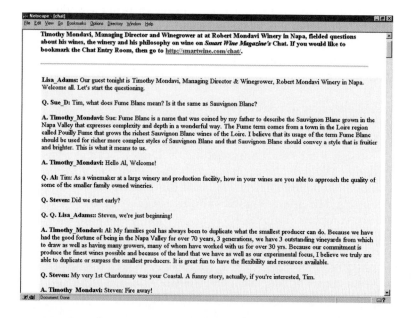

Newsgroups are governed by the subscribers; there are no *newsgroup police*. Newsgroup etiquette, or **netiquette**, is a list of simple guidelines that keep people from making mistakes. Want to sound like a newsgroup veteran when you venture into your first newsgroup? Here are some suggestions from Internet service provider America Online (AOL):

**netiquette**
A list of simple newsgroup guidelines that keep people from making mistakes.

- **Lurk**   Read the newsgroup without posting for a few weeks. This is known as *lurking*, and it will give you the flavor of the newsgroup.
- **Read the FAQ**   Find and read the newsgroup's FAQ, or list of frequently asked questions. It's the quickest way to learn the workings of a newsgroup. The FAQ can answer many of your questions, perhaps even some you haven't thought of yet.
- **Stay on the topic**   Know what is acceptable commentary and what is off-limits. Every newsgroup is a little different in what it talks about and how it does the talking.
- **Don't shout**   TYPING IN ALL CAPS IS CONSIDERED SHOUTING! It is easier to read a mix of upper- and lowercase letters.
- **Never, ever post** *MAKE MONEY FAST*   It doesn't work, it gets people really mad, and it's probably illegal.
- **Everyone hates commercials**   Be hesitant about posting advertisements or commercial messages. This also gets people mad.
- **Ignore** *trolls*   Some people get a thrill from posting *flames* (obnoxious messages) just to get a rise out of people. Sad, isn't it?
- **Don't** *spam*   Spam is posting the same message to dozens, even hundreds or thousands of unrelated newsgroups. No matter how important you think your message may be, don't spam. Think about it—if everyone posted messages on every topic, no one would be able to find the information they want. ■

**Internet Telephony**   **Internet telephony**, also known as **voice over the Internet** or **voice over IP** (IP stands for Internet protocol), features real-time voice conversations transmitted between computers on the Internet. Voice conversation is spoken into a microphone rather than into a telephone handset. From there it is broken into packets and transmitted in digital form to the recipient who in turn hears the conversation over computer speakers. Because the Internet is used, rather than a traditional telephone network, the caller avoids tolls charged by their phone company.

**Internet telephony/voice over the Internet/voice over IP**
Real-time voice conversations transmitted between computers on the Internet.

Special software is needed for Internet telephony. Although this technology shows promise and is being used on an experimental basis, it is still being perfected.

A discussion about the Internet's communication services can be confusing; some features overlap or at least sound similar. However, there are important differences for the users.

E-mail is delivered to your electronic mailbox automatically and the messages wait there until you are ready to read them. With e-mail, you have very little control over what you receive. People who have your e-mail address can send you whatever they wish.

A mail list will also deliver messages that appear automatically in your electronic mailbox, but this service is selective. You have to subscribe to a mailing list to get the messages.

Newsgroups and chat sessions are services that do *not* deliver messages to your mailbox. Instead, you must sign on to Usenet groups and chat sessions each time; then you can receive and send messages on the display screen of your computer while you are using it. Usenet newsgroups are bulletin boards; you access, review, and contribute information. Chat sessions, on the other hand, are like conversations; they are live, interactive discussion sessions. ■

Selected offices of the Automobile Association of America (AAA) have installed voice over IP. AAA, which provides emergency road service to its members, expects to improve its service with this new technology. The Internet will enable the association to route service calls more quickly and at a lower cost.

**Telnet**

A means users employ to communicate with their own systems through the Internet when they are away from their home location.

**Telnet**   The essence of the *network of networks* concept, **Telnet** is the network capability that permits remote sign-on from whatever computer you are currently using. With Telnet, any computer on the Internet can be accessed from any other computer on the Internet. If you are away from your college or organization, you can use Telnet to communicate with your own system back at your main location. All you need to do is use the Telnet capability and provide it with your Internet address. Telnet takes care of finding the system and connecting you.

## Retrieval Capabilities

The vast information resources on the Internet are of tremendous value, providing you can locate what you need. Retrieving information from the Internet is easy if you know the address of the Web site you wish to visit. However, there are many times when that is not the case. In these instances, special applications are used to aid in the retrieval of information. They include file transfer protocol, directories, search engines, portals, and webcasting (see Table 3.1).

**file transfer protocol (FTP)**

An Internet method that allows you to use a password to connect to another computer on the Net and transfer its files to your computer.

**File Transfer Protocol**   The **file transfer protocol (FTP)** communications method makes it possible to connect and transfer files to (upload) and from (download) a remote computer. Transfer to your own computer is easy, regardless of whether the file contains software, documents, or graphical information. Similarly, FTP helps you transfer files from your computer to the remote computer.

FTP preceded the development of the World Wide Web. Thus, there are programs specifically for FTP. However, as discussed later in this chapter, FTP transfers also can be conducted using the same browser software as that used to access the Web.

**Web directory**

A listing of information by category.

**keyword**

A string of letters or words that indicates the subject to be searched.

**Web Directories**   A **Web directory** contains lists of Web sites and their URLs, categorized by topic. To locate a Web site through a directory, you have to enter a **keyword.** The directory software in turn displays a list of categories fitting the keyword, with the corresponding Web site names or URLs that have the keyword in their title or description.

Directories are created and maintained by Internet sites specializing in general purpose Web directories, including Yahoo! and Excite. (See *Case Study,* "Do you Yahoo!?" at the end of this chapter.)

Special purpose directories are also created and posted on individual Web sites devoted to a topic. For instance, the Silicon Valley Web directory lists public and private organizations located in the high-tech region of Northern California by business category. Because each category name is a link, clicking on the category takes the user to a longer list of organizations within that category. You can see how the preclassified entries in a Web directory help users find sites quickly.

**search engine**

A program invoked from within the browser that scans the network by using a keyword or phrase.

**Search Engines**   When a directory is not available, **search engines** can be used to locate a Web site. Search engines are software programs that look through the Web to find sites matching the keyword entered by the user. The results are listed in an index according to a priority sequence that the search engine determines is the most appropriate for the keyword. The best or highest probability matches are displayed first. Users click on the highlighted link of a site to display its home page.

Among the most popular search engines are Google and Alta Vista, found at www.google.com and www.altavista.com. Each search engine is designed according to a processing method that the developers feel is most likely to produce the best results. Some also excel in searches conducted in languages other than English. Most people have a preference for a particular search engine depending on their experience and comfort level.

# CRITICAL CONNECTIONS 2

## HealthGrades: How Does Your Doctor Rate?

Choosing doctors and hospitals is an important but sometimes difficult task. Often we rely on word-of-mouth recommendations from friends, relatives, or colleagues. But how much do you *really* know about the successful treatment of patients by the recommended physician or hospital? Perhaps you could use information that rates the alternatives available to you.

HealthGrades.com is an Internet-based company that seeks to advance the quality of health care in the United States. HealthGrades promotes quality health care in the following ways: by informing consumers of the vast quality differences among the nation's hospitals, by assisting high-performing hospitals in promoting their programs, and by helping poor performing hospitals to improve their quality.

The company profiles more than 600,000 physicians and 5,000 hospitals. If you are interested in assisted medical care, for example, HealthGrades includes nearly 20,000 nursing homes and some 7,000 home health agencies. To address other health concerns, it evaluates 10,000 mammography clinics, 300 fertility clinics, 60,000 chiropractors, 150,000 dentists, 21,000 assisted-living centers, 75 birth centers, 3,000 hospice-care facilities, 8,000 acupuncturists, and 700 naturopathic physicians.

A five-star rating reflects top-notch care, a three-star rating reflects average care, and a one-star rating reflects poor care. In a recent report rating hospitals (updated annually), HealthGrades shows substantial differences in mortality rates for the treatment of heart attacks and strokes in one-star (poor) versus five-star (excellent) hospitals. According to the American Heart Association, heart attacks, strokes, and related cardiovascular diseases account for 60 percent of all deaths in the nation, killing more Americans annually than the next seven leading causes of death combined, including all types of cancer.

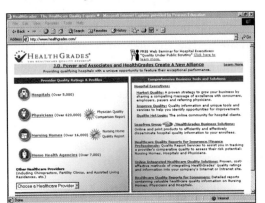

Seeking information to make an informed medical decision? An important step is visiting the leading Internet resource for medical profile information. Because HealthGrades is on the Internet, it is (like a good physician) always available, day or night.

---

**Portals**   A portal is a gateway or hub from which to visit other Web sites. It provides a single point from which to link to other sites meeting user needs. It may be a publicly accessed site, or it may be limited to use within a company.

Public portals began with ISPs, such as America Online (AOL). Over time, ISPs added more services in order to attract users back to the site more frequently. Hence, at a portal you can find an array of features including e-mail services, links to newsgroups, directories, search capabilities, and shopping. All of these features are designed to encourage users to come to the portal for any service they need. In this sense they are the gateway to the Web.

**Vertical portals** (or vortals) specialize in providing information related to a particular industry such as automobiles, healthcare, or investments. For example, vFoodPortal (www.vfoodportal.com) is a vertical portal serving the food industry (agriculture,

**vertical portal/vortal**
A Web site that specializes in providing information related to a particular industry such as automobiles, healthcare, or investments.

manufacturing, beverages, etc.) It provides a wealth of information, including directories, resources, job openings, training programs, and industry news (Figure 3.5).

Unlike vertical portals, which are narrower in scope, **horizontal portals** provide services and links to Web sites of interest to a wide variety of users. Because Yahoo! and AOL have added many services, they are now considered horizontal portals even though they began with more distinct roles.

**horizontal portal**
Provides services and links to Web sites of interest to a wide variety of users.

Webcasting    There are many effective retrieval tools for locating and viewing information on the Web. However, with most tools there is only one way to obtain the information: *The user has to go and get it* (that is, **pull** it) from the Web site by clicking on a link or entering a URL.

**pull**
To get something from a Web site by clicking on a link or entering a URL.

**Webcasting** is the prearranged and periodic delivery, or **push** of information of interest to a user's desktop automatically. Webcasting is a feature that can be selected on the leading browsers or an option that can be added through separate software applications loaded on the user's system. Pointcast and Backweb are well-known applications for webcasting. The software runs in the background of the user's PC. While the computer is being used for other work, the webcasting software shares the Internet connection to request updates from Web sites, or **channels,** the user has selected. As the update information arrives, it is either stored for later viewing, or the user may be notified by an audible sound or an e-mail message that the information has arrived. Once delivered, the new information can be viewed—whether or not the network connection is active.

**webcasting**
The prearranged and periodic delivery of information of interest to a user's desktop automatically.

**push**
The capability of a Web site for automatic Internet delivery of information, including software updates, to a user's desktop.

**channel**
A Web site designed to push information to a user's desktop.

Channels are simply Web sites, or portions of a Web site. Corporations are increasingly using channels to maintain the applications loaded on their users' computers. Here is how it works.

When a software company updates a piece of its software, it needs to let its customers know. A growing number of software manufacturers push these updates to a customer's information technology department. They push this information whenever it is ready, at defined intervals, or after notifying the company and receiving an okay to push the update. Once the software update arrives from the software manufacturer, the user's computing manager can in turn push the updates to all appropriate users via the company's internal network. Both the software company and its customer benefit by having the latest updates distributed in a timely manner and with the lowest possible cost.

Microsoft Corp. has begun using software update channels for users of its latest Windows releases. Whenever updates are ready for release, Microsoft sends a message to the users' computers over the software update channel. The user can decide to receive the updates then and install them immediately, receive the updates and install them at another time, or delay receiving the updates until later.

**FIGURE 3.5**
*vFood Vertical Portal*

**REALITY CHECK**
Today, the distinctions between types of portals are less visible. Many sites have combined functions in order to attract the greatest number of users. The category of a site is not as important. Rather, the big questions for individual users are: (1) Does the Web site have the necessary capabilities to meet your information search and retrieval needs? and (2) Is the site designed in a way that makes it easy to find the right information? ■

**Streaming**   Hollywood film producers and movie producers have made the Internet an integral part of the marketing campaign for introducing new movies. Whenever Sony Pictures, Time Warner, Walt Disney Pictures, Paramount Pictures, and others near the launch of a new movie, they put a video clip (a trailer, in Hollywood lingo) containing scenes and music from the movie on their Web site. Visitors can preview the movie by playing the video clip.

When files of audio and video information, like movie trailers, are pushed or pulled from the Internet, they are much larger than a text file. , At one time, users had to download the entire file before they could play or view it. Wait times could be lengthy. For instance, if you wanted to listen to a 10-minute video clip and were accessing the Internet over an ordinary phone line, you could wait more than an hour for the information to download to your computer.

That problem was solved by the introduction of streaming. **Streaming** (sometimes called **streaming media**) is a process in which you can listen to or view audio, video, or other media files as the downloading is occurring. When you click on a link to retrieve a media file, the contents of the file begin to flow across the Internet to your computer in a continuous stream—hence the name—of information packets. The audio or video contents are played as they arrive; it is generally unimportant that the contents of the file are still being transmitted from their source to your computer. (At times you may notice momentary pauses or disruptions, a result of heavy Internet traffic or a poor network connection.)

Thus, streaming is an on-demand retrieval and playing of a media file. Most streaming applications on the Web use prerecorded material. However, if desired, live broadcasts can also be streamed. For example, many publicly traded companies in the United States now broadcast quarterly reports about the company's performance to investors over the Internet using streaming media. As the presentations are being made live, the voices (and sometimes presentation slides) are transmitted over the Internet to anyone who is listening or viewing at the company's Web site. The presentations may also be captured and stored as a file for playing later.

Streaming also makes it possible for many users to retrieve the same file of audio, video, or other information simultaneously. For instance, the investor conference file can be used by, say, 100 people at the same time. One person may be 5 minutes into the file, another 5 1/2 minutes, another 7 minutes, and so on. Each is receiving a stream of information independent of the others.

To use streaming media, you must have streaming player software on your computer. This type of software, called a *plug-in* is associated with the browser you are using to access the Internet. (Browsers and plug-ins are discussed later in this chapter.)

The *Information Technology in Practice* feature, "Fans are Streaming for Major League Baseball," describes how fans can follow the live action of their favorite team, regardless of where they are at game time, simply by tuning in to the Internet.

## Shop, Buy, and Sell

For a growing number of users, the Internet provides a wealth of sites for online shopping. Automobiles, computers, airline tickets, clothing—just about anything can be bought or sold on the Internet. Online shopping is often called **electronic commerce,** or **e-commerce.** Because this is an important topic to businesses and users alike, a separate chapter is devoted to electronic commerce and the Internet (see Chapter 9).

**streaming/streaming media**
A format that enables an audio or video file or transmission to begin playing on the user's desktop even before the entire file is downloaded.

**electronic commerce/ e-commerce**
Online shopping.

# INFORMATION TECHNOLOGY IN PRACTICE

## Fans Are Streaming for Major League Baseball

**RealNetworks** Fans of major league baseball can now follow the live action of their favorite team from anywhere, over the Internet. For a fee, of course. For a subscription cost of less than $20, fans can listen to live audio webcasts of regular season Major League Baseball (MLB) games by logging on to MLB.com or real.com. The streaming software itself, created by RealNetworks, is free.[1] MLB Gameday Audio, the name given to the service, makes all home and away games of each of the 30 MLB teams (about 2,400 games) available for the season's fee. Versions of the game are also available in English, Spanish, and French.

In addition, MLB and Real-Networks offer subscribers the ability to search for and create customized video highlights of daily game coverage. This gives baseball fans and fantasy-league enthusiasts—who simulate owning and managing their own baseball team with *real* baseball players—to compile and review footage of their favorite teams and players on a daily basis. By providing archival access to every pitch from every game, this personalized video service will let individual subscribers choose the exact game highlights they want to watch.

The enthusiasm of Major League Baseball Advanced Media (MLBAM) and RealNetworks for the innovation was evident at the initial announcement:

"RealNetworks' partnership with Major League Baseball and MLBAM—offering full game audio, synchronized statistics, customizable video and condensed game playback content—will provide baseball fans worldwide with a resource for online entertainment that is second to none," said Rob Glaser, Chairman and CEO, RealNetworks, Inc. "Like the cable television industry did so effectively in the 1970s, RealNetworks is now opening up the Internet as the next mass medium for distributing great sports content. We are methodically building a critical mass of top-tier, Web-based sports content—and proving that subscription models on the Internet can and will be successful."

"We are thrilled to be working with RealNetworks to deliver the excitement of MLB action to Web fans worldwide," said Bob Bowman, president and CEO of MLBAM. "We hope that MLB.com and RealNetworks will set the precedent for the future of online sports entertainment."

Not all fans are as enthusiastic. Some consider Major League Baseball's Internet strategy to be a foul ball. After all, they say, information on the Internet should be free. The Internet is a public medium and not the property of any company.

So there you have it: a mass medium innovation in streaming games and information to baseball fans everywhere, for a nominal fee. Or is it a foul ball where fans will have to pay to follow their favorite national pastime over a public communications channel. You be the judge.

[1]RealNetworks is a software company whose applications enable users of personal computers and other consumer electronics devices to send and receive audio, video, and other multimedia content over the Web.

# The Internet Community

Just as the Internet is a network of networks, it is also a community of participants. The Internet's community consists of users, service providers, content providers, infrastructure providers, and Internet support agencies.

## Internet Users

*Users* are those who interact with the Internet to view, retrieve, or submit content. The number of users has been growing constantly since the Internet became public in the early 1990s and especially since it was made available for commercial use in 1994. The greatest initial use was in the United States. However, it is now accessible in more than 200 countries.

The rate of Internet use in the United States, like elsewhere in the developed world, continues to grow at a significant rate. Figure 3.6 illustrates this growth.

Who uses the Internet? We can tell a great deal by the languages of the online users (Figure 3.7). More than one-half of the 600 million or so Internet users rely on a language other than English for day-to-day communication. (By comparison, two-thirds of the world's economy—4 billion of the world's population of 6 billion people—is associated with non-English speakers.). Of this, approximately 34 percent use European languages, and 26 percent speak Asian languages.

Most surveys show that slightly more males than females use online access in North America (approximately 55 percent vs. 45 percent). Studies conducted by A.C. Nielson Media Research during the first half of the decade repeatedly indicate that the greatest number of online users use the Internet from home. For many people, the Internet has gone from a novelty to a highly useful utility.

## Service Providers

**Service providers** can be classified into two categories. **Internet service providers (ISPs)** supply access to the Internet by acting as the link between the user's computer and the Internet. An individual may dial the telephone number of the ISP or link through an *always-on* connection. (Chapter 8 discusses the technologies for accessing communications networks, like the Internet, in greater detail.)

ISPs typically charge a monthly service fee. At one time, the service fee provided up to a specified number of minutes/hours of time to be connected to the Internet. However, as the number of users and service providers alike increased, the monthly service fee has come to ensure an unlimited amount of time for Internet connection. The charges vary by whether the connection provides for high- or low-speed communications. Most ISPs include one or more unique e-mail addresses (discussed later in the chapter) in the monthly fee.

**Application service providers (ASPs)** are companies that develop, install, and operate (or *host*) an information technology application on the Internet for the user, charging a recurring fee for doing so. Because the application is on the Internet, it can be made available to anyone or any company having access to the Internet. ASPs offer the benefit of taking full responsibility for maintaining the service, ensuring that it is always available for use. The range of services can vary widely from creating and operating an individual or company site on the Internet to handling large volumes of transactions for a business.

The *Information Technology in Practice* feature, "OnStar Virtual Advisor Means In-Car Internet Access," describes how a voice-based, personalized Internet access service

**service providers or Internet service providers (ISPs)**
A company that sells communications services that enable users to access the Internet.

**application service providers (ASPs)**
Companies that develop, install, and operate (or *host*) an information technology application on the Internet for the user, charging a recurring fee for doing so.

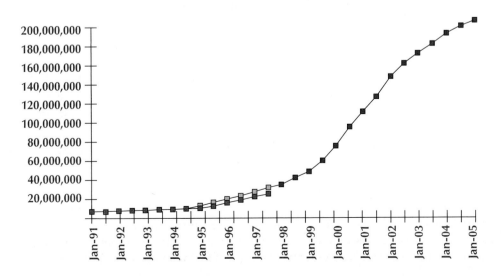

## Internet Domain Survey Host Count

**FIGURE 3.6**
*Growth of Internet Use*

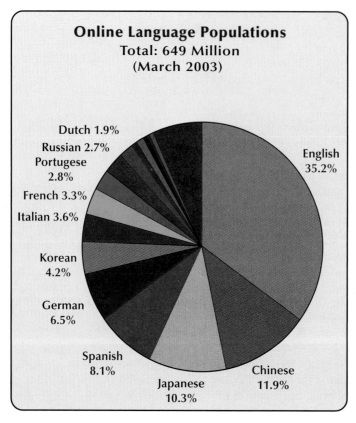

**FIGURE 3.7**
***Languages of Internet Users***

*Source:* Vilaweb.com, as quoted by <u>eMarketer</u>

available in selected American, Japanese, and German automobile models, provides security, safety, and information services to drivers.

## Content Providers

**content**
Information distributed over the Internet.

**content providers**
Individuals or companies that furnish the information available on the Internet.

Information distributed over the Internet is often referred to as **content.** When you access a site/location on the Internet, you typically do so for its content. Hence, **content providers** are the individuals or companies that furnish the information available on the Internet. Common examples include:

- CNN, the Cable News Network (www.cnn.com), provides users with written and video news stories that repeat or expand on information broadcast over the television stations of its cable network partners.
- Historic Augusta National Golf Club, home of the world renowned Masters Golf Tournament, hosts a wealth of color photographs, video clips, and records of golfers and past tournaments at www.augustgolf.com. In the spring of each year, when the Masters Tournament is in progress, users can also monitor the plays of their favorite golfers as they go from shot to shot throughout each day's round.
- Internal Revenue Service (IRS), a unit of the U.S. Department of Treasury, provides copies of all income tax forms as well as the rules and regulations associated with calculating and paying income taxes (www.irs.gov).
- TuCows, a content provider with one of the most unique names on the Internet, provides copies of software designed to be shared—distributed free or for a minimal charge. Check out TuCows (www.tucows.com) for thousands of shareware programs that can be transferred to your computer via the Internet.

# INFORMATION TECHNOLOGY IN PRACTICE

## OnStar Virtual Advisor Means In-Car Internet Access

U.S. drivers collectively spend more than 500 million hours a week in their vehicles. What good is the Internet if during the lengthy periods of time you spend in your automobile you cannot access it?

For many drivers, there is an option. It is called OnStar Virtual Advisor, a voice-based, hands-free personalized Internet access system. OnStar Virtual Advisor combines wireless communications, voice recognition, and text-to-speech translation to link users to the Internet. With this system, subscribers can access and process a wide array of information from the Web. Here are some examples:

- **E-mail**  Retrieve personal e-mail with the simple voice command, "Get my e-mail." Virtual Advisor *reads* the messages when prompted by the *read it* command. A user needing assistance can prompt the system at any time simply by asking, "What are my choices?"
- **News**  National news, headline news, world news, or business news services can brief drivers with a simple voice command.
- **Weather conditions**  Current and forecasted weather conditions are available for any U.S. or Canadian postal code. "Look up local weather" takes advantage of OnStar's ability to determine its location and then get information for that area.
- **Sports**  Updates are available for teams in women and men's

major league professional sports, college basketball, baseball, and football, as well as men's and women's golf, and auto racing.
- **Stocks**  Market information provides updates for stocks on the New York Stock Exchange, NASDAQ, and AMEX, as well as for most mutual funds. "Move to stocks" is all it takes to transfer from e-mail into this portion of the information service.

For security purposes, the individual activates the system by providing a four-digit personal identification number (PIN).

Each user is provided with a personalized home page. If desired, OnStar subscribers can tailor the information they wish to receive, either through an OnStar advisor or by signing on to the OnStar Web site from their home or office PC. For instance, individuals can preselect the stock or mutual funds about which they wish to receive information.

Virtual Advisor is a special service available to users who have the OnStar security, safety, and information service offered by General Motors. The service combines global positioning system (GPS) satellite communications technology and wireless communications to link the driver and vehicle with the OnStar Center. In essence, OnStar makes the vehicle itself a communications device. The phone unit embedded in the system is five times more powerful than the conventional handheld cellular phone. Its stronger signal means equipped vehicles can connect to the Internet and the OnStar Center from places that would be inaccessible with a cellular phone.

OnStar's three-button system limits the attention demands on drivers, so they can keep their eyes on the road and their hands on the wheel. The three buttons, integrated into the instrument panel,

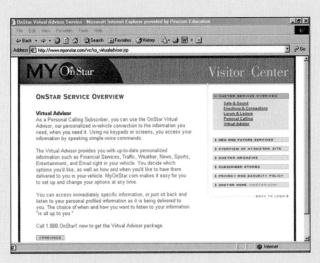

*continued*

the overhead console, or the rearview mirror enable the driver to: interact with OnStar to send or receive a call from the OnStar Center, send an emergency call that is treated as a priority, or initiate Virtual Advisor services. (The driver need only press one button to activate OnStar.) A hands-free microphone is built into the vehicle, and radio speakers carry the responses of the OnStar or Virtual Advisor, as well as personal-calling conversations.

OnStar and OnStar Virtual Advisor are available in many automobile models manufactured by General Motors, as well as Toyota Motor's Lexus series, Honda Motor Company's Honda and Acura models, and Volkswagen's Passat models.

## Infrastructure Providers

**network infrastructure providers**
Companies, such as telephone, cellular telephone, cable TV, and satellite transmission companies, that operate the network of communication channels that carry data and information to and from user and content locations.

Infrastructure providers are the companies that supply the resources to use the Internet. **Network infrastructure providers** operate the network of communication channels that carry data and information to and from user and content locations. These include telephone, cellular telephone, cable TV, and satellite transmission companies.

**Component infrastructure providers** supply the computer hardware and software that makes it possible to use, operate, or store and retrieve content from the Internet. For instance, the security software that prohibits unauthorized individuals from using a specific Internet site is an example of infrastructure software. Users typically are more aware of the components they can see and use compared to the network infrastructure, which is largely operated behind the scene.

**component infrastructure providers**
Companies that supply the computer hardware and software that makes it possible to use, operate, or store and retrieve content from the Internet.

## Internet Support Agencies

Although no one owns the Internet, a variety of agencies—committees and task forces—provide coordination by assigning names for the domains and promoting standards. Two of the most important are ICANN and IETF.

**Internet Corp. for Assigned Names and Numbers (ICANN)**
The nonprofit corporation that was formed to assume responsibility for the IP address space allocation, protocol parameter assignment, domain name system management, and root server system management.

The **Internet Corp. for Assigned Names and Numbers (ICANN)** is the nonprofit corporation that was formed to assume responsibility for the IP address space allocation, protocol parameter assignment, domain name system management, and root server system management. These functions were previously performed under contracts administered by the U.S. government. At ICANN, various members of the Internet community can come together, debate and discuss technical coordination and other policy issues related to the domain names and address allocation systems. Remember that the Internet is global and so each of the nations and regions of the world should be considered when decisions are made. ICANN was viewed as a more desirable alternative than a multinational governmental treaty organization, which because of the Internet's global character was considered the only other practical option. The private-sector consensus-development approach used by ICANN was believed to be quicker, more responsive to changing conditions, and more suitable to the development of effective global policies.

**Internet Engineering Task Force (IETF)**
A large international community of network designers, operators, vendors, and researchers concerned with the evolution of Internet architecture and the smooth operation of the Internet.

The **Internet Engineering Task Force (IETF)** is a large international community of network designers, operators, vendors, and researchers concerned with the evolution of Internet architecture and the smooth operation of the Internet. It is open to any interested individual.

The actual technical work of the IETF is done in working groups, which are organized by topic into several areas (e.g., routing, transport, and security). Much of the work is handled via mailing lists. The IETF holds meetings three times per year.

In addition, many universities and colleges manage large segments of the Internet's resources and conduct research in support of both the Internet support agencies and the vast community of users.

## Internet Addresses

Everyone and every computer on the Internet has a unique address—just like the telephone system—from which to send and receive messages. An Internet address has four parts: (1) the user's personal identification, (2) the name of the host computer, (3) the name of the institution or organization, and (4) the domain name (Figure 3.8). To understand the structure, it is best to begin with the computer's address.

## Domain Name System

Computers have numeric addresses consisting of strings of numbers known as their Internet protocol (or IP) address (e.g., 207.46.230.219, 207.171.181.16, 66.218.71.102, and 205.188.145.215). But it would difficult to remember all of the addresses. As a result, a **domain name system (DNS)** was created. **Domain names** are the familiar, easy-to-remember names for computers on the Internet (e.g., Microsoft.com, amazon.com, yahoo.com, and aol.com). Each domain name correlates to assigned IP addresses (e.g., 207.46.230.219 for Microsoft, 207.171.181.16 for amazon.com, 66.218.71.102 for yahoo.com, and 205.188.145.215 for aol.com). The purpose of the domain name system (DNS) is to make it possible to reach any computer in the world by simply entering its domain name.

The highest-level domain names (signified by the .XXX name at the end of the address) vary depending on the purpose of the organization to which they are assigned. For instance, .com, .net., and .org are open to all persons or organizations on a global basis. Other top level domain names are shown in Figure 3.9 Because of continuing Internet growth, additional domain names were created at the beginning of this decade.

Individual countries and geographically distinct territories have a country code for their top level domain name. For example, as shown in Figure 3.9, addresses in Japan end in .jp while those in the United Kingdom end in .uk. The local Internet community in the country or territory chooses the country code. Each country and global domain name has its own **registry.** However, the actual interaction with registrants (e.g., organizations seeking a domain name) is delegated to **registrars.** They process applications for assignment of domain names and submit approved names to the registry.

At the heart of the global domain name system are 13 special computers, called **root servers.** Root servers, coordinated by ICANN (see Figure 3.10), contain the IP addresses of all top level domain registries for both the global registries (e.g., .com, .net, and .org) and the country registries (e.g., .uk, .jp, and .br).

## Addresses on Host Computers

Together, the domain names form a tree growing downward from a root file on the Internet's root server system. As illustrated in Figure 3.11, amazon.com, yahoo.com, and aol.com appear under the .com top level domain. A university similarly is a *registrant* under the .edu domain.

In order for a business or a university to connect one or more of its computers—called a host computer—to the Internet, it must first apply for and receive a unique domain name. In turn, the university or business that provides your access to the Net will assign you a personal identification name. This personal ID is often a combination of your name and the

**domain name system (DNS)**
Computers have numeric addresses consisting of strings of numbers known as their Internet protocol (or IP) address (e.g., 207.46.230.219, 207.171.181.16, 66.218.71.102, and 205.188.145.215).

**domain name**
The familiar, easy-to-remember names for computers on the Internet that correlate to assigned IP addresses.

**registry**
A regional organization that allocates Internet addresses to requestors in that region.

**registrars**
Organizations delegated to accept and process Internet address applications and submit approved applications to the regional registrar.

**root servers**
One of 13 special computers distributed around the world that maintain the Internet addresses for all global and country registries.

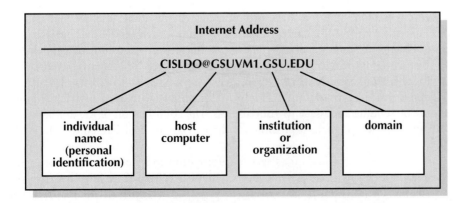

**FIGURE 3.8**
*Internet Addresses*

**FIGURE 3.9**

***Internet Domain Names***

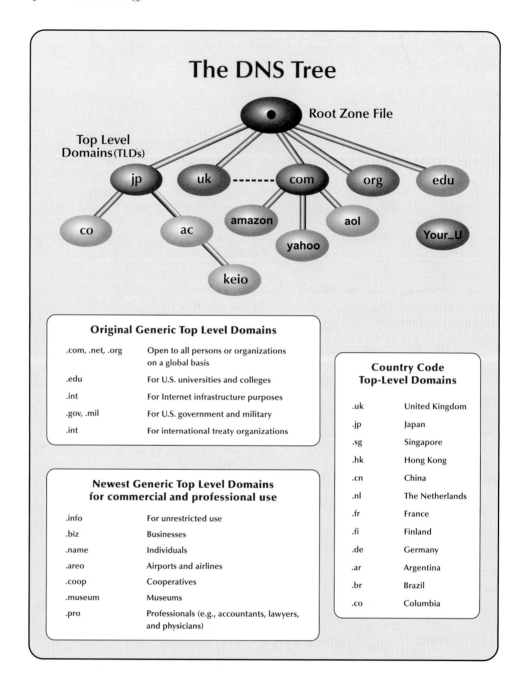

name of the network serving your location or work group within the organization. The unique domain name assigned to the host computer is included in your address. Your address is unique in the same way that your personal telephone number is unique.

**E-Mail Addresses**    You may have two different types of addresses: an e-mail address, and a unique address for information you display on the World Wide Web. Your e-mail address is associated with a unique set of letters and numbers—perhaps your name—followed by the @ sign and in turn followed by the domain name (e.g., wgates@microsoft.com, david.alexander@harvard.edu).

If someone has your Internet address they can locate you from anywhere in the world simply by sending a message to your address. The combination of the domain name system and root servers make it possible for the message to be delivered to you.

**uniform resource locator (URL)**
A document's address on the WWW.

**World Wide Web Addresses**    Pages of information and files at sites on the Internet are located through their **uniform resource locator (URL).** Each page has its own URL; if you enter the URL on your browser, the page will be displayed.

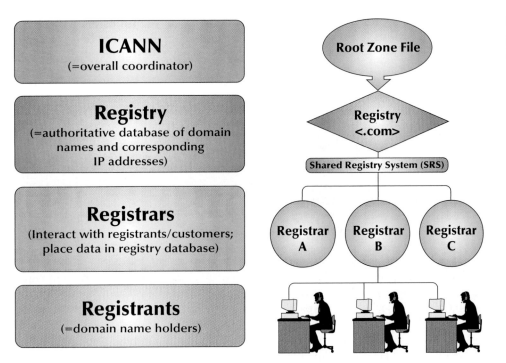

FIGURE 3.10

***Basic DNS Registry Structure***

**Components of URL**   The URL contains several components (see Figure 3.12):

- A protocol identifier–http://
- The letters www, for World Wide Web
- The unique registered domain name
- The registry name (e.g., .edu or .com)

However, it is no longer necessary to enter the protocol http:// before the address; this is automatically assumed to be the desired, or default, protocol. Hence, clicking the URL www.microsoft.com will display the company's home page, while www.amazon.com will display its home page. Since Web sites often contain large volumes of information, it is customary to organize the information into folders and files within folders. Hence, by including the organization structure in the URL, you can direct someone straight to the desired information within the site. For instance, to obtain information on the Microsoft Office software from the company's Web page, the URL is www.microsoft.com/office. The product support files for Microsoft Office can be found at www.microsoft.com/office/support. A specific document often will include its name and the format in which it was created (e.g., documentation.html, meaning it was created using the html format). In this instance, the

## The DNS Tree

FIGURE 3.11

***The DNS Tree***

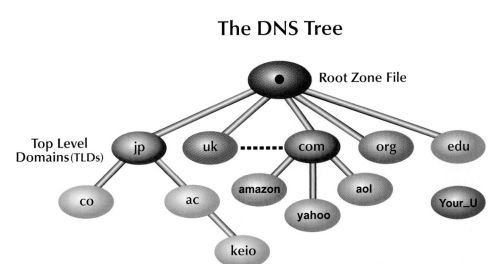

FIGURE 3.12

*Components of the URL*

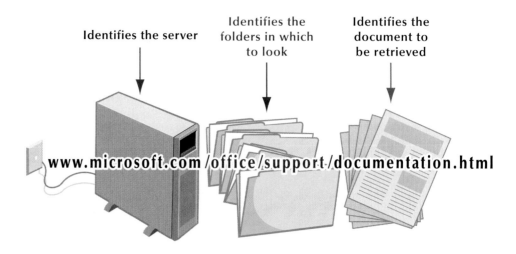

Identifies the server   Identifies the folders in which to look   Identifies the document to be retrieved

www.microsoft.com /office/support /documentation.html

URL would be www.microsoft.com/office/support/documentation.html. (Keep in mind, however, that because of the hyperlinks used with the World Wide Web, you can generally enter just the URL for the home page, and *click* to the files and documents without having to enter the complete URL.)

**FTP Addresses**   The URL address structure remains largely the same when retrieving or sending information involving an FTP site. However, the letters *ftp* will replace http in the URL. Hence, to reach Microsoft's FTP site, the URL becomes: ftp://ftp.microsoft.com (or simply ftp.microsoft.com).

**World Wide Web (WWW)/ the Web**
The set of interconnected electronic documents, or Web pages, that are linked together over the Internet.

**Web pages**
Interconnected electronic documents.

**hyperlinks**
Words and/or symbols highlighted by blinking, color, or underline that connect one document to another related document on the Web.

**World Wide Web**   The **World Wide Web (WWW)**–known to most users as simply **the Web**–is a set of interconnected electronic documents, called **Web pages**, which are linked together over the Internet. Web software searches the Web to find pages connecting keywords that are entered by the user. Special keywords in the pages of Web documents, called **hyperlinks**, connect or link documents to one another. Recognized on your computer display screen as words and symbols highlighted by color, underline, or blinking words and symbols, hyperlinks are your connection to other documents on the Web (Figure 3.13). By using Web software to follow the links in a document, you can jump to related information in any file on the Web. When you click on a hyperlink, the Web software processes the address contained in the hyperlink, connects to the location, and displays information from the linked location. Clicking on successive hyperlinks enables you to jump from location to

FIGURE 3.13

*Hyperlink Structure*

WWW pages. . . . . . . . . . . . . .

Hyperlinks between pages. . . . . . . . . . . .

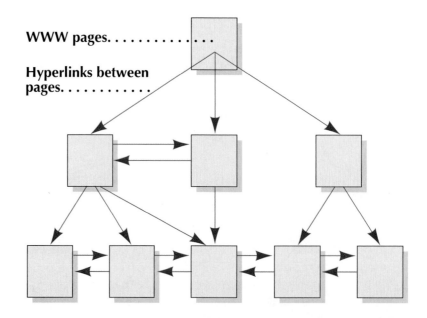

# INFORMATION TECHNOLOGY IN PRACTICE

## InnoCentive's Internet Stimulates Mind over Matter

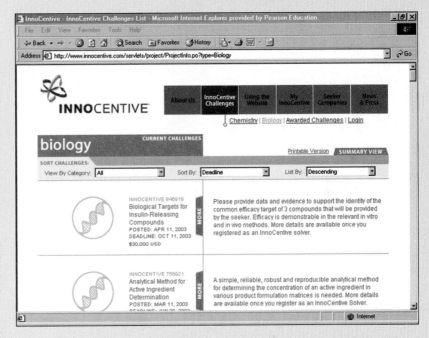

**INNO**CENTIVE®  There is nothing worse than being stumped by a problem when you *know* a solution exists. Eli Lilly, the highly regarded pharmaceutical manufacturer headquartered in Indianapolis, Indiana, experienced this situation and decided to do something about it. In the process, Eli Lilly has speeded the pace of scientific-based research and development for its industry.

Eli Lilly created a subsidiary, called InnoCentive, which takes its problems to the scientific world by way of the Internet. When its scientists run into a dead end while working on a chemistry, biology, physics, or toxicology problem, they may list it on the InnoCentive Web site.

InnoCentive is a virtual space where unsolved scientific problems can be seen and taken on by uniquely qualified scientists regardless of their geographic location or background. The Web site encourages scientists to quickly find problems that match their qualifications and then collaborate or work independently to solve the problem. In contrast to the traditional contract or grant, scientists work and submit solutions with the understanding that the best solution will produce a financial reward of up to $100,000.

The Internet is the means of communicating the scientific challenges to the research community.

Each problem is listed in the simplest possible terms. This protects the corporate secrets of the company submitting the problem and ensures that the nature of the problem is understood by those outside of the company. A summary of each problem is visible to anyone visiting the InnoCentive site. However, in order to view detailed information about a problem and gain access to a private online project room where final solution proposals are submitted, scientists must register with InnoCentive. Registration is free.

The company's Referral Rewards Program is designed to get scientists to encourage their colleagues to participate. It provides a $1,000 reward to any individual referring a scientist who eventually submits an accepted problem solution.

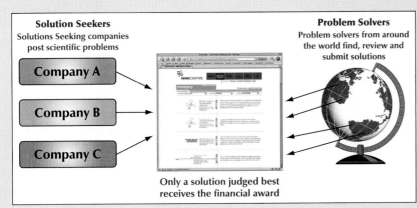

**Solution Seekers**
Solutions Seeking companies post scientific problems

Company A

Company B

Company C

Only a solution judged best receives the financial award

**Problem Solvers**
Problem solvers from around the world find, review and submit solutions

*continued*

InnoCentive is not just for Eli Lilly. Rather, any company can post problems that it wants to have researchers tackle. Confidentiality is guaranteed. The potential benefits for companies include the following:

1. Solutions to problems that may seem otherwise unsolvable
2. Faster solutions to problems at substantially lower costs
3. Multiple solutions that can be combined or scrutinized to provide the best possible resolution of the problem
4. An easy, convenient way to tap into the entire scientific global community
5. An efficient and effective alternative for expanding a company's capacity for scientific research and development

Scientific researchers enjoy these potential benefits:

1. A quick way to find unsolved problems matching their expertise
2. A means of leveraging under-utilized scientific capacity while simultaneously producing a financial reward
3. A way to collaborate on serious scientific problems and gain peer recognition for solutions they devise
4. Being able to do all of the above without developing proposals or becoming involved in sales efforts

InnoCentive's Internet efforts seem to address a previously unmet need. In the first year of its operation, more than 8,000 scientists registered on its site. More than 40 *unsolvable* problems were posted

on the site, with solution awards totaling in the millions of dollars.

Among the initial awards granted for solutions include the following:

- A retired chemist received $25,000 for submitting a breakthrough pathway for synthesis of a compound
- A biotechnology company received $15,000 for providing a solution to a Hydroxyprimidine challenge
- A graduate student received $30,000 for synthesis of a protected unnatural amino acid

InnoCentive's Internet site guarantees broad exposure of problem challenges to the scientific community. Or, as InnoCentive likes to say, it's about minds over matter.

---

location to obtain the information you want. The Web is the fastest-growing part of the Internet. For many people, the Web *is* the Internet, for that is the only part they use.

The *Information Technology in Practice* feature, "InnoCentive's Internet Stimulates Mind over Matter," illustrates how pharmaceutical manufacturer Eli Lilly & Company uses the power of the World Wide Web for advancing scientific research—even when its scientists are stumped with a problem.

# Browsing the World Wide Web

Electronic pages are the most distinguishing characteristic of the Web. Pages in a Web document are specially formatted files that can display text, graphical, and image information. They can also include clips of audio and video, which users can play if their computers are equipped with the necessary hardware and software.

Graphical browser software, introduced in the early 1990s, triggered widespread use of the Web by individuals, universities, companies, and government. With interest in the Web skyrocketing, it was inevitable that there would be a tremendous growth in Web pages. This section of the chapter describes: home pages and links to other pages; the HTML language; browser software; URL addresses; Web navigation; and plug-ins for Web browsers.

## One Home Page, Many Links

**home page**
The first page of a Web site, which identifies the site and provides information about the contents of electronic documents that are part of the site.

The **home page** is the first page you see when you access a Web site. It identifies the site and provides information about the contents of electronic documents that are part of the site (i.e., a table of contents or map). Often the home page uses graphical symbols or icons (in addition to text blocks) to highlight information and provide links to other pages.

Figure 3.14 shows the home page for the city of Paris. Notice how quickly you can identify the subject of this page. The city's name stands out because of its size, color, and the surrounding images of prominent statues in central Paris. Text in the middle of the page further identifies the subject and gives access to other pages at the site.

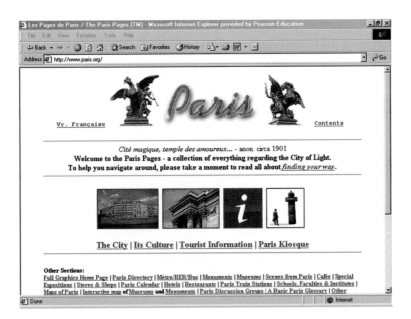

FIGURE 3.14

**Home Page for the City of Paris, France**

The Paris home page also contains links to other information. Eight of these links are visible; each contains an underlined word or phrase that signifies it is a hyperlink. For example, if you wanted to view the home page in the French language, you would click on the hyperlink *Vr.Française*. Or if you wanted a table of contents, you would click on *Contents*.

Images, or icons, are also used to signify hyperlinks on Web pages. Clicking on the image activates the hyperlink. The four images at the bottom of the Paris home page are hyperlinks that serve the same purpose as the text hyperlinks for *The City, Its Culture, Tourist Information*, and *Paris Kiosque*. These icons are also activated by a mouse click.

## Creating Web Pages Using HTML

The features of a Web page take shape when the user specifies the location and appearance of the information. A set of commands—**hypertext markup language (HTML)**—specifies the position, size, and color of text, the location of graphic information, and the incorporation of sound and video (Figure 3.15). HTML commands also identify the words or images that will serve as hyperlinks to other documents. When the computer processes files containing HTML commands, it creates and displays the page and prepares the hyperlinks.

HTML consists of a series of *tags* that set off sections of text that will appear on a Web page. Used in pairs, the tags mark the beginning and end of an HTML section (such as the head, title, or body areas of a page). Tags are recognized by their angle brackets (<>). An initial tag identifies the beginning of a section (<HEAD>) and a second tag, which includes a slash (/), signifies the end of the section (</HEAD>).

The basic structure of a page will conform to this standard sequence:

<HTML>
<HEAD>

This is the section of the document where the purpose of the page is described. The comments here are not for display by the browser; they are for informational purposes only.

</HEAD>
<BODY>

This is the section of the document that contains the information and graphical images the browser will display. It also contains hyperlinks to other Web pages.

</BODY>
</HTML>

Creating a Web page consists of preparing a document that includes the tags and a combination of text, hyperlink references, and graphics. Figure 3.15 lists the most common HTML commands used in creating Web pages.

**hypertext markup language (HTML)**

A set of commands that specifies the position, size, and color of text, the location of graphic information, and the incorporation of sound and video. HTML commands also identify the words or images that will serve as hyperlinks to other documents.

| TAG | DESCRIPTION |
|---|---|
| **Structure** | |
| <HTML> . . . </HTML> | Identifies the document as an HTML document and its beginning and end. |
| <HEAD> . . . </HEAD> | Identifies the head, one of two parts of an HTML document. |
| <BODY> . . . </BODY> | Identifies the body of the document, the other part of an HTML document. |
| <TITLE> . . . </TITLE> | Identifies the documents title. |
| <!- . . . -> | Sets off a comment within a document. (Browser software does not display comments on a Web page.) |
| <HEAD> . . . </HEAD> | Identifies the head, one of two parts of an HTML document. |
| **Block Elements** | |
| <H1> . . . </H1> | Identifies a first-level heading (the highest level) within the document. It is customary to use a level 1 heading as the first element in the body of an HTML document. |
| <H2> . . . </H2> | Identifies a second-level heading within the document. |
| <H3> . . . </H3> | Identifies a third-level heading within the document. |
| <H4> . . . </H4> | Identifies a fourth-level heading within the document. |
| <H5> . . . </H5> | Identifies a fifth-level heading within the document. |
| <P> . . . </P> | Sets off paragraphs within a document. |
| <CENTER> . . . </CENTER> | Centers the block (the content between the tags) on the page when it is displayed. |
| <TAB> | Describes the number of spaces to indent: e.g., <TAG INDENT = 5> will indent the text 5 characters until the end of the paragraph (no closing tag is required). |
| **Hypertext Links** | |
| <A> . . . </A> | Marks the start (HREF) or end (NAME) of a link: e.g., <A HREF=url>text to be highlighted as hyperlink</A>. |
| <H2> . . . </H2> | Identifies a second-level heading within the document. |
| **In-line Images** | |
| <IMG> | Used to place an in-line image into the page at the designated location: e.g., <IMG SCR=../image.gif"> where SCR indicates the file name, image.gif, containing the image to be embedded (there is no closing tag). |
| **Formatting** | |
| <P> | Start a new paragraph; insert a blank line. |
| <BR> | Start a new line. |
| <HR> | Insert a ruler line. |
| <B> </B> | Boldface type. |
| <I> </I> | Italic type. |
| <U> </U> | Underline. |
| <PRE> </PRE> | Maintains formatted space. (HTML will remove extra spaces, tabs, and blank lines except when instructed to retain preformatted spacing by the <PRE> tag.) |
| & | Inserts special character. |

**FIGURE 3.15**
*Common HTML Tags*

The HTML commands describing a page are stored on a Web server. When retrieved by browser software, they are processed to create the page and its links, which are shown on the user's display screen (Figure 3.16).

Software developers have created tools to assist people in preparing Web pages (Figure 3.17). Some of these tools provide sample HTML segments that users can modify to create a page without writing the HTML from scratch.

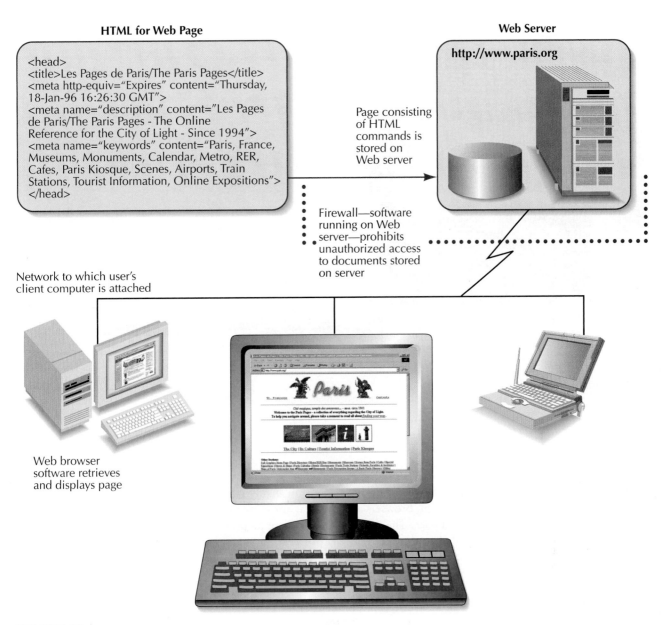

**FIGURE 3.16**

### *World Wide Web Page Structure*

A page displayed on a PC connected to the Web is the result of a creation using HTML that is stored on a Web server, retrieved and transmitted over interconnecting networks, and viewed on a PC using a Web browser.

## Browser Software

To take advantage of the graphical nature of the Web, you need a browser program.[2] **Web browsers** are client computer programs designed to locate and display information on the World Wide Web. With a Web browser you can display Web pages, jump between Web pages using hyperlinks, and search the Web for pages of topical interest. It was when graphical Web browser programs were introduced in the early 1990s, making the creating and viewing of electronic pages possible, that interest in the Web shot up. Individuals, universities, companies, and governments began to use Web pages to display information and invite communication with people on the Internet.

**Web browser**

Client computer program designed to locate and display information on the World Wide Web.

[2]Browser programs can usually be downloaded from the Internet and loaded on a PC or workstation. Some are available without charge.

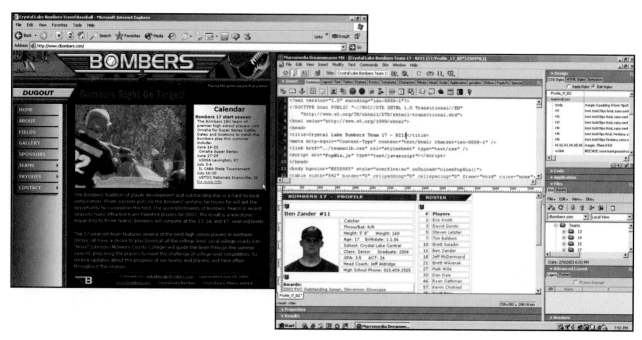

**FIGURE 3.17**

***World Wide Web Developer Tools***

The productivity of Web developers is improved by tools that automate large portions of the HTML creation process, including those involving text, graphics, animation, and audio/vidio components.

**graphical browser**

A type of browser used with the Web that displays both text and images within a page.

Typically, you activate Web browsers by clicking on an icon that is associated with the program. Browsers are graphical, meaning that they can display both text and images within a page. The image may be an icon, a photograph, or a drawing. Some pages also include animated images. **Graphical browsers** display a window consisting of the display and nine principal components (Figure 3.19).

---

 **REALITY CHECK**   Plenty of books are available that will familiarize you with HTML and help you create your own pages on the Web. Alternatively, you can use the Web itself to retrieve information on HTML and page construction. For example, you may want to search for *home page construction kit* or *Web page design.* ■

---

1. **Title bar**   Displays the name of the browser and the page currently displayed.
2. **Menu bar**   Contains the browser commands for creating, editing, navigating, and invoking special actions related to the page currently displayed.
3. **Net site**   Displays the address of the Web site for the page currently displayed.
4. **Toolbar**   Contains icons that represent frequently used commands included in the menu bar, such as:

   *Forward* Moves ahead to pages in the history list.

   *Backward* Moves back to pages in the history list.

   *Open file* Makes a file ready to use.

   *File store* Writes a copy of the current file to storage.

**FIGURE 3.18**
*Browser's Client Program*

*History list* Keeps track of all WWW pages visited in a particular session, thus providing the capability for a user to jump directly to any of those pages.

*Print* Prints a copy of the page currently displayed.

*Home page* Returns to the home page of the site at which the user is connected to the WWW.

5. **In-line Image**   Graphics embedded (at the page creator's option) in the page to enhance its appearance and visually convey information about the nature of the page.

6. **Hyperlinks**   Icon or text links (usually signified by an underline or different color) that can be selected to jump to another page.

7. **Status bar**   Displays the address of the highlighted link.

8. **Activity indicator**   An icon that signals the user that an activity, such as locating a WWW site or transmitting information from another location, is in process.

9. **Scroll bars**   Allow the user to move the window up or down for viewing information.

**FIGURE 3.19**
*Internet Explorer Graphical Browser*

## URL Addresses

As with all Internet locations, each Web page location has its own address. The uniform resource locator (URL) is the document's address on the WWW. The URL system is a consistent way to identify Web sites that all page developers use. The Paris home page (Figure 3.14), has the following URL: http://www.paris.org.

The URL is determined on the basis of the Internet address of the site. Its general format is illustrated in Figure 3.12 (on page 106). Hence, a browser pointed at the page identified by URL http://www.paris.org uses the hypertext transfer protocol (HTTP), the communication language employed by WWW clients and servers. When the browser connects to this page, it retrieves a file called *paris* in a directory named *org* (the abbreviation for organization).

## Navigating the Web

To take advantage of what the Web has to offer, you must know how to navigate from page to page. This is quite easy. You merely point the browser to a specific URL location. If you do not know the URL, you can search for information or scan a directory.

**Using Search Engines**   If you have ever *surfed* the Internet, then you are familiar with search engines. Without a URL or Web address, a search engine can help you locate a wealth of information on any subject imaginable. To get started, all you have to do is call up the search engine and then enter a keyword or phrase (Figure 3.20). For instance, if you want to search for information on World Cup Soccer, you simply enter the phrase "world cup soccer" (in any combination of upper-and lowercase letters) when prompted to do so by the search engine.

Many different search engines are available on the Web, most are free. Common search engines are Alta Vista (www.altavista.com), Google (www.google.com), Go (www.go.com), and InfoSeek (www.infoseek.com).

**Directories**   A Web directory is a listing of information by category. To find information in a directory, you click on the most important category; then you continue through successive choices, each with more specific options, until you find what you want.

Yahoo! is one of the most widely used directories. When you reach *Yahoo!* (www.yahoo.com), you see a subject list. Major headings include *Arts, Business and Economics, Computers and Internet, Education, Entertainment, Health,* and so forth. If you are

**FIGURE 3.20**

*Home Page for Google Search Engine*

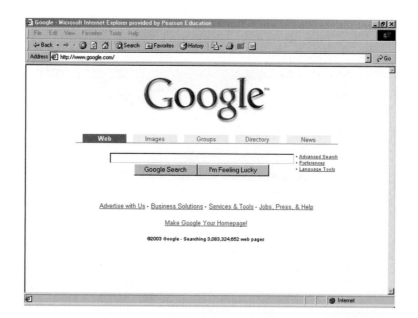

# CRITICAL CONNECTIONS 3

## Google Searches Behind the Portal Scene

Google

The best-known names in portals—America Online, Microsoft Network, and Yahoo!—gained their leading positions by their ability to respond effectively to visitor inquiries. Visit a portal, pose a query, and review the results. That is what users want. The portal that consistently satisfies the visitor's needs, gets repeat traffic. To the user, satisfying search requests are what portals are all about. To the portal, getting the most repeat visitors is the basis for its existence.

But what software powers the search process for each portal? A software company named Google can often be found behind the scenes. Google has provided the search engine that powers some or all of the information retrieval activities at the leading portal sites. Its less successful competitors include Inktomi, Overture, and Teoma.

Speed is an important characteristic for a search engine, and Google is one of the fastest. Even more important to many users is the engine's ability to provide results that are relevant to their needs. Google, like all other search engines, has its own process for seeking out sites with information that users want. Its unique PageRank technology relies on a complex ranking system based on the number of links to any given Web site. Each link is considered a *vote*. For example, if ABCnews.com links to a site, that site receives a vote. In processing a user query, Google claims its PageRank technology produces more relevant results than any of its competitors. Many users would agree.

---

interested in a topic related to *Business and Economics,* you click on this topic and a more detailed subject list will appear.

The key to using both search engines and directories effectively is to plan in advance. Know what subject list is likely to contain the information you are looking for, and consider which keywords will most accurately describe the topic.

Because a number of search engines are adding directory capabilities, the distinction between search engines and directories is becoming somewhat blurred. This causes no problem, however, as people can use whatever means they find most helpful for locating information on the Web.

## Plug-Ins for Web Browsers

**Plug-ins** are software programs that extend the capabilities of your Internet browser, giving it added features. The most common plug-ins add the ability to play audio samples (e.g., music) or view video movies from within your browser.

Plug-ins are generally available without charge and can be obtained by visiting the company Web site of the manufacturer and downloading the software. The second step of linking the plug-in to your browser generally requires no more than a click on the plug-in's icon. The software takes care of the rest. Table 3.2 summarizes the characteristics of the most common plug-ins.

**plug-ins**
Software programs that extend the capabilities of your Internet browser, giving it added features.

# A Final Word

The World Wide Web and the Internet are still in their relative infancy; you can be sure that many innovative uses for them will emerge in the next few years. People will find clever new ways to capitalize on their ability to incorporate sound, video, animation, and high-resolution graphics. We can only imagine what is to come!

**Table 3.2   Characteristics of Common Plug-Ins**

| PLUG-IN | NAME | MANUFACTURER | FEATURE |
|---|---|---|---|
| Get QuickTime Free Download | Apple QuickTime Player | Apple Computers | The Apple QuickTime plug-in lets you experience QuickTime animation, music, audio, and video objects directly in a Web page. |
| PDF Adobe | Acrobat Reader | Adobe Software | Software for sharing information. This plug-in lets you view and print (PDF) files. With Acrobat Reader, you can also fill in and submit Adobe PDF forms online. |
| macromedia FLASH PLAYER | Flash Player | Macromedia | Flash software provides graphics, animation, and entertainment on the Web. |
| Java | Java | Sun Microsystems | The Java plug-in allows you to run Java programs(called *applets*) inside your Web browser. Applets can perform animation, display graphics, play sounds, etc. |
| macromedia SHOCKWAVE PLAYER | Shockwave | Macromedia | Shockwave lets users experience quality interactive games, multimedia, graphics, and streaming audio on the Web. |
| Windows Media Player 9 Series FREE | Windows Media Player | Microsoft | Media Player lets you play streaming audio, video, animations, and multimedia presentations on the Web |
| real player | RealPlayer | RealNetworks | RealPlayer lets you play streaming audio, video, animations, and multimedia presentations on the Web. |

# CRITICAL CONNECTIONS

## 1  Part II: Hotmail Is Hot—And Free!

**Hotmail**   Even if it is free, you can still choose the right e-mail service for you. Not all e-mail services are alike. Hotmail, Yahoo! mail, Lycos Mail, and Mail.com—the leading free services—differ in the capabilities they offer. Among factors to consider is their ease of use, breadth of features, reliability in receipt or transmission of messages, and allocated storage space.

Some services support instant messages. Others differ in the speed at which Web pages are displayed on the screen. Storage allocations for holding messages also differ, ranging from two megabytes to six or eight megabytes. If you send and receive large volumes of messages, especially if they include photos and other graphics, the storage allocation will be a vital selection criterion.

At any rate, you can evaluate available services in terms of what features are most important to you. For instance, extra storage, personalized e-mail addresses, or the ability to transcribe e-mail into voice messages may be important for some users. Of course, the charges for each added service is a point of comparison as well.

Finally, free e-mail systems may serve as a backup in case of emergencies. If you cannot send or receive messages using your main e-mail provider, then a free e-mail service may be just the answer.

### Questions for Discussion

1. Why do free e-mail systems make their services available without charge? How do they pay for the cost of creating and maintaining the system if they give the services away without charge? (Visit some free e-mail sites to check this out firsthand.)
2. What emergencies involving a primary e-mail system might occur? Would you use a free-email account as a backup? Why or why not?
3. Consider the people you know, if any, who use free e-mail accounts. For what purposes do they use these e-mail systems?

## 2  Part II: HealthGrades: How Does Your Doctor Rate?

HEALTHGRADES'
THE HEALTHCARE QUALITY EXPERTS'

HealthGrades' search capability lets you quickly locate information. For instance, a search for hospitals that perform open-heart surgery in New York reveals a list of 11 hospitals. Each is rated according to the five-star ranksing system. A map and directions to each hospital also are available.

Choosing a hospital by clicking its name reveals additional details. You can find information describing the number of procedures performed annually, the state of its treatment facilities, and a performance comparison with national standards.

HealthGrades relies on data captured from other sources (such as Medicare records). It applies unique statistical models for each outcome (e.g., in-hospital deaths, major complications) and each patient cohort (e.g., coronary bypass surgery, total hip replacement–1st surgery) using logistic regression. Complete information on the grading methodologies for each category can be found on the Web site.

HealthGrades also provides reports to professional medical liability insurance underwriters for nursing homes, hospitals, and physicians that assist these companies in assessing risk and verifying background information.

### Questions for Discussion

1. What would determine whether you would use HealthGrades in selecting a physician or treatment facility for yourself, family, or friends?
2. What factors should you evaluate when considering the usefulness of HealthGrades' information?
3. What features besides grading and location information would you wish to see included in the HealthGrades site?

Does the fact that HealthGrades is found on the Internet influence your tendency to use or not use its services?

## 3  Part II: Google Searches Behind the Portal Scene

Google™
Portals may contract to use multiple search engines, each dedicated to different types of searches on the portal. For instance, general keyword searches may be powered by one search engine, while those handling *Yellow Page* searches (e.g., a search for all businesses supplying a certain type of product or service, say, apparel) may be powered by a different engine.

Search engines are often embedded within Web sites other than portals. For instance, you will find search engines within Web sites that sell books and music or that operate online auctions. The source of revenue for the search engines in these sites may not be a fixed fee or million-dollar contract, but rather a nominal charge for the users it refers to the site as a result of the search. For instance, a search engine company may charge a book company $.25 per click when a Web searcher jumps to its pages from the search engine. Charges ranging from $.05 to $.50 per referral are common.

Search engine providers are businesses just like the Web sites they serve. To stay in business, they too, must create revenue. Charges for the service are the means to that end.

### Questions for Discussion

1. How would users find information on the Internet if no search engines existed?
2. What factors do users value most when using a search engine to locate and retrieve information on the Internet?
3. If search engines imposed a small charge each time you conducted a Web search (e.g., $.50 per search), would you still use them to locate information?

## *Summary of Learning Objectives*

**1**  **Explain how individual computers and server computers interact on the Internet.**  A client computer—the computer on an individual's desktop—requests data and information from a server computer on the network. The requested data and information are transmitted to the client computer, where the recipient uses them as desired.

**2** **Describe the three types of capabilities of the Internet.** The Internet supports communication; retrieval; and shop, buy, and sell capabilities. Its communications capabilities allow the exchange of information between senders and receivers virtually anywhere in the world. Through the Internet's retrieval capabilities, individuals have access to data and information from other networks connected to the Internet. Use of the Internet for shopping, buying, and selling goods and services is often referred to as e-commerce.

**3** **Identify the 13 principal communication and retrieval capabilities of the Internet.** The Net's communications capabilities are e-mail, mailing lists, newsgroups, chat sessions, instant messages, Internet telephony, and Telnet. Its retrieval capabilities are FTP, Web directories, search engines, portals, webcasting, and streaming.

**4** **Summarize how the Internet knows the location of a particular user on the Net.** Everyone on the Internet has a unique address. That address consists of four components: a personal identification, a host computer identification, the name of the institution or organization, and the domain name. All Internet messages are routed to a location according to these address components.

**5** **Describe the use of pages on the World Wide Web.** Each WWW location consists of a series of pages or documents that contain text, graphics, images, and audio or video information. They may also contain links (called hyperlinks) to other pages. The home page is the main page at a specific location. All other pages are linked to the home page.

**6** **Explain the purpose of hyperlinks and their role on the World Wide Web.** Hyperlinks (or hypertext) are keywords that connect WWW locations. When a hyperlink is activated by clicking on the linked word, a jump to the connected location occurs without any need to use menus or other means to access the location. Pages containing hyperlinks are the most visible characteristic of the World Wide Web.

**7** **Describe the characteristics of browser software and relate them to the different types of information that can be included in a home page.** Browsers are client software programs that connect with servers on the Internet. Most WWW browsers are graphical, meaning they can display icons, graphics, and images. Individuals use the browser by clicking on hyperlinks or icons, or by entering addresses (URLs) on the Internet. The browser, in turn, makes the interconnection, transferring information from the network to the display screen of the client computer.

## *Key Terms*

application service provider (ASP)   99
channel   96
chat session/Internet relay chat (IRC)   91
client computer   87
client-server computing   87
component infrastructure providers   102
content   100
content providers   100
domain name   103
domain name system (DNS)   103
electronic commerce/e-commerce   97
e-mail/electronic mail   89
file transfer protocol (FTP)   94
graphical browser   112
home page   108
horizontal portal   96
hyperlinks   106

hypertext markup language (HTML)   109
instant messages   92
Internet/the Net   86
Internet Corp. for Assigned Names and Numbers (ICANN)   102
Internet Engineering Task Force (IETF)   102
Internet telephony/voice over the Internet/voice over IP   93
keyword   94
moderated   90
network infrastructure providers   102
newsgroups   91
netiquette   93
plug-ins   115
portal   92
pull   96
push   96

registrars   103
registry   103
root servers   103
search engine   94
server computer   87
service provider/Internet service provider (ISP)   99
streaming/streaming media   97
surf (surfing)   87
Telnet   94
uniform resource locator (URL)   104
Usenet/User's Network   91
vertical portal/vortal   95
Web browser   111
Web directory   94
webcasting   96
Web pages   106
World Wide Web (WWW)/the Web   106

## Review Questions

1. Was the Internet developed by public or private organizations? Who pays for the cost of operating the Internet today?
2. What is the significance of the name Internet?
3. Describe the characteristics of client and server computers. What is the relationship between client-server computing and the Internet?
4. What are host computers? How are host computers involved in the Internet?
5. Why are root servers important to the successful functioning of the Internet? How many root servers comprise the Internet?
6. How is an Internet address determined? Who assigns Internet addresses?
7. Describe the three types of activities possible on the Internet.
8. What are the characteristics of each of the communications capabilities of the Internet?
9. How are chat sessions and instant messages different?
10. Are Telnet and Internet telephony synonymous terms? Why or why not?
11. What is an FTP site and why would someone visit such a site on the Internet?
12. What benefits does streaming offer Internet users?
13. What five types of organizations comprise the Internet community? Briefly describe the characteristics of each organization type.
14. Why are ICANN and IETF important to the Internet?
15. Describe the purpose of a search engine. Who uses a search engine? What information must be provided before a search engine can work?
16. What is the difference between a search engine and a directory?
17. What is the most distinguishing characteristic of the World Wide Web?
18. When is HTML needed for the WWW? Who uses HTML?
19. How does a URL enable a Web user to find and retrieve information?
20. Describe the importance of pages for the World Wide Web. What contents are included in a page?
21. What is a home page? How is a home page created?
22. What role do plug-ins play in using the World Wide Web? With what software are they used?

## Discussion Questions

1. What characteristics of the Internet have made it so widely used globally?
2. Does anyone or any organization control the Internet?
3. What is your assessment of the domain naming system and the use of URLs on the Internet? Is the naming system easy to use or do you find it difficult to understand and apply on a day-to-day basis?
4. The Internet is in its infancy; it exploded onto the business scene relatively recently. Hence, companies are still learning how to capitalize on its features. What characteristics of the Internet do you feel are most important to business and why? Do you think every business, from the largest corporations to the smallest mom-and-pop stores should be Internet users? Why or why not?
5. Businesses have developed another use of the intranet to link selective business partners over the Internet. Access to these extranets is controlled in the same way as intranets so that only authorized companies can view company information. Develop three examples illustrating when a company might want to establish extranets to interconnect with outside companies.
6. What are examples of ways in which scientific organizations could use the Internet's FTP capability in conducting research? In what ways do you believe businesses could use the capability of FTP to service their customers? Do you think companies can deliver their products by means of FTP? Why or why not?

# Group Projects and Applications

## Project 1

Most regular Net users have a favorite search engine. Which one do you like best? To find out, perform the following activity with three or four members of your class.

Your goal is to answer one of the following questions:

- Which three companies in United States had the highest revenue last year? What are the three largest corporations in the world?
- In what year was the novel *Tom Jones* published? Who wrote it? Name two other English literary works also published that year.
- What area codes are used in metropolitan New York City and which counties use each of the codes?
- Which three New Jersey towns have the highest per capita income?
- In which museum is Edvard Munch's "The Scream" displayed? Which museum owns the largest collection of paintings by Grandma Moses?

Each member of your group should use a different search engine to find the answer to the question you have chosen. Some search engines to try:

- Alta Vista    www.altavista.com
- Google        www.google.com
- Go            www.go.com
- Infoseek      www.infoseek.com
- Yahoo!        www.yahoo.com

How long did each member of your group take to find the answer? Compare your answers with those of other groups. How do the various engines and directories differ? Are some more appropriate for particular types of research than for others? Report on the results of your searches to the class.

## Project 2

Subscribers to newsgroups often become members of a *virtual community* in which they exchange ideas and some-times develop friendships. Groups of four or five students should subscribe to and monitor the activities of a newsgroup for a period of two weeks. Choose any topic in which the group is interested, from the standard to the unexpected. At the end of two weeks, report to the class on the activities of your Usenet group. Is the group popular? What topics is it discussing? Have you begun to correspond with anyone?

## Project 3

Many companies have found it challenging to make money buying and selling products or services over the Internet. Setting up and maintaining a Web site can be expensive. Free sites, such as search directories, are often supported by advertising. However, advertisers may not be willing to advertise on the Net in the future unless they see a return on their investment.

Form a team and visit a local company that has a home page on the Internet. Interview someone in the information technology or advertising department about the company's Internet philosophy. Some questions you might ask:

- Who designed the company's site—a company employee or an outside expert?
- Who maintains the site? Who is in charge of answering any e-mail that comes through the site?
- Does the company advertise on the Web? If so, where? Who designed the advertisements? How much do the ads cost?
- How many *hits* does the company get on its ads? In other words, how many people see the ad each week or month? Has the company been able to make a direct connection between its sales revenue and its Internet ads?
- What are the company's plans for using the Internet in the future?

Prepare a two- to five-page written summary of the interview.

# Net_Work

## URLs Find Home

In this exercise, you will journey onto the Internet's World Wide Web, using the browser's rich capabilities. As you visit different Web sites, you will see dramatic differences between the ways each site's designer has chosen to display information.

To get started, sign onto the Internet. Click on the appropriate icon to activate the browser software. If you are using either the Netscape Navigator or Microsoft Explorer browsers, you will see one of these icons on your computer:

As soon as the browser is loaded and the Internet connection made, you will see a home page display. The address for the home page shown on the screen can be found on the browser's location line, near the top of the screen. Compare the address shown on the location line with the home page address—the URL—for your institution or service provider.

1. If your institution's home page URL is different, enter that URL in the location line (check your notes from the Net_Work application in Chapter 1, where you recorded the URL). Do this by clicking on the location line and keying the URL over the original URL. A new home page will appear on the screen. Move the vertical scroll bar on the right side of the page up or down to view the information clearly.

2. To see a different home page, enter the URL for Netscape Navigator: www.netscape.com. You can jump back and forth between the two home pages by clicking on the browser's *Back* or *Forward* button near the top of the display.

3. What are the differences between the home pages? Consider the size and style of the text information and note the use of color. What does the graphic image on Netscape's home page convey? Does the home page of your institution or service provider include graphics (perhaps a mascot, seal, or logo)?

4. What hyperlinks are embedded in each page? Hyperlinks are usually identifiable as text that is underlined or set off in a different color or as an icon.

5. Try the hyperlinks to see where they take you. Click on a hyperlink and you will jump to a new page. You may see hyperlinks on the new page as well. Click on another hyperlink to see where that takes you.

6. Now go back to your starting point, in one of two ways:

   a. Click, and the previous display will appear. Do this several times and you will see each of the preceding screens, until you come to your starting point.

   b. Click on the *house* icon, and the browser will jump directly to the home page.

7. Visit other interesting Web sites, checking their contents and their design. Which ones stand out in your mind and why? Which are the easiest to navigate? Which are most difficult? Which appear to have useful information? You might want to visit these sites:[3]

   **The U.S. Library of Congress**   lcweb.loc.gov
   **The Smithsonian**   www.si.edu
   **The White House**   whitehouse.gov
   **The U.S. Bureau of the Census**   www.census.gov
   **The Government of Canada**
   debra.dgbt.doc.ca:80/opengov/
   **The Government of Mexico**
   www.presidencia.gob.mx

8. For each site you visit, explore the hyperlinks. Behind each link you will find some interesting features. For example, you can send an e-mail message to the White House, view one of the Smithsonian's collections via its on-line images, test your knowledge of French as you explore information about Canada's legislative bodies, or get a glimpse of Mexico's rich heritage.

9. When you are finished, don't forget to sign off. Click on *File* on the menu bar. Then from the *File* menu, click *Exit*.

   The wide world of the Internet awaits your next sign-on!

[3]Web sites can be *busy* because of high use, in which case you might see an informative message displayed on your screen. Also, Web site operators may move their home page to a different URL, sometimes linking the old page to the new (when they do not, a message may state that the URL is no longer used).

# Cool Mobility

## On Assignment

Mark Goodman, *Cool Mobility's* human-resource officer, looks after the welfare of all employees at the company. Among the most important concerns are the areas of compensation and benefits (including vacation and sick days), health and safety, training and development, and recruitment. Goodman is enthusiastic about creation of the company's intranet.

Mr. Goodman wants to meet with you to learn your views on the company's Web site. Though his responsibilities require that he focus a great deal of attention on the employee intranet, he also is interested in the company's public site.

## In Consultation

Your discussion with Mr. Goodman includes his questions to you about the Internet and the intranet.

a. About the Internet site, Mr. Goodman wants to know the following:

1. What benefits does the company gain by having all visitors to its Internet site interact by means of a Web browser?

2. Since you have become familiar with *Cool Mobility's* home page, what is your assessment of the information it contains? Does it give visitors information about the features and functions they are likely to want to know about the site? Is any critical information missing?

3. Is the Web site easy to navigate for a first-time visitor seeking to go from page to page? Why or why not?

4. Are any plug-ins needed to take advantage of features on the home page?

b. Mr. Goodman is even more interested in your thoughts about ways the company could use its intranet to aid employees. He specifically asked about webcasting.

1. What are the potential benefits of webcasting in regard to the employee information and services available through our intranet? Could we improve our services on the intranet if we incorporated webcasting?

2. If webcasting is implemented, would the company have to acquire software to add that feature—or is the feature built into browser software? (You might want to conduct a search on the Internet if you need additional information to answer this question.)

# Case Study

## Do You Yahoo!?

**Yahoo**

Every day hordes of users turn to the Yahoo! Web site and search out information on the Internet. In fact, surveys show that Yahoo!'s zany name is the Internet's most widely recognized and valuable brand globally. It reaches some 250 million unique users in 25 countries and 13 languages. What is Yahoo!'s product? Pure information.

Yahoo! started in 1994 as a hobby for its creators, Jerry Yang and David Filo. Both were advanced graduate students at Stanford University, in the heart of California's Silicon Valley. Both were seeking a way to locate stuff on the obscure parts of the burgeoning Internet (as well as interesting ways to procrastinate while supposedly working on their dissertations). They began by compiling a list of every Internet site they visited, adding to the list each time a new site was located. Then they categorized them based on the information at the site. Related smaller categories were grouped into larger categories. Out of this grew the first navigational guide to the World Wide Web.

How does Yahoo! work today? First, the URLs of new Web sites are assembled. Most are received from individuals operating a Web site. If the operator

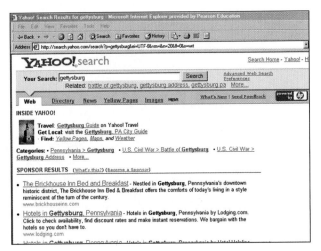

of a new site does not notify Yahoo! of its existence, it probably won't be listed. Rather than visiting Web sites manually, as the founders did, a spider does the work today. Spiders are simple software programs that crawl from link to link (the terms spider and crawler refer to the fact that they follow links on the Web). The spider enters the home page of a new Web site to read the text of the page, similar to the way a Web browser operates. Then, one of the many human classifiers at Yahoo! headquarters in San Jose, California looks over the Web site and determines how to categorize it. The site's URL is entered into directories for each relevant category. Today's directories span virtually any topic you can imagine and exceed many times over the number that could be maintained by hand.

If you have used a search engine, you know they operate based on the keyword or phrase you enter. Yahoo!'s software searches its directories and displays a set of sites with those keywords and phrases in the title and description.

Why have a Yahoo! at all? In a word, efficiency. The search engine organizes information about the contents of the site by topic. Storing data in directories reduces the search time by allowing large collections to be searched by many people simultaneously. Since the search engine orders sites by the relevance of their topic to the search term, users can locate and retrieve information much more efficiently than if they attempted to locate it themselves. They need only click on the Yahoo!-displayed link to the site, and the page displays on their browser.

From its earliest days, Yahoo! has relied on advertising to support itself. By selling valuable space on its pages to companies wishing to promote their products or services, it produces substantial revenue streams.

The founders quickly recognized that Yahoo! could be more than a check point on the way to someone else's Web site. They began to view the site as a full-fledged media site, with a potentially valuable brand name that could rival other media, including magazines, television, and radio.

Today Yahoo! is committed to enhancing the ability of people around the world to connect. It has augmented its original capability with a variety of new services, such as *Yahoo! Mail; Yahoo! Calendar; Yahoo! Chat; Yahoo! Clubs;* and *Yahoo! Photos.*

It also enables a wide variety of different commercial transactions, including *Yahoo! Shopping; Yahoo! Auctions; Yahoo! Finance;* and *Yahoo! Travel.* Yahoo! also works with many different partners to offer content and entertainment services in popular areas of interest such as *Yahoo! Sports; Yahoo! Music; Yahoo! Movies; Yahoo! News;* and *Yahoo! Games.*

*My Yahoo!* makes it personal by allowing users to customize the information appearing on the page they see when they visit Yahoo! You can choose to see only the news you want, track favorite stocks and sports teams, and automatically receive local weather forecasts.

Yahoo!'s overwhelming success is evident in the fact that it is

- The busiest portal, with more user time spent on Yahoo! than any other portal. (The average time spent is several hours per user each month. Average traffic, measured by number of pages viewed, exceeds 1.5 billion pages daily. At Yahoo! Japan, more than 200 million pages are viewed daily.)
- The number-one Internet network on corporate desktops, with more than a 70 percent reach in the U.S. workplace.
- The leading provider of Internet video and audio streaming solutions for corporate and consumer communications. It delivers thousands of live and on-demand corporate events, including product launches; financial briefings; and training and distance learning programs.
- The industry leader in online advertising, serving several thousand advertisers each month.

Recognizing that people everywhere are on the move, the ways of interacting with Yahoo! have been expanded. In addition to desktop PCs, its content and services can be obtained over wireless mobile phones, personal digital assistants, palm PCs, and two-way interactive pagers. As access to the Internet becomes possible through still other devices, you can be sure that Yahoo! will be there too. After all, its mission is to be the place to go to find anything, communicate with anyone, and buy anything. So, *do you* Yahoo!?

### Questions for Discussion

1. What factors account for the success of Yahoo!? Can its success be attributed to the fact that Yahoo! was the first of its kind to appear on the Internet?
2. Do you use Yahoo!? Why or why not?
3. Yahoo! went public in 1996 when it began trading shares in the company through the NASDAQ stock exchange. Why would investors buy stock in Yahoo? What factors would an investor use to assess the value of Yahoo!?
4. What other uses of Yahoo! are possible? What other ways might you expand Yahoo!'s use and value?
5. What are the greatest challenges facing Yahoo!?

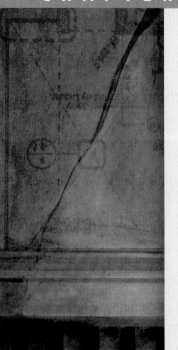

## LEARNING OBJECTIVES

When you have completed this chapter, you should be able to

1 Describe the components and purpose of the central processing unit (CPU).

2 Distinguish between primary storage (also called memory) and secondary storage (also called storage), and between RAM and ROM.

3 Describe the chips and boards that can be used to augment the CPU and main memory.

4 Explain the process by which computers use registers to process data.

5 List and explain the four determinants of processor speed.

6 Describe eight ways of increasing processing and computer speed.

# The Right Foundation for a Steinway Work of Art

STEINWAY & SONS

For more than 150 years, the name Steinway has been synonymous with the finest pianos. Works of art themselves, Steinway pianos are trusted by the world's leading pianists. In 1853, German immigrant Henry Engelhard Steinway founded Steinway & Sons in a Manhattan, New York, loft. Henry was a master cabinetmaker who built his first piano in the kitchen of his Seesen, Germany, home. By the time Henry established Steinway & Sons, he had already built 482 pianos. Over the next 40 years, Henry—and his sons, Henry Jr., Albert, C.F. Theodore, and Charles—developed and perfected the modern grand piano.

Today, you will not find information technology controlling the manufacture of Steinway grand pianos, for the art and tradition of handcrafting each Steinway continues. However, Steinway & Sons has chosen to use IT in one area where consistent precision improves the process of handcrafting the instrument.

Maintaining a constant climate in the factory is essential since more than 80 percent of a Steinway piano is wood. When the supplies of the spruce, rosewood, and maple used in making the Steinway arrive, they are air-dried for several weeks. Then the sheets of wood are placed in a computer-driven drying room, or kiln. Computer software and sensing devices continuously monitor and automatically adjust the temperature and humidity in the room until the moisture level in the wood reaches 6 percent, the level that craftspeople over the decades have found to be ideal. Thanks to the computer controls, craftspeople know the wood from the kiln will not splinter, peel, or warp during the stages that follow.

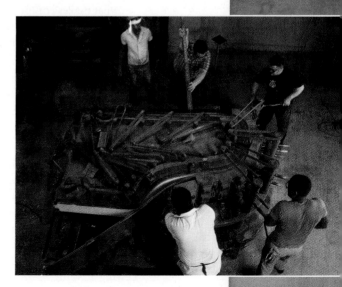

When the sheets reach the right moisture level, they are cut into sections measuring 6 inches wide and 8- to 10-feet long, to suit the various sizes of grand pianos. The sections are then moved to the part of the factory where the piano frames, or rims, are created. The signature shape of a grand piano rim is its straight left side that gives way to a rounded end (opposite the keyboard end) and a gracefully curving right side. Layers of wood are stacked and glued into a single form and carefully molded on a giant piano-shaped vise, called a rim-bending press, to create the elegant curves of the grand piano.

Once shaped, the rim is taken to a conditioning room where it sets for two months or more. Here, too, computer-controlled sensors monitor the temperature and humidity levels, continuously displaying the measurements on a supervisor's display screen. Any fluctuation in room conditions can be detected and adjusted quickly.

Steinway craftspeople find that they gain more precise results in cutting some of the wooden pieces with computer-controlled tools. Also, the programmability of the tools means that the cutting specifications can be changed rapidly to meet new requirements. In the factory's machining center, 10 computers control the machines (a fraction of the 85 machines that are used) that cut the wooden pieces that will later be fit into the piano.

After assembling the rest of the piano and the strings, and after applying the many coats of lacquer needed to produce the wood's rich finish, one step remains—tuning the strings. Although there are many digital tools for checking and adjusting the sound of each string, Steinways leaves this process to the ear of an expert. Every piano is *hand tuned* at least three times before it is ready for delivery.

So the next time you see a world-renowned pianist proudly seated at a Steinway grand piano, you'll have a little extra background information. You will know that the piano's creation began with getting the wood for the foundation just right, and that Steinway's use of information technology was key to enabling its experts to craft *their* work of art.

C hapter 2 explored the five components of a computer system: (1) hardware, (2) programs, (3) information, (4) people, and (5) procedures. By now, you have a sense of how these elements work together to help individuals and businesses perform more productively and effectively.

This chapter and the next will take a closer look at hardware components by building on what you learned in Chapter 2. We begin by taking a tour of the central processor to see what makes computers work. You will see how computers remember information and execute instructions, like those to sense and adjust the humidity in Steinway's kiln rooms. The final section of this chapter discusses how and why computers differ in processing speed. Chapter 5 concludes the discussion of hardware; it covers more on input and output devices and storage.

By the time you finish Chapter 4 and Chapter 5, you will have a working knowledge of how a computer functions–an important part of the know-how you will need to use information technology productively and effectively.

## The Central Processing Unit (CPU)

**central processing unit (CPU) or processor**
The computer hardware that executes program instructions and performs the computer's processing actions.

Recall from Chapter 1 that a computer is any electronic system that can be instructed to accept, process, store, and present data and information. At the heart of the computer's hardware are the software programs that extend the capabilities of your Internet browser, giving it added features. The **central processing unit (CPU)**, sometimes called the **processor**, executes program instructions and performs the computer's processing actions.

**integrated circuits/chip/microchip**
A collection of thousands or millions of transistors placed on a small silicon chip.

The CPU is a collection of electronic circuits made up of millions of transistors placed onto integrated circuits. **Integrated circuits** are also called **chips** or **microchips,** because the transistors are etched onto a small silicon chip. Each

**transistor** is an electronic switch that can be in one of two states: open or closed. (Numerically, a switch's closed state is described by the number 0, its open state by the number 1.)

Decreasing the size of transistors allows more transistors to be packed onto one chip. This process, called **integrating**, brought about the *PC revolution* in the 1980s and 1990s and is driving many of the advances in information technology today. Integrating makes it possible to place more of the CPU's components onto a single chip, thus eliminating the need for separate chips. Integrating greatly increases the speed of the computer.

Because processing is electronic, you cannot see what happens inside a processor. If you open the cover, you will not see moving parts, just as you do not see the electricity moving when you turn on the lights in a room.

Processors are designed and constructed in different ways. The processor for a PC is a single microprocessor chip. For larger systems, the processor consists of multiple circuit boards, each containing many chips. Figure 4.1 shows the two parts of the processor—the control unit and the arithmetic/logic unit.

The *Information Technology in Practice* feature, "*Moore's Law* Underlies IT's Evolution," describes one of the most important technical principles of IT. In fact, Gordon Moore's landmark observation continues to drive advances in computing some 35 years later.

## Control Unit

Computers *think* by using the on/off pulses of electric current. You might liken the **control unit**, the part of the CPU that oversees and controls all computer activities, to the human brain, which oversees and controls all of our actions, whether we are working, playing, or exercising.

All computer activities occur according to instructions the control unit receives. **Instructions** are detailed descriptions of the actions to be carried out during input, processing, output, storage, and transmission. A typical instruction might be to add two numbers together, to retrieve information for processing, or to print the results of processing. A wide range of instructions is embedded in such computer applications as retrieving the details of a specific transaction or transmitting data over a communications network.

The control unit does not actually execute the instructions, just as the brain does not actually do the working, playing, and exercising that make up many of our daily activities. Rather, it directs other processing elements to do so.

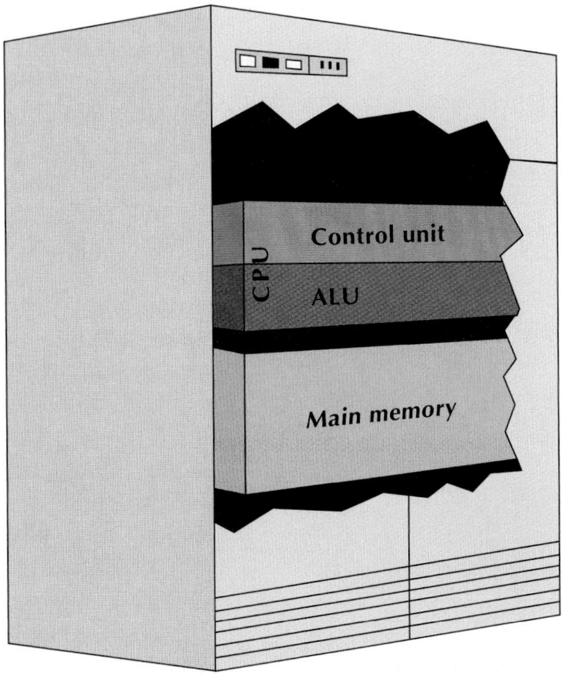

**transistor**
An electrical switch that can be in one of two states: open or closed.

**integrating**
The process of packing more transistors onto a single chip.

**control unit**
The part of the CPU that oversees and controls all computer activities according to the instructions it receives.

**instructions**
Detailed descriptions of the actions to be carried out during input, processing, output, storage, and transmission.

**FIGURE 4.1**

***The Components of the CPU***

In microcomputers, the control unit and the arithmetic/logic unit (ALU) are found together on a single microprocessor chip (see Figure 4.11). In larger systems, the control unit and ALU are usually found on separate boards. Note that main memory is not a part of the CPU.

# INFORMATION TECHNOLOGY IN PRACTICE

## Moore's Law—by Gordon Moore, *The Accidental Entrepreneur*—Underlies IT's Evolution

"The future of integrated electronics is the future of electronics itself. The advantages of integration will bring about a proliferation of electronics, pushing this science into many new areas.

Integrated circuits will lead to such wonders as home computers—or at least terminals connected to a central computer—automatic controls for automobiles, and personal portable communications equipment. The electronic wrist watch needs only a display to be feasible today."

So wrote Gordon Moore in *Electronics,* a little noticed magazine, in 1965. With these remarks, Moore (who later with Robert Noyce founded Intel Corp.), laid out the future of information technology—the future we are living today. His comments underlie the current characteristics of information technology, and they continue to suggest ways in which IT will evolve in the years ahead.

Moore's observations in the mid-1960s challenged conventional thinking. He believed, "With the unit cost falling as the number of components per circuit rises, by 1975 economics may dictate squeezing as many as 65,000 components on a single silicon chip." Even though the article's accompanying charts graphically illustrated how the path of chip integration would occur (see accompanying charts), these projections were unbelievable at the time. The press coined these forecasts, *Moore's Law.*

In 1965, few people—even those at the large computer manufacturing companies of the time like Control Data, General Electric, Honeywell, IBM, and Sperry Rand—thought about PCs or embedding chips in automobiles and appliances. The big manufacturers felt certain that the future was in bigger computers; that is where they focused their research and development teams. Today, with the exception of IBM, those large computer manufacturers are no longer in business.

Moore's Law is as important today as it was in 1965. The current wording of the law is as follows: "The number of transistors (and therefore the processing power) of chips will double every 18 months." This "law" describes the present state of technology and is viewed as the mission of the technology development teams at Intel and other high-tech manufacturers. The developers at these corporations seek to break down

the barriers of size, heat, and chip density that threaten to halt the advancement and development of the industry.

More than four decades later, Moore remains modest about his tremendous vision and the accomplishments he led at Intel. He frequently refers to himself as an accidental entrepreneur, as he did in an interview for *Forbes Magazine:* "The accidental entrepreneur like me has to fall into the opportunity or be pushed into it . . . Things have to line up right. Then the entrepreneurial spirit eventually catches on," he said. "We had no idea at all that we had turned the first stone on something that was going to be a $100 billion business."

Perhaps Moore *didn't* realize what he had started, but there is little doubt that it was his vision and insights that caused the *accident.* The technology industry and people the world over owe a great deal to Gordon Moore, *The Accidental Entrepreneur.*

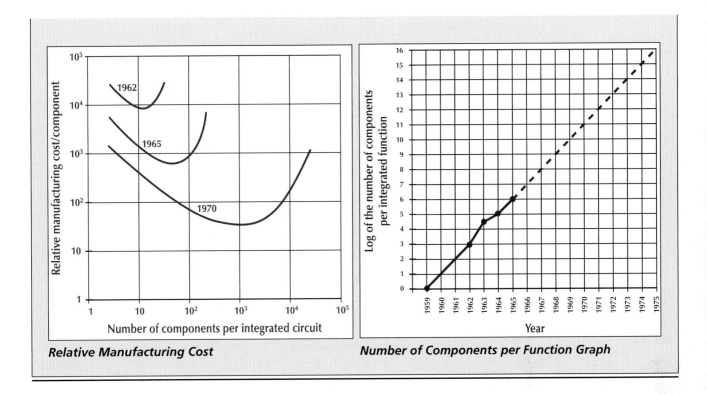

**Relative Manufacturing Cost**

**Number of Components per Function Graph**

## Arithmetic/Logic Unit (ALU)

The other component of the central processor is the **arithmetic/logic unit (ALU).** The ALU contains the electronic circuitry that performs arithmetic operations and logical operations, the two activities that underlie all computing capabilities.

*Arithmetic operations* include addition, subtraction, multiplication, and division. When a university's computer tallies the number of credit hours in a student's schedule or transcript, it is doing arithmetic. So is the post office's computer system when it sorts letters by the postal code in an address.

*Logical operations* compare one element of information to another. The comparison determines whether one item is greater than, less than, or equal to the other. The outcome of a logical comparison usually determines what type of processing occurs:

- **Greater Than (>)** The ALU compares two values to determine if one is greater than the other. For example, if the number of reservations for a specific flight on an airplane is greater than the number of seats on the plane, the computer will show that the flight is oversold. Actions can then be taken to ensure that all passengers reach their destination—perhaps another flight will be scheduled or passengers will be assisted in making reservations at another airline.
- **Less Than (<)** The ALU compares two values to determine if one is less than the other. For example, if the number of students registered for a class is smaller than the number of seats in the auditorium where the class is to be held, then the class is still open for registration.
- **Equal To (=)** The ALU compares two values to determine if they are equal or not. For example, if the amount of money submitted to a utility company for payment is equal to the amount of money owed, the computer will change the amount owed to show a zero balance.

Arithmetic and logical comparisons are possible because of computers' memory capability. But what exactly is memory?

**arithmetic/logic unit (ALU)**
The part of the CPU that performs arithmetic and logical operations.

# Memory

When the electronic calculator was introduced in the 1930s, it was viewed as a breakthrough because of its memory capability. Earlier mechanical calculators did not have the capacity to store data and information, but electronic calculators did—and so do their descendants, the various kinds of computers. This memory, which is composed of computer chips, can be used repeatedly by different applications.

The CPU interacts closely with memory, referring to it both for instructions and for data or information. However, memory is separate from the CPU.

As Figure 4.2 shows, memory space in a computer is used in five different ways:

1. To hold the computer's operating system program (e.g., Windows, DOS, UNIX, Linux, VM)—the software that oversees processing and acts as an interface between the hardware and the applications programs.
2. To hold application programs—word processing, spreadsheet, order entry, and inventory control programs.
3. To hold data and information temporarily (in *virtual memory)*, receiving from input devices data or information that is processed and sent to output devices during processing.
4. To store other data or information needed in processing in the working storage area.
5. To provide additional space as needed for programs or data. (If the computer has more memory than is needed for a particular application, the excess memory will go unused but remain available. Since the amount of memory needed may change during the processing of an application, it is useful to have excess memory.)

Now we need to distinguish between primary storage and secondary storage. **Primary storage**—also known as **primary memory**, **main memory**, **internal memory**, or simply **memory**—is storage within the computer itself. It holds data only temporarily, as the computer executes instructions. **Secondary storage** is memory that augments the primary memory. It is used to store data long-term. Typically, only a portion of the data in use resides in primary memory during processing. The remainder is kept in secondary storage until needed.

## Memory Size

Computers vary widely in the amount of primary memory they have. The size of this internal memory is measured by the number of storage locations it contains. Each storage location, or **byte**, has a predetermined capacity. In simplest terms, a byte is the amount of memory required to store one digit, letter, or character.

---

**primary storage/primary memory/main memory/internal memory**
Storage within the computer itself. Primary memory holds data only temporarily, as the computer executes instructions.

**memory**
Any device that can store data in a machine-readable format.

**secondary storage**
A storage medium that is external to the computer, but that can be read by the computer; a way of storing data and information outside the computer itself.

**byte**
A storage location in memory; the amount of memory required to store one digit, letter, or character.

---

**FIGURE 4.2**

***Primary Memory Allocation***

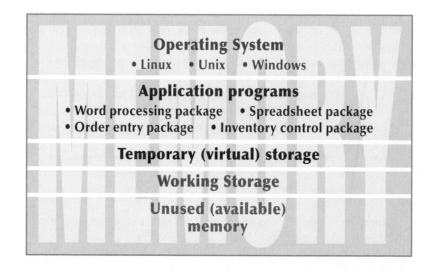

Operating System
• Linux   • Unix   • Windows

Application programs
• Word processing package   • Spreadsheet package
• Order entry package   • Inventory control package

Temporary (virtual) storage

Working Storage

Unused (available) memory

Bytes are generally measured by the **kilobyte** (also written **K-byte, KB,** or **K**)–which is 1,000 bytes;[1] **megabyte** (**M-byte, MB,** or **meg**)–1 million bytes; **gigabyte** (**G-byte, GB,** or **gig**)–1 billion bytes; and **terabyte** (**T-byte** or **TB**)–1 trillion bytes. Thus, a computer with *512 meg* has 512 million bytes of memory.

Personal computers have memory capacities in the megabyte range. For example, most desktop PCs have a main memory capacity of 128 megabytes to 1 gigabyte. Memory capacities for midrange, mainframe, and supercomputers are substantially higher.

Each byte is identified by a memory **address** that allows the computer to determine where an element of data or information is stored. (In some cases, a group of bytes may have an address.) As Figure 4.3 shows, memory addresses are similar in principle to the addresses of a house or building–they distinguish one location from another and make each one easy to find.

Figure 4.4 shows precisely how data are represented electrically using bits and bytes.

## RAM and ROM

Two types of main memory are *random-access memory* and *read-only memory*, with two variations on each type.

**RAM**   Main memory, the largest area of memory within the computer, is composed of **random-access memory**, or **RAM**, chips. *Random access* means that data or information can be written into or recalled (read) from any memory address at any time. With RAM, there is no need to start at the first location and proceed one step at a time. Information can be written to or read from RAM in less than 100 billionths of a second. However, RAM stores data and information only as long as the computer is turned on. The electrical currents that comprise the data and information cease when the power is turned off.

**kilobyte/K-byte/KB/K**
One thousand bytes.

**megabyte/M-byte/MB/meg**
One million bytes.

**gigabyte/G-byte/GB/gig**
One billion bytes.

**terabyte/T-byte/TB**
One trillion bytes.

**address**
An identifiable location in memory where data are kept.

**random-access memory (RAM)**
Memory that permits data or information to be written into or read from memory only as long as the computer is turned on.

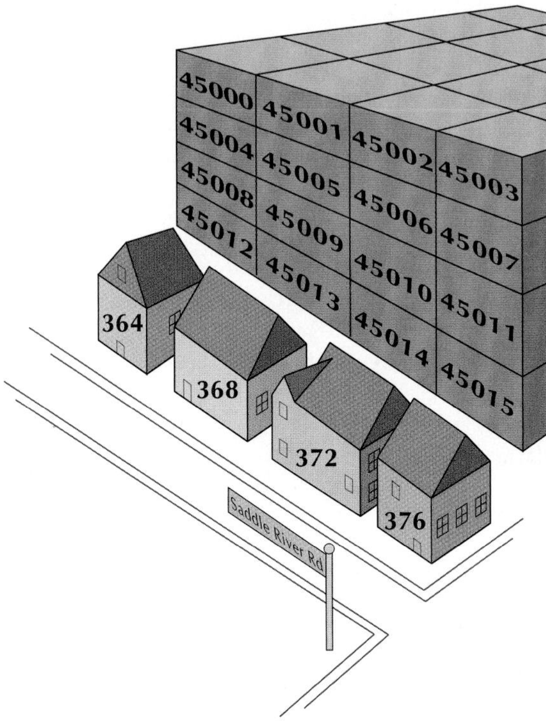

**FIGURE 4.3**

*Addresses in Computer Memory*

In main memory, bytes are identified by a memory address that allows the computer to determine where an element of data or information is stored.

---

[1]Although users of information technology generally equate K with 1,000, doing so is not strictly accurate. A kilobyte of memory is actually 1,024 bytes. If you hear someone referring to 640K of storage, the component actually has 655,360 (calculated as 640 × 1024) memory locations. Reference to 512 megabytes means the memory actually has 524,288,000 memory locations (i.e., 512,000K × 1024).

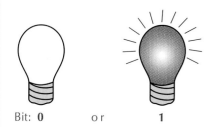

Bit: **0**     o r     **1**

a) Computers use bits and bytes to process and store data. Because they run on electricity, computers know only two things: on and off. This two-state system is called a **binary system.** Using single digits called **bits** (short for *bi*nary dig*its*), the computer can represent any piece of data. The binary system uses only two digits, 0 and 1. The 0 corresponds to the "off" state, the 1 to the "on" state.

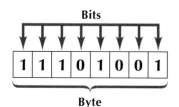

**Bits**

| 1 | 1 | 1 | 0 | 1 | 0 | 0 | 1 |

**Byte**

b) Single bits can't store all the numbers and characters that need to be processed and stored. For this reason, seven or eight bits are usually grouped together into bytes. Each byte generally represents one character.

When a character is entered through the keyboard, the processor accepts the character into main memory and translates it into coded form. It simultaneously shows the character on the display screen.

| Character | EBCDIC | ASCII |
|---|---|---|
| A | 1100 0001 | 100 0001 |
| B | 1100 0010 | 100 0010 |
| C | 1100 0011 | 100 0011 |
| D | 1100 0100 | 100 0100 |
| E | 1100 0101 | 100 0101 |
| F | 1100 0110 | 100 0110 |
| G | 1100 0111 | 100 0111 |
| H | 1100 1000 | 100 1000 |
| I | 1100 1001 | 100 1001 |
| J | 1101 0001 | 100 1010 |
| K | 1101 0010 | 100 1011 |
| L | 1101 0011 | 100 1100 |
| M | 1101 0100 | 100 1101 |
| N | 1101 0101 | 100 1110 |
| O | 1101 0110 | 100 1111 |
| P | 1101 0111 | 101 0000 |
| Q | 1101 1000 | 101 0001 |
| R | 1101 1001 | 101 0010 |
| S | 1110 0010 | 101 0011 |
| T | 1110 0011 | 101 0100 |

| Character | EBCDIC | ASCII |
|---|---|---|
| U | 1110 0100 | 101 0101 |
| V | 1110 0101 | 101 0110 |
| W | 1110 0110 | 101 0111 |
| X | 1110 0111 | 101 1000 |
| Y | 1110 1000 | 101 1001 |
| Z | 1110 1001 | 101 1010 |
| 0 | 1111 0000 | 011 0000 |
| 1 | 1111 0001 | 011 0001 |
| 2 | 1111 0010 | 011 0010 |
| 3 | 1111 0011 | 011 0011 |
| 4 | 1111 0100 | 011 0100 |
| 5 | 1111 0101 | 011 0101 |
| 6 | 1111 0110 | 011 0110 |
| 7 | 1111 0111 | 011 0111 |
| 8 | 1111 1000 | 011 1000 |
| 9 | 1111 1001 | 011 1001 |
| ! | 0101 0010 | 010 0001 |
| $ | 0101 1011 | 010 0100 |
| & | 0101 0000 | 010 0110 |

c) Two standard systems for representing data have been developed. **EBCDIC** (pronounced "eb-see-dick"), short for Extended Binary Coded Decimal Interchange Code, uses eight-bit bytes to represent a character. In EBCDIC, the capital letter S is represented by 11100010. **ASCII** (pronounced "ass-key"), short for American Standard Code for Information Interchange, uses seven-bit bytes to represent a character. In ASCII, the capital letter S is represented by 1010011. All characters—including upper- and lower-case letters—have a unique code in each system. EBCDIC is generally used in mainframes, ASCII in microcomputers.

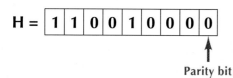

H =  | 1 | 1 | 0 | 0 | 1 | 0 | 0 | 0 | 0 |

**Parity bit**

d) A special bit called a **parity bit** is sometimes used to detect errors in the transmission of data. If a bit is lost during transmission, the total number of bits will be wrong, and the computer will be alerted that there is something wrong with a particular byte.

| Decimal | Binary | Hexadecimal |
|---|---|---|
| 0 | 0000 | 0 |
| 1 | 0001 | 1 |
| 2 | 0010 | 2 |
| 3 | 0011 | 3 |
| 4 | 0100 | 4 |
| 5 | 0101 | 5 |
| 6 | 0110 | 6 |
| 7 | 0111 | 7 |
| 8 | 1000 | 8 |
| 9 | 1001 | 9 |
| 10 | 1010 | A |
| 11 | 1011 | B |
| 12 | 1100 | C |
| 13 | 1101 | D |
| 14 | 1110 | E |
| 15 | 1111 | F |

e) Sometimes computer professionals find it easier to convert binary values to another number system, the **hexadecimal number system.** This system uses the digits 1–9 and the letters A–F. One hexadecimal digit is the equivalent of four bits. For example, hexadecimal B, which represents the number 11, may be easier to deal with than the binary number 1011, which also represents the number 11.

**FIGURE 4.4**

*Bits, Bytes, and Number Systems*

Two types of RAM are widely used. *Dynamic RAM (DRAM)* is the major memory component in virtually every computer. DRAM chips hold data and information dynamically. This means that the computer does not hold data and information indefinitely. Rather, it must continually refresh the DRAM cell electronically–several hundred times per second. In contrast, *static RAM (SRAM)* chips retain their contents indefinitely, without constant electronic refreshment. They are faster than DRAM, but are not as compact, and they use a more complicated design.

RAM chip technology is changing rapidly, both in capacity and packaging. RAM chips are available in 32M, 64M, 128M, and 256M. Larger versions–1G and beyond– will become popular in the future.

**ROM**   Like RAM, **read-only memory**, or **ROM**, offers random access to a memory location. However, ROM chips hold data and information even after the electrical current to the computer is turned off. Unlike the contents of a RAM chip, the contents of a standard ROM chip cannot be changed. Whatever is inserted into a location in a ROM chip when it is manufactured cannot be altered.

Typically, the start-up programs that run automatically when computers are first turned on are written into ROM. Since these programs–which load the computer's operating system and perform housekeeping checks, like ensuring that a keyboard is attached or that memory is functioning–are written into ROM, the instructions can be read again and again, but cannot be changed.

There are several variations on ROM. *Programmable read-only memory (PROM)* chips, first developed as a tool for testing a new ROM design before putting it into mass production, can be modified from their manufactured state, but only once. These modifications are not reversible. Data or information in *erasable programmable read-only memory (EPROM)* chips can be erased by bathing the chip in ultraviolet light, a process that dissipates the electric charges that created the original data or information values. *Electrically erasable programmable read-only memory (EEPROM)* chips are reprogrammed by electronically reversing the voltage used to create the data or information (rather than by using ultraviolet light).

Figure 4.5 summarizes the different types of memory chips.

**read-only memory (ROM)**
A type of storage that offers random access to memory and can hold data and information after the electric current to the computer has been turned off.

**FIGURE 4.5**

**Types of Memory Chips**

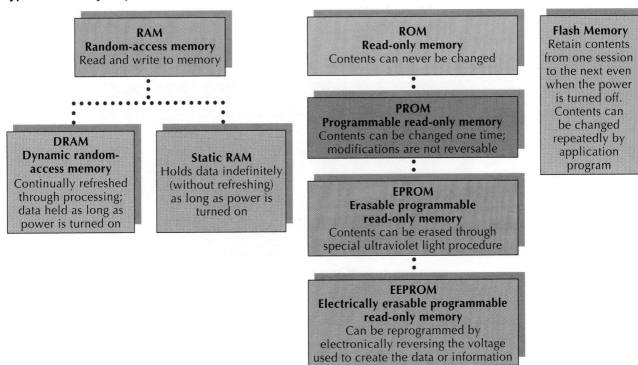

You will not see EPROM or EEPROM chips in business applications like spreadsheets or course registration systems. Generally, they are used only by engineers and designers who develop devices that contain embedded computers. When Hewlett-Packard develops a laser printer, for instance, its designers write the codes that control the printer's functions, paper-handling features, and type styles into EPROM or EEPROM. Using these special forms of ROM, they can rewrite the code without having to remanufacture the chip. When the design is complete and the printer goes into mass production, the EPROM or EEPROM is replaced with a ROM chip containing the final instructions.

The *Information Technology in Practice* feature, "Speedpass Turns Chips into Good Business Strategy," illustrates how Mobil Oil's keen insights into the capabilities emanating from advances in chip technology are producing valuable advantages for both consumers and dealers of energy giant Exxon Mobil.

## Flash Memory

**flash memory**
Memory that retains its contents even when electricity is turned off.

**Flash memory** is a type of EEPROM chip that is used more as a storage device than as RAM. It is solid-state memory (no moving parts), provides rapid storage and retrieval of data, and is small in size. It retains its contents even after the electrical power is turned off. Unlike with RAM, data and information stored in flash memory when the computer is on can be saved from one session of computer use to the next. Unlike with ROM, data and information held in flash memory can be erased and new details written in place by the application program.

Because of its flexibility in storing and changing all types of data and information, flash memory is commonly the technology for the *removable* memory sticks or memory cards used in digital cameras and game machines, or in PCMCIA memory (sometimes called solid state disks) for laptop computers (Figure 4.6)

Because it is more expensive than conventional hard disk storage (discussed in Chapter 5), computer and electronics designers select flash memory only for special purpose uses.

## PCMCIA Card Memory

**PCMCIA card/PC card**
A card designed to expand a computer's memory.

The Personal Computer Memory Card International Association (PCMCIA) was established in 1989 to formulate standards for the manufacture of memory cards for personal computers. The first cards manufactured according to the standards were designed to expand the memory of personal computers. Known originally as **PCMCIA cards,** and now as **PC cards**, these memory units are 2 by 3 inches (5 by 8 cm) in size and several millimeters thick. Since they are about the size of a credit card, they are also called *credit card memory.*

**FIGURE 4.6**

*Flash Memory, Used in a Variety of Computers and Electronic Devices, Is Available in Many Sizes and Shapes*

# INFORMATION TECHNOLOGY IN PRACTICE

## Speedpass Turns Chips into Good Business Strategy

**Speedpass** Speedpass is a valuable business-building tool at Exxon and Mobil service stations. Introduced in a market test by Mobil Oil Corp. in 1996 (Exxon and Mobile merged in 1999), the Speedpass payment system enables customers to buy gas quickly without the hassle of either going inside the station to pay for gas or having to fool with credit cards or PIN numbers at the pump. Best of all, it costs the customer nothing to have or to use a Speedpass device.

Speedpass uses an electronic reader located in the pump or register that *talks* with a device (a transponder) that can hang on your keychain, be affixed in your car, or even inserted in a watch. You simply drive into the station, and if you have a car tag transponder, when you come within 5 feet of the gas pump, the reader talks to the transponder, and the pump readies to fill your tank. If you have a key tag transponder or a Speedpass-enabled Timex™ watch, you simply wave your device in front of the

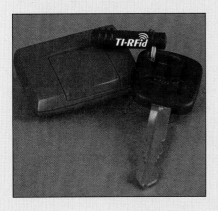

pump reader, and again, the reader talks to the transponder, and the pump readies to fill your tank. The Speedpass system knows who you are and how to charge your purchase. You still have to get out of your car and put the nozzle in your tank, but the rest is automatic. A receipt will print for you if that is your preference, and you do not even need to sign for the purchase.

The transponder, which is in the shape of a cylinder, is about an inch and a half in length and is about 3/8 of an inch wide, and contains a plastic-coated chip that stores a unique identification and security code. No customer personal or financial information is stored in the Speedpass device. Speedpass operates on a radio frequency that transmits this identification and security code. Your Speedpass device automatically—and immediately—communicates your payment preferences. Speedpass knows what credit or check card you wish to use, and even knows whether or not you want a receipt.

Mobil's intent was to make it easier for customers to purchase gas at its stations, and customers have found that with Speedpass it has. More than 1 million customers signed up for Speedpass shortly after the product was introduced, and another 5 to 6 million joined in the next few years. Speedpass also has international appeal. The system was an overnight success when introduced to Mobil customers in Singapore.

Mobil also finds that its Speedpass customers make more repeat visits to its stations each month than those who do not have Speedpass. Perhaps this is why some 8,200 Exxon and Mobil stations in the United States alone have signed on to offer the Speedpass technology, with more stations signing on every week.

The largely untapped potential for Speedpass is huge. In the Northeastern part of the United States, Speedpass is used in conjunction with highway toll roads, speeding the flow of traffic through tollbooths. In the Midwest, McDonald's Corp. uses Speedpass in many of its restaurants. Think of the other possibilities. It is easy to imagine other businesses such as convenience stores, hotels, and theaters accepting this form of payment. Here too, Speedpass could store customer preferences and purchase patterns. Underlying this clever technology is a basic principle: When you eliminate hassles and delays for your customer, you increase business.

When you turn on your computer, a power-on self-test brings all components to life. ROM chips are a key component of this test.

When the electrical (or battery) power to a computer, large or small, is turned on, the first thing the computer does is check itself to ensure that its components are connected and in working order. To **boot** the system thus means to turn on the power and let the built-in self-test run. Booting the system also activates the system's components to load the operating system into memory, ready for use. (The expression *booting* comes from the old adage "to pull oneself up by the bootstraps," which means "to take the initiative.")

The location of the beginning of the boot program is stored permanently in a set of ROM chips that contain the computer's basic input/output system **(BIOS).**[2] Thus, in a **cold boot (**meaning that the system is being turned on and started from an *off* state), the CPU invokes the ROM BIOS boot program, which in turn, runs the power-up self-tests and loads the operating system from disk storage. In a restart, or a **warm boot,** the BIOS knows the system is already running (data is written in a specific memory location checked by the BIOS) and skips the power-on test. ■

[2]In some computers, it may be possible to upgrade the BIOS of a computer. This is often advisable on older computers so that it can be made to handle new devices or use new standards. To change the BIOS, a special program supplied by the computer or BIOS manufacturer is needed.

**boot**

To turn on the computer system and let the built-in self-test run.

**cold boot**

The system is turned on and started from an *off* state). The CPU invokes the ROM BIOS boot program, which in turn, runs the power-up self-tests and loads the operating system from disk storage.

**warm boot**

In a restart, the BIOS knows the system is already running (data is written in a specific memory location checked by the BIOS) and skips the power-on test.

**FIGURE 4.7**

*PCMCIA Card Slots Expand the Communications Capabilities of Laptop Computers*

**board**

A hardware device onto which chips and their related circuitry are placed.

**system unit**

The hardware unit that houses a computer's processor, memory chips, ports, and add-in boards.

**system board/mother board**

The system unit in a microcomputer, located on a board mounted on the bottom of a computer base.

PCMCIA cards use flash memory, which is faster, more power-efficient, and more shock-resistant than either hard disk or diskette storage. Because of these features, PCMCIA memory cards, designed initially for use in laptop and notebook drives, are being used in desktop systems as well.

Ever since the introduction of portable laptop and notebook computers, developers have sought to expand the capabilities of these computers without adding size, weight, or devices that consume excessive power. They have also sought a means to allow customization of portable computers. To customize a desktop computer, users can add a card or adapter board. This is not possible with laptop and notebook computers because they have neither cases that can be opened nor expansion slots inside.

Slots for PCMCIA cards (Figure 4.6) have become the means for expanding the capabilities of laptops and notebooks. Already a wide variety of credit card adapters are available. By inserting the appropriate PCMCIA card, users can add to a laptop or notebook computer an external disk drive, CD-ROM, fax/modem, network interface, speakers, and cellular telephone (Figure 4.7)–the list of options becomes more extensive all the time. Thus PCMCIA cards have made it possible for people to personalize their laptop and notebook computers.

The *Information Technology in Practice* feature, "Silicon Valley's Computer Recycling Center™–A Pioneer in Environmental Protection," discusses the challenges and opportunities created when the many advances in IT lead consumers and companies to replace their computers with newer and faster systems.

## Inside the System Unit

Both the CPU and memory units can be augmented by combinations of chips and boards. A **board** is a hardware device onto which chips and their related circuitry are placed. To show you how the hardware components fit together, Figure 4.8 takes you under the hood of a PC.

In all computers, the processor is housed inside a hardware unit called the **system unit.** On mainframe or midrange systems, the system unit is typically a cabinet filled with circuit boards (Figure 4.9). On microcomputers, a single **system board** (also known as a **mother board**) is mounted on the bottom of the computer case and attached to an electrical power supply that generates the current needed to operate the computer. The system

**FIGURE 4.8**

***Under the Hood of a Personal Computer***

Inside this IBM personal computer are a disk drive, circuit board (with a microprocessor chip), and power supply. The display terminal, keyboard, and printer are all attached by plug-in cables.

board of a PC contains a processor chip, memory chips, ports, and add-in boards, in addition to the circuitry that interconnects all of these components (Figure 4.10). System units in larger computers can also contain all of these elements.

## Processor Chips

The **microprocessor** is, in essence, a *computer on a chip*–all the processing capabilities of the control unit and ALU reside on a single computer chip. The microprocessor is the smallest type of processor. It is sealed in a protective package and connected to a system board with pins (Figure 4.11 on page 140). Microprocessors gave rise to microcomputers, which use microprocessors for their CPU.[3]

**microprocessor**

The smallest type of processor, with all of the processing capabilities of the control unit and ALU located on a single chip.

**FIGURE 4.9**

***IBM s/390 Mainframe e-Server Enterprise Computer***

[3]The terms *microcomputer* and *personal computer* are often used interchangeably. *Microcomputer* is the accurate technical term. *Personal computer* refers to the way microcomputers are used.

# INFORMATION TECHNOLOGY IN PRACTICE

## Silicon Valley's Computer Recycling Center™— A Pioneer in Environmental Protection

The rapid evolution of computers has meant continuous sales for manufacturers as consumers buy new computers to replace those that have become outdated or are less than state-of-the-art. But this rapid evolution has also raised questions about what to do with the old computer systems. On the average, companies replace computers every three years. Each year the number of computers being replaced grows, so much so that the National Recycling Coalition (www.nrc-recycle.org) estimates that by 2007 some 500 million personal computers will have become obsolete. (That is approximately two PCs for every person in the United States.)

What should be done with old computers? Some can be reused and are passed along to schools and community organizations, where they are either disassembled and refurbished or put to use *as is*.

But often computers removed from use are obsolete or damaged beyond repair. What happens to these? Incinerating or discarding used computer equipment in landfills is not a good alternative. Computer equipment contains components that are toxic to the environment if not discarded properly. The glass in the cathode-ray tube used in computer monitors contains lead, which is highly toxic when buried in landfills. Multiply the 4-to-6 pounds of lead in each monitor by the number discarded annually, and the problem is quite large. Add to that the circuit boards and other computer components containing materials (such as copper chromium, gold, lead nickel, zinc, cadmium, steel, and plastic) that should not be carelessly discarded, and the challenge is monumental.

The answer is computer recycling. In 1991, the Computer Recycling Center™ (www.crc.org) was founded in California's high-tech Silicon Valley, just south of the San Francisco bay area. In 1992, with the help of a grant from the David and Lucille Packard Foundation (started by one of the founders of Hewlett-Packard Corp.), the Computer Recycling Center™ became a full-time center for collection, reuse, refurbishment, and recycling of computer components. Reuse of entire units is given highest

priority, followed by disassembly for reuse of parts, and finally recycling of the unusable parts (a significant percentage of which is incorporated into newly manufactured components). The innovative efforts of the Computer Recycling Center™ have triggered a growing network of reuse and recycling organizations.

Strategies to stimulate recycling are necessary, as computer recycling takes some effort. First, a center must be established. Next, the cost associated with getting the computer equipment transported to the center must be addressed. To deal with these and other issues, companies have established in-house recycling programs. For instance, Hewlett-Packard recycles more than 3-million pounds of electronic equipment *every month*. Computer manufacturers have also launched programs to encourage their customers to recycle their computers at the end of their useful life. Such well-known companies as IBM and Sony underwrite the cost of transporting used equipment to recycling centers. Concerned manufacturers have also redesigned components to make them easier to recycle.

These programs are voluntary; there are no laws in the United States mandating recycling. Laws will not be necessary, if companies and individuals act responsibly.

Silicon Valley's Computer Recycling Center™ pioneered computer recycling. Other organizations that offer or support recycling services include the following:

Electronic Industries Alliance
www.eia.org
Global Recycling Network
www.grn.org
Grassroots Recycling Network
www.grrn.org

Many state departments of environmental quality also have computer and electronics recycling programs.

**Intel and Motorola Microprocessors**   The most popular processor chips (Table 4.1) are manufactured by Intel, for Windows computers, for example. These chips have evolved over time, with each new chip gaining more capability and greater speed than its predecessor.

Programs are written to work with a specific microprocessor chip. Thus, the software packages written for Apple computers, which used Motorola chips until the mid 1990s and then PowerPC chips (discussed in the next section), cannot be used with computers that use Intel chips, without making substantial changes (see Table 4.2). However, software developers, ever mindful of people's desire to use the same software on both types of computers, are finding ways to develop software that will run on more than one family of chips.

Intel has also developed other microprocessor lines to support the varying computing requirements of companies and consumers. They include:

- **Intel Celeron processors**   Created for the lower-cost, economical PC market
- **Intel Pentium-M processors**   Intended for use in mobile systems, such as laptop computers
- **Intel Celeron-M processors**   For use in mobile systems in the lower-cost, economical laptop computing segment

**REALITY CHECK**   PCMCIA cards can instantly change a laptop computer's personality. For instance, if you want to connect your laptop PC to a network, you merely insert a PCMCIA card that provides a connection to a local area network.

If you later decide to run a multimedia application that requires both extra memory and a CD-ROM/DVD unit, you can change your notebook's personality again. Pull out the network card (it slips right out) and push a PCMCIA memory card into one slot and a CD-ROM/DVD interface card into a second slot. (Most laptops have at least two PCMCIA slots.)

PCMCIA cards allow people to continually change the features of their laptop computers without using any tools at all—not even a screwdriver. ■

FIGURE 4.10

*Intel System Board and Pentium IV Microprocessor Chip*

FIGURE 4.11

*Widely Used Microprocessors*

**Table 4.1 Evolution of Intel Pentium Family of Microprocessors**

| NAME | DATE INTRODUCED | TRANSISTORS | CLOCK SPEED UPON INTRODUCTION | DATA WIDTH | MIPS |
|---|---|---|---|---|---|
| 8080 | 1974 | 6,000 | 2 MHz | 8 bits | 0.64 |
| 8088 | 1979 | 29,000 | 5 MHz | 16 bits, 8-bit bus | 0.33 |
| 80286 | 1982 | 134,000 | 6 MHz | 16 bits | 1 |
| 80386 | 1985 | 275,000 | 16 MHz | 32 bits | 5 |
| 80486 | 1989 | 1,200,000 | 25 MHz | 32 bits | 20 |
| Pentium | 1993 | 3,100,000 | 60 MHz | 32 bits, 64-bit bus | 100 |
| Pentium II | 1997 | 7,500,000 | 233 MHz | 32 bits, 64-bit bus | NA |
| Pentium III | 1999 | 9,500,000 | 450 MHz | 32 bits, 64-bit bus | NA |
| Pentium 4 | 2000 | 42,000,000 | 1.5 GHz | 32 bits, 64-bit bus | NA |

- **Intel Xeon processors**   Designed for workstations and servers
- **Intel Itanium processors**   Designed for workstations and servers (employs parallel-computing technology and large memory-addressing capability)

**PowerPC Microprocessor**   The diversity of microprocessors has arisen for two reasons: (1) the objective of some manufacturers to achieve power and speed for a specific set of applications; and (2) the goal of some manufacturers to create a business advantage by carving out their own niche in the marketplace.

People using information technology, however, want to be able to focus on the application rather than on the underlying microprocessors. Software designers have tried to accommodate them. This has been most evident in the case of Apple Computers, which used Motorola microprocessors for many years, and Windows (sometimes called IBM-compatible) computers, which use Intel microprocessors. Since software designed to run on one computer could not be run on the other, separate programs had to be supplied. Thus, even a program with the same name (e.g., Microsoft

**Table 4.2 Evolution of Microprocessors for Macintosh Computers**

| NAME | DATE | CLOCK SPEED UPON INTRODUCTION | DATA WIDTH |
|---|---|---|---|
| Motorola MC68000 | 1982 | 8 MHz | 16 |
| Motorola MC68020 | 1984 | 16.7 MHz | 32 |
| Motorola MC68030 | 1987 | 20 MHz | 32 |
| Motorola MC68040 | 1989 | 25 MHz | 32 |
| PowerPC 603 | 1994 | 120 MHz | 64 |
| PowerPC 620 | 1994 | 133 MHz | 64 |
| PowerPC 750 | 1997 | 233 MHz | 64 |
| PowerPC G4 | 1999 | 500 MHz | 64 |
| PowerPC G4 with velocity engine | 2002 | 1 GHz | 128 |
| PowerPC G5 | 2003 | 2 GHz | 128 |

**FIGURE 4.12**

*Apple G4 PowerMac and PowerPC G4 with Velocity Engine Microprocessor*

**FIGURE 4.12**

*Apple G4 PowerMac and PowerPC G4 with Velocity Engine Microprocessor*

Word) would be written in two versions—one for the Macintosh and another for IBM-compatible PCs.

The PowerPC microprocessor—a product of the combined efforts of Motorola, Apple, and IBM—was designed to combine high-speed processing power with the ability to run both Apple Macintosh and IBM-compatible software. Both IBM and Apple have developed their own lines of computers based on the PowerPC microprocessor, regularly referred to as simply the *PowerPC* (Figure 4.12). Both can run proprietary operating systems (e.g., Mac OS), or they can run on software written specifically for the PowerPC that uses open standard operating systems (e.g., UNIX and Linux).

PowerPC microprocessors will continue to evolve. But they are not just for PCs. Because of their processing speed, smaller size, lower heat dissipation, and ability to run a wide range of software, they are being used in powerful workstations and servers, such as IBM's 6000 and e-server series, respectively. Apple computer also uses the PowerPC in its PowerPC G4, acclaimed for putting supercomputing power on the desktop. This computer, which uses dual 1 GHz PowerPC processors, hits very high computing speeds comparable to those attributed to some supercomputers (i.e., more than 15 gigaflops).

**Other Microprocessor Chips**   There are still other microprocessors in use today. AMD, of Sunnyvale, California, poses perhaps the most serious competition to Intel. Depending on the particular point in time, the company's Atlon XP series of microprocessors have been shown to outperform the Intel Pentium series. AMD microprocessors have been used as alternatives to Intel by such well-known PC makers as Compaq and IBM.

Many other vendors have also developed their own high-speed microprocessors, among them Digital Equipment Corp. (acquired by Compaq), Hewlett-Packard, MIPS Technologies, and Sun Microcomputers. These companies' computers are widely used and play an important role in business applications, though they are not nearly as commonly used as Intel and Motorola microprocessors are on desktop computers.

## Memory Chips

**single in-line memory module (SIMM)**

A multiple-chip memory card inserted as a unit into a predesigned slot on a computer's system board.

Originally, memory chips were installed onto the system board, eight chips at a time, by connecting the chip to the system board with pins. Memory chips now often come in modules. A **single in-line memory module**, usually called a **SIMM**, is a multiple-chip card (Figure 4.13) that is inserted as a unit into a predesignated slot on the system board. SIMMs of 62M, 128M, and 256M are common.

People choose laptop computers mostly for their processing and storage capabilities. However, battery power is also an important factor, especially if the purchaser expects to use the laptop on airplanes, in meetings, or at other times when it cannot be connected to an electrical outlet. Depending on their characteristics, laptop computers run from one to eight hours on a single battery charge.

Manufacturers of laptop computers have developed a special feature called **hibernation mode**, to minimize power usage and thus increase the time a battery charge will last. During hibernation mode, all computer tasks are suspended, and memory data, as well as the details of processing, are stored on the hard disk. The computer turns off, meaning no battery power is used. When the power turns on again, the computer automatically restores programs and data, resuming the task that was in process.

This power-saving feature is often automatically invoked when the cover of a laptop computer is closed, when its battery power gets low, or when the laptop is not used for a period of time. As laptop computers grow in popularity, you will see many more features developed to extend battery life. ◼

**hibernation mode**
The time during which all tasks are suspended and memory data and processing details are stored on the hard disk.

**Installed memory** is the amount of memory included by the computer's manufacturer on its memory board. **Maximum memory** is the highest amount of memory that a processor can hold.[4]

**installed memory**
The amount of memory included by a computer's manufacturer on its memory board.

**maximum memory**
The most memory that a processor can hold.

## Ports

Any device that is not part of the CPU or the system board—a keyboard, mouse, monitor, printer, telephone line, etc.—must somehow be attached to the computer. **Ports** are the connections through which input/output devices and storage devices are plugged into the computer (Figure 4.14). *Parallel ports* are typically used for connecting printers to PCs, whereas *serial* and *network* ports are usually used for interconnecting data communication devices. Each has a unique shaped connector (Figure 4.15).

When an input/output device needs to be plugged into the system unit and there is not a built-in port for it, a special add-in circuit board is plugged into an **expansion slot** on the system board. All systems have a practical limit to the number of ports that can be added.

**port**
A connector through which input/output devices can be plugged into the computer.

**expansion slot**
A slot inside a computer that allows a user to add an additional circuit board.

**FIGURE 4.13**
### *256M SIM Module*

[4]Three memory allocation ranges are found in microcomputers running Windows prior to 2000. *Conventional memory* is the memory managed by the operating system and in which application programs run. Once conventional memory was limited to 640K, but this barrier was crossed with the introduction of a new version of Windows in the mid-1990s. ROM-based instructions, the computer's operating system, and application and communications programs run in conventional memory. A limited number of operating systems use *expanded memory*—the usable memory beyond the old 640K threshold, up to 1 megabyte. Application software may also use expanded memory. *Extended memory* starts at 1 megabyte and extends upward. This memory is freely available to application programs. (*Note:* These three memory allocation ranges pertain to the Intel line of chips.) Windows systems since 2000 and all Apple systems treat memory as one segment without the above distinctions.

# CRITICAL CONNECTIONS 1

## Disney's FASTPASS®: All the Fun Without the Wait

**Disney**

Since its opening in 1971, a journey to Walt Disney World Resort near Orlando, Florida, has always meant plenty of fun, loads of excitement for visitors young and old, and—long lines. The fun and excitement still abound, but waiting in line has become a thing of the past—thanks to Disney's FASTPASS®, which uses IT to eliminate lines at popular attractions.

FASTPASS® allows visitors to sign up for a Disney attraction—a ride or a show—in advance. To do so, they stop by the entrance to the attraction and swipe their admission tickets through the magnetic reader in one of several computer-controlled kiosks. The kiosk displays the probable wait time, should the visitors choose to enter the line right away. It also offers them the option of coming back later with a FASTPASS®. For visitors who want to wait, the kiosk prints a ticket—a FASTPASS®—that indicates a future one-hour time window when they can return for the attraction and not have to wait in line.

FASTPASS® reduces the amount of time visitors spend waiting in lines to get into the most popular attractions. In doing so it also increases the value of their park admission ticket, by making it possible for them to see as much as 25 percent more attractions each day for the same admission price.

FASTPASS® has proven so successful in Florida's Walt Disney World that it has been implemented at Disney parks around the world, including those in Paris, Tokyo, and California. As the new Disney park opens in Hong Kong, you can count on it featuring not only Mickey and all the Disney characters but also FASTPASS®.

FIGURE 4.14

*Ports Commonly Included
on PCs*

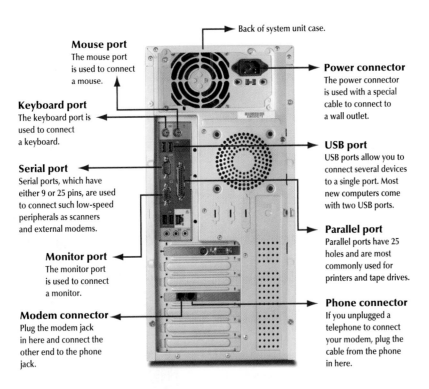

**Back of system unit case.**

**Mouse port**
The mouse port
is used to connect
a mouse.

**Keyboard port**
The keyboard port is
used to connect
a keyboard.

**Serial port**
Serial ports, which have
either 9 or 25 pins, are used
to connect such low-speed
peripherals as scanners
and external modems.

**Monitor port**
The monitor port
is used to connect
a monitor.

**Modem connector**
Plug the modem jack
in here and connect the
other end to the phone
jack.

**Power connector**
The power connector
is used with a special
cable to connect to
a wall outlet.

**USB port**
USB ports allow you to
connect several devices
to a single port. Most
new computers come
with two USB ports.

**Parallel port**
Parallel ports have 25
holes and are most
commonly used for
printers and tape drives.

**Phone connector**
If you unplugged a
telephone to connect
your modem, plug the
cable from the phone
in here.

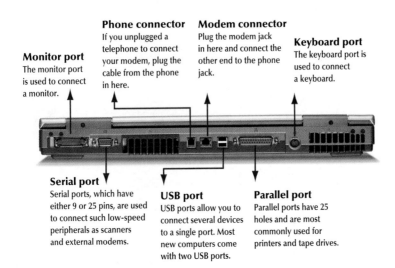

**Phone connector**
If you unplugged a
telephone to connect
your modem, plug the
cable from the phone
in here.

**Modem connector**
Plug the modem jack
in here and connect the
other end to the phone
jack.

**Keyboard port**
The keyboard port is
used to connect
a keyboard.

**Monitor port**
The monitor port
is used to connect
a monitor.

**Serial port**
Serial ports, which have
either 9 or 25 pins, are used
to connect such low-speed
peripherals as scanners
and external modems.

**USB port**
USB ports allow you to
connect several devices
to a single port. Most
new computers come
with two USB ports.

**Parallel port**
Parallel ports have 25
holes and are most
commonly used for
printers and tape drives.

## Universal Serial Bus

The **universal serial bus (USB)** port is one of the most recent additions to PCs. It was created as a general-purpose port that can connect up to 128 devices, all using the same connector. Many printers, scanners, handheld computers, and digital still and video cameras are manufactured today to use the USB capability for connecting to a PC.

USB ports are also *hot swappable*, meaning that devices can be plugged in or unplugged without having to shut down or reboot the system (something that could not always be avoided when changing devices in the past). Users appreciate the convenience hot swapping provides.

A USB version 2 specification (known as USB 2) that increases data transfer by a factor of 40 has been introduced. It uses the same cables as USB version 1 and is fully backward compatible so that any USB1 device can be connected to a USB2 port. From a user's perspective, USB 2 is just like USB 1, but with faster transfer speed.

Most PCs manufactured today, including laptop computers, have at least two USB ports built in.

**universal serial bus (USB)**
A recent addition to PCs that can connect up to 128 devices, ranging from computer disk storage to a variety of multimedia devices.

FIGURE 4.15

*Connectors and Cables Commonly Used with PCs*

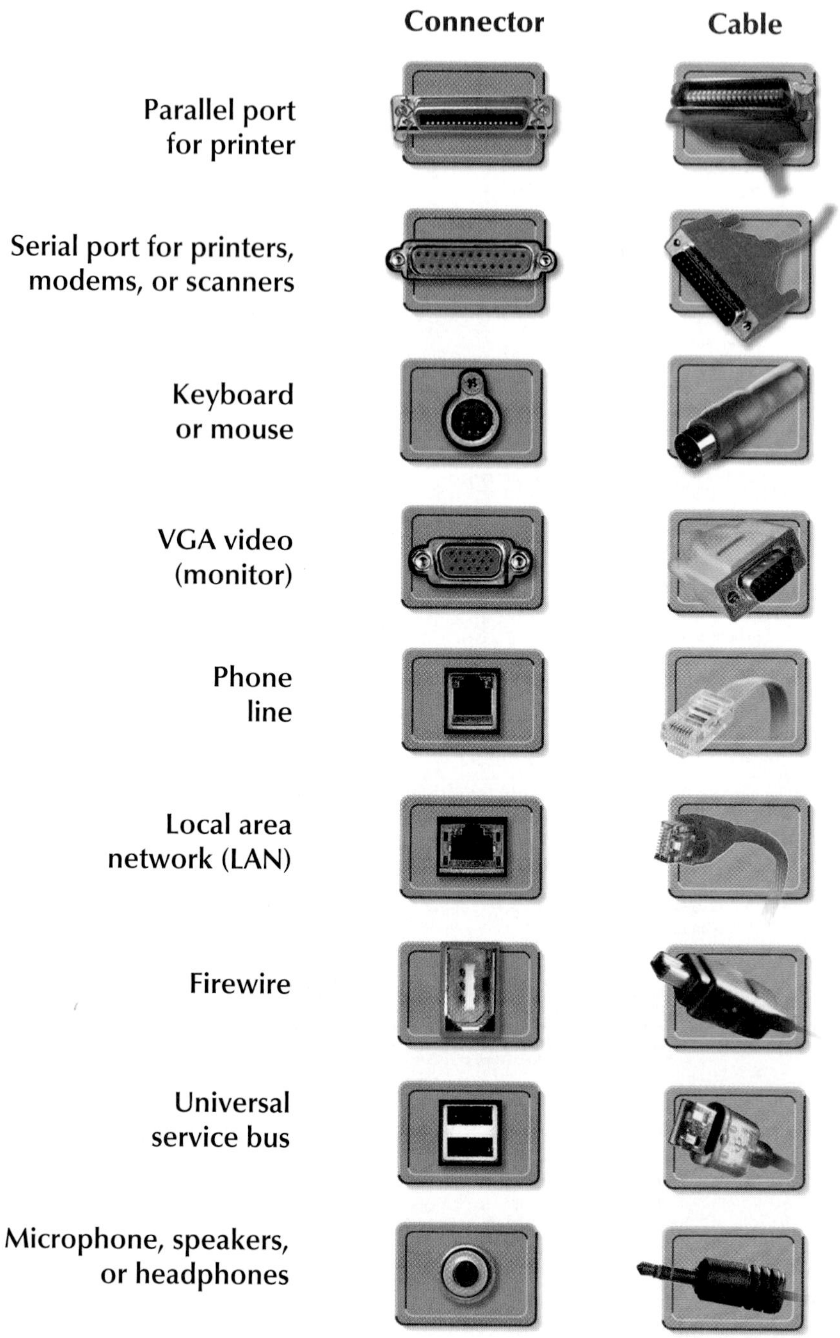

| | Connector | Cable |
|---|---|---|
| Parallel port for printer | | |
| Serial port for printers, modems, or scanners | | |
| Keyboard or mouse | | |
| VGA video (monitor) | | |
| Phone line | | |
| Local area network (LAN) | | |
| Firewire | | |
| Universal service bus | | |
| Microphone, speakers, or headphones | | |

## Add-In Boards

**add-in board**
A board that can be added to a computer to customize its features and capabilities.

Virtually all desktop microcomputers as well as midrange and mainframe computers have an *open architecture*, meaning that additional boards, called **add-in boards,** can be plugged into them by way of expansion slots to customize the computer's features and capabilities. Computers that do not have this capacity are said to have a *closed architecture*.

Table 4.3 lists several types of boards available, which can be added to today's microcomputers. The variety of add-in boards continues to expand as computer manufacturers find ways to meet users' demands for more capabilities.

The combination of desktop computers and customized add-in boards is helping to train healthcare providers in areas of medicine that are difficult to explain through usual methods of instruction. For example, the American Heart Association, in an effort to encourage doctors and medical students to study preventive medicine, has been offering medical schools, community health groups, and practicing physicians a computer-based

**Table 4.3  Types of Add-In Boards for Microcomputers**

| BOARD FUNCTION | DESCRIPTION |
|---|---|
| Accelerator board | Increases speed of computer |
| Controller board | Allows different printers and storage devices to be attached to computer |
| Coprocessor board | Includes special chips that speed up the system's overall processing capabilities |
| Display adapter board | Permits the use of computer displays by providing interaction with the processor board |
| Fax modem board | Enables the computer to send and receive facsimile images, data, and information |
| Memory expansion board | Extends the computer's memory capacity by adding additional sockets for memory chips |
| Network interface board | Enables the computer to be connected to a local area network |
| SCSI adaptor | Provides an interconnection for a variety of peripheral devices, including scanners, CD-ROM units, and DVD player/recorders. Also interconnects disk drives and scanners, using a SCSI interface (rather than using the more common IDE or USB interfaces) |
| Sound board | Contains chips and circuitry that translate data and information into sound output, including music; permits connection of speakers to computer |
| TV-tuner board | Enables computer to receive television signals |
| Video capture board | Enables the computer to capture full-motion color video and accompanying sound for processing and storage |
| Voice board | Provides the capability to translate stored data and information into spoken output. |

multimedia interactive application that focuses on the workings of the heart and bloodstream. Users load the system onto Apple or Windows/Intel computers outfitted with add-in boards that provide sound and animation capabilities. By providing an animated view of that organ pumping blood into arteries, the system lets users see the effect of high cholesterol levels in the bloodstream on the heart. Another system developed by High Techsplanations of Rockville, Maryland, allows surgeons to practice prostate surgery without cutting up cadavers (Figure 4.16).

Marketing professionals are also using add-in boards for market research and target marketing.

## Plug and Play

Inserting or removing memory, chips, or boards, as well as storage or peripheral devices, changes the configuration of a computer. In the past, computer users had to *inform* (or *tweak*) the computer of a change, either through entering commands or changing switch settings inside the computer. Plug-and-play capability is making that step unnecessary, and simplifying computing in the process.

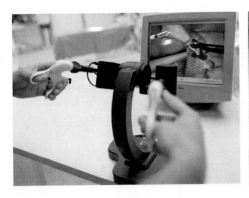
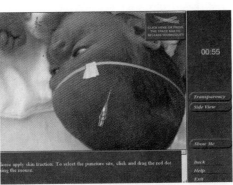

**FIGURE 4.16**

*Surgical Simulation Using Add-in Boards*

With **plug and play**, users can install devices into or remove them from a desktop computer, and the computer itself will sense the change and make any necessary internal adjustments. For example, if you install a graphics accelerator board in one of the computer's expansion slots, the computer will sense that it has been plugged in. Or if extra memory is plugged in, the computer will sense that it has been added. In either case, you can begin using—that is *playing*—immediately, without doing any *tweaking*. Plugging in new external devices too (a printer, for example) will also be sensed. It is easy to see why plug and play, first introduced as a feature of Apple Macintosh computers, was adopted as the norm on all computers.

# The Processing Sequence

By this point, you may be wondering exactly how a computer processes data. To understand this process, you need to know something about the machine cycle and the role of registers.

## The Machine Cycle

**machine cycle**
The four processing steps performed by the control unit: fetch, decode, execute, and store.

**instruction cycle (I-cycle)**
The first two steps of the machine cycle (fetch and decode), in which instructions are obtained and translated.

**execution cycle (E-cycle)**
The last two steps of the machine cycle (execute and store), which produce processing results.

All functions of information processing are directed by the control unit, which works with the ALU and memory to perform four steps:

1. **Fetch**   Obtain the next instruction from memory.
2. **Decode**   Translate the instruction into individual commands that the computer can process.
3. **Execute**   Perform the actions called for in the instructions.
4. **Store**   Write the results of processing to memory.

Collectively, these four steps are known as the **machine cycle**. The first two steps, in which instructions are obtained and translated, are called the **instruction cycle (I-cycle)**, and the last two steps, which produce processing results, are known as the **execution cycle (E-cycle)** (Figure 4.17).

**FIGURE 4.17**
***The Machine Cycle***

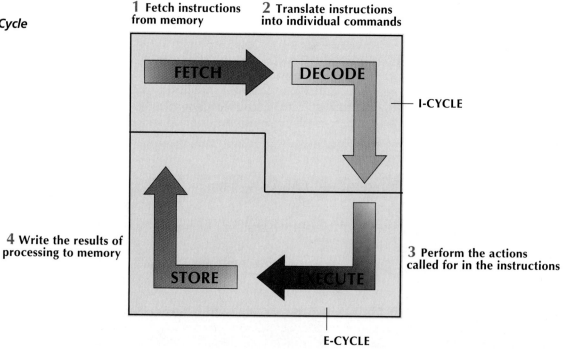

1 **Fetch instructions from memory**

2 **Translate instructions into individual commands**

I-CYCLE

4 **Write the results of processing to memory**

3 **Perform the actions called for in the instructions**

FETCH   DECODE   STORE   EXECUTE

E-CYCLE

## Registers

To execute the machine cycle, the control unit depends on **registers,** temporary storage areas in the processor (not in the main memory). Registers, which can move data and instructions more quickly than main memory, momentarily hold the data or instructions used in processing as well as the results generated. They also assist the ALU in carrying out arithmetic and logical operations.

There are four types of registers:

- **Storage registers**   temporarily store data that have been moved from memory and are awaiting processing or that are about to be sent to memory.
- **Address registers**   contain the address of the data to be used in executing an instruction.
- **Accumulators**   hold the results of computation as each arithmetic operation occurs. From the accumulator, the results are moved into main memory or to another register for additional processing.
- **General-purpose registers**   hold data, addresses, or arithmetic results.
    Registers are like staging areas. They are a place where preparations are made so that an activity will go smoothly once it is underway.

Consider the planning of a group trip. The organizer will tell members of the group to arrive at a specific location by a particular time. Some people will arrive earlier than others, of course, but all should be assembled at the specified location by the time the trip is due to begin. This is how registers work. They assemble all the data instructions so that the computer can perform its next machine cycle quickly and without a hitch.

> **register**
> A temporary storage area in the processor that can move data and instructions more quickly than main memory can, and momentarily hold the data or instructions used in processing as well as the results that are generated.

# Processor Speed

As noted in Chapter 1, one of the main reasons people use information technology is speed. Computers can perform millions of calculations per second consistently, accurately, and reliably.

Computer speeds are measured in **milliseconds** (thousandths of a second), **microseconds** (millionths of a second), **nanoseconds** (billionths of a second), or **picoseconds** (trillionths of a second). Processors and processor chips tend to operate at microsecond and nanosecond speeds, though new chips are emerging with picosecond capabilities. Secondary storage and input/output devices function at millisecond speeds.

Another way of describing speeds is by the number of instructions the processor can execute per second. **Millions of instructions per second,** or **MIPS,** ratings ranged from less than 100 MIPS for a typical desktop PC at the beginning of the 1990s, to more than 1 million MIPS for a comparable PC less than 10 years later. The instruction rate of mainframe and supercomputers is even higher. Computer speeds are constantly increasing; consumers expect every new computer model to have a higher MIPS capability. However, because computers do so many different tasks today, compared to the number they did in the past, ratings in terms of MIPs are not as meaningful as they were earlier.

Computing speed can also be measured in **megaflops,** or millions of floating point operations per second. *Floating point operations* is a technical term that refers to the floating of a decimal point from calculation to calculation. *Megaflops* is a measure of how many detailed arithmetic calculations can be performed per second.

The *Information Technology in Practice* feature, "Monsanto Uses Grid Computing as an Alternative to Supercomputers," discusses the way the company links the processing power of small computers instead of using expensive supercomputers to conduct scientific research.

> **millisecond**
> One thousandth of a second.
>
> **microsecond**
> One millionth of a second.
>
> **nanosecond**
> One billionth of a second.
>
> **picosecond**
> One trillionth of a second.
>
> **millions of instructions per second (MIPS)**
> The number of instructions the processor can execute per second—a measure of processor speed.
>
> **megaflops**
> Millions of floating point operations per second—a measure of how many detailed arithmetic calculations the computer can perform per second.

## Determining Processor Speed

What determines processor speed? In automobiles, greater speed comes from more engine power and greater fuel use. Aircraft engines produce higher speeds when they generate more thrust. But engine power, thrust, and fuel use have nothing to do with

# INFORMATION TECHNOLOGY IN PRACTICE

## Monsanto Uses Grid Computing as an Alternative to Supercomputers

**MONSANTO** imagine™ Monsanto Company, the large biotechnology firm headquartered in St. Louis, Missouri, is a leading provider of agricultural solutions to growers worldwide. An important part of its work focuses on crop protection. Monsanto scientists are exploring ways to restructure the genetic characteristics of foods, including rice, corn, and wheat, to make them more resistant to the extremes of weather. They also want to create food-growing techniques that offer a natural resistance to insects, which would help farmers reduce their use of pesticides and herbicides.

Monsanto's scientists seek to identify patterns they can match to other genetic information describing traits that are known to yield better crops. This biotechnology research requires the analysis of huge volumes of genetic data. Even when the analysis is conducted on the company's giant supercomputers, the analysis of a single gene can take four to eight weeks. In addition to limiting the number of discoveries possible during a year's work, the lengthy analysis time also uses up the computing time of a supercomputer.

Today, the elapsed time for genetic analysis has been reduced dramatically, thanks to grid computing, a computing method that can be more powerful and less expensive than using a supercomputer. Grid computing taps the combined power of hundreds of smaller, less costly computers that are linked together via the Internet and the company's own computer networks to create a computing grid.

Two factors are important in the emergence of grid computing. One is the power that exists in individual microprocessors, a direct result of Moore's Law at work (that is, the doubling of processing power every 18 months). The second is that most of the time, the processor in PCs and other computers is idle, waiting for its user to start an application, send an e-mail message, or take some other action. Grid computing puts the unused computer power to use. Both factors have been of enormous importance to Monsanto.

Searching to uncover new genes and learn their structure or sequence means examining a 10-terabyte research database. Rather than using software that processes the database in sequence, a tactic of the past, Monsanto's grid computing software peels off slices of the database and sends each set of data to computers on the grid. These computers process the data, transmit the analysis back to Monsanto, and take on the next data slice. Instead of weeks, the gene analysis can usually be completed in less than a day. Grid computing has enabled Monsanto to search for thousands of new genes each year, more than 50 times the number that was possible the supercomputer way.

You can think of the value of grid computing this way: In the agricultural era, farmers relied on horses for pulling the plows, harrows, and other farming implements they used to till the fields. If they needed more horsepower, they did not seek out a bigger horse—they hitched up more horses. It has taken the computing world a long time to appreciate the farmer's solution. Instead of seeking bigger computers to solve larger problems, companies are turning to the technique of hitching more *computing horses* to the network, creating a team of processors that can do the needed work.

computers. Four elements determine a computer's speed: (1) the system clock, (2) bus width, (3) word size, and (4) available memory.

**System Clock**   Because computers work at high speeds, synchronization of tasks is essential to ensure that actions will take place in an orderly and precise fashion. All computers have a **system clock**, a circuit that generates electronic pulses at a fixed rate to synchronize processing activities. Each time a pulse is generated, a new instruction cycle begins.

The clock speed varies by computer. Older computers ran at speeds measured in **megahertz (MHz)**–millions of pulses per second. Today's computers operate at **gigahertz (GHz)** speeds–billions of pulses per second. A computer with a clock speed of, say, 4 GHz would be dramatically faster than one running at 2 GHz and many, many times faster than one operating at 500 MHz. The higher the megahertz, the faster the computer (see Table 4.1 on page 141).

As a result of improvements in microprocessors, following Moore's Law, computer clock speeds have been doubling every 12 to 18 months. As Table 4.1 shows, the clock speed of the Intel 8088, among the first used in PCs, ran at just 4.7 MHz, a far cry from the 1 GHz speed first achieved and exceeded in the year 2000 and the multi-GHz speeds that users are now accustomed to.

**Bus Width**   For a computer to process information, the details must be moved internally–that is, within the computer. Data are moved from input devices to memory, from memory to the processor, from the processor to memory, from memory to storage, and from memory to output devices. The path over which data are moved is a bus, an electronic circuit.

There are two types of bus. An **input/output (I/O) bus** moves data into and out of the processor–that is, between peripheral units (such as input devices) and the central processor. A **data bus** moves data between the central processor and memory (Figure 4.18).

The width of the bus determines the amount of data that can be moved at one time. A 32-bit bus, for example, transmits 32 bits of data at a time. Greater bus width means faster movement of data.

**system clock**
A circuit that generates electronic impulses at a fixed rate to synchronize processing activities.

**megahertz (MHz)**
Millions of electric pulses per second—a measure of a computer's speed.

**gigahertz (GHz)**
Billions of pulses per second.

**input/output (I/O) bus**
A bus (electronic circuit) that moves data into and out of the processor.

**data bus**
A bus that moves data between the central processor and memory.

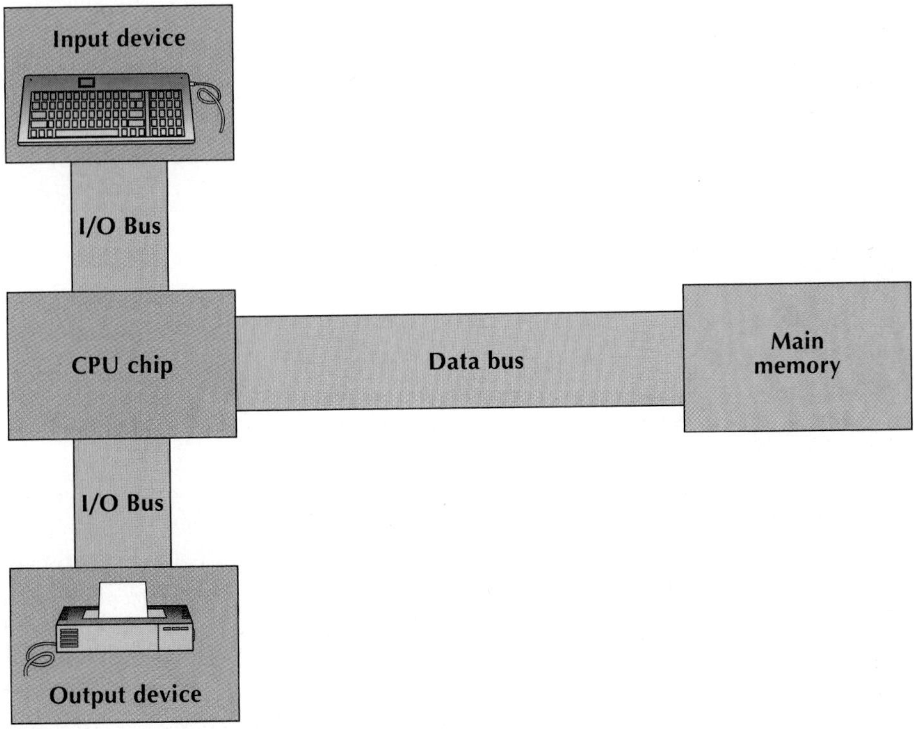

**FIGURE 4.18**

***The Two Types of Bus***

An input/output bus moves data into and out of the processor. A data bus moves data between units within the central processor.

# CRITICAL CONNECTIONS 2

## Hitachi's *Mu Chip:* The World's Smallest Wireless ID Device

When a product is successful, it gets copied. Although imitation is a fact of life in business, it is a constant source of frustration to brand managers of well-known lines such as Gucci, Escada, and Rolex. Cheap imitations can ruin a good brand, especially if buyers cannot detect a copy from the real thing.

Governments, too, are concerned about imitation. Every country must address counterfeit currency and the falsifying of other official documents such as passports and birth certificates. Merchants must address the possibility of copied gift certificates, and concert organizers must deal with the risk of forged tickets. All of these documents provide an attractive opportunity for counterfeiting, theft, forgery, and other criminal behavior.

Hitachi Ltd., a leading global electronics company headquartered in Tokyo, saw the problem and decided to do something about it. The company's engineers devised a way to better identify and authenticate products. They created the Hitachi *mu chip*, which can store ID information, yet is small enough (only 0.4 mm square) and thin enough to be embedded even in paper, as well as in clothing and product labels. The mu chip, to date, is the world's smallest wireless identification device. Because the identification information is embedded in the chip's memory during manufacturing, it provides high resistance to tampering.

The mu chip's ID information can help merchants and buyers distinguish a fake from the real thing. The device also could be used for antitheft and law-enforcement purposes. Its wireless feature (it *beeps*) means that the chip can identify its location when it receives an electronic signal to do so, which would make it useful as an antitheft device.

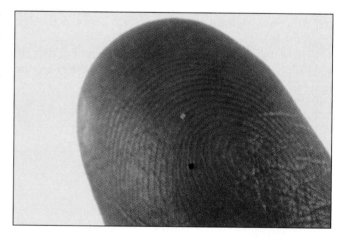

---

Most PCs have 32- or 64-bit buses, while servers and mainframe systems typically use 64-bit and 128-bit buses. Two bus standards are in widespread use. The Enhanced Industry Standard Architecture (EISA) is used on most Windows/Intel microcomputers. The second standard, the NuBus architecture, has been widely used on Apple Macintosh computers.

**word**
The number of bits a computer can process at one time.

**Word Size**   A **word** is the number of bits a computer can process at one time. Word size is measured in bits. An 8-bit word, for example, consists of 8 bits (8 electronic circuits). Alternatively, words are sometimes expressed in bytes. A 1-byte word contains 8 bits; a 2-byte word, 16 bits; and a 4-byte word, 32 bits (see Figure 4.4 on page 132).

The larger the word size, the faster the computer can process data and perform arithmetic and logic operations. Many micro and most midrange systems use 32-bit words; mainframes and supercomputers are built for 64-bit and 128-bit words. In contrast, most personal computers use 32-bit words (four 8-bit bytes), with the most powerful built around 64-bit word structures.

**Memory**   Often the amount of memory in a computer will influence the speed of processing even more than the clock cycle of the chip. For instance, a computer with a 2 GHz chip and 1 gigabyte of memory will more than likely outperform one with a 2.53 GHz chip and only 128 meg of memory.

The reason has to do with the amount of space that the operating system has to allocate to software, data, and the working storage area in which calculations are performed. If space is limited, the processor must spend precious extra time rearranging space in order to have a large enough area to do the work, in effect degrading the potential performance of the processor. With large memories, this space rearranging is not necessary, the work gets done more quickly, and the processing speed is faster.

## Increasing Computer Speed

The users of information technology are demanding more and more speed from computers. Processing and computer speed may be increased in eight ways: (1) through the use of greater chip density, (2) cache memory, (3) coprocessors, (4) accelerator boards, (5) RISC computing, (6) pipelining, (7) parallel processing, and (8) grid computing.

**Increased Chip Density and Integration**   Data and information move through the computer at faster than one-third the speed of light (which is 186,000 miles per second). Reducing the distance traveled even by a little can make a tremendous difference in the computer's speed. This fundamental principle underlies the continual emphasis on miniaturization of circuits and greater chip density, or the number of circuits on a single chip.

Exactly how many circuits can be packed onto a chip? The Intel 80386 chip (usually called the *386*), introduced in 1985, holds .25 million transistors. The Intel 80486 (commonly called the *486*), introduced in 1991, operates at speeds of 33 to 66 megahertz; executes at a speed of 54 million instructions per second; holds 1.25 million transistors; and integrates a CPU, input/output controller, high-speed graphics support, memory cache, and math coprocessor–all on a chip the size of your fingernail. The 486 is compatible with all of its predecessors; it can process applications software developed for earlier generations of chips and computers.

The Intel Pentium chip, the successor to the 486, was introduced in early 1993. This chip has more than 3 million transistors and operates at speeds exceeding 112 million instructions per second (see Table 4.1). An even more powerful Pentium II chip was introduced in 1997 followed by the Pentium III just two years later.

By 2000, chip speeds of the Pentium IV were already at 1.5 GHz on microprocessors comprised of more than 40 million transistors. If you apply Moore's Law, you know that by the middle of this decade chip speeds will easily exceed 6 GHz, with a processing capacity well in excess of 1 billion instructions per second, interacting with 1 gigabyte (or more) DRAM chips.

The photo essay at the end of this chapter shows the steps involved in creating these chips and microprocessors. The *Case Study*, "IBM and Nanotechnology: Advancing the IT Industry," shows how the company is creating breakthroughs that will advance both the processing speed and the density of chips used in computers.

**Cache Memory**   A special form of high-speed memory, called **cache memory**, eliminates the need to repeatedly move data to and from main memory. In systems without cache memory, the CPU sends data requests to main memory, where they are read and acted on. Main memory then sends the result back to the CPU. This process can be quite time-consuming if a large amount of information is stored in main memory.

Cache memory acts as a temporary holding/processing cell. As data requests pass between the CPU and main memory, they travel through cache memory and are copied there. Subsequent requests for the same data are recognized and captured by the cache memory cell, which fulfills the data request with the CPU. By decreasing the number of data requests to main memory, processing time is significantly reduced (Figure 4.19).

Because of the advantages offered by caching, microprocessors now include an area of *internal (or level-1) cache memory*. However, because space on microprocessors is precious and therefore the amount of cache there is limited, computers usually include

**cache memory**
A form of high-speed memory that acts as a temporary holding/processing cell.

## FIGURE 4.19

### How Cache Memory Works

a) The central processor sends a request to main memory, which accepts and acts on the request. When the data travel between the processor and memory, they travel through and are copied into cache memory.

b) Subsequent requests involving the original data are recognized by the cache memory and captured. The cache memory acts on the data requests and provides the response to the central processor. Because the data no longer travel on to the main memory unit, processing time is cut in half.

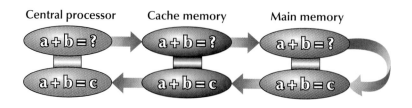

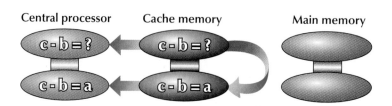

*external (or level-2) cache memory* on separate chips that plug into the system board. Level-2 cache, typically SRAM memory, is usually located close to the microprocessor.

**Coprocessors**   When a certain task is performed again and again, special-purpose chips can be designed to handle it quickly and efficiently. These chips, called **coprocessor chips**, are mounted on the processor board and function simultaneously with the primary processor chip. By taking processing work away from the main processor, they free the central processing unit to focus on general processing needs.

Among the most common reasons for adding coprocessors is to support increased security in data storage and transmission. Coprocessors in these cases perform the encryption and decryption of data, thereby creating coded data that would be difficult for unauthorized persons to interpret.

**Accelerator Boards**   An **accelerator board** is an add-in circuit board that increases a computer's processing speed by (1) using a clock speed that is faster than the CPU's, (2) using a faster processor chip, or (3) using an arithmetic/logic unit that speeds up floating point calculations. Any combination of these three is possible.

An accelerator board's characteristics depend on the nature of the work the board was designed to help accomplish. For example, floating point arithmetic is important to engineering and scientific applications. Thus, a PC used in those areas may be outfitted with an accelerator board that has a faster ALU. Or the computer may be outfitted with a specialized accelerator board, such as a graphics accelerator board. In most applications, accelerator boards yield speed increases of 200 percent to 400 percent.

The *Information Technology in Practice* feature, "*Wildfire Assistant* Gives Small Businesses Big Business Benefits" describes how high-speed processing, computer storage, and communication can be combined to aid small businesses (and large corporations, too).

**Reduced Instruction Set Computing (RISC)**   The quest for greater speed has prompted computer designers to rethink how computers should process instructions. One type of processing, **complex instruction set computing (CISC)** has been used since the earliest days of computing. CISC moves data to and from main memory so often that it limits the use of registers to store temporary data values. Calling on the memory so frequently results in slower overall performance, since a portion of the processor must coordinate and execute the instructions to move the data. (These instructions to move the data are called the **microcode**.)

In the 1990s, systems developers and manufacturers alike became concerned that CISC computing would impede information technology's advances. Hence, a second type of processing became popular. **Reduced instruction set computing (RISC)** processes data more simply. With RISC, data for the execution of an instruction are

**coprocessor chip**
A special-purpose chip mounted on a processor board; it is designed to handle common functions quickly and efficiently.

**accelerator board**
An add-in circuit board that increases a computer's processing speed.

**complex instruction set computing (CISC)**
A computing instruction set that moves data to and from main memory so often that it limits the use of registers.

**microcode**
The instructions that coordinate the execution of the instructions to move data to and from memory.

**reduced instruction set computing (RISC)**
A computing instruction set that takes data for the execution of an instruction only from registers.

# INFORMATION TECHNOLOGY IN PRACTICE

## *Wildfire Assistant* Gives Small Businesses Big Business Benefits

Information technology goes a long way toward abolishing the limitations that make small businesses small. An IT product that can greatly expand the horizons of a small business is the around-the-clock personal assistant for the traveler developed by Wildfire Communications Inc., of Lexington, Massachusetts. The *Wildfire Assistant* incorporates speech recognition, audio output, and telephone communication into a system built around a Pentium-class desktop computer. It is connected to the telephone system, but it is much more than a telephone answering machine. It incorporates voice mail and electronic messaging.

Besides answering and placing calls, Wildfire Assistant has processing capabilities that enable it to track down an individual who is traveling. Using call forwarding, the system can transfer an incoming call to the call-forwarded location of the intended recipient. (If the intended recipient is already on the phone, Wildfire Assistant will—if it has been told to do so—discreetly whisper the name of the caller, and the person can decide whether to take the call.)

This system has the ability to schedule appointments and then remind users of those appointments. An internal database stores schedule details that are perused to determine when events are scheduled as well as when new events can be planned.

Wildfire Assistant understands voice commands, too. When executives are traveling, they can call their office and verbally ask their assistant to look up and repeat telephone numbers and names; Wildfire will incorporate them. They can even verbally ask Wildfire to place the call for them.

Wildfire Assistant's capabilities can be tailored to companies of any size. Hence, a small company can easily gain the same features as a large business. Information technology in this case helps businesses overcome both distance and size limitations.

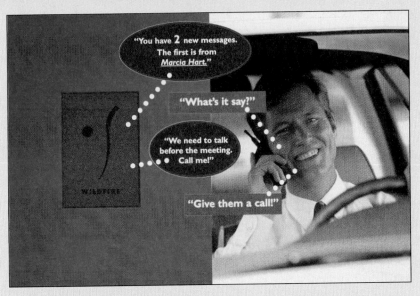

Wildfire is an electronic assistant that uses speech recognition to help busy people manage their daily telephone activities. The version of Wildfire now available through public telephone network carriers includes Intelligent Messaging™: Wildfire captures the caller's name and phone number, so the user can return the call by simply saying "give them a call"—nothing to write down, no number to dial.

taken only from registers. This simplifies—and accelerates—instruction processing greatly because the microcode is not needed. A separate set of instructions moves the data from memory to the registers.

Today this issue is of little concern, as CISC and RISC instruction sets are becoming more alike.

At the University of New Hampshire's Institute for the Study of Earth, Oceans, and Space, scientists use RISC-based workstations to transform data into three-dimensional graphics and animation—an imaging process called *visualization*. Since the speed of the RISC-system computers is much greater than that of the other computers used in the laboratory, the scientists can turn mountains of data into animated pictures relatively quickly. Visualization makes it possible to see how the ocean's tidal forces interact with the underwater landscape of the eastern coast of the United States and Canada and to simulate tides. These spectacular images are useful for managing fishing and sea life as well as regulating shipping and commercial fishing activities in the area.

**Pipelining** Computers traditionally were designed to complete the processing of one instruction before undertaking the next. However, computer engineers found that they could speed the entire processing sequence by **pipelining**. Pipelining means that a computer starts processing a new instruction as soon as the previous instruction reaches its next step in the processing cycle. With pipelining (as Figure 4.20 illustrates), before the CPU finishes processing the first instruction, the second, third, and fourth instructions are already being processed. In a computer not using pipelining, they would not be processed until the preceding instruction was fully processed. Because of the tremendous improvements in speed, processors today have built-in pipelining.

**pipelining**
A computer starts processing a new instruction as soon as the previous instruction reaches its next step in the processing cycle.

**sequential processing**
Processing in which the execution of one instruction is followed by the execution of another.

**parallel processing**
Processing in which a computer handles different parts of a problem by executing instructions simultaneously.

**single instruction/multiple data (SIMD) method**
A parallel-processing method that executes the same instruction on many data values simultaneously.

**multiple instruction/multiple data (MIMD) method**
A parallel-processing method that connects a number of processors that run different programs or parts of a program on different sets of data.

**Parallel Processing** Sometimes we do things in sequence, one step after another. For example, we assemble model cars and airplanes one careful step at a time. Other times, we do things simultaneously. For example, we walk, talk, and gesture as we share information with a colleague. Computers, too, can be designed to perform tasks sequentially or simultaneously.

Traditionally, computers have been designed for **sequential processing**–that is, processing in which the execution of one instruction is followed by the execution of another. Some computer designers have been developing **parallel processing**–that is, processing in which computers handle different parts of a problem by executing instructions simultaneously. In the end, the results of each parallel process are combined to produce a result.

Two types of parallel processing have emerged (Figure 4.21). **Single instruction/multiple data (SIMD)** methods execute the same instruction on many data values simultaneously. **Multiple instruction/multiple data (MIMD)** methods connect a number of processors that run different programs or parts of a program on different sets of data. Communication between the processors is essential to MIMD methods.

In New Haven, Connecticut, a team of scientists and physicians at Yale University is working to incorporate parallel processing into a computer that can monitor the

FIGURE 4.20

***Pipelining Speeds Elapsed Time for Computer Processing***

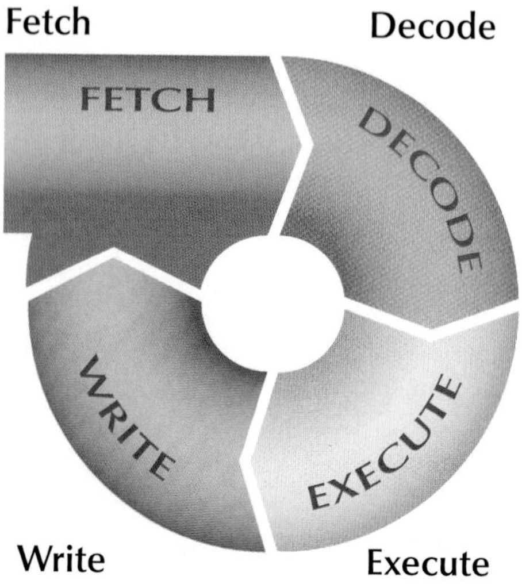


**Processing Without Pipelining**

An instruction must complete the entire machine cycle before another instruction begins processing

| | | | | | | | |
|---|---|---|---|---|---|---|---|
| Fetch Instr 1 | Decode Instr 1 | Execute Instr 1 | Store Results 1 | Fetch Instr 2 | Decode Instr 2 | Execute Instr 2 | Store Results 2 |

**Processing Using Pipelining**

A new instruction enters processing when the preceding instruction enters the next step in the cycle

| | | | | | | | |
|---|---|---|---|---|---|---|---|
| Fetch Instr 1 | Fetch Instr 2 | Fetch Instr 3 | Fetch Instr 4 | Fetch Instr 5 | Fetch Instr 6 | Fetch Instr 7 | Fetch Instr 8 |
| | Decode Instr 1 | Decode Instr 2 | Decode Instr 3 | Decode Instr 4 | Decode Instr 5 | Decode Instr 6 | Decode Instr 7 |
| | | Execute Instr 1 | Execute Instr 2 | Execute Instr 3 | Execute Instr 4 | Execute Instr 5 | Execute Instr 6 |
| | | | Store Results 1 | Store Results 2 | Store Results 3 | Store Results 4 | Store Results 5 |

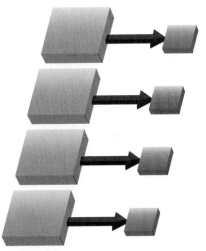

FIGURE 4.21

*The Two Types of Parallel Processing*

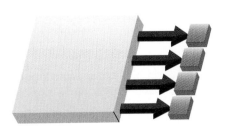

a) Single instruction/multiple data (SIMD) methods. In a SIMD computer, many data items are processed simultaneously by one instruction or by identical instructions on different processors.

b) Multiple instruction/multiple data (MIMD) methods. In a MIMD computer, multiple processors act independently on different data items.

condition of seriously ill patients. Currently, after a patient has surgery, nurses and physicians monitor the patient every few minutes, checking for changes in vital signs including blood pressure, heart rate, and breathing rate. However, even the most dedicated medical personnel may not be able to detect subtle changes in the patient's condition.

Using parallel processing techniques, separate processors within a computer will be assigned responsibility for monitoring vital signs. Still other processors will be interconnected with medical databases and with the patient's medical history in order to compare data from all of these sources and translate them into meaningful information for physicians and medical support staff. Because both medicine and the human body are complex, the system is necessarily complex. However, parallel processing promises to make this complexity manageable by turning over difficult coordination and analysis tasks to the computer.

Today, parallel processing is still the exception rather than the rule. In the future, computer systems of all sizes—from the smallest to the largest—will likely have parallel-processing capabilities. In fact, *massively parallel computers* are now beginning to appear. These computers contain hundreds of thousands—even millions—of microprocessors; they will be used in ways that were undreamed of only a few years ago.

Grid Computing   Capitalizing on the fact that processors are getting more powerful and that most are idle much of the time, computer experts want to extend parallelism in processing across geographically separated processors that are linked together. **Grid computing** harnesses idle time on computers and then uses them to provide processing for an application that needs more speed and capability than may be available on a single computer, even on a supercomputer.

Imagine the number of banks that have large computing systems. Even with the considerable processing that takes place after a bank closes, there is still a large amount of processing capability going unused. If connected to a grid, the unused power could be tapped by an unrelated company anywhere in the world for any number of processing tasks. In return for allowing another company to use its idle capacity at night, the bank might be given access to that company's extra computer capacity during its peak daytime hours.

Grid computing is emerging as a way of extending the capability of enterprises to gain computing speed and power. It promises to be an important technology for the future, and is one more example of the continuing advances in information technology.

**grid computing**
A process that harnesses idle time on computers and then uses them to provide processing for an application that needs more speed and capability than may be available on a single computer, even on a supercomputer.

# CRITICAL CONNECTIONS

## 1  Part II: Disney's FASTPASS®: All the Fun Without the Wait

Disney's FASTPASS® innovation reduces the need for visitors to stand in line to see popular attractions by providing a time window when they can return to enter the attraction with virtually no delay. The kiosks at each attraction using FASTPASS® know how many people are waiting to see an attraction at any time and use that information to suggest the best one-hour return time window for visitors.

Park visitors can only hold one FASTPASS® at a time. After using a FASTPASS® they can go to another popular attraction and get a new pass that informs them of the return time for that attraction. They can repeat this as many times as they like during their visit, but the computer system will not let anyone hold more than one FAST-PASS® at a time.

The kiosks that read the visitor tickets and print the passes are the visible part of the computer-based system that makes the FASTPASS® innovation work. Behind the scenes information is captured and processed to monitor the number of visitors to each attraction. The system knows the number of visitors that can visit an attraction each hour and compares that with the rate of requests when printing a FASTPASS® with the return time window.

### Questions for Discussion

1. What details must be kept in the Disney computer system in order for Fast Pass to work as described?
2. What IT components are needed to make the system work? Please describe.

3. How do visitors benefit from using Fast Pass?
4. How do Walt Disney World and other Disney parks benefit from using Fast Pass for their most popular attractions?

## 2  Part II: Hitachi's Mu Chip: The World's Smallest Wireless ID Device

Hitachi's *mu chip*–the world's smallest wireless identification device, measures only 0.4 millimeters square and is so thin that it can be embedded in passports, paper currency, and the labels of high-fashion products. Yet its cost (less than $.20 each) makes it attractive to companies and governments seeking to protect against imitations. Hitachi has overcome the size and cost barriers that have been the main obstacles to more aggressive use of embedded identification systems.

There is no guarantee that an innovation will be successful. Hitachi established a separate company, *Mu-Solutions*, to develop and expand the market for the chip. The company works with manufacturers of the electronic bar-code readers often found in retail environments to ensure that the equipment can read the chip's information.

### Questions for Discussion

1. What are the most important factors for the success of Hitachi's mu chip?
2. What other uses can you envision for the Hitachi chip? What advantages does the chip provide in each situation?
3. Is there a risk of invading consumer privacy if companies adopt the Hitachi chip? Why or why not?

# Summary of Learning Objectives

**1  Describe the components and purpose of the central processing unit (CPU).** At the heart of every computer is the *central processing unit (CPU)*, or *processor*, which executes program instructions and performs the computer's processing actions. The CPU is a collection of electronic circuits made up of thousands of *transistors* placed onto an *integrated circuit* (also called a *chip* or *microchip*). The two components of the CPU are the control unit and the arithmetic/logic unit (ALU).

**2  Distinguish between primary storage (also called memory) and secondary storage (also called storage), and between RAM and ROM.** *Primary storage* is

the storage within the computer itself. It is often referred to simply as *memory*. It holds data only temporarily, as the computer executes instructions. *Secondary storage*, external storage that augments primary memory, is used to store data over the long term. Often secondary storage is called simply *storage*.

*Random-access memory (RAM)* is memory that permits data or information to be written into or read from any memory address at any time. RAM stores data and information only as long as the computer is turned on. *Read-only memory (ROM)* also offers random access to data, but it can hold data and information after the electric current to the computer has been turned off.

**3** **Describe the chips and boards that can be used to augment the CPU and main memory.** Both chips and boards are used to augment the CPU and main memory. *Processor chips* contain all of the processing capabilities of the control unit and ALU on one chip. *Memory chips* are used to augment primary storage. *Add-in boards* allow users to customize their computer's features and capabilities.

**4** **Explain the process by which computers use registers to process data.** The processing sequence is a four-step process called the *machine cycle*. These four steps, all of which are directed by the control unit, are as follows: (1) *fetch*, or obtain the next instruction from memory; (2) *decode*, or translate the instruction into individual commands that the computer can process; (3) *execute*, or perform the actions called for in the instructions; and (4) *store*, or write the results of processing to memory. To execute the machine cycle, the control unit depends on *registers*, which are temporary storage areas in the processor.

**5** **List and explain the four determinants of processor speed.** Four elements determine processor speed: (1) the system clock, (2) bus width, (3) word size, and (4) available memory. All computers have a *system clock*, a circuit that generates electronic pulses at a fixed rate to synchronize processing activities. Clock cycles are measured in *gigahertz* and *megahertz*; the higher the cycle speed, the faster the computer. A *bus* is the path over which data are moved. The width of the bus determines the amount of data that can be moved at one time. Word size is measured in bits. A *word* is the number of bits a computer can process simultaneously. The larger the word size, the faster a computer can process data. Often, the amount of memory in a computer will also be an important factor in the speed at which results are produced.

**6** **Describe eight ways of increasing processing and computer speed.** Processing and computer speed may be increased in eight ways: through the use of greater chip density, cache memory, coprocessors, accelerator boards, RISC computing, pipelining, parallel processing, and grid computing.

*Greater chip density* means that a greater number of transistors are included on the surface of a chip. Chips with densely packed transistors run faster because the electronic signals take less time to traverse the circuits on the chip's surface.

*Cache memory* is a form of high-speed memory that acts as a temporary holding/processing cell and eliminates the need to move data to and from the main memory repeatedly.

*Coprocessors* are special chips designed to handle tasks that are performed often. By taking over this processing work from the main processor, they free the CPU to focus on general processing needs.

*Accelerator boards* are add-in circuit boards that increase a computer's processing speed. Packing more transistors on a chip—that is, creating greater chip density—results in greater computing speed.

*Reduced instruction set computing (RISC)* processes data more simply than complex instruction set computing (CISC). With RISC, data for the execution of an instruction are taken only from registers. This both simplifies and accelerates instruction processing.

Computers capable of *pipelining* increase computer speed by starting processing of a new instruction as soon as the current ones reach the next step in the processing cycle. Therefore, several instructions are in processing at any time.

With *parallel processing*, computers handle different parts of a problem by executing instructions simultaneously. In the end, the results of each parallel process are combined to produce a result.

*Grid computing* harnesses the idle time in computers that are linked together and uses it to provide processing for applications that need more speed and capacity than might be available in a single computer. Processing activities are divided among computers connected in the grid.

# Key Terms

accelerator board   154
add-in board   146
address   131
arithmetic/logic unit (ALU)   129
board   136
boot   136
byte   130
cache memory   153
central processing unit (CPU) or
   processor   126
cold boot   136

complex instruction set computing
   (CISC)   154
control unit   127
coprocessor chip   154
data bus   151
execution cycle (E-cycle)   148
expansion slot   143
flash memory   134
gigabyte/G-byte/GB/gig   131
gigahertz (GHz)   151
grid computing   157

hibernation mode   143
input/output (I/O) bus   151
installed memory   143
instruction cycle (I-cycle)   148
instructions   127
integrated circuits/chip/microchip   126
integrating   127
kilobyte/K-byte/KB/K   131
machine cycle   148
maximum memory   143
megabyte/M-byte/MB/meg   131

# Review Questions

1. Describe the importance of a computer's central processing unit.

2. What is the difference between data and instructions? Where are each processed in a computer?

3. Describe the role of the control unit and the two types of activities performed by the arithmetic/logic unit.

4. What is the role of primary memory in computing? What is the relationship between primary memory and the central processor? How does primary memory differ from secondary storage?

5. In what five ways is memory space used?

6. What is a memory address?

7. How do RAM and ROM differ from one another?

8. How are DRAM and static RAM alike? How are they different?

9. What is a system board? What does the system board of a PC contain?

10. Distinguish between a microcomputer, a microprocessor, and a microprocessor chip.

11. What is SIMM memory?

12. Describe the characteristic of flash memory. How is flash memory similar to or different from RAM or ROM?

13. In what forms is flash memory available for use in computers and other electronic devices?

14. Why are ports built into computers? What are two popular types of ports on computers?

15. Describe the purpose of the universal service bus (USB). What advantages does its *hot swappable* feature offer users?

16. What is an expansion slot? An add-in board?

17. Describe the purpose of PCMCIA cards. What advantages do these cards give to PC owners?

18. What is meant by *plug and play?* What advantages does plug and play provide to PC users?

19. What is the difference between a closed and an open architecture?

20. What are the four steps of information processing? How are these divided into the machine, instruction, and execution cycles of computing?

21. What is the role of registers in computing? Where are registers found?

22. Describe the purpose of each of the four types of registers.

23. Why are system clocks important to the speed of a computer? Why are they important to the performance of a microprocessor?

24. What are MIPS? What are megaflops?

25. What four features of a computer determine its processing speed?

26. Distinguish between an input/output bus and a data bus.

27. Why do computers contain cache memory? How do primary memory and cache memory differ?

28. What is a coprocessor?

29. How do accelerator boards increase processing speed?

30. How many transistors are found on Intel's Pentium chip? What is the speed of the Pentium chip?

31. What does RISC stand for? Why was RISC introduced into computing?

32. How does pipelining influence the speed of computer processing?

33. What is parallel processing? What are its potential benefits? What are the two types of parallel processing?

34. Describe the characteristics of grid computing. What benefits are gained by using grid computing?

# Discussion Questions

1. According to a United Kingdom survey conducted at the beginning of the decade by the Work Foundation, men make up two-thirds of all computer users. Moreover, the survey found that only one-third of women felt comfortable using computers and current information technology compared to 56 percent of men.

   What is your reaction to the survey's findings? Do you think the findings are representative of the differences between men and women in their use of information technology? That is, is there a gender difference with respect to IT? Why or why not?

   If your opinion is correct, what are the implications for the manufacturers of computer hardware and software?

2. One of the most notable trends in IT today is the availability of affordable micros with powerful processors, large amounts of memory, and the capacity to add boards that control sophisticated input/output devices.

   What potential business opportunities might this trend create? What difficulties might it create for businesses?

3. The availability of affordable high-power micros has spurred a trend toward downsizing, or moving business applications from mainframes to mini/midrange computers or PCs. Some companies, such as UPS and BankAmerica Corp., still maintain large data centers built around mainframes. Why do you think this is so?

4. Why is grid computing becoming important in computing applications? What feature of current computers is encouraging the development of grid computing? In other words, *should* businesses consider grid computing as a central part of their computing strategy?

5. Advertisements for microcomputers often list two amounts of RAM—the amount that comes with the computer and the maximum amount of memory that can be added. Why is this second figure important to a manager who is shopping for a computer?

# Group Projects and Applications

## Project 1

Visit a local computer store or conduct an Internet search of online computer retailers to learn about the pricing and features of currently available desktop and laptop computers. Focus specifically on the following computer features: (1) Microprocessor brand, model, and clock speed; (2) ROM memory; (3) cache memory; (4) hard disk storage capacity; (5) price; and (6) other features (such as software).

Prepare a report that summarizes the alternate configurations for computers arranged by the microprocessor brand, model, and speed used inside the desktop and laptop computer systems. Analyze the details in your report and describe the conclusions that should be drawn from your information about the variation in the computer features of the various manufacturers.

## Project 2

Flash memory is widely used in computer and electronic devices, primarily in the form of memory cards and memory sticks. Investigate the flash memory choices available to consumers in each of these categories, focusing on those available for use in the following products: (1) computers, (2) computer games, and (3) other devices.

| FLASH MEMORY TYPE | MEMORY MANUFACTURER | AVAILABLE FOR WHAT PRODUCT TYPE? | MEMORY SIZE | LOWEST PRICE FOUND |
|---|---|---|---|---|
|  |  |  |  |  |
|  |  |  |  |  |
|  |  |  |  |  |
|  |  |  |  |  |
|  |  |  |  |  |

(Include additional rows as needed.)

## Project 3

Suppose that your group wants to start a business. After actively investigating local market conditions, you decide to open one of the following businesses:

Choose one of these businesses, visit a local electronics or computer store (e.g., Best Buy, CompUSA, or Radio Shack), and talk to the staff about the information technology that is necessary to support your business. What software will you need? How much memory do these programs require? How

| TYPE OF BUSINESS | MAIN BUSINESS ACTIVITIES |
|---|---|
| Desktop publishing service | • Creation of résumés for people in the job market. |
| | • Design of both color and black-and-white flyers and newsletters for local organizations. |
| | • Typing/keyboarding services for publishing houses and local writers. |
| | • Preparation of multimedia-based Web pages for small businesses. |
| Tax preparation and accounting service | • Preparation of income tax returns for individuals and small businesses in the area. |
| | • Assistance with accounts payable and payroll for local companies. |
| Marketing support service | • Preparation and maintenance of mailing lists composed of the current customers of local department stores. |
| | • Preparation and maintenance of a database of customers' purchases, likes, and dislikes to use as the basis for a *relationship marketing* campaign for mail-order catalog companies. |

fast of a processor does your PC need? Will you require any add-in boards? Do you plan on networking your computer to other computers within your company or to any outside computers? If so, what kinds of equipment will you need?

## Project 4

Information technology advances so quickly that it is sometimes hard to keep up with the changes. With the members of your group, prepare a timeline showing the development of information technology over the last decade. Answer the following questions:

- How does the speed of the average desktop PC compare with that of one year ago? Two years ago? Five years ago? Ten years ago?
- How have the prices of PCs changed over the past 10 years?
- What can you now do on a PC that you could not do just two years ago?
- Read the "Information Technology" section in recent issues of *Business Week*. What are the latest developments in IT? Add these to your timeline.
- What IT developments seem probable over the next five years? Add a category titled "The Next Five Years" to your timeline, and list your predictions there.

# Net_Work

## Exploring New Microprocessors

The evolution of microprocessors is ongoing. Several times each year, the principal manufacturers release new versions. They also announce their intentions to release new microprocessors in the coming months, so that manufacturers, financial analysts, and consumers know what they can expect to see entering the market. In addition to providing information on processor speeds, they also include other details, such as cache size and expected pricing.

Using the Internet, conduct a search of the announcements by leading microprocessor manufacturers discussed in the chapter (posted at their Web sites) as well as at news sites (such as CNET). Then assemble the information you acquire into a table that includes the following elements:

Manufacturer
Microprocessor model
Announcement date (for newly released microprocessors) or expected release date (for processors not yet released)
Clock speed
Price to manufacturers of computers
Other specifications

After examining the information you have assembled, what is your conclusion about the relation between Moore's Law and the new microprocessors?

## USB Devices

After its release, the Universal Service Bus (USB) standard was quickly accepted as a preferred means for connecting devices to computer ports. The variety of devices using USB/USB2 has therefore grown rapidly.

Using the search capabilities of the Internet, conduct an investigation to identify the types of devices that can now be attached to desktop and laptop computers using USB. Prepare a table that lists the categories of devices using USB. For each category, include at least two manufacturer models, in the following format:

| USB Device | |
|---|---|
| CATEGORY | EXAMPLE MANUFACTURER & MODEL |
| | |
| | |
| | |

## Cool Mobility

### On Assignment

Within a few days of your meeting with each of them, Tina Fuentes (CEO) and Mark Goodman (human resources officer) happened to have lunch together. Each tells the other that they are impressed by the way you handled their questions. Your meetings inspired them, raising their interest in adding other features to the Web sites, a topic they intend to bring up with you during later meetings.

### In Consultation

Following his lunch with Ms. Fuentes, Mr. Goodman sends you an e-mail with questions related to their discussion about expanding the Web site's capabilities. Since they expect that the site's use by customers and employees will increase as the company grows, they want to be certain that the Web site is not too limited. Goodman summarized their concerns, as follows:

a. With the growing number of users, can the system accommodate everyone? Can employees and customers—using different brands of computers or running under different operating systems—be assured of interacting with the sites? Do users have to use the same choice of browser when they interact with www.CoolMobility.biz? Why or why not?

b. What data and information are most likely to reside on storage rather than in memory?

c. What factors, other than the speed of the communications link, will influence speed of interaction with the site?

## Case Study

### IBM and Nanotechnology: Advancing the IT Industry

IBM Corp., headquartered in Armonk, New York, has long been a leader in developing and delivering information technology products and services. While many associate the company's name with computers, software, and computer services, IBM is also one of the premier research and development companies in the industry. Products of its research have repeatedly changed the industry. Among the many innovations IBM has created and introduced are disk drives, semiconductor main memory, cache memory, relational databases, and the use of copper wiring (instead of conventional aluminum wiring) in microprocessors. IBM holds more than 30,000 patents worldwide. It spends more than 6 percent of its annual revenue on research and development.

IBM, like the rest of the IT industry, is facing a period of fundamental change. It has long been known that at some point theoretical or fundamental limits would dramatically slow or put an end to further miniaturization. Moore's Law, stating that the number of transistors that can be packed on a chip doubles every 18 months, has served as a guiding light of miniaturization for more than 30 years. Transistors are a key building block of electronic systems—they act as bridges that carry data from one place to another inside computer chips. The more transistors on a chip, the faster the processing speed.

It appears that the industry is reaching the limits of miniaturization. The combination of still smaller transistors and even faster speeds may become impossible to achieve. Even if chips can be made smaller, at some point smaller transistors may not perform faster, thereby halting progress. If this occurs, the industry will reach a period of maturity. The growth of technological performance and the growth of the industry itself will slow, unless breakthrough innovations are realized and moved from the research labs and put into full-scale production and use.

### Nanoscience

Among the hopes IBM and others in the industry have for transcending the limits of miniaturization is a rapidly evolving new branch of science known as nanoscience or nanotechnology. Nanoscience gets its name from nanometer, or one billionth of a meter. Nanoscience researchers are working at the molecule level,[5] often seeking to arrange molecules into new structures that

---

[5]Molecules are the smallest collection of atoms of a compound that retain the properties of that material. For example, water is made up of two atoms of hydrogen and one atom of oxygen (the chemist would say its formula is "H-two-O," and would write the formula as "$H_2O$"). It turns out that how these atoms are connected together is also important in determining the properties of the material.

Manufactured products are made from atoms. The properties of those products depend on how those atoms are arranged. If the atoms in coal are rearranged, a diamond can be created. If we rearrange the atoms in sand (and add a few other trace elements), we can make conventional computer chips.

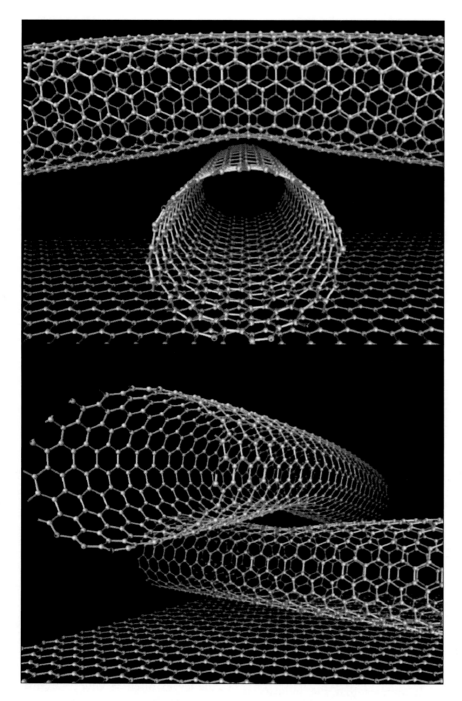

*500 times smaller* than today's silicon-based transistors and *1,000 times stronger than steel*. The tube-shaped molecules of IBM's carbon nanotubes are so thin that more than 50,000 bundled tubes take less space than the cross-section of a strand of human hair. (Of course, these structures are only visible through the lens of a powerful microscope.)

In addition to the impressive size characteristics, the transistors IBM has created using carbon nanotubes have been shown to have more than twice as much capacity to carry electric current as today's advanced silicon transistors. Hence the extreme levels of miniaturization coupled with impressive current capacity suggest that this advance by IBM scientists could have a profound impact on future chips and their performance.

## Nanostorage

Using another innovation in nanotechnology, IBM scientists have demonstrated a data storage density of a trillion bits per square inch—20 times higher than the densest magnetic storage available today. This remarkable density makes it possible to store 25 million printed textbook pages on a storage surface the size of a postage stamp.

In commenting on the breakthrough, Nobel laureate Gerd Binning (an IBM Fellow and one of the drivers of the project) said, "While current storage technologies may be approaching their fundamental limits, this nanotechnology approach is potentially valid for a thousand-fold increase in data storage density."

Compare this innovation with the increasingly popular flash memory, and the impact of the research is immediately apparent: Flash memory is not expected to surpass 1 to 2 gigabytes of capacity in the near term. In contrast, IBM's breakthrough in the use of nanotechnology could pack 10 to 15 gigabytes of data into the same tiny format, without requiring more power for device operation.

offer dramatic advantages for their recipients.

Applications of nanotechnology are beginning to move into commercial products. For instance, Levi, a leading garment manufacturer, is using nanofibers in new garments that resist stains. Spill a cup of coffee on a pair of slacks and you simply wipe it off. Nanoscience is also the foundation for breakthrough work in the creation of new life-saving miracle drugs.

## Carbon Nanotube Transistors

At IBM, researchers in nanotechnology are seeking to apply the science to new chip and storage technologies. They are achieving significant levels of success in the laboratory.

IBM researchers have created the world's first array of transistors out of carbon nanotubes—extremely tiny cylinders of carbon atoms measuring about 10 atoms (see photo). They are

## Technology Transfer

As impressive as these innovations are, IBM will not be using them in the chips and microprocessors you will see next year. Once innovations like these are created in the laboratory, additional research is needed to develop high-quality manufacturing technology for their mass production. Moreover, computer manufacturers will have to design new products around the technologies. Technology transfer—the process of transferring laboratory innovations into commercial use—takes years of additional research and development.

IBM's long history of research and development innovations suggests that odds favor the company's efforts to transfer its breakthroughs in nanotechnology into commercial use. Industry participants, observers, and consumers hope it is successful before IT reaches the limits of Moore's Law.

### Questions for Discussion

1. What is nanotechnology, and why are scientists actively investigating its possibilities?
2. What is the importance of nanotechnology to information technology developers and users?
3. What will likely happen if IT industry researchers do not find chip and storage breakthroughs before the limits of Moore's Law are reached?
4. Why is nanotechnology important to the future of IBM?
5. What factors favor the likelihood of IBM's success with nanotechnology? What factors could hinder IBM in its effort to create and commercialize innovations in nanoscience?

Microprocessors are built from sand and are constructed in layers consisting of circuits and pathways, doped silicon substrate, and silicon dioxide. ("Doping" the silicon allows it to conduct electricity well or not at all. This is important because computing is at heart an electrical process.) This photo essay describes the steps in creating the silicon wafer on which the circuits are created.

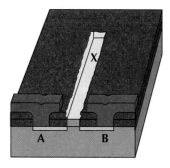

**(a) Transistor off**

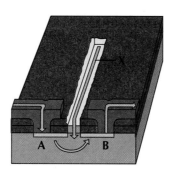

**(b) Transistor on**

**KEY:**
- Positively doped silicon substrate
- Silicon dioxide
- Negatively doped silicon
- Pathway X
- Circuit pathway
- Direction of electrical charge along pathway X
- Direction of electrical charge along circuit pathway

## STEP ONE: Designing the Microprocessor Chip

1. A microprocessor's design is created using a powerful desktop computer equipped with a design program. Each component of the microprocessor is drawn and positioned using a digitizing tablet that allows the designer to translate images on paper into an electronic format, with the resulting image appearing on a display screen. Today's microprocessors contain billions of transistors and circuits, each microscopic in size.

2. The microprocessor's design is transformed into a series of photo masks, one for each layer of the chip. A typical microprocessor design includes 20 or more different photo masks.

## STEP TWO: Manufacturing the Chip

3. The entire process of manufacturing and testing the microprocessor takes place in a Fab, short for fabrication facility. The fab's clean room is a workroom that is virtually free of dust—more than 100 times more sterile than a hospital operating room. Clean air continuously flows from every pore of the ceiling and through the holes in the floor. All of the air in the clean room is replaced several times every minute.

4. To avoid contaminating the atmosphere, all engineers and workers don special gowns (called "bunny suits") before they enter the clean room.

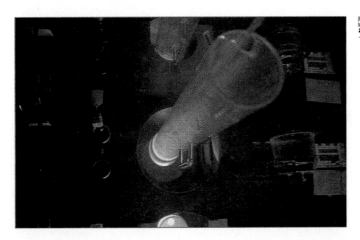

5. The first step in manufacturing is creating cylindrical silicon ingots. Silicon sand (hence the name silicon chip) is heated until it melts. The molten silicon, which contains almost no impurities or contaminants, is then grown into a cylindrical crystal that looks like a metal rod.

6. A diamond-tipped saw slices the silicon rod into very thin (3/1000 inch) disks, called wafers. The wafer, which may be 5" to 8" (13 cm to 20 cm) in diameter, is the base from which the microprocessor chips are built.

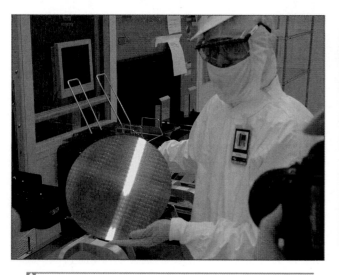

7. Wafers are sterilized and their surfaces polished to a shiny, mirror-like finish. Each square on the wafer is called a "die" and each microprocessor will eventually become the "brain" of a PC.

8. During *photolithography*, a gelatin-like substance called photoresist, similar to the film used in ordinary film photography, is deposited on the wafer's surface. A glass photo mask containing circuit patterns is held over the wafer and ultraviolet light is passed through the glass regions of the photo mask that do not contain the circuit pattern. A portion of the electronic circuit will subsequently be placed everywhere that the light exposes the photoresist on top of the wafer.

9. Wafers are taken into a "yellow room," so called because of the special yellow light used to illuminate the room. Here, after the resist is exposed, it is placed in chemicals to develop it. The exposed resist will remain on the wafer; the unexposed resist will be removed by the chemicals.

Next comes oxidization. Silicon heated and exposed to steam or dry oxygen (that is, oxidized silicon) will form silicon dioxide, more commonly known as glass. (An analogy: Iron exposed to oxygen forms rust; silicon "rust" is glass.)

Unexposed regions of the wafer can be oxidized to separate the electronic circuits.

Following oxidization, special materials are diffused or implanted into the wafer. These materials change the electrical properties of the silicon so that the electronic circuits (or switches) can be made.

After implantation comes deposition, in which liquid metal or other films are "sprayed" on the wafer. These films will later be selectively patterned, following the photolithography steps described in #8.

In the final manufacturing step, called etching, chemicals that selectively remove one type of material or another are used to etch away patterned regions of the wafer, leaving only the required circuit patterns.

**10.** An automated wet etch tool is used to clean the wafers of any excess process chemicals or contamination.

**11.** The preceding six-step process is repeated to "build" images and electrical circuits into the wafer. Metals deposited on the wafer are selectively etched to provide thin wires interconnecting the circuits.

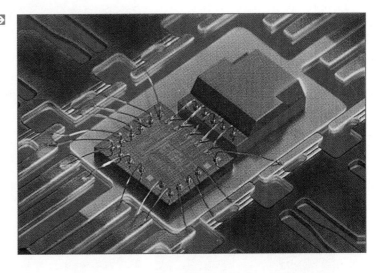

**12.** Technicians check individual wafers, which contain hundreds of individual chips, to make sure they are perfect. The rectangles near the center of the wafer are test circuits for monitoring the quality of the fabrication process.

**13.** Each wafer contains millions of transistors. The color-enhanced close-up photos show the sections of the chip and the bonding pads along the edges of the chip.

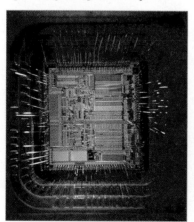

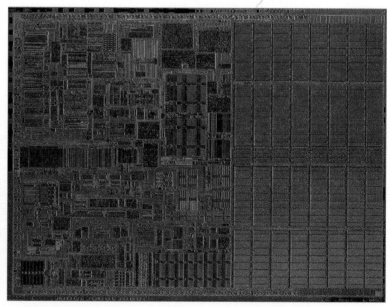

## Step Three: Testing the Microprocessor

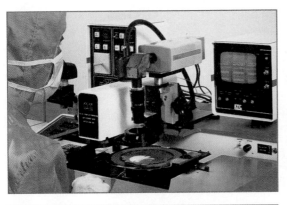

**14.** A wafer's yield is the number of good chips that result. Testing determines chip quality. During testing, large computer-controlled electronic testers determine whether a chip functions as it was designed. The chips that do function as designed are diced out of the wafers using diamond-tipped saws. Defective wafers are discarded.

## Step Four: Packaging the Microprocessor

**15.** By itself, the microprocessor chip is too fragile to be handled or used. Hence, it is mounted in a protective package. Each chip is bonded to a plastic base and the chip's wire leads are in turn wired to the electrical gold or aluminum leads on the package. The wire leads of the chip are thinner than a human hair. The microprocessor package is generally shaped in a square as a result of the dicing process.

**16.** During assembly of system (mother) boards, the leads of the microprocessor package are inserted into holes in the circuit board. Each lead contacts an electrical lead on the board, which is used to transmit to and receive electrical signals from other components mounted on the board.

# 5

# Storage and Input/Output Devices

## LEARNING OBJECTIVES

When you have completed this chapter, you should be able to

1   Discuss why people and businesses use storage, not just the computer's main memory, to store information.

2   Distinguish between the two main types of magnetic storage, and identify three types of magnetic disk storage.

3   Describe two alternatives for extending disk storage capacity in enterprises.

4   Explain why optical storage is of growing importance in computing and describe the most commonly used forms of optical storage.

5   Identify the seven most widely used input devices and describe how they are employed in computing.

6   Discuss the future of voice input and audio output devices as components of IT.

7   Describe the eight types of output devices and identify their uses in business.

# Dress for Success: Body Scanning by Brooks Brothers

*T*he clothes make the man—and the woman. Like it or not, it is well accepted that the selection and fit of the attire you choose for business can influence the impression you make and be a factor in your professional success. In certain settings, having well-tailored clothing is essential.

Brooks Brothers of New York City, a brand well known to men and women alike, has long been considered a bastion of men's style. The company has outfitted U.S. presidents, world political figures, and business executives in business and casual wear. Brooks Brothers features custom tailoring and offers premium off-the-rack suits, slacks, shirts, and more.

In most shops, getting custom tailoring is expensive and time-consuming, often requiring several fittings before the garments are just right. Several months can pass between the time an order is placed and the fitted garments are finished.

Brooks Brothers' *digital tailoring* is an innovation that provides the advantages of custom tailoring without the drawbacks. The system's digital body scan—the core of the innovation—is conducted right in the store. This process takes only 12 seconds; it uses a white-light scanning technology that produces an illumination level no different than that shed by regular light bulbs (it does not use laser beams). The scan captures an individual's measurements quickly and accurately. It creates a topographical map consisting of over 200,000 data points of the customer's body, rendering exact measurements—everything from the circumference of wrists, biceps, chest and neck, to the slope of shoulders and the curve of a seat. The data points are translated by computer software into approximately 45 tailoring measurements (collar size, sleeve length, waist, etc.).

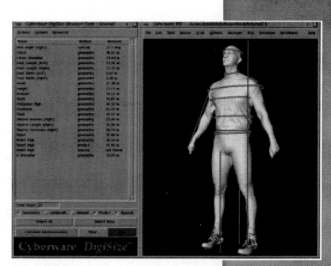

Brooks Brothers digital tailoring opens up a new world of choice. Suits, sport coats, blazers, pants, and dress shirts can be crafted from hundreds of the world's finest fabrics chosen from the company's many swatch books. Multiple-choice questions prompt the selection of every detail of the garment's design. For example, a customer can choose the shape of collar, number of buttons, and position of pockets, or defer to standard house styles.

The style, design, and measurement details are transmitted over secure networks to the company's East Coast factories where each garment is made. Finished items are returned to the store in two to three weeks—about the same amount of time needed by other stores to alter goods purchased *off-the-rack*.

Brooks Brothers maintains a customer's personal scan data, and details of any adjustments made after the delivery of garments, in its private database. Future orders can be placed and delivered even more smoothly.

Other companies, including famous mail order clothier Lands' End and blue-jeans manufacturer Levi Strauss, also offer women and men options for body scanning and custom-made clothing. However, none has advanced its capabilities to the extent of Brooks Brothers. Even so, it is increasingly evident that body scanning is only one technological innovation affecting fashion. Surely there are more to come.

*I*t is easy to forget that there is more to a computer system than a keyboard and a display monitor. All of the processing work is done *behind the scenes*. Computers use data to generate information, but very often the information for processing enters the computer from outside sources. In the opening case study, for instance, the customer's image was scanned as input to the computer. Processing also uses data stored within the computer.

This chapter continues the detailed tour of the hardware components of a computer that began in Chapter 4. The first part of the chapter discusses storage and its importance to business and personal computing. The second half of the chapter covers the many input and output devices commonly used with computers. As you will see, getting data and information into and out of a computer, whether from memory or storage, depends on having the right equipment.

The same caveat with which we began Chapter 4 applies to this material as well. The purpose of this chapter is not to make you an expert on equipment technology, but rather to familiarize you with the many technological options available today. Knowing which technology to use can make you both more productive and more successful.

## Storage

Recall that memory is the section within the computer's central processing unit that holds data, information, and instructions before and after processing. In contrast, **storage,** sometimes called **secondary storage** or **auxiliary storage,** is a way of storing data and information outside the computer. Storage is any external storage medium that can be read by a computer.

Storage is an integral part of information technology for three reasons:

1. *The contents of memory—RAM, for example—reside in the computer only temporarily* (see Chapter 4). Memory is used by many different applications. Between applications, the memory is, in effect, cleared and reassigned to the next application. Hence, any information or results obtained from an application must be stored outside of memory—that is, in storage.

2. *Memory holds data only while the computer is turned on.* When the computer is turned off, the contents of primary memory are lost if, as is typical, ordinary RAM is used.

3. *Memory is seldom large enough to hold the considerable volumes of data and information associated with typical business applications.* For instance, it would be impossible to hold the transcripts for all of the students at a large college or university in primary memory.

By doing what memory cannot, storage helps the computer process and store large amounts of information (Figure 5.1). At the same time, storage is

- **Reliable**   Storage retains its data when the power is turned off.

---

**storage**
The computer process of retaining information for future use.

**secondary storage/auxiliary storage**
A storage medium that is external to the computer, but that can be read by the computer; a way of storing data and information outside the computer itself.

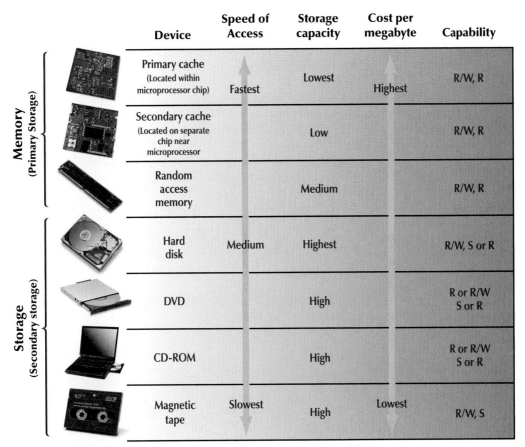

| Device | Speed of Access | Storage capacity | Cost per megabyte | Capability |
|---|---|---|---|---|
| Primary cache (Located within microprocessor chip) | Fastest | Lowest | Highest | R/W, R |
| Secondary cache (Located on separate chip near microprocessor | | Low | | R/W, R |
| Random access memory | | Medium | | R/W, R |
| Hard disk | Medium | Highest | | R/W, S or R |
| DVD | | High | | R or R/W S or R |
| CD-ROM | | High | | R or R/W S or R |
| Magnetic tape | Slowest | High | Lowest | R/W, S |

**FIGURE 5.1**

***Characteristics of Storage vs. Memory***

- **Economical**  Storage is cheaper than memory.
- **Compact**  Large volumes of data can be stored at high density.
- **Convenient**  Storage is easy to use and can transfer data rapidly (though not as fast as memory).

## Types of Storage

As you will see in the section that follows, storage can be described according to its different read/write and access characteristics.

**By Read/Write Capability**  Most storage alternatives are **read/write,** meaning a computer application can use the storage for both writing and reading data. Therefore, computers can record data or the results of processing, read the recorded data, or *re-record* on the same device.

Some storage, however, is read-only; a computer application cannot record or write data to storage. It can only read data recorded in advance on the storage medium. For instance, the tapes and CDs listeners play on a Sony Walkman or Diskman are examples of read-only storage and read-only devices. You can listen to them, but you cannot use the device to change their contents.

**By Access Capability**  Storage is also described by the manner in which it records and reads data. **Sequential storage** means that elements of data are read one right after the other. For instance, if details of sales transactions are written sequentially, the first is recorded, followed by the second, which is followed by the third. To read from sequential storage, the storage device begins with the first record, and then reads the second, and

**read/write**

A computer application can use storage for both writing and reading data.

**sequential storage**

Elements of data are read one right after the other.

then the third, and so on. You might liken sequential storage to the cassette used on tape recorders. You cannot listen to the third selection on the tape without first going past (by either listening to or fast forwarding past) the first two. This process is called **sequential access** capability; that is, the contents are accessed *in sequence*.

**Random access storage** has the capability for direct access to a set of data regardless of its location. Processing does not have to start at the beginning of the storage medium, although it can. For instance, you can jump to the third song on a CD without playing the first two. The CD player, in contrast to the cassette tape recorder, is a **random access device.**

Each type of storage has important applications, as you will see in the next section, which deals with storage technologies.

## Storage Technologies

The two main storage technologies are magnetic and optical. Both are in widespread use and promise to remain so. They differ in storage capacity, cost, and speed of accessing data and in their read/write and access capabilities (see Figure 5.1).

**Magnetic Storage**  Since the earliest days of computing, magnetism has played a central role in storing data and information. While disk storage is the form most commonly chosen today, **magnetic tape** was the first form of storage.

How exactly does magnetism store information? Data are stored on the magnetic medium by a **read/write head,** a device that records data by magnetically aligning metallic particles (iron oxide mixed with a binding agent) of the medium (Figure 5.2). These particles correspond to binary digits (alignment represents a binary one, nonalignment represents a zero). The *write head* records data and the *read head* retrieves them.

*Writing,* or *recording,* converts the contents of electronic circuits in primary memory into spots on the recording surface of the storage medium. Each spot, or pattern of spots, stores one piece of data. *Reading,* or *retrieving,* is not the reverse of this process in the sense that it does not change or move what is stored. Rather, it leaves what is stored intact. The read process senses the coded spots and interprets them as data.

**Optical Storage**  **Optical storage devices** use light rather than magnetism to store information. A beam of light produced by a laser is directed through a series of lenses until it is focused on the surface of a metal or plastic spinning disk. The disk's pattern of reflectivity, which corresponds to the data it carries, is an essential aspect of reading and writing data and information.

Optical disks use the same binary recording scheme that is used in all areas of information technology. During recording, a powerful laser beam makes a pit in the surface of the disk. The presence or absence of these laser pits corresponds to the 1's and 0's of

**sequential access**
The contents are accessed *in sequence.*

**random access storage**
The process of retrieving a particular record of information from any track directly.

**random access device**
The self-contained unit that holds and processes the disk.

**magnetic tape**
A magnetic storage medium in which data are stored on large reels of tape.

**read/write head**
A device that records data by magnetically aligning metallic particles on the medium. The write head records data and the read head retrieves them.

**optical storage device**
A device that uses a beam of light produced by a laser to read and write data and information.

**FIGURE 5.2**

***Recording Data from Magnetic Devices***

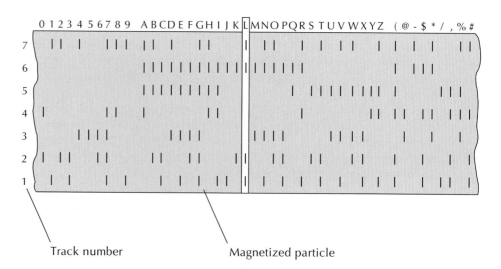

Track number          Magnetized particle

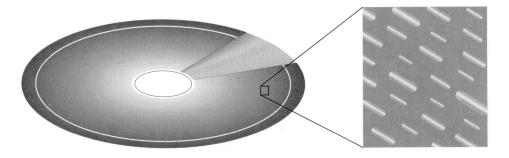

**FIGURE 5.3**
***The Topography of a Disk***
The pits on a prerecorded optical disk (detail) resemble parallel lines of regularly spaced ridges. Each of these pits is about .6 micron (0.6 millionth of a meter) wide. If 3,000 pits were lined up side by side, they would be about as wide as this letter o.

binary code. To read the stored information, a weaker laser beam scans the disk's surface, sensing the pattern of pits. The pattern is reflected back to a reader that interprets and sends the data to the central processor. Figures 5.3 and 5.4 illustrate how data are read from an optical disk.

## Magnetic Disk Storage

There are three types of magnetic disk storage: (1) flexible disks, (2) hard disks, and (3) disk cartridges.

**Flexible Disks** **Flexible disks**, also known as **diskettes** or **floppy disks**, were not the first magnetic disks used with computers (hard disks, discussed next, came earlier). However, they have long been associated with PCs.

In the early 1970s, as transistor chips became the dominant component of computer memories, engineers began seeking a way to preserve data even when the computer's power supply was turned off. (Recall from Chapter 4 that RAM chips are volatile, which means that their contents are lost when the computer's electrical current ceases.) Even the computer's operating system had to be reloaded if the computer was powered down.

Early attempts to store the operating system permanently in the computer's memory met with no success. Researchers tested all known storage devices, including hard disks, magnetic tape, and even phonograph records, to no avail.

The breakthrough came when an engineer on IBM's research team suggested using a very thin flexible disk–a disk so thin, in fact, that it would almost bend in half when held by one edge (hence the term *floppy disk*). Thinness was extremely important, for the researcher wanted to create a high-storage density on a six-inch disk (the standard at the

**flexible disk/diskette/ floppy disk**
A type of magnetic disk made of flexible plastic.

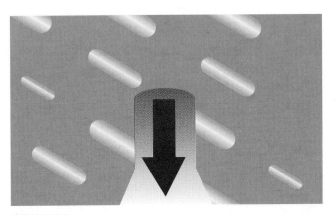 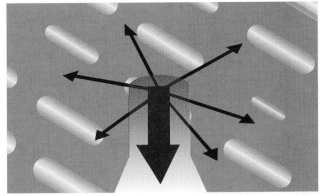

**FIGURE 5.4**
***The Land and the Pit***
**The land.** When a focused laser beam hits a flat space between pits—a land—much of its light is reflected straight back toward the detector. At the point where the laser strikes the disk, it has been focused to a spot about a micron in diameter. This diameter is only a little larger than the wavelength of the laser light. As a result, the beam, which was originally cone-shaped, assumes a cylindrical shape near its point of focus.
**The pit.** When the focused laser beam strikes the pit, much of the light is scattered sideways, so that very little is reflected back to the detector. Each time the beam moves from a land to a pit, the reflected light changes in intensity, generating a signal that can be decoded to reproduce the data written on the disk.

The key to the success of the flexible diskette *is not the disk.* Rather it is the holder.

The first disks produced by IBM's research team were so flimsy that they needed to be held in a foam-padded stiffener an eighth of an inch (3.18 millimeters) thick–thicker than the disk itself. After the flexible disk (stiffener and all) proved itself in tests, the question became how to pack the disk in marketable form. The answer was a custom-designed flexible plastic jacket. Today's flexible disks spin inside their own plastic sleeves. The inside of these sleeves is lined with a special nonwoven fabric that protects the diskette from abrasion and wipes it clean with each revolution. A small rectangular opening allows the read/write heads to write data or to retrieve data from the disk's surface.

The disk and packaging together are what we know as the *flexible diskette,* though *flexible* pertains only to the disk inside. Figure 5.5 illustrates additional features of the flexible diskette. ■

time was 14 inches) and to have the disk sit right next to the read/write head without causing damage to disk, data, or head.

The rest is history. Not only did the idea work, it revolutionized the way data are stored on computers. Today's flexible disks are inexpensive–less than $1 each–and reusable. Data can be written to and erased from them quickly and easily. They are commonly found in $3^1/_2$-, and 2-inch sizes, with the $3^1/_2$-inch size the most popular in business. Although their storage capacity is limited to 1.44 MB, they are convenient to use. Since they can be removed from one disk drive and inserted in another, they are also portable. Though they are convenient, low cost, and portable, they have limited storage capacity. Since, users are storing larger files, often because they contain audio or graphical information, floppy disks will be used less frequently in the future.

**Hard Disk**    **Hard disks** consist of platters, made of rigid aluminum, and read/write heads. Most hard drives are fixed disks, meaning that the platters and heads are sealed in a self-contained unit known as the **hard drive** or the **disk drive** (Figure 5.6). This is the device that holds and processes the disk. The read/write head alters the magnetic direction of the metallic particles coating the disk. Spots are magnetized or nonmagnetized in a coding scheme that corresponds to the on and off states of circuits (bits) in the processor. The disk drive records onto the hard drive in groups or **records,** which are sets of data about a single transaction (for example, the registration for a course or the payment of an invoice).

Most hard disks for PCs are sealed units containing both the storage medium and the read/write heads. Today's hard disks have gigabyte capacities. It is increasingly common to find PCs that store several hundred gigabytes of data.

**hard disk**
A type of secondary storage that uses nonflexible, nonremovable magnetic disks mounted inside the computer to store data or information.

**hard drive/disk drive**
The device that holds and processes the disk.

**record**
A grouping of data items that consists of a set of data or information that describes an entity's specific occurrence.

**FIGURE 5.5**

***Inside the Flexible Diskette***
A rigid plastic jacket protects the flexible magnetic disk. A spring-loaded door (open in this illustration) covers the jacket's access window. The door remains closed until the floppy disk is inserted into a disk drive, thus protecting the disk from dust and fingerprints. A metal hub, bonded to the underside of the disk, has one hole that serves to center the disk and another that spins it. Sliding the write/protect tab to open a hole in the corner of the jacket protects the disk from unintentional writing or erasure.

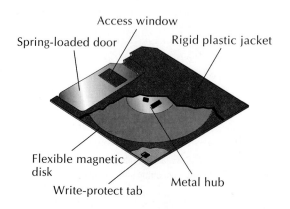

Access window
Spring-loaded door    Rigid plastic jacket
Flexible magnetic disk
Write-protect tab    Metal hub

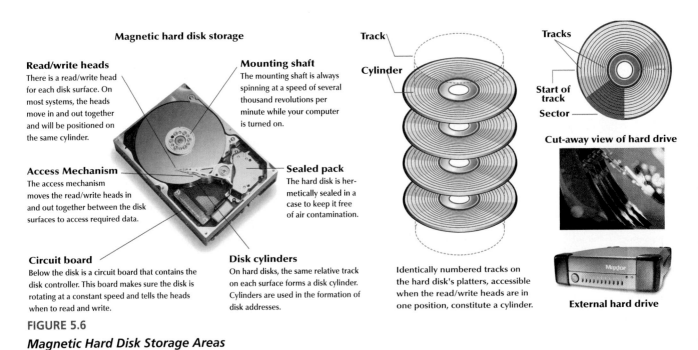

**FIGURE 5.6**

*Magnetic Hard Disk Storage Areas*

**Disk Storage Areas** The storage area of a magnetic disk is divided into **tracks,** concentric circles in which data can be stored (Figure 5.7). These tracks are often divided into **sectors** for easier access during reading and writing. The tracks have a specified recording density. Data are read from or written to a specific track as the disk is rotated by the disk drive at a constant speed of several hundred revolutions per second. (This speed is controlled by the disk drive built into the computer or attached to the computer by cable.) As the disk drive spins the disk continually, it positions the read/write heads over the proper track. Some disk drives on large mainframes and supercomputers position a read/write head over every track. The extra expense and complexity are justified because data can be retrieved much more quickly this way since there is no delay while the heads move from position to position.

**track**
The area in which data and information are stored on magnetic tape or disk.

**sector**
A subdivision of a track on a magnetic disk; used to improve access to data or information.

**FIGURE 5.7**

*Data Organization on Hard Disk*

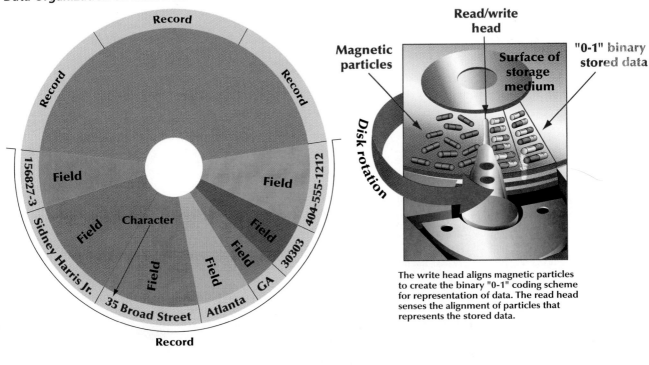

The write head aligns magnetic particles to create the binary "0-1" coding scheme for representation of data. The read head senses the alignment of particles that represents the stored data.

**REALITY CHECK** The decision to use aluminum in manufacturing hard disks came about only after a great deal of research. Researchers at IBM, where hard disks were also invented, first tested glass, plastic, brass, and magnesium, but discovered that disks made of these substances wobbled when run at high speeds, causing serious data loss and errors. Today, hard disks are made of aluminum laminates clamped together and heated in ovens, producing a highly reliable storage medium. ■

**cylinder**

A storage concept that refers to the same track location on each of the platters.

**head crash**

The situation that occurs when the read/write heads that normally float close to a magnetic disk's surface actually touch the surface.

**disk pack**

A stack of disks, enclosed in a protective plastic cover, that can be lifted onto or off a disk drive.

**random access storage/ direct access storage**

The process of retrieving a particular record of information from any track directly.

**hard disk controller**

A hardware interface that may be built into the hard drive itself, in the form of an expansion board, or a connection on the system board.

**integrated drive electronics (IDE)**

A standard electronic interface used between the bus or data path on a computer system board and the computer's disk storage devices.

Most disk drives contain multiple platters. Therefore, another storage concept–a cylinder–is used to describe areas of the disk. A **cylinder** refers to the same track location on each of the platters. Therefore, if there are 6 recording surfaces in a hard drive, cylinder 4 would consist of the set of track 4s from each surface (see Figure 5.8).

It is important to note that the read/write heads are supposed to *float* very close to the disk surface, but never actually touch it. If the read/write heads do touch the disk, the result is a **head crash.** The data stored at the point where the head touched the disk will be lost, and the head itself could be damaged (Figure 5.8).

Other disk units feature a **disk pack,** a stack of disks enclosed in a protective plastic cover that can be lifted onto or off the disk drive (Figure 5.9). A disk pack allows the user to remove and store disks easily. It is useful for making backup copies of information or programs, for separating databases onto different disk packs, and for storing very large databases when all the data will not fit on a single disk pack. Disk pack use has long been associated with mainframes and supercomputers.

Magnetic disk storage is **random access storage,** also called **direct access storage.** As indicated earlier, this means that a particular record of information can be retrieved from any track directly. The processor does not have to instruct the drive to start at the beginning of the disk and read each record sequentially. However, systems designers can create a sequential file and perform sequential storage and processing if they desire.

**Disk Controller Interfaces**    Hard disks communicate with the processor of a computer through a **hard disk controller,** a hardware interface that may be built into the hard drive itself, in the form of an expansion board, or a connection on the system board. The most frequent hard drive interfaces are:

- **Integrated drive electronics (IDE)**    The IDE interface is a standard electronic interface used between the bus or data path on a computer system board and the computer's disk storage devices. The IDE interface is based on the IBM PC Industry Standard Architecture (ISA) but is also in computers that use other bus standards.

**FIGURE 5.8**

*Head Crash*

The read/write heads float very near, but do not touch, the surface of the disk. A head crash occurs if the read/write heads touch the surface.

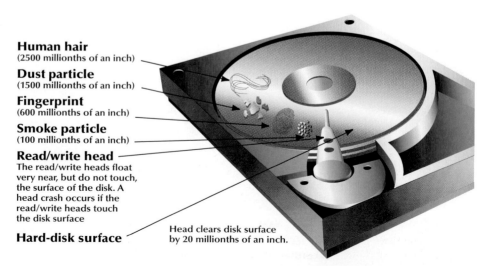

**Human hair** (2500 millionths of an inch)

**Dust particle** (1500 millionths of an inch)

**Fingerprint** (600 millionths of an inch)

**Smoke particle** (100 millionths of an inch)

**Read/write head** The read/write heads float very near, but do not touch, the surface of the disk. A head crash occurs if the read/write heads touch the disk surface

**Hard-disk surface**

Head clears disk surface by 20 millionths of an inch.

**FIGURE 5.9**

***Magnetic Disk Pack***

A removable disk pack contains multiple disks stacked around a hollow core. The stack slips onto a shaft in the disk drive.

IDE was adopted as a standard by American National Standards Institute (ANSI) in 1990. The ANSI name for IDE is *advanced technology attachment* (ATA). You may therefore see disk drives using this interface standard noted as IDE/ATA disks. Most computers sold today use an enhanced version of the IDE called *enhanced integrated drive electronics (EIDE)*. In today's computers, the EIDE controller is often built into the system board.

- **Small computer system interface (SCSI)** SCSI (pronounced *skuzzy*) was created to speed the transfer of data between hard disks and other peripherals. SCSI runs up to 40 megabytes per second, more than twice as fast as the EIDE interface. SCSI devices are connected using a SCSI card that fits in an expansion slot inside the computer. PCs purchased in retail stores and via mail order often do not include SCSI because of the extra cost, which would therefore raise the price retailers would have to charge. However, SCSI is often found in business and scientific computer systems where users have decided that having the highest data transfer speed is essential.

- **Universal service bus (USB)** USB is a recent addition to PCs that can connect up to 128 devices ranging from computer disk storage to a variety of multimedia devices. Recall from Chapter 4 that USB ports are also *pluggable (hot swappable)*, meaning that devices can be plugged in or unplugged without having to shut down or reboot the system. USB2 improved on USB, increasing data transfer by a factor of 40. Most PCs include USB interfaces as well as an IDE or SCSI interfaces.

- **FireWire** FireWire is one of the fastest peripheral interface standards ever developed. It is like USB in many ways, and the two interface technologies coexist on some systems, including Apple Macintosh. In contrast to USB, which is aimed at lower-speed input devices, FireWire connects higher-speed devices. Transferring data at up to 400 mbps, FireWire delivers data much more quickly than the popular USB peripheral standard. It is also hot-swappable. With its high data-transfer speed and *hot plug-and-play* capability, it is a commonly chosen optional interface for connecting external hard drives as well as multimedia devices, including digital audio, digital cameras, and video recorders. FireWire can support up to 63 devices.

**small computer system interface (SCSI)**
A device created to speed the transfer of data between hard disks and other peripherals.

**universal service bus (USB)**
A recent addition to PCs that can connect up to 128 devices, ranging from computer disk storage to a variety of multimedia devices.

**FireWire**
One of the fastest peripheral interface standards ever developed.

**Disk Cache**  Disk caching allows the system to store information that is frequently read from a disk in RAM. (Write caching is also provided with some disk caches.) PCs have disk cache built onto the hard drive. In the Macintosh, disk cache is part of the computer's RAM.

This process speeds up retrieval because it takes much less time to retrieve data from a disk cache than from a disk. When a PC needs to retrieve data from storage, it first checks the disk cache to see if the data is there (Figure 5.10). If not, it reads it from storage.

FIGURE 5.10
*Disk Cache*

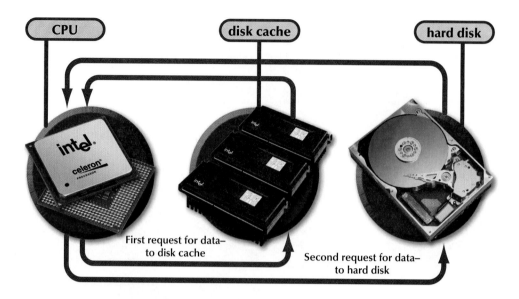

First request for data–
to disk cache

Second request for data–
to hard disk

Disk caching is used to manage large amounts of data. It improves retrieval time when used to prepare large documents with desktop publishing software or to perform calculations with spreadsheet software.

Note that disk cache, related to storage, is different than a computer's cache memory. (We discussed cache memory in Chapter 4.)

**disk cartridge**
The cartridge, a hard disk sealed in a protective package, is inserted into the disk drive for reading and writing data.

**Disk Cartridge**   **Disk cartridges** (Figure 5.11) offer most of the features of hard disks. Unlike hard disks, disk cartridges are removable. The cartridge–that is, the hard disk sealed in a protective package–is inserted into the disk drive for reading and writing data. When one cartridge is full, you replace it with another. Cartridges are often used to make backup copies of files and databases stored on hard disk.

The read and write capabilities of disk cartridges are the same as for hard disks.

**Extended Disk Storage Alternatives**   Although disk storage capacity continues to increase, the need for users to store large quantities of data is also escalating. Two innovations that provide extended disk storage are (1) RAID and (2) storage area networks.

**RAID**   The speed of reading and writing to disks has always been a concern. However, in today's computer applications, including those involving digital video and graphic images (discussed later in this chapter), large volumes of data are transferred to and from

FIGURE 5.11

*Magnetic Disk Cartridges*
The cartridge is removable; when one cartridge is full, it can be replaced with another.

storage. This fact, coupled with the use of faster and faster processors, has created the need for ever-greater storage capacity *and* faster read/write speeds.

At one time, large computer systems used 14-inch disk drives (both fixed and removable), which could store large volumes of data. However, large drives cannot rotate as fast as smaller dimension drives, and therefore the access times were not as quick. Attention turned to using combinations of smaller dimension drives that provided better access times. The result was the creation of RAID storage.

**Redundant arrays of independent disks (RAID)** consist of a set of small disk drives that work together as a single unit, known as an **array** of drives (Figure 5.12). The array provides performance, capacity, and reliability exceeding that of a single large drive. The array of drives appears to the computer as a single logical drive.

RAID is widely used in the server and mainframe configurations of large company data centers and to support Web sites. PCs generally do not use RAID as they do not need the extra speed, striping, or backup capabilities that RAID offers.

**Striping**   RAID technology uses **striping,** a method of combining multiple physical drives into one logical storage unit. Striping partitions the storage space of each drive into *stripes,* which can be as small as one 512-byte sector or as large as several megabytes. The stripes are interleaved across the disks so that the combined space is composed of alternate stripes from each disk (Figure 5.13).

In order to gain maximum read and write speed, the load must be balanced across all of the disk drives so that each can be utilized as much as possible. Most records can be evenly distributed across all drives by using software that manages the process with stripes that are large enough to ensure that each record falls entirely within one stripe. This keeps all drives in the array busy during times of heavy processing. All drives work concurrently and thus provide maximum rates of reading and writing of data.

**RAID Levels**   Several levels of RAID are possible, depending on the desired level of protection against loss of data or drive failure. The RAID level known as RAID 0 consists of a group of striped disk drives featuring striping of data across the subsystem's drive (Figure 5.14). While RAID 0 produces the desired read and write speeds, it offers no protection against the failure of one or more drives. Should one drive fail, the entire array fails and the data is lost. Since **fault tolerance,** the capability for a computer application to continue processing even if a disk drive fails, is often necessary, other forms of RAID were devised.

**redundant arrays of independent disks (RAID)**
A set of small disk drives that work together as a single unit.

**array**
A set of small disk drives that work together as a single unit. The array provides performance, capacity, and reliability exceeding that of a single large drive. The array of drives appears to the computer as a single logical drive.

**striping**
A method of combining multiple physical drives into one logical storage unit.

**fault tolerance**
The capability for a computer application to continue processing even if a disk drive fails.

**FIGURE 5.12**
*Redundant Array of Independent Disks (RAID)*

FIGURE 5.13

*RAID Storage Method Using Striping*

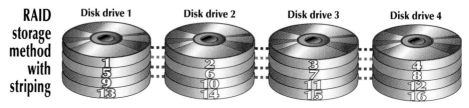

Data stripes from each disk drive are interleaved to create one logical drive.

**disk mirroring**

The most frequently used form of RAID; it uses pairs of drives within the array and duplicates the entire contents of a disk on a second disk.

RAID 1, also known as **disk mirroring,** is the most frequently used form of RAID. It uses pairs of drives within the array and duplicates the entire contents of a disk on a second disk. Data is duplicated on each pair as it is written. However, the pair appears to the computer as a single drive. All writes go to both drives of a mirrored pair so that the data on the drives is kept identical. Should one disk drive fail, the system automatically reads from the other one. RAID 1 disk drives are hot swappable, in this case meaning that the faulty drive can be removed for repair or replacement without shutting down the system.

FIGURE 5.14

*RAID Storage Levels*

**a. RAID 0**
**Nonredundant striped array**

**Data can be written simultaneously on every drive.**

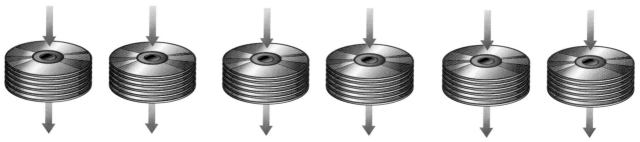

**Data can be read simultaneously on every drive.**

**b. RAID 1**
**Mirrored arrays**

**Duplicate data is written to pairs of drives.**

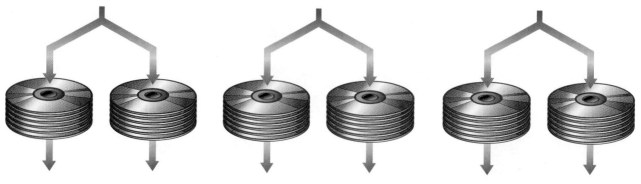

**Data can be read simultaneously on every drive.**

Some computer and disk manufacturers also offer other levels of RAID. Each provides alternative combinations of the features discussed above.

RAID has become the dominant method of disk storage on mainframe computers and large servers.

**Enterprise Data Storage and Storage Area Networks**  Estimates consistently show that the volume of data flowing through companies is *more than doubling every year,* and that both companies and individuals are storing greater quantities of that data. As proof, consider the number of pages displayed on company Web sites, plus all of the digital video and graphic images that are available, and of course e-mail. When you consider, too, that individuals are saving more of this space-eating information on their PCs, it is easy to understand the magnitude of the data explosion. Future needs will surely be even greater.

While the continual improvements in disk and tape storage capacities, and the addition of RAID, helps bolster storage capacity on a computer system or a server, it does not necessarily mean that the storage can be accessed by everyone needing the data. Companies are finding that more and more they need to take an enterprise-wide view of data storage needs. Storage area networks are increasingly the tool used to meet this requirement.

A **storage area network (SAN)** is a high-speed network or system that allows different kinds of storage devices, such as tape drives and disk arrays, to be shared by all users through network servers. Recall that data storage devices attached to a single computer or server is only accessible by users attached to that server (Figure 5.15). In a SAN environment, the storage devices are available to many servers and users via a high-speed communications link. (Communications networks are discussed in greater detail in Chapter 8.)

SAN offers important advantages for managing data from the enterprise view, including:

**storage area network (SAN)**
A high-speed network or system that allows different kinds of storage devices, such as tape drives and disk arrays, to be shared by all users through network servers.

- Sharing of a variety of storage devices by different systems having different configurations of hardware and software. For instance, each user may have a different operating system.
- Consolidation of storage resources. Data can be stored on the SAN and shared by everyone, rather than being duplicated on several independent computer networks.
- Independent computing and storage requirements. Storage capacities can be added for the entire enterprise without changing computers or servers.

**FIGURE 5.15**

***Storage Area Networks Increase Enterprise Data Handling Capabilities***

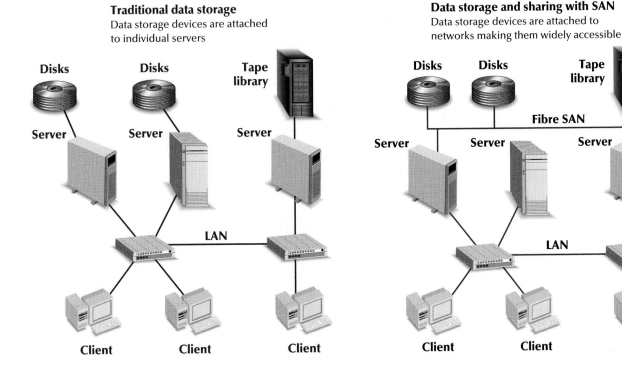

- Fault-tolerant data access is provided. A SAN makes it possible to mirror data, making multiple copies available.

Molson Breweries, founded in 1786 by John Molson on the banks of the St. Lawrence River in Montreal, is North America's oldest brewery. The company, with more than $2 billion in annual sales, consistently provides consumers with outstanding beers and has some of the most popular brands in the world. First-rate brewers and the highest quality ingredients are one reason for its continued success. Good business practices, enabled by excellent IT capabilities, are another.

Among Molson's most important IT applications is its transaction processing system, which handles the orders for its more than 25,000 customers. Another critical application is the company's ability to depend on gathering information from its marketing database.

Molson uses a SAN to share the data throughout the enterprise. It also uses the SAN to ensure that the company will always be able to take orders and coordinate shipping, for if these IT applications fail, business systems stop. The SAN incorporates RAID to fully secure and protect the data. Every five minutes, a backup copy of the data is sent to a remote server.

Molson's SAN also protects its investment in the computers and servers already installed. Even though some of its smaller servers have used their entire storage capacity, the systems remain useful. Because they are connected to the SAN, they have access not only to the enterprise data, but also to additional data storage capacity.

With the increasing tendency to store and share greater volumes of data, at Molson and elsewhere, it is likely that storage area networks will become very prominent in the information technology capabilities of many companies.

**Other Magnetic Disk Storage Systems**   Several variations on the different types of disks—removable USB drives, Zip disks, and SuperDisks—have emerged recently.

- **USB Drives**   (Figure 5.16) consist of flash memory (discussed in Chapter 4) and a USB connection. When connected to the computer's USB port, they can read and write data. Roughly the size of a stubby marker pen, they are highly portable and, depending on the capacity purchased, can store anywhere from a few hundred megabytes to many gigabytes of data.
- **Zip drives**   (Figure 5.17) are removable storage devices that use hard-shelled removable Zip disks, which are approximately four inches square and slightly thicker than the conventional diskette. Each Zip disk can store up to 750 MB of information, more

**USB drive**

Consisting of flash memory and a USB connection, it can read and write data when connected to the computer's USB port.

**Zip drive**

A removable storage device that uses hard-shelled removable Zip disks, which can store up to 750 MB of information.

**FIGURE 5.16**
*USB Drive*

**FIGURE 5.17**
*Zip Magnetic Disk Cartridges and Disk Drive*
The Zip disk is larger than a conventional diskette and can hold 500 times as much data.

than 500 times the storage capacity of traditional floppy disks. Plus, when loaded into the special Zip drive, information on the zip disk can be transferred between the disk and computer memory at 20 times the speed of a floppy disk. These features make zip disks extremely useful for storing backup copies of files and fast enough to run applications and multimedia. They bring a new dimension of flexibility to today's powerful PCs. Although zip disks cannot be used with conventional floppy disk drives, and the price of Zip disks is considerably higher than the price of conventional floppy disks, their convenience and storage capacity make them a popular secondary storage device.

- **SuperDisk**   is a storage alternative developed by Imation (originally part of 3M Corp.) that has a capacity of 120 MB. SuperDisk drives can also read ordinary floppy disks. This storage alternative is not widely used.

> **SuperDisk**
> A storage alternative developed by Imation (originally part of 3M Corp.) that has a capacity of 120 MB.

The *Information Technology in Practice* feature, "Checking In for Your Next Delta Flight . . . from Anywhere," describes how one of the world's leading international airlines combines rapid access to storage with passenger-accessible kiosks to speed the movement of passengers through its terminals. The airline also uses its information technology to provide special service to its SkyMiles® members, the airline's most valued frequent travelers.

## Magnetic Tape

On May 13, 2002, IBM announced that it had recorded 1 terabyte (TB) of data to a linear digital tape cartridge, storing nearly 10 times more data than any linear tape cartridge available at the time. One terabyte is equal to 16 days of continuously running DVD movies, or, according to IBM, 8,000 times more data than a human brain retains in a lifetime. This *laboratory demonstration* indicates the capacity that users will have with tape when IBM releases this technology to the market in the future.

The announcement coincided with IBM's 50th anniversary of magnetic tape storage that ushered in a new era of information processing. In May 1952, IBM introduced a tape drive that stored a total of 1.4 MB (equal to that of 1 floppy disk today) on a movie reel over 12 inches in diameter.

Magnetic tape storage was once the only magnetic storage medium available and thus was the primary choice for external storage. Once disk storage became available, tape became a medium for backing up and archiving data on large computers. Magnetic tape is also used heavily in storage area networks. It is also a backup alternative used by a small number of PC users.

**Tape for Large Systems and SANs**   Cartridges are the most commonly used form of tape storage today. The standard four-inch wide by five-inch long by one-inch thick cartridge (Figure 5.18) typically stores 20 to 40 gigabytes (GB), but in compressed mode can record 60 to 120 MB (3:1 compression). Extended capacity cartridges can store up to 200 MB.

Data are stored, or written, to the magnetic tape by a read/write head on the *tape drive*, a peripheral device that holds 10 or more cartridges that are individually retrieved for processing (Figure 5.19). Hence, a 10-cartridge tape facility can store from 200 GB to 1.2 TB of data.

Data are recorded in tracks that run the length of the tape.[1] Widely used tape drives write up to 256 tracks on a tape and can record at 14 MB per second.

The read/write head inside the tape drive alters the magnetic direction of the metallic particles coating the tape. The *transport mechanism* moves the tape back and forth. Reading and writing occurs as the tape passes over the heads (Figure 5.20). As with disk storage, the tape drive records onto the magnetic tape in groups or records.

MGM Mirage operates 19 resorts and entertainment properties across the United States and in Australia and South Africa. At one time it was running five different tape sites to back up its operating data. While the systems, which used thousands of tapes,

---

[1]On widely used IBM tape drives, the head element is composed of two groups of 16-track read/write heads. The tape drive writes 16 data tracks at a time to the end of the tape and electronically switches heads to write 16 different interleaved tracks and records back on the tape to the beginning. The head is then moved slightly to record the next set of tracks. A total of 256 tracks are thus recorded on the cartridge. The tape speed is 124 inches per second (3.14 meters per second) with search and rewind speeds of 198 inches per second (5 meters per second).

# INFORMATION TECHNOLOGY IN PRACTICE

## Checking in for Your Next Delta Flight . . . from Anywhere!

**△Delta** Delta Air Lines (www.
delta.com delta.com), the world's
second largest airline in terms of
passengers carried, and the leading
U.S. airline across the Atlantic, offers
some 6,000 flights each day to over
400 destinations in 76 countries.
Growing to this size is one measure
of success. However, the way passengers feel about Delta service is
sure to be a factor in sustaining its
success. Sheer passenger volume
presents challenges for Delta, specifically in its ability to check in passengers and baggage quickly. Delta's
business travelers in particular want
to travel hassle-free.

Among the innovations Delta
has recently added is a network of
self-service kiosks, currently available in nearly 100 U.S. airports. The
airline also offers wireless and *off-
airport* check-in services.

Although many airlines are
adding check-in kiosks to improve
operating efficiency, Delta's system
does more than simply let passengers check in and print out boarding passes.

Delta travelers can check in and
print boarding passes for originating and connecting flights up to
four hours before their departure.
In addition, they can select or
change seats, request to standby
for upgrades, check baggage,
change flights, request receipts for
e-ticket purchases, and find out
about possible flight delays or can-
cellations—all right from the touch-
screen of the easy-to-operate kiosk
(and without waiting in line to see a
Delta agent at the ticket counter).

The kiosk chosen by Delta
Technologies, the company's information technology subsidiary, is the
component that passengers see. It
contains interactive terminals that
feature Windows software and
touch screen user displays encased
in a weather-resistant plastic shell
with the *Delta blue* color molded
into the material. The microphone
that captures passenger voice information is hardly visible. Beneath the

cover is an eight-inch thermal
printer used for producing boarding
passes. Other components, such as
passport readers, CD-ROM units,
and biometric scanners can be
added at any time.

Members of Delta's SkyMiles®
frequent flier program can also
check in online over the delta.com
Web site, and print boarding cards
from their home or office before
they get to the airport (and they
are able to do so up to six hours
before their departure). Or if they
prefer to wait until they reach the
airport, SkyMiles medallion (higher
mileage) members can use a wireless PDA or mobile telephone to
handle their check-in. An automated voice system makes it
unnecessary for business travelers
to key in the information; they
need only state their flight and personal identification aloud and the
check-in system will capture and
process the details.

Delta passengers are delighted with the system's performance. It is fast and convenient, and the complexity of handling many passenger needs is hidden behind sophisticated IT components and applications. For example, the touch screen and voice interfaces keep the process simple.

Another reason for the passenger accolades is the full-service assistance. The kiosk, wireless access service, and Web site are all connected to Delta's worldwide ticketing and reservation system. This feature not only enables customers to retrieve all reservation details, but it also ensures that any changes initiated by passengers take effect immediately. As soon as passengers submit information, the system enters the details directly into the airline's active database. There is no delay.

The airline expects continued growth, meaning that the volume of passengers will continue increasing, even if the available space in the passenger terminals does not. Delta Air Lines IT innovations in check-in services not only speed passenger movement, they do so at lower operating costs. Electronic check-in is a win-win for all concerned.

# CRITICAL CONNECTIONS 1

## Federal Aviation Administration's *Black Box* Captures Aircraft Flight Information

The Federal Aviation Administration (FAA), which is responsible for enforcing air safety rules in the United States, requires every U.S. passenger aircraft that soars into the skies to carry two *black boxes:* a flight data recorder and a cockpit voice recorder. (Actually, these black boxes are usually bright orange today to make them easy to spot in wreckage.)

The flight data recorder (FDR), required since 1958, captures details of the plane's flight—including time, airspeed, direction, altitude, and fuel flow—that are useful for determining the aircraft's performance in the event of any type of failure. Initially, FDR information was recorded on 400-foot rolls of metal foil. Today, Mylar magnetic recording tape is used because it can record several hours of flight information in much less space.

The cockpit voice recorder (CVR) captures sound in the aircraft's cockpit, including conversations between the pilot and co-pilot, transmissions over the intercom, and background noise. CVR information is captured on separate channels and recorded on magnetic tape that automatically overwrites itself every half hour, so in the event of a disaster, only the last half hour of sound recorded in the cockpit will be retained.

Both devices are housed in durable steel cases that are able to withstand high temperature, sudden impact, and catastrophic explosions in order to protect the recorded information inside. After a catastrophic incident, a search is made for the cases and the tapes from the black boxes are removed for computer processing by the National Transportation Safety Board. Details from the recordings are used to reconstruct the situation that led up to the incident.

**FIGURE 5.18**
*Magnetic Tape Storage*

worked well, one person at each site was dedicated to overseeing the backup activities. The company was not able to back up its entire operation within a 24-hour period, jeopardizing its ability to recover should a disaster occur.

To improve its readiness and ensure adequate backup data, the company's IT department installed a SAN at its Las Vegas headquarters that included tape storage capabilities. Backup data is now transmitted over the SAN from the various locations for centralized storage at headquarters. The system not only improved the level of backup protection, it also enabled Mirage to cut the backup window to 12 hours even though the volume of data transmitted and stored continues to grow substantially.

**Tape for PCs**   On PCs, the quarter-inch-tape cartridge (QIC) was adopted first as an inexpensive storage medium for backing up data. QIC cartridges are similar to audiotape

**FIGURE 5.19**
*IBM 3590-E Enterprise Tape Drive*

**FIGURE 5.20**
*Magnetic Tape Transport Unit*

cassettes, with two reels inside, one with tape and the other for take-up. The reels are driven by a belt built into the cartridge. When they are inserted into a computer tape drive (Figure 5.21), a metal rod, or capstan, on the cartridge transport system pinches the tape against a rubber drive wheel, creating movement of the tape.

The QIC format records data linearly, in parallel tracks running the length of the tape. The number of tracks determines the tape's capacity. QIC tapes store approximately 10 GB of data and thus can store large portions of the data on a PC hard drive.

In 1998, Sony defined the *digital data storage* (DDS) standard that made it possible to use **digital audiotape (DAT),** originally created to provide CD-quality audio storage, to store computer data. DAT is a 4-mm tape and uses a different recording system (called helical scanning) similar to that found on videotape recorders.

Although it provides high storage capacity (approximately 40 GB), it is slower than the linear system used with QIC.

The latest tape alternative, **advanced intelligent tape (AIT),** was introduced in the late 1990s for use with PCs functioning as servers and with midrange systems. Innovations in both the tape medium and recording systems led to thinner, stronger tape. This enabled higher capacity (from 30 to 90 GB) and faster recording speeds (in excess of 15 mbps).

The most unique feature of the AIT format is the innovative emory-in-cassette (MIC) drive interface system devised by Sony. A 64 KB memory chip is built into the data cartridge. The data contained on the chip includes the tape's system log, search map, and other user-definable information, allowing data to be accessed immediately no matter what section of the tape is being accessed. The ability of the MIC to support multiple partitions and multiple load points drastically reduces the average time to access data—to fewer than 20 seconds compared to an average of over 100 seconds for conventional, competing technologies. It is likely that AIT will continue to advance for use with server applications.

Although tape storage technologies have benefited from impressive and continual advances, reading from and writing to magnetic tape is slow compared to other forms of storage. If a large number of records are stored, a relatively long section of tape will be required to record the data. When you want to recall a particular record, the search for it must begin at the beginning of the tape and proceed record by record—that is, *sequentially.* The computer may, therefore, need to scan several hundred feet of tape to find the record you want.

**digital audiotape (DAT)**
A 4-mm tape that uses a different recording system (called helical scanning), similar to that found on videotape recorders.

**advanced intelligent tape (AIT)**
Latest tape alternative that was introduced in the late 1990s for use with PCs functioning as servers and with midrange systems.

**FIGURE 5.21**

*PC Tape Drive Mounted in Tower Chassis with Tape Cassette*

Even so, magnetic tape remains an important storage alternative on computers of all sizes because it is relatively inexpensive (approximately $25 for a blank cartridge) and reliable. Also, users can store a tape cartridge on or off premises for a long time without worrying about data loss. These reasons explain why it is so widely used for creating archives to back up data in use.

Optical storage methods, which are discussed next, offer large storage capacity, but slower retrieval times.

## Optical Storage

The technology that made vinyl LPs obsolete by bringing us compact disks (CDs) for recorded music is bringing about a similar revolution in IT. While it does not make magnetic disk storage obsolete, optical storage does provide a storage option for high-density data and information. Optical storage has been one of the factors in the emergence of multimedia applications.

As with magnetic disks, information on optical disks is stored in circular tracks. Because a laser beam can be positioned extremely accurately, the tracks of data on an optical disk can be packed densely enough to provide immense storage capacities. A floppy disk will have from 25 to 100 tracks per inch and a hard disk several hundred, but a prerecorded optical disk will contain more than 15,000 tracks per inch. Yet any individual track can be identified and read easily.

The most commonly used types of optical storage today are CD-ROM and DVD.

**CD-ROM**    The **CD-ROM disk** (compact disk–read only memory) was originally adapted from audio disk technology. CD-ROMs come in several sizes (Figure 5.22), including:

- **Standard CD**    Measures 4.72 inches (12 cm) in diameter with a .59-inch (15 mm) diameter center hole. These CDs are the same size as CDs used for music. They have a storage capacity of up to 650 MB.
- **Mini-CD**    Measures 3.15 inches (8 cm) and offers a capacity of 185 MB. Mini-CDs have been available for a number of years. Most tray-loading CD players are already designed to handle 8 cm disks, having a recess in the tray that is exactly the right diameter to hold a mini-CD.
- ***Business Card* CD**    A variant on the mini-CD, sometimes also known as the **personal compact CD (PCD)**. It holds 20 to 60 MB, depending on the physical size of the CD. This CD gets its name from the appearance of an ordinary business

**CD-ROM disk**
Short for "compact disk–read only memory," an optical storage medium that permits storage of large amounts of information. CD-ROM disks can only be written to and cannot be erased.

**personal compact CD (PCD)**
A variant on the mini-CD, it holds 20 to 60 MB, depending on the physical size of the CD.

**FIGURE 5.22**

***CD-ROMs Come in Different Sizes***

# CRITICAL CONNECTIONS 2

## American Express' Optical Storage Creates Country Club Billing

**American Express**

If you have ever felt overwhelmed by a flood of monthly bills, consider the 3 million charge slips that pour into American Express Company for processing and storage every day. With this kind of volume, it is easy to understand why American Express has turned to an image-processing computer system that uses optical storage.

At American Express, the *images* are digital images of charge slips, which are created when the originals are scanned into the system at regional operations centers in Phoenix and Ft. Lauderdale. The digital images–complete with cardholder signatures–are stored on 12-inch optical disks; the flimsy paper originals are shredded. When cardholders' bills are prepared, the images are sorted by account number, and reduced facsimiles are printed eight to a page and enclosed with monthly statements prepared for billing via conventional data processing. The resulting service, called *enhanced country club billing* (ECCB), is unique in the industry and is very popular with American Express' 5.1 million corporate cardholders, who often need help in documenting their expense accounts.

The system also helps American Express. Paper handling is cut by a factor of 10, improving productivity and reducing the number of lost or mishandled charge slips, and the optical disks take less storage space than paper records. Moreover, the system both shortens the billing cycle and minimizes disputes about charges–so American Express gets paid sooner.

---

card, achieved either by cutting off two sides of the disc only, or by trimming all four sides so as to create a truly rectangular shape. This CD format is often used as a marketing tool, as a substitute for promotional print brochures. Instead of reading the print in a brochure, potential customers are encouraged to insert the CD in their computer to read the information or view animated demonstrations, video clips, or images.

CD-ROM offers several advantages:

- It is the least expensive way to store large amounts of data and information.
- CD-ROM disks are durable and easy to handle.
- Information can be stored on CD-ROM for many years. Because information cannot be erased from a CD-ROM disk, critical material is safe from being destroyed either accidentally or intentionally.
- Finally, CD-ROM disks can hold motion, video, audio, and high-resolution image information–essential features for multimedia applications.

CD-ROM also has its disadvantages:

- You cannot edit what is already written on the disk unless the data is on a special CD that allows rewriting. Thus, what is an advantage when you want to ensure that material cannot be changed is a disadvantage when you do want to make changes.
- CD-ROM disks retrieve data and information noticeably more slowly than magnetic disks do.

CD-ROM is often used to store large volumes of reference information, such as dictionaries, encyclopedias, and financial reports. Interior designers and illustrators use CD-ROM storage as a source of predrawn art and prepared photographs. They read drawings stored on CD-ROM into their computer's main memory and then embed them in the documents they are preparing. Similarly, engineers retrieve detailed blueprints from CD-ROM and copy them to main memory for their applications.

Two formats are in widespread use:

**CD-R disk**

A disk that allows users to write information to a disk only once but to read it many times (sometimes known as *worm* optical storage).

- **CD-R disks** allow users to write information to a disk only once, but to read it many times (sometimes known as *worm* optical storage). People use CD-R disks to store and retrieve archival information or historical data. Because CD-R systems do not allow the alteration of data once they are entered, CD-Rs are used where the security of data is essential–in distributing software where manufacturers want to protect against unauthorized copying, or in financial and legal documents, for example.

  CD-Rs are often used in banks. If anything is more important to a bank than accuracy, it is the ability to pass an audit. A bank must be able to show the details of its transactions, when they occurred, and the sequence in which they occurred. The *audit trail*–as the series of documents describing a transaction is called–is a permanent record that can serve as a legal document should the need arise. Countless banks now use CD-R optical disks to preserve their auditing activities. Transaction documents are imaged and recorded on CD-R disks. Once recorded, this audit trail cannot be altered in any way. Yet all of the details are readily accessible to the bank's personnel and can be retrieved easily through a computer network. CD-R technology helps banks fulfill their legal obligations to maintain audit trails, provide good customer service, and to maintain records efficiently.

  Depending on the software used, CD-Rs may be *multisession*. That is, they can be partially recorded in one session. In additional sessions, more data can be recorded on the CD. For instance, Eastman Kodak, of Rochester, New York, is a global leader with a long history of helping people take, share, enhance, preserve, print, and enjoy pictures. Among its most recent innovations is the *Kodak PhotoCD*. Developed for storing photographs taken by a digital camera, a consumer can record a set of photos to the CD. Later, additional photos can be added to the CD. However, the CD cannot be erased and rewritten.

  In contrast, when Microsoft issues software on a CD-R, it is designed to be a single session CD. The company does not want any alterations made to the software nor does it want additional data written to the CD.

**CD-RW disk**

A disk that combines the erase-ability and editing options of magnetic storage devices with the permanence, capacity, and reliability of optical storage.

- **CD-RW disks** combine the eraseability and editing options of magnetic storage devices with the permanence, capacity, and reliability of optical storage. CD-RW optical disks tend to be even more reliable than their magnetic counterparts (which are highly reliable). Unlike magnetic disks, CD-RW disks are immune to the harmful effects of stray magnetic fields that can erase data and information stored on magnetic storage media. Also, because they rely on light beams instead of mechanical heads to read and write information, they are immune to head crashes.

  Like CD-Rs, CD-RWs are multisession disks. That is, they can be partially recorded in one session and data can be recorded on the CD in later sessions. In addition, a CD-RW disk can be erased entirely and reused. University faculty members often use CD-RW disks to record the presentation slides, case studies, exercises, and video clips they use during a course. Often this is done in multiple sessions, where each session deals with a particular topic in the course. The next term they may rewrite some of the presentation material, where the newest version replaces the older version on the CD. They may also add revisions and supplementary material to that used in the first term. In this example, a faculty member is making use of both the rewrite and the multisession capabilities of CD-RW disks.

**CD recorder**

Also known as a CD writer or CD burner, this equipment is attached to a PC to create CDs.

CDs can only be created when a **CD recorder** (sometimes called a *CD writer* or *CD burner*) is attached to a PC. A CD drive that is a reader only cannot write CD-RW disks, though it may be able to read them.

The speed of CD drives varies, depending on the model purchased. When they were first introduced to the market, CD drives were designed to process data at a speed of 150,000 bps (i.e., 150 kbps). Drives quickly improved, and in the late 1990s were capable of *writing* at quad-speed (or four times as fast), and *reading* at 12 times the original speed (denoted as *4X/12X*). Within a few years, 10X/40X drives were widely used. They were soon followed by combination CD-ROM/DVD drives.

The use of CD-ROM is growing in all sectors of society. The U.S. Department of Defense, for example, has created a program called *computer-aided acquisition and logistics support (CALS)* to replace some of the massive printed documentation needed to operate and maintain complex aircraft systems. The department's goal is to put all of its aircraft manuals—many of which run to a thousand pages—on CD-ROM. The great virtue of CALS is that it allows pilots to view the documentation onscreen in the cockpit of an aircraft.

Boeing Aircraft, the largest aircraft builder in the world, has instituted a similar CD-ROM system to replace all operation and maintenance manuals for its civilian and military aircraft. At one time, when an aircraft was delivered, Boeing had to deliver thousands of pounds of paper documentation with it. Then it had to keep this documentation updated as enhancements and changes were made to the aircraft. Replacing this material with CD-ROM versions has resulted in faster and easier access to information for the operators of the aircraft.

**DVD** **Digital video disk (DVD)** is the newest generation of optical storage. It appears to operate the same way and has the same dimensions as a CD-ROM. In fact, CDs can be played on a DVD player (but not vice versa). Like CD-ROM, they do not wear out from playing (but can sustain physical damage) and are not susceptible to magnetic fields.

**digital video disk (DVD)**
The newest generation of optical storage. It appears to operate the same way and has the same dimensions as a CD-ROM but has a much larger capacity.

DVDs have a far greater storage capacity of up to 4.7 GB on one side. In addition, one side is divided into two layers, creating a dual layer recording format, which provides a capacity of up to 9.4 GB. DVDs can be recorded on both sides, making the overall capacity 17 GB. (The two-sided recording ability does not double the recording capacity because some of the capacity is reserved for other use.)

DVDs were developed to cope with the large amounts of data needed to store cinema-like quality audio and video, which is much better than is found on VHS videotape or via ordinary television broadcasts. Over two hours of high-quality video can be stored on a single side, single layer DVD. DVDs are widely used in multimedia applications.

The rapid data transfer speeds of DVDs (up to 12 mbps) make them attractive for storage of data. Because they can store and retrieve large volumes of data quickly, they rival some forms of disk storage.

DVD players are widely sold for connection to TVs for playing music and movies. Combination CD-RW/DVD drives are common on PCs. In addition, a large selection of a rewritable DVD form (called **DVD-RAM**) is available and can be used in PCs. As initial competing standards for storing DVD data are resolved, this storage technology will play an increasingly important role in IT applications.

**DVD-RAM**
A rewritable DVD form that can be used in PCs.

 **REALITY CHECK** The demand for CD-ROM storage is growing rapidly. Fortunately, CD-ROM disks can be duplicated in a factory by methods similar to those used to duplicate compact discs. First, a master is made with a laser beam, and then copies of that master are stamped out in a press. (Magnetic tapes and disks cannot be duplicated through mass production stamping. They must be copied individually by recording—a more time-consuming and costly process.) Mass production techniques are both a cause and an effect of the trend toward making CD-ROM drives a standard component on many computer systems, particularly microcomputers.

# Interaction with Computers: Input Devices

Storage and peripheral devices interact with computers through interfaces and ports. People use input and output devices connected to the ports to interact with the computer. Recall that input is the data or information entered into a computer, while output is the result of inputting and processing returned by the computer, either directly to a person using the system or to storage. **Input devices** are the means by which input is fed into the central processor. **Output devices** make the results of processing available outside of the computer.

The seven most commonly used input devices are (1) keyboards, (2) terminals, (3) scanners, (4) digitizers, (5) digital cameras, (6) digital camcorders, and (7) voice and sound input devices. Multimedia audiovisual devices are likely to be used more frequently in the future.

**input device**
A device by which input is fed into a computer's central processor.

**output device**
A device that makes the results of processing available outside of the computer.

## Keyboards

**keyboard**
The most common computer input device.

The most visible and common input device is the computer **keyboard,** as discussed in Chapter 2 (see Figure 2.2). All keyboards are used to enter data and text information into a computer, but computer keyboards differ in four ways:

1. **Characters**   Both alphabetic and symbolic keyboards are available; the choice depends on the country in which the computer is used. In Japan, a symbolic keyboard containing the characters of the Kanji language is the norm. In most other countries, an English-language keyboard is the norm, with U.S. and international versions available.
2. **Key Arrangement**   The arrangement of the keyboard's keys varies. The *QWERTY keyboard* (Figure 5.23) is the most common in English-speaking countries. This keyboard uses the conventional typewriter layout, in which the top row of alphabetic keys begins with the letters Q, W, E, R, T, and Y (reading from left to right).

**FIGURE 5.23**

***The QWERTY Keyboard***

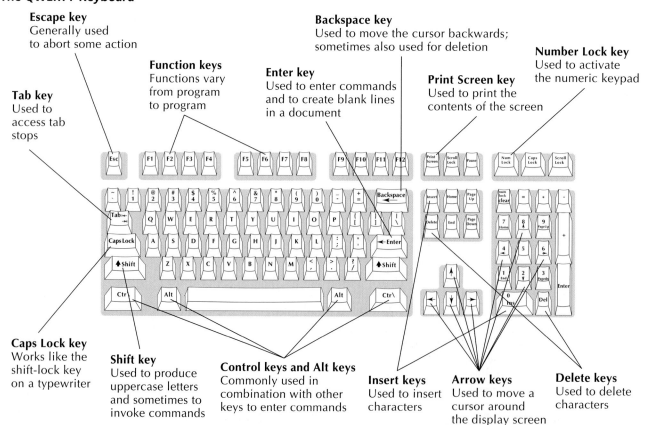

**Escape key**
Generally used to abort some action

**Backspace key**
Used to move the cursor backwards; sometimes also used for deletion

**Number Lock key**
Used to activate the numeric keypad

**Function keys**
Functions vary from program to program

**Enter key**
Used to enter commands and to create blank lines in a document

**Print Screen key**
Used to print the contents of the screen

**Tab key**
Used to access tab stops

**Caps Lock key**
Works like the shift-lock key on a typewriter

**Shift key**
Used to produce uppercase letters and sometimes to invoke commands

**Control keys and Alt keys**
Commonly used in combination with other keys to enter commands

**Insert keys**
Used to insert characters

**Arrow keys**
Used to move a cursor around the display screen

**Delete keys**
Used to delete characters

# CRITICAL CONNECTIONS  3

## Encyclopædia Britannica's DVD Version Lets Readers Explore the Possibilities

**Encyclopædia Britannica**

In 1768, three Scottish printers began publishing a compendium of knowledge, creating what grew to become the first English-language encyclopedia–*Encyclopædia Britannica*. Since that time, *Britannica* has gone through many revisions. The print version now contains more than 30 volumes.

Today's *Encyclopædia Britannica* is also published on DVD and included as part of the *Ultimate Reference Suite*. The information in the print version is included–all 75,000 articles, many written by Nobel laureates and other renowned contributors. But that is only the beginning. In addition to the encyclopedia, the DVD incorporates many digital features, including:

- **World Atlas**  Readers can take a tour of the world through more than 1,300 clickable maps linked to articles about countries, economies, cultures, and technologies.
- **Rich Multimedia**  The *Ultimate Reference Suite* is highly illustrated with 21,000 images, video clips, audio clips, and animation that bring topics to life.
- **Timelines**  History unfolds in 25 extensive timelines showing the people, events, and discoveries of the past, all in graphical form. Nearly 7,000 points on the timelines are hot linked to related articles for quick reference.

The reference suite also includes student and elementary versions of the encyclopedia; two dictionaries and thesauruses containing more than 500,000 definitions, synonyms, and antonyms; an interactive browser for brainstorming and exploring new topics; and a research organizer.

The entire *Ultimate Reference Guide*, including video, audio, and graphic images, resides on a single DVD that sells for under $100. The 30-volume print version, which includes a CD-ROM and a one-year subscription for support is priced at over $1,200.

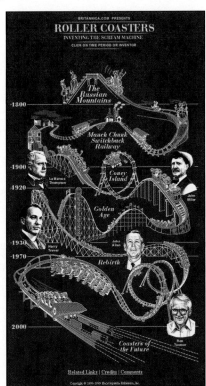

Many countries' languages contain special characters that are not used in English words–for example, *à, á, â, ã, ä, å, æ, ç, ñ, ø, è*, and i. Others have different alphabets. Keyboards used in these countries contain those characters and alphabets.

3. **Special-Purpose Keys** Certain keys are designed to assist the user to enter data or information (for example, the numeric keypad found to the right of the alphabetic keyboard section on many keyboards, as in Figure 5.23) or to control processing (the *Ctrl* and *Alt* keys). The uses of these special **function keys** vary from program to program. For example, the F7 key is used in one software package to invoke information to assist in using correct grammar and capitalization in a document, in another to turn text from bold to italics, and in another to print a report.

4. **Detachability** Most desktop computers have keyboards that can be detached from the rest of the computer system. Wireless keyboards that transmit data to the computer electronically are also popular.

Choosing a keyboard is often a personal matter. The touch, the placement of keys, and the presence or absence of a click when keys are depressed are factors that can affect a user's level of comfort with a computer.

Proper placement of the keyboard is also a factor in personal health. Frequent computer use sometimes leads to such physical problems as carpal tunnel syndrome and tendonitis (muscle stiffness in the wrists). To prevent these problems, several manufacturers have devised ergonomic keyboards (Figure 5.24). In contrast to the conventional fixed straight keyboard, ergonomic keyboards split in the middle so that the portion designed to be used by each hand can be positioned at an angle that corresponds to the natural position of that hand. Since the two sections of the keyboard are movable, they can be adjusted by the individual to a position that feels most comfortable.

The *Information Technology in Practice* feature, "What You Need to Know about Ergonomics," explains more about the importance of having the right physical setup when using IT.

## Terminals

A **terminal** is a combination keyboard and video screen that accepts input, displays it on the video screen, and displays the output sent by the computer to which it is attached. There are three common types of terminals (Figure 5.25):

1. **Dumb terminals** do not contain processing capability. (That is, they do not have control units or arithmetic/logic units. When they do, they are called *intelligent terminals*.) Therefore, they can only accept input from the keyboard and display information from the remote computer to which they are attached. Dumb terminals send whatever is entered through the keyboard to the main computer and display whatever they receive from the main computer without doing any processing (not even simple arithmetic).

---

**function key**

A key designed to assist the computer's user to enter data and information or to control processing.

---

**terminal**

A combination of keyboard and video screen that accepts input and displays it on the screen.

---

**FIGURE 5.24**

***The Ergonomic Keyboard***

## What You Need to Know About Ergonomics

Many computer-dependent workers have been disabled by carpal tunnel syndrome, an extremely painful condition due to damage in the nerves and tendons of the wrists. You can protect yourself (and the people you are managing) against this condition through *ergonomics,* the study of how human bodies interact with equipment in the workplace. The table below lists a few of the problems to watch for—and some solutions, should you encounter them.

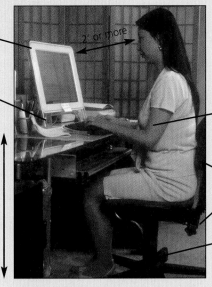

Top of screen should be no higher than eye level.

Monitor should allow tilt/swivel adjustment.

2' or more

Height of keyboard 23–28½" above floor.

Arms should bend down from the shoulders and into angles at the elbow.

Chair back and height should be adjustable

Feet should be flat on floor, with hips and knees bent at right angles.

| THE PROBLEM | THE HIGH-TECH SOLUTION | THE LOW-TECH SOLUTION |
|---|---|---|
| **Repetitive stress injuries (RSIs).** Painful nerve and tissue damage to the wrists and back caused by long hours at poorly designed computer workstations. Accounts for about half of all occupational illnesses; costs employers an estimated $7 billion in lost productivity and medical expenses. | Hire an ergonomics expert to recommend an ergonomically correct chair and computer desk with an adjustable keyboard insert. The chair should allow you to sit with your feet flat on the floor and provide good support for your lower back. The chair cushion should slope down in front, to avoid putting pressure on the backs of your legs. When the chair is properly adjusted, the keyboard should be raised or lowered so that you can type with your wrists and hands parallel to the floor. | Be sure you've adjusted your present chair for optimum support and conformity to your body, using a footrest or cushion if necessary. If the keyboard is too low, prop it up on books; if too high, either adjust the chair height or shorten the table legs. Buy a foam rubber wrist rest and use it during frequent short breaks. Better yet, stop work every 30 minutes and walk around the room for a minute or so. |
| **Electromagnetic emissions from computer monitors.** There is concern that prolonged exposure to these emissions can cause miscarriages, cancer, and other health problems. Research is ongoing. | If your monitor doesn't conform to the stringent Swedish MPR2 guidelines for electromagnetic emissions, buy one that does or switch to a laptop using an LCD (liquid crystal display) screen. As an interim measure, invest in an "antiradiation" screen. It won't block emissions, but some brands claim to cut 99% of electric radiation, and all reduce overhead glare. | Keep your screen at least at arm's length, where emissions are only one-sixth to one-eighth the strength they are when you work closer than four feet to the back or sides of a monitor (electromagnetic emissions are two times stronger there than in front). Turn the monitor off when you aren't using the computer. |
| **Eyestrain and related vision problems.** Vision difficulties caused by staring at the glare and flicker of a monitor for long periods affect an estimated 10 million Americans. | If your monitor produces noticeable flicker, replace it or your graphics board with one that creates a more stable image. To help prevent vision-related problems install an antiradiation or glare screen, and avoid staring at it. Replace overhead fluorescent lighting with indirect and table-top task lighting that uses incandescent bulbs. | Minimize glare by positioning the monitor at a right angle to the window and wear an eyeshade to block too-bright overhead lights. To keep eyes from drying out and to reduce neck strain, adjust the monitor so that the top of the screen is even with your eyes and you're looking down slightly. Take frequent work breaks. |
| **Sick building syndrome.** Flulike symptoms that show up in people when ozone emissions from laser printers and photocopiers, as well as indoor pollutants, accumulate in their work areas. | Hire a consulting engineer to evaluate the ventilation system and make recommendations for reconfiguring work areas to obtain better air flow. Buy an air purifier for your work area. | Don't work near printers and photocopiers, which give off electromagnetic emissions as well as ozone emissions. Keep lots of live plants around—they're great at soaking up indoor pollutants. |

**FIGURE 5.25**

**The Three Types of Terminals**

A The three most common types of terminals are dumb terminals, automated teller machines, and point-of-sale terminals.

2. **Automated teller machines (ATMs)**  are limited-function intelligent terminals that usually contain a small video display, a keyboard consisting of only a few keys, and perhaps a sound speaker. Banks have long used ATMs to dispense cash, accept deposits, and transfer funds between accounts. But the use of ATMs is growing in other areas as well. Airlines are now employing them to dispense tickets, state motor vehicle offices to issue drivers' licenses, and entertainment promoters to sell concert and theater tickets.

3. **Point-of-sale (POS) terminals**  are widely used in department, retail, and grocery stores. Designed to assist salespersons in conducting transactions, POS terminals feature special keys (such as Sale, Void, and Credit) and a numeric keypad similar to the one found on a calculator. They are usually connected to a computer that processes data entered by an employee, perhaps accepting a product or stock number and providing a price in return. Frequently, the data entered by employees into the system are also used to update product inventory information maintained on the computer to which the POS is connected.

The *Information Technology in Practice* feature, "Line Busting at Kroger—Do It Yourself!" describes the fast, self-service customer checkout system installed by this large grocery company. Kroger created the system by combining POS terminals and scanners.

## Scanners

**source data automation**

A method of data entry in which details enter computers directly from their written or printed forms without the intermediate step of keying.

**scanning**

The process of transforming written or printed data or information into a digital form that is entered directly into the computer.

Keying numeric and text data and information into a computer takes time and always includes the possibility of error. As anyone who has ever done any typing knows, it is easy to strike the wrong key. To avoid errors, many companies use **source data automation,** a method of data entry in which data enter computers directly from their written or printed forms without the intermediate step of keying. **Scanning**, which was discussed in Chapter 1, transforms written or printed data or information into a digital form that is entered directly into the computer.

Scanners are used in many industries, including the pharmaceutical industry, where it is extremely important to maintain adequate supplies. Patients expect a pharmacy to have the medicine they need when they take their prescription to be filled. On the other hand, pharmacies do not want to hold too large a supply of any medicine, not only because excess inventories take up room, but also because many drugs have a brief shelf life.

To help druggists maintain the proper inventory balance, San Francisco–based McKesson Corp. has developed a scanner system (see *Critical Connections 1,* Chapter 2). To place an order, the druggist passes a laser scanner over a shelf ticket in front of the item to be ordered. This single swipe of the scanner captures the product's name and the amount of it the pharmacist usually orders. These data are captured in a handheld computer that is later connected to a telephone line to McKesson's order department.

When the order arrives at McKesson, it is electronically transferred into the company's order-processing system. Because entries like this do not have to be keyed, mistakes are rare. When McKesson's employees fill the order, IT again plays a pivotal role. Strapped to the wrist of each employee is a combination portable computer,

# INFORMATION TECHNOLOGY IN PRACTICE

## Line Busting at Kroger—Do It Yourself!

Bar-code scanners revolutionized the retail industry when they were introduced in the 1980s. Today they are installed in countless organizations, helping to improve worker productivity and reducing mistakes during the checkout process.

Now another checkout innovation is taking hold in many stores, and it is causing line busting. It is self-checkout, where the customers do the work themselves and even pay for merchandise without the involvement of store personnel.

Kroger, headquartered in Cincinnati, Ohio, is one of the largest retail grocery chains, operating some 2,500 supermarkets and multi-department stores in 32 states. Kroger is among the leaders in introducing self-checkout systems, having installed them in the majority of its stores with successful results.

The self-checkout system includes a video camera that detects approaching shoppers, activating the system and the audio unit that greets them. It also includes a POS system with a touch-screen monitor that graphically guides the shopper through each step of the process. It instructs the customer to pass each item over the flatbed scanner that is built into the counter's surface. A beam of laser light is reflected off of the item's bar code onto a sensor that converts the pattern into data that can identify the item. The price for the item is retrieved from the store databases and added to the shopper's purchase tally.

Self-checkout units can weigh produce, but unless there is a bar code attached, they cannot tell, well, apples from oranges. Kroger's systems include colorful icons and illustrations, including onscreen product identification and voice assistance to help identify these items. (Clever researchers at IBM have developed a scanner, nicknamed *Veggie Vision*, that can identify fruits and vegetables without UPC bar codes. However, they are not yet in commercial use.)

In Kroger's self-checkout systems, the bagging area rests on a scale, the main purpose of which is to assist in preventing theft. The system knows the weight of each item and can detect when an item is put in the grocery bag without being scanned. When it detects extra weight, it alerts a store attendant.

The self-checkout system allows shoppers to use coupons, pay with cash, debit, or credit cards, and electronic benefits transfer (EBT). Its slip printer prepares a tape showing each transaction, any deductions for coupons inserted into the coupon bin, the amount paid, and any change due. The coin and bill dispensers issue the appropriate change for cash payments.

An attendant is available if shoppers have questions or should any difficulties arise. One attendant can supervise several checkouts simultaneously, providing labor savings for the store.

Behind the scenes each self-checkout system is connected to the store's network and servers. In addition to providing access to the pricing database, the system also tallies sales information and adjusts inventory details, as is the case with Kroger's manually operated POS systems.

Self-checkout systems typically cost $25,000 to $30,000 per unit, and are often installed in sets of four. Kroger finds that the labor savings and productivity benefits accumulate so that the systems pay for themselves in about a year.

However, the appeal of the self-checkout system is not universal. Customers that *do* prefer the self-checkout system consider it faster than the staffed checkout counters. They like not having to stand in line behind other shoppers and enjoy scanning and bagging their own groceries. Some of these customers even feel they are afforded more privacy by self-checkout. Still, a substantial number of shoppers think the traditional checkout process is faster. These customers also prefer to have someone else manage the scanning and bagging for them.

While not all customers choose the self-checkout option, Kroger's success with self-checkout has convinced management to retain the systems. They help both the company and some of its best customers achieve one of their primary objectives: line busting.

laser scanner, and two-way radio (Figure 5.26). Details of the order are transmitted by radio from the central computer to the wrist computer, telling the employee which item is needed and where it is located in the warehouse. When the order filler reaches the stock location, a quick point of the laser scanner at the shelf ticket confirms that the item is correct. When the worker pulls the stock, McKesson's inventory records are adjusted, and the pulled item is added to the customer's bill.

Clearly, both parties benefit from this system. The customer gets fast service, often receiving the item within 24 to 48 hours of placing the order. McKesson avoids costly errors (a mistake costs five to seven times more than a correctly filled order) and ensures accurate inventory and billing information—not to mention satisfied, repeat customers.

There are two types of scanning: optical character recognition and image scanning.

**Optical Character Recognition**    The term **optical character recognition (OCR)** refers to devices that can read information printed on paper and convert it into computer-processable forms. There are three types of OCR: optical mark readers, optical character readers, and optical code readers.

**Optical mark readers** recognize the presence and location of dark marks on a special form (Figure 5.27) as the form is scanned. Many standardized tests, such as the SAT, use this format. In answering questions, students blacken designated spots on the scannable test form. The completed form is read by an OCR scanner, which sends the student's responses to a processor that determines the number of right and wrong answers and computes the student's final score. Government and medical offices also use optical mark readers to take large surveys, for example, marketing research surveys and the U.S. Census. The efficiency and reliability of optical mark readers allow these organizations to capture a large volume of information in a consistent format.

**Optical character readers** recognize printed information rather than just dark marks. Optical character readers are often used by retail stores to read the product number of store merchandise, by libraries to read the call number of a library book, and by mail-order companies to read merchandise order numbers (Figure 5.28). Bank checks are processed by a special form of optical character reading called **magnetic ink character recognition.** The check, bank number, and customer account number—all of which are preprinted in magnetic ink on the check—are read optically or sensed magnetically (Figure 5.29).

**Optical code readers** are used by supermarkets and other large retail stores. When customers check out at the cash register, the items they selected for purchase are usually passed over a piece of glass covering an optical scanner, which reads the **universal product code (UPC)** printed on the package. The UPC is a bar code that identifies the product by a series of vertical lines of varying width representing a unique product num-

**optical character recognition (OCR)**
A technology by which devices read information on paper and convert it into computer-processable form.

**optical mark reader**
An OCR device that recognizes the location of dark marks on a special form as the form is scanned.

**optical character reader**
An OCR device that recognizes printed information rather than just dark marks.

**magnetic ink character recognition**
A form of optical character reading in which preprinted information written in magnetic ink is read optically or sensed magnetically.

**optical code reader**
An OCR device used to read bar codes.

**universal product code (UPC)**
A bar code that identifies a product by a series of vertical lines of varying widths representing a unique product number.

**FIGURE 5.26**

***Source Data Automation at McKesson***

Order fillers at McKesson Corp. use AcuMax wrist computers to locate inventory and bill customers' accounts directly.

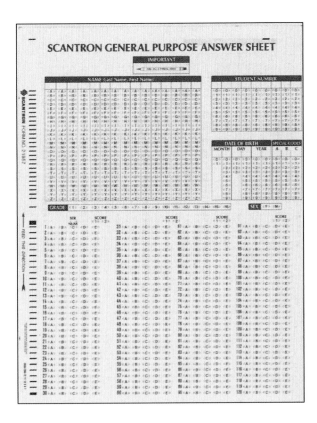

**FIGURE 5.27**

***Sample Optical Mark
Test Form***

Many standardized tests use optical
mark readers to determine scores. In
answering questions, the test taker
blackens a designated spot on the test
form, which is then read and graded
by an OCR scanner.

*Source:* Courtesy Scan-Tron Corporation

ber. This number is sent to a store computer, which contains pricing and inventory information. The price is rung up at the register, and in many systems the inventory information is updated at the same time. Alternatively, the checkout cashier may pass a handheld scanner (a *wand* or *gun*) over the UPC code (Chapter 2, Figure 2.4).

Catalina Marketing of Anaheim, California, has converted the supermarket checkout scanner into an effective marketing tool. The company connects a personal computer to each checkout scanner to capture information on a purchase as the customer is making it. Using quick processing, the computer can then issue the customer a coupon to promote additional purchases. Suppose, for example, the customer is buying cat litter. The computer, thus informed that the customer probably has a cat, will print out a coupon for a cat food the store (or manufacturer) wishes to promote. Say instead the purchase is a six-pack of Pepsi. The Coca-Cola Company, Pepsi's biggest competitor, may have arranged for Catalina's backroom computer to print out for the Pepsi customer a two-for-one coupon for a six-pack of Coke. Or Pepsi may have arranged for a half-off coupon for Frito-Lay potato chips to be printed out with a purchase of Pepsi (Frito-Lay is owned by Pepsi).

**REALITY CHECK** Until recently, the millions of students who took the SAT or a similar college-entrance exam annually sat in a large room with other nervous students. Each got a test booklet and an answer sheet on which they blackened the letter *a*, *b, c,* or *d* using a No. 2 pencil. This process is now largely obsolete.

Now students complete the standardized multiple-choice exams on a computer rather than blackening spots on answer sheets. The main advantage of this is convenience. (The tests are not any easier.) Instead of adhering to the traditional Saturday test schedule, SAT takers can now call test centers and make an appointment to take the test on any weekday. And instead of waiting six to eight weeks to find out their results, test takers (with enough courage) can ask the computer to flash the score as soon as they complete the exam. ■

N762-3

# YES! Send me 5 Books for 99¢ when I join

Please enroll me in *Doubleday Book Club* according to the risk-free membership plan described in the accompanying magazine. Send me the 5 BOOKS I've indicated, and my FREE GIFT. Bill me just 99¢, plus shipping and handling. I agree to purchase 4 more books in the next 2 years.

Please initial here_____

Choose your FREE GIFT here:
☐ Free Umbrella Tote Set #9159
   **or**
☐ Free Book
   (write book number)

0 1 2 3 4 5 6 7 8 9

If you select a book that counts as 2 choices, write the first 4 digits of the book number in one row of boxes and 9999 in the next.

**DOUBLEDAY**
B O O K   C L U B

85/86

**MONEY-SAVING OPPORTUNITY**
Send me the book indicated here. Bill me just $2.99, plus shipping and handling (books that count as two choices not eligible)

(write book number)

93286  85  86  9159  45

FALL 93

---

**image scanning**

Examining an image and translating lines, dots, and marks into digital form.

**flatbed scanner**

A large image scanner that works like an office photocopier.

**resolution**

The clarity or sharpness of an image.

**Image Scanning**   To scan drawings, entire documents, or photographic images, **image scanning** must be used. The scanner examines the images and translates its lines, dots, and marks into digital form.

**Flatbed scanners** (Chapter 2, Figure 2.2) work like office photocopiers. The flatbed scanner is attached by cable to an input/output port on the computer. The person doing the scanning places the photograph, drawing, or page of text face down on a glass plate on top of the scanner. As a bar of light, controlled by software, passes beneath the glass, the light is reflected off the printed image onto a grid of photosensitive cells. The number of light sensors in the scanner determines the quality of the scanner's optical **resolution**—that is, the clarity or sharpness of the image. A scanner with a resolution of 2,400 dots per inch (DPI), for example, contains 2,400 sensors in each inch of the scanning mechanism. The more DPI, the higher the resolution (the sharper the image). The flatbed scanners used with most PCs have resolutions ranging from 600 to 2,400 DPI. Scanners used by commercial printers have resolutions of 9,600 DPI and higher, providing much sharper images.

**FIGURE 5.29**

***Magnetic Ink Character Recognition***

Magnetic ink characters are located on the bottom line of a check. On the left side are the bank identification number and customer's account number. On the right side is the check amount, which is imprinted on the check after it has been cashed.

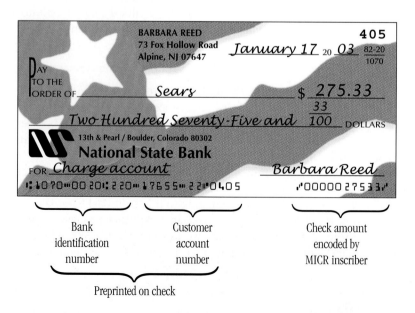

As the flatbed scanner's light bar moves down the page, the image data are collected dot by dot. Depending on the type of scanner, the data may be sensed as shades of gray or in 256 or more colors. When the image is transmitted from the scanner to the central processor, color information is included so that the image can be properly recreated for processing, display, or storage.

The benefits of image scanning are well known to Consolidated Freightways, a nationwide freight carrier. It used to take the company as long as three weeks to respond to a customer's inquiry about an invoice, a damage claim, or a complaint. All this time was needed to locate and assemble the documents required to answer the inquiry. Then, in the early 1990s, the company invested $10 million in an imaging system. All documents and correspondence related to a shipment are now scanned and stored in the company's computer system. Up to three years' worth of shipping and billing documents—more than 60 million pieces of paper—are accessible through the centralized system. Now, when a customer makes an inquiry—whether in writing or over the telephone—a customer service representative can get copies of all pertinent documents in approximately 10 minutes.

## Digitizers

A **digitizer** is an input device that translates measured distances into digital values that the computer can process. As the digitizing device moves, electric pulses inform the computer of the change in position. The computer responds by shifting an indicator, such as an arrow (→) or cross-hair cursor (⊕), to the same position as the digitizer.

Following are seven types of digitizers. With one exception (the stylus on a PDA) all must be connected to the computer by a communications cable.

1. The **mouse** (Chapter 2, Figure 2.2) is a familiar input device found with many desktop computers. As the ball on the underside of the mouse moves, the horizontal and vertical coordinates of the corresponding mouse cursor change. By checking these coordinates, the computer knows where the cursor is and displays the indicator in the appropriate place on the display screen.
2. The **touchpad** (Figure 5.30), an alternative to the mouse, is built into most laptop computers and can be attached to desktop computers. The small, flat pad senses the user's finger movement and downward pressure, moving the cursor in the corresponding direction on the display screen.
3. The **pointing stick** (see Figure 5.30, an alternative to the mouse and often used with laptop computers, directs the cursor across the computer screen. The growing use of laptop computers necessitated the development of a device more compact than the

**digitizer**
An input device that translates measured distances into digital values that the computer can process.

**mouse**
An input device with a small ball underneath that rotates, causing a corresponding movement of a pointer on a display screen.

**touchpad**
An alternative to the mouse that senses the user's finger movement and downward pressure, moving the cursor in the corresponding direction on the display screen.

**pointing stick**
A device that positions the cursor on the computer screen.

**FIGURE 5.30**

***Laptop Computers Often Include Both a Touchpad and a Pointing Stick***

mouse. The pointing stick, embedded in the notebook's keyboard above the *b* key, is used to position the cursor on the display screen. The motion of the cursor on the screen is controlled by the amount of pressure applied to the pointing stick (it does not actually move, but rather senses finger pressure). The speed at which the cursor moves corresponds to the amount of pressure on the stick.

When a computer is equipped with a pointing stick, the click buttons normally found on a mouse are located below the keys. As with a conventional mouse, the function of these click buttons is determined by the application program in use.

The pointing stick offers two advantages. First, it does not take any extra space, so you can use the laptop computer in tight spaces (such as on the serving tray of an airplane seat) where you would not have room to move a mouse to position a cursor. Second, you do not have to move your fingers from their typing position in order to use the pointing stick. Because of these advantages, a growing number of laptop manufacturers are adding the pointing stick, originated by IBM, to their computers.

Many leading manufacturers are now including both touchpads and pointing sticks in their laptop computers, thereby enabling users to select the one they prefer.

**light pen**

An input device that uses a light-sensitive cell to draw images and to select options from a menu of choices displayed on a computer screen.

4. The **light pen** (Figure 5.31) looks like a ballpoint pen, except that its ball is actually a light-sensitive cell. When the tip of the light pen touches a computer's display screen, the computer senses the pen's location on the screen and transmits this information to the processor. Movement by the light pen in any direction is sensed by the processor, which determines the meaning of the movement according to the application program in use. Light pens are used both to draw images and to select options from a menu of choices displayed on the screen.

**joystick**

An input device used to control the actions in computer games or simulations. The joystick extends vertically from a control box.

5. The **joystick** extends vertically from a pivot connected mechanically and electronically to a control box. It is often used to control computer games or simulations. As the joystick is moved up, down, right, left, or diagonally, it sends a signal to the computer's processor, which senses the distance and direction of the movement. These signals are incorporated as input data into the program, which then determines action status and steps to take. A visual display of the movement appears on the computer screen.

Want to fly a jet fighter without spending hours and hours of time training? Get the Microsoft *Flight Simulator.* This popular computer game provides the operator with a realistic simulation of the inside of an airplane cockpit, complete with moving dials and gauges. Grab the joystick, pull back on it, and you will feel yourself gaining altitude quickly. Look to the right or left on the screen and you will see a terrain with trees, buildings, and other objects getting smaller and smaller as you climb higher. Push the joystick to the right and you will begin a turn. Push it too far to the right, and you will be flying upside down.

**trackball**

An input device that consists of a ball mounted on rollers. As the user rotates the ball in any direction, the computer senses the movement and moves the cursor in the corresponding direction.

6. A **trackball** (Figure 5.32) is a ball mounted on rollers. As the user rotates the ball in any direction, the computer senses the movement in much the same way that it does with a joystick. Roll the ball to the left, and the cursor will move to the left. Roll the ball to the right, and the cursor will move with it. Many laptop computers use a trackball instead of a mouse. The click buttons, as on a mouse, are located next to the trackball.

**stylus**

A penlike instrument that is used to trace images on paper for translation into electronic form.

**digitizing tablet**

A device by which an image on paper can be translated into electronic form.

7. A **stylus** is used to trace images on paper for translation into electronic form. This is done on a **digitizing tablet** (Figure 5.33a) or on a handheld device (Figure 5.33b). As a pen-like stylus or cross-hair pointer is passed over the features of the drawing, the computer senses the dots and lines that compose the drawing and creates an electronic version in memory while displaying the information visually on the screen. Once the drawing is complete, the digitized form can be stored or modified.

Users of personal digital assistants (PDAs) rely on the stylus as the principal form of entering data. As the stylus is moved across the PDA's screen, the motion is transferred into letters, numbers, and images that are stored in memory.

Note that mice, joysticks, and trackballs all recognize movement and position, while light pens and digitizing tablets recognize the presence or absence of information as they move. Digitizing devices are in widespread use on computers of all sizes.

**FIGURE 5.31**
*Light Pen*

**FIGURE 5.32**
*Trackball*
The trackball is a popular alternative to the mouse and touch pad as an input device.

## Digital Cameras

Digital cameras are quickly gaining a foothold in photography. A **digital camera** captures a photographic image as a collection of tightly grouped dots. Each digital image is captured on light-sensitive memory chips that can store from approximately 24 to more than 100 images, depending on the make of the camera and size of its memory.

After digital images are captured, they can be copied into computer memory or stored on disk. These images can be printed or processed to change the size or alter the

**digital camera**
A device that captures a photographic image as a collection of tightly grouped dots that can be stored on disk or in memory.

**FIGURE 5.33a**
*A Digitizing Tablet in Action*
Digitizing tablets are often used in combination with graphic design programs. Here a clothing designer creates a sweater design. Once the original design is created, it can be stored in the computer's memory and modified later.

**FIGURE 5.33b**
*Using a Stylus to Enter Digital Information in a PDA*
Data can be entered into a PDA by using a stylus to write characters and numbers on the display screen, where they are recognized by the software. Or they may be entered by invoking an image of a keyboard and touching the sensitized letters and numbers with the stylus.

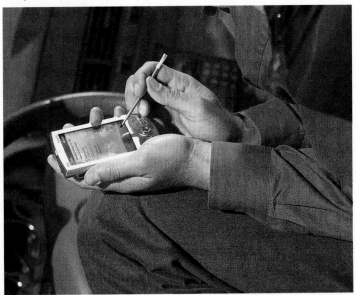

color of the dots, or even to remove them entirely. In addition, images captured by digital cameras can be transmitted over a communications link in the same way as an e-mail image.

A growing number of news photographers are relying on the digital camera because of the good quality of its photographs and the convenience of the digital form. Is a digital camera in your future? The combination of ever-high resolution and easy-to-use features, plus attractive pricing, is leading many people to buy them for home and business use. If you need to capture images for computer processing, there is a good chance that you will be using a digital camera soon.

The *Information Technology in Practice* feature, "Getting Beyond the Digital Photo Chain of Pain," describes how companies are seeking to help consumers adapt to digital photography and at the same time increase their sales of cameras.

## Digital Video Camcorders

**digital video camcorder**
Used to capture the sound and sight of events on videotape, information is recorded as individual bytes of information. Digital recording thus increases the quality of both audio and video.

Camcorders have been used for many years to capture the sound and sight of events on videotape. Until recently, all have been analog. Now widely available, **digital video camcorders** record information as individual bytes of information. Digital recording thus increases the quality of both audio and video. Since the images are a series of ones and zeros, they can be reproduced exactly the same way.

Digital camcorders (Figure 5.34) can be connected to computers making it possible to transfer the video to storage. There the video can be edited to add special effects or to remove unwanted segments, and can be viewed through playback software. Digital video segments can also be transmitted by e-mail or posted on Web pages.

The case study in Chapter 2, "CNN Digital Assets," describes how this global broadcast company is using digital video in daily program production. The case describes how digital video and all-digital production video capabilities are creating new opportunities for Cable News Network (CNN).

## Voice and Sound Input Devices

**voice input device**
An input device that can be attached to a computer to capture the spoken word in digital form.

Digitizing the spoken word is being done more and more to take advantage of the multimedia capability of computers. Spoken words are captured in digital form by **voice input devices** connected to the computer. A microphone is attached either to a voice expansion board that fits within an internal slot in the computer or to a special microphone jack on the computer. Special software controls the process of capturing and digitizing the human voice or any other sounds sensed by the microphone. Figure 5.35 explains how this process works.

**FIGURE 5.34**

***Digital Camcorder and Digital Video Cassettes***

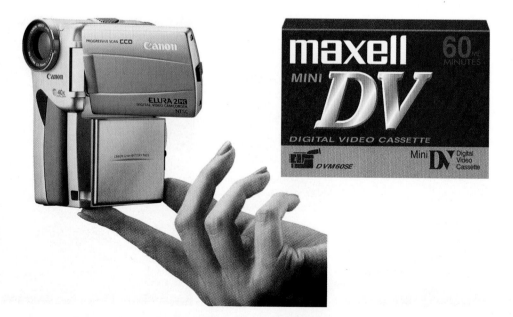

# INFORMATION TECHNOLOGY IN PRACTICE
## Getting Beyond the Digital Photo Chain of Pain

Taking photos with digital cameras is becoming more and more popular. Printing those images, however, has not caught on—at least, not yet.

The strategy behind the introduction of digital photos was clear. Camera makers would aggressively advertise digital photography while manufacturers of computers and printers would widely promote their products' ability to create colorful, high-quality prints. However, photo printing and the related sales of specialty papers and printer inks for this purpose has failed to meet initial expectations. This is because consumers at this point are transferring just a portion of the images they shoot to paper. Many are being stored on PCs in digital photo albums. A substantial number are also being transmitted to friends, relatives, and acquaintances via e-mail, but never printed. Others are simply erased because of imperfections and still others remain in the camera's memory indefinitely. Only a fraction of the photos taken with digital cameras ever appears on paper.

For many consumers, photo printing is, as the industry has labeled it, a *chain of pain.* Printing digital images at home, or even uploading them to an online printing service, is a hassle. Just think of the steps you must go through: To transfer photos from your camera to a PC, software must be loaded into your computer. Once transferred, you need to name and store the images. Before printing, you may want to edit the image. Then you must set the software

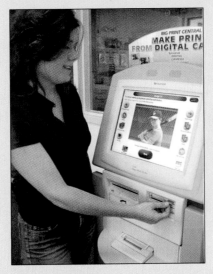

for image size and number of images to be printed per page. Only after loading the special photo paper can you finally print your photos. Compared to the old way of dropping off a roll of film or a single use camera for one-hour processing, the hassle of printing digital photos is indeed a pain.

It is no secret that the industry is seeking to overcome the chain of pain and stimulate the printing of digital photos. Kodak, Fuji, and Polaroid—companies long associated with photography—and digital camera maker Sony are installing digital photo kiosks in malls, discount stores (such as Wal-Mart), and camera stores. All you have to do is insert the chip, memory stick, CD, or diskette from your digital camera into the machine. The kiosk's easy-to-use software lets you select only the images you wish to print without the need to manage the steps of transfer, naming, or storage required on

your PC. In less than 30 seconds, out pops the final result.

If you wish, you can use the kiosk's software to edit the imperfections in images, add special effects, or remove the dreaded red-eye effect caused by electronic flashes.

There is little or no assistance at the kiosks, should you have questions or if you improperly insert your memory device. However, once you get beyond the questions of first-time use, the entire process is simple.

For consumer and industry alike there is good opportunity in digital photography if the chain of pain caused by one technology can be turned into gain by another.

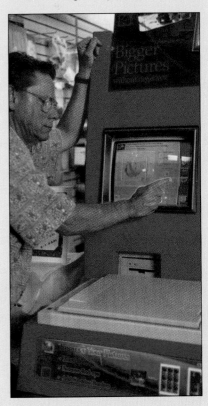

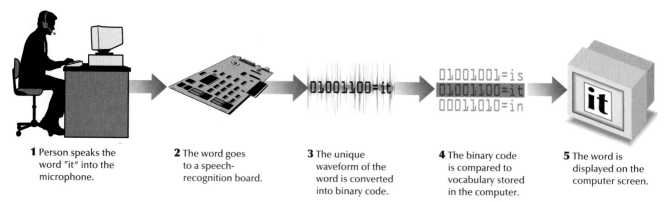

**1** Person speaks the word "it" into the microphone.

**2** The word goes to a speech-recognition board.

**3** The unique waveform of the word is converted into binary code.

**4** The binary code is compared to vocabulary stored in the computer.

**5** The word is displayed on the computer screen.

**FIGURE 5.35**

*Capturing and Digitizing Sounds*

The U.S. Transportation Command is integrating voice input devices to change the way it handles the movement of its aircraft around the world. When the organization's aircraft dispatchers are notified of bad weather or that an aircraft is running low on fuel, they must divert the plane to the airport that is closest to its current location. But since there are so many different airports, with varying capabilities for handling large and small aircraft, it is sometimes impossible for the dispatchers to recall instantly all of the information they need to direct the pilot.

For this reason, the organization is considering creating a voice input system to assist dispatchers. Then, when a fog rolls in, making it impossible for an incoming aircraft to land at its intended destination of, say, Frankfurt, the dispatcher will be able to speak into a microphone built into the control tower computer: "Give me a list of all airports within one hour of Frankfurt, Germany." Instantly, a list will appear on the screen. The dispatcher then can query the computer by voice again: "Which airport is closest and not closed because of weather?"

 **REALITY CHECK**  Until recently, research in voice, sound, and speech input advanced slowly because of technological limitations. Most English speakers have a vocabulary of approximately 20,000 words, but the earliest voice input boards could usually recognize fewer than 100. One problem was that a huge amount of storage was needed to hold a decent vocabulary list. Another was the length of time needed to search the list of words.

Massive leaps in storage technology (both for primary memory and for storage) and faster processors are solving these problems. Systems that have a vocabulary capacity of over 25,000 words are already in use on desktop computers. It is safe to assume that the technical barriers to voice input will continue to disappear.

But how and where would voice input be used? Delta Air Lines, discussed in an *Information Technology in Practice* feature earlier in this chapter, has incorporated voice input into its telephone reservation systems. Callers can choose to retrieve information from the system by pressing a number of their telephone touchpad or speaking the number into the phone: "For international reservations, press or say 1."

Certainly there are many situations where voice commands would be helpful. Would people want to give dictation to their computer and have the system transform their rambling speech into a polished document with correct spelling and good grammar? Would they like their automobiles to have a voice-controlled guidance system that replaces the dashboard and stick-shift levers? What about video arcade games—could voice control create a new dimension of entertainment?

It is not too early for you to start thinking about these possibilities. Few experts have yet to emerge in this area; perhaps you can be one of the first. ■

# Interaction with Computers: Output and Information Distribution Devices

Eight types of devices are used to display and distribute computer output: (1) monitors, (2) data projectors, (3) printers, (4) audio response units, (5) television, (6) plotters, (7) film recorders, and (8) digital cameras. Digital cameras were discussed in the previous section on input devices. This section describes the other seven devices.

## Visual Displays (Monitors)

A computer's visual display is its most visible component. Visual displays are usually called **video display terminals (VDTs) or monitors** (Figure 5.36). Until recently, monitors used with desktop PCs relied on conventional cathode ray tube (CRT) technology. Laptops, having smaller, flat display screens, used liquid crystal display (LCD)[2] technology. Today, manufacturers are offering large-size LCD flat-panel displays for use with PCs. The main advantages of these LCD displays are that they present a sharper, nonglare image, take up less desk space and are lighter.

Monitors also differ in size, color, resolution, bit mapping, and graphics standard.

- **Size**   Monitors come in many different sizes, from the small screen built into palmtops and laptops to the extra-large monitors used for special purposes. The standard monitor for personal computers is 15 to 17 inches (38 to 42 cm), measured diagonally, corner to corner. Large-screen monitors have been developed for use by engineers and illustrators, who need to examine fine details closely. These are commonly 19 and 21 inches (48 to 53 cm) wide and provide 45 to 60 percent more viewing area than standard monitors do.
- **Color**   Color monitors are the norm (see Figure 5.36). These **RGB displays** can create 256 colors and several thousand variations on them by blending shades of red, green, and blue (hence the term RGB display). **Monochrome displays** show information using a single foreground color on a contrasting background color (for example, white on black, black on white, amber on black, green on black).
- **Resolution**   Since all characters and images on a monitor are made up of dot patterns, the number of dots, or **pixels,** per inch determines resolution, or the sharpness

**video display terminal (VDT) or monitor**
A computer's visual display.

**RGB display**
A video screen display with the ability to create 256 colors and several thousand variations on these colors by blending shades of red, green, and blue.

**monochrome display**
A video screen display that shows information using a single foreground color on a contrasting background color (e.g., black on white).

**pixels**
The dots used to create an image; the higher the number of dots, the better the resolution of the image.

**FIGURE 5.36**

***Color Monitors Using CRT and LCD Technology***

---

[2]LCD displays consist of two sheets of polarizing material with a liquid crystal solution between them. An electric current passed through the liquid causes the crystals to align so that light cannot pass through them. Each crystal, therefore, is like an open or closed shutter, either allowing light to pass through or blocking the light.

of the image. A higher number of pixels means a sharper image. Common resolutions are as follows:

- 800 columns × 600 rows (800 × 600 = 480,000 pixels on the screen)
- 1,024 columns × 768 rows (786,432 pixels)
- 1,280 × 800 columns (1,024,000 pixels)
- 1,600 columns × 1,200 rows (1,920,000 pixels)

- **Bit Mapping**   A monitor may or may not have bit-mapping capabilities. With **bit mapping,** each dot on the monitor can be controlled individually. Graphics created through bit mapping are sharp and crisp, without unseemly jagged edges. Prior to the introduction of bit mapping, **character addressing** was the norm. Character addressing permitted only letters, numbers, and other preformed letters and symbols—no lines or curved images—to be sent to and displayed on the display screen.

- **Graphics Standard**   A graphics standard is one that combines resolution and use of color. A monitor's resolution and use of color are determined by a **graphics adapter card,** an interface chip on the system board or an add-in board between computer and monitor that performs according to one of several widely used PC standards: *super VGA* (SVGA), which is the most widely used and has the best resolution of all); *video graphics array* (VGA); *enhanced graphics adapter* (EGA); or *color graphics adapter* (CGA—the oldest and lowest-resolution standard). Similar standards exist for Macintosh and other computers.

**Multisync/multiscan monitors** are designed to work with a variety of graphics standards, automatically adjusting to provide the best possible resolution for the adapter card and computer configuration in use.

Resolution, color clarity, and graphics capabilities are steadily improving, making more sophisticated applications possible. Color and graphic displays on high-resolution monitors are changing the business of publishing (this entire book was designed and laid out using a color monitor), just as they are influencing the business of commerce and government.

## Data Projectors

**Data projectors,** connected to the computer's display output port by a data cable, are used to show the contents of a computer video display on a movie screen. In this way, large audiences can see the same information and animation as an individual seated in front of the monitor.

**Liquid crystal display (LCD) projectors** are a widely used data projector for small groups of fewer than 100 people (Figure 5.37). An LCD projector works on the principle of blocking light rather than emitting it. The brightness of the light (measured in lumens) determines how easily the images can be viewed in a room with ordinary lighting (as opposed to a darkened room). Projectors with ratings of 1,000 or higher lumens can generally be used in daylight presentations. Those with ratings of 2,500 and above provide exceptionally high quality projection.

LCD projectors remain expensive, with prices ranging from $2,000 to more than $10,000 according to the size, resolution, and lumens rating of the LCD projector.

**Digital light processing (DLP) projectors** are a better choice when projecting for large audiences in big auditoriums, hotel ballrooms, and concert halls. Lighting ratings on these projectors range from approximately 2,000 to more than 9,000 lumens. Image brightness is achieved by using an advanced *digital micromirror device* (DMD), an optical semiconductor chip that includes an array of microscopic aluminum mirrors that reflect light. This projector builds images on screen by digitally controlling the reflected angle of incident light, converging it with a prism and passing the image through a lens on to the screen. The DLP projector differs from that of an LCD projector in that it has a higher reflectance, and can use light more efficiently for higher brightness. The result is clear, sharp images and high contrast text as well as rich color in projected images.

---

**bit mapping**

A feature of some monitors that allows each dot on the monitor to be addressed or controlled individually. Graphics created through bit mapping are sharp and crisp.

**character addressing**

The precursor to bit mapping that allowed only full characters to be sent to and displayed on a VDT.

**graphics adapter card**

An interface board between a computer and monitor that is used to determine the monitor's resolution and use of color.

**multisync/multiscan monitors**

Monitors designed to work with a variety of graphics standards.

**data projector**

Equipment connected to the computer's display output port by a data cable that is used to show the contents of a computer video display on a movie screen.

**liquid crystal display (LCD) projector**

An LCD projector works on the principle of blocking light rather than emitting it. The brightness of the light (measured in lumens) determines how easily the images can be viewed in a room with ordinary lighting (as opposed to a darkened room).

**digital light processing (DLP) projector**

This projector builds images on screen by digitally controlling the reflected angle of incident light, converging it with a prism, and passing the image through a lens on to the screen. It has clear, sharp images and high contrast text as well as rich color in projected images.

# CRITICAL CONNECTIONS 4

## Wireless Electronic Shelf Tags Guarantee Uniform Prices

**Shaw's Supermarkets**

Shaw's Supermarkets Inc. operates nearly 200 stores in the six New England states of the United States, serving some 5 million customers weekly. Like its parent company, J Sainsbury plc. of London, Shaw's has found that electronic shelf labels benefit its customers and improve store efficiencies.

The introduction of bar coding and scanners in food stores put an end to store owners' need to price each item individually. However, since implementing this innovation, grocers have been caught between wanting to gain operating efficiency and wanting to meet their customers' desire to be sure they are paying the correct price for an item. Although some states require that the price continue to be marked on every item so there could be no question of the item's price, others allowed the price to be posted only on the shelf. Consumers were, understandably, quick to point out that discrepancies between the price on the shelf and the price charged at the checkout counter occurred too often. Shaw's believes that electronic shelf tags will meet the needs of both the consumer and the company.

Electronic shelf tags are a high-tech alternative to the adhesive paper labels on shelves. Their digital display shows the price, which is transmitted wirelessly from the store's database—the same database that the POS terminals at the checkout counter use for pricing information. Hence, this system ensures that when purchases are scanned at the checkout, the price will match the one displayed on the store shelf. Shaw's likes the fact that price changes can be implemented with a few keystrokes on the computer while eliminating the expense, hassle, and uncertainty of having labels simultaneously posted to show the new price.

## Printers

A printer is an output device that produces **hard copy**—paper output. Two general categories of printers are impact and nonimpact printers (Figure 5.38).

In **impact printing**, the paper and the device printing the character come into contact with each other. In **nonimpact printing**, there is no physical contact between the paper and the print device. Instead, the characters are produced on the paper through a heat, chemical, or spraying process.

**Nonimpact Printers**   Laser, ink-jet, and thermal printing are the most frequently used kinds of nonimpact printers (see Figure 5.39).

**hard copy**
The paper output from a printer.

**impact printing**
A printing process in which the paper and the character being printed come into contact with each other.

**nonimpact printing**
A printing process in which no physical contact occurs between the paper and the print device; the characters are produced on the paper through a heat, chemical, or spraying process.

**FIGURE 5.37**
*Data Projectors*

**laser printer**
A nonimpact printer that uses laser beams to print an entire page at once.

**ink-jet printer**
A printer that sprays tiny streams of ink from holes in the print mechanism onto the paper in a dot pattern that represents the character or image to be printed.

- **Laser printers,** due to their speed and capabilities, account for a large segment of the printer market. As the laser printer receives information from the central processor, it converts it into a laser beam (a narrow beam of light) that, in turn, encodes a photoconductor with the information. This process forms the character or image to be printed. The photoconductor attracts particles of toner, a black granular dust similar to that used in many photocopiers, which, when transferred to the paper, produces the full image. Finally, the image is fused to the paper by heat and pressure. The laser printer prints an entire page at once.

  The process is fast (from 10 to 50 pages per minute on the most commonly used laser printers) and can print both text and images. Black-and-white laser printers are widely used, and color laser printers are common in business and educational settings where multicolor documents (including visual transparencies) are needed to present data and information effectively. As prices continue to drop, color laser printers will be more attractive for consumer use.

- **Ink-jet printers** spray tiny streams of ink from holes in the print mechanism onto the paper (Figure 5.40). The spray makes up a dot pattern that represents the character or image to be printed. Because ink-jet printers create characters and images by spraying ink rather than by striking preformed characters against paper, they are often used

**FIGURE 5.38**
*Tektronix Printer*

**FIGURE 5.39**

*Printing Processes*

(a) Impact and (b) nonimpact printers.

## NONIMPACT/LASER PRINTING

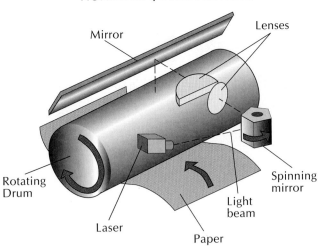

Mirror

Lenses

Rotating Drum

Laser

Light beam

Paper

Spinning mirror

## IMPACT/DOT MATRIX PRINTING

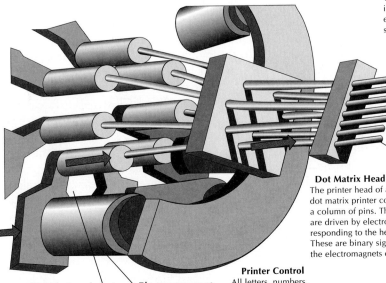

**Pin Patterns**
The pins strike an inked ribbon that marks the paper with dots. The head signals fire the pins in different combinations so that each character is made up of several vertical dot patterns.

Ribbon

Pins

Paper

**Dot Matrix Head**
The printer head of a dot matrix printer contains a column of pins. The pins are driven by electromagnets responding to the head signals. These are binary signals that turn the electromagnets on or off.

**Quality Printing**
Seven pins are shown here for simplicity; good quality printers have 24 pins. To improve quality, the head may pass over the paper again and print dots that overlap with those printed on the first pass.

Head signal

Electromagnet drives hammer

Hammer strikes pin

**Printer Control**
All letters, numbers, and other characters have standard codes that the computer sends to the printer. A chip in the printer converts these codes into signals that drive the printer head as it moves across the paper and prints the characters. The power drive board amplifies the chip signals. Special motors move the head and paper to the right positions.

Printer chip

Power driver board

Head signal

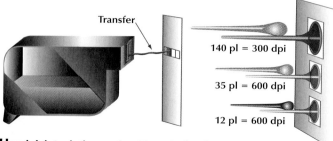

Transfer

140 pl = 300 dpi

35 pl = 600 dpi

12 pl = 600 dpi

**How ink-jet printing works** – The print head in an ink-jet printer contains four ink cartridges — one each for magenta, cyan, yellow and black. When output is to be formed, certain cartridges and nozzles are activated. Nozzles fire drops to transfer ink from print head to paper. This printer measures the transfer rate in picoliters (pl), a microscopic drop.

**FIGURE 5.40**

*Ink-jet Printing Process*

to create charts and graphs. The application software controls the information to be printed, and a controller within the printer oversees the actual printing process.

Both color and black-and-white ink-jet printers are in widespread use. Versions are available for PCs as well as for larger computer systems, the latter often referred to as *page printers* (Figure 5.41).

Versions of ink-jet printers designed specifically for photo-quality printing have become popular as the use of digital cameras and digital images has grown. These printers (Figure 5.42) produce colorful images on special paper designed to produce high-gloss or matte finishes. They also handle the traditional photo-size paper (e.g., 4 × 6 inches) as well as full sheets. Many models include a built-in reader into which the user can insert camera memory cards for processing by the printer.

The *Information Technology in Practice* feature, "Look Closely–Is It Produced by an HP Digital Innovation?" describes the many uses for HP ink-jet printers besides preparation of reports and correspondence.

**thermal printer**
A printer that heats a wax-based colored ink contained in the printer ribbon and transfers it to a special paper.

**Thermal printers** heat a wax-based colored ink contained in the printer ribbon and transfer it to a special paper. Three or four colored inks—usually yellow, magenta, cyan (blue), and black—are laid out in a repeating sequence of page-size panels along a length of the ribbon. Rollers sandwich the ribbon between the paper and a print head containing many small heating elements. These elements switch on and off, in correspondence to the characters and bits of information sent to the printer by the computer software. The paper must make four passes by the ribbon and heating element—one for each of the colors (Figure 5.43).

Thermal printing is slower than single-pass black-and-white printing, but faster than ink-jet printing for color. It is also much cheaper than color laser processes.

**FIGURE 5.41**

*IBM Page Printer*

**FIGURE 5.42**
***Photo-Quality Ink-jet Printer***
The resolution of photo-quality inkjet printers produces photographs rivaling those produced in traditional processing labs.

**Impact Printers**   Impact printers have existed for many years and have historically been very common in large and small computer configurations. Although they are being displaced by nonimpact printers, many are still used. Impact printers include line, dot matrix, and character printers (Figure 5.44):

- High-speed **line printers** have enjoyed widespread usage on large computers. They print a full line (up to 144 characters) at one time on continuous-form paper that can be up to 14 inches wide. Because of their high speed, which ranges up to several thousand lines per minute, they have been used in computer centers that routinely print large volumes of documents or very long reports. Since they are character-oriented, they are not suitable for printing images. (It should be noted that most computer line printers today are *non*impact, using laser or ink-jet technology. However, at one time *all* line printers were of the impact variety.)
- In **dot matrix printing,** the characters and images are formed by wire rods pushed against a ribbon and paper. A careful examination of the characters shows that each is actually a collection of small dots. Dot matrix printers have been used on systems of all sizes because of their speed, low cost, and simplicity.
- **Character printers** print one character at a time. In contrast to dot matrix and line printers, whose speed is rated at lines per minute, character printers are evaluated at the number of characters they print per second. (The slowest ones print approximately 30 characters per second, the fastest approximately 200.) Because the characters on a

**line printer**
A printer that prints a full line (up to 144 characters) at one time on continuous-form paper that can be up to 14 inches wide. Because of their high speed, which ranges up to several thousand lines per minute, line printers have been used in computer centers that routinely print large volumes of documents or very long reports.

**dot matrix printing**
A printer where the characters and images are formed by wire rods pushed against a ribbon and paper to create characters that are actually a collection of small dots.

**character printer**
A printer that prints one character at a time. Its speed is rated according to the number of characters printed per second.

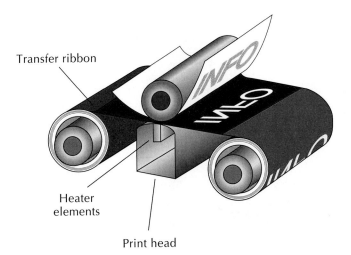

Transfer ribbon

Heater elements

Print head

**FIGURE 5.43**
***The Thermal Printing Process***
All thermal-wax-transfer printers work by heating four colored waxes and fusing them to a special paper. The print head melts tiny dots of color from a ribbon onto the paper. The paper must pass the ribbon and heating element four times—one pass for each of the four colors: cyan (blue), magenta, yellow, and black.

# INFORMATION TECHNOLOGY IN PRACTICE

## Look Closely—Is It Produced by an HP Digital Innovation?

Hewlett Packard, known for IT innovations since its founding in Palo Alto, California, brought laser printing to the desktop in 1984. Since then, HP has grown into the world's largest manufacturer of desktop printers. It has sold well in excess of 200-million laser printers. In addition, its lines of ink-jet printers, also introduced in 1984, have made color printing available to hundreds of millions of consumers. Its most recent photo-quality printer models have become natural companions to popular digital cameras, providing a convenient means of transferring digital images to high-gloss paper, fabric, film, and other media. It is no exaggeration to say that HP has revolutionized printing on the desktop.

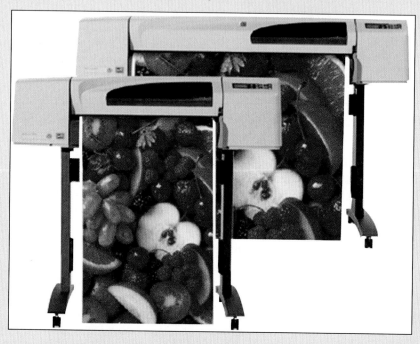

Despite these successes, HP is well aware that only a small fraction—less than 10 percent—of the trillions of pages that are printed each year are produced on desktop printers (whether from HP or other manufacturers). A large portion of the other pages comes off the rollers of commercial printing presses. HP has used its digital printing expertise to create entirely new products for the commercial world.

For instance, R.R. Donnelly, a large and well-known printer of college textbooks and trade books, has installed HP indigo digital printers in its book plants. There they are used to meet the *books on demand* needs of Donnelly's customers who want runs of, say, 1,000 copies printed quickly. Because the system is digital, it can be connected to the company's computer networks. Customers transmit digital manuscripts, complete with high-color photographs and detailed drawings, directly to Donnelly computers. When Donnelly is ready to print, it simply sends the manuscript from the computer to the HP digital printer that is also connected to the network. Full-color pages are instantly digitally printed, without the traditional intermediate steps of creating film.

HP's indigo digital presses can produce offset quality printing on

paper and other media up to 19.5 × 27.5 inches, in up to seven colors—commercial printing presses use four colors—at a rate of 2,000 sheets per hour, or 32,000 monochrome 8.5 × 11 inch sheets per hour (see photo). HP's indigo presses are ideal for on-demand book publishing.

What about the large colorful posters—complete with photographs of the stars—that promote the release of new movies? Or the signs touting soft drinks, or advertising for *can't miss* sales on clothing and jewelry? Then there are the eye-catching murals, vehicle graphics, window displays, and banners you see everywhere. At one time, these could only be produced by specialty printers. That was then.

Today, artists and designers can connect DesignJet printers to their computers. These printers operate like the familiar ink-jet printers found in homes and offices, but they do much more. DesignJet printers are able to produce vivid colors and print spectacular graphics on vinyl, canvas, film, and adhesive-backed paper and plastic. These media can be up to 42 inches wide. The DesignJet printers can also switch between two ink systems: one for media that will be displayed indoors and another that can tolerate unpredictable outdoor weather conditions. Built-in chips monitor the application of layers of ink from an unlimited pallet of colors, all the while ensuring the colors match precisely and positioning the dots of ink perfectly, to produce the razor-sharp details of the original design. Even more impressive, these results occur from a press that can fit a 300-foot roll of specialty paper and print at nearly 700 feet per hour.

HP revolutionized the production of professional-looking reports and sales materials in the office, and printing of photographs in the home with the advent of its laser and ink-jet printers. Now it is doing the same for the professional artist, graphic designer, and commercial publisher, providing all with premium results in minimal time. The next time you look at a colorful banner or poster, you will have to wonder whether it is a product of commercial printing presses or an HP innovation.

character printer are preformed on the ends of hammers or the petals of a wheel, character printers are not good for printing images. However, they have been widely used in the preparation of manuscripts and correspondence.

**Hertz Uses Wireless Technology for Car Returns**  When you rent a car, you want to receive a new car at a good price. Most people also want to return the automobile quickly and without hassle. Hertz Rent-A-Car, like many rental-car agencies, uses wireless POS terminals, called *instant return*, for credit-card customers at their airport locations; these terminals allow drivers to return cars quickly. When the driver pulls into the return lot, Hertz attendants read the vehicle's identification number from the sticker on the windshield, and key the number and a few other details into a handheld terminal (Figure 5.45). The vehicle number is transmitted to the Hertz computer inside the rental office, where information about the rental contract is retrieved from the computer.

In seconds, the computer displays the renter's name on the handheld terminal, calculates total rental charges, and sends a wireless message to the attendant's portable electronic printer. A few more seconds pass while the driver's receipt is printed. In less than a minute the rental transaction is settled, and renters are on their way to the airport gate.

## Audio Response Units

In the world of IT, the spoken word is increasingly being used as a form of output. Data or information is transformed into sound by an **audio response unit** (also called a **speech synthesizer**) in the following manner: Upon receiving instructions from the

**audio response unit/speech synthesizer**
An output device that transforms data or information into sound.

**FIGURE 5.44**

***Impact Printers and Sample Printouts***

In impact printing, the paper and the character being printed come into contact with each other. Although nonimpact printers are the standard, many businesses still use impact printers.

central processor, the audio response unit retrieves the prerecorded voice messages and sounds stored in the *voice unit,* wherein they are assembled and sent to a speaker.

Audio response units are at work today in all types of business settings. Many supermarkets have them attached to their bar-code scanners. As products are scanned, the response unit says the name of the product and its price aloud. Because they hear the price of an item, customers are assured that they are not being overcharged. Telephone companies and stock quotation services regularly use audio response units to give callers directory assistance and stock quotes, respectively. Both the firm and the individual caller benefit from this speedier and cheaper service. Many newer airports around the world are using audio response systems to assist passengers. For instance, when you move between the concourses connecting the approximately 200 gates at Atlanta's Hartsfield International Airport, one of the three busiest airports in the world, you do so on an easily accessible, complimentary shuttle train. A computer-controlled response unit announces the arrival of the vehicle at each gate and gives the traveler instructions on how to proceed from there. (It also controls the display of the same information in six different languages.)

**FIGURE 5.45**

***Handheld Broadcasts Running in Individual PC Windows***

The attendant keys the identification number from the windshield sticker into a handheld terminal. Information is transmitted to a computer, which displays the renter's name on the handheld unit and prints a receipt.

## Television

Television broadcasts can also be integrated into computer systems through the addition of special adapter boards. Partitions (or *windows*) of computer-display screens can show several television programs simultaneously (Figure 5.46). The latest news, business reports, or even closed-circuit TV can be shown, captured, and stored for later viewing.

Texaco uses several multimedia devices in its everyday operations. A good part of the company's profitability depends on getting information that managers need to determine when to buy and sell crude oil on the world market. Missing a breaking news item by just a few minutes can mean millions of dollars in lost opportunities. Texaco's trading room is equipped with high-speed computers that brokers use to create contracts electronically via a worldwide network. In one corner of the display screen is a window showing CNN in color, with full sound—the same live broadcast available on an ordinary color television. This use of IT and multimedia capability to obtain up-to-date news constantly gives Texaco's traders a solid advantage over competitors who still rely on delayed news broadcasts.

## Plotters

**Plotters** (Figure 5.47) literally draw image information, such as charts and graphs, line drawings, and blueprints of buildings. Just as if it were drawing by hand, a plotter creates every line and character, including shadows and patterns, stroke by stroke.

The process is fascinating to watch. The plotter arm takes a felt-tip pen from a holder containing one or more pens and, under direction from the computer, transforms electronic signals into marks on the page. The page may be of any size, from the common 8-1/2 by 11 inches or A4 (210 by 297 mm) to the very large commercial blueprints used in architecture, engineering, and construction.

Although once in widespread use for commercial applications, plotters have largely been replaced by large format ink-jet printers. The *Information Technology in Practice* feature focusing on HP, the leader in both plotter and ink-jet technology, illustrates why this has occurred.

**plotter**
An output device that draws image information (such as charts, graphs, and blueprints) stroke by stroke.

## Film Recorders

Color (35 mm) slides, transparencies, and other types of film output are produced on **film recorders** (Figure 5.48). Virtually anything that can be shown on a computer screen can be copied onto a film recorder. Under the control of a computer program, the film recorder transforms the electronic image on the screen into a film image. You might think of the film recorder as an electronic camera, setting the exposure and controlling the shutter to capture the electronic image on the computer screen on film.

**film recorder**
An output device that transforms an electronic image on a computer screen into a film image.

**FIGURE 5.46**

***Television Broadcasts Running in Individual PC Windows***

FIGURE 5.47

**Hewlett Packard DeskJet 350c Plotter**

Architects and other design professionals frequently use plotters to create detailed schematics of buildings, rooms, and floor plans.

Film recorders are being used by many businesses to prepare slide presentations in-house. (In days past, such presentations were developed almost exclusively by professional graphic artists using specialized tools.) Presentation software programs—used to create the shapes and images, enter the text, and control the color schemes—are widely available for under $500. If a company does not have its own film processor, it can store a copy of the presentation on disk and send it out to a slide-processing firm that will produce the color slides. The cost: $5 to $10 per slide.

Genigraphics, a world leader in computer-generated slides, transparencies, and color graphics, provides exactly this service. Using one of the many imaging packages that run on PCs, you can create the text, image, and color specifications of a professional-looking presentation right on your desktop. When finished, you can transmit the file to Genigraphics electronically over the Internet or via an ordinary dial-up telephone line, or you can copy the file to a diskette and mail it to Genigraphics. When it receives the file, Genigraphics transforms it into colorful output using film recorders, color laser printers, or other output devices. In 24 hours (or sooner if necessary), the results are back on your desk.

The technology for capturing digital images and for producing color slides and presentation transparencies is readily available. It is important to keep in mind, however,

FIGURE 5.48

**High Resolution Film Recorder**

**REALITY CHECK** As you pursue your career, you will probably see many poorly conceived slides and graphic presentations assembled by people who have the necessary tools—the PC and the presentation software package—to do the job. What they lack is the know-how that makes the difference between a good and a poor presentation. No amount of IT can conceal that their ideas are poorly conceived and their message is ineffective. The same is true with respect to IT. Know-how makes the difference between poor and effective use. ■

that the most important element of information technology is know-how. The most valuable resources of graphic artists are not the tools they use but rather their professional experiences and skills.

# CRITICAL CONNECTIONS

## 1  Part II: FAA's *Black Box* Captures Aircraft Flight Information

At the urging of the National Transportation Safety Board, the FAA now requires the recording of many more details (over 100 different flight parameters) on the FDRs. Digital signals are recorded once every second.

The newest black boxes use nonvolatile memory chips instead of Mylar tape. Lockheed Martin, which employs this form of information technology in both its FDRs and its CVRs, says these solid-state systems, which use no moving parts, are more likely than the old systems to stay intact in the event of a catastrophic incident.

**Questions for Discussion**

1. What benefits does nonvolatility in memory chips provide for FDR and CVR use?
2. What other benefits do memory chips provide in contrast to Mylar magnetic tape?
3. Which alternative do you believe is cheaper: a sense-and-record mechanism that uses magnetic tape or one that records on digital memory chips?

## 2  Part II: American Express' Optical Storage Creates Country Club Billing

**American Express** American Express is not the only company that is looking to image-processing systems to help it control a tidal wave of paper. Banks, too, are counting on image processing to stem the flood of 55-million checks that pass through their *back rooms* for processing and sorting every year. In fact, some banks are already charging higher fees to

customers who insist on getting back the originals of their canceled checks—as opposed to image-processed facsimiles—with their monthly statements.

**Questions for Discussion**

1. Courts have ruled that reproductions of documents are admissible as evidence as long as they *accurately reproduce the original*. Would this knowledge make you comfortable with a checking account statement that includes only image-processed facsimiles? What does your reaction and the reaction of your classmates imply for the future of a *checkless* society?
2. American Express, one of the first companies to adopt image processing and optical storage, likes to present itself as a leader in technology. How might this image help the company's marketing strategies?
3. In recent years, American Express has lost business because merchants and customers are turning to bank credit cards with lower interest rates, lower annual fees, and lower charges than those offered by American Express. How can ECCB help American Express fight back?

## 3  Part II: Encyclopædia Britannica's DVD Version Lets Readers Explore the Possibilities

**Encyclopædia Britannica** The DVD version of the *Encyclopædia Britannica* takes advantage of digital technology to bring topics to life with text and interactive multimedia information. It makes possible exploration of topics in ways that are simply impossible in the print version.

For example, suppose you are interested in creating a feature exploring the new boom in roller coasters.

(Recently, in one year alone, more than 100 new coasters were opened around the world, making a total of approximately 900 active roller coasters worldwide.) How would you examine this topic as an author for *Britannica*?

Here is what you will find on the DVD once you mount it on your computer:

- A well-written description (called *Roller Coasters: Inventing the Scream Machine*) that traces roller coasters from their origin in the Russian mountains during the 1800s until today. It includes the world's tallest *Superman the Escape* coaster in California.
- Vivid color photographs–they enlarge to fill the screen when clicked–that show the diversity of coasters, their cars fully loaded with screaming fun-seekers.
- An interactive gallery of the people who introduced the many innovations in the coaster's colorful history. It shares facts, insights and interesting bits of the colorful history around each inventor.
- An animation of the physics of coasters illustrating the importance of such elements as centrifugal force, acceleration stress, and friction.
- Video illustrations of the motion and safety technologies of the coaster from the earliest gravity-powered rides to the latest using electromagnetic waves. The video shows coasters running up, down, and through the loops associated with these exciting rides.

As you research roller coasters using *Encyclopædia Britannica*'s digital version, you can almost feel the excitement of being on one of the new-age hypertwisters. And this is only a partial list of what is on the DVD.

It is easy to see why DVDs are such an important component of IT. Best of all, they are still in their infancy of use. Who knows what other features will emerge from clever authors and developers?

### Questions for Discussion

1. What are the most important benefits of the DVD version of the *Encyclopædia Britannica* compared to its 30-plus volume print edition?

2. What is the impact of the high storage capacity of the DVD on the use of digital methods of presenting information?

3. Considering the roller-coaster example above, does the use of DVDs change the content of the information? Or does it simply illustrate the information's existing content more fully?

## 4  Part II: Wireless Electronic Shelf Tags Guarantee Uniform Prices at Shaw's Supermarkets

**Shaw's Supermarkets** New England-based Shaw's Supermarkets has found that its wireless digital shelf tags are an effective way to ensure that the shelf price matches the price shoppers pay upon checkout. The system has proven so effective that a number of states, including Connecticut and Rhode Island, which have item-pricing laws, have exempted retailers that install electronic shelf labels.

The electronic store labels not only contain large numbers and letters, but also additional space for notices of special programs, bundled offerings, or promotional messages. Both consumers and the company find the ability to display the additional information to be beneficial.

Although the technology for electronic shelf tags has been available for a number of years, it is only recently that Shaw's and other stores put them into use. They were not economical to use until their cost dropped to about $5 per tag.

### Questions for Discussion

1. What are the economic benefits of using wireless electronic shelf tags to Shaw's Supermarkets?

2. What is your opinion, as a consumer, of electronic shelf tags?

3. Since the tags can receive information transmitted from the store's computer, what other uses might be made of promotional message space on the tag?

## *Summary of Learning Objectives*

**1** **Discuss why people and businesses use storage, not just the computer's main memory, to store information.**   People and businesses use storage because (1) the contents of primary memory remain there only temporarily, (2) data vanish from primary memory as soon as the computer is turned off, and (3) primary memory is not large enough to contain the large volume of data and information associated with business applications.

**2** **Distinguish between the two main types of magnetic storage, and identify three types of magnetic**

disk storage.   The two main types of magnetic storage are magnetic tape and magnetic disk. Magnetic tape, the earliest form of magnetic storage, comes on large reels or cartridges. Magnetic disks come in three types: flexible (floppy) disks, hard disks, and disk cartridges.

**3** **Describe two alternatives for extending disk storage capacity in enterprises.**   Redundant arrays of independent disks (RAID) consist of a set of small disk drives that work together as a single unit, or array, of disks. They are widely used in mainframe and server, but not PC environments, to provide storage exceeding that of a single drive. Striping and disk mirroring are common techniques used with RAID. Storage area networks (SAN) are high-speed networks that allow the sharing of different kinds of storage devices, including disk arrays and tape drives, to be shared by users connected to the network.

**4** **Explain why optical storage is of growing importance in computing and describe the most commonly used forms of optical storage.** Optical storage is of growing importance in computing because it can store high-density data and information. The most common types of optical storage are CD-ROM, the least expensive way to store large amounts of information, and DVD, a larger-capacity medium that can store both images and sound. Neither CD-R nor DVD disks can be rewritten after they are created. Two alternative forms of optical disks, CD-RW and DVD-RAM permit computer users to write data or information onto the disks.

**5** **Identify the seven most widely used input devices and describe how they are employed in computing.** The seven most widely used input devices are as follows: (1) keyboards; (2) terminals, which are a combination of keyboard and video screens that accept and display keyed input and display the output sent by the computer to which they are attached; (3) scanners, which transform written or printed information (optical character recognition scanners) or photographic images, drawings, or entire documents (image scanners) into a digital form that is entered directly into the computer; (4) digitizers, which translate measured distances into digital values that the computer can process; (5) digital cameras, which capture photographic images on light-sensitive computer-memory chips; (6) digital video camcorders that capture audio and video as individual bytes of information; and (7) voice and sound input devices, which are attached to the computer to capture spoken words and other sounds in digital form.

**6** **Discuss the future of voice input and audio output devices as components of IT.** Voice input devices capture the spoken word in digital form. Research in voice, sound, and speech input advanced slowly until recently, because of technological limitations. With the development of new storage technologies and faster processors, this situation is changing. Audio response units, which transform data or information into sound output, are now in widespread use. The directory-assistance services of public telephone companies regularly use audio response units to give callers phone numbers.

**7** **Describe the eight types of output devices and identify their uses in business.** The eight types of output devices are as follows: (1) video displays or monitors; (2) digital cameras; (3) data projectors, for showing the contents of a computer display on a movie screen; (4) printers, which produce paper output (hard copy); (5) audio response units, sometimes known as speech synthesizers, which translate output into audible words and sounds; (6) television broadcasts, which can be displayed in a window on a computer display; (7) plotters, which draw image information, such as charts and graphs, line drawings, and building blueprints; and (8) film recorders, which transform the electronic image on the computer screen into a film image. The uses of these devices vary greatly, but all businesses use output devices in their computer systems.

## *Key Terms*

advanced intelligent tape (AIT)   191
array   183
audio response unit/speech synthesizer   219
bit mapping   212
CD-R disk   194
CD recorder   194
CD-ROM disk   192
CD-RW disk   194
character addressing   212
character printer   217
cylinder   180
data projector   212
digital audiotape (DAT)   191
digital camera   207

digital light processing (DLP) projector   212
digital video camcorder   208
digital video disk (DVD)   195
digitizer   205
digitizing tablet   206
disk cartridge   182
disk mirroring   184
disk pack   180
dot matrix printing   217
DVD-RAM   195
fault tolerance   183
film recorder   221
FireWire   181
flatbed scanner   204

flexible disk/diskette/floppy disk   177
function key   198
graphics adapter card   212
hard copy   213
hard disk   178
hard disk controller   180
hard drive/disk drive   178
head crash   180
integrated drive electronics (IDE)   180
image scanning   204
impact printing   213
ink-jet printer   214
input device   196
joystick   206
keyboard   196

## Review Questions

1. What features do primary and secondary storage have in common? How do these storage alternatives differ?
2. Why is storage needed in computing? In what way does storage offer users an advantage compared to memory?
3. Distinguish between sequential processing and random-access processing.
4. What are the two main storage technologies available to users?
5. What are the three main magnetic storage media?
6. What is a track-on magnetic tape? How does it differ from a track-on magnetic disk?
7. What does recording density mean?
8. What is the origin of the term *floppy disk?*
9. How do disk cartridges and diskettes differ?
10. When does a head crash occur and why is it undesirable?
11. Is magnetic tape an obsolete storage medium? Why or why not?
12. What is RAID storage, and why has this storage alternative been developed?
13. How do RAID storage systems differ in characteristics and in their use?
14. How do magnetic tape cartridges differ from magnetic disk cartridges?
15. What are SANs, and when are they used in IT applications?
16. Describe the characteristics of USB drives and Zip drives.
17. How do optical storage devices work? How do they differ from magnetic storage devices?

18. How do CD-ROM and DVD disks differ?
19. Is it possible to write data to CD-ROM or DVD disks? Explain the reasons for your answer.
20. What are the seven most frequently used input devices?
21. Why are scanners used in processing data and information? What is a flatbed scanner?
22. What is a digitizer? Name seven common types of digitizers.
23. What are the characteristics of digital cameras? How do digital cameras capture images, and what advantages does this method offer?
24. Describe the characteristics of digital video camcorders.
25. Describe the purpose of voice input and multimedia audiovisual input devices.
26. What is an audio response unit? When is such a device used?
27. What features distinguish one computer monitor from another?
28. How does an LCD monitor differ from a CRT monitor?
29. When are data projectors used? How do data projectors differ from one another?
30. What is the difference between impact printing and nonimpact printing?
31. Are laser printers impact or nonimpact printers? Explain your answer.
32. What are audio response units and when are they used in computing applications?
33. What is the purpose of a plotter? A film recorder?

## Discussion Questions

1. Lands' End, the well-known mail order apparel company, recently launched *my virtual model,* which enables men and women to order personalized, custom-manufactured chino trousers and slacks. Shoppers visit the Lands' End Web site (www.landsend.com) where they enter information they already know, including height, and weight as well as shoe, shirt, and sport coat or blazer size. The process takes about two minutes.

   Lands' End virtual model software uses this data to figure out how the weight is distributed on each person's individual body shape. The resulting measurements are used to adjust standard cutting patterns, enabling Lands' End to produce a customized pair of chinos. The finished, competitively priced garment is delivered to the customer in about two weeks.

   Compare the Lands' End virtual model process to the Brooks Brothers *digital tailor.* What advantages and disadvantages do each offer to the customer? To the company?

   If you were only going to order custom slacks, which process would you prefer and why?

2. Merrill Lynch & Company, a large New York broker, moved a large portion of its business-operating data to a storage area network. However, rather than creating and managing the SAN itself, it contracted with a third party to perform these services. By outsourcing the SAN to the contractor, Merrill Lynch anticipated savings of some 20 percent on the total cost of ownership of the storage network.

   Do you feel it is a good idea to store actual operating data (rather than backup data) on a storage area network? Why or why not?

   What factors should a company such as Merrill Lynch examine when considering whether to outsource its need to build, operate, and maintain its SAN or to create and manage a SAN itself?

3. When a user of the computer system at the Amoco Research Center accidentally deleted 940 files relating to the remodeling of Amoco's building, an administrator was able to restore the files in about half an hour, using the magnetic tape backup created every night at 1 A.M. Why do you think the administrator chose magnetic tape over magnetic disks for the backups?

4. As part of its effort to organize a mega-auction of real estate and other items to secure $800 million worth of loans from 136 failed savings and loan associations, the Resolution Trust Corp. (RTC) hired a consulting company to create a computer system. The system would let bidders review copies or images of the relevant legal documents, photographs, and surveys. What type of storage would you recommend for such a system? Why? What input and output devices would you recommend?

5. The Travelers Corp., an insurance firm based in Hartford, Connecticut, provides a toll-free number for consumers who want to learn the name of Travelers-approved doctors in their area or get a status report on their claims. Callers have the option of using a voice response system that extracts information from the computer files or speaking to a live operator who has access to the same files. Why do you think that many experts in the field are convinced that customers are coming to expect these options?

6. Industrial Light & Magic, Pacific Data Images, and Pixar are just a few of the companies using computer graphics to create special effects for big-budget motion pictures. How might these companies use each of the output devices discussed in this chapter?

## Group Projects and Applications

### Project 1

Conduct a survey of at least 10 medium and large manufacturing or service companies to understand the current role of magnetic tape storage in their IT services groups. Among the questions you should raise are the following:

1. Is any form of magnetic tape storage used for data associated with the company's computers or servers? Why or why not?

2. If the company does use magnetic tape, determine what forms (for example, cartridges, cassettes, reels) are used and why. Remember that the form may vary from one computer or server to the next—PCs vs. mainframes, for instance.

3. Has the type of tape storage in use at the firm changed in the last five years?

4. Is the use of tape storage increasing, decreasing, or staying about the same? What is the reason behind this finding?

5. Does the company use a storage area network? If so, are magnetic tape drives connected to the SAN?

These questions should form the basis for a written or verbal presentation of your findings. Additionally, you should add your observations of any other unique storage uses revealed during the investigation.

## Project 2

LCD technology has made it possible for companies to mount large, flat panel computer displays (42 inches or more in width) in public places that tend to draw large volumes of customer traffic. Since these LCDs can be connected to computer systems, either directly or through networks, they can display color and graphic information updating viewers on changes in status or conditions. They can also be used to guide viewers in what actions they should take and when.

Visit a combination of five or more shopping malls, transportation depots/stations/terminals, university student centers, athletic facilities (including health clubs), theaters, and movie houses. Analyze the possibilities for using large, computer-driven, LCD panels in these environments:

1. What information do you recommend displaying and for what purposes?
2. In what form should the information be displayed in each case and for what reason?
3. How would displaying information on the LCD help viewers? How would the display help manage the facility in which you recommend its use?

## Project 3

Refer to *Project 3* in Chapter 4. With your group, answer the following questions for the business you chose for that project:

- What type(s) of storage media will you need?

- Which type(s) of input devices will you use? Will your business have any need for handheld, palmtop, or laptop computers?
- Keeping in mind that high-resolution monitors are quite expensive, what type of monitor will your business use? What type of printer?
- How might your business use voice and sound input and output devices to increase customer satisfaction?

After completing *Project 3* in Chapters 4 and 5, you should have a complete *IT Plan* for your new business. Present this plan to the class.

## Project 4

Several companies offer specially designed ergonomic devices to help prevent repetitive stress disorders (such as carpal tunnel syndrome). Others provide special *adaptive devices* for people with a wide range of disabilities so they can work comfortably with IT.

With your group, investigate one of the following topics:

- Ergonomic workstations and equipment
- Input devices for people with disabilities
- Output devices for people with disabilities

Two good places to begin an investigation into adaptive technologies are the Americans with Disabilities Act Document Center (www.jan.wvu.edu/links/adalinks.htm) and the Apple Computer Disabilities Solutions Store (www.apple.com/disability).

Each group should present one or two *enabling technologies* to the class, explaining the technology and how it works. The presentations should discuss the price of these adaptive technologies and whether the price is a barrier to use.

---

## Net_Work

### Storage on the Web

An important reason for having copies of data in storage—magnetic or optical—is to ensure that there are backup copies in the event of a disaster of any kind, whether from electrical failure, hardware malfunction, software errors, or intrusion into the system by a hacker. Should a disaster occur, a copy can be loaded onto the system, thereby enabling a firm to restart its system with data it knows is accurate and reliable.

The Internet's World Wide Web has opened up new possibilities for storage of data. Web services are available that enable companies to transmit copies of data to the Web site where it is stored until such a time as it is needed. Furthermore, companies can keep the backup copies at the Web site current by transmitting new versions for storage.

Use a search engine of your choice to conduct an investigation on the Internet to identify sites that are offering backup storage services. Identify at least five different sites that you judge to offer attractive, but different, Web backup services. Prepare a report that outlines the differences with respect to the following:

1. Viability of using the Web as backup storage.
2. Variety of services offered by each of the companies you choose.
3. Actions you need to take to create and use backup storage.
4. Tools you need to have (or those the Web company provides) to create and use the backup storage.
5. Costs associated with each of the alternatives you have selected.

## When News Is Online

A growing number of newspapers are publishing online, taking advantage of the global reach of the Internet and World Wide Web as well as their unique capabilities for displaying information. Some newspapers make their pages available without charge, while others either require a monthly or annual subscription fee or charge for each viewing.

1. Search the Web and prepare a list of newspapers you find appealing. Note the URL for each one. Also indicate for each newspaper whether it requires a subscription fee or other charge for online viewing.
2. Peruse the pages of each online newspaper you chose to see the nature of the news it covers and how it is presented. Then consider the similarities and differences between each page you have viewed:
   - How does the contents vary by newspaper?
   - What characteristics of online newspapers do you find most appealing?
   - What information is better obtained from the print version of the paper?
3. The Web's pages are not just for viewing. You can also print them. Choose a newspaper page and by clicking on the print icon, and print a paper copy of it.
4. Do you think online newspapers will ever replace the printed version?
5. What are the advantages of publishing newspapers over the Web?

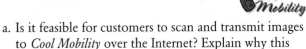

## On Assignment

Although the management team believes the innovative product features and services of *Cool Mobility* have already generated widespread consumer interest, it also wants to keep quality levels high even as it expands

The company's scanning process for drawings and art submitted by its customers uses commercial-quality scanners. However, in the interest of improving service, an option being considered is to enable customers to scan drawings and photos on home scanners. Once they are scanned, customers will transmit the images to *Cool Mobility* over the Internet (currently they send printed images by U.S. mail or courier, and *Cool Mobility* handles the scanning process).

## In Consultation

The company asks for your recommendation regarding the following alternative:

a. Is it feasible for customers to scan and transmit images to *Cool Mobility* over the Internet? Explain why this process will or will not work.
b. The company now scans all user submitted photos and drawings with a commercial-quality digital scanner. If image resolution is important to maintain the quality of *Cool Mobility*'s products, do you recommend that the company adopt the customer scanning option? Why or why not?
c. The company wants to consider other options that can used to capture or prepare images in digital form for submission over the Internet. What other IT devices do you think *Cool Mobility* should recommend for this purpose?

# *Case Study*

## Does FleetBoston Financial Have an Edge?

At one time, computer storage was so expensive and limited that system developers went to the trouble of saving space by storing only the last two digits of the year. This lead to the infamous year 2000, or Y2K, problem whereby computers were unable to tell whether the year '90 in transactions means 1890, 1990, or 2090. During the time leading up to 2000, many companies had to rework their computer applications to rid them of the dreaded Y2K fault.

Computer storage is now readily available and relatively low cost. As a result, company practices that determine when and how they store data on their computer systems are changing. In fact, the more innovative companies are seeking to capitalize on the ample and readily accessible storage on their computer systems to produce new products and services that enable them to grow their businesses.

FleetBoston Financial, headquartered in Boston, Massachusetts, is the seventh-largest financial holding company in the United States. A diversified financial services company with assets of approximately $200 billion, Fleet offers a comprehensive array of innovative financial solutions to 20-million customers in more than 20 countries and territories.

Fleet is using its IT resources to offer new services that are changing the way its customers pay their monthly bills. Among the most promising is its bill presentment and payment system, part of Fleet HomeLink$^{SM}$, the 24-hour online banking and investment system. With a few clicks, customers can pay bills, and have their bank account (also visible on their computer display) automatically reconciled.

Here is how it works. Customers can choose to pay service suppliers or bills from just about any other company through online banking.

Customers use the *bill payment* feature to authorize the bank to send payment from their account to the bill issuer. With the Fleet system, customers gain other conveniences, including the ability to

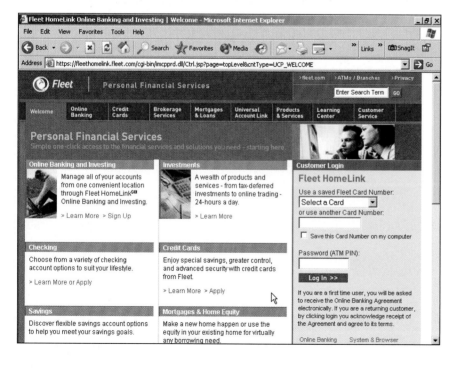

- Choose the account from which funds will be drawn.
- Schedule the date the payment is to be made.
- Set up automatic, recurring payments (such as a car loan).
- Schedule one-time future payments.
- View payment history.
- See when bills were paid.
- Cancel or change a payment up to 11:59 the night before the payment is scheduled to go out.

If customers wish to pay bills to companies that are not electronically linked to Fleet, the *pay anyone* feature will allow them to request checks to be sent to any billers, or even to individuals. With this feature, they can make payments to virtually anyone in the United States.

Once bills are approved by the HomeLink customer, Fleet takes care of preparing, processing, recording, and transmitting the payment. Its system maintains all of the billing and transaction details on its huge disk storage system. This way, the information is accessible to either billers or customers.

FleetBoston Financial's system has been called a *killer app* and is clearly the next step in online banking.

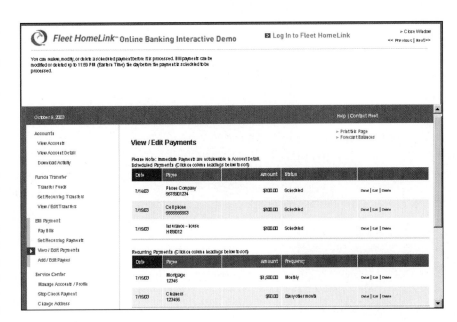

## Questions for Discussion

1. What benefits does FleetBoston Financial gain from the bill payment features in HomeLink? How should its management determine whether the investment in the system is paying off?

2. What processing activities are handled by the bank's computer system?

3. From the viewpoint of a bank customer, what are the advantages and disadvantages to bill payment?

4. Does the bill payment system give Fleet a long-term edge against competing banks that do not offer equivalent services?

# 6

# Personal and PC Databases

## LEARNING OBJECTIVES

When you have completed this chapter, you should be able to

1 Explain why databases are widely used.

2 Describe the main components of a database.

3 List and describe five objectives of database management systems.

4 Identify when a business should use a spreadsheet and when it should use a database.

5 Identify the seven-step sequence for developing database applications.

# Smithsonian's Image Databases
# Give Everyone Access to History

The Smithsonian Institution, in Washington, D.C., is the world's largest museum complex and research organization. Composed of 16 museums and galleries, as well as the National Zoo, the Smithsonian's exhibitions offer visitors a glimpse into its vast collection numbering over 142-million objects. The most important aspects of the country's evolution in art, history, and science are captured in the vast halls of the Smithsonian.

The Smithsonian's Office of Imaging, Printing, and Photographic Services (OIPP) is the institution's central photographic facility. The office maintains a library of approximately 1 million negatives and transparencies in an environmentally controlled cold storage room. Photographic images include the work of Smithsonian photographers dating from the late 1800s; they are continually augmented by the work of contemporary photographers. You can find photographs illustrating the changes in everyday household gadgets, along with cultural memorabilia from an earlier century. Just as easily, you can view illustrations of the latest innovations for peering into outer space. In addition, the museum houses a library of digital images, which include photographs taken with digital cameras. Databases of information are maintained about each library.

Documenting and keeping track of these images in a database is as important as their actual creation. Although the staff relies on computer processing, indexing can be complicated, especially when the database of information must be usable across different computers connected to the museum's network. Moreover, hundreds of new images are created every day, which means the database is always changing.

One enterprise database contains information about negatives and transparencies in the Smithsonian library. Each entry in the database

describes an image belonging to a museum or gallery, including caption information, a physical description, location, creator, and negative number (if available). Indices categorize the database contents, making it possible to identify individual and sets of images according to these descriptive details. The centralized index and image database can be searched by PCs attached to any of the servers residing on the museum's computer network.

A second enterprise database, the digital image library, is maintained online and includes not only the descriptive information, but also the actual digital images. Each day, Smithsonian photographers transfer their finished images into electronic folders, or *drop boxes*, on the servers in the museum or gallery in which they are working. An OIPP computer application retrieves and indexes the images, recording descriptive information including the creation date and characteristics of the image. The images are then electronically transferred over the network to the Smithsonian's enterprise database where they become part of the permanent collection. The process not only automates the capture and archiving of images, but it also provides quick access to any image file in the library.

OIPP uses a PC database as a front end to the enterprise database. The PC database system captures and processes the digital images. It also serves as a front end to the central negative and transparency library's database, maintaining a copy of the index on PCs for rapid access. This avoids having to interact with either the database or the museum network every time there is a need to retrieve information about an image. OIPP not only maintains the image libraries, but also makes prints and duplicate transparencies available to museum staff and to the general public, providing research assistance to those who request it. The museum also produces and sells educational products to collectors, schools, and libraries internationally.

The PC database captures orders and customer information. As orders are filled, the records in the database are updated to show the change in status. Order and customer records can be processed at any time to examine the level of activity and to highlight particular areas of interest.

The enterprise and PC database combination is an essential operation resource. The databases are instrumental in helping OIPP carry out its mission of collecting, preserving, and making available the official records of the Smithsonian Institution.

*A* database, as described in Chapter 2, is a collection of data and information describing items of interest, arranged in a manner that allows for easy access, retrieval, and use. This chapter and the next one explore the management and use of databases.

You'll explore the development and use of personal database systems in this chapter, beginning with the characteristics of database management systems and the reasons so many people and companies use them. We'll also discuss the process of creating databases and then using them to store, retrieve, and use data from them. An extensive an extensive example will demonstrate the power of PC database management systems.

## An Overview of Personal and PC Database Systems

**database management system (DBMS)**
A program that makes it possible for users to manage the data in a database in order to increase accessibility and productivity.

A **database management system** is software that enables you to create a database, to maintain its contents, and to retrieve and display data in reports and forms.

Traditionally, a database's contents have included text and numbers—hence the name *data*base. Increasingly, though, people and organizations are broadening their view of databases to include images, graphics, and voice. For example:

- California's Division of Motor Vehicles maintains a computerized driver's license database that includes drivers' names, addresses, and personal attributes (height, weight, birth date, etc.), along with their photographs and an image of their signatures.
- Many hospitals and medical centers—including Massachusetts General Hospital, the Mayo Clinic, and the Harvard Community Health Plan—have begun to maintain patient records in databases that include personal information, insurance and financial data, medical history, and medical images (such as X rays and electrocardiograms).
- Manufacturing and service companies like IBM, Wal-Mart, and General Motors are installing multimedia training systems that feature databases containing video clips, color slides, narrative (text) screens of information and instructions, self-tests, and voice narrations. These training systems use all of the trainee's senses (with the possible exception of smell; they are working on that).

The point is clear. People collect data and information because they expect it to be useful later—whether to identify drivers, to diagnose and treat medical problems, or to train employees. In other words, the all-important assumption underlying database creation is that data and information should be stored when they are expected to be useful in problem solving.

At one time, people focused primarily on storing data—numbers and text. However, with the advances in computers' storage capabilities over the last decade or so, the contents of personal and organizational databases have broadened. As a result, the terminology is gradually changing, too. The term **information repository**, or simply **repository**, may soon replace *database* as the name of this information resource. (We will stick with *database* in this chapter because it is still the most widely used term, but *repository* is almost certainly the term of the future.)

**information repository/repository**
A synonym for database.

## Reasons for Using Databases

Many of the databases you will encounter in organizations will be large multiuser systems developed and maintained by IT professionals. These database systems are known as **enterprise databases** (see Chapter 7).

A growing number of individuals, organization managers and staff members, entrepreneurs, and small-business owners are turning to smaller personal databases to boost their productivity. **Personal databases** typically reside on personal computers (hence the name **PC database**), and are designed to support a particular function. As the Smithsonian example illustrates, PC databases can be used in conjunction with enterprise databases. While PC databases generally are smaller (in terms of the volume of data they store) than enterprise databases, the database management software available to manage them is very powerful, offering users a vast array of capabilities.

PC databases offer advantages for storing, retrieving, sharing, editing, and distributing data.

**enterprise database**
Large multiuser database systems developed and maintained by IT professionals.

**personal database (PC database)**
Typically reside on personal computers and are designed to support a particular function.

**Storing Data** Data and information are useless unless there is an effective system for collecting, organizing, and storing them. The larger the volume of data, the greater the benefit of using a database system.

As you know, it is common business practice to exchange business cards the first time you meet someone. Keeping track of a business contact's name, telephone numbers, e-mail address, and the nature of their company's business is vital in order to follow-up with them. This is easy to do if you have only a handful of business cards. But as the number of cards in your stack grows, it becomes difficult and time-consuming to go through them each time you need to get in touch with one of those contacts. Establishing a database of names and addresses is a good solution to the *business card problem*. The more business acquaintances you have—and thus the more business cards you have collected—the greater the benefits from storing the details in a computer database.

Moreover, as an entry is made for each business contact, you might also include details that place them into a category. For example, a home builder might keep track of electricians, plumbers, roofers, and landscapers by their specialty along with the other details.

**Retrieving Data**  Databases make it easy to retrieve data quickly and flexibly. Getting the e-mail address off of the business card of a landscape firm is not difficult, providing you can put your hands on the card quickly. On the other hand, when you have thousands of cards, finding a particular e-mail address might be tough.

**query/querying**
A question to be answered by accessing the data in a database.

The process of posing a question (that is, a **query**) and retrieving data from the database is known as **querying** the database. Looking up the e-mail address of a landscape company (that is, *querying the database for a landscaper's e-mail address*) is quick if the company's descriptive details are entered into the database properly. To query the database, you simply key in the name of the company when prompted by the database software, and the software will locate and retrieve the company data for you.

What if you want the names and phone numbers of *all* landscape companies? When the database system is prompted, it will quickly sort through the details about every company to identify those that specialize in landscaping and retrieve the requested data. Or, if you want to know the names and phone numbers of only those landscape companies that are located outside of the city, you can pose the query to the system and have it retrieve details about a smaller group of companies.

Databases excel at quick and flexible retrieval of details. You can take the same information (e.g., names and phone numbers of landscape companies), alter one detail in a database query (e.g., change landscape companies to plumbers), and get a totally different retrieval result.

**editing**
Adding, deleting, or changing the data about companies.

**Editing Data**   **Editing** refers to adding, deleting, or changing the data about companies. In the normal course of business, companies change their street addresses, e-mail addresses, telephone numbers, and even their names. If you keep track of companies by filing paper business cards, then you either have to get a new replacement business card for the firm or write the changes on the original business card (if you can find it).

When stored in a computer database, editing data to reflect the changes is easier. You only have to retrieve the details about the company, enter the new data, and restore the edited information. The database system locates the company's data, makes the changes as directed, and permanently records the results.

**Organizing Data**   Even after the data is stored, it can be reorganized. For instance, if you decide to split the landscape category into two categories—say the categories of architectural landscaping and landscape services—you can simply recategorize the companies by adding the new categories and placing each firm in the proper category. The database does not have to be recreated nor do any records need to be reentered.

**Distributing Data and Information**   Once stored, the data can be used in many ways. Details can be shown on the computer display screen; or they can be printed as a report organized by company name, specialty, or phone number, for example. Alternatively, you can use the database to send a form letter to a number of recipients, inserting the name and address of each firm into the letter, thus personalizing it. Mailing labels can also be generated from the database contents. Both letters and labels can be printed in sequence by postal code; that way, the letters can be stuffed in the envelopes efficiently and grouped for mailing.

Since the database is in electronic form, backup copies readily can be made. Should the need arise, the entire database can be transmitted over a computer network.

The benefits of an electronic database over keeping track of hundreds or thousands of business cards are clear. Good organization means higher personal productivity.

The *Information Technology in Practice* feature, "SpeakWrite Shares the Spoken Word," describes how adoption of a personal database helps speechwriters find the right words for any occasion.

# INFORMATION TECHNOLOGY IN PRACTICE

## SpeakWrite Shares the Spoken Word

As founder of SpeakWrite, a small company that publishes quotations and speeches in Woodville, Ontario, Earle Gray has created an industry helping speechwriters find the right words for any occasion. Gray's company sells two products: *Canadian Speeches*, a collection of notable speeches given across Canada; and *Quotes, Notes and Anecdotes*, a potpourri of ideas that speakers can use to add sparkle to their presentations.

For a small mom-and-pop operation with limited resources, keeping up with technology can be daunting. In the last few years, Gray's company has had to change from one that was paper-based to one that is electronic. "We are running hard to stand still. But it is an exciting challenge and I enjoy it," Gray says.

In a sense, Gray, 70, a former newspaperman who started working in the days of linotype, is doing what he has always done: compiling and organizing information. However, technology has dramatically changed how that information is stored, retrieved and used. As much as any business, publishing has been revolutionized by technology.

Just as the *Encyclopedia Britannica* and other major reference publications have moved online, Gray has adopted technology to better serve his customers. "The big lesson that I have learned is the need to cope with change. If we had stayed with our original concept, we surely would not be in business today," he says. "It is hard

to anticipate what the next changes are going to be, but we are going to have to keep going with those changes."

When they started publishing in 1987, Earle and Joan Gray took what seemed like a giant leap into technology by purchasing an $11,000 laser printer. Their aim was to be one of the first periodicals in Canada to use desktop publishing.

By 1994, it became apparent that customers wanted a computerized version of their products. The Gray's son Gordon, a computer consultant, helped customize a version of FoxPro software, which SpeakWrite then used to market its collections to customers on floppy disks.

As CD-ROM technology emerged, the focus shifted again. Gray learned the workings of FileMaker Pro Developer Edition, software that allows his customers to access and to search the database electronically. By buying established software and updating regularly, the company found it easier to keep pace with technology than by pursuing a customized approach.

In January 2001, SpeakWrite launched its first Web site with daughter-in-law Cheryl handling duties as Webmaster. Using the Web site, customers can order products online. Subscribers will eventually receive passwords to download services as an alternative to receiving CD ROM or paper copies. The Web site also provides a brochure on the art of speechwriting and free research on recent *hot* topics.

The Grays not only use technology to deal with customers and manage their subscriber list, they also rely on it in their day-to-day operations. Gray and two part-time researchers scan mainstream publications looking for nuggets to include in *Quotes, Notes and Anecdotes*. Printed versions of major newspapers and magazines make up about 80 percent of their research material. However, they transfer the selected information to an electronic format.

SpeakWrite uses electronic data management capabilities to collect, store, and update over 1,700 speeches and 20,000 quotes and anecdotes collected over the years. Using technology, SpeakWrite is able to reduce production times, lower overall costs and increase customer satisfaction.

Understanding the needs of the customer is an integral part of SpeakWrite's success. Clients for *Canadian Speeches* are generally Canadian institutions, such as libraries and universities, who want access to in-depth reference material that can be searched electronically.

Customers for *Quotes, Notes and Anecdotes* include journalists, speechwriters, and language lovers. Most readers want to browse through a traditional publication. Although SpeakWrite serves customers around the world, more than half of them live in the United States. American customers are well represented partly because material from major U.S. sources is included in the publication and partly because an alliance with an American speechwriting newsletter, *The Executive Speaker,* has helped the Grays tap into the American market.

The Internet breaks down the limitations of geographical distance between client and customer, cre-

ating the opportunity for a small business in rural Ontario to share its words with people around the world. "With today's technology, there are no limits for a home-based business," Gray says. "Even

the United States is managed as a home-based business, with the President working out of his White House."

## Special-Purpose Databases

The preceding section presumes the database is maintained with powerful database management software that can be applied to just about any PC database you might imagine. This software is often known as a **general-purpose database system**. Chapters 6 and 7 will focus on these general-purpose database systems. However, before proceeding, it is useful to note that there are also special-purpose database systems.

**Special-purpose databases** are predesigned for a specific use. The structure and contents of the database along with the software for entering and retrieving data fit the intended purpose. Users typically cannot change either. Among the most common special-purpose databases are directories, commercial and government databases, and personal information managers.

**Directories**  Organize information on a particular topic and its subtopics. An index indicates where data about an item can be located. The most common example is a telephone directory, with entries consisting of individuals or company names and the addresses and telephone numbers where they may be located. E-mail directories include the names and e-mail addresses of individuals accessible over a computer network. Mailing databases are directories of names and addresses that can be searched or processed by name, address, or topic.

**Commercial and Government Topical Databases**  Topical databases pertain to a specific subject and contain data about that topic. Common examples include economic, statistical, financial, and literary databases.

**Economic databases** capture details related to the state of the U.S. economy (other nations have comparable databases). If you are interested in understanding national income levels, labor trends, price indices, current business indicators, and changes in industrial production, you want to check the wide variety of economic databases available from the federal government. Many of these databases also include information on economic activity in states and regions.

Statistics measure the level of activity and a means of comparing areas of activity. **Statistical databases** include the measurement data. For instance, STAT-USA, an agency in the Economics and Statistics Administration, U.S. Department of Commerce, assembles data produced by hundreds of separate offices and divisions of the government. Without STAT-USA, it would be almost impossible for individuals to find out what is available, much less obtain it and use it. Similarly, the World Health Organization makes available an array of statistical databases reporting measures such as population growth or decline, population health, and the rate of growth or decline in diseases.

**Financial databases** focus on areas of monetary and investment activity, including stock market trading, issuance of mortgages, real-estate transactions, corporate finance, and venture-capital investment activities. For instance, many university business and economic courses require that students be familiar with the Electronic Data Gathering, Analysis, and Retrieval system and Compustat databases.

The Securities and Exchange Commission (SEC) requires all public companies (except foreign companies and companies with less than $10 million in assets and 500 shareholders) to file registration statements, periodic reports, and other forms

---

**general-purpose database system**
A database maintained with powerful database management software that can be applied to just about any PC database.

**special-purpose database**
Predesigned for a specific use.

**directory**
A listing of information by category.

**economic database**
Capture details related to the state of the U.S. economy (other nations have comparable databases).

**statistical database**
Include the measurement data to measure the level of statistical activity and a means of comparing areas of activity.

**financial database**
Focus on areas of monetary and investment activity, including stock market trading, issuance of mortgages, real-estate transactions, corporate finance, and venture-capital investment activities.

electronically through EDGAR. Anyone can access and download this information for free.

Compustat, in contrast, provides annual financial and stock market activity on thousands of companies. Up to 20 years of financial history, with quarterly reports, are included in the database, making it possible to track the rise and fall in the value of companies.

**Literary databases** pertain to books, monographs, or reports, or to articles appearing in newspapers and magazines. Alternatively, a literary database may contain the actual publications themselves or links to the publications. These databases can be searched in a variety of ways, depending on their design. Among the most common uses of a literary database are searches to retrieve references to a specific topic, author, or publication.

You can find databases on virtually any topic of interest, including music, book reviews, art, business, and science. For instance, the *Computer and Information Systems Abstracts* database contains reference information and brief summaries of publications on such topics as software, automation, security, imaging, robotics, computer mathematics, and electronics. The *General Science Index* describes articles on astronomy, biology, botany, chemistry, zoology, and other sciences.

In contrast, the *ABI/INFORM Database* can be purchased in several different forms. One version contains an index of publications on business, economics, and technology. An alternate version contains the complete articles from these publications. Both versions are searchable by author, title, topic, date, and publication name.

Databases may reside on a PC, on a company or university network, or on the World Wide Web. PC versions are delivered on DVD, CD-ROM, or over the Internet. The features and contents are generally the same regardless of the means of access.

It is important to note that these are *flat file* databases: All of the data are stored in a single large file. In contrast, relational databases (discussed shortly) divide the databases into two or more tables and relate the tables.

**Personal Information Managers**   A **personal information manager (PIM)** contains preprogrammed features enabling users to manage data helpful in their personal activities. PIMs store thousands of records of information according to the predefined structure of the database. Users cannot change or restructure the database. PIMs are sometimes called **contact managers**.

Among the most common PIM features are the following:

- **Contacts**   Contains a phone book of names, addresses, phone numbers, e-mail addresses, and other personal details, including friends and business acquaintances. A single entry for one individual can be displayed or the entire set of contact data can be printed in a report. Often contact management software includes an option for automatically dialing a phone number stored in the database.
- **Calendar**   A day-by-day calendar spanning several years records the date and time of classes, meetings, and appointments. Each day can be subdivided to show event starting and ending times to the minute. Alternate views of the calendar data can be displayed to show events scheduled for a day, a week, and a month. The contents of a calendar database can be printed in any of these views.
- **To-Do List**   A working list of items to be completed. To-do entries can be organized according to priority and due date.
- **Memos and Notes**   Free-form information, including notes, comments, and thoughts that do not fit into the other categories. For instance, sales persons often use this area to note tidbits of information about a prospect, such as their alma mater, hobbies, and the names of their children.

These PIM features are built in to most personal digital assistants (PDAs) and palm computers. A wide variety of PIM software is available for PCs as well.

Typically, individuals using PDAs want to maintain a copy of the database on their PC. Data can be transferred from one to the other by performing a *hot sync* using a cable connecting the PDA and PC or by infrared transfer.

**literary database**
Pertain to books, monographs, or reports, or to articles appearing in newspapers and magazines. Alternatively, a literary database may contain the actual publications themselves or links to the publications.

**personal information manager (PIM)/contact manager**
Contains preprogrammed features enabling users to manage data helpful in their personal activities.

# CRITICAL CONNECTIONS 1

## Farmland Boosts Sales With IT

**Farmland**

When most people think of a farm in the United States, they picture a solitary tractor tilling the earth from dawn to dusk. But the modern U.S. farmer is also a major consumer, one who spends thousands of dollars on feed, fuel, and chemicals at the local farm cooperative. The co-op, in turn, buys its wares from distributors, such as Farmland Industries, which has thousands of salespeople crisscrossing the Midwest.

Because Farmland's salespeople tend to specialize in certain product lines, several might visit the same co-op. Farmland realized that this was a duplication of effort. Another more serious problem was that Farmland's salespeople did not know what their colleagues had or had not already sold and therefore often missed opportunities to sell farm supplies related to the products they specialized in.

The firm turned to IT for help. Most of the company's salespeople already had laptop computers with communication capability, which meant they could easily access a database of products and prices. The next logical step was to install a contact manager—a data management system designed to help salespeople manage their work—on the network.

Thanks to the recently installed network-based contact manager, Farmland's salespeople now use their laptops to tap into a centralized database and extract a complete account history for each customer, including a record of what colleagues sold that customer on their last sales calls.

## Database Terminology

General- and special-purpose database systems have the same objective: to make the contents accessible in the most efficient manner. Both can be described by a common terminology. Users rely on a precise terminology to describe the structure and details of a database. This terminology makes it possible to generalize across many different situations without getting bogged down in the jargon of a particular industry, company, or problem setting. Five of the most commonly used database terms are *entity, attribute, data item, record,* and *relation.*

**entity**
A person, place, thing, event, or condition about which data and information are collected.

**Entities and Attributes**   An **entity** is a person, place, thing, event, or condition about which data and information are collected. For example, universities and colleges collect information about several entities, including students, faculty members, courses, and degree programs. Information in a hospital database typically focuses on such entities as patients, physicians, nurses, and rooms. In business, entities include customers, suppliers, and orders.

Choosing entities is an important step toward understanding a problem and devising its solution, for the right entity must be agreed upon before a problem can be addressed effectively. For instance, to institute a new security system, a university needs the following data and information about each of its students:

| Entity | Data and Information (Attributes) | |
|--------|-----------------|------------------|
| Student | Name | Telephone |
| | Street address | Date of birth |
| | City | Residency status |
| | State | Emergency contact |
| | Postal code | Fingerprint |
| | Student ID number | Picture |

Each category of data or information describing the entity is called an **attribute.** An attribute is a *fact* about a student. The last two attributes of the student entity—fingerprint and picture—may surprise you because they are a different form of information from the other items, all of which can be recorded in text or numeric format. But remember that information can be composed of several different components, including data, text, graphics, sound, and images (Figure 6.1). In the future, other details may be added: voice prints, spoken phrases, and video segments.

**Data Items and Records**   Once the specific facts of an individual entity are stored in a database, they are known as data items. Hence, the university's name **data items** may include such entries as Thomas O'Rafferty and François La Fleur. A **record** is a grouping of data items. It consists of the set of data and information (data, text, sound, or image) that describes an entity's specific occurrence (or instance). Each record in a database describes one specific occurrence of an entity. For example, as Figure 6.2 shows, the record for the student Thomas O'Rafferty includes the data items describing one occurrence of this *student* entity.

Records hold the information about an instance—one record per instance. If the university used a paper-based system, it would probably create a paper record: a form or an index card for each student. Records stored in a computer database are usually maintained on magnetic storage rather than in memory.

The *Information Technology in Practice* feature, "Finagle A Bagel Uses CRM Database to Build Buyer Loyalty," illustrates the value of database software in the successful operation of a big-city business where competition is tough.

**Relations**   The most common type of database is a **relational database.**[1] This type of database structures information in a table format consisting of horizontal rows and vertical columns.

The table itself, called a **relation** or **file**, describes an entity. The rows of the relation are its records, or **tuples,** representing instances of interest. The relation's columns are its attributes, or **fields.**

Relations have four general characteristics:

1. Each column contains a single value about the same attribute.
2. The order of columns in the relation does not matter.

---

**attribute**
A category of data or information that describes an entity. Each attribute is a fact about the entity.

**data item**
A specific detail of an individual entity that is stored in a database.

**record**
In a database, a designated field used to distinguish one record from another.

**relational database**
A database in which the data are structured in a table format consisting of rows and columns.

**relation/file**
The table in a database that describes an entity.

**tuples**
The rows of a relation. Also called records.

**fields**
The column of a relation. Also called attributes.

---

**FIGURE 6.1**

***The Components of Information in a Database***
In addition to data and text information, a database can contain graphic, sound, and image information.

---

[1]Other types of databases were common in the past, notably hierarchical and network database structures (see Chapter 7), which are still sometimes found in mainframe and midrange computer applications. However, because relational databases are currently the predominant type across all classes of computers, large and small, we will not discuss the other types here.

**FIGURE 6.2**

***Database Terminology***

Each record in a database specifies one instance of an entity. Here, the specific instance of the student entity is Thomas O'Rafferty.

**FIGURE 6.2**

***Database Terminology***

Each record in a database specifies one instance of an entity. Here, the specific instance of the student entity is Thomas O'Rafferty.

## ENTITY: STUDENTS AT NEW YORK UNIVERSITY

**General record structure for student entity**

**Specific record**

Attributes/ fields:
- Student name
- Street address
- City
- State
- Postal code
- Student ID
- Telephone
- Date of birth
- Residency
- Contact

Data items:
- Thomas O'Rafferty
- 1201 Sixth Avenue
- New York
- New York
- 10020-3021
- 102347654
- 212-555-6760
- 01-17-69
- Commuter
- Deborah O'Rafferty

3. The order of rows in the relation does not matter.
4. Each row is unique—one row cannot duplicate another.

As Figure 6.3 shows, all the records in a relation contain the same number of data items. However, there can be any number of records in the relation, and they can be entered in any order. (Processing will retrieve information in a particular sequence if the application requires that.)

*A word of advice:* Do not let the different terms confuse you. People often alternate between these formal and common names for database components:

| Formal Name | Common Name |
|---|---|
| Attribute | Field |
| Tuple | Record |
| Relation | Database or file |

We will use the more common names throughout this book. However, you should be familiar with the formal terms, particularly if you interact with systems analysts or other information technology professionals.

**FIGURE 6.3**

***The Elements of a Relation***

### STUDENT RELATION

| Name | Student ID Number | Street Address | City | State | Postal Code |
|---|---|---|---|---|---|
| Gorzynski, John | 253054720 | 71 West Washington | Chicago | Illinois | 60602-1634 |
| Markus, Lewis | 762027721 | 22 Ocean Blvd | Atlantic City | New Jersey | 08103 |
| Martin, Carol | 934841834 | 33 Hightower Lane | Montgomery | Alabama | 36116 |
| O'Rafferty, Thomas | 102347654 | 1201 Sixth Avenue | New York | New York | 10020-3021 |
| Patterson, Jane | 376358722 | 440 Holcomb Lane | Atlanta | Georgia | 30338-1538 |

*Attributes or Fields* (column headers)

*Records or Tuples* (rows)

# INFORMATION TECHNOLOGY IN PRACTICE

## Finagle A Bagel Uses CRM Database to Build Buyer Loyalty

CRM or Customer Relationship Management is a hot topic among retailers and restaurateurs. Large companies have been using databases to assist them in marketing their products and managing their customer service for a long time. But don't think this valuable business-building tool is available only to big firms. The power of information technology, including CRM, is available to companies of all sizes.

Finagle A Bagel, a Boston-based chain of bagel bakeries and cafes utilizes state of the art technology to manage a diverse customer base and to drive top-line sales. Finagle's "Frequent Finagler Program," is an ASP application that serves as both a loyalty and stored value program. Guests earn 'Finagler Points' for every dollar spent and receive rewards at the 20, 50, 75 and 100 point levels. Guests may also opt to put money on their cards and spend their Finagle Dollars over time. The stored value option also replaces the company's paper gift certificates automatically tracking the redemptions and the outstanding liabilities through the database.

Laura Trust, Co-President of Finagle A Bagel gives the Frequent Finagler Program high marks: "The

program works. It helps us drive sales. It also gives us a way to manage our promotions, understand our guests' buying patterns, provide vendors information about the products our guests choose, and track how our guests use our stores." And does the program work! In less than one year, Finagle A Bagel has built a customer database of over twenty thousand Frequent Finaglers. Thirty percent of all in-store transactions are associated with a Frequent Finagler and best of all the average Frequent Finagler transaction is 20% higher than the average transaction for non Frequent Finaglers.

In addition to driving sales, Finagle A Bagel utilizes Frequent Finagler information from a guest service standpoint. Heather Robertson, Director of Marketing, and her Guest Relations Team respond to all guest comments, however the additional information gleaned from the Frequent Finagler database enhances all guest follow-up. Now, whenever a guest calls, their Frequent Finagler Number is entered into the system. All of the guest's transaction history, the specific store visited and the dollars spent are immediately available. You can imagine the impression it makes on guests when Robertson or another member of her team is able to discuss with the guest their past history with the company. Such a capability not only makes it possible to follow up on inquiries but also builds unbeatable customer loyalty.

Each guest who calls in with a comment traditionally received a

coupon for a free sandwich or a dozen bagels, thanking them for their feedback and giving them an opportunity to come and try Finagle a Bagel again. With new releases of the Frequent Finagler software—paper coupons and manual coupon tracking systems become obsolete. Adding 'comp' or 'coupon' dollars to a Frequent Finagler card replaces the need for paper coupons. It tracks redemption automatically and even allows Robertson to follow up once the rewards have been redeemed. "So Mr. Jones, did you enjoy your Santa Fe Smoked Turkey Melt?" Robertson also has the added benefit of getting a new Frequent Finagler Card in a guest's hand if they do not yet have one.

From an IT standpoint the program integrates seamlessly with Finagle a Bagel's Point of Sales system. Regina Jerome, Director of IT at Finagle comments: "One of the most important aspects of our Frequent Finagler program is that all information is gathered during our normal transaction process. Guest cards are swiped at the POS terminal at transaction time—and the system does the rest."

The program also allows the guests to "register" their card online. Finagle a Bagel entices the

guest to do so by offering a free half dozen of bagels when the guest registers a card. In return, the guest provides their name, address and other demographic information that the company uses to further market the company's new specials, up coming events or to send a guest who has not used their card in a while a coupon or other incentive to come back to the store.

From a marketing, sales, accounting and IT perspective, implementing the current Frequent Finagler program has turned out to be a valuable business decision at Finagle A Bagel.

## The Objectives of Database Management Systems

Obviously, it is much better to *manage* data and information than to allow them to just accumulate. Managing data is precisely the objective of the various personal **database management system (DBMS)** packages now on the market. The most popular of these packages are listed in Table 6.1.

Database management systems provide users with these tools: a **data definition language (DDL)**, which allows users to define the database; a **data manipulation language (DML)**, which lets users store, retrieve, and edit data in the database (a query language is a type of data manipulation language); and a variety of other capabilities (discussed later in this chapter) that help users increase their productivity.

Managing data means taking deliberate actions guided by specific objectives. Database management systems are designed to achieve the following five objectives:

1. Integrating databases.
2. Reducing redundancy.
3. Sharing information.
4. Maintaining integrity.
5. Enabling database evolution.

You might think of these as both problem-*solving* and problem-*avoiding* objectives.

**data definition language (DDL)**
A tool provided in a database management system that allows users to define the database.

**data manipulation language (DML)**
A tool provided in a database management system that allows users to store, retrieve, and edit data in the database.

**Integrating Databases** Because the data and information needed to solve a particular problem often reside in several databases, problem solvers must be able to integrate databases. Database management systems allow the merger of separate files, created at varying times or by different people.

**REALITY CHECK** Knowledge entails more than collecting facts and details. Indeed, collecting data is not nearly as important as arranging those data in a useful way. A good database organizes all the data relevant to an entity and gives its users the ability to assess a situation and determine the proper course of action.

For example, a university's database will contain data on individual students including name, date of birth, major, elective courses taken, grade point average, extra-curricular activities, and expected date of graduation. *Knowledge* comes from assembling and synthesizing these details in a way that allows you to answer questions like the following:

- Is this individual someone you would recommend to a prospective employer?
- Do you think this person will graduate on time?
- Is this person highly creative and innovative?

The answers to these questions are not contained as facts in the database. Rather, they are derived from an analysis of the facts contained in the database. Knowledge comes from making use of data and information when they are relevant to the situation at hand. ■

| Table 6.1 Popular PC Database Management Systems | | |
| --- | --- | --- |
| SOFTWARE PACKAGE | MANUFACTURER | VERSIONS AVAILABLE |
| Access | Microsoft | Windows and Macintosh |
| FileMaker Pro | Apple | Windows and Macintosh |
| Visual FoxPro | Microsoft | Windows and Macintosh |
| Interbase | Borland | Windows and Linux |

Integration is often done to process an inquiry or to create a report. Suppose that the university we discussed earlier wants to generate a report listing all courses, instructors, and the office numbers and office hours of each instructor. As Figure 6.4 shows, the DBMS prepares this report by integrating information retrieved from separate databases. In integrating databases, specialized databases such as a course database and an instructor database are maintained. Yet the benefits of processing them together are achieved.

**Reducing Redundancy**  Duplication of information between databases is termed *redundancy.* When files are developed independently, some data and information may be repeated in the databases, and unfortunately, these multiple copies sometimes become inconsistent. Because the data and information in databases are updated or changed at varying times, often by people who are not aware of the existence of other databases with the same information, only one copy may be altered. The others will be out-of-date and therefore inaccurate.

In well-managed databases, most data items are not duplicated. Rather, the DBMS extracts copies of the information from the appropriate databases to produce the necessary report.

Not all redundancy is bad, however. Information that is common to different databases makes possible the integration of descriptions and the preparation of reports. In the student/course/instructor example, for instance, several data items, such as the course name Music 340 and instructor G. Kris, are included in all databases (Figure 6.4). Figure 6.5 identifies those areas where redundancy is and is not necessary.

**Sharing Information**  An important advantage of databases (as described earlier) is that they allow the sharing of information among many people in various locations. Hence, achieving the sharing of information is also an objective of database management. The *information-sharing* capabilities of database management software mean that information can be stored once and then retrieved any number of times by any authorized user of the database. This capability both reduces overall storage needs and helps to ensure consistency in the information obtained by people working in different areas of the same organization.

Information sharing also means that the same information can be shared by different applications. The alternative, having a different set of information for each application, would lead to redundancy and, most likely, inconsistency between the different sets.

**Maintaining Integrity**  Database management systems play an important role in database security. When a database is *secure,* access to its information is controlled so that only authorized people can retrieve or process it. Security is important, especially when personal information (such as salary history and telephone numbers) is involved.

A DBMS also helps to ensure database *reliability,* meaning that the information in the database is accurate and available when needed. A DBMS forces people to take precautions to ensure that the information they are entering into the database is correct. It also makes them maintain backup copies of the database in case of loss or damage.

A database that is both secure and reliable is said to have *integrity.*

**FIGURE 6.4**

***Integrating Databases to Produce a Report***

Database management systems frequently integrate information from separate databases into a special report.

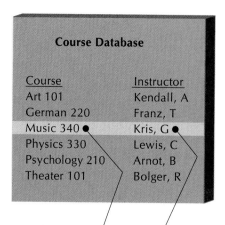

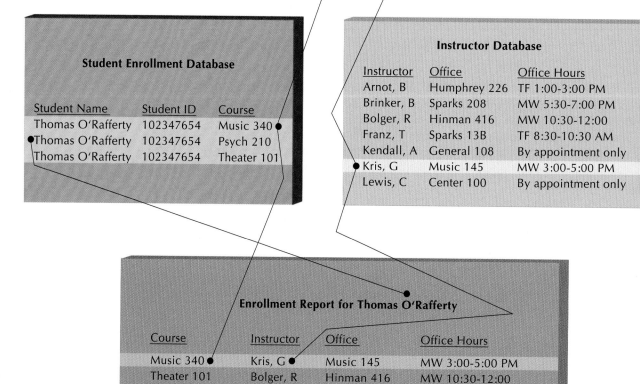

**Course Database**

| Course | Instructor |
|--------|-----------|
| Art 101 | Kendall, A |
| German 220 | Franz, T |
| Music 340 | Kris, G |
| Physics 330 | Lewis, C |
| Psychology 210 | Arnot, B |
| Theater 101 | Bolger, R |

**Student Enrollment Database**

| Student Name | Student ID | Course |
|--------------|-----------|--------|
| Thomas O'Rafferty | 102347654 | Music 340 |
| Thomas O'Rafferty | 102347654 | Psych 210 |
| Thomas O'Rafferty | 102347654 | Theater 101 |

**Instructor Database**

| Instructor | Office | Office Hours |
|-----------|--------|-------------|
| Arnot, B | Humphrey 226 | TF 1:00-3:00 PM |
| Brinker, B | Sparks 208 | MW 5:30-7:00 PM |
| Bolger, R | Hinman 416 | MW 10:30-12:00 |
| Franz, T | Sparks 13B | TF 8:30-10:30 AM |
| Kendall, A | General 108 | By appointment only |
| Kris, G | Music 145 | MW 3:00-5:00 PM |
| Lewis, C | Center 100 | By appointment only |

**Enrollment Report for Thomas O'Rafferty**

| Course | Instructor | Office | Office Hours |
|--------|-----------|--------|-------------|
| Music 340 | Kris, G | Music 145 | MW 3:00-5:00 PM |
| Theater 101 | Bolger, R | Hinman 416 | MW 10:30-12:00 |
| Psych 210 | Arnot, B | Humphrey 226 | TF 1:00-3:00 PM |

**Enabling Database Evolution**   Databases are not stagnant. They evolve because the environment in which they are used—home, campus, or office—is constantly changing. Databases change in two ways:

- **Content**   The data items in current records change, new records are added, and existing records are deleted.
- **Structure**   The data items that make up a record change the database's logical structure, either because fields are added or deleted, because data items' characteristics change (for example, more space is needed for a data item than is currently allocated), or because the way the database is stored physically changes.

**FIGURE 6.5**

**Database Redundancy—Necessary and Unnecessary**

The student's street address, city, state, and postal code are not needed in the student enrollment database. Since each student's ID number is unique, that is enough to ensure that two students with the same name will not be confused.

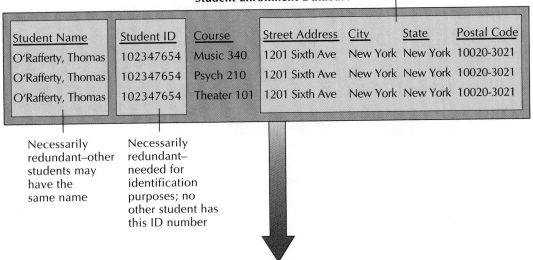

**Student Enrollment Database**

Unnecessarily redundant—not needed for identification purposes, contained in another database, and likely to change

| Student Name | Student ID | Course | Street Address | City | State | Postal Code |
|---|---|---|---|---|---|---|
| O'Rafferty, Thomas | 102347654 | Music 340 | 1201 Sixth Ave | New York | New York | 10020-3021 |
| O'Rafferty, Thomas | 102347654 | Psych 210 | 1201 Sixth Ave | New York | New York | 10020-3021 |
| O'Rafferty, Thomas | 102347654 | Theater 101 | 1201 Sixth Ave | New York | New York | 10020-3021 |

Necessarily redundant—other students may have the same name

Necessarily redundant— needed for identification purposes; no other student has this ID number

**Master Student Database**

| Student name | Student ID | Street Address | City | State | Postal Code |
|---|---|---|---|---|---|
| Markus, Lewis | 762027721 | 22 Ocean Blvd | Atlantic City | New Jersey | 08103 |
| O'Rafferty, Thomas | 102347654 | 1201 Sixth Avenue | New York | New York | 10020-3021 |
| Patterson, Jane | 376358722 | 440 Holcomb Lane | Atlanta | Georgia | 30338-1538 |

Appropriate place for address information

# CRITICAL CONNECTIONS 2

## Associated Press Relies on Databases for its Information Business

**Associated Press**

Since it was founded in the 1840s, the Associated Press (AP) has been a principal supplier of news to the world's newspapers. Every day, from its headquarters in New York City's Rockefeller Center, AP sends out a wealth of information—some 20 million words, equivalent to half the content of the *Encyclopedia Britannica*—to its 8,500 member newspapers, government agencies, television and radio stations, and private news agencies.

Since the beginning of the decade, AP has used the Filemaker Pro database to provide information to its subscribers. Its editorial databases are accessible over the Web to subscribers who in turn link these databases to provide information via their own Web sites. So, people who view the news on their hometown newspaper's Web site might very well be linked by the Internet to the AP wire service's Filemaker Pro database system, a personal database management system created for the PC.

# INFORMATION TECHNOLOGY IN PRACTICE

## IT in Private Practice Is Making the Rounds

Dr. Hagelyn Wilson has been practicing medicine for more than 30 years in her hometown of Montgomery, Alabama. In 1957, when she decided to become a physician, many of the residents of Montgomery who knew her thought the idea laughable. What made the daughter of a southern black preacher think she could successfully pursue a career in medicine? The answer was her personal determination and a supportive family.

When Dr. Wilson is asked what she thought about the steep odds against her getting into medical school and ultimately becoming a physician—and the odds against a young black woman in the 1950s were indeed formidable—she does not hesitate. "I never really thought about it," she says. "There were a lot of people who gave me a hard time, but I never let them get me down. I believe you can do almost anything with enough faith and discipline."

Dr. Wilson's practice centers on patients and personal attention. Six mornings a week are reserved for seeing patients in the office. The afternoons are reserved for home visits. (Dr. Wilson is the only physician in Montgomery who regularly sees patients in their homes.)

When Dr. Wilson began her practice, a computer in a doctor's office was unheard of. Even as

late as 1990, she was without a computer. Then a patient gave her one as payment for treatment. Neither Dr. Wilson nor her staff had any notion of how to use a computer, but they were determined to learn. Every Sunday afternoon they came into the office to practice, initially with word processing and spreadsheets. Soon Dr. Wilson learned how to create computer procedures and passed her knowledge along to her staff. Within a month or so, information on all of her regular patients had been incorporated into a spreadsheet: names, addresses, medical history, and billing information.

Recently, Dr. Wilson upgraded to a new computer and began using software she obtained from health insurance providers Medicaid, Medicare, and Blue Shield, which made it possible to submit insurance claims electronically. This reduced the insurers' payment time from 6 weeks to less than 30 days.

Today, Dr. Wilson's practice relies on database applications written by her son, who is an IT professional. The online patient databases he has developed have the capability to monitor the treatment of her patients. These records are linked to an accounting database that is used with other office procedures. Dr. Wilson encourages her staff to familiarize themselves with the capabilities of IT, and she pays the cost of their attendance at seminars and workshops to develop their skills.

The use of IT has enhanced not only her practice, but also the well-being of her patients who receive quality medical care at an affordable cost. IT enables Dr. Wilson to contain the cost of maintaining records—a savings she passes along to her patients in the form of lower fees. She also stays on top of medical developments through her computer, and she uses her computer to stay in touch with other physicians. She particularly enjoys discussions of recent medical advances that go on over the Internet, since attending medical conferences is too expensive for a doctor with her kind of practice.

Information technology and databases are no substitute for a good doctor making the rounds and visiting patients at home when they need her. However, they can certainly make a caring physician even better at her profession.

Database changes happen every day. This is not a problem if provision is made for the evolution of the database. Only when people find that they cannot adjust the database to fit new circumstances is there a problem. Database management systems give users the capability to modify the database and to avoid inflexibility. The *Information Technology in Practice* feature, "IT in Private Practice Is Making the Rounds," describes how Dr. Hagelyn Wilson, of Montgomery, Alabama, developed a database system to monitor the treatment of her patients.

## Database or Spreadsheet—What's the Difference?

Lotus 1-2-3 and Microsoft Excel, the spreadsheets that swept the PC world in the early 1980s, actually integrated three basic functions: an electronic spreadsheet, database management, and business graphics. Since then, many people have tried to use these spreadsheet packages to build personal databases, only to find that what they really need is a database management system.

**Three Basic Questions**    How do you decide whether you should use a spreadsheet or a database management system in your work? Simply ask yourself these three questions:

1. **What do I need to do with the data?**   Much of a spreadsheet's power comes from its embedded formulas, which let you explore the numerical relationships between business variables such as cost, price, and profit. The spreadsheet is therefore an ideal tool for performing *what if* financial analyses and forecasts. The database, in contrast, is designed to collect, store, and retrieve data items that are structured in a particular way. Although database management systems can perform mathematical functions (such as sums and averages), their main strength is their ability to maintain the *relationships* among data items.

2. **How much data do I need to store?**   Spreadsheets do have *find* and *search* functions that help users retrieve specific records, but the process can be slow and cumbersome if the spreadsheet is very large. A small-store owner might find it practical to record accounts payable in a spreadsheet, while a major credit-card company would find it more practical to use a database.

3. **How important are the data?**   Data and information are often described as the lifeblood of the modern organization. With them, managers can carefully monitor the organization's performance and plan for the future. In some situations, data and information have life-and-death consequences; a record of patient drug allergies is one such situation. Other data, such as sales forecasts and employee salaries, are so sensitive and confidential that if they get into the wrong hands, the organization or individuals could be harmed. Hence, it is important that data be both accurate and protected from unauthorized users.

A spreadsheet does not offer much help here, for anyone who can access the spreadsheet file can also read—or change—the data it contains. A database management system, in contrast, contains many functions a spreadsheet cannot perform, including (but not limited to) those that are designed to eliminate common data entry errors and protect the data from unauthorized users. (You will read more about these functions later in this chapter.)

**Spreadsheets and DBMSs: A Team for the Future**   Spreadsheets and databases both have a valuable role to play in the modern organization. At many firms, for example, corporate data are warehoused in a multiuser database system and safeguarded by a database management system. Authorized users, however, can use queries to download a copy of specific data into their desktop computers, where they can use a spreadsheet to perform *what if* analyses. Or, alternatively, they can use a PC and a spreadsheet to collect raw data, which are then transferred into the multiuser database system. (Au Bon Pain, an international chain of French-style cafés, uses this arrangement.) Clearly, knowledge workers of the future will need to know how to use both spreadsheet and database software.

# Developing Database Applications

**database application**
A computerized database routine for collecting, retrieving, or manipulating data to meet recurring needs.

Like the process of developing a spreadsheet application, the process of developing a **database application** is a form of problem solving. It proceeds in a deliberate fashion, with one action leading to the next in the most efficient and effective manner possible. Database-application development can be viewed as a seven-step sequence (Figure 6.6):

1. Study the problem.
2. Determine the requirements.
3. Design the database.
4. Create the database.
5. Design the application.
6. Create the application.
7. Test the application.

In the sections that follow, we will use a problem commonly faced by student association offices on university campuses to illustrate each phase of the database development process.

## Study the Problem

Studying a problem involves determining its characteristics and the ways that database creation and processing can help solve it.

The problem is as follows: The Student Association Office (SAO) at the University of Ithaca is responsible for keeping all members of all student clubs informed of membership requirements and special events. At present, the director's office maintains a file of index cards on which names, addresses, telephone numbers, and other personal information are recorded. However, there are now nearly 50 organizations on campus, each with 25 to 50 members, and the director wants to develop a better system.

After studying the problem, the director and his staff decide to develop a database for the SAO. Using the student database in the university's student records office would make their job much easier, but university policy dictates that this database can be used only for official university business. It is not available to social and service organizations.

**FIGURE 6.6**

***Database Application Development Sequence***

The seven steps in database application development are common to all database development projects, whether large or small.

| STEP | DESCRIPTION |
|---|---|
| Study the problem. | Describe the system's data entry (input) requirements, inquiry requirements, and output requirements. |
| Determine the requirements. | Determine the problem's characteristics and how database creation and processing can assist in solving the problem. |
| Design the database. | Identify entities of interest, determine the data or information that describes them, and determine which data items will be used to distinguish one entity from another. |
| Create the database. | Name the database; establish the database structure (field names, types, widths, and decimal positions; field indexation). |
| Design the application. | Develop data entry, report generation, and query-processing methods. |
| Create the application. | Write the programs to perform data-processing tasks. |
| Test the application. | Evaluate the application's processes and procedures to ensure they are performing as expected. |

# INFORMATION TECHNOLOGY IN PRACTICE

## Chicago Public Schools' KidStart Database Manages a Summer's Work Experience

"Chicago's corporate involvement is an important part of this program because for many youth it is their introduction to the world of work. These jobs offer young people the chance to network with people who could become lifetime mentors."
—Mayor Richard M. Daley

Summer is an important time for high school students. For some, it is a vacation from day-to-day school activities. For many others, however, the summer offers a chance to gain valuable work experience through on-the-job internships.

For more than a decade, Chicago's Mayor Richard M. Daley and the City of Chicago Public Schools have provided a summer internship program for high school students. During its initial stages, school officials helped to place students in jobs at various city agencies, such as the Chicago Public Library and Chicago Park District. To be considered, students completed written applications that school officials reviewed to match qualified students with agency needs.

The City's early success convinced school officials to expand the program. To do so, officials worked with local companies to create nearly 1,000 summer jobs. When the expanded program was publicized, more than 30,000 student applications were submitted, creating a massive data management challenge for the program's administrators. To avoid the trouble and expense of manually entering data from hard-copy applications into a spreadsheet or database, officials created an online application process.

The Chicago School's program directors decided that the only logical approach was to create a database of the students' personal information. Working with Microsoft Access database software, the program staff created an online database, which they named KidStart. The database incorporated Web application forms for both students and prospective employers. Now instead of completing paper forms that require a subsequent data-entry step, applicants can key job or personal information into the electronic form displayed on their computers. When completed, they need only click the submit button, and the information is transmitted to the school office. The computer processes the information and flags any missing or incorrect information that applicants can correct. Then the application details are entered directly into the KidStart database.

A similar process is followed for the more than 100 companies now participating in the program. Since employers have been able to enter their information online, rather than filling out and mailing paper application forms, the number of available jobs can be accessed quickly and efficiently.

The database system provides more than just efficient online data entry. Once entered, the student's information can quickly be linked electronically to academic data on file in another school system database and to a database containing the job and skills information needed by employers. Program directors then view a combined set of information (without creating a new file) to select students with the background, qualifications, and interest that fit employer preferences.

The KidStart database provides important advantages as well. For instance, KidStart staff can now easily add information about job placement, work experience, and employer comments. They can also process the database periodically to monitor how participation in KidStart affects academic performance. The database's flexibility means that other uses can occur as the need arises, all without reentering or copying data. Not only are data entry costs avoided, but the database system plays an integral role in helping Chicago kids get a jump on a summer's worth of experience.

Because the director's office already uses personal computers, the director and staff decide the database should be created and maintained on a PC. Before they plunge into the development tasks, they check to ensure that two essential conditions are met:

* The designated PC on which the database will be established has adequate storage capacity for the database and for the computer-based procedures that will be needed to use the database.
* The database management software they plan to use will run on the designated PC, and the system's main memory and disk storage capacity are sufficient.

Once these conditions are met, they can determine the application's requirements.

The *Information Technology in Practice* feature, "Chicago Public Schools' KidStart Database Manages a Summer's Work Experience," is another example of how database management capabilities helped an education program meet its growth objectives.

## Determine the Requirements

The database's *requirements* are the capabilities the system must have for capturing, storing, processing, and generating data and information. These include input/data entry requirements, query requirements, and output requirements. Determining requirements begins with the formation of a project committee to oversee the effort. In the SAO example (University of Ithaca), this committee includes managers, informed staff members, and students. Bringing these three groups together should ensure that all meaningful ideas are considered.

The project committee evaluates the manual system of index cards currently in use with the objective of determining which features work well and which are inefficient. Because database applications have a way of generating additional uses after they are developed, committee members also try to identify possible future uses of the data and information that will be included in the database. For example, the committee may decide that a likely new use of the database will be to keep track of the location of student club members after they graduate.

After much discussion, the committee formulates the following requirements. People using the new system must be able to

* Enter and maintain records in the database.
* Prepare reports listing all members of student clubs
    −in alphabetical order.
    −in postal code order.
    −in alphabetical order by name of student club.
* Prepare mailing labels.
* Process queries to display or print information about a particular club member who is identified either by name or by student ID number.
* Make copies of the database for backup purposes.
* Protect the database from unauthorized use.

The committee members agree that they can design a new application that meets all of these requirements.

## Design the Database

With the requirements set, the project leader can turn to the design process. Database design consists of three activities:

* Identifying the entities of interest.
* Determining the attributes that describe the entity of interest.
* Determining which data items will be used to distinguish one entity from another (for retrieval purposes).

For the student club database, the primary entity is the student member. The most important attributes describing the members are

- Name:
  - –Last name
  - –First name
  - –Middle initial
- Student ID number.
- Student club/society name.
- Room number (in student club facilities).
- Year of graduation.
- Office held in student club (if any).

Office staff members want to be able to retrieve information from the database using the individual's name (last name, then first name), but they expect that in some instances it will be necessary to rely on the individual's student ID number. As in Figure 6.7, each student will have a unique ID number to ensure that students with the same last and first names are not confused. These three data items–last name, first name, and student ID number–are all used as **index keys** or **search keys**. When the user specifies a search key, the database management software searches through the database to locate the record containing the specified data item.

**index key/search key**
A data item used by database management software to locate a specific record.

## Create the Database

Creation of a database entails naming the database and defining its structure, which consists of five elements (Figure 6.7):

1. Names of the individual fields (attributes).
2. Type of information stored in each field.
3. Maximum width of information stored in each field.
4. Number of decimal positions allowed in each field (when appropriate).
5. Whether or not each field will be indexed.

**Field Names**   Field names distinguish one field from another. The guidelines for naming the fields are contingent on the data management software used. For example, in the popular Microsoft Access database system, field names:

- Can be up to 64 characters long.
- Can include any combination of letters, numbers, spaces, and special characters except a period (.), an exclamation point (!), an accent grave ('), and brackets ([ ]).
- Cannot begin with leading spaces.
- Cannot include control characters (ASCII values 0 through 31).

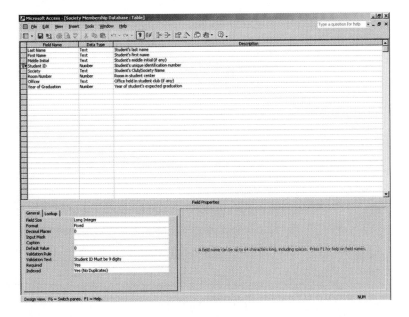

**FIGURE 6.7**

*Database Structure for Student Club Database (Using Microsoft Access)*

The project committee decides to use Microsoft Access to create the SAO's database. The database will contain eight fields with the following names: last name, first name, middle initial, student ID, society, room number, officer, and year of graduation.

**Field Types**    In addition to naming each field, database creators must specify the type of data the field will hold. The most popular database systems permit six different types of data (Figure 6.8):

1. **Character**    The letters A–Z, the numbers 0–9, and any other characters on the keyboard (such as & and #). Most fields contain character, or alphanumeric, information. (The terms *character* and *alphanumeric* are used interchangeably.) Numbers treated as character data cannot be used in arithmetic or computation and are for identification purposes only (student ID numbers, for example).
2. **Numeric**    Any integer (that is, any whole number, such as 1, 2, 50, or 100) or any number with a decimal point or a minus sign (2). Unlike alphanumeric data, numeric data can be used in arithmetic processes.
3. **Floating point**    Decimal numbers (such as 1.5, 2.33, 50.84, and 100.992). Floating point numbers are used when greater precision is needed. They can speed arithmetic processing when the numbers are very large.
4. **Logical**    Only a single character–Y or y (yes), T or t (true), N or n (no), or F or f (false). Some systems allow entry of yes-or-no values and convert them to true-or-false values when storing the data in the database.
5. **Memo**    Text information consisting of alphanumeric characters. Memo fields are designed to hold long blocks of text, often several thousand characters in length.
6. **Date**    In the form mm/dd/yyyy (month/day/year). For example, a birth date of January 3, 2002, can be described as 01/03/2002. The data management system inserts the slash (/) character.

Many database management systems include image and graphic data types as well.

**Field Width**    The width of the field specified in the database structure determines how long, in characters, each field can be. For some fields, like the logical, date, and memo fields, length is predetermined by the database management system. Other field lengths are specified by the database designer. For instance, the chosen length of the student ID field will depend on the number of characters the university includes in all student identification numbers. University of Ithaca uses nine-digit student ID numbers, so the width of the student ID field is nine characters.

**FIGURE 6.8**

***Field Types***

The six most common field types are listed here. A growing number of database management systems can also include image and graphic field types.

| FIELD TYPE | DESCRIPTION | EXAMPLE |
|---|---|---|
| Character or alphanumeric | Alphabetic or special characters and numbers (cannot be used in arithmetic processes). | O'Rafferty 12001 Sixth Avenue |
| Numeric | Any integer or any number with a decimal point or minus sign (can be used in arithmetic processes). | 540 -12 4.7 |
| Floating point | Decimal numbers (typically used in applications involving frequent multiplication and division). | 128.6 |
| Logical | One space used to indicate True or False, or Yes or No. | Tt Ff Yy Nn |
| Memo | Text data used to explain or annotate other details contained in the record, frequently at length. | "Details captured by Jerri Olenburg during interview with student on April 14." |
| Date | Calendar date in the format mm/dd/yyyy (month, day, year). | 07/15/1999 |

**Decimal Positions**   When decimal data will be included in the database, the designer specifies the number of positions to allow after the decimal point. If a field will describe money, it is customary to have two decimal positions (for example, the monetary figure $34.78 has two decimal positions). The SAO at University of Ithaca does not need to use decimal numbers in its database, so the relevant fields have decimal positions of zero.

**Indexation**   **Indexing** is the structural element that permits the database system to find fields and records in the database. The designer must specify which fields will be used for retrieval so that the database management system can create an index of key fields and storage locations. Once the designer chooses the respective fields, the database management system does all of the work. Figure 6.9 shows that the project committee has chosen to index last name, student ID, and society. The *yes* at the bottom of the screen means that the field will be indexed. A *no* would mean that it will not.

**indexing**
A database system's capability to find fields and records in the database.

## Design the Application

Database processing includes many features that make data and information accessible to people and that help safeguard the existence of the database. It is during the application design step of the development process that these features are determined. The most important of them are the methods for data entry, report generation, and query processing.

**Data Entry**   Database creation, as we just saw, is the process of establishing the database's structure by defining the database's different fields and their characteristics. **Data entry** is the process of *populating* the database with data and information. During data entry, new records are added to the database by providing the details for each field in the record. At the University of Ithaca, data entry methods will determine how all of the student club details, such as last name, first name, and student ID, will be entered into the database.

**data entry**
The process of populating a database with data and information.

**Data entry forms** are custom-developed video displays used to enter and change data in a database. Forms can be very basic, or they can be designed to look like the paper forms and reports that the database will generate. Figure 6.9 shows two different data entry forms. The form at the top asks the user to enter data directly, using field names as a prompt. The form at the bottom has been specially designed and formatted for ease of use and aesthetic appeal.

**data entry form**
Custom-developed video display used to enter and change data in a database.

**FIGURE 6.9**
**Two Data Entry Forms**

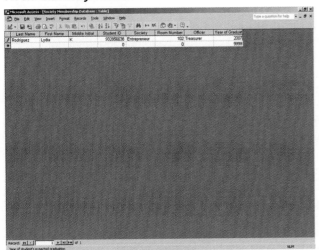
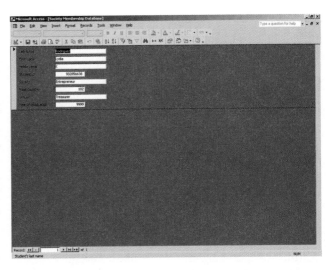

# INFORMATION TECHNOLOGY IN PRACTICE
## Kinion Furniture Links Database to Long-Standing Software Systems

Since 1982, Kinion Furniture of McMinnville, Oregon has been crafting handmade solid wood furniture. The company works primarily with cherry, but can build furniture in black walnut, eastern hard maple, or other hardwoods. Many of Kinion's standard designs can be modified to meet unique customer specifications. The company ships to customers throughout the United States.

For years, Kinion Furniture has relied heavily on its small-business accounting and manufacturing software acquired from a well-known commercial software vendor. The system maintains order and financial details and produces tracking documents used in the company's manufacturing area. Tracking orders is especially important for Kinion since the order-to-delivery cycle is 12 to 16 weeks (characteristic of the furniture industry as a whole) and most orders include custom specifications.

In 1990, Kinion opened a showroom in Portland, some 40 miles from company headquarters. When the showroom first opened, salespeople in Portland would write customer furniture orders and place them in a new order file. A copy also went in an *outbox* where it stayed until someone made the 40-mile trip to McMinnville. Several days typically passed before a paper copy of the sales order reached the manufacturing area in McMinnville.

Since the lead time on orders is long, it was not unusual for customers to return to the showroom to change or add to their order. Each time this happened, a salesperson would have to locate a paper copy of the order, make the

changes, and call the McMinnville shop to alert its staff to the changes. The shop in turn would have to locate the order, make the changes, enter them into the computer system, and call the salesperson to confirm that the change had been received and entered into the order.

The long lead time also meant customers often called to inquire about the status of their order. Showroom staff had trouble getting status information from the manufacturing shop, which made it difficult to respond to customer inquiries.

After several years of operating this way, Kerry Kinion, vice president and son of founder Gary Kinion, decided the order process had to be streamlined and that the two locations must be linked electronically. However, he did not want to disturb the existing accounting and manufacturing software systems that were working effectively.

The solution was to create an order-entry system for the Portland showroom. The order-entry system was built using PC database software. From then on, all customer and order details were entered into the database by sales staff. The system produced a sales order for the

showroom and transmitted the details electronically to the company's manufacturing system over a high-speed communication line installed with the new system. No more hand carrying of paper copies of order forms.

The showroom application provides other advantages as well: Showroom staff can retrieve cut lists, drawings, and other materials residing on Kinion's manufacturing server when they want to share information with customers in real time. The system also keeps a record of each customer interaction and every update to a customer's order. Even e-mail activity is recorded. Everyone likes the fact that information can be exchanged between the systems without the need to rekey any details.

Kinion's database-driven order-entry system has streamlined the order-entry process, saving precious time for waiting customers, even as it has improved the efficiency of tracking orders throughout the manufacturing process. Best of all, the order-entry application was added without disturbing the already installed software and without adding redundant data.

The data-entry portion of application design involves determining the method and sequence in which the data are entered. Typically, data are still entered through the keyboard, but scanners, microphones, and light pens are being used more frequently.

The *Information Technology in Practice* feature, "Kinion Furniture Links Database to Longstanding Software Systems," describes how a PC database can be used both as a data-entry tool and as a means to transform essential parts of the company's business activities.

**Report Generation**  A *report* is a printed or onscreen display of data or information in the database. Some reports are simply a list of the records in the database, one record after the other; others contain only certain elements of the database (Figure 6.10). Most of the time, however, a report is more than just a list. A good report organizes data into a form that is meaningful and helpful.

Reports are most useful when they

- Contain the records that meet the recipients' needs.
- Contain only the information that is needed from the records.
- Present information arranged in a sequence that fits the users' needs (perhaps in alphabetical order or grouped by category according to the contents of particular fields).
- Have the date of preparation, titles that identify the purpose of the report, and headings that identify the contents of the rows and columns of information.
- Have numbered pages, with the title repeated on each page when reports are lengthy.

In a well-designed report, such as that shown in Figure 6.11, information appears where users expect it; headings and titles are clear and useful. The focus is on the information rather than on the design itself, which is hardly noticed.

| LASTNAME | FIRSTNAME | INITIAL | STUDENT_ID | SOCIETY |
|----------|-----------|---------|------------|---------|
| JAMISON | JULIETTE | R | 535460299 | ENTREPRENEUR |
| HUNT | MARTHA | L | 325937742 | ENTREPRENEUR |
| RODRIGUEZ | LYDIA | K | 932856638 | ENTREPRENEUR |
| LING | MAI | T | 535257812 | ENTREPRENEUR |
| GONZALEZ | RAMON | | 285339934 | STUDY ABROAD |
| MARKS | DAVID | M | 883226077 | STUDY ABROAD |
| CHO | JOHN | D | 488249931 | STUDY ABROAD |

**FIGURE 6.10**

***Unformatted Database Printout***

This report is simply a report of certain elements of the student club database. It contains information from the database, but is not organized usefully.

**CLUB MEMBERSHIP**

Page No.  1
08/08/04

| SOCIETY | LASTNAME | FIRSTNAME | INITIAL | STUDENT_ID |
|---------|----------|-----------|---------|------------|
| ENTREPRENEUR | HUNT | MARTHA | L | 325937742 |
| ENTREPRENEUR | JAMISON | JULIETTE | R | 535460299 |
| ENTREPRENEUR | LING | MAI | T | 535257812 |
| ENTREPRENEUR | RODRIGUEZ | LYDIA | K | 932856638 |
| STUDY ABROAD | CHO | JOHN | D | 488249931 |
| STUDY ABROAD | GONZALEZ | RAMON | | 285339934 |
| STUDY ABROAD | MARKS | DAVID | M | 883226077 |

**FIGURE 6.11**

***Formatted Database Report***

This report contains the same data as the printout in Figure 6.10, but it is organized alphabetically by club and by Student's last name.

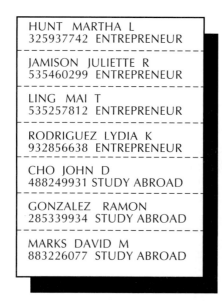

```
HUNT  MARTHA  L
325937742  ENTREPRENEUR
- - - - - - - - - - - - - - - - - - - - -
JAMISON  JULIETTE  R
535460299  ENTREPRENEUR
- - - - - - - - - - - - - - - - - - - - -
LING  MAI  T
535257812  ENTREPRENEUR
- - - - - - - - - - - - - - - - - - - - -
RODRIGUEZ  LYDIA  K
932856638  ENTREPRENEUR
- - - - - - - - - - - - - - - - - - - - -
CHO  JOHN  D
488249931  STUDY ABROAD
- - - - - - - - - - - - - - - - - - - - -
GONZALEZ   RAMON
285339934  STUDY ABROAD
- - - - - - - - - - - - - - - - - - - - -
MARKS  DAVID  M
883226077  STUDY ABROAD
```

Database systems also can generate output in the form of labels. At the University of Ithaca, items from the database are printed on mailing labels or on labels for file folders and reports (Figure 6.12).

**Query Processing**   Recall that a *query* (also called an *inquiry*) is a question that guides the retrieval of specific records in a database. In solving problems, it is common to pose *who are* or *how many* queries. In the student club example, for instance, the SAO may ask

Who are the members of the Entrepreneur Club?

How many students expect to graduate this year?

Who are the members of the Entrepreneur Club who expect to graduate this year?

An important part of designing a database application entails establishing the form of the queries. Figure 6.13 shows how a database management system processes the query, "Who are the club members who graduated after 2000?" The fields at the bottom of the screen in Figure 6.13 are the fields that the database will use to retrieve the necessary data. The > symbol in the *year of graduation* field is called a **relational operator**. Relational operators tell the database system to make a comparison to call up the requested data. The most commonly used relational operators are listed in Table 6.2.

**relational operator**

A symbol that tells a database system to make a comparison to call up the requested data.

**FIGURE 6.13**

***Query for Retrieval of Selected Data***

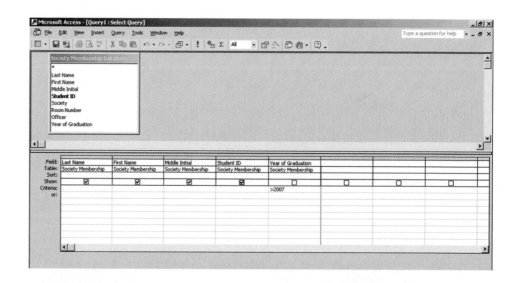

**Table 6.2  Commonly Used Relational Operators**

| RELATIONAL OPERATOR | COMPARISON |
|---|---|
| < | Less than |
| > | Greater than |
| = | Equal to |
| <> OR # | Not equal to |
| <= | Less than or equal to |
| >= | Greater than or equal to |

Of course, you could review each record in the database, one by one. But this would not be an efficient use of your time. Well-designed database systems allow users to search them quickly and accurately. The *Information Technology in Practice* feature, "Parents in a Pinch Make the Right Link," describes how this child-care firm relies on its PC database to match care providers with families seeking help.

## Create the Application

Most microcomputer-based database systems contain a set of commands that can be combined to carry out the desired processing activities. Database applications contain procedures for the following processing actions:

- Add records.
- Delete records.
- Edit records.
- Process queries.
- Prepare reports.
- Make copies of the database (for backup purposes).
- Process information: Carry out calculations.
- Process information: Sort information into a particular sequence.

Figure 6.14 shows the processing menu on the SAO's student club database.

During application creation, the actual programs to perform these database-processing tasks are created. There are two common methods for creating database-processing

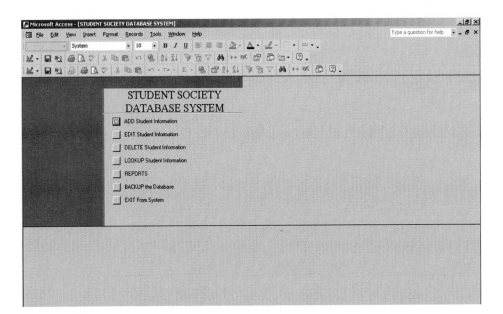

**FIGURE 6.14**

***Database Menu for Selection of Processing Actions***

Using the main menu of the student club database system, the user can add, edit, delete, or retrieve student records; prepare reports; back up the database; or exit from the system.

# INFORMATION TECHNOLOGY IN PRACTICE

## Parents in a Pinch Make the Right Link

Parents in a Pinch Inc., headquartered in Brookline, Massachusetts (a suburb of Boston), specializes in providing child-care services. Since 1984, it has been providing short-term backup child care, regular ongoing in-home child care, group child care for special events, and backup child care as a corporate benefit. The two important resources at the heart of Parents in a Pinch are warm individuals who love and understand children, and the databases that are used to match child-care providers with families who need a babysitter or a nanny.

Each day staff members match dozens of families with care providers. Making the right match means managing a lot of information. Capturing data on job applicants, past and present care providers, and clients is only the beginning. Keeping the data updated is essential so that the records always show assignments as well as personal contact information.

To have access to its services, families must first register by completing an online form at www.parentsinapinch.com. The form captures important family information, including background information on parents and children, as well as details about the days and time when child-care support will be needed. Paper applications can also be completed and submitted. The details enter an applicant PC database.

Information on prospective providers is captured in a separate database. Most individuals interested in providing child care complete an application on a computer in the company's office, though some may fill out a paper application. The information, which describes their background and experience, personal attributes, and availability, is entered into an applicant database. Parents in a Pinch staff then interview the applicant and check references. Individuals must also complete a three-hour orientation that covers agency procedures, professional methods, and practices regarding health and safety for infants and children. Once a prospective provider is approved for employment, the information can be transferred easily into the active-provider database, with no manual data reentry.

Parents in a Pinch staff use the three PC databases—the job applicants database, active-provider database, and the client database—to identify appropriate matches and analyze business needs. The databases also help the company spot trends to which they can respond, such as whether they need to recruit more child-care providers for evening jobs, for a particular night of the week, or for group events.

Each day the staff retrieves data about clients, jobs, and providers to create a match. Parents and providers have an opportunity to speak with one

another before the provider comes to the family's home. When an agreement is made, a query of the database retrieves provider and client names along with the fees and hours per week to which they have agreed. These details are electronically pasted into a contract. There is no need to enter the information manually.

The databases are also integrated with other applications. For instance, data is routinely imported from the databases to a spreadsheet program used to create charts of the company's month-to-month income, volume of business, and number of nanny jobs filled. Details can also be inserted into e-mail messages transmitted to clients or providers, notifying them about special classes periodically offered by Parents in a Pinch.

Though Parents in a Pinch specializes in providing personal child-care services, its database resources make it possible to keep the focus on providing good service without getting bogged down in repetitious data entry or time-consuming searches of records. The capabilities of the software selected for managing the data makes it possible to transfer details between databases, to match information across databases, and to import details from the databases to word processing, spreadsheet, and e-mail programs. By using these capabilities to keep pace with their growing workload, the staff of Parents in a Pinch is not distracted from committing its energy to providing good service.

applications on microcomputers. In **custom programming**, programmers write detailed procedures using the commands and functions built into the database management software. Every step of each application must be specified in detail. In **application generation**, programmers use menus and simple commands to describe the components, or objects, that constitute the application to an *application generator*—a system program that creates the set of detailed commands to perform the procedures as they have been defined.

The trend is toward developing increasingly powerful application generators so that users can concentrate on the problem to be solved rather than on the detailed programming procedures needed to produce the information. The steps taken in designing the Student Association Office database, such as creating the processing menu and input form, resulted in the creation of a set of detailed commands. These commands were not visible because they were developed and managed by the Microsoft Access software.

**custom programming**
In a database system, the writing of detailed procedures using the commands and functions built into the database management software.

**application generation**
In a database system, the use of menus and simple commands to describe the application to a system program that creates the set of detailed commands.

### Test the Application

No application design is complete until it is tested. Testing entails using sample data to verify that the results come out as expected. Almost certainly, testing will reveal mistaken assumptions, incorrect procedures, or errors in completing a particular stage of design and development. Obviously, then, failure to test an application can lead to serious problems.

## A Final Word

The example used in this chapter to illustrate the development of a database system involved a fairly simple database. But whether the application is a student club directory; a business database intended to manage day-to-day contacts with customers and suppliers; or the processing of important transactions; the steps for creating the database are the same. The capabilities of database management systems can make people much more effective—but only if the appropriate steps are followed in creating and using the database.

# CRITICAL CONNECTIONS

## 1 Part II: Contact Manager Helps Farmland Boost Sales

**Farmland** In addition to allowing Farmland's salespeople to share valuable account histories, the contact manager helps them maintain a customer address book, schedule sales calls, create to-do lists, track expenses, and set up a special *tickler* file to remind them of important dates and appointments. The contact manager also lets salespeople create extra displays of demographic information to support their sales presentations. Says the firm's network manager, "Our goal is to turn our salespeople into consultants. If a salesperson can have the account's information, then the salesperson can know the needs of the co-op rather than just selling one product."

When a new edition of the contact manager software was released, with additional tracking and analysis features, Farmland's salespeople capitalized on the new capabilities. Now they can use the built-in scheduling feature to record the time they spend with each customer and to make com-

ments about the sales call. At the end of the week, they send in summary reports to regional managers, who track their performance and then work closely with those salespeople who are not top performers.

### Questions for Discussion

1. How can Farmland's sales staff use the contact manager to meet its needs for up-to-date pricing data?
2. How can the contact manager make Farmland's sales staff more efficient? How can the contact manager make the staff more responsive to the needs of Farmland's customers?

## 2 Part II: Associated Press Relies on Databases for its Information Business

**Associated Press** AP's database system allows for easy distribution of news reports to its 8,500 member newspapers, government and private news agencies, and broadcasters. In addition to capturing stories of breaking news events, AP also uses its database management capabilities to store, process, and distribute vast amounts of raw data. For instance, it uses its Filemaker Pro database system to maintain census data and demographic information, obtained from the Commerce Department, on virtually every town and city in the United States. AP is also creating a database based on the Federal Bureau of Investigation's Uniform Crime Report containing crime statistics for most U.S. towns.

Rapid retrieval and processing of vast amounts of data is essential if the Associated Press is to continue its long history as a supplier of news to the world's news

agencies. Beneath the surface, its database is an essential tool for searching and retrieving the facts that make up each news story.

### Questions for Discussion

1. How does the Associated Press use its database system to effectively manage data?
2. What database management features do you feel are most important to AP in meeting the varying demands of its member firms?
3. What are the challenges of storing and processing large databases at the Associated Press?

## Summary of Learning Objectives

**1 Explain why businesses use databases.**   After people, a business's most important resources are data and information. The reasons people and businesses use databases include storing, retrieving, editing, organizing, and distributing data.

**2 Describe the main components of a database.** The five most common terms used to identify the components of a database are (1) entities, (2) attributes, (3) data items, (4) records, and (5) relations. An *entity* is a person, place, thing, event, or condition about which data and information are collected. Each category of interest in an entity is an *attribute* of that entity. A *data item* is a specific piece of data or information about an entity's attributes that is entered into the database. A *record* is a grouping of data items. A *relation* is the table (consisting of rows and columns) in a database that describes an entity.

**3 List and describe the five objectives of database management systems.**   Database management systems have these five objectives: (1) integrating data-

bases, (2) reducing redundancy, (3) sharing information, (4) maintaining integrity, and (5) enabling database evolution.

**4 Identify when a business should use a spreadsheet and when it should use a database.**   If a business has only a small number of variables to record or needs an application that will examine the numerical relationships between business variables, such as costs and profits, it should use a spreadsheet. If a business has many records structured in a particular way or needs to put security measures in place to protect the data, it should use a database.

**5 Identify the seven-step sequence for developing database applications.**   There are seven steps to developing a database application: (1) study the problem, (2) determine the requirements, (3) design the database, (4) create the database, (5) design the application, (6) create the application, and (7) test the application.

## Key Terms

# Review Questions

1. What is a database?
2. How do relational and flat-file databases differ?
3. Discuss the meaning of the term information repository as it relates to a database.
4. Identify and describe the four reasons people and enterprises use databases.
5. What is a query? What purpose does it serve?
6. Databases consist of entities, data items, records, and relations. Describe the meaning of each and include an example that illustrates each database component.
7. What are the formal terms for fields, records, and databases?
8. Identify and describe the five objectives of database management systems.
9. Why is the ability to integrate databases valuable in problem solving?
10. Why should redundancy in databases be managed? Should redundancy be altogether eliminated from databases?
11. What two components constitute database integrity?
12. In what two ways can databases change?
13. In deciding whether to use a spreadsheet or a database, what three questions should you ask yourself?
14. What seven steps are involved in developing a database application?
15. What three activities take place during database design?
16. List the five elements of a database structure.
17. What six types of data can a database field hold?
18. What is the difference between database creation and data entry?
19. What data or information must a database report contain to be useful?
20. Distinguish between custom programming and application generation.

# Discussion Questions

1. The Smithsonian Institution case study describes the use of a combination of PC databases and enterprise databases by the institute's Office of Imaging, Printing, and Photographic Services (OIPP). The PC database serves both as a front end to the enterprise databases and as an operational database itself. It captures and processes information on digital photographs that is subsequently submitted for inclusion in an enterprise database. In addition, the PC database is used to capture and store order and customer information.

    What are the advantages and disadvantages of using PC databases in the manner employed at OIPP?

2. The chapter feature on Kinion Furniture describes the use of a PC database as a front end to the company's manufacturing system. When customers place orders at the retail showroom, the salesperson enters order details into the PC database and at the same time transmits the details to the company's manufacturing system. Reread the discussion of Kinion Furniture and then:

    a. Identify the entities about which data must be captured for the Kinion Furniture sales process.

    b. What attributes are important for each entity identified and therefore what data items should be included in the database?

    c. On what attributes do you want to index the database for retrieval purposes? Explain the reasoning behind each of your selections.

    d. What data item should be designated as the order database's primary key? Why?

3. When Mary Ann Morley was hired as a human resources assistant at the American Pharmaceutical Association in Washington, D.C., one of her first assignments was to collect the data managers needed to reschedule all salary reviews for January and prorate each employee's new salary. (At the time, salaries were reviewed at 75 different dates throughout the year, based on each employee's starting date.) Morley accomplished the task with a relational database for human resources departments. What data items or fields do you think she included in each row or tuple of her database? Explain your answer.

4. How does Morley's use of the database illustrate the benefits of using a database in business?

5. Levi Strauss & Company maintains a PC-based interactive computer network called OLIVER (Online Interactive Visual Employee Resource) that allows employees to tap into a mainframe database in order to review their total compensation packages. Which function of a database management system do you think would be most important in creating this type of application?

6. OLIVER uses a series of easy-to-use menus to help employees learn about their benefits, including health care, disability, and pension earnings. Why do you think the system's designers chose this access method?

# Group Projects and Applications

## Project 1

Parents in a Pinch, discussed in an *Information Technology in Practice* feature in this chapter, specializes in child-care services. To do so, it depends heavily on database processing.

Reread the Parents in a Pinch feature and then identify *three relational databases* needed to support the company's activities described in the feature.

1. For each database,
   a. Name the database.
   b. Identify the data items needed in the database according to the use described.
   c. Describe the data type (text, numeric, image) and the number of characters (that is, the field width) that should be allowed for each data item.
   d. Indicate whether the field should be used as a key.
   e. Identify the primary key.

| DATA ITEM NAME | KEY FIELD | DATA TYPE | DATA ITEM SIZE |
|---|---|---|---|
|  |  |  |  |
|  |  |  |  |
|  |  |  |  |

Primary key is _____

2. What databases and which data items in each should be used to answer the following queries:
   a. Do we have sufficient care providers to meet child-care needs for Friday and Saturday evenings?
   b. Who are the approved Spanish speaking care providers available for weekday work?

## Project 2

Your marketing company, Market Concepts Unlimited, has just landed a major new account. The Travel Shop is a chain that sells luggage and travel books; it operates in 10 malls and shopping centers. The Travel Shop has embarked on a massive new marketing program and has asked your company to create a database of all of its customers and what they purchase. It plans to do the following:

1. Keep track of all credit-card purchases. Because the Travel Shop uses scanners, it can keep a record of the luggage and travel book titles sold to each credit-card number. From the credit-card company, the Travel Shop can get the following customer information: name, street address, town, state, zip code, sex, age, types of pets, type of computer, yearly annual income, number of children, and ages of children.
2. Determine what types of luggage sell best in individual areas. For cash sales, cashiers will ask customers for their zip code, which they will then enter before each transaction. For credit purchases, the Travel Shop can get the zip code from the credit-card company.
3. Embark on a direct-mail campaign offering volume discounts. People who spend over a certain amount each month will receive a gift certificate equal to 10 percent of their purchases.

Your group is in charge of database design at Market Concepts Unlimited. Brainstorm the possibilities and answer the following questions:

- What types of information/reports should the database be able to generate?
- What entity(ies) will be used in the database?
- Which attributes will be used to describe the entity(ies)? Which of these fields will use characters? Which will be numeric? Which will be logical?
- How might a spreadsheet be integrated with the database package?
- Suppose the Travel Shop wishes to sell more travel books through mail order. Which attribute(s) will it want to extract from the database to create a mailing list?
- Now suppose the Travel Shop is thinking about offering a discount on *carry-on* luggage. In which attribute(s) will the company be most interested?

# Net_Work

## Yellow Page Databases

Yellow pages are specialized databases that seek to bring buyers and sellers of products and services together. Buyers use yellow pages to locate companies quickly, while sellers believe that advertising in these databases can help them reach larger target markets compared to other methods of advertising.

A variety of companies now offer yellow-page services on the Internet. Conduct a search of the Internet and select the three yellow-page services that you feel offer the most useful features to sellers. For each,

a. Describe the features of the service that you feel distinguish each yellow-page site.

b. For each yellow-page service, describe the database structure that you believe underlies the services, that is, list the entities and attributes that are included in the database.

c. What data items are used as search keys in each database?

## Online University/College Library

Visit your university's online library databases (or that of another university library) to determine what resources it makes available to students and faculty. Determine whether the following services are available and what details a user must provide to locate library information via each service:

- **Find articles.** Does the database include full-text articles from general and scholarly journals? If so, approximately how many journals can be accessed online? What information must be provided to locate a *specific article*? To locate articles on a *specific topic*?

- **Find citations.** Can users locate citations to articles in printed journals and other publications found at your library or other libraries with which the university interacts? What information must a user enter to find citations?

- **Find reference information.** Does the library offer access to online encyclopedias, directories, and other reference titles? What details must a user enter to use the reference information if looking for general information on a topic?

- **Find recommended Web sites.** Does the library link users to other Web sites as a means of aiding their search for information? Describe the data a user enters to obtain links to other Web sites having information related to the topic.

What is your overall assessment of the library's methods for locating and retrieving information in its online databases? What are the benefits to students and faculty conducting online searches? What are the limitations of searching databases online?

## Journey into Cybercruiting

In the scramble to snare top-notch talent, a growing number of companies, like individual job seekers, are posting job information databases stored on the Internet. While companies have not dropped the conventional methods of recruitment, many are finding that cybercruiting–posting jobs on World Wide Web sites and in news groups–extends their reach into different geographic areas. It also allows them to make a good deal of information available to a prospective candidate instantly, via online access, which saves them the cost of preparing and distributing printed materials. The drawback is that designing an effective Web page takes time and resources.

The best way to assess the benefits and drawbacks of cybercruiting is to visit Web sites designed for this purpose. Among the most active and best-known sites are

- **Careerbuilder.com** (www.careerbuilder.com) Provides the ability to search for candidates by their area of specialty and location. Job seekers can post resumes and search the employer database for job openings of interest.

- **Monster** (www.monster.com) Provides job listings, a résumé database, and career counseling. The Monster Global Network reaches into many other countries to aide in matching individuals and companies with interests outside of Monster's U.S. base.

- **Hotjobs, a service of Yahoo!** (www.hotjobs.com) Seeks to match both companies and individuals nationally and internationally. Includes a feature, MyHotjobs! that enables individuals to obtain customized information focused on their specific interests.

- **Medzilla.com** (www.medzilla.com) Specializes in jobs in health care and the sciences, including biotechnology.

1. What information is typically found on an organization's recruiting home page?
2. What assistance is offered to candidates regarding their résumés?
3. What assistance do these Web sites provide for companies seeking to recruit candidates?
4. Based on your review of these Web sites, would you say cybercruiting tends to attract a certain type of job candidate, or do you think it is an effective means to reach all types of candidates? Explain the reasons for your answer.

## Cool Mobility

### On Assignment

While talking to *Cool Mobility's* CIO James Marsalis, you mention your coursework in database design and processing. You also indicate your belief that good database design is essential to creating effective IT applications.

### In Consultation

At the conclusion of your discussion, Marsalis asks you to examine the databases that hold customer and order data.

a. Orders are created only when placed by a customer. That is, there are no orders that do not have customers.

Also, a customer may place an order for one or more mobile phones. Each phone order includes details of the model, ring tone, logo or image, and service plan. Prepare an entity relationship diagram describing customers and orders.

b. Currently each order contains all customer data, such as name, address, and payment details. Marsalis asks you if it would be better to maintain separate databases for customers and orders. What is your answer and what are the underlying reasons?

c. If you were to undertake a design of CoolMobility.biz's databases, without knowing details of the current design, where would you store and maintain details about each model mobile phone, calling plan, ring tone, and logo? Keep in mind that these product and service options change, as current choices are replaced by new products, services, and features.

## Case Study

## Johnson Controls Captures Database Information with PDAs

**Johnson Controls**

Behind the scenes of every large office building and enterprise campus is an often invisible, but highly important facility-management process. Facility management is the practice of coordinating the physical workplace with the people and work of the organization. Businesses and institutions have come to realize that maintaining a well-managed and highly efficient building improves employee welfare as well as the effectiveness of the enterprise. As a result, facility managers have witnessed an increase in their responsibility to provide an attractive workplace for employees.

Johnson Controls is a $20 billion manufacturing and service company headquartered in Milwaukee, Wisconsin. Its controls group is focused on providing customers with a quality building environment. The group designs, manufactures, installs, services, operates, and maintains mechanical and electrical systems that control energy use, heating, ventilating, air conditioning, lighting, security, and fire management for nonresidential buildings.

Johnson Controls has facility-management responsibilities for the entire campus of Hewlett-Packard in Palo Alto, California. The HP campus provides workspace for thousands of managers and staff members.

Routine inspections are a regular part of facility management at the HP campus. Inspections are conducted by walkthroughs during which a building or facility manager carefully examines the rooms, corridors, and external areas of a building. For a long time, detailed paper checklists guided inspectors in their scrutiny of the structure and condition of a facility. The sheets signaled them to examine a wide range of factors, including state of repair, ease of access for handicapped and non-handicapped individuals, air quality, temperature, protection against intrusion, access to emergency exits, and many more. A careful walkthrough can easily result in the collection of as many as 1,000 points of information for each building.

Capturing the necessary inspection data at the HP campus was a time-consuming process for Johnson Controls. The post-inspection process was also a concern, as the details had to be transcribed from paper inspection forms to a spreadsheet—an error-prone process—where they could be analyzed. Then building deficiencies were assigned to staff members for correction and monitored for completion. Entries in the spreadsheet enabled managers to track the completion of assigned activities.

The traditional walkthrough and post-inspection process followed by Johnson Controls (and the industry as a whole) was time-consuming and inefficient. Its managers thought there had to be a better way. Being in the midst of one of the world's high-tech leaders, its managers witnessed all sorts of interesting things happening with information technology.

Perhaps some of the *high-tech thinking* rubbed off on the Johnson Controls facility experts, for they devised an innovative solution involving PC databases to streamline the inspection and maintenance process. Today the company's facility management staff inspects the buildings in the HP campus equipped with personal digital assistants (PDAs). When the company's inspectors go to a particular building, they open an easily navigated form on the PDA display. The on-screen form guides them during the walkthrough, enabling them to enter a rating score for each building component. Navigation between the screens of the PDA is simple and intuitive, making the entire process much easier than it was with page after page of paper forms.

Once an inspector has completed the walkthrough, the information on the handheld computer can be transferred directly into a PC database for processing and analysis. The inspector needs only to place the PDA in a cradle and press the synchronization button. Data in the PDA is transferred over the connecting cable to a PC where it is stored in a PC database. The old error-prone manual data-entry steps are eliminated; the process occurs in a matter of seconds.

Since the data is digital and in a database, building information can be reorganized in different ways, making it easy to compare information. For instance, all of the air-quality ratings or temperature levels for the buildings can be reviewed together. Then the data can be resorted to identify recurring situations common across several buildings in the campus. Worker names can be entered to reflect assign-

ments for each maintenance condition, with expected completion dates.

Having the information in the database makes it possible for Johnson Controls to also process the information into reports that are suitable for display on the HP intranet. The Web-based displays enable HP staff members to easily view conditions and required maintenance on the buildings.

By applying these information technology resources to its facility management process, Johnson Controls can fulfill its responsibilities with improvements in speed and accuracy while reducing operating costs. In the end, its use of IT has resulted in improved working conditions for Hewlett-Packard employees who are hard at work on the next generation of information technology.

## Questions for Discussion

1. If you were a facility inspector for Johnson Controls, what would be your assessment of using the PDA in place of paper inspection sheets? Would you find it desirable or undesirable? Why?
2. What productivity benefits does the combination of a PC database and the personal digital assistant (PDA) offer for the Johnson Controls facility management process? Does use of the database system result in any loss of flexibility?
3. What benefits does storing inspection data in a PC database have compared to its capture on paper inspection forms? Are there any disadvantages to using a PDA and a PC database to manage the HP campus facilities?

# Enterprise Databases and Data Warehouses

## CHAPTER OUTLINE

## LEARNING OBJECTIVES

When you have completed this chapter, you should be able to

1 Identify the reasons organizations choose to share databases and the functions of a database management system.

2 Explain the difference between relational and object-oriented databases and their uses in business.

3 Describe the differences between schemas, views, and indexes.

4 Discuss the benefits of client/server computing.

5 Differentiate between shared and distributed databases.

6 Explain why enterprises establish data warehouses and how they differ from data marts and enterprise databases.

7 Distinguish between a database administrator and a systems programmer.

8 Discuss database administration procedures and concurrency procedures and explain why these are an essential part of a shared database system.

# Ritz-Carlton Luxury Begins with Customer Customization

People like to hear their name, and guests at any of the luxurious Ritz-Carlton hotels hear their name often. At the door, bellhops greet arriving guests by name, even though they may never have seen them before. The attendant in the reception area also uses guests' names when speaking to them.

Guests who have stayed at a Ritz-Carlton in the past will find that many of their preferences are seen to—even before they arrive. When a repeat guest gets to her room, for example, she may find that it is set up with the feather pillows she enjoys and two complimentary bottles of her favorite chilled mineral water. When she arrives in the hotel's restaurant for dinner, she will find that it has stocked the special variety of wine she favors. Now *this* is service—the kind of service that makes you want to stay at a Ritz-Carlton hotel *every* time you travel.

Your repeat business is just what Ritz-Carlton management and staff are working hard to earn. Through its personalized attention to detail, Ritz-Carlton seeks to be the premium worldwide provider of luxury travel and hospitality services. Information technology plays a central role in the hotel's delivery of its superior service.

The Ritz-Carlton Hotel Company manages more than 30 luxury hotels in North America, Europe, Asia-Pacific Rim, the Caribbean, Africa, and the Middle-East. Its hotels are repeatedly awarded the prestigious four and five-star designations from the Mobil Travel Guide and other ratings groups, a distinct measure of its top performance and high level of customer service.

The Atlanta-based luxury hotel chain is the only hotel to ever win the coveted Malcolm Baldrige National Quality Award. In fact, the Ritz-Carlton, the only service company to win the award twice, is recognized for its exceptional achievement in the practice of total quality management principles.

To cultivate customer loyalty, the Ritz-Carlton focuses on *customer customization*—its way of arranging the individuality of the guest experience in the midst of serving large numbers of people. It does this by *tracking* guest preferences rather than *reacting* to them.

The Customer Loyalty Anticipation System (CLAS) database is at the heart of this experience. Created by a cross-functional corporate and hotel team, this guest recognition database is the company-wide tool used to meet and anticipate repeat customers' preferences and requirements. The database is structured so that guest information can be retrieved in many ways besides the usual guest name and reservation confirmation number.

The system consists of a Windows-based application running Informix database management software. Hundreds of thousands of customer files are maintained in the enterprise database, each accessible through a communication network linking all of its properties. Hence, the information captured at one Ritz-Carlton property is available to staff at all other hotels, an essential feature since customer customization relies on the gathering and sharing of extensive data.

So how does the staff at Ritz-Carlton make such a good impression the moment a guest arrives? The bellhop relies on a daily printout of expected guests and their distinguishing characteristics to greet returning guests by name. At the reception desk, the attendant asks a few casual questions to make the guest comfortable: "Where did you come in from? How long will you be staying with us?" Using the CLAS database while the guest is responding, she quickly determines who the guest is, verifying this with "You're Ms. Harris, correct?"

Ms. Harris's room is equipped to suit her personal preferences because on the last visit her request for feather pillows was noted in her CLAS guest profile. The chambermaid noticed two empty mineral water bottles each morning while cleaning the room. She noted that on a *Guest Preference Card.* These details were entered into the CLAS database.

This scenario is repeated many times each day. Accessible to all Ritz-Carlton hotels worldwide, the enterprise database enables hotel staff to anticipate the needs of returning guests and take actions to deliver the premier service they have come to expect.

E nterprise databases are designed to be shared by many users throughout an organization in much the same way as people in the same building can share computers, printers, and communications networks. Whether across the hall or in different cities, states, and countries, people can share enterprise data to make effective use of available resources and to become more productive. If, for example, a group of related businesses shares a set of data, each business will have the same view of a customer, supplier, resource level, or business transaction.

This chapter will examine the sharing and distributing of data among multiple persons. The chapter begins with a discussion of the principles of data sharing and distribution. Then it examines the structure of relational and object-oriented databases. Throughout the chapter, you will see how data can be organized and stored to meet the needs of database users. You also will see the opportunities that client/server computing and Web databases offer and the importance of good procedures. Finally, you will see that the sustained usefulness of shared databases is dependent on the people who manage them.

## The Principles of Data Sharing

**database**
A collection of data and information describing items of interest to an organization.

**entity**
A person, place, thing, event, or condition about which data and information are collected.

**enterprise database**
A collection of data designed to be shared by many users within an organization.

As discussed in Chapter 6, a **database** is a collection of data and information describing items of interest (sometimes called **entities**) to an organization. Data are collected on such entities as people, places, things, events, and conditions (Figure 7.1). Each *data item* in the database—whether numeric, text, image, graphic, or sound—describes an *attribute* of the entity. In contrast to a personal database, created for an individual's use, an **enterprise database** is a collection of data designed to be shared by many users within an organization.[1]

[1] The organization may be a work group, department, business unit, or an entire firm.

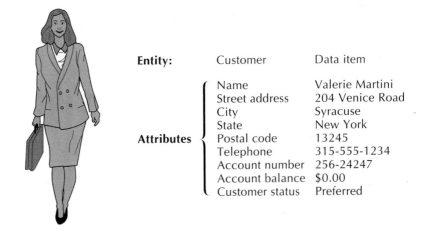

| Entity: | Customer | Data item |
|---|---|---|
| | Name | Valerie Martini |
| | Street address | 204 Venice Road |
| | City | Syracuse |
| | State | New York |
| **Attributes** | Postal code | 13245 |
| | Telephone | 315-555-1234 |
| | Account number | 256-24247 |
| | Account balance | $0.00 |
| | Customer status | Preferred |

**Instance of entity as database record**

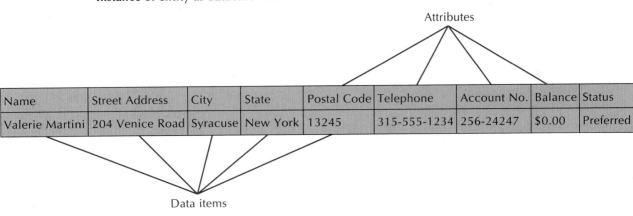

| Name | Street Address | City | State | Postal Code | Telephone | Account No. | Balance | Status |
|---|---|---|---|---|---|---|---|---|
| Valerie Martini | 204 Venice Road | Syracuse | New York | 13245 | 315-555-1234 | 256-24247 | $0.00 | Preferred |

Attributes

Data items

**FIGURE 7.1**

**Entity Description in a Database**

The "customer" entity includes nine attributes and a data item for each attribute.

## Why Share Data?

Capturing, storing, and maintaining data in a database is an expensive process. In fact, managers who examine the human, physical, and financial resources they have invested in compiling their organization's data find that data collection and maintenance are very costly indeed. Thus, it makes sense to use this important resource as often as possible and to manage it as effectively as possible. To do so entails making sure that all members of the organization who need the data will have access to them.

Sharing data means that all persons in the enterprise will work from the same set of data items for an entity. This consistency is important to the organization's short-term and long-term success. Imagine the problem on a university campus if the campus book-store used an enrollment figure from the registration database to order books for a course while the course instructor knew that many more students had been allowed to add the course to their semester's studies.

When databases are shared, two facts quickly become evident: (1) people need differ-ent data from the database; and (2) people often need the same data, but organized in different ways. You will see later in this chapter how these needs can be met, even if users and databases are at different locations.

## Database Management Systems

**database management
system (DBMS)**
A program that makes it possible
for users to manage the data in a
database in order to increase
accessibility and productivity.

Databases are used by different applications and for multiple purposes. **Database management systems (DBMS)** are programs that make it possible for users to manage the data and to increase productivity. Through the DBMS, the data are accessed, maintained, and processed.

The database management system program operates in conjunction with the other programs running in a computer system, including the application program, operating system, and network operating system (Figure 7.2). It maintains the structure of the data and interacts with the other programs to locate and retrieve the data needed for processing. It also accepts data from the application program and writes it into the appropriate storage location.

**The Functions of Database Management**   As discussed in Chapter 6, database management is meant to accomplish five objectives. A brief review will be useful here.

1. **Integrating Databases**   Through database management, individual databases created at various times or by different people, can be joined, partly or entirely, to provide the information required to solve a problem or deal with a business issue.
2. **Reducing Redundancy**   Unnecessary or undesirable duplication of data across databases can be eliminated through database management. Some redundancy, however, is desirable if it assists the people using the databases.
3. **Sharing Information**   People at remote locations can share stored data that are made accessible to them.
4. **Maintaining Integrity**   Good database management ensures the integrity of the database by allowing controlled access to information, providing security measures, and ensuring that data are available when needed.
5. **Enabling Database Evolution**   A database management system helps to ensure that the database will be able to evolve to meet the changing requirements of its users.

The database management system achieves these objectives through database creation, database inquiry, database updating, and database administration (see Chapter 6 if you need to review these terms).

# Enterprise Database Structures

All databases, whether shared or not, must be defined. Definition starts with creation of a graphical enterprise data model which in turn serves as a foundation for describing the schema, the formal definition of a database's structure.

**FIGURE 7.2**

***Relationship of DBMS to Other Programs in Computer Memory***
A DBMS works in conjunction with the other programs running in a computer system.

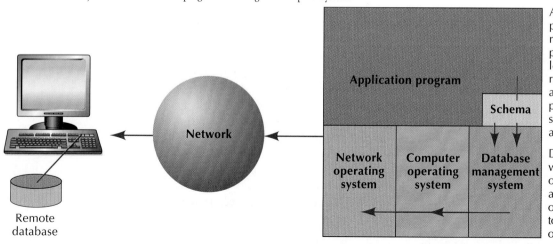

# CRITICAL CONNECTIONS 1

## Bridgestone/Firestone's Unified Database

**Firestone**

Bridgestone and Firestone, two well-known brands of automobile tires, are manufactured by Firestone Tire and Rubber Company of Akron, Ohio. The company also operates a network of more than 2,000 tire and service centers across the United States.

For years, the service center managers had followed the practice of entering the name and address of those customers *who paid for service by credit card* into a database. Later these customers were sent a promotional mailing that encouraged them to visit the store for other vehicle services. The practice proved so successful that Firestone decided to create a unified database capturing information on *all* of its customers.

Today, all Firestone stores use the same point of sale (POS) system. Whenever any customer purchases tires or service, the store manager enters customer information (name, address, telephone number, vehicle information, method of payment, and service transaction details) into the POS terminal. The details are electronically transmitted to company headquarters where they enter its enterprise database. The database is processed to send reminders to customers about rotation or replacement of tires, or other periodic services that should be performed on their vehicle.

## Enterprise Data Model

An **enterprise data model** is a graphical representation of the items (the entities) of interest about which data is captured and stored in the database. Enterprise databases typically store data about multiple entities, so the data model also shows the relation between the entities. For this reason, the data model is sometimes termed an **entity relationship** data model.

Large databases may store data about a large number of entities. However, the principle of data modeling is the same regardless of the number of entities and whether the database contains scientific, medical, engineering, financial, or business data.

Among the most common activities of business is the acceptance and processing of orders submitted by customers. Each order specifies one or more items the customer seeks to purchase. At any point in time, a customer may have several active orders at a company.

The entities in this database are *customers, orders,* and *items* (goods or products) ordered. In a graphical model (Figure 7.3), the entities are shown along with the *association* or *relationships* between them:

1. Each *customer* places one or more uniquely identified *orders*. Similarly, each *order* is associated with one specific *customer* (that is, two different customers cannot submit the uniquely identified order).

2. Each *order* contains one or more *items*.

**enterprise data model/entity relationship**

A graphical representation of the items (the entities) of interest about which data is captured and stored in the database.

**FIGURE 7.3**

*Entity Relationship Model Shows Relations Between Customers and Orders*

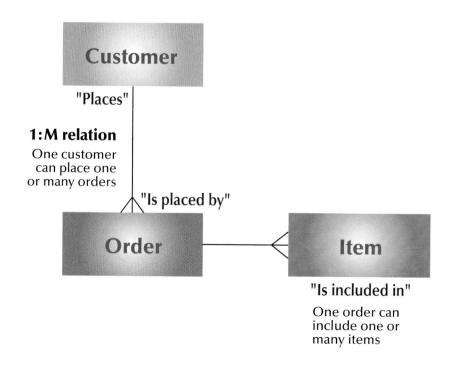

The entity-relationship model shows three entities and two associations between them. The lines between entities indicate there is an association. Database designers by convention use the crowfoot ( ⅄ ) at end of the line to indicate that the entity may have one or more occurrences of the entity. Hence, the crowfoot above the order entity in Figure 7.3 shows that a customer may have one, two, or many orders in process at a time with an enterprise. Similarly, any order may be for one or many unique items. The relationship is termed a *one-to-many relationship*. In contrast, a uniquely identified order can only be associated with one customer, which is a *one-to-one relationship*.

Since a complex database may include data on many different entities, with many associations between them, the graphical representation of the enterprise data model can itself become quite complex. Database designers may spend hours developing the right data model before they begin actually creating the database.

Keep in mind that the enterprise data model is only a graphical representation, and it is used as an aid to understanding the associations that the database must support.

Since relational databases are the most widespread type of database in use, the enterprise data model is usually a guide to understanding what relations must be created. The schema describes the resulting structure.

## Schema

**schema**
The structure of a database.

The formal name for the definition of a database structure is its schema. The **schema** describes the names and attributes of each entity about which data are collected and stored. It provides a structure only; it does not include data items (the customer's name or address, for example). You might think of the schema as the framework that outlines the structure of the database, with the database's entities and the relations between them fitting within that framework. Figure 7.2 shows the schema's relationship to other items in computer memory.

Each database has only one schema. Different databases use different schemas.

**relational database**
A database in which the data are structured in a table format consisting of rows and columns.

**Schema for Relational Databases**  Recall from Chapter 6 that **relational databases** are made up of data structured in a table format (a *relation*) consisting of rows and columns. The horizontal rows of the relation are called *records* or *tuples*. The vertical columns are the *attributes*, or *fields*, and contain *data items* of a record. The term *record* can also refer to a grouping of data items that describes one specific *occurrence* of an entity. For example, a customer database includes records of all relevant data for each customer. Throughout this chapter, we will use this second definition of record.

The schema for a relational database identifies the database by a unique name and describes the relations contained within the database. A relation, in turn, is defined by its data items, each of which is identified by a name, type (such as numeric or text), and length specification. In this manner, the schema gives a distinct structure to the relational database. The schema in Figure 7.4 shows customers, orders, and item relations.

**Schema for Object-Oriented Databases**   A newer type of database that is emerging alongside relational databases is the **object-oriented database**. An object is a focal point about which data and information are collected. Hence, the customers and orders in a data model—items we called *entities* when discussing relational databases—are treated as object classes in an object-oriented database (Figure 7.5). Object-oriented database systems store descriptive data and information about each object in an object class. (**Object** refers to an individual instance in a **class**.)

Data and information can be stored about both entities and objects. However, unlike relational databases, object-oriented databases also store **actions** (also called **methods**), instructions, or short programs telling the database how to process the object to produce specific information. For instance, a customer object could store the method for determining a customer's credit-worthiness. In a student database, the student object might include the method for determining the student's grade point average.

The U.S. brokerage and investment firm Shearson Lehman Brothers has created an object-oriented database as the basis for many of its business activities. In this database are account objects (customers), contract objects (management agreements between Shearson Lehman and firms that have signed investment contracts), and security objects (the descriptive details of stocks, bonds, and stock options). Each object contains the descriptive data you would expect (names, addresses, prices, etc.). Each also contains information describing when and how to purchase an investment instrument. Thus, an individual account (the object) can buy a security, just as if a broker were initiating the action, but without human intervention.

Object-oriented databases offer the capability to store more sophisticated types of data and information than relational databases do. For example, such complex information as three-dimensional diagrams, animated video clips, and photographs do not fit easily within the row-and-column structure of relational databases. However, because both data and processing instructions are part of object descriptions, such information can be handled in an object-oriented database.

Both U.S.-based Boeing Aircraft Company and England's British Aerospace Ltd. use object-oriented databases to maintain data about the design, components, and maintenance of their multimillion-dollar aircraft. These object databases store detailed schematic drawings of the planes' interiors, exteriors, and electronic components, including their extensive cable and wiring systems. Manufacturing and cost information is also included in the databases.

Before moving to object-oriented databases, both companies maintained their data on groups of separate databases. This system was costly and inefficient because it made it difficult for designers and engineers to get a complete picture of the repercussions of a particular action. For example, if the cost of a component changed, a project engineer would first have to search the component database to see where and in what quantity

**object-oriented database**
A database that stores data and information about objects.

**object**
A component that contains data about itself and how it is to be processed.

**class**
A set of objects that share a common structure and a common behavior.

**action/method**
An instruction that tells a database how to process an object to produce specific information.

**Customer relation**

| Account No | Name | Address | City | State | Postal Code | Telephone | Balance | Status |
|---|---|---|---|---|---|---|---|---|
| | | | | | | | | |

**Order relation**

| Order No | Account No | Item No | Quantity | Price |
|---|---|---|---|---|
| | | | | |

**Item relation**

| Item No | Item Description | Price | Quantity on Hand |
|---|---|---|---|
| | | | |

DATABASE SCHEMA

**FIGURE 7.4**

*Schema for Customer-Order Relationship*

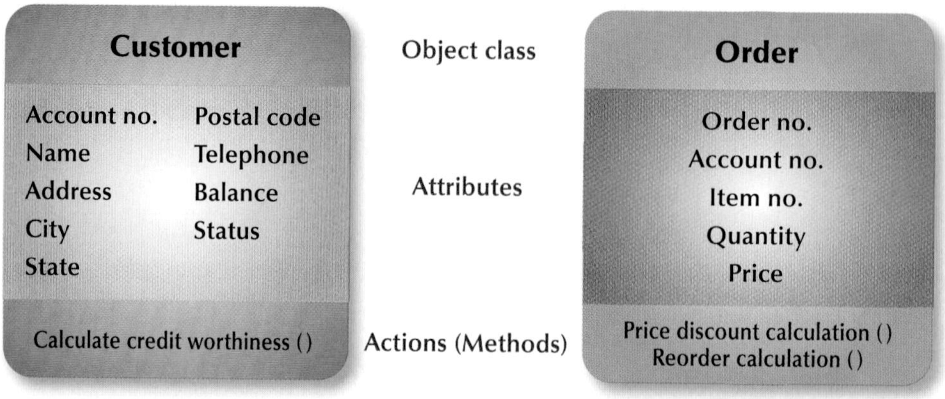

**FIGURE 7.5**

*Classes in an Object-Oriented Database Featuring Customer and Order Objects*

that component was being used. Then the engineer would have to search the order database to see if the component was being used in a specific aircraft configuration. Finally, the engineer would have to go to the manufacturing database to retrieve construction and assembly details related to the component. The process was both time-consuming and error-prone. Today, drawings, cost, manufacturing, and assembly details regarding a component are all combined in the object database. Data and information are available much more quickly, and the cost of managing data and information is lower.

The *Information Technology in Practice* feature, "Chubb Insurance Objects Streamline Preparation of Cross-Border Quotes," describes how this leading insurance underwriter relies on an object-oriented database to prepare quotations for complex insurance policies for everything from precious jewelry and art to international cargo shipments.

**Other Database Schemas**    Two other types of database schemas are worthy of mention here. *Hierarchical databases* store data in the form of a tree, where the relationship among data items is one-to-many (that is, one data item is linked to several other data items). In *network databases,* the relationship among the data items can be either one-to-many or many-to-many (that is, several data items are linked to several other data items). Detailed explanations of these types of databases are beyond the scope of this discussion. It is enough to say here that hierarchical and network databases store data in a way that makes access to them faster for certain types of queries and slower for others.

## Views

When a database is created, it is designed and stored according to a designer-determined structure of relations. As noted earlier in this chapter, however, users of shared databases often want to organize the data differently from the way in which they are stored. Database management systems address this need.

**view**

A subset of one or more databases, created either by extracting copies of records from a database or by merging copies of records from multiple databases.

Users who want to organize data and information differently from the way in which they are stored in the database can use views to do so. A **view** is a subset of one or more databases, created either by extracting copies of records from a database or by merging copies of records from multiple databases.[2] Like databases themselves, views have names and records composed of data items. As Figure 7.6 shows, multiple views of data can be extracted from the database and used in any application, including calculation, sorting, and generation of reports and other output.

In one sense, a view is simply a logical grouping of data. It gives the appearance that data have been moved or combined to meet processing requirements, although the database's physical structure (schema) has not been altered. Savvy marketers purchase large databases and create views to help them target advertising campaigns, as the *Information Technology in Practice* feature, "Database Marketing: The Personal Art of Persuasion," explores in detail.

[2]In some organizations, views are called *subschemas*—or sets of the scheme. In effect, subschemas (views) partition the database among applications.

# INFORMATION TECHNOLOGY IN PRACTICE
## Chubb Insurance Objects Streamline Preparation of Cross-Border Quotes

Chubb Corp., headquartered in Warren, New Jersey, traces its roots back to the spring of 1882, when Thomas Caldecot Chubb and son Percy opened their marine underwriting business in the seaport district of New York City. Having collected $1,000 from each of 100 prominent merchants to start their venture, they focused on insuring ships and cargoes. The Chubbs were adept at turning risk into success, often by helping their policyholders prevent disasters in the first place. By the turn of the century, Chubb had established strong relationships with the insurance agents and brokers who placed their clients with Chubb underwriters, and the original subscribers enjoyed a substantial return on their investment in the young company. Today, Chubb's revenues rank it among the top 10 publicly traded insurance organizations in the United States.

With more than 13,000 employees throughout North America, Europe, South America, and the Pacific Rim, Chubb serves property and casualty customers from more than 130 offices in >30 countries. The company works closely with 8,000 independent agents and brokers worldwide.

Like any insurance company, its success depends on its ability to drive down expenses and at the same time grow in its areas of expertise and interest. Among Chubb's distinctions in the highly competitive insurance industry is its longstanding ability to create custom insurance products for its personal and business customers. The company also creates specialty programs for affinity groups, such as broadcasters and law firms, and cargo shippers. Chubb's ability to create unique products for customers quickly, while keeping costs low, distinguishes it from many of its competitors and is a fundamental reason underlying its continued growth.

A characteristic of the industry is the tremendous diversity in the laws for insurance coverage. They differ from state to state and between countries, meaning that a policy written for coverage in, say, New York, may not be sold in California.

To manage the complex task of creating personal lines of insurance for consumers, Chubb created a system known as *Masterpiece®*. At the heart of the system is an object-oriented database that serves as a central resource for packaging homeowner, vehicle, excess liability, and valuable article (jewelry and art, for example) coverage together into a single custom policy. Rather than storing product rules for each state—a common conventional database design practice—Chubb's system encapsulates the rate and rule information for each state into *rate and rule book* business objects (like blueprints in an office designer's handbook).

Masterpiece consists of more than 1,000 classes and approximately 18 methods per class. Each method is comprised of some 10 lines of computer program code.

For instance, when insuring jewelry, the insurance object classes Masterpiece will include classes such as precious stones, gold jewelry, and silver jewelry. Methods associated with the class precious stones include valuation of diamonds, assessing the risk of loss, determining allowable coverage, and calculating the premium. For instance, the method for valuing a diamond takes into account the size, clarity, and cut of the diamond.

When it is necessary for Chubb's agents to create a new policy, they enter information about the customer's needs (for example, the type of insurance and amount of coverage desired) into the Masterpiece system. Masterpiece retrieves the relevant insurance objects and uses the stored methods describing state regulatory constraints to process the application, preparing a premium quote for the customer.

Business objects offer the benefit of reusability. For instance, if several states have the same laws for treatment of, say, homeowners insurance, the relevant object can be used to prepare policies in each state. Without this, separate business rules would have to be individually crafted for the states.

The object-oriented technologies that reside behind the scene of this busy insurance company, go unseen by executives, agents and policy holders. Yet each benefits from Chubb's innovative use of business objects and their incorporation into object-oriented databases, for they provide a foundation from which solid business benefits can be delivered. The results are measurable improvements in customer service, less elapsed time in preparing policy quotations, reduction in back office expense, and impressive revenue growth. At Chubb, when the *objective* is creation of business benefits, the means to their achievement is often *business objects*.

At one time, object-oriented databases were evolving as a distinct type of database. Today, object features are being built into relational database management systems. It is likely this trend will continue, with the predominant database management system becoming an *object-oriented-relational database management system*.

**FIGURE 7.6**

### *Views Extracted from Relational Database*

Data from a relation can be extracted and used in many applications.

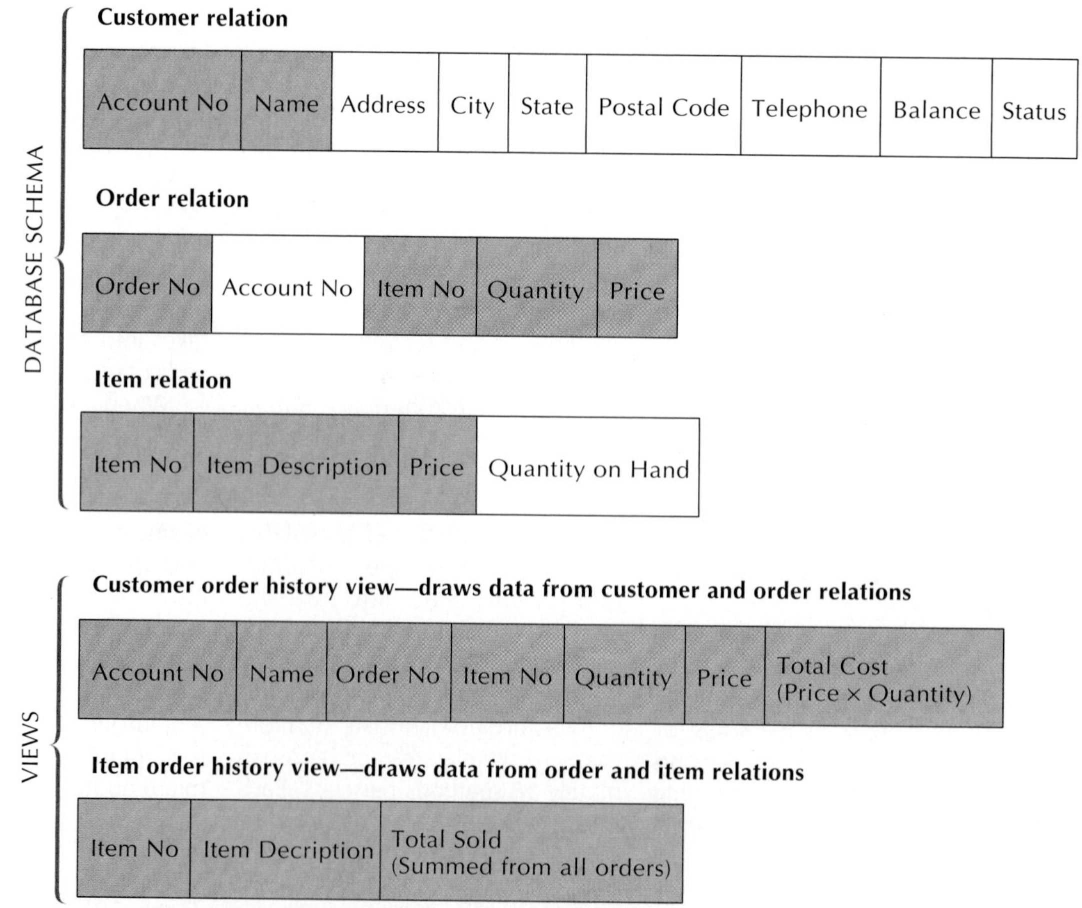

DATABASE SCHEMA

**Customer relation**

| Account No | Name | Address | City | State | Postal Code | Telephone | Balance | Status |
|---|---|---|---|---|---|---|---|---|

**Order relation**

| Order No | Account No | Item No | Quantity | Price |
|---|---|---|---|---|

**Item relation**

| Item No | Item Description | Price | Quantity on Hand |
|---|---|---|---|

VIEWS

**Customer order history view—draws data from customer and order relations**

| Account No | Name | Order No | Item No | Quantity | Price | Total Cost (Price × Quantity) |
|---|---|---|---|---|---|---|

**Item order history view—draws data from order and item relations**

| Item No | Item Decription | Total Sold (Summed from all orders) |
|---|---|---|

 **REALITY CHECK**  Object-oriented technology promises to be the basis for many types of applications in the future. The object-oriented concept of combining data and processing instructions is now being embedded in programs (object-oriented programs) and application development procedures (object-oriented design), as well as in databases.

We can draw an analogy between objects and Lego blocks, the plastic building blocks that snap together. Each Lego can be attached to any other Lego to build any type of structure—a house, a barn, a skyscraper, a car, or a medieval castle. Should the builder decide partway through the process to change the structure's design, she can either add more Lego blocks to the current design or reassemble the blocks in a different way. Objects can be used in a similar way. Although they are different on the inside, they are like Legos on the outside—they are an assortment of objects that can be assembled in many different ways. Therefore, applications can be created quickly and efficiently by connecting individual objects to create a desired result. ▪

---

Viewing capabilities provide many benefits to business users.

- Views allow users to examine data in different ways without changing the physical structure of the database.
- Users can make changes in the data in a view while leaving the data in the database in its original form.
- Database security is maintained because individuals and applications can be kept away from sensitive data since they will process from the views rather than from the database itself. Sensitive or protected data are not included in a view.
- Views shield users from changes in the physical database (for example, the restructuring of records so that they reside in a different location or a different sequence).

Views from multiple databases can be combined to meet business requirements. The State of Georgia Department of Revenue, for example, has linked several different databases in an effort to collect the state sales and withholding taxes owed by businesses. During the processing of income tax refund checks, department staff members use personal and business ID numbers to link records showing an individual's business income tax, the sales tax the state received from the business, and the withholding tax it received from the company's employees, even though each database is maintained by a separate system and a different agency (Figure 7.7). When the Department of Revenue's computer determines that a refund is due to an individual, it checks with the other databases before cutting the check. If it finds a match with a record describing sales tax owed by the same person through his or her business, it automatically applies the refund to the sales tax debt. At the same time, it sends the individual a message saying, "We have determined that you still owe sales tax and have applied your income tax refund against that obligation." Before the state acquired this ability to interrelate databases, a large amount of sales taxes went uncollected.

## Indexes

An important advantage offered by databases and a DBMS is flexibility of retrieval. Views provide users with a way to assemble data from different databases. Indexes make it possible to retrieve data in different sequences and on the basis of different data items.

An **index** is a data file that contains identifying information about each record (the record key) and its location in storage. The **record key** is a designated field used to distinguish one record from another. For example, the record key by which university students are typically identified is a unique student ID number. Each number is unique in that it is assigned to only one student.

A DBMS is able to automatically build and use indexes according to specifications prepared by the database administrator, whose role is discussed later in this chapter. When

**index**
A data file that contains identifying information about each record and its location in storage.

**record key**
In a database, a designated field used to distinguish one record from another.

# INFORMATION TECHNOLOGY IN PRACTICE

## Database Marketing: The Personal Art of Persuasion

Mass markets, mass merchandising, mass media. To many people, these phrases define marketing. They think of big companies seeking to appeal to massive groups of people through print or broadcast messages. For some companies, that image of marketing is true. But for a sizable number of others, it is inaccurate, and has been so for some time.

Many of the world's leading companies view their customers, current or potential, not as a large, anonymous group with uniform taste, but rather as individuals with unique needs and desires. For these companies, database marketing is a means for serving people even as the firms benefit.

Database marketing combines the availability of databases of customer and consumer information with sophisticated new software capable of extracting valuable marketing information. Do not confuse database marketing with direct-mail marketing, in which large name and address lists are used to mail catalogs, brochures, applications, and announcements by the thousands (even millions). Database marketing focuses on the individual, not the addressee.

Sophisticated companies try continually to capitalize on their strengths in order to close the gap

between themselves and their customers, to provide more tailored services, and to fill a niche where needs are not being met. Of course, they want to keep their existing customers—and perhaps woo more business from them—even as they win over new customers. But to do that, they must know the wants and needs, as well as the likes and dislikes, of individual buyers. They must personalize the art of persuasion. And that is where database marketing comes in.

A restaurant's software, for example, might extract from its cus-

tomer database the information that your birthday is approaching. It automatically addresses and mails a birthday card to you with the gift of a complimentary birthday dinner. Of course, the restaurant expects

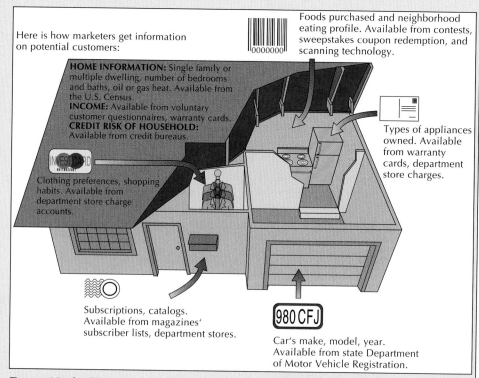

Here is how marketers get information on potential customers:

**HOME INFORMATION:** Single family or multiple dwelling, number of bedrooms and baths, oil or gas heat. Available from the U.S. Census.

**INCOME:** Available from voluntary customer questionnaires, warranty cards.

**CREDIT RISK OF HOUSEHOLD:** Available from credit bureaus.

Clothing preferences, shopping habits. Available from department store charge accounts.

Subscriptions, catalogs. Available from magazines' subscriber lists, department stores.

Foods purchased and neighborhood eating profile. Available from contests, sweepstakes coupon redemption, and scanning technology.

Types of appliances owned. Available from warranty cards, department store charges.

Car's make, model, year. Available from state Department of Motor Vehicle Registration.

### Target Marketing

Modern technology is transforming mass marketing into target marketing. By utilizing information from a variety of sources, companies can focus their sales efforts on specific consumer groups.

*Source:* Tribune Media Services

you to bring along some friends to help you celebrate your birthday—so it will have the chance to attract new customers even as it pleases an old one with a free meal.

Other examples abound. Take Goodyear Tire Company, which sends you a message offering free rotation of the tires you purchased from it several months back. Interestingly, the card arrives just when you have run up enough miles to need a rotation to get the best wear out of your tires. Is there a gimmick here? No. The rotation is free, but the company knows that if other things on your car need attention, you will probably have them done at the same time, giving more business to Goodyear.

Delta Air Lines sends out announcements of special services being offered at its new European terminal. The message goes only to

those frequent fliers who regularly travel to Europe.

Then there is Brady's, a San Diego–based chain of men's clothing stores, which asks customers to complete a card noting their size and style preferences. From these cards, Brady's creates a database its salespeople use to identify which customers should be reminded about sales. The same database yields information ensuring that every Brady's shopper gets a birthday card containing a discount coupon worth $15. The result? Even though Brady's cut its advertising budget by 60 percent, its sales increased by 10 percent. The chain expanded from two to five stores in just two years.

Finally, there is the grocery chain that has designed a system to determine what products people purchase as they check out, and then offer coupons on the spot for

complimentary store-brand products. The idea is that if people sample a product they never thought of buying, they may like it enough to add it to their shopping list next time. (Besides, freebies usually stimulate customer loyalty.)

Companies are learning to take advantage of valuable databases they already own from recording business transactions or from customer information supplied on warranty cards. With the help of the right software, marketers can analyze these details to identify opportunities for reinforcing customer loyalty or increasing sales.

Marketing indeed involves the art of persuasion, but the style of persuasion is changing. The trend is away from brute force selling to the masses toward meeting the real needs and wants of customers in a way that benefits both customer and company.

**FIGURE 7.7**

***Using a View to Span Multiple Databases at the State of Georgia Department of Revenue***

By linking several databases, the State of Georgia Department of Revenue can collect taxes owed before it issues refund checks.

**Department of Revenue cross–database view, created by using common data fields of personal tax ID number and business tax ID number**

| Name | Personal tax ID number | Business tax ID number | Amount of refund* | Business tax due* | Sales tax due* | Withholding tax due* |
|---|---|---|---|---|---|---|
| | | | | | | |

* Value determined by calculation

an application, by providing the record key, requests the DBMS to retrieve a record, the DBMS quickly searches the index to find the right record key. It then accesses the database to locate and retrieve the record so that it can be processed by the application.

As Figure 7.8 shows, the index and search process takes place *behind the scenes* as part of processing. Therefore, neither the index nor the search is visible to an individual user. Information about the student can be obtained by requesting the database to locate and retrieve the record for the person with a specific ID number. To speed retrieval, the database system searches an index containing all student ID numbers and location information for each record associated with the student's ID, and then retrieves data and information directly from the specified location. Indexes eliminate the need to search all records in a database to find the one needed.

**The FedEx Index**   FedEx, the Memphis, Tennessee–based overnight shipping company, believes that *the information about a package is as important as the delivery of the package itself.* The company uses an index to keep track of the location of each package shipped through its system. The company's central enterprise database at corporate headquarters in Memphis is accessible to all FedEx drivers and telephone agents throughout the world. When a customer connects over the Internet or calls in to inquire about the location of a package, FedEx can provide a speedy response. Here is how it is done.

Each package is identified by a unique number (called a tracking number), by the name of the individual and company shipping the package, and by the recipient. Five million packages enter the system every day. A huge database (more than 100 billion bytes) holds the details of all packages entering the system.

Customers seeking to track a package over the Web must enter the package's tracking number, which is in turn used to retrieve information from the database. If a customer calls in to ask, "Has my package been delivered?" and does not know the package's tracking number the database must be searched.

FedEx creates multiple indexes for its tracking database, one each for the tracking number, sender's name, sender's company, recipient's name, and recipient's company. When a customer calls with an inquiry, a customer-service rep asks for the tracking number. If the customer has this number handy, the rep can enter it into the computer and immediately display the shipment information on the video screen. If the caller does not have the tracking number, the rep will ask for shipper or recipient information and have the DBMS search through the appropriate index to obtain the desired information. The system also checks the name phonetically in case the correct spelling was not provided (for example, Andersen, Anderson, and Andersson sound the same).

**FIGURE 7.8**

***Using an Index to Retrieve Data***

An index uses a record key—in this case, a student ID number—to locate and retrieve a record for processing.

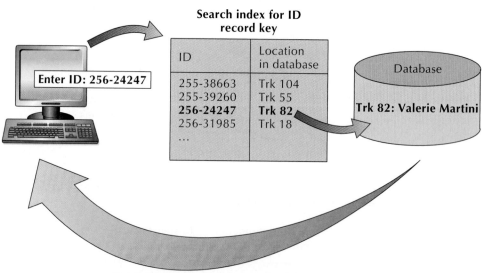

**Search index for ID record key**

| ID | Location in database |
|----|----------------------|
| 255-38663 | Trk 104 |
| 255-39260 | Trk 55 |
| **256-24247** | **Trk 82** |
| 256-31985 | Trk 18 |
| ... | |

Enter ID: 256-24247

Database

Trk 82: Valerie Martini

**Retrieve copy of data from database and place in main memory**

There is no question that DBMS capabilities help FedEx give its customers the service they expect when, as the company's slogan says, "It's absolutely, positively gotta be there overnight."

# Client/Server Computing

Businesses should avoid having separate databases created and maintained by different application systems. *Islands of automation,* a term the IT trade uses to describe situations in which databases and applications cannot share related data, should also be avoided.

The sharing of data can be facilitated through file server computing (see Chapter 2). A **file server** is a computer containing files (including databases) that are available to all users interconnected on an office network, which is a local area network (LAN). Workstations connected to the LAN can request and receive data and information from the server. Figure 7.9 provides an illustrated review of how file server computing works. Success with file servers, coupled with advances in desktop computing capabilities, has led to **client/server computing**.

Client/server computing combines distributed processing and multiuser systems with database systems. All data and information retrieval requests and responses pass over the network. As Figure 7.10 shows, client/server computing can use a multilevel distributed architecture to retrieve information from databases outside of the user's immediate network.

Client/server computing differs from host-based computing (see Chapter 8) in several ways. In a host-based architecture, data and information are stored, and applications run, on a central computer. People log onto the computer using a dumb terminal (or a microcomputer functioning as a dumb terminal) and run applications by a teleprocessing link. The terminal itself adds nothing to the processing. In client/server computing, in contrast, individual desktop computers play a significant role in processing. In essence, the application is running on the user's desktop rather than on a remote computer. The **client**—that is, the desktop workstation—plays the lead role, initiating and

**file server**
A computer containing files that are available to all users interconnected on a local area network.

**client/server computing**
A type of computing in which all data and information retrieval requests and responses pass over a network. Much of the processing is performed on the server and the results of the processing are transmitted to the client.

**client**
In client-server computing, a desktop workstation.

**FIGURE 7.9**
*Data and Information Retrieval Using File Server Computing*

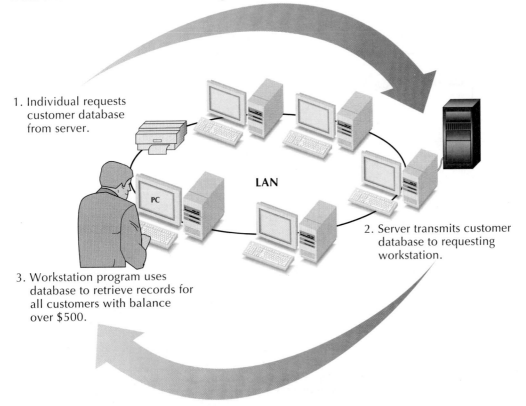

1. Individual requests customer database from server.

LAN

2. Server transmits customer database to requesting workstation.

3. Workstation program uses database to retrieve records for all customers with balance over $500.

**REALITY CHECK**
FedEx's tracking system uses neither an uncommon type of information technology nor custom-made hardware or software. Rather, the company relies on the same information technology that is available to any business or organization. Nonetheless, FedEx provides the combination of good service and reliable information that its customers want.

The point to be taken from this example is one that bears repeating. The benefits of information technology do not come from IT itself. Rather, they come from the manner in which the technology is used. FedEx is so successful because it has been able to identify its customers' needs and then use IT effectively to meet them. Computers, communications, and know-how are all equally important to the company.

Of course, you have to keep moving ahead or competitors will catch up with you. FedEx is at the moment receiving strong challenges from UPS and other competitors. In some areas, its competitors have even taken the lead in the use of IT. ■

---

**server**

A computer that hosts a network and provides the resources that are shared on the network.

driving the processing by requesting selected data and some processing from the main computer, or **server**. Once the server has performed the requested tasks—the requested data, information, and the results of processing are transmitted back to the client.

**Client/Server Computing at Burlington** Burlington Coat Factory, headquartered in Burlington, New Jersey, operates more than 300 retail outlets throughout the United States and Mexico. The company relies on a client/server computing architecture to link all of its stores and distribution centers to headquarters. Point-of-sale cash registers are interconnected through a LAN to a powerful workstation that acts as a store processor (Figure 7.11). The store processor is a file server for the cash registers, providing product and pricing information while capturing each consumer's purchase for inventory information.

**FIGURE 7.10**

***Multilevel Client/Server Architecture***

Client/server company can use a multilevel distributed architecture to retrieve information from databases outside of the user's immediate network.

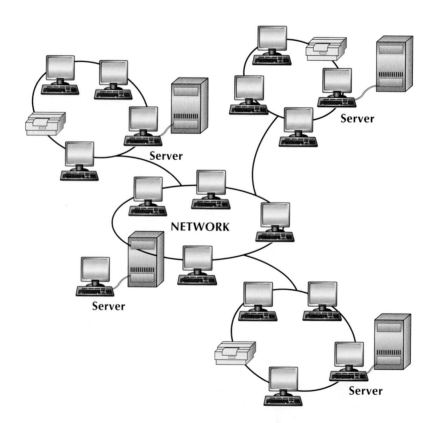

**FIGURE 7.11**

***Client/Server Computing
at Burlington Coat Factory***

Burlington Coat Factory relies on
client/server computing to link more
than 200 stores throughout the
United States and Mexico.

a) Point-of-sale terminals at Burlington's stores are
interconnected through a LAN to a workstation that
acts as a store processor. Each store processor is also a
gateway to the central host computer in New Jersey.

b) The host computer receives information from the
individual stores and processes incoming data, updates
company databases, and redirects transactions. The
same information can then be used to automatically
replenish stock at an individual store. The host computer even prints out the price tags and mailing labels.

# CRITICAL CONNECTIONS 2

## Zagat's Famous Restaurant Surveys Are Web Enabled

### Zagat

If *foodies* are stumped while trying to find the perfect restaurant while in any of 45 cities
away from home, they often turn to the well-known Zagat restaurant guide. Since publishing its first survey in New York City in 1979, Zagat has set a new standard for rating
restaurants. Unlike competitors, Zagat's ratings do not depend on the opinions of professional food critics. Instead, they rely on the ratings of thousands of consumer experiences.

Here is how the Zagat process has worked since the beginning. Each year, several hundred to several thousand Zagat's surveyors visit the restaurants, experiencing the food and
environment, and evaluating the overall dining experience. Once a year, they fill out an
online survey in which they respond to questions and also include their own narrative
description of the restaurant. The surveys are collected by Zagat, and the details are
entered into a database. Zagat's staff processes the database entries by city to capture the
ratings of each restaurant in that city. Then it issues a new *Zagat Survey* for the top food
and entertainment resources.

Department managers who need inventory, sales, or other information interact with the system by means of PCs. Each store processor is also a communications gateway to the central host computer in New Jersey.

Burlington's headquarters system is composed of a battery of processors that receive information from stores via a satellite-based communications network. The headquarters system processes incoming transaction data, updates company enterprise databases, redirects transactions—such as Visa/MasterCard authorization requests—to destinations outside the company, and accepts responses.

Burlington's client/server system provides rapid response to processing requests while linking different IT devices together, both within individual stores and across the country. The system has the added benefit of being extremely reliable: There are so many different components and links in the network that it is unlikely that processing in the Burlington system as a whole will fail.

## The Benefits of Client/Server Computing

Client/server computing offers several benefits to its users. Most important, the server computer processes database requests and the client computer takes the results and works with them. Since as much of the processing as possible is performed on the server before the requested data and information are transmitted to the client, the client receives only the specific information requested—not complete files or large sections of databases—and can begin processing that information immediately.

Figure 7.12 shows how this process works in a consumer banking setting. When a bank employee at a client computer wants to send a personalized letter to all customers with balances over $500, the employee sends a request from her workstation program to

**FIGURE 7.12**

**Data and Information Retrieval Using Client/Server Computing**

In client/server computing, specific information—not complete files or huge sections of databases—is transmitted from the server to the client.

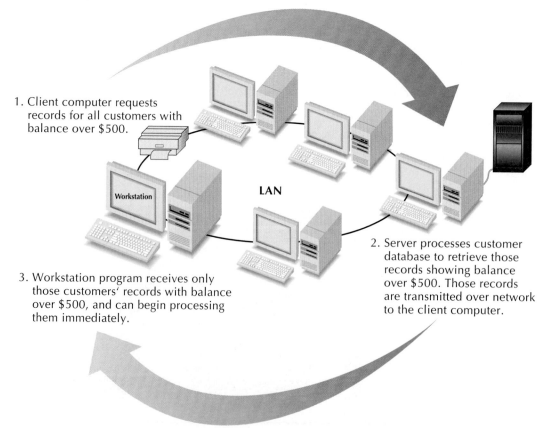

1. Client computer requests records for all customers with balance over $500.

2. Server processes customer database to retrieve those records showing balance over $500. Those records are transmitted over network to the client computer.

3. Workstation program receives only those customers' records with balance over $500, and can begin processing them immediately.

LAN

Workstation

the server asking the system to review the customer database. The server processes the database to identify all customers meeting the $500 criterion, and then transmits only the records of those customers to the client workstation. The employee's program extracts name, address, and balance information from the data and inserts them into a customized letter prepared through the word-processing program on the client workstation. Without the shared processing between client and server, either entire databases would be copied from one system to another or repeated requests would be necessary to retrieve names and addresses.

In addition to saving time and money, client/server computing can make users more productive by ensuring their access to the information they need when they need it. Client/server computing allows many users to share common data resources, including files and databases as well as computer storage and printers. Sharing data and information eliminates the need for personal management of data and/or peripheral devices. Finally, client/server computing allows the integration of geographically distributed users and computing resources into a cohesive computer and communications environment. All of these advantages result in faster access to data and information for users, better service for customers, quicker responses to changes in the business environment, more efficient business processes, fewer errors, and, in general, higher levels of productivity.

For more information on the best-known client/server system, review Chapter 3, which discussed the Internet and the World Wide Web.

**Client/Server Computing in Action: AMR Corp. and CSX Corp.**   When companies turn cargo over to a shipper for transport to a customer, they frequently lose contact with the goods. Unlike FedEx, most shipping companies do not have a computerized tracking system that allows them to retrieve shipping and delivery information online so they can know the exact location of the boat, plane, or railcar carrying their goods. AMR Corp.–the parent company of American Airlines, and CSX Corp.–one of the largest land, ocean, and rail cargo shippers in the world–have teamed up to remedy this problem by developing the Encompass system for tracking the movement of freight worldwide. With this system, the status of any shipment can be determined from the time the goods leave the shipper's freight dock until they arrive at their final destination.

Establishing the Encompass system required linking manufacturers, shippers, and third parties worldwide, each of which had its own computing and communications systems and its own databases. To link all of these different systems, the designers of Encompass turned to client/server computing (Figure 7.13). AMR and CSX provide their

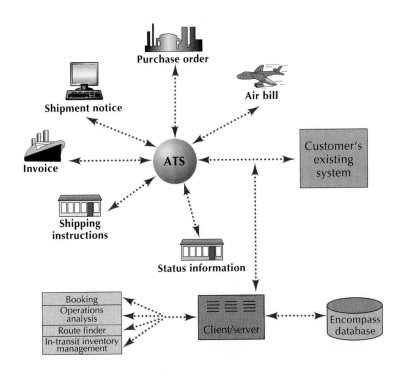

**FIGURE 7.13**

***The Encompass System***

With the Encompass system, shippers and carriers can determine the status of their shipments from the time the goods leave the dock until they arrive at their final destination.

# INFORMATION TECHNOLOGY IN PRACTICE
## Estimating Databases Take the Guesswork out of Fixing Dings and Dents

Selling cars is a big business around the world. So is fixing them. Wherever you go, body shops that do the repairs to remove dings and dents have backlogs of work. Preparing reliable estimates of the costs of repairs takes time, but also brings in repeat business. Yet it sometimes requires inspired guesswork to know just how something will need to be fixed—and thus how much a repair will cost. To eliminate much of this guesswork, a number of automobile dealerships in the United Kingdom, along with insurance companies (such as Royal Insurance and Guardian Insurance) and several car rental companies, use a sophisticated estimating system called Glassmatix.

Glassmatix, a system developed by Glass's Information Services, features PartBase, a parts and labor times look-up system. PartBase contains more than 26,000 exploded parts diagrams and 1,000 model specific vehicle images, and corresponding part numbers and prices from more than 30 manufacturers. The repair labor time estimates are provided by an insurance industry-sponsored research center in Thatcham, England, and part prices provided by the manufacturers. The parts and labor database is updated monthly. Glass provides the know-how to integrate the information and computer software so that quick and accurate estimates can be prepared.

The system works like this. An estimator in a body shop examines a banged-up vehicle to determine what damages must be repaired. The estimator looks up the car parts in the Glassmatix system. Then Glassmatix III calculates the labor and materials needed for the entire repair process. It displays an accurate estimate, which can be printed on body shop's stationery or electronically transmitted to the repair center where the work is being performed.

Say the damaged car needs a new door, replacement of several windows, a new side molding, and a new front fender. Using the Windows interface on the Glassmatix system, the estimator enters parts and vehicle descriptions, enabling the system to find each item in PartBase.

Next the desktop computer assembles the parts information and determines the cost of all repairs, including parts and labor. Once the full cost of repairing the damaged car has been estimated, the system determines whether the car is worth repairing and makes its recommendation to the estimator. Finally, Glassmatix suggests a preferred order in which to make the repairs to minimize labor costs.

The Glassmatix system includes the capability to keep track of the value of cars and to determine when repairs exceed a dealer-specified level—say, 35 percent or so of the value of the car—they are probably not worthwhile. Another module, called eSalvage, provides a unique Internet based salvage disposal system for cars that are not worth repairing. The eSalvage system offers salvage buyers access to an electronic trading module, enabling sellers of salvage, including insurance companies, to trade over the Internet.

Glass's Information Services has developed a related IT capability it calls Glassimage. Also designed to be used in preparing repair estimates, this system is portable, so it can be taken to an accident scene (or anywhere else the damaged vehicle is located). Glassimage can scan photographs or videotape images and transmit the images over the Internet or by a telephone link to the body shop, where the images are viewed by estimators.

Glassmatix is a valuable resource that eliminates the need for estimators to spend time running down parts costs or haggling over labor estimates. Other systems of this nature are emerging throughout Europe and North America. Because dings and dents occur everywhere there are cars, and because the databases can be modified to incorporate details about cars used in a specific region, along with local labor costs, there is no limit to where in the world this system can be used.

customers (clients) with software that can be used on the clients' computers to request tracking information from servers in the Encompass network. Clients can book shipments, determine the route over which their freight will travel, manage their inventory in transit by determining its location and scheduled arrival dates, evaluate their own shipping activities through an operations analysis module, and even evaluate the performance of the transportation companies. They can also prepare essential shipping documents (air bills, shipment notices, purchase orders, shipping instructions, invoices, etc.). Online databases, high-speed communications networks, and powerful servers make it possible for all of these activities to occur in real time. (Review the definitions of real time and batch processing in Chapter 2, if necessary.)

The benefits of the Encompass system to AMR and CSX are enormous. Like FedEx, they are offering a capability that is attracting new customers, thus increasing their business. While other companies struggle to catch up, AMR and CSX plan to stay several steps ahead of competitors by constantly adding features and capabilities. Good people and know-how lead to the creation of systems like Encompass.

Workstations together with good database management practices can improve business practices in many ways. The *Information Technology in Practice* feature, "Estimating Databases Take the Guesswork Out of Fixing Dings and Dents," illustrates the power of desktop computers and network connections in what many people consider to be a low-tech industry.

## Databases on the Internet

**Web-based integration** makes data from enterprise databases available to users connecting through the Internet (including enterprise intranets and extranets). The FedEx illustration examined earlier, which enables customers to trace their packages over the Internet, is an example of Web-based integration.

How does it work? The FedEx Web server (Figure 7.14) accepts user queries initiated from its Web browser and translates them into other queries that are processed to retrieve the appropriate data from the database. Using the results, the Web server creates and displays a new Web page containing the data requested by the user.

**Web-based integration**
Makes data from enterprise databases available to users connecting through the Internet (including enterprise intranets and extranets).

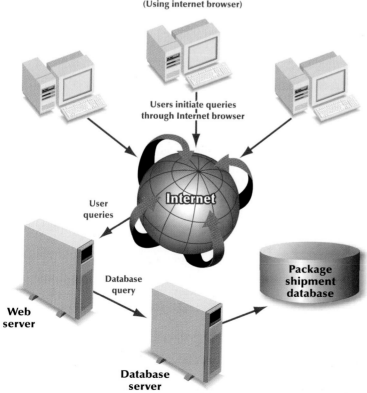

**User client computers**
(Using internet browser)

Users initiate queries
through Internet browser

User
queries

Database
query

**Package shipment database**

**Web server**

**Database server**

FIGURE 7.14

*Web-Enabled Database Processing*

Because of ever-increasing use of the Internet and browsers, it will be increasingly common for enterprise databases to be linked to the Internet via Web servers. Web-based integration may be used for centralized enterprise databases or in a distributed database environment.

# Distributed Databases

Enterprise databases are almost always shared among many users and applications. These **shared databases** can also be distributed. A **distributed database** is a database whose data reside on more than one system in a network. These data can be accessed, retrieved, or updated from any node in the network. Distributing data provides the needed data and information at a specific location, while allowing those same data to be used at other locations in the organization as well.

Anyone using distributed databases need not be aware of the location of the database because the application programs, communications software, and database management systems will automatically interact to identify, locate, and retrieve the data and information the user needs.

## Partitioning and Replication

Databases may be distributed in two ways: partitioning and replication. With **partitioning**, different portions of the database reside at different nodes in the network. To partition effectively, the database designer divides the database into the logical or meaningful subsets needed to support a specific type of application or business usage. The actual storage location of each database partition is known to the database management system but is not something the database user needs to be concerned about.

When a database contains data that are included in another database, it is said to be *replicated*. **Replication** is designed to speed the retrieval of data and, in turn, speed processing. It is particularly useful if certain parts of the database are required repeatedly for processing at different locations in a network. Avoiding continual transmission of information requests and the subsequent transmission of the requested data minimizes delay and perhaps lowers network or communications costs.

**Partitioning and Replication at Crédit Lyonnais**   A good example of partitioning and replication can be seen at Crédit Lyonnais, one of the best-known banks in the world. Headquartered in Paris, it has more than 1,800 branch offices serving some 6 million customers throughout France. The heart of the bank's operation is a multilevel distributed system that includes a distributed customer database, interconnected local area networks, and multiple mainframe data centers that each run other banking databases.

Every Crédit Lyonnais branch office includes a communication network that links tellers, customer service representatives, loan officers, and the branch's managers. Each branch office, in turn, is linked to one of 18 regional centers, where midrange computers maintain a portion of a partitioned customer database (Figure 7.15). This relational database contains personal and financial profiles of the bank's customers in that region. Because the regional centers are linked to one another by multiple private digital communications lines, each center has access to database partitions at any of the other centers. (Prior to the creation of this system in 1992, each center maintained its own separate database. These databases were neither compatible with one another nor accessible to bank personnel outside the region.)

In addition, each regional center is linked by communications lines to data centers running mainframe computers in the cities of Lyons, Tours, and Paris. These three centers have access to all of the regional database partitions, store account balance information, and handle the processing of customer loan applications.

This combination of a multilevel distributed system and partitioned databases has made data and information accessible to Crédit Lyonnais personnel when and where needed. The structure has an additional benefit: the potential to develop new business. For example, while tellers are assisting a customer to deposit a check or make a withdrawal from a savings account, they can retrieve the customer's profile from the regional

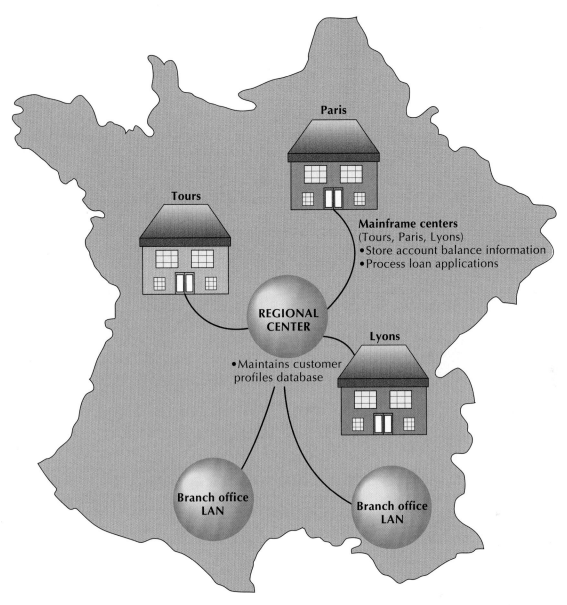

**FIGURE 7.15**

*Crédit Lyonnais's Distributed Database System*

Crédit Lyonnais's distributed database system spans 1,700 branch offices, 18 regional centers, and 3 mainframe centers.

center and have it right in front of them on-screen. This information enables tellers to determine whether the customer is a candidate for other bank services, which they can explain while serving the customer at the bank window.

All parties benefit from the system. Bank employees make more efficient use of their time because they do not have to deal with paper records and printed reports. Customers get better service; if they have a question about a past transaction while they are at the bank window, the teller will be able to answer it by looking at their customer profile on-screen. Customers can also view their banking information via the Internet. Managers benefit from the system because it lets them spend more time developing customer relations and new banking services and less time handling special cases or managing cases of missing information.

## Distribution Strategies

Database designers decide to partition or replicate by choosing the strategy that best fits the manner in which an organization conducts its business. The two most common distribution strategies are geographic and functional.

**geographic distribution strategy**
A database distribution strategy in which the database is located in a region where the data and information are used most frequently.

**functional distribution strategy**
A database distribution strategy in which the database is distributed according to business functions.

In a **geographic distribution strategy**, a database, or database partition, is located in a region where the data and information will be used most frequently. Crédit Lyonnais, with its databases partitioned across 18 regions, uses a geographic distribution strategy. Each partition is accessible to bank employees in all regions.

A **functional distribution strategy** stresses processing functions over physical location. For example, it is common for business units to distribute databases according to business functions. Figure 7.16 illustrates how a company might use a computer network to distribute the various components of its database. The sales database includes the names and addresses of current and potential customers; the manufacturing database holds the schedules for the production and assembly of finished goods; the inventory control database holds inventory records of materials, parts, and finished goods; and the accounting database holds records of revenues due the company and monies to be paid out.

Functional distribution strategies are effective only when communications networks interconnect each database or partition. If, for example, salespeople do not know what products are scheduled for manufacturing (information in the manufacturing database) or which customers' accounts are overdue (information in the accounting database), they will not be able to function effectively. Throughout the business world, executives, managers, and staff members are increasingly recognizing the interdependence of business functions. Multiuser networks make communication among the various business functions faster and easier than once thought possible.

The *Information Technology in Practice* feature, "Lithonia Lighting's Distributed Database Drives Business End-to-End," describes how this large corporation combines its database and network capabilities to make its agents efficient, and in turn, the company an industry leader.

## Designing a Distributed Database

The principle of high-tech/high-touch emphasizes the importance of considering the *people* side of information technology. This idea stresses that in general, IT works best when it adjusts to people, not when people have to adjust to it. This simple principle applies just as much to the design of distributed databases as it does to the design of software packages for individual users.

**FIGURE 7.16**

*Functional Distribution of a Database*

A functional distribution strategy stresses processing functions over physical location.

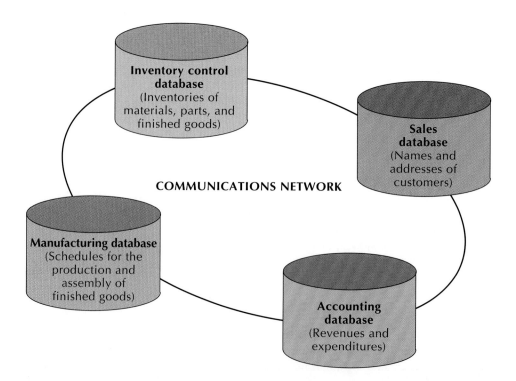

# INFORMATION TECHNOLOGY IN PRACTICE
## Lithonia Lighting's Distributed Database
## Drives Business End-to-End

**LITHONIA LIGHTING** An *Acuity* Brands Company — Lithonia Lighting is North America's largest manufacturer of lighting equipment for commercial, industrial, outdoor, and residential applications. Headquartered in Conyers, Georgia (just outside of Atlanta), Lithonia operates 15 manufacturing facilities in the United States, Canada, and Mexico and maintains seven distribution centers and a North American network of regional warehouses.

Lithonia employs 8,000 people in production, distribution, sales management, marketing, and administration. In addition, more than 1,000 independent sales agents operating out of some 200 offices represent Lithonia Lighting throughout the United States, Canada, and Mexico. Although they are not employees of Lithonia, the sales agents representing the company are essential to its marketing success. Agents work with engineers and designers in their respective regions to choose the company's lighting products.

At the heart of Lithonia's operating activities is its order-fulfillment system for order entry, distribution, and shipping. For many years, the centralized database at the core of this system resided on the company's mainframe system. However, in order to support the company's continued growth and as a way of providing better support to the sales agents in the field, the company migrated to a distributed database operating on networked servers.

Today, more than 100 instances of the company's order-fulfillment database are installed in field locations. Using a custom-designed order-processing interface, the sales agents enter orders into the database residing on servers in their offices. Once entered, the system logs the orders in the database and transmits the details to the enterprise database at Lithonia's headquarters. The headquarters database contains an enterprise-wide view of all products, sales, and customer data. (Agents can access the enterprise database if their local database is inaccessible for any reason.)

At headquarters, the orders are reviewed and replicated to servers at one of the company's 15 manufacturing locations, where the items will be manufactured, or to a distribution center where items are kept in stock. Each site maintains an order database running on its local server.

Small computers mounted on the forklifts at each manufacturing and distribution center have wireless connections to the database. When the order-fulfillment system's shipping module transmits product and shipping information to the forklift, the computer signals the operator to retrieve the items and prepare the order for shipment. As the order is shipped, information to update the enterprise database is transmitted to headquarters and in turn to the appropriate sales-agent database.

If at the point of shipment or at any other time the contents or status of an order changes, the system automatically updates the database in the agent's office. Keeping sales agents informed means they always have the means to provide current and accurate information to customers.

The enterprise database is also the principal source of information used in the company's executive information system. Lithonia's executives rely on an information *dashboard* that presents status indicators to keep them abreast of the status of sales and manufacturing activities. A data-warehouse function, also linked to the enterprise database, enables executives to plan and forecast manufacturing needs by providing sales information by product, region, and other categories of interest.

Lithonia's network of facilities and independent agents, mirrored by a network of distributed databases, means the company is well positioned to achieve its continued growth.

The secret to making distributed databases effective is to keep their operational details invisible to their users. People using a database should be able to focus on the customer, supplier, or other business opportunity without having to worry about which database to use, how it is structured, or where it is located. The database management system should handle the technical details *behind the scenes* so users do not have to think about how the DBMS works. For instance, a **database directory**–a requirement for shared databases–keeps track of the location of data and information so that users do not have to. This directory may be centralized, partitioned, or replicated.

The vast public telephone network does an excellent job of applying the principle of high-tech/high-touch. To make a telephone call, all you need to do is pick up a mobile phone (or the receiver of a desk phone) and dial a few numbers. The telephone network does the rest. It translates the telephone number for processing by the network, retrieves routing information from the appropriate partition (the public phone system does not have a single centralized directory), and uses the routing to connect you. In short, it manages the entire process while you wait for your party to pick up the receiver at the other end. The public phone system uses a distributed database to make your life easier.

**Other Design Factors**   Distributed database designers are influenced by six factors besides the need for ease of use:

1. **Storage Costs**   Duplicating data in multiple partitions increases storage costs. Hence, designers must carefully monitor the volume of data in the distributed database and associated directories.

2. **Processing Costs**   Because the cost of processing data and information rises as the extent of database distribution increases, designers must ensure that the database is distributed only to those who will use it.

3. **Communication Costs**   The distribution of data increases the need for communication between nodes and, consequently, the costs of communication. The designer must ensure that these costs are justified by improvements in the business activities they support.

4. **Retrieval and Processing**   The location of data, coupled with the architecture of the communications network, determines response time (for example, elapsed time due to retrieval and processing). Database designers must be aware that wider distribution will increase response time if data and information must be assembled from several remote locations. If, on the other hand, the data needed most often are located at or near the node requiring those data, retrieval and processing time may diminish substantially.

5. **Reliability**   Designers must safeguard both the existence of and access to important databases. Higher levels of reliability often mean higher costs because database partitions, which allow retrieval of duplicated information maintained at another node if one node breaks down, must be duplicated.

6. **Frequency of Updates and Queries**   Designers generally locate databases at those locations that update the databases most frequently. If processing requires retrieval of data and information in response to queries rather than just for updates, local storage of a database or directory at a node may not be justified.

Although cost-cutting is a recognized fact of business life today, merely minimizing costs is not enough to guarantee success for a distributed database. For a distributed database to be truly useful, the IT professional who designs it must weigh storage costs, processing speed, and reliability against the frequency of use of the database and the manner in which it is used (entering or changing data as opposed to retrieving data). The more frequently the database is used, the more important it is to evaluate these criteria properly.

**database directory**
The component of a shared database that keeps track of data and information.

## Data Warehouses and OLAP

Databases are designed to support ongoing transaction processing, which occurs as an organization carries out its day-to-day activities. Retrieval of data must be rapid in order to keep pace with the activities. These activities are often termed **online transaction**

**online transaction processing (OLTP)**
Transaction-oriented applications design for direct data entry and retrieval of information by users connected to the system.

processing (OLTP). The Crédit Lyonnais banking system features OLTP. In OLTP, the database is linked to the processes to provide current status details, such as the current balance in a customer's account for Crédit Lyonnais.

While databases are effective for maintaining current status information, they are not necessarily useful for examining patterns, trends, or the history of activities. This is why many organizations are instituting data-mining processes using data warehouses and data marts for online analytical processing.

## Online Analytical Processing

**Online analytical processing (OLAP)** is database processing that selectively extracts data from different points of view. For instance, a Crédit Lyonnais manager might need to know the pattern of new deposits and withdrawals for its largest customers, by region and type of account.

In contrast, a medical researcher can request that data be analyzed to display the number of influenza cases for elderly patients during the month of January; compare figures with those for the same disease during the month of July; and then see a comparison of nonelderly patients during the same periods of time. To facilitate this kind of analysis, OLAP uses multidimensional data. That is, each data attribute (such as specific disease, type of patient, care provider, geographic region, and time period) is a separate dimension. Data warehouses and data mining are the data source used in OLAP to discover previously unrecognized relationships between activities and events (those between data items).

**online analytical processing (OLAP)**
Database processing that selectively extracts data from different points of view.

## Data Warehouse

A **data warehouse** is a large data store, designed for inquiries, that combines details of both current *and* historical operations, usually drawn from a number of sources. It may also contain data from external sources, including local or regional economic and demographic data acquired from public or private sources. Data warehouses typically contain several terabytes of data (1 terabyte equals 1,000 gigabytes), with the largest ranging to 50 terabytes in size.

Data warehouses do not replace enterprise databases. How do data warehouses differ from application-oriented databases? Frequently, the databases associated with transaction-oriented systems focus on a *single type of current enterprise activity* and are designed to support related transactions in the most efficient manner (Table 7.1). To enable managers to deal with *multiple enterprise activities,* and hence several databases, a data warehouse draws details from multiple databases over a period of weeks, months, and years of activities. Since data warehouses combine both current and historical data from various sources, they are much larger than ordinary operational databases (Figure 7.17).

The *Information Technology in Practice* feature, "Data Warehouse Powers French Railroad System," describes how the French railroad system relies on its data warehouse to keep track of the travel needs for the citizens of France.

**data warehouse**
A large data store, designed for inquiries, that combines details of both current *and* historical operations, usually drawn from a number of sources.

| Table 7.1  **Comparison of Enterprise Databases and Data Warehouses** | | |
|---|---|---|
| | **ENTERPRISE DATABASE** | **DATA WAREHOUSE** |
| Subject Focus | Data are stored with a function or process orientation. | Data are subject oriented, reflecting multiple views of functions and processes. |
| Temporal Focus | Data are recorded as current transactions or to reflect current events. | Data reflect an historical orientation spanning several periods of time. |
| Volatility | Updates to data are routine and may be frequent. | Data does not change (i.e., details are *read-only*). However, additional data may be added to the warehouse, reflecting additional time periods or areas of interest. |

**Enterprise
databases**

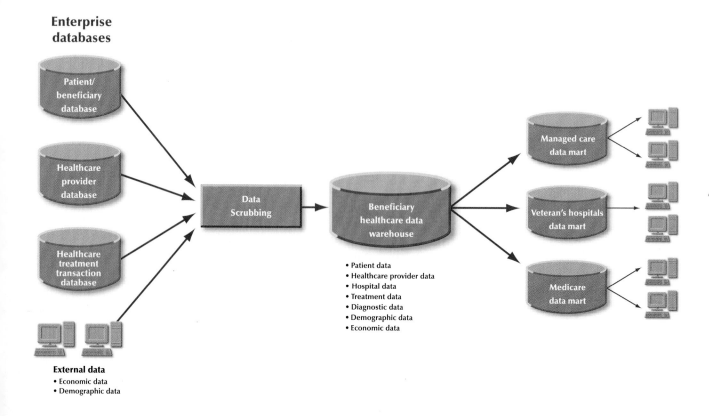

**FIGURE 7.17**
*Data Warehouses and Data Marts Support Analysis and Decision Making*

## Data Mining

**data mining**

Uses software designed to detect information *hidden* in the data.

The objective of OLAP and the use of data warehouses is to identify patterns, trends, and rules that are embedded in the activities, products, or services of an enterprise. The process of scanning the data warehouse in this fashion is known as **data mining**. Data mining uses software designed to detect information *hidden* in the data. When properly identified and incorporated into management decision making, the resulting information can improve service quality, increase competitiveness, enhance revenues and profits, and transform enterprise processes.

The Health Care Financing Administration (HCFA), an agency within the U.S. Department of Health and Human Services, headquartered in Baltimore, Maryland, assists 75 million American beneficiaries who are disabled or have low income with health insurance coverage. HCFA does not provide health care. Rather, its 10 regional offices around the United States interact with both healthcare providers and beneficiaries.

HCFA is responsible for the dual challenges of ensuring beneficiaries get the best care possible while also protecting against waste or improper use of taxpayer-provided funds. In so doing, the agency receives data from many sources, including beneficiaries, healthcare providers, managed-care agencies, and other government agencies such as the Social Security Administration. HCFA relies on a data warehouse to analyze the quality and cost of care and to detect patterns and trends in health care. For instance, the data warehouse enables HCFA to explore such important multidimensional issues as:

- Average Medicare (health insurance for the elderly) reimbursement per beneficiary
- Trend in recovery time for patients receiving treatment in managed-care programs compared to national trends

# INFORMATION TECHNOLOGY IN PRACTICE

## Data Warehouse Powers French Railroad System

Many people have childhood memories of trains and railroads. Some remember the distant, lonesome whistle of a diesel engine heard across open farmland. Others—usually older people—associate railroads with a giant fire-breathing, smoke-belching *iron horse* chugging down the tracks, dragging a load of freight behind it. Although the golden age of railroads is the inspiration for many colorful memories, today's reality is very different.

For a contemporary railroad to be successful and profitable, its executives must be expert at more than running trains. They have to know how to manage the entire system effectively, know who is riding on their trains, and understand the usage patterns of their customers. They have to recognize that there is no such thing as an average train.

One of France's most prized possessions is its national rail system. The French National Railroad—the Société Nationale des Chemins de Fer Français, or simply SNCF—operates some 1,600 trains daily, rolling from the northern coast, bordering on the English Channel, to the southern coast, where France spills into the Mediterranean Sea. The French are particularly proud of the SNCF's bullet trains, the Train à Grande Vitesse (TGV). The 400 daily TGV trains are not only sleek in appearance—a far cry from the chugging steam-puffing iron locomotives that have been the train's image around the world—but also whip around the country at average speeds of 300 kilometers per hour. In fact, the TGV holds a world speed

record for a train (more than 515 kilometers per hour).

New designs and engineering advances are responsible for the high speeds and many traveler comforts enjoyed by people riding the TGV. But information technology and data warehousing are responsible for the high passenger revenues and effective daily use of these trains.

Recognizing the necessity to make better use of its trains, meet passenger demand, and fund continued expansion of the TGV, SNCF officials determined they had to analyze the details of their operations more effectively. Accordingly, they set up a data warehouse that runs on a special database computer to support strategic decision support analysis.

Prior to creating its data warehouse, SNCF managers treated all TGV lines the same, using a rigid fare control system that had passengers paying comparable fares for trips of similar distances, regardless

of whether the tickets were purchased well in advance or at the last minute. With data warehousing, SNCF officials can analyze data in new ways by regularly reviewing current and historical details on reservations, fleet management, marketing, and accounting systems for each train. For instance, its marketing analysts can tell when and where passengers on the train from Paris to the coastal city of Rennes purchased their tickets, how much they paid for them, and whether they ordered meals en route or booked rental cars at their destinations.

Data warehousing has also enabled SNCF to create a yield management system similar to that pioneered by U.S. airlines. Yield management enables officials to analyze the patterns and trends associated with each train and to understand customer behavior with more precision, avoiding the need to rely on averages.

…

Officials can now customize the prices and services for each train. Instead of assuming the average train has a certain percentage of no-shows and an average ticket price, the data warehouse system lets them more accurately anticipate how many people will request first-class and coach seats on a particular train on a given day, as well as predict the number of no-shows. With this information in hand, SNCF officials can determine whether to offer a certain number of discount seats on the train and what percentage of seats should be overbooked to counter the no-shows. The result: maximum revenue is collected for each trip.

SNCF's data warehouse has allowed French railroad officials to make better-informed decisions while creating an infrastructure for reusing data in numerous ways. Best of all, it has increased revenues and improved flexibility in meeting passenger needs. In France, there is no such thing as an average train.

Before data are stored in the data warehouse, they are scrubbed. *Data scrubbing* software validates the data for correctness (for example, validation of date or detection of duplicate transactions) and transforms it into a consistent format that enables effective data mining (so that all dates are expressed in the same format and duplicate transactions are removed).

- Average inpatient hospital stay for pneumonia patients in managed-care programs vs. treatment by private physician
- Total number of office visits by age and geographic region

HCFA's repeated need to pose such queries, combined with the size and scope of these inquiries, and the need to incorporate external data for some queries, necessitates the creation of data warehouse.

## Data Marts

**data marts**
Processed to focus on a specific area of activities or isolated scientific or commercial processes

Smaller, narrowly focused versions of a data warehouse, called **data marts**, are processed to focus on a specific area of activities or isolated scientific or commercial processes. For instance, the Health Care Financing Administration, discussed above, might determine it needs to establish data marts to study managed care, treatment at veteran's hospitals, and patient care under Medicare (see Figure 7.17).

Enterprise databases, data warehouses and data marts are all important and valued resources for the enterprise. Hence, the people who create them are specialists.

# People

The people who work with enterprise databases include the applications programmers and the end-users. The applications programmers embed database interaction instructions in application programs. This facilitates communication with end-users, who interact directly with the database, data warehouse, or data mart. In addition, two types of IT professionals are closely connected to enterprise database development and management: the database administrator and the systems programmer.

## Database Administrator

**database administrator (DBA)**
The IT professional responsible for managing all the activities and procedures related to an organization's database.

The IT professional with the most extensive database management responsibilities is the **database administrator (DBA)**, sometimes called the *data administrator*. The database administrator is responsible for managing all activities and procedures related to an organization's database. In some organizations, the database administrator is one person. In others, a team fulfills this function, with each team member responsible for some aspect of the data administration procedures.

## Systems Programmer

Organizations that use large, complex databases may have a systems programmer, a software and hardware specialist who works with the physical details of the database and the computer's operating system. The systems programmer organizes the data on magnetic

# CRITICAL CONNECTIONS 3

## Jiffy Lube Mines Customer Data

**Jiffy Lube**

Jiffy Lube, a wholly owned subsidiary of Pennzoil-Quaker State Company, started in 1979 as an association of seven automotive service centers. Today, the company has over 2,200 service centers in the United States and Canada, featuring quick oil changes and lubes. Jiffy Lube centers service about 30 million cars annually.

A large portion of Jiffy Lube's success depends on the ability of its service centers to create repeat business. Hence, the company maintains a large database in which it keeps records of the millions of vehicles it has serviced by customer. Database entries record the frequency with which owners bring their vehicles for service as well as the services that are performed.

For more than a decade, Jiffy Lube has followed the marketing practice of mailing promotional coupons to its past customers. Within 75 to 90 days following the servicing of a vehicle—the length of time it takes the average driver to accumulate the recommended number of miles between oil changes—its owner receives a promotional dollars-off coupon along with a reminder that it is time to service the vehicle again. A high percentage of drivers return as a result of the promotion.

Even with the repeated success of the promotional campaign, the company's marketing directors wondered if they were capitalizing on the rich information embedded in its large enterprise database.

disk (or other storage medium) according to a structure determined by the database designer. The systems programmer also determines the optimal way to arrange records and objects in storage, and creates indexes and other devices for retrieval in conjunction with guidelines established by the database administrator.

Database administrators' primary responsibility is managing the database. This task occupies virtually all of their workday. Systems programmers spend only a portion of their time on database-related activities. The rest of their time is spent working with the operating system, managing the network, and handling other types of hardware and software matters.

# Procedures

A *procedure* is a step-by-step process or set of instructions for accomplishing a specific result. The procedures associated with databases are grouped under the general heading of **database administration procedures**.

## Database Administration Procedures

Database administration means managing the database. This entails doing what is necessary to develop and safeguard the database in the most beneficial way.

**database administration procedures**
The procedures associated with managing a database.

Procedures for data administration include six areas of responsibility:

1. **Database Planning**    Like any valuable resource, a database must be planned. Planning includes being aware of and understanding business needs and user requirements, selecting the DBMS, developing standards for usage, and outlining security strategies.

2. **Database Design**    To be as useful as possible, the database must be carefully designed. Designers define the records and objects—including the schema, data names, and length specifications—that make up the database.

3. **Database Creation**    The database design is only a framework. The database becomes a reality when data are entered into the design and saved on a storage device.

4. **Database Maintenance**    As users' needs and demands change, the database may need adjustment. New records or objects may be added or changes may be made to the existing structures. Database maintenance pertains to the *structure* and *organization* of the database. Maintenance of the *contents* of individual records (the data items) is the responsibility of those using the database, not the database administrator.

5. **Analysis of Usage**    Managing a database means monitoring how and when it is used. If data and information retrieval patterns change, the database administrator may decide that adjustments (maintenance) are needed to restructure the database to meet new user requests.

6. **Creation and Monitoring of Security Procedures**    The existence and integrity of the database must be safeguarded at all times. Developing, implementing, and monitoring security procedures are important parts of database administration.

Much of a database's value comes from the procedures the database administrator uses to develop and maintain the database. These responsibilities are quite different from those of individual users or systems programmers.

## Concurrency Procedures

**concurrent data sharing**
A database procedure that allows several users to access the database simultaneously.

**nonconcurrent data sharing**
A database procedure that allows individuals to access a database only when no other person or application is processing the data.

Whenever more than one user has access to a database, there is a chance that several people will want to access the database simultaneously. With **concurrent data sharing**, users can do exactly that. With **nonconcurrent data sharing**, individuals can use the data in a database only when no other person or application is processing the data. The database is shared but *not simultaneously* by different people.

In developing a database or an application, the systems designer or database administrator must determine what type of sharing is to be permitted. With concurrent data sharing, if two or more people try to retrieve and change existing records simultaneously, the result can be chaos. To understand why this is so, consider the following example:

1. Travel Agent A retrieves from the database a copy of the inventory record for seats available on Flight 10 to London on November 28. The record shows him that five coach seats remain for sale.

2. At virtually the same instant, Travel Agent B retrieves a copy of the same record. Her goal is to book seats for her clients, who are traveling to London on November 28.

3. *Both* travel agents are proceeding based on the availability of five seats. Neither one knows that the other is using a copy of the record or preparing to book seats on the same flight.

4. Travel Agent B's customers give the go-ahead for the reservation first, so B books seats for her four customers. The database system writes the change into the database, noting the names of the customers and adjusting seat inventory to show one remaining seat.

5. Travel Agent A's screen still shows five seats available. Agent A wishes to book a party of three for the flight to London. If the database allows him to do so, and then shows two remaining seats available (the original five minus the three he just sold), two passengers of the seven booked by A and B will be stranded without seats.

Systems developers can use several different strategies to avoid this type of situation. First, they can choose not to allow concurrent sharing. Second, they can decide to partition the database, with each partition assigned to one user or group of users. If different users access separate portions of the database independently, concurrent data sharing will be avoided. Third, they can partition database processing, a strategy that entails assigning the database to a particular user for a period of time (perhaps mornings rather than afternoons, or odd-numbered days rather than even-numbered days). But since travel agents need access to flight information 24 hours a day, none of these strategies would be right for them.

When concurrent data sharing is essential, the proper procedures must be developed to avoid the type of debacle described in our flight-booking example. The most common of these concurrency procedures is **record locking**. When a record is being used by one person, it is locked and another user cannot access or alter it. The record is unlocked when the initial user finishes processing the record. Locking and unlocking occur automatically. Today's airline reservations systems use record locking to ensure that seats are not sold more than once. To revert to our example, Travel Agents A and B *cannot* sell the same seats on the same flight simultaneously because while one agent is assigning the seats, the other is prevented (locked out) from entering a sales transaction for those seats.

**File locking** is another common concurrency procedure. It is used in systems that store unstructured information and have file-level sharing. For example, in a word-processing or spreadsheet system, the principal document processed is a file. If file locking is specified by the designer, only one user or application will be able to use a specific document at a given moment.

Whenever record locking is used, there is a chance that two or more users will find themselves in a **deadlock**, a situation in which each user of the database is waiting for the others to free (unlock) the record. Although deadlocks are rare, the DBA must develop procedures for dealing with them. Typically, the solution is for the DBMS to detect the occurrence of the deadlock and issue a message to the users asking them to release the record or reenter the details of their transaction.

**record locking**
A concurrency procedure that prohibits another user from accessing or altering a record that is in use.

**file locking**
Used in systems that store unstructured information and have file-level sharing.

**deadlock**
A situation in which each user of a database is waiting for the others to unlock a record.

# A Final Word

Shared and distributed data create many opportunities for businesses to serve customers and conduct day-to-day activities. However, as in all areas of information technology, computers and communications systems provide only potential capabilities. It is up to the firm's people to determine how and when IT can be used to achieve the desired results.

# CRITICAL CONNECTIONS

## 1 Part II: Customers Benefit From Bridgestone/Firestone's Unified Database

**Firestone**

Firestone's unified enterprise database contains information on all tire and service transactions at any service center, regardless of the customer's form of payment. Firestone uses the database to monitor store performance and to send promotional information to its customers.

Customers benefit directly from the company's enterprise database, for they can access it over the Internet. Their vehicle's entire record of services performed at a Firestone store is available for their review. This feature is available without cost or any effort on the customer's part, since the data is entered by Firestone staff at the time of service. (Of course, services performed elsewhere are not part of the database.)

When Firestone recently encountered a manufacturing problem leading to flaws in some of its tires, it decided a recall was necessary. Because of the unified database, Firestone was able to process the database by the type of tire purchased during the time period when the manufacturing flaw occurred. It then sent recall notices to all customers who had purchased the flawed tire, instructing them to visit any Firestone center for free replacement of the tires. The replacement process was carried out quickly and with a high level of customer satisfaction.

## Questions for Discussion

1. How does the customer benefit from Firestone's unified enterprise database?
2. Would having your vehicle's history available over the Web be an incentive for you to use a Firestone service center?
3. If Firestone did not maintain a unified customer-service database, how would it have recalled the flawed tires?

## 2 Part II: Zagat's Famous Restaurant and Entertainment Surveys Are Web Enabled

**Zagat**

Zagat's successful formula for surveying a city's top restaurants has made it a reliable source of information for food aficionados across the United States. Due to customer demand and the reliability of its survey and database methods, Zagat has expanded into publishing ratings for hotels, resorts, and spas across the United States as well as guides to nightlife in leading American cities.

Recently, to handle the increased volume of surveys, Zagat has implemented a Web-enabled system for capturing surveyor opinions. Now surveyors can use their PCs to submit their opinions online to a Zagat site on the Internet. The opinions are automatically captured in a database residing on Zagat's file server, thereby eliminating the need for paper and transfer of opinions into electronic form (paper surveys, however, are still accepted). A surveyor's opinions remain online until the end of a survey period, thereby enabling surveyors to retrieve and edit their comments anytime. At the end of the annual survey period, Zagat processes the database to tally the votes, review the written opinions, and produce a new guide. Zagat's Web-enabled survey process has not only been successful, but is providing a means for increasing the survey content it gathers electronically.

## Questions for Discussion

1. What benefits are gained from the Web-enabled survey process?
2. Does the Web-enabled survey process change the purpose or contents of Zagat's ratings database?
3. Do you feel the ability of surveyors to submit and then later edit their opinions online changes the quality of the Zagat restaurant and entertainment guides? Why or why not?

## 3 Part II: Jiffy Lube Mines Customer Data

**Jiffy Lube**

Each time customers bring their vehicle to a Jiffy Lube center for servicing, the staff member handling the servicing makes an entry of the visit in the company's enterprise database. While use of the database for sending promotional reminders always proved successful, the company's marketing directors sought to gain additional leverage from the amount of customer information in the database.

Jiffy Lube created a data warehouse that enables corporate and store managers to analyze the buying practices of its customers and design-focused promotional campaigns. By processing the more than 50-million records in the data warehouse using special data mining software, Jiffy Lube is able to group customers into segments and create special offers to meet their needs. For instance, if a customer only visits for oil changes and never purchases any other services, a special offer can be sent to encourage a visit for transmission service or to have the fuel injectors of their vehicle cleaned. Management then tracks the offer's effectiveness.

The data warehouse is also accessible at the store level over its Internet connection. Store managers can use the data warehouse to conduct their own analysis based on criteria appropriate to their respective regions. The Web site enables them to build on their resulting analysis by creating custom mailings for customers who have not visited recently or who are candidates for other services.

Jiffy Lube's experience with data warehouses at the enterprise and store levels demonstrates how analytical processing is an effective tool in building its business. It not only aids in keeping current customers in a highly competitive business but also enables management to use insights gained from its analysis to increase the amount of services it provides for its most valued customers.

## Questions for Discussion

1. What capabilities does Jiffy Lube's data warehouse provide that are not feasible from routine processing of its enterprise database?
2. Is the company's database and its data warehouse best described as centralized or distributed? What is the reason for your answer?
3. What factors should be evaluated to determine whether Jiffy Lube is getting a sufficient return for its investment in data warehouse and data mining activities?

## *Summary of Learning Objectives*

**1** **Identify the reasons organizations choose to share databases and the functions of a database management system.** Organizations choose to share databases because data collection and maintenance are very expensive. Managing these data effectively entails making sure all members of an organization who need them have access to a consistent set of data. The five functions of a database management system (DBMS) are (1) integrating databases, (2) reducing redundancy, (3) sharing information, (4) maintaining integrity, and (5) enabling database evolution.

**2** **Explain the difference between relational and object-oriented databases and their uses in business.** Relational databases consist of data structured in a table format consisting of rows and columns. Object-oriented databases store data and information about objects. Unlike relational databases, object-oriented databases can store actions—instructions telling the database how to process the object to produce specific information. Object-oriented databases offer the capability to store more sophisticated types of data and information than relational databases do.

**3** **Describe the differences between schemas, views, and indexes.** A schema is the structure of a database. A view is a subset of one or more databases, created either by extracting copies of records from a database or by merging copies of records from multiple databases. An index is a data file that contains identifying information about each record and its location in storage.

**4** **Discuss the benefits of client/server computing.** Client/server computing combines distributed processing and multiuser systems with database systems. All data and information retrieval requests and responses in client/server computing pass over the network. This offers several benefits to users. Because much of the processing is performed on the server, specific information—rather than complete files—is transmitted to the client. In addition to saving time and money, client/server computing makes users more productive by ensuring their access to information when they need it.

**5** **Differentiate between shared and distributed databases.** A shared database is one that is shared among many users and applications. A distributed database is a shared database whose data reside on more than one system in a network. These data can be accessed, retrieved, or updated from any node in the network.

**6** **Explain why enterprises establish data warehouses and how they differ from data marts and enterprise databases.** Data warehouses are large data stores that combine details of both current *and* historical operations, usually drawn from a number of sources. They may also contain data from external sources, including local or regional economic and demographic data acquired from public or private sources. In contrast to enterprise databases, which support ongoing transaction processing for an organization's day-to-day activities, data warehouses are designed for inquiries to support research and analysis. Data marts are smaller, narrowly focused subsets of a data warehouse focusing on a specific activity or process area.

**7** **Distinguish between a database administrator and a systems programmer.** The IT professional with the most extensive database management responsibilities is the database administrator (DBA), who is responsible for managing all the activities and procedures related to an organization's database. A systems programmer is a software and hardware specialist who works with the physical details of the database.

**8** **Discuss database administration procedures and concurrency procedures and explain why these are an essential part of a shared database system.** Database administration procedures include six areas of responsibility: (1) database planning, (2) database design, (3) database creation, (4) database maintenance, (5) analysis of usage, and (6) creation and monitoring of security procedures. In addition, concurrency procedures allow more than one user to access a database simultaneously. All these procedures are an essential part of a shared database system because they provide for an efficient, well-managed database and increased worker productivity.

# Key Terms

action 275
class 275
client 283
client/server computing 283
concurrent data sharing 300
database 270
database administration procedures 299
database administrator (DBA) 298
database directory 294
database management system (DBMS) 272
data marts 298
data mining 296
data warehouse 295
deadlock 301

distributed database 290
enterprise database 270
enterprise data model 273
entity 270
entity relationship 273
file locking 301
file server 283
functional distribution strategy 292
geographic distribution strategy 292
index 279
method 275
nonconcurrent data sharing 300
object 275
object-oriented database 275

online analytical processing (OLAP) 295
online transaction processing (OLTP) 294
partitioning 290
record key 279
record locking 301
relational database 274
replication 290
schema 274
server 284
shared database 290
view 276
Web-based integration 289

# Review Questions

1. What is a database? Why are databases shared?

2. What is the purpose of a database management system (DBMS)?

3. Describe the components of an entity relationship diagram. What is the purpose of an entity relationship diagram in the process of developing an enterprise database?

4. What is a database schema? How many schemas does each database have?

5. Discuss the relationship between an entity relationship model and the schema for a relational database.

6. How are relational and object-oriented databases different? What is an object? An action?

7. Describe the relationship between classes and methods in object-oriented databases.

8. How are object-oriented databases evolving in practice?

9. What is the purpose of a database view?

10. What is the difference between a database schema and a database view?

11. What is the function of an index?

12. What is client/server computing? What are its benefits?

13. Describe the relation between client/server computing, communications networks, and shared databases.

14. What is a distributed database? How is it related to or different from a shared database?

15. Define the two ways of distributing databases. How may a database be distributed between different locations?

16. What benefits do businesses gain from distributing databases?

17. Describe the difference between a functional distribution strategy and a geographic distribution strategy.

18. Discuss the factors that must be considered in designing a distributed database.

19. What is OLAP? How does it differ from OLTP?

20. Why do enterprises create data warehouses?

21. What is the source of a data warehouse's contents?

22. Why can't an enterprise database fulfill the functions of a data warehouse?

23. Describe the relation between a data warehouse and a data mart.

24. Why do organizations create data marts?

25. How is data mining performed and what tools are needed to carry it out?

26. What is Web-based integration, and how does it involve enterprise databases?

27. What trends underlie Web-enabled enterprise databases?

28. Describe the responsibilities of a database administrator and a systems programmer.

29. Describe the six areas of responsibility in data administration.

30. What is the difference between concurrent and nonconcurrent data sharing?

31. What is record locking and why is it used in shared database processing? What is a deadlock and how does it occur?

# Discussion Questions

1. The combined networks and services of CNN, the global television broadcast company headquartered in Atlanta (see "CNN Digital Assets" in Chapter 2) are available to more than 1 billion people in more than 212 countries and territories. CNN has over 40 bureaus around the world, each created to enable reporters, journalists, and camera operators to be near the areas likely to be the center of news.

   When events in the field and interviews are captured on film, the video content is transmitted back to Atlanta where it is edited, indexed, and added to a centralized enterprise database. Producers and editors of all network programs, whether originating in Atlanta, New York, Washington, London, or elsewhere, draw from the same central database to prepare the content for broadcast programs. This includes those distributed broadcasts over satellite channels as well as via the Internet (CNN Interactive).

   a. What advantages does CNN's practice of maintaining a centralized database of video/news offer the network?

   b. How could CNN maintain the video/news database as a distributed database, with the video content remaining at each of the global bureaus?

   c. What advantages and disadvantages would CNN encounter if it maintained a globally distributed video/news database?

2. Review the *Information Technology in Practice* feature, "Data Warehouse Powers French Railroad System."

   a. How does a data warehouse enable SNCF to make better decisions about running the railroad?

   b. In addition to questions related to ticket process and overbooking, what other issues can management address with its data warehouse?

   c. It is often said that without data warehouses, even companies with well-designed database systems spend too much time locating data and not enough time analyzing it. How can data warehouses overcome this problem?

3. Even though the Internet is widely used in business and government, organizations frequently treat Web pages as nothing more than a series of billboards containing colorful graphics or as attractive brochures. Yet, many really useful applications can be delivered over the Internet when they are designed to process and present valued information—information that often resides in enterprise databases. By connecting Web pages to databases, organizations can improve the depth, quality, and timeliness of information to customers and other interested parties.

   With so much to be gained, why haven't more organizations made the link between enterprise databases and Web pages displayed on the organization's Internet site?

4. Allegheny Ludlum Corp., a Philadelphia-based manufacturer of special steel and metals, is using IT to achieve above-average growth rates. A network that links the firm's plants in six states provides a steady flow of data and information from the shop floor to the marketing department.

   One of the company's recent strategies has been to move to relational database management systems. Why might Allegheny Ludlum want to consider instead a move to object-oriented databases? What management tool might help the company evaluate the advantages of moving to an object-oriented structure?

5. Texas-based retailer Neiman Marcus recently equipped its 27 stores and two warehouses with a set of client/server systems that will record point-of-sale data on a server within each store as well as on a host computer at central headquarters. One goal is to automate the *client book* that each sales associate presently keeps on the tastes and preferences of long-standing customers. What measures can the IT staff take to protect this confidential client data from the snooping eyes of unscrupulous employees and still ensure that sales associates have the information they need to do their jobs? What benefits does the new client/server system offer to the retailer's upper-level managers, and how might these offset the need to implement stringent security measures?

# Group Projects and Applications

## Project 1

A consulting company wishes to create an enterprise database focused specifically on its consulting projects. This database will be used to monitor project activities, the assignment of its consultants to specific projects, and to support billing of customers.

Every consultant has a name, address, birth date, employee ID, and office location. All projects have a project name, project ID, start date, and expected completion date.

All projects must have one or more consultants assigned to them and a consultant may be assigned to more than one project. However, a consultant also may not be assigned to any project at a given time. Every consultant who is assigned to a project has a specified billing rate. However, the billing rate may vary by project.

Draw an entity relationship diagram that will describe the relationships that must be incorporated into the company's project management practices.

## Project 2

Many companies are finding that enterprise databases can provide additional value to their firms if they are made accessible over the Internet's World Wide Web, that is, if they are *Web enabled*. As a result, Web enabling of legacy systems (systems, often residing on mainframe systems that have been installed and in operation for many years), and related enterprise databases is increasingly common in established companies.

Conduct interviews with a sample of manufacturing, retail, and wholesale distribution companies to determine their interest and experience in Web enablement of legacy systems. Include in your interview the following questions:

a. Which legacy systems and databases have the company chosen to Web enable and why?
b. What were the principal reasons the company decided to pursue a Web-enablement strategy for its existing systems?
c. What process was followed in creating a Web front end for these systems?
d. What has been the principal impact on the structure of the database? On use of information contained in the database?
e. What group includes the greater number of users of the Web-enabled systems: internal users or external users?

Prepare a summary of your investigation process and the results obtained. What conclusions do you draw from your investigation?

## Project 3

Arrange to visit a company or government organization that has implemented an enterprise database to learn how it manages the database. Inquire about:

a. The use of data administrators, including their responsibilities and their reporting relationship within the organization. Is there one data administrator for the database?
b. The background and experience of the data administrator.

## Project 4

A growing number of companies are creating data warehouses to gain better insight into the buying habits of their customers, and to identify ways to improve their customer relationship management (CRM). Identify four to six companies that have created data warehouse projects and arrange to interview a manager involved in the project.

Include the following questions in your interview:

a. What is the relationship between the company's CRM strategy and the creation of a data warehouse?
b. What is the focus or subject of the data warehouse?
c. Who uses the data warehouse—the sales force, call center agents, or marketing managers? What information do they seek?
d. How does current transaction data become part of the data warehouse?
e. What external data does the company include in its data warehouse, and what steps are taken to bring about its integration?
f. What has been the impact of traffic to and from the warehouse on the company's network infrastructure?
g. How does the company go about backing up the data warehouse? How often does it run a backup process?
h. What data cleansing/data scrubbing procedures does the company use?
i. What data mining, statistical analysis, and online analytical processing (OLAP) tools does the company use?

Prepare a PowerPoint presentation that describes your investigation and the results you obtained. Also include questions you have identified that merit further investigation.

## Project 5

Once your name is entered into a database, it becomes part of a massive marketing and direct-sales system. To find how names are transferred from one company to another through databases, a group of students should perform the following experiment.

Each member of the group should request a free catalog or publication. When you make the request, vary the spelling of your name. For instance, if your name is Cathy Jones, make the request under Cathi Joans. If you are John Smith, temporarily become Jon Smyth. Over the next several weeks, watch your mailbox for unsolicited advertisements bearing your assumed name.

What kinds of marketing material are you receiving? How are these materials related to the original material you requested? For example, if you requested a catalog of children's toys, you may soon find yourself receiving offers from children's portrait studios and children's book clubs, as well as coupons from diaper and toy companies.

Each member of the group should report on his or her findings to the class at the end of the semester.

## Project 6

In a group, visit a small or large company in the area. The group should then break up and individually interview various people involved with the company's database activities. One group member should interview the company's database administrator to learn more about the job. Specific questions you might ask include the following:

- What activities occupy the bulk of your time?
- How big is your database—that is, how many records does it contain?
- Is the database relational or object-oriented?
- In what ways is the database used?
- How long has the database existed? Is it fairly static, or is it expanding?
- How many workers do you support?
- What are the benefits of the distributed database to the company?
- Do you use client/server computing?
- What procedures do you follow daily, weekly, monthly?
- What are the biggest challenges of your job?

Other members of the group should interview people who use the database. Ask the following questions:

- What exactly is your job? What are your responsibilities?
- How do you use the database in the course of a day?
- How exactly do you access the data you need? Are some data classified as *confidential* or off-limits to you? If so, why?
- How does the database administrator support your efforts?
- Do you have a *wish list* for the database? Would you like the database to include views or indexes that do not currently exist? Why?

Prepare a two- to five-page summary of your interviews. Be sure to write thank-you notes to the people you have interviewed.

## Net_Work

1. Because of the growing interest in data warehouses, data marts, and data mining, many specialized vendors now provide the necessary technology. In addition, enterprise database software companies have expanded their capabilities to provide data warehouse-related products.

   You have been appointed head of a team to conduct an investigation, using the Internet, to identify potential vendors that could be of assistance for a data warehouse project. Classify the vendors by the categories of software or tools they provide. Keep in mind that a vendor may provide software or tools in more than one category.

   Prepare a report that (1) identifies and describes each category you have identified, (2) lists the principal vendors in each category, and (3) describes the differences between vendors in each category.

2. The Internet is often thought of as a huge network that interconnects people and companies. However, it also provides access to a wide range of databases. Among the publicly accessible databases on the Internet are telephone directories from around the United States and other countries of the world.

   Using any of the search engines available on the Internet (see Net_Work, Chapter 3), locate and provide the URL for any of the following databases:

   Any directory of toll-free (800 or 888) telephone numbers
   Any airline flight schedule
   Any library online card catalog
   Any theater or sports team schedule of performances or games

## Cool Mobility

### On Assignment

CIO James Marsalis appreciates the diligence with which you tackle assignments and the care you take in preparing your analyses and recommendations across a broad range of IT issues. He is consulting with you more and more, seeking your insights on questions that come to him from other employees.

### In Consultation

During your meeting, Mr. Marsalis expresses a great deal of interest in the characteristics and uses of the company's enterprise databases, especially the order database. Part of

your discussion focuses on the handling of data for the orders submitted at CoolMobility.biz. The other part concerns use of the enterprise order data for market research.

A. In preparation for a meeting on IT applications as they relate to the company's databases, Mr. Marsalis asks you to do the following:

   1. Prepare a schema for the order database. The schema should describe the data items that comprise the record. The company's order database includes customer information. Individuals and enterprises become customers once they submit an order.

In some instances, you may have to determine item specifications by examining actual data via the company Web site.

2. You should be certain to indicate which data item serves as the primary record key.

3. Also indicate what, if any, secondary keys should be defined in the schema and when they will be used.

B. Grace Ma, the director of marketing, uses the order database as a source of product summary information. The details on active and historical orders in the database reveal which products sell the most and at what time of the year.

However, now Ms. Ma wants to periodically process the company's active and historical order data to detect unnoticed trends in customer buying habits. She also has expressed interest in linking the customer's postal code to information on the economic characteristics of the area where the individual resides. Can this be accomplished using the company's order database, or do you recommend construction of a data warehouse suitable for data

mining purposes? Both Ma and Marsalis will want to know the reasoning behind your recommendation.

C. Inquiries submitted to the company by visitors to the company's *Contact Us* Web page are currently sent directly to a printer in the marketing department where a copy is printed and reviewed by a staff member. The printed copy is the *only* record of the inquiry.

During your conversation, Ms. Ma indicates that this is a poor practice. She also points out that it would quickly prove inefficient as the number of inquiries increases with the company's growing business. Noting that some areas of the inquiry are unstructured, she asks you to do the following:

1. Examine the option of capturing the inquiries in a structured database. Is it feasible to capture and store the inquiries? If so, how will the unstructured portions of the query be included in the database?

2. Other than preserving a digital copy of the inquiry, what are the benefits to the enterprise of maintaining a database of inquiries?

---

# Case Study

## Lands' End Databases Drive Direct Sales

LANDS'END
DIRECT MERCHANTS

Lands' End, headquartered in Dodgeville, Wisconsin, is one of the top direct retailers in the world. The company is well known for its traditionally styled clothing for the family, for its soft luggage, and for its products for the home. It operates in North America, the United Kingdom, Europe, and Japan, but

can serve customers anywhere in the world. A direct merchant, Lands' End deals directly with textile mills and manufacturers, eliminating the markups of intermediaries. Lands' End passes the savings on to its customers who it deals with directly—by phone, mail, fax, or the Internet—anywhere in the world. Customers benefit from lower prices as well as from more accessible and convenient shopping.

With annual sales in excess of $1.6 billion, Lands' End enjoys a reputation for high-quality products, superior customer service, and an ironclad guarantee of satisfaction. Lands' End offers one of the simplest guarantees in the industry—GUARANTEED. PERIOD.® The company allows customers to return items at any time, for any reason, for refund or replacement.

Among the most important business tools at Lands' End are its customer catalogs and its databases. The

colorful, highly illustrated catalogs have long been the primary means of contact with customers and are essential tools underlying its successful history. (The company's highly profitable Web site also features the items included in its catalogs.) Each catalog represents a Lands' End sales channel and is associated with particular types of customers. Among the catalogs it distributes are:

- ***The Lands' End Catalog*** Classic casual clothing for men and women.

- ***Lands' End Men*** A complete line of finely tailored clothing for men, from suits, ties, and dress shirts to more casual office attire.

- ***Lands' End Women*** Finely constructed, tailored clothing for the working woman; and casual classics that remain staples from season to season.

- ***Lands' End Women 18W–26W*** Clothing perfectly proportioned to fit women 18W–26W. Along with style and reassuring quality, this collection features rich, natural fibers, beautiful colors, and unsurpassed value.

- ***Lands' End Kids*** Quality clothing, freshly styled, to dress kids from head to toe. These fun, colorful classics fit newborns to pre-teens.
- ***Lands' End for School*** Uniforms and school-appropriate clothing, designed to meet dress-code requirements, in sizes for kids and adults, including Spiritwear, embroidered with your logo for sports, clubs, and organizations.
- ***Lands' End Home*** High-quality, classically styled products for the home, with a focus on honest value instead of promotional *white sales.*
- ***Lands' End Business Outfitters (Corporate Sales)*** Offers the Lands' End brand as a compelling option in clothing personalized with state-of-the-art embroidery for company incentives, rewards, gifts, and group apparel.

The Lands' End enterprise databases are also tools essential for its success. Among the most important for its sales processes are the product inventory, product pricing, and customer databases. Because of their importance to the company's livelihood, management invests substantially to maintain and safeguard these databases.

The company has not always had an enterprise customer database. For many years, Lands' End had been successful with a decentralized business model in which operating units were responsible for developing and applying their own marketing strategies. The business units also maintained their own customer databases. Although this strategy was highly successful, management of the company sought to grow the company by using its customer information more effectively. It was certain the company would be able to increase customer loyalty and in turn increase revenue. The company also wanted to address the always-present threat of other retailers using ever-more aggressive tactics in an attempt to entice away its valued customers.

Lands' End's management decided to centralize the customer data into an enterprise-wide customer database that could be shared by all business units. The enterprise database it created resides on a dedicated server (a database server) and includes more than 12-million active customers as well as some 33-million names on its complete mailing list. The enterprise database permits the company to create focused marketing campaigns that cut across all Lands' End channels, brands, and catalogs worldwide.

Creating an enterprise-wide customer database did more than produce a giant database. It resulted in substantial other benefits, including the ability to:

1. Maintain *one* customer database rather than multiple databases that often contained redundant or inconsistent information, and resided in separate business areas of the company. The result of having one customer database is consistent information about customers and their past purchases.
2. Enable marketing managers to have a better understanding of customer behavior across all channels by processing the database. Customer histories are centralized—marketing managers can know past purchases and can explore buying tendencies.
3. Shift its marketing emphasis from a product-centered strategy ("How can we create a successful marketing campaign for these products?") to a customer-centered strategy ("What products are likely to be of greatest interest to these customers?"). The database is the basis for analyzing historical customer experiences and preferences spanning several years.
4. Coordinate marketing efforts, avoiding poorly targeted catalog mailing while also creating opportunities to cross-sell. Cross-selling involves assisting customers normally shopping from one catalog to find items of interest in other catalogs.
5. Avoid customers receiving and immediately discarding unwanted catalogs because they have no personal relevance. Such cases are all too common among direct marketing merchants. Unwanted catalogs are a nuisance to the recipient and a waste of time and money for the company.

The company now mails more than 270 million catalogs annually and at the same time has reduced the mailing to customers not likely to buy from that particular catalog. Its average sales transaction per customer has risen by a substantial percentage across all channels. The added insight into customer needs and buying behavior has highlighted promising new lines of business. For Lands' End, an enterprise focus on its customers is more than a data management tool—it is a business-building resource.

### Questions for Discussion

1. What are the benefits to Lands' End of developing a shared enterprise database to replace the separate databases maintained and used by the individual business units?
2. What are the challenges of combining the contents of separately developed and maintained databases into a single enterprise database?
3. What entities and relations should comprise the company's customer database?

# *Fed Ex*

*S*ince its founding by Fred Smith, FedEx (originally Federal Express) has seen the value of time in helping its customers to distinguish their products and services. By helping its customers to be successful, the company has continually increased its success. Because of its innovative leadership, company-wide dedication to customer satisfaction, and effective use of information technology, FedEx became the first U.S. service company to win the highest honor in American business, the Malcolm Baldridge National Quality Award.

FedEx's information technology not only ensures its customers receive prompt, reliable service, but it is so unobtrusive you hardly ever see it. Here is a peek behind the scenes.

Handling over 3 million packages daily requires the largest all-cargo fleet in the industry. The FedEx Express fleet, based at the main hub in Memphis, Tennessee, includes more than 650 aircraft.

In the night skies above Memphis, a string of FedEx planes stretches beyond the horizon. One lands and another takes off every minute. Inside those hundreds of planes are thousands of containers. Every one of the millions of packages carried on a typical day is urgently needed somewhere else.

Neither the sender nor the receiver can afford to worry about whether or not it will be delivered. FedEx's control system starts when a company calls to request pickup of an outgoing package or when a package is dropped off at one of the company's 1,200 service centers, its 8,200 authorized shipping centers, or the more than 43,000 drop box locations. The airbill attached to each package is more than just a shipping label, for it also contains billing information, an important identification number, and a bar code incorporating that identification number. You might even think of it as the package's unique fingerprint.

As soon as a driver accepts the package, the bar code is scanned using a handheld scanner developed especially for FedEx. From that moment on, the package is in the FedEx system, where its every move is tracked by effective use of information technology. The highly regarded Supertracker, used by drivers for many years, is being replaced with the custom-designed PowerPad PDA.

As soon as an aircraft lands at Memphis, FedEx staff members unload it, moving packages secured by huge nets and wheeling shipping containers holding thousands of packages from the aircraft to the sorting facility.

As soon as a package hits one of the rapidly moving conveyors, it is whisked past a scanner that reads the bar-code tracking information. As it moves down the conveyor, it is routed to a staging area where it is prepared for loading onto another aircraft that will carry it onward toward its destination city. Every package is scanned electronically at least 12 times as it moves from the pickup to delivery through a series of laser scanners used throughout the FedEx network.

When FedEx's aircraft arrive at the destination city, packages are unloaded and scanned in a regional sorting center. Then they are loaded on the vehicle best suited for ultimate delivery to the customer.

Any customer can check on the location of his or her package by calling a FedEx customer representative who with a few mouse-clicks can look at the customer record using an online workstation. Or the customer can check FedEx's World Wide Web site on the Internet where, with one-click access, complete information on the package is instantly available. (You can also use the Web to schedule a pickup.) While customers can access the FedEx Web site from their PC or laptop computer, a growing number do so via handheld PDAs. With Palm PDAs, FedEx customers can access the nearest dropoff location and track shipments through the FedEx network.

What can customers ship via FedEx? Letters, packages … even automobiles. Just about anything that "absolutely positively" needs to be at the destination overnight. FedEx is successful because it helps its customers to be successful. But the company knows that it has competitors who are just as dedicated to their customers and equally committed to providing top-notch service. Hence, you can expect that additional innovations, and even more creative uses of information technology, are in the making.

# Enterprise and Personal Communications Networks

## CHAPTER OUTLINE

## LEARNING OBJECTIVES

When you have completed this chapter, you should be able to

1   Identify the reasons that multiuser systems are used in business.

2   Describe eight network service applications used in enterprises.

3   Discuss the three types of communications networks and the advantages offered by each.

4   Discuss the two types of communications channels used in networks and the ways that computers interconnect with them.

5   Identify the five transport technologies that are in widespread use in physical channel networks.

6   Describe the four forms of wireless communications.

7   Explain the role of a network operating system.

8   Discuss the activities involved in network administration.

9   Explain the three types of enterprise architectures and the advantages offered by each.

# NASDAQ Network Survives 9/11 Test

The Nasdaq, located in the Wall Street area of New York City, is the world's largest electronic stock market. It does not operate a hectic open-pit-trading floor replete with boisterous traders. Instead, it trades through its sophisticated computer and telecommunications network. This method of trading must be working—the trading volume on Nasdaq has surpassed the trading volume of the New York Stock Exchange for many years.

The Nasdaq is building the world's first truly global stock market, electronically and Internet-accessible, and open to anyone in the world, 24 hours a day. More than 500 financial firms (known as market-makers) trade on Nasdaq. Real-time trade data is transmitted to some 1.3 million users in over 80 countries.

Now people in Canada, Europe, and Japan—and soon those in Asia, Latin America, and the Middle East—can invest electronically in companies that trade over Nasdaq. Trading on Nasdaq is not limited to any fixed number of participants. This allows a large number of firms with widely different trading technologies to connect to the Nasdaq network and compete on an equal basis. By continuing to shape the new world of investing, Nasdaq is challenging the very definition of what a stock market is—and what it can be.

Nasdaq's data center consists of a family of separate systems for quotations, negotiation, trading, and reporting—all with backup processing and storage capabilities. These systems can produce up to 2,000 quotations per second, and they have handled the trading of more than 3 billion shares of stock in a single day. Nasdaq's network consists of more than 7,000 computers at more than 2,500 sites, all connected to the servers of market makers that provide information to traders.

Nasdaq also operates a Web site, Nasdaq.com. With an average of more than 7 million pages viewed each day, it is among the most popular financial sites on the Internet. The Nasdaq Web site consists of more than 400 Intel-based servers running Windows software. Investors can log on to Nasdaq.com and see how Nasdaq and other financial markets are performing, obtain quotations for stocks and other financial instruments, and view business and financial news and commentary.

The infamous September 11 terrorist attacks on the World Trade Center in New York City's Wall Street area put Nasdaq's communications architecture to its most intense test. During the attacks, many land line and wireless communications links in the Wall Street area failed. Well-known telecom companies lost key cell towers and voice switches near the site of the destruction. The reduced number of working network channel circuits were overwhelmed with much greater call volumes and network traffic as a result of people anxiously seeking to contact friends, family, and business associates.

Despite the destruction in the area, Nasdaq's network was unfaltering. Three reasons account for the continued network service: good planning and foresight, a distributed network architecture, and high-quality backup facilities.

Nasdaq's IT capabilities were designed for resilience in the fact of any conceivable type of failure. They include dual data centers, housed in different locations, and redundancy in its vastly distributed communications networks. Workstations connect to Nasdaq through at least 20 different points of presence, each with *at least* dual connections to Nasdaq's primary and secondary data centers outside of New York City and in Maryland.

Since the communications network is the heart of its day-to-day business and a central factor in accomplishing its trading mission, Nasdaq ensured that its central points of success *and* vulnerability—its communication and computing capability—were designed to withstand the toughest test. Though it could never have been anticipated during network planning, that test turned out to be 9/11.

*C*ommunications networks and IT are not luxuries but essentials in the Information Age. Information technology's communications capability provides the means for overcoming two important business barriers: distance and time. Geographic distance can hinder an enterprise's ability to deliver its product or service, monitor activities of competitors, maintain information flow between the organization and its employees, or have a physical presence in an area. Time barriers cause delays in meeting the company's goals and the customer's needs.

Network communications capabilities take on special importance when they are employed to overcome these barriers and gain a business benefit. They add value to people and the enterprise when they are used to conduct activities in ways and at locations that would be otherwise impossible.

## Principles of Communications Networks

**communication**
The sending and receiving of data and information over a communications network.

A hallmark of the Information Age is the astonishing advances in **communication,** which involves the sending and receiving of data and information over a communications network. Communications networks are the foundations of **multiuser systems,** which (as defined in Chapter 2) are systems in which more than one user shares hardware, programs, information, people, and procedures. IT professionals often refer to using a network as *resource sharing.* Here we take a close look at the need for communications networks and the role they play in enterprise and personal communications.

**multiuser system**
A communications system in which more than one user share hardware, programs, information, people, and procedures.

### Need for Communications Networks

It became clear in the 1980s that people liked using PCs, which offered several advantages over mainframes. With microcomputers, people could get quick access to data and information from their desks. They could also tailor the computer and software they used to their personal needs. Nonetheless, some managers—even some IT professionals—questioned the wisdom of heavy business investment in PCs. They claimed that PCs were underutilized. Either the PC merely emulated the dumb terminal it replaced (meaning that the built-in processing capabilities of the PC went largely unused), or it was used for a limited number of activities and for just a few minutes a day.

That was then. Now, in the twenty-first century, PCs in all their forms (including laptop and handheld computers) are being used in ways undreamed of only a decade or so ago. Many people work at them all day long, every day. Computers are constantly increasing in speed, storage capacity, and reliability while shrinking in size and cost. This *PC revolution* was brought about by several major trends in the business world, the most important of which are listed in Table 8.1.

Driven by the need to compete effectively in a global market, companies dispersed their executives and other employees throughout the world, at both company facilities and customer locations. And they turned to IT professionals for help in answering these pressing questions:

* How can we get our products to market more quickly?
* How can we more effectively share information, both internally and with other companies?

The answer was better coordination, which meant finding ways to overcome time and distance barriers between organizations and between people within organizations. Communications networks provide those capabilities.

## Role of Communications Networks

A **communications network** is a set of locations, or **nodes**, consisting of hardware, programs, and information that are linked together as a system that transmits and receives data and information. When a computer is connected to another computer, both are part of a network. Networks may link people across relatively short distances, or they may span wide areas. (The different types of networks are discussed in detail later in this chapter.)

It has become much easier to connect computers for multiuser activities. For this reason, communications networks are common today in both large and small organizations. These networks enable people and organizations to share and transmit important data and information and, in the process, to overcome barriers created by geographic distances.

Communications networks can be used in any or all of these four roles (see Table 8.2):

**communications network**
A set of locations, or nodes, consisting of hardware, programs, and information linked together as a system that transmits and receives data and information.

**node**
A communication station within a network.

| Table 8.1 Trends Driving Enterprise Networks in the Twenty-First Century |
|---|
| A growing awareness of the *international nature of science, engineering, business, and entertainment,* and the emergence of global commerce. |
| A heightened awareness of the importance of *speed* in responding to the needs and desires of consumers, customers, and suppliers, regardless of their location. It is imperative today to ensure that products and services are available when needed. |
| A new awareness that *alliances*—partnerships among enterprises—can be created so that all parties to the alliance benefit from mutual cooperation. |
| An awareness that people have to know what is happening in other areas of an enterprise, not just their own department. Instead of being concerned solely with their assigned departmental tasks, people are increasingly thinking about *cross-function processes.* Entire processes have been redesigned so that individuals focus on the complete set of tasks making up the process from beginning to end rather than on just the activities that fall within their work area. |
| A new *emphasis on the role of those companies and agencies with which the enterprise interacts,* either as customers or suppliers. Suppliers are now recognized as an integral part of an enterprise's success or failure and the satisfaction of its customers. |

| Table 8.2    **The Role of Communications Networks** | |
|---|---|
| Send and receive messages or documents electronically | • Electronic mail (e-mail)<br>• Voice mail<br>• Electronic document exchange<br>• Electronic commerce<br>• Electronic funds transfer<br>• Internet/WWW<br>• Videotex |
| Hold meetings involving participants who are at different locations | • Video conferencing<br>• Work group conferencing<br>• Internet/WWW |
| Share and distribute documents or information from a repository | • Internet/WWW |
| Establish an electronic presence | • Internet/WWW<br>• Videotex |

- Sending and receiving messages or documents electronically
- Holding meetings involving participants who are at different locations
- Sharing and distributing documents or information from a repository
- Establishing an electronic presence

These roles are fulfilled through *network services,* those applications that businesses can choose to provide on their communications networks.

The Internet and World Wide Web (WWW) applications, discussed in detail in Chapter 3, illustrate each of the roles of a communications network. Recall that an individual linked to the Internet—and its most frequently used feature, the World Wide Web—can send and receive documents of all types, including those containing sound, animation, video, and colorful graphics. Hence, you will find the Internet playing a growing role in company communications. Already it is being used more often to communicate within a company (a network application known as an *intranet*) and between companies and organizations.

## Network Service Applications

**network services**
The applications available on a communications network.

The applications available on a communications network are called **network services.** This section discusses the eight most frequently used network applications in business: (1) electronic mail, (2) voice mail, (3) videoconferencing, (4) work group conferencing, (5) electronic bulletin boards, (6) electronic funds transfer, (7) electronic data interchange, and (8) videotex.

### Electronic Mail

You probably know the game of *telephone tag.* You call someone, only to find that he or she is not in. So you leave a message. The person returns your call just when you have stepped out—to run an errand, attend a meeting, or get a cup of coffee—and leaves a message for you. When this sequence is repeated regularly, both parties can become very frustrated.

*Electronic mail,* sometimes called *e-mail,* and voice mail (discussed in the next section) are designed to avoid telephone tag and to overcome the communication barriers created by time and distance. E-mail is a service that transports text messages from a sender to one or more receivers. It ensures that your message is delivered and not lost in a mailroom or message center. When you send a message from your computer, the network transmits it to the proper destination and inserts it into the recipient's electronic mailbox, an area of space on magnetic disk in the server or host computer that is allocated for storing an individual's messages.

The recipient need not be at the computer when e-mail arrives. When the intended recipient of the message returns to the computer, he or she will be alerted, often by a flashing note, that a message is waiting in the **electronic mailbox.** The recipient can then display the message on the screen and decide whether to print it, send a response, store it for later review, or pass it along to another individual on the network.

E-mail messages that are stored on the network can be replayed at a later date. They can also be *broadcast*—that is, sent to a number of individuals simultaneously. The sender need only type the message into the system, enter the identification names of the intended recipients, and instruct the network to send the information. The e-mail system does the rest (Figure 8.1).

People can acquire e-mail capabilities in three ways: by purchasing an e-mail package, by subscribing to a public information service, and by using a university network.

- **E-mail software packages can be purchased and loaded onto a network.** Some of the packages available for the different types of networks are listed in Table 8.3. These software packages are purchased for a one-time fee. A copy is needed for each workstation that will send and receive messages.
- **E-mail capabilities are also available through commercial public data services.** For a monthly subscriber fee, plus a variable charge based on usage, you can have a mailbox established on the network. Using your identification name, others connected to the public network can send messages to you. The most widely used public data services offering e-mail are America Online (AOL), Earthlink, and Yahoo. These services, sometimes called information utilities, are based in the United States but are accessible around the world.

**electronic mailbox**

An area of space on magnetic disk in a server or host computer that is allocated for storing an individual's e-mail.

**FIGURE 8.1**

### *E-mail Network and Mailboxes*

Electronic mail sent via a network can be stored, replayed, and broadcast to other nodes on the network.

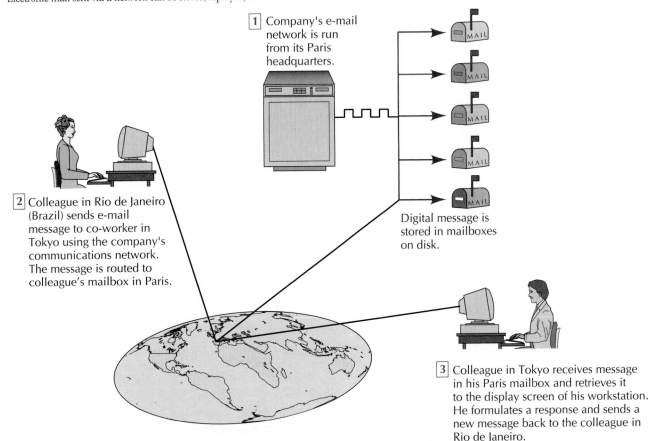

1 Company's e-mail network is run from its Paris headquarters.

Digital message is stored in mailboxes on disk.

2 Colleague in Rio de Janeiro (Brazil) sends e-mail message to co-worker in Tokyo using the company's communications network. The message is routed to colleague's mailbox in Paris.

3 Colleague in Tokyo receives message in his Paris mailbox and retrieves it to the display screen of his workstation. He formulates a response and sends a new message back to the colleague in Rio de Janeiro.

**REALITY CHECK**   The broadcast capability of e-mail is a feature included in the software that manages many networks. Broadcasting is not unique to communications networks, however. You are already familiar with this capability from two other communications media—radio and television. The terms *radio broadcast* and *television broadcast* mean that the same transmission (music, news, or multimedia information) is sent to all receiving nodes that are turned on at the time. E-mail has one advantage over radio and television broadcasting, though. An e-mail transmission can be sent to many different nodes simultaneously or it can be directed to a specific location. ■

- **University faculty and students can interconnect with the university's computer network.**   The network, in turn, is connected to external communications networks such as the Internet (including the World Wide Web). From their desktop PCs, faculty members can exchange messages and documents with other faculty within the university and with faculty members at other institutions around the world. A growing number of businesses are also linking to the Internet to send and receive messages.

Accenture, a global consulting firm, has an e-mail system that is representative of the e-mail systems used in large companies across the globe. Thousands of consultants and staff members throughout Europe, Asia, the South Pacific, and North and South America are connected to Accenture's e-mail system. A consultant can send an e-mail message to a client simply by typing in the individual's name or computer address and the message. The network locates the individual and transmits the message to the recipient's mailbox, where it is held until the client is ready to read it.

Accenture's e-mail system is used for much more than electronic conversation, however. It also drives business opportunities and new-product ideas. When consultants, project managers, or members of Accenture's management team have questions about a problem they are wrestling with, they broadcast a message across the network. For example, say the following message is sent out: "An important Accenture customer wishes to interconnect its home office in Atlanta, Georgia, with a manufacturing site in Jakarta, Indonesia, but has not worked with any communications carriers servicing that region. What experiences have Accenture partners and staff members had with any carriers providing service in the area, good or bad? What advice do you have about approaching the carriers?" In a few hours, the individual who transmitted the message will probably have a wide variety of detailed responses to the inquiry in his or her electronic mailbox—responses that will help the customer get accurate and timely advice from Accenture on

| Table 8.3 | Widely Used E-Mail Software Packages |
|---|---|
| Eudora Express | A popular application used to interconnect desktop computers with the Internet |
| GroupWise | A widely used enterprise application that usually operates over a local area network |
| MSN/Hotmail | A Microsoft Web-based e-mail service |
| Netscape | An e-mail application running within the well-known Netscape Internet browser |
| Outlook | A Microsoft e-mail application that is included with Windows software packages |
| Pine | A shareware program, developed at the University of Washington, designed for use with the Internet |
| PROFS | An acronym for Professional Office Systems, an IBM software package used for many years with host-based networks. White House staff members were among the first users of this package. PROFS is seldom used now, having largely been replaced by the preceding alternatives. |

how to capitalize on an important business opportunity. Moreover, the electronic conversation can continue between selected team members as additional questions are posed or as more complex problems arise.

## Voice Mail

Messages created in *text* form are sent through a network via e-mail. But businesses also use **voice mail** systems, which capture, store, and transmit spoken messages. Voice mail systems use an ordinary telephone connected to a computer network. A sender enters a message by speaking into the telephone, and this message is transformed from analog to digital form (digitized) and then stored in the recipient's voice mailbox (Figure 8.2). Later, the recipient can use a phone to dial into the system and retrieve the stored message, which is reconverted to analog signals and played back over the telephone. As with e-mail, voice messages can be broadcast to others on the network, stored on the network, or replayed.

Voice mail systems are available worldwide, some from computer vendors, others from providers of telephone equipment, and still others from telephone companies or **PTTs (post, telephone, and telegraph companies**–a general term for telephone companies outside the United States). Many of these systems run on a local or wide area network. However, some organizations keep their voice mail system separate from their computer networks.

Although voice mail is quite popular, some people are reluctant to use its capabilities because they do not like talking to a computer or a recording. Others find the process of retrieving or replaying messages too cumbersome. IT professionals will need to address these concerns if voice mail is to continue to expand.

When the events of 9/11 disrupted business and personal travel plans, the airlines were suddenly faced with massive ticketing and schedule changes. Every airline faced the monumental problem of handling incoming calls from passengers as well as communicating fundamental schedule changes to customers. United Airlines sought to use its call centers to contact already booked customers but quickly realized that the challenge was overwhelming. Staff members recognized that trying to catch customers in their office or at home could take weeks. The airline needed a better, faster solution.

United Airlines turned to an automated calling system that delivered *personalized* messages to customers' homes. The voice mail system was able to call the customers' home phones and communicate a high-quality voice message. It included touch-tone confirmation and message replay features to assist customers in verifying the message. The system had the ability to sense answering machines and voice mail systems in order to leave the message on these systems. United's ability to implement this system quickly

**voice mail**
A system that captures, stores, and transmits spoken messages using an ordinary telephone connected to a computer network.

**PTTs (post, telephone, and telegraph companies)**
A general term for telephone companies outside the United States.

**FIGURE 8.2**
***How Voice Mail Works***

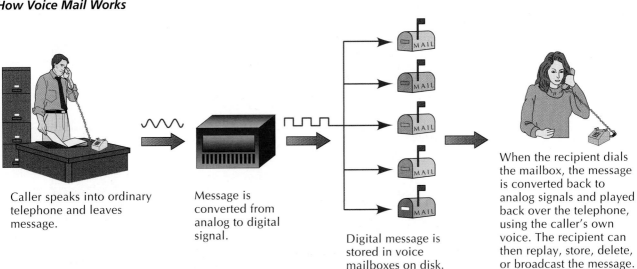

Caller speaks into ordinary telephone and leaves message.

Message is converted from analog to digital signal.

Digital message is stored in voice mailboxes on disk.

When the recipient dials the mailbox, the message is converted back to analog signals and played back over the telephone, using the caller's own voice. The recipient can then replay, store, delete, or broadcast the message.

met both customer and airline needs, with a fraction of the time and cost compared to making live outbound calls.

Many voice mail systems are evolving into **unified messaging systems.** These systems offer users the ability to manage several communications media, including telephone, fax, e-mail (including those from the Web), and voicemail through a central message manager (Figure 8.3). Rather than having to check each message source individually, unified messaging makes it possible to receive them from a single site. Users can connect to the unified messaging system, which may be operated by a company's IT group or by an outside service. Using virtually any communications device (for example mobile telephone, laptop computer, Internet browser, or pager), they can view, listen or organize the message, choosing to forward, copy, store, erase or take other actions with it. The popularity of unified messaging, a recent communications innovation, is growing rapidly, proving to be a valuable tool for busy professionals.

## Videoconferencing

Audio and visual communications come together in **videoconferencing,** a type of conferencing in which video cameras and microphones capture sight and sound for transmission over a communications network (Figure 8.4). Videoconferencing makes it possible to conduct meetings with the full participation of group members who are hundreds, even thousands, of miles apart. People interconnected this way see one another *live* on large display screens.

Videoconferencing is more than a two-way audio and video system, though. Because computers can be linked to the videoconferencing network, documents and images stored on magnetic or optical devices are accessible to conference participants. Information retrieved from a central database or entered into a computer or server linked to the network can be transmitted to all conference locations simultaneously. And the parties to the videoconference do not have to use computers or terminals to participate in discussions. Rather, they can express their ideas verbally, with microphones capturing their comments and passing them to the network for transmission.

**unified messaging systems**
Offers users the ability to manage several communications media, including telephone, fax, e-mail (including those from the Web), and voicemail through a central message manager.

**videoconferencing**
A type of conferencing in which video cameras and microphones capture the sight and sound of participants for transmission over a network.

**FIGURE 8.3**
*Unified Messaging*
Rather than having to check each message source individually, unified messaging makes it possible to receive them from a single site

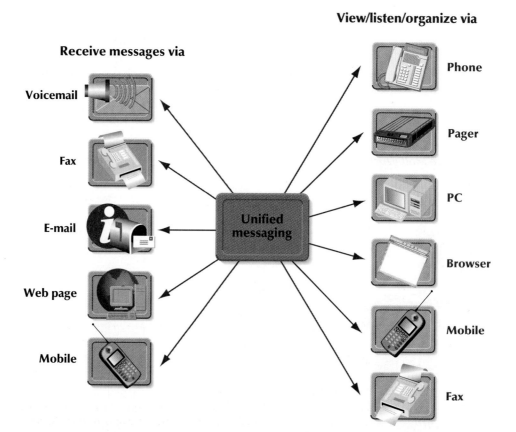

**Receive messages via**

Voicemail

Fax

E-mail

Web page

Mobile

**View/listen/organize via**

Phone

Pager

PC

Browser

Mobile

Fax

Unified messaging

**FIGURE 8.4**

***Vidoeoconferencing***

Pediatric cardiologists at the University of Kansas Medical Center use video-conferencing equipment to monitor the heartbeat of a patient 300 miles away. The screen on the left shows the patient's electrocardiogram.

Air Products Europe, headquartered outside London, frequently conducts videoconferences with its home office in Allentown, Pennsylvania. A videoconference facility at each site uses satellite communications to put executives and managers separated by the Atlantic Ocean in touch with one another. The facilities, which cost less than $100,000 each, have not only eliminated many time-consuming cross-ocean trips but have also increased communication and information sharing among key executives. Air Products Europe's executives say they can no longer imagine running their business without videoconferencing.

Kmart, the $36 billion U.S. discount retailer with some 1,500 stores nationwide, operates a videoconferencing system linking its store managers to its headquarters in Troy, Michigan. The company regularly broadcasts live satellite transmissions from Troy to all of its stores. Interactive presentations by senior executives enable store managers out in the field to pose questions by telephone and hear immediate responses over the network.

A growing number of enterprises are turning to webcasting as a vehicle for conducting video conferences. **Webcasting** uses the reach of the Internet to link people from anywhere in the world into a conference. They need not be at a specially equipped facility, as with traditional video conferencing, but rather can be anywhere they can use the Internet. The entire conference can be viewed via their computer or PDA display screen, and they can express their comments through built-in or individual attached digital Web cameras and microphones.

Webcasting takes advantages of the capability of browser software to display several windows simultaneously. Hence, a web cast participant's display screen may include a window for video, one for a Power Point slide presentation, another for video clips, and still another for live real-time chatting (Figure 8.5). Webcasting makes it possible for colleagues, vendors, investors or customers to participate in briefings, demonstrations, training, or marketing events, all without leaving home. An enterprise may choose to conduct its own web cast or to work with a service provider specializing in conducting web casts.

## Work Group Conferencing

**Collaborative conferencing,** also called **work group conferencing,** uses a type of software package called groupware to organize an electronic meeting in which participants' computers are interconnected from their various locations. The participants may be in the same room, linked by a local area network, or geographically dispersed and interconnected over a wide area network. The electronic conference centers on the entry of ideas, comments, suggestions, and the retrieval and display of information. Typically, each participant interacts through a microcomputer directly linked to a computer acting as a server (servers

**webcasting**
Uses the reach of the Internet to link people from anywhere in the world into a conference.

**collaborative conferencing/ work group conferencing**
A type of conferencing that uses a software package called groupware to interconnect participants' computers at their various locations. Participants interact through a microcomputer directly linked to a server and their comments are broadcast to all others taking part in the conference.

**FIGURE 8.5**

*Webcasting*

Webcasting uses the reach of the Internet to link people from anywhere in the world into a conference. The use of multiple windows on a display screens permits simultaneous viewing of live images of participants and various forms of information.

are discussed later in this chapter). The individual's typed comments are then broadcast to other participants in the conference and stored for later analysis (Figure 8.6).

Work group systems are ideal for bringing far-flung individuals together via the network to tackle a problem. The group gets the benefit of shared thinking and distribution of information without the costs and time involved in travel.

Groupware and videoconferencing capabilities will likely be merged into a single service in the not-too-distant future. Experts expect this type of conferencing to retain the name *groupware* or *group support systems.*

## Electronic Bulletin Boards

**electronic bulletin board**

A network service application that allows messages and announcements to be posted and read. It is accessed by dialing a telephone number and interconnecting with the bulletin board through a modem.

**Electronic bulletin boards** came into widespread use along with desktop computers and have since moved to the Internet. The electronic version of a bulletin board is similar to the bulletin board at the supermarket where you post or read messages and announcements. To use an electronic bulletin board, you simply dial into the board over a communications link and leave a message, a file, or a program. Others dialing into the bulletin board can retrieve the information and copy it into their system.

**FIGURE 8.6**

*Work Group Conferencing*

Groupware facilitates the online sharing of information between participants in a conference, whether they are across the room or around the world.

Creating a stand-alone bulletin board requires only four things: a computer, a telephone line, a bulletin board program, and a telephone modem. Callers can dial the telephone number of the bulletin board and interconnect with it through the modem. The bulletin board program monitors who is calling, connects the caller, inserts or copies information, and disconnects the caller at the end of the session. Many bulletin board programs also provide password screening to ensure that only approved individuals can gain access to the files and databases maintained within the system.

Today, bulletin boards are almost always designed to be accessible over the Internet. As discussed in Chapter 3, which focuses on the Internet, a Web site dealing with a specific topic is created and users can visit the site to share and retrieve information.

Electronic bulletin boards are commonly used to share information among members of clubs and organizations (Figure 8.7). However, many companies are finding them to be an excellent vehicle for distributing product and service information to actual or potential customers. Best of all, the cost of creating a bulletin board is low: Good software is available for under $100.

Before software giant Microsoft markets a new-generation Windows operating system, it tests the software for several years to ensure that both its features and its performance will be suitable for the intended users. Because changes are made continually throughout the months prior to its release for public sale, Microsoft needs quick and efficient ways to keep software testers around the world informed as well as a way to distribute program changes.

Microsoft originally began this practice by maintaining a private computer bulletin board it established on the CompuServe network. Today it uses a Web site. Testers access the site and, with the proper identification information, can peruse any of the following messaging sections and libraries about the new system:

- **Messaging Sections**
  **Forum News**   Announcements and news posted by Microsoft
  **Open Discussion**   Technical support from Microsoft support engineers and peer-to-peer interaction among tester sites, regardless of international location
- **Libraries**
  **Upload Bug Reports**   Tester submission of problem reports to Microsoft
  **Software Changes**   Updates and files posted by Microsoft that testers could download to their computers

The beneficial freewheeling exchange of information and software that goes on throughout the extensive testing period for the next Windows software generation would not be possible without this network application.

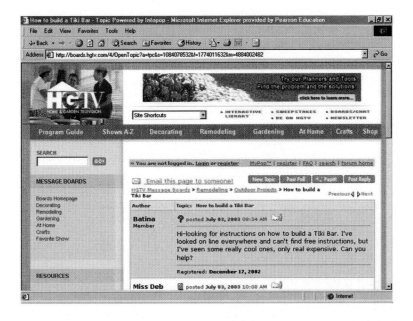

**FIGURE 8.7**

***Electronic Bulletin Boards***

Electronic bulletin boards are often used to share information among members of a community, club, or organization. Many companies also use them to facilitate communication among their employees and to distribute product and service information to their customers.

## Electronic Funds Transfer

Within the world's banking community, information is transferred much more often than money is. Seldom do actual coins and paper currency move. But *information about money transfers* moves all the time—often instantaneously.

**electronic funds transfer (EFT)**

The movement of money over a network.

**Electronic funds transfer (EFT)** is the movement of money over a network. In banking, a clearinghouse accepts transfer transactions and settles accounts for both the sending bank and the receiving bank. Automated teller machines also make use of EFT.

EFT settles credit-card transactions by transferring funds between the seller and the issuer of the credit card. It is also used to deposit payroll checks and government support checks directly into an individual's bank account. It is certain that there will be even less movement of actual cash in the future as more funds are transferred electronically.

The electronic movement of money (or, rather, information about money) depends on communications networks. Of particular importance here are networks of automated teller machines (ATMs), which provide customers with access to their money around the clock at thousands of locations away from the bank itself. An international automated teller network called the PLUS ATM network enables cardholders to obtain cash almost anytime and anywhere by using their credit or debit cards on any ATM machine.

Say you are getting ready for an evening out with friends: dinner and a bit of late-night entertainment. A quick look at your wallet tells you that you need more cash to make it through the evening. No problem. You simply stop by an ATM on your way to dinner. These machines seem to be everywhere today. They are made possible by reliable and efficient communications networks. When you stop at the ATM of your choosing, you insert your plastic credit or debit card (they are becoming virtually indistinguishable), enter your identification information, and specify the amount of money you want. The cash and a receipt of the transaction are dispensed immediately. Behind the machine, the details of the transaction are routed over an invisible communications network of processors back to your bank, where they are stored on magnetic disk, and your account is adjusted to reflect the transaction. The ATM you used probably did not belong to the bank, but rather was part of a large network, such as PLUS which offers similar services and capabilities.

The PLUS network is large. Some 800,000 PLUS ATMs are scattered throughout nearly 130 countries and territories of the world. More than 1 billion cards can access the PLUS worldwide network.

A single connection to the PLUS network (Figure 8.8) allows the network's customers, which include banks and a vast array of merchants, to use their ATMs to service their customers. PLUS can capture Visa, Discover, American Express, Diners Club, the Armed Forces Financial Network, CIRRUS, and MasterCard transactions in the United States, plus a wide assortment of credit and debit cards from around the world.

For the individual consumer, PLUS provides convenience in the form of ready access to money anytime. For the banks and merchants who use the system, PLUS provides services that help them satisfy their customers. In addition, they get online processing and settlement of sales and credit transactions, along with management and statistical reporting, from PLUS.

All parties benefit from the rapid transfer of funds through such networks. Their usage around the world continues to grow (Figure 8.9).

Debit cards, an alternative to the familiar credit cards, were designed to eliminate the need for people to carry money. When making a purchase, the cardholder inserts her debit card into an electronic reader (Figure 8.10) and keys in her personal authorization number, thereby directing her bank to transfer funds equal to the amount of purchase from her account to that merchant's bank. The transfer, which occurs immediately, is an information exchange: A message is sent over the network interconnecting the debit card reader, the cardholder's bank, and the merchant's bank telling each bank to change the information describing the amount of money in each account.

**electronic data interchange (EDI)**

A form of electronic communication that allows trading partners to exchange business transaction data in structured formats that can be processed by applications software.

## Electronic Data Interchange

E-mail is the transmission of text messages. **Electronic data interchange (EDI)**, in contrast, is a form of electronic communication that allows trading partners to exchange

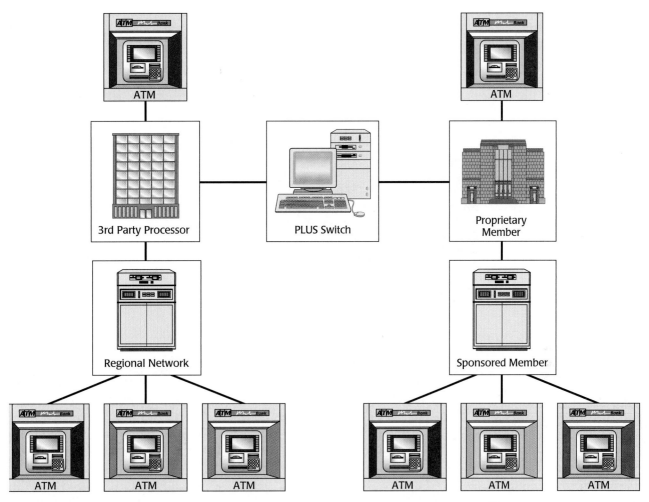

**FIGURE 8.8**
***ATM Network Configurations***

**FIGURE 8.9**
***ATM Networks Link Regional, National, and International Banks***

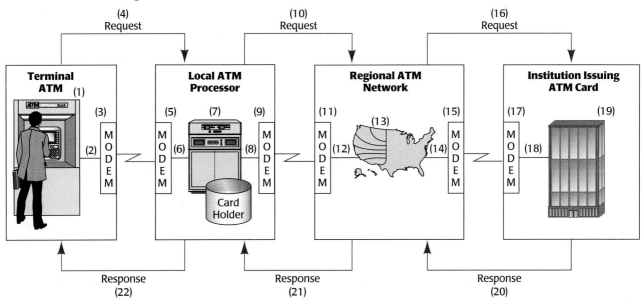

business transaction data in structured formats that can be processed by applications software. In industries from transportation to automobile manufacturing to retailing, companies are using EDI to reduce the time needed to transfer business information and to obtain products and services. Approximately one-third of all business documents, including purchase orders, invoices, and payments, are moved by EDI (Figure 8.11).

EDI often uses network service providers that offer communications services designed specifically for EDI. *Translation software* interacts with the computer to transform data from the format stored in a company's database into a form that can be transmitted. Translation software on the other end changes the received information into the form required by the receiving company.

In the pharmaceutical industry, California-based Bergen Brunswig Corp., a unit of AmeriSource Bergen Corp. (Figure 8.12), relies on its EDI-based Electronic Partnership Program to maintain strong links with its suppliers. The purchase orders and subsequent invoices and payments that Bergen Brunswig interchanges with its vendors account for nearly all of the merchandise distributed by the company. The company's business goal of dealing electronically with 100 percent of its suppliers is based on its desire to develop more accurate and timely ordering practices that will reduce inventory levels and

**REALITY CHECK** Do not be surprised to see people using cash even less frequently in the future. Although the well-established credit card already substitutes for cash in many instances, and debit cards will become more and more common, another alternative is in the offing: *digital cash.* Every year, more than $2 trillion is spent worldwide on purchases of $10 or less. Many of these transactions involve a face-to-face exchange of coins and paper money. Digital cash is emerging as an alternative for those who neither want to pay by credit nor draw small amounts of money out of their account through debit cards. Here is how it works: You buy a card that contains a predetermined digitally recorded value. Then each time you purchase something, you pay for it by having the amount deducted from the balance on your cash card.

Digital cash began in the form of public telephone and transit cards, which are widely used in many European cities. For example, each time you make a phone call, you insert the cash card into the appropriate slot on the public telephone. At the end of the call, the digital reader inside the telephone deducts the cost of the telephone call from the balance on your card and writes a new balance—digitally, of course. Digital cash is on the way. ■

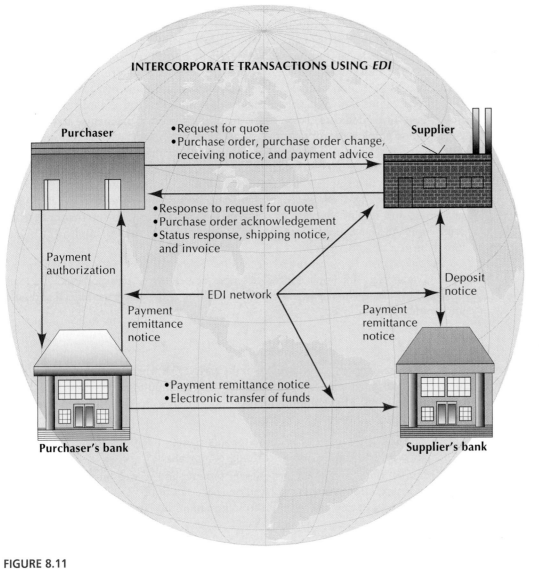

**FIGURE 8.11**

***Electronic Data Interchange***

EDI greatly simplifies business transactions by allowing trading partners to exchange data in structured format.

**FIGURE 8.12**

***Bergen Brunswig***

Many firms dedicate sizable staffs to tracking orders, payments, or shipping papers, working against diverse time zones and business customs.

improve cash management. In an industry where the average after-tax profit is less than 1.5 percent, electronic opportunities can mean the difference between a profit and a loss. The time needed to process orders also diminishes when EDI is used: Drug wholesalers using EDI have reduced the order/delivery cycle by over 50 percent.

The role of EDI is rapidly increasing in international commerce. Two obstacles dramatically affect the more than $2 trillion of international trade that takes place annually: the enormous flow of paperwork and delays in the transit of goods and information. Many firms dedicate sizable staffs to tracking orders, payments, and shipping papers; these employees work against diverse time zones and business customs. Some estimates suggest that the flow of paperwork in international trade creates costs equal to 7 percent of the value of the product traded. In this area, then, the benefits of EDI can be enormous. When shippers, transporters, customs agents, and customers send documents electronically, they overcome the barriers posed by geographic distance. This saves time and money. Because EDI makes such a difference in international trade, some companies have told their suppliers to *link up or lose out*—that is, implement EDI or lose them as a customer.

The *Information Technology in Practice* feature, "Schneider National's Success Depends on Innovative Network Applications," describes how this large transportation and logistics company has reached new performance levels through effective use of EDI and satellite communications links.

## Videotex

**videotex**

A two-way, interactive, text-only service operating on mainframe computers that combines a video screen with easy-to-follow instructions.

British Telecom gave birth to **videotex** in the early 1970s when it developed a two-way, interactive, text-only service operating on mainframe computers. The system, which preceded development of the public Internet and World Wide Web, quickly evolved to include two essential features:

1. An easy-to-use interface that allows people to select options through successive menus providing choices and English-like commands.
2. Medium-resolution graphics that present product and service information visually. On videotex, information is displayed one page at a time. People using videotex systems can both review and respond to information displayed on their computers or terminals.

This interactive system was used to provide a variety of business services:

- Sony Corp. created a sales support videotex system that allows personnel to place orders, fill out expense accounts, and receive messages. Sales agents respond to information displayed on the screen by filling in an electronic form or by answering inquiries with short statements.
- The Motor Vehicle Department of British Columbia (Canada) videotext system was designed to test driver's license applicants. Multiple-choice questions regarding driving laws and practices are presented on the videotex screen at the testing center. As applicants responded to each question, the system checked their responses against the correct answers stored on the host computer. Would-be drivers passed the videotex portion of the exam before proceeding with a road test.
- In the 1980s, the Buick Motor Division of General Motors created a database of more than 2,000 videotex pages describing automobile specification and design options. Interacting through a computer terminal, a salesperson and customer together selected different options and determined the price and availability of the vehicle. The initial success of this Electronic Product Information Center (EPIC) led to an advanced version that allows people to see the automobile with chosen color, trim, and options displayed on the screen. When sales staff and customers were not using EPIC, the system automatically displayed a series of videotex advertising pages.

At one time, videotex was growing into a data communications network for home shopping whereby customers were able to peruse video display catalogs of merchandise, complete with price and product specifications. If they wished to buy something, they entered their order and payment information directly into the videotex system, and the

# INFORMATION TECHNOLOGY IN PRACTICE
## Schneider National's Success Depends on Innovative Network Applications

**SCHNEIDER NATIONAL** Schneider National Inc., founded in 1935 and still privately owned, is the leading provider of premium truckload and companion train or ship (that is, intermodal) services with annual revenues in excess of $2 billion. As North America's largest private truckload carrier, headquartered in Green Bay, Wisconsin, Schneider National moves freight and offers innovative services that are designed to solve customers' transportation needs. In its transportation network, Schneider National (which often refers to itself as *the orange, on-time machine*) currently operates its own 14,000 trucks and 40,000 trailers and has partnerships with over 6,000 carriers. Its bright orange trucks travel more than 5-million-loaded miles per day. Schneider's services, operated out of 36 locations in North America, are used by two-thirds of Fortune 500 companies.

Schneider's backbone communications network is comprised of a mix of frame-relay transport technology and dedicated high-speed T-1 wide area network connections, coupled with an Ethernet backbone for the local area network at its headquarters campus. Schneider also relies heavily on two-way satellite links, EDI networks and the Internet for other communications needs.

Schneider National is widely recognized for its effective use of IT and network communications, having received the industry's most prestigious awards for its innovations. Its fully integrated satellite tracking systems give the company and its customers real-time visibility to shipments by its VSAT-equipped trucks. Each time a truck is electronically polled, by sending a signal to the truck's VSAT in order to determine its location, the location information is immediately updated in Schneider's *Track and Trace* database. Truck pollings are automatically generated every two hours or customer service representatives can poll a truck on demand to determine its location. Updates can be received from shippers, carriers, and consignees, as well.

Schneider is also testing an application that tracks the status of its trailers. Using GPS (Global Positioning System) satellite equipment that feeds status information, Schneider is able to determine the location of a trailer and whether it is full, empty, or still hooked to a tractor.

Schneider National is widely recognized for its leadership in EDI implementation in the trucking industry. It has more than 1,200 trading partners (customers and other transportation companies) with which it exchanges EDI transactions through a value-added network (VAN) or on a secure Internet connection. Its volume of EDI activity is high, including the following:

- More than 1 million EDI transactions processed per month
- 5,000 loads per day are offered (that is, tendered) by customers
- 3,000 invoices per day electronically received by customers

The company relies on transportation-industry-set EDI transaction standards for load tendering, response to load tendering, shipment status notification, freight bill, and remittance advice. Virtually all shipping notices (called waybills) sent electronically to railroads partnering with Schneider National are in the industry-standard format.

Because the benefits EDI are substantial for all participants, Schneider's EDI team assists new customers in adopting EDI at no charge. It has created a set of implementation guidelines including transaction specifications based on transportation industry standards and best-practice information. This way, trading partners can get up and running with EDI quickly and effectively.

The bulk of Schneider's business is conducted through EDI because it allows companies to transport large volumes of data in a standardized format. However, the Internet is of growing importance. In fact, Schneider's IT managers have stated that all of the company's future services will be built

"to execute within a browser," that is, to capitalize on the Internet and Internet browser software (such as Internet Explorer and Netscape Communicator). The goal is to run the entire shipping transaction—order offer, acceptance, pickup, delivery, billing, payment, and reporting, by way of the Internet.

Schneider has created a set of Internet shipping tools (programs) and a secured Internet site (www.schneider.com). More than 2,000 Schneider customers use the Web site to manage their transportation, including tender-

ing loads, tracking a shipment's progress and retrieving documents, all with the click of a mouse. No telephone inquiries are needed.

Schneider National's justly earned reputation for getting freight from here to there is a direct result of its innovative use of communications networks. You might say the company's success lies in two intertwined networks—a physical network of over-the-road trucks and an electronic network of information. Both were built for service and impact.

payment funds were transferred automatically from their bank account to the vendor (Figure 8.13). Cable television companies provided most of the videotex shopping services.

Although videotex is still in use in parts of the world, the trend is to move these applications onto the Web where they will be easily accessed over the Internet. These business-to-consumer and business-to-business applications, included within the broader category of e-commerce, are discussed in greater detail in Chapter 9.

The eight network application services discussed here are providing businesses and the people they serve with an effective means for overcoming time and distance barriers. In many cases, the network is the system, for it not only connects sites, but also directs the movement of information, routing it from one location to another. Without the network, there could not be a system for collaboration, exchanging messages, or moving other types of data and information.

But what exactly is a communications network and how do PCs, ATMs, and other devices work with a network? Just how do they interconnect devices and people across the hall or around the world? The next section examines these questions.

**FIGURE 8.13**
*Videotex*

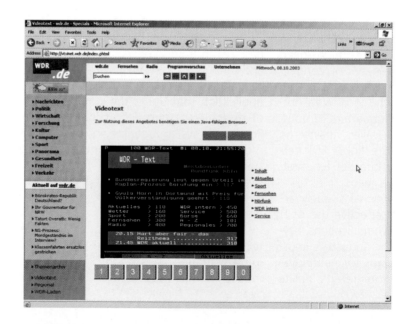

# Types of Networks

Networks come in three configurations, or **topologies** (Figure 8.14). The type of connection and the span of the network define the three types of networks: (1) wide area, (2) local area, and (3) metropolitan area.

**topology**

A network configuration, or the arrangement of the nodes or workstations of a network in relation to one another.

## Wide Area Networks

When companies and governments must interconnect sites dispersed across states, countries, or continents, they develop **wide area networks (WANs).** The following companies make use of WANs:

**wide area network (WAN)**

A network that connects sites dispersed across states, countries, or continents.

- London-based British Petroleum runs a worldwide WAN linking its data centers in order to provide information about oil and exploration, energy distribution, and chemical research and development to employees around the globe (Figure 8.15). The network links hundreds of company sites in North and South America, Europe, and Asia. The company's main data center in Glasgow, Scotland, is linked by communications channels to major business centers in Aberdeen, Glasgow, London, and Stavanger (Norway); U.S. hubs in Houston, Cleveland, and Anchorage; and South American hubs in Caracas (Venezuela) and Bogotá (Colombia). Business centers in Moscow and Jakarta (Indonesia) can also communicate with the main data center in Glasgow through the firm's wide area network. The network is designed to enable individuals at any location to operate as if they were at the host computer site.
- Toys *R* Us operates a WAN that links the following: some 700 toy stores in the United States; more than 500 international toy stores in Europe and Asia; more than 400 Kids *R* Us and Babies *R* Us stores; and 42 Imaginarium stores. The system is designed to allow 30,000 employees to share inventory and sales information and to send messages to one another via electronic mail. This multilevel network interconnects each store to one of 19 regional centers located around the world. Information is then routed from the center to company headquarters in Paramus, New Jersey. Toys *R* Us is

**FIGURE 8.14**

### *The Topology of Networks*

The topology of a network is its shape—the arrangement of the nodes or workstations of a network in relation to one another. In determining which structure to use, network designers consider the distance between nodes, the frequency and volume of transmissions, and processing capability at each node.

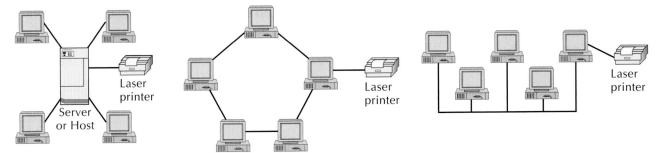

The *star topology* interconnects many different sites through a central computer system (a server). The central computer is typically a mainframe. Nodes may be other mainframes, midrange systems, or microcomputers. Sending a message from one node to another entails sending the message to the central server or host computer first, which receives and retransmits the message to the intended destination.

In the *ring topology,* each node is connected to an adjacent node. There is no central node. A message is sent from one node through the network. Each location examines the identification code in the message (which is inserted by network software) and accepts the message if it has the code. Otherwise, it transmits the message to the next node. The process continues until the message reaches its destination.

The *bus topology* is a linear network—a "data highway," so to speak. All nodes tap onto the bus. Data transmissions from one node are sent to every other node on the network. Each node examines the identification code, accepting those messages containing its code and ignoring the others.

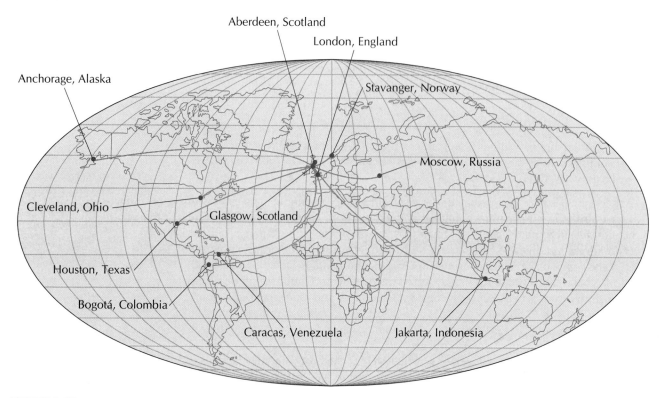

**FIGURE 8.15**

*British Petroleum's Global Wide Area Network*

London-based British Petroleum's WAN linking its data centers and providing information to employees around the globe. The network links hundreds of sites in North and South America, Europe, and Asia to the company's main data center in Glasgow, Scotland.

also building a special network that will eventually allow the direct broadcast of information to each store via satellite.

- Levi Strauss, the San Francisco–based clothing manufacturer and retailer, has a PC-based cash register in each of its stores. A network known as Levi Link captures all sales transactions, and at the end of the day, it sends details of these sales to a computer at headquarters. There the information is analyzed to determine what has been sold, which items must be shipped to replenish inventory at the store, and what goods need to be manufactured. Levi Link helps to keep the stores fully stocked, thus giving them a sales advantage over competitors that use manual inventory methods.

In the Levi Strauss example, information must travel over distances that are far too long to be spanned by a single cable linking one location to another. For this reason, *teleprocessing* is frequently used in wide area networks. The telephone lines used to link different sites to a central computer are generally not owned by the company, but rather are leased from a telephone or communications company. Another type of transmission link for wide area networks, called fiber-optic cables, will be discussed later in the *Network Channels* section.

A company furnishing public communications transmission services for voice and data transmission is called a **common carrier.** The most visible common carriers in the United States are AT&T, WorldCom, and Sprint. Common carriers in other countries include BT (formerly British Telecom) in the United Kingdom, France Télécom, Duetsch Telecom in Germany, and Nippon Telephone and Telegraph (NTT) in Japan.

**common carrier**

A company that furnishes public communications facilities for voice and data transmission.

**Bandwidth**   The speed at which information is transmitted over a communications medium is determined by bandwidth. A greater bandwidth means that more information is sent through a medium in a given amount of time. The bandwidth of a network is measured (indirectly) by the bits of data transmitted per second:

# CRITICAL CONNECTIONS 1

## Havertys Furniture Redesigns Network for Top Performance

**Havertys Furniture**

Havertys Furniture Companies Inc., with annual sales of more than $500 million, is the fourth largest independent furniture dealer in the United States. Its three data centers support the company's 129 stores located throughout 14 Southeastern states.

All Havertys stores are connected to the company's data centers for order entry, inventory management, and other business applications. As a result of the company's growth and increased business volume, its original communications network—featuring leased communications lines—was characterized by unacceptably slow response times. As much as 10 seconds passed before the system responded to transactions entered by store sales and clerical staff, all because of the network.

Since the data centers feature IBM equipment, the company wanted to retain IBM's System Network Architecture (SNA) in its new communications network. Havertys' IT group ultimately installed a new network featuring TCP/IP protocol over a frame-relay communications channel for its SNA computers. The network met the need for speed and reliability while also enabling Havertys to standardize on a single networking protocol across all of its computing applications.

- **Kilobits per Second (kbps)**   Thousands of bits of information per second
- **Megabits per Second (mbps)**   Millions of bits per second
- **Gigabits per Second (gbps)**   Billions of bits per second

Hence, a transmission at 56,600 bits per second, a common speed for dial-up transmission of data from a PC to a server or mainframe over a wide area network, is said to be at 56.6 kilobits per second.

Corporations often develop high-speed WANs that transmit over networks using a **T-carrier,** a very high-speed channel designed for use as the backbone of a network and for point-to-point connection of locations. A *backbone* is a high-speed transmission link that interconnects lower-speed networks or computers at different sites. Transmission rates for U.S. T-carriers are as follows: T-1 lines at 1.544 mbps; T-2 at 6.312 mbps; T-3 at 44.736 mbps; and T-4 lines at 274.176 mbps. Outside of the United States and Japan, T-carriers are known as *PCM carriers.*

After fiber optics were invented in the late 1970s to early 1980s (thereby enabling data to be sent over glass fibers rather than copper cables), AT&T began to use lasers to transmit the digital information as a beam of concentrated light, thus greatly increasing speeds. (The speed of light is much faster than the speed of electricity.) You may also hear about OS-1 and OS-3, which refer to fiber-optic channels. These channels serve the same function as T-carriers, but are given a different name because of their circuitry and

**T-carrier**

A very-high-speed channel designed for use as the backbone of a network and for point-to-point connection of locations.

resulting bandwidth. The OC-1 is one pair of optic cables. It can transmit slightly faster than a T-3, at 51.840. The OC data rates are as follows:

| | |
|---|---|
| OC-1 | 51.840 mbps |
| OC-3 | 155.250 mbps |
| OC-9 | 466.560 mbps |
| OC-12 | 622.080 mbps |
| OC-18 | 933.120 mbps |
| OC-24 | 1.244 gbps |
| OC-36 | 1.866 gbps |
| OC-48 | 2.488 gbps |
| OC-96 | 4.976 gbps |
| OC-192 | 10 gbps |

Optical cables have a much farther range than the T-carrier systems. On T-carriers, repeaters (devices that receive and resend digital messages) are needed every mile to keep the signal strength up and the noise down. Optics can have a range of up to 40 miles before a repeater is needed. The higher the speed, the shorter the distance is without a repeater. Also, up until recently, optics have used one color of light (red), to transmit data. Sprint, a telecommunications service provider, and Lucent Technologies, a telecommunications equipment company, developed a system to use 16 colors of light on a *single* fiber. That would be equivalent to 16 OC-1s in a *single* pair of optic fibers (currently, OC-48 is 50 fibers, each way, for a total of 100 fibers in the bundle). With this new technology, one fiber can handle 829.44 mbps, thereby providing a tremendous increase in bandwidth.

## Local Area Networks

**Local area networks (LANs)** interconnect computers and communications devices (printers, fax machines, and storage devices) within an office, series of offices in a building, or campus of buildings (Figure 8.16). They typically span a distance of a few hundred feet up to several miles. The network components (the LAN's nodes), including the cable linking the devices, are generally owned by the company using the network.

LANs are generally comprised of desktop computers, servers, storage area networks (SANs) and the printers designed to work with them. A desktop computer connected to a network may be called a **workstation** (alternatively, it may be called a *node* or a **client**). The computer that hosts the network and provides the resources that are shared on the network is called the **server.** The server provides services to each of the worksta-

**local area network (LAN)**
A network that interconnects computers and communications devices within an office or series of offices; typically spans a distance of a few hundred feet to several miles.

**workstation/client**
A desktop computer connected to a network.

**server**
A computer that hosts a network and provides the resources that are shared on the network.

**REALITY CHECK**    To put bandwidth in perspective, consider the following examples. A standard page of typed correspondence contains approximately 275 words—about 2,000 bytes or 16,000 bits (recall that a byte equals 8 bits) of information, including punctuation, spaces, and blank lines. Transmitting one page of correspondence over a standard modem takes approximately 6 seconds. Sending the page of correspondence at the faster voice transmission rate of 56 kbps takes .28 seconds. Using a high-speed network transmitting at, say, 1.544 mbps, would shorten transmittal time to 1/100 of a second.

Suppose you wanted to transmit 600 pages of this book over a wide area network. Assuming that each page contains 3,000 bytes (24,000 bits) of information, it would require

- At 2,400 Bps (a common dial-up speed in the past)—7,000 seconds (116 minutes, or approximately 2 hours).
- At 56,000 Bps—300 seconds (5 minutes).
- At 1.544 mbps—10.8 seconds. ∎

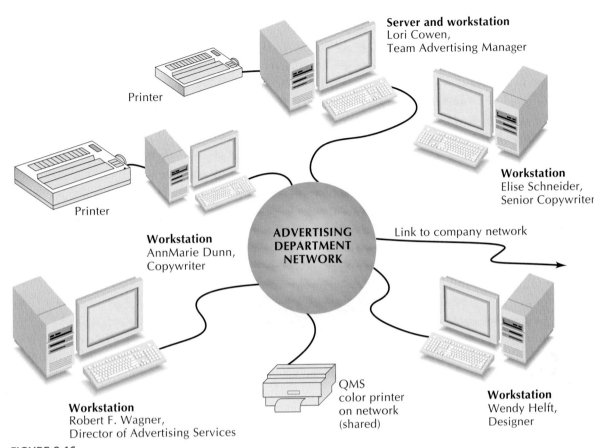

**FIGURE 8.16**

*A Local Area Network in an Advertising Department*

tions attached to it. When workstations, that is PCs, access a server, they can use *(execute)* the software residing on the server or process data in a file or database on the server.

The server typically has more primary memory and storage capacity and a higher processing speed than the other computers on the network. Some networks have multiple servers, either to provide a backup in case one is not working or to distribute databases more quickly for faster access to information.

A **file server** is a computer containing files available to all users connected to a LAN. In some LANs, a microcomputer is designated as the file server. In others, a computer with a large disk drive and specialized software acts as the file server. (See Chapter 7 to review *client/server computing.*)

LAN transmission speeds generally range from 1 to over 100 mbps. However, several leading networking companies are seeking to develop LAN technology that will operate at speeds of 10 gbps. LAN speeds should increase as new transmission technologies are developed.

The *Information Technology in Practice* feature, "Bethlehem Steel's Campus Networks Pay Off in Tough Times," shows how campus-wide LANs give this major steel producer an edge over global competition.

## Metropolitan Area Networks

**Metropolitan area networks (MANs),** which have evolved from LAN designs, transmit data and information over longer distances (approximately 30 miles, or 50 kilometers) and may do so at greater speeds (up to 200 mbps) than is possible with LANs. Moreover, MANs are often designed to carry more diverse forms of information than LANs, including combinations of voice, data, image, and video. MANs are usually optimized for voice and data transmission.

**file server**

A computer containing files that are available to all users interconnected on a local area network.

**metropolitan area network (MAN)**

A network that transmits data and information over citywide distances and at greater speeds than a LAN.

# INFORMATION TECHNOLOGY IN PRACTICE
## International Steel Group's Campus Networks Payoff Big in Tough Competitive Times

International Steel Group (ISG) is one of North America's largest integrated producers of steel with annual shipping capability in excess of 16 million tons. ISG has operating facilities in ten states including fully integrated steel works in Cleveland, Ohio; East Chicago and Burns Harbor, Ind.; and Sparrows Point, Md. It produces a wide variety of steel mill products including hot-rolled, cold-rolled and coated sheets, tin mill products, carbon and alloy plates, rail carbon and alloy bars and large diameter pipe. Its principal markets include automotive, construction, machinery and equipment, appliance, containers, service centers, rail and pipe.

Most U.S. integrated steel manufacturers have faced tough times due to high quality global competitors who are able to deliver steel at comparatively low prices. Price conscious buyers have many choices since global steel makers are seeking to generate business and grow their revenue in a worldwide market having excess supply. For ISG, standing up to competition means finding ways to improve efficiencies and enhance product quality, all while delivering products that meet the needs of current and potential new customers.

IT plays an important role in steel making and in managing costs. A steel making plant is actually a large campus of buildings and storage areas. Telecommunications networks connect these physically adjacent locations. Typically, such areas require one or more local area networks and bridging, routing, and

transmission equipment to meet a variety of operating needs. For example, the Sparrows Point campus-area network consists of some 17 miles of fiber optic cable that weaves around six mills, steelmaking areas, and office buildings on the 23-acre campus. The network backbone operates at 100Mbps while the links inside the mills and those running to desktops operate at 100Mbps and 10Mbps respectively. More than 1,200 PCs and several hundred process computers controlling steel making are attached to the network.

ISG's investment in high speed networks, occurring in the face of cost cutting elsewhere, demonstrates management's judgment that it can't allow networks to degrade or it will make the competitive situation even more difficult. It also illustrates how its communication networks can improve the company's operations. For instance, real-time video applications were recently added for environmental and safety monitoring. Steelmaking is known to have inherent risks such as fires and physical damage to facilities from heat. To detect the occurrence of problems quickly, the company has positioned industrial quality video cameras in hazardous

areas throughout the plant, each connected to the company's virtual LAN. Employees can view the cameras from any location.

The network is setup to be fully redundant so that it can recover damage to any transmission link (a cable cut, for example) in less than two seconds. Every camera, as well as any other node, has two possible routes for transmitting across the network. The campus network uses a virtual LAN topology to isolate traffic. Four logical networks—industrial control, supervisory control and data acquisition, video, and general office—all run on the same backbone system. Each is isolated from the other. A Virtual LAN controller can change or add workstations or process controllers and manage bandwidth allocation more easily than with separate physical LANs. Network management software keeps track of virtual LAN activity and overall transmission traffic on the physical backbone.

Because ISG can use its network to manage steelmaking, it is able to minimize the number of workers it needs in the process, thereby providing cost benefits and limiting risks to personal safety. Its campus network is recognized as a vital operating resource and an essential competitive tool.

MANs do not operate over telephone lines. Rather, to obtain the combination of high-speed performance and citywide transmission (hence the name *metropolitan* area network), fiber-optic cables are generally used as the transmission medium. SONET (synchronous optical networking standard) is a high-speed (45 mbps to 1.5 gbps) network specification using fiber-optic channels. It is often used to obtain both the high-speed performance and the multimedia transmission capabilities that people want in metropolitan networks.

Denver, Colorado, known as the mile-high city because of its elevation in the Rocky Mountains, is also becoming known for its high-speed network links using metropolitan area networks. The network links the city's major facilities, including the Denver International Airport, and transmits data over an OC-3 ATM channel (discussed later) at 155 mbps. The network carries data, voice, and video transmissions. Denver's MAN will eventually support telemedicine and videoconferencing applications as well and will connect more than 5,000 users in some 300 government buildings. The MAN delivers faster performance times than the other available alternatives.

# Network Channels

How are networks put together? This section describes the hardware components of networks and the devices used to interconnect different networks.

## Communications Channels

A **communications channel**, also called a **communications medium**, links the different components of a network. There are two categories of communications channels: (1) physical channels and (2) wireless (also called cableless) channels.

**communications channel/ communications medium**
The physical or cableless media that link the different components of a network.

 **REALITY CHECK**

In recent years, the combination of faster computer processing, larger storage capabilities on smaller computers, and high-speed computer networks has led to a distinct trend toward computer downsizing. Applications that were previously run on shared mainframes are being moved to servers and midranges; applications that were once run on midranges are now often run on powerful PCs. Yet all these different computers can be linked together by communications networks. Thus, downsizing means more than moving applications to smaller computers; it also means interconnecting different computers in a distributed environment.

The appeal of downsizing is closely tied to costs: Midrange computers are cheaper than mainframes; PCs are cheaper than midranges. But there is more to downsizing than lower costs. Companies that take advantage of the power now available in smaller computers while standardizing applications across the organization see application performance improve. Why? Because if they move an application to its own dedicated computer, people can use it whenever they need it; they don't have to wait for another application to finish running on a shared computer. Response time for data and information retrieval is noticeably faster—an important benefit in a time when speed to market is a critical element of a firm's success.

Downsizing is not a fad; it is a trend. It is fueled by the quest for greater speed in business and commerce and enabled by the continuing advances in information technology. ■

**Physical Channels**   Physical channels are wires or cables along which data and information are transmitted. There are three types of physical channels: twisted pair, coaxial cable, and optical cable (Figure 8.17).

As mentioned earlier, teleprocessing gave rise to the use of telephone wires as a popular medium for transmitting data and information between multiple user sites. They remain the most popular medium today, whether strung from telephone poles, run through underground conduits, or embedded in the walls of buildings. Often referred to as a **twisted pair**, this telephone wire medium consists of strands of copper wire that are twisted in pairs. Because the twisted pair channel was developed for the transmission of voices and text, IT professionals refer to this medium as a *voice-grade channel*.

Twisted pair channels transmit at a variety of speeds, from as slow as 110 Bps to as fast as 100 mbps. The *feasible speed* of transmission is established by the carrier, independent of the data or information transported on the channel. The *actual speed* of transmission is determined by the hardware attached to the medium and the programs managing the communications process.

**Coaxial Cable**   **Coaxial cable**, sometimes called just **co-ax,** consists of one or more central wire conductors surrounded by an insulator and encased in either a wire mesh or metal sheathing. Co-ax offers higher transmission speeds than voice-grade lines and a capability for transmitting all types of information effectively (not just voice and text). If you have cable television, you are using coaxial cable to receive the broadcast programs without interference.

Coaxial cable comes in two types: (1) baseband cable and (2) broadband cable. **Baseband cable,** which carries a single communication or message at very high megabit speeds, is often used in local area networks. **Broadband cable** carries multiple signals—data, voice, and video—simultaneously; each signal can be a different speed. Cable television uses broadband cable. Both types of coaxial cable achieve bandwidths of more than 100-megabit speeds. These speeds will continue to increase through advances in networking technology.

**Fiber-Optic Cable**   **Fiber-optic cable** is the newest type of physical communications channel. As introduced earlier, this high-bandwidth transmission medium uses light as a digital information carrier. Glass fibers, rather than wire, are the transmission medium. Because the glass fibers are much thinner than wire, many more fibers can be packed into

**twisted pair**
A physical communications channel that uses strands of copper wire twisted together in pairs to form a telephone wire.

**coaxial cable/co-ax**
A physical communications channel that uses one or more central wire conductors surrounded by an insulator and encased in either a wire mesh or metal sheathing.

**baseband cable**
Carries a single communication or message at very high megabit speeds, is often used in local area networks.

**broadband cable**
Carries multiple signals—data, voice, and video—simultaneously; each signal can be a different speed.

**fiber-optic cable**
A physical communications channel that uses light and glass fibers.

**FIGURE 8.17**

***Physical Communications Channels***
Physical communication channels transmit data and information along a wire or cable.

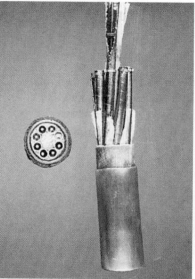
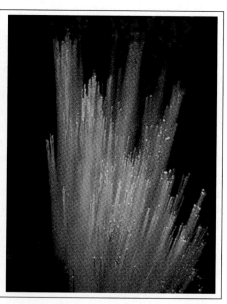

a cable, with each transmitting at much higher speeds than twisted pairs or coaxial cable. And because laser (light) beams, rather than electricity, carry the data and information, fiber-optic cables are immune to electrical interference within buildings or when strung near electrical lines.

The costs of manufacturing, installing, and maintaining fiber-optic cables are lower than those for wire channels. These advantages, combined with the benefits of high transmission speeds, make it easy to see why the use of fiber optics has grown at a rapid rate worldwide. Indeed, most telephone companies now install only fiber-optic cable when they lay new lines to expand their networks. Hence, if you make a telephone call or transmit data over a telephone line, there is a good chance your message will be sent over fiber-optic cables, at least part of the way to its destination.

The term *line* is a carryover from the days when all data communications were carried by twisted-pair lines. IT professionals use the term today to refer to all communications media, both physical and wireless.

**Wireless Channels**   The four most common types of **wireless** (also called *cableless*) transmission channels are microwave, satellite, infrared, and radio waves. Depending on the company's needs, these media may be used alone or in conjunction with each other and the three types of physical channels. Wireless channels are an important predominant network medium for pen-based and tablet computers as well as personal digital assistants. Experts predict that they will also be used more frequently for other types of computers.

**Microwave**   This form of transmission uses high-frequency radio signals to send data and information through the air, without wire or cable connections between sites, all in a fraction of a second. **Microwave** signals can be transmitted using terrestrial stations or communications satellites. With terrestrial stations, relay towers stationed approximately 30 miles apart receive and retransmit communications to link source and destination sites. The path between each tower must be unobstructed, though, because the signals are sent in a straight line (Figures 8.18a and 18b). For this reason, microwave stations are often located on the tops of buildings in metropolitan areas or at the peaks of mountains and hills in remote regions.

**Satellite**   The preferred method of transmission of information between sites when large distances must be spanned or when obstructions are in the way is by **satellite.** With this type of cableless transmission, the significance of distance disappears. Each communication is beamed from a microwave station to a communications satellite that is in a fixed orbit relative to Earth (or a *geosynchronous* orbit) 22,000 miles *above* Earth. Transmissions are relayed from one sending earth station to another or to multiple earth stations (Figure 8.18b).

Another type of satellite, **low-earth-orbit satellites (LEOs)** are also being deployed. Because they circle Earth at a distance far closer (approximately 900 miles/1,500 kilometers in altitude) than other satellites, LEO satellite systems offer significant advantages

**wireless**
Wireless channels transmit data using radio signals send through air or space rather over wire or optical cables.

**microwave**
A cableless medium that uses high-frequency radio signals to send data or information through the air.

**satellite**
A cableless medium in which communications are beamed from a microwave station to a communications satellite in orbit above the earth and relayed to other earth stations.

**low-earth-orbit satellite (LEO)**
Because they circle Earth at a distance far closer than other satellites, LEO satellite systems offer significant advantages: they do not have the comparatively long propagation delays, do not require use of bulky, expensive, directional antennas, less expensive to produce and and launch into orbit. However, greater numbers are needed to provide coverage for a geographic area because they do orbit closer to Earth.

---

 Most office buildings have a communications network running through their offices. A **private branch exchange (PBX),** or **computer branch exchange (CBX),** is a private telephone system designed to handle the needs of the organization in which it is installed. Telephones—that is, stations or extensions—are interconnected with the network. Calls coming into the organization from outside lines are processed through the PBX, which switches the call to the appropriate internal extension. Calls originating inside the organization are routed by the PBX to an available outside line.

Because most PBX systems today are computer based—microprocessors manage the switching activities and keep track of the location of various extensions—PBX implicitly means CBX. ▪

**private branch exchange (PBX)/computer branch exchange (CBX)**
A private telephone system designed to handle the needs of the organization in which it is installed.

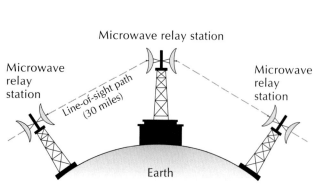

**FIGURE 8.18A**

***Terrestrial Transmission***

In terrestrial microwave transmission, dish-shaped antennas 30 miles apart relay signals from one to another. Paths between relay stations must be unobstructed.

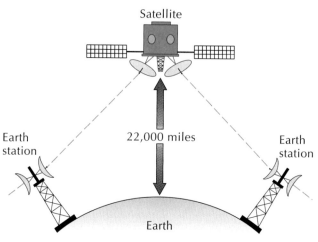

**FIGURE 8.18B**

***Satellite Transmission***

In satellite microwave transmission, a satellite orbiting approximately 22,000 miles over the earth acts as a relay station that transmits a signal from one earth station to another.

over high-altitude, geosynchronous (GEO) systems for the delivery of mobile services. For instance, they do not have the comparatively long propagation delays inherent in GEO systems that produce the echo effect, and they do not require use of bulky, expensive, directional antennas, which must point or be pointed at a satellite. They are also less expensive to produce and launch into orbit. However, greater numbers are needed to provide coverage for a geographic area because they do orbit closer to Earth.

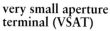

**very small aperture terminal (VSAT)**

A satellite earth station with an antenna diameter of under one meter.

Of growing importance are **very small aperture terminals (VSATs),** which have been integrated into corporate networking strategies at an increasing rate in recent years. A VSAT is a fairly inexpensive satellite earth station (it costs only a few hundred dollars), with an antenna diameter of less than 1 meter (40 inches). VSATs enable companies to use networks in creative and effective ways because the earth station can be installed just about anywhere and still maintain contact with the orbiting satellite.

In the United States, Schneider National, the large long-haul trucking company discussed in the *Information Technology in Practice* feature earlier in this chapter, was the first to equip its trucks with VSATs (Figure 8.19). Mounted on top of drivers' cabs, these receivers allow the company to communicate with its drivers anywhere and at any time. Company dispatchers simply determine the location of the trucks and send messages to drivers instructing them to make additional pickups, to change delivery schedules, or to perform any other tasks that would make the company more effective. Schneider pays for access to an orbiting public communications satellite. Its transmissions are sent to the satellite and then beamed to the truck, all in a matter of seconds.

**infrared**

A cableless medium that transmits data and information in coded form by means of an infrared light beamed from one transceiver to another.

**transceiver**

A combination transmitter and receiver that transmits and receives data and information.

**Infrared**   **Infrared** communications occur via a combined transmitter and receiver, or **transceiver.** Data and information are transmitted in coded form by means of an infrared light beamed from one transceiver to another. Infrared systems are limited to a single area, such as an open retail store space or a large room, because the transmitter and receiver must be in sight of each other. Infrared communications between different areas or buildings can be achieved only if they are close to each other (no more than 220 yards or 200 meters apart) and only if the transceivers are in windows of the buildings, visible to each other.

Kroger Company, a large supermarket chain based in Cincinnati, Ohio, has installed a series of infrared transceivers on the ceilings of some stores and equipped shopping carts with flat screen display terminals. As shoppers wheel their carts through the store, the transceiver senses their presence and transmits advertising and pricing information to the screen on the cart (Figure 8.20). In the produce department, the screen suggests innovative ways to cook seasonal fresh vegetables. As the consumer enters the frozen food section, the display shows information about special prices and this week's sales. In the

# CRITICAL CONNECTIONS 2

## XM Satellite Radio Lets Listeners Tune In . . . Nationwide!

Exploring the radio dial may never be the same, thanks to XM Satellite Radio, headquartered in Washington, D.C. The spirit and the passion that made radio fun during

its Golden Era (when teens and their parents huddled around the old vacuum tube radio to catch breaking world news, listen to baseball's World Series or tune in to the latest Swing tune release) is now reborn in all-digital sound and delivered coast-to-coast. For around $10 a month, subscribers can choose from continuous programming on 70 music channels plus 30 channels of news, talk, sports, and entertainment—100 basic channels in all, with over 35 commercial-free channels. To top it off, XM Satellite Radio comes with the crystal clear, hiss-free sound that only a digital channel can deliver.

XM is using today's satellite network technology to transform radio, an industry that has seen little technological change since *FM* was introduced, almost 40 years ago.

XM uses two high-power satellites and a network of terrestrial repeaters—ground-based electronics equipment that receives and retransmits the satellite signals to augment its satellite signal coverage. Special chipsets and XM radios are widely available; anyone can sign up and tune in to XM. Want to give it a try? Go to www.xmradio.com/programming/full_channel_listing.jsp.

**FIGURE 8.19**

### *Very Small Aperture Terminal Communication at Schneider National*

A receiver mounted on top of Schneider National's truck cabs (left) allows drivers and headquarters to communicate anywhere and at any time. Schneider pays for access to an orbiting public communications satellite, from which its messages are beamed to its drivers' trucks (right).

**FIGURE 8.20**

*Infrared Marketing*

VideOcart's supermarket system pioneered the use of infrared to sense the presence of shopping carts and transmit advertising and pricing information to a screen on the cart. The cart offers supermarkets the opportunity to call attention to new items, products on sale, and coupon specials. Shoppers can use the VideOcart to locate hard-to-find items and favorite products.

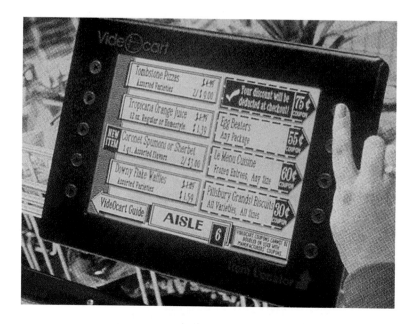

snack food area, the consumer is reminded about upcoming televised sporting events and the need to stock up on extra snacks for the family to enjoy while watching them. The added expense of installing 30 to 40 transceivers in each store is justified, Kroger managers say, by advertising revenues and the extra sales generated.

**radio wave transmission/ radio frequency (RF) transmission**

A cableless medium that uses frequencies rented from public radio networks to transmit data and information.

**Radio Waves**    **Radio wave transmissions,** sometimes called **radio frequency (RF) transmissions,** use transmission frequencies rented from public radio networks in a region. The company or individual user pays a monthly fee for airtime and transmits information at the assigned frequency. A transmitter sends information to a receiver designed to accept the same frequency. Radio wave transmissions are not practical for transmitting large files or databases because of their relatively low transmission speeds (see Table 8.4).

Governments in different countries regulate radio frequencies in different ways and assign the frequency ranges for varying purposes. In general, governments have not reserved any RF transmission frequency for local area network use.

There are two major players in the worldwide public radio network market. In the United States, Motorola and IBM have created a joint venture, called the ARDIS Company. In Europe, RAM Mobile Data Company uses a mobile data network system developed by the Swedish company Ericsson AB. Each of these companies provides a

| Table 8.4    Transmission Speeds of Communications Channels | |
|---|---|
| **CHANNELS** | **TRANSMISSION SPEEDS** |
| Twisted pair | Over 100 mbps |
| Coaxial cable | 140 mbps |
| Fiber-optic cable | Over 2 gbps |
| **WIRELESS (CABLELESS) CHANNELS** | **TRANSMISSION SPEEDS** |
| Microwave | 275 mbps |
| Satellite | 2 mbps |
| Infrared | 275 mbps |
| Radio waves (RF transmissions) | 275 mbps |

series of public radio channels in major metropolitan areas that are available to users for a monthly fee that covers rental of airtime and transmission equipment. The network companies run and maintain the network.

Otis Elevator uses a public radio network to transmit information to its field service staff. Maintenance and service personnel can send and receive information about parts and procedures for servicing an elevator or diagnosing a problem. The company finds the network an effective way of routing personnel from one service call to the next (Figure 8.21).

In the United States, Otis's system has other benefits as well. Because the company can stay in touch with service employees throughout the day, it does not have to assign the day's service calls in the morning or rely on telephone calls to do so throughout the day. Instead, it is able to manage the entire service team in the most efficient way possible, responding to customer emergencies that arise during the day and accommodating a service call that takes a little longer than expected. Both customer and company benefit from this wireless network.

## Communications Channels for WANs and MANs

Three different communications channels are widely used by companies creating wide area or metropolitan area networks. These are public-access networks, private networks, and value-added networks.

**Public-Access Networks** U.S. telephone companies and the world's PTTs—that is, the common carriers—maintain certain networks for use by the general public: hence the term **public-access networks.** Specialized carriers also operate other focused services, such as making satellite communications links available to the public. All carriers interconnect their networks with other networks to give their customers a seamlessly integrated single network. The complete set of public-access networks is often called the **switched network** (also called **circuit switched**), so named because the telephone company operates and maintains the switching centers that make it possible to transmit a call or information from its origin through the nodes of the network to its destination. *Switched access* refers to communications access over a switched, nondedicated line. This means that the line—the circuit—is assigned to a different caller each time, and the completion of a call requires the carrier to switch between different lines to create a link between the caller and the desired destination of his or her call.

A growing number of networks are being designed to use **packet switching.** In a packet-switched network, relatively small units of data called **packets** are routed through a network to the destination address contained within each packet. Breaking

**public-access networks**
A network maintained by common carriers for use by the general public.

**switched network/circuit switched**
The complete set of public access networks, so named because the telephone company operates and maintains the switching centers that make it possible to transmit data and information.

**packet switching**
A network communication method in which messages are divided into packets. Each packet is then transmitted individually and can even follow different routes to its destination.

**packet**
A piece or section of a transmitted message that contains both data and address information enabling the network to deliver the packet to its intended destination.

**FIGURE 8.21**

***Otis Elevator's Service Network***

Otis Elevator uses a public radio network to transmit information to its field service staff. Maintenance personnel can send and receive information about parts and procedures via a portable handheld computer.

communication down into packets allows the same channel to be shared among many users in the network. This type of communication between sender and receiver is known as *connectionless* (rather than *dedicated*). Most traffic over the Internet uses packet switching; the Internet is basically a connectionless network.

**Private Networks**   When organizations transmit large volumes of information regularly, it may be more economical and effective for them to lease lines from a common carrier than to use a public-access network. When an organization agrees to lease a line for a period of time, the carrier will *dedicate* that line to the company, meaning it will reserve it for the exclusive use of that company. Hence, **leased lines** are sometimes called **dedicated lines.** Networks comprising dedicated lines are known as **private networks.**

**Value-Added Networks**   BMA public data communications network that provides basic transmission facilities plus enhancements (such as temporary data storage, error detection and correction, conversion of information from one form to another, and electronic mail service) is called a **value-added network (VAN).** The VAN provider generally leases the transmission channels from a common carrier and then creates the *value added* to its customer by investing in and operating the network so that the customer does not need to do so.

## Communications Channels for LANs

Local area networks seldom use public switched networks or satellite transmission channels because these do not provide much distance between nodes. Although wireless methods are increasingly popular, fiber-optic, coaxial cable, and even twisted pair lines remain common methods of connecting the nodes of a LAN. In most cases, the company simply has the cables installed on its premises by a wiring contractor. When companies and institutions expect a large number of people to use their LAN, they often build either a high-speed transmission facility called a **backbone network** or an arrangement of such facilities. When developed as part of a wide area network, the channels are often T-carriers.

Georgia State University and the Georgia Institute of Technology (Georgia Tech), both in Atlanta, and many other leading universities have developed backbone networks for their entire campuses. Communications cables buried in the ground run near all campus buildings and laboratories. Each backbone serves as a conduit that connects lower-speed communications lines or dispersed communications to computing devices. The lower-speed components move data onto the backbone, where they are transported to the intended destination at high speed. At the destination, the data move off the backbone to the lower-speed network and eventually to their intended recipient.

## Connecting to the Channel

A communications medium provides only the *capability* to transmit and receive information. It is entirely separate from the other hardware components of the computer system: computers, printers, or other devices that determine *what* and *when* to communicate. Different devices are used to connect computers to WANs and LANs.

In WANs using the public telephone network, special devices called **modems** connect computers to the communications medium and translate the data or information from the computer into a form that can be transmitted over the channel. The term *modem,* a contraction of *modulation-demodulation,* describes the device's operations. Computers generate digital signals (combinations of the binary zero and one), but voice-grade lines transmit analog signals. The modem on the transmitting end translates the digital signal into analog form so it can be transmitted. On the receiving end, another modem transforms the analog signal back into a digital form that the computer can process (Figure 8.22). When the channel is digital, a *digital modem* is needed. If the channel consists of coaxial cable, a *cable modem* is needed instead.

**leased line/dedicated line**
A communications line reserved from a carrier by a company for its exclusive use.

**private network**
A network made up of leased (dedicated) communications lines.

**value-added network (VAN)**
A public data communications network that provides basic transmission facilities plus enhancements (e.g., temporary data storage and error detection).

**backbone network**
A transmission facility designed to move data and information at high speeds.

**modem**
A device that connects a computer to a communications medium and translates the data or information from the computer into a form that can be transmitted over the channel. Used in WANs.

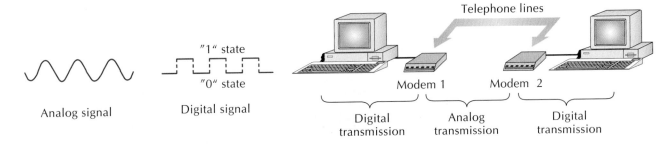

| Analog signal | Digital signal | Digital transmission — Analog transmission — Digital transmission |
|---|---|---|

The signals sent along a communications medium can be digital or analog. The phone system carries **analog signals**—continuous waves—over a frequency range.

Most types of computing equipment use **digital signals,** which code data into blocks of zeroes and ones.

When a computer sends data to a modem for transmission at a specified speed, it represents the digital blocks of zeroes and ones electrically as −5 and +5 volts, respectively. The modem changes, or **modulates,** the electrical signals into two analog frequency tones. It converts zeroes into a frequency of 2025 cycles per second (2025 hertz) and ones into a frequency of 2225 cycles (2225 hertz) per second.

This process is reversed at the receiving end of the transmission, where a second modem converts the analog signals back into digital signals.

**FIGURE 8.22**

***Converting Digital Signals to Analog Signals Using a Modem***

Modems come in several different forms. *External modems* consist of circuit boards mounted inside a protective case and interconnected with the computer through a cable that plugs into a port on the computer (Figure 8.23a). *Card* or *internal modems* are circuit boards that can be pushed into a slot in the computer (Figure 8.23b). The communications line connects to both types through a plug on the modem. The speed of the modem determines how quickly data and information will be transmitted on the line.

**Multiplexers** that are used to connect terminals to an analog communications line also convert data from digital to analog signals and vice versa. These devices allow a single communications channel to carry simultaneous data transmissions from the many terminals that are sharing the channel.

In the most commonly used LANs, both the devices and the network channels transmit digital information. Thus, there is no need for a modem. A circuit board called a **network interface card (NIC)** plugs into the computer, printer, or other device, thus becoming part of the device itself (Figure 8.24). In PCs, laptops, and some PDAs, the NIC is often integrated into the system board, thereby eliminating the need for a separate card. The network channel, in turn, connects to the interface card by way of a special plug spliced to the cable. If a wireless channel is used, the NIC contains the transceiver for sending and receiving information.

The network card and the cable type used in the LAN must agree, so the choice of cable is affected by the network card (or vice versa). If an office area is wired for coaxial cable, the computer must be equipped with interface cards that will interconnect with coaxial cable.

**multiplexer**

A device that converts data from digital to analog form and vice versa in order to allow a single communications channel to carry simultaneous data transmissions from the many terminals that are sharing the channel.

**network interface card (NIC)**

A circuit board used in LANs to transmit digital data or information.

## Interconnecting Networks

Because communications networks vary so widely in type and structure, it is common for companies to operate many different networks. Distributed processing presumes multiple networks, and it is likely that people will want to interconnect networks to share information and other resources. We have discussed how computers and communications devices are interconnected, but how do networks themselves interconnect? It all depends on whether the networks are the same or different types and whether they are managed by the same or different software.

**FIGURE 8.23A**

### Broadband Modem

PCMCIA modems inserted into PCs make it possible to use communication software transmit a fax or send and receive e-mail.

**FIGURE 8.23B**

### Broadband Modem

Broadband modems give users high-speed internet access. Cable modems connect PCs to the Internet through a cable TV network while DSL modems connect to the public telephone system.

**bridge/router**

A device that interconnects compatible LANs.

**gateway**

A device that connects two otherwise incompatible networks, network nodes, or devices.

**Bridges** and **routers** are devices that interconnect LANs, making it possible to send information from a device on one network to a device on another network. Routers are the means by which local area networks connect to the Internet. In essence, both take packets of information transmitted on one LAN and move them to another LAN. Hence, the two LANs can be treated essentially as one big LAN.

**Gateways** interconnect two otherwise different and incompatible networks, network nodes, or devices. The gateway performs conversion operations so that information transmitted in one form on the first network can be transformed into the form required for transmission to its destination on the second network (Figure 8.25).

**FIGURE 8.24**

### Network Interface Cards

A circuit board called a *network interface card* plugs into the computer, printer, or other device, thus becoming part of the device itself. The network channel, in turn, connects to the interface card by way of a special plug spliced to the cable.

**FIGURE 8.25**

***Interconnecting Networks with Bridges and Gateways***

*Bridges* interconnect compatible LANs, making it possible to send information from a device on one network to a device on another network. *Gateways* connect otherwise different and incompatible networks.

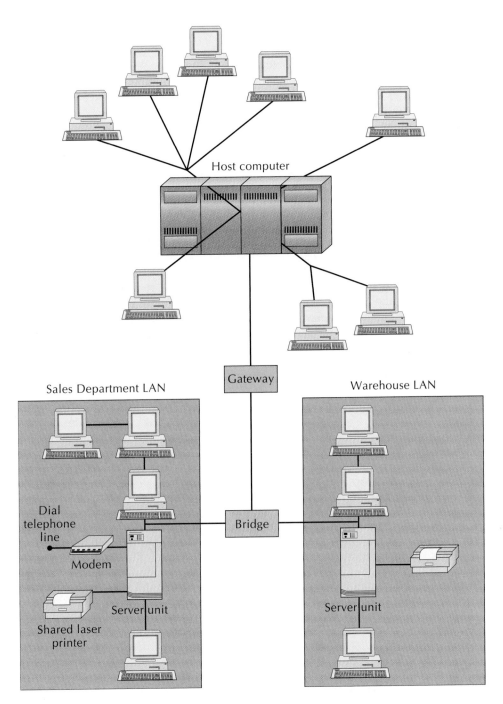

# Physical Network Transport Technology

The network transport technologies incorporated into a physical channel network strategy determine the type of data that can be transmitted, whether the channel is dedicated or shared, and the rate at which transmission occurs. Five transport technologies are in widespread use, including (1) frame relay, (2) ATM, (3) DSL, (4) ISDN, and (5) SMDS. The choice of transport technology will depend on the planned use of the network and on the technology available in a specific geographic region (availability varies by region).

## Frame Relay

**Frame relay** is a widely used way of sending data over a wide area network (WAN) to connect LAN, SNA, Internet, and even voice applications. Data streams are divided into frames (that is, packets) with each containing an address that the network uses to deter-

**frame relay**
A way of sending data over a wide area networks in which data are divided into frames (i.e., packets) with each containing an address that the switched network uses to determine its destination.

mine its destination. The frames travel through a series of switches within the frame-relay network in order to reach their destination.

The form of packet switching used in frame-relay networks is well suited to PCs and workstations that operate using intelligent protocols, including TCP/IP and SNA. As a result, frame relay provides high transport speeds and the reliability needed for many enterprise communications applications.

The frame-relay network is often depicted as a cloud (Figure 8.26) because the network is not a single physical connection between endpoints. Rather it is a *virtual circuit*— a logical path within the network. Although a specified level of bandwidth is allocated to the network on a continuing basis, the transmission of a message causes the network to allocate bandwidth on a packet-by-packet basis, with enough capacity to meet the transmission needs.

Frame-relay technology was developed in response to the demand for networks that could transmit graphics, rather than just text, intermittently at high speeds between powerful PCs and servers. Frame relay was also a direct result of the need to support the growing use of LANs and client/server computing.

Transmission speeds commonly available for frame-relay channels are 56 kbps, 384 kbps, 1.536 mbps, and 45 mbps.

The *Information Technology in Practice* feature, "Tower Automotive Uses Frame Relay for Flexible Product Designs," describes how this global automotive supplier relies on its frame-relay network to meet customer needs in the face of competitive challenges.

**FIGURE 8.26**

**Frame Relay Network**

Data travel in frames (i.e., packets) through a series of switches within the frame relay network in order to reach their destination

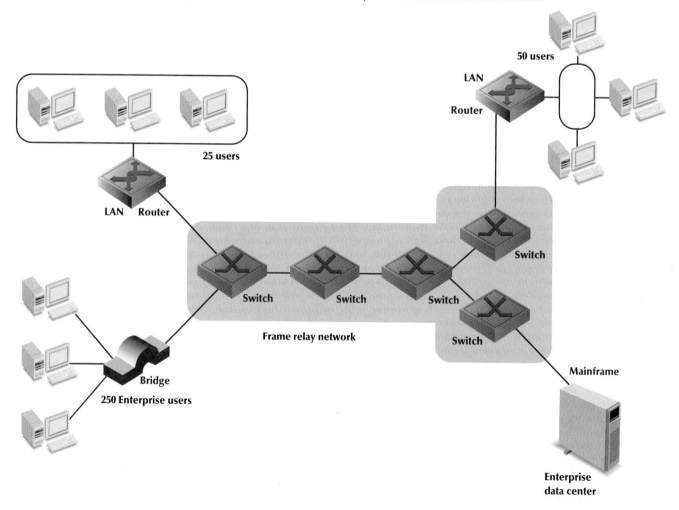

# INFORMATION TECHNOLOGY IN PRACTICE

## Tower Automotive Uses Frame Relay for Flexible Product Designs

Tower Automotive Inc., with annual revenues of $2.5 billion, is a global designer and producer of structural components and assemblies used by every major automotive equipment manufacturer. Its well-known customers include Ford, DaimlerChrysler, GM, Honda, Toyota, Nissan, Fiat, Hyundai, Kia, BMW, and Volkswagen Group. The company produces a broad range of structural components and assemblies, many of which are critical to the structural integrity of a vehicle. Its products include body structures and assemblies; lower vehicle structures; suspension modules and systems; and suspension components. Many of the company's stamped, formed, and welded components and assemblies are attached directly to the frame of an automobile at the manufacturer's vehicle assembly.

Tower aspires to be the global supplier of choice in its segment of the auto industry. Achieving this objective depends on its ability to design and develop the products auto manufactures want. In order to be close to its customer technical centers and manufacturing centers, Tower Automotive's 16,000 employees reside in 15 countries.

The company offers its customers full product development capabilities ranging from design and analysis to prototype and testing as well as manufacturing, supported by communication between the company's Grand Rapids, Michigan, headquarters and its technical centers and manufacturing sites.

The first stage of product development begins when an engineer generates drawings that meet manufacturer specifications. The principal IT tools in this process are powerful desktop computers equipped with computer aided design (CAD) software. CAD files contain a great amount of detail, enough so that they in effect contain a virtual version of the auto part or component that will eventually be manufactured. Hence, they also occupy a substantial amount of storage. This factor was an important consideration when the company designed

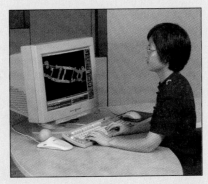

the communications network it uses to transmit files between worldwide customer and company sites. Large CAD files traveling over a network consume lots of bandwidth, which could slow down the transmittal process in a poorly designed network.

Tower's WAN connects with its distributed local area networks (LANs), and centralized company data sites 24 hours a day, 7 days a week at more than 30 North American sites and at over 70 sites worldwide.

The network's frame-relay transport technology handles the large volume of *voice and data traffic* between Tower's customers and its suppliers, and enables Internet access from anywhere in the world.

At the core of the frame-relay network is an asynchronous transfer mode (ATM) switching backbone that provides the high-speed reliability needed to transport the large CAD files without congestion—even if many engineers transmit at the same time. Because the need for engineers to send and receive CAD files is intermittent, the packet management system in the network's design accommodates *bursty* traffic. The Frame/ATM network is scalable, meaning that additional transmission capacity is added dynamically when unusually large volumes of data are transmitted. This capability means that the company can count on sufficient bandwidth always being available when needed.

The company's IT group is ever on the lookout for new communications technologies that will enable it to add capabilities or improve services for its global activities. For instance, it is developing voice over IP service—voice calls will automatically be converted to IP packets—for its Apodaca, Mexico, site and with its European sites. It is also looking

at IP-enabled frame relay. This service will allow many more interconnections without the need to preconfigure the network (that is, it will not be necessary to preprogram routers on specific routes). The overall communications environment will be easier to operate, having more built-in capabilities for automatically adjusting capacity to meet transmission needs.

In the automobile industry, where just-in-time manufacturing (that is producing the right vehicle at just the right time to meet demand) is becoming the norm, both Tower and its customers must be able to count on reliable communications networks that have the needed capacity. When it comes to networks, *just in time* means reliable transmission anytime, anywhere, and with the capability to transport anything.

## ATM

**asynchronous transfer mode (ATM)**

A data transmission method using switched networks in which a message containing data, voice, or video is divided into fixed length cells.

The growing desire to transmit message containing voice, video, and data over a single network led to the development of the **asynchronous transfer mode (ATM)** data transmission technology. Data sent over ATM channels is divided into fixed length cells (of 53 bytes each) that are transported to the destination and reassembled. Because the cells are of fixed length, data can be transported in a predictable manner. That means a network manager can determine in advance the performance characteristics of voice or video applications. This is the reason that ATM is ideally suited to support the convergence of voice, video, and data.

ATM is a switched technology (Figure 8.27). Since transmission is routed through a switch, rather than on a shared channel, ATM provides dedicated bandwidth for each connection with flexible bandwidth speeds. Access speeds in ATM networks are typically from 1.544 mbps to 622 mbps.

## DSL

**Digital subscriber line (DSL)**

Offers high-speed data access over the single pair of the *ordinary copper lines* used with basic voice-grade telephone service.

**Digital subscriber line (DSL)** technology offers high-speed data access over the single pair of the *ordinary copper lines* used with basic voice-grade telephone service. DSL is designed to transport a large volume of data through *the last mile* of telephone connections—the twisted pair channels that run to most homes (Figure 8.28). DSL channels are point to point, running from a home to the local telephone company's switching substa-

**FIGURE 8.27**

***Asynchronous Transmission Method***

Data sent over ATM channels are divided into fixed length cells.

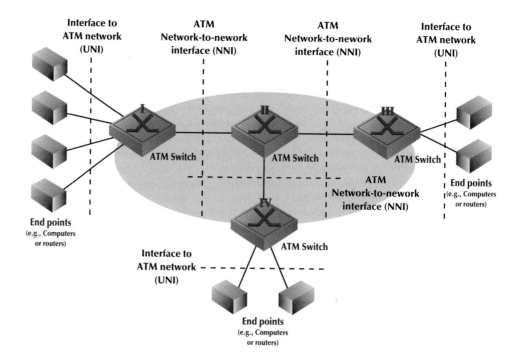

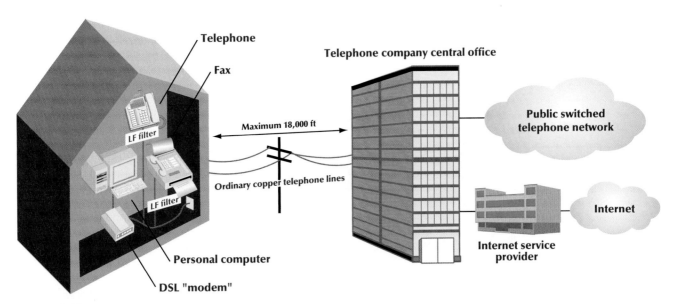

**FIGURE 8.28**
A digital subscriber line provides high-speed data transmission over ordinary copper telephone lines.

tion. Because the channels are restricted to lengths less than 18,000 feet, users must be located near their telephone company's switching substation. Because DSL technology uses a wide frequency range, it is possible to have simultaneous voice and data use of a single copper connection.

A DSL modem establishes a connection from one end of a copper wire to the other end. The signal does not pass into the telephone switching system. At the phone company office, the voice frequency data is stripped off and routed into the normal telephone-switching network. The data frequency transmission is handed off to a LAN/WAN (but never to the voice network) connected to an ISP (the telephone company or a private service provider) that may then route the data onto the Internet. This is how home users are able to connect to the Internet via their DSL service.

**Asymmetric digital subscriber line (ADSL)** is the most commonly used form of DSL. The service is termed *asymmetric* because the downstream (to the subscriber from the central office) data transmission rates are much greater than the upstream (from the subscriber to the central office) speeds. Accordingly, it is an especially good fit for Internet access, where typically small data messages are sent in order to retrieve large data files from the Web. ADSL is a point-to-point, not switched service.

DSL is *always on,* meaning that the channel is always ready to send or receive data. There is no need to dial a remote number and wait for modems to synchronize and establish a connection.

**Very high speed DSL (VDSL)** also provides transport of data over copper twisted pair lines at even higher speeds, ranging from 13 mbps to 55 mbps. Both symmetric and asymmetric upstream/downstream transmission rates are possible. However, the permissible distance is much shorter than DSL, usually between 1,000 and 4,500 feet. For this reason, its use is generally limited to small businesses operating in metropolitan areas where the user is near a telephone-company substation.

## ISDN

**Integrated Services Digital Network (ISDN),** developed in the 1970s, was designed as a *next generation* telephone system integrating voice and data onto one line and capable of transporting *digital* data over *analog* lines. It is available in two forms. The ISDN *Basic Rate Interface (BRI)* is a standard connection often chosen for homes and small businesses. It provides two channels for simultaneous connection of any combination of voice, data, and facsimile (Figure 8.29). When used for data, it can transmit at speeds of 64 and 128 kbps.

**asymmetric digital subscriber line (ADSL)**

The most commonly used form of high speed digital subscriber line (DSL) Internet access characterized by higher receiving (upstream) transmission rates compared to sending (downstream) transmissions.

**very high speed DSL (VDSL)**

Provides transport of data over copper twisted pair lines at even higher speeds, ranging from 13 mbps to 55 mbps.

**Integrated Services Digital Network (ISDN)**

A *next generation* telephone system integrating voice and data onto one line and capable of transporting *digital* data over *analog* lines.

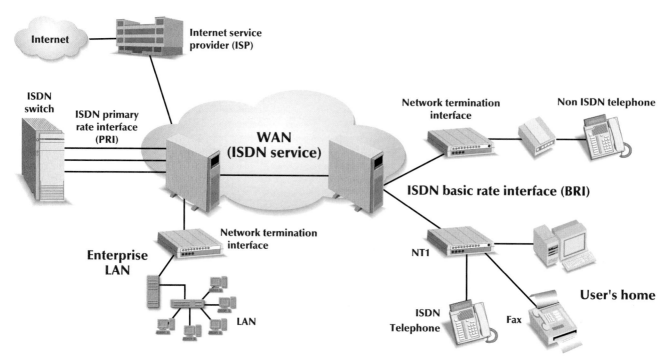

**FIGURE 8.29**

*Integrated Services Digital Network*

Integrated services digital network (ISDN) is an international communications standard for transmitting data, voice, and video over digital telephone lines or ordinary telephone wires.

ISDN *Primary Rate Interface (PRI)* provides 30 channels that transport at 64 kbps each. When used together, they transport at a combined speed of 1920 kbps.

Although a dial-up service, ISDN connections to the telephone network occur very quickly (generally in one to two seconds). Their digital transmission capability and fast speed, compared to ordinary dial-up service, makes them useful for connecting PCs, for remote teleworking, and for video conferencing.

ISDN has been most popular in Europe and parts of Asia. Today, ISDN is being replaced by DSL.

## SMDS

**Switched Multimegabit Data Services (SMDS)**

A high-speed, packet-switched transport technology that can operate over copper or fiber channels.

**Switched Multimegabit Data Services (SMDS)** is a high-speed, packet-switched transport technology that can operate over copper or fiber channels. Subscribers pay only for the time actually used and can purchase different levels of transport speed, ranging from 1.54 mbps (to 44.736 mbps (34 mbps in Europe) to a feature sometimes known as *bandwidth on demand*). Although the network is shared (it is a switched service), transport speed for the variable length packets is guaranteed at the level purchased.

Companies can connect client/server systems and local area networks to an SMDS (Figure 8.30), thereby supporting e-mail, intranet, and Web applications. The subscriber model makes it possible for an enterprise to connect additional network as the need arises. However, if networks expand beyond the metropolitan area of the service provider, transmission must be switched to a long-distance carrier, which can introduce additional cost and complexity.

# Wireless Communications Networks

The capability for wireless communication has in the past decade or so gained interest for a wide range of IT applications (though its planning began in the 1940s). Four wireless forms are of particular interest: (1) cellular communications service, (2) wireless LANs, (3) Bluetooth personal area networks, and (4) wireless data networks. Virtual pri-

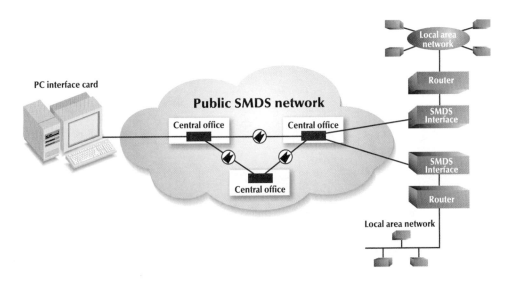

**FIGURE 8.30**

***Switched Multimegabit
Data Service***

Switched multi-megabit data service
enables users to acquire different service levels as needed.

vate networks are often incorporated into wireless communications as a means of providing security in message transmission.

## Cellular Communications Service

The wireless technology for **cellular communications service** transmits radio messages between a mobile device (such as a mobile telephone, PDA, or wireless laptop) and
a cell site. The service has evolved from analog to digital, with exciting innovations
emerging in *next generation* systems.

**Cellular Radio System**   Cell sites contain a radio transceiver, a base station controller
that sends and receives messages from mobile devices, an antenna, and a tower (Figure
8.31). The cell site is linked to a cellular switch, called a **mobile telecommunications switching office (MTSO).** The MTSO is linked by a wire channel to a telephone-switching office (Figure 8.32) that is part of the public switched telephone network (PSTN).

   Because the distance the radio message can travel is limited, cellular communications
services depend on (1) a network of cell sites that receive and send messages and (2) the
ability of the communications service to transfer mobile devices from one cell site to
another as the transmitting device moves about. The MTSO places calls from land-based

**cellular communications
service**

A wireless technology that transmits radio messages between a
mobile device (such as a mobile
telephone, PDA, or wireless laptop)
and a cell site.

**mobile telecommunications
switching office (MTSO)**

The switch used in a cellular
(mobile) telephone system that
links the cell tower to a traditional
telephone switch in the public
switched telephone network
(PSTN).

**FIGURE 8.31**

***Cell Tower Showing
Antennae***

Cell towers send and receive messages
from wireless devices.

**FIGURE 8.32**

*Cellular Radio System*

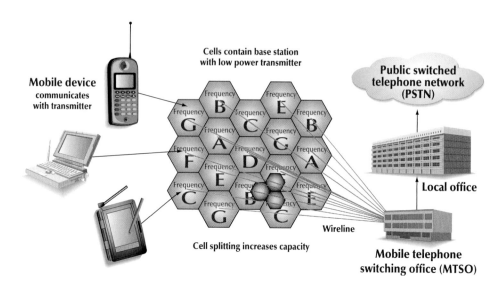

telephones to wireless customers, switches calls between cells (cellular radio and conventional wireline telephony use circuit switching) as mobiles travel across cell boundaries, and authenticates wireless customers before they make calls.

**Analog and Digital Cellular Service** The first public cellular communications services available, introduced in the 1980s, used analog access technologies. However, in the 1990s, second generation digital access technologies were introduced (Table 8.5). In fact, *three* different digital access technologies were introduced, each offering a different advantage with respect to transmission capabilities. Though digital services did not immediately replace analog service, some parts of the world adopted digital access technologies more quickly.

Mobile telecommunications companies in Europe and Asia developed large customer bases faster than in the United States. The European Union adopted the Global System for Mobile Communications (GSM) access technology, developed by the telecommunications company Groupe Spéciale Mobile, as a standard. This factor is often thought to explain why Europe developed a large base of cellular customers (between many different wireless service providers) more quickly than the United States. Using the GSM network, it is possible to drive from Rome to Helsinki and make calls on the same cell phone along the way. The telephone registers on the cellular network of the country in which it is switched on, and the GSM network automatically updates its location throughout the journey. Incoming calls are automatically rerouted through the multicountry network. Similar capabilities are available for fax and data transmission.

Asian countries followed suit. Their adoption of GSM has made it relatively easy for customers to use cellular services in communications between continents.

The U.S. companies providing public wireless service stayed with analog service longer than Europe and Asia. They also chose to use the **time division multiple access (TDMA)** and **code division multiple access (CDMA)** digital standards rather

**time division multiple access (TDMA)**

A digital cellular transmission technology that divides a radio frequency into time slots and then allocates slots to an individual device's conversation or message, there by distinguishing it from other transmissions.

**code division multiple access (CDMA)**

A digital cellular transmission technology that encodes each device's conversation or message with a unique identification code to distinguish it from other transmissions.

| Table 8.5 Cellular Access Technologies | |
|---|---|
| **ANALOG** | **DIGITAL** |
| **AMPS**—Advanced Mobile Phone System; developed by AT&T in 1983 | **TDMA**—Time Division Multiple Access: Allocates time slot to mobile device |
| **FDMA (used in AMPS)**—Frequency Division Multiple Access: Allocates a frequency to mobile device | **CDMA**—Code Division Multiple Access: Allocates code sequence to mobile device |
| | **GSM**—Global System for Mobile Communications: The most widely used cellular access technology in the world |

than GSM. By not settling on a common standard, many industry observers feel that U.S. service providers were responsible for the country's falling behind the rest of the world in adoption of digital cellular services. By the turn of the century, leading U.S. cellular service providers, led by AT&T Wireless and Cingular Wireless had introduced widespread changeover to GSM.

**Next Generation Cellular Service**   First- and second-generation analog and digital cellular services offered tremendous convenience for mobile users. However, they also had a severe limitation: transmission speed. Compared to dial-up computer transmissions, which were operating at 56.6 Kbs, cellular service transported data at only a much slower 9.6 Kbs. Though very effective for voice conversations, this limitation handicapped users wishing to send and receive large volumes of data involving laptop computers and PDAs.

Meanwhile, around the year 2000, cellular service providers began experimenting with new generations of access technologies. **Generalized packet radio service (GPRS),** sometimes known as 2.5 generation (or 2.5G) started to rollout in Europe and Asia in 2001 and in the United States during 2002. GPRS offered advantages of improved speed, with transmission rates of up to 115 Kbs. In addition, the GPRS network used packet switching rather than circuit switching. Packet switching meant the transmission networks service providers could use their networks more efficiently by simultaneously sharing a circuit between more customers. It was therefore expected that users would keep their mobile devices turned on because they would incur charges *only when transmitting packets,* rather than when they were connected to the network. Industry observers predicted that GPRS service would be added to GSM services, providing better services for users and increased revenue for service providers.

Beginning in 2001 in Japan and parts of Europe, **third-generation service (3G)** began to roll out, albeit with only a few service providers. A 3G network uses packet switching and transmits at higher bandwidths that provide faster downloads of information. Transmission rates range from 384 Kbs to 2 Mbs, depending on the location of the user. Although the cellular and mobile applications that will take advantage of 3G capabilities are still being developed, it is expected that they will include video applications and mobile access to the Internet.

Cellular networks are built around public telephone networks and include links to the public switched telephone network.

## Wireless LANs

Companies are also using wireless technologies to construct local area networks, or **wireless LANs (WLANs)** because they enable staff members to move around the building with laptops, PDAs, and other wireless devices and still connect to the enterprise's local area network without a wire. Wireless LANs transmit data using radio frequencies instead of cables. Their use is growing rapidly both because of the interest in mobile communication (the necessary equipment is widely available at low cost) and because standards have emerged to make creation of these networks relatively simple.

**Components**   Two hardware components are needed to create a wireless LAN: wireless network interface cards (NIC) and access points. A wireless NIC performs the same function as a wireline NIC: interconnecting a laptop or other device to the local area network. However, instead of sending the message over a wired channel, it is transmitted as an airborne radio signal. **Access points** are devices that convert wired LAN signals into radio frequency. They accept and transmit within a limited range. Actual distance depends on the environment in which the WLAN is operating. Many wireless LAN developers suggest that access points generally have a reliable range of approximately 300 to 500 feet indoors and up to 1,000 feet outdoors (the signal degrades and is unreliable at longer distances).

Wireless LANs are used in office buildings and in large campus areas. They can also be set up at home allowing multiple users to share access to an Internet connection (Figures 8.33a and 8.33b).

**generalized packet radio service (GPRS)**
GPRS (or 2.5G) features higher speed transmission rates than preceding telecom generations and uses packet switching rather than circuit switching, to transmit messages.

**third-generation service (3G)**
Uses packet switching and transmits at higher bandwidths that provide faster downloads of information—rates ranging from 384 Kbs to 2Mbs, depending on the location of the user.

**wireless LAN (WLAN)**
Local area networks that transmit data using radio frequencies instead of cables.

**access point**
A device that converts wired LAN signals into radio frequency.

**FIGURE 8.33A**

*Wireless Access Point*

Wireless LANs transmit data to an access point using radio frequencies. A cable connects the access point to the network by cable.

**802.11 Wireless Ethernet**   The 802.11 standard is a family of wireless standards for transmission of messages using the Ethernet LAN protocol. The 802.11b standard, released by the Institute for Electronics and Electrical Engineers (IEEE) in 1999 is a wireless local area network protocol enabling high-speed access to the network. It operates at speeds up to 11 mbps, depending on distance.

The 802.11a standard was released several years later. It increased performance to 54 mbps and more. (Other variants of 802.11, featuring higher speeds and capabilities for interconnecting wireless components, are also under development.)

Wireless LANs using the 802.11 protocol are sometimes referred to as *Wi-Fi* networks. *Wi-Fi* stands for *wireless fidelity,* meaning high-quality transmissions over wireless links.

A trend for use of WLANs is the establishment of wireless LAN *hot spots* and community networks. A growing number of airports and airport lounges are establishing wireless networks that enable travelers with wireless devices to check in with the airline, connect to the Internet, and check e-mail.

**FIGURE 8.33B**

*Wireless LAN Architecture*

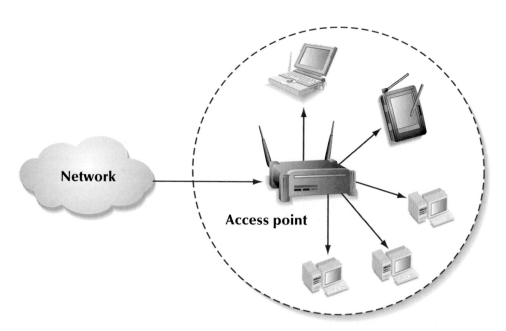

Starbucks Coffee Company, the Seattle-based specialty coffee retailer has installed wireless hot spots at more than 2,300 of its stores. The high-speed service enables patrons to connect to the Internet at speeds of *up to 50 times faster* than with a dial-up Internet connection. Starbucks believes that its wireless hot spots are good for business; they encourage customers to quickly and easily check e-mail, download files they need for an upcoming meeting, surf the Web, and get work done in coffeehouse comfort. Returning frequently for coffee and connections seem to go hand in hand at Starbucks. (Chapter 9 describes Starbucks' electronic commerce technology.)

The *Information Technology In Practice* feature, "FedEx Thrives on Wireless Communications," illustrates the manner in which this global courier company designs and uses wireless LANs.

**Wireless LAN Security**   In spite of good fidelity, two problems can occur with wireless LANs: signal interference and signal interception. If too many users are online in an area—in a building or a neighborhood—the frequency over which their devices transmit messages can become overcrowded. Unfortunately, this in turn may mean that radio frequency signals become susceptible to interception by other parties, whether intentionally or unintentionally. Therefore, most Wireless LANs use the **wired equivalent privacy (WEP)** system of security protection. WEP is a standard for encrypting data (that is, converting the data into a protective code) over an 802.11b wireless network. Its 40 or 128 bit encryption standard offers some protection, but it is not completely secure. A better alternative for highly sensitive wireless messages is through a virtual private network.

**wired equivalent privacy (WEP)**
A system of security protection that is a standard for encrypting data (converting the data into a protective code) over an 802.11b wireless network.

## Bluetooth Personal Area Networks

**Bluetooth personal area network** is another wireless technology for communicating between devices. The Bluetooth protocol enables short-range radio links (30 feet or 10 meters) between devices, such as between a PC and a laptop, or a PDA and a printer. Hence the name **personal area network.** Devices equipped with a Bluetooth component are termed Bluetooth-enabled.

Although Bluetooth-enabled devices are likely to become more common, they will not replace wireless LANs. The greater distance over which WLANs can be used, and their interconnection with an enterprise LAN, enables greater flexibility for users.

**Bluetooth personal area network/personal area network**
A wireless technology for communicating between devices that enables short-range radio links (30 feet or 10 meters) between devices, such as between a PC and a laptop, or a PDA and a printer.

## Wireless Data Networks

The heavy demand for high-speed mobile access for high-use applications such as e-mail with large attachments and corporate intranets has stimulated the creation of a focused wireless solution. The response from telecom service providers is **wireless data networks (WDNs).** These networks, which use cellular communications services, are intended to support mobile users seeking to interconnect with networks using wireless laptops and PDAs and have the following additional features: breadth of coverage, high transmission speed and reliability, security, the ability to send and receive large files,

**wireless data networks (WDNs)**
Networks that use cellular communications services to support mobile users seeking to interconnect with networks using wireless laptops and PDAs.

**REALITY CHECK**   You might be wondering how *Bluetooth* got its name. The technology is named after Danish Viking and King, Harald Blåtand. Blåtand means dark complexion and is translated as Bluetooth in English. (He got his name from his very dark hair, unusual for often light-haired Vikings.) Blåtand, who lived in the latter part of the tenth century, united Denmark and Norway—hence the inspiration for the name *Bluetooth*. (Bluetooth *unites* devices.)

There is another often-shared explanation for King Harald's nickname, but it is less likely to be true. Proponents of this story claim that the Viking loved blueberries; he ate so many his teeth became stained with the color, leading to the name Bluetooth.

# INFORMATION TECHNOLOGY IN PRACTICE
## FedEx Thrives on Wireless Communications

FedEx, headquartered in Memphis, Tennessee, began delivering packages in 25 U.S. cities in 1973. Today it transports upwards of 6-million packages daily, generating annual revenues of more than $20 billion (see the *Photo Essay,* "Inside FedEx" at the end of Chapter 7).

FedEx is first and foremost a network company. It operates a network of airplanes, a network of trucks, networks of courier vans, and vast telecommunications networks, all intersecting to speed customer deliveries. Two types of packets move through the network: shipper parcels and packets of information.

It is no surprise then that information technology and network communications has been at the heart of FedEx since its first day of operation. Recognizing the importance of having reliable computer processing and network communications around the clock, FedEx created a multi-data center strategy. Its three main data centers are in Memphis (where it has two data centers 35 miles apart) and in Colorado Springs, Colorado, each well secured. All are interconnected with fiber and other high-speed communications links. Should the need arise, FedEx operating system can be shifted from one data center to the other in a matter of moments.

Much of the network communications at FedEx is wireless. But this is not a recent development, for the company built a wireless capability back in the 1970s when it first used voice networks for dis-

patching drivers and delivering customer shipping details to the company's order-entry system and databases (captured on the driver's handheld wireless scanners.) These networks were later converted for digital transmission. Wireless soon became a necessity to run FedEx networks in the most efficient and reliable manner.

Wireless networks are now pervasive throughout the company, albeit with different transport technology than in the 1970s and 1980s. The twenty-first century FedEx has some 600 WLANs throughout the company running 802.11b, later upgraded to 80211a. More than 10,000 access points are scattered throughout company facilities to provide the necessary wireless access.

To take advantage of its wireless resources, FedEx is in the process of rolling out next generation scanners to replace the trusty SuperTracker scanners that its drivers have used for many years. The new scanners

will feature Bluetooth technology and will have a two-dimensional scanning capability. Its sales and field personnel are outfitted with laptop computers equipped with wireless capabilities.

FedEx has assembled a vast knowledge about wireless networks, including widely shared awareness among IT staff members that characteristics of a wireless network vary substantially from those of a fixed network. Any time a wireless communications solution is created, systems developers must design the application with awareness that there will be brief periods of time when the application will be disconnected. For instance, the surrounding environment of the wireless user is a key factor in determining the location of access points. For example, a building containing a large proportion of steel or a room with line-of-sight obstacles or radio-wave absorbing materials—such as cardboard or heavy fabric—near an access point will likely cause disruption to wireless transmissions. Hence, the company's application designers must write software in such a way that the application will not lose all of the data if there is a blip in communication linkage.

User expectations must be managed differently, too. Users must realize that the benefits of portability associated with wireless come with the drawback of more sensitivity to their location when seeking to send or receive messages.

In spite of the success that FedEx has had with its *private* wireless networks over more than two decades, the company is considering a shift to use of more *public* networks. Why? Public wireless networks have become very reliable and are widely available. Moreover, transmission speeds keep going up even as their costs come down. As next generation transmission technologies and their new performance characteristics emerge, the company will shift more of its vast communication traffic to public networks. Having the most effective and efficient communications networks is a key success factor and underlies its very existence. After all, FedEx is a network company.

and ease of connection to the network. Also, in many instances, WDNs have an *always on* capability that avoids the need to sign on to a network and enter passwords for user authentication each time a message is sent or an e-mail retrieved. In addition, many users seek integration of the wireless data network with the wireless LAN networks at their enterprise.

Among the most frequent users of wireless data networks are mobile managers and workers who rely on wireless Palm Pilot and Compaq iPaq PDA or the RIM Blackberry (Figure 8.34). Special versions of these devices have a wireless capability built in, so it is not necessary to add a modem or wireless network card. A service fee, ranging from $10 to $100 per month, enables the user to interconnect with a wireless data service provider (Figure 8.35) that operates a private packet data network. The service provider in turn interconnects with the user's enterprise network. WDN service providers typically offer WLAN service and can provide VPN service as well.

Although thousands of U.S. organizations already subscribe to wireless data networks, this service is still in its infancy. With the evolution to the higher bandwidths, a result of 2.5G and 3G services, it is likely that their use will grow dramatically.

**Virtual Private Networks**  **Virtual private network (VPN)** technology was developed to enable client systems to securely connect to servers over the Internet. VPN's powerful encryption and user authentication methods have proven extremely successful

**virtual private network (VPN)**
A network constructed of public channels to connect client computers to servers, incorporating encryption and other security mechanisms to ensure that only authorized users can gain access and that the data cannot be intercepted.

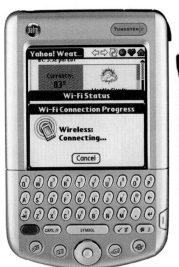

**FIGURE 8.34**

***Devices Commonly Used on Wireless Data Networks***

Palm Pilot, Compaq iPAC, and RIM Blackberry are among the most commonly used devices to interconnect with wireless data networks.

**FIGURE 8.35**

***Wireless Data Network***

Wireless data network enables users
of mobile devices to have wireless
connections to their enterprise
network.

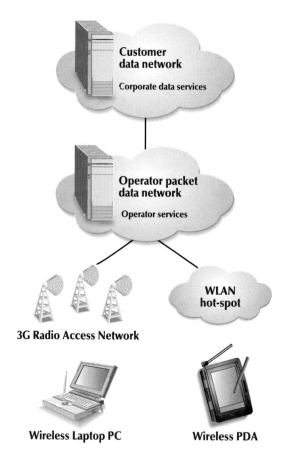

in providing security for message transmissions. Hence, VPN is being adopted in wireless LAN environments.

VPN works by establishing a secure, private connection (that is, a one-to-one connection) between the mobile device and a VPN gateway (Figure 8.36). In essence, each mobile device on the network communicates with an access point over a dedicated VPN tunnel—what appears to the user to be a private channel even though the network is shared. Packets traveling from one device to another over the mobile network must first pass through the sending clients' VPN tunnel, past the access point, and then out the VPN gateway. The packets then travel over the *wired* LAN to another VAN gateway where they are encrypted before being transmitted to the mobile device via a wireless access point. By placing the VPN gateway behind the access point, companies can ensure that all communications that go over the air are protected.

Security on a VPN is accomplished by two levels of encryption: password and data. Password encryption is the assumed minimum level of security, with data encryption—a more intense measure—providing second-level security. Additional security may be obtained by encrypting not only the data, but the originating and receiving network addresses as well. Such encryption methods allow users to tunnel through public networks in a manner that provides the same level of security formerly available only in private networks.

The VPN connection is an addition, not a replacement, to the network. VPN creates a tunnel between two end points, protecting against intrusion for packets traveling over the link. The (private) tunnel is created inside an already existing larger public network, and from the user's perspective, he or she appears to be operating within a distinct and independent system of interconnecting lines or channels. While security advantages are obvious, the organization also benefits. A VPN offers the same capabilities that would exist in a private network, but overall expenses are reduced with the shared infrastructure.

# CRITICAL CONNECTIONS 3

## MasterCard's IP Virtual Private Network Redefines Its Global Processes

**MasterCard**

MasterCard began in the late 1940s when several U.S. banks started giving their customers specially-issued paper that could be used like cash in local stores. In 1951, the Franklin National Bank in New York formalized the practice by introducing the first real credit card. Since its origin, MasterCard has been responsible for many innovations in the payments industry and continues to create innovative ways to pay for purchases. It has expanded globally to such an extent that no other payment card is accepted in more locations around the world. MasterCard also features the MasterCard/Cirrus ATM network, the world's largest. In 1987, MasterCard became the first payment card to be issued in the People's Republic of China.

Network bottlenecks, fluctuations in processing volume, and ensuring the security of transactions are among the most important concerns for MasterCard's enterprise network managers. Although MasterCard has operated a global communications network for many years, global events caused the company to seek ways to increase network security as it was upgrading the capacity of its network.

MasterCard implemented a virtual private network (VPN) using the Internet Protocol, the first such network in the credit-card payments industry. The VPN network, which operates in more than 60 countries, not only provides essential security of transactions but also ensures added reliability. Network reliability is essential with innovative payment products such as smart cards, which include the features of credit cards *plus* electronic cash.

With credit-card transactions, if a link is down between the card issuer and a merchant, the merchant will check a MasterCard database to see if a customer is creditworthy. But there is no database that says how much cash a smart card has stored on it. The network has to be accessible for card verification anywhere, any time, every time, and without delay. There is no room for failure.

FIGURE 8.36

*Virtual Private Network Architecture*

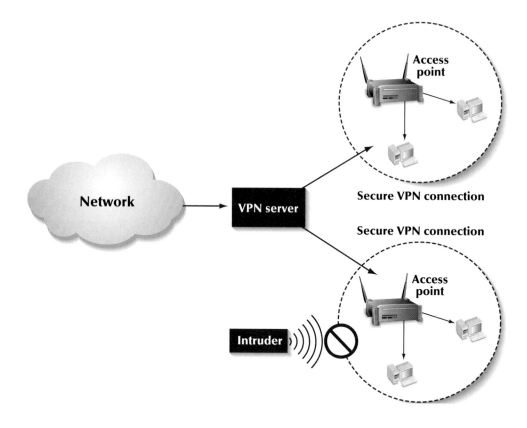

# Network Operating Systems

**network operating system (NOS)**

A software program that runs in conjunction with the computer's operating system and applications programs and manages the network.

Every computer that runs a network must have a **network operating system (NOS),** a software program that runs in conjunction with the computer's operating system and applications programs and manages the network. Like computers, networks cannot function without their operating system (Figure 8.37).

The NOS communicates with the LAN, WAN, or MAN hardware, accepting information transmitted from one device and directing it to another. It also manages the sharing of peripherals and storage devices, keeping track of the location of the devices and who is using them at a particular moment. Some widely used network operating systems are listed in Table 8.6.

## Protocol and Communications Control

**protocol**

The rules and conventions guiding data communications, embedded as coded instructions in the network software.

Every conversation, whether interpersonal or electronic, needs to proceed in an orderly fashion. How do computers know when and how to talk to one another? The rules and conventions guiding data communications are embedded as coded instructions in the network software. This **protocol** performs the following tasks:

FIGURE 8.37

*Network Operating System in Relation to Other Software*

A network operating system runs in conjunction with a computer's operating system and applications programs and manages the network.

| Application program | | |
|---|---|---|
| Network operating system | Computer operating system | Other programs (for example, database management system) |

| Table 8.6 Widely Used Network Operating Systems | |
|---|---|
| System Network Architecture | The IBM network structure for linking applications on mainframes, large e-servers, and midrange systems. |
| Apple Talk | Apple Computer's network operating system introduced in the early 1980s for Apple Computers, Macintosh computers and its personal digital assistants. |
| Novell Netware | The most widely used network operating system for microcomputers. |

- Signals the receiving computer that another computer wants to send a message.
- Identifies the sender.
- Transmits messages in blocks, if it detects that each block is received as it is sent.
- Retransmits a message, if it detects that the previous attempt was not successful.
- Determines when an error occurs and recovers from the error so that transmission can continue.
- Signals the receiver at the end of the transmission that no more messages will follow.
- Terminates the connection.

Many protocols have been established as standards in the use of information technology in WANs. The most common of these are SNA (IBM's system network architecture), TCP/IP protocol suite (Transmission Control Protocol/Internet Protocol for large-scale, high-speed backbone networks), X.25 (for public data networks), and X.400 (for electronic mail between different types of computers). In local area networks, two protocols are in widespread use: carrier sense multiple access (CSMA) and token ring. Table 8.7 summarizes the differences between these protocols, and Table 8.8 explains some other terms used in communications control.

Since protocol is needed between different components in communication, network designers developing communications use a seven-layer *open system interconnection (OSI) model* (Figure 8.38). Computer applications programs, network operating systems, and transmission protocol are defined within the OSI model, constituting what network professionals refer to as the *system network architecture.* (People using communications networks need not worry about these layers since they are handled by the software and network personnel.)

| Table 8.7 LAN Protocols | |
|---|---|
| Carrier Sense Multiple Access (CSMA) | The CSMA protocol follows the rule "Don't begin transmitting without first listening on the network to see if anyone else is using it. If not, send the message." A variation on CSMA, called *carrier sense multiple access with collision detection (CSMA/CD)*, is designed to avoid the case where two PCs begin to transmit at the same time, each thinking it is the only network user. The CSMA/CD protocol says, in effect, "Listen before you transmit *and* while you transmit. If you detect someone else using the network (a collision), wait for the other transmission to stop and then start your message again." The CSMA and CSMA/CD protocols are built into the Ethernet network developed by Xerox Corporation for LANs and into the LANs used by Apple Computer and some IBM systems. |
| Token Ring | The token ring protocol, so named because it is used with a ring topology, is based on a simple rule often invoked at large meetings: "Don't speak unless you have the microphone." When implemented as a LAN protocol, a token (string of bits) rather than a microphone is sent around the network. If no one is transmitting, the token is available for a member of the network to take and begin transmitting. When the transmission is completed, the token is sent back to the network so that another computer can retrieve it. With only one token, there cannot be any collisions, because protocol allows transmission only when a computer is holding the token. The token ring protocol is used often in IBM and Novell LANs. |

| Table 8.8 | **Communications Control Terminology** | | | |
|---|---|---|---|---|
| **TYPES OF TRANSMISSION LINES** | | | **TYPES OF TRANSMISSION** | |
| Simplex Lines | Transmit data in one direction only (either send or receive). | Asynchronous Protocol | Data are transmitted one character at a time. Transmissions of data bits is preceded and followed by special start-stop sequences. | |
| Half-Duplex Lines | Transmit data in either direction, but in only one direction at a time (alternate between send and receive). | Synchronous Protocol | Transmission is continuous. The transmitting receiving terminals must be synchronized — that is, in phase with each other. A clock (usually in the modem) governs transmission by determining when each data bit is sent. | |
| Full-Duplex Lines | Send and receive data simultaneously. | | | |

## Network Administration

**network administration/ network management**

The management of a network, consisting of those procedures and services that keep the network running properly.

The management of a network, usually called **network administration** or **network management,** consists of procedures and services that keep the network running properly. An important part of network management entails making sure that the network is available (or *up and running*, as IT professionals say) when employees and managers need it. Other network administration activities are

- Monitoring the network's capacity to ensure that all transmission requirements can be met.
- Adding capacity to the network by increasing bandwidth, interconnecting additional nodes, or creating and interconnecting additional networks.
- Training people to use the network effectively.
- Assisting IT professionals in writing applications that will make good use of the network's capabilities.
- Backing up the network software and data regularly to protect against the failure of the network or any of its components.

**FIGURE 8.38**

***Open System Interconnection (OSI) Model***

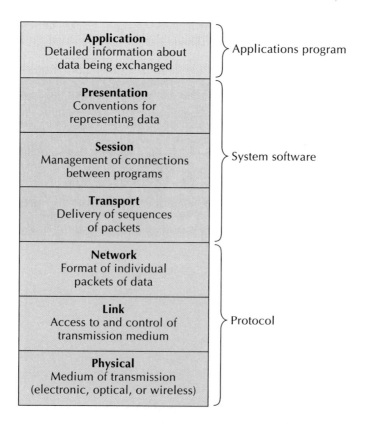

- Putting security procedures in place to make certain that only authorized users have access to the network, and ensuring that all security procedures are followed.
- Making sure that network personnel can respond quickly and effectively in the event of a network operational or security failure.
- Diagnosing and troubleshooting problems on the network and determining the best course of action to take to solve them.

As in business in general, the success of a network depends on the people who design and manage it. Network specialists include *network designers,* who specify the necessary features of the network and oversee its construction and installation; *network administrators,* who manage the day-to-day operations of the network; and *network security personnel,* who develop and oversee the use of procedures designed to protect the integrity of the network and ensure that is used in the intended manner and by authorized persons only. In large organizations, these roles are usually filled by different people. In smaller firms, one person may have multiple responsibilities.

# Enterprise Architectures

A communications **architecture** is the structure of a communications network; it determines how the various components of the communications network are structured, how they interact, and when cooperation between the system's components is needed. There are three types of enterprise system architectures: (1) centralized architecture, (2) distributed architecture, and (3) architectures that combine elements of centralized and distributed systems.

## Centralized Architecture

In a **centralized architecture,** all network hardware and software are found at a central site, usually in a computer center or a *server farm*—a center consisting of servers. Centralized computing is also called **host-based computing.** The central computer (or set of computers linked together at a single site) performs all processing and manages the network—that is, it hosts the network (Figure 8.39). It may retrieve information from a database, store new information, or accept and transmit information from one individual to another. All security protection works through the central server or host computer, which validates individual passwords and restricts the activities that individual users are

**architecture**
The structure of a communications network, which determines how the various components of the network are structured, how they interact, and when cooperation between the system's components is needed.

**centralized architecture**
A communications architecture in which a computer at a central site hosts all of the network's hardware and software, performs all of the processing, and manages the network.

**host-based computing**
Centralized computing.

Host computer

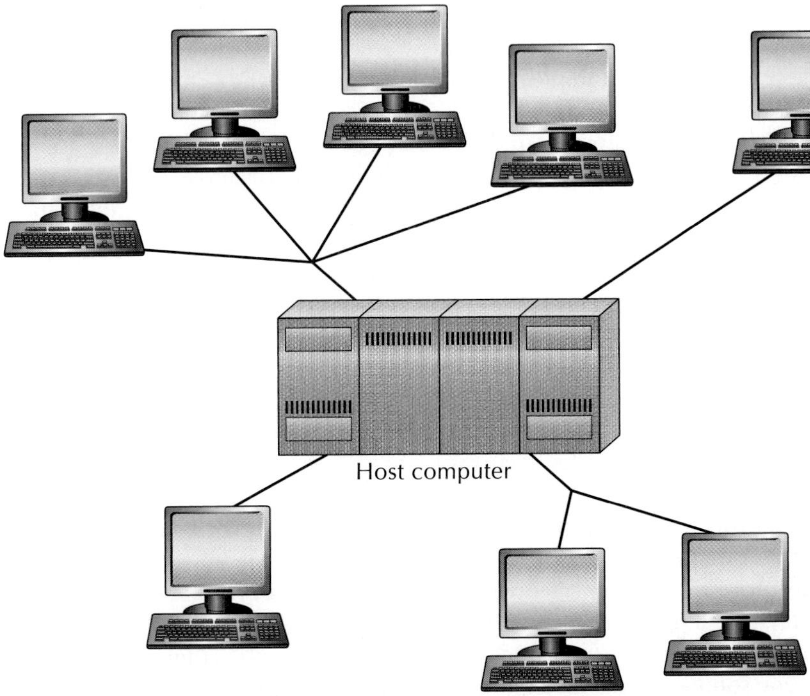

**FIGURE 8.39**

***Centralized Architecture***

In a centralized architecture, all network hardware and software are found at a central site, usually in a computer center. The central computer performs all the processing and hosts the network.

allowed to perform. IT staff members make backup copies of information and programs from the original versions, which reside on the host computer.

Throughout the 1960s, 1970s, and most of the 1980s, information technology was largely centralized. Organizations ran their applications on centralized mainframe or minicomputers located in data centers. Initially, dumb terminals—a display and keyboard without a processor (see Chapter 4)—were connected to the mainframe by a cable. For this reason, the terminals could not be too far away from the computer center. Users had to come to the computer center to use the computer, hauling their work with them.

A major advance in network technology came in the late 1960s, when computer manufacturers devised ways for people to connect with the centralized computer through telephone lines. This **teleprocessing** capability was an important advance in IT because the central computer's processing power and storage capacity could now be accessed and shared by many people from many locations simultaneously. People could remain at their work location and still use the host computer's processing capabilities. Figure 8.40 explains in detail how telephone communication works.

By the 1970s, minicomputers had enabled small and medium-sized companies to establish computer networks without having to invest in expensive mainframe computers. Minicomputers could serve as hosts, provided the volume of processing to be done was not so large as to overwhelm the processing and storage capabilities of the computer. Some companies also began using **front-end computers,** minicomputers loaded with special programs to handle all incoming and outgoing communications traffic in a host-based centralized system (Figure 8.41). A front-end mini frees the host computer to carry out the processing, storage, and retrieval tasks for which it is best suited.

## Distributed Architecture

As these changes came about, business and government leaders began to challenge IT professionals, saying, in effect: Our people are distributed, so our information and our processing capabilities must be, too. Therefore, we would like to find out the following:

- How can we get more value from our current IT capabilities?
- How can we interconnect different systems to achieve maximum efficiency?
- How can we make different computer and communications systems work together?

The answer to all of these questions was distributed architecture. In a **distributed architecture,** computers—supercomputers, mainframes, midrange systems, and microcomputers—reside at different locations, rather than in a single data center, and are interconnected by a communications network. The computer at each location primarily serves the needs of that location. The distributed computers work together through the network, retrieving information from some locations within it and acting as a source of information for other locations in the network.

A distributed architecture supports **distributed processing,** in which an application runs on one or more locations of the network simultaneously (Figure 8.42). In a distributed processing system, the hardware, software, or information needed for the application may be physically located at a different location. **Distributed databases** (discussed in Chapter 11) are databases that reside on more than one computer system in a distributed network. Each component of the database can be retrieved, processed, or updated from any node in the network, rather than through a central host computer only.

Kmart uses a very large distributed architecture (Figure 8.43). All of its stores use point-of-sale bar code scanning on all items that pass through the checkout counter. By means of its satellite link, this purchase information is transmitted immediately to merchandise buyers at the company's Troy, Michigan, headquarters and to a large number of the company's suppliers. Credit authorization for customers paying by credit card is also obtained through this communications link, thus speeding the checkout process while ensuring that the card is valid.

Each Kmart store is interconnected with one of the company's 12 distribution centers nationwide, where inventory records are maintained. Sales information is transmitted continuously between the stores and the distribution centers' computers. In addition, Kmart's key suppliers have invested in their own computer systems that let them

---

**teleprocessing**

The processing capability made possible by connecting desktop computers to a remote computer through telephone lines.

**front-end computer**

In a centralized system, a minicomputer loaded with special programs to handle all incoming and outgoing communications traffic.

**distributed architecture**

A communications architecture in which the computers reside at different locations and are interconnected by a communications network.

**distributed processing**

Processing in which an application runs on one or more locations of the network simultaneously.

**distributed database**

A database that resides in more than one system in a distributed network. Each component of the database can be retrieved from any node in the network.

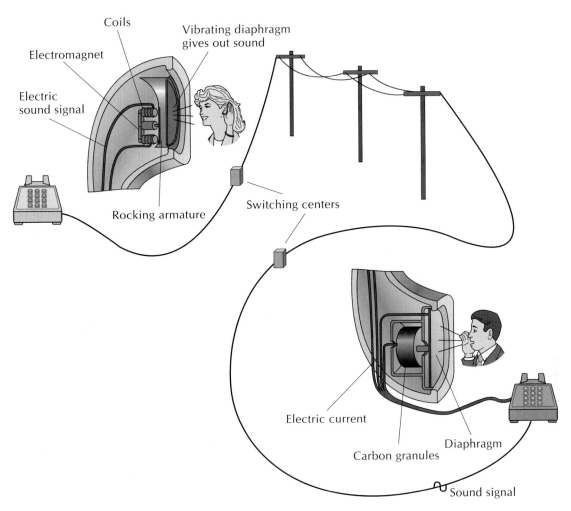

**FIGURE 8.40**

### *How Telephone Communication Works*

When you speak into the telephone, a small microphone in the handset captures the sounds through a vibrating diaphragm, causing the electrical current flowing through the microphone to vary. From the handset, these electrical signals are sent over metal telephone wires. In the public telephone network, the electrical signals may be translated into light signals that are beamed over fiber-optic lines (see Figure 8.17). Alternatively, they may be converted into radio signals transmitted over radio networks or by microwave (see Figures 8.18A and 18B).

How does a telephone call or data communication transmission get to the right place? How are so many conversations and messages sent over a communications network? Today's communications systems convert speech into digital form—the same digital codes used in computer systems. Using *multiplexing,* several messages can be packed together and sent simultaneously on the network. The messages are divided into blocks that are sent in very short intervals. Built into each block of data are identification and routing codes. When these are read by the digital switching components that are part of the network, the message can be switched from one line to another, perhaps repeatedly, so that it reaches its intended destination. Because data move at the speed of electricity or at the speed of light (186,000 miles per second), a message reaches its destination in a fraction of one second.

The identification codes make it possible to keep one message distinct from another and to ensure that the right data are sent to the proper destination. At the destination, a *demultiplexor* unpacks the various streams of data and routes the message blocks back to the correct telephone.

These same principles apply in computer communications (see Figure 8.22).

electronically monitor inventories at Kmart's distribution centers. Now they can automatically replenish the stock, without awaiting approval from Kmart, when supplies run low. Even small suppliers can take advantage of these distributed capabilities. The total cost (for hardware and software) needed to set up this type of system is under $15,000.

## Combining Architectures

One type of architecture is not always better than the other. Each has benefits and drawbacks. For example, centralized systems are easier to manage because of the central location. Distributed systems, though more difficult to manage, place information at the

**FIGURE 8.41**

*Centralized Architecture Using a Front-End Computer*

A front-end computer allows the host computer to carry out the processing, storage, and retrieval tasks for which it is best suited.

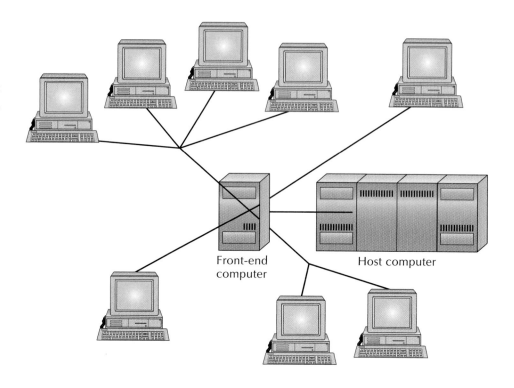

Front-end computer

Host computer

**hybrid network**

A communications architecture that combines centralized and distributed architectures to take advantage of the strengths of both.

locations where it is used most often while ensuring that other nodes in the system have access to it.

To take advantage of the benefits of both configurations, companies sometimes combine architectures. In general, these **hybrid networks** mesh centralized teleprocessing and distributed features. In hybrid networks, the computer at the top of the system (usually a mainframe or large server) controls interaction with all of the devices attached directly to it. The host does not, however, directly control those computers interconnected at lower levels of the network (Figure 8.44).

**Hybrid Networks in the Airline Industry** Hybrid networks can take many forms. Some companies, for example, have combined networks that span vast geographic regions with others that link desktop computers within a single building. One such system was developed for use in the airline industry during the 1980s and 1990s, when many European airlines suddenly confronted heightened competition from deregulated U.S. airlines. To stay in business, their managements concluded, these airlines would have to expand beyond their national borders. Doing so was a challenge, however, for two main reasons.

First, at that time (before the Internet), travel agents—independent businesspeople who receive a commission on every sale of a ticket for an airline—sold the majority of airline tickets. Travel agents sold tickets for virtually all of the world's airlines, so they often tended not to promote a single carrier. Second, no single European airline had the resources to develop its own network to interconnect the travel agents in the many countries to which it flies. The system development and operations costs were prohibitive. Nonetheless, each airline had to find a way to share information with travel agents about schedules, fares, and reservations.

Out of this necessity evolved an alliance among more than 20 airlines (including Air France, Iberia, Lufthansa, and SAS) and the network-based Amadeus system. Through this network, the airlines and a vast array of travel agents throughout the world shared flight information. Development of the Amadeus network provided the foundation for other network-based travel services. For example, Amadeus could be used to book reservations for ferry and Hovercraft crossings, trains, and automobile rentals.

The strength of Amadeus is its hybrid network. Each airline, hotel, or other business enterprise connected to Amadeus continues to operate its own computer network. Some of these individual networks are centralized, while others are distributed; some span large

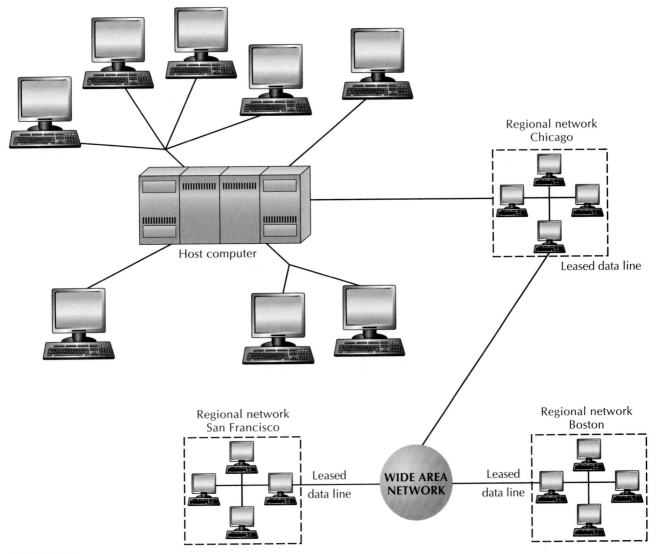

**FIGURE 8.42**

**Distributed Architecture with Distributed Processing**

In a distributed architecture, computers reside at different locations, rather than in a single data center, and are interconnected by a communications network.

areas, while others span small areas; all use different combinations of computers, programs, and screen displays. Amadeus links all of these individual networks.

Amadeus continues to exist some two decades later. However, the rise of the Internet and e-commerce has triggered all airlines to develop Web sites through which bookings can be made. Hence, traveler usage of Amadeus, which itself has a Web site, is not at its earlier levels.

The combination of business alliances with a hybrid network architecture has changed the way international airlines compete and the markets they serve. But communications networks are also of great interest to societies. In fact, an industry-sponsored study conducted by the Iacocca Institute at Lehigh University in the early 1990s recommended the creation of a nationwide communications network to link factories across the United States, with the goal of boosting the global competitiveness of U.S. manufacturers.

Under plans developed as part of the Iacocca study, the Factory America Net was to allow most companies to interconnect with the network. For example, a company developing a new product will be able to send a message across the network asking suppliers to provide information on their ability to manufacture a component or to provide a service needed for the new product. The creation of **virtual companies**–business

**virtual company**

A company that joins with another company operationally, but not physically, to design and manufacture a product.

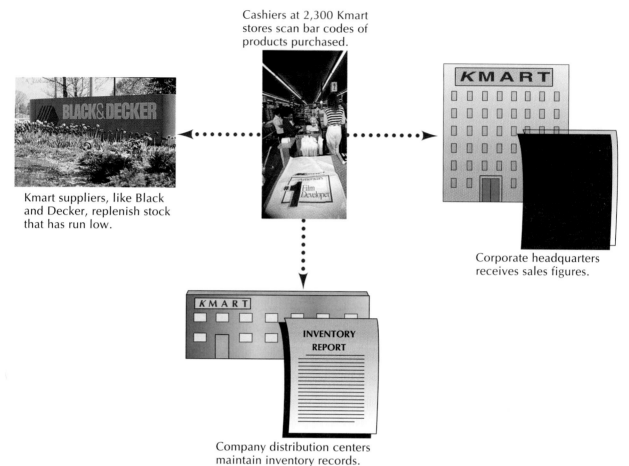

Cashiers at 2,300 Kmart stores scan bar codes of products purchased.

Kmart suppliers, like Black and Decker, replenish stock that has run low.

Corporate headquarters receives sales figures.

Company distribution centers maintain inventory records.

**FIGURE 8.43**
*Kmart's Distributed Database*

**FIGURE 8.44**
*Hybrid Architecture*
Hybrid architecture combines centralized and distributed features. The computer at the top of the network (here the mainframe) controls interaction with all the devices attached directly to it. The host does not control the computer interconnected at lower levels of the network.

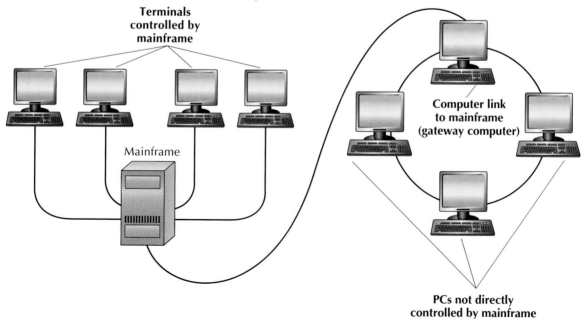

Terminals controlled by mainframe

Mainframe

Computer link to mainframe (gateway computer)

PCs not directly controlled by mainframe

enterprises that come together operationally, but not physically, to design and manufacture a product—is expected to be one result of this hybrid network.

The essence of the Factory America Net has been created through a variety of different Internet applications and will undoubtedly evolve as the concept takes shape through Web applications. It is long-term in scope, designed to be an integral component of U.S. manufacturing strategies in the twenty-first century.

## A Final Word

As you leave this chapter, one point should be clear: Communications networks are an essential component of IT. If you can't link up, you can't communicate, and you will probably lose out. That is the reality of business today.

## CRITICAL CONNECTIONS

### 1 Part II: Havertys Furniture Redesigns Network for Top Performance

**Havertys Furniture** Havertys Furniture Company's new network, featuring the TCP/IP protocol over a frame-relay transport channel, achieved new levels of speed and performance. This company's experience shows the impact the choice of protocol and transport technology can have on overall network performance without any change in computer equipment or applications. Without the change, the system response would not only have continued to be poor, but company officials believed that frustration of sales and clerical staff would have continued to grow, ultimately resulting in lost business and misplaced orders.

The change in the structure of its communications network also enabled Havertys to lower its network expenses. The company's frame-relay-based system cost dramatically less than the leased lines it had been using, which produced an extra benefit on top of the improved response time for business transactions.

#### Questions for Discussion

1. How does a network's response time influence the willingness of individuals to use a communications network?
2. What characteristics of a communications network influence the response time that users encounter when sending and receiving data?
3. How did the TCP/IP protocol, when used with a redesigned network, enable Havertys to integrate LAN, Internet, and intranet message traffic?
4. What conclusions do you draw from the Havertys Furniture Company's experience concerning the importance of choosing the right mix of technologies when creating an enterprise network?

### 2 Part II: XM Satellite Radio Lets Listeners Tune In . . . Nationwide!

 XM Satellite Radio is using satellite communications networks to redefine radio. Market data show strong demand for radio service—more than 75 percent of the U.S. population (age 12 and older) listens to the radio daily, and over 95 percent listens to the radio weekly. However, many radio listeners have access to only a limited number of radio stations and listening formats offered by traditional AM/FM radio. With XM, 100 channels of crystal clear digital music, news, sports, and entertainment are available. Because XM relies on satellite transmission channels, its broadcasts are available virtually anywhere. Moreover, a program's signal doesn't fade as the listener drives away from the city center.

Specially equipped radios having the receiver and antenna to pick up the programs can be mounted in an automobile or positioned on a desk or counter top. They are available at major electronics retailers throughout the United States. These radios not only accept satellite transmissions, but they also feature a small screen displaying information about the music or other program being broadcast. Programs not only include special broadcasts originating in XM's studios, but also draw on stations from throughout the United States. For example, someone in California who enjoys listening to a famous New York City station's special broadcast of jazz is likely able to tune in to that station on XM radio.

XM Satellite Radio, licensed by the Federal Communications Commission, seeks to become the premier nationwide provider of audio entertainment and information programming for reception by vehicle, home, and portable radios. Its clever use of satellite technology and its ability to reach audiences anywhere may be just what it needs to turn the vision into reality. XM provides a premium service to radio fans seeking a step up in reception quality and breadth of news and entertainment choices when they want to turn on and tune in.

### Questions for Discussion

1. What advantages does use of satellite channels give to XM Satellite Radio listeners compared to traditional radio broadcast channels?
2. What special requirements are there to listen to XM?

Why do you suppose there is not a large number of radio broadcast companies like XM Satellite Radio?

## 3   Part II: MasterCard's IP Virtual Private Network Redefines Its Global Processes

**MasterCard** MasterCard's global VPN provides all-important network security and operational reliability. But that is only the beginning. Because MasterCard VPN uses a public infrastructure to run a network that is essentially private, the company is able to change network capacity to cope with seasonal fluctuations. Its VPN has eliminated the processing bottlenecks that caused delay in card verification transaction handling. At the same time, the VPN has added the flexibility to meet shifting activity levels. The bandwidth-on-demand feature allows MasterCard to expand network capacity during peak-volume times.

Using the Internet protocol (IP) in the network not only provides the transmission and network efficiency that comes with packet-based messages, but it also supports future expansion. Because of the IP's open standard, MasterCard can be assured of system flexibility to support any new payment applications it will devise in the future.

### Questions for Discussion

1. What are the most important characteristics of VPNs for MasterCard?
2. How does MasterCard's VPN provide flexibility in the capacity and bandwidth of its global processing network?
3. What are the most important characteristics of the Internet protocol in achieving MasterCard's network processing objectives?

## *Summary of Learning Objectives*

**1** **Describe eight network service applications used in enterprises.**   The eight network service applications most frequently used in business are (1) electronic mail, (2) voice mail, (3) videoconferencing, (4) work group conferencing, (5) electronic bulletin boards, (6) electronic funds transfer, (7) electronic data interchange, and (8) videotex.

Electronic mail, or e-mail, is a service that transports text messages from a sender to one or more receivers via computer. Voice mail systems capture, store, and transmit spoken messages. They do not use computer keyboards, but rather a telephone connected to a computer network. Videoconferencing is a type of conferencing in which video cameras and microphones capture sight and sound for transmission over networks. Large display screens show the other parties in the conference–*live*. Work group conferencing uses a type of software package called groupware to organize an electronic meeting in which participants' computers are interconnected from their various locations. Each participant interacts through a microcomputer directly linked to a main computer; comments are broadcast to all participants in the conference. Electronic bulletin boards are similar to the bulletin boards at the supermarket where messages and announcements are posted and read. Users of an electronic bulletin board dial into the board over a communications link and leave a message, file, or program.

Others dialing into the bulletin board can retrieve the information and copy it to their system. Electronic funds transfer (EFT) is the movement of money over a network. Electronic data interchange (EDI) is a form of electronic communication that allows trading partners to exchange business transaction data in structured formats that can be processed by applications software. Videotex is a two-way, interactive, text-only service operating on mainframe computers that provides a video screen with easy-to-follow instructions.

**2** **Discuss the three types of communications networks and the advantages offered by each.**   The three types of networks are (1) wide area networks (WANs), designed to span large geographic regions; (2) local area networks (LANs), which interconnect desktop computers and communications devices within an office or series of offices; and (3) metropolitan area networks (MANs), which use fiber-optic cables to transmit various types of information around a city or metropolitan region.

**3** **Discuss the two types of communications channels used in networks and the ways that computers interconnect with them.**   Two types of communications channels are used in networks: (1) physical channels and (2) cableless channels. The physical channels (twisted pair, coaxial cable, and optical cable) use a wire or cable along which data and information are transmitted. The cableless channels (microwave, satellite, infrared, and radio frequency transmission) are wireless transmission media.

In WANs, modems connect computers to the communications channel and translate the information from the computer into a form that can be transmitted over the channel. In LANs, a network interface card is used.

**4 Identify the five transport technologies that are in widespread use in physical channel networks.**
The five transport technologies in widespread use are (1) frame relay, (2) asynchronous transfer mode (ATM), (3) digital subscriber lines (DSL), (4) integrated services digital network (ISDN), and (5) switched multimegabit data services (SMDS). The choice of transport technology depends on the planned use of the network and on the technology available in a specific geographic region.

**5 Describe the four forms of wireless communications.**
The four widely used wireless communications forms include (1) cellular communications service, (2) wireless LANs, (3) Bluetooth personal area networks, and (4) wireless data networks. Cellular communications services, which typify mobile telephone service, are evolving from analog to digital service, with new generations offering higher transmission speeds. Wireless LANs are increasingly used to augment traditional LAN use in the enterprise, giving users greater mobility while enabling them to access the network. The Bluetooth personal communications network technology provides wireless access to devices, albeit over a range of 30 feet (10 meters) or less. Wireless data networks are frequently used by individuals seeking to send and receive data (especially e-mail) via PDAs and wireless laptop computers. These networks are operated by a third party who interconnects with the user's enterprise network.

**6 Explain the role of a network operating system.**
Every computer that runs a network must have a net-

work operating system (NOS), a software program that manages the network and runs in conjunction with the computer's operating system and applications programs.

**7 Discuss the activities involved in network administration.** Network administration, or management, consists of all of the procedures and services that keep the network running properly. One important aspect of network administration entails making sure that the network is available when users need it. Other parts of the network administrator's job are monitoring the network's capacity to ensure that all transmission requirements can be met; adding capacity to the network when necessary; conducting training to prepare individuals to use the network; assisting IT professionals in writing applications; backing up the network software and data regularly; putting security procedures in place; ensuring that network personnel can respond quickly to an operational or security failure; and diagnosing and troubleshooting problems on the network when they occur.

**8 Explain the three types of enterprise architectures and the advantages offered by each.** In a centralized architecture, all network hardware and software are located at a central site where the central computer, or host, performs all of the processing and manages the network. Centralized systems are easy to manage. In a distributed architecture, computers reside at different locations and are interconnected by a communications network. Distributed architecture places information at the locations where it is used most often while ensuring that others in the system have access to it.

To take advantage of the benefits of both types of architecture, companies can choose to combine them in a hybrid architecture. Here, a mainframe controls interaction with all of the devices attached directly to it. The host does not, however, directly control those computers interconnected at lower levels of the network.

## Key Terms

access point 357
architecture 367
asymmetric digital subscriber line (ADSL) 353
asynchronous transfer mode (ATM) 352
backbone network 346
baseband cable 340
Bluetooth personal area network 359
bridge 348
broadband cable 340

cellular communications service 355
centralized architecture 367
circuit switched 345
coaxial cable/co-ax 340
code division multiple access (CDMA) 356
collaborative conferencing 323
common carrier 334
communication 316
communications channel/communications medium 339

communications network 317
digital subscriber line (DSL) 352
distributed architecture 368
distributed database 368
distributed processing 368
electronic bulletin board 324
electronic data interchange (EDI) 326
electronic funds transfer (EFT) 326
electronic mailbox 319
fiber-optic cable 340
file server 337

## Review Questions

1. What are the two principal purposes of a communications network?
2. What trends related to network use are driving enterprises today?
3. Define *communications network*. What is a node and of what does it consist of in a communications network?
4. Discuss the nature of communications architecture and distinguish among the three types of communications architecture. What advantages and disadvantages does each type offer to business?
5. Identify and briefly describe the eight most widely used network service applications involving enterprise networks.
6. How do host computers and front-end computers differ? What purpose does each serve in a communications network? Is each a required component of a network?
7. Describe the distinguishing characteristics of a WAN, LAN, and MAN. Under what circumstances do companies use each type of network?
8. What are the two types of communications channels?
9. Identify the three types of physical communications channels. Which has been in use for the longest period of time?
10. Describe the four types of cableless communications media.
11. How do LEOs and GEOs differ and what are the advantages and disadvantages of each?

12. Explain the differences among public-access networks, private *leased line* networks, and value-added networks. What advantages does each offer to business?
13. Do LANs use the same types of communications channels as WANs? Explain.
14. What is the purpose of a modem? A network interface card?
15. Why do businesses sometimes want to interconnect their communications networks? What are the two means for doing so? What determines which method of interconnection will be used?
16. How do circuit switched and packet networks differ from one another? Why have packet networks grown in use?
17. Five network transport technologies are in widespread use. Identify each and describe their distinguishing characteristics.
18. What factors determine the selection of a particular transport technology for use in an enterprise network?
19. What advantages does DSL offer for accessing the Internet from a computer at home?
20. Describe the four wireless forms for data communication. Which forms are most likely to be used for voice communications? Why?
21. What is a cellular communications service?
22. How do cellular radio systems and the public switched telephone network interconnect?

23. Can a wireless network using cellular communications service act as the backbone of a wide area data network? Why or why not?

24. How did users and service providers benefit when a shift was made from first- to second-generation cellular access technologies?

25. What are the three 2G cellular access technologies in use today? Which one is most widely used globally? Why is this the case?

26. How do 2G, 2.5G, and 3G cellular access technologies differ from one another?

27. Describe the characteristics of generalized packet radio service. How does this compare with 2G wireless networks?

28. Two hardware components are needed to create a wireless LAN. What are they and what function does each serve?

29. Describe the advantages and disadvantages of wireless LANs.

30. Identify the characteristics and relationship between 802.11a, 802.11b, and Wi-Fi.

31. Why is wired equivalent privacy useful in wireless LANs?

32. Are wireless LANs and Bluetooth personal area networks substitutes for one another? That is, can these wireless network technologies be used interchangeably? Why or why not?

33. What are the distinguishing characteristics of wireless data networks? Who are the principal users of such networks and why do they use them?

34. What is a VPN and what purpose does it serve?

35. Do VPNs replace ordinary WANs and WLANs? Explain the reason for your answer.

36. Describe the role of a network operating system in a communications network. How is it different from a computer operating system? Does using one eliminate the need for the other?

37. What responsibilities are entailed in network administration?

38. How are electronic mail and voice mail different? What advantages does each system offer?

39. What is unified messaging and how does it differ from voice mail? What advantages does unified messaging provide to professionals who are on the move from place to place and use a variety of different communication tools?

40. How does webcasting differ from video conferencing?

41. Describe electronic data interchange. What is the relationship between electronic data interchange and a value-added network?

## Discussion Questions

1. Wal-Mart, the Bentonville, Arkansas discount retailer is well known both for its size and for its *everyday low prices*. A key reason the company is able to keep prices low is because of its use of EDI to interact with its suppliers. Wal-Mart uses EDI to transmit order, shipment, and payment information electronically over VANs. To be a Wal-Mart supplier, a company must be able to interact with a VAN.

   Wal-Mart recently announced that soon all suppliers, large or small, will have to replace their EDI systems using VANs; all EDI transactions will soon be conducted over the Internet. What advantages and disadvantages does this change have for Wal-Mart? Will the change help or hurt current Wal-Mart vendors and potential new Wal-Mart suppliers? Why?

2. The capability for individuals or enterprises to conduct web casts is now widely available. What role could webcasting play in acquiring or sharing information from prospective investors or buyers of a new product or service *while it is under development?* In these instances, what advantages does webcasting provide over video conferencing and one-on-one personal visits with each investor or buyer? What do you think the future holds for webcasting in business? In university and executive education?

3. NSPs are in the business of constructing and operating wireline and wireless communications networks, which they make available to companies for a fee. However, the level of security varies between the networks provided by NSPs. Often, enterprises contracting with an NSP must add their own security features in order to ensure their transactions and messages are safe from unauthorized detection or use.

   What are the advantages and disadvantages of using a network service provider as a substitute for an enterprise building that operates its own wide area network?

   Should NSPs have a legal obligation to offer customers only networks that are fully secure from unauthorized intrusion and interception of transactions and messages? Why or why not?

4. Consider the possibility of widespread installation of wireless LANs and access points in public areas such as stores, shopping areas, and airports. Is this likely to be a growing trend in the United States? Why or why not?

   Next, discuss the advantages and disadvantages of having widespread availability of wireless LANs in the areas mentioned above. What possible uses would be made of these networks, and by whom?

5. E-mail is widely used by individuals and within public and private organizations. Its capabilities have been

perfected over two decades. In the meantime, usage of wireless networks for communication by individuals and organizations is skyrocketing, driven by attractive prices, ever-improving reliability, and a wide selection of PDAs and mobile phones.

What is the future of e-mail? Will its use increase? Will the growing usage of wireless PDAs impede its growth? Might both coexist, with each growing even more in usage? What factors underlie the reason for your opinion?

6. Matson Navigation Company, a 110-year-old company that operates ships carrying cargo between the West Coast of the United States and Hawaii, uses electronic mail, fax, and local area networks linked to a mainframe to track containers on its ships and on the 600 trucks that pass through its terminal gates daily. What type of network architecture is Matson using? What type of network is it using?

7. The Internet, today a maze of thousands of networks around the world, was originally created in the mid-1960s to facilitate the sharing of information between researchers at government agencies and universities. Now that millions of private enterprise employees exchange electronic mail on the Internet every day, company officials often stress that none of these messages involve confidential data. Why would officials emphasize this point?

8. Managers typically spend between 30 percent and 70 percent of their time in meetings. Why might this fact be inspiring companies to use work group conferencing?

## Group Projects and Applications

### Project 1

As you know, enterprise communications networks can be configured in a variety of different ways. Contact or visit the network manager in a large retail, grocery, or hotel company of your choice. Interview the manager about the nature of the company's WAN. Note the number of locations on the network and the number and variety of devices attached to the WAN.

Secondly, discuss the choice of transport technologies and protocol features in the company's network. Inquire about the reason for the selection of these alternatives, noting what other alternatives were not selected.

Thirdly, discuss the company's future plans for its WAN. What enhancements and changes does the network manager foresee and why?

### Project 2

Arrange to interview—in person, by telephone, or via e-mail—the network security manager for a regional or national financial services firm (such as a bank, a brokerage firm, or a credit card company). First, interview the manager about the company's wide area and local area network characteristics, including transport technologies, volume of message traffic, and the devices interconnected to the network. Also determine whether any wireless links are included in the networks.

Second, explore the nature of security concerns in the enterprise network. Inquire about the company's use of virtual private networks and other security provisions that are included in the network's design.

Prepare a PowerPoint presentation outlining the characteristics of the company, the nature of your investigation, and your findings in each of the areas of inquiry.

### Project 3

With a partner, visit a company in one of the following industries, which all make use of large-scale computer networks:

- Transportation
- Retailing
- Manufacturing

Interview the network manager or someone in the IT department. What are the benefits of a wide area communications network to the company? What types of applications run on the network? What type of architecture is used? What functions does the network operating system perform? What business challenges does the company face, and how is the network helping to meet those challenges?

Prepare a two-page report summarizing your findings. Exchange reports with another group, then read and critique each other's report. Try to answer any questions that the other group may have.

### Project 4

All parts of the United States have both local and long-distance telephone carriers. Contact a representative from one of these providers to discuss the company's position on developing additional communications capabilities for the nation's business and commerce infrastructure. What kinds of breakthroughs are expected over the next few years? What are the company's long-term plans? How will both businesses and private citizens benefit from these new technologies?

If possible, invite the representative to speak to your class. Before the lecture, the class should brainstorm a list of questions to ask the rep.

# Net_Work

## Comparing Cellular Service Alternatives

Competing cellular communications service providers are offering many different wireless service plans as a way of acquiring new business. The prices and features of these plans can vary dramatically.

Using the Internet, conduct an investigation of the differences in plans. You may choose to visit the Web sites of wireless service providers in your area. Or, you may find it beneficial to visit one or more of the Web sites designed to offer comparative information, such as

www.point.com
www.getconnected.com
www.letstalk.com
www.myrateplan.com
www.cellmania.com

Be certain to compare the alternative plans on price as well as other possible differences outlined in this chapter's discussion.

Using the information gathered during your analysis, prepare a brief report summarizing the differences between the calling plans offered by the service providers. Indicate the conclusions you have drawn from your fact-finding investigation.

## Wireless Data Services

A growing variety of PDAs are manufactured or can be equipped with the capability to interconnect with wireless data services. Both the PDAs and the available services provide differing features designed to meet personal preferences and individual needs.

Compare the features of *wireless versions* of the Palm Pilot, Compaq iPAQ, and RIM Blackberry. Prepare a table that outlines the similarities and differences in features. Be sure to include such features as price and functions. If a user is only interested in sending and receiving a large volume of e-mail messages, would one PDA be more desirable than the others?

Next, investigate the wireless data services that are available for use with each PDA. Prepare a summary of the economic and functional differences between each service. Indicate whether the service can be used with all three of the PDAs mentioned above, or only one.

## More Collaboration on the World Wide Web

There is growing interest in Web-based collaboration software. CU-SeeMe (pronounced See You, See Me), an Internet software program created by Cornell University and its collaborators, was the first program that made it possible to conduct desktop conferencing over the Web. Anyone with a Macintosh or Windows computer and a connection to the Internet can use CU-SeeMe to videoconference (for conferences, broadcasts, or chats) with another site located anywhere in the world. Best of all, multiple parties can do so right from their own desktop computers. (If you wish to learn more about this program, you can do so at www.cuseeme.com or www.cuseemeworld.com.)

Since then, other software and online services have been developed to support collaboration. Using any of the leading search engines, conduct an investigation on the Internet to identify at least five other software programs and Web services currently available for collaboration.

Using the information acquired during your investigation, prepare a summary table that outlines the similarities and differences between each alternative.

# Cool Mobility

## On Assignment

The company's internal network features a PC on every desk. Each PC is connected to a local area network (LAN) by fiber-optic cable that runs to the network router. The router for each LAN in turn is linked to a large server where shared software and databases reside.

## In Consultation

Mark Goodman has been inquiring about the feasibility of installing wireless communications capabilities within the human resource department. This way, he says, people working on laptop computers could remain connected to the company network even when they take their computers into a conference room. (Currently employees must disconnect their laptop computers from the cable at their desks.)

a. What hardware and software components will have to be added to the company's network in order to enable employees to link to the intranet by a wireless channel?

Other than expense, are there any drawbacks to implementing a wireless LAN access alternative for those employees who use laptop computers?

b. Besides wireless LAN, what other wireless communications transmission method could be considered to interconnect laptop computers to the network? What equipment would be needed to make the link?

# Case Study

## Boeing Stays on Top—with Wireless Networks and Jumbo Jets

**Boeing Company**

The Boeing Company is the world's leading aerospace company, with its heritage mirroring the history of flight stemming from a long tradition of technical excellence and innovation. The global reach of the Chicago-based company, with annual revenues in excess of $58 billion, includes customers in 145 countries, employees in more than 60 countries and operations in 26 states. Every day its aircraft and its networks connect passengers, partners, and employees. For instance:

- In the next 24 hours, 3-million passengers will board 42,300 flights on Boeing jetliners carrying them to nearly every country on earth.
- In the next 24 hours, more than 15,000 Boeing suppliers in 81 countries will provide parts and services for Boeing products and the infrastructure that designs, builds, sells, and supports them.
- In the next 24 hours, Boeing will send 4,650 shipments of spare parts to airline customers worldwide.
- In the next 24 hours, 8-million e-mail messages will be exchanged among employees in the Boeing network.

Boeing has been the world leader in commercial flight for more than 40 years, with more than 14,000 commercial jetliners in service worldwide, which is roughly 75 percent of the world fleet. The main commercial products consist of the 717, 737, 747, 757, 767, and 777 families of jetliners

and the Boeing Business Jet. Its 747, 767, and 777 models have rightly been dubbed *jumbo jets* because of their huge size and large passenger and freight capacity. The Boeing 747, built at the company's Everett, Washington, factory, is the largest passenger aircraft in the sky. In fact, the Wright Brothers' first flight at Kitty Hawk, North Carolina, could have been performed within the 150-foot (45-m) economy section of a 747-400. Its wings cover an area large enough to hold 45 medium-size automobiles; the aircraft itself is as tall as a six-story building.

Passengers often wonder how an aircraft the size of these jumbo jets *can fly*. Engineers, who gasp at the fact that each consists of more than 6-million parts and in excess of 170 miles of wiring, wonder *how they can be manufactured*. You can be sure that good design, sharp project managers, and

the right tools play a crucial role in ensuring that the aircraft performs as expected.

Inside the giant 98-acre hanger where these aircrafts are made, you can see the skeletons of partially completed 747s and the other jumbo jets. Giant cranes move about on a network of some 30 *miles* of overhead track. Trucks, forklifts, and bicycles drive back and forth across the factory floor on indoor *streets* created by painted lines.

Information technology is at the heart of many of the tools used at Boeing's jumbo jet manufacturing facility. Workers rely on computers to access digital encyclopedias of schematics, blue prints, instructions, and drawings. However, you will not see networking cables connecting the workers' computers to Boeing's mainframe computers where these digital documents reside. (Imagine the challenges of stringing and protecting conventional Ethernet cables in a warehouse this size, where a cable could be cut by a moving vehicle or by a careless worker.) Instead, Boeing counts on a wireless LAN using the 802.11b wireless protocol (Wi-Fi). Here is how it works.

Mobile Boeing workers can view aircraft information on their laptop PC or PDA from anywhere in the hangar or the surrounding outside area. When they enter a query or parts request into their laptop, the computer translates the request into a radio signal and transmits it via the wireless Internet connector built into the PC or PDA. The signal is picked up by an antenna and sent through an access point on the factory network. The access stations, mounted 75 to 100 feet in the air across the factory ceiling, transmit the request at more than 11 mbps to a Boeing mainframe computer attached to the factory network. The query and subsequent response that are sent back across the wireless network takes less than a second (except for detailed graphical information that might take 1 or 2 seconds longer).

Since wireless transmissions are not inhibited by walls or the shells of aircraft under construction, workers can count on using their wireless devices regardless of their location. This characteristic, which enabled them to be mobile, caused usage to grow rapidly once the network was installed. It removed many information retrieval and communications hassles in the manufacturing process. It eliminated the need for technicians to climb down from the scaffolding and walk to a PC at the edge of the factory floor, wait in line, and then

print instructions or order a part. Instead mobility means they can use the network regardless of where they are working.

Moreover, manufacturing managers and workers can respond to emergency requests immediately, for messages reach them anywhere at the Boeing manufacturing facility. Waiting for people to check voice mail messages or download e-mail at their desk is a thing of the past.

As workers grew accustomed to the network and increased their usage, additional applications were implemented. Today the Boeing Wi-Fi factory network delivers multimedia and animation files that demonstrate complex manufacturing procedures. Workers using the multimedia demonstrations can be guided in how to perform a manufacturing step and how to verify the quality of the result. Without this support, they would need someone's on-the-spot assistance or have to leave the work site to get guidance.

The Wi-Fi network is triggering still other innovations. For instance, combined advances in wireless network communications and miniaturization of PC components has led to the development of wireless goggles by industry IT manufacturers. Boeing has tested the goggles and envisions their use by workers who will be able to view blueprints, drawings, and animated information. The goggles will eliminate workers having to glance away from their work to view information on their laptop or PDA.

Phil Condit, Boeing's Chairman and CEO, is a strong supporter of wireless networks and worker mobility. He foresees the day when airports, too, will be full of wireless networks, even to the point of having wireless chips on passenger luggage that can be

detected in the baggage area. In referring to possibilities of wireless networks and mobile communications, during an address to the Economic Club of Chicago, he said, "Here is why I think this all works, and I believe this is the key: People migrate to systems that are convenient, economic, and reliable . . . I believe being mobile and connected also is changing the way we work and play . . . ."

Condit also stresses, "We are moving into a civilization that is linked by mobility and bandwidth and will be linked by infrastructure systems. We are moving from a world marked by relative independence to one with real interdependence."

Boeing's wireless manufacturing network is paying substantial dividends for the company and its workers because it meets their combined needs, with benefits for all. As with all forms of information technology, implementing enterprise networks leads to use and usefulness only when they are judged practical in the operating activities of managers and staff.

### Questions for Discussion

1. What features and capabilities of Boeing's wireless manufacturing network led to its widespread adoption by workers in the manufacturing hangar?
2. How has Boeing benefited from its wireless network?
3. What are the components of the manufacturing network?
4. What components would be needed to implement the wireless airport baggage management system envisioned by Phil Condit?
5. Do you agree with Condit's assessment and vision of wireless and mobile networks?

C H A P T E R

**9**

# Electronic Commerce and Electronic Business

## LEARNING OBJECTIVES

When you have completed this chapter, you should be able to

**1** Describe the meaning of electronic commerce.

**2** Identify the two principal segments of electronic commerce.

**3** Describe the seven advantages that participants in electronic commerce enjoy compared to traditional commerce.

**4** Distinguish between the four business-to-consumer forms of electronic commerce.

**5** Discuss supply chain integration and the reason companies are making it an e-commerce objective.

**6** Identify the characteristics of electronic procurement.

**7** Explain the purpose of electronic exchanges and identify the three forms that have emerged.

# UPS: Moving at the Speed of Business in Electronic Commerce

First-time visitors to the lobby of UPS world headquarters in Atlanta are sure to smile when they notice *Package Car No. 1*, the very first UPS delivery van. Nearby, hangs a portrait of founder Jim Casey, who launched the company in 1907. His inspirational words are etched into the stone wall: *Our horizon is as distant as our mind's eye wishes it to be.* On the horizon for today's CEO is the intention of *growing a global footprint across the entire supply chain of business.* That horizon is very near.

The famous brown trucks of the largest package carrier in the world are a familiar, reassuring sight around the world. Filled with valuable goods, UPS *package cars* reliably deliver packages large and small to waiting recipients. That is UPS, at least the part of UPS that is most familiar to outsiders. But UPS is much more than an efficient and reliable package carrier. Casey's words have never been truer or more important than they are today, for they surely explain why electronic commerce is so important to UPS—and to its customers. E-commerce is an essential part of the UPS strategy, and UPS is a pivotal element in the Internet sales and e-commerce success of many of its customers. Here is why.

Behind the brown truck and the delivery scenes is an efficient, highly engineered logistics system—a success story in itself. Through its carefully located global distribution centers, the company moves packages from origin to destination with speed and remarkable predictability. UPS guarantees on-time delivery of both air and ground shipments.

The company's famous, often displayed slogan—*moving at the speed of business*—is more than just a marketing motto. It expresses the company's challenge, opportunity, and commitment to its customers participating in or depending on a business world that is increasingly focused on electronic commerce. UPS is responsible for delivering more than half of all of the products sold by the book shops, toy stores, and online computer sites that typify electronic commerce purchases by consumers. It makes no sense for a company to be able to quickly take an order online if it cannot also deliver that order quickly and reliably. So, behind the scenes of a company's electronic commerce activities you are likely to find UPS.

Moving packages is one thing. Keeping the information about those packages moving *and* accessible is quite another matter. UPS has been refining this capability for over a decade. Drivers for some time have carried an electronic clipboard, called a *delivery information acquisition device* (DIAD). This is a combination computer and communications device that captures and simultaneously transmits package information. As soon as customers sign for delivery of a package in an electronic window on the DIAD, the signature is transmitted and available on the company network. Customers can view the signature, and any other information describing the movement of a particular package, online at the UPS Web site.

Customers can also use the ever-popular Palm Pilot PDA to check in with UPS. By merely touching the UPS shield on the Palm Pilot display screen, an individual can check the status of a UPS shipment simply by entering the tracking number. Its status will be displayed on the Palm Pilot's screen. Or, they can locate the nearest UPS drop-off location by entering a postal code. Location information is immediately displayed.

With today's high-velocity business activities—locally, nationally, and globally—it is important to move packages *and* information at the speed of business. Now that is UPS.

*W*ithout a doubt, electronic commerce is a high-priority topic in IT business today. Long established and start-up companies alike are examining the ways electronic commerce can affect or renew their business. As you will see, electronic commerce is not only changing the way products and services are bought and sold, it is changing the very nature of these items.

This chapter examines the many facets of electronic commerce and illustrates why the topic is on the agenda and minds of countless enterprise managers today. The first section of the chapter describes the key characteristics of electronic commerce. It discusses its benefits and illustrates how online innovator Amazon.com became an early leader and a company that is watched closely even today. This section also examines the ongoing evolution of electronic commerce both in the United States and throughout the developed world.

Subsequent sections of this chapter examine the different forms of electronic commerce, including both consumer-oriented and business-oriented commerce. Electronic commerce is far from a fad; it is a force causing fundamental shifts in the way individuals and companies engage in and carry out commerce.

**electronic commerce (e-commerce)**

Use of communication networks, including the public Internet, to conduct commercial transactions between businesses or with consumers.

# What Is Electronic Commerce?

**Electronic commerce (e-commerce)** is the buying, selling, and exchange of information about products and services over public or private communications networks. A substantial proportion of e-commerce occurs on the public Internet. However, it also takes place over private intranets and extranets. E-commerce is an important aspect of *IT;* buyers and sellers participate in e-commerce by interconnecting to communications networks through desktop computers, PDAs, mobile telephones, and other electronic devices. It is also an important element of *business* because large and small companies consider the possible benefits of e-commerce an essential part of their strategy to be successful, regardless of the segment in which they participate.

## Types of Electronic Commerce

Electronic commerce consists of two segments: business-to-consumer and business-to-business. Both are of growing interest to established large and small businesses. In addition, each segment includes many start-up companies seeking to serve the segment and grow their organizations.

**Business-to-Consumer E-Commerce**   Because of widespread newspaper and media coverage, you have probably heard much about **business-to-consumer (B2C) e-commerce,** that is, electronic commerce carried out by an enterprise in order to serve its *consumer* customers. Here consumers shop and buy over the public Internet, using the browser on their PC to access the company's business Web site where products and services are offered for sale. Consumers scan the company's online product information, select the items they wish to purchase and pay for them, typically with credit or debit cards or prepaid gift certificates.

The business in turn processes the Web order, delivering the product or service according to address information provided by the customer (Figure 9.1). It may be delivered electronically if it is a digital information product, such as software or an electronic *e-book.* Physical products are delivered in the usual way, perhaps using UPS.

Many companies in the business-to-consumer segment were *born on the Internet,* that is, established specifically to create and serve consumers using the Internet as their

**business-to-consumer (B2C) e-commerce,**
Electronic commerce carried out by an enterprise in order to serve its *consumer* customers.

FIGURE 9.1

*Business to Consumer Buying and Fulfillment Cycle for a Pure Internet Company*

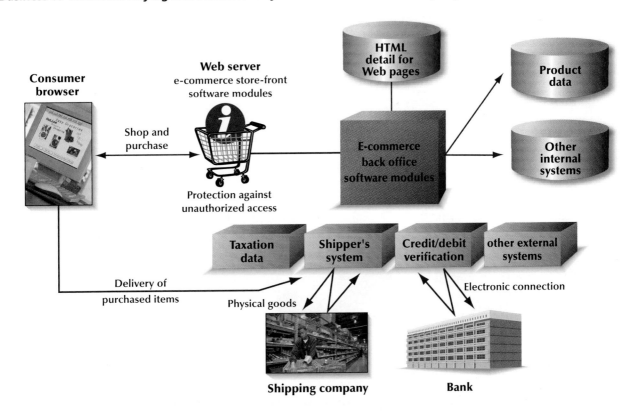

commercial medium. They are *pure Internet companies,* meaning they conduct business transactions *only* over the Internet. (Pure Internet companies are often termed *dot-com* companies because they have the Internet's .com designation included in their names.) Many dot-com companies were launched to enter the business-to-consumer sector. While a large proportion failed (they offered little value to consumers or were poorly marketed and never really got off the ground) some have dramatically changed consumer and business practices.

For instance, Amazon.com, one of the best-known B2C companies was launched as a bookseller operating only over the Internet. Similarly, the online druggist Drugstore.com, and the travel companies Expedia and Travelocity were created as Internet companies.

On the other hand, the *Wall Street Journal Interactive* newspaper, e-Schwab brokerage, and Delta.com airline e-commerce were started as new arms of well-established traditional companies. These are *not* Internet-only companies. However, the Internet is an essential component of their B2C e-commerce business.

**business-to-business (B2B) e-commerce**

Companies doing business electronically with other businesses.

**Business-to-Business E-Commerce** **Business-to-business (B2B) e-commerce,** as the name suggests, refers to companies doing business with other businesses. Buyers interact electronically with their *upstream* suppliers (see Figure 9.2) to obtain the parts, materials, resale goods, and services they need to carry out the activities of their businesses. In contrast, suppliers interact with their *downstream* customers who buy products and services they offer for sale.

Many of the same practices common with B2C e-commerce are followed. For instance, product information is displayed online for review by buyers who enter transactions over the Internet. However, as discussed later in this chapter, added innovations are enabling business buyers to dramatically alter systematic buying patterns and at the same time create highly efficient relations with their suppliers.

## Benefits of E-Commerce

Widespread interest in e-commerce stems from the seven principal advantages (Table 9.1) that participants enjoy:

1. **Geographic Reach** Distance is not a barrier for e-commerce participants. Consumers have the ability to use their link to a communications network to search for products, services, or information regardless of the seller's geographic location. Similarly, sellers can offer products, services, and information to potential buyers

**FIGURE 9.2**

*Goods, Information, and Funds Flow Upstream and Downstream in the Supply Chain*

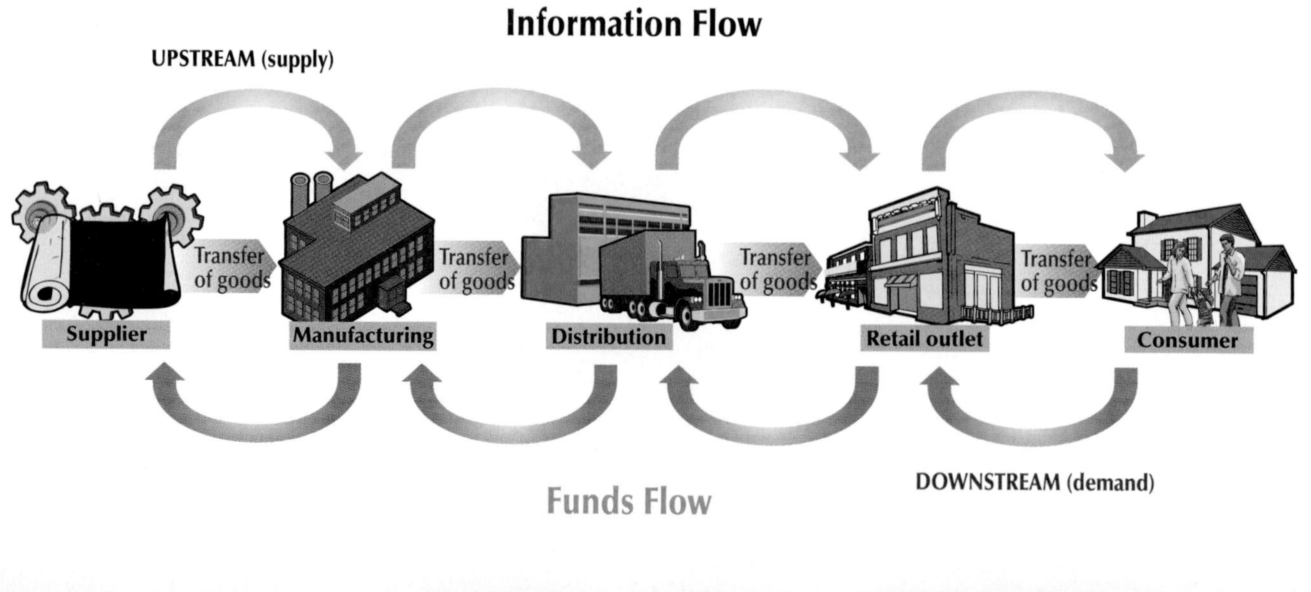

# Information Flow

UPSTREAM (supply)

| Supplier | Transfer of goods | Manufacturing | Transfer of goods | Distribution | Transfer of goods | Retail outlet | Transfer of goods | Consumer |

DOWNSTREAM (demand)

Funds Flow

**Table 9.1   Benefits of Electronic Commerce**

| BENEFIT | EXAMPLE |
|---|---|
| Geographic Reach | Geographic distance does not create a barrier to reaching and serving customers electronically or for interacting with suppliers. |
| Speed | Near-instant exchange of information means the interaction between buyer and seller takes place at rapid speed. |
| Productivity | Individuals are more productive when they can do more work in a segment of time. Spending less time getting information means more time available for its use, therein producing greater efficiency. |
| Information Sharing | Virtually any form of information—text, audio, video, graphics, or animation—can be transmitted to recipients located on the network. |
| New Features | New features can be added to products and services offered over communications networks, including personalization, automatic notification of activities, and instant delivery. |
| Lower Costs | The cost of business is reduced when companies and individuals can be reached quickly and without respect to geographic distance, while improved efficiencies result from electronic information exchange. |
| Competitive Advantage | Those companies that develop and implement an effective electronic commerce strategy have business advantages over others in their industry that cannot over similar products, services, or operating capabilities. |

anywhere in the world. For instance, UPS, which participates in the delivery of products emanating from B2C and B2B e-commerce transactions, enables its customers to track shipments destined for any global buyer. Both buyer and seller can track the shipment over the Internet regardless of where they are located.

2. **Speed**   The interaction between buyer and seller takes place almost instantly. Information is transmitted at the speed of the digital communications channel, where only seconds elapse during an exchange. Hence, all participants benefit by the rapid speed with which information can be transmitted or received.

3. **Productivity**   Being able to search for and locate information online quickly increases the *productivity* of individuals and companies. They gain efficiency because more *work* can be done in a segment of time. Since less time is spent getting information, more time can be given to using the information, making decisions, or conducting business transactions. More work in less time means higher productivity.

4. **Information Sharing**   Information in electronic form–text, audio, video, graphics, or animation–can be transmitted anywhere with equal ease. Because electronic information sharing is easier than sharing information in most other ways, it occurs freely and frequently in e-commerce. For instance, news broadcaster CNN makes its news available all over the world and in a variety of electronic forms to anyone having Internet access. The variety of digital formats, including audio, video, and animation, are far greater than could ever be achieved by facsimile or voice messages.

5. **New Features**   E-commerce participants constantly find more product features and services that they can offer over communications networks–items that would be prohibitive in traditional business activities. These features include personalizing information and prices, automatically notifying shoppers of the arrival of new items, instantly delivering video clips online, and so on. Companies and individuals are attracted to the companies that offer these new features.

6. **Lower Costs**   The cost of conducting business and distributing all forms of information is reduced because of the digital communications links that characterize e-commerce methods. Cost advantages are substantial when information on Web sites

is accessible to both companies and individuals quickly and without the need for a firm to print and mail documents. Similarly, the cost of processing online transactions is dramatically lower because the work can be carried out instantly by computer rather than delayed for later processing by expensive clerical staff.

7. **Competitive Advantage**    Those companies having effective e-commerce capabilities generally are able to compete more successfully to gain business and customers. Products and services can be offered to more buyers and in a manner that benefits, and perhaps improves the competitiveness, of buyer and seller. This is why firms having the capability to participate in e-commerce enjoy a valuable business asset today. Of course, the opposite is true as well: Companies that do not have the capability for e-commerce are at a distinct competitive disadvantage when others in their industries do.

A growing number of companies—both new and old—are creating innovative practices that differentiate themselves from competitors while enabling them to capitalize on e-commerce's benefits. A tremendous opportunity may exist in industries where buyers perceive products and services to be about the same regardless of where they are acquired.

Consider, for instance, how many places consumers are able to buy the same book title, music CD, airline ticket, or software program. Moreover, because most potential buyers understand these products very well, they need little assistance in selecting and using them.

However, if a seller stands out because it makes it possible for the buyer to acquire it in a more convenient, quicker, or less expensive way, the buyer will likely give its business to that seller. Companies that understand how to use e-commerce's benefits can often create an edge for themselves, thereby obtaining the buyer's business.

## Amazon.com's Early E-Commerce Success

A good book and Amazon.com go hand in hand. Together, they are an important example of the broad appeal of e-commerce.. Amazon.com, among the best known of all pure Internet companies, came into business initially by offering a huge selection of books—many times more than any *brick and mortar* (traditional) bookstore could possibly stock (Figures 9.3A and 9.3B). The company later expanded to include music CDs and other products and services. Amazon guarantees rapid delivery and uses its lower operating costs to keep prices at least 10 percent to 30 percent below those of its traditional competitors. Moreover, consumers benefit by added convenience: They do not have to go to a bookstore. They can shop over the Internet anytime, day or night, from their home or elsewhere, and have a book delivered to their doorsteps in 1 to 3 days.

**FIGURE 9.3A**
*Amazon's "Store Front"*

**FIGURE 9.3B**
*Traditional Bookstore's "Store Front"*

While Amazon's prices, convenience, and selection are attractive, the Internet company offers still more advantages. Take its special services, customized to fit individual shopper needs. Here is what Amazon does Using the shopper's choice of paper, Amazon.com will giftwrap a purchase and ship it anywhere in the world. It will even enclose a signed card with a personal note written by the buyer. This special service is widely used by shoppers who wish to purchase gifts for local or distant friends. It is so easy to buy and send gifts this way that you have to wonder why every company does not offer these options.

There is more. Extensive information about books is available online. If consumers wish, Amazon.com will keep them abreast of newly published books in their areas of interest. When a new book is published, customers receive a note, via e-mail, informing them of the book's publication. The message may even include early reviews of the book. Or it may indicate that several chapters of the book are *posted* on the company's Web page where excerpts can be read online or downloaded for later viewing. If a reader likes the excerpt, the book can be purchased on the spot by a few clicks of the mouse and be delivered within a matter of days.

Amazon also offers electronic books, or e-Books. Because e-books are digital, readers can download them easily and quickly onto a PC, laptop computer, or PDA. Amazon is building a growing library of e-books that can be instantly downloaded, ready for viewing whenever and wherever the reader chooses. It is easy to see why Amazon.com is among the most frequently mentioned B2C e-commerce companies in the world. However, Amazon is only one of many; there are many others that have also capitalized on the advantages of electronic commerce. Other examples will be covered in the rest of this chapter.

## Growth of E-Commerce

Granted, most business is still carried out in traditional fashion, with people going to stores or businesses and buying from salespersons. However, e-commerce is of growing importance because it is altering the way people search out and acquire products and services.

Figure 9.4 illustrates the growth of e-commerce activity. At the beginning of the millennium, technology researchers predicted that e-commerce would reach at least $1.3 trillion. It is estimated that B2C commerce will grow to more than $180 billion by the middle of the decade—a dramatic increase from the approximately $20 billion at the beginning of the millennium.

FIGURE 9.4

*Growth of Electronic Commerce*

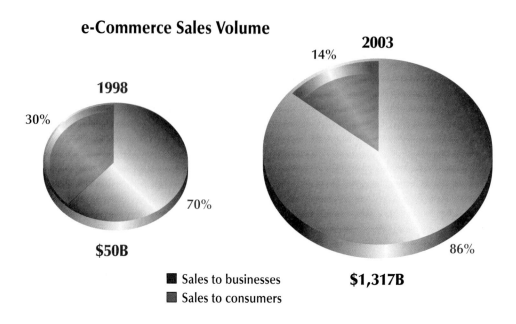

**e-Commerce Sales Volume**

1998

30%

70%

$50B

2003

14%

86%

$1,317B

■ Sales to businesses
■ Sales to consumers

The size of the B2B sector for e-commerce is much larger than B2C commerce, and it is growing even more rapidly. The approximately $60 billion in B2B commerce conducted at the beginning of the decade is expected to grow to well over $1 trillion by the middle of the decade.

E-commerce activity grew first in the United States and within a few years spread to other countries with growth in Internet usage (Figure 9.5). Western Europe and Japan are the leading countries. However, Singapore and Hong Kong are among the Asian regions experiencing the most rapid growth in e-commerce now.

Because of the vast reach of the Internet and other telecommunications networks, and since e-commerce provides many benefits to both business and consumers, there is little question it will be widely used internationally. It is playing an increasingly greater role in business and trade around the world. Those companies, and countries, that participate enjoy many potential opportunities. Those who are unable to link up will surely lose out.

For instance, Singapore's TradeNet, an e-commerce application that allows traders to submit electronic documentation before a ship or plane nears the port, means the shipper obtains advance clearance and approval before arrival. This dramatically reduces the time spent in port, benefiting the shipper, recipient, and the port. Singapore itself is also able to successfully compete with other ports in the region that are seeking the same shipping business, a direct result of the capability of its e-commerce application to link up with shipping companies electronically. (See Chapter 1 feature on TradeNet.)

FIGURE 9.5

*Internet Users by Region*

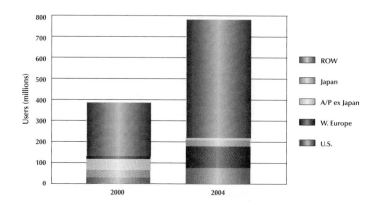

# Business-to-Consumer E-Commerce Applications

Historically, shopping has taken many forms. Depending on their needs, consumers might shop at a store, in a mall, at an open-air market, or through mail-order catalogs. In order for e-commerce to be useful (and successful), it must meet the needs of consumers who *still* have these traditional options available to them.

Four common e-commerce forms are widely used in the B2C sector: (1) online retailing, (2) electronic markets, (3) portals, and (4) online services.

## Online Retailing and Electronic Storefronts

To many consumers, retail shopping means a visit to a clothing or sporting goods store, shopping for groceries at a nearby supermarket, or browsing an automobile dealer's car lot in search of a new car. It also means going to the store, strolling its aisles, eyeing the goods on the store shelves, and checking the product to see that it has the right features.

In **online retailing** (or e-commerce retailing–*e-tailing*), shoppers *still* visit a store and check out the products. However, the store is reached over the Internet. The home page is the **electronic storefront.** Its aisles, counters, and displays of goods are pages on the World Wide Web, visible through a browser. Hence, *getting there* means locating the online store's home page.

When shoppers visit Amazon.com, they find selections of books and other goods displayed at the company's storefront, that is, its Web site. Shoppers browse the books available by an electronic display of their titles, descriptions, reviews, and perhaps reader comments. If they decide to make a purchase, they indicate their choice, usually by clicking on the book's title, and provide the payment and mailing information. The purchase and payment transaction is processed over the Internet, by the company's software.

What if the shopper is interested in groceries rather than books? Is this an area where e-commerce is likely to be widespread? Because there is widespread awareness that for many people *time* is in short supply–they do not like to give up time to visit the supermarket–some e-commerce experts predict that online grocery shopping will flourish.

Peapod is a well-known online grocer that has been operating over the Internet for some time. As an online retailer, Peapod must provide the same online shopping capabilities as other e-tailers, whether they feature groceries, books, or airline tickets.

**online retailing**
Shoppers visit a store over the Internet and check out the products.

**electronic storefront**
Home page of an online retailing business.

---

**REALITY CHECK**   Frequently you will hear the words e-commerce and e-business used interchangeably. Strictly speaking, there is a difference. If you visit the Web site of a company and search for a product, review a catalog, or place an order, you are experiencing its *e-commerce* capability. *E-commerce* therefore refers to online transactions, such as for sales and exchange of information.

In contrast, *e-business* is the entire process of supporting the transaction activities, and the back office support processes needed to carry out the activities initiated online. Hence, the speed with which a company fills an order initiated online depends on the sophistication of its e-business processes–the interconnection of inventory management, shipping, billing, and customer management with online transactions. You can generally tell how much attention a company has paid to its e-business capability: If you can place an order online, but cannot determine whether the item is in stock and can be shipped immediately, it is likely that the firm's e-business systems have not been carefully developed.

Throughout this book, e-commerce is used to refer to both the online transaction *and* the e-business activities. ■

Figure 9.6 shows the Web page of Peapod. When a visitor clicks on the icon *Groceries for your home* and selects a city, Peapod's electronic storefront appears. The *Browse the Aisles* button reveals that the Peapod store is arranged in aisles (dairy, frozen foods, beverages, etc.) just like a traditional grocery store. Each aisle contains the items in the corresponding category. Shoppers can choose to visit or skip any aisle in the store.

Shoppers visiting a traditional brick-and-mortar grocery store would most likely take a shopping cart with them as they go around the store, placing each grocery item in the cart as they make their selections. Online grocers use an *electronic shopping cart*, that is, a list of items selected.

## Electronic Markets

**electronic markets (e-markets)**

A collection of individual shops accessible through a single location on the World Wide Web

Electronic markets are a second common B2C application. **Electronic markets (e-markets)** are a collection of individual shops accessible through a single location on the World Wide Web. E-markets can be compared to a neighborhood shopping mall. In fact, they are sometimes referred to as *electronic malls* or *cybermalls*. Companies join an e-market because of the one-stop shopping convenience for buyers, and because of the services the market operator offers. Each individual storefront can be visited at the e-market. The market operator's home page displays information on each store comprising the marketplace. Inside each store, which shoppers can visit by clicking on its name or corresponding icon, there are displays of its products or information describing its services. The market operator processes purchases, and ships the purchases to the buyer. In turn, the storeowner pays a fee, often including a percent of the sales revenue, to the e-market operator for providing the services.

Electronic markets can be attractive to buyers seeking to locate goods or services when they do not know how to find businesses serving their need. They are attractive to sellers when its managers do not wish to create and maintain their own e-commerce site, yet still want to have an Internet site to offer for commerce. (They choose an e-market that has enough visibility among consumers to draw shoppers to the site.)

Electronic markets can grow quite large. Some of the best-known e-markets, such as America's Choice Mall (www.choicemall.com) (Figure 9.7) and Home Shopping 2000 (www.homeshopping2000.com) include thousands of stores.

**auctions**

Shoppers make bids to determine the sale price of an item rather than relying on predetermined, fixed prices.

Some electronic markets use **auctions** to determine the sale price of an item rather than relying on predetermined, fixed prices. Bids are submitted for each item by inter-

**FIGURE 9.6**

***Grocery Shopping at Peapod***

 **REALITY CHECK**

E-commerce stores, created on the Internet, are sometimes called *cyberstores*, depicting their presence in cyberspace. In contrast, traditional stores are frequently referred to as *brick-and-mortar* facilities. The reference originates with the construction method and exterior of many traditional buildings.

**Brick and mortar** has grown to mean any physical store or building, regardless of how it is constructed or where it is located. If it is not in cyberspace, it is *brick and mortar.* ■

**brick and mortar**

Any physical store or building, regardless of how it is constructed or where it is located.

---

ested shoppers. There are three types of online auctions. In traditional **forward auctions** (sometimes called a *Yankee auction*), shoppers make offers for (that is, *they bid on*) a desired item, with the knowledge that the seller will take the highest offer. If a shopper notices that another bidder has offered a higher price, the shopper may choose to submit a different, higher bid. The process is repeated until one bidder—the highest bidder—is left at the end of the auction.

**forward auction**

Shoppers bid on a desired item with the knowledge that the seller will take the highest offer.

**FIGURE 9.7**

***Choicemall.com Electronic Market***

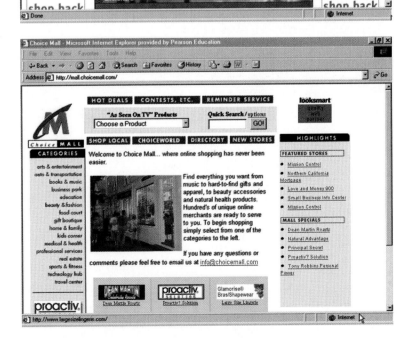

**reverse auction**

The direct opposite of a traditional auction. The bidders list their product or service requirements and the maximum price they are willing to pay for it. Potential sellers who can provide the good or service reverse bid against each other by posting their bids for buyers. The bidder offering the requested products or services at the best price wins the bid.

**Dutch auction**

On electronic markets, the market operator displays a *high* opening price for an item and asks for buyers willing to pay the price. At prespecified intervals, the price is lowered until a bidder is willing to pay the displayed price.

**portal**

A gateway or hub site, such as Yahoo!, that provides chat rooms.

A **reverse auction** is the direct opposite of a traditional auction. The bidders list their product or service requirements (say a five-day Caribbean cruise) and the maximum price they are willing to pay for it. Potential sellers (e.g., the cruise company participating in the e-market or the e-market operator) post their bids for buyers.

**Dutch auctions** originated in the flower markets of the Netherlands. The market operator selects a batch of flowers to be sold, sets and displays a *high* opening price, and asks for buyers willing to pay the price. At prespecified intervals, the price is lowered. This process continues until a bidder indicates a willingness to pay the displayed price.

Auctions have become very popular in e-commerce, especially with certain e-commerce sites.

## Portals

When shoppers visit an online retailer or e-market frequently, they will either know its Internet address or they will have the address bookmarked on their Internet browser. But with so many e-commerce sites, many will not be familiar to shoppers. How do shoppers find a site that they need when they may not even know it exists?

What is a problem for some is an opportunity for others, which is why innovative entrepreneurs created the third B2C application category. A **portal** is a Web site that provides a single point of access from which shoppers can locate and connect to other Web sites meeting their needs, whether for shopping, services, or content.

The earliest portals were *search engines*. Upon prompting a search engine by entering key words, shoppers receive a response consisting of suggested answers to their inquiry. The responses are arranged in sequence, with those that the search engine software thought meet the inquiry the best displayed first. Each response typically includes a brief description and a hyperlink to the Web site located by the search engine (Figure 9.8). (See Chapter 3 for more information on hyperlinks.)

Today's portals offer five functions. In addition to the search capability, the first function, portals provide a second important function: access to *specialized functions*. For instance, they will link the shopper directly to e-markets where certain types of goods and services are offered for sale. Or they may link to sites that run auctions, such as eBay.com. Still others may link to Web sites that aggregate medical information, including WebMD and the Online Health Network.

The third function performed by a portal is *personalization of content*. Portals make it possible for individuals to indicate the type of information they want to receive. The portal then monitors the Internet to detect the addition of information on that topic to the Internet. It transmits an e-mail notification when that occurs. *My Yahoo!* and *MyExcite!* are among the best-known examples of portals providing this function.

**FIGURE 9.8**

*Portals Provide a Starting Point in the Search for Products and Services*

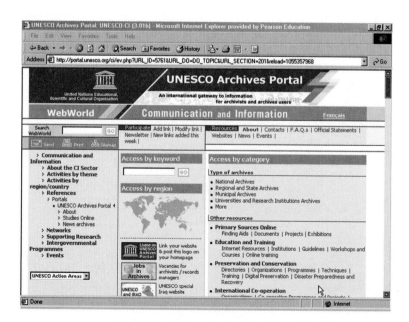

# CRITICAL CONNECTIONS  1

## Priceline Rewrites the Rules with Its Demand Collection System

**Priceline.com**

Priceline.com has pioneered a unique breed of e-commerce known as a *demand collection system* that enables *consumers* to use the Internet to save money on a wide range of products and services while enabling *sellers* to generate incremental revenue for items that might otherwise go unused. Launched in April 1998, this new form of transaction service was created to leverage the unique attributes of the Internet for the benefit of consumers and businesses.

Through its *Name Your Own Price*[SM] services, Priceline.com enables consumers to make purchase offers for goods and services at the prices they want to pay. It collects consumer demand in the form of individual customer offers (guaranteed by a credit card) for a particular product or service at a price set by the customer. In return, consumers agree to varying degrees of flexibility in the brand and product features they receive for their price. *Name Your Own Price* can be directed to airline tickets, hotels and resorts, rental cars, long distance phone service, vacations, cruises, and new and used cars.

Once Priceline.com receives a consumer's purchase offer, it tries to find a participating business willing to sell its product at the consumer's desired price. Consumers are notified when an agreement is arranged with the seller or service provider. All arrangements are final. Neither seller nor buyer engages in any additional negotiations.

**content aggregator**
An e-commerce portal that assembles information (that is, content) from a variety of sources, organizing the information into a form that is useful to visitors to the Web site.

**infomediary**
A Web site that locates, retrieves, and organizes specialized information for potential users. The term is a composite of information and intermediary.

**electronic banking/ cyberbanking**
Customers conduct their banking activities without going to a physical bank office.

**virtual bank**
Operates exclusively over the Internet.

Fourth, portals establish *communities of interest,* linking individuals together who have interest in similar content topics. For instance, *Yahoo! Financial's* discussion includes information, comments and opinions on money and investment topics. People who have joined the community by submitting their online addresses can receive information and participate in the discussion. Real-time chat options are also provided within communities of information by some portals.

Portals are sometimes called by the functions they perform: search engine, **content aggregator** (meaning that the portal's software assembles, or aggregates, information), or **infomediary** (a software intermediary that locates, retrieves, and organizes information.)

## Online Services

The range of online services offered over the Internet is growing constantly as enterprising new and established firms develop their e-commerce capabilities. Many e-commerce companies have been created to provide services to consumers. This section discusses four online consumer services: (1) electronic banking, (2) personal finance and bill payment, (3) securities and investments, and (4) travel services.

**Electronic Banking**   Through **electronic banking,** also known as **cyberbanking,** customers conduct their banking activities without going to a physical bank office. Millions of people are initiating e-banking every year at those financial institutions that have been first to offer it to customers. It is highly likely that all banks will soon offer e-banking as part of their everyday services.

Electronic banking has been evolving for some time, with early innovators creating proprietary software in the 1980s. These banking systems enabled customers to gain access to their accounts using dial-up telecom links. It was not until the mid-1990s that several new banks entered the world of e-commerce as *virtual banks.* A **virtual bank** operates exclusively over the Internet (Figure 9.9). Among the first were Security First Network Bank and NetBank. These banks were offering the same wide range of services provided by traditional banks, including checking, savings and money market accounts, debit and credit cards, automated teller machine (ATM) service, and loans. However, they were doing so on the Internet, thereby assuring customers 24-hour-a-day access to account information.

Supplementing online convenience, virtual banks focused on improving service efficiency, transferring savings to customers in the form of higher returns and lower loan costs. Because they do not have brick-and-mortar branches, the banks operate at significantly lower costs than traditional banks while offering the same personal financial services to customers.

**FIGURE 9.9**

*Virtual Banks Operate over the Internet*

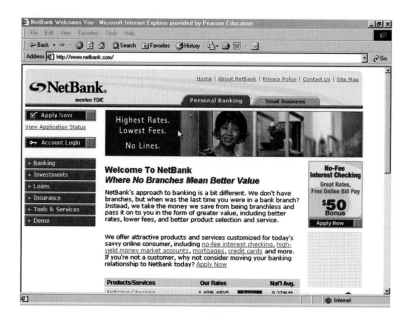

Realizing that some virtual banks were successful in signing up tens of thousands of customers, traditional banks began rolling out Internet banking services for any of four different reasons. Some did this as a defensive move so that virtual banks would not be able to raid their customers. Some did so primarily because their customers were asking for these services. Still others launched online banking so they could later launch new revenue-generating services, such as online bill payment (discussed next).

The fourth reason was because of the potential to offer banking services at lower costs. According to industry statistics complied by the American Banking Association and other industry groups, the average payment transaction on the Internet is costs only about $.01. This compares with $.26 for a transaction done through a PC banking service where customers use the bank's software, $.54 for a telephone-banking service, and $1.07 for a bank-branch transaction.

**Personal Finance and Bill Payment**   As online banking has grown, many customers have become accustomed to handling other personal finances online, including receipt and payment of bills. Consider that every month the average person receives at least 10 to 20 bills for services such as natural gas, electric, telephone and Internet access, rent or mortgage, and credit cards. Each time the process is generally the same: The service provider prints the monthly bills, stuffs them in an envelope, applies postage, and mails them to the consumer. The consumer process generally goes like this: Bills arrive; they are opened and examined; and then they are stacked up until *bill paying time.* Ultimately a check is written for each bill and placed in an envelope ready to be stamped and mailed. Finally, the service provider gets the invoice back, processes the checks, and credits the accounts. This same cycle is repeated billions of times each year throughout the United States.

Electronic bill receipt and payment has emerged with the hope of simplifying this process for those consumers who are interested. The five principal forms in use include (see Figure 9.10):

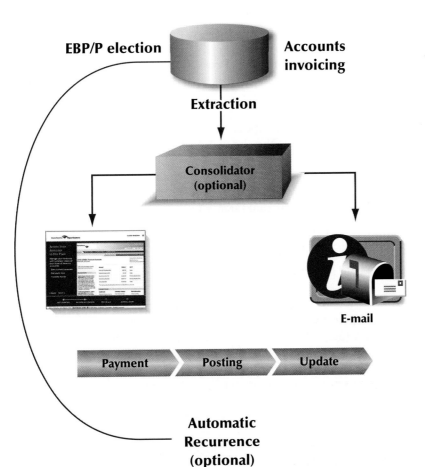

**FIGURE 9.10**

*Bill Presentment for Online Receipt and Payment of Bills*

1. **Automatic Transfer of Bank Loan and Mortgage Payments** Customers of Bank of America, among the largest of U.S. banks, and USAA Bank, can direct that the banks automatically transfer a set amount of money from their accounts for their monthly payments. This benefits both bank and customer because the payments are handled more quickly and there is no need to exchange paper (i.e., invoices and checks).

2. **Automatic Payment of Utility Bills** It has become commonplace for natural gas, electric, and telephone companies to enable customers to pay their monthly bills (which vary in amount from month to month) directly from their bank accounts on a prespecified date. The bank automatically transfers the amount of the bill for that month from the customer's account to the utility company, eliminating the need for customers to write a check—paper or electronic—to pay the bill.

3. **Online Bill Payment** As part of their home-banking service, Chase Manhattan, Fleet Financial Boston, Wells Fargo, and many other banks provide their customers with the capability to pay many other bills online, in addition to utility bills. Customers set up a list of bills they typically pay. After they receive the merchant's paper bill each month, the customer goes online to direct the bank to pay the appropriate amount to participating companies. As part of the process, the customer specifies the date on which the bank is to make the payment. On that date, the bank transfers funds from the customer to the merchant's account without any additional action needed on anyone's part. No transfer occurs during the month unless the customer tells the bank to make the payment.

4. **Electronic Bill Presentment** Innovative companies are giving customers the option of *receiving* their bills via their Internet bank accounts. Customers can choose to receive bills through e-mail or by the company posting their monthly bills on its secured Web site. Customers can privately access, review, and pay their bills. Customers of Cox Communications, one of the largest broadband communications service providers in the United States, can choose to receive their monthly cable, local and long-distance telephone statements electronically on their personal computers and pay them with a click of the mouse, thereby instructing their banks to make the payments.

**intermediary**
In virtual banking, serves both merchant and consumer to streamline the billing and payment process.

**bill consolidator**
Receives bills from merchants and assembles them into a uniform format for each consumer.

5. **Combined Electronic Bill Presentment and Payment** To further streamline the billing and payment process, this new service involves an **intermediary** that serves both merchant and consumer. A **bill consolidator** receives bills from merchants and assembles them into a uniform format for each consumer. In turn, the consumer reviews and approves all of the bills before they are paid electronically. America Online (AOL), the world's largest Internet service provider, along with financial software maker Intuit have combined forces to provide a bill presentment service to utilities, credit-card companies and other billers. They will also scan paper bills into an electronic format for presentment. Consumers can then view their bills online and have their banks transfer the funds for payments by a click of the mouse.

All forms of electronic bill payment are growing in consumer appeal. By the middle of the decade, nearly 50 percent of all U.S. households are expected to bank online—greater than a 400-percent increase over the rate in 2000.

**Securities and Investments** In December 1999, a milestone in the trading of securities over the Internet was exceeded when the value of Charles Schwab, the biggest online broker, passed that of Merrill Lynch, the traditional U.S. broker then considered the largest securities group in the world. This watershed event shows how far the trading of stocks and other securities over the Internet has come. In 1996, there were an estimated 1.6 million online trading accounts. By the year 2000, the number soared to some 20 million, an amount that continues to grow. By the middle of the decade, it is expected to have tripled.

Consumers have moved to online trading because of its convenience and low fees for conducting a trade—frequently less than $30—compared to charges from traditional brokers. Similarly, the low operating costs and high volumes of online trading have caught the eye of even established brokers.

# CRITICAL CONNECTIONS 2

## Quicken Takes Financial Management Online

**Quicken**

Quicken is a widely used financial services software product developed by Intuit Inc., a leading provider of business and financial management solutions for small businesses, consumers and accounting professionals. This inexpensive program, designed for desktop computers and selected PDAs, enables individuals to organize their finances, manage investments, and plan for the future.
Its many functions include the following:

- Balance personal checkbook and pay bills
- Bank and pay bills online
- Create budgets, reports, and graphs
- Track personal retirements investments including 401(k)'s and individual retirement accounts (IRAs)
- Track employee stock options
- Plan for retirement, a new home, and other future expenses
- Track tax deductions and prepare estimates of payroll tax withholdings
- Transfer financial data to Intuit's *TurboTax* program, designed to assist individuals in preparing local and state income tax forms

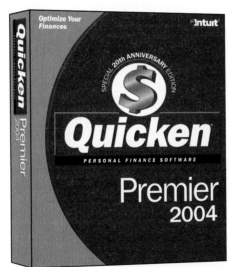

Online displays show information in familiar formats, such as checkbook registers, bank account deposit and withdrawal summaries, and listings of bills received as well as the date and amount paid.

Quicken uses the data communications features of PCs to connect to the Internet and to interact with the operating systems at many banks. Hence, an individual's personal banking data can be downloaded directly from the official bank records, ensuring that all financial records (deposit records, balances, bills payments, etc.) are synchronized. Quicken is fully in step with a growing trend for people to move their financial management and activities online.

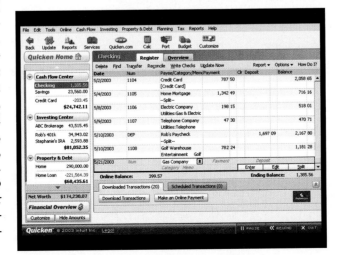

Brokerages with online operations not only trade securities for their customers, but also use their Web sites to offer research, real-time price quotes, and securities portfolio management services (Figure 9.11). Nonetheless, most online traders acknowledge that they will need to enhance their service offerings if they are to prosper in the highly competitive market.

The *Information Technology in Practice* feature, "E-Trade Takes Trading Online," describes the services of the popular online-only brokerage that began serving customers in 1992.

**Travel Services**    Airlines are rushing to capitalize on e-commerce as they seek to deal directly with customers and to reduce their operating costs. In the process, the survival of the traditional ticket-booking intermediary—the travel agent—is threatened.

When airline tickets are booked through a travel agent, the airline pays a commission to the travel agent for the services performed. The value of those commissions adds up for both large and small airlines. For instance, before it began developing its Web site where passengers could book their own tickets online, American Airlines was spending more than $1 billion annually on travel-agent fees, making commissions the third biggest expense after fuel and salaries. American Airlines' situation is representative of that faced by all major U.S. carriers. With airline traffic expected to double by the year 2015, reducing these costs is a big concern at American and elsewhere.

Sensing the huge growth in airline travel, e-commerce travel sites have also emerged, including expedia.com, travelocity.com, and travelweb.com. They offer travelers the flight schedules of many different airlines, worldwide, whereas individual airlines usually offer only their schedules and those of other airlines that cooperate with them as partners. These e-commerce travel sites also help consumers make hotel, car rental, and entertainment reservations (Figure 9.12). Online agencies receive a commission from each company for whom they book a reservation. Since the agencies can span vast geographic distances, the business potential is substantial.

If travelers books through an online reservation site and use electronic rather than paper tickets, the cost to the airline drops by more than 80 percent, to about $1 per ticket. You can see why the airlines are doing all they can to get ticket booking done over their Web sites.

Today, many travelers use online sites to *look up* flight information, but not to actually book the reservation. Less than 20 percent of bookings occur online, although the number is growing. Hence, airlines are offering extra incentives to get travelers to make their travel plans online, including awarding extra frequent-flier points for online bookings and providing exclusive services for corporate and

**FIGURE 9.11**

*Electronic Brokerages Provide Online Training and Information Services*

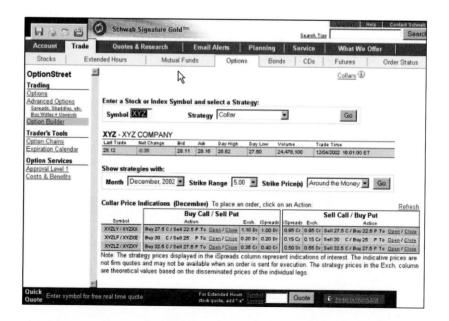

# INFORMATION TECHNOLOGY IN PRACTICE

## E-Trade Takes Trading Online

Up-to-the-minute information and easy online access have fueled the explosion of a new segment of the brokerage industry: online trading.

In 1992, E-Trade Securities Inc., one of the original all-electronic brokerages, was born and began to offer online investing services through AOL and other online service providers. When www.etrade.com was launched on the Internet, demand for E*Trade's services exploded, marking the start of a revolution in investing practices. Today, virtually all brokerages are preparing online trading strategies.

E-Trade traces its roots back to 1982 when Bill Porter, a physicist and inventor with more than a dozen patents to his credit, began providing online quotations and trading services to other investment firms, including Fidelity, Charles Schwab, and Quick & Reilly. As the value of these services grew, Porter began to question the need for individual investors to pay industry-standard fees for stock

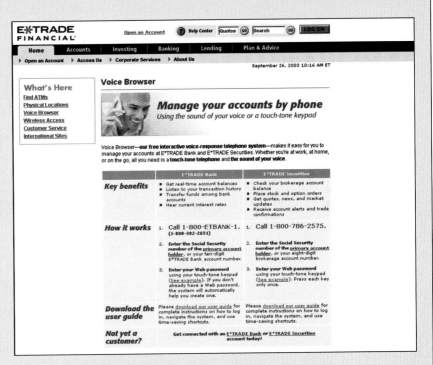

transactions. Looking at the evolution of desktop computers, he envisioned the day when most people would have their own computers and, with the right services, could conduct their investment activities through them.

Today, customers can open an E-Trade cash account and use it to trade stocks, mutual funds, bonds, and options online. They can access their accounts in many ways, including from E*Trade's Web account, AOL, CompuServe, Prodigy Internet, Microsoft Investor, WebTV, and direct modem.

When investors wants to buy or sell stocks but are away from their PCs, they can still execute transactions. TELE*MASTER is a special telephone investing system that accepts entry of trading instructions through speech recognition, where investors submit their instructions verbally. Alternatively, they can choose to use the touchtone keys on the telephone to enter trading details.

Fast trading action is only one feature E-Trade offers. Many other customer services have helped the company reach its industry leadership position. Free real-time quotes (up to 100/day) ensure that anyone can always know the latest trading price of a security. In addition, E-Trade customers can receive stock alerts, breaking news, performance charts and analysis plus high-powered research reports. Many more services are available, including portfolio management, retirement planning, and IRA account management.

E-Trade ensures that an investor's money is always at work. If it is not invested in a stock or other security, it earns daily interest in money market fund accounts. Free unlimited checking and cash transfer services make it easy to move money into and out of trading accounts. Credit cards, with no annual fee and a generous credit line up to $100,000 are also available (with the ability to view statements and pay bills online).

E-Trade's free e-mail service enables its investors to send and receive e-mail messages from home, work, or anywhere in the world that they can connect to the Internet. An advanced junk mail-blocking (or spam-blocking) feature assures investors that they are not bombarded with junk mail.

In a business that some observers consider high risk—investing in stocks and bonds—the firm helps protect customer assets. Securities in an E-Trade account are automatically protected up to $100 million free of charge. The Securities Investor Protection Corp. (SIPC) provides up to $500,000 of coverage, and the National Union Fire Insurance Company provides an additional $99.5 million of coverage.

If you want to invest in the new economy, and know which company's stock you want to buy, then why pay a broker for advice? Because so many people feel that way, brokerage firms that handle investor trades over the Internet are taking off.

frequent-flier travelers. Online agencies frequently send e-mail messages to past customers and Web-site visitors, offering special prices and other incentives aimed at turning *lookers into bookers.*

# Functions Performed by B2C e-Commerce Site

As the preceding sections have illustrated, an e-commerce Web site must be able to perform certain functions. This section discusses four common functions of B2C sites: (1) catalog and content management, (2) shopping and checkout, (3) back office processing, and (4) advertising. Depending on the purpose of the site, some or all of these functions will be performed.

## Catalog and Content Management

**content**
Information distributed over the Internet.

When you visit the electronic storefront of an e-commerce site, you see the site's **content,** that is the set of Web pages consisting of text, images, interactive forms (such as order forms) and information about the products or services. As you can imagine, an important part of the e-commerce site's value is having the right content displayed in a useful format.

Catalog shopping has been an important part of commerce for many years. For instance, mail-order shoppers are accustomed to selecting merchandise from colorful cat-

**FIGURE 9.12**

*Online Travel Reservation Services Aid Ticket Booking*

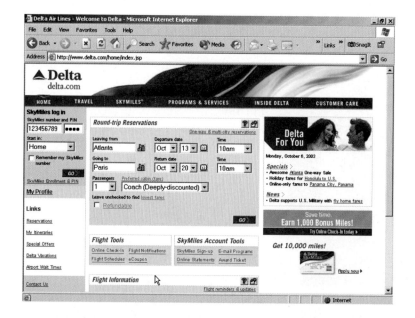

 **REALITY CHECK**   A few years ago, observers wondered if people would buy a car online. Then, most auto-related sites merely provided information about buying and financing cars. Today, with growing interest from both consumers and automobile manufacturers in actually buying or leasing cars online, there are new worries. Will online sales be legal?

In most states, legal barriers prevent some auto sales to consumers. That is because state franchise laws in some cases ban manufacturers from selling over the Internet. In effect, the dealership and the car-buyer must reside in the same state. Manufacturer-owned *stores* are illegal.

The purpose of such laws, when passed years ago, was to protect consumers from unscrupulous out-of-state sellers who could not be summoned into a state court of law in the event of a consumer complaint. Some consumers today feel that the law is actually working against them by protecting a state's dealers from out-of-state competition. They fear the laws are thereby keeping auto prices higher, meaning that consumers are being hurt, not helped. The choice of purchasing vehicles from e-commerce sites on the Internet, they claim, would open up competition for auto sales in the state, leading to lower prices and more purchase choices. ▪

---

alogs they receive from merchants. The catalogs identify, describe, and illustrate the merchandise, and its index aides in locating items within its pages. Because the mail-order company's entire business centers on its catalog, a great deal of effort goes into having the right catalog content and presentation.

Similarly, an e-commerce site is often centered on a catalog—an online catalog. The catalog's purpose remains the same: to describe the products and services available online. Instead of an index, the storefront includes a *search capability* that locates and displays an item based on keywords you supply (see Figure 9.13). As illustrated earlier in the discussion of Peapod, a grocery store's Web content consists of information on food and household items, perhaps organized by category. Similarly, the catalog of an online computer store will likely include the different categories of computers, software, and accessories. For each item, the catalog includes descriptive information and prices.

Online catalogs can be customized to a particular customer. For instance, companies that buy frequently from Dell Computer will have a customized catalog displayed when they visit *Dell Online.* Each company's custom catalog, which Dell refers to as *Premiere Pages,* includes only those items that the company wants its employees to choose from

**FIGURE 9.13**

*Online Catalogs Provide Buyer Access to Product and Service Information*

along with specially negotiated prices. Dell Computer has found the use of customized online catalogs so compelling to its customers that it maintains thousands of catalog versions online, each tailored to specific customers.

## Shopping and Checkout

After shoppers view product information and decide to buy certain items, they click on an icon that indicates they are ready to make their purchases. (Icons include instructions such as, *Buy Now* or *Place in Shopping Cart*.) This places the items in a *virtual* shopping cart—a table in memory that keeps track of the items including the quantity of each item for purchase.

At checkout time, the list is examined and the total of all purchases is calculated, including sales tax, if applicable. Shoppers pay for their purchases, usually by providing a credit, debit, or smart card number, a gift certificate, or a company purchase order authorization.

## Back Office Processing

**back office**
Deals with the final steps in the sale.

The **back office** deals with the final steps in the sale, including the following:

- **Processing Customer Payment**   When payments are made by credit, debit, or smart card, the transaction and payment information is transmitted to the appropriate banking system where approval is granted and the funds transferred, usually electronically, to the seller's own bank. Payments made via gift certificates or purchase orders are transferred to the company's accounting office.
- **Updating Inventory Records**   The quantity of items sold in a transaction is deducted from inventory records. If processing is done in real time, the most desirable choice, the adjustment reflecting the lower quantity on hand is made immediately. Otherwise, the adjustment to inventory will be made several hours later when all inventory adjustments for the period are made in one batch.
- **Preparing Item for Distribution**   For those digital products that will be delivered online (such as a computer software program), the company's back office process transmits the product electronically to the customer. Products that will be delivered in the traditional way are packaged for shipping and transferred for transport to the customer's location.

Although the back office activities are the last portion of a sales transaction, they may be the most important factor in creating satisfied customers who are willing to return again and again.

## Advertising

Advertising involves the display of messages and information that are designed to lead to sales. For some companies, advertising generates revenue when it lets potential customers know about their products and services, and stimulates them to buy. For others, displaying the advertising messages themselves is their source of revenue.

Four forms of advertising are common in B2C e-commerce: (1) search engine links, (2) banner ads, (3) interactive marketing, and (4) e-mail.

**Search Engines**   Search engines play a role in advertising when they direct a shopper to specific sites following a request for information. The search engine processes the shopper's keyword and the link to a site displayed for selection. (See Chapter 3 for more on search engines.)

**Banner Ads**   When visiting a site, shoppers see advertisements for products or services offered at that site as well as those offered at other sites. Usually these are *banner ads*, small rectangular notices that appear in a position on the display screen where they are likely to be noticed. The ad may identify a company or a product, or it may display a teaser question designed to get the shopper's attention (Figure 9.14).

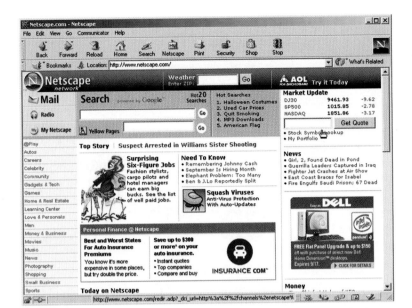

**FIGURE 9.14**

*Banner Advertisements Are Designed to Be Noticed in the Midst of Other Information Displayed on a Web Page*

Banner ads occur in three forms. Different predefined banner ads may appear on each page displayed at a site. Or, those displayed on a page may change every few seconds, at random. Third, banner ads may change depending on the position of a cursor over a keyword or the entry of a keyword for a search request. In each case, clicking on the banner ad will link shoppers directly to the company or to information about the product.

Companies frequently pay operators of other e-commerce sites to have their advertisement displayed and linked. While a set fee may be established, the actual fee for advertising usually depends on *impressions*–how frequently the banner ad is selected. Costs are usually priced per thousand impressions, and range from $.02 to $.20 per impression. Hence, a banner add that is clicked 10,000 times in a month, where the company agreed to pay the host site $20 per thousand impressions (that is $.02 per impression) will have a monthly cost of $200.

**Interactive Marketing** **Interactive marketing** is the use of custom advertising prepared to fit the profile of a specific visitor to a site. Information provided by the visitor (name, e-mail address, or company information) is recorded and used to tailor the message. On a subsequent visit, the information may be used again to determine what advertising to display.

A special case of interactive marketing is **interactive coupons.** An interactive coupon (Figure 9.15) is offered online. Since a site's visitors are considered the best prospect for a sale, issuing coupons that entitle them to free samples or discounted prices often stimulates a purchase. Usually shoppers are required to provide information about themselves in return for the coupon. The coupons can be printed on the spot or transmitted by e-mail. (Sometimes a company will send the coupon via regular mail, and send it with novelties or gadgets.)

**E-Mail** E-Mail is commonly deployed as a tool for advertising. Some companies choose to announce special prices or new products by sending messages to potential buyers or to past Web site visitors. For example, during a recent holiday season, bookseller Barnes and Noble online sent an e-mail message to past customers offering a discount for purchases made before the holiday.

Unsolicited advertising by e-mail, which is known as **spam,** is usually viewed as an undesirable e-commerce practice, and often a violation of the recipient's privacy. Companies who spam potential buyers seldom develop a loyal customer base in this way, often earning their ire instead. The most privacy-conscious companies now ask visitors to their Web sites for permission to send them information via e-mail. Their messages also include instructions telling them how to opt out of receiving future e-mail.

**interactive marketing**
The use of custom advertising prepared to fit the profile of a specific visitor to a site.

**interactive coupon**
Offered online.

**spam**
Unsolicited advertising by e-mail.

**FIGURE 9.15**

*Interactive Marketing
Customizes Advertising
to the Viewer*

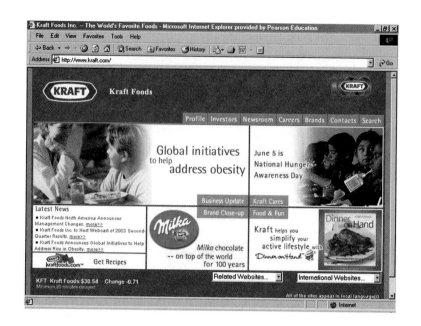

E-mail spam has become such a nuisance that information service providers and manufacturers of virus scanning software now routinely seek to detect and eliminate spam messages. (Chapter 14 discusses privacy and security in more detail.)

# Business-to-Business E-Commerce Applications

As mentioned earlier, B2B e-commerce is conducted between two or more business enterprises. Typically one company is a seller of products or services and the other is a buyer. Third parties—intermediaries—may also be involved to assist in the exchange or the delivery of products or services. The most prominent B2B applications are in supply-chain management, electronic procurement, and electronic exchanges.

## Supply Chain Management

The Internet and B2B e-commerce are permanently altering the interaction between the manufacturers, suppliers, and customers who comprise the supply chain. Hierarchical relations are being replaced by collaboration and integration between participants. This is occurring both because IT has made it possible and because companies are under increasing pressure to improve the way in which they receive, handle, or distribute goods and materials. As a result, many companies are seeking to:

- Reduce the inventory of goods they keep on hand without influencing their ability to meet the demand for those goods.
- Cut the cost of keeping goods on hand.
- Reduce replenishment times.
- Slash transportation costs associated with delivering goods.
- Eliminate or contract out activities that do not add value to the company or its customers.

In so doing, businesses are also rethinking the way they deal with their suppliers or the role they play as a supplier themselves.

**supply chain**
The flow of parts, components, materials, funds, and information between a company's sources and its customers.

**supply chain management**
The oversight of activities interconnecting suppliers and buyers.

**Supply Chain Characteristics**   A company's **supply chain** is the flow of parts, components, materials, funds, and information between a company's sources, on the one hand, and its customers, on the other. **Supply chain management** is the oversight of activities interconnecting suppliers and buyers (Figure 9.16). It encompasses a broad range of activities that span the sourcing of parts, components, materials and services, the production of goods, the distribution of finished goods, and the interaction with the

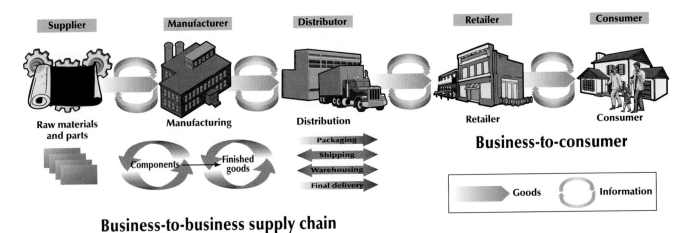

**Business-to-business supply chain**

FIGURE 9.16

*Components of a Business-to-Business Supply Chain*

 **REALITY CHECK**

Conducting e-commerce activities over the Internet allows buyers and sellers to easily span vast distances, often crossing national borders. However, cultures and legal systems are not as easily spanned. A company's managers learn quickly that each country in which they seek to do business may have different practices and unique laws—laws that prohibit some activities and require the performance of others. Here are a few examples:

- Online shoppers in many countries pay by the minute for the time they connect to the Internet for e-commerce. Hence, their perceived savings from buying products and services online may differ from shoppers in North America. U.S. shoppers, for instance, pay a fixed monthly telephone fee for local telephone service. A local call enables them to interconnect with the Internet for as long as they wish, without a per minute fee, to shop or surf the Web for information.
- Buyers want to shop for products that are priced in their local currency (Euros, Sterling, Yuan, etc.) regardless of the e-merchant's home country. Moreover, the prices must take into account local tax policies.
- Products that are legal and saleable online in one country (such as over-the-counter drugs or bottled wine) may be illegal in another country, even though online shoppers can view them on the e-commerce site. It is the responsibility of the seller to know and obey another country's laws.
- National laws may require that Web sites on the Internet display information in the language of that country, regardless of the languages used by the merchant or visitors to the online information display. France, for example, enforces legislation requiring all companies with offices in the country to include French language pages (in addition to any pages in other languages).
- Frequently, shoppers want to buy only from their national merchants and not from foreign companies. International companies may therefore be at a disadvantage even though their Web pages are accessible in the country.
- Local customs determine whether a customer is willing to pay for purchases by credit card, debit card, smart card, or another form of electronic currency. (Or custom may dictate that they not submit online payments under any circumstances).

It is the responsibility of the e-commerce merchant to know and accommodate local laws and customs and to build the Web site accordingly. ■

buyer (and in some cases the ultimate consumer) at the point of sale. Any point in the chain is an opportunity to add or reduce cost, elapsed time, and quality.

Supply chains also have competitive aspects. If one company has a more efficient and timely supply chain than another, it may pull customers away from competitors that are less efficient.

Industrial-era supply chain management focused on *stocking of items* to be used in manufacturing or for sales. In that era, effective inventory practice meant buying stock at good prices and far enough in advance to ensure sufficient on-hand quantities to meet manufacturing or resale requirements (to avoid shortages) without overstocking (thereby avoiding excesses). In essence, supply chain management systems were *inventory driven*. Eventually managers grew to realize that this was not an ideal way to manage supply chains, as inventory built up in many places: in warehouses and inventory areas, on factory floors, and on trains, boats, and trucks. All inventory takes up space, ties up money, and carries the risk of becoming obsolete, lost, stolen, or damaged. If companies avoid the need for inventory, they can prevent these disadvantages and problems.

Changing business conditions have put tremendous pressure on firms to cut down on excessive supply chain costs. Information technology and innovative e-commerce practices are providing the means to do so, making it possible to shift the emphasis from inventory-driven systems to demand-driven systems. Rather than being driven by forecasts of expected needs to *push* goods through the company's supply chain, today's advanced supply chain designs hope to enable buyer demand to *pull* goods through the supply channel (Figure 9.17). Here is how.

**Supply Chain Software**   Supply chain management software helps businesses reach beyond their company walls to connect with suppliers, distributors, and retailers, to change the way they conduct routine business. This type of software is a proven tool for helping companies shift activities in the various stages of making and selling products to business partners; that way, these activities can be performed more efficiently—*to everyone's benefit.*

**FIGURE 9.17**

***Push vs. Pull Strategy***

**Push Strategy "Make and sell"**
Goods are manufactured and placed in inventory. Manufacturing is driven by forecast. Sales force and sales promotions encourage buyers to select goods from inventory when possible. Buyer purchase orders may be driven by forecast or replenishment needs.

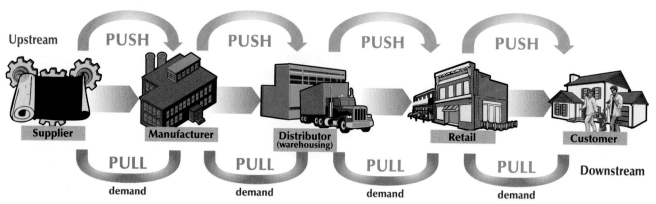

**Pull Strategy "Sell and make"**
Goods are manufactured in response to actual demand and shipped to buyer. Sales force and sales promotions encourage buyers to select goods from inventory when possible. Buyers provide sales information to manufacturers who in turn determine timing and need for replenishment.

Traditional business models have relied on push strategies. Interest is growing in implementing more efficient "pull" strategies.

Supply chain management software typically contains some or all of these components:

- **Capacity Requirements Planning**   The planned and actual orders for goods are matched with the production capability of the enterprise. This software also tracks production load by order status.
- **Demand Planning Module**   The need for goods is determined based on past performance and historical trends. Specific manufacturing requirements are then formulated to determine how much of an item to manufacture.
- **Manufacturing Planning Module**   The available facilities and manufacturing resources are examined to determine the production capacity that is available. If the software module determines that company's overall resources are a *constraint* that will prohibit the firm from meeting planned demand, it signals a need to either adjust plans or to acquire additional capacity.
- **Distribution Planning Module**   The module evaluates the ability of a firm to replenish its stock of goods as they are used up. It analyzes the supply of parts, components, materials, and other supplier resources that are available to the company. Inventory levels are also examined to ensure that the supply of goods will be adequate to support manufacturing.
- **Logistics Planning Module**   This module focuses on the planning and control of the forward and reverse flow and storage of goods between the manufacturer (or other point of origin) and their ultimate destination.
- **Transportation Planning Module**   This module determines the best way to warehouse and ship products, taking into account cost-effectiveness and responsiveness to customer needs.

Good supply chain management systems seek to balance supply chain and demand. Therefore, the *entire* supply chain—from the initial supplier to the end buyer—is examined, not just a single company's needs. Good supply chain practices focus on the *interactions* of supply chain members, seeking to produce results that benefit all participating companies and their customers.

The *Information Technology in Practice* feature, "At Ford, E-Commerce Strategy Redefines a Century of Success," describes how this pioneering auto manufacturer is focusing on supply chain management to change the way it manufactures cars and trucks.

**Supply Chain Integration Strategies**   **Supply chain integration** is the synchronization of all parties involved in making a product or delivering a service in order to meet buyer, seller, and customer needs. It requires unprecedented information exchange, coordination, and collaboration between participants, and an end-to-end view of supply-chain activities. It emphasizes levels of performance that are mutually beneficial to all. At the heart of supply chain integration is the Internet.

The most widely used strategies are *efficient consumer response* and *vendor-managed inventory*.

**Efficient Consumer Response**   Efficient consumer response is a partnership strategy in which general merchandise retailers and their suppliers work together to respond more quickly to consumer needs by sharing sales information. The strategy grew out of research conducted by the retail grocery industry where a typical supermarket stocks many, many products—usually more than 50,000 different items—some of which have very short shelf lives. It has since been adopted in other industries.

In an **efficient consumer response** supply chain strategy (also known as **continuous replenishment**), data and information on products are captured at the point of sale and shared with suppliers periodically (usually daily) so that both can work together to jointly forecast future demands for replenishable items, monitor trends, and detect opportunities for new items. Both parties use electronic data interchange (whether involving value added networks, or VANs, or via the Internet) or extranets to speed the flow of information. A synchronized system reduces the need for the three separate replenishment cycles (see Figure 9.18) that typically make up the supply chain: store to consumer, distributor to store, and manufacturer to distributor.

**supply chain integration**
The synchronization of all parties involved in making a product or delivering a service in order to meet buyer, seller, and customer needs.

**efficient consumer response/ continuous replenishment**
Data and information on products are captured at the point of sale and shared with suppliers periodically (usually daily) so that both can work together to jointly forecast future demands for replenishable items, monitor trends, and detect opportunities for new items.

# INFORMATION TECHNOLOGY IN PRACTICE

## At Ford, E-Commerce Strategy Redefines a Century of Success

The twentieth century was, in retrospect, the *century of the automobile*. More than any other invention or innovation, it changed the way people live, how they work, and the companies and industries in which they work.

The twenty-first century has begun as the *century of the Internet* and electronic commerce. At Ford Motor Company, headquartered in Michigan, the Internet and e-commerce are playing an essential role as the company redefines the meaning of success in the twenty-first century.

It is fitting that Ford, one of the major U.S. automakers, has so vividly embraced the Internet and its ability to change both the company and its industry. After all, it was Ford that made history with its twentieth-century innovations. Ford virtually created the automobile industry on October 1, 1908, when it introduced the famous Model T automobile, which quickly won the approval of millions of owners. The first year's sales broke all records. On October 13, 1913, mass production of the automobile began, an innovation of founder Henry Ford that was to change the auto industry for the entire century. The moving assembly line, replacing an individual-stage assembly method, immediately improved the speed of assembly. This reduced elapsed time from 12 hours and eight minutes to a mere one hour and 33 minutes. In 1914, Ford produced 308,162 cars—more than all other auto manufacturers com-

bined. It was also in 1914 that Ford, which previously manufactured the Model T in black, red, blue, green, or gray, further streamlined the production process by ensuring that the Model T was *available in any color so long as it is black*. By 1921, Model Ts accounted for 56.6 percent of global auto production.

Mass production served Ford well. Yet as Ford's leaders look ahead today, they see a much different industry—an industry where e-commerce is enabling the company to redefine the most fundamental assumptions it has made throughout its history.

Ford believes the auto industry practice of pushing vehicles through the supply channel and ultimately finding ways to successfully sell those to consumers *must* give way to a *pull* strategy wherein customers determine the vehicles they want. That is, they pull their choice through the supply channel by

placing an order that determines what is manufactured and when.

Ford has created an e-commerce business group, *ConsumerConnect,* to develop and implement an e-commerce capability that makes the pull strategy possible. Partners are playing pivotal roles in the implementation of Ford's e-commerce strategy: Oracle (e-commerce and database software), Cisco (routers for the Internet), Yahoo! (search and portal services), and TeleTech (call-center specialist) are developing the systems to deliver highly personalized and customized services for loans, warranty services, vehicle repairs, all while keeping abreast of buyers' lifestyles and driving habits.

Although the customer is an important beneficiary, Ford's e-commerce strategy is also intended to benefit the suppliers, through redesign of the supply chain. Among the e-commerce features planned by the ConsumerConnect group is an online trading site,

than $8 billion. Ford e-commerce planners are even considering establishing an auction site where other participants in the auto industry will be able to buy and sell everything from parts and components to office and maintenance supplies.

Although Ford Motor Company was highly influential in the development of the automobile during the last century, it plans to redefine its role in the twenty-first century. Management recognizes that its e-commerce strategy will be an important influence on its success in the future. Look for many new features of e-commerce at Ford.

dubbed auto-exchange, where Ford's 30,000 suppliers can be linked to the company for rapid, online communication as well as better prices and faster delivery. Participants will not only know what a Ford production line is assembling on a given day, but will play a role in keeping Ford supplied with parts and materials (using techniques such as vendor-managed inventory and electronic procurement) to meet production plans. Experts project that the savings in reduced paper shuffling could exceed $1 billion while a full implementation of e-procurement could increase savings to more

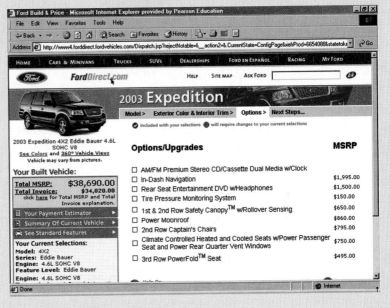

The consumer's purchase is detected when the product is scanned at the checkout counter using a point of sale (POS) system. Manufacturers automatically receive the details electronically, via electronic data interchange (EDI). A computer-assisted ordering system determines when replenishment items should be ordered. Companies implementing this strategy usually seek to automatically generate and transmit reorders using POS data rather than relying on sales forecasts to guide them. This form of supply chain integration increases reorder frequency and stimulates faster replenishment rates that enable companies to reduce their inventory on hand and at the same time decrease the number of sales lost to out-of-stock conditions. Overall, reorder costs, inventory costs, over and under stock costs, and elapsed time are reduced, usually by more than 50 percent. All participants, including the consumer, benefit (Table 9.2).

Many companies are seeking to simplify the replenishment process and streamline the supply chain by dealing directly with the manufacturers. That is, they are seeking to

# Information Flow

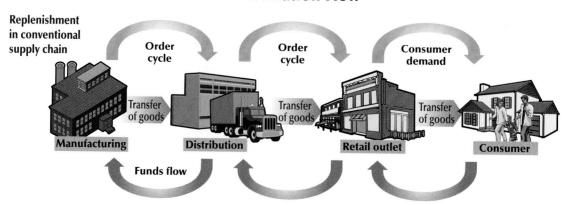

**Replenishment in conventional supply chain**

Order cycle

Order cycle

Consumer demand

Transfer of goods — Manufacturing

Transfer of goods — Distribution

Transfer of goods — Retail outlet

Consumer

Funds flow

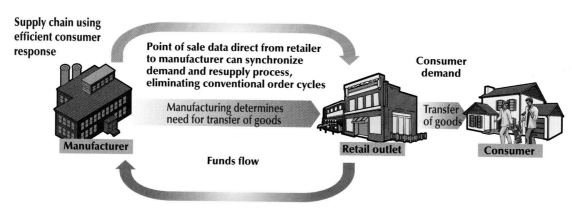

**Supply chain using efficient consumer response**

**Point of sale data direct from retailer to manufacturer can synchronize demand and resupply process, eliminating conventional order cycles**

Consumer demand

Manufacturing determines need for transfer of goods

Transfer of goods

Manufacturer

Retail outlet

Consumer

Funds flow

## Manufacturer benefits
- Reduced shipment variation
- Lower finished product inventories
- Increased volume due to improved fill rates
- Reduction in raw materials inventories
- Damage/returns reduction
- Reduction in packaging materials inventories
- Reduced administration
- Improved return on assets
- Lower deductions

## Retailer benefits
- Reduced inventory
- Improved inventory turns
- Improved service levels/fill rates
- Improved cash flow
- Reduced administration
- Improved return on assets
- Less damage handling
- Product freshness
- Lower deductions
- Improved invoice error rates

**FIGURE 9.18**

*Efficient Consumer Response Version of Supply Chain Leads to Synchronized Replenishment of Goods*

**disintermediation**

Name given to removing intermediaries (like brokers and distributors) from the supply chain.

eliminate the brokers and distributors—often called intermediaries—with whom they have been dealing. **Disintermediation** is the name given to removing intermediaries (like brokers and distributors) from the supply chain (Figure 9.19). The rationale of these companies is as follows: If they buy in large quantities and can deal direct via electronic links, there is no need to involve an intermediary or distributor who only receives and redistributes goods.

Companies will increasingly eliminate an intermediary if they do not believe that it offers useful or valuable services, or if it is deemed to unnecessarily increase time and cost to the supply and replenishment process.

**vendor-managed inventory**

Companies deal directly with vendors, that is, manufacturers or suppliers.

**Vendor-Managed Inventory** Under **vendor-managed inventory,** companies deal directly with vendors, that is, manufacturers or suppliers. The decision of when to replenish goods is *turned over to the supplier*—the vendor. Vendors in turn take responsibility for ensuring that the level of inventory on hand at a company is adequate to meet

**Table 9.2  Benefits of Implementing Efficient Consumer Response System**

| EXPENSE TYPE | SAVINGS WITH ECR |
|---|---|
| Cost of goods | Reduced product losses due to damage, reduced manufacturing expense (less overtime, better capacity utilization), lower packaging expense (fewer promotional packs, variety reduction), more efficient raw material purchasing. |
| Marketing | Reduced trade and consumer promotion administration expense, fewer product introduction failures. |
| Selling/Buying | Less field and headquarters resources (fewer special pricing deals, automated ordering, reduced deductions, simplified administration). |
| Logistics | More efficient use of warehouses and trucks, cross-dock flow through distribution, reduced warehouse space requirements. |
| Administration | Reduced clerical and accounting staff. |
| Store Operations | Automated ordering, higher sales per square foot. |

Source: Adapted from Kurt Salmon Associates Inc., "Efficient Consumer Response: Enhancing Consumer Value in the Grocery Industry."

demand from customers, but not so large as to be excessive, entailing great merchandise costs and the need for more storage space.

This is controversial. Opponents say it is risky to let sellers determine the quantity of goods a buyer should purchase. Proponents say that picking the right supplier and monitoring their performance minimizes any risk. It is highly likely this strategy will gain momentum as more attention is focused on supply chain integration.

Global discount retailer Wal-Mart has found many benefits to dealing directly with vendors and giving them substantial responsibility for inventory replenishment. Using these methods, it has become an industry leader in supply chain integration. (This chapter's *Case Study*, "Wal-Mart's Retail Link Connects its Supply Chain," describes in detail the company's e-commerce capabilities and how its supply chain integration strategy benefits both customers and suppliers.)

**FIGURE 9.19**

*Disintermediation Eliminates Unnecessary Intermediaries from Supply Channel*

**Distributor is "disintermediated" from supply channel when . . .**

Buyer does not judge that value is added by dealing with a member of supply channel (e.g., a distributor).

Information technology provides effective means of interacting directly with other channel members, avoiding intermediaries.

# E-Procurement

**Electronic procurement (e-procurement)** systems give employees access to catalogs of products and services from multiple suppliers. The catalogs listing items, descriptions and illustrations, and prices of items that employees need to do their work, are accessible using PCs on the company's intranet or other communications network. Each catalog may be customized to list the items the company wishes its employees to choose from, along with prenegotiated prices for each. For instance, e-procurement systems enable employees to buy office supplies by choosing from online catalogs. Frequently the system can tap directly into the vendor's inventory management system, so employees can have immediate information about the price and availability of the product or service.

All companies have expenditures for two types of goods: **Direct spending** is to obtain materials or components from suppliers for use in the manufacture of a product or delivery of a service. The preceding supply chain integration examples focused on instances of direct spending. In contrast, **indirect spending** buys goods and services that support operation of the company as a whole (horizontal exchanges, discussed in the next section, typically sell indirect goods and services). These items are sometimes referred to as **maintenance, repair, and operations (MRO)** items. The types of indirect spending shown in Table 9.3 do not directly appear in a product or service, but they make their production or delivery possible. They are necessary to run the company effectively.

**E-Procurement Objectives**   In the past, it has been necessary for companies to choose between centralized purchasing that is expensive, but provides good control and leverage with vendors, or decentralized purchasing that is convenient for employees but does not always lead to the best buying habits for the company. Electronic procurement provides the best of both.

Greater attention is being given to the manner in which indirect procurement activities occur, with the following objectives:

- **Reducing Purchasing Costs**   The cost of preparing and processing purchasing orders to procure such items as office supplies, temporary workers, catering, computer hardware, and software is very high. The cost of preparing and processing a purchase order in a typical company exceeds $100, regardless of the value of the goods bought. Hence, a company ordering, say $50 worth of office supplies, may actually spend $150 to obtain the goods, including both the goods themselves and the purchasing costs.
- **Providing Employee Self-Service**   Company intranets and communications networks make it possible for employees to review online catalogs and other product

| Table 9.3   Indirect Spending Buys Maintenance, Repair, and Operations (MRO) Goods and Services |
| --- |
| Office Equipment & Supplies |
| Computers and IT Equipment |
| Piping, Electrical, HVAC Supplies |
| Legal and Professional Services |
| Utilities and Communications |
| Catering and Food Services |
| Material Handling Supplies |
| Nuts, Bolts, Nails, and Screws |
| Advertising and Marketing Supplies |

or service information in determining which vendors or suppliers they want to use. Moreover, they can prepare and submit electronic (not paper!) purchase orders from their desktop computer and transmit them to the supplier for fulfillment.

- **Increasing Leverage with Suppliers** If businesses aggregate their department purchases into company-wide purchases from a single vendor, their enterprise's buying volume usually entitles them to better prices and delivery conditions.

**E-Procurement Software** E-procurement systems can be designed to span a variety of different vendors and need not be limited to a single supplier catalog. Hence, from their desks employees can choose from a variety of supplier alternatives and still enjoy the benefits of online buying. Once the buying decision is made, the order can be submitted electronically from their PCs.

If items in the order require approval by the purchasing department (perhaps because their value exceeds a predetermined threshold), the order can be routed electronically to purchasing for online review and approval, and subsequently transmitted to the vendor.

E-procurement systems also benefit vendors that are able to cultivate an online buying relationship. Receiving orders electronically eliminates the exchange of paper documents and also speeds the buying cycle. Moreover, vendors can transfer the order electronically within their own company network. And, when the products are delivered to the buyer, the invoice can be transmitted electronically, further compounding the benefits by speeding the entire accounting and payment process.

E-procurement processes usually have a valuable byproduct in the form of reports that summarize company spending with a particular supplier, for a specific product or service, for an important project, or by departments or cost centers. Managers have at their hand more resources to use in streamlining purchasing and procurement activities.

## Electronic Exchanges

Sometimes companies seek to lower the price of parts, components, and supplies by participating in electronic exchanges. **Electronic exchanges** (also known as *electronic markets* or **B2B hubs**) are commerce sites on the Internet where buyers and sellers can come together to shop, exchange information, or carry out transactions to buy or sell products and services. Exchanges are structured according to one of three models: (1) public, (2) consortia-led, and (3) private exchanges (Figure 9.20).

**Public Exchanges** In a **public exchange** (sometimes known as an **independent exchange**), a third party—the *market maker*—operates the electronic market, displays the market's information content, and provides electronic tools for conducting trade.

The focus of an exchange describes its objective of serving a specific industry or serving multiple industries. Exchanges have vertical or horizontal objectives.

**electronic exchange/ B2B hub**

Commerce sites on the Internet where buyers and sellers can come together to shop, exchange information, or carry out transactions to buy or sell products and services.

**public exchange/ independent exchange**

A third party—the *market maker*—operates the electronic market, displays the market's information content, and provides electronic tools for conducting trade.

**FIGURE 9.20**

*Evolution of e-Procurement and B2B Exchanges*

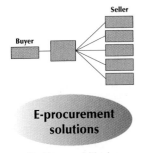

**E-procurement solutions**

Desktop requisitioning and buying from online catalogs

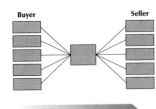

**Independent exchange**

Independently owned trading exchange

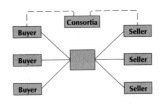

**Consortia backed exchange**

Consortia owned trading exchange

**Private exchange**

Private, invitation only trading exchange centered on a specific sponsoring company and its trading partners

# CRITICAL CONNECTIONS 3

## GE Global eXchange Service Provides Worldwide E-Procurement

**GXS**

GE Global eXchange Services (GXS), part of GE Information Services, a wholly owned subsidiary of electronics giant General Electric Company, operates one the largest B2B e-commerce networks in the world, connecting more than 100,000 trading partners. The network spans more than 50 countries.

GXS electronic procurement systems assimilate all supplier information into a single catalog. An individual company's negotiated pricing terms are integrated directly into the catalog and automatically displayed when accessed by employees. A *Favorites* page can be created for frequently ordered items and a *Special Request* option enables buyers to make purchases of items not included in the regular catalog.

Because GXS customers often have many global locations, the system is designed to span national boundaries and cultures. Different buyers in a company can select their preferred languages, currencies, date formats, and make other adjustments that suit their local practices. Different procurement approval rules can also be incorporated into the process to fit the unique needs of a specific company division or department.

GXS processes some 1 billion transactions for goods and services annually, valued at more than $1 trillion.

## GXS Marketplace Architecture

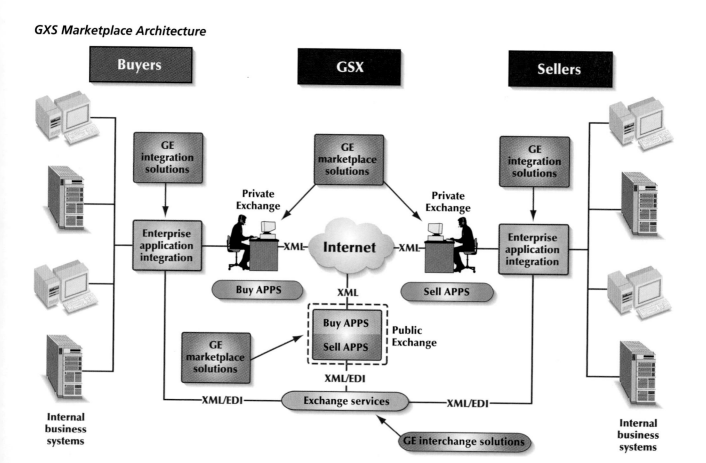

**Vertical Exchanges** **Vertical exchanges** are structured to serve members of a specific industry (Figure 9.21). The products and services offered in the market are likely to be of interest only to industry members. Companies that develop electronic markets in a particular industry do so because they have extensive knowledge of the industry and have the insight to provide the type of assistance that buyers and sellers within the industry are seeking. Examples of vertical e-market companies include:

* **E-Steel.com** An online exchange where buyers and sellers can initiate, specify, negotiate, and close transactions for the sale of rolled, coated, or bar steel. The marketplace represents more than 1,000 companies, including steel mills, service centers, fabricators, and distributors residing in more than 70 countries.
* **PlasticsNet.com** A leading electronic marketplace designed to simplify and streamline buying and selling for the plastics industry. Several hundred thousand items are included in the product directory. Shoppers can find resins and materials, equipment and supplies, and training materials. Visitors to the e-market can also view and bid on surplus products offered at auction through the site.
* **WaterOnline.com** A market offering everything for the movement, storage, and treatment of water. This public exchange is also a source for technical information, job postings, training, and calendar of industry events.
* **Medibuy.com** Offers healthcare purchasing professionals a fast, convenient, worldwide source for medical/surgical products, supplies, and equipment. The market provides two ways to purchase and sell products. Buyers can submit electronic requests for proposals (eRFPs) for all equipment and supplies used in the healthcare environment that are in turn distributed to all qualified vendors. Or, buyers can bid at electronic auctions where used equipment, excess inventory, and refurbished items can be bought or sold.

Vertical exchanges are most attractive to companies within industries that are very fragmented, because in these industries it is otherwise necessary to deal with a number of different companies to obtain needed services or products.

**vertical exchange**
Structured to serve members of a specific industry.

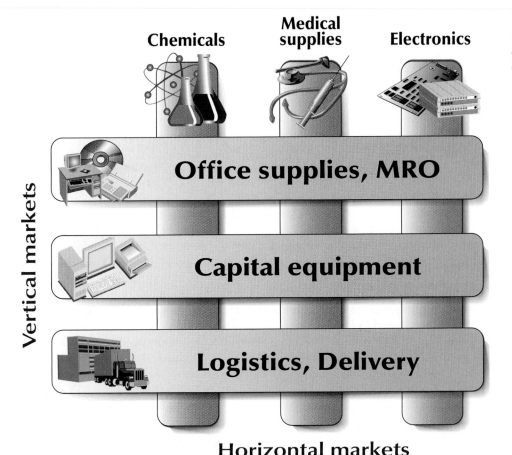

**FIGURE 9.21**

***Vertical and Horizontal Structures in Electronic Markets***

The vertical e-market exchange is most valuable if it becomes a single source for buyers and sellers alike. In this case, the market creator benefits the buyer by establishing a catalog containing products from many different sellers, giving the buyer more sources and greater choices than is possible in traditional markets. Buyers can obtain the products, services, and information they want at a single exchange rather having to contact each seller individually. Similarly, sellers gain the efficiency of having the exchange represent them to many more customers than they would be able to reach directly in other ways. The seller typically pays the exchange operator a small fee for the e-commerce services. It seems that everyone—buyer, seller, and e-market operator—win in this situation.

**horizontal exchange**
Seek to simultaneously serve the interests of companies across different industries. Customers seek their services because of functional expertise rather than industry expertise.

**Horizontal Exchanges** **Horizontal exchanges,** in contrast, seek to simultaneously serve the interests of companies across *different* industries. Customers seek their services because of *functional expertise* rather than industry expertise.

Representative examples of horizontal exchanges include the following:

- **IMark.com** Buying and selling used equipment
- **Employease** Employee benefits administration
- **MRO.com** Maintenance, repair, and operating procurement
- **BidCom** Project management
- **YOUtilities** Energy management

Horizontal exchanges are attractive when they offer a broad selection of products and services or a wide range of potential buyers, and an efficient means of conducting a buy or sell transaction.

**Future of Public Exchanges** Launched in the heady days of Internet dot-com mania, most public exchanges faced huge ongoing technology investment expenses even as they sought to grow customer participation and revenue. For most, profitability after their founding was well in the future, with expenses vastly exceeding revenue. The very public nature of the exchange's openness to anyone wishing to participate worked against the model. Potential participants did not come to the market, for fear of exposing sensitive information about their prices, capacities, and business activities. As a result, many of the thousands of exchanges that existed at the beginning of this decade have faded into dot-com history, a clear signal that these independent market places may become extinct.

The *Information Technology in Practice* feature, "Chemdex: An E-Market that Organized a Fragmented Supply Chain," describes the operation of a vertical market in the life sciences industry. While this exchange received a great deal of attention, like many developed during the same time period, it was not able to generate sufficient business to continue in operation. In the end, it suffered the same fate that fell to many public exchanges.

**consortia-led exchange**
Industry players combine forces to create a common forum for the exchange of goods and services.

**Consortia-Led Exchanges** Fear of independent, public exchanges among established brick-and-mortar firms led some of these traditional firms to create consortia to build e-markets. In a **consortia-led exchange,** industry players combine forces to create a common forum for the exchange of goods and services. These exchanges, whose controlled access limits suppliers to those chosen by the operator, share the principal objective of driving down costs for everyone. Examples include the Covisant exchange in the auto industry (created by GM, Daimler-Chrysler, and Ford) and Orbitz in the airline industry (backed by American, United, Delta, Northwest, and Continental Airlines). Their success depends in part on the ability of the competing companies who comprise the consortium to work toward common objectives in backing the exchange.

Orbitz was started as a way to lower the cost to the airlines of selling tickets over the Internet, especially through public exchanges such as Travelocity and Expedia. The sponsoring airlines thought that with their own consortia-exchange, they could drive down the cost of tickets by having passengers book at Orbitz rather than at the other exchanges or through travel agents. Hence, they promised to give Orbitz the right to sell virtually every type of discount ticket they offered to the public or through public exchanges.

Orbitz widely promotes the low-fare discount tickets and generates several billion dollars annually in revenue for its investors. Unfortunately for the airlines (but not necessarily for the passengers), the widely publicized fares are having the effect of providing

# INFORMATION TECHNOLOGY IN PRACTICE

## Chemdex: An E-Market That Organized a Fragmented Supply Chain

Biotech is a multi-billion dollar industry loaded with intellectual horsepower—some 500,000 scientists worldwide. Look closely, and you will find that the scientists depend on a highly fragmented supply chain for supplies, because that portion of the industry is made up of thousands of businesses, including large multinational companies (like 3M and CN Biosciences) as well as small businesses. Just finding out who provides various supplies is a time-consuming hassle. It often requires a review of individual, well-worn, out-of-date catalogs from several different suppliers distinguished by dog-eared pages and Post-it Note place markers. For the buyer, this means individual orders, shipments, and payments; and perhaps more cost than most buyers realize.

Others looking at this situation see the hassle as an opportunity. To David Perry and Jeff Leane, cofounders of Palo Alto-based Chemdex, the fragmented biotech supply chain was pure opportunity. Armed with a business plan, and $15 million in funds from the venture capital firm Kleiner Perkins Caufield & Byers, they set out in 1997 to change industry practice, benefiting both customers and suppliers in the industry. Unfortunately, they were unable to generate the necessary income to keep their operation afloat.

The Chemdex electronic market served the needs of pharmaceutical, biotechnical, and academic institutions. Its e-commerce capabilities included an extensive online, electronic marketplace offering a wide range of life science products, such as biological and chemical reagents, lab supplies, instruments, and equipment. The e-procurement capabilities offered at the Chemdex Web site streamlined the buying and selling process for both customers and participating manufacturers.

At the Chemdex marketplace you could find biological chemicals and reagents (antibodies, enzymes, cell culture media, molecular biology reagents, and organic and inorganic chemicals). Lab supplies, instruments, and equipment were also available; this created a convenient one-stop source for all lab needs.

Searching through the thousands of products was easy. A search engine made it possible to compare hundreds of thousands of products, locating them by name, product category, supplier name, supplier catalog number, or any keyword that might be in a product description.

Suppliers benefited as well. Their product and service information was displayed online, in an electronic market that was well known and easily accessible over the Internet. Chemdex also offered a suite of solutions designed to link suppliers to the market through efficient, well-integrated business processes. The Chemdex Web catalog manager gave suppliers the capability to submit and post catalog descriptions, or to delete and change information about their products directly online.

As orders were placed at the Web site, Chemdex transmitted them to each supplier. Suppliers, in turn, shipped the items directly to the customers. The customer support group at Chemdex monitored each step in the order fulfillment process, immediately notifying customers by e-mail of any exceptions, such as when unexpected out-of-stock or backorder conditions occurred.

There was no up-front cost to have products listed in the Chemdex marketplace. The only cost was a nominal transaction fee that was charged when a customer ordered items from a supplier.

Customers were able to easily reorder supplies by duplicating an order that had been previously submitted. It was easy—just clicking a *duplicate* button on the order status page took care of this. Frequently ordered products, or any product in the catalog, could be placed on a list of *favorites*. Customers could recall their list of favorites with a single mouse click, and quickly add one or more of the items on the list to an order. Payments could be made with credit cards or by preapproved Chemdex charge accounts.

For those who enjoyed paging through printed catalogs of thousands of biotech products and suppliers, Chemdex did not have much appeal. On the other hand, for others who wanted to check out products and suppliers quickly, Chemdex online was the answer.

Although Chemdex's operating and IT capabilities were top-notch, it ceased operation because of insufficient need for its services. Even the best-conceived e-commerce concepts must survive the test of generating enough customer demand. In the end, Chemdex could not do so.

complete pricing information in a public place, thereby reducing the fares the airlines are now able to charge for regular tickets. Meanwhile, Orbitz's expenses are outpacing the revenue it generates.

Large corporations that have established consortia-led exchanges must also balance cutting their costs via electronic commerce and being perceived as using the exchange to unfairly pressure suppliers into reducing prices–a move that may ultimately hinder the suppliers' very survival. Consortia-backed exchanges that pressure suppliers into excessively squeezing their margins could also face scrutiny from government regulators concerned about antitrust violations.

**Private Exchanges**    Enterprises that favor electronic procurement but want to avoid participating in public exchanges for fear of openly disclosing prices, inventory levels, and operating capacities, are moving to create private exchanges. A **private exchange** is an Internet-based trading forum (i.e., an electronic market) implemented by a *single company* with a *select group of suppliers and customers*. It is often linked to a company's in-house IT systems and is only open to those enterprises that are invited to participate. (This means companies disclose information selectively rather than publicly.) Private exchanges are viewed as threats to both independent and consortium-based exchanges.

A private exchange provides an electronic way to share its aggregate buying requirements, define product specifications, negotiate with suppliers, and establish a contract. In addition, the private exchange gives suppliers an accurate view of customer product needs for the contract period, enabling it to more carefully assess its own manufacturing and inventory needs. Yet neither gives up sensitive information to competitors or competitor's suppliers.

Cisco Systems, well known for the routers it sells for creating LANs and the Internet, operates a private exchange for invited customers and distributors. Customers wanting to purchase its routers can connect to the private exchange, configure a router to their unique needs, and check for price and availability. Cisco verifies the viability of the proposed configuration, and an authorized distributor participating in the private exchange provides information pricing and availability. A sales agreement is struck and the routers are shipped to the customer. Neither the customer, nor the distributor, nor Cisco System discloses any information publicly.

Private exchanges have other inherent advantages that public e-markets may never acquire:

- Owners of the private exchange regulate customer and supplier access, excluding competitors or suppliers to competitors.
- Owners can direct trading partners to the private exchange through pricing incentives or by alternatives for streamlining business processes that will benefit all participants.
- Private exchanges can be tailored to serve specific products, in contrast to public exchanges which must be general purpose and able to accommodate many companies.
- Private exchanges can be secured through limited access and encryption of messages.

Private exchanges are still in their infancy. It is likely that they will receive a great deal of attention in the next few years as enterprises seek to refine and grow their capabilities in B2B electronic commerce.

# A Final Word

Electronic commerce is changing the way customers and companies, and buyers and sellers, think about business. New products and services are one result. The way buyers and sellers engage one another is also evolving rapidly. Executives and managers who do not embrace these innovations or who do not have the vision to see the future of e-commerce, may soon find their success threatened. In many cases, the threat has already surfaced. The question is not *whether* companies will be reshaped as a result of electronic commerce, but rather *when* and *how*. In the future, it is likely that all companies will have to be e-commerce companies to some extent in order to survive.

---

**private exchange**
An Internet-based trading forum (i.e., an electronic market) implemented by a single company with a select group of suppliers and customers.

# CRITICAL CONNECTIONS

## 1 Part II: Priceline Rewrites the Rules with its Demand Collection System

**Priceline.com**  Priceline.com's *Name Your Own Price* services enable consumers to submit purchase offers over the Internet for goods and services at the prices they want to pay. Consumers agree to hold their offers open for a specified period of time to enable Priceline.com to fulfill their offers from inventory provided by participating sellers. Once fulfilled, offers cannot be canceled. By requiring consumers to be flexible with respect to brands, sellers and/or product features, Priceline.com enables sellers to generate incremental revenue without disrupting their existing distribution channels or retail pricing structures.

Priceline.com is a unique form of commerce. It is not an auction or a reverse auction, since there is no competition among buyers or sellers to set the price. Priceline.com is not an aggregator. Each buyer's offer is handled as it is received, and individuals have just as much (if not more) buying power than they would as part of a group.

Because Priceline.com does not publish accepted prices, and does not identify a seller until after the sale is completed, it is an effective and efficient outlet for businesses to move excess or perishable inventory without affecting their retail pricing structure.

## 2 Part II: Quicken Takes Financial Management Online

**Quicken**  The widely used Quicken financial management software features a data communications capability that enables its users to initiate financial transactions on their PCs and PDAs and have theses transactions synchronized with their bank records. Approximately 3,000 financial institutions have developed links in their day-to-day IT applications in order to enable customers to download personal banking and financial information into the Quicken program on their PCs. The data communications alternatives include:

- **Direct Connect**  The fastest, easiest way to connect with a financial institution. *Direct Connect* allows individuals to access their account information, pay bills, transfer money, and send other instructions to their institution right from within Quicken.
- **Web Connect**  Automatically enter transactions and update balances in Quicken simply by logging onto the financial institution's Web site and clicking the *Download to Quicken* button.

Intuit continues to extend Quicken's capabilities and the very meaning of its name. Today users can obtain Quicken credit and debit cards associated with MasterCard or Visa, arrange mortgages and loans, and more. PIN number access helps keep financial information private.

By looking at the growth of services around Quicken, it is easy to see that it is becoming a preferred platform for personal financial management—one that can connect and communicate with institutions offering traditional financial services. Where will Quicken go next?

### Questions for Discussion

1. What features of Quicken appear to be most attractive to its users?
2. How significant is Quicken's data communications capability and its ability to interconnect with banking systems?
3. Why do you think so many banks have made it possible for Quicken users to connect and download data from their systems?
4. Is it possible that Quicken will grow to rival traditional banks?

## 3 Part II: GE Global eXchange Service Provides Worldwide E-Procurement

**GXS**  The B2B e-commerce networks of GE Global eXchange Services connect more than 100,000 trading partners around the world. In addition to the company's catalog-based electronic procurement services, GXS also operates business-to-business exchange services. It provides three exchange services:

- **Industry Marketplace**  An independent B2B exchange, hosted by GXS, that links many different buyers with many vertical or cross-industry suppliers (i.e., many-to-many buying/selling relationships).
- **Private Marketplace**  A privately owned one-to-many Extranet hosted by GXS that enables a company to use company-specific business processes in acquiring products and services from selected suppliers and trading partners; transactions involving the private marketplace can be closely integrated with the company's internal business systems (i.e., one-to-many buying relationships).
- **Express Marketplace**  A GXS hosted B2B exchange where companies can conduct immediate buying or selling activities using only a Web browser and a PC (no other hardware or software is needed); pricing may be determined through buyer-requested quotations from suppliers or via reverse auctions.

The GXS marketplace combination is designed to offer a buying exchange that meets the needs of every type of buyer, large or small seeking immediate (i.e., spot buying) or ongoing relationships with sellers in the more than the 50 countries it serves.

## Questions for Discussion

1. What are the most attractive features of GXS' electronic procurement service?

2. Do you think GXS needs to operate three different forms of B2B exchanges?

3. Why would buyers or sellers use the GXS services instead of developing their own e-procurement or B2B exchange capabilities?

4. What business and e-commerce challenges does GXS encounter as a result of offering its services worldwide?

# Summary of Learning Objectives

**1 Describe the meaning of electronic commerce.** Electronic commerce (e-commerce) is the buying, selling, and exchange of information about products and services over public or private communications networks. Transactions may occur over the public Internet or on private intranets and extranets.

**2 Identify the two principal segments of electronic commerce.** E-commerce is generally categorized as business-to-consumer and business-to-business commerce.

**3 Describe the seven advantages that participants in electronic commerce enjoy compared to traditional commerce.** *Geographic reach* enables an enterprise to serve customers and interact with suppliers virtually anywhere with *speed* that enables near instant interaction with trading partners. *Productivity* improvements mean that a greater volume of work can be completed. *Information sharing*, including text, audio, video, graphics, or animation, and *new features* in products and services may enable firms to use e-commerce to achieve a *competitive advantage* even as they *lower costs*.

**4 Distinguish between the four business-to-consumer forms of electronic commerce.** *Electronic retailing* enables shoppers to make purchases over the Internet from a seller's home page, which functions as its storefront. *Electronic markets* enable shoppers to visit a collection of stores in a market comparable to an online shopping mall. *Portals* are Web sites that provide a single point of access from which shoppers can locate and then connect to other Web sites meeting their needs. *Online services* span a range of services, including online banking, personal finance and bill payment, securities and investments, and travel services.

**5 Discuss supply chain integration and the reason companies are making it an e-commerce objective.**

A company's supply chain (for example the flow of parts, components, materials, funds, and information from manufacturers and vendors) is integrated when all of the activities of all parties are synchronized and when there is coordination and collaboration between participants and an end-to-end view of all activities. E-commerce enables firms to implement the strategies of efficient consumer response and vendor-managed inventory as a way of achieving supply chain integration.

**6 Identify the characteristics of electronic procurement.** Employees are able to initiate purchasing activities with multiple suppliers from their networked desktop PCs, often using online catalogs for purchasing of indirect goods and services. E-procurement eliminates paper documents while also reducing purchasing costs, providing employee self-service, and increasing leverage with suppliers.

**7 Explain the purpose of electronic exchanges and identify the three forms that have emerged.** Electronic exchanges are commerce sites on the Internet where buyers and sellers come together to shop, exchange information, or carry out transactions, typically with the assistance of a third party (the market maker). In *public (independent) exchanges*, the third party creates and operates the market, keeping it open to anyone. Public exchanges may have a vertical or a horizontal industry focus. With *consortia-led exchanges*, collaborating companies combine forces to establish a market for the exchange of goods and services with selected suppliers. A *private exchange* is an Internet-based trading forum implemented by a single company with a select group of suppliers and customers. All electronic exchanges seek to streamline the buying and selling process for participants.

# Key Terms

auctions  392
back office  404
bill consolidator  398
brick and mortar  393
business-to-business (B2B) e-commerce  386
business-to-consumer (B2C) e-commerce  385
consortia-led exchange  418
content  402
content aggregator  396
continuous replenishment  409
cyberbanking  396
direct spending  414
disintermediation  412
Dutch auction  394

efficient consumer response  409
electronic banking  396
electronic commerce (e-commerce)  384
electronic exchange/B2B hub  415
electronic markets (e-markets)  392
electronic procurement/e-procurement  414
electronic storefront  391
forward auction  393
horizontal exchange  418
independent exchange  415
indirect spending  414
infomediary  396
interactive coupon  405
interactive marketing  405
intermediary  398

maintenance, repair, and operations (MRO)  414
online retailing  391
portal  394
private exchange  420
public exchange  415
reverse auction  394
spam  405
supply chain  406
supply chain integration  409
supply chain management  406
vendor-managed inventory  412
vertical exchange  417
virtual bank  396

# Review Questions

1. What is electronic commerce? How is it distinguished from e-business?

2. Two segments comprise e-commerce. What are they and what are the distinguishing characteristics of each?

3. Describe the seven principal advantages e-commerce offers to those who participate.

4. How significant is e-commerce expected to be over the next few years in terms of commercial activities? Which segment comprises the largest portion of e-commerce activity?

5. What are the four common consumer-focused e-commerce forms? Briefly describe each.

6. There are three forms of auctions. What characteristics distinguish each?

7. In electronic banking, also known as cyberbanking, transactions can be conducted at traditional or virtual banks. How are these types of banks different and what advantages and disadvantages does each offer its customers?

8. There is growing interest in electronic bill payment. Describe the characteristics of the five principal forms of electronic bill payment, indicating when each form is used and the advantages it offers.

9. Does electronic bill payment also include electronic bill presentment? Why or why not?

10. Describe the four functions provided by e-commerce Web sites.

11. What are interactive ads and how do they differ from banner advertisements?

12. Why is spam considered an undesirable aspect of advertising?

13. What is a business-to-business supply chain?

14. What is supply chain management and what components may be included in software aimed at assisting in management of the supply chain?

15. Discuss the objectives of supply chain integration and the two strategies commonly used in integrating the supply chain.

16. How do indirect and direct spending differ from one another?

17. Why is electronic procurement of interest to enterprises? What advantages does it offer to an enterprise? To its employees?

18. Describe the features and characteristics of electronic procurement systems.

19. Electronic exchanges are of growing importance in business-to-business e-commerce. What is an electronic exchange and what are the three common forms of electronic exchanges?

20. What are the advantages and disadvantages of participating in an electronic exchange from the viewpoint of the buyer? From the viewpoint of the seller?

21. How do vertical and horizontal exchanges differ from one another?

22. Which form of private exchange is increasingly favored by buyers? Why is this the case?

## Discussion Questions

1. Which, if any, of the following items would you purchase online and what features must the e-commerce Web site include for you to do so? Alternatively, which of the following transactions would you *never* conduct online and why?

   a. Airline ticket

   b. Field level seats to the World Series

   c. Hotel room reservation in the capital city of a distant country

   d. Pizza to be delivered to your door

   e. Autographed copy of a rare leather-bound book published in 1913

   f. Diamond ring at 35 percent below the normal price in stores for a comparable quality item

   g. A new automobile produced by a well-known global auto manufacturer

   h. Automobile insurance (annual policy)

   i. Group medical insurance (annual policy)

   j. A 14-day cruise to Antarctica (all expenses, lodging, and food included)

2. Do you believe there will be a day when all *active* consumers age 15 or older will routinely purchase *some items* online, over the Internet? If so, why and by what date will this be achieved? What types of items will be so purchased? If you think that this will never be the case, why not?

3. What form of e-commerce is likely to account for the greatest portion of online buying and selling in *your state* over the next five years: B2C e-commerce, or B2B e-commerce? What is the explanation and supporting information underlying your conclusion?

4. E-commerce emerged originally through EDI and more recently has evolved through the Internet's spectacular growth. Many EDI-oriented systems that previously relied on VANs are now migrating to Internet EDI. It is safe to say that without these information technologies, there would not be anything called electronic commerce.

   On the other hand, B2C e-commerce focuses primarily on interaction with customers and the marketing and delivery of products and services to them. In some instances—for digital products and services—delivery is actually made through the Internet and other communications links.

   For B2B e-commerce, the principal focus is on supplier relationship, inventory management, manufacturing, and similar functional areas within an enterprise. At the same time, creating or participating in private and public exchanges (i.e., B2B hubs) typically involves other operating functions within an enterprise.

   a. Given the substantial and growing importance of e-commerce to the different activities in an organization, where should the responsibility for developing and carrying out the e-commerce strategy of an enterprise lie? In the information technology group, the marketing group, the supply chain group, or elsewhere? Why?

   b. If an enterprise pursues both B2B and B2C e-commerce, should an enterprise have more than one e-commerce group, each with the resources to develop its own plan and Internet presence? What is the reason underlying your viewpoint?

5. Vendor-managed inventory is a form of supply chain integration that has proponents and opponents. The pressures to reduce costs and delays in supply chains are well understood, and thus is a force supporting innovations such as vendor-managed inventory. Of course, it may be understandable that some company managers are uncomfortable with turning inventory management over to suppliers.

   Are you a proponent or opponent of vendor-managed inventory? (*It depends* is not an acceptable answer.) What are the reasons you hold your position?

6. With the growth of the Internet and electronic commerce, there is an emergence of Internet-only banks. NetBank, one of the first Internet-only financial institutions, provides banking and mortgage lending services to retail and commercial customers. As an Internet bank, NetBank benefits from a low-cost delivery system. Because it does not have brick-and-mortar branches, it does not have the overhead expense of traditional banks. These cost savings allow NetBank to offer its customers an ideal banking arrangement: low cost, even no-fee banking, plus exceptional, higher interest rates on deposits.

   a. Given these benefits, is banking through an Internet bank attractive to you as a consumer?

   b. In general, what, if any, factors make banking with Internet-only banks attractive? What, if any, factors might make Internet banking unattractive to consumers?

   c. What do you think is the future of Internet-only financial institutions like NetBank? Why?

# Group Projects and Applications

## Project 1

Identify three to six companies in an industry of your choice. Arrange to interview (in person or by telephone) the chief information officer (CIO) or a senior IT manager concerning the company's activities involving electronic commerce. Learn about the extent to which the company is pursuing e-commerce and its reason for doing so. Plan your questions in advance. Among the questions you might ask are the following:

1. Does the company have a strategy for including e-commerce in its day-to-day activities? If so, what is it and how was it developed?

2. Does the company have a director of e-commerce? If so, in which department is that individual located? Is e-commerce the full-time responsibility of the individual? If not, what are the reasons for not creating the position of director of e-commerce?

3. Is the company's strategy focused on B2C or B2B activities? What is the evidence of this?

4. What role, if any, does the company's Web site play in its e-commerce strategy?

5. What factors will company management evaluate to determine whether its e-commerce strategy is successful or not?

Prepare a written report that discusses the similarities and differences between the companies' e-commerce strategies. Are the companies alike or different with respect to their outlook and development of e-commerce? What are the reasons behind the conclusions your team has drawn?

## Project 2

There appears to be growing interest in online banking, bill presentment, and bill payment. Select four banks in your area and visit each one. Talk with bank officers to learn about each bank's e-commerce capabilities as they relate to banking services. During the course of your interview, acquire the following information:

1. Does the bank offer Internet banking? If so, what banking functions are available over the Internet? Are those functions available via a Web site or by some other means (for example a dial-up connection directly to the bank's computer system)? What ordinary banking functions are *not* available over the Internet? Is there a service charge associated with its Internet banking services?

2. What services does the bank offer for receiving and paying bills online? Why does the bank *offer or not offer* bill presentment and bill payment? If the bank offers bill payment, can a customer pay *any* bill online? What service charges must customers pay if they participate in bill presentment? What are the requirements for a customer to use the bank's bill payment services? What is the bank's outlook for online bill presentment and bill payment?

## Project 3

Select a medium or large size utility (such as a natural gas company, an electricity company, or telephone-service provider), in your region that has chosen to develop e-commerce capabilities to link with its suppliers and vendors. Determine the intent behind the company's B2B strategy and seek to identify the factors that brought it about. How long have the company's B2B initiatives been in progress?

Next, inquire about the impact its B2B capabilities have had on the company's internal processes, activities, and operations. What areas have been affected the most and which have been influenced the least?

Third, determine what impact the company's B2B activities have had on its relations with suppliers and vendors. Have supplier activities changed? If so, how? If not, why not? Is there a role for public or private B2B exchanges? What is the overall impact of the company's B2B e-commerce activities on supply chain efficiency and why has this result occurred?

Prepare a slide presentation that introduces the company and its background, its B2B strategy, and the results that have been achieved to date. The presentation should also include your assessment of why the results you identified have been achieved and what other opportunities you believe the company should or will consider in the future.

## Net_Work

1. Visit Amazom.com on the Internet and examine the characteristics of the Web site that supports customers wishing to shop online. Notice the services offered, the information available to shoppers, and the process for making a purchase. Notice also any aids to make the shopping and purchasing process enjoyable and efficient.

   a. From an e-commerce viewpoint, what are the distinguishing features of the Amazon.com Web site?

   b. What tools does Amazon's Web site provide to aid the shopper?

   c. What categories of products can shoppers purchase from Amazon?

   d. What business is Amazon really in?

2. An example frequently used to illustrate the characteristics of B2C e-commerce is the process of shopping for and buying automobiles over the Internet. Autobytel is one well-known Internet company. However, there are other online car-buying sites.

   a. Conduct an investigation to identify Web sites that provide information to aid consumers who are seeking to buy or sell automobiles, *but do not actually sell automobiles.* Prepare a written summary of at least three different such Web sites. Identify the Web sites and provide their URLs, and compare the information and features offered by each of them. Finally, present your assessment of the usefulness of each site in helping consumers to buy or sell an automobile.

   b. Now search the Internet to identify three Web sites *other than autobytel* through which consumers can purchase automobiles. Investigate each site and compare the services they offer to shoppers. In your written analysis, identify each Web site. Then describe the features of each site, indicating which

sites have the same features as autobytel and which have different features. Note also which Web sites have electronic links to actual automobile dealers. Finally, indicate which Web site, in your opinion, would be most likely to stimulate a shopper to use the site to purchase an automobile online.

3. Locate two e-commerce sites on the Internet that conduct either horizontal or vertical B2B markets. What characteristics make it a B2B (rather than aB2C) market? Who are the intended participants in each B2B market? In addition, note whether the market is designed to assist buyers or whether it is primarily focused on sellers. Finally, which features (other than a good Web page design) are likely to encourage visitors to participate or not participate in the B2B market?

4. The end-of-chapter *Case Study,* "Wal-Mart's Retail Link Connects Its Supply Chain," notes that the company chose not to participate in industry-organized public online exchanges (i.e., B2B markets). Its management thought that its relationship with current and prospective suppliers and the features of *Retail Link* were generating greater benefits to Wal-Mart than they could obtain by participating in an industry B2B market.

   a. Chose a single industry and investigate the public online exchanges operating on the Web to support B2B buying and selling in the industry. Identify at least three such public exchanges.

   b. Determine whether the B2B market is designed to benefit buyers or sellers, indicating the reason for your determination.

   c. What are the most useful and beneficial features of the online exchange and why would a buyer or seller use them?

## Cool Mobility

### On Assignment

Companies that excel in conducting business over the Internet know that two characteristics of a Web site play an important role in generating sales and satisfying customers. The Web site should make it easy to shop for goods and services, and it should inform the customer when the item they wish to order will be delivered.

### In Consultation

Visit several commercial sites on the World Wide Web that sell directly to consumers (such as those selling personal computers, clothing, and books). Examine the way the sites assist shoppers. Then answer the following requests:

A. CEO Tina Fuentes wants you to compare the way other online commerce sites display product information, or content.
   1. What categories of product content are displayed at CoolMobility.biz?
   2. Is it easy to select and submit your content choices for processing? Why or why not?
B. Ms. Fuentes also wants to see a feature added to CoolMobility.biz that informs buyers when their custom mobile phones will be ready for shipment. Typically, orders are shipped in 24 to 48 hours, provided the mobile phone the customer selected is in inventory at the company. If it is not, then the normal shipping time is 5 to 7 days.

What front or back-office processing steps would have to be added to incorporate the shipping notification feature into the Web site?

---

## Case Study

# Wal-Mart's *Retail Link* Connects Its Supply Chain

Founder Sam Walton launched Wal-Mart Stores Inc. in 1962 when he opened the first store. Today it is the world's largest retailer. Annual sales exceed $220 billion and growth continues at a rate of 12 percent to 15 percent each year. The company operates 3,200 facilities in the United States and more than 1,100 units in Mexico, Puerto Rico, Canada, Argentina, Brazil, China, Korea, Germany, and the United Kingdom. More than 100-million customers per week visit Wal-Mart stores worldwide.

Wal-Mart's discount stores, known for low prices every day, offer a variety of quality, value-priced general merchandise and a pleasant, convenient shopping experience. The stores range from 40,000 to 125,000 square feet displaying more than 80,000 unique items in family apparel, automotive products, health and beauty aids, home furnishings, electronics, hardware, toys, sporting goods, lawn and garden items, pet supplies, jewelry, and housewares.

While the consumer public knows Wal-Mart for its everyday low prices, business analysts, shareholders, and IT experts admire its efficient logistics management and the responsive supply chain that links the company with its vendors. Today its B2B e-commerce capabilities are pivotal in its continuing supply-chain success.

Instead of focusing only on its stores and distribution centers, where it has always been adept at moving and stocking products, Wal-Mart management in the 1990s began to delve into the entire product replenishment process. It studied the cost incurred in the supply chain and the speed at which goods are placed onto shelves once they arrive at the store.

Continued improvements in its global supply chain, using a system known as *Retail Link*, is a big factor in its ability to sell merchandise to consumers at deep discount prices and still make a fair profit.

## Retail Link

In a typical commerce supply chain, there exists simultaneously at least two sets of data—demand data and supply data. However, in most companies, the enterprise and its suppliers have different views of the data, making it difficult to align buy and supply plans between parties. This problem

reduce their costs, which translates into lower costs for Wal-Mart and better prices for its customers.

## Business-to-Business Exchanges

When B2B electronic markets became popular, retail industry groups began constructing the online exchanges, operating over the Internet, as a way of obtaining lower prices from suppliers. By requiring competing vendors to offer prices through the B2B exchange, using features like reverse auctions, retailers thought they could drive their cost for goods even lower. Even though suppliers were not enthusiastic about the prospect of reduced profit margins, it was widely held that if enough retailers joined the industry exchanges, vendors would have no choice but to participate. Otherwise, they would lose business.

Wal-Mart, and other large and influential companies such as Intel and Dell, refused to join industry-sponsored, public exchanges. Wal-Mart chose instead to use Retail Link and its other IT capabilities for its competitive advantage. Moreover, its management believes that it is to the advantage of the company and its customers to work more closely with

has been widespread for years, even though the computer and communication technology is available to overcome it.

Retail Link has been a source of competitive edge for Wal-Mart since 1991 when it was created. It was upgraded to a browser-based Web-enabled system in 1997. Today it is regarded as the best system that has been implemented for supplier collaboration via the Internet and as instrumental in building strategic relationships with key manufacturers.

As sales transactions occur in its stores, Wal-Mart's IT systems capture the sales data, item by item for every customer passing through its checkout stands. This routine step is the start of Wal-Mart's system of creating *supply chain visibility*. The Retail Link system captures the details on more than 10-million daily transactions and stores them in what is thought to be the biggest data warehouse—more than 100 terabytes of data—in use anywhere. The day's transaction data for every Wal-Mart store is available by 4 A.M. the next morning, all accessible to the company's vendors over the Internet.

Retail Link lets the company's more than 10,000 global suppliers view and sort individual and group store sales data at an item level. The huge data warehouse has the capacity

to store 104 weeks—two years—of historical data integral in planning inventory and shipping. Wal-Mart's suppliers can see exactly what consumers bought in a particular shopping trip. Having actual item-level sales data, rather than relying on estimates and forecasts, provides the visibility to know what occurred and when it happened, and to in turn tailor manufacturing and shipping activities to real events, replenishing inventories as needed. Vendors can thus

existing suppliers rather than using a public exchange simply to beat down the prices of products offered by current or new suppliers. There is a growing belief that Wal-Mart's success has validated its view about public B2B exchanges.

## Supply Chains as Competitive Weapons

Wal-Mart's enormously successful supply-chain strategy and its Retail Link are fostering new ways of thinking about competition. Pointing to its success, analysts are saying that in the retail industry (and in other industries) competition is no longer *business against business*. Rather, it's *supply chain against supply chain. Live*

sales data and supply-chain visibility helps Wal-Mart increase its efficiency and lower its prices still further. At the same time, it is able to find new vendors, bring new products into its store mix, and aid suppliers in delivering the right product to the right store at the right time. With highly competitive supply chains, and systems like Retail Link, is there any question that the best will get better?

### Questions for Discussion

1. What characteristics of Wal-Mart's Retail Link underlie its many accolades?
2. Do you think other companies should develop and implement such systems?
3. How does Wal-Mart create supply chain and inventory visibility? What information technology components make this possible?
4. What is your assessment of Wal-Mart's decision not to participate in industry-sponsored public B2B exchanges? What facts underlie your assessment?
5. Do you agree that e-commerce and innovative use of information technology is creating a climate where supply chains, not companies, compete against one another? Why or why not?
6. If e-commerce evolves to competing supply chains, will consumers lose in the long term? Why or why not?

# Launching Information Technology Applications Projects

## LEARNING OBJECTIVES

When you have completed this chapter, you should be able to

1 Describe the origin of IT applications in business and understand why they have become so prominent.

2 Identify the distinguishing characteristics of an IT application.

3 Explain the benefits of IT applications to users and enterprise.

4 Explain how a systems project begins and how its desirability is determined.

5 Describe the six phases of the **systems development life cycle**.

6 Explain the importance of continual evaluation and evolution in IT systems.

# Sabre Connects the Travel Industry

S abre, headquartered in the Dallas suburb of Southlake, Texas, with employees in 45 countries, is a leading IT provider for the worldwide travel industry. Its IT applications give the company an important competitive advantage, enabling it to connect more than 60,000 travel agencies. The agencies in turn serve their traveling customers through online access to route, schedule, and pricing information on some 400 airlines. Sabre also provides information on over 50,000 hotels, more than 50 car-rental companies, nine cruise lines, 33 railroads, and more than 200 travel-tour operators. Sabre, which

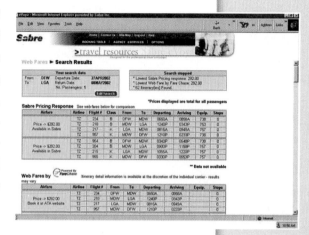

began as part of American Airlines, demonstrates the way well-designed IT applications evolve over months and years of use. Even though it is a highly visible success story, Sabre's evolution experienced its share of project-management disappointments.

Originally, Sabre was designed to help American gain a competitive edge over other airlines. It was first conceived in 1959 as an internal system that would link the airline's offices and ticket counters. Sixteen years later, American Airlines CEO Robert Crandall and CIO Max Hopper realized that Sabre could be used as more than a communications system within the airline. They began marketing the system to travel agents, the people who sell the most tickets for the airline industry. After American expanded Sabre's capabilities to make it a convenient tool for booking reservations on *all* airlines, a large portion of the country's travel agents were quickly sold on the system. American also successfully implemented a policy of charging other airlines a nominal *booking fee* when travel agents made reservations on their flights through the Sabre system. Today, American receives hundreds of millions of dollars of revenue annually because independent travel agents process flight reservations on other airlines through Sabre.

During the 1980s, when deregulation increased competition in the U.S. airline industry and changed it almost overnight, Crandall stepped forward again. Recognizing Sabre's potential for use in other kinds of programs, he came up with the American Advantage Frequent Flier program—a computer-based marketing strategy that encourages travelers to

431

fly with American by rewarding them with points redeemable for free travel. American's frequent flier program has millions of members and has created tremendous loyalty toward American among travelers. In addition to enticing travelers to fly with American Airlines to obtain the benefits of its frequent flier program, the Sabre system allows the airline's management to adjust its fares rapidly in response to competitors' ticket prices.

However, the story does not end there. Seeking to capitalize further on Sabre's enormous capabilities, AMR Information Services (AMRIS—AMR Corp. is the parent of American Airlines) in 1988 announced plans to create a hotel, car rental, and travel reservation system, called *Confirm.* A budget of $125 million was established for the project. Four companies agreed to participate as partners in developing and using Confirm: AMR, Marriott, Hilton Hotels, and Budget Rent A Car System Inc. The partners formed the International Reservations and Information Consortium (INTRICO) to oversee the development of Confirm and to market the system to the travel industry. The original plans for Confirm called for more than 3,000 programs running on two large mainframes at AMRIS' data center. The systems were to communicate with various hotel and rental car airport reservations centers and to store data in a large, centralized database.

In October 1992, AMR announced that it was suspending development of Confirm. According to industry reports, the project was running well behind schedule and the partners disagreed about the system's features and functions—one partner had reportedly provided a set of specifications that stood literally six feet high. After the failure of the project, the partners made many charges and countercharges about their original expectations, the development process, the feasibility of the system, and the capabilities of development personnel.

Sabre was a success and Confirm a disappointment. Why? The Confirm concept was attractive and appeared to make creative use of IT. Yet, in the end, the project collapsed because the partners failed to manage the development of a shared IT system.

American and Sabre developers went on to add more features and capabilities to the Sabre systems. Many of the ideas that they proposed for Confirm were eventually added to Sabre.

In 1996, Sabre became a public company through its initial public offering of stock and its listing on the New York Stock Exchange. During that year, it also launched Travelocity, the first site to offer travel reservations and comprehensive destination and event information on the Internet.

Since then, the company has continued to build on its 40-year history of advances in IT applications. Its reservation, inventory management, and flight operations systems benefit many industry partners, including the airlines and travelers. Clearly, effective IT use is the basis for Sabre's competitive advantage.

*T*his chapter discusses the development of IT applications, focusing on how they are launched and the set of activities that occur after the launch. It also discusses the development of both personal and enterprise systems. (The terms *personal system* and *single-user system* are used interchangeably.) The first section of the chapter describes the characteristics of IT applications. Then, the author looks at the impact these systems can have on productivity, effectiveness, and creativity. The last section examines the process of developing an IT application. (Chapter 11 discusses the tools and techniques IT professionals use for developing applications.)

# What Is an IT Application?

An IT application is the software and procedures that are combined with data, networks, and hardware to meet specific user or enterprise requirements. As discussed in Chapter 6, single-user systems are usually composed of a PC or workstation, various input and output devices, and programs that are tailored to the specific needs and wants of one individual. **Single-user systems,** frequently called **personal systems,** free their users from time-consuming routines and procedures so they can focus on the creative aspects of their work. Because personal systems are so cost-effective, they are important tools in both personal and business activities.

**Enterprise systems,** introduced in Chapter 7, usually involve the same types of components as personal systems, plus servers or mainframes, databases and networks. They are generally shared systems, meaning systems in which two or more users share computers, communications networks, and applications.

## Origin of IT Applications

In the early days of IT—the 1950s through the 1970s—information technology was synonymous with large computers and vast communications networks. Single-user systems were unheard of in IT applications. At that time, computing meant spending large sums of money (often millions of dollars) to set up an IT system, hiring specialists to run it, and keeping support personnel nearby (or at least on call) to clean, adjust, and repair the system's components. In acquiring an IT system, an organization knew it was making a substantial financial commitment.

Technological progress and innovation in the last two decades changed many aspects of computing. Large computers are still in widespread use and will be for years to come. However, personal computers—designed for individual users—are now everywhere. Because of advances in electronics and engineering over the last two decades, PCs have powerful capabilities. Also, as a result of strong competition in the computer industry, they are widely available at affordable prices. Today, PCs are the dominant source of IT capability in many organizations. In fact, most universities, colleges, and training centers around the world now assume that students either own or have ready access to personal systems—that is, PCs and software.

## Characteristics of Personal Systems

Three characteristics distinguish single-user systems (Figure 10.1). Personal systems are: (1) designed for hands-on usage, (2) tailored to an individual's requirements and preferences, and (3) used to improve personal performance.

**Designed for Hands-On Usage**   Single-user systems are **hands-on systems**—meaning the user actually operates the system, enters data and information, directs the processing, and determines which types of output will be generated. Because individual users direct the processing, they can watch, control, and adjust the activities as they occur, and can even stop processing if a change must be made. In contrast, large-scale shared systems are usually running at a remote location, often a great distance away from the individuals using the system.

The artist who draws an illustration on-screen using a mouse or other pointing device is a hands-on user. So is the writer who enters text using a keyboard and then prints the text on a laser printer. The sales trainer who creates a multimedia sequence of text, voice, sound, and animation on a PC by assembling a combination of keyboard entries, prestored music and art, and scanned images is also a hands-on user.

The information generated by a single-user system is usually stored within the system or on an attached secondary storage device. In large multiuser systems, the information may reside at remote locations, not under direct user control.

**single-user system/personal system**
An IT system used by only one person. A system that stands alone and is not interconnected with other companies or shared by other people.

**enterprise system**
Usually involves the same types of components as a personal system, plus server or mainframe, database, and network. It is generally a shared system.

**hands-on system**
A system in which a user enters data and information, directs processing, and determines the types of output to be generated.

**configuration**

The specific combination of hardware and software in a system.

**Tailored to Personal Requirements and Preferences**   Single-user systems are tailored to the needs of their users.

- The hardware configuration chosen determines the system's speed, power, and capacity. For example, special effects designers may configure their personal systems to feature high-resolution color graphics, high-speed *flicker-free* animation, and stereo sound generation.
- The programs installed on the system create its *personality*. Load one combination of programs and the system fulfills the requirements of a professional copywriter or novelist. Load a different set and it is ready to assist a medical researcher.

Personal preference plays an important role in personal systems. Some people like to rely on a keyboard, while others prefer to use pointing devices for entering instructions and invoking processing activities. The choice of how to tailor a single-user system is, of course, personal.

**Used to Improve Personal Performance**   Ultimately, the value of personal systems is that they make individual users better at what they do. Whether individual users work at home, in an office, or as part of a team, the purpose of single-user systems is the same: to assist individuals in carrying out their activities. This book looks at many examples of how personal systems can improve performance.

**FIGURE 10.1**

*The Characteristics of Single-User Systems*

Frank Serafine of Serafine FX uses a single-user system to concoct sound effects for major motion pictures. To capture noises, Sarafine has jammed microphones in Jacuzzis, up air conditioners, and through sewer drains, then transferred the samples to a keyboard linked to a Macintosh personal computer.

**Tailored to personal preferences**—To help synchronize the sound effects to the movie, Serafine has tailored his work studio to include not only keyboards and computers but also a large movie screen.

**Used to improve personal performance**—Serafine's personal system lets him quickly and easily alter sounds to achieve the desired effect. "Once the music is in the system," he says, "it's like Silly Putty. I can bend every sound."

**Hands-on usage**—Serafine operates the various components of the system himself.

## Characteristics of Enterprise Systems

Enterprise systems also provide for hands-on operation of users, enable the tailoring of selected features, and improve personal performance. However, they have additional characteristics as well (Table 10.1).

**Designed for Shared Use**   As indicated earlier, enterprise systems are designed for shared use by many types of users. Internal users include executives, operating managers, departmental, and clerical staff. Their purpose in using the system will of course vary, depending on their jobs. Some rely on the reports produced by these systems. Others enter information into the system that triggers the processing of transactions and that is ultimately included in reports produced for management. IT professionals are users too, whether they are adding enhancements to the applications themselves or monitoring system usage. Of course, e-mail may be essential to many enterprise system users.

External users may be customers, dealers, distributors, or others who interact with the system via its Web site or by way of other online interconnections. The features that enable their usage may be a significant factor in the system's overall success, as you will see.

**Designed for Sharing Data Resources**   Databases are also shared in enterprise systems. Although it is feasible to develop separate databases for every application, it is rarely desirable to do so. In fact, it is a common occurrence to launch systems projects that have the objective of combining or integrating databases so they can be shared by several enterprise applications.

**Designed to Connect a Variety of Users**   The varying types of users are generally not hands-on users of the actual computers or servers at the core of the network. Rather, they use PCs, PDAs, or various wireless devices to connect to the central computers or servers. Connecting users, via communications links (including the Internet, intranets, or extranets) is an essential feature of enterprise systems. Connections may be local, within a single enterprise and a single building, or they may be global, whereby individuals and computers at distant company locations are connected. Moreover, companies themselves may be interconnected via an IT application, sharing data and exchanging operating information. (Global networks and interconnecting users are discussed in Chapter 9.)

**Designed for Larger Size and Scope**   Enterprise systems feature large volumes of transactions entering the processing stream and many users. Compared to personal systems, the volume of data processed, stored, and retrieved is likely to be many times higher as well. That, coupled with the likelihood that communication networks will connect a variety of users, means that the size of the computer, input/output, storage, and communication facilities will be much greater. The overall scope of enterprise systems is thus much greater than personal systems.

| Table 10.1   Characteristics of Personal and Enterprise Systems | | |
|---|:---:|:---:|
| **CHARACTERISTIC** | **PERSONAL SYSTEM** | **ENTERPRISE SYSTEM** |
| Designed for hands-on usage | X | X |
| Used to improve personal performance | X | X |
| Tailored for personal preference and performance | X | X |
| Designed for shared use | | X |
| Designed for sharing data resources | | X |
| Designed to connect a variety of users | | X |
| Designed for larger size and scope | | X |

rezztytfww

## Impact of IT Applications

When properly designed, IT applications have three main effects: (1) improved productivity, (2) greater effectiveness, and (3) increased creativity.

**productivity**
The relationship between the results of an activity (output) and the resources used to create those results (inputs).

**Improved Productivity** **Productivity** is mentioned often in this book. As discussed in Chapter 1, productivity is a measure of accomplishment—the amount of work that can be accomplished with a given level of effort. If you want to accomplish more work in a period of time, or if you want to complete a specific task or project more quickly, then you are concerned about productivity.

Formally defined, productivity is the relationship between the results (output) of an activity, a work process, or an organization, and the resources (inputs) used to create those results. Productivity can be measured by dividing the outputs by the inputs. A higher ratio means a higher level of productivity.

Productivity can be increased in three ways:

1. **Activities are completed more quickly.** Person A (or enterprise A) is more productive than person B (or enterprise B) if A can complete a task in less time than B.
2. **More activities are completed in a particular period of time.** Person X (or enterprise X) is more productive than person Y (or enterprise Y) if X can complete more activities than Y in the same amount of time.
3. **Activities are completed with fewer resources.** If enterprise Z can conduct manufacturing, inventory management, and other business processes with fewer resources (people, space, financing, vehicles, etc.) than before, then enterprise Z has increased its productivity.

Personal systems are designed to raise personal productivity—that is, to permit activities to be completed more quickly, allow more activities to be completed in a particular period of time, or allow a task to be completed with fewer resources. Single-user software packages for creating spreadsheets or personal database systems (Chapter 6) are all designed to increase productivity. For this reason, they are often called **personal productivity software.** To aid the user, personal productivity software is increasingly making use of artificial intelligence tools. The *Information Technology in Practice* feature, "Artificial Intelligence Moves into Personal Productivity Software," further illustrates this point.

**personal productivity software**
Software packages that permit activities to be completed more quickly, allow more activities to be completed in a particular period of time, or allow a task to be completed with fewer resources.

Enterprise systems that share data and link managers and staff members in different parts of the firm are designed to raise enterprise productivity. Sharing data, exchanging information, connecting workers, and managing business and work processes—characteristics of enterprise systems—should improve overall enterprise performance compared to the results that would occur without these actions.

Two warnings are in order. First, productivity gains from working faster should not come at the expense of quality. If working faster causes mistakes, those mistakes will have to be corrected and the time used to do that may cancel out the gains from working faster. Moreover, when quality suffers, an organization's reputation can be quickly damaged. Second, an organization's productivity gains should not come at the personal expense of workers. If an organization chooses to use PCs simply to force more work out of its employees, any apparent gains are likely to be short-lived. People will tire of the

**FIGURE 10.2**

***Productivity: A Measure of Accomplishment***

**Commonly used input measures:**
Hours of work required to complete a task
Management time
Equipment investment
Consulting services
Total project budget
Art supplies

OUTPUTS
INPUTS

**Commonly used output measures:**
Number of clients visited
Number of reports produced
Length of time to complete report
Number of contracts negotiated
Amount of profit per completed contract
Number of drawings completed

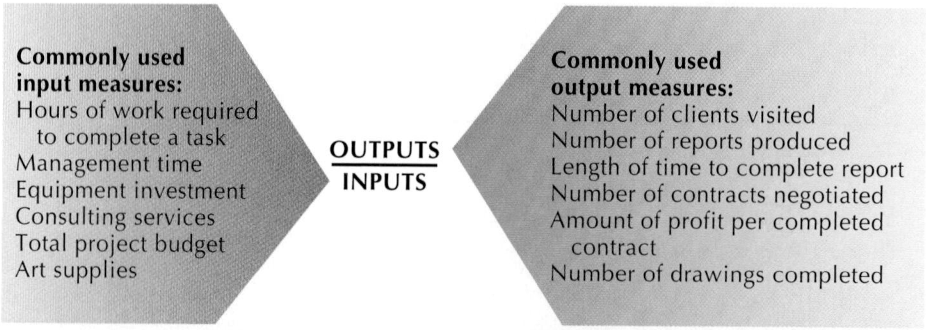

# INFORMATION TECHNOLOGY IN PRACTICE

## Artificial Intelligence Moves into Personal Productivity Software

If you use today's powerful personal productivity software, you have probably encountered artificial intelligence (AI), a complex field with two main branches. The first branch continues the quest, begun in the late 1950s, to unravel the mysteries of human thought, speech, vision, and hearing. The second, sometimes called applied intelligence, looks for ways to build these human capabilities into computer programs, including some of the software that runs on today's personal computers. There are three AI tools:

1. The algorithm is a collection of rules and step-by-step procedures used to identify patterns and perform tasks such as playing chess, spell-checking, or approving credit applications.
2. The neural network tries to simulate the way the web of neurons in a living brain processes, learns, and remembers information. Instead of passively following rules and algorithms, neural networks observe patterns, form associations, and learn by example and by trial-and-error. In one lab, for example, a robot taught itself to swing, arm over arm, from the ceiling like a gibbon—but only after it fell several times. In the business world, corporations are now using neural networks to detect credit-card fraud, predict the performance of stocks, and schedule airplane maintenance.
3. Fuzzy logic got its name from its ability to solve problems involving ambiguous data and

inexact instructions that do not fit the true-false patterns of traditional computer logic. Fuzzy logic is most often used today in controllers embedded in computers, automobile components, consumer electronics, and home appliances. However, it is also being used in decision-support systems in business, finance, and medicine.

Together, these tools promise to create an exciting new generation of silicon servants.

AI tools are already making computers easier to use. Here are a few examples:

- **Handwriting Recognition** People who cannot use or do not want to use computer keyboards have been intrigued by the idea of pen-based computing. This is part of the appeal of the personal digital assistant (PDA) since its introduction in 1993. To make it work, designers had to develop handwriting recognition software, another type of pattern recognition. The first generation of this software used algorithms, with mixed success. The next generation will use neural networks.
- **Speech Recognition** Another type of pattern recognition, speech recognition, can use algorithms, neural networks, fuzzy logic, or a combination of all three AI tools.
- **Expert or Knowledge-Based Systems** These systems use a large database of rules and algorithms to analyze problems and

make decisions. Although expert systems are common in corporations and hospitals, they are also found in desktop software. One example is the grammar checker. Another is a system called *Mavis Beacon Teaches Typing*, which covers both conventional and Dvorak keyboards. This software uses an expert system to assess the user's skill level and progress. (If *Mavis* senses you are getting frustrated or tired, she will suggest a break or a typing-related game.)
- **Software Agents** A software agent goes beyond providing online help to offer interactive advice or instructions. Microsoft pioneered this technique. Its *Wizards* software agent leads users, step by step, through complex procedures, such as adding a chart to an Excel spreadsheet. A related Excel feature, *Tip Wizards*, analyzes the way users work and suggests more efficient techniques. Agents are also available in such products as *Microsoft PowerPoint* (presentation graphics), *Microsoft Word*, and *WordPerfect for Windows*.

General Magic in Mountain View, California, created Telescript, a software language that can be used to create and dispatch software agents to the Internet's electronic marketplaces and for interactive television. Given relatively vague instructions (e.g., *Find the best price for a two-week cruise to Alaska, leaving the first week of June*), the agent will do your shopping and report back, letting you make the final decision. There are other emerging applications of neural networks and fuzzy logic, and along with them the promise of innovative and unique ways to use information technology.

In the future, experts predict, software agents will play a bigger role in computing—anticipating their users' needs, sensing when they require help, and taking over routine or often-repeated tasks.

As neural networks and fuzzy logic become more common, users may be able to tell their computers to *do what I mean* (DWIM) instead of *do what I say* (DWIS).

pressure and will seek ways to cut corners in order to meet production goals. The results may be product defects, shoddy service, careless mistakes–lower quality.

When the consulting firm Gestion y Control de Calidad (GCC) conducted a study of quality in Spain several years ago, it found that the cost of defective products and services in the average Spanish company was equivalent to 20 percent of sales. This was four times higher than the level in Japan and Germany, two countries known for their high-quality products and services. The Spanish have invented the word *chapuza* to describe mistakes made through carelessness and neglect.

Proud of both their heritage and their country, the Spanish resolved to fix the quality problem. They started with their biggest national industry, tourism, which was in a state of crisis. For decades, Spain had been an international holiday playground for all of Europe, hosting visitors seeking to relax, play, and enjoy sports. But a decade or so ago, tourism was falling off. Spain's chief tourism official, Ignacio Fuejo, examined the problem and decided that the main reason for the crisis was the poor price-quality ratio. Recognizing that prices were not going to fall, Fuejo declared, "The only solution is to improve quality." Quality programs, workshops, and training programs were launched with wide participation throughout the tourism industry.

Fuejo's initiatives have paid off. Since the start of the initiative, Barcelona hosted the Summer Olympics and Seville held the World Expo (Figure 10.3). Visitors from around the world enjoyed the hospitality of these and other Spanish cities, while millions more learned about Spain through television programs and discussions with returning visitors. Today, Spain's reputation as a place to visit is better than ever. *Quality,* not quantity, remains the watchword for the tourism industry: the Spanish know that if the quality is there, the quantity (of visitors) will follow.

Spanish banks, auto manufacturers, and companies in many other industries have picked up the initiative, developing their own programs to enhance quality while maintaining productivity levels.

**Greater Effectiveness**    Some people are described as *effective workers, effective managers,* or *effective speakers.* Some security procedures are considered *really effective.* What exactly does *effectiveness* mean?

**effectiveness**
The extent to which desirable results are achieved.

**Effectiveness,** as described in Chapter 1, entails doing the right things to accomplish a task. It is the extent to which desirable results are achieved. People are effective when they take actions that produce desirable results. An effective speaker presents ideas, stories, and illustrations in a manner that not only captures and holds the attention of an audience but also makes a point memorably. The speaker seems to say the right things in just the right way.

Personal systems improve individual effectiveness when they help people do the right things. Perhaps a spreadsheet package helps an analyst perform a more extensive analysis of alternatives to produce a high-impact result, or a graphics package helps an artist create magazine illustrations that have more realistic characters and scenery. Both people have used their personal systems to increase their effectiveness.

Enterprise systems improve effectiveness when they help work groups, teams, and department staffs do the right thing, whether in ordering materials, manufacturing products, or delivering services. For example, Sabre's travel reservation system aids the airlines in booking reservations, assigning seats, and processing payments in the right way. In the end, both passengers and the airline benefit.

**FIGURE 10.3**

***Increasing Quality in Spain's Tourism Industry***
Spain's quality initiative has made it a more popular vacation spot than ever before.

**Increased Creativity and Innovation**   Creativity is hard to define, but most people agree that it entails a high degree of artistic or intellectual inventiveness. Some people are born with creative ability; others have to work at it.

Actually, everyone is creative in his or her own way. The challenge is to identify your creative areas and then find a way to unlock the inventiveness inside you. Personal systems can help by providing tools that do routine work while you focus on the creative aspects of the activity. For example:

- A particular artist's strongest skills are design, layout, and use of color. Drawing images is not her strong point. A combination of clip art and scanned images can help her overcome this weakness so that she can focus on deciding what to illustrate and how to create the desired image and message.
- A musician likes to compose music sitting at his keyboard. He finds it distracting to have to stop to write down the notes as he is composing. Using special software, he can compose music by playing it on an electronic instrument, and the software will take care of printing the notes or displaying them on a screen. The composer is free to work at creating music without pause because the PC is capturing the information and performing the appropriate processing.
- A journalist has a much greater flair for describing natural disasters than for spelling and grammar. A personal system equipped with word-processing software allows her to enter her ideas and observations almost as quickly as she thinks of them, and then go back and make revisions—repeatedly if necessary. She can use automatic checking and correction software to ensure that her creative flair is correct to the word, letter, and period.

We seldom think of financial analysts and other businesspeople as creative in the same way as artists and writers. Yet assembling investment packages, arranging financing for investments, and suggesting financial portfolios is creative work when done well. Creative financial analysts do not want to be bothered with calculating returns on investment, payback periods, or payment and interest rates while working on ideas for new products or packages. They use PC software to handle the calculations for them.

In enterprises, the term innovation is generally used rather than creativity. Some enterprises are known for their innovativeness, and the way they use IT to bring out that innovativeness. *Innovation* is the invention of new technologies, products, and production processes. It the result of successfully exploiting creative ideas. For example, the ideas of Crandall and Hopper at American Airlines led to the innovation of using IT to create new uses of the Sabre system, online ticket booking by travel agents, and a frequent flier program that drew more customers to the airline. The enterprise has benefited from these systems innovations for many years.

Productivity and effectiveness are both important in business, but the terms are not interchangeable. *Productivity* is concerned with *quantity* of work, the time or effort needed to produce a result, and the resources used in producing an output. *Effectiveness*, in contrast, is concerned with the *quality* of results.

A single-user system gives you a personal advantage only if you learn to use the system to your benefit. The key concept here is leverage—doing what you do best, while using IT to compensate for your weaknesses. This idea draws on the principles of productivity and effectiveness.

For example, if you are a financial analyst, your single-user system should be configured to help you become a better financial analyst. That is the primary goal. But if you are weak at writing reports, your system should also have the tools—the software—to help you become a better writer. Prestored report formats, appendixes, and illustrations that can be used repeatedly, along with the other writing support features of a word-processing program, can help you compensate for your writing weaknesses.

Do not think of an IT application as another name for *computer*. Think of it, rather, as a package of tools specifically designed to help individuals or enterprises be the best at what they are or what they want to be. ◼

# The Origin of Enterprise System Projects

**Systems development** is the process of examining a business situation; designing a system solution to improve that situation; and acquiring the human, financial, and IT resources needed to develop and implement the solution. **Project management** is the process of planning, organizing, integrating, and overseeing the development of an IT application to ensure that the project's objectives are achieved and that the system is implemented according to expectations. Before development of an enterprise IT project can begin, a project proposal must be prepared by users or systems analysts and submitted to a steering committee.

## Project Proposal

The **project proposal** is a critical element in launching the systems study. Although its form varies from firm to firm, the proposal should always answer the following questions:

- What specifically is the problem?
- What details describe the problem?
- How significant is the problem?
- What is a possible solution to the problem?
- How will IT help to solve the problem?
- Who else knows about this problem and who else should be contacted?

Whether the proposal has been triggered by a single event or by a recurring situation is also an important consideration. For example, at AMR, managers and executives noticed that their major customers—business travelers and their travel agents—nearly always booked more than one type of reservation at a time. In addition to airline reservations, business travelers often require hotel and car-rental reservations. AMR saw a business opportunity in creating a shared system capable of handling all types of reservations simultaneously. The resulting Sabre success story demonstrates the wisdom behind this system proposal.

## Steering Committee Review

Most companies do not let individuals launch shared systems projects on their own. Rather, they direct that project proposals be submitted to a **steering committee.** The committee, usually made up of people from various functional areas of the business (such as executives in marketing, accounting, purchasing, inventory control, manufac-

# CRITICAL CONNECTIONS 1

## Personalize Your Message with American Greetings' CreataCard

americangreetings.com℠

Custom calls for recognizing special occasions—birthdays, holidays, and important achievements—with a greeting card. Each year, retailers stock and sell millions of carefully designed greeting cards for almost every occasion. For decades, this is how it was done: people would visit a store and choose from an array of cards the one that best expressed their sentiment.

Although many people still prefer the convenience of mass-produced greeting cards, now there are options available for those who want a more personal touch. American Greetings, headquartered in Cleveland, Ohio, has made it possible to send personalized cards using the capabilities provided by today's information technology. If you have a personal computer and access to the Internet, you can download a sample version of American Greetings CreataCard software, or you can purchase the complete program at a computer retailer. This software will enable you to personalize cards, as well as stationery, certificates, and invitations. You can craft thoughtful personal messages and print them at home on a color ink-jet printer. American Greetings makes available a wide array of high-quality, electronic card designs that have colorful photographs and illustrations on the front and space for personal messages inside. They are personal because you can add your own special touch to them. You can change not only the text but you can also select alternate artwork.

Using their PC and the software, which includes a variety of electronic card designs, customers can create a unique message for that special person whenever the need arises. The available card designs span nearly every topic, including *A Little Romance; Oh, Baby; Birthday Fun; For Cat Lovers; Over the Hill; Hot Stuff for Him; Hot Stuff for Her;* and *Thoughts to Live By.* (New electronic card designs are always available for ordering through the Internet.)

turing, sales, and information systems), determines if the project is desirable and should be pursued.

## The Systems Analyst

Recall that the term *systems analyst* is used very broadly to refer to a person who develops all or a portion of an IT application. However, IT professionals distinguish among systems analysts, systems designers, and programmer/analysts, all of whom have different responsibilities. **Systems analysts** are responsible for working with users to determine a system's requirements and to describe the features needed in the system. **Systems designers** are responsible for doing the technical work of designing the system and its software. **Programmer/analysts** are responsible for determining system requirements

**systems analyst**
The IT professional responsible for working with users to determine a system's requirements and for describing the features needed in the system.

**systems designer**
The IT professional responsible for doing the technical work of designing the system and its software.

**programmer/analyst**
A person who has joint responsibility for determining system requirements and developing and implementing the systems.

and developing and implementing the systems. In essence, they act as programmers, systems analysts, and systems designers.

Some systems analysts are identified as **Web developers.** These analysts are expected to have additional capabilities that enable them to use their expertise in creating IT applications that will involve the Internet or company intranets and extranets, Web browsers (including Microsoft's *Internet Explorer* or Netscape's *Navigator*), and the display of information using browsers. Often Web developers need to have the additional capability of developing multimedia components for Web-enabled IT applications. (Chapter 12 discusses the development of multimedia applications.)

In the business world, it is very often the systems analyst who sees the development of a shared IT application through—from original conception to finished product. For this reason, the rest of the chapter focuses primarily on the activities of the systems analyst.

# The Systems Development Life Cycle

The proposal submitted to the steering committee is the first step in systems development. The **systems development life cycle (SDLC),** outlined in Figure 10.4, is the set of activities that brings about a new IT application. The SDLC is a problem-solving process. It consists of six phases:

1. **Problem Recognition/Preliminary Investigation** Defining and investigating the problem.
2. **Requirements Determination** Understanding the current system and the new system's requirements.
3. **Systems Design** Planning the new system.
4. **Development and Construction** Creating the new system.
5. **Implementation** Converting to the new system.
6. **Evaluation and Continuing Evolution** Monitoring and adding value to the new system.

Each of these stages is discussed in detail in the sections that follow.

## Problem Recognition/Preliminary Investigation

Most businesses have more requests for systems development activities than they can possibly support. Hence, the first activity in the systems development life cycle—problem recognition/preliminary investigation—is conducted at the direction of the steering committee.

The purpose of the **preliminary investigation** is to examine the project proposal in order (1) to evaluate its merits and (2) to determine whether it is feasible to launch a project that will address the issues it raises. During the preliminary investigation, systems analysts work to clarify the proposal, determine the size and scope of the project, assess the costs and benefits of alternative approaches, and determine the project's general feasibility. They then report their findings to the steering committee along with a recommendation.

Systems analysts assess three types of feasibility: (1) operational, (2) financial/economic, and (3) technical feasibility.

**Operational Feasibility**   A project is judged *operationally feasible* if it will meet the business's operating requirements and will have a desirable effect on the company. If the project requires changes in current procedures, those changes must be acceptable for the project to be judged operationally feasible.

For example, United Parcel Service (UPS), the world's largest and most successful package delivery service, saw its business threatened by the growth of FedEx's overnight service. UPS decided to examine the feasibility of expanding its business services to include both overnight package delivery and more effective use of its distribution and delivery capabilities. It conducted an investigation to determine if its operations, delivery procedures, and IT capabilities could be expanded to guarantee next-morning delivery. The company's executives and employees knew that developing a guaranteed-overnight business was desirable; they wanted to be sure it was feasible.

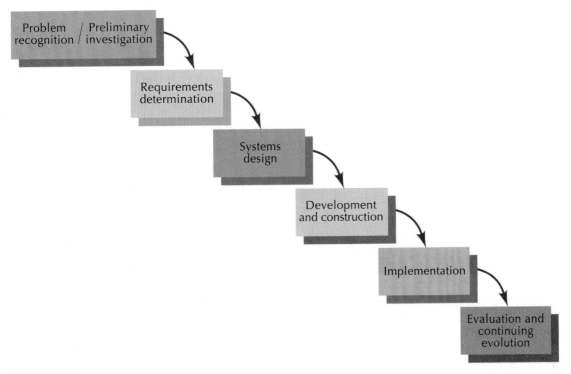

**FIGURE 10.4**

### *The Systems Development Life Cycle*

The systems development life cycle begins with problem recognition but never really ends, for the new system must be continually monitored and evaluated after it has been put in place.

**Financial and Economic Feasibility**  Even if the proposed system is operationally feasible, it must be a good financial investment for the business to undertake it. In other words, the project's benefits should exceed its costs. Benefits would be increased business, lower costs, and fewer errors. The costs would be: the expense of conducting a full systems investigation; the cost of hardware, communications links, and software for the application being considered; and the cost to the business if the proposed system is *not* developed.

The UPS vision depends on information technology, not just for moving packages, but also for moving information. UPS executives recognized that enhancing communication between the drivers of its 50,000 trucks and the company's distribution centers was important for improving the UPS delivery system. They also wanted to provide customers with real-time information (see Chapter 2) about the location of their packages. A five-year $1.6 billion effort was launched to accomplish these goals. Because UPS is a successful, well-managed $23 billion company, an investment of this magnitude was financially feasible.

**Technical Feasibility**  A project is technically feasible if the systems analyst can answer the following questions with *yes:*

- Does the firm have the necessary computer and communications technology to do what the proposal suggests? If not, can it acquire this technology?
- Does the proposed hardware (whether currently installed or to be acquired) have the capacity to store and transmit the data and information required for the new system?
- Will the proposed system provide adequate responses to inquiries, regardless of the number of individuals who will use it?
- Can the system be expanded at a later date?
- Does the proposed system guarantee accuracy, reliability, ease of access, and data security?

To determine the technical feasibility of linking its customers, drivers, and distribution centers, UPS contacted the operators of the largest cellular networks (see Chapter 8). After much discussion, the company was convinced it could improve its distribution system with wireless communications. Working with four carriers—McCaw Cellular Communications, GTE Mobile Communications, PacTel Cellular, and Southwestern Bell Mobile Systems—UPS established a custom-designed nationwide network.

Thanks to the *TotalTrack* systems, UPS drivers are connected to the cellular network through handheld computers attached to a combination cellular modem/telephone (Figure 10.5). The handheld computer automatically dials the closest carrier, which then interconnects to the UPS private network and the company's data center. Information about the pickup, delivery, or location of any package can be transmitted over the network.

UPS' cellular system was completed on time and within the $150 million budget allocation. Since implementing the system, UPS has transformed itself into a successful overnight package carrier while continuing to expand its highly efficient and profitable parcel service. It has duplicated virtually all of FedEx's features and services in the overnight parcel business, including Saturday morning delivery. (Until recently, UPS delivered only Monday through Friday.) IT was the vehicle for turning the company's vision into reality. The UPS story continues to evolve, with new IT applications and communications devices being added all the time. The ongoing IT evolution ensures it will be an interesting company to watch for years to come.

Not all systems development proposals are feasible, of course. And not all proposals judged infeasible are worthless. Sometimes a proposal is sent back to the originator with a request for more information, and then reexamined. At other times, the preliminary investigation of a proposal reveals opportunities to change business processes and activities in a way that both improves the business and eliminates the need to invest in a new information system. In these cases, the proposal and its preliminary investigation contributed to the business's ultimate goal: increased success for the organization.

Given the complexity and time-intensiveness of the SDLC, there is a potential for significant error. The *Information Technology in Practice* feature, "The SDLC: Avoiding Problems Before They Occur," offers a list of the most common problems encountered in systems development. Forewarned is forearmed.

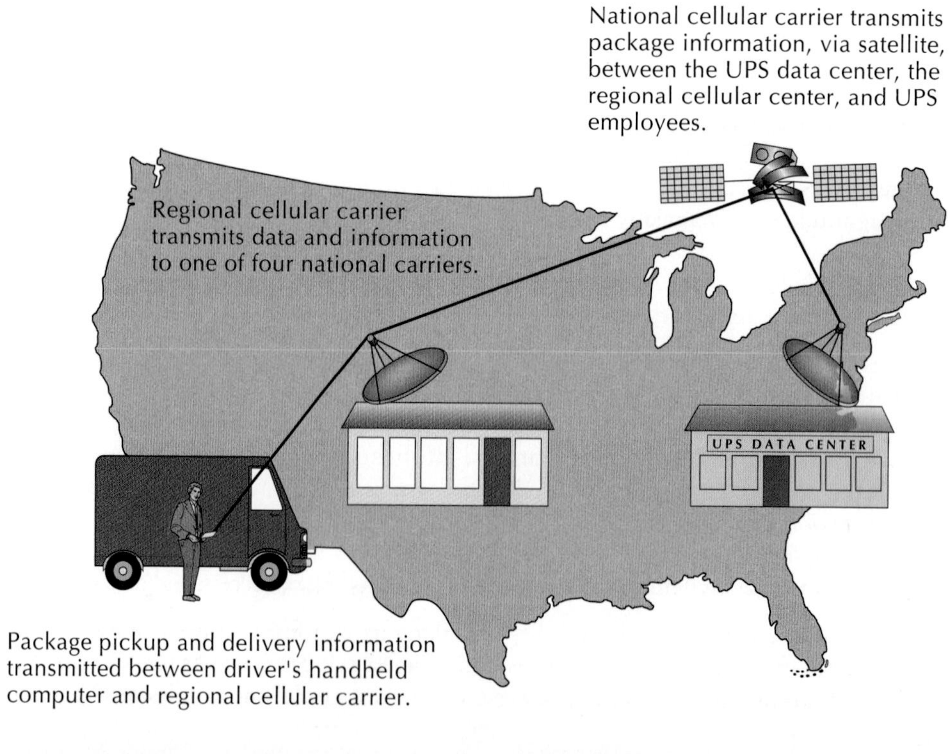

**FIGURE 10.5**

**United Parcel Service's Cellular Network for Package Tracking**

UPS's new $150 million communications network has helped it compete with its major rival, Federal Express.

National cellular carrier transmits package information, via satellite, between the UPS data center, the regional cellular center, and UPS employees.

Regional cellular carrier transmits data and information to one of four national carriers.

UPS DATA CENTER

Package pickup and delivery information transmitted between driver's handheld computer and regional cellular carrier.

## Requirements Determination

A **requirement** is a feature that must be included in a system. This feature may be a way of capturing or processing information, a method of interacting with the system, a processing activity or result, a piece of information displayed or printed as a result of processing, or a function that can be performed to safeguard data and information. For UPS, the requirement was guaranteed overnight delivery and package tracking. For AMRIS, the requirement (never fulfilled) was the connection of business partners to allow them to share information and assist their customers.

During the **requirements determination** phase of the systems development life cycle, the systems analyst studies the current business situation, collecting and analyzing data and information to determine who is involved, what data and information are used, and how the current system can be improved. Requirements determination should address either or both types of improvement: process improvement and business improvement.

**Process Improvement**    A **process** is a structured activity that leads to a set of results (in systems terms, an *output*). The structure of the process specifies its sequence of activities and the flow of work from beginning to end. Processes cut across business functions, spanning department and location boundaries. A company's order-fulfillment process, for example, depends on the ability of its manufacturing, inventory, shipping, and accounting departments to work together to ship a customer's order and bill the account in a timely and accurate fashion.

**Process improvement** addresses the question, "Can we improve the way we work?" Before improvements to a system can be made, the systems analyst must know how activities are performed now, which procedures are effective, and which processes need improvement. Table 10.2 lists the questions that an analyst attempts to answer in evaluating a process. It is useful to think of the process as having a customer—an individual or a group who receives the benefits or results of the process. Depending on how well the process is performed, the customer will be satisfied or dissatisfied.

The fast pace of today's business, coupled with the competitive pressures and customer expectations of high-quality products and services, is causing managers and executives in many organizations to review all of their business processes. Reshaping business processes, often called *reengineering*, simultaneously seeks to remove barriers that prohibit an organization from providing better products and services and to help the organization capitalize on its strengths.

Reengineering is just one part of the *RE phenomenon*. Businesses are *re*designing, *re*tooling, *re*making, *re*shaping, *re*structuring, *re*organizing, *re*establishing, *re*building, and *re*positioning to gain an advantage in the extremely competitive global marketplace. IT plays an important role in reengineering business processes. The five steps involved in the reengineering process are outlined in Figure 10.6.

**requirement**
A feature that must be included in a system.

**requirements determination**
The second phase of the systems development life cycle, in which the current business situation is studied to determine who is involved, what data and information are needed, and how the current system can be improved.

**process**
A structured activity that leads to a set of results (output).

**process improvement**
An improvement in the way a business works.

| Table 10.2    **Evaluating a Business Process** |
| --- |
| What is being done? |
| How is it being done? |
| How frequently does it occur? |
| How great is the volume of transactions or decisions? |
| How well is the task being performed? |
| Does a problem exist? |
| If a problem exists, how serious is it? |
| If a problem exists, what is the underlying cause? |
| Who is affected by the business process or work activity under construction? |

# INFORMATION TECHNOLOGY IN PRACTICE
## The SDLC: Avoiding Problems Before They Occur

The U.S. General Accounting Office (GAO) is a federal agency charged with monitoring the performance of other federal agencies. Among the agencies it monitors are the National Weather Service, Federal Aviation Administration, Patent and Trademark Office, Department of Justice, Department of Education, NASA, Internal Revenue Service, Department of Defense, and Department of Veterans Affairs. Because the federal government uses many IT applications and dedicates large amounts of financial and human resources to each application, the GAO frequently examines the development of the applications to determine whether the projects are on schedule, within budget, and producing the intended results. Such information is highly useful both for evaluating project managers and for developing future IT projects.

The GAO has identified 10 problems that occur repeatedly in the development and use of IT applications. In order of frequency, they are as follows:

1. Inadequate management of the systems development life cycle.
2. Ineffective management information as a result of poor systems procedures.
3. Flaws in systems security, integrity, and reliability.
4. Inability of multiple systems to work together.
5. Inadequate resources to accomplish goals.
6. Cost overruns.
7. Schedule delays.
8. Systems not performing in the intended manner.
9. Inaccurate or incomplete data and information.
10. Difficulty in accessing data and information.

Such a list points to the importance of effective project management.

Improper management of SDLC can turn a systems project into a money-devouring monster. The best defense against cost overruns is strong project management from start to finish.

Improper management of the systems development life cycle can turn a system project into a money-devouring monster. The vest defense against cost overruns is string project management from start to finish.

**Business Improvement** The capabilities of a business can be expanded through business improvement. Requirements determination addresses the question, "Can we improve our business?" The UPS example clearly illustrates how information technology can improve a business.

IT plays a central role in business improvement in four general ways: It helps firms offer new products and services; it speeds up business processes; it reduces the cost of products and services; and it helps firms enter new regions or markets.

| Step 1: Review | During the review of business processes, the systems analyst should document activities in the current process, determine what value or benefits are added by performing the process, and identify opportunities for improvement. |
| --- | --- |
| Step 2: Redesign | Reengineering is often most successful when company personnel are able to take a fresh look at how they carry out activities. Challenging traditional assumptions about the reasons for doing things in a particular way often leads to process redesign. The frequent result is processes that are simpler, less time-consuming, and more effective than those they replaced. |
| Step 3: Reorchestrate | Redesign suggests new ways to do business. Reorchestration is the transition to those new ways. Realignment of responsibilities, adjustment of quality control procedures, and implementation of new methods are essential. Reorchestration also entails addressing the concerns of individuals who are directly affected by the changes. Failure to deal with human concerns may render reengineering efforts unsuccessful. |
| Step 4: Reassess | Measurement of results documents the impact of reengineering. Some changes may be better than expected, while others may need rethinking. Only by evaluating the results can the impact of the reengineering process be determined. |
| Step 5: Recycle | Reengineering is not a one-time activity. Because opportunities and the competitive environment change constantly, rethinking business processes is always an agenda item for an organization's leaders. |

**FIGURE 10.6**

**The Reengineering Process**

Reengineering means overhauling business processes and organization structures that limit the competitiveness, efficiency, and effectiveness of the organization.

**Offering New Products and Services** This type of business improvement arises when businesses identify and then meet the previously unrecognized wants and needs of their existing or potential customers.

The Regional Bell Operating Companies (RBOCs) in the United States (BellSouth, Qwest, SBC, and Verizon) and Post, Telephone, and Telegraph (PTT) administrations in Europe and the Far East are using their IT capabilities to offer many new services to customers. Among the first value-added services were call forwarding (in which calls are automatically rerouted to the recipient's actual destination rather than to the number dialed) and call waiting (in which a signal alerts a customer that a call is waiting to come over a link already in use). Since then other services, such as auto redial of busy numbers and information services (e.g., weather updates and sports scores), are also available for an additional fee.

There are other new services in various stages of development by telephone companies, including the delivery of movies, the monitoring of home security systems, and the reading of electric and gas meters. Customers benefit from the new, more convenient services, and the telephone companies earn higher revenue and develop a larger customer base.

**Speeding Up Business Processes** Compressing the time it takes to do business can increase efficiency or produce a substantial competitive advantage. As both FedEx and UPS know well, the ability to move information quickly and effectively can give companies an edge in taking business from their competitors.

The benefits of speeding up business processes are not limited to service industries. Manufacturing companies have also reaped business advantages from speeding up their operations. When the time needed to complete a task is compressed, the risk of errors is reduced because decisions are made closer to the point when action is taken. Less risk usually means that businesses need to tie up fewer resources as a precaution against mistakes and poor cost or demand estimates.

Toyota Motor Corp. of Toyota City, Japan, competes worldwide on the basis of time. The company invented the *Toyota production system,* which aims to use the same manufacturing process to make many different models of automobiles in small quantities. An essential component of this system is what is known as *just-in-time production* (Figure 10.7). Toyota can take an order for a custom-manufactured automobile and deliver the vehicle within the same week. Many of Toyota's competitors require four to six weeks to manufacture and deliver a custom-ordered vehicle.

Toyota has compressed the manufacturing process by simplifying each step and by ensuring that the workers on the assembly line have all the information they need to

*Just-in-Time Manufacturing at the Toyota Plant in Toyota City, Japan*

Toyota's JIT system ensures that all assembly line workers have parts at hand when needed. The parts and assembly lists for each vehicle are prepared by computers that retrieve information from company databases. This information is shared through the company communications network with suppliers, who deliver the parts "just in time" for worker installation in the vehicle.

assemble the car ordered by the customer. Doing things right the first time results in fewer delays and less time spent on reworking improperly assembled vehicles.

At Toyota, compressing time also means more accurate scheduling and closer relations with suppliers. The company uses IT to receive and assemble all dealers' orders electronically. The parts and assembly lists needed to build each vehicle are prepared by computers that retrieve details from the company's databases. This information is then shared through Toyota's communications network with suppliers, who deliver the parts and assemblies, often several times daily, *just in time* for workers to install them in the vehicles. This system allows Toyota to deliver a customer's choice of automobile much faster than competitors can, even while maintaining high standards of quality. Scheduling parts delivery closer to manufacturing time also means the company needs less production space and ties up less of its money in inventory.

**Reducing the Cost of Products and Services**   Reduced costs give companies great flexibility in their pricing policies. If a competitor decides to compete by lowering the price of a product, the company can respond and still make a profit. *Price wars* occur when businesses compete solely on the price they charge customers. In the end, the company that has the lowest costs is usually in the best position. No business really wins in a price war—unless it is able to drive a competitor out of the industry—because reduced prices usually decrease profits, which are needed to finance future operations and expansion. Even the customer, who benefits from a price war in the short run, may lose out in the long run if companies drive each other out of business or if the survivor later raises prices. IT, when used to help reduce costs of products or services, plays a central role in business improvement.

**Entering New Regions or Markets**   Companies can improve their businesses by using their IT capabilities to enter new geographic regions. For example, both FedEx and UPS found that a growing number of their business customers were expanding into new international regions. Accustomed to overnight package delivery in the United States, these customers expected the same capability abroad, whether in Canada or Mexico, Europe or the Far East. They also expected the same level of accountability—the same ability to find out the location of a package at any moment. After identifying these requirements, both companies expanded their delivery capabilities and the capabilities of their tracking systems to cover packages shipped to international destinations.

Business improvement has the greatest impact when it enables a company to launch a new product or service that competitors cannot duplicate quickly or at all. Businesspeople call this type of improvement a *preemptive strike*. By launching a preemptive strike, a company can capture the market for the product or service, satisfying customers' desires so swiftly and to such an extent that they have no desire to switch to other products later.

# CRITICAL CONNECTIONS 2

## Volkswagen Parts Online in Mexico

**Volkswagon in Mexico**

Volkswagen is known around the world as a high-quality, moderately priced German automobile. Six generations of drivers have grown up with Volkswagen's familiar logo and its ever-present VW Beetle.

Because there is such a high demand for Volkswagen cars, they are manufactured in several countries around the world, including Mexico. When the North American Free Trade Agreement (NAFTA) took effect, the potential U.S. market for Volkswagen automobiles made in Mexico prompted Volkswagen managers to take a new look at the company's operations there. They found that the manufacturing process at Volkswagen-Gedas NA, the company's Mexican subsidiary, was turning out high-quality cars, as they expected, but the spare parts operation (accounting for the sale of more than 1 million Volkswagen parts annually) was not of the same caliber.

Most Volkswagen dealers had to submit their parts orders on a diskette; only a few had online access to the company's ordering system. Processing and fulfillment often took two weeks, which was clearly unacceptable in the quickly changing post-NAFTA business climate. Rapid development of a system for reliable parts ordering and fulfillment for the 200 dealers in Mexico became the challenge for Volkswagen.

American Airlines launched a preemptive strike when it implemented its computerized reservation system and related frequent flier program. Even though other airlines have tried to emulate this system, few have been successful. AMR retains approximately 25 percent of the U.S. market for travel agent and fee-based reservation processing, while the more than 50 remaining carriers fight it out for the rest.

The *Information Technology in Practice* feature, "Maersk Sealand's Charlotte Terminal Automation System," describes how this global shipping company used information technology to streamline operations and gain an edge in the highly competitive shipping business.

## Systems Design

A system's *design* is the set of details that describe how the system will meet the requirements identified during requirements determination. The process of translating requirements into design specifications is known as **systems design.**

Systems design has three steps: (1) preliminary (conceptual) design, (2) prototyping, and (3) detailed (physical) design.

**systems design**
The third phase of the systems development life cycle, in which requirements are translated into design specifications.

**Preliminary (Conceptual) Design**   The preliminary design of a system specifies its distinguishing characteristics, conceptualizing the functions it will perform and how they will occur. Current systems capabilities will influence the design.

The preliminary design typically specifies the following:

- Whether the system will be distributed or centralized.
- Whether the system will be developed by the company's staff members, by outside contractors, or by purchasing a software package.
- Whether processing will use online or batch procedures.
- Whether data communications networks will be developed.
- Whether applications will run on PCs, PDAs, servers, mainframes, or some combination of these.
- The data and information that will be generated and the reports that must be produced.
- The files or databases needed for the system to function.
- The number of users and locations supported by the system.
- The capacity of storage devices.
- The number of printers and communications links among individuals, customers, suppliers, and others who will interact with the system.
- The personnel needed to operate the system.

After the preliminary design is prepared, it is presented to the users and to the steering committee for approval. Any necessary changes are made before the design moves into the prototype phase.

Diamond Star Motors Corp., located in Normal, Illinois, was created as a joint venture between Chrysler Corp. of Detroit, Michigan (now DaimlerChrysler), and Japan's Mitsubishi Motors Corp. in 1985. Diamond Star later became a subsidiary of Mitsubishi Motors. The company, which produces Mitsubishi and DaimlerChrysler automobiles, now has more than 3,000 employees.

Manufacturing activities at Diamond Star are patterned after Mitsubishi Motors' practices in Japan. Production associates begin their workday at 6:30 A.M. with stretching exercises (performed to music piped throughout the building). All employees, including managers and the 50-person IT staff, wear the same uniform: gray pants and maroon shirts bearing the company logo over the left pocket and the employee's name over the right (Figure 10.8).

Originally, Diamond Star intended to duplicate the manufacturing and business processes of the Mitsubishi plant in Okazaki, Japan. It quickly determined, however, that copying that plant's computer and communications systems was much easier than transplanting its business processes and related IT applications. Analysts discovered, for example, how dramatically different Japanese finance and accounting practices are from those in the United States. For instance, some Japanese companies budget in six-month cycles—on the premise that shorter budget periods give businesspeople better control over resources, enable them to forecast more accurately, and allow them to respond more rapidly to fluctuations in business—while U.S. companies generally draw up 12-month annual budgets.

**FIGURE 10.8**

***Shared IT Applications at Diamond Star Motors***

All Diamond Star employees, including managers and assembly line workers, wear the same uniform. This standard is part of the company's team-oriented approach to automobile design and assembly. Using sophisticated design programs linked to the company's network, engineers can communicate directly with the assembly line to create prototypes of the parts they've designed.

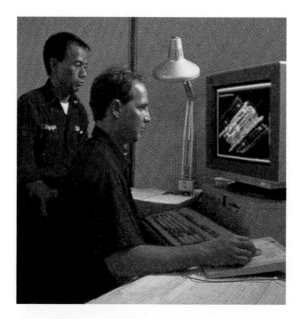

# INFORMATION TECHNOLOGY IN PRACTICE

## Maersk Sealand's Charlotte Terminal Automation System

Maersk Sealand, one of the leading liner shipping companies, is the world's largest provider of containerized transport services. Its service network spans six continents, with operations in more than 100 countries. Maersk Sealand operates more than 250 vessels and 800,000 containers.

The Sealand service integrates a transportation network of ships, railroads, barge lines, and trucking operations, all aimed at moving goods into and out of the world's ports in large steel box-like containers. Prior to its acquisition by Maersk, Sealand was part of CSX Corp. During that time, it invented containerized ocean shipping and was the first company to launch trans-Atlantic and trans-Pacific service, as well as intermodal stacktrain service across North America.

The shipping industry is highly complex, with millions of tons of freight moving on and off trans-

portation vessels and vehicles daily. From the time a shipment of cargo leaves its home port to the time it arrives at a customer destination, many companies and agencies are involved, including multiple transportation companies and various government officials. Just keeping track of the location of each container, however important, is difficult. Locating a container in a shipping yard can be more difficult

than tracking its journey across the ocean.

The Maersk Sealand port facility at Charleston, South Carolina, is a showcase for the shipping company's use of information technology. A growing business (daily truck traffic in and out of the company's facility doubled in just three years) can turn from an opportunity into a problem if expansion results in slower customer service or delays in delivering and picking up freight. The Charleston yard is divided into a series of rows and slots (see photo), and a combination row-and-slot number serves as a container's *address*. With space for 3,500 tractor trailer–sized containers in the yard, locating the right container or the optimal spot to store an incoming container is a challenging task.

A new terminal automation system (TAS), the result of a carefully formulated reengineering plan, has changed the way Sealand runs its container business at the Charleston yard. The old system was successful,

but the new system has provided both improvements and new opportunities. Lower costs are only one of the benefits the company and its customers receive from the system.

Each container entering or leaving Maersk Sealand's Charleston shipyard is inspected for damage. Under the old system, drivers signed a paper inspection form describing the condition of the entering or departing container. Typically, the process, including wait time, required 50 to 60 minutes per driver.

Gate forms were counted manually and information from the form was entered into a terminal and transmitted by a communications network to a mainframe computer in Jacksonville, Florida. Having accurate information necessitated careful checking of details as they were keyed in, since the form was the only record of container condition and location.

The key to Maersk Sealand's terminal automation system today is the handheld computer. The visual inspection of the container still occurs in much the same way, but that is about all that has been retained of the old system. When a driver arrives at the gate entrance to the terminal, the cargo's con-

tainer number is entered directly into the handheld computer (see photo). Details—the container's owner, its contents, condition, and storage location—are retrieved and displayed on the computer screen. An inspection form is created, which the driver signs; then the form is transmitted electronically to the company's central computer system. The manual shuffling of forms and the need to enter details through a keyboard have been eliminated.

Maersk Sealand's automated terminal system is so easy to use that a training period of less than an hour is all new gate agents need to become comfortable with the handheld computer and the system.

The benefits of TAS for the company include swifter movement of containers in and out of the shipyard and a substantial

decrease in the time it takes to load and unload ships. Since containers can be located faster, ships can enter and leave the port more quickly, resulting in lower costs and higher revenues. Reengineering through information technology has made it possible for the container yard to handle doubled cargo levels in half the time, opening up the opportunity for even more spectacular growth in the future.

Maersk Sealand's use of IT has not only improved productivity in the Charleston shipyard, it has built new business. Customers acknowledge that they do more business with the company than with other terminal operators because of its ability to get their drivers in and out of the terminal faster, which means each driver can be responsible for more loads per day.

To launch the conceptual designs for the 30 new systems needed by the new company, Diamond Star's IT staff had to become familiar with the different cultures and business practices in the two countries. Some IT staff members spent time in Japan (from 2 to 10 weeks) to become familiar with the Japanese systems. In the end, not only did they design interfaces between each partner's computers to accommodate the different budgeting and reporting practices, but they also developed IT applications to run one of the most sophisticated automated manufacturing lines in the world. This line includes an online vehicle tracking system that tells workers the location of every vehicle, an online vendor broadcasting system designed to ensure that parts arrive just in time for installation in a vehicle, and more than 100 assembly line robots (550 plant-wide). Diamond Star's assembly line is more than 20 percent automated (10 percent is the norm in most automotive plants with the same capacity); a specially designed computer helps to run and manage it.

**prototype**
A working model of an IT application.

**Prototyping**  A **prototype** is a working model of an IT application that, compared to a complete system, is relatively inexpensive to build. Although it usually does not contain all the features of, or perform all of the functions that will be included in the final system, the prototype has enough elements that people can use the system and quickly determine their likes and dislikes. Also, the prototype can help determine if key features

Experience is an important factor in identifying systems requirements. Junior analysts tend to accept what they hear, see, or read about current business processes. But with seasoning, they recognize that processes change whenever an analyst becomes involved in a business situation because people tend to behave differently under scrutiny. They often change their actions to conform to the observer's expectations (a tendency called the *Hawthorne effect*). They may also exaggerate the difficulty of a task or objective.

That is why experienced analysts use a variety of sources and methods (discussed in the next chapter) to gather information. They compare the information obtained in one way or from one specific source with that obtained in other ways. They also seek to get inside the business or industry they are studying. Frequently, people will not inform an analyst of the details surrounding a business or industry practice. This is seldom an intentional withholding of information. Rather, the information is usually so integral to the process that the individual does not realize the systems analyst is unaware of it. Experienced analysts know how to get at this information.

Systems analysis entails more than simply gathering information and studying tools, techniques, and technologies. It requires gaining knowledge and insight and using these to identify and solve problems. ◼

---

are missing from the design. If, for example, those using the prototype complain that the capabilities for certain types of processing or for handling exceptional situations are not built into the design, the system's requirements can be expanded.

The value of the component method shows up during prototyping. Developers can insert prewritten components into the prototype quickly and give the system to users. In fact, they can insert alternate components into the prototype to determine which design meets users' business needs most effectively.

Application prototyping has two primary uses. First, it is an effective method of clarifying the requirements that must be built into a system. Reviewing written specifications is not nearly as effective as working with the features firsthand. Second, prototypes are useful for evaluating a system's features. Users' reactions to methods of interacting with the system (through a keyboard or mouse, for example, or by touching a menu option with a finger) and the arrangement of information on a computer display can be gauged quickly and easily by watching an individual sit down at a workstation and use the application (Figure 10.9).

As Figure 10.10 shows, the prototype is part of an *evolutionary* system. New information acquired from users during prototyping can be applied to modify the physical design early in the development process. Modified prototypes can then be reevaluated. Making changes to a prototype is much less costly than altering an application once it has been fully developed and implemented.

**Detailed (Physical) Design**    The detailed, or physical, design of a system specifies its features. The accompanying documentation consists of definitions explaining the characteristics of the system, its processing activities, and the reports and charts it can generate. Detailed design specifications, which might call for new program instructions to be written, new components to be created, or the use of prewritten components, usually are prepared in the following sequence:

- **Output: Information and Results** Because output is the reason for developing a system in the first place, it is usually the starting point for the detailed design. In the output design, the type, contents, and formats of reports and display screens are defined using **layout descriptions**—charts that show the exact location of data and information on the screen and in a printed report (Figure 10.11). If a prewritten output component is used (say, for a report or document, such as an invoice or payroll check), an output layout may already be suggested.

**layout description**
A chart that shows the exact location of data and information on a computer screen or in a printed report.

FIGURE 10.9

*Application Prototyping*

IBM's Software Usability Laboratory allows systems design and development personnel to monitor people's reactions to a system prototype. Listening to future users' reactions to and concerns about the new system is an important component of the system development process.

- **Input: Data and Information for Processing** Once they know the requirements, designers work back to determine what processing activities are needed to produce the output and which data and information will be provided as input by people using the system.
- **Stored Data: Databases and Files** If data are not keyed, scanned, or otherwise entered as input by a system user, and are not transmitted to a computer by an electronic link, they may be retrieved from a stored database or file. Figure 10.12 shows the various input components of a sales system and their origins, all of which are specified in the detailed design.
- **Processing and Procedures** Methods are determined for achieving computing results and arranging data and information into a desired sequence. These methods are the *processing requirements*. Also important is the establishment of procedures for

FIGURE 10.10

*Steps in the Development of a System Prototype*

After preliminary investigation and requirements determination, a prototype is created. Like systems themselves, prototypes undergo evaluation, development, and change.

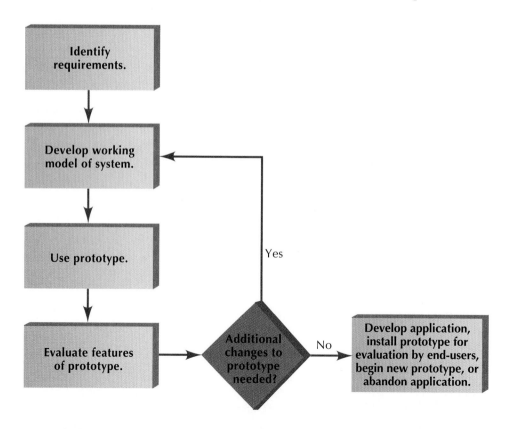

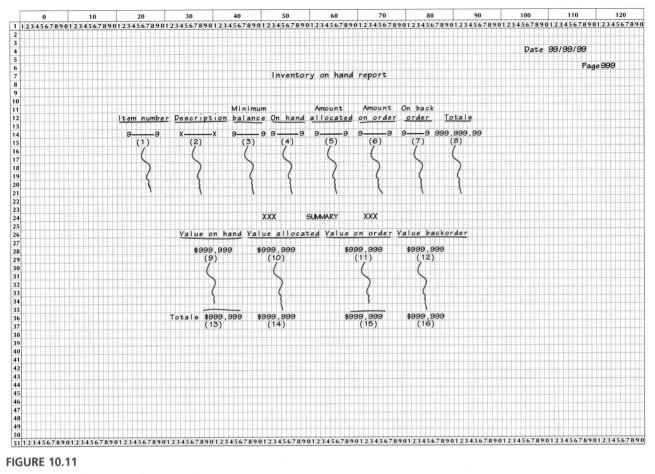

**FIGURE 10.11**

*Layout Form for Printed System Output*

Layout descriptions, sometimes drawn on paper and other times at the display screen, are used in physical design to show the exact location of data and information in a printed report and on screen. The layout form shown here was used to prepare the format of an inventory-on-hand report.

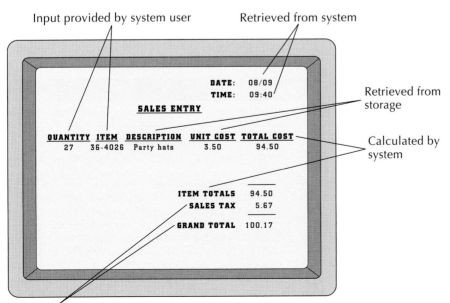

**FIGURE 10.12**

*Input Components of a Sales System and Their Origins*

Data that are not entered by a user into the system may be automatically retrieved from a database or file stored in the system.

the people using the system. Table 10.3 shows some important systems procedures specified during detailed design. These include actions taken to back up files and maintain system security.

- **Controls** In a shared system, individual users have responsibilities for activities and specific actions. Controls describe these responsibilities. For example, if transactions are accumulated into batches before processing, control information describes how the batches are identified, when they are processed, what files and databases they use, and how the computer operator determines that the batches have been properly processed. In the American Airlines system, controls describe how the weekly batches of ticket payments submitted by each agent will be audited for accuracy and processed within the system.

Confirm's design called for the crafting of over 3,000 programs because of the many different activities necessary to manage cross-country business transactions. Some of Confirm's many design requirements are detailed in Figure 10.13.

Throughout the design process for any system, designers examine many alternatives to ensure that the desired features are included, to meet every business requirement, and to fit within the budgetary constraints of the project.

## Development and Construction

During development and system construction, the system is actually built. That is, physical design specifications are turned into a functioning system. The principal activities of this phase of the SDLC are the acquisition of software and services, computer programming, and testing (Figure 10.14).

**Acquisition of Software and Services** Increasingly, systems incorporate prepackaged software and services originating outside the company. During construction and development, systems designers may acquire software packages that perform specific functions (such as data management, security, or backup) or special services (for example e-mail, electronic data interchange, or voice mail) and incorporate them into the overall system design.

Communications software and network services are usually acquired rather than developed in-house. During design and construction, systems analysts work with communications carriers to design the network characteristics (such as the locations to be interconnected and transmission speeds, as well as management, backup, and error-detection procedures).

**Programming** After the company has acquired software and services, computer programmers turn processing specifications into software. The software created for the system will perform its capture, generation, processing, storage and retrieval, and transmission functions.

| Table 10.3 | Design of Systems Procedures |
|---|---|
| **TYPE** | **DEFINITION** |
| Data entry procedures | Procedures for capturing data and entering them into the system. Identify which data originate from specific screens, with specific documents, input devices, or individuals. |
| Run-time procedures | The steps the system's user or operator takes to achieve the desired results. Identify the files and programs that must be included with the system. |
| Error-handling procedures | The actions a user or operator must take when unexpected or unacceptable results occur. Describe the steps to take when an error is detected or processing is disrupted for any reason. |
| Security and backup procedures | The actions taken to protect the system, data, information, reprograms against accidental or intentional damage. Specify when and how to make duplicate copies of data and programs or actions to take to prevent sabotage. |

| Input | Output/Reports | Stored data | Processing/Procedures | Controls |
|---|---|---|---|---|
| •Entry of reservation details for airlines, automobiles, or hotels. | •Printed acknowledgments of reservations. | •Transactions already entered into the system. | •Descriptions of how transcaction data are used to update files and databases or generate reports. | •Methods for detecting invalid charges or credits. |
| •Entry of a wide variety of rates and charges for airline seats, automobiles, or hotel rooms. | •Printed tickets or invoices. | •Customer, travel agent, airline, automobile, or hotel characteristics. | | •Steps for authorizing changes to charge rates and authorization codes in the system. |
| •Entry of changes to previously entered data and information. | •Printed reports summarizing the allocation of resources (airline seats, automobiles, or hotel rooms). | •Description of facilities, vehicles, or aircraft available to users of the system. | •Procedures for accepting, validating, and processing transactions. | •Description of facilities, vehicles, or aircraft available to users of the system. |
| •Entry of inquiries to retrieve information about a specific transaction, individual, flight, vehicle, or hotel. | •Printed current status information or historical descriptions of the business activities of a customer, travel agent, or hotel. | | •Procedures for backing up the system to safeguard sensitve data and infomation. | |
| •Entry of requests to print reports, display information, or transmit details from one location to another. | | | •Procedures for restarting an application that is interrupted for any reason. | |

**FIGURE 10.13**

**The Detailed Design of Confirm**

The design of AMRIS's Confirm system called for more than 3,000 programs. Some elements of the design, based on requirements determination, are listed here.

Programming may be done in-house or by outside contractors. In the latter case, the contractor is given the specifications and prepares the necessary software according to a development and delivery schedule set up by the client firm. Depending on the system, portions of the software may be delivered as they are completed, or the entire set of programs may arrive in one package when the development process is complete.

**Testing**   Once the system is constructed, it must be tested to determine if it (1) performs according to specifications, (2) performs as users expect it to perform, and (3) detects errors that halt processing or produce erroneous results. During **software testing,** software programs are used with special experimental data files called **test data** to ensure that the software will not fail—that is, will not produce unexpected or incorrect results or interruptions in processing. The test data are created to determine whether the

**software testing**
The testing of software programs to ensure that the software will not produce unexpected or incorrect results or interruptions during processing.

**test data**
Experimental files used to test software.

**FIGURE 10.14**

**Development and Construction of a System**

Development and construction—the fourth stage in the SDLC—entails three activities: computer programming, acquisition of software and services, and testing.

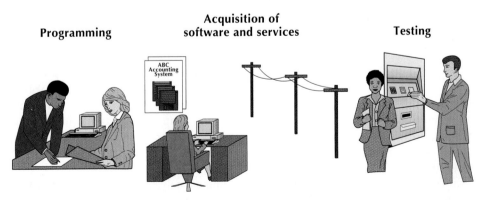

| Programming | Acquisition of software and services | | Testing |
|---|---|---|---|
| Have computer programs written by company personnel or by outside contractors. | Acquire and install prepackaged software purchased from outside sources. | Acquire communications links and network services needed for new system. | Test software, procedures, and features of new system. |

system will process them correctly. The systems analyst examines the processing results to see if they match expectations.

In **system testing,** the complete system—software, procedures, and guidelines—is tested. Also tested is the compatibility between different software modules that are to be used together in the system (such as a data input module, a communications module, and a report-writing module).

After UPS developed its wireless network, it performed many different tests. It checked (1) the reliability of the handheld computer in extremely hot and extremely cold temperatures and in both high and low humidity; (2) the clarity of network transmissions under different weather conditions; (3) the speed at which drivers could enter data through the keyboard; (4) the system's response rate if a large number of drivers entered data simultaneously; and (5) the system's response if a driver entered an unauthorized transaction code or entered only a portion of the data needed to process a transaction. UPS worked with a small number of drivers to test the system before deciding to go ahead and equip all drivers with wireless devices.

## Implementation

During the implementation phase of the SDLC, the new system is installed and put into use. New systems often bring many changes to a business, including new business procedures, different individual responsibilities, and adjustments in the flow of information. Thus, three important aspects of implementation are (1) training, (2) site preparation, and (3) conversion strategies.

**Training**   Even experienced computer users need to become familiar with the features of a new system. During **training,** IT professionals show people how to use the system and how to keep it running and reliable. Training covers all aspects of using the system, from routine procedures to periodic actions (such as replacing printer cartridges) to emergency operations (such as the steps to take if system security is breached).

People tend to think of *training* as the training of end-users who are part of a work group. But IT professionals also need training when a new application is installed because they often have to know both the user's procedures and the administrator's procedures to keep the network, server, or other components up and running.

**Site Preparation**   Sometimes new systems require new equipment and furniture and the construction of additional facilities—for example, new electrical wiring, air-conditioning systems, lighting systems, and security systems. **Site preparation** includes these and all other activities involved in preparing for the installation of a new system.

---

**system testing**
The testing of a complete system—software, procedures, and guidelines.

**training**
The process by which people are taught how to use a system.

**site preparation**
The activities involved in preparing for the installation of a new system.

---

**REALITY CHECK**   Have you ever realized that good designs are hardly noticeable? When you get into an automobile, the car's physical features are pretty much the way you expect them to be. The speedometer, fuel gauge, and warning lights are in the same vicinity in most automobiles. So are the controls for the lights and windshield wipers. In each case, you reach for them without giving it a second thought. If the seat's position, steering wheel's tilt, or mirror's angle is not just right, you can make the necessary adjustments quickly and easily. These are all hallmarks of a good design.

In contrast, a bad design is noticed almost immediately. You can probably think of instances when you had to fumble around to find the release for the hood, the gas tank cover, the ignition, or the headlight control switch. When the design is right, you do not give it a second thought; when it is wrong, your life is made more difficult. This is as true for computers and communications systems as it is for cars. ■

# CRITICAL CONNECTIONS 3

## Milwaukee Electric Tool's Web Site Meets Different Buyer Requirements

Milwaukee Electric Tool Corp. is a leading producer and seller of heavy-duty portable electric tools and accessories. Quality and the name Milwaukee have been synonymous in the power-tool industry since the company's founding in 1924. As the only electric-tool manufacturer in the United States exclusively targeting the professional tool user, Milwaukee's reputation is based on producing reliable, durable and high-quality power tools and accessories.

The company's first Web site, intended primarily for information sharing, was designed to provide information about the company, its history, and its products. Although it met those needs quite well, after several years company management decided that by building a new Web strategy, it could creatively use the Internet as an effective sales and marketing tool.

The requirements for Milwaukee Electric Tool's Web site consisted of two parts: (1) the consumer side, where the Web would provide consumers and the general public with information about the company's products, active promotional programs, and the location of dealers and sales outlets in the customer's vicinity, and (2) a business-to-business side featuring a secured extranet that would enable distributors to search the product catalog and place orders for tools and equipment.

During the feasibility investigation, the company determined it had to revise its operational business systems in order to support the sale of items to distributors over the Web. The investigation revealed that the evolution of its existing systems over the year, each with its own structure for data, had created incompatibilities that prevented them from sharing and exchanging data. Hence, the company selected and installed an enterprise-resource-planning (ERP) system that provided the database structure that would support its Web strategy.

---

Site preparation may be minimal or it may be extensive. If a new system requires the replacement of existing PCs with more powerful models, changes in the work site may not be needed. The old computers are simply unplugged and carried away, and the new ones are installed in their place. However, if a local area network is being installed in an office for the first time, site preparation may entail running communications cables, building a cable connection room, and installing cable plugs in the wall.

When UPS decided to install handheld computers and modem/telephone links in its delivery trucks, it had to train drivers how to use them, of course. But the company also had to prepare the connections and mount the devices in the trucks, as well as prepare communications facilities at its data center.

**Conversion Strategies** A **conversion plan** describes all of the activities that must occur to change over to a new system. It identifies the persons responsible for each activity, and includes a timetable for the completion of each event. The plan also includes the following measures of accountability: ensures that each activity is completed; specifies

**conversion plan**
A description of all the activities that must occur to change over to a new system.

and verifies dates on the conversion schedule; lists all databases and files to be converted; identifies all of the data and information that are required to build databases and files for the system; lists all new procedures that will go into use during conversion; and outlines all of the controls that will be used to ensure that each activity occurs properly.

Analysts can choose from four conversion strategies in implementing the new system (Table 10.4). Each strategy has advantages and disadvantages.

**direct cut over strategy**
A conversion plan in which people abruptly stop using an old system and immediately begin using a new one.

1. When time is tight or when no dramatic changes are being made in work processes or responsibilities, the analyst may choose a **direct cut over strategy,** in which people stop using the old system and jump right into using the new one. This conversion method can be risky if there are any serious problems or misunderstandings about the new system. However, it does offer a major benefit: When people are forced to use a new system right away rather than gradually, they tend to work hard to ensure its success.

**parallel systems strategy**
A conversion plan in which the old and the new system are used together for a period of time, with the old system being gradually phased out.

2. In a **parallel systems strategy,** both the old and new system are used together for a period of time, with the old system being gradually phased out. This conversion method offers the greatest security when people are unsure of the usefulness or reliability of the new system. In these cases, people appreciate the comfort of knowing they can fall back on the old system. Yet this advantage can also be a disadvantage if people feel the new system is taking away some of their important responsibilities or personal prestige. Then they may not try very hard to make it work. In fact, they may even want it to fail.

**pilot conversion strategy**
A conversion plan in which a working version of a new system is implemented in one group or department to test it before it is installed throughout the entire business.

3. The **pilot conversion strategy** is often used when the new system involves new business methods or drastic changes in work processes. Under this method, a working version of the system is implemented in one group or department. People know they are using a new system and that their experiences and suggestions may lead to changes in the system. When no more changes are needed and the system is judged complete, it is installed throughout the entire business. The advantage of this approach is that the system can be fully tested in one area of the business before it is put into full use throughout the company. However, while pilot programs avoid the risk of encountering a prob-

| Table 10.4 | **Conversion Strategies** | | |
|---|---|---|---|
| **METHOD** | **DESCRIPTION** | **ADVANTAGES** | **DISADVANTAGES** |
| Direct cut over strategy | The old system is abruptly replaced by the new one. The organization relies fully on the new system immediately. | Forces users to make the new system work. There are immediate benefits from new methods and controls. | There is no other system to fall back on if difficulties arise with new system. Requires the most careful planning. |
| Parallel systems strategy | The old system is operated along with the new system for a period of time, but is phased out gradually. | Offers greatest security. The old system can take over if errors are found in the new system or if usage problems occur. | Doubles operating costs. The new system may not get a fair trial. |
| Pilot strategy | Working version of the new system is implemented in one part of the organization. Based on feedback, changes are made and the system is installed in the rest of the organization by one of the other methods. | Provides experience and testing before implementation. | May give the impression that the old system is unreliable and not error-free. |
| Phase-in strategy | The new system is gradually implemented across all users. | Allows some users to take advantage of the system early. Allows training and installation without unnecessary use of resources. | A long phase-in may cause user problems whether the project goes well (overenthusiasm) or not (resistance and lack of a fair trial). |

**REALITY CHECK**

IT professionals, particularly systems analysts and computer programmers, use the word *bug* to mean an error or an unintended result. They will say, for example, "There's a bug in the software and it causes the program to fail if we report $0.00 sales for the day." They will then talk about *debugging* the program. You may wonder how they came up with this term.

Here is how it happened. Grace Murray Hopper, one of the pioneers in the computer field, was working in her laboratory one day, running a program she had developed. When the program produced an unexpected result, she tried to determine the cause. After rechecking the program's processing logic and convincing herself it was correct, she began looking elsewhere.

In those days—the 1940s and 1950s—computers were quite different. They did not use transistors and chips, but rather mechanical relays that opened and closed. Hopper glanced at one of the relays and saw that it was not fully closed, even though the program logic dictated that it should be. Upon closer scrutiny, she found that a moth had become trapped in the relay—and this intruder was preventing completion of the circuit and correct execution of the program. She pulled it out, and her program ran properly.

So the origin of the term *bug* was a real bug. ■

---

lem that affects a large number of people in the company, they may give the impression that the old system is unreliable and therefore make those still using it uneasy.

4. When it is impossible to install a new system throughout an entire organization or department at one time, the **phase-in strategy** is used. The conversion of databases, training of personnel, and installation of hardware and software are staged over a period of time ranging from weeks to months, depending on the system. Some people begin to use the new system before others do. Thus, the phase-in method allows some users to take advantage of the system early on. The disadvantage is that long phase-ins can create user problems whether the project goes well or not—overenthusiasm if it seems to be going well, and refusal to give it a fair trial if it does not go well at first.

> **phase-in strategy**
> A conversion plan in which a new system is gradually phased in throughout the organization or department over a certain period of time.

UPS did not acquire its wireless communications capabilities all at once. Rather, it pilot-tested a few handheld computers and the cellular link to determine if they would work as expected. When evidence showed that they would, the company proceeded to roll out the system to all of its drivers, region by region. The pilot test proved the concept and the technology worked; a phase-in of the system followed.

## Evaluation and Continuing Evolution

Once the system is implemented, analysts perform systems evaluation to identify its strengths and weaknesses. They want to determine if the system can deliver the expected level of usability and usefulness and provide the anticipated benefits.

Enterprise systems are often used for many years. However, during that time, the organization, the people using the system, and the business environment will change, as will the available IT components themselves. Therefore, all systems need to undergo continuing development, with features added and capabilities augmented as new or improved technologies are introduced.

# A Final Word

Large-scale systems can take long periods of time to develop. On the other hand, some aspects of development may go more quickly than others. For example, designing a Web page—positioning enterprise logos, navigation buttons, and blocks of information—will usually take far less time than the development of back-end features such as the structure of databases or the design of processing logic.

The manner in which an application development process is launched can have substantial influence over the likelihood of a project's success. For instance, poorly defined requirements at the beginning will likely hinder the performance of all other activities in the development process.

# CRITICAL CONNECTIONS

## 1   Part II: Personalize Your Message with American Greetings' CreataCard

americangreetings.com℠   The popularity of CreataCard has led American Greetings to introduce these alternatives:

1. **Add-a-Photo** This software enables you to place a photo of your choice on or in any card you choose from the 1,000 or so available cards. How? Drop your film off at any participating local developer or retailer, or mail it to a development center. The developer will place your photos online, protected by a password. You will be notified when your photos are online and ready for use. Then, when visiting the American Greetings Web site, you can link to the photos, view thumbnails (small copies of the full-size images), and choose the one(s) you want inserted into a greeting card. The software product also allows you to add photos to card designs using a scanner, CD-ROM photo disk, or digital camera.
2. **Send Cards Electronically** You can visit the American Greetings Web site (www.americangreetings.com) to prepare animated greetings that are sent by e-mail via the Internet.
3. **Mail Delivery** At the Web site, you can personalize a card, and American Greetings will print and mail it for you.

### Questions for Discussion

1. Would you use the American Greetings CreataCard program? Why or why not?
2. What characteristics of CreataCard make it attractive for individual users?
3. What are the apparent limitations and drawbacks of the *Add-a-Photo* and e-mail alternatives?

## 2   Part II: Volkswagen Parts Online in Mexico

**Volkswagon in Mexico**   In designing a new spare parts order and fulfillment system in Mexico, Volkswagen turned to the World Wide Web. The design chosen provides for the submission of Volkswagen dealer orders from any PC running a Web browser. Orders are submitted over the Web directly to the spare-parts center; the system calls for shipments to the dealers within 24 hours instead of two weeks.

Service, not cost savings, was the driving force behind the new design. Yet, both dealer and company also wanted cost benefits. As use of the system grows, both expect to benefit from lower inventories and, consequently, lower inventory management costs.

Volkswagen's Web-based ordering system gives its users access to parts information anytime and anywhere there is a Web-access point. By providing such good service behind the scenes, the business systems are supporting the Volkswagen name and increasing opportunities to sell Volkswagen cars.

### Questions for Discussion

1. Were you surprised that Volkswagen decided to use the World Wide Web as a basis for its new parts system?
2. What features of the Web make it attractive or unattractive for widespread business use?
3. Why should more rapid parts fulfillment reduce inventory levels for both dealers and Volkswagen?

## 3   Part II: Milwaukee Electronic Tool's Web Site Meets Different Buyer Requirements

*Milwaukee*   When Milwaukee Electric Tool decided to implement a Web strategy to support both consumer and business-to-business activities, it found that the feasibility of doing so was hindered by a legacy of operational business systems. The structure of data used in each of the system was inconsistent and incompatible. In order to make it feasible to share data between the systems, the company installed an enterprise resource planning system. The new software provided the consistency of data to integrate order entry, pricing, inventory, and order-fulfillment systems. It also ensured that order status and customer history reports would be accu-rate, whether emanating from the Web or traditional sales channels.

After the system was in use, the company determined that its dealers needed a *ship immediate* service alternative for orders entered over its extranet. It also determined that it should provide links for consumers visiting the Milwaukee Electric Tool Web site; that way, people could place orders at the site and have the order transferred to the dealer that would fill the order. Dealers welcomed the idea of a *sell through* feature for potential customers.

Milwaukee Electric Tool has continued to increase the volume of business that it generates over its Web site, as well as the support it offers to consumers and other visitors. Identifying the right requirements and developing a good systems design have proven to be invaluable in the success of the Web strategy.

### Questions for Discussion

1. What is your opinion of Milwaukee Electric Tool's decision to treat its consumer and its business-to-business Web strategies separately?

2. Why was it important for Milwaukee Electric Tool to ensure that it had a consistent structure of data, learned during the feasibility study, before it embarked on the process of designing the Web system?

3. Do you think Milwaukee Electric Tool's requirements determination was incomplete since it did not identify the need for *ship immediate* and dealer sell-through services in advance?

## Summary of Learning Objectives

**1** **Describe the origin of IT applications.** In the early days of data processing, large computers and vast communications networks were the norm. Although these large systems are still in widespread use, technological progress in the 1980s and 1990s, coupled with increased affordability, has made personal systems the dominant source of IT capability in many organizations.

**2** **Identify the distinguishing characteristics of an IT application.** Single-user systems are (1) designed for hands-on usage, (2) tailored to an individual's requirements and preferences, and (3) used to improve personal performance.

**3** **Explain the benefits of IT applications to users and enterprises.** When properly designed, single-user systems have three main effects: improved productivity, greater effectiveness, and increased creativity and innovation. Increasing creativity is a benefit associated with personal systems, while increases in innovation are benefits generally associated with enterprise systems.

**4** **Explain how a systems project begins and how its desirability is determined.** A systems project begins with a project proposal. The proposal is a result of problem or opportunity recognition. The completed project proposal is submitted to a steering committee, usually made up of people from different functional areas of the business. The steering committee determines whether or not the project is desirable.

**5** **Describe the six phases of the systems development life cycle.** The six phases of SDLC are as follows: (1) problem recognition/preliminary investigation–the definition and investigation of the problem; (2) requirements determination–the process of understanding the current system and the new system's requirements; (3) systems design–planning the new system; (4) development and construction–creating the new system; (5) implementation–converting to the new system; and (6) evaluation and continuing evolution–monitoring and adding value to the new system.

**6** **Explain the importance of continual evaluation and evolution in IT systems.** Because individual and enterprise needs change, systems must evolve to meet those needs. To remain effective, the users and systems developers must keep abreast of changing user and business needs, as well as the latest advances in information technology.

## Key Terms

configuration 434
conversion plan 459
direct cut over strategy 460
effectiveness 438
enterprise system 433
hands-on system 433
layout description 453
parallel systems strategy 460
personal productivity software 436
phase-in strategy 461
pilot conversion strategy 460
preliminary investigation 442

process 445
process improvement 445
programmer/analyst 441
productivity 436
project management 440
project proposal 440
prototype 452
requirement 445
requirements determination 445
single-user system/personal system 433
site preparation 458
software testing 457

steering committee 440
system testing 458
systems analyst 441
systems design 449
systems designer 441
systems development 440
systems development life cycle (SDLC) 442
test data 457
training 458
Web developer 442

## Review Questions

1. What is a single-user system?
2. How did single-user systems originate? Why are mainframe systems not considered single-user systems?
3. What are the three characteristics of single-user systems?
4. What is a *hands-on user*?
5. What is productivity? List three ways in which productivity can be increased.
6. How can single-user systems aid productivity?
7. What is personal productivity software?
8. Describe the importance of effectiveness and the role of single-user systems in improving effectiveness.
9. How are productivity and effectiveness different?
10. Define the concept of leverage.
11. Describe the purpose and contents of a systems development project proposal. Who initiates this proposal? Who reviews it?
12. Describe the purpose of a steering committee. Who serves on the committee? What role does the committee play in the development of an IT application?
13. What are the six phases of the systems development life cycle?
14. Describe the purpose of problem recognition and preliminary investigation. Who performs this investigation?
15. What three types of feasibility are assessed during the preliminary investigation phase of the systems development life cycle?
16. What is a systems requirement? What is requirements determination?
17. What is the difference between process improvement and business improvement? What is their relation to requirements determination?
18. Identify and discuss four types of business improvement that can be created through effective use of IT.
19. What are the differences between preliminary design, prototyping, and detailed design?
20. What three activities are involved in systems development and construction?
21. Discuss the purpose of testing. What is the difference between software testing and system testing?
22. What is implementation? List and describe three important aspects of implementation.
23. What four conversion strategies are available to systems analysts?
24. What is systems evaluation?

## Discussion Questions

1. Steering committees serve an essential role in helping the enterprise select the right mix of IT applications to meet operating needs. Consequently, the choice of steering committee members is an essential component in the committee's success and in the success of the enterprise's overall IT use. Committee members must be able to understand the importance of IT to the enterprise and also be able to judge the quality of a project proposal.

   a. What criteria should be used in selecting the overall mix of members for an enterprise IT steering committee?

   b. Should the steering committee be headed by an IT professional or by a manager/executive who is not part of IT department? What is the reason for your recommendation?

   c. If the IT group recommends against approval of a proposed project, but operating managers in the enterprise wish to have it developed just the same, should the steering committee be empowered to make the final decision—even if it means directing the IT group to develop a project it does not support?

2. A veteran IT developer at a large consumer products company has stated, "The systems development life cycle is of way of thinking—not a way of working. Activities overlap, especially in large systems. Not all aspects of a project will be completed at the same time. Moreover, a good project manager will not hold up one part of a team, making it wait for the other team members to complete their activities. Hence, different team members may simultaneously be working on different parts of the SDLC."

   a. Do you agree that the situations described by the IT veteran are bound to occur? Why or why not?

   b. If the IT veteran *is* correct (regardless of your opinion in a.), what is the value of the SDLC model?

3. A manager in an area outside of the IT group is a vocal critic of creating IT application prototypes. He has openly and repeatedly stated that, in his opinion, creating prototypes means that the systems developer does not know what users want or how an application will perform. He stresses that the need to create a prototype is an indication that the project team does not

have complete information on user and enterprise requirements.

What position do you hold concerning IT application prototypes? Do you agree or disagree with the manager? Create an argument to support or challenge the manager's viewpoint on the value of creating IT application prototypes.

4. Corporate Fact Finders, DataSearch, and InfoQuest are all *information brokers,* companies that do library and online database searches to meet their clients' research needs. For their services, information brokers are paid $40 to $300 an hour. If you were a freelance information broker, what requirements would your single-user system have to meet?

5. CompUSA and a number of other national computer chains offer regular training classes. Why are these training classes important to current and potential customers? Why might you take a training class during the preliminary investigation stage rather than waiting until you actually buy and install a single-user system?

# *Group Projects and Applications*

## Project 1

Using telephone interviews, conduct an investigation of IT project management. Contact at least 12 project managers who are responsible for the development of IT projects. The project managers may be employed in corporations, consultancies, government agencies, software development companies, or contract programming companies.

Through your interviews, learn what a project manager does, noting any differences between the types of enterprises in which you conduct your investigation. Prepare a profile of the activities of IT project managers. The profile should describe the variety of activities with which they are involved, those, which are most critical to the project's success, and the activities that are most troublesome. Also note which activities or stages of the project are most difficult or take the most time for project managers.

Prepare a written report summarizing the firms and project managers you contacted and the insights you gained from your investigation. Be sure to include your assessment of the importance of project management to the successful launch and completion of an IT application project.

## Project 2

Visit a sample of manufacturing and service companies in your area to learn first-hand about the IT applications used by the enterprise. Focus on the essential applications for day-to-day operations.

Prepare a summary of your investigation noting the following:

1. What essential operating applications are used within each company?

2. Approximately when was each operating application originally installed?

3. To what extent has each application been changed or modified since it was installed?

4. What conclusions do you draw about the evolution of IT applications once they are implemented?

## Project 3

With a group, visit a small- or medium-sized business in your area. Different members of the group should interview someone in each of the company's different departments—accounting management, marketing, finance, production, and so forth—regarding the personal system on their desks. Ask the following questions:

- How is your system designed for hands-on usage?
- How have you tailored the system to your personal requirements and preferences?
- How does your system differ from that of a colleague who does essentially the same job that you do?
- Has your system helped you improve your personal performance? Has it increased your productivity, effectiveness, and creativity? If so, how?
- What suggestions would you make for setting up a personal system? Any *must-haves?* Any pitfalls to avoid?

Present the results of your interview to the class. Be sure to write a thank-you note to the people you have interviewed.

## Project 4

In groups of five, brainstorm a business that you would like to establish in your area. For example, you might decide that you could open and operate a CD/tape store profitably near your campus, or you might think of starting a childcare service for professionals in your area. To run your business effectively, you will want to set up a personalized computer system.

The Small Business Administration (SBA), a branch of the U.S. government, was set up to assist small-business owners. The SBA's advisors can help you develop a marketing plan, put you in touch with other local businesspeople, and assist you in securing bank loans and other financing. They can also help you determine what types of IT will be most helpful to you.

After deciding on the type of business you would like to open, contact an SBA representative in your area and ask for assistance in setting up your personal productivity system. You can visit the SBA's home page on the World Wide Web (www.sba.gov) to find the office nearest you.

Share the advice you have received with the class.

## Project 5

Write up a plan for developing a personal system suited to the business you chose to start in Project 4. Follow the outline in this chapter, and be sure to specify the following:

- The problem(s) you are trying to solve.
- The feasibility of your proposed solutions.
- The operational, program, and storage requirements your system will need (use the checklist in Figure 10.6).
- The way you will test your system before using it.

## Net_Work

1. The ability to manage projects is an essential skill for many systems developers. However, the need for managing projects successfully is not unique to the IT profession. If affects many positions. Hence, special project management applications have been developed to aid in planning and controlling the activities comprising a project and in completing those activities and projects on time and within budget.

   Using the Internet, investigate the array of project management applications available. Compare the features and capabilities of each project management program, noting ways for identifying and scheduling activities comprising the project, the interrelation and sequencing of those activities, and the means of determining completion dates and adherence to schedules. Note also which applications are designed for individual use and which support shared use in team environments.

   Prepare a presentation that summarizes the essential features that all project management software must contain. Then list the project management programs you identified, noting the common and unique features of each as well as the computing and network platforms on which they operate. If possible, indicate the approximate cost of each program.

2. The position of Web developer emerged as an important IT professional with the advent of the Internet's World Wide Web. As organizations have incorporated the Web into their business systems, they have sought to capitalize on its capabilities for display of information, the use of multimedia presentations about the enterprise, and to process business transactions initiated through browsers.

   Conduct an investigation on the Internet into the skills required to be a Web developer. Visit at least three Web sites that post IT position openings for different companies. Examine the position announcements seeking Web developers.

   a. What skills, training, and background characteristics are generally required for the Web-developer position?
   b. What responsibilities are Web developers expected to fulfill for the advertised positions?

   c. Compare the number of Web-developer positions posted with the number of systems-analyst positions. What similarities and differences do you detect? Based on the number of listings you find, which position appears to have more openings? Why do you think that is the case?
   d. Based on the information you have assembled, what is your expectation about the future of the Web developer position within the field of information technology?

3. A growing number of computer buyers are finding it easy and worthwhile to shop for a computer on the Web. Companies such as Dell, Gateway, and Hewlett-Packard have built a substantial business by selling direct to company and private purchasers.

   Since Web-based computer sales do not involve face-to-face discussions with retail salespersons, a company's Web site must anticipate and address customer questions. At the same time, it must make it easy for potential buyers to shop for computers and configure their systems properly. Buyers must also be able to place the order, receive confirmation, and arrange payment over the Web, or call the company and complete the order verbally over the phone. In either case, good design of the sales site is essential to business success.

   To see the way in which Dell, Gateway, and Hewlett-Packard have chosen to develop their Web sites, you can visit each company at its respective URL:

   **Dell Computers** www.dell.com
   **Gateway** www.gateway.com
   **Hewlett-Packard** www.hp.com

   In comparing these companies' methods, consider the following questions:

   1. What assistance does each company provide in selecting the features of a personal computer?
   2. How do the companies vary in the way they inform you of the price of a specific computer?
   3. With which companies can you place an order for a computer over the company's Web site? What is the procedure for placing the order?

## Cool Mobility

### On Assignment

At the beginning of your consulting residency, both CEO Tina Fuentes and CIO James Marsalis indicated they wanted you to keep an eye out for products or services that you believe they should add. They said to make suggestions so long as you not only propose what to do but also suggest ways to make it happen.

### In Consultation

The more familiar you have become with *Cool Mobility's* business and IT capabilities, the more impressed you are with the company's innovative product strategies. Admit it: You're hooked, you're connected, you're wireless. You bought a top-of-the-line custom-designed mobile phone. It has all the little extras, including a display with your university's official crest, and it plays a distinctive ring tone to signal an incoming call. Then the novelty wore off. It was not as cool as you once thought. There are a few features you would like to change, but currently the Web site does not offer these services.

a. You would like to propose a project that will offer a service allowing customers to replace the face plate on their mobile phone with one of a different color and with one containing different photos or images. The proposal will also include the ability for customers who have previously bought a phone from *Cool Mobility* to connect to the Web site and download and install a new ring tone to their phone.

   Write a project proposal to add the services described above. Be sure that the proposal answers the six questions that are always answered in a well-developed proposal.

b. Drawing on your skills in IT project development practices, outline the steps to be taken to evaluate the feasibility of an IT project to add these new services to the Web site. Be sure to include the specific questions you wish to see answered regarding each type of feasibility.

## Case Study

JOHN DEERE

### John Deere's Life Cycle of Innovation and Improvement

Deere & Company, founded in 1837, is a story of continuous innovation and product enhancement. John Deere himself developed the world's first commercially successful, self-scouring steel plow, an innovation that revolutionized the world of farming and agriculture. The company grew from a one-man blacksmith shop into a worldwide corporation that today does business in more than 160 countries and employs approximately 43,000 people worldwide. It is the world's leading manufacturer of agricultural and forestry equipment and a leading supplier of construction equipment and equipment used in lawn, grounds and turf care.

The company, with annual revenues in excess of $13 billion, is guided today, as it has been since

1837, by John Deere's original values: a commitment to product quality, customer service, business integrity, and a high regard for individual contribution. The company strives to create shareholder value through its pursuit of continuous improvement and profitable growth. Improving the quality of its products has been important since the company's beginning. When it was suggested one time to the company's founder that customers had to take what the company produced, Deere replied, "No, they don't have to take what we produce. If we don't improve our product, somebody else will." This spirit of John Deere lives on in the company today in the products it manufacturers and in the way it conducts its business activities.

In addition to its high quality and durable equipment, John Deere's success can also be attributed to its loyal dealers. Dealers interact with equipment buyers and thus are responsible for the sales of the company's products and the spare parts needed for maintenance of the equipment. John Deere pays special attention to the way it serves its dealers (who also sell its competitor's equipment), always seeking to improve the support it provides. By doing so, it aims to assist in improving their revenue and in turn the company's own sales.

Several years ago, as part of its e-commerce strategy, John Deere created an extranet called JDPoint. Both dealers and the company liked the features of JDPoint, finding it much

faster and more accurate than the previous methods of telephone calls and faxes. Dealers used JDPoint to retrieve information on prices, inventory, and parts, and to submit orders.

The system was developed and operated on its own Web server. The Web server displayed all information and accepted and processed inquiries from dealers. The Web server in turn interconnected with the company's legacy IT applications—well-established systems that handle *mission critical* activities such as tracking product and parts inventory, managing order fulfillment, scheduling manufacturing, and keeping track of financial and accounting transactions. The legacy systems operate on the company's mainframe computer.

JDPoint was very successful. It was used by over 4,000 of its nearly 6,000 dealers. During a typical month, over 350,000 order lines were generated over JDPoint, accounting for one-third of all spare-parts sales. Even so, John Deere management thought that the system could be improved and in so doing stimulate even greater sales for the company.

John Deere's e-business manager was appointed project manager and given responsibility for investigating alternatives for improving JDPoint. Since the system was an important parts ordering tool, the e-business manager sought out employees in the company's parts division to learn their ideas for improvement. Members of the division drew up a list of some 30 requirements to be considered as enhancements to

the system. The list detailed ways to improve the performance, scalability, maintainability, and reliability of JDPoint, thereby offering better dealer support.

The list included a requirement to create a single IT structure in which the front-end Web components and the back-end legacy systems would use the same computing and operating system platforms. The requirement was intended to eliminate separate *islands of automation*— the Web server and the mainframe— each having incompatible operating systems and unique maintenance needs.

After reviewing the list of requirements, the project manager decided to conduct a feasibility study that

would investigate whether the desired systems enhancements and the migration of the Web server to the same type of IT platform as the mission critical (i.e., legacy) system could be achieved. The feasibility study explored the possibility of running both the Web front-end and legacy systems on the same operating system, thereby improving overall maintainability, while achieving virtually 100 percent uptime. In addition, it sought to determine whether the system's manageability and maintainability would improve. The investigation also sought to ensure that the system's capacity could scale up with the company's objective of driving more business through JDPoint.

The project manager appointed a project team and assigned the responsibility for conducting the investigation. An external consultant from a consultancy well known for its expertise in e-commerce systems in manufacturing environments was retained and included as a member of the team.

The investigation concluded that meeting the requirements was feasible. It was also concluded that packaged software could be acquired to carry out the project, thereby avoiding the need to assign in-house pro-

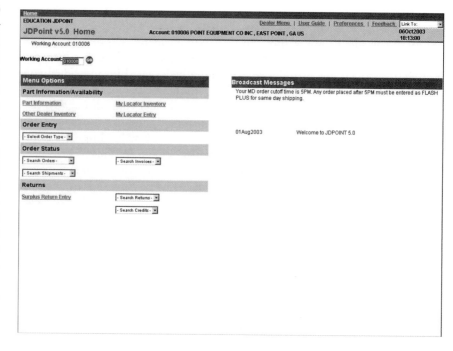

grammers or retain outside contractors to write custom software.

After assessing a broad selection of available software, the JD team selected an e-commerce application that met the project's requirements and could run on the same type of computer and use the identical operating system as the legacy systems.

Even though the analysts were confident in the characteristics of the chosen application software, they wanted to be certain that it would fulfill the company's needs. Hence, the team conducted *proof-of-concept* testing. During this phase, JDPoint was transferred to a new server and operating system, and tests were made to ensure that the application would perform as expected. It did.

Even though the proof-of-concept tests were successful, the project manager wanted to ensure the system would meet its dealers' requirements. It had to be easy to use and prove to be efficient and reliable. A live pilot study of the new system was conducted. Twenty-five North American dealers were given access to the new system. They were asked to use it in their daily activities and to note any features that did not function as they expected. They were also asked to note any discrepancies they encountered when entering orders or retrieving information. Throughout the pilot study, the project team measured improvements in speed and system availability compared to the previous version of JDPoint. At the end of the pilot study, the project team determined it a success and moved to the next step—the rollout to its dealers.

The rollout was phased in over a period of more than six months. During the initial rollout, some 800 dealers in the United States, France, Germany, and the United Kingdom adopted and began using the new JDPoint. With the initial rollout a success, John Deere continued rolling out the several thousand other sites over the ensuing six months. At the end of the effort, the project was judged a success, so much so that the project manager reported that "Team members from John Deere's Computer Operations and the Parts Division did an outstanding job of developing and porting this application to the new platform."

## Questions for Discussion

1. Did the John Deere project team use a systems development life cycle approach to the enhancement of JDPoint? Explain the reason behind your response.
2. What is your assessment of the approach John Deere took in developing the enhancements to its JDPoint?
3. Do you think the project team was overly cautious in conducting a feasibility study followed by a proof-of-concept study and pilot study? Why or why not?
4. What benefits do you think the project manager sought by including experienced consultants on the project team?
5. Is the John Deere example a model that other companies should follow when launching a systems project involving enhancement to an existing application? Why or why not?

# 11 Creating Enterprise Applications

## LEARNING OBJECTIVES

When you have completed this chapter, you should be able to

1 Describe the principal functions and roles of a systems analyst.

2 Identify the characteristics of shared systems.

3 Discuss the changing process for developing information systems applications.

4 Describe the tools and techniques available to systems analysts for collecting data and developing IT applications.

5 Summarize the purpose and characteristics of unified modeling language (UML).

6 Explain the roles of the four types of IT systems development professionals.

# Objects Are Key to New Services at Empire Blue Cross Blue Shield

Empire Blue Cross Blue Shield (BCBS), of Albany, New York, serves over 4 million members and has some 85,000 healthcare providers registered in its network. Empire's business is complex because it serves four different categories of customers, each with different needs. Its customers include patient members, physicians, brokers (who create and sell the company's insurance packages), and employers who provide coverage as part of the benefit package they offer to their employees.

As a result of mergers and acquisitions, common to the healthcare insurance industry in recent years, Empire BCBS was operating with six different membership, billing, and claims-processing systems. Consequently, Empire felt its customer service was slow and the company's operating costs were high. In addition, the enterprise IT group had to support and maintain six times as many systems as would be the case in a centralized enterprise.

Empire also judged its systems to be excessively dependent on paper forms and cumbersome approval processes. Patient members, physicians, and brokers alike routinely had to make several inquiries to the company's call center, often tolerating long *holds* and repeated transfers until they reached a representative who could effectively address their questions.

Led by the company's management team, including its CIO, Empire BCBS established broad requirements for a new IT system. For its customers, it wanted to streamline and improve the services, reduce delays in responding to inquiries, speed the payment processing, reduce the time needed to create new policies and insurance contracts. It wanted to merge the six existing systems and consolidate legacy applications while overhauling its customer services.

However, management did not want to simply reengineer its existing paper processes. Rather, it had a vision of a paperless customer self-service process, whereby any of its four customer types could use the Internet to go online, 24 hours a day. They wanted patients to have the capability to enter or change personal information or check on the status of a health-insurance claim. It wanted to give physicians the capability to instantly verify patient coverage or submit claims for processing. Employers should be able to enroll new employees online and verify their coverage. Empire also thought its brokers should have the capability to assemble and price coverage programs, tailoring features and determining policy quotations while online.

As the project was launched, teams were established to focus on each customer type. Through a combination of interviews, meetings with staff groups, and review of processing guidelines, each team created scenarios that documented business processes for each customer group. The analyses revealed many opportunities for streamlining customer processes.

One team focusing on the brokers took over a conference room, creating a color-coded map of the sales process. It found, for instance, that brokers who wanted to prepare a new policy proposal had to follow an 80-step, paper driven process that spanned 25 to 30 days. Unknown before the analysis was the fact it included more than 30 redundant audit processes.

After considering all of the facts surrounding BCBS processing, the teams determined that the customer groups could be serviced online through four unique customer portals. On the customer side, the only requirement was that they have an ordinary Internet browser on their computer.

The emerging concept also specified that all portals use a common infrastructure that included consolidated membership, billing, and claims processing systems. Each portal would link to Empire's operational systems. Yet each would have a separate view of the enterprise database, adjusted to the processing needs of the particular customer segment.

The Empire IT team quickly determined that achieving the vision was technically and economically feasible. However, it also recognized that because of the uniqueness of the vision, coupled with the complexity of the health-insurance environment, they would not be able to acquire *off-the-shelf* package software.

After further investigation, Empire decided to adopt an object-oriented development environment. The team, with outside consultants retained for the project, built sets of reusable components that could be incorporated into Web application servers. The servers were designed to present Web page content to customers visiting the portals while also interconnecting with back-end processing systems.

As the new system took shape, the Empire team sought to make each portal easy to use and responsive to customer needs. Along with the self-service features, each portal also included an innovative *click to talk* feature. If customers became stuck during use of the portal, a simple click with their mouse would connect them to the Empire call center where a representative could aid them in completing the transaction. Since the system could sense the type of customer and nature of the processing taking place, it was able to direct them to an assistant most skilled in their area of interest. Empire's real-time collaboration system for responding to Web-initiated requests, a first for an enterprise of its size, has proven effective in streamlining activities and improving service for the benefit of everyone.

Empire tested the member application by first rolling it out to its own employees. Adjustments and enhancements were made according to their experiences. Subsequently it was implemented for the general membership. Members had the option of registering to use the online portal or continuing to interact with Empire through the call center. The initial signups were only a small fraction of Empire's more than 4 million members. However, as word of the portal spread, the pace of registrations began to pick up.

Empire's system-development methodology has proven itself repeatedly. It features development and reuse of object components and iteration through successive versions of individual portals, making adjustments according to customer experience. Moreover, it has been a key success factor in achieving Empire's vision of carrying out streamlined operating activities online using the resources of the Web. Future plans call for further integration of online processes with sound management and effective operating systems.

*A*t some point in your career it is likely that you will be involved in the development of IT applications. If you are pursuing a career as an IT professional, you may be part of a development team or even the project leader. If you are a manager or staff member (an IT user), you may be consulted by IT professionals who want to involve you in the development activities for applications you will later use.

This chapter looks inside the process of developing enterprise IT applications. The first part of the chapter describes the alternatives for creating an IT application. Some alternatives come from outside the enterprise. The second part discusses the tools available to systems analysts. The third section explores the unified modeling language, an approach to creating applications that is gaining a great deal of support. Because just having the right tools is not enough, the chapter closes with a discussion of the skills that good systems analysts need to work effectively with businesspeople and to create effective applications.

The purpose of this chapter is not to teach you to create an IT application or to be a systems analyst. Rather, it is designed to give you a good idea of what systems analysts do and how to work with them to develop effective IT applications.

# Developing Open Shared Systems

Recall that in enterprise systems, two or more users share computers, communications technology, and applications. The introduction of an enterprise system into a work group or organization affects everyone who interacts with the application or receives information generated by the system. For this reason, enterprise systems are usually not developed by individual staff members, but rather by the organization's information technology group. This group goes by various names, including the information systems department, the management information systems (MIS) department, and the information resources group.

## Development Alternatives

The information technology group can take any of three approaches to developing an application:

1. **Build the application itself.**  Assemble a team of analysts, designers, and programmers who formulate the specifications for an application and write the computer software needed to fulfill the specifications.

2. **Purchase a prewritten application.**  Assign to a team of IT professionals the responsibility for searching out a prewritten software package that performs the specified functions and can be purchased from a commercial supplier or vendor. Many vendors specialize in the development, marketing, and support of applications designed to meet business needs.

3. **Contract out the application development.**  Under this approach, the company hires a software development firm (large or small) that specializes in writing computer and communications software. Either a legal contract or an informal working agreement is constructed that specifies what the software should do along with the features it should contain. The firm may decide to hire a software development

company to either formulate specifications for a system and then prepare software to meet those specifications or to write software that meets specifications provided by the company. A price for the services is agreed on, either a lump sum to be paid when the application is completed or a specified per-hour price.

The *Information Technology in Practice* feature, "Xerox's IT of the Future: Not a Copy of its Legacy," discusses how one well-known company has embarked on a new course to manage its information systems practices.

Considering the importance of IT in business, it should not surprise you that many companies use all three approaches, although there is a growing emphasis on the purchase and contract options.

Strictly speaking, a shared system is one in which two or more individuals use the same computer, interconnected to the system by communication links. They also share applications, data, and information. At a growing rate, shared systems are open systems.

## Open Systems for Sharing

**open system**
A software system that performs on different computer and communications hardware.

Shared systems depend on being open to different hardware and software. **Open systems** are software systems that perform on different computer and communications hardware. They are built on standard operating systems—that is, operating systems that can be easily purchased and used with a variety of different computers or communications systems—and work with the different user interfaces. Windows and Unix are examples of standard software systems. Windows is the de facto operating system for PCs, and is used more than any other operating system. It is *not*, however, open, as Microsoft holds the code as a proprietary resource, meaning that other developers cannot modify or add to the code. Likewise, Apple Computer has maintained its operating system as a proprietary resource, usable only on its computers. In contrast, Unix and, more recently, Linux have been released as nonproprietary operating systems. Both can be used on a wide variety of computers, both stand-alone and shared.

**interoperability**
The perfect exchange of data and information in all forms (data, text, sound, and image, including animation) between the individual components of an application (hardware, software, network).

**Interoperability** is the perfect exchange of information in all forms (data, text, sound, and image, including animation) between individual components of an application (hardware, software, network). With interoperability, the same application can operate on two different kinds of computers, yet perform the same task and have identical-looking interfaces. In other words, the components can differ in their origin (manufacturer or supplier), size (e.g., desktop computer or mainframe system), operation (including communication protocol or individual software program), or location (in the same room or across the continent). Interoperability requires open systems. (Chapter 12 discusses interoperable applications in greater detail.)

Interoperability is closely related to software portability, another desirable characteristic associated with open systems. This means information technology applications and information can be moved relatively easily between computers of varying size (for example, mainframe, midrange, or PC) and brands (for example, IBM, Apple, Compaq, Dell, and HP). An important, but subtler, benefit of software portability is that people also become somewhat portable. For instance, experts in the design and use of Lotus Notes applications can apply that expertise to systems running on any size or brand of computer. They are not constrained to a particular computer environment. (Prior to open systems, this was often a severe constraint on IT professionals.)

One reason Microsoft's software is the defacto standard is because it is available to run on a variety of computer systems. Recognizing the desirability and benefits of interoperability and software portability, Microsoft's Windows products are designed to be used on many computers besides desktop systems (servers, for example). This is not only a wish of Microsoft, but it is also the wish of many IT professionals responsible for developing and supporting enterprise systems.

Business and individual IT users want to acquire software more quickly, owing in part to the rapid pace of business change and in part to the ever-increasing number of effective ways in which to use information technology. Moreover, the demand is high for more powerful capabilities, preferably at a lower cost.

# INFORMATION TECHNOLOGY IN PRACTICE

## Xerox's IT of the Future: Not a Copy of Its Legacy

THE DOCUMENT COMPANY Xerox Corp., the Stamford, Connecticut,

**XEROX**®

company that redefined the way people around the world copy documents, has redefined its own manner of developing and managing information technology globally. In 1994, Xerox's chairman signed a $3.2 billion 10-year contract with the systems integration firm Electronics Data Systems (EDS) Corp. Owing to the success of the company's outsourcing agreement, in Fall 2001 the contract was extended five years, taking it through 2009.

Xerox's decision to shift a substantial portion of its IT responsibility to EDS is unique in two ways: scope and intention. First, the Xerox-EDS contract is the largest-ever global outsourcing contract. EDS has assumed responsibility for Xerox's information technology in the areas of computing, communications, and software management. To fulfill this huge responsibility, EDS has created a global strategic business unit that handles only Xerox IT activities. Some 1,700 of Xerox's 2,700 IT employees were shifted over to EDS, in addition to half of the $600 million Xerox was spending annually on information technology.

The other unique aspect of the Xerox decision is that it is viewed by top management as a means of transforming Xerox's IT activities. As soon as the company turned over the operation and maintenance of existing systems

to EDS, it started to focus on new systems development initiatives. Outsourcing freed up Xerox's remaining systems development staff: No longer compelled to devote the vast majority of their time to maintaining existing systems (often termed legacy systems because they have been in use for years), they were able to devote themselves to development activities focused on the Xerox of the future.

Behind this effort is an IT structure that mirrors Xerox's goal of putting customers first. The technology and infrastructure that is taken for granted in the United States is not supported all over the world. Xerox relies on EDS to manage its systems changes and to maintain its large computer system. EDS handles global strategic decisions such as architecture and new applications developments internally, allowing Xerox to focus on the needs of worldwide employees and customers.

In the process Xerox is rethinking —reengineering—its most basic business processes, giving particular attention to development of a

global sales and marketing process that is seamless from one country and region of the world to another. Dispersed as it is, Xerox presents such a unified front that it has swept every major quality commendation—from the Malcolm Baldrige Award to the Deming Prize. Xerox offers a consistent level of service to its customers, putting an overall strategy together and then tailoring it to local areas.

The IT transition is nearly complete and the system is running at 700 sites worldwide. It is a typical client/server system that features industry-standard Windows-based software. As a result, worldwide customer-service reps can better serve remote regions.

Xerox's mix of information technology applications, along with supporting computer and communication systems, is also in transition. A new architecture—hardware, software, networks, and data and information—is being developed to support the company's worldwide business objectives. Open systems, interoperability, and client/server computing are key elements in the company's IT future.

# CRITICAL CONNECTIONS   1

## Does Linux's Open-Standard Strategy Have a Chance Against Microsoft?

In August of 1991, Linus Torvalds, then a young computer science student in his home country of Finland, placed an announcement on the World Wide Web that he intended to create a universal computer-operating system. Moreover, he indicated that since this was merely a hobby, he would make it available for free. In October, he released the operating system, which he dubbed Linux 0.01. With the announcement, Torvalds asked other programmers to lend a hand, contributing enhancements and modifications that would make the system more workable.

By December 1991, Torvalds had so many submissions from innovative programmers from all over the world that he released Linux 0.1, the number signifying enhancement to the still young operating system. Linux had been born—and with it the global programmer community's interest in creating a continually evolving open-source operating system skyrocketed. The system would be available for Intel-based computers, Apple Macintosh, and other computer brands.

Several software vendors, such as Red Hat and Caldera became involved. They bundled the Linux operating system with graphical interfaces and other useful applications. Versions of Linux operating on a client PC and on servers were widely available. In fact, experts have repeatedly shown that Linux on a server outperforms Windows server software and other operating systems (such as UNIX) when running on the same model computers.

Today there are thousands of applications running on Linux worldwide, including those featuring the most popular Internet protocols as well as e-mail.

So, even as information technology is aiding individuals and organizations to be more innovative, IT professionals are continually seeking more creative ways to develop software. The most promising innovation at the moment is the dramatic shift from the traditional view of software development as a craft to an approach known as software assembly that makes use of the principles of software reuse and object-oriented design.

## Shifting Development Model

The analogy of how a building is constructed illustrates the differences between the craft and component approaches to information systems development (Figure 11.1).

**Craft Approach**   Under the *craft approach*, a builder determines the size and principal features of the building (number of rooms, size of each room, height of ceilings, number of windows, location of doors, type of flooring, and so on). Then each item needed to construct the building is prepared: Lumber is cut to the right size to create the frame, rafters, and beams (the structures supporting floors, walls, and ceilings).

The crafting continues as more visible features are designed. The size and appearance of each door are determined by considering how the room will be used and what items will be moved into and out of it. The size and appearance of windows are also deliberately chosen. Then the doors and windows are crafted from pieces of wood and glass (or whatever other materials are preferred). The process continues, step by step, until every item needed for the building project is identified, designed, crafted, and installed.

A crafted design provides a custom result with interesting individualized details. The problem with this approach is that it is both time-consuming and expensive. That is why the craft approach was abandoned for most construction in the industrialized world in favor of the assembly approach.

**Assembly Approach**   In the construction industry today, the norm is the *assembly* of buildings based on extensive use of *components*.[1] The erection of a building starts with a model outlining the structure's principal dimensions and features. Working from that model, contractors and subcontractors add key elements incrementally. Selections are made from catalogs of *predesigned* components: windows, doors, lighting fixtures, cabinets, and flooring (even the most lavish custom-designed facilities draw heavily on

**FIGURE 11.1**

### *Home Building Via Craft Approach Versus Assembly Approach*

For the craft approach, craftsmen make, by hand, each element of the roof. Under the assembly approach, preconstructed components are selected and lifted into place when needed.

[1] *Component method* here does not refer to prefabricated construction, in which all needed items are preselected, precut, and delivered together from a single source. The builder using the component method still chooses individual components and arranges to acquire them, possibly from a variety of sources.

components). Few elements are created from scratch. Since crafting special components is extremely expensive and time-consuming, builders only craft custom components when catalog options are unsatisfactory. If that is the case, careful advance scheduling is essential in order to avoid delays on other parts of the project.

The component-based modern construction industry suggests several practices that may be advantageous to IT professionals when they are creating information systems:

- *Division of labor* or the specialization of activities.
- *Purchasing standardized components* from outside suppliers rather than crafting them individually.
- *Hiring specialized experts* to do substantial parts of the work.

As the assembly approach to IT becomes more widespread in businesses, the development of information systems will change in this direction.

**object**
A component that contains data about itself and how it is to be processed.

**Objects** are components that are further refined. Objects contain data about themselves—data that tell how the object is to be processed. IT professionals term this feature *encapsulation,* meaning that the object includes information describing both the data and how the data are processed.

The *Information Technology in Practice* feature, "At Reuters, Objects Aid Accuracy and Business Growth," describes how a 140-year-old news agency is capitalizing on object-oriented design principles to build IT applications.

## Building IT with Components

When the concept of components is adapted to the IT world, components become functional units that can be plugged into a framework or surface, such as desktop windows (Figure 11.2). Individual components can be added incrementally to augment the application's utility. Each component can be inserted into the framework at the desired place. For example, the icon for a spreadsheet program can be dragged to the desired location or window on the computer user's desktop (the way a door can be inserted into a building at the desired location in a chosen wall).

One sign that the component approach is gaining ground in the IT environment is the appearance of program-generation tools that enable the designer to specify boxes and option groups (Figure 11.3) without needing to write the program code to use them. Other examples are business elements (purchase orders and invoices) and control elements (such as communications interfaces) of desktop software packages. Just around the corner are catalogs containing hundreds of prewritten and packaged components available to developers (whose jobs will increasingly focus on assembly of programs and applications).

**FIGURE 11.2**

*Design Tools Allow Developers to Insert Application Components into a Window*

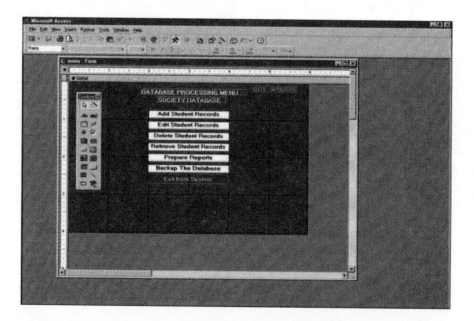

# INFORMATION TECHNOLOGY IN PRACTICE

## At Reuters, Objects Aid Accuracy and Business Growth

**REUTERS** Reuters, a century-and-a-half-old independent global news agency, provides information to financial and news organizations around the world: text, graphics, photographs, and video clips. Its customers use that information to make multimillion-dollar investment decisions. An investor in Tokyo, for instance, may rely heavily on an online display of information retrieved from the Reuters system to determine whether to acquire a large block of stocks recently issued for public sale. Or a television producer in France may incorporate a Reuters report on falling prices on Le Bourse (the Paris Stock Exchange) into its nightly business news. Business-persons like these expect the information supplied by Reuters to be both accurate and reliable. Customer confidence is essential to the company's image; accuracy and reliability are critical components of the Reuters system.

More than 200,000 individuals in over 125 countries use the Reuters system. Reuters does not aim to just pass along well-presented information to these subscribers. Much of the information the agency transmits comes from various independent sources, and Reuters believes that to fully serve its customers, it must ensure that the information is accurate.

To guarantee reliability while at the same time ensuring that its systems can be adjusted quickly as trading and investment rules change, Reuters chose an object-oriented design. Here is how the systems work for investment activities.

Objects are types of investment instruments: securities, interest-bearing notes, derivatives, and so on. The data describing the investment are part of an object, as are the type of activity involving the object and its origin. Hence, a derivative object (a type of investment) will include details to identify that it was traded as an option (a type of derivative) at a specific time on, say, the Paris Bourse. Reuters also designed the object to contain rules that are used to ensure the details are correct. Some are quite simple: The bid price at which an institution will buy shares must be less than the ask price. Others are more complicated, perhaps describing the manner in which a night trade (occurring after the exchange closes) is reported or specifying how to validate a complex trade, such as a put or call option.

Whenever Reuters receives information on an investment transaction, the system processes it using the rules contained in the object relating to that type of transaction. The built-in processing logic helps validate the transaction for Reuters, ensuring that the agency will pass along only accurate information to its subscribers. Because the system has an object-oriented design, whenever rules change, the IT professionals responsible for the system need only change the object involved—which is much easier than having to check an entire system for possible adjustments to procedures. The object-oriented design helps both Reuters and its customers build their businesses. After all, that is what business IT is all about.

| Icon | Tool Name | Control Purpose on a Form or Report |
|------|-----------|-------------------------------------|
| | **Select Objects** | Select, move, size, and edit controls |
| | **Label** | Display text, such as a title or instructions; an unbound control |
| | **Text Box** | Display a label attached to a text box that contains a bound control or a calculated control |
| | **Option Group** | Display a group frame containing toggle buttons, option buttons, or check boxes; can use Control Wizards to create |
| | **Toggle Button** | Signal if a situation is true (button is selected or pushed down) or false |
| | **Option Button** | Signal if a situation is true (black dot appears in the option button's center) or false; also called a radio button |
| | **Check Box** | Signal if a situation is true (X appears in the check box) or false |
| | **Combo Box** | Display a drop-down list box, so that you can either type a value or select a value from the list; can use Control Wizards to create |
| | **List Box** | Display a list of values from which you can choose one value; can use Control Wizards to create |

Using the option tool in Microsoft Access allows the designer to create an option component for processing

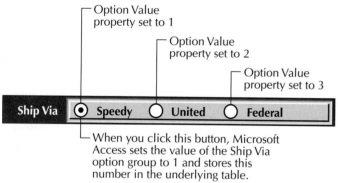

Option Value
property set to 1

Option Value
property set to 2

Option Value
property set to 3

Ship Via   ⦿ Speedy   ○ United   ○ Federal

When you click this button, Microsoft Access sets the value of the Ship Via option group to 1 and stores this number in the underlying table.

**FIGURE 11.3**

***Object Design Tools Enable Developers to Specify System Components***

A sample of object design tools included in the Microsoft Access database system.

## Managing the Development Process

The development of enterprise systems is an important business activity because of the challenges it presents to the firm. When a firm embarks on a shared system development project, it must keep in mind the following points:

1. An enterprise is dependent on IT for its success.
2. Introducing a new system means introducing a change to the enterprise.
3. Shared systems mean multiple viewpoints.
4. IT can create a competitive edge—or take it away.
5. Systems analysts (Chapter 2) must understand the needs of enterprise, but managers and users must also understand the needs of systems analysts.
6. Both systems analysts and users must anticipate problems that can arise with the new system.

7. Systems analysts must design the system to use the computer and communications capabilities available within (or that can be acquired by) the organization.

Every development project must be managed well to achieve the desired results. Even a company that does a good job generally of managing projects can fail if it does not pay attention to the details of the specific project, as the ill-fated Confirm project described in the previous chapter shows. Using the right tools (at the right time) is essential to the development process.

# The Systems Analyst's Tools and Techniques

**Systems analysts** use a variety of techniques to collect data, including interviews, questionnaires, document examination, observation, and sampling. They also use tools like system flowcharts, dataflow diagrams, data dictionaries, and computer-aided system engineering to describe systems and document business processes. All of these techniques and tools help systems analysts become more productive and effective and deliver a better final product.

## Data Collection Techniques

To assemble the details needed to determine system requirements, analysts use any combination of five data collection techniques: interviews, questionnaires, document examination, observation, and sampling.

1. **Interviews**   Analysts conduct interviews with a variety of persons (managers, staff members, employees, customers, and suppliers) to gather details about business processes. Interviews give the analyst the opportunity to learn why current procedures are followed and to hear suggestions for improvements. In a **structured interview,** the analyst prepares the questions in advance and asks each interviewee the same set of questions. In an **unstructured interview,** the analyst may also prepare questions in advance, but will often vary the line of questioning according to the participants' background and the answers they give to preceding questions. Unstructured interviews encourage interviewees to bring up ideas or worries that do not fit into any structured area of questioning.

2. **Questionnaires**   When an analyst must contact a large group of people, **questionnaires** can be a useful way to collect factual information and opinions. Analyzing the responses should give the analyst important insights into the system or business process and often identifies individuals who should be interviewed.

3. **Document Examination**   Analysts should recognize that a great deal of important information already exists in company documents. **Document examination,** also called **record inspection,** is the review of manuals, reports, and correspondence about the system or opportunity under investigation. By inspecting samples of sales slips, order forms, and worksheets, analysts can also learn a great deal about how work is done and how errors are made.

4. **Observation**   If a systems analyst wants to know what steps an employee takes in performing a task, how long a task takes, or whether prescribed procedures are easy to use and work as expected, **observation**—actually watching the activities take place—may be the best way of collecting information. This technique often reveals information that cannot be obtained in any other way.

5. **Sampling**   With **sampling,** the analyst collects data and information at prescribed intervals, or may meet with some of the system's users to get a sense of the effectiveness of current procedures. For example, a sample of 10 percent of the staff that interact directly with customers may tell the analyst a great deal about the views held by the entire staff. Or the analyst could decide to examine one out of every 10 orders to determine the kinds of items that are typically ordered and in what quantity.

**systems analyst**
The IT professional responsible for working with users to determine a system's requirements and for describing the features needed in the system.

**structured interview**
An interview in which the questions are prepared in advance and each interviewee is asked the same set of questions.

**unstructured interview**
An interview in which the questions may be prepared in advance, but follow-up questions vary, depending on the interviewees' background and answers.

**questionnaire**
A sheet of questions used to collect facts and opinions from a group of people.

**document examination/ record inspection**
The review of company documents about a system or opportunity under investigation.

**observation**
The process of watching an activity take place to collect information about that activity.

**sampling**
The process of collecting data and information at prescribed intervals.

Any of these techniques can yield valuable information about systems requirements. Most analysts use a combination of them to gain the best information possible.

Recall the UPS example in Chapter 10. The example describes a wireless network that enables the staff at a company facility to communicate with its drivers (and vice versa) whenever the need arises. If you were the analyst responsible for developing the UPS wireless system, what details would you have wanted and how would you have collected them? You probably would have used all of the data collection techniques just described to gather the system information you needed. You might have conducted structured interviews with drivers, distribution center employees, and managers to determine the biggest problems in tracking and delivering packages. You might also have conducted unstructured interviews to solicit personal observations, opinions, and suggestions for capitalizing on previously unrecognized opportunities or responding to challenging problems.

In addition, you might have used questionnaires to survey a large number of people (including employees, customers, and suppliers) on very specific questions. Likes, dislikes, and the appropriateness of policies and procedures are among the issues you might have addressed through questionnaires.

Riding with drivers and working with distribution personnel would have given you firsthand information about the nature of these people's jobs and the situations they encounter daily. Observing the tasks they perform, the routines they follow, and the time it takes them to complete specific planned and unplanned tasks would have given you valuable insights into productivity.

Using the techniques of record inspection and sampling, you would have examined shipping notices and airbills as well as customer account records. These techniques would have allowed you to see which types of customers ship packages most often and on what days activities are heaviest.

Of course, your entire investigation would probably have begun with a review of UPS' written procedures and policies describing the handling of packages.

## System Flowcharts

**system flowchart**
A graphical description of a business process or procedure using standard symbols to show decision logic.

Of all of the systems analyst's tools, system flowcharts are the easiest to use and understand. A **system flowchart** is a graphical description of a business process or procedure that uses standard symbols to show (1) the sequence of activities that take place in a process; (2) the data, information, or documents that are input to the process or generated (output) as a result of the process; and (3) the decisions that are made at each point in the process. Figure 11.4 describes the most commonly used symbols in system flowcharts.

System flowcharts describe *logic*—the decisions made within a process that determine which course of action will be followed. A sample system flowchart for order processing is shown in Figure 11.5. A more complex process would have several different process sequences.

## Dataflow Diagrams

**dataflow diagram (DFD)**
A chart showing the movement of data through a system.

A **dataflow diagram (DFD)** shows the movement of data through a system. The primary emphasis of a DFD is on the flow of data and information between people and processes and the changes that take place within a process. Like a system flowchart, a DFD shows data and information entering, leaving, or stored within the system. Unlike a system flowchart, however, it does not show decision logic. Different documents used within a system are represented in the DFD, but the conditions under which each is used are not. The DFD does not include anything not directly related to the *flow* of data.

DFDs use four symbols: (1) arrows, (2) circles or rounded rectangles, (3) squares, and (4) open rectangles. The functions of each are explained in Figure 11.6. The labels on each DFD symbol describe the system element.

FIGURE 11.4

*Symbols Used in System Flowcharts*

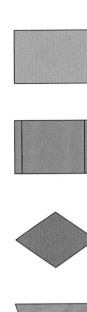

**Process:**
Indicates any processing performed by computer.

**Predefined processing:**
Indicates a process not specifically defined in the flowchart (defined in another flowchart).

**Decision:**
Indicates a point in the process where a decision must be made to determine further action.

**Manual operation:**
Indicates an operation performed off-line.

**Input/output:**
Indicates an input/output operation.

**Document:**
Indicates a printed document (input or output).

**Off-line storage:**
Represents data stored off-line.

**Magnetic disk:**
Represents data stored on magnetic disk.

**Magnetic tape:**
Represents data stored on magnetic tape.

**Communication link:**
Indicates transmission of data by any communication method.

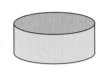
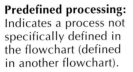

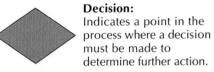
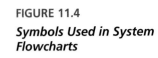

Figure 11.7 is a dataflow diagram illustrating the order and invoice-handling procedure at a well-known mail-order company. Note that it describes the processes but does not indicate when they are performed (for example, every Monday or on the 1st and 15th of each month). Dataflows or *vectors* (arrows) represent groups of data (order, payment, and shipment data), documents (orders, invoices, and other documents), or types of information (management approval/disapproval and so forth). Notice that the dataflows do not indicate *how* the information is carried; they do not tell us whether the information is communicated by telephone, e-mail, or personal messenger. This may surprise you. However, remember that the purpose of a DFD is to describe the movement of data, not the devices causing the movement.

Figure 11.7 shows that customers submit orders and payments (settlement data) to the company. The principal information processes in this system, all identified by numbers, are entering orders (1.0), processing orders (2.0), producing invoices (3.0), posting payments (4.0), and maintaining accounts receivable (5.0). When orders are received from customers, they are approved or disapproved by management. Details of approved orders are processed and recorded in an order log. The order is then prepared in production for shipment. An invoice is also prepared, with one copy serving as a packing slip accompanying the order. Another copy is used in preparing accounts receivable. Periodically, the records of accounts receivable are processed to adjust balances in accordance with payments and finance charges, as well as to provide management with an accounts-receivable report.

**DFD Levels**   There are different levels of dataflow diagrams. A system-level DFD describes an entire system in summary form (Figure 11.7 is a system-level DFD). A second-level DFD *explodes* processes to show more detail. Processes in a second-level DFD may, in turn, be exploded further to show more details and subprocesses. This method of exploding processes in a dataflow diagram to show ever more detail is called

**FIGURE 11.5**

***System Flowchart for Order Processing***

The system flowchart pictured here is used by a retail firm for its catalog sales. The two points in the process at which decisions must be made are indicated by diamond shapes.

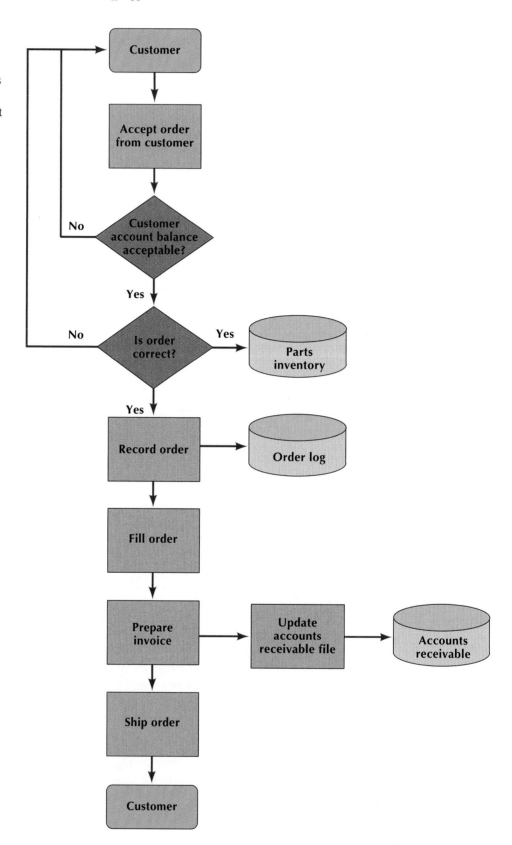

| SYMBOL | MEANING | |
|---|---|---|

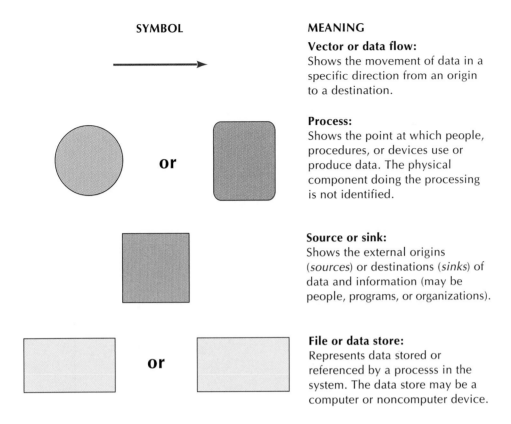

**Vector or data flow:**
Shows the movement of data in a specific direction from an origin to a destination.

**Process:**
Shows the point at which people, procedures, or devices use or produce data. The physical component doing the processing is not identified.

**Source or sink:**
Shows the external origins (*sources*) or destinations (*sinks*) of data and information (may be people, programs, or organizations).

**File or data store:**
Represents data stored or referenced by a processs in the system. The data store may be a computer or noncomputer device.

**FIGURE 11.6**
*Symbols Used in Dataflow Diagrams*

**leveling.** Numbers on each DFD identify the diagram level. Figure 11.8 shows three exploded processes from the DFD in Figure 11.7. DFD 2.1 describes order-handling details, DFD 3.1 shows post-payment processing, and DFD 4.1 describes accounts-receivable processing.

**leveling**
The process of exploding processes in a dataflow diagram to show more detail.

## Data Dictionaries

When system analysts develop dataflow diagrams, they also typically create a **data dictionary** (sometimes called a **repository**), which is a catalog that lists and describes all of the types of data flowing through a system. A data dictionary used in dataflow analysis contains the following two components: data elements and data structures. **Data elements** include data names, alternate names (aliases), and length allowances. The set of data elements used together and the name that collectively identifies the set is the **data structure.**

For example, look at the word *invoice.* Although this word has a specific meaning in business, the *invoice* data structure may be defined differently from one company to the next. The system in use at a particular company will have a data dictionary that defines the data elements that are included in that company's *invoice* data structure. (Whether *invoice* refers to a paper document or to an electronic format does not matter.) Figure 11.9 shows the data elements used by the Drazien Publishing Company's data dictionary to define *invoice.*

Analysts use data dictionaries for the following five reasons:

1. To manage detail in large systems.
2. To give a common meaning to all system elements.
3. To document the features of a system.
4. To facilitate evaluation of the system and determine where changes should be made.
5. To locate errors and to find omissions.

Because they define the meaning of each data element in a system, data dictionaries are an important accompaniment to DFDs. They are also an integral component of computer-aided systems engineering tools, which are discussed in the next section.

**data dictionary/repository**
A catalog that lists and describes all the types of data flowing through a system. Composed of data elements and a data structure.

**data element**
The component of a data dictionary that includes data names, alternate names, and length allowances.

**data structure**
The set of data elements used together and the name that collectively identifies the set.

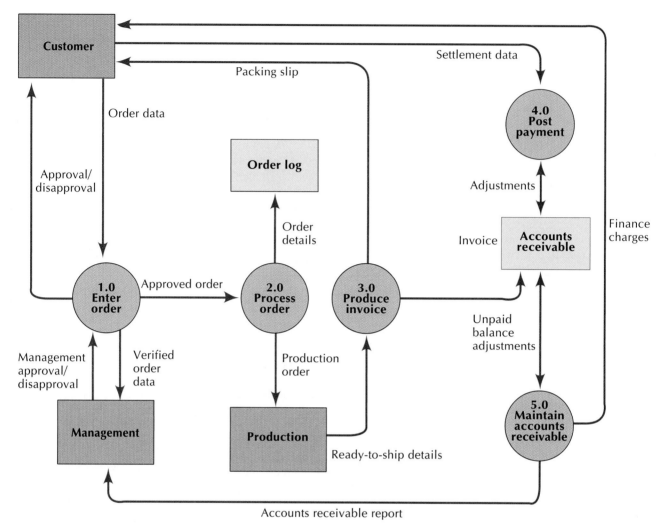

**FIGURE 11.7**

***Dataflow Diagram for Order and Invoice Handling at a Mail-Order Company***

This dataflow diagram includes five principal information processes: 1.0—order entry; 2.0—order processing; 3.0—invoice production; 4.0—posting of payments; and 5.0—maintenance of accounts receivable.

---

 **REALITY CHECK**   If you have ever watched architects at work, you know that they work from blueprints—exact detailed plans for the building they are designing. (The name comes from the white lettering on blue paper.) Every building's design consists of a series of blueprints, from the general to the very specific. Some show the shape of the building and its floor plan; others show locations of electrical outlets and ducts and pipes for heat and air flow.

A quick glance at a blueprint usually leaves those of us outside the profession overwhelmed by the symbols and technical terms. Yet, should you decide to build a house or create a layout for a new office, you can very easily learn what the key symbols and terms on an architect's blueprint mean (e.g., the size of a door, the positioning of windows, and the location of closets and storage areas). Think of system flowcharts and dataflow diagrams in the same way. They may appear quite abstract at first, yet if you learn how to read them, you will find that they provide a great deal of useful information. ■

FIGURE 11.8

*Exploded Dataflow Diagram*

System-level DFDs can be exploded to show more detail and subprocesses.

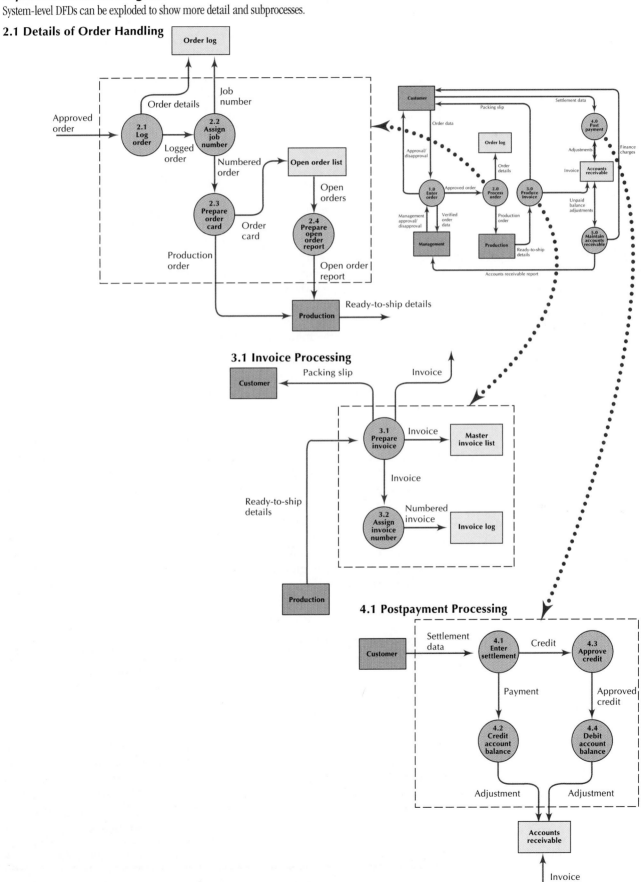

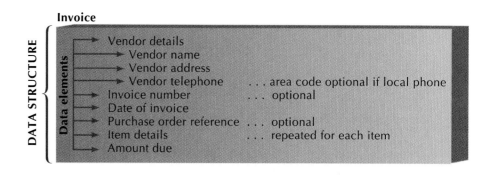

## Computer-Aided Systems Engineering (CASE)

The newest and most powerful tools available to the systems analyst use a computer's vast processing and storage capabilities. These **computer-aided systems engineering** or **computer-aided software engineering** tools, also known as **CASE** tools, are designed to improve the consistency and quality of systems while automating many of the most tedious and time-consuming systems tasks. CASE tools are used both to develop systems and to design the system's software.

The characteristics, capabilities, and components of CASE tools vary among the different brands available for purchase, some of which are listed in Table 11.1. However, most CASE tools contain the following features:

- **Charting and Diagramming Tools**   Because systems analysts spend a great deal of time analyzing data and processes, CASE tools typically include the capability to produce dataflow programs (both system-level and exploded views), data structure diagrams, and system flowcharts.
- **Centralized Information Repository**   A *centralized information repository* is a dictionary containing the details of all system components (data items, dataflows, and processes). The repository also includes information describing the frequency and volume of each activity. For example, if analysts need to know the high and low estimates of the number of invoices likely to be processed on a given day, they can retrieve the information from the central repository.
- **Interface Generators**   Recall that an *interface* is the means by which a person interacts with a computer. *Graphical interfaces,* such as those used by Microsoft Windows, or the Apple Macintosh, employ pictures and images. *Text interfaces,* such as those used in the many digital library systems on college and university campuses, employ keywords and phrases to instruct the system in processing. Interface genera-

| Table 11.1   Leading CASE Tools | |
| --- | --- |
| **CASE TOOL** | **DISTRIBUTED BY** |
| EasyCASE Professional for Windows | Visible Systems |
| PowerDesigner | Sybase |
| Rational Software | IBM |
| System Architect | Popkin Software and Systems, Inc. |
| Tau | Teleogic |
| Visible Analyst | Visible Systems Corp. |
| Visual Paradigm for UML | Visual Paradigm Software |

tors provide the capability to prepare sample user interfaces so that the creator can examine their features before composing the final version. Interface generators allow analysts to present and evaluate many different interfaces and to make changes quickly and easily.

- **Code Generators**  These tools automate the preparation of computer software. Although code generators are not yet perfected, many automate 75 to 80 percent of the computer programming needed to create a new system or application.
- **Project Management Tools**  As discussed previously, development projects must be carefully managed to ensure that all tasks are completed properly and on time. Project management tools enable the project manager to schedule analysis and design activities, allocate people and other resources to each task, monitor schedules and personnel, and print schedules and reports summarizing the project's status. Figure 11.10 summarizes the features of CASE tools.

**Front-End, Back-End, and Integrated CASE**  As Figure 11.11 shows, CASE tools are often categorized by the systems development life cycle (SDLC) activities they support. **Front-end CASE tools** automate the early (front-end) activities in systems development—namely, requirements determination and systems design. In these early phases, they help analysts describe process characteristics and record and analyze dataflows and processes. Front-end CASE tools' built-in charting capabilities relieve the analyst of the important but time-consuming task of drawing dataflow diagrams.

**Back-end CASE tools** automate the later (back-end) activities in systems development, developing detailed information from general system descriptions. Some back-end CASE tools are code generators, translation tools, and testing tools.

**Integrated CASE (I-CASE) tools** span activities throughout the entire SDLC. They incorporate analysis, logical design, code generation, and database generation capabilities while maintaining an automated data dictionary. I-CASE is actually a family of tools, all accessible from the same computer program and display screen. A sample I-CASE screen is shown in Figure 11.12.

Because of the complexity of integrating all of the activities of the SDLC, only a few integrated CASE tools have been created. However, more integrated tools will probably

**front-end CASE tool**
A CASE tool that automates the early (front-end) activities in systems development.

**back-end CASE tool**
A CASE tool that automates the later (back-end) activities in systems development.

**integrated CASE (I-CASE) tool**
A CASE tool that spans activities throughout the entire systems development life cycle.

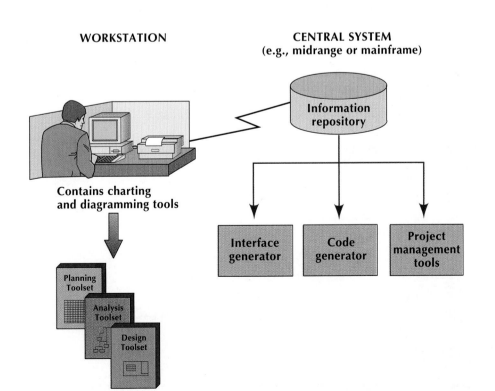

**WORKSTATION**

**CENTRAL SYSTEM**
(e.g., midrange or mainframe)

Contains charting and diagramming tools

Information repository

Interface generator

Code generator

Project management tools

Planning Toolset

Analysis Toolset

Design Toolset

**FIGURE 11.10**

***CASE Tool Features***

Although the capabilities of CASE tools differ among the packages available for purchase, most contain the features shown here.

**SEQUENCE OF SYSTEMS DEVELOPMENT ACTIVITIES**

**Front-end development**                                                    **Back-end development**

| Analysis ——————— Design ——————— | Development and Construction ——————— | Implementation ——————— | Evaluation and Continuing Evolution |

(Preliminary investigation)
(Requirements determination)

**Front-end CASE tools**
Analysis tools
Charting tools
Tools for logical design

**Back-end CASE tools**
Code generator tools
Translation tools
Testing tools

**Integrated CASE tools**

**FIGURE 11.11**

*Types of CASE Tools*

emerge as IT professionals continue their quest for tools that link all the activities associated with systems development.

# Unified Modeling Language

As discussed earlier in this chapter, the use of components are building blocks in the construction of buildings and software. Of course, it is easy to see that no one would dream of undertaking the construction of a building (whether using components or not) without blueprints to guide those working on the project. Can you imagine what would result if a contractor tried to construct an office tower without detailed drawings of the design? Any contractor would want drawings of the building's structure, its electrical wiring, and its plumbing. Moreover, the blueprints would use standardized symbols and systems to note important details for the contractors to read.

For the same reason, many information technology developers rely on the widely accepted design method, **unified modeling language (UML).** UML has become the standard vehicle for visualizing, describing, and documenting the details of an IT application. While systems analysts invest a great deal of time becoming familiar with the features of UML, it is useful to describe some of the most important components used in constructing an IT application. The following section looks at actors, activity diagrams, use case diagrams, use case descriptions, and class diagrams.

**unified modeling language (UML)**
The standard vehicle for visualizing, describing, and documenting the details of an IT application.

**FIGURE 11.12**

*Display Screens of I-CASE Tools*

Display contents are specified and arranged using the screen design tool. Modeling components enable developers to communicate designs using free-form modeling. References across models are dynamically updated. Data and process specifications are embedded within the models.

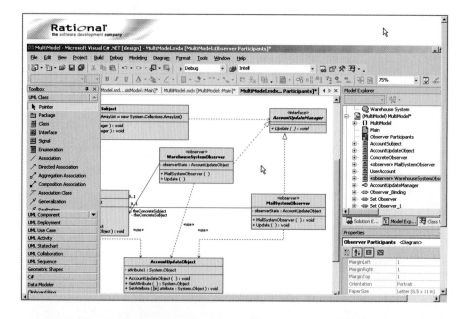

 **REALITY CHECK** Although CASE tools offer many valuable features and can assist the systems analyst in myriad ways, they are not a substitute for a good systems analyst. A great deal of the analyst's work is based on understanding what questions to ask, deciding when to probe more deeply into a business situation, and knowing which people to contact and how to get information. Systems design is a creative activity: It takes insight and innovative ideas to produce a well-designed application, and these are not qualities that can be automated. Automated tools will not replace good analysts, but they can make good analysts even better and more effective. ■

## Actors

As you recall from the preceding sections, structured analysis methods and CASE tools do not focus on the people who play a role in a system. UML, on the other hand, explicitly identifies **actors,** *anyone or anything* that will interact with the application. Hence one of the questions an analyst must ask during the analysis and design of an application is, *Who or what will inter<u>act</u> with the system?* The actor is *outside* the system, and may be an individual performing a specific role or even another application. Actors will *trigger* the system, perhaps by initiating a transaction or retrieving something from the system.

Graphically, actors are represented as stick figures. Each is labeled according to the role it plays, uniquely distinguishing it from other actors.

In Figure 11.13, actors include the following:

- **Customer** An individual who purchases and pays for a product or returns a product for credit.
- **Order Fulfillment System** The set of activities that accepts and processes orders or returns from customers.
- **Accounts Receivable System** The set of activities that processes payments submitted by customers.

Each interacts with the three activities within the boundary of the system, that is, to (1) buy items, (2) return items, and (3) pay for items.

## Activity Diagrams

**Activity diagrams** show the flow of control in an application. They consist of actions (represented by rounded rectangles) that transition to the next action when the first is completed. Unlike dataflow diagrams, they focus on *activities* rather than data. Arrows show the transition from one activity to the next. Actions can occur individually or in

**actor**
Anyone or anything that will interact with the application.

**activity diagram**
Shows the flow of control in an application.

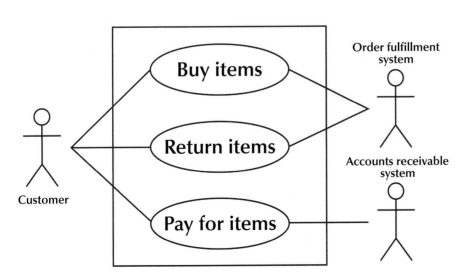

**FIGURE 11.13**

***Actors in Mail Order Use CASE***

parallel. For instance, Figure 11.14 shows the activities that make it possible for customers to make purchases. The system's processing of orders depends on the preparation of product catalogs that are mailed to customers and also posted on the enterprise Web site.

How do activity diagrams differ from the flowcharts discussed earlier? You can use an activity chart early in the analysis process to determine what activities are occurring, and later in the design process to describe the actions that must occur. The diagrams need not be developed at the detailed level of a programming flowchart, nor do they need to show decision or processing logic as is common in system flowcharts.

## Use Case Diagrams

**use case**

Identifies the sequence of activities performed for an actor.

A **use case** identifies the sequence of activities performed for an actor. An effective way of identifying use cases is to study each of the actors, asking the question, *Why does this actor want to use the application?* In a commercial setting, their roles may vary from, say, customers who buy products and services through the system, to sales agents who enter transactions, to an accounting system that tracks payments and receipts. In a university system, the actors might be students who register for courses, registrars who maintain the schedule of courses offered during a specific term, and the course-registration system.

**use case diagram**

Provides context for the system, illustrating the actors, the use cases, and the flow or interaction between use cases and actors.

Graphically, a *use case* is illustrated as an oval. Use cases are documented in two ways: as a use case diagram and as a use case description. A **use case diagram** provides context for the system, illustrating the actors, the use cases, and the flow or interaction between use cases and actors. It also shows what is inside the system and what is outside,

**FIGURE 11.14**

*Activity Diagram Showing Flow of Control*

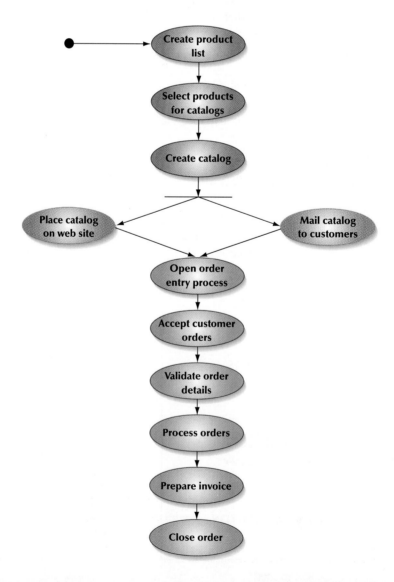

while providing a model of what a system does to satisfy a request. Typical system boundaries might include an IT application, a work group, a department, or an entire enterprise. In Figure 11.13, the actors (customer, order fulfillment system, and accounts receivable system) interact with the system activities of *buy items, return items,* and *pay for items*). Arrows identify the specific action/system interaction.

## Use Case Description

A **use case description** (Figure 11.15) describes the use case in ordinary language, including its identifying name and actors. It also includes the typical course of actions and the system response to each action. Developers may include cross-references to other diagrams as well.

Figure 11.15 is a use case description for the *customer transaction*. It also includes the typical course of events—the system response for each of the three actor activities.

**use case description**
Describes the use case in ordinary language, including its identifying name and actors.

## Class Diagrams

Object classes were discussed in Chapter 7 as part of the discussion of enterprise databases. In UML, **class diagrams** describe an object class, including the class name, attributes, and methods. Figure 11.16 includes class diagrams for the customer and order object classes. The diagram identifies the class and includes attributes and actions (methods) for each class.

**class diagram**
Describes an object class, including the class name, attributes, and methods.

## Other UML Diagrams

UML includes a variety of other diagram specifications that can be used according to the needs and preferences of systems developers. Among these alternatives are the following:

- **Sequence Diagram**  Shows the interaction of objects, arranged in time sequence. Sequence diagrams illustrate the steps carried out in completing an activity or process.
- **State Transition Diagram**  Shows the life cycle of an object, indicating how it changes as a result of different events within the system. State transition diagrams can

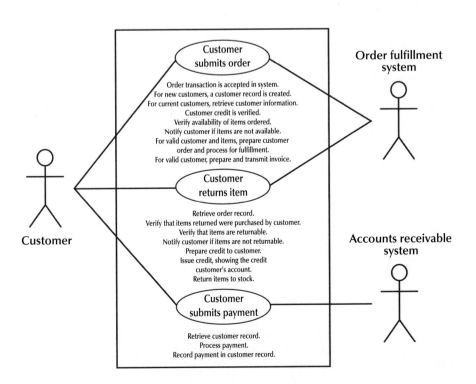

**Customer transaction**

**FIGURE 11.15**
*Use Case Description*

**FIGURE 11.16**

*Class Descriptions for Customer and Order Objects*

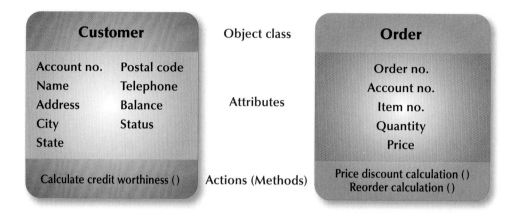

also be applied to use cases and to classes at a high level (that is, a general level) or at a very detailed level, comparable to that needed for describing processing logic in computer source code.

- **Component Diagram**   Shows the dependency between system components (for example, the necessary use of selected software components to complete an activity).

While this book will not discuss UML in detail, it is important to recognize that this language can be extended, with systems developers adding other diagrams and symbols that will assist them in analyzing use requirements, documenting an existing system, or designing a new application.

## Automation of UML

Although UML can be used manually—where developers keep track of actors, and create and maintain use cases and the many descriptive diagrams—it is more effective when automated. Systems developers in most moderate and large-size enterprises use an automated version of UML (an IT application) that relies on computer processing and storage of the details, and their sharing among developers who are interconnected through intranets or other forms of computer networks.

Automated UML tools are very helpful because they store and process the system descriptions. They also routinely check for missing information (such as an actor referenced in one part of the application that has not been defined in the system), inconsistent references to activity diagrams, or use cases that are never referenced in the system. You can imagine the value of having these types of validation and processing activities performed quickly, automatically, and consistently. After all, blueprints for IT applications, like those for office towers, are only useful if they are accurate and reliable.

The *Information Technology in Practice* feature, "Ceridian's Object Methods Deliver ResponsePlus.Net Ahead of Schedule," describes how this human-resources service company used a well-known automated UML tool in a complex two-year development project, bringing it in ahead of schedule.

# IT Development Personnel

Because systems analysts are the central people in the development of enterprise IT applications, this chapter has focused on their activities. This section takes a closer look at the job they do, the roles they play, and the skills that are critical to their success. This chapter also discusses the other IT professionals with whom systems analysts work—the chief information officer, computer programmers, and outside contractors.

## The Systems Analyst: The Key Roles

Systems analysts play several roles. As noted, they play a major *development role* in analyzing enterprise activities and formulating solutions. However, they also play an important *facilitating role*. Good analysts recognize the value of eliciting information from

# INFORMATION TECHNOLOGY IN PRACTICE

## Ceridian's Object Methods Deliver ResponsePlus.Net Ahead of Schedule

Ceridian Corp., headquartered in Minneapolis, is one of the leading human-resource service companies in the United States. It frees up companies to succeed in their primary area of business by providing innovative managed business solutions in the areas of human-resource management, payroll, tax filing, time and attendance management, benefits administration, and employee effectiveness services.

At one time the company, which operates in more then 20 metropolitan areas across the United States, could be described as a distributed enterprise. Each office operated individually, almost as independent businesses. Ceridian's IT was characterized by multiple customer databases, with offices using different computing platforms.

Ceridian management determined that it could improve customer service, address growing competitive challenges, and streamline operating activities if it integrated the diverse business systems, redesigned legacy systems, and used the capabilities of the Internet where appropriate. A project manager was appointed and an enterprise development team created for the multi-year project and the application known as ResponsePlus.net. The project team of developers, analysts, and software testers, was itself distributed. Team members resided in four different locations—in the Northeast, Northwest, Upper Midwest, and Southeast.

Working from the overall requirement of creating a single,

uniform customer database (1) shared by all Ceridian locations, (2) interconnected with the other appropriate enterprise systems, and (3) accessible from PCs running Microsoft Windows, the team began with a blank slate. It was up to the team to decide which tools, methods, and technologies (including programming and object languages) to use in defining detail requirements and meeting project objectives.

Because of the size and scope of the project and the location of its members, the ResponsePlus.net team decided to use an automated development tool. It also determined that taking an object-oriented approach and creating reusable components would prove highly beneficial. Since many of the team members were already familiar with the Rational Rose design tool (widely used by IT professionals), it was adopted as the object tool for the project. Other companion tools from Rational

software were also used as needed.

Before the team could proceed, it had to get a handle on detailed requirements for ResponsePlus.net. It quickly decided that applying the UML and creating and capturing use cases in a repository was the most efficient way to identify and track requirements across Ceridian offices. Having the automated tools proved to be highly beneficial as the number of requirements in the repository grew and evolved during the investigation. Since the repository was online, team members could share details regardless of their geographic location.

As the requirements became clear and the team moved to the development phase, members foresaw that they would dramatically reduce development time by several months if they created both their application models and data models using Rationale Rose. In turn, they were confident the software source code for the application

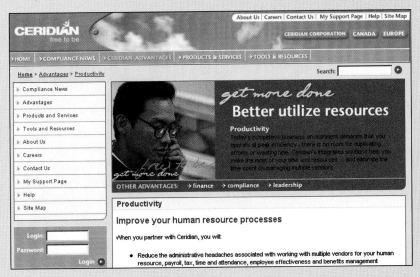

could be generated automatically. The data modeling tool proved especially useful, as the data structures contained especially complex parent/child entity relationships, often consisting of many levels of relationships. Team members modeled the relationships as different object classes in Rational Rose. The models in turn helped them determine the structure of the database they would later create.

As the team began building its own objects, it relied on its software tools and the models for generation of code, with great success. In the first three months of the project, the team generated source code for more than 300 objects, each with several stored proce-

dures (such as for adding, changing, deleting, or translating documents). Even more important, the automated tools ensured that the objects used consistent data names, regardless of which team member was overseeing the code generation. Testing of the code was efficient because team members could focus on processing logic rather than on resolving inconsistent data names. Moreover, when changes were necessary, the code could be regenerated from the stored modeling information.

When the project was completed, more than 750,000 lines of source code were generated in appropriate languages (such as Visual Basic, C++, SQL, and XML).

Automatic generation accounted for some 90 percent of the total software needed for the project.

The Ceridian team successfully completed a complex project of nearly two-years duration that required creation of a new database, replacement of five legacy systems, and integration with other standing IT applications. In a world where even moderate scale projects are often late and over budget, the fact that the Ceridian team brought the system in ahead of schedule and under budget is ample evidence of the benefits that result from equipping well-trained, committed team members with the right development tools.

people who will use IT to perform a job or manage a business process. These people, in fact, are the best sources of information about problems, solutions, and obstacles to solutions. Part of the analyst's job, then, is to facilitate the exchange of this information.

Developing and implementing information technology means change. People need to learn new or altered work processes (and perhaps even new computer and communications systems), and they must take on different responsibilities. Although change can be exciting, people often resist it, particularly if they do not see a reason for the change. Thus, the systems analyst's role also includes the vitally important one of **change agent.** In this role, the analyst acts as a catalyst for change and as a liaison among different parties involved in the creation and implementation of change.

The change agent's role is often depicted in the form of a three-step model (Figure 11.17). These three steps are (1) *unfreeze*—communicate with people about the reason for change to reduce potential resistance; (2) *change*—implement new activities, procedures, and applications; and (3) *refreeze*—ensure that people accept and use the new processes and procedures. In each of these roles, the systems analyst is directly involved in the business. Developing IT application systems, therefore, demands knowledge about the enterprise activities in which the applications will be used and how these systems can be changed to meet the enterprise's needs.

**change agent**
A person who acts as a catalyst for change.

**FIGURE 11.17**

***Model of Change Agent's Role***

In addition to working as a change agent, systems analysts play a development role and a facilitating role.

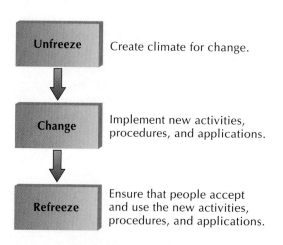

Unfreeze — Create climate for change.

Change — Implement new activities, procedures, and applications.

Refreeze — Ensure that people accept and use the new activities, procedures, and applications.

The end-of-chapter *Case Study*, "WiPro Sets Pace for Indian IT Application Development," describes the increasing interest in outsourcing the development of enterprise software. Within IT organizations, this tendency creates a significant change compared to traditional practices. However, implementation of outsourcing within an enterprise can fail if the systems developers are not supportive of the change.

As another example, consider professional sports. In the United States (and in Japan), the national pastime is baseball. In Europe and South America, it is soccer. Throughout the world, professional sports have become big business. Many teams not only use IT to manage their business but also employ IT professionals—including systems analysts.

Systems analysts in the baseball business have to know about more than computers, communications systems, and software if they are to contribute to the success of their organization. They also have to know the *business* of baseball and be prepared to change the hardware and software they use whenever a change is necessary to support the players, coaches, and team managers.

Take the Los Angeles Dodgers. The Dodgers' information technology department (yes, the team has an IT department, as do most major league teams) is responsible for maintaining applications that keep track of the more than 300 major and minor league players throughout the Dodger organization. Each player is accounted for as a company asset. When the team acquires a player, its accounting system is adjusted to add him to the organization's list of assets. When another player is traded, a different transaction takes place. As the players' value to the organization changes, the records are adjusted to show this change in the asset value.

The Dodgers' systems analysts have also repeatedly modified the team's IT applications to handle new business practices: multiyear signing bonuses, salaries paid over many years (even after the player has retired or moved on to another team), special injury clauses, and incentive bonuses (paid for achieving a specified performance level).

**Professional Skills**   The most successful systems analysts have these five professional skills: (1) problem-solving skills, (2) the ability to focus on outcome, (3) creativity, (4) the ability to plan and run meetings, and (5) excellent interpersonal communication skills.

**Problem Solving**   The problem-solving process, introduced in Chapter 1, seeks to close the gap between the current situation and the situation that is desired. Analysts play a key role in initiating the process by asking, *What is wrong?*, *What is the cause of the problem?*, and *What is the effect?*

**Outcome Thinking**   Good analysts complement their problem-solving skills with an ability to focus on outcome. They do this by asking: *What result is desired?*, *Forgetting about constraints for a moment, what is the ideal result?*, or *What is your vision of the way things should be?* This emphasis on outcome has the virtue of stressing the positive. More importantly, it recognizes the limitations of focusing solely on problems by pushing people to think about possibilities rather than impossibilities.

**Creativity**   Creative people look at the same thing everyone else looks at, but they see something different. To be creative is to generate ideas, and that cannot be done without forgetting about constraints (at least temporarily), relaxing rules, and allowing alternatives to rise to the surface of the mind. Most of us are not born innovators; we do not ordinarily consider ourselves to be highly creative. Yet, we recognize the power of good ideas and know how quickly they can turn a difficult situation into an exciting opportunity.

Good systems designs are often creative designs. UPS' decision to use wireless communications to link drivers to the company's data center was creative. It also made good business sense because it allowed the company to offer new services that benefit customers and add to the company's business.

**Meeting Skills**   Recall that one of a systems analyst's roles is to facilitate information exchange. For this reason, knowing how to plan and run a meeting efficiently is a critical skill in the analyst's repertoire. Good meeting skills determine the value of the information that analysts capture from people involved in the meeting.

Good meetings begin with an agenda of the topics to be addressed and are structured in a way that allows all attendees to participate. Questions must be carefully crafted to elicit the desired information. Effective analysts also find ways to create enthusiasm among a meeting's participants, fostering an atmosphere in which people *want* to participate and share ideas.

Today, more and more meetings are using electronic support tools. Group conferencing networks (discussed in Chapters 8 and 9) tend to foster more interaction among people. In a regular group discussion, only one person speaks at a time, but through a network many people can express their ideas. Electronic meeting tools also keep participants anonymous so that people feel free to speak up without worrying what others will think of their ideas. As the capabilities of these tools continue to evolve, electronic meeting systems are likely to become as important a tool in systems analysis and design as dataflow diagrams and flowcharts are today.

**Communication Skills**   Good communication skills are essential for effective person-to-person discussions. The analyst needs to be able to discuss ideas with users without lapsing into technical jargon and to understand what they are saying while recognizing what they are not saying. Then, the analyst must know how to assemble all of this information. Indeed, the analyst's ability to listen to people and understand their ideas and opinions is critical to the success of shared IT applications. Misstated systems requirements resulting from misunderstandings about business activities account for over half of the reasons that IT applications have to be changed after they have been implemented.

## The Chief Information Officer

**chief information officer (CIO)**

The person given the responsibility of managing and developing the firm's information technology capabilities.

In many businesses, one person is given the responsibility for managing and developing the firm's information technology capabilities. In large organizations, this person is often called the **chief information officer (CIO).** (Some firms use instead the title IT director or director of information systems.) The position generally has the corporate rank of vice president (Figure 11.18). In smaller businesses, the individual responsible for man-

**FIGURE 11.18**

### *Organization Chart for Typical Information Systems Department*
In large organizations, the chief information officer generally holds the rank of corporate vice president.

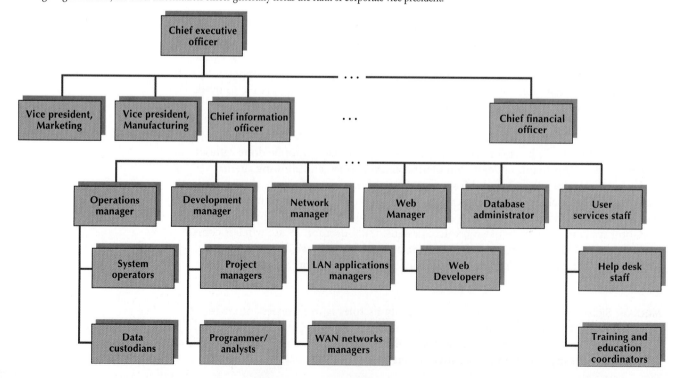

aging and developing the company's capabilities may have additional responsibilities. Hence, it is not uncommon to find IT management come under the controller, finance director, administrative coordinator, or operations manager in a smaller company.

Systems analysts generally work for a CIO or for a director of development, who, in turn, reports to the person responsible for managing the firm's IT capabilities. Communications about the firm's business plans flow to the analyst through these people. The quality of communication can be an important determinant of the firm's effective use of information technology for process or business improvement.

## Computer Programmers

As noted earlier, *programmers* are responsible for turning detailed specifications into computer software that processes data and information effectively and works with other computer programs (computer-operating systems, network-operating systems, database-management systems, etc.). They are also responsible for *documenting* the program, developing written explanations of how and why certain procedures are coded in specific ways and how the system can be used in the business. Analysts and programmers interact continually during the development of a system, usually serving jointly on the project team.

# CRITICAL CONNECTIONS 2

## Colgate-Palmolive: The Right Applications for the Right Time

*Colgate*

Colgate-Palmolive Company, the global consumer products giant headquartered in New York City, New York, was built on the principle of always having the right product for the consumer. Its successful track record, and its well-known brand names including Ajax, Mennen, Softsoap, Hills, Colgate, and Palmolive, have pleased customers for nearly 200 years.

Yet, in today's competitive business world, having the right product is no longer enough. Colgate's new mandate for success—having the right product in the right place at the right time—has changed the way the company conducts its business. Colgate would not be so successful today if its CIO had not ensured that the company integrated information technology into its business processes, for IT plays a pivotal role in the company's relations with customers and in the management of its own manufacturing processes.

The CIO of Colgate oversees the design of essential new information technology applications characterized by electronic links to its major customers. These applications enable it to constantly monitor the sales of its products at such retail giants as Wal-Mart, Kmart, and Target. The systems are designed so that transaction details are transmitted from the store's point-of-sale terminals directly to Colgate. Similar IT applications link Colgate with its key suppliers.

## Systems Contractors

Most large organizations have computer programmers (or programmer/analysts) on permanent staff. Smaller firms often retain outside programming services on a contractual basis.

In some cases, an organization will hire outside consultants to manage the development of a system. This strategy is common when the organization chooses not to assign any of its own personnel to the project or when it determines that it will be more expedient to have a third party handle the development. The term **systems contractor** is used to describe all types of outside personnel who contract with a company to develop IT applications. Some contractors are very small—even one-person shops. Others are worldwide, with offices in many cities.

A particularly important type of systems contractor is the **systems integrator,** an IT professional whose job originated in the recognition that business uses information technology components from a variety of sources and with a diverse set of name plates (hence the importance of interoperability, discussed earlier in this chapter). Systems integrators are retained to take the responsibility for acquiring hardware, software, and network capacity for an application, as well as for implementing that application. They may play any number of roles: consultant, engineer, designer, procurement expert, programmer, system tester, implementer, or maintainer. They may even oversee the ongoing operation of the system. At times, systems integrators develop custom computer programs; at other times, they contract with another firm. Among the best-known systems integrator firms are EDS, Accenture, IBM Global Services, and Computer Sciences Corp. (CSC).

Systems contractors often become experts by gaining years of experience with companies before starting their own consulting firms or joining an established consulting firm. Yet, many others go directly from college into training for IT consulting. Accenture has its own way of educating its more than 45,000 employees about IT. New recruits hired by Accenture (at an average age of 25) spend their first three to four weeks training in the company's local office. Then they head off to one of Accenture's four training centers: St. Charles, Illinois; Manila, the Philippines; Singapore; or Veldhoven, the Netherlands. There they learn Accenture's methodologies for determining systems requirements, developing application specifications, and preparing computer programs.

**systems contractor**
An outside person or firm that contracts with a company to develop IT applications.

**systems integrator**
A type of systems contractor who is retained to take responsibility for acquiring hardware, software, and network capacity for an application, as well as for implementing the application.

# CRITICAL CONNECTIONS 3

## Electronics Giant Sends Its Software Out

**Circuit City**

Circuit City Stores Inc., of Richmond, Virginia, is a large and highly successful electronics retailer. Its people are well informed about the products they sell—thanks partly to Circuit City's back-office systems, which manage the merchandise so that salespeople always know what is in stock in their store as well as in other stores within the region.

Getting good products to sell and keeping salespeople up-to-date have never been problems for Circuit City. However, getting enough good people to create all the application systems in the company's development plan proved just about impossible.

Finally, the company's IT directors faced the reality that in order to meet Circuit City's business needs, they would have to outsource selective computer applications, beginning with an accounting application. The company hired an external contractor, who, in turn, retained programmers working in offices in Bangalore, India, to write the computer code. The outsourcing contractor assumed full responsibility for meeting the specifications provided by Circuit City's IT staff and for on-time delivery at a specified price.

The experience was such a success for Circuit City that the company has incorporated outsourcing into its overall IT development strategy. This has proved to be an excellent way to gain access to high-quality personnel without having to hire them directly.

*Personal people* is an Accenture credo. The firm recognizes that individuals are as different from one another as the countries, cultures, and corporations in which they work. Hence, Accenture seeks to draw out individual differences in its new hires and show them how to turn these personal qualities into strengths when dealing with clients. Trainees also learn valuable business skills: how to interact with clients, how to work on a project team, and how to understand a business or an industry. Not all of the training is technical, however. New hires are often out in the woods near the training center, climbing rope ladders, or planning strategies to make their team a winner in a competitive outdoor game.

Because Accenture sees education as a career-long activity, visits to the four centers are not just for new recruits. Depending on the areas in which they work, Accenture consultants can expect to spend from 300 to 750 hours at one of these facilities every year. Continual improvement is a critical ingredient in the makeup of Accenture consultants and the systems they develop. You, too, should make training a career objective, whether you work as a developer or as a user of information technology.

## A Final Word

Business benefits from IT only when the right combination of information technology is used in the best way for the particular company. Because the combination of IT resources that are most effective for one firm may not be as useful for another, the development process must be managed to ensure that both IT applications and capabilities fit the firm.

## CRITICAL CONNECTIONS

### 1 Part II: Does Linux's Open-Standard Strategy Have a Chance Against Microsoft?

 Linux, the open standard-operating system that grew out of Finnish-born Linus Torvald's hobby, distributed free and enhanced by volunteer programmers, has captured the imagination of the IT community. It is also getting attention from governments and commercial enterprises. The governments of the People's Republic of China, France, and Germany, not wishing to be tied to or overly dependent on Microsoft, actively promote Linux because it is open-source software. A host of other federal governments around the world, as well as U.S. state governments, are starting to adopt Linux in government offices and in schools.

Several large companies have endorsed Linux and are selling computers equipped with the software. For instance, industry leader IBM offers a wide range of computers loaded with Linux. Retailing giant Wal-Mart also sells PCs preloaded with Linux software.

Linux has made the greatest impact as an operating system for servers—in 2003 it was generally estimated to have between from 15 to 20 percent of the market. Moreover, its market share has been rising, even though Microsoft still holds the largest portion of the market. Linux's market share for desktops remains very small, although interest increases each time Microsoft announces the possibility of price increases for its Windows operating system.

Linux creator Linus Torvalds, now a faculty member at MIT (and still guiding the global programming community), remains a staunch supporter. He freely expresses his belief that the trend toward open software is unstoppable. Many industry observers agree.

#### Questions for Discussion

1. What benefits does Linux provide to companies wishing to use open-standard software?
2. What are the drawbacks to Linux usage?
3. Why do you suppose there is so much interest in Linux?
4. Should Microsoft, which has a huge, global base of Windows PC and server users, consider Linux a threat to the industry-leading position it holds with its proprietary operating system? Why or why not?

### 2 Part II: Colgate-Palmolive: The Right Applications for the Right Time

*Colgate* Manufacturing schedules at Colgate factories are linked both to what is selling and to what is in the company's inventories. Even the raw materials mixed into a product are monitored as they are used. Whenever workers overseeing a manufacturing activity mix a batch of a product, they enter a few details describing the batch into a personal computer at their workstation. These details are then transmitted to the servers running the systems that make up Colgate's corporate nerve center. The systems immediately go to work, looking up the manufacturing recipe and then adjusting the inventory levels of all the ingredients that were used in the batch mixture. Suppliers hundreds of miles away also receive the details for the ingredients they provide so they can keep Colgate's supply of those ingredients at just the right level (just as Colgate does with its customers).

As Colgate knows, having good information technology is not enough to be successful in business today. Developing the right IT applications (in the right way) to solve the right problems goes to the very heart of business success.

### Questions for Discussion

1. What advantages do you think Colgate Palmolive's CIO brings to the process of identifying and developing the company's IT applications?
2. How do the responsibilities of Colgate Palmolive's operating managers, its CIO, and its systems analysts differ?
3. How does Colgate Palmolive benefit by linking its IT applications with those of its suppliers?
4. Do Colgate suppliers benefit by the integration of their systems with the company? Why or why not?

## 3 Part II: Electronics Giant Sends its Software Out

**Circuit City**   Circuit City executives believe that outsourcing will play an increasingly important role in the future of IT at the company because they still cannot hire enough highly qualified professional staff to meet business needs. However, they recognize that not all projects should be outsourced. To be a candidate for outsourcing, a project must have well-articulated objectives and its specifications must be spelled out in detail. The company has also found that having the outsourcing firm develop completed portions of the project every few weeks is another important ingredient for success.

When a project is being developed away from company premises by persons who are not employees, some companies do not pay enough attention to the project. Circuit City found it necessary to closely manage development activities for outsourced applications. Even more important, the company discovered, it was paying personal attention to the developers working on the project even though they are not permanent company employees. Outsourcing, it seems, does not eliminate the need to maintain interaction with project team members in order to ensure that the resulting systems include the right features.

### Questions for Discussion

1. What is outsourcing and why has it emerged as an important option in developing IT applications?
2. Within some companies, outsourcing is viewed this way: *Outsourcing is no different from letting people do business-related work on their PCs at home. In either case, they are away from the office. Yet, they can be quickly contacted by telephone or e-mail.* Do you agree or disagree with this view of outsourcing? Explain the reasons for your answer.

## *Summary of Learning Objectives*

**1** **Describe the principal functions and roles of a systems analyst.**   Systems analysts are responsible for working with users to determine a system's requirements and to describe the features needed in the system. The systems analyst sees the development of a shared IT application through, from original concept to finished product.

**2** **Identify the characteristics of shared systems. Shared systems are distinguished by the characteristics of openness and interoperability.**   Open systems use software programs that can run on different computer and communications hardware. They are built on nonproprietary operating systems. An application is interoperable when it can run in an identical fashion on different computer systems.

**3** **Discuss the changing process for developing information systems applications.**   Application development is shifting from a craft approach, in which each feature is uniquely designed, to an assembly approach, in which prewritten components are selected and integrated into the structure of an application. Components are characterized by reusable designs, meaning that a component can be used in multiple systems.

**4** **Describe the tools and techniques available to systems analysts for collecting data and developing IT applications.**   Systems analysts use a variety of techniques to collect data. The most common of these are interviews (both structured and unstructured); questionnaires; document examination (also called record inspection); observation; and sampling. The tools most commonly used by systems analysts to design systems are systems flowcharts—graphical depictions of a business process or procedure that show decision logic; dataflow diagrams (DFDs)—graphs that show the movement of data through a system; data dictionaries—catalogs that list and describe all of the types of data flowing through the system; and computer-aided systems engineering

(CASE) tools–tools that automate many of the most tedious and time-consuming systems tasks.

**5** **Summarize the purpose and characteristics of the unified modeling language (UML).** UML has become the standard vehicle for visualizing, describing, and documenting the details of an IT application. It features components useful to the systems analyst seeking to understand the requirements for a new application. Among the components are actors, activity diagrams, use case diagrams, use case descriptions, and class diagrams. Frequently, automated tools are used to create, maintain, and interrelate these and other UML components.

**6** **Explain the roles of the four types of IT systems development professionals.** In addition to their development and facilitating roles, systems analysts play the important role of change agent as they interact with the company's chief information officer, computer programmers, and systems contractors. The CIO is the one person in an organization responsible for managing and developing the firm's information technology capabilities. Computer programmers are charged with turning detailed specifications into computer software and with documenting the program. Systems contractors are outside personnel who contract with a company to develop IT applications.

## Key Terms

activity diagram   491
actor   491
back-end CASE tool   489
change agent   496
chief information officer (CIO)   498
class diagram   493
computer-aided systems engineering/
   computer-aided software
   engineering/CASE   488
data dictionary/repository   485
data element   485
dataflow diagram (DFD)   482

data structure   485
document examination/record inspection
   481
front-end CASE tool   489
integrated CASE (I-CASE) tool   489
interoperability   474
leveling   485
object   478
observation   481
open system   474
questionnaire   481
sampling   481

structured interview   481
system flowchart   482
systems analyst   481
systems contractor   500
systems integrator   500
unified modeling language (UML)   490
unstructured interview   481
use case   492
use case description   493
use case diagram   492

## Review Questions

1. What is systems development? How are systems projects initiated?

2. What are open shared systems? Why is the principle of openness desirable?

3. How do interoperable applications differ from those that do not have interoperability? What benefits does interoperability offer?

4. How do the craft and assembly approaches to systems development differ?

5. What role are software components playing in the development of information technology applications?

6. Discuss the desirability of the concept of reusability as it applies to software. What is the principal element that makes reusability possible?

7. Name the five data collection techniques used by systems analysts.

8. Distinguish between a system flowchart and a dataflow diagram.

9. What is leveling? Why is it useful in documenting dataflows?

10. What are the two components of data dictionaries?

11. Describe the features that most CASE tools have. What are the three kinds of CASE tools?

12. What is the unified modeling language and what objectives underlie its development?

13. How does the purpose of UML differ from constructing and using dataflow diagrams?

14. Discuss the meaning of *actors* in an IT application. Why do systems analysts using UML seek to identify them as part of the process of systems analysis and design?

15. Describe the most important UML components used in constructing an IT application.

16. What five skills should a systems analyst possess?

17. With which other IT professionals are systems analysts likely to work?

18. How do systems contractors differ from systems integrators? When is each likely to be involved in the development of an enterprise IT application?

## Discussion Questions

1. Is development of enterprise applications a craft that depends on the insights and skills of the systems analyst? Or is it a predictable process that tends to be more like a science based on engineering? What are the reasons behind your belief? Use examples of systems development activities or experiences to support your belief.

2. An IT industry observer has expressed the opinion that systems analysis is a creative process, not an engineering-like process. On the other hand, automated tools, including CASE tools and automated systems using UML tend to force the use of an engineering model. They say these tools do not allow for innovation, nor do they take into account the change process so important in implementing a new application.

   a. Do you agree that systems analysis is a creative process? Why or why not?

   b. Do you agree that automated systems development tools do not allow for innovation in the systems development process? Why or why not?

   c. Do automated tools take into account the change process that is part of the successful creation and implementation of an IT application?

3. Should companies be advised to select a mission-critical application as their first object-oriented application, or should they select a small-scale test application initially to gain experience? Explain your answer.

4. It has been said that systems analysts only get answers to the questions they ask. If they do not ask about something, they will not have adequate information. Do you agree with this assertion? Independent of whether or not you agree, how can analysts be certain they know all of the important details associated with the requirements that must be addressed in the features of an enterprise IT application?

5. A growing number of companies have opened custom-designed laboratories for usability testing. At these labs, end-users can evaluate new IT systems and suggest improvements. Where and how do these usability tests fit into the system development life cycle?

## Group Projects and Applications

### Project 1

Working in a team, contact 10 or more systems analysts from at least three different companies, and interview them in person, by telephone, or by e-mail using a set of structured questions. Inquire about the manner in which they conduct systems investigations and construct enterprise applications. Your inquiry should address the processes followed, means of assembling and validating requirements information, and the manner in which they turn requirements into features included in the new application. Be sure to ask how they validate that the application in fact meets user and enterprise requirements *before* the application is implemented.

In addition, find out which tools the systems developers use and which ones they have tried and discarded. What automated tools do they use? What automated tools do they seek to evaluate?

What conclusions do you draw about the manner in which analysts develop enterprise IT applications?

Summarize your findings in a written report or a slide presentation.

### Project 2

Visit with the CIOs of several medium and large size companies. Select a mix that includes both manufacturing and service companies. Inquire about the alternative strategies for developing new enterprise applications. Do they tend to craft their own, buy, or contract with an outside source for their development? What factors determine which alternative is selected for an individual application? To what extent does the need for a new application to interconnect with existing applications influence the means of development?

### Project 3

- Many computer-consulting firms offer companies help in developing shared IT applications. In small groups, contact a computer-consulting firm in your area and ask a project manager to sit down with you and discuss the process of developing a shared enterprise IT application from scratch. Ideally, you will be talking about a project that the firm has just completed. Ask the following questions:

- What problem were you called in to solve?
- What kinds of different people worked on the project team? What are their skills and responsibilities?
- Did the development of the shared system follow the six-phase process outlined in Figure 11.5? Did any of these six phases occur simultaneously? If so, which ones?
- What were the biggest challenges encountered in designing the system?
- How did employees react to the system after it was set up? Did you need to go back and redesign any parts of it to accommodate employees' needs?
- What steps do you take to satisfy your customers? How do you continue to support the system after you have created it and trained the client's employees?
- If possible, ask for copies of any flowcharts or dataflow diagrams the consulting firm used in developing the system, and share these with the class. Can other groups figure out the purpose of the shared application by examining these flowcharts?

## Project 4

This is a group research project. Groups of four or five persons choose one of the following industries (each group should choose a different industry):

- Airlines
- Publishing
- Advertising
- Health and beauty aids
- Computers
- Women's apparel
- Management consulting

- Accounting
- TV production

Research the top three or four companies in each industry. Then answer the following questions:

- Does each of these companies have a CIO?
- To whom does the CIO report?
- Within each industry, do those companies with a CIO perform better than those companies without?
- What is the CIO's background? What other jobs did that person hold (include any previous titles held within the company)?
- What is the CIO's annual compensation package? (At least obtain a salary range.)
- What is the CIO's mission? What improvements has the CIO made in the organization?
- Present the results of your search to the class.

## Project 5

The class breaks into an even-numbered set of groups. Half the groups brainstorm a new business they would like to start—one that will need to use a shared IT application. (You might choose to start a firm in one of the industries listed in Project 4.) The other groups take the role of IT consultants who have been hired to develop the system.

Role-play the meeting between the entrepreneurs and the consultants. The consultants should be prepared to ask questions regarding the entrepreneurs' goals, and the entrepreneurs should be willing to challenge the consultants to create an effective, efficient system.

## Net_Work

1. The standards associated with UML are overseen by the Object Management Group (OMG). It is an open-membership, not-for-profit consortium that produces and maintains the IT industry's specifications for interoperable enterprise applications.

   Research the OMG to determine the nature of the organization's membership and the activities it has underway with respect to UML and other IT development tools and methods. Is OMG a significant force in creating and communicating standards for systems development tools? What enhancements has it announced for UML beyond those described in this chapter? What other tools and methodologies is OMG developing besides UML? Prepare a summary of your findings.

2. Conduct a survey of the automated tools commercially available to aide developers of IT applications. Determine whether there is a large or a limited number of such tools available for purchase. Select a subset of those tools you identify and examine the similarities and differences between them. Classify them according to their features and capabilities, and the operating system/computer platform on which they run. Also seek to determine which ones are most widely used by IT professionals.

# Cool Mobility

## On Assignment

Both Grace Ma, director of marketing, and James Marsalis, CIO, know of your recommendation to add sales capabilities to the company's Web site. Ma is interested in determining the potential demand for the new products and services, while Marsalis wants to be certain that the capabilities can be added to the existing system. Both have encouraged you to assemble the necessary information to discuss your recommendation in more detail.

## In Consultation

Following the discussions with Ma and Marsalis, you undertake the next stage in your investigation, applying proven systems analysis tools and techniques.

a. Describe the data collection process you would follow to determine whether there is a need and justification to add sales capabilities to CoolMobility.biz. More specifically, you would like to enable the selling of faceplates and ring tones (for mobile phones) on the Internet site. Be sure to indicate what information you are seeking and where or from whom information will be acquired. Keep in mind that your investigation may require that you seek information from sources outside of the company.

b. Create an activity diagram showing the actors that interact with the CoolMobility.biz Internet site. Use standard symbols to show the actors, activities, and transitions between activities.

c. Once you have completed the activity diagram describing the current system, indicate how you would modify the activity diagram to add features allowing customers to purchase and pay for new face plates or download ring tones for their mobile phones.

d. Create a use case diagram that describes the customer buying process for the system if it is modified to include current product sales as well as the additions you are proposing for face plates and ring tones.

# Case Study

## WiPro Sets Pace for Indian IT Application Development

**WiPro**

WiPro Technologies, based in Bangalore, India, is known as the country's premier IT company and as a global player in IT application development. The 57-year-old company has focused intensely on IT since the 1980s when it moved into software and electronics. Its contract services span application development and maintenance, business process outsourcing, package implementation, systems integration, and IT consulting and services.

WiPro is well positioned for the growing tendency for companies to outsource IT application development and support activities. Gartner Group, a highly respected IT research firm, projects that by the second half of this decade, nearly half of all U.S. enterprises will engage consulting firms or conduct pilot studies to determine the benefits of outsourcing IT services. The reasons vary from gaining access to experienced software experts, shifting the task of application development outside of the company, and reducing the cost of developing and maintaining applications.

WiPro has already established a solid reputation in IT outsourcing. It

counts among its customers well-known companies in many industries from around the world including the following: Boeing, Ericsson, Toshiba, Cisco, Seagate, United Technologies, Best Buy, IBM, Microsoft, NCR, Thames Water, and Sony. WiPro has 28 customer-dedicated development centers across India, Europe, and the United States. It also has 21 offices in the United States, Canada, Finland, Taiwan, France, and the United Kingdom. Enterprise IT directors like the fact that the quality of the software and services WiPro delivers is high. Moreover, since the language of the developers is English and because software specifications and application code can readily be transported over the Internet or over high-speed telecommunication links, communication between WiPro and its clients is easy and efficient. The city of Bangalore, the site of WiPro's headquarters, plays an important role in its success. Bangalore is India's high-tech center; it is often compared to

California's Silicon Valley. Many leading IT companies have software development operations there, including the U.S. firms of Cisco, Oracle, SAP, and Sun Microsystems. The city's population includes a huge number of well-trained engineers, including many veterans with global experience. In addition, universities in Bangalore alone graduate 25,000 engineers annually, almost equal to yearly graduates from colleges and universities in the United States. India as a whole each year produces more than 200,000 software and computer-science engineers.

Bangalore is well established as a research center, with some 230 global multinational companies operating facilities in the city's research parks. This fact, plus active support from the government of India, means seasoned software developers and engineers are likely to continue to migrate to Bangalore.

The tendency of companies to contract software development to

offshore firms in India (including WiPro's Indian rivals InfoSys Technologies and Tata Consultancy Services) is well established. However, WiPro knows that as it continues its successful growth it will have to distinguish itself from those firms that only produce computer code or operate software support call centers, and it will have to compete head to head with the likes of big league IT consultants such as IBM, EDS, and Accenture in order to land the biggest contracts. Hence, it is complementing its software knowledge by developing industry expertise. Company leaders believe that understanding how companies operate within their industry will enable WiPro to be not just a service provider, but also a knowledge center. Judging from its recent contracts, the company's strategy seems to be on target. Sony, Japan's electronic giant, awarded WiPro a multimillion-dollar contract to write IT applications for its computer and electronics plants. As part of the award it expressed the hope that WiPro can emerge as a service provider that can design *business processes* for Sony in such day-to-day operating areas as supply-chain procurement and product development.

### Questions for Discussion

1. Do you agree with the assertion of the Gartner Group that soon nearly one-half of all U.S. enterprises will be engaged in or evaluating IT services?
2. What factors might cause a CIO to seek an outsourcing arrangement whereby responsibility for the development of software would be delegated to WiPro?

# 12 Creating Web-Enabled Applications

## CHAPTER OUTLINE

## LEARNING OBJECTIVES

When you have completed this chapter, you should be able to

1 Describe the three principal forces behind the interest in creating Web-enabled applications in enterprises.

2 Distinguish between the purposes of HTML and XML in Web-enabled applications.

3 Explain how XML aids in creating interenterprise IT applications.

4 Identify the six advantages of XML.

5 Explain the potential benefit of Web services to enterprises IT applications.

6 Identify and describe the three tools that facilitate the use of Web services.

# VISA Builds on its Legacy

*V*isa cards are the world's most widely used form of *plastic* payment—some $2 trillion worth of products and services are purchased annually using Visa cards. The card has a worldwide market share of 60 percent, which is greater than that of all other major payment cards combined. More than 1 billion Visa-branded cards are in circulation, accepted at more than 27 million locations in 144 countries.

Visa, headquartered in San Francisco, is jointly owned by more than 21,000 member financial institutions around the globe. Though it does not offer cards or financial services directly to consumers and merchants, it plays a pivotal role in advancing new payment products and technologies on behalf of its members.

Visa operates the world's largest and most sophisticated consumer payments processing system, with enough communications lines to encircle the globe nearly 400 times. The network, known as VisaNet, processes over 3,700 transactions every second during its peak season, and is capable of handling transactions denominated in 160 different currencies.

Always seeking to improve member service while also bolstering its position against competing payment cards, Visa decided to build an application to itemize charges to Visa corporate cards. The application would enable its valued corporate customers to refine the processing of business expenses that employees paid via Visa by automatically transmitting itemized charges to the proper corporate expense category. Corporate customers would enjoy streamlined expense management and improved efficiency in auditing cardholder activities. Visa itself would also benefit since the new application would produce detailed reports enabling product managers to better understand the spending patterns of corporate customers.

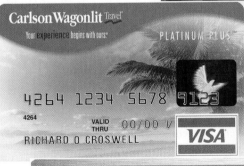

Adding the corporate-customer enhancement meant Visa had to modify its well-established legacy IT applications to capture and process additional transaction details. Its systems developers identified thousands of data elements—airline tickets, restaurant meals, hotel-room charges, state and local sales-tax

charges, taxi fares—that would now be captured to properly categorize the transaction details. Visa not only had to devise a way for capturing the processing of the transactions on its end, but it also had to establish reporting standards that merchants and customers could adopt—their computer applications would also be affected by Visa's new application.

The development team initially considered using well-understood electronic data interchange (EDI) standards for the application. EDI means that developers would have to develop document standards to accommodate each type of corporate transaction, a large undertaking in itself.

After additional investigation, the developers decided that altering and interconnecting legacy systems at both Visa and its merchant customers provided challenges that could not be met by an EDI solution. Instead, Visa's developers embraced XML, a standard language that had been created to extend the capabilities of the Internet and World Wide Web, enabling them to interconnect with legacy systems. Visa created a series of XML specifications that defined the feasible data elements for the corporate transactions. It published the specifications and began working with its customers to adopt the specifications in their systems. With a legacy environment as broad as that of Visa, the ability to interconnect corporate expense applications spanning many enterprises is a critical ingredient in IT success.

*I*t is widely recognized that the Internet has had a dramatic affect on personal and professional lives, and on the way enterprises distribute information. Its impact continues to grow. In the process, is it is influencing the nature of the IT applications that developers are creating. Moreover, it is altering the way these applications are used. This chapter explores the impact of the Internet and World Wide Web on Web-enabled enterprise IT applications.

In addition, a growing number of IT applications are emerging for operation *between or across* enterprises. The preceding chapters in this book focused on the development of applications for use *within* enterprises. This chapter shows how XML and Web services are making it possible to share data and interconnect applications across enterprises. As you will see, the creation of Web-enabled applications is changing both the nature of IT applications and the manner in which they are developed.

## Forces Behind Web-Enabled Systems

**Web-enablement**
The tendency of systems developers to incorporate features of the Internet in enterprise systems.

The tendency of systems developers to incorporate features of the Internet in enterprise systems is generally known as **Web-enablement.** Web-enabled systems are emerging for the following three principal reasons: (1) widespread use of browsers, (2) preserving value in legacy systems, and (3) creating interenterprise applications.

### Widespread Use of Browsers

It is difficult to identify any IT application—even e-mail—that has captured the attention of individual users and IT professionals more than Web browsers have. As a result, there is a huge installed base of computers loaded with Web browser software. Microsoft's Internet Explorer and Netscape Navigator are the most widely used.

Why have Web browsers gained such a large foothold on the world's computers? Among the most common reasons are the following:

- **New computers shipped with Web browsers**   Most new computers are sent to users with one or more Web browsers preloaded. As a result, the browser is ready to use as soon as the computer is removed from the box and connected to the Internet or the enterprise's communications network. There is no need to decide whether to acquire and install the software.

- **Large installed base of browser users**   Because of their widespread availability, the number of individuals and enterprises using browsers is huge. The vast majority of the more than 500 million PCs in use (Figure 12.1) have active Web-browser users.
- **Browsers appearing on other IT devices**   Their popularity on the PC is leading to their use for handheld information technology devices. Many personal digital assistants (PDAs) and mobile phones are being equipped with browsers, thereby making them Web-enabled. Industry observers expect the number of Web-enabled handsets to skyrocket (Figure 12.1).
- **Intuitive features**   Individuals need little training to understand how to use a Web browser. After only a few minutes of explanation, a first-time user usually adapts to its features and capabilities. Usage quickly becomes intuitive.
- **Flexibility**   Web browsers can be adjusted in appearance and capability to suit the needs of a wide array of users. Many add-on features can be incorporated into the browser through **plug-ins,** software programs that extend the capabilities of the browser in a specific way (for example, adding the ability to play audio samples, view video clips, or animated demonstrations from the browser).

**plug-ins**
Software programs that extend the capabilities of your Internet browser, giving it added features.

- **Universal front-end application**   Web browsers' functional advantages, coupled with their widespread adoption, have created interest among systems developers to use browsers as a universal front-end, or interface. Developers are increasingly using browsers as the means of interacting with enterprise systems as well as the Internet.

## Legacy Systems

There is widespread interest in Web-enabling legacy systems, with browsers serving as a new interface. As discussed in Chapter 7, **legacy system** refers to the many mainframe, midrange, client/server, or PC applications that are used to manage business functions such as finance, accounting, manufacturing, and human resources, but were deployed before the emergence of the Internet in enterprise applications. In most organizations, legacy applications have evolved over many years at a substantial cost. Unfortunately, they often impede interenterprise applications (discussed next) because they are a patchwork of mainframe, midrange, and PC applications, both centralized and distributed, under dispersed control. Legacy systems may also consist of entrenched data-management platforms that contains proprietary, custom-designed software. They can be fragmented by geography, incompatible databases, and even mergers of enterprises and business units. Moreover, the user interfaces are often awkward, seldom having the graphical features that users have grown accustomed to on their PCs.

**legacy system**
Refers to the many mainframe, midrange, client/server or PC applications that are used to manage business functions.

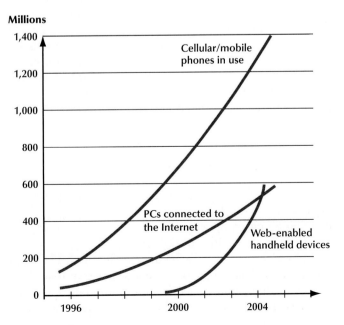

**FIGURE 12.1**

*Growth of Alternative IT Devices*

Despite these disadvantages, legacy systems are still relied on heavily for running enterprises on a day-to-day basis. This is why many enterprises judge it important to preserve the vitality of legacy systems by evolving and modernizing them. Web-enablement is a common tactic for enhancing the usefulness of legacy systems and for integrating them with other applications.

## Interconnected Enterprises

As highlighted in the discussion of e-commerce (Chapter 9), it is also becoming commonplace for enterprises to interconnect their business systems with IT applications running at other enterprises. For example:

- As the leading manufacturer of PCs, Dell Computer Co. thrives on efficient operations, which it can turn to great advantage over its competitors in the form of lower prices. When Dell takes a PC order (a computer and monitor), whether over the Web or via telephone, it electronically transmits details of the orders to various suppliers (such as its supplier of computer monitors). The monitor manufacturer is responsible for shipping a monitor to Dell's customer at the same time as Dell ships the computer. Dell and its monitor supplier are so interconnected that they are dependent on each other for their success.
- A leading insurance company needed to speed up its quotation process for new policies. However, the company maintained only part of the data needed. Other details are maintained by third parties, including a credit-rating service, to which the company had contracted for services. In order to deliver the new quotation process, the company developed a Web-enabled system that interoperated with an IT application at the credit service. The new application operates seamlessly even though it spans multiple company boundaries.

The *Information Technology in Practice* feature, "Cisco Systems Interconnects Suppliers in its Ecosystem," describes how this leading Internet-focused company has created an enviable record of success by integrating its business systems with those of its key manufacturing partners.

The key to enterprise integration is **interoperability,** the bringing together and sharing of data across applications. The seamless, end-to-end integration of IT applications provides for interconnecting enterprises as described in the above examples.

The greatest obstacle to interoperability is heterogeneous applications. Since the applications are developed by different organizations, often at various points in time, there is seldom much commonality in their design or features. They are thus **heterogeneous applications,** to the extent they may be written in different programming languages, run on different types of computers, and use varying communications networks and transmission methods. The ability of an enterprise to overcome the barriers of heterogeneous applications usually determines whether interoperability can become a reality or will remain just an interesting concept.

Two prominent strategies have emerged for Web-enabling applications and for end-to-end integration of interenterprise applications. The remainder of this chapter describes the characteristics of these two strategies: extensible markup language and Web services.

**interoperability**
The perfect exchange of data and information in all forms (data, text, sound, and image, including animation) between the individual components of an application (hardware, software, network).

**heterogeneous applications**
May be written in different programming languages, run on different types of computers, and use varying communications networks and transmission methods.

## Extensible Markup Language

As useful as the Internet is, its role has been limited to information delivery. Hypertext markup language, or HTML (see Chapter 3), is the principal means for describing how to present information on the World Wide Web. HTML consists of tags that set off sections of text. It describes how a Web browser should arrange text and position images on a Web page. Through HTML, for example, you indicate font style and color choice, as well as whether or not to use boldface or italic. HTML's ease of learning and use has been an important force behind the vast array of Web-page designers.

# INFORMATION TECHNOLOGY IN PRACTICE

## Cisco Systems Interconnects Suppliers in Its Ecosystem

Cisco Systems, headquartered in San Jose—the heart of California's Silicon Valley—is viewed as the worldwide leader in networking for the Internet. It designs and sells the routers, switches, and network management software that many companies have selected for use in constructing their private networks and connecting them to the Internet.

Cisco has been among the fastest growing companies in history, largely because of the way it chose to build its business around the Internet. The Internet isn't just Cisco's business; it's how Cisco does business. It created a new form of supply chain, called *ecosystem*, which seamlessly links customers, contract manufacturers, and other supply-chain partners using the power of Internet technology.

Cisco recognized early on that it could not recruit as many key technology experts or invest in the full range of manufacturing facilities it would need to be successful. Hence, it began to cultivate close relationships with other companies. However, it did not seek just suppliers, it sought partners. Cisco asked these partners—manufacturers, assemblers, distributors, resellers, and transportation companies—to integrate their supply chains with its own, and to interconnect their business systems, including key IT applications. The result was an automated order-acceptance and fulfillment process.

Cisco's manufacturing system incorporates more than 30 plants globally. However, few are owned by the company. Most are owned and operated by suppliers—partners in the ecosystem—who make all of the components, perform more than 90 percent of the subassembly work, and carry out well over half of all final assembly. When a product is finished, the Cisco supplier notifies a transportation company interconnected in the ecosystem and ships it directly to the customer, without a Cisco employee ever touching the product.

Ecosystem members do not rely on faxes, e-mail, or phone calls to coordinate their activities. Everything is done electronically, and there are few opportunities for errors. Information sharing occurs in real-time, with the entire supply chain operating from the same information. By providing direct access to process participants, Cisco reduces the time it must spend updating information both internally and with the suppliers, which ultimately enables an expedited process flow. Any change in one part of the supply chain can be known in other parts immediately.

Cisco's partners connect with the company through a supply-chain extranet known as Manufacturing Connection Online (MCO). It is Web-enabled, uses the technologies of the Internet, and interconnects companies for end-to-end integration. Companies use MCO to gain access to Cisco's Enterprise Program, a company-wide planning and control application. By connecting their systems with the enterprise program, suppliers can receive and directly monitor customer orders and ship products. The system enables all partners to minimize delivery times, excess inventory, and errors, while improving customer satisfaction year after year.

Cisco is not only a leader in manufacturing for the Internet, but is also an exemplar in using the Internet to interconnect companies in its ecosystem. It is hard to imagine Cisco without the Manufacturing Connection Online and its inter-enterprise systems. They are as much a reason for its success as the products and services it delivers through these connections.

However, the preceding section reveals that as experience with the Internet grows, individual and enterprise users want to do more than merely display information. Organizations may want to use the Web to control scientific instruments connected to the Internet, or to transmit patient medical records between physicians, or to accept and process online buying orders from customers, among other uses. HTML does not have the capability to meet these needs. For instance, the details of a patient's medical record presented via HTML can be *viewed* on a display screen, but they cannot easily be *processed*.

Recognizing the need to use the Web in new ways, the World Wide Web Consortium (W3C) created a new markup language, the **extensible markup language (XML).** (W3C is the organization that oversees the development of specifications, guidelines, and tools to lead the Web to its full potential.) XML is a set of rules for creating tags to describe data and thereby provide more flexible and adaptable use of Web data. It is called **extensible** because developers can design their own customized markup languages for describing data. (Technically speaking, XML is a *metalanguage*—a language for describing other languages.) It is limitless, meaning that virtually any piece of data in a Web-enabled system can be described by XML.

The *Information Technology in Practice* feature, "Data-Farber Cancer Institute Serves its Community Using XML," is a good illustration of the value of XML in distributing medical data to a wide audience, regardless of the information technology a recipient uses.

## Structure of XML

XML, like HTML, uses pairs of tags to identify Web data. However, the XML tags specify the actual content (rather than the presentation format) of the data so that the receiving system can read and process the data. Pairs of tags surround the details to which they apply.

In HTML, the tag

first class

means to present the words first class in bold type: **first class.** However, it provides no context and therefore no meaning for the words. Someone viewing the data might interpret it as referring to the first meeting of a university class for the new term.

Contrast this with the increased usefulness of an XML tag, as follows:

<ticket class>first class</ticket class>

When included in, say, an airline reservation system, it is evident that this data item pertains to the class of ticket, that is, a first class rather than an economy ticket. (Note that XML labels the data, *indicating what it is*—describing its contents. In contrast, HTML labels the data, *indicating how it should be presented,* but does not describe its contents.)

As this simple example illustrates, an XML element is made up of a start tag, an end tag, and the data in between. The start and end tags describe the data within the tags, which is considered the value of the element.

Tags can be nested. This feature makes it possible to specify a complete record of data to an application. Figure 12.2 contains an XML specification for the data in a reservation record. It consists of data items identifying the flight number, date, origin, destination, and so on.

Because XML is extensible, developers can design their own document types and thus are not limited to the predefined tags of HTML. Moreover, the designs can be tailored to the exact needs of the intended audience. Hence, documents intended for use by manufacturers and sellers in a retail environment would be designed much differently than those for use by, say, physicians, therapists, and clinic staff in a medical application.

The XML tags and the process for interpreting them can be transmitted anywhere. Web browsers and IT applications, such as airline-reservation systems and travel-agent systems, can follow the programmed rules for processing and presenting the data.

## XML Advantages

XML has six important advantages (Table 12.1) over HTML. In addition to be being Web-based and extensible, two very important characteristics, XML enables independent computer systems to interact with one another and to exchange, interpret and process data even if they run different operating systems. Moreover, the applications may be written in different programming languages.

Fourth, XML makes it possible to integrate applications created by different developers, that is, end-to-end integration, as discussed earlier. Business partners—buyers and sell-

# INFORMATION TECHNOLOGY IN PRACTICE
## Dana-Farber Cancer Institute
## Serves Its Community Using XML

The mission of Dana-Farber Cancer Institute is to provide expert, compassionate care to children and adults with cancer while advancing the understanding, diagnosis, treatment, cure, and prevention of cancer and related diseases. An affiliate of Harvard Medical School and a Comprehensive Cancer Center designated by the National Cancer Institute, the institute provides training for new generations of physicians and scientists. It also designs programs that promote public health particularly among high-risk and underserved populations, and it disseminates innovative patient therapies and scientific discoveries that target communities across the United States and throughout the world.

The institute serves a community of patients, physicians, and researchers. More than 700 physicians and researchers are linked to the institute. An important part of Dana-Farber's mission is providing easy access to up-to-date information about the different types of cancers, possible treatments, clinical trials, and ongoing developments in research. Its Web-enabled system is used to transfer clinical data and view images of cells and tissues, while providing security for

sensitive scientific research and protecting patient privacy.

In addition to making information on its own research available, Dana-Farber developed a process that retrieves information updates from the online systems of the National Cancer Institute (NCI). As each update arrives, it is converted into an XML format that ensures the data can be distributed electronically to a wide audience, regardless of the information technology they are using. The reformatted research summaries are

then made accessible via Dana-Farber's Web site.

The automated retrieval and XML conversion process avoids expensive, time-consuming manual updating processes. By maintaining the research summaries in XML format, the institute ensures that its community members can access the data in multiple ways and search for information based on their areas of interest. Above all, the process ensures that recipients have the most up-to-date and reliable information available.

ers—can exchange data, with XML defining the format for the data so that sending and receiving applications can share and process the same data.

Fifth, XML is a public format, not the proprietary development of any company. Its public nature means there is no license fee or charge for its use.

Sixth, XML has widespread vendor support. XML is supported by both Microsoft and Netscape browsers. Software vendors are incorporating XML features into database

```
<?xml version="1.0"?>
 <reservations>
  <flight number="DL56">
   <date>"10122004"</date>
   <origin>Tokyo</origin>
   <destination>Atlanta</destination>
   <passenger>Migel Gutierrez</passenger>
   <frequent flier>"3116545682"</frequent flier>
   <ticket class>first class</ticket class>
   <seat assignment>4F</seat assignment>
  </flight number>
 </reservations>
```

systems and a variety of enterprise application programs. Its features are increasingly found in scientific, supply chain, manufacturing, and online retailing applications, among many others.

## Document Type Definition

**document type definition (DTD)**

Defines the vocabulary (or standard) to make the data easily understandable and useable.

XML provides an application an independent way of sharing data. However, if several parties, such as teams of scientific researchers, physicians, or business-trading partners, will regularly exchange data via Web-enabled applications, they may want to work out an advance agreement on the data they will share, although doing so is optional. **Document type definition (DTD)** defines the vocabulary (or standard) to make the data easily understandable and useable. (You might think of it as a *dictionary* or *schema* that enables everyone using XML documents to be sure they are speaking in the same terms.)

A DTD is a formal description of a specific document, written in XML declaration syntax. It sets out the names that are used for the different types of elements, where they may occur, and how they all fit together. For example, companies in the airline industry might want to create a DTD so that all participating enterprises will know the Web data is in a consistent format. For the document type to be able to describe *lists* which contain *items*, the relevant part of the DTD (Figure 12.3) might contain the following:

```
<!ELEMENT List (Item)+>
<!ELEMENT Item (#PCDATA)>
```

This defines a list as an element type containing one or more items (indicated by the "+" sign); it defines items as element types containing just plain text (Parsed Character Data or PCDATA).

| Table 12.1   **XML Advantages** |
| --- |
| Web-based |
| Extensible |
| Computer and software platform independent |
| Facilitates end-to-end application integration |
| A public, license-free standard |
| Has widespread vendor support |

**REALITY CHECK**

Even prior to the emergence of XML, Web sites could still capture data. Doing so requires displaying a blank form online. Visitors to a site complete the blanks in the online form by keying in the requested data. Then the Web application swaps the completed form to the enterprise's Web server where it pastes the form into a database or determines how to extract data from the form. Depending on the application, a form might be swapped back and forth several times.

In addition, only the application for which the form was designed has the details of the form's design. Only that application knows the arrangement of the form and the meaning of the details entered into each blank in the form. Hence, the form is useless to any application other than the one for which it was designed.

The benefits of XML are substantial. Because XML adds meaning and context to the data, it enables an application to process the data on the spot. Less swapping also means reduced traffic on the Internet and at the same time reduced work for the Web server that would otherwise have to send and receive the data.

---

An application reads the DTD before it processes an arriving Web document so that it knows the sequence in which every element type ought to come and how each relates to the other.

In a sense, a DTD provides applications with advance notice of what names and structures can be used in a particular document type. An application designer, relying on a DTD, can thus assume that all documents that belong to a particular type will be constructed and named in a consistent and conformant manner.

A developer may choose to write a new DTD to meet unique application needs. However, thousands of DTDs are already in existence. Industry associations are establishing DTDs by having companies in the industry agree on a standard for sharing/interchanging data. For example, RosettaNet is a nonprofit consortium of supply-chain trading partners. Its members include companies such as American Express, Hewlett Packard, Microsoft, Oracle, and United Parcel Services. RosettaNet has established DTDs that enable trading partners to communicate using XML.

Similarly, Open Buying on the Internet (OBI) is a consortium of companies dedicated to developing and deploying a standard for Internet-based procurement. OBI members, such as Boise Cascade, DuPont, Visa, and Johnson & Johnson, established DTDs facilitating XML use in open-vendor, computer, and operating system-neutral purchasing systems.

**FIGURE 12.3**

*Sample DTD*

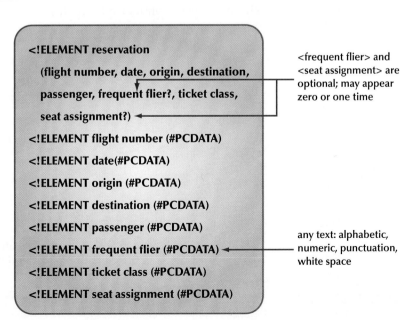

Oasis, the Organization for the Advancement of Structured Information Standards, is a nonprofit international consortium. It is developing XML definitions in partnership with the United Nations' UN/CEFACT, the UN body for Trade Facilitation and Electronic Business.

## Presentation Using XML Style Sheets

**XML stylesheet language (XSL)**

Created by developers or publishers of XML data to manage the display and presentation of information in a document.

One of the XML's advantages is the separation between content and the presentation of the data. However, when developers or publishers of XML data (such as the publisher of an airline flight schedule) want to manage the display and presentation of information in a document, an *XML style sheet* is created using **XML stylesheet language (XSL)**. XSL is used to define how the XML file should be converted so that it can be seen in the required format in the browser.

For example, in the XML file a developer might declare a Tag called

**<showbold>This is the Heading Text </showbold>** ,

and also want to show the text inside these tags in a different font and color. In this case then, the XSL file would declare it as

**<xsl:template** match= **showbold** >
    <font color= #FF0000 face= Arial size= 3 >
       **<xsl:apply-templates/>**
    </font>
**</xsl:template>**

As soon as the tag *showbold* is encountered during processing the XML file, the text—*This is the Heading Text*—is replaced with a different font size (Arial 3) and color (FF0000, which is the code for red) in bold. Note that the tag *showbold* is not part of the standard HTML; it is defined here as a custom tag.

XML style sheets are especially useful when a developer wants to control the appearance of the output and when the appearance will vary depending on whether it is presented on a full-size computer terminal or a smaller PDA display screen.

## Processing XML

The XML components include the XML document, DTD, and XLS style sheet. Processing occurs when an application scans the XML document and the DTD (called *parsing*) to identify the data. XML style sheets are processed to determine the format for presenting or displaying the data (Figure 12.4). The results may be presented in a Web browser display. Alternatively, they may be transmitted to another application where the data are used to carry out the application's processing activities.

**FIGURE 12.4**

*Processing of XML Components*

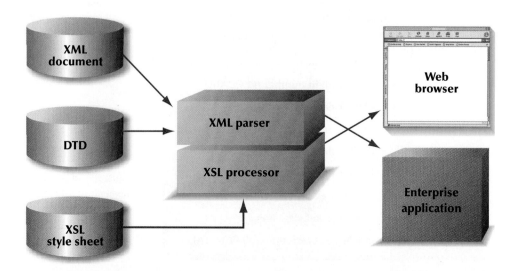

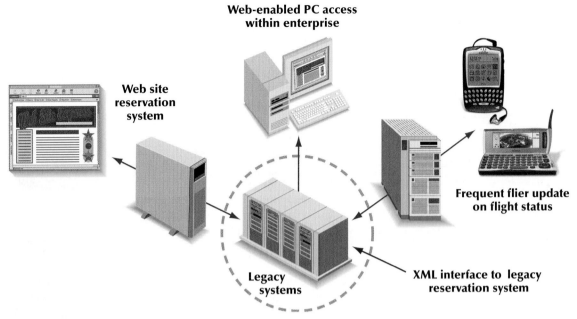

**FIGURE 12.5**
*XML Interface for Web-enabled Legacy System*

Figure 12.5 illustrates XML's use in the airline-reservation system example. Airline systems characteristically rely on long-established legacy systems for managing flight schedules and passenger reservations. Yet many airlines have developed the capability for online ticketing over the Internet, and for transmitting flight updates for display on passenger PDAs and mobile phones. XML and a small processing program provide an interface with the legacy system and a means for Web-enabling the reservation application.

XML's benefits are stimulating widespread interest in its use for many types of enterprise applications; it will continue to grow well into the future.

# Web Services

**Web services** are modular Internet applications that perform a very specific function or task. Because they are written to conform to a standard technical format, they can be interconnected and seamlessly integrated with other Web services to form a Web-enabled application. They represent a direction for the future.

**Web services**
Modular Internet applications that perform a very specific function or task.

## Web Services Principle

Web services have been evolving since the commercialization of the Internet, though most users have been unaware of their significance. Take Yahoo!, the popular Internet portal. A first-time visitor to Yahoo! quickly notices the wide variety of services offered at the site including the following: weather reports, financial services, travel information, games, and more. The valued combination of services it offers makes Yahoo! among the most frequently visited sites on the Internet.

While the services are attributed to Yahoo!, in reality, most of them are only *accessible* at Yahoo!, *not actually created by* Yahoo!. Other application developers offer the services, making them available through Yahoo!

This example illustrates the principle behind Web service. As with Yahoo!, independent developers create application modules, (analogous to the weather, financial, and travel services) and make them accessible to other developers over the Internet. Other developers select and incorporate those modular applications and use them as components in their enterprise or applications. However, like Yahoo!, the module's software code is not actually *embedded* in the application. Rather, it is *interconnected*, with the software remaining at the provider's Web site.

Many IT industry experts believe that Web-enabled applications will incorporate Web services at a growing rate. However, in order for this to occur, those creating applications must be assured of having the following:

- Uniform protocol for invoking a Web service
- Descriptor or definition of a Web service
- Registry where Web services can be located

## CRITICAL CONNECTIONS   1

### Telenor's Web-Enabled Service Meets Customer Needs—24 Hours a Day

Telenor is the leading telephone, broadband, Internet, and television-service provider in Norway. In Norway, as in many Scandinavian countries, a high percentage of citizens are interconnected with the Internet and routinely access the Web. Telenor wanted to use the Web as a means of improving service to its customers while also reducing service costs in the face of increasing competition. The company sought to automate its customer service processes, creating a complete self-service solution that would be available 24 hours a day.

Telenor developed a Web-enabled system that links to its legacy systems. Customers no longer have to wait on *hold* before speaking to customer service assistants. Through Telenor's online self-service system, customers can do the following:

- Order new services, including voice and high-speed Internet access
- Review special-service offers
- Adjust or cancel their subscriptions or change address information
- Check their telecommunication usage on a daily basis
- View invoices for services and obtain explanations of charges
- Pay invoices
- Arrange delayed payments for invoices
- Contact Telenor by e-mail

The service is popular with customers. Telenor finds it delivers services faster, more accurately, and at reduced costs.

**Table 12.2   Technologies of Web Services**

| TECHNOLOGY | ACRONYM | FUNCTION |
|---|---|---|
| Extensible Markup Language | XML | XML is a set of rules for creating tags that describe the layout and content of Web data |
| Simple Object Access Protocol (sometimes known as Services Oriented Architectural Protocol) | SOAP | Protocol for invoking remote Web service objects using XML |
| Universal Discover, Description, and Integration | UDDI | XML-based public directory service that provides information about available Web services |
| Web Services Description Language | WSDI | Protocol that describes the capabilities of a Web service object |

The IT industry has developed tools that provide these assurances, including SOAP, WSDL, and UDDI, all of which are discussed next. Together with XML, they comprise the core technologies of Web-enabled applications (Table 12.2).

The *Information Technology in Practice* feature, "L'Oréal's Shop-in-a-Shop Links its Web Sites to Retail Partners," describes how this global cosmetics company relies on Web services to interconnect with its valued business partners around the world.

## Simplified Object Access Protocol

**Simple object access protocol,** or **SOAP,** is the protocol used by an application to invoke a Web service located on another computer. (SOAP is sometimes translated to mean *services-oriented architecture protocol.*) It thus enables communication between applications (that is, objects) elsewhere on an enterprise's intranet or on the public Internet, regardless of what type of computer the application may be running on (Figure 12.6). Hence, SOAP plays a pivotal role in enabling heterogeneous systems to interoperate seamlessly.

**simple object access protocol (SOAP)**
The protocol used by an application to invoke a Web service located on another computer.

**FIGURE 12.6**

***Interplay Between Web Service Participants***

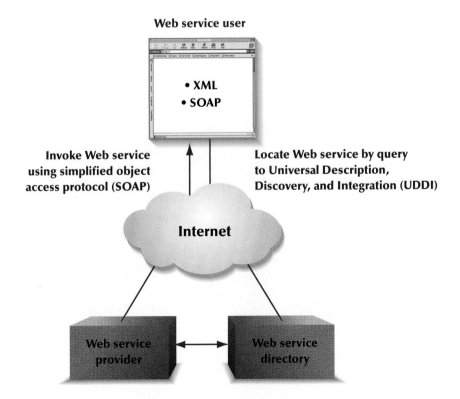

Web service user

• XML
• SOAP

Invoke Web service using simplified object access protocol (SOAP)

Locate Web service by query to Universal Description, Discovery, and Integration (UDDI)

Internet

Web service provider

Web service directory

Publish Web service description

# INFORMATION TECHNOLOGY IN PRACTICE
## L'Oréal's Shop-in-a-Shop Links Its Web Sites to Retail Partners

The L'Oréal Group, headquartered in Paris, seeks to contribute to the beauty of women and men all over the world, providing everyday solutions intended to enhance their sense of well-being. It is the number-one cosmetics company in the world, present in 130 countries with a worldwide turnover of more than $12 billion and a staff of almost 50,000. The group focuses on the following activities: hair color, hair care, skin care, make-up, and perfumes.

L'Oréal offers consumers all over the world a culturally diverse portfolio of brands such as L'Oréal, Garnier, Maybelline, Redken, Lancôme, Helena Rubinstein, Biotherm, Vichy, La Roche-Posay, Soft Sheen Carson, Matrix, Kiehl's, Shu Uemura, Ralph Lauren, Giorgio Armani, and Cacharel. The group's brands are present in every distribution channel including the following: mass market, professional hair salons, selective distribution, pharmacy, Internet, and mail order.

Research laboratories located in France, the United States, and Japan focus on skin, hair, and color: More than 110 original molecules have been developed by L'Oréal's laboratories and are used in the group's products; more than 3,000 new formulas are launched every year.

L'Oréal actively uses the World Wide Web to promote its brands, serve the consumer, and aid in distribution of its products to the upscale retailers that are among its direct customers. The company maintains *several hundred* Web

sites as a vehicle for marketing its family of brands across a wide array of countries. The features and functions of each Web site vary according to the culture in which a particular brand appears, as well as the level of information technology in use in the country where the site is accessible.

The company's many upscale retail partners play a critical role in L'Oréal's success. Many have their own Web sites and independent e-commerce capabilities. The company wanted to assist independent retailers in promotion and sale of its products, providing consumers with the experience of shopping at the retailer's online site. Yet it wanted to do so without sacrificing control over any aspect of the L'Oréal experience. The design specifications it created for the system called for high-quality merchandising includ-

ing both localization (for the culture and country) and personalization (for the retailer and customer), as well as catalog management and integration with partner business systems. It also wanted to maintain one location for product information—on its own servers—so that any changes in product information would be available to all partners at the same time.

L'Oréal created its Shop-in-a-Shop, a concept and capability that enables its Web sites to integrate with the e-commerce sites of its retail partners. Its developers designed the sites to convey a feeling similar to a customer's visit to a specialty cosmetic counter in upscale department stores. Consumers can browse the site, investigating the large variety of cosmetics *on display.* When the shopper selects a product for purchase, it is

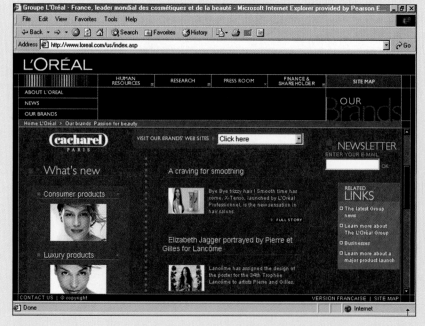

added to the shopping basket at the retailer's site, where the checkout and payment process takes place.

Behind the scenes, L'Oréal created XML Web services to integrate its system with retailer Web sites. This enables each retailer to electronically retrieve product, cosmetic, and skin-care information as well as graphics and images residing on L'Oréal Web sites, and integrate the information into its own Web site. An XML Web service also exposes the complete L'Oréal catalog to the retailer for search and retrieval of information. Because it is a Web service, L'Oréal has achieved its objective of operating one set of information that it maintains, which is available to a virtually unlimited number of retailers. Its effective use of its Shop-in-a-Shop and a Web services strategy means that the company can expand and improve the service with the knowledge that the all-important retailer can readily interconnect to L'Oréal.

**FIGURE 12.7**
*A SOAP Response Message*

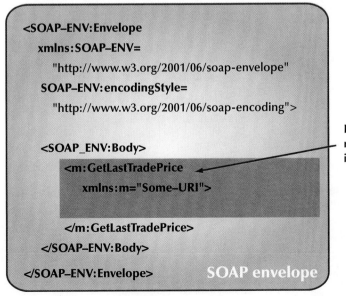

A SOAP response message

*Source:* IBM.

A SOAP message object, stated in XML, is sent to the remote Web service asking for processing. In turn, the Web service performs the processing and responds with the *result* of running the method. (Figure 12.7) For instance, an airline might want to make a freight tracking service available to its commercial customers. Rather than having each customer embed the code for entering shipment numbers and other tracking details, the airline may choose to establish a Web service that contains the computer code for tracking shipments. By this means, the customer need only have its program sent a SOAP message containing the shipment information to the airline's computer. It will activate the Web service that tracks and reports back the shipment's location.

The application developer invoking a Web service does not deal with the technical details (such as the language in which it is programmed or the operating system or type of computer on which it is running) of the service. The application developer's only concern is that the Web service produces and then returns the correct result in the expected format.

SOAP thus frees the developer from worrying about writing programming code to produce the result or the details of how the Web service is implemented on the remote computer. SOAP is being developed through W3C, thereby ensuring it will, like XML, evolve as a public, license-free standard.

## Web Services Description Language

**Web services description language (WSDL)**

Describes the capabilities offered by a specific Web service as well as the protocols and formats the service uses.

How do developers creating an application know what functions a specific Web service performs? **Web services description language (WSDL)** describes the capabilities offered by a specific Web service as well as the protocols and formats the service uses. The WSDL for a Web service dealing with stock quotations would define the service and indicate the locations where this service is available. Additional details would indicate the data that must be provided and the results that would be returned. WSDL uses XML to describe the data (Figure 12.8). Web service developers would use special tools to construct the complete WSDL for a service, thereby avoiding the need to write the detailed line-by-line specifications needed to define the service.

## Universal Description, Discovery, and Integration

**universal description, discovery, and integration (UDDI)**

A worldwide directory for registering, finding, and using Web services.

How do developers locate the capabilities of a specific Web service? **Universal description, discovery, and integration (UDDI)** is a worldwide directory for registering, finding, and using Web services. Via the UDDI, creators of Web services can publish their services, and application developers can discover and use their services (Figure 12.9) Many companies have lined up to contribute to and support UDDI, including such diverse firms as Accenture, Cargill, Dell, IBM, Microsoft, Sabre, SAP, and SUN.

**FIGURE 12.8**

*Web Services Description Language (WSDL)*

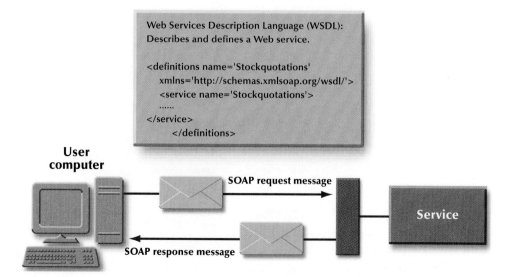

Web Services Description Language (WSDL): Describes and defines a Web service.

```
<definitions name='Stockquotations'
    xmlns='http://schemas.xmlsoap.org/wsdl/'>
    <service name='Stockquotations'>
    ......
</service>
    </definitions>
```

User computer

SOAP request message

Service

SOAP response message

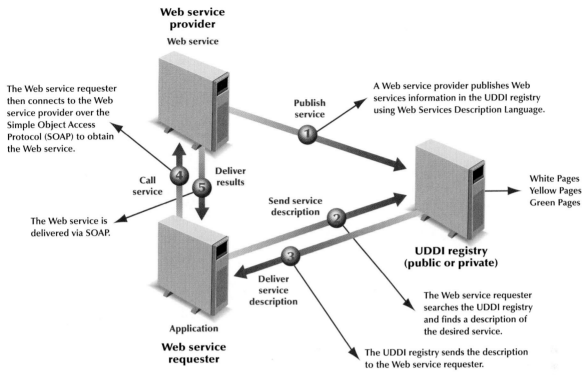

The Web service requester then connects to the Web service provider over the Simple Object Access Protocol (SOAP) to obtain the Web service.

The Web service is delivered via SOAP.

**Publish service**

A Web service provider publishes Web services information in the UDDI registry using Web Services Description Language.

White Pages
Yellow Pages
Green Pages

**UDDI registry (public or private)**

The Web service requester searches the UDDI registry and finds a description of the desired service.

The UDDI registry sends the description to the Web service requester.

**FIGURE 12.9**

*Universal Description, Discovery, and Integration (UDDI)*

(UDDI) provides a way to find Web services via a services registry.

## CRITICAL CONNECTIONS 2

## InterKnowlogy Develops Web Service to Aid San Diego Drivers

Southern California's highways are well known for the high volume of traffic they carry. Drivers often have difficulty deciding on any given day which route to their destination may be the best to take to avoid traffic jams or accidents that might be tying up traffic. Radio announcements, the usual source of information, provide a solution for only a fraction of the drivers.

InterKnowlogy, an IT development company located near San Diego, California, decided to do something about distributing traffic information around the city. It decided to create and host an interactive Web site at its company headquarters. It created a Web service that enables commuters to retrieve up-to-the minute traffic information from their cars. Using mobile, handheld devices, such as mobile phones, drivers can easily query the Internet application to check the current traffic speed on any freeway travel route. It is easy to see why InterKnowlogy's innovation is becoming indispensable for many area commuters.

**yellow pages**
Describe the services offered by UDDI.

**green pages**
Describe how an application can use the Web services.

The directory is maintained in several versions. UDDI's *white pages* contain contact information about Web service providers (the companies publishing their Web service), including Web site addresses. Its **yellow pages** describe the services offered by the company. UDDI's **green pages** describe how an application can use the Web services. It includes technical information about where the service is located and the characteristics and features of the service. UDDI messages are transmitted via SOAP.

# A Final Word

The Internet and the World Wide Web have had a profound impact on the distribution of information in professional and personal settings. Yet in many ways, the greatest impact is still to come. Enterprises large and small are seeking ways to capitalize on these innovations, both for existing legacy systems and in the creation of new applications. The widespread interest in creating Web-enabled applications will undoubtedly continue to grow, fueled by new technologies such as XML. At the same time, a vigorous evaluation of Web services is underway as companies seek to determine how they can avoid redeveloping application modules and services that have already been created by other developers. One point is clear. The use of Web-enabled applications within organizations—to create end-to-end integration between enterprises—is here to stay.

# CRITICAL CONNECTIONS

## 1 Part II: Telenor's Web-Enabled Service Meets Customer Needs—24 Hours a Day

 Telenor's Web-enabled service links customers directly to the company's legacy service and billing systems that support its telecommunications, Internet, and television services. By automating its support services, customers can now log on to the company's Web portal. Using a secure password, they can query the system about services, adjust their service subscriptions, and make payments.

The back end of the service system consists of well-established, mission-critical legacy systems. Telenor uses XML-based Web services and SOAP to integrate the online site with the back-end systems. Without Web services, it would have been very difficult for the company to create the online service portal.

### Questions for Discussion

1. As a customer of Telenor, how would you feel about having the online service capability available anytime you need it, rather than having to speak with a customer-service assistant?
2. What benefits does Telenor's Web-enabled system return to the company?
3. Why is SOAP an important tool for integrating the company's legacy systems to its Web portal?

## 2 Part II: InterKnowlogy Develops Web Service to Aid San Diego Drivers

InterKnowlogy's Web service enables San Diego drivers to query the company's Internet site from any mobile device, checking the current traffic speed on any of the city's freeways. The system is designed to query the CalTrans traffic-information Web site where it retrieves newly updated traffic data. The Web service pulls the traffic-speed data from the database and, with the help of SOAP, exposes it as XML content that can be returned to the InterKnowlogy Web site.

Drivers query the Web service by transmitting the identity of the selected freeway and direction of travel. The Web site in turn transmits the traffic information in a form that can be displayed on the driver's mobile device.

InterKnowlogy hosts the Web service as a benefit to the public. It does not receive any funds for its efforts, nor does it offer to sell the service.

### Questions for Discussion

1. What characteristics of InterKnowlogy's traffic reporting service qualify it as a Web service?
2. What benefits does XML provide in the retrieval of traffic information from the CalTrans traffic database?
3. As a San Diego driver, what would be your assessment of the InterKnowlogy traffic-information service?

# Summary of Learning Objectives

**1 Describe the three principal forces behind the interest in creating Web-enabled applications in enterprises.** First, the widespread use of browsers has fueled several factors, as follows: They are virtually always shipped with new computers; there is a large installed base of browser users; and they are appearing on other IT devices. In addition, they have intuitive features and offer a level of flexibility that makes them attractive as a universal front-end for applications. Second, there is widespread interest in using the Web as a front end to legacy systems. Third, it is becoming commonplace for enterprises to interconnect their business systems using Web-related capabilities.

**2 Distinguish between the purposes of HTML and XML in Web-enabled applications.** HTML, long associated with the display of information on Web pages, focused on information presentation—what the information looks like when presented. In contrast, XML is a set of rules for *describing* the information or data itself.

**3 Explain how XML aids in creating interenterprise IT applications.** XML tags identify Web data, specifying the actual content of the data so that a system can read and process the data. As a result, data created in one application can be interpreted and processed in another application, thereby supporting the development of interenterprise applications that exchange data.

**4 Identify the six advantages of XML.** XML is Web-based, and it is extensible, meaning that application developers can design their own customized markup languages for describing data so that other applications can use the data. In addition, XML enables independent computer systems to interact, thereby fostering end-to-end application integration. Because XML is a public for- mat, not the proprietary property of any company, it enjoys the widespread support of many software vendors.

**5 Explain the potential benefit of Web services to enterprise IT applications.** Web services enable independent developers to create applications or modules and make them accessible to other developers over the Internet. The modules can be interconnected with an application—the actual program code remains at the originating developer's location—making it unnecessary for each developer to independently create identical modules. Web services facilitate the sharing of software modules.

**6 Identify and describe the three tools that facilitate the use of Web services.** Simple object access protocol (SOAP) is a protocol for invoking remote Web service objects using XML. Universal description, discovery, and integration (UDDI) is an XML-based public directory service that provides information about available Web services. Web services description language (WSDL) is a protocol that describes the capabilities of a Web services object. Collectively SOAP, UDDI, and WSDL makes it feasible for developers to learn and share Web services created by other developers.

# Key Terms

## Review Questions

1. Describe the characteristics of a Web-enabled application.
2. What three forces are behind the widespread interest in Web-enabled applications? Briefly describe each force.
3. A growing number of IT application developers are seeking to use Web browsers for more than just interaction with the Internet. Why do they have this interest?
4. What are legacy systems and how do they come about? In most enterprises, are legacy applications of low value in day-to-day operations? Why or why not?
5. What is the challenge of seeking to interconnect enterprises when doing so involves linking heterogeneous applications?
6. What is XML, and why has it been developed?
7. Both HTML and XML are languages associated with the Internet. How are they similar in structure? How do they differ in purpose and use?
8. Why should enterprise application developers be interested in XML if the application they are creating will process data received from a business partner's IT application? What benefits could XML offer to the developer?
9. List and explain the six advantages of XML.
10. Describe the purpose of DTDs. How are they related to XML? Is their use mandatory if an enterprise is using XML in an application?
11. What is the relation between XML, XML style sheets, and XSL? When is XSL used in relation to an enterprise application?
12. How might XML overcome some of the undesirable features of a legacy system?
13. Describe the principle of Web services.
14. To use a Web service, must an application developer embed the program code of the Web service in an enterprise application? Why or why not?
15. What is SOAP and what is its role in the use of Web services?
16. How do potential users of Web services learn of their existence and availability?
17. Describe the purpose of WSDL. What is its relation to UDDI?
18. What role do white pages, yellow pages, and green pages play in the use of Web services?

## Discussion Questions

1. Although there appears to be widespread interest in Web services among systems developers and IT managers, there are also opponents. They point out that there is no official services standard and so at best, a de facto standard will emerge from one or more vendors. They say since it is unclear which vendors will be supportive of the standard, it is risky for systems developers to place too much confidence in Web services.

   Opponents also claim that Web services were initially conceived as suitable for low-value transactions (like calculating interest paid on loans and mortgages). However, the emphasis on using such services for inter-enterprise or e-commerce transactions of high value to an enterprise makes no sense. Users of Web services have very little information to validate the usefulness or reliability of these services. For this reason alone, opponents say that an enterprise concerned about security and reliability should not even consider Web services.

   What is your position? Do you side with the proponents or the opponents of Web services? What factors underlie the position you hold?

2. Who is responsible for the quality of a Web services application? For instance, suppose a developer reviews the documentation for a published, registered Web service. Based on the information and assurance of the Web-service creator, the developer decides to incorporate the service into a key application.

   After several weeks of using the Web service, the developer determines that the service does not perform properly. In fact, the service has caused the adopting company to lose a substantial sum of money through malfunctions the creator unknowingly incorporated into the Web service. Should the developer have a legal claim against the Web-service creator for damages equal to at least the money lost? Why or why not?

   Suppose the developer learns that the creator of the Web service knowingly included a component that would cause any user of the service to lose money through its use. Should a user have a legal claim against the Web-service creator? Why or why not?

## Group Projects and Applications

### Project 1

Visit with the systems developers at several nearby corporations or government agencies to learn whether they have an installed base of legacy systems. If you find they do not operate legacy systems, find out why they are different from so many other organizations that have such systems.

If the developers indicate they do have a set of legacy systems running, ask them to identify the functions of those applications. Are they critical to the mission of the enterprise? Also ask them how the applications came to be legacy systems. Then explore with them the challenges of operating and maintaining the legacy systems.

Prepare a summary of your findings in the form of a PowerPoint presentation that you can present to others or post on a Web site.

### Project 2

Arrange to interview, in person or by telephone, a set of IT managers at the headquarters of retail and manufacturing companies to learn about their view on the importance of XML. Pose a set of questions that will enable you to determine whether they are using or are considering using XML in any applications within the enterprise. If so, explore the reasons they are doing so. If not, determine the extent to which they have evaluated the potential of XML and why they do not see a role for XML in their future.

a. Compare the findings across the different types of organizations. Are the views consistent regardless of the type of enterprise, or do they vary?
b. Prepare a summary of your findings.
c. Include in the summary your assessment of the future of XML in retailing and manufacturing industries.

## Net_Work

1. As discussed in this chapter, the World Wide Web Consortium creates Web standards. Its mission is to *lead the Web to its full potential,* which it does by developing technologies (specifications, guidelines, software, and tools) that create a forum for information, commerce, inspiration, independent thought, and collective understanding.

   Visit the Web site of the W3C and learn more about its activities.

   a. What principles underlie W3C's activities?
   b. What are its membership requirements?
   c. What activities does W3C have underway that are related to further development of XML?

2. The growth of Web services depends on the extent to which key vendors support their development as well as

the availability of the types of services that application developers need. A wide variety of information is available on the Internet to gain insight into these concerns.

a. Using the Internet, conduct an investigation to assess the support for XML and Web services by visiting the Web sites of a sample of IT vendors. Include in your investigation such vendors as IBM, Sun Microsystems, and Microsoft as well as other important vendors of your choosing.
b. In addition, search for and visit a set of Web-service registries to determine the availability of such services.
c. Prepare a written summary of your findings, including your assessment of the future of Web services.

## Cool Mobility

### On Assignment

*Cool Mobility* accepted an earlier proposal you submitted to add products and services to its Web site. A project team was formed by CIO James Marsalis to undertake the enhancements. The team will write the software, make the necessary database modifications, and manage the testing and implementation process.

Once implemented, a well-used system often leads to requests for enhancements. This is as true for applications running on a company intranet as it is for other applications.

## In Consultation

The expertise you have demonstrated has led to more frequent inquiries from both managers and IT staff members who are seeking your opinion. Today you received the following inquiries concerning both Internet and intranet applications.

a. *As our business has grown, we have not only been selling mobile phones at a faster rate, but also the frequency of reorders—needed to restock our inventory—has increased. Though the reorder process is only moderately time-consuming, we want to avoid the possibility of forgetting to send in an order once it is prepared.*

During an IT staff meeting, one of the Web developers mentioned the possibility of using XML as a way of electronically linking with the computerized order systems used by the companies that supply the mobile phones. The analyst suggested that XML messages—containing company and order information—could be transmitted automatically to the vendors. The vendors, in turn, would process the messages, and resupply the company. If the message is coded using XML, any vendor should be able to process it.

Is this true? Should the company consider XML as a tool for transmitting electronic resupply orders to the vendors? Should any vendor be able to accept and process an XML message?

b. *Cool Mobility* has decided that, like the giant retailer Wal-Mart and a growing number of other retailers doing business on the Internet, it will collect sales tax for the orders it processes, turning the revenue over to the appropriate government agency. The sales tax is calculated as a percentage of the amount of the sale. However, the tax rate varies by the state and locale where the buyer lives. This means that there are several *thousand* state and county taxing authorities in the United States. Moreover, tax rates change throughout the year.

When you heard the company's plan for collecting taxes, and that they were wrestling with a way to keep track of the local tax rates, the possibility of using Web services for this purpose immediately came to mind. Before offering an opinion to Marsalis, you want to be certain your idea is correct. Hence, you conduct your own investigation, including a search of the Internet.

1. Is the calculation of sales taxes a good Web-service application? Why or why not?
2. Are Web services available on the Internet for sales-tax calculation?

c. This must be your day for Web service questions, for another inquiry came in from the human-resources department. The department uses the intranet to keep employees informed about contributions to their retirement accounts, known as 401(k) accounts. Currently, each employee can view a spreadsheet-like report that summarizes month-by-month contributions to an investment account that increases or decreases in value according to trends in the stock market. Adjusted values of the investment are reported every three months.

The inquiry from human resources asked whether there is a way to maintain in real-time employees' 401(k) balance and investment information. You immediately decided to check out the feasibility of using a Web service, posing the question: Are Web services available that will automatically update employee retirement investment summaries? How can such services be incorporated into human-resource services so that employees can view current balance information from their PCs?

---

## Case Study

## Dollar Rent a Car's Web Services Fuel Business Growth

Dollar Rent a Car, a subsidiary of Dollar Thrifty Automotive Group Inc., is one of the world's largest car-rental agencies. It maintains a fleet of over 78,000 vehicles available at more then 260 suburban and on-airport rental car locations at all major airports throughout the United States. It has approximately 430 worldwide locations in 26 countries, with a significant presence in Australia, Canada, the Caribbean, and Latin America. Through its alliance with Sixt rent a car, Dollar offers service in more than 25 additional countries covering Europe, the Middle East, and Africa. Dollar worldwide headquarters is located in Tulsa, Oklahoma.

Dollar has long maintained a worldwide reservation system, known as *Quick Keys,* running on a mainframe computer. The mainframe enables the company to handle the high volumes of rental transactions that occur during peak rental periods.

Customers interacted with the reservation system in two ways: Some corporate customers submitted reservation requests as EDI transaction documents. Others, including leisure travelers, submitted reservations through the dollar.com Web site.

Dollar, like other rental-car agencies, had long received the majority of its reservations through referrals transmitted electronically from large airline-reservation systems, such as Sabre and Apollo. Since these and other corporate and government reservations were submitted as EDI transactions, Dollar paid a transaction fee for each reservation that it received.

The company sought to increase the volume of reservations and to create direct links to potential new customers. Dollar's goal was to reduce the dependence on airline-reservation systems and avoid paying transaction fees. To do so, management decided to develop an electronic link so that corporate and government customers could, like leisure travelers, interact with the Quick Keys reservation system via the Internet rather than by EDI.

Dollar's advanced information technology group initially planned to provide the customer link via the company's Web site. However, one of the group managers suggested the company consider using XML Web services to link customers with Quick Keys. In order to demonstrate the potential of Web services, a team of developers constructed a working prototype. The prototype, which was created and put into use in just two weeks, provided the capability for customers to send rate inquiries and reservations to Dollar using SOAP requests.

The development group quickly concluded that the Web services strategy offered many benefits to Dollar. For instance, team members agreed that it provided a new channel for customer interactions that ultimately accounted for millions of dollars of new revenue annually. In addition, it enabled the company to put into place an adaptable interface to its legacy reservation system. Developers were confident that exposing the

reservation system as an XML Web service would provide a standard interface that could be used by many other IT applications, both internal and external at the company.

The adaptable interface provided by the Web-services strategy was tested when the company decided to support the receipt of rental rate requests and reservations transmitted from Palm Pilot PDAs. Using the previously created XML Web service, Dollar developers were able to construct and implement the PDA connection to Quick Keys is less than six weeks, much faster than could be achieved with any other alternative.

A few months after that (during which time Dollar replaced its Web server with a new version of the server operating system) the company's marketing department requested that the IT group extend the reach of the company's Web site. Marketing wanted to have it accessible by *all mobile devices* (both wireless PDAs and mobile phones). Time was of the essence, as Dollar wanted to be the first to announce wireless access to its reservation system.

Interconnecting mobile devices with a Web site was known to be a challenging task. Each mobile device is unique, featuring distinctive hardware and software technology. Dollar's IT developers wanted to avoid writing unique Web pages for each mobile device, so they checked various soft-

ware vendors to learn what programs were available to create the necessary Web links. However, they quickly concluded that the vendors could not deliver the software rapidly enough. Moreover, they decided that the vendor's prices were excessive.

One of the developers took up the challenge and in just 30 days created a Web site for mobile devices. The Web site was designed to interconnect with the company's existing XML Web services, and in turn the Quick Keys reservation system.

XML Web services have proved beneficial to Dollar Rent a Car on multiple occasions, extending the life of its legacy reservation system. The company is well positioned to seek new customers and grow its lines of business without having to worry whether it has the information technology necessary to support its growth.

### Questions for Discussion

1. What advantages do Web services provide for Dollar Rent a Car?
2. How have Web services extended the value of the company's legacy rental reservation system?
3. What role does SOAP play in Dollar's reservation system today?
4. From the viewpoint of a Dollar customer, is the company's creation of XML services a good idea? What advantages or disadvantages do XML Web services provide to Dollar customers?

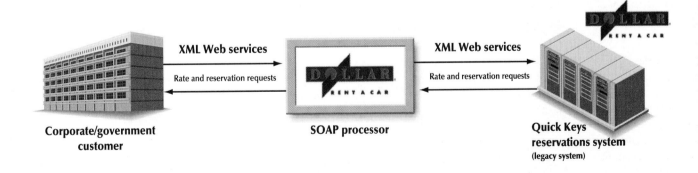

Corporate/government customer — XML Web services — Rate and reservation requests — SOAP processor — XML Web services — Rate and reservation requests — Quick Keys reservations system (legacy system)

# Information Systems in the Enterprise

## LEARNING OBJECTIVES

When you have completed this chapter, you should be able to

1 Define and explain the purpose of information systems.

2 Describe the six types of business information systems and know when each is used.

3 Summarize the purpose of computer-integrated manufacturing systems and manufacturing cells.

4 List and describe five specialized types of computer-integrated manufacturing systems.

5 Describe the distinguishing characteristics of enterprise resource planning systems and explain why so many large enterprises have implemented these systems.

6 Discuss the ways in which information technology may play a strategic role in an enterprise.

# GE Plastics Tracks Performance Using a Digital Dashboard

*G*E Plastics, a division of General Electric Corp, is a leading global manufacturer and distributor of plastic resins and related products that are used throughout the appliance, automotive, information technology, and building and construction industries. People often use products containing GE plastics without even realizing it.

GE Plastics, like its parent company, is known for its ongoing stream of product innovations and for having effective management systems. Among its recent products is Lexan®, an innovative polymer film technology that GE hopes the automotive industry will adopt widely. Lexan has qualities that fit perfectly with what automakers need to replace many painted parts on today's cars. Plastic is lighter than painted steel (good for fuel economy), holds its shape well (meaning less dents and dings), and will not rust.

A recent management tool, the digital dashboard, enables GE Plastics managers to be apprised of how its products, such as Lexan, and the operating units that make them, are performing. A *digital dashboard* (also known as a *digital cockpit*) is a software program comparable in function to an automobile dashboard or an aircraft cockpit. The software displays easy-to-read activity performance measures (like digital gauges on an auto dashboard) that permit an observer to quickly check whether an activity's performance is at, above, or below expectations. Additional detail explaining the summary measures, including charts and graphs, can easily be displayed if needed.

Creation of a digital dashboard starts when GE Plastics executives determine the eight to 10 key performance measures (such as sales revenue, number of orders taken, pricing quotations, and levels of inventory) that will provide the best indicators of how well the division is operating at any point in time. Thresholds for acceptable performance levels are also identified so they can be built into the system.

Next, a method for collecting the necessary data is devised so that as events occur (such as completion of a sale or adding stock to inventory), the details describing those events can be captured and automatically entered into the enterprise's information systems.

At the corporate level, the GE corporate digital dashboard reports the information from each of the divisional dashboards. Like the dashboards used within each business unit, the key indicator data is color coded when it is shown on the dashboard—green for good performance and red for a performance measure that is below its target. It includes tabs containing graphs, and the capability to display screens of details that explain the divisional results. The contents of the corporate dashboard tell so much about overall company performance that its viewing is restricted to fewer than 50 executives.

Company and division managers find that the dashboards enable them to assimilate a large volume of detail and transaction data because results are shown in a concise, meaningful form. In addition, the dashboards allow managers to keep abreast of major developments as they occur and to detect potential problems before they get out of hand. Weekly and monthly reports do not provide this capability because they appear *after* problems occur, not *as they are occurring.* In fact, the digital dashboards have proven so efficient that GE Plastics and some other divisions have even eliminated their weekly performance reports.

*T*his chapter examines the activities of many successful enterprises that are using IT to run their businesses and to manage their manufacturing activities. First, this chapter looks at the various types of enterprise information systems now in use throughout the business world. Second, it focuses on the applications of IT automation in manufacturing industries. You also will see how *enterprise resource planning systems* integrate the data and information in a way that cannot be duplicated by independent enterprise systems. The last section of the chapter explores the competitive value that information systems can provide an enterprise when developed for strategic purposes.

# Enterprise Information Systems

Recall that an **information system** is a system in which data and information flow from one person or department to another. Frequently, the term **enterprise information system** (or **business information system**) is used to refer to the family of IT applications that underlies the activities of running and managing a business (including the people and procedures associated with the applications). The six types of information systems commonly used in business enterprises are as follows: (1) transaction processing systems; (2) management reporting systems; (3) decision support systems; (4) group support systems; (5) executive support systems; and (6) expert support systems.

## Transaction Processing Systems

Enterprises exist by managing transactions, which are events that involve or affect the enterprise. Transactions are at the heart of every company's business process (Figure 13.1a and Figure 13.1b).

Processing transactions efficiently and accurately is what keeps an enterprise running smoothly. If a company cannot accept or fulfill orders, record its sales, manage its inventory, bill for its products or services, collect money, meet payroll needs, or maintain income-tax records, it will not stay in business for long. A **transaction processing system (TPS)** is a shared system that uses a combination of information technology and manual procedures to process data and information and to manage transactions. With a TPS, each transaction is handled according to standard company procedures. The characteristics of TPS are summarized in Table 13.1.

**TPS at Price Chopper Supermarkets**   Price Chopper Supermarkets is a regional grocery chain in the northeastern United States. In conjunction with its key suppliers, it has developed an efficient TPS for processing delivery information. When deliveries arrive at a store, the driver connects a handheld computer to a communications cable on the loading dock. Invoices for the delivery are automatically transmitted to a store computer, which immediately checks the invoices for correct pricing and delivery authorization, using details downloaded daily from a purchasing and product authorization database at company headquarters.

---

**information system**

A system in which data and information flow from one person or department to another.

**enterprise information system/business information system**

Used to refer to the family of IT applications that underlies the activities of running and managing a business.

**transaction processing system (TPS)**

A shared business information system that uses a combination of information technology and manual procedures to process data and information and to manage transactions.

**a)** Stopping for fast food at a bodega in the "Little Havana" section of Miami.

**b)** Registering for the new semester's classes at the Registrar's office at Suffolk University.

**c)** Signing a lease at a Citroën dealership in Paris.

**d)** Purchasing tickets for a ride on a San Francisco cable car.

**FIGURE 13.1**

***Business Transactions***

Businesses exist by managing transactions, the events that involve or affect the enterprise. Transaction processing systems can help to manage a wide variety of transactions, from registration for a university course to lease signings at an auto dealership.

Meanwhile, as the products are carried into the store, the receiving manager counts the goods, entering the actual quantity delivered into another handheld computer connected to the store computer by FM radio signals (Figure 13.2). The computer immediately compares the driver's counts to the receiving manager's counts. Any discrepancy can be adjusted while the supplier is still at the delivery dock.

Each day, the invoices from the many deliveries made to the store are uploaded from the store computer to an accounts-payable system at headquarters. This system processes each invoice to detect errors or discrepancies and notifies the store manager of any problems. After verification, the invoices go into the company's accounts payable cycle.

| Table 13.1 Characteristics of a Transaction Processing System |
|---|
| Processes a high volume of similar business transactions. |
| Supports multiple users in routine, everyday transactions. |
| Uses relatively simple procedures to control processing and to ensure accuracy. |
| Produces documents and reports. |
| Updates files and databases. |

**FIGURE 13.2**

*The Transaction Processing System at Price Chopper Supermarkets*

When deliveries arrive at Price Chopper Supermarkets, drivers use handheld computers to transmit invoices and pricing information to both the store's computer and company headquarters. Meanwhile, as the products are delivered into the store, the receiving manager counts the goods, entering the actual quantity delivered into another handheld computer connected to the store computer by FM radio signals.

**The Transaction Processing Sequence and TPS Output and Reports** A transaction processing system can process either online or in batches (see Chapter 2). Figure 13.3 summarizes the processing sequence and the five types of output produced during transaction processing including (1) action documents, (2) detail reports, (3) summary reports, (4) exception reports, and (5) updated master data.

**action document**

A document designed to trigger a specific action or to signify that a transaction has taken place.

- **Action documents** are documents designed to trigger a specific action or to signify that a transaction has taken place. At Price Chopper, for example, invoices are action documents intended to result in the payment of money. When a utility company produces a customer's monthly bill, it, too, is creating an action document designed to result in the payment of money. Similarly, state motor vehicle departments process their files regularly to determine who must renew their car registrations during a particular month, and then send out an action document prepared by the system. Airlines' reservation transactions lead to action documents in the form of printed tickets and, in some cases, boarding passes with the individual's seat assignment.

**detail report/transaction log**

A report describing each processed transaction.

- A **detail report,** sometimes called a **transaction log,** contains data describing each processed transaction. It includes enough details to identify the transaction and its most important characteristics. For example, if the transaction is the payment of an invoice, the detail report will list the transaction and indicate the amount of money paid, the check number or cash reference, the date of the transaction, and the individual or company making the payment. If any questions arise during or after processing, the transaction log serves as a ready reference.

**summary report**

A report that shows the overall results of processing for a period of time or for a batch of transactions and includes a grand total for all listed transactions and the average transaction amount.

- A **summary report** shows the overall results of processing for a period of time or for a batch of transactions, and includes a grand total for all listed transactions and the average transaction amount. It lists in summary form the transactions that took place. Different versions of the report may be produced for various recipients. For example, a grocery store may produce one summary report for the bookkeeper, another for the receiving manager, and others for department managers. If any of these people want additional data or information, they can request detailed reports, which also can be tailored to individuals.

**exception report**

A report that lists unusual, erroneous, or unacceptable transactions or results.

- An **exception report** lists unusual, erroneous, or unacceptable transactions or results. An exception is any activity that falls outside normal guidelines or expected conditions. One Price Chopper exception report, for example, lists supplier prices that are different from those in the database, items delivered that the store normally does not carry, and items delivered that were not ordered. The exception report is designed to call attention to the discrepancy and trigger an action to deal with it.

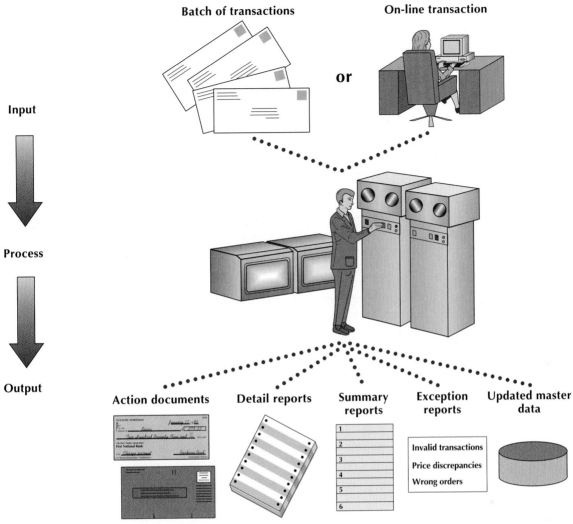

**FIGURE 13.3**
*The Transaction Processing Sequence and TPS Output*

- Transaction processing systems also generate **updated master data.** When a transaction is processed, all records in the system must be adjusted. When a customer makes a payment, for example, the database must be adjusted to show a decrease in that customer's account balance. When a supplier moves, the database must be updated to include the new address and telephone number. The people using the system should always be informed when master data change. In most cases, the detail report will include a summary of these changes.

  Error-free transaction processing is essential. Because the data and information produced by transaction processing are used in the company's other business systems, a mistake in transaction processing can have a multiplier effect throughout the organization.

**updated master data**
An adjustment of all records in a system in response to a processed transaction.

## Management Information Systems

**Management information systems (MIS)** are designed to provide managers with information useful in decision making or problem solving. For example, the manager of a furniture store needs to make many decisions concerning the purchase and replenishment of stock. These decisions include determining how much merchandise to order, whether a particular supplier is too expensive or carries low-quality products, and whether to continue offering certain products or services. The manager may also need to

**management information system (MIS)**
A business information system designed to produce the information needed for successful management of a structured problem, process, department, or business.

solve the problems of high labor costs or equipment repair costs. Management information systems can help address these problems by retrieving and processing the data generated through transaction processing.

A person uses a management reporting system by requesting it to produce a certain report. Typically, the format and content of all reports are predetermined when the application is designed. The application simply retrieves the necessary data and information from a database or master file, processes them, and automatically presents the results in the specified format. For example, a Price Chopper district manager who wants to monitor the produce sales of all stores in her district may have a report designed for that purpose and produced regularly. Each time it is prepared, the format will be the same, with the data and information reflecting recent business activity.

Management information systems are designed to produce information needed for successful management of a process, department, or business. They support recurring decisions when information needs have been determined in advance. Table 13.2 summarizes the characteristics of management information systems.

The opening case describes how GE Plastics uses digital dashboards, a form of executive information system (discussed shortly), rather than paper reports, to receive information on the performance of its operating units. Information presented via the dashboard summarizes performance for key indicators of success. In addition, graphic and detailed information forms are also available. The dashboard was designed to reduce the need for paper reports while speeding the ability of management decision makers to detect and deal with unexpected situations quickly.

**TicketMaster's Online Ticket Inventory**   For millions of people, making plans to attend a concert, play, or sporting event begins with a visit to TicketMaster, the world's leading ticketing company, a division of USA Interactive. TicketMaster, headquartered in Los Angeles, annually sells consumers some 100 million event tickets through 19 worldwide telephone call centers and more than 3,500 retail ticket-center outlets, and over the Internet at www.ticketmaster.com. TicketMaster serves more than 8,000 clients worldwide, acting as the exclusive ticketing service for hundreds of leading arenas, stadiums, theaters, and performing-arts venues.

Consumers and clients alike depend on TicketMaster to maintain comprehensive and reliable ticket inventory control across all sales channels. Producing periodic reports summarizing ticket-sales transactions and monitoring the sales agents is an essential service for the company and its clients alike.

TicketMaster also evaluates its sales agents to ensure that they are meeting expected quality levels. Until recently, TicketMaster's sales centers used a paper-based system to track its agents' performance. Documents were compiled by hand into Microsoft Excel spreadsheets. Preparing a report summarizing the activities at all sales centers meant manually combining the details from many different spreadsheets. It was evident to all that the manual information system would increasingly become an obstacle to the company's growth.

The automated management information system that was subsequently implemented is designed to electronically accept and assemble information from the sales centers. The new system not only replaced the tedious and error-prone paper system, but it

| Table 13.2   *Characteristics of a Management Information System (MIS)* |
| --- |
| Uses data captured and stored as a result of transaction processing. |
| Reports data and information rather than details of transaction processing. |
| Assists managers in monitoring situations, evaluating conditions, and determining what actions need to be taken. |
| Supports recurring decisions. |
| Provides information in prespecified report formats, either in print or on-screen. |

also had the effect of speeding up the entire process. Whereas TicketMaster previously produced sales reports once a month, it is now able to produce reports to monitor its agents every 10 days. The result? The company realized even higher quality and productivity levels without the hassle of manual data handling procedures. Both consumers and clients benefit from the improved information system.

The *Information Technology in Practice* feature, "Hallmark's MIS Makes the Very Best Possible," shows how important a management information system is to Hallmark, a leading greeting card company and its 40,000 retailers.

# INFORMATION TECHNOLOGY IN PRACTICE

## Hallmark's MIS Makes the Very Best Possible

Hallmark Cards Inc., founded in January 1910 and headquartered in Kansas City, Missouri, is best known for helping people express their feelings and touch the lives of others. The Hallmark brand's reputation for quality was established early in the company's life through its uncompromising attention to detail. Since 1944, Hallmark has maintained its slogan, *When You Care Enough to Send the Very Best*. The company achieved distinction through its products, its network of specialty retail stores, national advertising, and as sponsor of the *Hallmark Hall of Fame*, television's most honored and enduring dramatic series.

Hallmark merchandise, including everyday and seasonal greeting cards, holiday ornaments, collectables, wrapping paper and bows, can be found in some 42,000 company-owned and franchised retail stores in the United States. The stores—6,000 to 10,000 square feet each—typically carry more than 40,000 items, some originating at Hallmark and others supplied by hundreds of other manufacturers.

Having the right variety of greeting cards containing just the right message for any special occasion is a key factor in Hallmark's success. Hence, Hallmark employs a creative staff of some 800 artists, designers, stylists, writers, editors, and photographers. Together they generate more than 23,000 new and redesigned greeting cards and related products per year.

Still, Hallmark's large selection of creative cards is not enough to ensure the company's success. The line of Hallmark products is highly diverse, yet the shelf life of most holiday cards is limited to a few weeks before and a few days after the specific holiday. Since retail card displays change constantly, it is essential that each store be always freshly stocked with the proper mix of greeting cards. Refreshing store displays, which means replenishing rapidly selling cards and removing old ones, is time-consuming. Yet the actions at the store level drive the entire Hallmark sales and replenishment process. The company relies on its effective IT capabilities to track merchandise from the production line to the point of sale in order to ensure its operations are efficient and profitable. Its management information system keeps track of sales and ensures the

right mix of products is on hand in the stores and in inventory.

At the store level, customer sales transaction data and information are captured by point of sale (POS) scanners. Hallmark links these operational systems with its headquarters information system. Sales data from the stores are fed into MIS where they are processed. Sales are analyzed to determine buying patterns and project demand. Using these results, the system is able to automatically order replacement products for shipment to the stores.

Hallmark also carefully manages its pipeline of merchandise and products so that it can be assured of meeting consumer demand. To do so, its information system processes data describing past manufacturing and distribution activities to determine which products had greater than expected demand (i.e., which store orders went unfulfilled). The system then suggests adjustments in production.

Hallmark's impressive record of having just the right greeting for those wishing to send *the very best* is a result of two important resources—its creative designers and its effective management information system.

# Decision Support Systems

A **decision support system (DSS)** is an information system designed to assist in decision making by managers who are wrestling with unique situations. When the decision process is relatively unstructured—that is, the extent to which certain variables influence an activity or outcome is initially not clear, and/or only part of the information needed is assembled in advance—the DSS helps structure the problem by providing the needed information. A quantitative model of the situation is created using the DSS, and information is processed to determine the impact of variables included in the model. Typically, the uniqueness of the issues and the breadth of the problems will require the system to retrieve and process data from several files and databases and to use data provided online by individual decision makers simultaneously.

Because information needs are not known at the beginning of a unique situation, the reports and displays generated by DSS are not designed in advance. Instead, the user will generally request the processing of data and the generation of information through such inquiries as *How many _____ have this characteristic?*, *Under what circumstances did this occur?*, or *What if _____ occurs?* Frequently, getting some information raises additional questions, which, in turn, creates the need for more information. For this reason, a DSS must have greater flexibility than a management reporting system. The characteristics of decision support systems are summarized in Table 13.3.

**DSS in the U.S. Congress** Every time the U.S. Congress sets out to reevaluate revenue generation and the tax system, it faces a different situation. The economy has changed, new legislation affecting revenues is in effect, and the spending needs of the government have altered. Before it can begin preparing a new tax package, Congress must determine the intent of the new legislation (for example, to raise more revenue, to stimulate business spending on new plant and equipment, to attract more investment to business research and development, or to encourage more personal savings).

Analysts working for Congress can then formulate models for evaluating a new tax or revenue proposal and evaluate them through their decision support system. For example, finding out that a change in investment tax credits will have an undesirable effect on the economy may cause them to adjust and then reevaluate a proposed tax credit. Alternatively, determining that a change in tax rates will affect middle-class savings negatively may cause them to readjust the proposed tax rates. DSS software makes it possible to change the components of the model easily, recalculating them to determine the likely effects of different proposals (Figure 13.4).

Keep in mind that every tax package is different. The creation of each new package involves determining what new information is needed. These characteristics suggest the need for a decision support system rather than an information or transaction processing system, in which reporting needs have been predetermined.

# Group Support Systems

A **group support system (GSS)** permits people to process and interpret information as a group, even if they are not working face-to-face. Like a DSS, a GSS supports people working in situations that are not fully structured. In these kinds of situations, an impor-

| Table 13.3    Characteristics of a Decision Support System |
| --- |
| Assists people who make decisions where information requirements are not known in advance. |
| Supports problem solving and decision making where the situation is only partly structured. |
| Provides information needed to define and solve the problem. |
| Works both with files and database, as well as with people working online with the system. |
| Provides information in a format determined by the recipient at the time of need. |

# CRITICAL CONNECTIONS   1

## DSS Helps Build Energy-Efficient Homes

**DSS**

For years, energy designers and researchers have been devising techniques for building comfortable homes that can slash heating and cooling bills by 30 to 50 percent. But the techniques are not flooding the market, partly because of resistance by the construction industry. Many builders, used to building *to code* or to meet minimum standards, find it hard to justify the extra cost of energy-efficient construction. Others simply lack the engineering skills necessary to adopt the new techniques. This may change by the turn of the century, thanks to a number of programs designed to teach builders the new techniques and introduce them to a variety of new software tools.

Take the Energy Crafted Home Program, a trademarked program sponsored by several utilities and created with the help of a Harvard engineer. Most of the techniques taught at the program's seminars focus on ways to tighten the home's *envelope*—the boundary formed by the walls, ceilings, windows, and foundation. But make the envelope too tight, and you may let moisture or indoor pollutants build up. Looking at a building as a total system is really too much for the human brain to encompass all at once, say some engineers. But with the aid of computers, engineers can do just that.

The two simplest decision support software tools designed for this purpose are Builder Guide, from the Passive Solar Industries Council, and REM/Design, which was created by Architectural Energy Corp., of Boulder, Colorado. Both programs rely on a description of the home, climate data, and local utility rates to calculate the home's annual peak heating and cooling loads, energy costs, and so on. With the aid of the software, builders can compare the potential costs and savings associated with alternate construction techniques and floor plans.

tant part of problem solving involves conducting an analysis and determining what information is needed to make a decision.

Unlike in DSS systems, however, in GSS systems information is generated by the system in response to questions posed by group members. Online interaction is an essential GSS feature. Individuals usually work at networked computer workstations, entering questions, ideas, suggestions, and comments that are shared electronically with other

**FIGURE 13.4**

***Decision Support Systems in the U.S. Congress***

The decision-making process in the U.S. Congress—which is sometimes considered agonizingly slow—has been helped along by a decision support system. Congressional analysts are now using DSS generators to evaluate the effects of new tax and revenue proposals on businesses, taxpayers, and the economy.

group members, sometimes anonymously. (Chapter 8 and the *Photo Essay* at the end of the chapter discussed an important part of group support systems–groupware software.)

Many companies have constructed specially designed group support rooms called *decision rooms* (Figure 13.5a). Similar in style to conference or boardrooms, these facilities feature a large screen for display of information, individual workstations networked together, and a seating arrangement in which the group members can see one another. Another type of group support room uses a *remote decision network* (Figure 13.5b) format. Group members at remote locations are linked by a communications network that allows them to share databases, models, and GSS software. They enter their questions, ideas, and comments through a workstation; the network then displays these to other group members.

GSS sessions are typically managed by a facilitator who serves as an intermediary between the system and the group. This person is responsible for administering the group's activities and for keeping the group focused on the problem at hand. The facilitator draws out ideas and makes sure that no individual dominates the discussion.

Unlike the other business information systems discussed so far, a GSS does not produce traditional printed reports. Rather, the questions, comments, and ideas of each group session are captured in a database that can later be printed and reviewed. Frequently, the most important result of a GSS session is a decision, or series of decisions, about how to solve a problem or capitalize on an opportunity. Table 13.4 summarizes the characteristics of a group support system.

**GSS at Marriott**   Business travelers are among Marriott Hotels' most important customers. One reason Marriott is so successful is that it meets the needs of these travelers, even though they change from year to year. Periodically, Marriott assembles handpicked hotel managers, heads of housekeeping, front-desk personnel, catering managers, room-service coordinators, and bellhops to compare experiences regarding their guests. The meeting is conducted with a group support system, wherein hotel personnel enter their thoughts and criticisms regarding current capabilities and ideas for new services. For example, they may tell about encounters with guests in which they provided, or could not provide, an important service the guests wanted.

**FIGURE 13.5**

### *Group Support Rooms*

Users of a GSS can be linked together in a decision room or through a remote decision network.

**(a) Decision room**

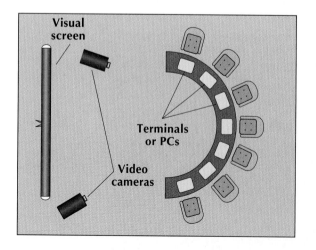

**(b) Remote decision network**

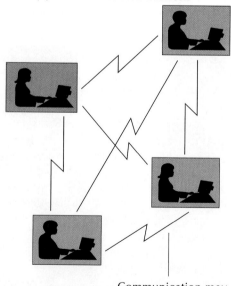

Communication may be through local or wide area network

| Table 13.4   **Characteristics of a Group Support System** |
| :--- |
| Supports situations that are not fully structured. |
| Assists in analyzing the problem under consideration. |
| Is used by groups or teams rather than individuals. |
| Emphasizes communication and generation of ideas and information. |
| Permits communication among team members at different locations, who participate through communications networks. |
| Involves a facilitator who keeps the group focused on the problem at hand and draws ideas out of group members. |
| Generates a database of the group's questions, comments, and ideas rather than a traditional report. |

Because the entries are made anonymously, Marriott finds that the rank or pay level of the employee is not a deterrent to sharing ideas. (Without anonymity, hourly-wage desk attendants might feel intimidated by a hotel general manager.) When the ideas and comments are displayed visually, they are discussed openly, without knowledge of their origin, so the group can evaluate them honestly. You can see how such Marriott service features as voice mail, rentable portable computers, and cordless telephones might have originated through GSS sessions.

## Executive Support Systems

The activities of top-level executives in business and government are often quite different from those of middle managers and staff members. Rather than focusing on a single business process or an individual product or service line, as most middle managers do, executives spend most of their time meeting the challenges and opportunities that will affect the enterprise's future. When a serious problem arises—for example, an industrial accident or the potential loss of an important customer—they are also likely to be involved in determining the cause, dealing with the effect, and preventing the problem's recurrence. Executives also spend a good deal of their time on activities external to the company. Uncovering new market opportunities, monitoring the activities of competitors, and keeping an eye on impending legislation are among executives' principal external concerns.

As you can probably guess, and as Figure 13.6 shows, executives spend much of their time in meetings. In fact, they spend very little time in their offices and have precious few moments of quiet time in which to contemplate the intricate plans and strategies they must put into effect. When they are in their offices, they need to be briefed on enterprise developments quickly and in a way that provides them with useful and well-focused information. An **executive support system (ESS),** sometimes called an **executive information system (EIS),** is an interactive information system designed to fill exactly this need. An ESS encompasses a broad spectrum of enterprise activities, presenting information on everything from entire business units to product and service lines to customers and suppliers.

Behind the scenes, the ESS software retrieves data and information from a variety of databases within or external to the company. Some ESS's are designed to display information on the company's stock prices (if the stock is publicly traded), current orders booked, and market prices of important materials. (An airline executive will want to know the cost of fuel, for example, while an executive at an appliance manufacturer will undoubtedly monitor current steel prices.) The ESS may also include a communications link for retrieval of information from sources external to the company, such as Dow Jones News/Retrieval and similar services. Some systems also include DSS-like capabilities that let executives test *what if* strategies and compare alternatives. Often companies combine DSS, GSS, and ESS. A sample menu screen from an ESS developed by the Comshare software company appears in Figure 13.7.

**executive support system (ESS)/executive information system (EIS)**

An interactive business information system designed to support executives that is capable of presenting summary information on company and industry activities.

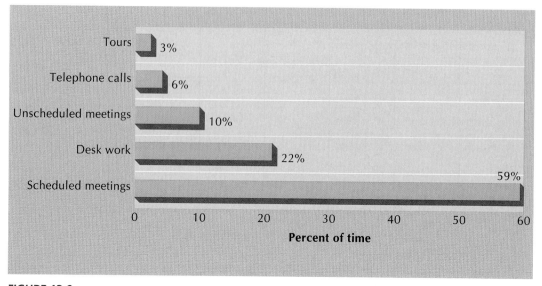

**FIGURE 13.6**

***How Executives Use Their Time***

Executives spend, on average, about 70 percent of their time in meetings.

ESS software includes powerful processing capabilities. These capabilities are necessary to boil down large volumes of performance details to a few screens that will allow the executive to grasp the status of events and assess key business indicators quickly. The summaries are usually presented in a standard format and rely heavily on business graphics to display results and relationships between business variables.

Although an ESS generally displays feature summaries only, the data supporting these summaries are quickly accessible. The report on each display screen is usually linked to detailed information that is available by clicking on an icon or entering a command. These supporting data can be presented in numeric or graphic form and displayed on-screen or printed. Table 13.5 summarizes the characteristics of an executive support system.

The digital dashboards in use at GE Plastics and General Electric Corp. headquarters, as described in the beginning of this chapter, are good examples of ESS. They contain the summary and critical performance information, in multiple formats, that executives need. Each display screen also provides access to additional details that explain the results. Because these features make dashboards effective management tools, it is likely that this form of executive support system will be used at a growing rate in enterprises.

**FIGURE 13.7**

***Executive Support System (Comshare)***

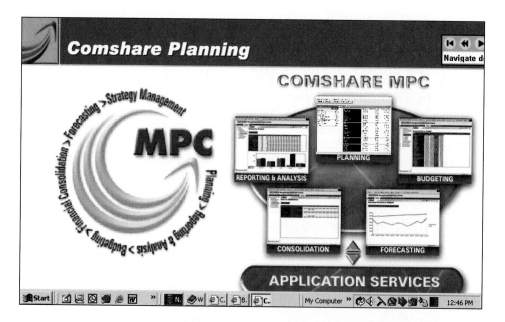

| Table 13.5  **Characteristics of an Executive Support System** |
| --- |
| Offers quick, concise updates of business performance. |
| Permits scanning of data and information on both internal activities and the external business environment. |
| Highlights significant data and information in summary form. |
| Allows the user to access data supporting the summary information. |

## Expert Support Systems

An **expert support system,** or simply **expert system,** uses business rules, regulations, and databases to evaluate a situation or determine an appropriate course of action. These systems are designed to capture and consistently apply the expertise of a human specialist in a particular field. Because they are so specialized, expert systems are limited in application scope. Nonetheless, they are extremely powerful. They are commonly used in such diverse areas as medical diagnosis, manufacturing quality control, and financial planning. The *Information Technology in Practice* feature, "Con-Way Uses Expert System for Dispatchers," describes how this large trucking enterprise improved the service it offers customers while increasing the efficiency of its dispatchers and drivers by implementing an expert dispatching system.

Expert systems usually process data provided by people interacting with the system through workstations. Alternatively, they may be part of a transaction processing system, analyzing data and information included in business transactions. When automobile makers assemble vehicle orders, for example, they may use an expert system to review the orders' option packages to ensure they are appropriate. An expert system will know that if a vehicle is built to include both air-conditioning and a towing package that will allow it to pull a trailer, it must have an oversize radiator, a heavy-duty alternator, and a transmission cooler. The expert system will review the order details and report any discrepancy from the rules, thereby preventing costly mistakes. In essence, the system incorporates the specialized knowledge of an auto design engineer to produce the finished product (Figure 13.8).

**expert support system/expert system**
A business information system that uses business rules, regulations, and databases to evaluate a situation or determine an appropriate course of action.

**FIGURE 13.8**

### *Expert System Embedded in Order Entry Portion of an Auto Manufacturing System*

An expert system embedded in an auto manufacturing system will review all order details and report any discrepancy from the rules of manufacturing or good engineering.

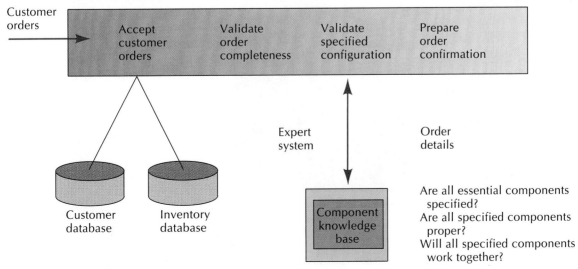

# INFORMATION TECHNOLOGY IN PRACTICE

## Con-Way Uses Expert System for Dispatchers

There can be no guesswork in the highly competitive commercial trucking industry. Peek inside a busy freight terminal—many are the size of several football fields—and you will see heavily loaded forklifts bustling across a loading dock. Each forklift driver knows exactly where to find a pallet of freight and when to load it on a particular truck. Each lift swiftly carries cargo pallets and boxes to the many empty trailers simultaneously being readied for their next delivery run.

Eliminating guesswork in loading and moving freight overnight is the responsibility of the linehaul dispatchers. They consolidate freight orders for specific destinations, assign drivers and trucks, and draw up routes, and create pickup and delivery schedules.

Con-Way Transportation Services Inc., a $2.1 billion transportation and services company, provides an array of business-to-business freight delivery services and logistics solutions. From the outset, Con-Way, headquartered in Ann Arbor, Michigan, has operated around the following four fundamental business principles: (1) respond to customers' needs for direct service and complete coverage of interstate and intrastate markets with regional next-day and second-day delivery; (2) provide consistent, reliable on-time service; (3) empower employees with responsibility for satisfying customers and delivering profitable performance; and (4) share the rewards of success with employees through incentive compensation beyond regular pay.

Today the Con-Way regional carriers offer premium direct next-day service in more markets and to more destinations than any other less than truckload (LTL) carrier. The Con-Way network is designed primarily to support its customers'

increasingly common *just-in-time* shipping strategies and advanced integrated logistics programs.

For years, Con-Way's linehaul dispatchers worked just like those at competing companies: Each sought to match tons of freight, comprising tens of thousands of individual shipments, with trucks that would be routed across all 50 states. Routes change from day to day, depending on customer shipments. The dispatcher had to assign each truck to do the following: carry deliveries to one or more of the over 440 locations the company serves; drop its freight; and return to its origin.

The time-consuming nature of the linehaul function means creating routes and assigning loads before all the day's orders are known. Fulfilling other responsibilities adds even more complexity: making good on the promise of overnight, on-time customer delivery; assigning loads to maximize a trailer's space; creating truck routes that cover the fewest miles; and making sure the drivers are back home at the end of the daily run. Working around bad weather and highway hazards add still more complications.

Though linehaul dispatching has always been somewhat of an art (dispatchers often take over a full year to fully learn the job), Con-Way's management decided to create an expert system—a linehaul automation system—to aid in the scheduling process. It was hoped the system would optimize the routing, loading, and delivery processes while minimizing costs and mistakes.

Con-Way's proprietary automated linehaul system allows the company to move commercial trucking faster than its competition.

Since there was little documentation describing the process, systems developers began with the linehaul dispatchers, interviewing each to identify the business rules, most effective practices, and problem-solving methods they use. They captured the insights of the dispatchers and created rules and instructions describing the processes and logic of the best dispatching practices.

Dispatchers now use Con-Way's expert linehaul system in the following way. Throughout the day, details of each incoming pickup order from customers are captured and recorded, including the origin and destination as well as the weight and dimensions of the freight. The expert system examines order details, looking for any unusual characteristics. It flags questionable shipment data, calling it to the dispatcher's attention for verification so that discrepancies can be resolved before loading time.

Con-Way's linehaul system includes a set of rules and guidelines (taking into account factors influencing cost, elapsed time, delivery times, and customer priorities) that result in the load and route specifications for the day's freight that will move that night.

**Welcome to the Con-Way.com Demo Site!** | **Register here!** | Thursday, October 9th

FasTrac *Go* | QuickTools *Go* | PowerTools *Go* | con-way

Click for Information ▼ | [ ] | Select a QuickTool ▼ | RapidReports ▼

**Activity Summary Report (OutBound)**

ROAD SYSTEMS INC (CSE) Acct Code: ROAXXLLR000
2001 S BENTON SEARCY, AR 72143
As Of 10/9/03 8:25:23 AM
Select a new Location

Download as spreadsheet | Format to Print

Click on the highlighted links to view detail information.

| Day Period | Ships | Total Wght | Total Dollars | Avg Wght | Avg Miles | % Load | Cost % | % | % |
|---|---|---|---|---|---|---|---|---|---|
| Oct03 | 2 | 255 | $328 | 128 | 1,070 | 50.0% | 50.0% | 0.0% | 100.0% |
| Sep03 | 13 | 13,063 | $4,644 | 1,005 | 854 | 69.2% | 30.7% | 0.0% | 53.8% |
| Aug03 | 16 | 16,347 | $6,468 | 1,022 | 777 | 68.7% | 25.0% | 6.2% | 50.0% |
| Jul03 | 7 | 6,968 | $2,189 | 995 | 649 | 57.1% | 42.8% | 0.0% | 28.5% |
| Jun03 | 7 | 8,359 | $2,130 | 1,194 | 609 | 57.1% | 42.8% | 0.0% | 57.1% |
| May03 | 10 | 8,629 | $2,778 | 863 | 776 | 40.0% | 60.0% | 0.0% | 50.0% |
| Apr03 | 13 | 7,951 | $2,822 | 612 | 737 | 61.5% | 38.4% | 0.0% | 61.5% |
| Mar03 | 8 | 3,635 | $1,240 | 454 | 754 | 87.5% | 12.5% | 0.0% | 37.5% |
| Feb03 | 15 | 22,515 | $6,252 | 1,501 | 861 | 80.0% | 20.0% | 0.0% | 40.0% |

The expert system seeks an optimal result for all concerned by combining its knowledge of freight information, origin and destination details, and equipment capabilities to create a sequence for loading trailers. This system seeks to make the best use of trailer space while reducing handling. It even considers the most common causes of damage to freight and ways to avoid these problems when it creates its loading instructions.

Con-Way's expert system makes its experts—the linehaul dispatchers—more efficient. They not only complete their scheduling task in a matter of minutes (it used to require *hours*), but they are able to accept customer orders later into the day. *CIO* magazine, an IT trade magazine, reported that the system, which cost more than $3 million, paid for itself within its first two years of use. Clearly, customers and Con-Way alike benefit from providing their experts with an expert system.

The heart of most expert systems is a database of rules called a **rule base** or **knowledge base**. The rule base is often expressed in the form of IF/THEN statements. The expert system at the auto plant described in the last paragraph, for example, might include a rule that says the following:

**rule base/knowledge base**
A database of rules in an expert system.

IF the vehicle requires a trailer package,
And it will have air-conditioning,
THEN check to ensure it will have the following components: oversize radiator, heavy-duty alternator, and transmission cooler.

The ultimate result of using an expert system is the diagnosis of a problem or determination of the cause of a problem. It may or may not include a recommendation for appropriate action. Unlike a TPS or MIS, expert systems generally do not produce formal detailed reports. (Table 13.6 summarizes the characteristics of an expert system.)

| Table 13.6  **Characteristics of an Expert Support System** |
| --- |
| Diagnoses problems and may recommend a course of action. |
| Captures data and applies the expertise of a human specialist to a situation. |
| Has a limited scope of application. |
| Relies on rule base. |
| Processes data entered by people interacting with the system as well as details retrieved from other information systems. |

# IT for Manufacturing Automation and Control

The challenge and opportunity of managing a business unit or company today lie in removing the barriers that were erected when the Industrial Age brought about specialization. As noted throughout this book, information technology is helping enterprises integrate their business processes and revolutionizing the way businesses operate.

A similar revolution is taking place on the floors of manufacturing companies. Production systems have changed dramatically since the Industrial Age. Today's factory finds people working in teams and relying heavily on computer and communications systems. **Computer-integrated manufacturing (CIM)** uses computers to link automated processes in a factory to reduce design time, increase machine use, shorten the manufacturing cycle, cut inventories, and increase product quality. In computer-integrated manufacturing, machines work together in groups known as **manufacturing cells.** Parts and materials are moved between cells by automated guide vehicles, automated machines, and materials-handling systems consisting of trolleys and carriers that move along guide wires or on conveyors. For most manufacturing companies today, the question is not whether to implement computers into their manufacturing processes, but when.

In essence, CIM fits the IT model used throughout this book. Recall that information technology has the following three components: computers; communications; and know-how (see Chapter 1). Computers are at the heart of many manufacturing systems and are the source of the artificial intelligence embedded in lathes and machine tools. Computers control the actions and movements of arms, wheels, gears, and conveyors, and examine process results. Database management systems store and retrieve manufacturing data and information, including product specifications, drawings, production procedures, setup instructions, and multimedia training documents.

Communications also play a central role in manufacturing industries. Wide area networks link factories across the country and fixed and wireless LANs interconnect work areas within the same facility.

The know-how needed for a successful CIM system is the same as that for any other IT application. All of the people involved with the system—analysts, communications specialists, database administrators, and IT managers—are responsible for developing the procedures that keep the system in sync with business needs while safeguarding the firm against the loss of data, information, or processing capability. Using a CIM system properly means having the know-how to use the system to the firm's best advantage.

*Computer-integrated manufacturing* is a general, all-inclusive term used for computerized manufacturing systems. This section describes the following five specialized types of CIM: (1) material requirements planning and manufacturing resource planning; (2) computer-aided design and manufacturing; (3) flexible manufacturing; (4) robots; and (5) computer vision systems.

## Material Requirements Planning and Manufacturing Resource Planning

Manufacturing management is as important to a company's success as the quality of the products it makes and the manner in which it produces them. **Material requirements planning (MRP)** is the core of the entire production management process. Most man-

---

**computer-integrated manufacturing (CIM)**

A manufacturing system that uses computers to link automated processes in a factory to reduce design time, increase machine utilization, shorten the manufacturing cycle, cut inventories, and increase product quality.

**manufacturing cell**

A group of machines working together in computer-integrated manufacturing.

**material requirements planning (MRP)**

A system that tracks the quantity of each part needed to manufacture a product; essentially, an important component of MRP II.

 Companies in different parts of the world approach automation differently. Experts believe that U.S. and Japanese firms tend to address problems first at the level of the manufacturing floor, and then proceed to a full systems analysis and design effort. In contrast, the sequence in most European companies is to examine the full system first, and then break it down into individual processes and department functions. As a result, companies in different parts of the world have different priorities in using IT. Most Japanese firms implement CIM only when doing so is economically justifiable. Many U.S. companies follow a similar strategy, qualified by the American emphasis on short-term returns on investment. European companies tend to focus on long-term manufacturing strategies, installing systems without so much emphasis on short-term gain. ■

ufactured products are made from a range of individual components. MRP systems keep track of the quantity of each part needed to manufacture a product. They also coordinate scheduled manufacturing dates with the lead time needed to have components delivered and assembled.

**Manufacturing resource planning (MRP III)**[1] systems are essentially advanced versions of MRP systems that tie together all of the parts of an organization into the company's production activities. MRP III systems include the following six essential subsystems (Figure 13.9):

1. **Bill of Materials Management** A bill of materials is the list of parts used in manufacturing an item. A sample bill of materials and an assembly order for a swimming pool filtration system are shown in Figure 13.10. When a manufacturing company receives an order for a product, the system examines the bill of materials for the product and compares it to its current parts inventory. If necessary, additional parts will be procured so that the ordered product can be manufactured.

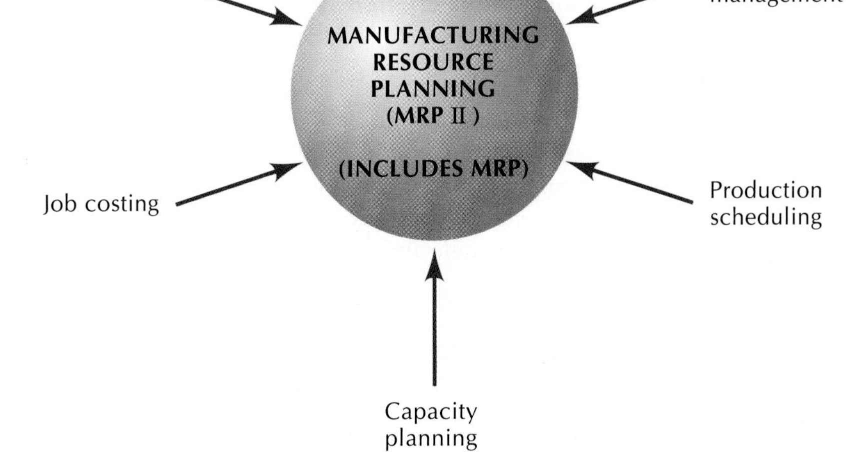

**manufacturing resource planning (MRP III)**
An advanced MRP system that ties together all the parts of an organization into the company's production activities.

**FIGURE 13.9**

***The Components of Manufacturing Resource Planning***
Do not confuse manufacturing resource planning (MRP II) with material requirements planning (MRP). MRP is an important component of MRP II.

[Diagram: Manufacturing Resource Planning (MRP II) (Includes MRP) with Bill of materials management, Inventory management, Cash planning, Job costing, Capacity planning, Production scheduling]

[1]MRP has evolved through various versions, each designated by generation number. MRP III includes a focus on distribution and logistics management that is not part of MRP II. In addition, there are MRP PC versions designed to run on personal computers. MRP PC is typically used in small enterprises.

**Bill of Materials**

Assembly number:  31436402
Assembly description:  SWIMMING POOL FILTRATION SYSTEM
Drawing number:
Structure change:                                                           Drawing size:

| Item number | Description | Type | Source | Unit of measure | Quantity/ assembly | Structure change | Dept. assembled in | Oper. assembled on |
|---|---|---|---|---|---|---|---|---|
| | | | | | | | | |

**Assembly Order**

Assembly number:        31436402
Assembly description:  SWIMMING POOL FILTRATION SYSTEM
Order quantity:            50

Order number:  62566

| Item number | Description | Unit of measure | Quantity per assembly | Expected quantity |
|---|---|---|---|---|
| 531674 | SCREW | 01 | 6 | 300 |
| 531690 | WASHER | 01 | 5 | 250 |
| 728419 | SCREW | 01 | 5 | 250 |
| 1431478 | SEAL | 01 | 2 | 100 |
| 3519794 | MOTOR | 01 | 1 | 50 |
| 3572133 | SPRING | 01 | 2 | 100 |
| 31436130 | PUMP SHAFT ASS'Y | 01 | 1 | 50 |
| 31436301 | SET COLLAR | 01 | 1 | 50 |
| 31436315 | CLAMP MOUNTING | 01 | 1 | 50 |
| 31436338 | SHIFTER COLLAR | 01 | 1 | 50 |
| 31436345 | SCREW | 01 | 4 | 200 |

**FIGURE 13.10**

***Bill of Materials and Assembly Order for a Swimming Pool Filtration System***
A bill of materials is essentially a recipe for a product. It specifies the necessary ingredients, the order in which they should be combined, and how many of each ingredient are needed to make one batch of the product.

2. **Inventory Management**   Inventory production schedulers keep track of what parts are on hand and on order. Using this information in conjunction with the bill of materials and the customer order, they determine which components must be ordered from suppliers. The manufacturing resource planning system helps inventory schedulers work with this information to determine the earliest date that manufacturing can begin.

3. **Production Scheduling**   A company's production schedule specifies the planned use of its factory facilities and the quantity of items to be produced. Manufacturing resource planning allows production schedulers to examine the current schedule and to determine when additional activities can be incorporated into the schedule without overloading plant capacity.

4. **Capacity Planning**   Each tool, machine, production line, and worker in a factory has a capacity—usually measured in output per hour. Manufacturing resource planning helps schedulers to incorporate manufacturing capacity into their schedules.

5. **Job Costing**   The level of costs and the sequence in which they will be incurred in manufacturing are extremely important to a business's bottom line. Manufacturing resource planning systems keep managers aware of both expected and unexpected costs throughout the production process.
6. **Cash Planning**   Business planning includes ensuring that the company has sufficient cash flow to pay for materials and for workers. Manufacturing resource planning systems record the company's sources and uses of cash, both planned and actual.

Many types of report are produced by each component of the MRP system.

**Manufacturing Resource Planning at Raychem**   Raychem Corp.'s manufacturing facility outside of Vancouver, British Columbia, makes wiring systems that carry electrical power and control signals to various airplane devices. Because of the wide variety of aircraft designs in the industry, Raychem's manufacturing processes vary greatly. Planning production and managing the details with paper forms—the way all companies managed the production process in the past—is extremely time-consuming.

To cut down on the paper shuffling, Raychem has installed a paperless manufacturing system designed around client/server network (review Chapter 8 if necessary). In this manufacturing resource planning system, production data and information are stored on servers that are accessible to a variety of workstations and manufacturing tools. The system is interconnected with a computer-aided design and manufacturing system (discussed in the next section). Both planners and designers work online, retrieving information from the system's databases and devising production plans to meet the diverse needs of the company and its customers. Because so much of the work is done through networked workstations, paper reports are not generated very often. Also included in Raychem's system is a rule-based expert system used to create wiring design and manufacturing specifications and a design database that allows designers to draw on previous specifications.

As production occurs, the system captures data on the amount of time needed to set up machines and assembly lines and the amount of scrap materials produced. These data are fed back into the materials-planning and job-costing subsystems to improve subsequent jobs.

## Computer-Aided Design and Manufacturing

For many years, automated manufacturing systems were synonymous with MRP. Today, computer-aided design and computer-aided manufacturing are also important components of most manufacturing systems. Product designers and engineers working on **computer-aided design (CAD)** systems use a powerful computer graphics workstation outfitted with programs that allow them to draw design specifications on the display screen. Manipulating a light pen, scanner, or mouse, they can specify the product's dimensions and show its lines, indentations, and other features with precision. Each element of the design appears on the screen as it is specified. Changes can be made quickly by adding, removing, or altering details on the drawing (Figure 13.11).

Since CAD tools usually work in three dimensions, the designer can specify and see the height, width, and depth of the product right on the screen. Designs can be rotated, tilted, and turned upside down so that every angle is visible for inspection. When a design is complete, it is stored on disk, ready for review, editing, or printing at any time.

CAD designs are frequently transmitted to **computer-aided manufacturing (CAM)** systems, which rely on IT to automate and manage the manufacturing process directly. Using the CAD database, CAM software controls the tools and machines on the factory floor to manufacture the product designed on the CAD system.

CAD/CAM systems require access to many computer and communications programs. For example, CAM systems obtain detailed product design information from the CAD databases and bills of materials from manufacturing resource planning systems. They communicate with the machines on shop floors by way of high-speed, sophisticated communications networks.

**computer-aided design (CAD)**
A system that uses a powerful computer graphics workstation to enable product designers and engineers to draw design specifications on a display screen.

**computer-aided manufacturing (CAM)**
A system that relies on IT to automate and manage the manufacturing process directly.

**a)** To improve its material handling and control system, Litton studied the design, spacing,
and layout of the machinery in use on the manufacturing floor.

**b)** Litton's designers then created a 3-D graphic simulation
of the manufacturing floor using CAD/CAM software. By
manipulating the simulation on- screen, they were able to
experiment with new floor layouts and manufacturing techniques without building costly prototypes.

## Flexible Manufacturing

**flexible manufacturing**
A manufacturing system that
automatically sets up machines for
the next job, thus reducing setup
time and making smaller job runs
feasible.

CAM improves the efficiency of the entire manufacturing process by automatically setting up machines for the next job. This capability, known as **flexible manufacturing,**
often reduces setup time by 75 percent while improving product quality by 75 to 90 percent. Shorter setup times make smaller job runs feasible, providing more flexibility in
scheduling while also reducing manufacturing lead times and the amount of inventory
kept on hand.

**Flexible Manufacturing at Flextronics**   Singapore-based Flextronics is the world's
second-largest contract manufacturing firm. Its 18,000 employees, like those in other
contract manufacturing companies, make electrical components, including printed circuit boards and chips, for such name-brand information technology companies as Cisco

# CRITICAL CONNECTIONS 2

## Boeing Takes Off with CAD Software

**Boeing
Company**

Quick: What has more than 3 million parts and can fly? It is the Boeing 777, the world's
largest twin-engine jetliner. This is the first commercial airplane ever to be designed completely with CAD software. (Boeing's huge system included eight mainframe computers,
2,200 engineering workstations, and more than 5,400 engineering and technical employees during the peak design period.) In fact, because the plane was designed entirely on
computer, engineers could *preassemble* it digitally, skipping the expensive and time-
consuming stage of building physical mockups.

With the help of CAD software and powerful workstations, engineers can factor stress,
inertia, and weight analysis—represented as colored, shaded, three-dimensional solids on
their screens—into designs. But the software is also an important communications tool.
With it, everyone on the design team has access to the same set of engineering drawings
needed to coordinate improvements and refinements as the design moves through the
various stages. This capability is essential to Boeing's team-style approach to design.

Product design itself usually accounts for only 5 to 8 percent of a product's total cost, but the decisions made by product designers typically account for *60 to 70 percent* of a product's total cost. Discovering during actual production that a product is too difficult to build or that its constituent materials are too costly to use can mean serious problems. So can learning that the product contains features that will make it difficult to sell.

**Concurrent engineering** can solve these problems before they happen. In a concurrently engineered project, teams of people from different departments take a *process view* of the product—that is, they focus simultaneously on parts, components, manufacturing, and testing. Design engineers, cost experts, manufacturing engineers, and marketing staff members all work together to manage the design and development process. As each design detail is considered, so are its manufacturing, cost, and market characteristics. Ernst & Young, a U.S.-based international consulting firm, estimates that concurrent engineering typically shaves total product cost by 20 percent.

Concurrent engineering requires team members to work across their departmental functions to evaluate the activities of many departments. This is just the beginning. Now emerging is the capability for companies to link their design teams, through communications networks and CAD systems, to machine tools located in a factory down the road or across the country. These factories can turn preliminary designs into prototypes that team members evaluate as part of the design process. ■

**concurrent engineering**
A design and manufacturing method in which team members work across their departmental functions to evaluate the activities of many departments and manage the product development process.

---

Systems, Hewlett-Packard Company, Microsoft, Motorola, and Palm Inc. These companies (known as original equipment manufacturers—OEMs) choose to outsource manufacturing of electronic components rather than build and operate their own factories; this is because the contract manufacturers have the facilities and skills to create the custom components at low cost while maintaining high quality levels.

At Flextronics, no single OEM accounts for as much as 10 percent of its total business. The company seeks to maintain its diversified customer base so it is not overly dependent on any company for its own success. In some instances it will manufacture high volumes of products having little variation. Other production runs will be low volume with a high degree of variability between each manufacturing run. This means that its factories must be flexible—more flexible than those of the company's customers. Flextronics factories need to operate the printed circuit board fabrication, injection plastics design and molding machines, and manufacturing lines for one customer; then they need to shift them over to do the same for another customer. Flexible manufacturing makes for an extremely flexible, fast-moving, competent global organization. Without this capability, Flextronics would probably not exist.

## Robots

A **robot** is a computer-controlled device that can physically manipulate its surroundings (Figure 13.12). On assembly lines, *pick-and-place robots* are usually programmed to carry out the following four functions: (1) move to the location of a part; (2) grasp the part; (3) move to the location where the part will be used; and (4) release their grip on the part. More sophisticated versions of robots, currently under development, will have the ability to *sense*—that is, to gather information about their immediate environment—through a variety of sensing devices and to analyze this information and determine the proper course of action to take.

Although the combination of increased computer power and decreased cost will undoubtedly lead to greater sophistication and capability in robots, do not expect robots to look like those you have seen in science-fiction movies. Industry has not yet given robots an *almost human* appearance, nor is it working terribly hard to do so. Most robots look exactly like what they are—programmable machines. Some have manipulator arms

**robot**
A computer-controlled device that can physically manipulate its surroundings.

**a) In veterinary medicine**—Dr. Hap Paul developed a computer robot that drills a hole in a dog's femur so that a metal joint can be implanted to replace the natural joint.

**b) In laboratories**—Robots are widely used to select and move test tubes so that lab technicians do not have to come in contact with the tubes' contents.

**c) In manufacturing**—Pick-and-place robots are frequently utilized to move parts into hard-to-reach areas.

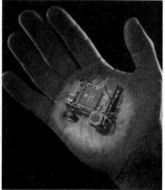

**d) In computer systems themselves**—Mobile Robot Group's "Squirt" robot is used to repair the interior components of computers and other electronic systems.

and grippers *(arms and fingers),* and others have computer vision systems *(eyes;* discussed below). However, they remain machines—with no personality or will of their own.

## Computer Vision Systems

In manufacturing, product quality and consistency are essential for two reasons. First, customers today will not accept poor-quality products. They do not have to; competition ensures that most manufactured products will be available from more than one company. Second, poor quality costs the company money and damages its profitability.

**computer vision system**
A system that uses computer sensors to detect shapes, images, and varying levels of detail.

**Computer vision systems** are rapidly becoming an important tool to improve quality and consistency. Often used for recognition of parts and automated assembly of finished goods, these systems employ computer sensors to detect shapes, images, and varying levels of detail, which they then compare with data stored in memory. Depending on the logic programmed into the system, they can detect the presence or absence of a match and signal other devices in the manufacturing cell to take corrective action. Computer vision systems are also frequently used to scrutinize finished products to detect imperfections and defects.

Vision capabilities are often embedded in robots. The integration of computer vision systems with robots increases the types of activities that robots can perform.

**Computer-Integrated Manufacturing at Saturn**  At the Saturn automobile plant near Nashville, Tennessee, more than 7,000 workers and managers are living out one of the greatest experiments in manufacturing. After an investment of eight years and $3.5 billion, Saturn automobiles began rolling off the assembly line in 1991. In the decade that followed, it manufactured more than 2 million vehicles. Saturn has earned the highest overall rating for customer service in studies conducted by independent industry research organizations—higher than even the most expensive luxury auto brands.

From the beginning, the goal of General Motors, Saturn's parent company, has been to use an innovative manufacturing process to build world-class small cars priced below comparable cars sold by Japanese automakers. To achieve this objective, GM's top managers were willing to break loose from GM's manufacturing traditions. They began the break by combing the world for the best, most efficient manufacturing practices. (Seeking out the world's best practices in any area is known as *benchmarking*. The best practice becomes a benchmark against which a firm can compare its own performance.) In designing their new system, Saturn's designers, managers, and executives borrowed ideas from such widely admired companies as Hewlett-Packard, Volvo, McDonald's, Nissan, and Kawasaki (along with 155 others).

Saturn's manufacturing cells, complete with robots (boasting computer vision systems) and automated guidance vehicles, can do only so much to make a quality automobile on time and within expected cost parameters, however. As in so many other companies, Saturn's success depends on its people and how deeply they are involved in and committed to the process. Saturn's management and assembly workers function as a team, sharing ideas and exchanging information. Information technology plays an important role by making the information accessible and by interconnecting people and machines. Still, the role of IT is secondary to that played by the people of Saturn.

The Saturn experiment is working. Saturn automobiles are selling extremely well. Saturn even opened a second manufacturing plant, employing 2,600 workers, in Wilmington, Delaware. The plant also uses the proven manufacturing methods pioneered in Tennessee.

Cheered by the huge demand for Saturn cars from dealers and consumers, the company has several new models on the drawing board.

# Enterprise Resource Planning System

**Enterprise resource planning (ERP) systems** are large scope, unified application programs that integrate many of the transaction processing and information systems application features discussed in the preceding sections of this chapter. Companies choosing to implement an ERP system may use the system to integrate processes and activities performed in different functions within the enterprise, such as accounting, sales, manufacturing, and inventory management.

**enterprise resource planning (ERP) system**
Large scope, unified application program that integrates many transaction processing and information systems application features.

## ERP Characteristics

ERPs are *unified* if someone in the enterprise's, say, accounting department can look at the details of an order to see whether it has shipped. *Unified* also means the information everybody uses is common. There is one inventory number for an item, one value for monthly sales, a single manufacturing schedule, and only one accounts receivable number within the enterprise.

ERP systems *integrate* these usually separate applications by using a database that is shared by all of the application programs (Figure 13.13). When a customer-service representative takes a sales order, its details are entered into the common database and are immediately available to the other application functions where it is needed (for example, in the manufacturing backlog, the credit system, and the shipping schedule). ERP systems work in real time. Databases are updated as changes occur, and the new status is available for everybody to use to manage their part of the business. This means that the exact status of everything is always available.

If desired, ERP systems can also span a company's globally distributed business units. In these instances, they can present data and information in multiple languages

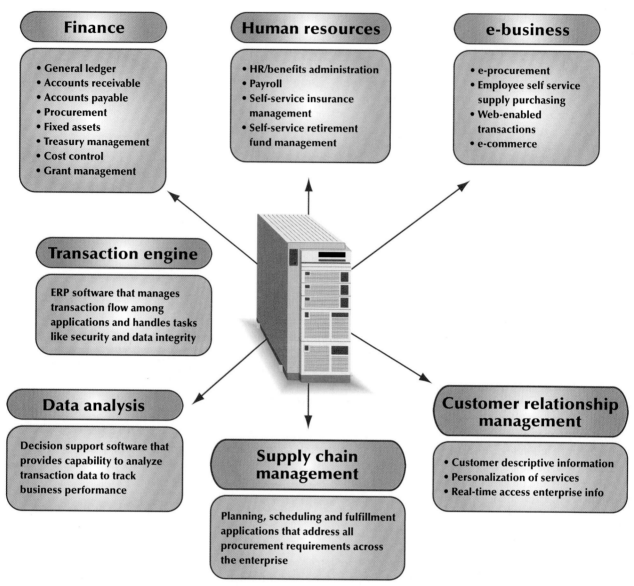

**FIGURE 13.13**

*Enterprise Resource Planning System Integrates Functions*

and currencies. For instance, a U.S. user in a company that stores and ships products in Japan can immediately see exactly how much of a particular product is at the warehouse in Japan and what its value is in yen or dollars.

## ERP Modules

ERP systems are often modular in nature (Figure 13.14). This gives the company the alternative of implementing modules for separate business functions in an evolutionary fashion.

Corning Inc., headquartered in upstate New York, is a global, technology-based corporation that has evolved from producing glass and cookware in past decades to operating in the following three broad business segments: telecommunications fibers and cable systems; advanced materials (including glass ceramic and polymer technologies) and information display components for computer displays; projection systems; and televisions. The company's 12 business units operate approximately 40 plants in 20 countries.

Each business unit manages its own sales planning, order management, manufacturing and other supply-chain operations. To aid the units' autonomous operations but

# R/3 Core Business Processes

**FIGURE 13.14**

*Modular Structure of
SAP's R/3 ERP Software*

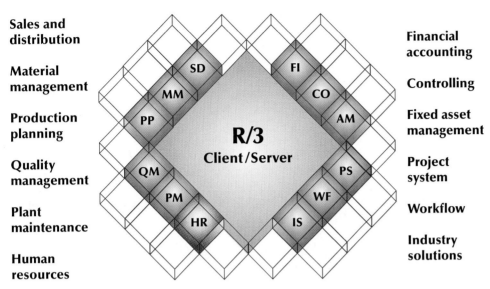

Sales and
distribution

Material
management

Production
planning

Quality
management

Plant
maintenance

Human
resources

SD

MM

PP

QM

PM

HR

**R/3**
**Client/Server**

FI

CO

AM

PS

WF

IS

Financial
accounting

Controlling

Fixed asset
management

Project
system

Workflow

Industry
solutions

*Source:* Adapted from SAP, Inc.

maintain a unified view of the enterprise across business areas and at the corporate level, Corning implemented the PeopleSoft ERP system. Since the emphasis is on managing the supply-chain activities as well as employee benefits, the company implemented the following four PeopleSoft modules: (1) supply-chain management; (2) procurement; (3) finance; and (4) human resources. The company knows it can add other modules to its ERP as the need arises.

Because of the scope and level of integration associated with ERP systems, they are much more complicated to implement than individual IT applications. The implementation period can be lengthy because the enterprise business processes are generally adapted to the procedures and capabilities included in the ERP system. Many managers and employees may be affected as a result, which sometimes creates challenging *change management* situations. (Chapter 11 addresses the issue of change and IT.) The end-of-chapter *Case Study,* "Nestlé's ERP System Implementation Is About Managing Change," describes how CIO Jerri Dunn stressed the importance of managing change as a critical element in the introduction of an ERP system. She repeatedly emphasized to her staff that just having good tools and applications is not enough to guarantee a successful implementation result.

# Strategic Role of IT

Information technology applications have strategic importance when they change the way a firm competes, providing a capability so valuable that they enable the firm to gain a substantial advantage—a competitive advantage against its competitors. These applications are often known as **strategic information systems.** This section explores the following five aspects of strategic importance as they relate to IT applications: (1) competitive advantage; (2) generic competitive strategies; (3) competitive forces; (4) value chains; and the (5) role of strategic information systems in an enterprise.

## Competitive Advantage

**Competitive advantage** occurs when an enterprise has the ability to outperform rivals on a primary performance goal—often profitability—or some other dimension. For instance, a firm may use or trade profitability to gain market share; invest in creation of products, services, or technology; increase customer satisfaction; enter international markets; or acquire other companies.

**strategic information
system**

Information technology application that changes the way a firm competes, providing a capability so valuable that it enables the firm to gain a substantial competitive advantage against its competitors.

**competitive advantage**

Occurs when an enterprise has the ability to outperform rivals on a primary performance goal—often profitability—or some other dimension.

# INFORMATION TECHNOLOGY IN PRACTICE

## Merrill Lynch's Classic Success from Strategic Use of IT

In the 1970s, the brokerage firm of Merrill Lynch, headquartered in New York, faced the same challenge as any other brokerage: High net-worth investors typically use several brokers, and thus a firm enjoys only a portion of the investor's business and resulting commissions. Seeking ways to capture a greater proportion of the business of such investors—the most desirable of all clients—Merrill Lynch wanted to create a unique capability that would benefit both investor and firm, thereby enabling it to draw more high-investor business.

In 1977, Merrill Lynch announced its *cash management account* (CMA). Under a single umbrella, CMA provided a consolidated account for securities and mutual funds, including credit in the form of a standard margin account. CMA account holders could withdraw funds through checks or VISA credit cards. Among the most distinguishing features was the automatic investment of cash and dividends in a Merrill-Lynch managed money market fund.

CMA could not have been possible without the firm's partnership with BankOne. The bank processed checks written by Merrill Lynch

customers and issued the VISA bank cards, services that brokerage houses were prohibited from offering at the time.

Merrill Lynch's innovation capabilities paid off only because the brokerage firm could also create the necessary software to integrate the diverse activities, keep track of all customer transactions, automatically perform daily sweeps of cash into working money market accounts, and maintain an integrated security program across all accounts.

Although brokers were initially unable to see the potential payoff from CMA, they responded when

the brokerage firm offered commission incentives. Once they realized their own income potential, brokers found CMA to be one of their most persuasive selling tools. The number of CMA accounts jumped from a handful in the first couple of years to 180,000 in 1980 and over 1 million accounts in 1983. More than 450,000 new accounts were also brought into the firm.

CMA remains a high-payoff innovation in the competitive brokerage business. Growth and attraction of new customers continues today.

Recognizing IT's strategic role is not a recent development. Information technology has been growing in strategic importance over the past three decades, across virtually all industries. The *Information Technology in Practice* feature, "Merrill Lynch's Classic Success from Strategic Use of IT, describes how this large brokerage firm created one of the earliest strategic applications of information technology, using it effectively as a competitive tool. The *cash management system* featured efficient transaction processing, innovative services, and an integrated database to strengthen its relationship with the most desirable investors. In doing so, it was able to gain an edge over other brokerage firms competing for the same type of investor.

Today many of the most admired and successful enterprises use their information technology capabilities to good competitive advantage. For example, Wal-Mart's highly effective Retail Link system (discussed in Chapter 9), which connects the giant retailer with suppliers, is a formidable competitive tool. Retail Link includes the capability to share daily sales data captured by the POS transaction processing system in each store with its suppliers. Interconnecting the suppliers with the sales data improves the efficiency of Wal-Mart's operation and is therefore a competitive advantage (in the form of lower costs and in turn lower consumer prices) over its competitors. Retail Link is a means by which Wal-Mart is able to pursue its competitive strategy. At the same time, the sharing of data gives participating suppliers a way to achieve greater efficiencies within *their* enterprise as well. Even more, the Retail Link technology gives Wal-Mart leverage with its suppliers. Its suppliers would knowingly give up something of value–a high volume of business and important market/sales information–if they walked away from their Wal-Mart relationship.

## Competitive Strategies

A **competitive strategy** is the means by which a firm seeks to gain an advantage over its competitors. The most widely held view of competitive strategy in practice emanates from the work of Michael Porter at the Harvard Business School. He suggests that to be successful, enterprises should follow one or more of these three general competitive strategies: provide low-cost products or services; practice product differentiation; and focus on a market niche (see Figure 13.15). Each strategy can lead to successful performance if it is the right strategy for a given corporation–customer–competition combination. The skills, resources, and organizational requirements of each strategy are summarized in Table 13.7.

**competitive strategy**
The means by which a firm seeks to gain an advantage over its competitors.

**Low-Cost Leadership**   This strategy is aimed at outperforming other enterprises in the same industry by providing suitable quality in the firm's products or services at a lower cost than that of comparable products or services of competitors. Cost leadership is generally achieved by such techniques as careful management of overhead and buying or production costs, selective advertising and merchandising strategies, and pinpoint marketing to customers. Lower costs generally mean that an enterprise can earn acceptable returns on investments even when competitors assume more aggressive pricing strategies.

Wal-Mart uses effective management and IT practices to enable it to acquire the products it sells and to operate its stores at the lowest possible *cost*. In turn, it typically is able to *price* its goods lower than its competitors. As Wal-Mart says, *Low prices always!*

**Low-cost leadership** offers an enterprise great flexibility in dealing with any suppliers that raise their prices to the firm, as well as buyers seeking to drive down the prices they pay. In addition, the enterprise enjoying a low-cost leadership position is better able to deter potential competitors, because in addition to the other startup challenges, any company wishing to enter the industry will have to develop strategies to deal with the leader's low costs. Unless the wishful entrant has unique advantages, such as an edge in raw materials availability, new efficient manufacturing or distribution processes,

**low-cost leadership**
Offers an enterprise great flexibility in dealing with any suppliers that raise their prices to the firm, as well as buyers seeking to drive down the prices they pay.

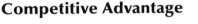
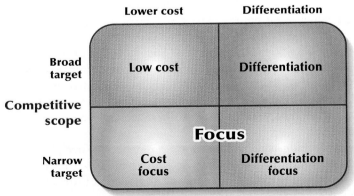

**FIGURE 13.15**

*Three Generic Competitive Strategies*

| Table 13.7 | Generic Competitive Strategies in Business |
|---|---|
| **STRATEGY** | **DESCRIPTION** |
| Low-cost leadership | • Outperform other firms in the industry by providing products or services at a lower cost than competitors while sustaining or exceeding quality and service levels they provide. |
| | • Provides competitive advantage when dealing with suppliers and buyers, and when offering substitute products or services. |
| Product differentiation | • Provide a product or service that is generally recognized as distinct from competitors. |
| | • Results in brand loyalty and avoids the necessity to take a low-price position; also effective in competing against substitutes. |
| Focus on a market niche | • Identify and compete in a market segment in which competitive advantage may be gained by concentration on a specific buyer group, product line, or geographical area. |
| | • Provides advantage of better service to customers, often at lower costs, while producing better customer loyalty. |

or particularly effective management practices, the chances for success in penetrating a market dominated by a low-cost leader are minimal.

Pursuing a low-cost strategy may require that the enterprise design its products for ease in manufacturing and that it is highly effective in its use of raw materials. Enterprises that can do so, may gain a substantial advantage over competitors that are not able to employ these practices.

**differentiation**
A product that is perceived by customers as having unique features in comparison to competitive items.

**Product Differentiation**  A product having **differentiation** is one that is perceived by customers as having unique features in comparison to competitive items. Differentiation can create brand loyalty among customers that will defeat the competitive thrust of rival firms. Because loyal customers may be willing to pay higher prices to have their preferred product, the need for taking a low price position is lessened. These factors all work together to establish a barrier to competitor entry into the market.

A differentiated product is less vulnerable to substitutes—there may be no comparable alternatives—and it establishes a basis for leverage against suppliers who adjust their prices in attempts to lure customers. However, at the same time, brand loyalty and higher prices may result in lower market shares for the firm marketing the differentiated product or service. Even if product superiority is acknowledged, customers may not be willing to pay the premium price, thereby affecting market share.

Merrill Lynch differentiated itself by providing integrated financial services for its most desirable investors. The Merrill Lynch cash management account not only became a valued and visible brand in itself, it also resulted in substantial loyalty from investors. In the end, the investors, the brokerage firm, and its brokers benefited from this differentiated product—to the detriment of competing brokerages.

**market niche**
A focal point for a product or service; it is a subset of the entire industry or segment of the market.

**Focus on a Market Niche**  A **market niche** is a focal point for a product or service; it is a subset of the entire industry or segment of the market. Firms that pursue the competitive strategy of concentrating on one or more market niches aim to serve a specific buyer group, segment of a product line or market, or geographical area.

This strategy is suggested when a firm believes it is better able to serve a narrow target area than an entire industry. For example, a bank may decide to focus on industrial customers, rather than competing in the mass consumer market. Or, an airline may attempt to gain strategic advantage by its shrewd ability to manage the shipment of cargo rather than passengers.

The *Information Technology in Practice* feature, "E-Trade Links Business and IT Strategy," illustrates how this financial services firm came into being by focusing solely on investors who wished to manage their buying and selling of stocks over the Internet. The feature also illustrates how E-Trade's strategy evolved as it served customers in its niche.

# INFORMATION TECHNOLOGY IN PRACTICE

## E-Trade Links Business and IT Strategy

When E-Trade processed its first stock market trade in the early 1990s, it did so as one of the first completely electronic brokerage firms in the United States. From its first day of business, all E-Trade interaction with customers was conducted through Internet service providers—initially America Online and CompuServe. Customers gravitated toward the brokerage firm because they could easily execute stock trades from their PCs 24 hours a day, 7 days a week, which was a rare capability at the time. In the early days, transaction fees and brokerage commissions accounted for nearly all the firm's revenues. By 1996, the firm's executives had formulated a vision to diversify beyond the brokerage business by linking a forward-looking business strategy with an effective information technology strategy.

Today, E-Trade Group Inc., with corporate offices in Menlo Park, California, is a diversified financial services company that offers a wide range of financial products and services under the brand E-Trade Financial. The group's strategy is to create value for customers and competitive advantage by using information technology to provide brokerage, banking and lending products, primarily through electronic delivery channels. Today only 30 percent of its revenue comes from brokerage fees.

E-Trade serves retail, corporate, and institutional customers, and operates in multiple countries around the world. Retail customers can move money electronically between brokerage, banking, and lending accounts and have access to physical touchpoints that include walk-in E-Trade centers in selected cities, smaller financial offices in many Target retail stores, and over 15,000 E-Trade automated teller machines (ATMs) located throughout the United States. Corporate clients use the firm's employee stock plan administration and options management tools. Institutional customers enjoy access to a broad range of brokerage products and services, including cross-border trading and independent research.

E-Trade divides its business into the following four segments: domestic retail brokerage; wealth management (which is combined with domestic retail brokerage); banking; and global and institutional.

E-Trade's *domestic retail brokerage* segment includes online investing and trading; automated order placement and execution of market and limit equity orders; streaming quotes; advanced trading platforms for active traders; personalized portfolio tracking; charting and quote applications; access to nearly 3,000 non-proprietary and proprietary mutual funds; bond trading and proprietary bond funds; access to separate account money management; individual retirement accounts; college savings plan products; real-time market commentary, and real-time quotes and news.

E-Trade's *wealth management* segment includes mutual fund operations; the E-Trade Business Solutions Group Inc. (BSG); and other services focused on retirement

Member FDIC

TOTAL PROTECTION
GUARANTEE
FIND OUT MORE ›

## *Banking just got better.*

**Introducing our new Online Banking service designed with your interests in mind.**

You asked and we listened. We've enhanced our Online Banking service to make it even easier to find and use the features you care about most.

*View Online Banking demo*

### Simpler.
*Keep track of your money in real time, anytime.*

View up-to-the-minute **balances and transactions**, and check your **projected balances** for the next seven days. You can manage your accounts 24 hours a day online or with our automated phone service at 1-800-ETBANK-1 (1-800-382-2651).

### Better.
*Organize your financial life.*

With features like **customizable transaction reports** going back two years, our online **Bill Pay** service, and **online check views**, it's easy to keep track of your money.

programs, college savings plans, and delivery of electronic advice and money management.

E-Trade's *banking* segment offers a range of products insured by the Federal Deposit Insurance Corp. (FDIC), including certificates of deposit, money market and savings accounts, and interest-bearing checking accounts. Services also include a range of lending products including first- and second-variable and fixed-rate mortgages; home-

equity loans; and other consumer loans to finance automobiles, marine, and recreational vehicles.

E-Trade's *global and institutional* segment provides online retail brokerage services to international retail customers, as well as financial services to institutional investors.

Today E-Trade offers much more than a set of products and services. It distinguishes itself from other companies that offer the same products and services by the fact that it

can integrate all of the services, providing consolidated financial statements electronically. This capability stems from E-Trade's birth as an online company focused entirely on use of information technology as the channel to serve its customers. As it grew and diversified, adding new products and opening physical office locations, E-Trade's executives never lost sight of their fundamental objective of linking the firm's business and IT strategies.

## Competitive Forces

The competitiveness of an enterprise is often determined by factors that seem beyond its control; that is, they are elements outside of the firm. However, competitive advantage actually grows out of the use of strategies that enable the firm to alter competition in its favor in spite of the outside forces.

Competitive forces (Figure 13.16) include the following: the industry's other competitors; the bargaining power of buyers; the bargaining power of suppliers; the threat of substitute products; and the threat from potential entrants to the industry. To a great extent, the strength or weakness of these forces determines the profitability of the industry because they influence the prices, costs, and investments the firms must make. Strong buyer influence, for example, may force an enterprise to keep its prices low. The threat of substitute products or services may also force the enterprise to maintain low prices.

**FIGURE 13.16**

*The Five Forces Influencing the Advantage a Firm Can Gain*

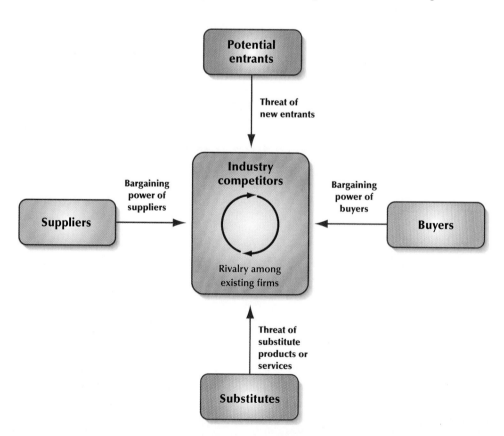

Some industries have loyal buyers, few competitors, and a limited threat from substitutes. The soft-drink industry in the United States, for example, is certainly one that comes to mind in meeting these criteria. Two companies dominate the industry.

Similarly, the PC industry is increasingly becoming consolidated among a handful of manufacturers. Today, there are fewer than half as many companies manufacturing PCs compared to a decade or two ago.

On the other hand, the airline industry in the United States must be continually concerned with the impact of competitive forces. Any of the many competing airlines can quickly lower fares to attract travelers. Moreover, a new airline can enter the industry by leasing aircraft and going into business with the offer of low fares to popular destinations. In these cases, an incumbent airline may have to either match the lower fares or forgo some of its passenger business.

The competitive playing field of these distinctive industries is very different and so are the strategies of the firms. Soft-drink firms rely heavily on advertising and the creation of image, and on occasion engage in special price promotions.

While in the PC industry it would be quite easy for a new company to come into existence by buying standard components from the industry's global chip and board manufacturers, a new firm might have difficulty becoming successful if it could not keep prices below those of the incumbent companies that already have valued brand names and attractive prices. At the same time, the laptop computer segment must be wary of the dangers posed by PDAs. A substantial number of laptop computer users are finding that they can do many things on new model PDAs (including sending and receiving e-mail, maintaining customer name and phone directories, and preparing notes and messages) for which they previously needed a laptop. In this sense, PDAs are a threat as a substitute product for laptop computers.

## Value Chain

Research in competitive strategy has shown that competitive advantage cannot be understood by looking at the firm as a whole. Rather, it is a result of the many activities that go on within the enterprise and in interaction with other organizations or entities outside the firm. Thus, the value chain is a powerful tool for understanding the factors underlying the generic low-cost, differentiation, or focused competitive strategies at work in an enterprise.

A **value chain** is a set of activities that are relevant to understanding the bases of cost and potential sources of differentiation in a firm. Gaining and sustaining competitive advantage depends on the ability of the firm to understand how its value chain fits in the overall value system that includes both buyers and suppliers.

**value chain**
A set of activities that are relevant to understanding the bases of cost and potential sources of differentiation in a firm.

**Components of the Value Chain** The value chain consists of primary and support activities (Figure 13.17). **Primary value-chain activities** are the basic business processes fundamental to any industry. **Support value-chain activities,** as the term suggests, are those activities that occur to facilitate the primary activities. The value chain categories are as follows:

**primary value-chain activities**
The basic business processes fundamental to any industry.

**support value-chain activities**
Those activities that occur to facilitate the primary activities.

### Primary Activities
- **Inbound Logistics** The activities of receiving, storing, and distributing materials and other items that serve as input to the products or services of the organization; *Examples:* Handling and accounting for raw materials and inventory
- **Operations** The activities that transform input into final products or services; *Examples:* Manufacturing and packaging of products; operation of a retail store chain
- **Outbound Logistics** The activities that facilitate collecting, storing, and distributing the finished product to buyers; *Examples:* Fulfilling orders and shipping goods to buyers.
- **Marketing and Sales** The activities that facilitate or induce the purchase of the product or service by buyers; *Examples:* Creating and displaying advertising about the company and its products or services; product pricing practices; creating and maintaining a company sales force

FIGURE 13.17
*The Value Chain*

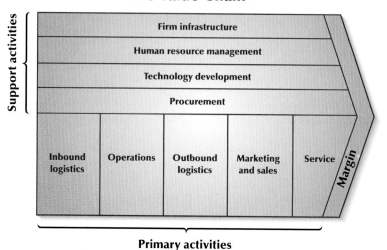

# The Value Chain

**Support activities**

| Firm infrastructure |
| Human resource management |
| Technology development |
| Procurement |

| Inbound logistics | Operations | Outbound logistics | Marketing and sales | Service | Margin |

**Primary activities**

- **Service**   The activities associated with providing service to enhance or maintain the value of the product or service; *Examples:* Maintaining facilities, machines, and parts

### Support Activities

- **Procurement**   The acquisition of purchased inputs for use in the primary activities in the value chain; *Examples:* Purchasing of raw materials, supplies, machinery, and buildings
- **Technology Development**   The broad range of activities created to improve the product or service and the processes that make them possible; *Examples:* Conducting research to create new equipment and machines; installation of new communications networks
- **Human Resource Management**   The activities involved in recruiting, training, and compensating personnel; *Examples:* Hiring IT application developers; negotiation of compensation and benefits specified in union labor contracts
- **Firm Infrastructure**   The activities that support the entire value chain, rather than just individual activities; *Examples:* Creating business strategy and management control systems; designing quality management systems

Each activity should be evaluated for its potential impact on competitive advantage.

**Value Chain and Performance**   The value chain is a tool that can be used to analyze the linkage between activities in an enterprise, with the intent of identifying ways to create a competitive advantage in the following two ways: (1) to optimize the performance and (2) to coordinate activities.

*Optimizing performance* is said to occur when the firm decides to invest additional resources in the design of a product to increase quality, increase the durability of component parts, or reduce the cost of providing services.

In the laptop computer segment of the PC industry, both IBM and Apple Computer believe that buyers are willing to pay a premium price for the optimum performance their product provides through the unique software-driven capabilities and exceptionally high quality parts and components.

Those who pursue heightened *coordination* recognize the competitive opportunity provided by closely integrating activities. Reducing manufacturing costs through just-in-time delivery of materials and components to the manufacturing floor—meaning that inventory levels are kept very low—requires coordination among the value chain activities of manufacturing operations, inbound and outbound logistics, and service. For example, Wal-Mart achieved coordination between actual sale of goods and their rapid replenishment by vendors in its supply chain through its application of IT (its Retail Link system).

## Creating a Strategic Role for Information Systems

The preceding examples illustrate how information technology can provide strategic value to an enterprise. Managers and staff in an enterprise often find it useful to determine whether information technology can be developed to serve a strategic role by a asking the following five questions. Does the firm's IT strategy apply resources to

- **Change the basis of competition?**   Dell Computer's order entry and manufacturing systems enable it to offer consumers custom-manufactured PCs *and* low prices, something that its competitors have been unable to match.
- **Build barriers to new entrants?**   The use of Microsoft Windows on an extremely high percentage of PCs creates a formidable barrier for any company seeking to introduce a competing operating system. To enjoy success, a potential competitor would have to find a way to get Windows users to remove that system and replace it with its software.
- **Build in switching costs to customers?**   Merrill Lynch's CMA integrates a variety of products and services in a way that offers valuable service and monetary advantages to those customers choosing to sign up for the program. The program's benefits deter investors from switching their business to other brokerage firms because they would give up benefits they value.
- **Strengthen a firm's power in dealing with suppliers?**   Because of its large quantity of purchases and because it captures, stores, and shares POS data with its vendors, Wal-Mart has buying power when dealing with those companies. The results are visible in the low product prices it is able to offer its customers.
- **Generate or serve as new products?**   The *Wall Street Journal* has published a print version for many years, including special editions for European and Asian subscribers. With the growth of the Internet, the publisher determined that it could reach additional subscribers by creating a new product in the form of an online version of the newspaper. For an annual subscription fee, online readers can view and print the current day's newspaper. They can also retrieve news stories that appeared in previous issues of the *Wall Street Journal*.

The results that these and other companies have achieved demonstrate the value of IT as a competitive tool. Hence, IT's strategic role is likely to be of growing importance in the future.

## A Final Word

Information technology plays a pivotal role in the way companies develop or change their business practices. Whether in the office, on the manufacturing floor, or on the front line with customers and suppliers–information technology provides many advantages through its ability to capture, process, store, and distribute information. Clearly, starting from scratch has its advantages. However, it is the organization's people and the know-how they possess that will determine whether a company can capitalize on the business opportunities presented by new IT capabilities.

# CRITICAL CONNECTIONS

## 1 Part II: DSS Helps Build Energy-Efficient Homes

**DSS**   Decision support software like BuilderGuide and REM/Design offers builders the advantage of helping them *sell* the new techniques to home buyers by showing them the savings in energy costs. But this software also helps *potential* home owners, who may need a larger mortgage to cover the higher costs of energy-efficient construction. They may use the programs' output to qualify for an energy-efficient mortgage because the projected savings on utilities will leave them more money for a larger loan payment.

### Questions for Discussion

1. Explain how BuilderGuide and REM/Design fit the definition of a decision support system.
2. The Energy Crafted Home Program is sponsored by a consortium of New England utility companies. Why do you think a utility company would sponsor a program designed to reduce energy consumption?
3. Output from software packages like BuilderGuide and REM/Design may eventually be used to create a national standard similar to the *energy guide* now found on all appliances. What might this mean for home builders as a professional group?

## 2 Part II: Boeing Takes Off with CAD Software

**Boeing Company**   Boeing's commitment to CAD software goes back to the mid-1980s, when CAD was limited mainly to use in design work. By 1989, though, Boeing's management decided the company needed to go a step further—to *digital preassembly*—if it was going to make its billion-dollar investment in CAD pay off. In digital preassembly, parts that would once have been put together in an actual-size handmade mockup are assembled, instead, on the computer screen. When Boeing did this, at the end of the third design stage for the Boeing 777 in May 1991, it discovered 2,500 interferences—places where parts did not fit together or fit so closely that they could not be reached by maintenance workers. By fixing such glitches on the screen, Boeing expected to minimize changes, errors, and the resulting rework by 5 percent—not bad on a multibillion-dollar project.

### Questions for Discussion

1. How is Boeing's CAD-based engineering system similar to other business information systems? How is it different?
2. What would be your primary concern in installing a CAD system like Boeing's?
3. Why is engineering quality especially important to a company like Boeing?

# Summary of Learning Objectives

**1   Define and explain the purpose of information systems.**   An information system is a system in which data and information flow from one person or department to another. Business information systems are the IT applications that underlie the activities of running and managing a business.

**2   Describe the six types of business information systems and explain how each is used.**   There are six types of business information systems. Transaction-processing systems (TPS) are shared systems that use a combination of IT and manual procedures to process large volumes of data and information and to manage transactions. Management reporting systems, also called management information systems (MIS), are designed to provide managers with information useful in structured decision making or problem solving. Decision support systems (DSS) are used to assist in making decisions where the decision process is rela-

tively unstructured and/or only part of the information needed is structured in advance. Group support systems (GSS) permit people to process and interpret information as a group, even if they are not working face-to-face. Executive support systems (ESS), also called executive information systems (EIS), are interactive information systems designed to brief company executives on company and industry developments quickly. Expert support systems, or simply expert systems, use business rules, regulations, and databases to evaluate a situation or to determine an appropriate course of action.

**3   Summarize the purpose of computer-integrated manufacturing systems and manufacturing cells.**   Computer-integrated manufacturing (CIM) uses computers to link automated processes in a factory to reduce design time, increase machine use, shorten the manufacturing cycle, and increase product quality. In

CIM, machines work together in groups called manufacturing cells. Parts and materials are moved between cells by automated guide vehicles, automated machines, and materials-handling systems.

**4** **List and describe five specialized types of computer-integrated manufacturing (CIM) systems.** The five types of CIM used in manufacturing are as follows: (1) material requirements planning and manufacturing resource planning; (2) computer-aided design and manufacturing; (3) flexible manufacturing; (4) robots; and (5) computer vision systems. Material requirements planning (MRP) systems keep track of the quantity of each part needed to manufacture a product. Manufacturing resource planning systems are advanced versions of MRP systems that tie together all parts of an organization into the company's production activities. Computer-aided design (CAD) systems use computer graphics workstations outfitted with programs that allow designers and engineers to draw specifications on the display screen. Computer-aided manufacturing (CAM) systems rely on IT to automate and manage the manufacturing process directly. Robots are computer-controlled devices that can physically manipulate their surroundings. Computer vision systems use sensors to detect shapes, images, and varying levels of detail, which they then compare with data stored in memory.

**5** **Describe the distinguishing characteristics of enterprise resource planning systems and explain why so many large enterprises have implemented**

these systems. ERP systems are *unified* when they enable everyone to have uniform information, thereby ensuring each person has the same view of activities occurring throughout the enterprise, regardless of the department in which they reside. ERP systems make this possible by *integrating* usually separate applications through a database that is shared by all of the application programs

**6** **Discuss the strategic role information technology may play in an enterprise.** Information technology takes on strategic importance when it is used by an enterprise in a manner that assists in seeking a competitive advantage over competitors. Competitive advantage occurs when a firm is able to outperform rivals on a primary performance goal. It typically pursues one of the following three generic competitive strategies: being the low cost provider; offering differentiated services; or focusing on a specific niche in the market. By studying the primary and support activities comprising a firm's value chain, managers can identify activities where business process performance can be optimized or where improved coordination can lead to improved performance. Strategic IT applications may play a pivotal role in dealing with the following five forces that comprise a specific industry: (1) competitive rivalry among existing firms; (2) bargaining power of buyers; (3) bargaining power of suppliers; (4) threat of substitute products or services; and (5) threat of new entrants.

# Key Terms

action document 536
competitive advantage 557
competitive strategy 559
computer-aided design (CAD) 551
computer-aided manufacturing (CAM) 551
computer-integrated manufacturing (CIM) 548
computer vision system 554
concurrent engineering 553
decision support system (DSS) 540
detail report/transaction log 536
differentiation 560
enterprise information system/business information system 534

enterprise resource planning (ERP) system 555
exception report 536
executive support system (ESS)/executive information system (EIS) 543
expert support system/expert system 545
flexible manufacturing 552
group support system (GSS) 540
information system 534
low-cost leadership 559
management information system (MIS) 537
manufacturing cell 548
manufacturing resource planning (MRP III) 549

market niche 560
material requirements planning (MRP) 548
primary value-chain activities 563
robot 553
rule base/knowledge base 547
support value-chain activities 563
strategic information system 557
summary report 536
transaction processing system (TPS) 534
updated master data 537
value chain 563

## Review Questions

1. What is an information system?
2. What is a transaction? Why is transaction processing so important to successful business processes? Why do businesses have transaction processing systems?
3. Describe the five types of output produced during transaction processing.
4. Describe the characteristics of management reporting systems. What types of reports do they produce?
5. When do businesses use decision support systems? What are the three different types of decision support systems?
6. How do group support systems differ from decision support systems? When are group support systems used?
7. How do executive support systems help executives spend their time effectively? What types of information do executive support systems generate?
8. What is an expert system? Why are knowledge bases an essential component of expert systems?
9. Describe the purpose of computer-integrated manufacturing.
10. What is a manufacturing cell?
11. Describe an MRP III system's capabilities and subsystems.
12. Explain the characteristics of CAD and CAM systems. Are CAD and CAM synonyms for one another?
13. What is concurrent engineering?
14. What are robots used for?
15. What competitive advantages does flexible manufacturing offer a company?
16. How are computer vision systems used to monitor and maintain quality?
17. What are enterprise resource planning (ERP) systems and what benefits do they provide to firms choosing to implement them?
18. Why is the implementation of ERP systems often challenging?
19. When do information systems take on strategic importance?
20. How do strategic information systems differ from enterprise information systems?
21. When does competitive advantage occur for an enterprise, and according to what three competitive strategies might a firm chose to use IT to seek an advantage?
22. Describe the five competitive forces that influence the ability of an enterprise to gain a competitive advantage.
23. What is a value chain and what are the components that comprise it?
24. Describe the purpose of studying a firm's value chain.
25. When seeking to evaluate the potential strategic role of information technology in an enterprise, what five questions should managers explore?

## Discussion Questions

1. Companies are increasingly seeking to obtain strategic benefits from the information systems they implement. At the same time, there is a growing tendency toward (1) buying and installing packaged software available to any other company, and (2) outsourcing the development of software to a company specializing in software creation.

    a. Do you feel information systems created by the use of packaged software can be applied to differentiate an enterprise from its competitors, thereby creating a competitive advantage? Explain the reasons behind your answer.

    b. Can information systems have strategic value if the development of the software is a result of outsourcing? Why or why not?

2. ERP systems are often described as being difficult to implement. There are also many stories circulating that tell of companies where ERP systems failed.

    a. What characteristics of ERP systems might make them difficult to implement within a company?

    b. When ERP systems succeed or fail, do you believe it is because of the features of the system, the existing operating processes of the enterprise seeking to install the system, or the implementation procedures used by the IT or project manager? Explain the reason for your conclusions.

3. A survey of IT managers by The Yankee Group, a market research firm, found that the primary goal of IT managers is the integration of manufacturing, engineering, and business groups. What business and IT trends do you think underlie this goal?

# Group Projects and Applications

## Project 1

Arrange to visit (in person, by telephone, or using e-mail) with a member of the IT staff in a company that has implemented an enterprise resource planning (ERP) system. Interview the staff member to learn about the ERP system, then answer the following questions:

a. Why did the company choose to install an ERP system?

b. How did the company go about selecting the particular ERP system it is using? Who was involved in the selection team?

c. Did the company have to alter its business processes in order to implement the ERP system? Why or why not?

d. What was the rationale behind the ERP system's selection and implementation?

e. Has the ERP system met the company's expectations?

f. What advice can the IT staff member offer to other companies considering adoption of an ERP system?

## Project 2

Select an industry of your choosing and conduct an investigation to determine what information systems capabilities are essential in the industry. That is, other than routine internal accounting and financial reporting systems, what information systems applications must a new competitor have in order to enter the industry successfully? Why are the systems you identified essential from a competitive perspective?

Considering the information systems applications you identified and using the insights gained from your analysis, answer the question: *Do information systems in your selected industry present a barrier to entry for firms wishing to enter that industry?* Explain the reasoning behind your answer.

## Project 3

With a partner or group, visit a company that uses one or more business information systems. Find out what each of these systems does by interviewing various managers and employees using the following framework. Present your findings to the class.

| SYSTEM TYPE | QUESTIONS TO ASK |
|---|---|
| Transaction processing systems | • In what kinds of transactions does your company routinely engage?<br>• What types of action documents does the system generate?<br>• What types of exceptions show up in your exception reports? |
| Management reporting systems | • What types of reports does the system generate?<br>• Where do the data in the management reporting system come from?<br>• Which managers have access to the system? |
| Decision support systems | • What types of problems is the DSS designed to help solve?<br>• Does the company use an institutional DSS?<br>• Can you provide a recent example of a decision that has been made with the help of a DSS? |
| Group support systems | • How has the GSS helped employees improve their productivity?<br>• How often do you use the GSS?<br>• How large does the decision need to be for the GSS to be used?<br>• Does your company have a decision room?<br>• Who serves as facilitator during group meetings? |
| Executive support systems | • Who has access to the executive support system?<br>• What types of information are included in the ESS? |
| Expert systems | • Who programmed the expert system? Is it updated as new knowledge comes to light?<br>• Who uses the system, and for what reasons?<br>• How much do workers rely on the expert system, and how much do they rely on their own experiences and hunches? |

## Project 4

Visit a manufacturing company that uses CAD/CAM technology. (Very often these companies are profiled in the business pages of your local newspaper.)

Spend some time on the shop floor, watching how the machines work.

- Does the company use robots?
- Flexible manufacturing?
- Computer vision systems?
- How expensive was the technology?
- Has it significantly improved productivity and profitability?

Present your findings in a two-page report. If possible, bring in photographs, brochures, or schematics to share with the class.

## Project 5

Technology sometimes replaces human workers; this *unemployment* effect is occasionally cited as one of technology's drawbacks.

Conduct a debate on the pros and cons of technology. Two groups of four individuals each should debate the issue. The first group speaks in favor of technology, the second against it. After the first person from each side has spoken, the second questions the opponent's arguments, looking for holes and inconsistencies. The third individual attempts to answer these arguments. The fourth presents a summary of each side's arguments. Finally the class votes on which team has offered the more compelling argument.

## Net_Work

1. Many airlines have developed online booking capabilities whereby travelers can investigate flight routes and ticket prices over the Internet and without the involvement of travel agents. Select three airlines and visit their online reservation sites to evaluate the features and capabilities offered there.
   a. How are the airlines' reservation sites similar and how are they different?
   b. Are the reservation capabilities offered at any of the sites strategic? Why or why not?
   c. Do any of the online reservation sites contain features that could give the airline a competitive advantage over its rivals? Explain.

2. Companies wishing to install an ERP system can choose from systems offered by several different companies. Some companies focus only on ERP software. Other companies produce a variety of software in addition to ERP systems.
   a. Conduct an investigation to identify at least six different ERP systems currently available. For each, identify the manufacturer and indicate whether it produces any software other than ERP systems.
   b. Choose two of the ERP systems identified in your search and compare their capabilities and features. Summarize your findings in a table of ERP system features.

3. A variety of sites on the Internet contain directories of decision support systems. Each site identifies the DSS and indicates a Web site containing additional descriptive information.
   a. Using a search engine of your choosing, locate a DSS directory on the Web.
   b. Choose an industry or specialty of interest to you (such as medicine or personal investments) and find at least two decision support systems that are focused on that industry.
   c. Follow the hyperlinks to the Web sites for the two decision support systems you have chosen. Investigate the features of each DSS. Summarize and compare the capabilities of each system.

# *Cool Mobility*

## On Assignment

CEO Tina Fuentes has shown time and time again that she is highly supportive of the role information technology plays in the day-to-day activities of *Cool Mobility*. You have heard her comment often on the importance of executing routine business transactions in an efficient and effective manner. She has paid close attention to the features of the company's Internet site that support the processing of sales transactions.

You know first-hand that she also stresses to the managers that they should take advantage of the company's IT capability to manage their operating areas effectively and to detect unusual situations before they turn into problems. In addition, you have heard Fuentes refer to CoolMobility.biz as the company's competitive weapon on the Internet.

## In Consultation

Apparently Fuentes' leadership in the use of IT is highly influential on company managers. Your new assignments reflect both operational and strategic uses of the company's IT.

a. Mark Goodman, director of human resources, wishes to receive a monthly report on employee time worked and time missed, whether due to illness (sick days) or vacation. Currently employees use the intranet to obtain forms to report each activity. They submit the completed form for processing by the company's computer-based transaction-processing system. The system stores the time worked for each employee in a database that is used for payroll and other processing activities.

You have been asked to design a layout for a monthly management information system report on employee time worked. The report should show week by week the number of hours worked, any sick days used, and days of vacation taken for each employee. (Although employees are paid when they take vacation days and sick days, those days do not count as days worked.). The normal workday is eight hours and employees are scheduled to work five days per week.

In addition to the report design, also describe or draw a flow diagram indicating how the weekly transaction data is used to produce the monthly report.

b. Using an Internet search engine, visit at least three other sites on the Internet that sell mobile phones. Compare the characteristics of the phones they sell, regardless of the brand, with those offered by *Cool Mobility*. Using your strategic thinking capability and insight into competitive strategy, what competitive advantages does *Cool Mobility* have over its competitors? Do the competitive sites you examined offer any services or features related to their phones that place *Cool Mobility* at a competitive disadvantage? Describe the role IT plays in the competitiveness of *Cool Mobility*.

c. Using the in-depth knowledge you have gained about *Cool Mobility* and its use of the Internet to interact with and sell to its customers, draw a value chain showing the company's primary value-chain activities. Analyze its value chain and identify where *Cool Mobility* adds value for its customers.

# Case Study

## Nestlé ERP System Implementation Is About Managing Change

Nestlé is Switzerland's largest industrial company. It is also the world's largest food company, with a total workforce of approximately 230,000 people in some 468 factories worldwide. Nestlé products are available in nearly every country around the world.

Nestlé opened its first U. S. facility in Fulton, New York, to make milk, food, and cheese. In 1907, the Fulton plant began making milk chocolate and today produces a variety of Nestlé chocolate products. In the ensuing years, other products and brands were developed within the company or through acquisitions, and the company managed some of the nation's more popular brands.

In 1990, the company unified and reorganized what had developed as a collection of independent brands, creating Nestlé USA. But the company's years of autonomous operation provided a steep hurdle for management's efforts to introduce common practices and benefit from economies of scale in manufacturing and day-to-day operations. Subsequently, the CEO established the goal of creating one Nestlé—to transform the separate brands into one highly integrated company.

A USA team, consisting of key stakeholders—executives in charge of critical business functions, such as finance, product distribution, and manufacturing—identified the need for business process reorganization, which would mean changing the way the company conducted its business activities. The team presented Nestlé USA executives with a summary of the current operations, pointing out areas where better coordination was needed, such as in multiple company relationships with customers, independent factory purchasing from the same suppliers, and multiple general ledger systems across the divisions. The executive team agreed that substantial process reengineering was needed to achieve its performance objectives.

An essential part of the reorganization required integrating the company's information across the operating units. Hence, information technology became a centerpiece in the reengineering effort, with the expectation that an ERP system was needed to achieve the organization's objectives.

Nestlé USA chose the SAP enterprise resource planning system. Although the CIO, Jeri Dunn, briefed the management team on the significance of changing both the business processes and the operations culture of the enterprise, and warned of the many months the transition would take, many still considered it simply a software project, not a dramatic change in business practices and processes.

A plan was put in place for Nestlé to implement given SAP modules—purchasing, financial management, sales and distribution, accounts payable, and accounts receivable, along with a supply-chain management application purchased from an independent software vendor. A deadline for implementing the software and associated process changes was also established.

The deadline for *installing* the new modules was met. However, within a few months, there was chaos in the business units affected. Workers did not understand how to use the new system, nor did they understand the new processes. The divisional executives, who were just as confused as their employees—and even more frustrated—did not go out of their way to help. Nobody wanted to learn the new way of doing things. Morale dropped sharply as turnover skyrocketed, exceeding 75 percent in some units.[2]

The CIO stepped in to take full charge of the project and soon gathered key Nestlé USA stakeholders at a three-day off-site retreat. The group reaffirmed the importance of the project (although the CIO decided to switch one component of the system, selecting a different supply-chain application). She also decided that the implementation process would have to be restarted. The team developed a new schedule for full integration of SAP. This time, with Dunn's encouragement, the team determined it would have to take the necessary steps to gain support from key division heads and be certain that all employees know what changes were occurring, why they were important, how they would benefit, and how the changes would be carried out.

During the ensuing weeks, an end-state design was completed for the system, giving the project team a clear roadmap to follow. A director

[2]Worthen, Ben, Nestlé's ERP Odyssey, *CIO* magazine (May 15, 2002).

of process change, brought on board for the project, was given responsibility for acting as liaison between the operating units and the project team. Frequent meetings were held with division heads, and employees were surveyed to determine how they were dealing with changes. On one occasion, the survey information convinced the CIO to delay the rollout of one module for several months until the employees were ready to use it.

The ERP system was installed and implemented, providing common databases and business processes as envisioned. The resulting improvement in demand forecasting for Nestlé products is producing a substantial return on investment.

Complex IT applications, like ERP systems, require long implementation periods because they touch so many functions within an enterprise. However, as Nestlé USA found, just having the right application tools may not be enough. In the end, the success of an application has a great deal to do with how well the change process is managed.

## Questions for Discussion

1. What factors make ERP systems unique compared to other enterprise applications?
2. Why are ERP systems more complicated to implement than other IT applications?
3. How does an effective change management process aid the likely success of an ERP implementation?
4. If ERP systems are so complex and are also difficult to implement successfully, why have so many enterprises adopted them?

# 14 Issues in Information Technology

## LEARNING OBJECTIVES

When you have completed this chapter, you should be able to

1 Identify the types of security breaches an enterprise should protect against and describe the five results that might occur if it does not.

2 Describe the most likely sources of security breaches.

3 Describe 10 ways to protect a system against intrusion.

4 Describe the six categories of security measures and identify those most effective in protecting against intrusion.

5 Identify the two methods of virus detection used by virus detection software.

6 Explain the IT professional's obligation to provide continued access to computers and networks, and describe the four methods used to ensure IT reliability.

7 Explain how the term *privacy* applies to information technology and why privacy is an important issue today.

8 Describe the importance of ethics in the use of information technology, and identify seven ethical issues associated with the use of IT in business.

9 Discuss the legal issues surrounding software piracy and three methods that have been used to prevent software piracy.

10 Describe the concern over piracy of digital content.

# Attack on Internet Creates Cybersecurity Fear

On October 21, 2002, hackers attacked the servers that are at the core of the Internet. In what security experts agree was a carefully organized effort, 13 root servers, key to the Internet's naming system, were flooded with messages, overwhelming them with traffic. The attack was global in nature—the root servers are distributed throughout the world; some root servers are located in Europe, the United Kingdom, and Asia.

The hackers did not focus on a particular Web site or individual service providers. Rather, it was deemed an attack on the Internet itself. Root servers run the global system of domain names and Internet addresses. They are responsible for matching Internet addresses with user requests. Observers called it the largest, most targeted attack ever seen.

Investigators had little doubt that the intent was to cripple the Internet. In this sense, the attack was a failure. While service was interrupted on nine of the 13 Internet root servers, most Internet users did not notice a difference in normal Internet response time during the one-hour duration of the attack. The fact that attackers were unable to shut it down is an endorsement of the Internet's robustness.

On the other hand, many security experts believe that a distributed attack of this magnitude *could have been catastrophic* if it had been sustained for a longer period of time. Internet services could have been denied to millions of users had the attack gone on.

Attempts to bring down *individual* servers are not unusual. Hackers regularly try to disrupt servers on which companies, schools, and governments maintain their Web sites by overloading them with useless information. Consequently, government and business security experts monitor their systems around the clock to detect and foil hackers, attempting to stop them before they can interrupt Internet or Web operations. In spite of this security, attacks have on occasion been so fierce that they have brought down such well-known Web sites as amazon.com, Yahoo!, and eBay.

However, this attack was rare because it targeted all 13 Internet root servers. Experts admit there is little that can be done to prevent such an attack if is conducted by well-equipped, highly trained, and determined attackers. Novices or Internet hobby users are unlikely to be able to launch an attack of this magnitude. They would not have access to the information technology components needed to pull this off: Sufficient network bandwidth and multiple speedy computers can simultaneously transmit messages in rapid-fire fashion to the root servers.

The world's news media has repeatedly carried government warnings and sounded alerts about cybersecurity threats. Information technology experts, enterprise security planners, and governments generally take the issue seriously. While it may be that the Internet itself is too robust to be taken down easily, there is little doubt that attacks on Web sites will continue, with varying degrees of success. Without sufficient protective action, many enterprises will sooner or later encounter serious incidents.

*C*ompanies that make information technology available for use by individuals or within an enterprise are expected to assume responsibility for protecting IT resources from accidental or intentional harm or destruction. Moreover, there is a general expectation by society that the IT will be used properly. These responsibilities and obligations constitute the issues in information technology.

This chapter examines the following issues of public and private concern with respect to IT: (1) security, (2) reliability, (3) privacy, (4) ethics, and (5) piracy. These issues are not likely to go away. In fact, with society's growing dependence on IT, they will be all the more visible and important in the coming years.

# Security

IT security is one of the hottest and most important topics facing users and providers of information technology. Until recently, many users did not consider security a serious challenge. They believed that if their servers and mainframe computers were inside a protected facility, with access limited only to authorized users, they were unlikely to encounter a breakdown, or **breach,** in security. However, with widespread use of PCs, PDAs, and wireless devices, coupled with the broad interest in use of the Internet and other computer networks, the image of computing secured in a protected site is no longer realistic. Hence the broad interest from executives, managers, and other users in securing the enterprise's information technology.

This section examines the meaning of IT security and concerns about breaches in security. It also discusses programs and tools for protecting the security of IT assets.

**breach**
A breakdown in security.

## What Is Security?

**Security** refers to safeguarding and protecting an enterprise's information technology assets. The four principal areas include the following:

1. **Site Security**   Computer centers and rooms where IT processing activities occur or where IT resources are housed and stored.
2. **Resource Security**   Equipment and facilities, software and systems, and databases of the enterprise.
3. **Network Security**   Communications networks, including local area networks, wide area networks, intranets, extranets, and their access to the Internet.
4. **Service Security**   Assurance that the IT services of an enterprise will always be available and accessible by authorized users.

**security**
Safeguarding and protecting an enterprise's information technology assets.

A **security program** describes the policies and protective measures that will be used, the responsibilities of individuals involved in maintaining security, as well as the responsibilities of those who abide by established security policies.

**security program**
The policies and protective measures that will be used, the responsibilities of individuals involved in maintaining security, as well as the responsibilities of those who abide by established security policies.

There is no such thing as a fully secure IT facility. It should always be assumed that if individuals are fully determined to do so at any cost, they can probably find a way to break through an enterprise's IT security protection. Hence, security programs are designed to **harden** a potential IT target, making the level of effort greater than the value of breaking into a system, network, or facility.

## Types of Security Breach

Security programs seek to protect an enterprise from two different forms of breaches. Protection against **intrusion** seeks to deter attacks from outside or inside an enterprise, including misuse of IT assets by an employee. This includes detecting an intrusion when it occurs and assessing its impact (such as evaluating data or software integrity).

Protection against **interception** is aimed at preventing the capture of data and information transmitted over an enterprise network or other communications link. It encompasses data transmissions over fixed or wireless networks and seeks to safeguard network activities involving computers, PDAs, and other handheld devices.

## Results of Security Breach

The results of a security breach, whether through intrusion or interception, can be classified into the following five categories:

1. **Destruction of Resources** Damaging equipment and facilities; erasing data and software.
2. **Corruption of Data and Applications** Altering software and IT applications so they produce incorrect or invalid results when they are used; corrupting stored data to make it unusable or unreliable.
3. **Denial of Services** Depriving, usually intentionally and temporarily, an enterprise or its users of the services they would normally expect to have, usually involving a network service (such as e-mail) or access to a location on the network (such as a Web site).
4. **Theft of Services** Using the processing capabilities of a service provider without paying for its use.
5. **Theft of Resources** Illegally copying or downloading data, software, music, movies, or other digital content; or stealing any of these items outright from an IT facility.

The opening case study, "Attack on Internet Creates Cybersecurity Fear," describes the potentially catastrophic nature of a **denial-of-services attack.**

## Sources of Security Breach

Attempts to breach security typically arise from four sources: employees, hackers, terrorists, and viruses.

**Employees** Current or former employees are a common source of security violations. Disgruntled individuals who are unhappy with the enterprise or its managers—perhaps because they feel they have not received a position, salary, promotion, title, or some other treatment they deserve—may decide to *get even* by attacking their employer's IT assets. Intrusion may, for example, occur in the form of a disgruntled employee sabotaging equipment or embedding destructive instructions into a computer application.

Alternatively, employees may take advantage of their position or their knowledge of an application or database by intercepting information and using it in an unauthorized manner. Whether the data is captured because it has value in its own right (perhaps for other damaging uses) or is sold, as illustrated in the identify theft case that follows, the enterprise is vulnerable unless it protects against employee breaches of security.

**harden**
Designing a security program to a potential IT target, making the level of effort greater than the value of breaking into a system, network, or facility.

**intrusion**
Forced and unauthorized entry into a system.

**interception**
Aimed at preventing the capture of data and information transmitted over an enterprise network or other communications link.

**denial-of-services attack**
Depriving, usually intentionally and temporarily, an enterprise or its users of the services they would normally expect to have, usually involving a network service (such as e-mail) or access to a location on the network (such as a Web site).

**identity theft**

Loss of personal identity through a security breach.

**hacker**

A person who gains access to a system illegally.

The *Information Technology in Practice* feature, "FTC Warns of Dangers of Identify Theft," describes the capture and sale of personal identity information and the damage that can be inflicted by an employee's unauthorized use of the IT resources. **Identity theft,** growing in frequency, is particularly serious since it can ruin an individual's finances, credit record and personal credibility. The feature also discusses actions individuals should take to prevent the loss of their personal identity through a security breach they do not even know has occurred.

Hackers   A **hacker** is a person who gains access to a system illegally usually through a network, although sometimes hackers physically enter a computer or network facility.

Some people like to call themselves *hackers,* referring not to their ability to break into computers and networks, but rather to their technical skill at computer programming and at making a system perform in innovative and productive ways. Criminal hackers who break into systems also have good technical skills, but have chosen to apply them in undesirable (often illegal) ways. When they decide to do damage, the results can be devastating.

The number of hackers around the world has grown substantially over the past decade, primarily because of greater access to powerful desktop computers in schools, in offices, and at home. More computers, coupled with easily accessible network and communications capabilities, mean more hackers of all ages.

**Hacking Leads to Jail Time**   One of the most highly publicized cases involved Kevin D. Mitnick (Figure 14.1), a 31-year old computer intruder who had been previously convicted of computer crimes. Mitnick broke into the computers of Tsutomo Shimomura, a computational physicist in San Diego, California, stealing hundreds of pages of Shimomura's sensitive research on cellular telephone security. He was tracked down and captured by Shimomura. Mitnick was ultimately convicted of violating federal laws dealing with violations of IT security. After serving a prison sentence and a probation period in which he was forbidden to use computers, Mitnick wrote a book, *The Art of Deception: Controlling the Human Element of Security,* which describes how hackers use staff to bypass security hardware and software. Mitnick supports each of his observations with case studies and analyses.

**Hunting Down a Hacker**   In detecting security breaches, noticing even the smallest *loose end* can be helpful, as Clifford Stoll found out. When astrophysicist Clifford Stoll (Figure 14.2) joined the Lawrence Berkeley Laboratory, a university research laboratory outside of San Francisco, he knew he would be responsible for managing a dozen main-

**FIGURE 14.1**

*Kevin Mitnick, Once the FBI's Most Wanted Hacker*

# INFORMATION TECHNOLOGY IN PRACTICE

## FTC Warns of Dangers of Identity Theft

 The U.S. Federal Trade Commission (FTC) is regularly flooded with concerns from individuals about the dangers of identity theft and reports about the harm individuals have suffered from the experience. One of the fastest growing crimes in the United States, identity theft occurs when someone steals an individual's name, social security number, credit-card information, or other personal information, using it to create false identities. With the identity, they are able to commit fraud or theft.

The commission describes some of the ways that identity thieves' work:

- They open a new credit-card account, using an individual's name, date of birth, and social security number. When they use the credit card and do not pay the bills, the delinquent account is reported on *the individual's* credit report.
- They call a credit-card issuer and, pretending to be the individual whose identity they have stolen, change the mailing address on their credit-card account. Then, the imposter runs up charges on the account. Because the bills are being sent to the new address, the individual may not immediately realize that there is a problem.
- They establish cellular phone service in an individual's name.
- They open a bank account in the name of the stolen identity and write bad checks on that account.

The commission's identity theft program tracks cases of identity theft, noting the tactics used by criminals. They reaffirm what has long been known: The threat from insiders seeking to use their access to sensitive information in electronic databases for unauthorized use is greater than the danger from hackers. Those who commit identity theft know closely guarded passwords, have easy and repeated access to the information systems that contain sensitive personal data, and understand how to use the system to retrieve details of individual identities and financial histories. They can enter and leave the system without anyone questioning their reason for doing so. Moreover, compared to hackers who break into a system, there is not a trail of activity that must be electronically concealed.

In *one instance* alone, federal investigators estimate that some 30,000 victims lost money, not to mention the months of misery they endured and the legal fees they paid as they worked to clear their names, reestablish credit, and solve other problems caused by the thieves. A ring of criminals used stolen passwords to download credit reports that were in turn sold to other criminals. The standard reports contained all the necessary information—personal bank accounts, credit cards, mortgage information, social security numbers—they needed to assume the identities of the thousands of victims. As is usually the case, these people did not know they were being victimized until the

scheme had been active for weeks and sometimes months.

It is evident that identity theft is a clear threat to personal privacy. However, it also highlights (and in some cases raises questions about) the priority companies must put on securing individual records from unauthorized or inappropriate use.

The FTC recommends that individuals take actions to protect themselves. It suggests that everyone regularly receive reports of their credit histories (at least annually) from the three U.S. private credit reporting agencies: Equifax, Experian, and TransUnion. The histories should be reviewed for any irregular activities. In addition, misspelled names, wrong addresses, and incorrect entries may be indicators of fraudulent activities.

FTC officials also suggest the following IT-related actions:

- Update virus-protection software regularly to prevent malicious programs from entering PCs, PDAs, and other electronic systems.
- Do not download files or click on hyperlinks sent from unknown persons or sources. Opening a file could expose your system to a computer virus that could permit another party to capture data from your Internet and message traffic.
- Install a firewall program, especially if you use a high-speed Internet link to which your computer is connected 24 hours a day.
- Use a secure browser that encrypts or scrambles information

you transmit over the Internet, thereby guarding the security of online transactions.

- Do not store financial information on a laptop computer unless absolutely necessary in order to minimize any risks should the computer be lost or stolen or used by someone else.

The FTC also warns everyone to be wary of e-mail requests that appear to be from their Internet Service Provider (ISP) stating that their "account information needs to be updated" or that "the credit card you signed up with is invalid or expired and the information needs to be reentered to keep your account active." Do not respond without checking with your ISP first. According to information received by the FTC, *this may be a scam.*.

With identity theft on the rise, everyone needs to be on guard to protect against their personal information falling into the hands of criminals.

---

frame computers (interconnected to thousands of other systems over more than a dozen networks) and over 1,000 user accounts. An additional computer was dedicated to gathering statistics and sending monthly bills to the laboratory departments using the machines.

Stoll began his second day at work by reviewing the computer usage records for the previous day. He quickly found that the books did not balance: There was a 75-cent shortfall on a bill of several thousand dollars. Someone must have used a few seconds of computing time without paying for it.

Puzzled, he dug into the scrambled code of the accounting software. When he could not find an explanation for the discrepancy, Stoll became more puzzled. Several days later, Stoll found another accounting imbalance of a few cents and a 5-minute discrepancy between the amount of computer time logged and the amount actually charged to user accounts. Digging further, Stoll decided that an intruder had entered a lab computer from a network. He thought the intruder had found a loophole in the system's security that would allow him to enter the system and become a *privileged user.* You become a privileged user by logging onto the computer with the system manager's password. Once inside, you can establish new passwords, open access paths, and generally roam through the system, changing records and databases at will.

Stoll was a fan of a then-popular movie called *War Games,* in which a teenage hacker broke into a Pentagon computer and nearly started a global nuclear war. Stoll was not worried about someone getting in to damage the lab's computers, but he wondered if he was living through a real-life version of *War Games.* What did the hacker want and what were his intentions?

**FIGURE 14.2**

***Clifford Stoll: Spy Catcher***

Stoll, an astrophysicist, noticed a 75-cent discrepancy in the computer access time billed to his lab. He eventually traced the discrepancy to a mysterious secret agent in Pittsburgh, a spy ring in Germany, and the former Soviet Union's secret police.

Stoll watched as the hacker came into the system repeatedly and erased his own tracks—except for the telltale accounting discrepancies. After monitoring the hacker's activities for several days, Stoll wrote a program that logged all of the hacker's activities. He continued to let the intruder wander through the system while he carefully recorded every keystroke.

For over a year, Stoll stalked the elusive, methodical hacker as he prowled the Berkeley lab network and accessed the computer networks of more than a half-dozen national agencies, burrowing into sensitive information about military programs. Eventually, Stoll traced the hacker's origin to Hanover, Germany.

Next, Stoll set up a sting operation, tempting the intruder into accessing a set of data and then transmitting it to another location. The sting uncovered a spy ring in Germany linked to a mysterious agent in Pittsburgh. The spy ring was selling computer secrets to the former Soviet Union's secret police, the KGB, for cocaine and tens of thousands of dollars.

Stoll's experience, while extraordinary, points to the threat of criminal intrusion into ordinary computer systems. In his many television and newspaper interviews, Stoll always makes the point that computer espionage is the most important IT security issue facing enterprises.

**More Examples of Hacking**   Consider these other representative examples of hacking[1]:

- The United Press International (UPI) wire service reported that two Staten Island, New York, youths were arrested on charges of invading and disrupting the computerized voice-mail system of a Massachusetts company. Their activities cost the firm $2.4 million. The youths used their home computer to dial into the system and obtain the system password. They then changed the passwords for various units in the system, resulting in the loss of important messages and numerous business transactions. The youths allegedly attacked the Massachusetts firm because it had failed to send them a poster that was supposed to accompany a paid subscription for a computer-game magazine published by the company.
- Australia's Compass Airline reported that its reservation system was being jammed. On one day alone, the new airline company received more than 25,000 calls. A computer had been used to dial the airline's reservation number repeatedly, and then abort the call when the line was answered. The airline's CEO emphasized that Compass did not believe the culprit was a rival airline.
- *The Independent,* a London newspaper, reported that at least five British banks were blackmailed by a group of hackers who had broken into the banks' central computer over a six-month period. This was the largest and most sophisticated breach of computer security ever experienced by British banks. The electronic break-ins, with their implicit threats of stealing information or sabotaging the systems by planting false data or damaging the banks' complex information systems, could have caused chaos for the banks. The hackers demanded substantial sums of money in return for showing the banks how their systems were penetrated.

The increased frequency of hacking, coupled with the newness of computer crime as an issue of law, has forced governments to draw up special legislation. In 1984, the U.S. Congress passed the Computer Fraud and Abuse Act. This federal legislation, which is supplemented by state statutes, was a first step in positioning the judicial system to deal with the problem.

**Terrorists**   The U.S. Federal Bureau of Investigation (FBI) distinguishes hackers, who conduct nuisance or financially motivated attacks on systems, from terrorists. A **terrorist** is someone who conducts a "premeditated, politically motivated attack against information, computer systems, computer programs, and data, which results in violence against non-combatant targets by sub-national groups or clandestine agents." Terrorists may also destroy information technology for the sheer purpose of creating fear among employees, customers, suppliers, or others, especially when it makes people wonder what might happen next.

**terrorist**

Someone who conducts a "premeditated, politically motivated attack against information, computer systems, computer programs, and data, which results in violence against non-combatant targets by sub-national groups or clandestine agents."

---

[1]*Software Engineering Notes.* Vol. 16, No. 1, pp. 20–22.

Terrorist attacks, also known as **cyberterrorism,** might target facilities that rely on IT to produce the services they produce. Potential terrorist targets in this category include electricity-producing power plants, water purification facilities, and aviation control systems. Financially motivated terrorists attacks target banks and stock exchanges.

**Computer Viruses**   Sometimes intrusion occurs by way of software. A computer **virus** is a hidden program that alters, without the user's knowledge, the way a computer operates or modifies the data and programs stored on the computer. The virus is written by individuals intent on causing damage or wreaking havoc in a system. It is called a *virus* because it reproduces itself, passing from computer to computer when disks or files are shuttled from one computer to another (Figure 14.3). A virus can also enter a computer via an e-mail message when a file to which it has attached itself is downloaded from a remote computer over a communications network. An infected file will continue to spread the virus each time it is used.

Each virus has its own characteristics—its own *signature*—as computer experts say. Some destroy irreplaceable data by writing gibberish over the disks they infect. Others take control of the operating system and stop it from functioning. Still others embed commands into the operating system, causing it to display messages on the computer screen. The worst forms of virus are much more subtle, moving through data and changing small amounts of detail in selected files so unnoticeably that they are difficult to detect.

All types of computers are vulnerable to viruses, but PCs are particularly vulnerable because most were not designed with computer security in mind. The next generation of PC is being developed with much greater concern for virus detection and security in general.

## Security Measures

Six categories of security measures are commonly used to provide enterprise security. Their selection depends on the level of security needed. This section looks at (1) general security policies and procedures, (2) virus protection software, (3) digital signatures, (4) encryption, (5) firewalls, and (6) proxy servers.

**General Security Policies and Procedures**   Preventing security breaches, including unauthorized access to a system, requires excellent physical security as well as good security policies and procedures. Hiring honest, reliable people is an obvious starting point. Figure 14.4 illustrates 10 additional techniques helpful in deterring intrusion and interception. These techniques are as follows:

1. **Change access passwords frequently**   Users should be required to enter personal identification codes and individually assigned code words in order to access the system. Passwords should be kept strictly confidential.
2. **Restrict system use**   Users should be given access to only the functions they need to use, rather than full-system access.
3. **Limit access to data**   Users should be allowed to access only the data they need to perform processing within their area of responsibility.
4. **Set up physical access controls**   Access cards and *biometric devices*—which recognize voice patterns, finger or palm prints, retinal eye patterns, and signatures—are among the most effective physical security systems (Figure 14.5). It is difficult to fool these systems.
5. **Partition responsibilities**   Critical functions involving high risk or high value in the data being processed should be separated so that more than one person must be involved to perform the processing. Database and network administrators should be given separate (but important) responsibilities for controlling access to the system.
6. **Encrypt data**   Changing the appearance of data through scrambling and coding makes it more difficult to use information even if a hacker is able to access it.

7. **Establish procedural controls**   When clearly stated security procedures guide users and IT staff members, it is more difficult to breach security.

8. **Institute educational programs**   There is no substitute for well-informed staff members. Security education programs stress the threat of intrusion, explain hackers' methods and tactics, and provide guidelines on how to respond when intrusions are detected.

9. **Audit system activities**   In an *audit,* independent parties review transactions and computer processing to analyze their origin and their impact on the system, as well as to determine that these activities were approved and performed by authorized individuals.

10. **Log all transactions and user activities**   Keep a record of each activity and the individual responsible for that activity.

Some companies supplement these techniques with call-back security. Here is how it works: When callers dial into the system, they provide the telephone number from which they are calling. (The system may also sense the calling number automatically.) The person calling then hangs up, and the system, after verifying that the telephone number is valid and authorized, calls the person back. Call-back security adds a valuable layer of protection to the 10 techniques described above.

**FIGURE 14.3**

### *The Spread of a Computer Virus*
Educational programs and the implementation of procedures are important steps in preventing the introduction and spread of viruses throughout a computer system.

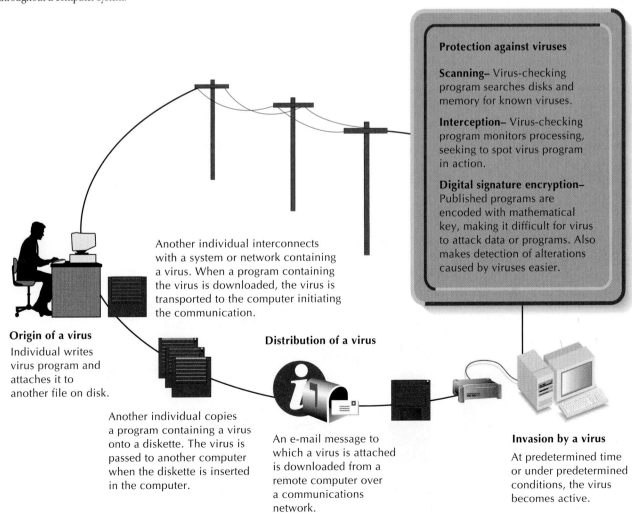

**Protection against viruses**

**Scanning–** Virus-checking program searches disks and memory for known viruses.

**Interception–** Virus-checking program monitors processing, seeking to spot virus program in action.

**Digital signature encryption–** Published programs are encoded with mathematical key, making it difficult for virus to attack data or programs. Also makes detection of alterations caused by viruses easier.

Another individual interconnects with a system or network containing a virus. When a program containing the virus is downloaded, the virus is transported to the computer initiating the communication.

**Origin of a virus**
Individual writes virus program and attaches it to another file on disk.

**Distribution of a virus**

Another individual copies a program containing a virus onto a diskette. The virus is passed to another computer when the diskette is inserted in the computer.

An e-mail message to which a virus is attached is downloaded from a remote computer over a communications network.

**Invasion by a virus**
At predetermined time or under predetermined conditions, the virus becomes active.

# CRITICAL CONNECTIONS   1

## NIPC Tackles U.S. Security Concerns

U.S. citizens generally expect their government to play a central role in protecting them against those who violate their legal rights and to take appropriate actions to protect the public's interest. However, the open debate process associated with passage of legislation means that the creation of appropriate regulations, including those related to IT security, usually lags behind events that demonstrated their need.

With the rise in the rate of hacker, virus, and denial-of-service attacks, the U.S. government has established a line of defense against cyber criminals and cyber terrorists. The National Infrastructure Protection Center (NIPC) addresses Internet-related security concerns in the following three areas:

1. Hackers and cyber vandals
2. Spies, criminals, and crime rings that attempt to steal classified data
3. Foreign nations that can potentially wage a sophisticated electronic war

**FIGURE 14.4**

*Ten Protection Schemes to Deter Hackers*

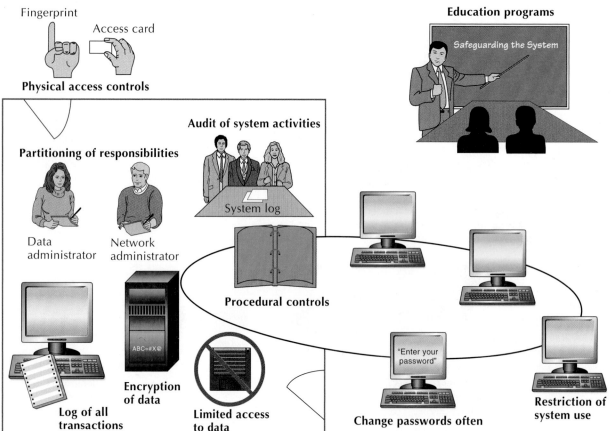

**FIGURE 14.5**

***Access Cards and Biometric Detection Devices***

Access cards have been used as security devices for several years. Growing in popularity are biometric detection devices, which grant access to an area or system by recognizing physical characteristics.

**a)** Comdisco's security access cards are used widely throughout business and industry. Card keys are distributed to authorized individuals. The programming of the card key restricts the individual's access to only those areas he or she is authorized to enter.

**b)** Courtesy Recognition System's Handkey security system, used in many government buildings and prisons, reads palmprints.

Despite these precautionary measures, some hackers do manage to break into even the best-guarded systems. When a hacker has penetrated a system, it is important to determine whether any damage or theft has occurred and to recognize that there is a *trapdoor*—an undetectable way of entering the system that bypasses the security system (Table 14.1). Stoll's experience with an intruder entering his system through a trapdoor, discussed earlier, reveals how even the smallest discrepancy in system performance could be a telltale sign of an intruder.

**Virus Protection Software** Although computer viruses are a fairly recent phenomenon, more than a thousand of them are already known, some bearing such exotic names as Code Red, Naked Wife, Melissa, the Michelangelo Virus, and the Christmas Virus (Table 14.2).

To protect their systems against viruses, companies must buy virus detection software, programs that scan the computer's disks to detect the virus. The two principal methods of virus detection are scanning and interception.

*Scanning programs* search memory to detect a virus. Most programs alert the user when a virus has been detected. The user can then signal the program to destroy the virus and, if possible, repair the data. *Detection programs* work behind the scenes, monitoring processing activities and signaling the user when a virus tries to infect the system.

Detecting and stopping viruses early is critical to maintaining data integrity. Novell—a Provo, Utah, software publisher and the largest supplier of office networks for personal computers in the United States—found this out the hard way. A few years back, it had to send out letters to approximately 4,000 of its customers warning them that it had accidentally shipped them infected copies of a disk for updating their network software. The virus in question became known as *Stoned III*. This virus is known for disabling every computer it infects.

Novell traced this debacle to a specific part of its manufacturing process, but admitted that it was unable to determine how the virus had infected its software in the first place. It later traced the origin of the virus to Europe just three months before the company produced and shipped infected disks. Somehow, the virus had traveled to the United States, on disk or via computer network, and crept into the Novell manufacturing process. To prevent a recurrence of this or similar problems, Novell acquired special digital-signature software that makes it far more difficult for viruses to spread undetected on the company's network software releases.

| Table 14.1 | Types of Computer Crimes |
|---|---|
| Data Diddling | Changing data and information before they enter a system. |
| Data Leakage | Erasing or removing databases and files from a system without indicating that they were removed or leaving any trace they ever existed. |
| Eavesdropping | Using electronic surveillance devices to *listen in* on electronic transmissions or to capture content of transmissions. |
| Logic Bomb | A program designed to execute when certain conditions occur. Designed to sabotage system data, programs, or processing (see also *Time Bomb*). |
| Piggybacking | Gaining access to a system or process by using the passwords or access codes of an authorized system user. Alternatively, taking over a terminal or workstation in use by an authorized user, perhaps while the person has stepped away from the system momentarily. |
| Salami (Data) Slicing | Developing or modifying software to capture small amounts *(slices)* of money in a transaction and redirecting them to a hidden account. The amounts are so small they go unnoticed, but can accumulate to a substantial sum in large-volume transaction-processing systems. |
| Scavenging | Searching trash cans—either figuratively, through a computer system icon, or literally, in a computer center—to find discarded data and information or program details. Used to obtain confidential information or to learn the structure of a program. |
| Time Bomb | A program designed to execute on a specific date. The program monitors the computer's internal clock/calendar. When the preset date arrives, the program comes to life, causing its damage. |
| Trapdoor | An illicit and unknown point of entry into a program or network that can be used to gain access to the system. |
| Trojan Horse | A program that appears to do one thing, but actually does something very different. Named after the Trojan horse of ancient Greek lore because the program masquerades as a harmless application and then does its damage after it is loaded onto a disk or into computer memory. |
| Wiretapping | Using any device to capture data transmission electronically or to *listen* in on network conversations, especially those transmitted through wireless methods or over copper wire. |
| Zapping | Damaging or erasing data and information to programs. Usually possible because the criminal is able to bypass security systems. |

**digital signature encryption**
Relies on a mathematical coding scheme designed to foil a virus's attempt to attack programs and data.

**Digital Signatures**   **Digital signature encryption,** a recent but increasingly used technology, relies on a mathematical coding scheme designed to foil a virus's attempt to attack programs and data. The easily transmitted electronic signature can be used to authenticate the identity of a message's sender or document's signer.

The Electronic Signatures in Global and National Commerce Act (often referred to as the e-signature bill), which went into effect in 2000, specifies that the use of a digital signature is as legally valid as a traditional signature written in ink on paper. The law does not specify a particular digital signature technology. Hence, IT vendors and service providers are exploring alternative methods to verify a person's legal identity, including the use of personal smart cards, PDA encryption devices, and biometric verifications.

The law, which only applies to electronic transactions in the United States, is expected to encourage companies to develop procedures for using e-signatures. Doing so will have the result of speeding routine business activities and reducing the costs of mailing and handling paper contracts and other commercial and legal documents.

**Encryption**   When the concern is protecting against interception of data (such as during the transfer of data over communication links), an effective security measure is to encrypt the data. With *encryption* a mathematical algorithm is used to convert the data into an enciphered form, known as *cipher text*. The algorithm uses *key*, a variable value, to

## Table 14.2  Infamous Computer Viruses

| NAME | WHAT HAPPENS WHEN VICTIM USES AN INFECTED PROGRAM OR DISK |
|---|---|
| Code Red | A worm that attacks Web servers running selected server software. While it does not affect an end-user's PC, all Internet users can feel the worm's effects (e.g., requested Web pages being defaced or unavailable). |
| Klez | When the virus runs, it attempts to turn off antivirus protection on the system, thereby compromising security. It may also transmit files from the infected machine, thereby sharing confidential information with the recipient machine. |
| Loveletter | Distributes itself via e-mail, with the subject line *résumé;* the message does not contain any text, though it includes an attachment named *résumé.txt.vbs.* When the attachment is opened, a résumé may appear on the user's display screen; meanwhile the virus is running in the background, infecting and retrieving information from the system. |
| Naked Wife | The W32/Naked@MM virus that is spread using the Outlook e-mail program. Infected e-mail can come from addresses that the recipient recognizes and contains a file attachment named *NakedWife.exe,* which appears to be a movie. When run, it copies itself to a TEMP directory and displays a window entitled *Flash* which reads *JibJab loading.* |
| AnnaKournikova Virus | The virus VBS/SST is spread using the Outlook e-mail program. Infected e-mail can come from addresses that the recipient recognizes and contains a file attachment named AnnaKournikova.jpg.vbs. When run, the script copies itself to the WINDOWS directory as *AnnaKournikova.jpg.vbs* and attempts to mail a separate e-mail message to all individuals in address book. |
| Stealth | Attacks the boot sector of a disk, causing the system to hang or lock up. |
| Stoned (aliases: *Hawaii, New Zealand, Marijuana, Smithsonian, Homo*) | At one time this was the most common virus in the United States. May display message, *Your PC is Stoned—LEGALIZE MARIJUANA.* May damage disk directory and file allocation table (FAT—a disk directory the computer needs to retrieve files). |
| Michelangelo | A mutation of the Stoned virus. Destroys content of the hard disk on March 6, the anniversary of the artist's birth in 1475. Gained national publicity in 1992, helping to raise public awareness of the growing threat of computer viruses. |
| Christmas (aliases: *XA1, XMAS*) | On April 1, the virus destroys the file allocation table. Between December 24 and January 1 of any year, the screen is filled with a picture of a Christmas tree. |
| Friday the 13th (aliases: *Jerusalem B, PLO Virus 1808, 1813, Israeli Virus, Pay Day, Anarkia, Arab Star, Black Friday, Hebrew University, Mendoza*) | The first computer virus identified; caused widespread panic at Hebrew University of Jerusalem in July 1987. System slows dramatically. If virus is in memory on any Friday the 13th, it will delete every program executed. *Black Box* appears on the lower left side of the screen and scrolls up as the screen scrolls. |
| Whale (alias: *Mother Fish*) | A *stealth virus* that uses layers of encryption and can infect files in 32 different ways. Slows system down; display flickers. Decreases available memory. Using system command to fix disk errors will damage files. |
| Casino (variant: *Casino B*) | On the 15th of January, April, or August, screen displays a message that the FAT has been destroyed, even though the virus has saved a copy in memory. Offers users a *last chance to restore your precious data* by playing a slot machine game. If users lose, virus wipes out FAT. Casino-B variant destroys FAT whether user wins or loses game. |
| Falling Letters | Ten minutes after the virus is loaded into memory, all the characters on the screen fall to the bottom. Infects only floppy disks. |
| Disk Killer (alias: *Ogre*) | Damages disk; destroys files on floppy disks. May cause unexpected formatting of disk. Displays message *Disk Killer . . . Warning! Don't turn off the power or remove the diskette while disk killer is processing! PROCESSING! Now you can turn off the power.* Once a certain number of disks have been infected, reformats hard drive, erasing all files. |
| MisSpeller (aliases: *Type Boot, Mistake*) | Causes misspelled words in printed documents, even though the on-screen spellings are correct. |
| Zero Bug (alias: *Palette*) | Display shows a smiley-face character, which eats all the zeros. |
| Frère Jacques | Causes misspelled words in printed documents, even though the on-screen spellings are correct. |
| Code 252 | Flashes screen message, *You are infected with a virus. Ha, Ha, Ha. Now erasing all disks. Ha,Ha, Ha,* although no files are actually erased. |
| T4-A, T4-B | Damages or deletes application and system files by trying to change the startup code or overwriting the file. |

*Sources:* Based on McAfee.com, 2003; Central Point Software, *Central Point Anti-Virus Users Manual,* Chap. 8, Virus Dictionary, pp. 71, 77, 79–83, 85, 92, 98, 107, 110; Michele Hasson, Virus Alert, *MacUser,* November 1992, pp. 268–269; and Christopher O'Malley, Stalking Stealth Viruses, *Popular Science,* January 1993, pp. 54–58, 92.

translate the message into its disguised cipher text form. The complexity of the key is a factor in determining the level of security built into the cipher text (Figure 14.6). For example, if the code only translates each letter and number into a different letter or number (for example, if an a becomes a b, or a 2 is translated as an r) it would be relatively easily to decode the message.

Three methods of encryption are in widespread use: *public key infrastructure, pretty good privacy,* and *virtual private network.*

**Public Key Infrastructure**   The **public key infrastructure (PKI)** method creates two keys—a public key and a private key—using the same algorithm. A *certificate authority* is a firm that issues and manages security credentials and public keys for message encryption. The private key is given only to the requesting enterprise and is not shared with anyone. In contrast, the public key is made available in a directory that all parties can search. Thus a sender wishing to transmit a secured message searches a *digital certificate* directory to find the recipient's *public* key, using it to encrypt the message. When the recipient receives the encrypted message, the recipient decrypts it with its *private* key. In addition to encrypting messages for security, senders can authenticate themselves to recipients, so they know who really sent the message. This is done using their private keys to encrypt a digital certificate.

The *Information Technology in Practice* feature, "For the Best IT Security, RSA Makes the Code Public", discusses an innovative application of public key encryption for thwarting intruders seeking to capture electronic transmissions.

[The financial services industry developed the **secure electronic transaction (SET),** an adaptation of public key encryption and the digital certificate (which the industry calls an *electronic wallet*) for securing financial transactions over the Internet. MasterCard, Visa, Microsoft, and Netscape were among the most active developers of SET. With SET, a customer (i.e., user) is given an electronic wallet (a digital certificate) and a transaction is conducted and verified using a combination of digital certificates and digital signatures.

**Pretty Good Privacy**   **Pretty good privacy (PGP)** is a popular program used to encrypt and decrypt e-mail and to encrypt digital signatures, so the recipient knows the transmission was not changed along the way.

If you want to use PGP to protect your e-mail, you download a freeware/shareware version or purchase a relatively inexpensive copy and install it on your computer system. It contains a user interface that works with most popular e-mail programs. The public key included as part of the PGP program must be registered with a PGP public-key server, so that others with whom you exchange messages will be able to find your public key.

**Virtual Private Network**   A **virtual private network (VPN)** is a way to use a public telecommunication infrastructure, such as the Internet, to provide secure communication between individuals or client computers at remote locations and an enterprise network. A VPN works by using the shared public infrastructure while maintaining privacy through security procedures and **tunneling protocols**. By encrypting data at the sending end and decrypting it at the receiving end, the protocols send the data (and if an enterprise chooses,

**public key infrastructure (PKI)**
A public key is made available in a directory that all parties can search. Thus a sender wishing to transmit a secured message searches a *digital certificate* directory to find the recipient's *public* key, using it to encrypt the message.

**secure electronic transaction (SET)**
An adaptation of public key encryption and the digital certificate (which the industry calls an *electronic wallet*) for securing financial transactions over the Internet.

**pretty good privacy (PGP)**
A program used to encrypt and decrypt e-mail and to encrypt digital signatures, so the recipient knows the transmission was not changed along the way.

**virtual private network (VPN)**
A way to use a public telecommunication infrastructure, such as the Internet, to provide secure communication between individuals or client computers at remote locations and an enterprise network.

**tunneling protocols**
By encrypting data at the sending end and decrypting it at the receiving end, the protocols send the data (and if an enterprise chooses, the originating and receiving network addresses as well) through a *tunnel* that cannot be *entered* by data that is not properly encrypted.

**FIGURE 14.6**
*Encryption Procedure for Protecting Data and Messages*

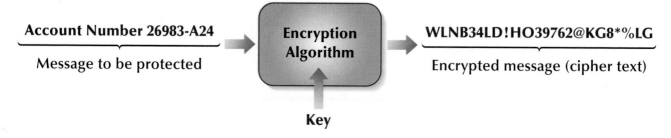

# INFORMATION TECHNOLOGY IN PRACTICE

## For the Best IT Security, RSA Makes the Code Public

Growth in the transmission of digital information has changed the encryption of data and information from an obscure specialty of spies, government agencies, and academics to an essential working tool for business. Electronic eavesdropping in general, and the scanning of documents in particular, leaves no mark on the transaction. Hence, it is difficult to detect when there has been a compromise of data and information.

RSA Data Security Inc., founded in Silicon Valley, south of San Francisco, and now headquartered in Bedford, Massachusetts, came out with an innovation that has changed the way companies encrypt data and information. The company controls the patents for this crucial software that manages the scrambling and unscrambling of computer messages.

Before RSA's innovation, the traditional encryption system used a secret coding method (called a key or cypher) known only to the sender and the recipient. Cryptography, as this method is known, is very protective—so long as the key is safeguarded. Once the code is broken, or is no longer secret, transmissions using that coding method are no longer protected.

RSA uses a public-key cryptography method, which allows sender and receiver to exchange messages without getting together beforehand to determine the key. This method relies on two keys: a public key, available to anybody; and a private key, known only to the recipient. The public key is used to encode the message. However, the message can be decoded and read only with the private key.

**The RSA Public Key Concept**

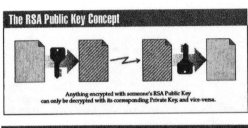

Anything encrypted with someone's RSA Public Key can only be decrypted with its corresponding Private Key, and vice-versa.

**The Conventional System: DES**

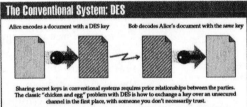

Alice encodes a document with a DES key        Bob decodes Alice's document with the *same* key

Sharing secret keys in conventional systems requires prior relationships between the parties. The classic "chicken and egg" problem with DES is how to exchange a key over an unsecured channel in the first place, with someone you don't necessarily trust.

**Authentication: The RSA Digital Signature**

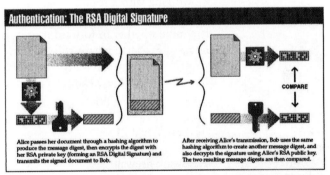

COMPARE

Alice passes her document through a hashing algorithm to produce the message digest, then encrypts the digest with her RSA private key (forming an RSA Digital Signature) and transmits the signed document to Bob.

After receiving Alice's transmission, Bob uses the same hashing algorithm to create another message digest, and also decrypts the signature using Alice's RSA public key. The two resulting message digests are then compared.

**Privacy: The RSA Digital Envelope**

1. Alice encodes the document with a random DES key.

2. Alice looks up Bob's RSA public key in her network directory, and uses it to encrypt the DES key.

3. The encrypted document & key together form the RSA Digital Envelope. Only Bob's RSA private key can open this envelope "addressed" to him.

**The RSA Public Key Concept**

Anything encrypted with someone's RSA Public Key can only be decrypted with its corresponding Private Key, and vice-versa.

People wishing to receive coded messages can freely distribute the public key. Those corresponding with them use the public key to prepare their coded message. However, only with the private key can the message be decoded.

The strength of RSA's coding methodology has been proven in the market, where some millions of copies of the software have been sold. It has widespread support from the information technology industry, including such well-known firms as Apple Computer, AT&T, IBM, Microsoft, Motorola, and Sun Microsystems. Its huge customer base spans the world.

the originating and receiving network addresses as well) through a *tunnel* that cannot be *entered* by data that is not properly encrypted. (See Chapter 8 for more on VPNs.)

**firewall**

A special-purpose software program located at a network gateway server.

**Firewalls** Firewalls (Figure 14.7) are seen as the essential perimeter defense for access over data communications channels, whether wired or wireless. A **firewall** is a special-purpose software program located at a network gateway server. It is designed to protect the users of a private network by blocking messages from users on other networks when the message is determined to contain potentially harmful programs or data.

Working with a router program, a firewall examines each packet arriving on the network. It evaluates the packet's origin, destination, purpose, contents, and attachments to determine whether to forward it to its destination. Often executable programs or attachments of excessive length will be filtered out, judged by the firewall to have potentially harmful contents. Firewalls can protect against intruders from the outside or snoops from inside who are seeking access via an intranet.

**FIGURE 14.7**

*Firewall Protecting Against Unauthorized Access to a Private Network*

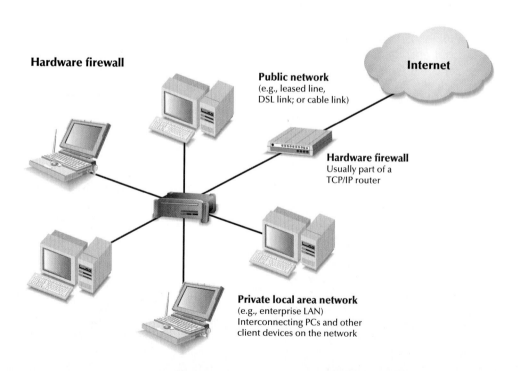

Hardware firewall

Public network
(e.g., leased line, DSL link; or cable link)

Internet

Hardware firewall
Usually part of a
TCP/IP router

Private local area network
(e.g., enterprise LAN)
Interconnecting PCs and other
client devices on the network

**FIGURE 14.7 continued**

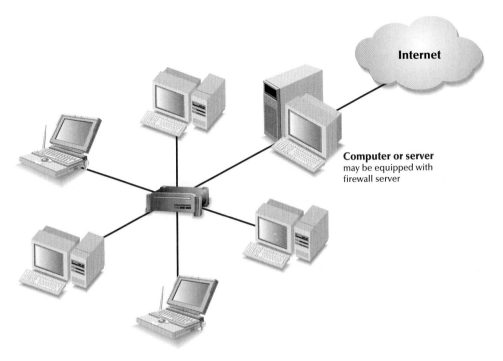

**Computer or server**
may be equipped with
firewall server

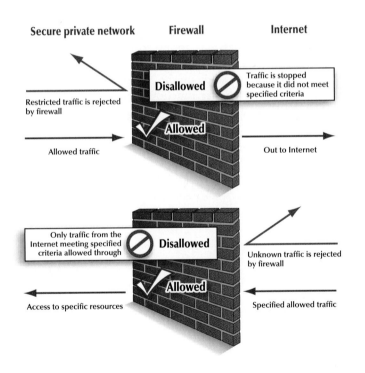

Secure private network          Firewall          Internet

Disallowed

Traffic is stopped
because it did not meet
specified criteria

Restricted traffic is rejected
by firewall

Allowed

Allowed traffic                                    Out to Internet

Only traffic from the
Internet meeting specified     Disallowed
criteria allowed through

Unknown traffic is rejected
by firewall

Allowed

Access to specific resources                   Specified allowed traffic

In the past, firewalls have been separate programs that users and network managers acquire and load on their systems. However, they are increasingly being built into operating systems (for example, in Microsoft's Windows and Sun's Solaris) and into communications devices such as routers used in local and wide area networks.

**Proxy Servers**   Proxy servers are often used to provide security for Internet applications (Figure 14.8). A **proxy server** acts as an intermediary between a PC and the Internet, separating an enterprise network from an outside network. It often operates in conjunction with a firewall and usually contains a cache that stores previously downloaded Web pages.

**proxy server**

Acts as an intermediary between a PC and the Internet, separating an enterprise network from an outside network.

When a proxy server receives a user's request for Internet access (such as retrieving a Web page request), it examines the request to assure it is valid for a particular user, and then looks in cache for a previously downloaded copy of the Web page. If it finds the page, it returns it to the user without needing to forward the request to the Internet. If the page is not in the cache, the proxy server requests the Web page from the Internet and forwards it to the user when it arrives. The proxy server is invisible to a user and does not noticeably change the speed with which a Web page is retrieved. The functions of proxy, firewall, and caching can be in separate server programs or combined. For example, a proxy server may reside in the same computer with a firewall program or it may be on a separate server, forwarding requests through the firewall.

There is no magic solution that guarantees absolute security. IT managers must assume that a determined terrorist, an aggressive hacker, or a newly created and potent virus may breach the system's security. Therefore, they must take steps to ensure system reliability.

## Reliability

**reliability**
The assurance that computers and communications systems will do what they should when they should.

As companies become dependent on IT, they also become dependent on the continued availability of their computers and communications systems. With that dependence comes the expectation that the service provider—whether an in-house IT professional or a hired IT service—will take the necessary precautions to ensure that service cannot be interrupted. **Reliability** is the assurance the system will do what it should when it should.

There are currently no laws explicitly governing service reliability. However, because of the importance of IT to business operations, society generally treats service loss as a breach of trust.

In Chapter 8, the opening case study on the Nasdaq network illustrates how building in system reliability kept the exchange functional in the face of a catastrophic event, namely the terrorist attacks on the World Trade Center.

**FIGURE 14.8**
*Proxy Servers*

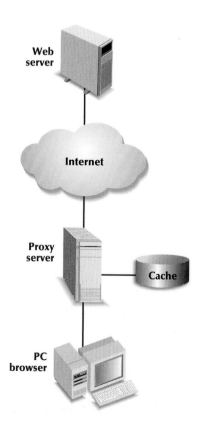

## Ensuring IT Service Reliability

Service reliability can be addressed at the following four levels: (1) fault-tolerant computers, (2) uninterruptible power-supply systems, (3) disaster recovery plans, and (4) off-site backup facilities.

The most reliable system is one that never fails. **Fault-tolerant computers** are designed with duplicate components so that if one component fails (a fault), an identical component will take over—usually without the user even realizing a fault has occurred. Many computers are not fault-tolerant, nor do they need to be. However, when applications must run 24 hours a day nonstop, the extra cost of a fault-tolerant computer is easily justified. Many air-control systems and bank automated-teller systems rely on fault-tolerant computers.

Because electrical power disruptions so often underlie a loss of computing capability, one of the most effective safeguards is the installation of **uninterruptible power supply (UPS) systems**. UPS systems ensure the continued flow of electricity, produced by private generators or from storage batteries, when the primary source fails. They are the second level of protection against computer failure. UPS systems help countless data centers ride out the many hurricanes that strike the East Coast of the United States.

The third level of protection is the development of a disaster recovery plan. Organizations should always assume that service will be lost at some point. When this occurs, the objective is to minimize the loss. **Disaster recovery plans** are procedures for restoring data lost when a system stops functioning. For computer networks, they include procedures for bypassing a failed segment of a network by using other communications lines.

The fourth level of protection against computer failure is the creation of an **off-site backup facility**. This is a computer center, often owned by the company, away from the company's main facility (Figure 14.9). **Hot sites** are fully equipped computer centers to which a company takes its backup copies of data and software to resume processing. **Cold sites** are facilities outfitted with electrical power and environmental controls (heating and air-conditioning), ready for the company to install a computer system (Figure 14.10). Often several different companies share hot and cold sites, each assuming there is little likelihood that they will ever need to use the site at the same time.

A common mistake in reliability planning is to focus on internal concerns and overlook external causes. Because companies rely heavily on computer networks and outside software suppliers, the possibility of system failure caused by external sources must be considered. AT&T and Revlon found this out the hard way.

**fault-tolerant computer**
A computer designed with duplicate components to ensure reliability.

**uninterruptible power supply (UPS) system**
A system that ensures the continued flow of electricity when the primary source of power fails.

**disaster recovery plan**
A procedure for restoring data lost when a system stops functioning.

**off-site backup facility**
A backup computer center located away from a company's main facility.

**hot site**
A fully equipped backup computer center to which a company can take its backup copies of data and software and resume processing.

**cold site**
A backup facility outfitted with electrical power and environmental controls so that it is ready for a company to install a computer system.

**FIGURE 14.9**

*Disaster Recovery Facility*

Most disaster recovery facilities are created to ensure an uninterrupted flow of electricity in case of emergency. The buildings are usually nondescript from the outside: what's inside (see Figure 14.10) is much more important. The 151,000-square-foot facility shown here houses multiple hot and cold sites.

**FIGURE 14.10**

***Hot and Cold Sites***

Given the need for computer reliability and the possibility of natural disasters, several companies have gone into the business of providing off-site backup facilities for companies that do not want to build their own. One of the most successful of these companies is Comdisco, whose rentable hot and cold sites are pictured here.

**a)** Hot sites are fully equipped computer centers to which companies take backup copies of their data and software to resume processing.

**b)** Cold sites are outfitted only with electrical power and environmental controls but are ready for companies to install computer systems at a moment's notice.

**System Failure at AT&T**  AT&T suddenly and without warning encountered a series of telephone system breakdowns around the United States. During a two-week period, telephone service to approximately 10 million customers was disrupted. This caused serious problems for businesses that depend on telephone service for their daily transactions.

AT&T sprang into action as soon as it detected trouble, assigning more than 200 technicians and engineers to work around the clock to identify and remedy the mysterious bugs causing the loss of service. It turned out that the problem was not caused by AT&T but rather by a small supplier to the communications giant. This company's products had been incorporated into the AT&T network to control switching in the system at enough places around the United States, so that when they began failing, the impact was felt nationwide. Neither AT&T nor its customers had ever experienced or planned for a failure of this type. AT&T's reputation for reliability was damaged in the short run, but its awareness of the impact of failure reached an all-time high.

**Disruption at Revlon**  Ethical concerns and IT reliability issues come together quite often. They did so disastrously for Revlon, the internationally known maker of cosmetics headquartered in New York, several years ago.

Revlon signed a contract with software supplier Logisticon of Santa Clara, California, to use Logisticon's inventory management software. Then Revlon complained that the software was not performing according to expectations and informed Logisticon that it would withhold a $180,000 scheduled payment for one portion of the contract and intended to cancel outright the other portion of the contract, valued at $600,000.

Logisticon allegedly decided to *repossess* the software because Revlon had not made the scheduled payments. To do so, it gained access to Revlon's computers over the telephone and activated commands that disabled the software. Revlon charged Logisticon with activating viruses (discussed in detail later in this chapter) that had been planted in the software, making the data incomprehensible. (Logisticon acknowledged disabling the software, but denied using viruses or destroying Revlon's data.)

The disruption to Revlon's computers affected two main distribution centers in Phoenix, Arizona, and Edison, New Jersey, halting approximately $20 million in scheduled product deliveries and idling several hundred workers. Revlon termed Logisticon's actions *commercial terrorism*.[2]

# Privacy

You have probably filled out countless forms and applications in your life: applications for college or university admission, magazine subscription cards, credit-card applications, and job applications. You have also provided information to local, state, and government bodies, including income tax agencies, the motor vehicles registration bureau, the health insurance bureau, and the social insurance coverage bureau.

[2]"Revlon Sues Supplier over Software Disabling," *New York Times*. October 25, 1990, pp. C1 and C4.

# CRITICAL CONNECTIONS 2

## Your Background: It's Just Business

Kroll Background America Inc., a professional investigation firm in Nashville, Tennessee, specializes in searching public records to locate information about people. If you apply for a job, your prospective employer may contact Kroll Background America to run a check on you. All the firm needs is a check, usually for a nominal fee, and your signature, indicating you have authorized the company to conduct the background check.

Here is a sampling of the information Kroll Background America can assemble on you in that preemployment check:

- Address verification
- Credit check
- Civil litigation, federal
- Civil litigation, state
- Criminal record
- Driving record
- Military record (if any)
- National law-enforcement submission
- Real property transactions
- Social security number verification

All of these details are available to anyone who knows how to search public records.

Do you know what information Kroll Background America could find out about your records?

---

Where is that information now? Who has control of it? Who has access to it and for what purpose? Is there a chance the data is being used in ways you did not intend or have not authorized? Who knows about your personal history because they have access to data you once provided to someone else?

## What Is Privacy?

As used in the field of information technology, **privacy** refers to how personal information is collected, used, and protected. The privacy issue did not arise with the advent of computers; in an earlier time, the taking of photographs caused serious concern about the invasion of personal privacy. However, the enormous capabilities of IT to store and retrieve data have amplified the need to protect personal privacy. Some consumer advocates have suggested that privacy protection will be the leading consumer issue in the coming years.

Some of the most heated privacy debates have been instigated by advances in telecommunications. Among the more controversial questions are the following:

- Is the use of automated equipment to originate phone calls or to collect caller information an invasion of privacy?
- Should telephone companies restrict the use of caller ID, which tells the recipient of a call the number of the calling party?
- Is the telephone company's ability to know the location of an individual using a cellular phone an invasion of that person's privacy?

**privacy**
In IT, the term used to refer to how personal information is collected, used, and protected.

## Privacy Legislation

To protect individual privacy, national legislatures have passed several important laws. The principal U.S. privacy legislation is summarized in Table 14.3. All of these laws focus on government records and have little influence over individual companies except as they do business with the federal government.

In 1973, the U.S Department of Health, Education, and Welfare (now the Department of Health and Human Services) issued a publication entitled *A Code of Fair Information Practices* that set forth rules designed to protect personal privacy within government agencies. The code's guidelines state the following:

1. There must be no personal data record-keeping system whose very existence is a secret.
2. There must be a way for people to access the information about them in a record and find out how that information is used.
3. There must be a way for people to prevent information about themselves obtained for one purpose from being used or made available for other purposes without their consent.
4. There must be a way for people to correct or amend a record of information about them.
5. Any organization creating, maintaining, using, or disseminating records of identifiable personal data must ensure their reliability and must take reasonable precautions to prevent misuse of the data.

The *Code of Fair Information Practices* served as the basis of the Privacy Act of 1974, the principal law still governing privacy protection within the federal government.

## Spam and Privacy

**spam**
Unsolicited e-mail.

**Spam** is unsolicited e-mail. It is often sent as bulk mail, transmitted to a large number of recipients whose names are drawn from mailing lists on the Internet. To the receiver, it is generally viewed as junk e-mail, a nuisance at best. Good e-mail etiquette (that is, *netiquette*) says to avoid sending spam. Spam on the Internet is generally equivalent to unsolicited automated telephone marketing calls (except that automated telephone marketing systems are illegal in many states).

**opt-in e-mail/permission-based e-mail**
If customers check a box agreeing to receive postings about the company's products, they have actually given approval for the mailing.

Some e-mail deemed to be unsolicited is, in fact, e-mail that people knowingly or unknowingly agreed to receive when they registered with a Web site. If they checked a box agreeing to receive postings about the company's products, they have actually given approval for the mailing. This is known as both **opt-in e-mail** and **permission-based e-mail.**

| Table 14.3    Major U.S. Privacy Legislation | |
|---|---|
| **LEGISLATION** | **DESCRIPTION** |
| Fair Credit Reporting Act (1970) | Allows individuals access to their credit records, to receive printed reports of the contents free of charge, and to challenge the contents in the event of errors. |
| Freedom of Information Act (1970) | Allows citizens access to data that have been gathered about them by federal agencies. |
| Privacy Act of 1974 | Allows people to determine what information is collected about them, to prevent records obtained for one purpose from being used for another purpose, to have access to — and copies made of — information about them, to correct or amend records, and to file civil suits for damages that occur through willful or intentional actions by individuals or organizations collecting the information. |
| Electronic Communications Privacy Act of 1986 | Protects the privacy of electronic messages sent through public networks. |

Nonetheless, spam is irritating people. Surveys of Internet users have shown that more than 80 percent of recipients detest the growing volume of unsolicited e-mail messages they are receiving. Porn spam, and unwanted solicitations for home mortgages and loans, investments, and real estate are ranked as the most irritating by two-thirds or more of survey respondents.

There is a cost on the Internet as well, as spam increases the volume of traffic moving across the network, slowing response time for other messages. In addition, Internet Service Providers and corporations have to invest in additional servers and communication links resources just to maintain the level of service their customers and users expect. The expense of doing so is growing.

In an attempt to deflect criticism of spam, some companies are including notices in their unsolicited messages giving recipients the opportunity to opt out. A representative notice is as follows:

> Anti-Spam Policy Disclaimer: Under Bill s.1618 Title III passed by the 105th U.S. Congress, mail cannot be considered spam as long as we include contact information and a remove link for removal from this mailing list. If this e-mail is unsolicited, please accept our apologies. Per the proposed H.R. 3113 Unsolicited Commercial Electronic Mail Act, further transmission to you by the sender may be stopped at no cost to you!

It is not surprising that a ground swell of privacy advocates and others are calling for legislation to protect the privacy of Internet users. However, the issues are not simple. Who should be responsible for abuse of e-mail through spam? The sender? The Internet service provider used by the sender? Moreover, should spam legislation be passed at the state level (where the majority of states are already assembling laws)? Or should one uniform bill, pertaining to all states, be passed at the federal level? What about spam that originates from outside of the reach of U.S. legislation? These issues will surely be addressed and resolved in the years ahead.

# Ethics

Spam is as much an ethics issue as it is one of privacy. Most records stored by companies and other nongovernmental organizations are not covered by existing privacy laws. Thus, a company's policy on privacy matters depends primarily on its ethical policies.

**Ethics** are the standards of conduct and moral behavior that people are expected to follow. *Personal ethics* pertain to people's day-to-day activities in private life; *business ethics* pertain to their actions in the world of business, including how they deal with colleagues, customers, and anyone else with whom their firm interacts. Some have argued that it is impossible to draw a boundary line between personal ethics and business ethics because one's personal ethics should always influence, and in the end outweigh, one's business ethics.

**ethics**
The standards of conduct and moral behavior that people are expected to follow.

There is an important distinction between ethical behavior and legal behavior. Ethical behavior refers to *expected* actions, while legal behavior refers to required actions. An action may be legal but unethical, or ethical but illegal.

Companies today are challenged by many questions of ethics arising from the widespread use of information technology. These issues are not limited to IT professionals, but involve everyone in the company who provides data to, or uses information from, the company's IT systems.

## Ethics and IT Usage in Business

Among the most urgent ethical issues that businesses must confront today are the following:

1. **E-Mail Privacy**   Do the contents of an e-mail system operated by a company, and intended for use by its employees, belong to the company? May the company do with those contents whatever it deems appropriate?

2. **Software Licenses**   What are the ethical requirements for acquiring and monitoring conformance to *software licenses*, which allow a company to use programs

developed by another company? Are the ethical requirements here different from the legal requirements?

3. **Software Copyrights**   What are a company's obligations for determining who owns a software copyright? When is the company's obligation for enforcing software copyrights different from an individual's obligation to abide by a software copyright?

4. **Hardware Access**   Under what circumstances is access to a company's computer and communications hardware ethical? When is it unethical?

5. **Intellectual Property Ownership**   When an information system contains ideas, writings, expressions, and other items considered to be the intellectual property of an individual, what obligations does the operator of the system have to safeguard the property? What is intellectual property and how is its ownership determined?

6. **File Access**   Under what circumstances is use of a file or database unethical?

7. **Data Ownership**   Who owns the data in a company's information system? The company, because it invested its resources to capture and store the data, or the individual or company described by the data?

Some IT directors and professionals dissent from the view that ethics in information technology is a major problem. Aside from questions related to computer software—and these are actually legal issues—most cannot recall more than a handful of instances when ethical problems have surfaced. Some researchers paint a contrasting picture, one that emphasizes the threat of ethics violations. They point out, for example that company business codes seldom address computing and communications issues. They also suggest that IT professionals generally do not take an active enough role in defining ethics as a critical concern in the Information Age, and that university and college faculty members need to do more to create an awareness in students that users of computers and communications systems have certain ethical responsibilities.

## An Ethics Challenge

To get an idea of the ethical challenges managers and employees face, consider how you would answer these 10 questions:

1. Is it right or wrong for managers to access the files or databases of people in their department or on their project team?

2. If data and information are stolen or illegally copied from a company's computer systems, should the IT director be held legally responsible for the loss?

3. If data and information are stolen or illegally copied by an outsider using the company's communications network, should the IT director be legally responsible for any resulting damage to the network?

4. If a company has a policy stating that its e-mail system is to be used only for company activities, does that company have the right to monitor its employees' e-mail messages?

5. Does a company have an obligation to inform its employees that their e-mail could be monitored?

---

Both users and developers of information technology tend to focus primarily on IT's capabilities for assisting them in a particular business situation. They are so caught up in the power of IT that their first inclination is to ask: "Can IT help solve this problem?" or "Can IT do this?" And if the capabilities are affirmed, their position is implicitly, "If the system can do it and the payoff is right, then let's do it."

From an ethical standpoint, a more appropriate question to ask before developing an IT system is "Should the system do this?" If the answer is yes, then the system's capabilities can be determined. When ethics come first, implementing IT takes on a completely different perspective. ■

---

6. Should IT directors be held accountable for software licensing violations by members of their department or development teams? If the copyright holder of a program decides to press charges for damages, including lost revenue, resulting from illegal copying of the software, should the IT director be liable for a fine or prison time if a court finds in favor of the software owner?

7. If an employee copies company software for personal use at home, should the company have the right to terminate the employee? If an employee copies company software for use at home to work on company business, but without receiving formal permission to do so, should that employee be terminated?

8. If an individual uses an illegal copy of copyrighted software without realizing either that it is an unauthorized copy or that it is copyrighted, should that individual be subject to legal action? Are people who discover that they have used an illegal copy ethically bound to report their infringement to the copyright owner?

9. Should a company be obligated to notify its employees in advance when a check will be made to see what software is loaded on their system and whether the company owns the software?

10. Do personal ethics take precedence over business ethics? If someone decides that a company's ethical practices are wrong based on his or her personal ethical standards and is fired for failing to follow company guidelines, should that person be compensated for the loss of employment?

This short list could easily be expanded to include hundreds of similar questions. Users of information technology confront these kinds of questions daily, and *wrong* answers can have major consequences. This is an important issue that may never be completely resolved.

The *Information Technology in Practice* feature, "Are Cookies Dangerous to Your Health?" explores the issues surrounding the common practice of Web site software writing information on the hard drive of a visitor to the site without the visitor's explicit permission or awareness.

**Developing a Code of Ethics**    Because it is impossible to list all of the possible questions that could arise in a business situation, many companies have created a general *code of ethics* to guide the behavior of their employees. Among the IT professional groups that have established codes of ethics are the New York-based Association for Computing Machinery, part of whose code of ethics is reprinted in Figure 14.11, and the Association of the Institute for Certification of Computer Professionals in Des Plaines, Illinois.

Donn B. Parker, senior management consultant at SRI International in Menlo Park, California, and a leading expert on computer ethics, encourages IT professionals and users to adhere to the following ethical guidelines:

- **Informed Consent**    When in doubt about the ethics of a particular action, inform those whom your action will affect of your intentions and obtain their consent before proceeding.
- **The Higher Ethic**    Take the action that achieves the greater good.
- **Most Restrictive Action**    Use as your basis for deciding whether to take action (or avoid taking action) the assumption that the most severe damage that could happen will happen.
- **Kantian Universality Rule**    If an action (or failure to act) is not right for everyone to commit, then it is not right for anyone to commit.
- **Descartes' Change In Rule**    A sufficient change in degree produces a change in kind. Although many small losses may be acceptable individually, when added together, they may result in an unacceptable total loss.
- **The Owner's Conservative Rule**    Assume that others will treat your assets as if they are public domain. Explicitly declare that the products of your efforts and your property are either private or public in reasonably visible ways.
- **The User's Conservative Rule**    Assume that any tangible or intangible item belongs to somebody else unless an explicit declaration or convention identifies it as in the public domain or authorized for your use.

# INFORMATION TECHNOLOGY IN PRACTICE

## Are Cookies Dangerous to Your Health?

Surfing the Net can provide a wealth of information—not to mention amusement—about companies, products, and services. Best of all, you can visit company sites all over the world without physically leaving your desk. The Net will take you there. However, there is one thing about surfing the Net you may not know: In the course of your travels along the Net's many links, you may pick up a few cookies. *These* cookies may not be good for you. It depends on the intentions of their creator.

*Cookies* are bits of data and information that some Web servers store on your computer's hard drive during your visit to a Web site, so that when you return to that site, the server can read the cookies and in the process know how often you visit the site, which pages you look at, and what actions you take.[3]

How do these servers know that it is *you* returning? Actually, you provide this information unknowingly. Net browsers have a section listing your name, Internet address, and organization (it is usually found under the preferences section of the option menu on your browser). As you enter a site, the server software may request your browser to transmit your identity (or prompt you for the information before letting you continue). By combining your identity with information it reads from the cookie stored on your system from a previous visit, the server can tell who you are, when you last visited the site, how often you visit it, and what you like to see there.

Does this bother you? Should it bother you? Is this any different than a charitable organization noting the name and address on your check whenever you make a voluntary donation? (Your visit to a Web site is voluntary, too.)

[3]Not all Web sites deposit cookies on your hard drive. Some Web browsers, such as Netscape Communication Corp.'s Navigator, display a message alerting you that a cookie is present. Microsoft's Internet Explorer allows you to set the level of acceptance for cookies.

---

Leaders in many companies and professional associations agree that a code of ethics is necessary for every business, but they often disagree that a special code of ethics *for information technology* is needed. These people are not speaking against ethics in IT. Rather, they are pointing out that IT ethics must be part of the company's overall code of ethics because IT is so pervasive today that it is a major part of most companies' practices.

In recent years, the concept of social responsibility has been advanced as a counterpart to ethics. A company that exercises **social responsibility** attempts to balance its commitments—not only to its investors, but also to its employees, its customers, other businesses, and the community or communities in which it operates. McDonald's Corp. for example, established Ronald McDonald houses several years ago to provide lodging for families of sick children hospitalized away from their home areas. Sears and General Electric support artists and performers.

**social responsibility**
The concept that businesses need to balance their commitments to investors, employees, customers, other businesses, and the communities in which they operate.

## Digital Piracy

Ethical issues apply as much to the use of digital content and software as they do to the characteristics of each that companies deliver. Like data and information, software is a valuable component of a business system: It is the element that oversees processing and transforms data into a useful form. Since commercial software is often perceived as expensive, it is often pirated. So is digital content.

**FIGURE 14.11**

***Excerpt from the Association for Computing Machinery's Code of Ethics***
Code of Ethics and Professional Conduct

### Association for Computing Machinery

*General Moral Imperatives:*
- Contribute to society and human well-being.
- Avoid harm to others.
- Be honest and trustworthy.
- Be fair and take action not to discriminate.
- Honor property rights including copyrights and patents.
- Give proper credit for intellectual property.
- Respect the privacy of others.
- Honor confidentiality.

*More Specific Professional Responsibilities:*
- Strive to achieve the highest quality, effectiveness, and dignity in both the process and products of professional work.
- Acquire and maintain professional competence.
- Know and respect existing laws pertaining to professional work.
- Accept and provide appropriate professional review.
- Give comprehensive and thorough evaluations of computer systems and their impacts, including analysis of possible risks.
- Honor contracts, agreements, and assigned responsibilities.
- Improve public understanding of computing and its consequences.
- Access computing and communication resources only when authorized to do so.

*Organizational Leadership Imperatives:*
- Articulate social responsibilities of members of an organizational unit and encourage full acceptance of those responsibilities.
- Manage personnel and resources to design and build information systems that enhance the quality of working life.
- Acknowledge and support proper and authorized uses of an organization's computing and communications resources.
- Ensure that users and those who will be affected by a system have their needs clearly articulated during the assessment and design of requirements. Later the system must be validated to meet requirements.
- Articulate and support policies that protect the dignity of users and others affected by a computing system.
- Create opportunities for members of the organization to learn the principles and limitations of computer systems.

*Source:* Courtesy Association for Computing Machinery, Inc.

*Piracy* is the making of illegal copies of copyrighted information. **Digital piracy** is the illegal copying of digital products and information. Two forms are of the greatest concern: software piracy and piracy of digital content.

**digital piracy**
The making of illegal copies of copyrighted information.

## Protecting Against Software Piracy

**Software piracy** is the making of illegal copies of software. Software piracy is one of the most serious issues in IT today because it is so widespread that it is responsible for an enormous loss of revenue to software originators. Manufacturers and software industry groups estimate that as many as seven illegal copies are made for every legal copy of software sold by retailers.

Although no software protection method is foolproof, three methods are widely used in the IT industry to avoid piracy: (1) copyright protection, (2) copy protection, and (3) site licensing.

**software piracy**
The making of illegal copies of software.

**Software Copyright Protection**   A **copyright** protects original works against unauthorized use, including duplication, provided the owner visibly displays a notice of copyright on the product. The copyright notice is similar across many countries, although not all countries acknowledge the right of copyrighted ownership. Under the Universal Copyright Convention adopted by most nations, the copyright notice consists of three elements:

1. The symbol © (in the United States, the additional word Copyright or the abbreviation Copr. can also be used).
2. The year of publication of the work.
3. The name of the copyright owner.

**copyright**
Legal protection of original works against unauthorized use, including duplication.

Copyright protection has been used for many years to protect books, magazines, music, and other original works (Figure 14.12). Today, it also applies to computer software, databases, CDs and DVDs, and is the principal legal protection against duplication or outright theft of original ideas embodied in computer programs. Well-known programs such as Word, Access, Eudora Mail, and Acrobat are copyrighted and therefore protected by law from unauthorized copying or use.[4]

When Microsoft Corp. releases new versions of its Windows operating system, it works with law-enforcement officials to seize pirated versions of the software. Even before the program is widely distributed, law-enforcement officials typically seize tens of thousands of illegally packaged copies. CDs, documentation, and the packaging itself are usually duplicated and wrapped in cellophane to look like the real thing.

**copy protection**
A software protection scheme that defeats attempts to copy a program or makes the copied software unreliable.

**Copy Protection** Software developers and vendors have tried many schemes to make software copying impossible. **Copy protection** schemes involve hardware or software features that defeat attempts to copy a program or make the copied software unreliable.

**FIGURE 14.12**

***Copyright Page***

Copyright notices range in length from a single symbol, date, and name to an entire page of information. Copyright pages in books often contain information in addition to the copyright line. Included on the page shown here are (top to bottom): editorial staff credits, copyright information, printing information, the publication's international standard book number (ISBN), and international divisions of the publishing company.

Library of Congress Cataloging-in-Publication Data
Senn, James A.
   Information technology in business : principles, practices, and opportunities / James A. Senn.–3rd ed.
      p. cm.
   Includes bibliographical references and indexes.
   ISBN 0-13-143626-0
   1. Business–Data processing.   2. Information storage and retrieval systems–Business.   3. Information technology.   I. Title: Business.   II. Title.
HF5548.2.S4366      2004
650'.0285–dc22                              2003021914

**Publisher and Vice President:** Natalie E. Anderson
**AVP/Executive Editor:** David Alexander
**Project Manager:** Kyle Hannon
**Editorial Assistant:** Robyn Goldenberg
**Senior Marketing Manager:** Sharon M. Koch
**Marketing Assistant:** Danielle Torio
**Permissions Supervisor:** Suzanne Grappi
**Manufacturing Buyer:** Arnold Vila
**Design Manager:** Maria Lange
**Art Director:** Patricia Smythe
**Interior Design:** Kathryn Foot
**Cover Design:** Bruce Kenselaar
**Cover Illustration/Photo:** Chris Cheadle/Getty Images, Inc.–Stone Allstock and Ryan McVay/Getty Images–Image Bank
**Manager, Print Production:** Christy Mahon
**Composition/Full-Service Project Management:** Caryl Wenzel and Sue Katkus, PreMediaONE, A Black Dot Group Company
**Photo Research Coordinator:** Kathy Zander, PreMediaONE, A Black Dot Group Company
**Photo Research:** Rae Grant, Judy Mason, and Billie L. Porter
**Printer/Binder:** RR Donnelley-Willard

Credits and acknowledgments borrowed from other sources and reproduced, with permission, in this textbook appear on page C-1.

Microsoft® and Windows® are registered trademarks of the Microsoft Corporation in the U.S.A. and other countries. Screen shots and icons reprinted with permission from the Microsoft Corporation. This book is not sponsored or endorsed by or affiliated with the Microsoft Corporation.

**Copyright © 2004, 1998, and 1995 by Pearson Education, Inc., Upper Saddle River, New Jersey, 07458.**
Pearson Prentice Hall. All rights reserved. Printed in the United States of America. This publication is protected by Copyright and permission should be obtained from the publisher prior to any prohibited reproduction, storage in a retrieval system, or transmission in any form or by any means, electronic, mechanical, photocopying, recording, or likewise. For information regarding permission(s), write to: Rights and Permissions Department.

**Pearson Prentice Hall™** is a trademark of Pearson Education, Inc.
**Pearson®** is a registered trademark of Pearson plc
**Prentice Hall®** is a registered trademark of Pearson Education, Inc.

Pearson Education LTD.                         Pearson Education Australia PTY, Limited
Pearson Education Singapore, Pte. Ltd          Pearson Education North Asia Ltd
Pearson Education, Canada, Ltd                  Pearson Educación de Mexico, S.A. de C.V.
Pearson Education–Japan                         Pearson Education Malaysia, Pte. Ltd
Printed in the United States of America

**PEARSON**
Prentice
Hall

10 9 8 7 6 5 4 3 2 1
ISBN 013-143626-0

---

[4]Copyright owners can choose to allow others to use their copyrighted work. In such cases, a credit line indicating that use is authorized is attached to each copy of the work. Copyright owners may require the payment of a royalty for use of the work.

No copy protection scheme developed so far has proven foolproof. Even worse, copy protection has hindered the copying of software by individuals who have legally purchased a program and want to make a backup copy to protect against damage to the original copy. Making a backup copy is usually in most software license agreements. To avoid antagonizing users who have legally purchased the software, most software vendors have dropped attempts at copy protection. However, they still vigorously pursue legal action against software pirates under the copyright laws.

**Software Site Licensing**    To assist large-volume users of programs and at the same time avoid software piracy, many software developers offer **site licenses.** Under these agreements, the purchaser (typically a company, university, or government agency) pays a fee to the manufacturer to make a specified number of copies of a particular program (and in some cases, its documentation). In turn, the buyer agrees to keep an accurate record of who makes the copies and the computer or network on which they are installed.

**site license**
An agreement under which a software purchaser pays a fee to the manufacturer to make a specified number of copies of a particular program.

Both parties benefit from site licenses. Purchasers gain the convenience of making legal copies when necessary, and for an average cost that is substantially (usually more than 50 percent) lower than the retail cost of the software. Sellers gain large adoptions of their software programs while discouraging pirated use of their software within an organization.

## Public Domain Software

Not all software is copyrighted. Noncopyrighted software that can be used by the general public is known as **public domain software.** The individuals or companies who wrote, and therefore own, the software have chosen to make their programs available to anyone who wants to use them.

**public domain software**
Any noncopyrighted software that can be used by the general public.

**Shareware** combines the best features of copyrighted software and public domain software. Like public domain software, shareware is given away and freely distributed. However, the developers retain ownership and ask users to register with them and to pay a nominal fee for using the program. Registering allows users to receive notices of updates to the programs, and the nominal fee supports the continued development of the software.

**shareware**
Software that is given away and freely distributed. The developer retains ownership, asks users to register with the owner, and requests a nominal fee for using the program.

Sometimes a company or individual will offer software for a very small fee. This encourages people to use the software freely while simultaneously publicizing the issuer's claim of ownership. When you pay even $1, you are acknowledging that the issuer owns the software.

## Digital Millennium Copyright Act

In 1998, the Digital Millennium Copyright Act was signed into law. The Act was designed to implement the treaties signed in December 1996 at the World Intellectual Property Organization (WIPO) Geneva conference. It also addresses other copyright matters that Congress judged to need attention.

The law sets out the actions of individuals and enterprises that violate the intentions of the copyright laws. It also clarifies who has legal responsibility and liability for copyright enforcement. Figure 14.13 summarizes the key features of the legislation.

## Piracy of Digital Content

The general availability of high-speed Internet connections, CD and DVD recorders, and portable devices equipped with substantial memory, triggered widespread interest in recording and playing digital content, especially music and movies. During the dot-com era that began in the late 1990s and carried on into the early days of the twenty-first century, Web sites were also created for distributing digital content.

Napster, created by 19-year-old Shawn Fanning in 1999, quickly become popular on college campuses as one of the first sites to facilitate the sharing of music and

**FIGURE 14.13**

*Key Features of the Digital Millennium Copyright Act*

The Digital Millennium Copyright Act signed into law in 1998 addresses copyright issues agreed to at the World Intellectual Property Organization (WIPO) Geneva conference.

The legislation contains provisions that

- Make it a crime to circumvent antipiracy measures built into most commercial software.

- Outlaw the manufacture, sale, or distribution of code-cracking devices used to illegally copy software. (However, the cracking of copyright protection devices is permitted to conduct encryption research, assess product interoperability, and test computer security systems.)

- Provide exemptions from anticircumvention provisions for nonprofit libraries, archives, and educational institutions under certain circumstances.

- Generally limit Internet service providers from copyright infringement liability for simply transmitting information over the Internet.

- Assert that service providers are expected to remove material from users' Web sites if that material appears to constitute copyright infringement.

- Limit liability of nonprofit institutions of higher education—when they serve as online service providers and under certain circumstances—for copyright infringement by faculty members or graduate students.

- Require that "webcasters" pay licensing fees to record companies.

- Require that the Register of Copyrights, after consultation with relevant parties, submits to Congress recommendations regarding how to promote distance education through digital technologies while "maintaining an appropriate balance between the rights of copyright owners and the needs of users."

- State explicitly that "[n]othing in this section shall affect rights, remedies, limitations, or defenses to copyright infringement, including fair use...."

## CRITICAL CONNECTIONS 3

## CNN Watermarks Show When Copying Occurs    CNN

Thwarting counterfeiting and proving authenticity are centuries-old concerns, most often associated with currency and legal documents. However, these concerns have taken on new importance in the Information Age.

Atlanta-based Cable News Network (CNN) transmits its programs all over the globe, via satellite (see *Case Study,* Chapter 2). The network also produces special features that are shown only in select regions of the world. Because of the uniqueness of each program, CNN needs to guard against unauthorized interception, copying, or rebroadcast. Hence, it takes all of the usual and customary protection measures for its programs, including copyrighting the content and scrambling (i.e., encrypting) the transmittal signal.

To that end, it embraced the age-old practice of adding watermarks to its property—albeit in digital form. Watermarks are faint words or symbols that have traditionally been used with paper stock. They become visible when the document is held up to the light. Since illegal copies of the document do not have the watermarks, they are a useful device for certifying the origin, ownership, and authenticity of a work.

CNN's watermark—inserted throughout the entire length of each program—is a computer-generated digital signal consisting of the letters CNN appearing in the lower right-hand corner of the picture.

movies over the Internet. Both copyrighted and copyright-free files were on the site. Soon, users from all over the world visited Napster to check out the wide range of material it featured. Napster was controversial since it enabled people to use the Internet to share music without having to purchase their own copy of a CD. After downloading the Napster software, individuals could locate music recorded in the digital MP3 format. They only had to key in the name of the artist or the title of the music they wanted. A list of the available music appeared on the display screen, and from it they could choose the selection of interest and download it to their hard drive. Once on the hard drive, they could play the music as often as they wished, burn it onto a CD, or transfer it to a portable music player, all without ever having purchased the CD.

Some colleges moved quickly to ban Napster because of its bandwidth drain on campus communications networks. So many students were downloading music that transmission speeds slowed dramatically, interfering with normal network use.

As you can imagine, Napster also became a target for music and movie companies who viewed its popular site as nothing more than a digital tool for aiding criminals. Its distribution practices, they said, amounted to unauthorized use of copyrighted material under U.S. and international law. The music industry also attributed falling sales in music CDs to rampant sharing over the Internet.

A U.S. court ruling that Napster was violating copyright law effectively put it out of business. However, the outcry against digital sharing has not subsided; instead it has grown. As DVDs, along with DVD burners, make it possible to store full-length motion pictures on a single disk have become popular, concern has increased that widespread sharing of copyrighted digital movies will take place.

DVDs are already protected by a digital wrapper that prevents them from being copied. And after heavy lobbying by the entertainment industry in the United States, a federal statute was passed that makes it illegal to break such digital safeguards, even to make a personal copy, or an excerpt for research purposes—something consumers have taken for granted in the past.

The end-of-chapter *Case Study,* "What Constitutes Digital Piracy?" explores the actions being taken to define legal copying of digital content and defend against illegal actions.

The piracy of software and digital content is an issue that will undoubtedly receive greater attention as information technology use becomes more widespread and its capabilities more sophisticated with each new generation of hardware, software, and services.

## A Final Word

The issues discussed in this chapter affect everyone, either directly or indirectly. The most important points to take from these discussions are simple: Be aware of possible misuses and take responsibility for safeguarding the IT resources under your control.

# CRITICAL CONNECTIONS

## 1 Part II: NIPC Tackles U.S. Security Concerns

**NIPC**

NIPC addresses Internet-related security concerns and was created as a direct result of increasing threats to IT security in the United States. NIPC is staffed by members of the FBI, the Departments of Defense and Treasury, and the CIA. The agency and its staff have five principal functions:

1. Detect security threats and issue public alerts.
2. Maintain a database that consists of information on all intrusion cases, sharing the information broadly to avoid redundant investigations, and analyzing events to detect patterns and commonalities.
3. Conduct investigations of IT-related intrusions, working in collaboration with local, national, and international authorities.
4. Provide support to other agencies as a means of deterring criminal activities and assisting in prosecuting criminals.
5. Conduct security training for cyber investigators and protectors of infrastructure in both the public and private sector.

It is widely held that NIPC activities will prove to be an essential component of a long-lasting and effective national Internet security strategy.

### Questions for Discussion

1. What factors brought about the creation of NIPC?
2. What functions and characteristics of NIPC, if any, do you think will serve to deter cyber crime? Why?
3. Do you think the existence of NIPC will improve IT security practices in government and private enterprises?

## 2 Part II: Your Background: It's Just Business

*The Risk Consulting Company*

A great many publicly accessible documents and government agency databases and information sources are computerized, so you would think searching them would be easy for Kroll Background America. However, most of this material is not linked to a network or to the Internet, and thus cannot be searched from remote locations. Instead, someone must go to the right address and locate the room where the records reside. That can be a bit challenging, even for the pros.

### Questions for Discussion

1. Are you concerned about the large amount of information that companies can find out about you (or anyone) in public records? If so, what is behind your concern?
2. Does the Internet pose a new threat to personal privacy with respect to the use or distribution of public information?
3. Should use of the Internet to retrieve public information be regulated by law? What are the arguments for and against such regulations?

## 3 Part II: CNN Watermarks Show When Copying Occurs

**CNN**

To protect against unauthorized use of its programming content, the copyrighting and scrambling of signals have been part of the programming process since CNN's origin. However, these are merely protections, not guarantees, against unauthorized use. Since capturing, copying, and distributing copies of information, including digital transmissions, are tasks that information technology can do with ease, CNN inserted a digital watermark showing the network's letters, making it visible whenever a program is copied.

The watermark is embedded among the electronic signals of the program in a manner that does not interfere with the quality of the picture or the sound. Yet it is impossible to remove the watermark without damaging or erasing segments of the program. The watermark is therefore visible proof that a program has been copied.

In the Information Age, the value of intellectual property will continue to increase. So will unauthorized and illegal attempts at copying and duplication. Digital watermarks are an important weapon in the war against theft of intellectual property.

### Questions for Discussion

1. Do you think CNN is putting the watermark on to prevent unauthorized users from using programs without the network's permission?
2. Do *you* think the watermark will prevent unauthorized use or misuse of its content?
3. In order to prevent piracy of digital content, which is more effective—watermarking video material, or passage and enforcement of tough piracy laws?
4. Applying the principle of watermarks, are there similar *markings* that can be used to prevent the unauthorized distribution and use of digital music?

# Summary of Learning Objectives

**1 Identify the types of security breaches an enterprise should protect against and describe the five results that might occur if it does not.** Enterprises must protect against intrusion, attacks on the enterprise from outside or inside; and interception, the capture of data and information transmitted over a communications network. If the safeguards against these types of security breaches are inadequate, five different types of problems can occur: destruction of enterprise resources, corruption of its data and applications, denial of services, theft of services, and theft of resources.

**2 Describe the most likely sources of security breaches.** Breaches generally occur from four sources: employees, hackers, terrorists, and viruses. Employees are a very common source as individuals seek to *get even* with their organization or decide to take advantage of their knowledge or position to use a system or its data in unauthorized ways. Hackers are persons who seek to gain access to a system illegally, usually through a network. Terrorists conduct nuisance or financially motivated attacks on a system based on political motivation. Terrorist attacks against IT are often termed cyberterrorism. Computer viruses are hidden programs that alter, without the user's knowledge, the way a computer operates or modify the data and programs stored on the computer.

**3 Describe 10 ways to protect a system against intrusion.** Ten common ways to protect a system against intrusion are as follows: change access passwords frequently; allow workers access to only the system functions they need to use; permit workers to access only the data that they need to use; establish physical security systems; separate critical processing functions so that more than one person must be involved in them; encrypt data by scrambling or coding information; adopt procedural controls; keep staff well informed through education programs; audit system activities; and keep a log of all transactions and user activities. Some systems also use callback security.

**4 Describe the six categories of security measures and identify those most effective in protecting against intrusion.** The six categories include the general security policies and procedures of an enterprise and the use of virus protection software. In addition, digital signatures are often used to authenticate the identity of a message's sender or document's signer. Encryption applies a mathematical system to code and uncode data and messages in case they would be intercepted. Firewalls protect against incoming messages that might contain potentially harmful programs or data. Proxy servers act as an intermediary between a PC and the Internet, separating an enterprise network from outside networks.

**5 Identify the two methods of virus detection used by virus detection software.** All types of computers are vulnerable to viruses, hidden programs that alter (without the user's knowledge) the way a computer operates or that modify the data and programs stored on the computer. To protect against them, companies must buy and use virus detection software. There are two methods of virus detection. Scanning programs search the computer and main memory to detect a virus. Detection programs monitor processing activities and signal the user when a virus tries to infect the system.

**6 Explain the IT professional's obligation to provide continued access to computers and networks, and describe the four methods used to ensure IT reliability.** As companies become dependent on IT, they become dependent on the availability of their computers and communications systems. With this dependence comes the expectation that the service provider—whether an IT professional or a hired IT service—will ensure that service cannot be interrupted.

Four methods are used to ensure IT reliability. Fault-tolerant computers are designed with duplicate components so that if one component fails, the duplicate automatically takes over. Uninterruptible power-supply systems ensure the continued flow of electricity, produced from a backup source, when the primary source fails. Disaster recovery plans help to restore data lost when a system stops functioning. Off-site backup facilities provide a backup computer center away from the company's main facility.

**7 Explain how the term *privacy* applies to information technology and why privacy is an important issue today.** Privacy, as the term is used in information technology, refers to how personal information is collected, used, and protected. Although privacy has always been an important issue, the enormous capabilities of IT to store and retrieve data have amplified the need to protect personal privacy.

**8 Describe the importance of ethics in the use of information technology and identify seven ethical issues associated with the use of IT in business.** In the United States, most records kept by companies and nongovernmental organizations are not covered by privacy laws. Therefore, people must rely on a company's ethical policies for protection of private information. Seven ethical issues that businesses must confront are electronic mail privacy, software licenses, software copyrights, hardware access, intellectual property ownership, file access, and data ownership.

**9** **Discuss the legal issues surrounding software piracy and three methods that have been used to prevent software piracy.** Software piracy is the making of illegal copies of software. Three methods are used to protect against it. Software copyright protection safeguards original works against unauthorized use, including duplication, provided the owner visibly displays a notice of copyright on the product. Copy protection schemes either defeat attempts to copy a program or make the copied software unreliable. Software site licensing is used to assist large-volume users of programs and at the same time avert piracy by allowing purchasers of software to make a specified number of copies of a particular program.

**10** **Describe the concern over piracy of digital content.** Digital content refers to music, movies, and other information that is coded in digital form. The owners of digital content are generally protected from unauthorized copying by copyright laws. However, the MP3 music format, the high-storage capacity and widespread use of recordable CDs and DVDs, coupled with general access to high-speed networks, has led to concerns for widespread distribution, or piracy, of copyrighted digital content. Both Web sites and special software have been created for assisting in the piracy of digital content, creating concern among copyright holders. A variety of legislative actions are emerging to address such piracy.

## Key Terms

breach   576
cold site   593
copy protection   602
copyright   601
cyberterrorism   582
denial of services attack   577
digital piracy   601
digital signature encryption   586
disaster recovery plan   593
ethics   597
fault-tolerant computer   593
firewall   590
hacker   578
harden   577

hot site   593
identity theft   578
interception   577
intrusion   577
off-site backup facility   593
opt-in e-mail   596
permission-based e-mail   596
pretty good privacy (PGP)   588
privacy   595
proxy server   591
public domain software   603
public key infrastructure (PKI)   588
reliability   592
secure electronic transaction (SET)   588

security   576
shareware   603
security program   576
site license   603
social responsibility   600
software piracy   601
spam   596
terrorist   581
tunneling protocols   588
uninterruptible power supply (UPS) system   593
virtual private network (VPN)   588
virus   582

## Review Questions

1. What is IT security?
2. Describe the purpose of hardening an IT resource that might encounter security threats..
3. Against what two forms of security violations do enterprises seek to protect themselves?
4. When there is a security breach, what five categories of problems may result?
5. How does a denial-of-services attack differ from a theft of services attack?

6. Describe the characteristics of identity theft and the manner in which this problem can occur. Why is identity theft such a serious security violation?
7. Identify the three sources from which security problems in an enterprise are likely to occur.
8. What are hackers and what is their role in system intrusion? Is system intrusion a crime?
9. Describe 10 techniques for deterring computer intrusion by hackers.

10. What is a computer virus? How does a virus originate? How does it spread?

11. Name the two techniques used to detect the presence of a computer virus.

12. What is a firewall and what role does it serve in providing IT security?

13. How do proxy servers differ from firewalls?

14. Describe the characteristics and differences between digital signatures and digital certificates.

15. What are PKI and PGP and how does each work?

16. Why is there a growing concern among IT users and others over spam? What kind of issue is it—a security, legal, or ethical issue?

17. What does the word *privacy* mean as applied to information technology? Why is privacy a concern among those using IT and those affected by the use of IT?

18. Describe the five privacy provisions outlined in the Code of Fair Information Practices.

19. What are ethics? Can personal ethics be separated from business ethics?

20. Identify and explain seven ethical issues related to the use of IT in business.

21. Describe the ethical guidelines that Donn B. Parker of SRI International encourages IT professionals and users to adopt.

22. Why do companies have an obligation to ensure continued access to computer and communications systems once they have been made available to users?

23. Describe the four methods of ensuring IT service reliability.

24. What is piracy? What is software piracy?

25. Describe three methods that companies can use to protect their software from piracy.

26. How does copy protection differ from copyright protection?

27. Describe the differences between copyrighted software and public domain software.

28. Explain why piracy of digital content has become such a widely discussed issue in the past few years. What are examples of digital content piracy?

29. To what types of individuals or organizations is the piracy of digital content of greatest concern? Why?

## *Discussion Questions*

1. There are two alternative opinions about how to handle a security situation that involves hackers. One view holds that hackers should always be prevented from entering a network or system. It is based on the belief that if they are thwarted in their attacks, they will eventually give up and *go away*.

   The other view suggests letting hackers enter a system, observing both how they breach security and the IT resources they seek to locate. This view is based on the assumption that following a hacker's moves will enable the firm to detect security weaknesses that are unknown so that they can be fixed while also revealing the resources an intruder regards as most valuable.

   Which view has more merit? What risks are associated with implementing either view as the IT network security policy in an enterprise?

2. Companies often hire highly skilled former hackers to proof their security policies and procedures. Do you think this is a good idea? Why or why not?

3. Should an Internet service provider be responsible for preventing spam emanating from its site? Why or why not?

   Independent of your response above, does an ISP have any financial or other liability

   (1) if it *does establish* or enforce policies preventing its occurrence, but some of its customers commit serious spam violations anyway?

   (2) if it *does not* have policies or procedures to prevent its occurrence and its customers commit serious spam violations?

4. Should penalties be assigned to those who commit Internet spam? If not, why not? If yes, what types of penalties do you think should be assigned and by whom? (If you believe they should be, at what point are penalties in order? After one event to one person . . . or one event to hundreds of persons, or hundreds of occurrences?)

5. It is fairly easy to eavesdrop on cellular and cordless phone conversations because most of these messages are carried on analog radio waves that can be picked up by inexpensive radio-frequency scanners. For this reason, Apple Computer has instructed its employees never to discuss confidential matters over these devices. What might increased use of cellular phones mean to you as a private citizen? As a manager?

6. What ethical issues are raised by the practices of credit reporting agencies, such as TRW Information Services and Equifax Credit Information Services? Can you suggest any solutions for these issues?

7. A broken water pipe interrupted the electrical service at the Chicago Board of Trade Clearing Corp. In less than an hour, the company's manager of quality assurance had to put her disaster recovery plan in action. This involved shifting people and computer tapes to a backup site in a nearby suburb, where they spent four days coordinating recovery activities that kept all normal business activities operating. Why are such plans essential for businesses? Do different types of businesses need different types of recovery plans?

In a published survey, *PC Computing* magazine found that 64 percent of respondents thought it permissible for company managers to search employees' hard drives for illegal copies of software. Do you agree that this activity is permissible? Explain your answer.

## Group Projects and Applications

## Project 1

The widespread use of e-mail in the business and personal lives of employees in many companies has caused firms to establish policies regarding use of e-mail, the ownership of e-mail contents, and other rights the company has regarding e-mail. Arrange to visit with company representatives having the responsibility for administering e-mail policy in their firm. In arranging the visit, you will have to determine the location of that individual (e.g., the company's communications network group or its legal affairs department).

Arrange interviews with at least five companies. In advance of your visit, prepare a set of interview questions that can be used to inquire and learn about the companies' e-mail policies and the manner in which they are administered. Be sure to include questions that explore the reason underlying the initial creation of the policies and probe to determine whether all employees have heeded the policies.

When you have completed the interviews, prepare a summary outlining the findings of your visits. The summary should highlight areas where the policies are similar and where they are different.

As part of your summary, include your own assessment of the policies in force at the sample companies. In what areas do you agree or disagree with the company policies? Indicate the reasons underlying your agreement or disagreement.

## Project 2

Contact a sample of companies in your area to determine whether the firms have designated individuals with responsibility for ensuring ethical use of the companies' IT resources. If so, arrange to visit with those individuals to learn details of the policies the reason for their creation, and whether the policies are actively enforced in the respective companies.

Compare your findings from the different companies.

## Project 3

Contact security specialists in banks and credit-card processing centers in your region to learn about the procedures the companies have in place to protect against interception of data transmitted to or from the firm. Be aware that they may be unwilling to discuss some aspects of their security procedures.

Inquire specifically about the use of data encryption in business and network transactions. Do the companies use encryption as a security tactic? If so, what encryption forms do they use? What are examples of the type of data they handle through encryption?

If a particular company does not use encryption, seek to determine why it has not found such protection methods necessary. Does it use an alternate protection method in place of data encryption? Why or why not?

## Project 4

Using the print and digital publications of your institution's library, as well as the back issues of leading newspapers and IT magazines, seek to identify at least six serious IT security breaches that have been reported in the last two years.

a. Summarize the nature of each breach, identifying the means by which the breach was accomplished.
b. What was the effect of the breach and who was most significantly affected?
c. Could the breach have been prevented if the *victim* had followed the security precautions outlined in this chapter? Why or why not?

d. What conclusions about the application of IT security practices and procedures can be drawn from the instances you have identified?

## Project 5

In groups of five persons each, brainstorm a list of technology-based products and/or practices that may lead to a loss of privacy. Then suggest how these items could have positive uses.

A designated person should collect each group's list and then write all of the items on the blackboard. The class will then conduct a straw poll, with each person voting *for* or *against* each item.

After the poll, the class should discuss the following issue: What separates the *acceptable* technologies from the *unacceptable* technologies?

## Project 6

Each individual should bring to class a *code of ethics* from a real-world company. Then break into small groups to discuss these individual codes, addressing the following questions:

- Does the code specifically mention the ethical use of technology? If not, write a paragraph to address the ethics of using technology in a responsible manner.
- Do you consider these codes to be generally effective? What, if anything, would you change about them?

## Project 7

It is widely known that software piracy is a major problem in the international arena. U.S. software companies have reported that millions of unauthorized copies of their most important products have turned up in European and Asian markets.

In groups of three, conduct some research into this growing problem. Each person in the group should research and report on one of the following topics:

- Software piracy in Asia
- International law and policies regarding software piracy
- Proposals to decrease software piracy
- Built-in antipiracy protection in software

## Project 8

A recent *Fortune* magazine cover story asked, "Who's Reading Your E-Mail?" Most companies have a policy stating that e-mail is considered a corporate asset and that employee privacy is therefore not guaranteed in this area.

Do employees have the right to privacy in their e-mail, or do employers have the right to read any documents prepared by their workers? Two groups of four students each should debate the issue. The first group takes the employer perspective; the second group takes the employee perspective. After the first student from each side has spoken, the second student questions the opponent's arguments, looking for holes and inconsistencies. The third student attempts to answer these arguments. The fourth student presents a summary of each side's arguments. Finally, the class votes on which team has offered the more compelling argument.

## Net_Work

1. Because of the increasing concern in the growth of e-mail spam, there has been growing interest in legislation at both the state and national levels in the United States to protect Internet users and service providers. Other countries are exploring legal remedies for those who spam as well.
   a. Using the Internet, conduct a search to obtain data on public opinion regarding spam. Prepare a summary that describes the most different viewpoints and the extent to which those viewpoints are widely held.
   b. Then continue your research, searching for information on current antispam laws or proposed legislation at the national and state levels. Prepare a set of tables that summarize the legislative activity at each governmental level. Include in the table a summary of the features of the legislative activities, associating each feature with one or more legislative proposals in which it is included. Using the table, what conclusions do you draw about the intent of the legislation?
   c. Finally, compare the legislative activities with the data you assembled on public opinion regarding spam. Do current and proposed laws support the public's opinion regarding spam? Why or why not?

2. Conduct a visit to the Web sites of at least six leading Internet service providers to learn their policy for preventing and discouraging spam. Does the information on the ISP Web sites indicate what actions it takes

against customers who are spamming by using e-mail services provided by the ISP?

3. PGP software is widely used to protect against interception of e-mail messages. Conduct your own investigation to determine the representative alternatives available to individuals wishing to implement PGP. In summarizing the findings of your sample, include the cost of the software, the most popular e-mail systems with which it operates, and other important or distinguishing characteristics of each software product.

4. Among the most intense debates centered on the Internet are those concerning security of transactions and the protection of privacy. Hence, great efforts are being made to protect the identity of people using the Net to make purchases. Similarly, companies have developed various ways to ensure that individuals and companies alike can transact business over the Internet and exchange money or credit information securely. (See Chapter 9 to review the discussion of online payments.)

Several different methods of securing transactions have come to the forefront. They include methods for exchange of cash as well as variations on credit-card transactions. To review the differences among them, visit the following Web sites:

- **PayPal** (www.paypal.com)  Provides new concept in payment systems, one that combines computerized convenience with security and privacy in a way that could be considered to some an improvement on paper cash.
- **Verisign's CyberCash** (www.cybercash.com)  An electronic wallet that can be used on the Internet is a distinguishing characteristic of this company's products.
- **MasterCard** (www.mastercard.com)  This worldwide processor of credit-card transactions has staked out its place on the Internet, promising that "when you do need cash, you can have instant access to it absolutely anywhere" through MasterCard.

After visiting each of these sites and reviewing the information provided there, do a comparison by answering the following questions:

a. What product does each company provide?
b. What are the distinguishing characteristics of each company's product?
c. Can these products be used only on the Internet?
d. Which products do you feel offer (1) the greatest security and privacy protection, and (2) the greatest convenience for consumers?

# Cool Mobility

## On Assignment

"Your residency is nearly complete," says CEO Tina Fuentes. Looking across the conference table at you and CIO James Marsalis, she adds, "We have been good for each other. *Cool Mobility* has benefited tremendously from your consulting skills and your deep understanding of IT. From the beginning, we asked you to assess our IT use and capabilities. You have been open and candid in expressing your observations and opinions on CoolMoblity.biz. That has been very helpful."

Marsalis, leaning forward as if to signal the intensity behind the remark he was about to make, adds, "You not only brought benefits to us today, but you have planted seeds that will grow and flower tomorrow. On top of that, the insights you shared into emerging practices and advances in IT have shown us that we cannot rest on our current success. As you said many times, there is no magic in IT. The magic comes from *insight*—the insight to know when and how to use IT's capabilities in innovative ways. Of course, we still have to execute everything well."

Talk about making your day—such praise from the CEO and CIO together! It feels great to do a good job and be appreciated for it.

Secure in knowing that your grasp on IT practices and opportunities is firm and that you have a career reference from successful executives, you are ready to move to the next adventure in your career . . . just as soon as you finish one last assignment.

## In Consultation

You are secure within yourself . . . but you know that an IT application can never be too secure. There is always a need to safeguard information and property. Apparently, Grace Ma was thinking along the same lines when she consulted you about the following matters.

a. Current customers who visit CoolMobility.biz can view information about their mobile phone usage by signing on to the Web site. The current sign-in process, appearing on the home page, requires that they enter the telephone number of their mobile phone and a password of any form and length that they chose when opening the account.

Says Ma, "Do you think our sign-on procedure adequately protects customer-specific information stored in our system? I would like your assessment and recommendations.

b. "I'm concerned about these denial-of-service problems that have popped up from time to time with the Internet. If current and potential customers cannot reach our Internet site, we're out of business. The *Cool Mobility* home page is our *front door* to the company. I know you have not had a chance to evaluate our security strategy in detail, but tell me: What security methods and practices should we have in place to protect us to the greatest extent possible against denial-of-service attacks made against our Web site? If we are already following your recommendations, does that *guarantee* we are protected against a denial-of-service attack? Let me know *what* you think and *why* you hold that opinion.

c. "A few weeks ago, Mark Goodman asked you about my interest in using our customer and order database for marketing research purposes. I plan to associate customer information with income and demographic information I have purchased from the U.S. govern-

ment. Specifically, I wish to link a customer's postal code to the government database, so we can determine the income and demographic characteristics of people living in that area. Of course, this information will be used only within the company.

"Do you think I am violating any privacy laws or principles if I institute this practice? It is quite common in many companies, you know. I am *very* interested in hearing both your opinion and your insights on this.

d. "Oh, one other question before you go." Ma just will not let you get away. "You know, all of our employees are connected to our intranet through their PCs and the LAN. It's a good practice, but quite frankly I am concerned about the growing problem in this country with identity theft. By making our intranet so easy to use I hope we are not opening ourselves up to identity theft. Can we build any feature or IT component into our system that will prevent identify theft? What do *you* think? (I promise . . . that's my last question before you go!)"

## Case Study

### What Constitutes Digital Piracy?

The Motion Picture Association of America (MPAA) and its international counterpart, the Motion Picture Association (MPA) serve as the voice and advocate of the American motion picture, home video, and television industries, domestically through the MPAA and internationally through the MPA. Today, these associations represent not only the world of theatrical film, but serve as leaders and advocates for major producers and distributors of entertainment programming for television, cable, home video, and future delivery systems not yet imagined. They, together with Recording Industry Association of America (RIAA), its music industry counterpart, are fighting hard to maintain their copyright protection against illegal copying and sharing of digital content over the Internet.

**Napster**

Napster, created in 1999 as one of the first sites to facilitate the sharing of music and movies over the Internet, became popular very quickly. Visitors from all over the world accessed the Napster Web site to peruse the copyrighted and copyright-free files that were posted on the site. Napster became controversial almost instantly because it enabled people to use the Internet to share music without having to purchase their own copy of a CD. Within months, the U.S. courts ruled against Napster's sharing practices.

Since the court ruling against Napster, other file-sharing services have emerged in its place. They include Gnutella, Kazza BV in the Netherlands, iMesh in Israel, Bluster in Switzerland, and WinMix of Belgium. As these examples suggest, the trend in new sharing services is to locate them outside of the United States.

The sites created after Napster do not store copyrighted material. Rather, they facilitate sharing between users by creating a network through which data files of users' choosing can be shared. There is a legal debate over whether making it possible to share copyrighted material, without actually receiving, storing, or transmitting it, is a violation of law.

Understandably, industry groups are pursuing every legal avenue, citing not only the laws they believe are being violated, but also reporting substantial damage to copyright holders in lost revenue and lower sales. Jack Valenti, chairman and CEO of MPAA, has been among the most outspoken against peer-to-peer file sharing:

> There are many in my country who have a curious philosophy which essentially has turned upside down an ancient civic morality which informs us that it is wrong to take what does not belong to

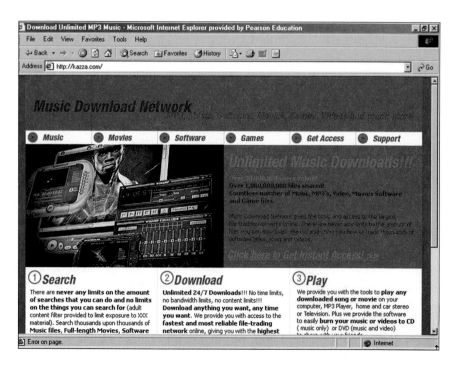

you, without the consent of the owner. It is wrong to shatter the civic contract which binds together a free society. It is wrong to embrace a tattered moral mind-set that declares whatever is on the Internet ought to be *free* to everyone. It is wrong to illegally download movies, scorning payment to their authors and copyright holders, and find asking permission of the owner a kind of foolishness that only the stupid would engage in. It is wrong to insist that the new digital world is one where no one pays for anything.

> A research firm in my country recently reported that 400,000 to 600,000 movies are being illegally downloaded *every day* in America.

> So I say to you if ever there was a single issue which ought to unite the creative communities of the world, directors, writers, producers, actors, studios, production companies engaged in film, television, and home video arenas, it is the great issue of digital piracy. Those who

steal movies—*steal* is a harsh word but it precisely defines the act—off the Internet or by illegally copying DVDs, are open-minded. They steal any movie, no matter its national, ethnic or cultural origin. If it is a popular film, it is fair game for theft.

Valenti's harsh words reflect the view of many in the entertainment industry. Similarly, the RIAA blames a sharp decline in the sale of recorded music directly on the popularity of file sharing on the Internet. Comparable entertainment associations in other countries hold similar positions.

The U.S. Congress proposed legislation dealing directly with Internet file sharing. A bill introduced in the House of Representatives proposes that copyright holders be allowed to search an individual's PC for downloaded copyright music and movie files, and to take actions to prevent the files from being shared with anyone. While the bill would not allow entertainment agencies to erase, remove, or damage files, it would protect them against any legal penalty for *disabling, interfering with, blocking, diverting, or otherwise impairing* the ability of individuals to share, swap, or exchange copyrighted music and movie files over the Internet.

The Congressman authoring the bill views sharing of copyrighted files as pure theft. "Copyright owners should have the same rights as other property owners" he stated.

Since the ruling against Napster, entertainment companies must trace alleged violators one-by-one, identifying both the individual and the Internet service provider that is providing the communication channel. In turn, they try to convince the ISP to terminate the individual's service or cooperate with the company in other ways to stop the file sharing. ISPs have been reluctant to participate.

The proposed legislation has created an outcry among Internet users and others who claim violation of legally guaranteed protection against unreasonable search of personal property. In response, members of Congress have introduced legislation taking counterpositions. For instance, one legislative proposal seeks to make it legal for individuals to make copies of digital versions of copyrighted music and movies and store or display it on any device of their choosing. Another proposal aims to make it legal to evade copy-protection schemes embedded in digital media (e.g., CDs and DVDs). The proposal also seeks to allow *fair use* copying of copyrighted material, allowing the copies to be used in presentations, research projects, and the like.

Settlement of this sensitive issue is likely to take years and involve countless legal proceedings and appeals of court decisions. There is little question that the ultimate decisions will influence the development of the Internet and copyright law for decades to come.

## Questions for Discussion

1. Based on the information above, do you believe that sharing digital files over the Internet is a problem for the IT industry? Explain the reasoning behind your thinking.

2. Do you believe that file-sharing sites, such as Napster and its successors, should be allowed to distribute or facilitate the distribution of copyrighted music, movies, and the like over the Internet? Why or why not?

3. Should the practice of embedding anti-copying schemes in digital content products, such as CDs and DVDs, thereby prohibiting consumers who have purchased them from making copies for their own personal use be allowed or prevented by law? Why?

**accelerator board** An add-in circuit board that increases a computer's processing speed.

**access point** A device that converts wired LAN signals into radio frequency.

**action document** A document designed to trigger a specific action or to signify that a transaction has taken place.

**action/method** An instruction that tells a database how to process an object to produce specific information.

**activity diagram** Shows the flow of control from one activity to the next in an application, representing activities by rounded rectangles and transitions to the next activity by arrows.

**actor** Anyone or anything that will interact with the application.

**add-in board** A board that can be added to a computer to customize its features and capabilities.

**address** An identifiable location in memory where data are kept.

**advanced intelligent tape (AIT)** Latest tape alternative that was introduced in the late 1990s for use with PCs functioning as servers and with midrange systems.

**Agricultural Age** The period up to the 1800s, when the majority of workers were farmers whose lives revolved around agriculture.

**analog audio** Sound transmitted by acoustic, mechanical, or electrical frequencies or waves; the normal version of sound.

**anonymous FTP site** A public FTP site that does not require you to use a special password to gain access.

**antivirus software** Scans incoming e-mail messages, documents, and other information to detect viruses that may be attached, alerts the user to the presence of a virus, and offers alternatives for removing the virus.

**application generation** In a database system, the use of menus and simple commands to describe the application to a system program that creates the set of detailed commands.

**application program/application** A program or a combination of programs written for a specific use.

**application service provider (ASP)** A company that develops, installs, and operates (or *hosts*) an information technology application on the Internet for the user, charging a recurring fee for doing so.

**Archie** A server that lists the contents of anonymous FTP sites.

**architecture** The structure of a communications network, which determines how the various components of the network are structured, how they interact, and when cooperation between the system's components is needed.

**arithmetic/logic unit (ALU)** The part of the CPU that performs arithmetic and logical operations.

**array** A set of small disk drives that work together as a single unit. The array provides performance, capacity, and reliability exceeding that of a single large drive. The array of drives appears to the computer as a single logical drive.

**asymmetric digital subscriber line (ADSL)** The most commonly used form of high speed digital subscriber line (DSL) Internet access characterized by higher receiving (upstream) transmission rates compared to sending (downstream) transmissions.

**asynchronous transfer mode (ATM)** A data transmission method using switched networks in which a message containing data, voice, or video is divided into fixed length cells.

**attribute** A category of data or information that describes an entity. Each attribute is a fact about the entity.

**auction** Online shoppers make bids to determine the sale price of an item rather than relying on predetermined, fixed prices.

**audio** Sound. The two forms of audio are analog and digital.

**audio response unit/speech synthesizer** An output device that transforms data or information into sound.

**authoring** The sequence of activities used to create a multimedia production: deciding on purpose, content, and components, and incorporating them into a presentation.

**authoring system** The set of software tools used to create a multimedia presentation.

**backbone network** A transmission facility designed to move data and information at high speeds.

**back-end CASE tool** A CASE tool that automates the later (back-end) activities in systems development.

**back office** Deals with the final steps in the sale.

**backup copies** Extra copies of information or software made to protect against losses.

**backup procedure** A procedure that describes how and when to make extra copies of information or software to protect against losses.

**bar code** A computer-readable code consisting of bars or lines of varying widths or lengths.

**baseband/baseband cable** One of two types of coaxial cable, which carries a single communication or message at very high megabit speeds, often used in local area networks.

**batch processing** The grouping and processing of all transactions at one time.

**bill consolidator** Receives bills from merchants and assembles them into a uniform format for each consumer.

**BIOS** The computer's basic input/output system.

**bitmapped image** A paper photograph that has been digitized.

**bit mapping** A feature of some monitors that allows each dot on the monitor to be addressed or controlled individually. Graphics created through bit mapping are sharp and crisp.

**block** The writing of one or more records onto a section of magnetic tape.

**Bluetooth personal area network** A wireless technology for communicating between devices. The Bluetooth protocol enables short-range radio links (30 feet or 10 meters) between devices, such as between a PC and a laptop, or a PDA and a printer.

**board** A hardware device onto which chips and their related circuitry are placed.

**boot** To turn on the computer system and let the built-in self-test run.

**breach** A breakdown in security.

**brick and mortar** Any physical store or building, regardless of how it is constructed or where it is located.

**bridge/router** A device that interconnects compatible LANs.

**broadband/broadband cable** Coaxial cable that carries multiple signals—data, voice, and video—simultaneously; each signal can be a different speed. Cable television uses broadband cable.

**browser** *See* Web browser.

**build** The animation technique that displays text one line at a time in a multimedia slide presentation.

**business graphics** Charts, graphs, and maps that are created using special graphics packages that translate data into visual representations.

**business information system** The family of IT applications that underlies the activities of running and managing a business.

**business processes** Collections of activities, often spanning several departments, that take one or more kinds of input and create a result that is of value to a company's customers.

**business-to-business (B2B) e-commerce** Companies doing business with other businesses.

**business-to-consumer (B2C) e-commerce** Electronic commerce carried out by an enterprise in order to serve its *consumer* customers.

**byte** A storage location in memory; the amount of memory required to store one digit, letter, or character.

**cache memory** A form of high-speed memory that acts as a temporary holding/processing cell.

**capture** The process of compiling detailed records of activities.

**CD-R disk** A disk that allows users to write information to a disk only once but to read it many times (sometimes known as *worm* optical storage).

**CD recorder** Also known as a CD writer or CD burner, this equipment is attached to a PC to create CDs.

**CD-ROM disk** Short for "compact disk–read only memory," an optical storage medium that permits storage of large amounts of information. CD-ROM disks can only be written to and cannot be erased.

**CD-RW disk** A disk that combines the erase ability and editing options of magnetic storage devices with the permanence, capacity, and reliability of optical storage.

**cell** In an electronic spreadsheet, the intersection of a row and a column.

**cell address/cell reference** The intersection of a particular row and column in an electronic spreadsheet.

**cell pointer** The cursor in an electronic spreadsheet.

**cellular communications service** Transmits radio messages between a mobile device (such as a mobile telephone, PDA, or wireless laptop) and a cell site.

**cellular telephone** A device used to send and receive voice communications and computer and fax transmissions while allowing users freedom of movement.

**centralized architecture** A communications architecture in which a computer at a central site hosts all of the network's hardware and software, performs all of the processing, and manages the network.

**central processing unit (CPU)/ processor** The computer hardware that executes program instructions and performs the computer's processing actions.

**change agent** A person who acts as a catalyst for change.

**channel** While the computer is being used for other work, the webcasting software shares the Internet connection to request updates from Web sites, or channels, the user has selected.

**character addressing** The precursor to bit mapping that allowed only full characters to be sent to and displayed on a VDT.

**character printer** A printer that prints one character at a time. Its speed is rated according to the number of characters printed per second.

**chat session/Internet relay chat (IRC)** A live interactive discussion where all parties are actually on the network, interacting through their computers.

**class** A set of objects that share a common structure and a common behavior.

**class diagram** Describes an object class, including the class name, attributes, and methods.

**chief information officer (CIO)** The person given the responsibility of managing and developing the firm's information technology capabilities.

**client** In client-server computing, a desktop workstation.

**client computer** The computer that accesses the information stored on a server computer.

**client-server computing** A type of computing in which all data and information retrieval requests and responses pass over a network. Much of the processing is performed on the server and the results of the processing are transmitted to the client.

**coaxial cable/co-ax** A physical communications channel that uses one or more central wire conductors surrounded by an insulator and encased in either a wire mesh or metal sheathing.

**code division multiple access (CDMA)** A digital cellular transmission technology that encodes each device's conversation or message with a unique identification code to distinguish it from other transmissions.

**cold boot** The system is turned on and started from an *off* state). The CPU invokes the ROM BIOS boot program, which in turn, runs the power-up self-tests and loads the operating system from disk storage.

**cold site** A backup facility outfitted with electrical power and environmental controls so that it is ready for a company to install a computer system.

**collaborative conferencing/workgroup conferencing** A type of conferencing that uses a software package called groupware to interconnect participants' computers at their various locations. Participants interact through a microcomputer directly linked to a server and their comments are broadcast to all others taking part in the conference.

**columns** The vertical elements in a spreadsheet.

**common carrier** A company that furnishes public communications facilities for voice and data transmission.

**communication** The sending and receiving of data and information over a communications network.

**communications channel/ communications medium** The physical or cableless media that link the different components of a network.

**communications infrastructure**   The underlying structure of technical facilities and institutional arrangements that supports communication via telecommunications, broadcasting, film, audio and video recording, cable, print, and mail.

**communications network**   A set of locations, or nodes, consisting of hardware, programs, and information linked together as a system that transmits and receives data and information.

**communications program**   A program that manages the interaction between a computer system and a communications network and the transmission of data, programs, and information over the network.

**competitive advantage**   Occurs when an enterprise has the ability to outperform rivals on a primary performance goal—often profitability—or some other dimension.

**competitive strategy**   The means by which a firm seeks to gain an advantage over its competitors.

**complex instruction set computing (CISC)**   A computing instruction set that moves data to and from main memory so often that it limits the use of registers.

**component infrastructure provider**   A company that supplies the computer hardware and software that make it possible to use, operate, or store and retrieve content from the Internet.

**computer**   An electronic system that can be instructed to accept, process, store, and present data and information.

**computer-aided design (CAD)**   A system that uses a powerful computer graphics workstation to enable product designers and engineers to draw design specifications on a display screen.

**computer-aided manufacturing (CAM)**   A system that relies on IT to automate and manage the manufacturing process directly.

**computer-aided systems engineering/ computer-aided software engineering (CASE) tools**   A set of tools used in systems development to improve the consistency and quality of the system while automating many of the most tedious and time-consuming systems tasks.

**computer crime**   The unauthorized use of a computer system or theft of system resources for personal use.

**computer engineer**   An IT professional who designs, develops, and oversees the manufacturing of computer equipment.

**computer-integrated manufacturing (CIM)**   A manufacturing system that uses computers to link automated processes in a factory to reduce design time, increase machine utilization, shorten the manufacturing cycle, cut inventories, and increase product quality.

**computer programming language**   A series of commands or codes that a computer can translate into the electronic pulses that underlie all computing activities.

**computer vision system**   A system that uses computer sensors to detect shapes, images, and varying levels of detail.

**concurrent data sharing**   A database procedure that allows several users to access the database simultaneously.

**concurrent engineering**   A design and manufacturing method in which team members work across their departmental functions to evaluate the activities of many departments and manage the product development process.

**configuration**   The specific combination of hardware and software in a system.

**consortia-led exchange**   Industry players combine forces to create a common forum for the exchange of goods and services.

**consumer electronics**   Electronic devices used to satisfy people's needs and wants rather than to manufacture products or deliver services.

**consumer-to-consumer (C2C)**   Electronic commerce where consumers buy or sell goods and services from each other, aided by an intermediary such as an electronic auction site on the Web.

**contact manager**   *See* personal information manager (PIM).

**content**   Information distributed over the Internet .

**content aggregator**   A e-commerce portal that assembles information (that is, content) from a variety of sources, organizing the information into a form that is useful to visitors to the Web site.

**content line/edit line**   The line of an electronic spreadsheet's control panel indicating the data or information being keyed into the active cell of the spreadsheet.

**content provider**   An individual or company that furnishes the information available on the Internet.

**continuous replenishment/efficient consumer response supply-chain strategy**   Data and information on products are captured at the point of sale and shared with suppliers periodically (usually daily) so that both can work together to jointly forecast future demands for replen-

ishable items, monitor trends, and detect opportunities for new items.

**control unit**   The part of the CPU that oversees and controls all computer activities according to the instructions it receives.

**conversion plan**   A description of all the activities that must occur to change over to a new system.

**coprocessor chip**   A special-purpose chip mounted on a processor board; it is designed to handle common functions quickly and efficiently.

**copy protection**   A software protection scheme that defeats attempts to copy a program or makes the copied software unreliable.

**copyright**   Legal protection of original works against unauthorized use, including duplication.

**current cell/active cell**   In an electronic spreadsheet, the cell in which the user is currently working.

**custom programming**   In a database system, the writing of detailed procedures using the commands and functions built into the database management software.

**custom software**   Software written specially for a particular business.

**cyberbanking**   *See* electronic banking.

**cyberterrorism**   Terrorist attack on computer facilities in companies that rely on IT to produce their services.

**cylinder**   A storage concept that refers to the same track location on each of the platters.

**data**   Raw facts, figures, and details.

**database**   A collection of data and information describing items of interest to an organization.

**database administration**   The management of a database.

**database administration procedures**   The procedures associated with managing a database.

**database administrator (DBA)**   The IT professional responsible for managing all the activities and procedures related to an organization's database.

**database application**   A computerized database routine for collecting, retrieving, or manipulating data to meet recurring needs.

**database directory**   The component of a shared database that keeps track of data and information.

**database management program**  A program that allows users to store information as interrelated records that can be retrieved quickly.

**database management system (DBMS)**  A program that makes it possible for users to manage the data in a database in order to increase accessibility and productivity.

**data bus**  A bus that moves data between the central processor and memory.

**data center/computer center**  A facility at which large and midrange computer systems are located. These systems are shared by many users who are interconnected with the system through communications links.

**data communication**  The transmission of data and information through a communications medium.

**data definition language (DDL)**  A tool that allows users to define a database.

**data dictionary/repository**  A catalog that lists and describes all the types of data flowing through a system. Composed of data elements and a data structure.

**data element**  The component of a data dictionary that includes data names, alternate names, and length allowances.

**data entry**  The process of populating a database with data and information.

**data entry form**  Custom-developed video display used to enter and change data in a database.

**dataflow diagram (DFD)**  A chart showing the movement of data through a system.

**data item**  A specific detail of an individual entity that is stored in a database.

**data manipulation language (DML)**  A tool that allows users to store, retrieve, and edit data in a database.

**data marts**  Processed to focus on a specific area of activities or isolated scientific or commercial processes.

**data mining**  Uses software designed to detect information *hidden* in the data.

**data processing**  The process of handling data and transforming them into information.

**data projector**  Equipment connected to the computer's display output port by a data cable that is used to show the contents of a computer video display on a movie screen.

**data structure**  The set of data elements used together and the name that collectively identifies the set.

**data warehouse**  A large data store, designed for inquiries, that combines details of both current *and* historical operations, usually drawn from a number of sources.

**deadlock**  A situation in which each user of a database is waiting for the others to unlock a record.

**decision support system (DSS)**  A business information system designed to assist in decision making where the decision process is relatively unstructured and only part of the information needed is structured in advance.

**denial of services attack**  Depriving, usually intentionally and temporarily, an enterprise or its users of the services they would normally expect to have, usually involving a network service (such as e-mail) or access to a location on the network (such as a Web site).

**desktop computer**  The original form of PC, designed so that the keyboard and display unit, and sometimes the processing unit, sit compactly on the surface of a desk or table.

**desktop publishing (DTP) program**  A program that combines text and image-handling features with document-design capabilities.

**detail report/transaction log**  A report describing each processed transaction.

**development procedure**  A procedure that explains how IT professionals should describe user needs and develop applications to meet those needs.

**differentiation**  A product that is perceived by customers as having unique features in comparison to competitive items.

**digital animation**  A method for making an object appear to move across a computer screen.

**digital audio**  Sound transmitted by discrete binary pulses; the computerized version of sound.

**digital audio tape (DAT)**  A 4-mm tape that uses a different recording system (called helical scanning), similar to that found on videotape recorders.

**digital camera**  A device that captures a photographic image as a collection of tightly grouped dots that can be stored on disk or in memory.

**digital light processing (DLP) projector**  This projector builds images on screen by digitally controlling the reflected angle of incident light, converging it with a prism and passing the image through a lens on to the screen. It has clear, sharp images and high contrast text as well as rich color in projected images.

**digital piracy**  The making of illegal copies of copyrighted information.

**digital signature encryption**  Relies on a mathematical coding scheme designed to foil a virus's attempt to attack programs and data.

**digital subscriber line (DSL)**  Offers high-speed data access over the single pair of the *ordinary copper lines* used with basic voice-grade telephone service. DSL is designed to transport a large volume of data through *the last mile* of telephone connections—the twisted pair channels that run to most homes

**digital video camcorder**  Used to capture the sound and sight of events on videotape, information is recorded as individual bytes of information. Digital recording thus increases the quality of both audio and video.

**digital video/digital motion video**  The presentation of data and information as moving images that can be processed by computer or transmitted over communications networks.

**digital video disk (DVD)**  The newest generation of optical storage. It appears to operate the same way and has the same dimensions as a CD-ROM but has a much larger capacity.

**digitizer**  An input device that translates measured distances into digital values that the computer can process.

**digitizing tablet**  A device by which an image on paper can be translated into electronic form.

**direct cut over strategy**  A conversion plan in which people abruptly stop using an old system and immediately begin using a new one.

**directory**  A listing of information by category.

**direct spending**  To obtain materials or components from suppliers for use in the manufacture of a product or delivery of a service.

**disaster recovery plan**  A procedure for restoring data lost when a system stops functioning.

**disintermediation**  Name given to removing intermediaries (like brokers and distributors) from the supply chain.

**disk cartridge**  The cartridge, a hard disk sealed in a protective package, is inserted into the disk drive for reading and writing data.

**disk mirroring**  The most frequently used form of RAID, it uses pairs of drives within the array and duplicates the entire contents of a disk on a second disk.

**disk operating system (DOS)**  A combination of programs that coordinates the actions of a computer, including its peripheral devices and memory.

**disk pack**  A stack of disks, enclosed in a protective plastic cover, that can be lifted onto or off a disk drive.

**distributed architecture**  A communications architecture in which the computers reside at different locations and are interconnected by a communications network.

**distributed database**  A database that resides in more than one system in a distributed network. Each component of the database can be retrieved from any node in the network.

**distributed processing**  Processing in which an application runs on one or more locations of the network simultaneously.

**division of labor**  Separation of a work process into component tasks, with different workers specializing in each of the tasks.

**documentation**  An instruction manual that accompanies software. Also, a technical, detailed written description of the specific facts of a program.

**document examination/record inspection**  The review of company documents about a system or opportunity under investigation.

**document type definition (DTD)** Defines the vocabulary (or standard) to make the data easily understandable and useable.

**domain name**  The familiar, easy-to-remember name for a computer on the Internet that correlates to an assigned IP address.

**domain name system (DNS)** Computers have numeric addresses consisting of strings of numbers known as their Internet protocol (or IP) address (e.g., 207.46.230.219, 207.171.181.16, 66.218.71.102, and 205.188.145.215).

**dot matrix printing**  A printer where the characters and images are formed by wire rods pushed against a ribbon and paper to create characters that are actually a collection of small dots.

**downloading**  The transfer of information from a central system to a desktop computer.

**drive**  The device containing a secondary storage medium's read/write unit.

**Dutch auction**  On electronic markets, the market operator displays a *high* opening price for an item and asks for buyers willing to pay the price. At prespecified intervals, the price is lowered until a bidder is willing to pay the displayed price.

**DVD-RAM**  A rewritable DVD form that can be used in PCs.

**economic database**  Captures details related to the state of the U.S. economy (other nations have comparable databases).

**editing**  Adding, deleting, or changing the data about companies.

**effectiveness**  The extent to which desirable results are achieved.

**efficient consumer response supply-chain strategy/continuous replenishment**  Data and information on products are captured at the point of sale and shared with suppliers periodically (usually daily) so that both can work together to jointly forecast future demands for replenishable items, monitor trends, and detect opportunities for new items.

**electronic banking/cyberbanking** Customers conduct their banking activities without going to a physical bank office.

**electronic bulletin board**  A network service application that allows messages and announcements to be posted and read. It is accessed by dialing a telephone number and interconnecting with the bulletin board through a modem.

**electronic commerce/e-commerce** Online shopping.

**electronic data interchange (EDI)** A form of electronic communication that allows trading partners to exchange business transaction data in structured formats that can be processed by applications software.

**electronic exchange/electronic market/B2B hub**  Commerce sites on the Internet where buyers and sellers can come together to shop, exchange information, or carry out transactions to buy or sell products and services.

**electronic funds transfer (EFT)**  The movement of money over a network.

**electronic mailbox**  An area of space on magnetic disk in a server or host computer that is allocated for storing an individual's e-mail.

**electronic market (e-market)**  A collection of individual shops accessible through a single location on the World Wide Web.

**electronic procurement (e-procurement) system**  Give employees access to catalogs of products and services from multiple suppliers.

**electronic spreadsheet**  An automated version of the manual spreadsheet, created and maintained by a spreadsheet program.

**electronic storefront**  Home page of an online retailing business.

**e-mail/electronic mail**  A service that transports text messages from a sender to one or more receivers via computer.

**enterprise database**  A collection of data designed to be shared by many users within an organization.

**enterprise data model/entity relationship**  A graphical representation of the items (the entities) of interest about which data is captured and stored in the database.

**enterprise information system**  Used to refer to the family of IT applications that underlies the activities of running and managing a business.

**enterprise resource planning (ERP) system**  Large scope, unified application programs that integrate many transaction-processing and information systems application features.

**enterprise system**  Usually involves the same types of components as a personal system, plus server or mainframe, database, and network. It is generally a shared system.

**entity**  A person, place, thing, event, or condition about which data and information are collected.

**entity relationship**  *See* enterprise data model.

**ethics**  The standards of conduct and moral behavior that people are expected to follow.

**exception report**  A report that lists unusual, erroneous, or unacceptable transactions or results.

**execution cycle (E-cycle)**  The last two steps of the machine cycle (execute and store), which produce processing results.

**executive support system (ESS)/ executive information system (EIS)** An interactive business information system designed to support executives that is capable of presenting summary information on company and industry activities.

**expansion slot**  A slot inside a computer that allows a user to add an additional circuit board.

**expert support system/expert system** A business information system that uses business rules, regulations, and databases to evaluate a situation or determine an appropriate course of action.

**extensible markup language (XML)** Developers can design their own customized markup languages for describing data.

**fault tolerance** The capability for a computer application to continue processing even if a disk drive fails.

**fault-tolerant computer** A computer designed with duplicate components to ensure reliability.

**fiber-optic cable** A physical communications channel that uses light and glass fibers.

**fields** The columns of a relation. Also called attributes.

**file locking** Used in systems that store unstructured information and have file-level sharing.

**file server** A computer containing files that are available to all users interconnected on a local area network.

**file transfer protocol (FTP)** An Internet method that allows you to use a password to connect to another computer on the Net and transfer its files to your computer.

**film recorder** An output device that transforms an electronic image on a computer screen into a film image.

**financial database** Focus on areas of monetary and investment activity, including stock market trading, issuance of mortgages, real-estate transactions, corporate finance, and venture-capital investment activities.

**firewall** A special-purpose software program located at a network gateway server.

**FireWire** One of the fastest peripheral interface standards ever developed.

**flash memory** Memory that retains its contents even when electricity is turned off.

**flatbed scanner** A large image scanner that works like an office photocopier.

**flexible disk/floppy disk/diskette** A type of magnetic disk made of flexible plastic.

**flexible manufacturing** A manufacturing system that automatically sets up machines for the next job, thus reducing setup time and making smaller job runs feasible.

**formula** An electronic spreadsheet instruction describing how a specific computation should be performed.

**forward auction/Yankee auction** Online shoppers bid on a desired item, with the knowledge that the seller will take the highest offer. Shoppers may choose to submit a different, higher bid until the highest bidder is left at the end of the auction.

**fractal method** An image compression method that stores images in pixel blocks and matches those blocks with fractal shapes whose identifying numbers constitute a mathematical formula that is used to regenerate the image.

**frame relay** A way of sending data over a wide area networks in which data are divided into frames (i.e., packets) with each containing an address that the switched network uses to determine its destination.

**front-end CASE tool** A CASE tool that automates the early (front-end) activities in systems development.

**front-end computer** In a centralized system, a minicomputer loaded with special programs to handle all incoming and outgoing communications traffic.

**function** A formula built into electronic spreadsheet software that will automatically perform certain types of calculation.

**functional distribution strategy** A database distribution strategy in which the database is distributed according to business functions.

**function key** A key designed to assist the computer's user to enter data and information or to control processing.

**gap** In magnetic storage, a space left before and after a block so that the tape drive can stop without skipping over any data.

**gateway** A device that connects two otherwise incompatible networks, network nodes, or devices.

**generalized packet radio service (GPRS)** GPRS (or 2.5G) features higher speed transmission rates than preceding telecom generations and uses packet switching rather than circuit switching, to transmit messages.

**general-purpose database system** A database maintained with powerful database management.

**generation** The process of organizing information into a useful form, whether as numbers, text, sound, or visual image.

**geographic distribution strategy** A database distribution strategy in which the database is located in a region where the data and information are used most frequently.

**gigabyte/G-byte/GB/gig** One billion bytes.

**gigahertz** Billions of pulses per second.

**Gopher** A server that organizes descriptions of information located on the Internet in the form of easy-to-use hierarchical menus.

**graphical browser** A type of browser used with the Web that displays both text and images within a page.

**graphical user interface (GUI)** A link to an operating system that allows users to use icons rather than command words to start processing.

**graphics adapter card** An interface board between a computer and monitor that is used to determine the monitor's resolution and use of color.

**green pages** Describe how an application can use the Web services.

**grid computing** A process that harnesses idle time on computers and then uses them to provide processing for an application that needs more speed and capability than may be available on a single computer, even on a supercomputer.

**group support system (GSS)** A business information system that permits people to process and interpret information as a group, even if they are not working face-to-face.

**hacker** A person who gains access to a system illegally.

**handheld computer** A name for a PDA and a Palm PC that is descriptive of the size and the fact that people can hold them in one hand as they enter and retrieve information with the other.

**handheld scanner** An inexpensive handheld alternative to the flatbed image scanner.

**hands-on system** A system in which a user enters data and information, directs processing, and determines the types of output to be generated.

**hard copy** The paper output from a printer.

**hard disk** A type of secondary storage that uses nonflexible, nonremovable magnetic disks mounted inside the computer to store data or information.

**hard disk controller** A hardware interface that may be built into the hard drive itself, in the form of an expansion board, or a connection on the system board.

**hard drive/disk drive** This is the device that holds and processes the disk.

**harden** Designing a security program to a potential IT target, making the level of effort greater than the value of breaking into a system, network, or facility.

**hardware** The computer and its associated equipment.

**hardware/computer hardware/devices** The computer and its associated equipment.

**head crash** The situation that occurs when the read/write heads that normally float close to a magnetic disk's surface actually touch the surface.

**heterogeneous application** May be written in different programming languages, run on different types of computers, and use varying communications networks and transmission methods.

**hibernation mode** The time during which all tasks are suspended and memory data and processing details are stored on the hard disk.

**high-definition television (HDTV)** A television system that uses digital technologies to present sound and images over high-quality television screens.

**home page** The first page of a Web site, which identifies the site and provides information about the contents of electronic documents that are part of the site.

**horizontal exchange** Seeks to simultaneously serve the interests of companies across different industries. Customers seek the services because of functional expertise rather than industry expertise.

**horizontal portal** Provides services and links to Web sites of interest to a wide variety of users.

**host-based computing** Centralized computing.

**hot site** A fully equipped backup computer center to which a company can take its backup copies of data and software and resume processing.

**hybrid network** A communications architecture that combines centralized and distributed architectures to take advantage of the strengths of both.

**hyperlinks** Words and/or symbols highlighted by blinking, color, or underline that connect one document to another related document on the Web.

**hypertext** A multimedia text display system in which words or phrases are highlighted to signal that clicking on them will reveal additional information. Also called hyperlinks.

**hypertext markup language (HTML)** A set of commands that specifies the position, size, and color of text, the location of graphic information, and the incorporation of sound and video. HTML commands also identify the words or images that will serve as hyperlinks to other documents.

**icon bar** The line of an electronic spreadsheet's control panel that shows the icons (pictures) used to invoke frequently used commands.

**identity theft** Loss of personal identity through a security breach.

**illustration program** A program in which the computer screen becomes a drawing board on which artists translate their ideas into visual form.

**image compression** A technique for reducing the size of stored images.

**image scanning** Examining an image and translating lines, dots, and marks into digital form.

**impact printing** A printing process in which the paper and the character being printed come into contact with each other.

**implementation** The fifth phase of the systems development life cycle, in which the new system is installed and put to use.

**independent exchange** *See* public exchange.

**index** A data file that contains identifying information about each record and its location in storage.

**indexing** A database system's capability to find fields and records in the database.

**index key/search key** A data item used by database management software to locate a specific record.

**indirect spending/maintenance, repair, and operations (MRO)** Buys goods and services that support operation of the company as a whole.

**Industrial Age** The period from the 1800s to 1957, when work processes were simplified through mechanization and automation.

**infomediary** A Web site that locates, retrieves, and organizes specialized information for potential users. The term is a composite of *information* and *intermediary*.

**information** An organized, meaningful, and useful interpretation of data.

**Information Age** The period that began in 1957, in which the majority of workers are involved in the creation, distribution, and application of information.

**information processing** A general term for the computer activity that entails processing any type of information and transforming it into a different type of information.

**information repository/repository** A synonym for database.

**information society** A society in which more people work at handling information than at agriculture and manufacturing combined.

**information superhighway** A communications network spanning a nation, carrying data and information traffic.

**information system** A system in which data and information flow from one person or department to another.

**information system/management information system (MIS)** A business information system designed to produce the information needed for successful management of a structured problem, process, department, or business.

**information technology (IT)** A term used to refer to a wide variety of items and abilities used in the creation, storage, and dispersal of data and information. Its three main components are computers, communications networks, and know-how.

**information technology professional** A person who is responsible for acquiring, developing, maintaining, or operating the hardware associated with computers and communications networks.

**infrared** A cableless medium that transmits data and information in coded form by means of an infrared light beamed from one transceiver to another.

**ink-jet printer** A printer that sprays tiny streams of ink from holes in the print mechanism onto the paper in a dot pattern that represents the character or image to be printed.

**input** The data or information entered into a computer or the process of entering data or information into the computer for processing, storage and retrieval, or transmission.

**input device** A device by which input is fed into a computer's central processor.

**input/output (I/O) bus** A bus (electronic circuit) that moves data into and out of the processor.

**input/output controller** A data controller with its own memory and processor that regulate the flow of data to and from peripheral devices.

**installed memory** The amount of memory included by a computer's manufacturer on its memory board.

**instant message** A sort of combination of real-time chat and e-mail that has grown rapidly since it was introduced in the late 1990s; a typed conversation, in which snippets of text are rapidly exchanged over the Internet, with each snippet appearing on the recipient's screen as soon as it is sent and disappearing when a messaging session is closed.

**instruction cycle (I-cycle)**   The first two steps of the machine cycle (fetch and decode), in which instructions are obtained and translated.

**instructions**   Detailed descriptions of the actions to be carried out during input, processing, output, storage, and transmission.

**integrated CASE (I-CASE) tool**   A CASE tool that spans activities throughout the entire systems development life cycle.

**integrated circuit/chip/microchip**   A collection of thousands or millions of transistors placed on a small silicon chip.

**integrated drive electronics (IDE)**   A standard electronic interface used between the bus or data path on a computer system board and the computer's disk storage devices.

**integrated services digital network (ISDN)**   A *next generation* telephone system integrating voice and data onto one line and capable of transporting *digital* data over *analog* lines.

**integrating**   The process of packing more transistors onto a single chip.

**interactive coupon**   Offered online.

**interactive marketing**   The use of custom advertising prepared to fit the profile of a specific visitor to a site.

**interactive multimedia presentation**   A multimedia presentation in which information is presented dynamically–that is, it can be shown in many different sequences, depending on the viewer's instructions.

**interactive television (ITV)**   A television with a keyboard, storage capability, and the capacity to transmit and receive vast amounts of information.

**interception**   Aimed at preventing the capture of data and information transmitted over an enterprise network or other communications link.

**interface**   The means by which a person interacts with a computer.

**intermediary**   In virtual banking, serves both merchant and consumer to streamline the billing and payment process.

**Internet Corp. for Assigned Names and Numbers (ICANN)**   The nonprofit corporation that was formed to assume responsibility for the IP address space allocation, protocol parameter assignment, domain name system management, and root server system management.

**Internet Engineering Task Force (IETF)**   A large international community of network designers, operators, vendors, and researchers concerned with the evolution of Internet architecture and the smooth operation of the Internet.

**Internet/Net**   A communication network that is itself a connection of many other networks.

**Internet relay chat (IRC)/chat session**   A live interactive discussion where all parties are actually on the network, interacting through their computers.

**Internet service provider (ISP)**   Supply access to the Internet by acting as the link between the user's computer and the Internet. An individual may dial the telephone number of the ISP or link through an *always-on* connection.

**Internet telephony/voice over the Internet/voice over IP**   Real-time voice conversations transmitted between computers on the Internet.

**internetworked**   The linking of several networks.

**interoperability**   The perfect exchange of data and information in all forms (data, text, sound, and image, including animation) between the individual components of an application (hardware, software, network).

**intrusion**   Forced and unauthorized entry into a system.

**joystick**   An input device used to control the actions in computer games or simulations. The joystick extends vertically from a control box.

**JPEG (Joint Photographic Expert Group) format**   An image compression method that stores images in pixel blocks embedded with information that makes possible the regeneration of the image.

**jump**   To suspend the display of the current screen and immediately display a new screen; direct navigation.

**keyboard**   The most common computer input device.

**keywords**   A string of letters or words that indicates the subject to be searched.

**kilobyte/K-byte/KB/K**   One thousand bytes.

**know-how**   The capability to do something well.

**knowledge**   An awareness and understanding of a set of information and how that information can be put to the best use.

**knowledge workers**   Workers involved in the creation, distribution, and application of information.

**label**   A piece of descriptive information pertaining to a row or column of an electronic spreadsheet.

**laptop computer/notebook computer**   Smaller versions of microcomputers that are designed for portability. All of their components, except a printer, are included in a single unit.

**laser printer**   A nonimpact printer that uses laser beams to print an entire page at once.

**layout description**   A chart that shows the exact location of data and information on a computer screen or in a printed report.

**leased line/dedicated line**   A communications line reserved from a carrier by a company for its exclusive use.

**legacy system**   Refers to the many mainframe, midrange, client/server, or PC applications that are used to manage business functions.

**leveling**   The process of exploding processes in a dataflow diagram to show more detail.

**light pen**   An input device that uses a light-sensitive cell to draw images and to select options from a menu of choices displayed on a computer screen.

**line printer**   A printer that prints a full line (up to 144 characters) at one time on continuous-form paper that can be up to 14 inches wide. Because of their high speed, which ranges up to several thousand lines per minute, line printers have been used in computer centers that routinely print large volumes of documents or very long reports.

**liquid crystal display (LCD) projector**   An LCD projector works on the principle of blocking light rather than emitting it. The brightness of the light (measured in lumens) determines how easily the images can be viewed in a room with ordinary lighting (as opposed to a darkened room).

**literary database**   Pertains to books, monographs, or reports, or to articles appearing in newspapers and magazines. Alternatively, a literary database may contain the actual publications themselves or links to the publications.

**local area network (LAN)**   A network that interconnects computers and communications devices within an office or series of offices; typically spans a distance of a few hundred feet to several miles.

**low-cost leadership**  Offers an enterprise great flexibility in dealing with any suppliers that raise their prices to the firm, as well as buyers seeking to drive down the prices they pay.

**low-earth-orbit satellite (LEO)** Because they circle Earth at a distance far closer than other satellites, LEO satellite systems offer significant advantages: they do not have the comparatively long propagation delays, do not require use of bulky, expensive, directional antennas, less expensive to produce and launch into orbit. However, greater numbers are needed to provide coverage for a geographic area because they do orbit closer to Earth.

**machine cycle**  The four processing steps performed by the control unit: fetch, decode, execute, and store.

**macro**  A time-saving miniprogram, identified by a name and a series of keystrokes, that is used to perform commonly repeated actions.

**magnetic disk**  A general term referring to two types of storage disk: the flexible/floppy disk and the hard disk.

**magnetic ink character recognition** A form of optical character reading in which preprinted information written in magnetic ink is read optically or sensed magnetically.

**magnetic tape**  A magnetic storage medium in which data are stored on large reels of tape.

**magnetic tape cartridge**  Magnetic tape encased in a protective shell. The cartridge can be removed from the tape reader for storage or shipment to another location.

**mainframe**  Larger, faster, and more expensive than a midrange computer, this computer is used for several purposes simultaneously.

**maintenance, repair, and operations (MRO)/indirect spending**  Buys goods and services that support operation of the company as a whole.

**management reporting system/ management information system (MIS)** A business information system designed to produce the information needed for successful management of a structured problem, process, department, or business.

**manufacturing automation protocol (MAP)**  A protocol used by factory designers to provide a common language for the transmission of data.

**manufacturing cell**  A group of machines working together in computer-integrated manufacturing.

**manufacturing resource planning (MRP II)**  An advanced MRP system that ties together all the parts of an organization into the company's production activities.

**market niche**  A focal point for a product or service; it is a subset of the entire industry or segment of the market.

**material requirements planning (MRP)**  A system that tracks the quantity of each part needed to manufacture a product; essentially, an important component of MRP II.

**maximum memory**  The most memory that a processor can hold.

**megabyte/M-byte/MB/meg**  One million bytes.

**megaflops**  Millions of floating point operations per second—a measure of how many detailed arithmetic calculations the computer can perform per second.

**megahertz (MHz)**  Millions of electric pulses per second—a measure of a computer's speed.

**memory/primary storage/main memory**  Storage within the computer itself. Primary memory holds data only temporarily, as the computer executes instructions.

**menu bar**  The line of an electronic spreadsheet's control panel that contains the commands for working with worksheets, creating graphics, and invoking special data-processing actions.

**method/action**  An instruction that tells a database how to process an object to produce specific information.

**metropolitan area network (MAN)** A network that transmits data and information over citywide distances and at greater speeds than a LAN.

**microcode**  The instructions that coordinate the execution of the instructions to move data to and from memory.

**microcomputer/personal computer/PC**  A computer that is relatively compact and usually found on a table or desktop.

**microprocessor**  The smallest type of processor, with all of the processing capabilities of the control unit and ALU located on a single chip.

**microsecond**  One millionth of a second.

**microwave**  A cableless medium that uses high-frequency radio signals to send data or information through the air.

**MIDI (musical instrument digital interface) audio**  A form of digital audio in which objects containing sound created by musical instruments are stored in computer-processible form.

**midrange computer/minicomputer/ mainframe**  A computer used to interconnect people and large sets of information. More powerful than a microcomputer, the minicomputer is usually dedicated to performing specific functions.

**millions of instructions per second (MIPS)**  The number of instructions the processor can execute per second—a measure of processor speed.

**millisecond**  One thousandth of a second.

**mixing**  An editing process in which two or more audio files are integrated during playback.

**mobile telecommunications switching office (MTSO)**  The switch used in a cellular (mobile) telephone system that links the cell tower to a traditional telephone switch in the public switched telephone network (PSTN).

**model**  A plan that simulates the relationships between events or variables.

**modem**  A device that connects a computer to a communications medium and translates the data or information from the computer into a form that can be transmitted over the channel. Used in WANs.

**moderated**  A mailing list in which the messages are first screened by an individual to determine their suitability given the purpose of the list.

**monochrome display**  A video screen display that shows information using a single foreground color on a contrasting background color (e.g., black on white).

**mouse**  An input device with a small ball underneath that rotates, causing a corresponding movement of a pointer on a display screen.

**multimedia PC**  A system that contains standard PC features but also has the capability to handle audio, video, animation, and graphics.

**multimedia presentation**  The seamless integration, through information technology, of different forms of information, including text, sound, still and animated images, and motion video.

**multimedia slide show**  A multimedia presentation in which information is displayed in a predetermined sequence, one slide at a time.

**multimedia system**  A computer system that can process multiple types of information simultaneously.

**multiple instruction/multiple data (MIMD) method**  A parallel-processing method that connects a number of processors that run different programs or parts of a program on different sets of data.

**multiplexer**  A device that converts data from digital to analog form and vice versa in order to allow a single communications channel to carry simultaneous data transmissions from the many terminals that are sharing the channel.

**multisync/multiscan monitors**  Monitors designed to work with a variety of graphics standards.

**multiuser system**  A communications system in which more than one user share hardware, programs, information, people, and procedures.

**nanosecond**  One billionth of a second.

**navigation**  A capability of interactive multimedia presentations that allows the viewer to move around within the presentation.

**netiquette**  A list of simple newsgroup guidelines that keep people from making mistakes.

**network administration/network management**  The management of a network, consisting of those procedures and services that keep the network running properly.

**network infrastructure provider**  A company, such as a telephone, cellular telephone, cable TV, and satellite transmission company, that operates the network of communication channels that carry data and information to and from user and content locations.

**network interface card (NIC)**  A circuit board used in LANs to transmit digital data or information.

**network operating system (NOS)**  A software program that runs in conjunction with the computer's operating system and applications programs and manages the network.

**network services**  The applications available on a communications network.

**newsgroup**  A discussion area where any user can post a message (i.e., provide information, ask questions, or express opinions) to the group and read the responses from others.

**node**  A communication station within a network.

**nonconcurrent data sharing**  A database procedure that allows individuals to access a database only when no other person or application is processing the data.

**nonimpact printing**  A printing process in which no physical contact occurs between the paper and the print device; the characters are produced on the paper through a heat, chemical, or spraying process.

**notebook computer/laptop computer**  Smaller versions of microcomputers that are designed for portability. All of their components, except a printer, are included in a single unit.

**object**  A component that contains data about itself and how it is to be processed.

**object-oriented database**  A database that stores data and information about objects.

**object-oriented programming**  Software development combining data and procedures into a single object.

**observation**  The process of watching an activity take place to collect information about that activity.

**off-site backup facility**  A backup computer center located away from a company's main facility.

**online analytical processing (OLAP)**  Database processing that selectively extracts data from different points of view.

**online retailing/e-commerce retailing/e-tailing**  Shoppers visit a store over the Internet and check out the products.

**online transaction processing (OLTP)**  Transaction-oriented applications design for direct data entry and retrieval of information by users connected to the system.

**open system**  A software system that performs on different computer and communications hardware.

**operating system**  A combination of programs that coordinates the actions of a computer, including its peripheral devices and memory.

**operations procedure**  A procedure that describes how a computer system or application is used, how often it can be used, who is authorized to use it, and where the results of processing should go.

**optical character reader**  An OCR device that recognizes printed information rather than just dark marks.

**optical character recognition (OCR)**  A technology by which devices read information on paper and convert it into computer-processable form.

**optical code reader**  An OCR device used to read bar codes.

**optical mark reader**  An OCR device that recognizes the location of dark marks on a special form as the form is scanned.

**optical storage device**  A device that uses a beam of light produced by a laser to read and write data and information.

**opt-in e-mail/permission-based e-mail**  If customers check a box agreeing to receive postings about the company's products, they have actually given approval for the mailing.

**output**  The results of inputting and processing data and information returned by the computer, either directly to the person using the system or to secondary storage.

**output device**  A device that makes the results of processing available outside of the computer.

**outsourcing**  A business practice in which firms use freelancers and consultants, rather than in-house staff, for selected activities.

**packet**  A piece or section of a transmitted message that contains both data and address information enabling the network to deliver the packet to its intended destination.

**packet switching**  A network communication method in which messages are divided into packets. Each packet is then transmitted individually and can even follow different routes to its destination.

**palm PC**  A version of the microcomputer about the size of a pocket calculator, used today for a small number of functions, such as maintaining personal calendars, name-and-address files, and electronic worksheets.

**palmtop computer**  The smallest and most portable computer, typically used for a limited number of functions, such as maintaining a personal calendar or address file.

**parallel processing**  Processing in which a computer handles different parts of a problem by executing instructions simultaneously.

**parallel systems strategy**  A conversion plan in which the old and the new system are used together for a period of time, with the old system being gradually phased out.

**partitioning**  A method of database distribution in which different portions of the database reside at different nodes in the network.

**PC database/personal database**
Typically resides on personal computers and is designed to support a particular function.

**PCMCIA card/PC card** A card designed to expand a computer's memory.

**pen-based computer** A tabletlike computer controlled with a special pen.

**peripheral equipment** A general term used for any device that is attached to a computer system.

**permission-based e-mail/opt-in e-mail** If customers check a box agreeing to receive postings about the company's products, they have actually given approval for the mailing.

**personal area network/Bluetooth personal area network** A wireless technology for communicating between devices that enables short-range radio links (30 feet or 10 meters) between devices, such as between a PC and a laptop, or a PDA and a printer.

**personal compact CD (PCD)** A variant on the mini-CD, it holds 20 to 60 MB, depending on the physical size of the CD.

**personal computer/PC/microcomputer** A relatively compact type of computer, the most common of all, for use in business and at home.

**personal database/PC database** Typically resides on personal computers and is designed to support a particular function.

**personal digital assistant (PDA)** A portable computer generally used as a personal aid.

**personal information manager (PIM)/contact manager** A database that enables users to manage data helpful in their personal activities by storing thousands of records of information in a predefined structure.

**personal productivity software** Software packages that permit activities to be completed more quickly, allow more activities to be completed in a particular period of time, or allow a task to be completed with fewer resources.

**phase-in strategy** A conversion plan in which a new system is gradually phased in throughout the organization or department over a certain period of time.

**picosecond** One trillionth of a second.

**pilot conversion strategy** A conversion plan in which a working version of a new system is implemented in one group or department to test it before it is installed throughout the entire business.

**pipelining** A computer starts processing a new instruction as soon as the previous instruction reaches its next step in the processing cycle.

**pixels** The dots used to create an image; the higher the number of dots, the better the resolution of the image.

**platform** The computer foundation on which applications are built. The two most common platforms for PCs are IBM-compatibles and Apple Macintosh.

**plotter** An output device that draws image information (such as charts, graphs, and blueprints) stroke by stroke.

**plug and play** The ability to install devices into a computer when the computer itself makes any necessary internal adjustments.

**plug-in** A software program that extends the capabilities of your Internet browser, giving it added features.

**pointing stick** A device that positions the cursor on the computer screen.

**port** A connector through which input/output devices can be plugged into the computer.

**portal** A gateway or hub site, such as Yahoo!, that provides chat rooms.

**post, telephone, and telegraph (PTT)** A general term used for the government-controlled telephone company in a country other than the United States.

**preliminary investigation** The first phase of the systems development life cycle, in which the merits and feasibility of a project proposal are determined.

**pretty good privacy (PGP)** A program used to encrypt and decrypt e-mail and to encrypt digital signatures, so the recipient knows the transmission was not changed along the way.

**primary storage/primary memory/main memory/internal memory** Storage within the computer itself. Primary memory holds data only temporarily, as the computer executes instructions.

**primary value-chain activities** The basic business processes fundamental to any industry.

**privacy** In IT, the term used to refer to how personal information is collected, used, and protected.

**private branch exchange (PBX)/computer branch exchange (CBX)** A private telephone system designed to handle the needs of the organization in which it is installed.

**private exchange** An Internet-based trading forum (i.e., an electronic market)

implemented by a single company with a select group of suppliers and customers.

**private network** A network made up of leased (dedicated) communications lines.

**problem** A perceived difference between an existing condition and a desired condition.

**problem solving** The process of recognizing a problem, identifying alternatives for solving it, and successfully implementing the chosen solution.

**problem solving cycle** The five-step sequence of activities designed to address and solve problems in a structured way.

**procedure** A step-by-step process or a set of instructions for accomplishing specific results.

**process** A structured activity that leads to a set of results (output).

**process improvement** An improvement in the way a business works.

**processing** The process of converting, analyzing, computing, and synthesizing all forms of data or information.

**processor/central processing unit (CPU)** A set of electronic circuits that perform the computer's processing actions.

**productivity** The relationship between the results of an activity (output) and the resources used to create those results (inputs).

**program** A set of instructions that directs a computer to perform certain tasks and produce certain results.

**programmer/analyst** A person who has joint responsibility for determining system requirements and developing and implementing the systems.

**project management** The process of planning, organizing, integrating, and overseeing the development of an IT application to ensure that the project's objectives are achieved and the system is implemented according to expectations.

**project proposal** A proposal for a systems project prepared by users or systems analysts and submitted to a steering committee for approval.

**protocol** The rules and conventions guiding data communications, embedded as coded instructions in the network software.

**prototype** A working model of an IT application.

**proxy server** Acts as an intermediary between a PC and the Internet, separating an enterprise network from an outside network.

**public-access network** A network maintained by common carriers for use by the general public.

**public domain software** Any non-copyrighted software that can be used by the general public.

**public exchange/independent exchange** A third party—the *market maker*—operates the electronic market, displays the market's information content, and provides electronic tools for conducting trade.

**public key infrastructure (PKI)** A public key is made available in a directory that all parties can search. Thus a sender wishing to transmit a secured message searches a *digital certificate* directory to find the recipient's *public* key, using it to encrypt the message.

**pull** To get something from a Web site by clicking on a link or entering a URL.

**push** Prearranged and periodic delivery of information of interest to a user's desktop automatically.

**query/querying** A question to be answered by accessing the data in a database.

**query by example (QBE)** A query format in which the user fills in the blanks with simple commands or conditions.

**query language** A computer language that forms database queries from a limited number of words.

**questionnaire** A sheet of questions used to collect facts and opinions from a group of people.

**radio wave transmission/radio frequency (RF) transmission** A cableless medium that uses frequencies rented from public radio networks to transmit data and information.

**RAM disk** A disk created in primary memory that offers instant direct access to the data stored on it.

**random-access device** The self-contained unit that holds and processes the disk.

**random-access memory (RAM)** Memory that permits data or information to be written into or read from memory only as long as the computer is turned on.

**random-access storage/direct access storage** The process of retrieving a particular record of information from any track directly.

**read only** A type of disk that information can be read from but not written onto.

**read-only memory (ROM)** A type of storage that offers random access to memory and can hold data and information after the electric current to the computer has been turned off.

**read/write** A computer application can use storage for both writing and reading data.

**read/write head** A device that records data by magnetically aligning metallic particles on the medium. The write head records data and the read head retrieves them.

**real-time processing** The processing of each transaction as it occurs.

**record** A grouping of data items that consists of a set of data or information that describes an entity's specific occurrence.

**record key** In a database, a designated field used to distinguish one record from another.

**recording density** The number of characters per inch at which a drive writes data.

**record locking** A concurrency procedure that prohibits another user from accessing or altering a record that is in use.

**recovery procedure** An action taken when information or software must be restored.

**reduced instruction set computing (RISC)** A computing instruction set that takes data for the execution of an instruction only from registers.

**redundant arrays of independent disk (RAID)** A set of small disk drives that work together as a single unit.

**reengineering** The reshaping of business processes to remove barriers that prohibit an organization from providing better products and services and to help the organization capitalize on its strengths.

**register** A temporary storage area in the processor that can move data and instructions more quickly than main memory can, and momentarily hold the data or instructions used in processing as well as the results that are generated.

**registrar** Those who process applications for assignment of domain names and submit approved names to the registry.

**registry** The record of both global and country domain names kept by the local Internet community in each country or territory.

**relational database** A database in which the data are structured in a table format consisting of rows and columns.

**relational operator** A symbol that tells a database system to make a comparison to call up the requested data.

**relation/file** The table in a database that describes an entity.

**reliability** The assurance that computers and communications systems will do what they should when they should.

**replication** A method of database distribution in which one database contains data that are included in another database.

**requirement** A feature that must be included in a system.

**requirements determination** The second phase of the systems development life cycle, in which the current business situation is studied to determine who is involved, what data and information are needed, and how the current system can be improved.

**resolution** The clarity or sharpness of an image.

**retrieval** The process by which a computer locates and copies stored data or information for further processing or for transmission to another user.

**reverse auction** The direct opposite of a traditional auction. The bidders list their product or service requirements and the maximum price they are willing to pay for it. Potential sellers who can provide the good or service reverse bid against each other by posting their bids for buyers. The bidder offering the requested products or services at the best price wins the bid.

**RGB display** A video screen display with the ability to create 256 colors and several thousand variations on these colors by blending shades of red, green, and blue.

**robot** A computer-controlled device that can physically manipulate its surroundings.

**root server** Thirteen special computers coordinated by ICANN that contain the IP addresses of all top level domain registries for both the global registries (e.g., .com, .net, and .org) and the country registries (e.g., .uk, .jp, and .br).

**router** A device that interconnects compatible LANs.

**rows** The horizontal elements in a spreadsheet.

**rule base/knowledge base** A database of rules in an expert system.

**sampling** The process of collecting data and information at prescribed intervals.

**satellite** A cableless medium in which communications are beamed from a microwave station to a communications satellite in orbit above the earth and relayed to other earth stations.

**scanning** The process of transforming written or printed data or information into a digital form that is entered directly into the computer.

**schema** The structure of a database.

**scroll bar** A bar located at the right or bottom of the computer screen that allows the user to move around the screen—up, down, left, or right.

**search engine** A program invoked from within the browser that scans the network by using a keyword or phrase.

**secondary storage/auxiliary storage** A storage medium that is external to the computer, but that can be read by the computer; a way of storing data and information outside the computer itself.

**sector** A subdivision of a track on a magnetic disk; used to improve access to data or information.

**secure electronic transaction (SET)** An adaptation of public key encryption and the digital certificate (which the industry calls an *electronic wallet*) for securing financial transactions over the Internet.

**security** Safeguarding and protecting an enterprise's information technology assets.

**security procedure** A procedure designed to safeguard data centers, communications networks, computers, and other IT components from accidental intrusion or intentional damage.

**security program** The policies and protective measures that will be used, the responsibilities of individuals involved in maintaining security, as well as the responsibilities of those who abide by established security policies.

**security software** Software that is designed to protect systems and data.

**sensitivity analysis** The analytical process by which a computer determines what would happen if certain data change.

**sequential access** The contents are accessed *in sequence.*

**sequential processing** Processing in which the execution of one instruction is followed by the execution of another.

**sequential storage** Elements of data are read one right after the other.

**server** A computer that hosts a network and provides the resources that are shared on the network.

**server computer** The computer that contains data and information that can be accessed by a client computer.

**service provider** *See* Internet service provider (ISP).

**shared database** A database shared among many users and applications.

**shared system** A system in which two or more users share computers, communications technology, and applications.

**shareware** Software that is given away and freely distributed. The developer retains ownership, asks users to register with the owner, and requests a nominal fee for using the program.

**simple object access protocol (SOAP)** The protocol used by an application to invoke a Web service located on another computer.

**single in-line memory module (SIMM)** A multiple-chip memory card inserted as a unit into a predesigned slot on a computer's system board.

**single instruction/multiple data (SIMD) method** A parallel-processing method that executes the same instruction on many data values simultaneously.

**single-user system/personal system** An IT system used by only one person. A system that stands alone and is not interconnected with other companies or shared by other people.

**site license** An agreement under which a software purchaser pays a fee to the manufacturer to make a specified number of copies of a particular program.

**site preparation** The activities involved in preparing for the installation of a new system.

**small computer system interface (SCSI)** A device created to speed the transfer of data between hard disks and other peripherals.

**social responsibility** The concept that businesses need to balance their commitments to investors, employees, customers, other businesses, and the communities in which they operate.

**software** The general term for a set of instructions that controls a computer or a communications network.

**software package** An application that focuses on a particular subject, such as word processing, and is sold to businesses and the general public.

**software piracy** The making of illegal copies of software.

**software testing** The testing of software programs to ensure that the software will not produce unexpected or incorrect results or interruptions during processing.

**source data automation** A method of data entry in which details enter computers directly from their written or printed forms without the intermediate step of keying.

**spam** Unsolicited advertising by e-mail.

**special-purpose database** Predesigned for a specific use.

**spoken information** Information that is conveyed by sound.

**spreadsheet** A table of columns and rows used by people responsible for tracking revenues, expenses, profits, and losses.

**spreadsheet program** A software package used to create electronic spreadsheets.

**spreadsheet/worksheet** A table of columns and rows used by people responsible for tracking revenues, expenses, profits, and losses.

**statistical database** Includes the measurement data to measure the level of statistical activity and a means of comparing areas of activity.

**steering committee** A group of people from various functional areas of a business that determines whether a systems development project proposal is desirable and should be pursued.

**still image** A paper photograph; an analog image.

**storage/secondary storage/auxiliary storage** The computer process of retaining information for future use.

**storage area network (SAN)** A high-speed network or system that allows different kinds of storage devices, such as tape drives and disk arrays, to be shared by all users through network servers.

**strategic information systems** Information technology applications that change the way a firm competes, providing a capability so valuable that they enable the firm to gain a substantial competitive advantage against its competitors.

**streaming/streaming media** A process in which you can listen to or view audio, video, or other media files as the downloading is occurring.

**striping** A method of combining multiple physical drives into one logical storage unit.

**structured interview** An interview in which the questions are prepared in advance and each interviewee is asked the same set of questions.

**stylus** A penlike instrument that is used to trace images on paper for translation into electronic form.

**summary report** A report that shows the overall results of processing for a period of time or for a batch of transactions and includes a grand total for all listed transactions and the average transaction amount.

**SuperDisk** A storage alternative developed by Imation (originally part of 3M Corp.) that has a capacity of 120 MB.

**supply chain** The flow of parts, components, materials, funds, and information between a company's sources and its customers.

**supply chain integration** The synchronization of all parties involved in making a product or delivering a service in order to meet buyer, seller, and customer needs.

**supply chain management** The oversight of activities interconnecting suppliers and buyers.

**support value-chain activities** Those activities that occur to facilitate the primary activities.

**surfing** Moving among a number of networks that are linked together, or internetworked.

**Switched Multimegabit Data Service (SMDS)** A high-speed, packet-switched transport technology that can operate over copper or fiber channels. Subscribers pay only for the time actually used and can purchase different levels of transport speed

**switched network** The complete set of public access networks, so named because the telephone company operates and maintains the switching centers that make it possible to transmit data and information.

**system** A set of components that interact to accomplish a purpose.

**system board/mother board** The system unit in a microcomputer, located on a board mounted on the bottom of a computer base.

**system clock** A circuit that generates electronic impulses at a fixed rate to synchronize processing activities.

**system construction** The fourth phase of the systems development life cycle, in which the system is actually built.

**system flowchart** A graphical description of a business process or procedure using standard symbols to show decision logic.

**systems analyst** The IT professional responsible for working with users to determine a system's requirements and for describing the features needed in the system.

**systems contractor** An outside person or firm that contracts with a company to develop IT applications.

**systems design** The third phase of the systems development life cycle, in which requirements are translated into design specifications.

**systems designer** The IT professional responsible for doing the technical work of designing the system and its software.

**systems development** The process of examining a business situation, designing a system solution to improve that situation, and acquiring the human, financial, and information technology resources needed to develop and implement the solution.

**systems development life cycle (SDLC)** The six-phased set of activities that brings about a new IT application.

**systems engineer** An IT professional who installs and maintains hardware.

**systems integrator** A type of systems contractor who is retained to take responsibility for acquiring hardware, software, and network capacity for an application, as well as for implementing the application.

**systems programmer** A software and hardware specialist who works with the physical details of a database and the computer's operating system.

**system testing** The testing of a complete system—software, procedures, and guidelines.

**system unit** The hardware unit that houses a computer's processor, memory chips, ports, and add-in boards.

**tablet PC** A wireless personal computer (PC) that enables individuals to use a stylus or digital pen retrieve and display information on a touch screen or take notes using natural handwriting.

**T-carrier** A very-high-speed channel designed for use as the backbone of a network and for point-to-point connection of locations.

**teleprocessing** The processing capability made possible by connecting desktop computers to a remote computer through telephone lines.

**Telnet** The means users employ to communicate with their own systems through the Internet when they are away from their home location.

**template** A worksheet containing row and column labels, and perhaps formulas, but not necessarily any values. It is distributed to people as a guide for analyzing problems or providing data.

**terabyte/T-byte/TB** One trillion bytes.

**terminal** A combination of keyboard and video screen that accepts input and displays it on the screen.

**terrorist** Someone who conducts a "premeditated, politically motivated attack against information, computer systems, computer programs, and data, which results in violence against noncombatant targets by subnational groups or clandestine agents."

**test data** Experimental files used to test software.

**text-based browser** A type of browser used with the Web that displays only text information, either a line at a time or a full screen at once.

**thermal printer** A printer that heats a wax-based colored ink contained in the printer ribbon and transfers it to a special paper.

**third-generation service** Uses packet switching and transmits at higher bandwidths that provide faster downloads of information; transmission rates ranging from 384 Kbs to 2 Mbs, depending on the location of the user.

**thumbnail** The display of miniature images of each slide in a multimedia slide presentation so the designer can check them for sequence.

**time division multiple access (TDMA)** A digital cellular transmission technology that divides a radio frequency into time slots and then allocates slots to an individual device's conversation or message, thereby distinguishing it from other transmissions.

**title bar** The line of an electronic spreadsheet's control panel that contains the program name and sometimes the name of the file in use.

**topology** A network configuration, or the arrangement of the nodes or workstations of a network in relation to one another.

**touchpad** An alternative to the mouse that senses the user's finger movement and downward pressure, moving the cursor in the corresponding direction on the display screen.

**track** The area in which data and information are stored on magnetic tape or disk.

**trackball** An input device that consists of a ball mounted on rollers. As the user rotates the ball in any direction, the computer senses the movement and moves the cursor in the corresponding direction.

**training** The process by which people are taught how to use a system.

**transaction processing system (TPS)** A shared business information system that uses a combination of information technology and manual procedures to process data and information and to manage transactions.

**transceiver** A combination transmitter and receiver that transmits and receives data and information.

**transistor** An electrical switch that can be in one of two states: open or closed.

**transmission** The computer process of distributing information over a communications network.

**tunnel protocols** By encrypting data at the sending end and decrypting it at the receiving end, the protocols send the data (and if an enterprise chooses, the originating and receiving network addresses as well) through a *tunnel* that cannot be *entered* by data that is not properly encrypted.

**tuples** The rows of a relation. Also called records.

**twisted pair** A physical communications channel that uses strands of copper wire twisted together in pairs to form a telephone wire.

**unified messaging system** Offers users the ability to manage several communications media, including telephone, fax, e-mail (including those from the Web), and voicemail through a central message manager.

**unified modeling language (UML)** The standard vehicle for visualizing, describing, and documenting the details of an IT application.

**Uniform Resource Locator (URL)** A document's address on the WWW.

**uninterruptible power supply (UPS) system** A system that ensures the continued flow of electricity when the primary source of power fails.

**universal description, discover, and integration (UDDI)** A worldwide directory for registering, finding, and using Web services.

**universal product code (UPC)** A bar code that identifies a product by a series of vertical lines of varying widths representing a unique product number.

**universal serial bus/universal service bus (USB)** A recent addition to PCs that can connect up to 128 devices, ranging from computer disk storage to a variety of multimedia devices.

**universal service** The principle, established in telecommunications, whereby it is assured that anyone who wants a basic service can receive it at low cost.

**unstructured interview** An interview in which the questions may be prepared in advance, but follow-up questions vary, depending on the interviewee's background and answers.

**updated master data** An adjustment of all records in a system in response to a processed transaction.

**uploading** The process by which information is sent from a PC to a mainframe.

**USB drive** Consisting of flash memory and a USB connection, it can read and write data when connected to the computer's USB port.

**use case** Identifies the sequence of activities performed for an actor.

**use case description** Describes the use case in ordinary language, including its identifying name and actors.

**use case diagram** Provides context for the system, illustrating the actors, the use cases, and the flow or interaction between use cases and actors.

**Usenet/User's Network** A system of worldwide discussion groups, not an actual physical network.

**users/end users** The people who use IT in their jobs or personal lives.

**utility programs/utilities** Special programs used to perform tasks that occur repeatedly during processing.

**value** A number that is entered into a cell of an electronic spreadsheet. It may be an integer, a decimal number, or a number in scientific format.

**value-added network (VAN)** A public data communications network that provides basic transmission facilities plus enhancements (e.g., temporary data storage and error detection).

**value chain** A set of activities that are relevant to understanding the bases of cost and potential sources of differentiation in a firm.

**vendor-managed inventory** Companies deal directly with vendors, that is, manufacturers or suppliers.

**Veronica** An internet program that uses keywords to search Gopher menus.

**vertical exchange** Structured to serve members of a specific industry.

**vertical portal or Vortal** A Web site that specializes in providing information related to a particular industry such as automobiles, healthcare, or investments.

**very high speed DSL (VDSL)** Provides transport of data over copper twisted pair lines at speeds ranging from 13 mbps to 55 mbps but at much shorter distance than DSL, usually between 1,000 and 4,500 feet.

**very small aperture terminal (VSAT)** A satellite earth station with an antenna diameter of under one meter.

**videoconferencing** A type of conferencing in which video cameras and microphones capture the sight and sound of participants for transmission over a network.

**videodisk** An optical read-only storage medium.

**video display terminal (VDT)/monitor** A computer's visual display.

**videotex** A two-way, interactive, text-only service operating on mainframe computers that combines a video screen with easy-to-follow instructions.

**view** A subset of one or more databases, created either by extracting copies of records from a database or by merging copies of records from multiple databases.

**virtual bank** Operates exclusively over the Internet.

**virtual company** A company that joins with another company operationally, but not physically, to design and manufacture a product.

**virtual private network (VPN)** A network constructed of public channels to connect client computers to servers, incorporating encryption and other security mechanisms to ensure that only authorized users can gain access and that the data cannot be intercepted.

**virus** A hidden program that alters, without the user's knowledge, the way a computer operates or that modifies the data and programs stored on the computer.

**voice input device** An input device that can be attached to a computer to capture the spoken word in digital form.

**voice mail** A system that captures, stores, and transmits spoken messages using an ordinary telephone connected to a computer network.

**voice over IP/Internet telephony/voice over the Internet** Real-time voice conversations transmitted between computers on the Internet.

**wand** An input device used to read a bar code and input this information directly into a computer.

**warm boot** In a restart, the BIOS knows the system is already running (data is written in a specific memory location checked by the BIOS) and skips the power-on test.

**WAVE audio** A form of digital audio that captures sound through sampling.

**Web-based integration** Makes data from enterprise databases available to users connecting through the Internet (including enterprise intranets and extranets).

**Web browser** Client computer program designed to locate and display information on the World Wide Web.

**webcasting** The prearranged and periodic delivery of information of interest to a user's desktop automatically (chapter 3). Uses the reach of the Internet to link people from anywhere in the world into a conference (chapter 8).

**Web developer** Expected to have additional capabilities that enable him or her to use expertise in creating IT applications that will involve the Internet or company intranets and extranets, Web browsers, and the display of information using browsers.

**Web directory** *See* directory.

**Web enablement** The tendency of systems developers to incorporate features of the Internet in enterprise systems.

**Web pages** Interconnected electronic documents.

**Web services** Modular Internet applications that perform a very specific function or task.

**Web services description language (WSDL)** Describes the capabilities offered by a specific Web service as well as the protocols and formats the service uses.

**Wide Area Information Servers (WAIS)** A retrieval method that searches databases

on the Internet and creates a menu of articles and manuscripts containing the keywords provided.

**wide area network (WAN)** A network that connects sites dispersed across states, countries, or continents.

**Winchester disk drive** A disk drive that contains a read/write head, an access arm, and a disk in one sealed unit.

**Windows** A single-user operating system that allows several programs to be operated simultaneously.

**wireless/cableless** Wireless channels transmit data using radio signals send through air or space rather over wire or optical cables.

**wireless data network (WDN)** Networks, which use cellular communications services, intended to support mobile users seeking to interconnect with networks using wireless laptops and PDAs; have breadth of coverage, high transmission speed and reliability, security, the ability to send and receive large files, ease of connection to the network, and many have an *always on* capability.

**wired equivalent privacy (WEP)** A system of security protection that is a standard for encrypting data (converting the data into a protective code) over an 802.11b wireless network.

**wireless local area network (WLAN)** LANs using wireless technologies because they enable staff members to move around the building with laptops, PDAs, and other wireless devices and still connect to the enterprise's local area network without a wire. Wireless LANs transmit data using radio frequencies instead of cables.

**word** The number of bits a computer can process at one time.

**word processing (WP) program** A program that allows the user to enter, change (edit), move, store, and print text information.

**work-group conferencing** *See* collaborative conferencing.

**work processes** The combination of activities that workers perform, the way they perform those activities, and the tools they use.

**workstation/node/client** A desktop computer connected to a network.

**World Wide Web/WWW/the Web** A set of interconnected sites on the Internet that are use the Hypertext Transfer Protocol (HTTP). The electronic documents on these sites, called Web pages, can be found and retrieved using the Internet.

**XML style sheet language (XSL)** Created by developers or publishers of XML data to manage the display and presentation of information in a document.

**yellow pages** Describe the services offered by UDDI.

**Zip disk** Similar to diskettes, but housed in a hard plastic case; they store from 70 to 175 times more than diskettes and data can be stored and retrieved more quickly than from diskettes.

**Zip drive** A removable storage device that uses hard-shelled removable Zip disks, which can store up to 750 MB of information.

**Chapter 5**   **173** Logo used with permission of Brooks Brothers; **173** Copyright ©1995–2000 Cyberware, Incorporated; **175** *a,b:* Courtesy of Intel, *c:* Courtesy of Micron, *d:* Courtesy of Maxtor, *e,f:* Courtesy of IBM, *g:* Courtesy of Hewlett-Packard; **179** *a,b:* Courtesy of IBM, *c:* Courtesy of Maxtor; **181** Courtesy of IBM; **182** *a:* Courtesy of Intel, *b:* Courtesy of IBM, *c:* Courtesy of Maxtor; **182** *bottom:* Courtesy of IBM; **183** *left:* Courtesy of Hewlett-Packard; **183** *right:* Courtesy of Iomega; **186** *left:* Courtesy of Iomega; **186** *right:* Courtesy of Iomega; **188** Logo used with permission of Delta Airlines; **188** *top and bottom:* Courtesy of Delta Airlines; **189** Allied Signal Division of Honeywell; **190** *top left:* Courtesy of Quantum; **190** *top right:* Courtesy of IBM; **190** *bottom left:* Courtesy IBM; **190** *bottom right:* Courtesy IBM; **191** Courtesy of Hewlett-Packard; **192** ©Erv Schowengerdt; **197** *left:* ©Erv Schowengerdt; **197** *right:* Copyright ©1998–1999 Encyclopædia Britannica, Inc.; **198** Courtesy of Microsoft; **199** ©Gary Conner/PhotoEdit; **200** *left:* Corbis; **200** *center:* George Shelley/Corbis; **200** *right:* Paul Slater/Corbis; **201** Logo used with permission of Kroger.; **201** ©Sonda Dawes/The Image Works; **202** McKesson Corporation; **203** Scantron Corporation; **204** Courtesy of Doubleday Direct; **205** Courtesy of IBM; **207** *top left:* Courtesy of Logitech; **207** *top right:* Courtesy of Microsoft; **207** *bottom left:* Joseph Nettig/Stock, Boston; **207** *bottom right:* Courtesy of Hewlett-Packard; **208** *left:* Courtesy of Canon Corporation; **208** *right:* Courtesy of Maxell; **209** *top:* ©Kathy Zander; **209** *bottom:* ©Michael Newman/PhotoEdit; **211** *both:* Courtesy of Hewlett-Packard; **213** Courtesy of NCR; **214** *top:* Courtesy of Hewlett-Packard; **214** *bottom:* Courtesy of Xerox; **215** Redrawn from *The Way Things Work* by David Macaulay, pp. 348–349. Compilation copyright ©1988 by Dorling Kindersley, Ltd. Text copyright ©1988 by David Macaulay and Neil Ardley. Ilustrations copyright ©1988 by David Macaulay. Reprinted by permission of Houghton Mifflin Co. and Dorling Kindersley, Ltd.; **216** *top:* Courtesy of Hewlett-Packard; **216** *bottom;* Courtesy of IBM; **217** Courtesy of Hewlett-Packard; **218** *top and bottom:* Courtesy of Hewlett-Packard; **219** Courtesy of Hewlett-Packard; **220** *top:* Courtesy of IBM; **220** *bottom:* ©Michael Newman/PhotoEdit; **221** Copyright ©1995–2003 Hauppauge Computer World, Inc. All rights reserved.; **222** *top:* Courtesy of Hewlett-Packard; **222** *bottom:* www.ccg.germany.com; **230** *top:* Photodisc/Getty Images; **230** *bottom:* ©FleetBoston Financial; **231** ©FleetBoston Financial.

**Chapter 6**   **233** *top:* ©Lee Snider; Lee Snider/CORBIS; **233** *center:* Photographic History Collection, National Museum of American History, Smithsonian Institution. Negative Number: 89-7710; **233** *bottom left:* Photographic History Collection, National Museum of American History, Smithsonian Institution. Negative Number: 86-2205; Photographic History Collection, National Museum of American History, Smithsonian Institution. Negative Number: 83-4644; **241** SISCO (Security Identification Systems Corporation™); **243** *both:* Courtesy of Finagle A Bagel; **248** Lloyd Gallman; **253** ©Microsoft Corporation; **255** *both:* ©Microsoft Corporation; **256** Courtesy of Kinion Furniture; **258** ©Microsoft Corporation; **259** ©Microsoft Corporation.

**Chapter 7**   **269** Courtesy of Ritz-Carlton Corporation; **273** ©Michael Newman/PhotoEdit; **277** Logo used with permission of Chubb Insurance; **277** *top:* ©PhotoEdit; **280** ©Tony Freeman/PhotoEdit; **285** *top left and right:* David Male/Burlington Coat Factory; **285** *bottom left:* ©Erv Schowengerdt; **285** *bottom right:* ©Royalty-Free/CORBIS; **288** Courtesy of Glass Information

Systems, Ltd.; **293** Logo and photo ©2003 Lithonia Lighting, a division of Acuity Lighting Group, Inc.; **297** ©Georgina Bowater/CORBIS; Courtesy of Jiffy Lube; Courtesy of Lands' End; **299** ©Jiffy Lube; **308** Logo and photo ©2003 Lands' End, Inc. Used with permission.; **309** ©2003 Lands' End, Inc. Used with permission.; **310** *left:* Courtesy of FedEx Corp.; **310** *right:* Etienne de Malglaive/Gamma Press; **311** *top:* Courtesy of FedEx Corp.; **311** *center:* ©Jeff Greenberg/The Image Works; **311** *bottom:* Courtesy of FedEx Corp.; **312** *top left, center left and bottom left:* Etienne de Malglaive/Gamma Press; **312** *top right:* Bill Gallery/Stock, Boston; **312** *center right:* John Madere; **312** *bottom right:* Courtesy of FedEx Corp; **313** *top left:* Nubar Alexanaian/Stock, Boston; **313** *top right:* Courtesy of FedEx Corp; **313** *center left and right:* Courtesy of FedEx Corp; **313** *bottom:* John Madere.

**Chapter 8**   **315** *top:* ©Jean Miele/CORBIS; **315** *bottom:* ©Allan Tannenbaum/The Image Works; **323** Eli Reichman; **324** *top:* ©R.W. Jones/CORBIS; **324** *bottom:* ©William Taufic/CORBIS; **325** ©2003 Scripps Networks, Inc. All rights reserved.; **328** ©Ken Glaser/Index Stock Imagery, Inc.; **329** The Image Reader; **331** Logo and photo used with permission of Schneider National; **332** ©vtxnet.wdr.de; **335** Courtesy of Haverty's; **338** *top:* ©Paul A. Souders/CORBIS; **338** *bottom:* Copyright ©Wonderfile Corporation 2003. All rights reserved.; **340** *left:* AT&T Archives; **340** *center:* AT&T Bell Laboratories; **340** *right:* Sperry Corporation; **343** *top and center:* Delphi; **343** *bottom left and right:* Courtesy of Schneider National, Inc.; **344** VideoCart, Inc.; **345** United Technologies-Otis Elevators; **348** *top left:* Courtesy of International Business Machines Corporation. Unauthorized use not permitted.; **348** *top right:* Courtesy of Motorola; **348** *bottom left and right:* Courtesy of International Business Machines Corporation. Unauthorized use not permitted.; **351** *both:* Courtesy of Tower Automotive (www.towerautomotive.com); **355** ©Johnny Crawford/The Image Works; **358** *left:* Courtesy of Starbucks Co.; **358** *right:* Courtesy of NETGEAR; **360** Bill Gallery/Stock, Boston; **361** *left:* Courtesy of Palm Computing; **361** *center:* Courtesy of Hewlett-Packard; **361** *right:* Courtesy of Blackberry; **363** *bottom:* Courtesy of MasterCard; **363** *top:* www.newscom.com; **380** ©George Hall/CORBIS; **390** *both:* Source: IDC Internet Commerce Market Model, version 5.0.

**Chapter 9**   **383** *all:* Courtesy of United Parcel Services Incorporated; **385** *left:* ©Ed Bock/CORBIS; **385** *right:* ©Neema Frederic/CORBIS SYGMA; **388** ©2002 Amazon.com, Inc. All rights reserved.; **389** ©Erv Schowengerdt; **392** ©1990-2003 Peapod, LLC. All rights reserved. Used with permission of Peapod Inc.; **393** *both:* ©1999-2002 QCommerce Inc. All rights reserved.; **394** UNESCO.org; **395** All material herein ©1998-2003 priceline.com Incorporated. All rights reserved.; **396** ©2003 NetBank, Inc. All rights reserved. Used with permission of Netbank.; **399** *both:* ©2003 Intuit Inc. All rights reserved.; **400** Charles Schwab & Co., Inc.; **401** Logo and screen courtesy of E*TRADE. E*TRADE Financial and the E*TRADE logo are registered trademarks of E*TRADE Group, Inc. or its subsidiaries. All rights reserved. **401** *bottom:* AP Photo/Stephan Savoia/Wide World; **402** Courtesy of Delta Airlines; **403** ©Harry and David. All rights reserved. Harry and David® is a registered trademark.; **405** ©Netscape Communications Corporation; **406** ©2001 Kraft Foods, Inc. All rights reserved.; **410** ©Hulton-Deutsch Collection/CORBIS; **411** *top:* ©Corbis; **411** *bottom:* ©2003 Ford Motor Company. All rights reserved.; **427** ©2001 Wal-Mart.com USA, LLC. All rights reserved.; **428** *both:* ©2001 Wal-Mart.com USA, LLC. All rights reserved.

**Chapter 10** **431** *top:* www.newscom.com; **431** *bottom:* ©Tony Freeman/PhotoEdit - All rights reserved.; **434** Friedrich Cantor/Onyx/Outline Press Syndicate, Inc.; **439** ©Teri Stratford; **441** Logo used with permission of AG.com; **441** ©Erv Schowengerdt; **446** ©Michael Witte; **448** ©Charles O'Rear/CORBIS; **449** ©Jack Kurtz/The Image Works; **450** Diamond Star Motors, Inc.; **451** *top and bottom:* Courtesy of Maersk Sealand/Nick Souza, Photographer; **452** Courtesy of Maersk Sealand; **454** Courtesy of International Business Machines Corporation. Unauthorized use not permitted.; **459** Logo and photo used with permission of Milwaukee Electric Tool Corp.; **467** Logo used with permission of John Deere & Company; **468** *top:* ©Dorothy Burrows/Leslie Garland Picture Library/Alamy; **468** *bottom:* Photo and illustration courtesy of Deere & Company, Moline, IL.

**Chapter 11** **475** *all:* Courtesy of Xerox Corporation. Xerox & The Document Company are registered trademarks of Xerox Corporation.; **476** *right:* ©James A. Sugar/CORBIS; **476** *left:* Courtesy of Red Hat; **477** *left:* Mike Siluk/The Image Works; **477** *right:* ©Mark E. Gibson; **478** ©Microsoft Corporation; **490** ©IBM Rational®; **495** ©2003 Ceridian Corp.; **499** ©Erv Schowengerdt; **499** Logo used with permission of Colgate-Palmolive, Inc.; **506** Courtesy of WiPro; **507** Courtesy of WiPro.

**Chapter 12** **509** *all:* www.newscom.com; **515** ©Pete Saloutos/CORBIS; **515** Logo used with permission of the Dana-Farber Cancer Institute.; **520** Used with permission of Telenor ASA.; **522** ©L'Oreal Group; **525** Concept City/eStock. Used with permission of Interknowlogy, LLC.; **531** ©Dollar Rent a Car.

**Chapter 13** **535** *top left:* David Dietz/Stock, Boston; **535** *top right:* ©Susan van Etten/PhotoEdit – All rights reserved; **535** *bottom left:* Greg Meadows/Stock., Boston; *bottom right:* Mike Mazzaschi/Stock, Boston; **536** Bill Houlton, Intermec; **539** Logo used with permission of Hallmark Cards.; **541** ©Reuters NewMedia/CORBIS; **544** Copyright 2003 Geac Computer Corporation Limited; **546** Used with permission of Con-Way Transportation Services; **547** Used with permission of Con-Way Transportation Services; **552** *both:* ©Lon Harding; **554** *top left:* Ken Kobre/Words and Pictures; **554** *top right:* Ted Horowitz/The Stock Market/CORBIS; **554** *bottom left:* ©Richard Nowitz/The Stock Market/CORBIS; **554** *bottom right:* ©Louis Psihoyos/Matrix International; **558** ©Merrill Lynch & Co., Inc.; **559** Adapted from Michael Porter, *Competitive Advantage,* The Free Press, 1985; **561** E*TRADE Financial and the E*TRADE logo are registered trademarks of E*TRADE Group, Inc., or its subsidiaries. All rights reserved; **562, 564** Adapted from Michael Porter, *Competitive Advantage,* The Free Press, 1985.

**Chapter 14** **575** ©Phil Martin/PhotoEdit; **578** ©J. Bounds-RNO/CORBIS SYGMA; **580** Liaison/Getty Images; **585** *both:* Comdisco Disaster Recovery Services; **589** RSA Security; **593** Comdisco Disaster Recovery Services; **594** *left:* Comdisco Disaster Recovery Services; **594** *right:* Comdisco Disaster Recovery Services; **595** Logo used with permission of Kroll Worldwide.; **600** "Compatible" by Diana Ong/SuperStock; **604** ©David Young-Wolff/PhotoEdit; **613** The MPAA and MPA logos are reproduced with their permission.; **613** ©Wally McNamee/CORBIS; **614** Copyright 2001 OSMB, LLC. All rights reserved.

# Name, Company, and Product Index

## A

ABC network, 30
ABI/INFORM Database, 239
Accenture, 320–321, 500–501, 507, 524
Access (Microsoft), 245, 253, 254, 480, 602
The Accidental Entrepreneur, 128
AcuMax wrist computers, 202
Acura model (Honda), 102
Adobe Systems, 33, 61, 116, 602
Advanced Mobile Phone System (AMPS), 356
Aetna U.S. Healthcare, 4
Air France, 32, 370
Air Products Europe, 323
Airborne Express, 32
Airbus, 51
Ajax, 499
Alta Vista search engine, 94, 114
amazon.com, 103, 384, 386, 388–389, 391, 575
AMD Atlon XP, 140, 142
America Online (AOL)
    bill presentment, 398
    chat rooms, 91
    domain names, 103
    e-mail and, 319
    E-Trade and, 401, 561
    instant messaging, 92
    as portal, 115
    as public network, 19
    public portals, 95, 96
American Airlines
    American Advantage Frequent Flier program, 431–432
    client/server computing, 287
    innovation, 439
    multiuser systems, 69
    Orbitz and, 418
    preemptive strike, 449
    Sabre system, 431
    training, 31–32, 51–52
    travel services, 400
American Banking Association, 397
American Express Company, 193, 223, 326, 517
American Greetings, 441, 462
American Heart Association, 146–147
America's Choice Mall, 392
AmeriSource Bergen Corp., 328
AMES, 101
AMR Corp., 287–289, 432, 440, 449
AMR Information Services (AMRIS), 432, 457
Apollo system, 530
Apple Computer
    graphical interfaces, 488
    interoperability and, 474
    LAN protocols, 365
    microprocessors and, 139–142
    optimizing performance, 564
    PC DBMS packages, 245
    plug-ins, 116
    RSA Public Key, 590
    Unix operating system, 474
Apple iBook, 16
Apple iMac, 16
Apple Macintosh, 148, 152, 181, 212

Apple QuickTime Player plug-in, 116
Apple Talk, 365
Architectural Energy Corp., 541
Armed Forces Financial Network, 326
The Art of Deception (Mitnick), 578
Associated Press (AP), 247, 261–262
Association for Computing Machinery, 599, 601
Association of the Institute for Certification of Computer Professionals, 599
AT&T, 334, 335, 590, 593–594
AT&T Wireless, 357
Augusta National Golf Club, 100
Automobile Association of America (AAA), 94

## B

Babies R Us, 333
Bank of America, 398
BankOne Corp., 66, 558
Barnes and Noble, 405
BBC network, 30
Bell, Alexander Graham, 19
Bell Atlantic, 22
Bellsouth, 447
Bergen Brunswig Corp., 328–329
Best Buy, 507
BidCom, 418
Big Science Company, 4
Binning, Gerd, 164
Biotherm, 522
BITNET academic network, 91
Blåtand, Harald, 359
Blue Cross Blue Shield (BCBS), 471–473
Blue Mountain supercomputers, 18
Bluster, 613
BMW, 351
Boeing Aircraft Company, 51, 195, 275, 380–381, 507, 552
Boise Cascade, 517
Borland, 245
Bowman, Bob, 98
Brady's clothing stores, 281
Bridgestone tires, 273, 301–302
British Aerospace Ltd., 275
British Airways, 31, 32, 66–67
British Petroleum, 333, 334
British Telecom, 330
Brooks Brothers, 173–174
BT (British Telecom), 334
Budget Rent A Car System Inc., 432
Builder Guide DSS, 541
Burlington Coat Factory, 283–286
BusinessWeek, 85

## C

Cable News Network (CNN)
    case study, 82–83
    as content provider, 100
    e-commerce and, 387
    IT and, 30
    watermarks, 604, 606
Cacharel, 522
Caldera, 476
Canadian Speeches, 237
Carey, Maria, 22
Cargill, 524

CargoProf, 43–44, 53
Casey, Jim, 383
Catalina Marketing, 203
Catalyst catalog, 91
Caterpillar, Inc., 28–29
CBS network, 30
Celeron processors, 140
Cerf, Vincent, 87
Ceridian Corp., 495–496
Charles Schwab, 398, 401
Chase Manhattan, 398
Chemdex, 419
Chevron Texaco, Inc., 25
Choicemall.com, 393
Chrysler Corp., 450
Chubb Corp., 276, 277–278
Chubb, Percy, 277
Chubb, Thomas Caldecot, 277
CIA, 606
Cingular Wireless, 357
CIO Magazine, 5
Circuit City Stores, Inc., 500, 502
CIRRUS, 326
Cirrus ATM network, 363
Cisco Systems, 31, 410, 420, 507, 513, 552–553
Citroën, 535
City of Chicago Public Schools, 251
CN Biosciences, 419
CN Tower (Toronto), 41
CNET Networks, 85–86
CNN Airport Channel, 82
CNN Headline News, 82
CNN International, 82
CNN.com, 82
Coca-Cola Company, 69, 203
Colgate, 499
Colgate-Palmolive Company, 499, 501–502
Comdisco, 585
Compaq, 15, 16, 142, 474
Compaq iPaq PDA, 16, 361
Compaq Tablet PC, 16
Compass Airline, 581
Comprehensive Cancer Center, 515
CompUSA, 61
CompuServe, 325, 401, 561
Compustat, 238, 239
Computer and Information Systems Abstracts (database), 239
Computer Fraud and Abuse Act, 581
Computer Recycling Center, 138–139
Computer Sciences Corp. (CSC), 500
Computer Security Institute, 5
The Computer Shopper, 86
Comshare software company, 543–544
Condit, Phil, 381
Confirm reservation system, 432, 457
Consolidated Freightways, 205
ConsumerConnect, 410
Continental Airlines, 43–44, 69, 418
Control Data, 128
Con-Way Transportation Services, Inc., 546–547
Corning, Inc., 556–557
Courtesy Recognition Systems, 585
Covisant exchange, 418
Cox Communications, 398
Crandall, Robert, 431–432, 439
CreataCard software (American Greetings), 441, 462

# Subject Index